C000097588

The
Restaurant
Guide

ENJOY 30% OFF LEISURE BREAKS

Choose from over 50 hotels in locations the length and breadth of the country. Whether you are planning a short romantic interlude, a family break or a few days shopping you are sure to find a Corus hotel to suit you. Corus hotels are fresh, bright and stylish with an enthusiastic approach to service and a commitment to getting the simple things right every time.

To book please call us on **0870 609 6180** to make your reservation quoting *The AA Restaurant Guide*. For a copy of our Escapes brochure please call **0870 2400 111** or visit **www.corushotels.com**

Prices from just £35 Dinner, Bed and Breakfast per person per night
Terms and Conditions Offer valid for a 30% discount on the Leisure Times full rate, based on two people sharing a twin or double room for a minimum of two nights on dinner bed and breakfast Packages. This offer is valid until 22nd December 2006 (excluding 23 December 2005 to 2 January 2006 and bank holidays except at short notice) and is subject to availability. Bookings must be made by calling 0870 609 6180 and quoting *The AA Restaurant Guide*. This offer cannot be used in conjunction with any other discount, offer or promotion. See Corus hotels Leisure Times for full terms and conditions.

CREDITS

This 13th edition published 2005
© Automobile Association Developments Limited 2005. Automobile Association Developments Limited retains the copyright in the current edition © 2005 and in all subsequent editions, reprints and amendments to editions. The information contained in this directory is sourced entirely from the AA's information resources. All rights reserved. No part of this publication may be reproduced, stored in a retrieval system, or transmitted in any form or by any means - electronic, photocopying, recording or otherwise - unless the written permission of the publishers has been obtained beforehand. This book may not be sold, resold, hired out or otherwise disposed of by way of trade in any form of binding or cover other than that in which it is published, without the prior consent of all relevant Publishers. The contents of this book are believed correct at the time of printing. Nevertheless, the Publisher cannot be held responsible for any errors or omissions, or for changes in the details given in this guide, or for the consequences of any reliance on the information provided by the same. This does not affect your statutory rights. Assessments of AA inspected establishments are based on the experience of the Hotel and restaurant Inspectors on the occasion(s) of their visit(s) and therefore descriptions given in this guide necessarily dictate an element of subjective opinion which may not reflect or dictate a reader's own opinion on another occasion. See page 5 for a clear explanation of how, based on our Inspectors' inspection experiences, establishments are graded. If the meal or meals experienced by an Inspector or Inspectors during an inspection fall between award levels the restaurant concerned may be awarded the lower of any award levels considered applicable. The AA strives to ensure accuracy of the information in this guide at the time of printing. Due to the constantly evolving nature of the subject matter the information is subject to change. The AA will gratefully receive any advice from our readers of any necessary updated information.

Please contact
Advertisement Sales: advertisingsales@theaa.com
Editorial Department: lifestyleguides@theaa.com

Front cover photos sourced from www.seafish.org.
Thanks to Handpicked hotels for the images on p5 and p6 (Nutfield Priory, Redhill and Woodlands Park, Stoke d'Abernon)

Photographs in the gazetteer provided by the establishments.
Typeset/Repro: Keenes, Andover
Printed by Trento Srl, Italy.
Restaurant descriptions have been contributed by the following team of writers: Cathy Fitzgerald, David Halford, David Hancock, Julia Hynard, Denise Laing, Olivia Laing, Philip Moss, Portia Spooner, Allen Stidwill, Mark Taylor and Jenny White. Researcher: Ed Hutton.

Published by AA Publishing, a trading name of Automobile Association Developments Limited, whose registered office is Fanum House, Basing View, Basingstoke, Hampshire RG21 4EA.
Registered number 1878835.
A CIP catalogue for this book is available from the British Library.
ISBN-10: 0-7495-4623-9
ISBN-13: 978-0-7495-4623-6
A02391

Maps prepared by the Cartography Department of The Automobile Association. Maps © Automobile Association Developments Limited 2005.
This product includes mapping data licensed from Ordnance Survey® with the permission of the Controller of Her Majesty's Stationery Office. © Crown copyright 2005. All rights reserved. Licence number 399221.

This product includes mapping based upon data licensed from Ordnance Survey of Northern Ireland® reproduced by permission of the Chief Executive, acting on behalf of the Controller of Her Majesty's Stationery Office. © Crown copyright 2005. Permit number 40462.

Republic of Ireland mapping based on Ordnance Survey Ireland Permit number MP000105.
© Ordnance Survey Ireland and Government of Ireland.

CONTENTS

How the AA Assesses for Rosette Awards

The AA's Rosette award scheme was the first nationwide scheme for assessing the quality of food served by restaurants and hotels. The Rosette scheme is an award, not a classification, and although there is necessarily an element of subjectivity when it comes to assessing taste, we aim for a consistent approach throughout the UK. Our awards are made solely on the basis of a meal visit or visits by one or more of our hotel and restaurant Inspectors, who have an unrivalled breadth and depth of experience in assessing quality. They award Rosettes annually on a rising scale of one to five.

One Rosette
- Excellent local restaurants stand out in their local area
- Food prepared with care, understanding and skill
- Good quality ingredients
  Of the total number of establishments with Rosettes around 50% have one Rosette.

Two Rosettes
- The best local restaurants • Higher standards
- Better consistency • Greater precision apparent in the cooking
- Obvious attention to the quality and selection of ingredients
  About 40% of restaurants have two Rosettes.

Three Rosettes
- Outstanding restaurants demanding recognition well beyond local area
- Selection and sympathetic treatment of highest quality ingredients
- Timing, seasoning and judgement of flavour combinations consistently
- Excellent intelligent service and a well-chosen wine list
  Around 10% of restaurants have three Rosettes.

Four Rosettes
- Cooking demands national recognition
  Dishes demonstrate: • intense ambition • a passion for excellence
- superb technical skills • remarkable consistency
- appreciation of culinary traditions combined with desire for exploration and improvement
  Around fifteen restaurants have four Rosettes.

Five Rosettes
- Cooking stands comparison with the best in the world
- Highly individual voices • Breathtaking culinary skills
- Setting the standards to which others aspire
  Around six restaurants have five Rosettes.

So what makes a restaurant worthy of a Rosette Award?

For our Inspectors, the top and bottom line is the food. The taste of a dish is what counts for them and whether it successfully delivers to the diner what the menu promises.

A restaurant is only as good as its worst meal. Although presentation and competent service should be appropriate to the style of the restaurant and the quality of the food, they cannot affect the Rosette assessment of such, either up or down. The summaries on the left attempt to explain what our Inspectors look for, but are intended only as guidelines. The AA is constantly reviewing its award criteria and competition usually results in an all-round improvement in standards, so it becomes increasingly difficult for restaurants to reach award level. For more detailed Rosette criteria, please see www.theAA.com

AA Classifications and Awards

Where the following AA ratings appear under 'Rooms' in the guide, the establishment has been inspected under nationally recognised Classification schemes. These ratings ensure that your accommodation meets the AA's highest standards of cleanliness with the emphasis on professionalism, proper booking procedures and a prompt and efficient service.

AA Star Classification

★ If you stay in a one-star hotel you should expect a relatively informal yet competent style of service and an adequate range of facilities, including a television in the lounge or bedroom and a reasonable choice of hot and cold dishes. The majority of bedrooms are en suite with a bath or shower room always available.

★ ★ A two-star hotel is run by smartly and professionally presented management and offers at least one restaurant or dining room for breakfast and dinner.

★ ★ ★ A three-star hotel includes direct dial telephones, a wide selection of drinks in the bar and last orders for dinner no earlier than 8pm.

★ ★ ★ ★ A four-star hotel is characterised by uniformed, well-trained staff with additional services, a night porter and a serious approach to cuisine.

★ ★ ★ ★ ★ Finally, and most luxurious of all, is the five-star hotel offering many extra facilities, attentive staff, top quality rooms and a full concierge service. A wide selection of drinks, including cocktails, is available in the bar and the impressive menu reflects and complements the hotel's own style.

★ AA Top Hotels

The AA's Top Hotels in Britain and Ireland are identified by red stars. These stand out as the very best and range from large luxury destination hotels to snug country inns. To find further details see the AA's website at www.theAA.com

AA Diamond Awards

The AA's Diamond classification covers bed and breakfast establishments only, reflecting guest accommodation at five grades of quality, with one Diamond indicating the simplest and five Diamonds the upper end of the scale. The criteria for eligibility are guest care and quality rather than the choice of extra facilities. Establishments are vetted by a team of qualified inspectors to ensure that the accommodation, food and hospitality meet the AA's own exacting standards. Guests should receive a prompt professional check in and check out, comfortable accommodation equipped to modern standards, regularly changed bedding and towels, a sufficient hot water supply at all times, good well-prepared meals and a full English or continental breakfast.

RED DIAMONDS are awarded to the very best places in the three, four and five Diamond ratings.

🍴 Restaurants with Rooms

A restaurant that also offers accommodation. Most have 12 bedrooms or fewer, and public areas may be limited to the restaurant itself. No Star or Diamond rating is shown in the guide but bedrooms reflect at least the level of quality normally associated with a two-star hotel. A red symbol indicates a restaurant with rooms that is amongst the AA's top hotels in Britain and Ireland.

AA Restaurants of the Year

Potential restaurants of the year are nominated by our team of full-time Inspectors based on their routine visits. In selecting a Restaurant of the Year, we look for somewhere that is exceptional in its chosen area of the market. Whilst the Rosette awards are based on the quality of the food alone, Restaurants of the Year takes into account all aspects of the operation.

Winner for England
The New Angel, Dartmouth
p119 ◉◉◉

The wonderful, half-timbered Tudor exterior catches the eye on Dartmouth's waterfront. The interior is simple yet stylish, with an open-to-view kitchen adding drama on the ground floor with a quieter dining option upstairs. Impeccable French-orientated cooking in the expert hands of John Burton-Race shows polished strength and skill, with great deference and intelligence given to the simple treatment of the very best and freshest ingredients, especially fish.

Winner for London
Le Cercle p278 ◉◉◉

A discreet entrance leads to a surprisingly large and airy subterranean restaurant. Le Cercle (sister to Club Gascon p257) is at the cutting edge of 21st-century gastronomy, offering French cooking in tapas-sized, grazing portions, ideal for all-day dining. The cuisine is firmly rooted in classical France, with refined presentation in miniature. Cheese is taken very seriously here, with a glass window into the kitchen showing the cheese chef at work.

Winner for Scotland
étain, Glasgow p580 ◉◉

Accessed by street lift or through the Zinc bar, this contemporary restaurant is located at the top of a glass-fronted building. The interior is styled in wood, leather and earthy colours – typically Conran – with shiny pewter-clad pillars (*étain* means pewter in French). Very competent modern British cooking here with powerful French overtones, clear technical skills, high quality Scottish produce and strong flavours. There's a daily carte with a vegetarian option and a six-course epicurean menu.

Winner for Wales
Gilby's Restaurant, Cardiff
p620 ◉

Something of a Cardiff institution, Gilby's is set in a converted 18th-century tithe barn close to the fast-growing Culverhouse Cross shopping area. It's popular and bustling with a modern open-plan kitchen, yet the decor is traditional. High ceilings and original beams characterise the split-level dining areas. The lengthy, populist, modern menus offer something for everyone, with fish taking centre stage with a wonderful selection on display.

Fish is the dish

Seafood is one of the healthiest and most delicious foods that you can choose when eating out. With thousands of tantalising dishes to choose from, ranging from Champagne and oysters to mouthwatering fish pie, there is literally a dish for every occasion. There are around 100 exciting varieties of seafood available to buy in the UK, so there is plenty of opportunity to be more adventurous and try a wider range of seafood.

Why not try beer battered New Zealand hoki and chunky chips or succulent langoustines next time you eat out?

UK's Best Seafood Restaurant 2006

The top seafood restaurants in England, Northern Ireland, Wales and Scotland have been presented with the prestigious title of Best Seafood Restaurant, sponsored by the Sea Fish Industry Authority (Seafish). The award-winning restaurants were selected following a rigorous search of some of the top seafood restaurants in the UK. The UK's Best Seafood Restaurants 2006 can be found in this guide by looking for the 'Best Use of Seafood' logo.

Good Seafood Served Here

Over 250 restaurants in this guide specialise in seafood dishes. Finding these outlets is easy; they are all marked with a fish symbol that indicates 'Best Use of Seafood'. All of these restaurants have been visited by AA Inspectors to ensure that the menu features a wide range of seafood dishes.

Sea Fish Industry Authority
18 Logie Mill, Logie Green Road, Edinburgh EH7 4HG
Tel: 0131 558 3331 Fax: 0131 558 1442
E-mail: marketing@seafish.co.uk Website: www.seafish.org

AA Seafood Restaurants of the Year

In conjunction with Seafish, the Sea Fish Industry Authority. We have sought out some of the restaurants that make the most of seafood on their menus.

Winner for England
West Beach Restaurant, Bournemouth (see p140)

Enjoying a prime seafront location a few metres from the pier, West Beach Restaurant has a smart, contemporary feel, and floor to ceiling windows to maximise the sea views. An open-plan kitchen lets you watch the food being prepared, and you can dine outside in summer. Open from breakfast to dinner, the menu focuses on high quality fish and seafood, delivered daily from Newlyn, Brixham and Billingsgate markets.

Winner for Scotland
Tolbooth, Stonehaven (see p542)

Once a prison and excise house, the Tolbooth is reputedly the oldest building in Stonehaven, and is ideally located on the harbourside. Some fish is still landed here, and the boats come and go to the rhythm of the tides and seasons. Enjoy the fine views from the first floor dining room and peruse the options on the blackboard menu, where you'll find the day's catch cooked with flair and integrity.

Winner for Wales
The Shed, Porthgain (see p643)

The name gives a good indication of what to expect here! Set on the quay in this remote and unchanged old port, the restaurant is a tearoom by day, offering sandwiches and home-made cakes, but in the evening the upstairs dining room is transformed into a small quayside bistro. The owner's husband catches much of the fish himself, and The Shed has a well-deserved and growing reputation for fresh fish well cooked.

Winner for Northern Ireland
The Quays Pub & Restaurant, Portavogie (see p659)

Set on the most easterly point of Northern Ireland, midway down the Ards Peninsula, the Quays is ideally located, with views of the Irish Sea and the harbour where the fish is landed. It's a modern split level restaurant, warmly decorated, with a menu to suit all tastes but specialising in fish, most of which is local.

Best Use of Seafood

The following restaurants have received a symbol for Best Use of Seafood sponsored by Seafi

Providing over 3000 of the most distinctive
wines from around the world, encompassing
the greatest Burgundian Domaines to the
smallest artisan producers

Winner of the International Wine Challenge for
'Fine & Rare Wine Merchant of the Year'
and 'Burgundy Merchant of the Year'

Award Winning Wine Merchant
Trevor Hughes of T & W Wines

"Best at the Best"
Jancis Robinson

Importers of one of the world's greatest
wine producers, Willi Opitz.Austria

Possibly the largest selection
of half bottles in the world

Send for
our 150 page
catalogue today
or view online at
www.tw-wines.com

T&W Wines Limited
tation Way, Brandon, Suffolk IP27 0BH. Tel 01842 814414
ebsite: www.tw-wines.com - Email: contact@tw-wines.com

Wine Trends

So what are this year's most popular wines? What does the diner prefer to drink pre-dinner? And what's the next up-and-coming wine region to watch out for? These are some of the questions that our 1,000 restaurants were asked.

New Zealand and South Africa were mentioned most in terms of increased wine sales, followed by Australia, Spain, Chile, and Italy. This reflects the continuing trend of dominant market share and popularity that New World wines have achieved in recent years. Interestingly however, when asked to name the next up-and-coming wine producing region, the Old World countries fared much better, with French regional wines, Spain and Greece mentioned the most.

As Britain is the largest export market for Champagne it came as no surprise that the majority of our entrants listed it as the most popular choice as an aperitif followed by wine, with spirits a distant third.

Over the last few years we have been gauging the industry's view on screwtop wines. Clearly these are becoming commonplace in the retail sector with little consumer resistance and it is with great interest that we noticed the majority of restaurants and hotels surveyed now list screw-capped wines.

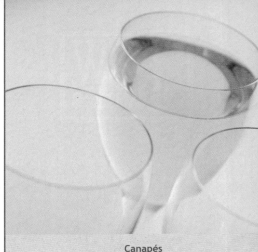

Canapés
Gosset Grande Réserve Champagne,
Multi Vintage £40.00

Pressing of Foie Gras with apple jelly, roasted fig
and plum chutney with toasted brioche
Tin Shed 'Wild Bunch' Riesling 2003 Eden Valley,
Australia £21.00

Pithivier of Orkney Scallops with beurre blanc
Chassagne Montrachet, Olivier Leflaive,
Premier Cru 1998 £48.00

Roasted saddle of New Forest Venison with
McSween Haggis Dauphinoise and a rich red wine
sauce, roasted beetroot and seasonal vegetables
Sangiovese, Seghesio, Sonoma Coast 2001 £38.00

Munster cheese with a compôte of shallots and
grapes, wheat wafers and oat cakes
Riesling, Cuvée Frederic Emile, Trimbach 1997 £45.00

Strawberry and passion fruit panacotta with
vanilla bean ice cream
Off the Rack Chenin Blanc, Plantagenet 2003 £21.00

Freshly brewed coffee and petits fours
Alvear PX Solera, 1927 Montilla £24.00

The AA Wine Award

This year's wine award attracted an excellent response with approximately 1,000 entries, from which three national and one overall winner (who gets an all-expenses-paid trip to Willi Opitz's vineyards at Illmitz in Austria's Burgenland) were chosen. All 1,800 or so rosetted restaurants in the guide were invited to submit their wine lists. From these, the panel selected a shortlist of around 135 establishments who together with all previous winners are highlighted in the guide with the 'Notable Wine List' symbol. The short-listed establishments were then asked to choose wines from their list (within a budget of £50 per bottle) to accompany a challenging menu (see above) designed by Nick Scade from The New Mill at Eversley in Hampshire, the 2005 overall Wine Award winner.

Wine Award Winner for England & Overall Winner
The Harrow at Little Bedwyn
(see p485)

Judges' comments on the winning list included "a list you just don't want to put down", "a list of pure passion and enthusiasm for wine" and "depth in every area". Proprietors Roger and Sue Jones have created a stunning wine list, which is beautifully presented and laid out, easy to navigate and includes concise tasting notes for each wine. Wine selections throughout are of the highest quality and also offer much interest and diversity, with some even exclusive to The Harrow. There are over twenty wines by the glass available including Gosset, Krug and Dom Perignon 1996. The Harrow holds regular wine events including tastings, gourmet and wine dinners and also produces a customer newsletter that features various wine updates.

See left for the overall winning selection of wines from The Harrow to accompany the menu devised by Nick Scade.

Wine Award Winner for Scotland
The Cross, Kingussie (see p594)

Well-established restaurant with rooms run by David and Katie Young offers an interesting, varied and high-quality wine list. Their list begins with a very useful short-list page and has other notable features such as a section on second wines of Bordeaux, a personal selection of Tuscan Reds, Rioja and Quinta do Crasto, a strong half-bottle list, and an excellent selection of pudding wines, with several recommended specifically to accompany chocolate.

Wine Award Winner for Wales
The Bell at Skenfrith (see p640)

17th-century former coaching inn, now restaurant with rooms, offers guests a highly impressive wine list created by proprietor William Hutchings. Interest and quality fills each page and an informative and personal tasting note accompanies every wine. Thirteen wines available by the glass are particularly well chosen and offer great value. Half bottle choices are extensive as is the separate list of pudding wines and a stunning range of vintage cognacs.

The AA would like to thank Nick Scade for his help in this year's judging.
The AA Wine Awards are sponsored by T&W Wines Ltd 5 Station Way, Brandon Suffolk IP27 0BH
Tel: 01842 814414 email: contact@tw-wines.com web: www.tw-wines.com

The Proof of the Pudding

BY DENISE LAING

MOST PEOPLE WOULD THINK TWICE BEFORE DRIVING FROM THE WILDS OF EXMOOR TO URBAN KENT JUST FOR LUNCH, BUT FOR THE AA RESTAURANT INSPECTOR SUCH ACTIVITIES ARE ALL IN A DAY'S WORK. WITH PUNISHING SCHEDULES THAT REQUIRE THEM TO STAY OVERNIGHT IN HOTELS AND GUEST HOUSES, MAKE DAY VISITS FOR UNHERALDED INSPECTIONS, AND OFTEN EAT BOTH LUNCH AND DINNER TO ASSESS ROSETTE RATINGS AND ROSETTE POTENTIAL, THEY CAN OFTEN FIND THEMSELVES MILES AWAY FROM WHERE THEY NEED TO BE THE NEXT DAY. A RELIABLE CAR, A GLOBAL PLOTTING SYSTEM AND A HANDS-FREE TELEPHONE FOR LAST MINUTE BRIEFINGS ARE ESSENTIAL TO GET THEM ACROSS SWATHES OF COUNTRY TO THEIR NEXT ASSIGNATION. ONCE THEY ARRIVE AT THEIR DESTINATION, A KEEN INTEREST IN FOOD AND A WELL-HONED KNOWLEDGE OF THE CATERING INDUSTRY WILL SEE TO THE REST. THESE PEOPLE LITERALLY EAT FOR A LIVING, AND THEIR STANDARDS, LIKE THEIR HOPES, ARE ALWAYS HIGH.

People often envy the glamorous lifestyle of a restaurant inspector, and their licence to eat the best food in the country at prices that most couldn't, or would choose not to, afford. Yet the price they have to pay for this privilege is that not all the food is wonderful. For every impressive restaurant visited, an untold number have to be dismissed as not up to the required standard. When I shadowed four AA restaurant inspectors as they went about their daily work, it was a relative rarity to see their eyes really light up and hear them declare that a meal, a dish or a combination of flavours was superb. More often they are required to munch their way through pretentious food that is overly ambitious, poorly timed, ill-judged and, worst crime of all these days, made from ingredients that are less than fresh, far from local and with scant regard for the seasons, whatever the menu might claim. Pleasant culinary surprises can come from unexpected places, and conversely, restaurants that have been flagged up and celebrated can be disappointing.

The proof of the pudding might be in the eating, as they say, but a well-trained AA inspector takes several other factors into account when assessing a restaurant. First impressions matter, and the staff who greet diners and show them to their table will be making an unconscious contribution to the outcome of the inspection. A pleasant manner, a little friendly conversation, and offers of help with the menu and wine list will all impress. The ambience and decor are taken into account too, along with an assessment of the sort of clientele the establishment attracts and how well it caters for them, and all of this will be reflected in the description that appears in the Guide. But it's the food that really counts towards a rosette, and the well-honed palate of the restaurant inspector must be ruthlessly honest.

In one two-rosette restaurant somewhere in the North of England, a February starter of grilled fresh asparagus immediately caused raised eyebrows. Why offer such a dish when fresh asparagus is not available naturally in this country until early May? A dessert of chocolate tart with clotted cream and 'fresh' strawberries was similarly dismissed. Even Dover sole with a choice of three sauces was criticised: flat fish are not at their best in winter when the roe is present and the flavour is poor, apparently; but to offer a variety of sauces instead of designing the ideal pairing showed a lack of commitment to getting the best out of every dish. The wine list here was another surprise; previously the undisputed star of the show with hundreds of well-chosen bins, it had shrunk to a few dozen bottles. We soon found the reason for the less than impressive food too: the fêted owner had moved on, taking his wine business with him, and the restaurant now had new owners. The old magic had gone out of the place, and it had become just another restaurant serving mediocre food and wine. Solution? Remove the rosettes.

In another restaurant, four rosettes this time, the inspector enthused over a winning starter of lobster ravioli with cauliflower purée and lobster Cognac sauce. This was not just ordinary ravioli, I was informed, but home made, and wafer thin; the lobster was meaty and juicy, the sauce gave the dish a real kick, and the purée spooned over the top was nearly the consistency of a sauce – a superb achievement! But even better was to come in the form of braised oxtail stuffed with pancetta and celeriac purée, with baby beetroot and roasted silverskin onions, and a foie gras mousse drizzled over the top. The mousse had permeated through the pancetta and purée, thus bringing the whole thing together as a glorious composite. This was one of the chef's signature dishes, and the 'Wow factor' was there in spades! Listening to the inspector deconstruct it was a fascinating experience: stuffed oxtail is notoriously difficult to make, and most kitchens shy away from the task despite the end result being so worthwhile. As the house speciality here, it demanded the laborious boning of several oxtails a day – an art in itself – followed by time-consuming stuffing and slow cooking. It was served with delicate little accessories that made the tongue, and the spine, tingle. This was the epitome of four-rosette dining, and the rating was assured for another year. I soon realised that this is why attention paid to minutest details helps to make legends of chefs. This particular chef was bemused when the inspector asked about a hint of vanilla that she had detected in her main dish, but he suddenly remembered that a vanilla pod had been briefly used in the stock made some days previously. Impressive knowledge from the AA inspector too.

A four-star London hotel with a one-rosette restaurant turned up unexpected trumps for one highly experienced inspector. The young head waiter and sommelier brought this place to life with their charm, helpfulness and service. Dishes were described in knowledgable detail, and recommendations made. We were asked for our wine preferences, and suitable bottles were suggested until we indicated that we would only require a glass each. Without an eyebrow twitch or snooty sniff the sommelier changed tack and helped us choose successfully. He seemed genuinely pleased at our satisfaction. Even more impressive was the food, an unsung list of memorable dishes that now demanded the free use of superlatives from the inspector (and that doesn't happen too often I was assured!) Sautéed fillet and braised shin of beef with parsnip purée and wild mushroom à la crème was acclaimed as a triumph of imagination and execution. The fillet was perfectly cooked, rare, tender and full flavoured. The braised shin melted in the mouth and was separated from the fillet by a good potato fondant. Some ceps brought an interesting texture to a light cream sauce, whilst a creamy parsnip purée introduced a striking and welcome balance. Without dissembling, the inspector could honestly assure the waiter that, yes, the dish was indeed a good one. Despite the lack of weekday custom, the ambitious new chef was producing cutting-edge dishes that were about to achieve recognition of their worth.

The enthusiasm and dedication of the AA restaurant inspectors never waned while I was with them, despite the occasional disappointment. Their obvious respect for the more than 1,800 restaurants commended in The Restaurant Guide, and their mission to encourage the highest standards at every level of cooking, were truly impressive. I decided that eating to live was a lot easier than living to eat, and left them all plotting their next meals.

Subscribe to

WAITROSE
FOOD
ILLUSTRATED

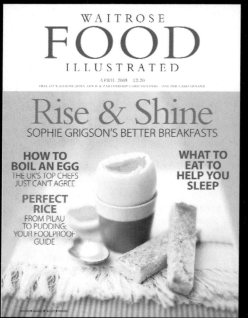

+

Waitrose Food Illustrated is the award-winning magazine for people who love food and drink. It provides a monthly feast of seasonal and regional produce, inspiring recipes, international food stories and restaurant reviews, as well as mouthwateringly sumptuous photography. *AA Restaurant Guide* readers who subscribe to the magazine will not only receive a copy each month for a year, delivered to their door, but will also receive a free folder (worth £6.95) in which to keep all their favourite recipes. All this for the special price of £19.80 – a saving of 25 per cent. Bon appetit!

EXCLUSIVE TO *AA RESTAURANT GUIDE* READERS: SUBSCRIBE TO *WFI* FOR JUST £19.80 (USUALLY £26.40), AND PICK UP A FREE RECIPE FOLDER, WORTH £6.95

CALL 01795 414930

Quote 'AA Guide offer'

OFFER IS LIMITED TO FIRST-TIME UK-BASED SUBSCRIBERS, AND IS VALID UNTIL 15 SEPTEMBER 2006.

AA Chefs' Chef 05-06

The annual poll of all the chefs in *The Restaurant Guide*. Around 1,800 of the country's top chefs vote to recognise the achievements of one of their peers from a shortlist chosen by the AA's team of Inspectors.

THIS YEAR'S WINNER IS GERMAIN SCHWAB, PROPRIETOR OF WINTERINGHAM FIELDS (SEE PAGE 233), AN INTERNATIONALLY RENOWNED RESTAURANT WITH A BATTERY OF PRESTIGIOUS AWARDS LOCATED IN RURAL NORTH LINCOLNSHIRE. GERMAIN'S FASCINATION WITH FOOD AND HIS LIFELONG DEDICATION TO HIS CRAFT IS REFLECTED IN HIS ACCURACY, CONSISTENCY AND ATTENTION TO DETAIL, ADDING UP TO A MAGICAL EXPERIENCE FOR THE DINER.

Germain comes from the Jura region of Switzerland, where he grew up in a farming community and began his apprenticeship in a local restaurant where he found that 'the odd tap on the head with a casserole worked wonders for the learning process'. This is not a technique Germain has adopted in his own management style, which is one of encouragement and nurturing, enabling him to build up a strong brigade of dedicated professionals.

In 1971 Germain moved to England, eventually working at The Chesterfield, The Dorchester and Robert Carrier's, before returning to Switzerland at the age of 25 as head chef at the Hotel Mont Cervin, Zermatt. After four years here he met his English wife Annie and the couple returned to the UK to open a small restaurant 10 miles from York, which they operated successfully for two years. In 1987 they moved into Winteringham, taking a year to renovate the property, a beautiful 16th-century manor house.

Germaine and Annie have been at the forefront of developing youngsters in the industry, giving their time to training, judging competitions and charitable activities. They command the highest respect from everyone in the industry and are down-to-earth, hard working and genuinely nice people.

'No one expects a restaurant of this calibre to be nestled in the wilds of Lincolnshire.'

'It's your dedication, skill and passion that creates the establishment, but don't reach for the top if you can't sustain it.'

Germain Schwab

Previous Winners

Raymond Blanc
Le Manoir aux Quat' Saisons, Great Milton, Oxford *p391*

Shaun Hill

Heston Blumenthal
The Fat Duck, Bray *p34*

Jean-Christophe Novelli
Novelli at Auberge du Lac, Welwyn *p209*
Novelli in the City *p263*

Gordon Ramsay
Restaurant Gordon Ramsay, London SW3 *p294*

Rick Stein
The Seafood Restaurant, Padstow *p75*

Marco Pierre White

Kevin Viner

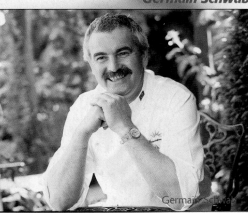

Germain Schwab

How to Use the Guide
Sample Entry

1
2 — ANYTOWN MAP 12 AB34
3
4 — 🏵🏵 **Stylish Restaurant** ──────── 24
                                    ─── 23
5 — *European*   🍾🐟🍴 **NEW** ─ 22
   Victorian country house dining   ─ 21
   ☎ 0855 888 32516 Green Lane GL51 9ES

6 —

7 — **MENU GUIDE** Spicy Cornish crab tagliatelle • Dublin Bay
   prawns on black rice , with a lemon sauce • Lemon peel parfait.
8 — **WINE GUIDE** ♀ VT de Extremadura 1999 £11.50 • ♀ Bierzo
   Mencius £13.50 • 10 bottles over £20, 5 bottles under £20 • 8 by
   the glass (£5-£7)
9 — **PRICE GUIDE** Fixed D £15 • starter £3.50-£5 • main £6.50-
   £12.50 • dessert £4.50-£6 • coffee £2.50 • service added 10%
   PLACE: Country house hotel set in wooded grounds on the
   outskirts of the village. The restaurant's blue decor lends a
   contemporary feel to an otherwise classic setting.
   FOOD: The menu combines English tradition with French flair: a
   meal could include warm salad of butter-roasted quail with
   kumquat and cashew nuts followed by rosettes of beef tenderloin
   and wild mushroom with foie gras croûte on a beef tea.
   OUR TIP: Book a window seat and enjoy the sea views.
10 — **Chef:** Keith McAllister **Owners:** Pageant Hotels **Times:** 12.30-2/7.30-9.30,
11 —   Closed L Sat **Notes:** Vegetarian available, Civ Wed 60 **Seats:** 65,   20
   12   Pr/dining room 40 **Smoking:** N/Sm in dining room, Air con   19
13 14 — **Children:** Menu **Rooms:** 33 (33 en suite) ★★★ **Directions:** From A6   18
       to Clapham turn R into Green Lane **Parking:** 60 ──────────   17
15 — **e-mail:** woodlands.manor@pageant.co.uk **web:** www.pageant.co.uk

16 — ⚹ **The New Local Restaurant** 24, High Street
   ☎ 01256 786787 Bright and frequently bustling bistro with cheerful
   polo shirted staff and a short blackboard menu

---

3   Restaurant name

4   🏵 The AA Rosette Award
    Main entries have been awarded one or
    more Rosettes, up to a maximum of five.
    See page 4 for an explanation of how
    they are graded.

5   The food style of the restaurant in bold
    italics, followed by a short summary
    statement.

6   Restaurants awarded AA rosettes are
    invited to enhance their entry with up to
    two photographs.

7   Typical menu dishes, prices may also be
    given.

8   Best-selling white and red wine, along
    with the number of wines under and
    over £20, and the selection by the glass.

9   Prices for fixed lunch and dinner (where
    available) along with à la carte dishes,
    coffee and mineral water. Service charge
    information. Note: Prices quoted are a
    guide only, and are subject to change
    without notice.

10 The names of the chef(s) and owner(s).
    These are as up-to-date as we could
    make them at the time of going to press,
    but changes in personnel often occur,
    and may affect both the style and quality
    of the restaurant.

11 Additional information: e.g. availability of
    vegetarian dishes.

12 Establishments that do not allow
    smoking in the dining room may allow it
    elsewhere.

13 If the establishment is in any of the AA's
    accommodation schemes, the number of
    rooms and the rating are shown. See
    page 5 for further details.

14 Children's portions, age restrictions etc.

15 E-mail addresses and websites

16 Neighbourhood restaurants and quality
    chains are worth a look. These are not
    inspected.

    🇮🇹 Italian   ⚹ Global
    ♀ Wine Bar   🍺 Pub
    ☕ Café & Tea Shop
    ⑦ Other

17 Parking details

18 Directions are given wherever they have
    been supplied by the establishment.

---

1   The map reference for the atlas section at the back of the
    guide. The map page number is followed by the National
    Grid Reference. To find a location, read the first figure
    horizontally and the second figure vertically within the
    lettered square. For Central London and Greater London,
    there is an 8-page map section starting on page 240.

2   Restaurants are listed in country and county order, then by
    town and then alphabetically within the town. There is an
    index by restaurant at the back of the book and a similar one
    for the Central & Greater London sections on pages 235-239
    with plan references.

19 Number of seats in the restaurant, followed by private dining room (Pr/dining room).

20 Opening and closing times of the restaurant, and the days of the week the restaurant is closed, with seasonal closures. Note that opening times are liable to change without notice. It is always a good idea to telephone in advance to avoid disappointment.

21 🚜 Best Use of Local Produce

22 **NEW** Indicates that an entry is new to the guide this year.

23 🐟 Best Use of Seafood. See explanation on page 8.

24 🍷 Notable wine list

All establishments take major credit cards, except where we have specified otherwise.

Where current details of opening times and prices etc. do not appear in an entry, this is because the establishment has not supplied us with up-to-date information. This is indicated by an italic establishment name. All information is correct at time of print and may change without notice.

Guide dogs for the blind and assist dogs should be accepted in a restaurant, but please check beforehand.

Website Addresses

Website addresses are included where they have been supplied and specified by the respective establishment. Such websites are not under the control of The Automobile Association Developments Limited and as such The Automobile Association Developments Limited has no control over them and will not accept any responsibility or liability in respect of any and all matters whatsoever relating to such websites including access, content, material and functionality. By including the addresses of third-party websites the AA does not intend to solicit business or offer any security to any person in any country, directly or indirectly.

Service Charge

We asked restaurants the following questions about service charge:

• Is service included in the meal price, with no further charge added or expected?

• Is service optional – charge not automatically added to bill?

• Is service charge compulsory, and what percentage?

• Is there a service charge for larger groups, minimum number in group, and what percentage?

Their responses appear under the Price Guide in each entry.

Please note: many establishments automatically add service charge to the bill but tell the customer it is optional.

FACILITIES FOR DISABLED GUESTS

The final stage (Part III) of the Disability Discrimination Act (access to Goods and Services) came into force in October 2004. This means that service providers may have to consider making permanent physical adjustments to their premises. For further information, see the government website www.disability.gov.uk/dda.

The establishments in this guide should all be aware of their responsibilities under the Act. We recommend that you always telephone in advance to ensure that the establishment you have chosen has appropriate facilities.

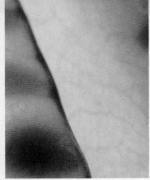

Why not search online?

Visit **www.theAA.com** *and search around 8,000 inspected and rated hotels and B&Bs in Great Britain and Ireland. Then contact the establishment direct by clicking the 'Make a Booking' button...*

...it's as easy as that!

Whatever your preference, we have the place for you. From a farm cottage to a city centre hotel — we have them all.

AA

The Top
Ten Per Cent

Each year all the restaurants in the AA Restaurant Guide are awarded a specially commissioned plate that marks their achievement in gaining one or more AA Rosettes. The plates represent a partnership between the AA and Villeroy & Boch – two quality brands working together to recognise high standards in restaurant cooking.

Restaurants awarded three, four or five AA Rosettes represent the Top Ten Per Cent of the restaurants in this guide. The pages that follow list those establishments that have attained this special status.

Villeroy & Boch in the restaurant

Villeroy & Boch is Europe's best selling tableware brand and, with its renowned tiles and bathrooms division, the company is also the world's leading ceramics manufacturer. At prestigious restaurants and hotels around the globe, Villeroy & Boch is the first choice of discerning chefs and restaurant managers, who choose Villeroy & Boch china, glassware and cutlery for its stunning design and uncompromising quality.

Villeroy & Boch in your home

Villeroy & Boch is no stranger to the domestic dining table either! Since 1748, brides and grooms have chosen the brand as much for the reputation and status of the name as for the quality and diversity of the designs. But the appeal of Villeroy & Boch is not limited to wedding lists. China cutlery and glass bearing the Villeroy & Boch name is simply chosen by people who want the best!

Villeroy & Boch in the future

Villeroy & Boch is leading the way in creative shaped design and is continuing to develop new products for its immensely popular New Wave tableware range.
Launching this year is 'New Wave Premium' and 'New Wave Premium Gold', two elegant bone china tableware collections continuing the New Wave theme. 'New Wave Premium Gold' is an opulent collection with accents of gold adding a decadent look to the table.
Villeroy & Boch also launches three new bold and colourful New Wave Caffè designs 'Fashionista', 'Chocolate Drops' and 'Jungle', ideal for the breakfast table or as gifts.

Villeroy & Boch for every occasion and every home

Formal or relaxed, patterned or plain, cutlery, glass and china from Villeroy & Boch suits every occasion and every budget. It will give lasting pleasure time and again, and is available from quality stores throughout the UK. Call 020 8875 6060 or visit www.villeroy-boch.com for more information.

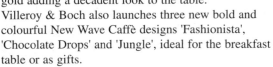

LONDON

@ @ @ @ @
Mandarin Oriental Hyde Park, Foliage
66 Knightsbridge, SW1
020 7235 2000

Pétrus
The Berkeley, Wilton Place,
Knightsbridge, SW1
020 7235 1200

Restaurant Gordon Ramsay
68 Royal Hospital Road, SW3
020 7352 4441

ENGLAND

@ @ @ @ @
BERKSHIRE
The Fat Duck
High Street, BRAY, SL6 2AQ
01628 580333

LINCOLNSHIRE
Winteringham Fields
WINTERINGHAM, DN15 9PF
01724 733096

OXFORDSHIRE
**Le Manoir Aux Quat'
Saisons**
GREAT MILTON, OX44 7PD
01844 278881

LONDON

@ @ @ @
The Capital
Basil Street, SW3
020 7589 5171

Tom Aikens
43 Elystan Street, SW3
020 7584 2003

Aubergine
11 Park Walk, SW10
020 7352 3449

Orrery
55-57 Marylebone High Street
WI
020 7616 8000

Pied à Terre
34 Charlotte Street, W1
020 7636 1178

Sketch
9 Conduit Street, W1
0870 777 4488

Thyme
The Hospital,
24 Endell Street, W1
020 7170 9200

LONDON, GREATER

@ @ @ @
Chapter One
Farnborough Common,
Locksbottom, BROMLEY,
BR6 8NF
01689 85484

ENGLAND

@ @ @ @
BERKSHIRE
Waterside Inn
Ferry Road, BRAY, SL6 2AT
01628 620691

Vineyard at Stockcross
Stockcross, NEWBURY,
RG20 8JU
01635 528770

CUMBRIA
L'Enclume
Cavendish Street, CARTMEL,
LA11 6PZ
01539 536362

DEVON
Gidleigh Park
CHAGFORD, TQ13 8HH
01647 432367

GLOUCESTERSHIRE
**Le Champignon Sauvage
Restaurant**
24 Suffolk Road,
CHELTENHAM, GL50 2AQ
01242 573449

GREATER MANCHESTER
Juniper
21 The Downs,
ALTRINCHAM, WA14 2QD
0161 929 4008

RUTLAND
Hambleton Hall
Hambleton, OAKHAM
LE15 8TH
01572 756991

SHROPSHIRE
Hibiscus
17 Corve Street, LUDLOW,
SY8 1DA
01584 872325

SCOTLAND

@ @ @ @
CITY OF EDINBURGH
Restaurant Martin Wishart
55 The Shore, Leith,
EDINBURGH
EH6 6RA
0131 553 3557

PERTH & KINROSS
Andrew Fairlie at Gleneagles
AUCHTERARDER, PH3 1NF
01764 694267

WALES

@ @ @ @
CEREDIGION
Ynyshir Hall
EGLWYSFACH, Machynlleth
SY20 8TA
01654 781209

REPUBLIC OF IRELAND

@ @ @ @
DUBLIN
**Restaurant Patrick Guilbaud
Merrion Hotel,**
21 Upper Merrion Street
01 6764192

LONDON

@ @ @
E14
Ubon by Nobu
34 Westferry Circus,
Canary Wharf
0207 719 7800

EC1
Club Gascon
57 West Smithfield
020 7796 0600

EC2
Aurora
Great Eastern Hotel,
Liverpool Street
020 7618 7000

SE3
Chapter Two
43-45 Montpelier Vale
Blackheath Village,
020 8333 2666

SW1
Mju at Millennium
Knightsbridge
17 Sloane Street
020 7201 6330

Nahm
The Halkin Hotel, Halkin Street
020 7333 1234

One-O-One
Sheraton Park Tower,
101 Knightsbridge
020 7290 7101

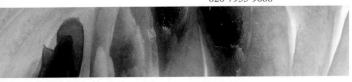

Zafferano
15 Lowndes Street
020 7235 5800

SW3
Rasoi Vineet Bhatia
10 Lincoln Street
020 7225 1881

SW7
The Bentley Kempinski
    Hotel
27-33 Harrington Gardens
020 7244 5555

SW17
Chez Bruce
2 Bellevue Road,
Wandsworth Common
020 8672 0114

W1
Angela Hartnett at The
    Connaught
Carlos Place
020 7592 1222

The Berkeley Square
7 Davies Street, Berkeley
Square
020 7629 6993

L'Escargot -
    The Picasso Room
48 Greek Street
020 7439 7474

Le Gavroche Restaurant
43 Upper Brook Street
020 7408 0881

Gordon Ramsay at
    Claridge's
Brook Street
020 7499 0099

The Greenhouse Restaurant
27a Hay's Mews
020 7499 3331

Hakkasan
No 8 Hanway Place
020 7927 7000

Lindsay House Restaurant
21 Romilly Street
020 7439 0450

Locanda Locatelli
8 Seymour Street
020 7935 9088

Nobu
19 Old Park Lane
020 7447 4747

The Square
6-10 Bruton Street
020 7495 7100

Umu
14-16 Bruton Place
020 7499 8881

W6
The River Café
Thames Wharf, Rainville Road
020 7386 4200

Royal Garden Hotel,
Tenth Floor Restaurant
2-24 Kensington High Street
020 7361 1910

WC2
Savoy Grill
The Savoy Hotel
Strand
020 7592 1600

◉ ◉ ◉
Monsieur Max
133 High Street, Hampton Hill,
HAMPTON, TW12 1NJ
020 8979 5546

The Glasshouse
14 Station Road,
KEW TW9 3PZ
020 8940 6777

McClements Restaurant
2 Whitton Road,
TWICKENHAM TW1 1BJ
020 8744 9610

ENGLAND
◉ ◉ ◉
BERKSHIRE
Fredrick's Hotel Restaurant
    Spa
Shoppenhangers Road,
MAIDENHEAD, SL6 2PZ
01628 581000

L'Ortolan
Church Lane, SHINFIELD
RG2 9BY
0118 9888 500

BRISTOL
Michael Caines at
    The Bristol Marriott Royal
College Green
BS1 5TA
0117 925 5100

BUCKINGHAMSHIRE
Hartwell House Hotel,
    Restaurant & Spa
Oxford Road, AYLESBURY,
HP17 8NL
01296 747444

The Compleat Angler
Marlow Bridge
MARLOW, SL7 1RG
0870 4008100

Waldo's Restaurant
    Cliveden
Cliveden Estate,
TAPLOW, SL6 0JF
01628 668561

CAMBRIDGESHIRE
Midsummer House
    Restaurant
Midsummer Common,
CAMBRIDGE, CB4 1HA
01223 369299

The Pink Geranium
Station Road, MELBOURN,
SG8 6DX
01763 260215

CHESHIRE
The Arkle
The Chester Grosvenor & Spa
Eastgate, CHESTER, CH1 1LT
01244 324024

Co DURHAM
Seaham Hall Hotel
Lord Byron's Walk, SEAHAM,
SR7 7AG
0191 516 1400

CORNWALL & ISLES OF SCILLY
Well House Hotel
St Keyne, LISKEARD
PL14 4RN
01579 342001

The Seafood Restaurant
Riverside, PADSTOW
PL28 8BY
01841 532700

Driftwood
Rosevine, PORTSCATHO
TR2 5EW
01872 580644

St Martin's on the Isle
Lower Town, ST MARTIN'S,
TR25 0QW
01720 422092

Terrace Restaurant at Talland Bay
TALLAND BAY,
PL13 2JB
01503 272667

CUMBRIA
Rampsbeck Country House Hotel
WATERMILLOCK, CA11 0LP
01768 486442

Gilpin Lodge Country House Hotel & Restaurant
Crook Road, WINDERMERE,
LA23 3NE
01539 488818

Holbeck Ghyll Country House Hotel
Holbeck Lane,
WINDERMERE,
LA23 1LU
01539 432375

DERBYSHIRE
Fischer's Baslow Hall
Calver Road, BASLOW,
DE45 1RR
01246 583259

The Old Vicarage
Ridgeway Moor, RIDGEWAY,
S12 3XW
0114 247 5814

DEVON
22 Mill Street
22 Mill Street,
CHAGFORD, TQ13 8AW
01647 432244

The New Angel
2 South Embankment
DARTMOUTH, TQ6 9BH
01803 839425

The Horn of Plenty
GULWORTHY, PL19 8JD
01822 832528

Lewtrenchard Manor
LEWDON, EX20 4PN
01566 783222

DORSET
Summer Lodge Country House Hotel, Restaurant & Spa
EVERSHOT,
DT2 OJR
01935 482030

Stock Hill Country House Hotel
Stock Hill, GILLINGHAM,
SP8 5NR
01747 823626

GLOUCESTERSHIRE
Buckland Manor
BUCKLAND, WR12 7LY
01386 852626

The Greenway
Shurdington, CHELTENHAM,
GL51 4UG
01242 862352

Lords of the Manor
UPPER SLAUGHTER
Cheltenham, GL54 2JD
01451 820243

5 North Street
5 North Street,WINCHCOMBE
GL54 5LH
01242 604566

HAMPSHIRE
Le Poussin @ Whitley Ridge Country House Hotel
Beaulieu Road,
BROCKENHURST
SO42 7QL
01590 622354

36 On The Quay
47 South Street, EMSWORTH,
PO10 7EG
01243 375592

Chewton Glen Hotel
Christchurch Road,
NEW MILTON, BH25 6QS
01425 275341

JSW
1 Heath Road, PETERSFIELD,
GU31 4JE
01730 262030

HEREFORDSHIRE
Castle House
Castle Street, HEREFORD,
HR1 2NW
01432 356321

HERTFORDSHIRE
The Grove
Chandlers Cross,
RICKMANSWORTH,
WD3 4TG
01923 296015

ISLE OF WIGHT
George Hotel
Quay Street, YARMOUTH,
PO41 0PE
01983 760331

KENT
Apicius
23 Stone Street
CRANBROOK TN17 3HF
01580 714666

Read's Restaurant
Macknade Manor, Canterbury
Road, FAVERSHAM
ME13 8XE
01795 535344

Thackeray's
TUNBRIDGE WELLS,
TN1 1EA
01892 511921

LANCASHIRE
Northcote Manor
Northcote Road, LANGHO,
BB6 8BE
01254 240555

The Longridge Restaurant
104-106 Higher Road,
LONGRIDGE, PR3 3SY
01772 784969

LINCOLNSHIRE
Harry's Place
17 High Street, Great Gonerby,
GRANTHAM, NG31 8JS
01476 561780

MERSEYSIDE
Fraiche
11 Rose Mount, Oxton Village,
BIRKENHEAD
CH43 5SG
0151 652 2914

NORFOLK
Morston Hall
Morston, Holt, BLAKENEY,
NR25 7AA
01263 741041

NORTH YORKSHIRE
Devonshire Arms Country
**   House Hotel**
BOLTON ABBEY, BD23 6AJ
01756 710441

Swinton Park
MASHAM, Ripon, HGA 4JN
01765 680900

Yorke Arms
RAMSGILL, HG3 5RL
01423 755243

Middlethorpe Hall Hotel,
**   Restaurant & Spa**
Bishopthorpe Road,
Middlethorpe, YORK,
YO23 2GB
01904 641241

NORTHAMPTONSHIRE
Fawsley Hall
Fawsley, DAVENTRY
NN11 3BA
01327 892000

SHROPSHIRE
Mr Underhills Restaurant
Dinham Weir, LUDLOW
SY8 IEH
01584 874431

Overton Grange
**   Country House**
Old Hereford Road, LUDLOW,
SY8 4AD
01584 873500

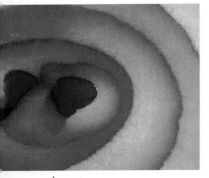

Old Vicarage Hotel and
**   Restaurant**
WORFIELD, WV15 5JZ
01746 716497

SOMERSET
The Royal Crescent Hotel
16 Royal Crescent, BATH,
BA1 2LS
01225 823333

Andrews on the Weir
Porlock Weir, PORLOCK,
TA24 8PB
01643 863300

Charlton House
Charlton Road, SHEPTON
MALLET, BA4 4PR
01749 342008

Castle Hotel
Castle Green, TAUNTON,
TA1 1NF
01823 272671

Little Barwick House Ltd
Barwick Village, YEOVIL,
BA22 9TD
01935 423902

SOUTH YORKSHIRE
Richard Smith at Thyme
32-34 Sandygate Road,
SHEFFIELD, S10 5RY
0114 266 6096

SUFFOLK
Hintlesham Hall Hotel
HINTLESHAM, IP8 3NS
01473 652334

SURREY
Pennyhill Park Hotel &
**   The Spa**
London Road, BAGSHOT,
GU19 5EU
01276 471774

Drake's
The Clock House, High Street,
RIPLEY, GU23 6AQ
01483 224777

WARWICKSHIRE
Mallory Court Hotel
Harbury Lane, Bishop's
Tachbrook, ROYAL
LEAMINGTON SPA,
CV33 9QB
01926 330214

WEST MIDLANDS
Paris Restaurant Patrick
**   McDonald**
109-111 Wharfside Street
Mailbox, BIRMINGHAM
B1 IRF
0121 632 1488

Simpsons
20 Highfield Road, Edgbaston,
BIRMINGHAM B15 3DN
0121 454 3434

WEST SUSSEX
Ockenden Manor
Ockenden Lane, CUCKFIELD,
RH17 5LD
01444 416111

Gravetye Manor Hotel
EAST GRINSTEAD, RH19 4LJ
01342 810567

The Camellia Restaurant at
**   South Lodge Hotel**
Brighton Road,
LOWER BEEDING, RH13 6PS
01403 891711

WEST YORKSHIRE
Box Tree
35-37 Church Street
ILKLEY LS29 9DR
01943 608484

Anthony's Restaurant
19 Boat Lane
LEEDS, LS1 5DA
0113 245 5922

WILTSHIRE
Lucknam Park
COLERNE, SN14 8AZ
01225 742777

The Harrow at Little
**   Bedwyn**
LITTLE BEDWYN, SN8 3JP
01672 870871

Whatley Manor
Easton Grey, MALMESBURY
SN16 0RB
01666 822888

WORCESTERSHIRE
The Lygon Arms
High Street, BROADWAY,
WR12 7DU
01386 852255

JERSEY

◉ ◉ ◉
Atlantic Hotel
Le Mont de la Pulente
St Brelade JE3 8HE
01534 744101

Bohemia
The Club Hotel & Spa
Green Street
ST HELIER, JE2 4UH
01534 880588

Longueville Manor Hotel
ST SAVIOUR, JE2 7WF
01534 725501

Carlton House Hotel
Dolycoed Road, LLANWRTYD
WELLS, LD5 4RA
01591 610248

SCOTLAND

◎ ◎ ◎
ABERDEENSHIRE
Darroch Learg Hotel
Braemar Road, BALLATER,
AB35 5UX
013397 55443

ANGUS
Castleton House Hotel
Castleton of Eassie, GLAMIS,
DD8 1SJ
01307 840340

ARGYLL & BUTE
Isle of Eriska
ERISKA, PA37 1SD
01631 720371

Airds Hotel
PORT APPIN, PA38 4DF
01631 730236

DUMFRIES & GALLOWAY
Knockinaam Lodge
PORTPATRICK, DG9 9AD
01776 810471

EDINBURGH
Norton House Hotel
Ingliston, EDINBURGH,
EH28 8LX
0131 333 1275

FIFE
Cellar Restaurant
24 East Green, ANSTRUTHER
KY10 3AA
01333 310378

The Peat Inn
PEAT INN, KY15 5LH
01334 840206

The Road Hole Grill
The Old Course Hotel,
ST ANDREWS, KY16 9SP
01334 474371

The Seafood Restaurant
The Scores
ST ANDREWS KY16 9AS
01334 479475

HIGHLAND
The Three Chimneys
COLBOST, IV55 8ZT
01470 511258

Inverlochy Castle Hotel
Torlundy, FORT WILLIAM,
PH33 6SN
01397 702177

The Cross
Tweed Mill Brae,
Ardbroilach Road
KINGUSSIE, PH21 ILB
01540 661166

The Boath House
Auldearn, NAIRN, IV12 5TE
01667 454896

PERTH & KINROSS
Kinnaird
Kinnaird Estate, DUNKELD,
PH8 0LB
01796 482440

SOUTH AYRSHIRE
Glenapp Castle
BALLANTRAE, KA26 0NZ
01465 831212

Lochgreen House
Monktonhill Road, Southwood
TROON, KA10 7EN
01292 313343

STIRLING
Roman Camp Hotel
CALLANDER, FK17 8BG
01877 330003

**WEST
DUNBARTONSHIRE**
De Vere Cameron House
BALLOCH, G83 8QZ
01389 755565

WALES

◎ ◎ ◎
CONWY
Tan-y-Foel Country House
Capel Garmon,
BETWS-Y-COED, LL26 0RE
01690 710507

**The Old Rectory
    Country House**
Llanrwst Road, Llansanffraid
Glan Conwy, CONWY,
LL28 5LF
01492 580611

Bodysgallen Hall
LLANDUDNO, LL30 1RS
01492 584466

NORTHERN IRELAND

◎ ◎ ◎
Co BELFAST
Restaurant Michael Deane
34-40 Howard Street, BELFAST,
BT1 6PF
028 9033 1134

Co DOWN
Shanks
The Blackwood, Crawfordsburn
Road, BANGOR, BT19 1GB
028 9185 3313

REPUBLIC OF IRELAND

◎ ◎ ◎
Co CORK
Longueville House Hotel
MALLOW
022 47156/47306

Sheen Falls Lodge
KENMARE
064 41600

Co KILDARE
The K Club
STRAFFAN
01 6017200

Co WEXFORD
Marlfield House Hotel
GOREY
055 21124

England

Restaurant of the Year for England
The New Angel, Dartmouth

(see p119)

BEDFORDSHIRE

BEDFORD MAP 12 TL04

Knife & Cleaver

British

Satisfying dining in well-kept conservatory

☎ 01234 740387 The Grove, Houghton Conquest MK45 3LA

MENU GUIDE Potted Woburn ham, leek & mustard Pithiviers • Whole baked turbot • Mandarin crème brûlée

WINE GUIDE ♀ Chablis Château Maligny Chardonnay £19.50 • ♀ Santa Helena Cabernet Sauvignon £15 • 36 bottles over £20, 33 bottles under £20 • 22 by the glass (£2-£4.95)

PRICE GUIDE Fixed L £12.95 • Fixed D £22 • starter £4.25-£7.95 • main £10.95-£23.50 • dessert £4.50 • coffee £1.85 • min/water £3 • Service optional • Group min 10 service 10%

PLACE: Situated in the village centre, this 17th-century inn restaurant has historic links to John Bunyan and acquired its wood panelling from old Houghton Hall; the model for House Beautiful in *The Pilgrim's Progress*. The light and airy dining room is an attractive Victorian-style conservatory overflowing with plants. **FOOD:** Uncomplicated, modern British dishes prepared from high quality local ingredients. Typically you could begin with marinated herring and potato salad and follow with black pudding in puff pastry with a caramelised apple and sage sauce. **OUR TIP:** A good choice of fresh fish and seafood **Chef:** Chris Bishopp **Owners:** Mrs P & Mr D Loom **Times:** 12-2.30/7-9.30, Closed 26-30 Dec, BHs-dinner only, closed L Sat, closed D Sun **Notes:** Sun lunch 3 courses £15.95, Vegetarian available, Smart Casual **Seats:** 65, Pr/dining room 12 **Smoking:** N/Sm in restaurant, Air con **Children:** Menu, Portions **Rooms:** 9 (9 en suite) ♦♦♦♦ **Directions:** Just off A6, 5m S of Bedford. Follow brown tourist signs from A6. Opposite church in village. M1 junct 12-13 **Parking:** 35 **e-mail:** info@knifeandcleaver.com **web:** www.knifeandcleaver.com

Woodlands Manor Hotel

British, European

Fine dining in secluded Victorian manor house

☎ 01234 363281 Green Ln, Clapham MK41 6EP

MENU GUIDE Puy lentil & foie gras soup • Magret of duck, creamed Savoy cabbage • Caramel bavarois

WINE GUIDE ♀ Macon Villages Caves de Lugny £16.75 • ♀ Fleurie Château de la Verne £22.75 • 16 bottles over £20, 26 bottles under £20 • 8 by the glass (£3.50-£5.50)

PRICE GUIDE Fixed L £10 • Fixed D £30-£40 • starter £4.50-£5.50 • main £13.95-£26.50 • dessert £5.95-£7.95 • coffee £2.95 • min/water £3.50 • Service optional

Woodlands Manor Hotel

PLACE: Traditional in style, this country-house hotel offers a warm welcome. With its high ceilings and large bay windows, the restaurant is classic in design and the panelled drawing room has large, comfortable sofas for pre-dinner drinks. Classical music and flower arrangements enhance the formal atmosphere. **FOOD:** Familiar English dishes are presented with classical French panache: a roast chicken terrine, as a starter, may be served with a bee pollen salad, and followed by a roast fillet of sea bass with an apricot and white bean purée and vanilla jus. **OUR TIP:** Enjoy a stroll around the well-tended grounds **Chef:** Neil Falzon **Owners:** Signature Hotels **Times:** 12.30-2/7.30-9.30, closed L Sat **Notes:** Civ Wed 90 **Seats:** 65, Pr/dining room 40 **Smoking:** N/Sm in restaurant **Children:** Menu **Rooms:** 33 (33 en suite) ★★★ **Directions:** From A6 to Clapham turn right into Green Lane **Parking:** 60 **e-mail:** reception@woodlandsmanorhotel.com **web:** www.signaturegroup.co.uk

Villa Rosa Ram Yard MK40 1AL ☎ 01234 269259 Bustling, family-run Italian.

FLITWICK MAP 11 TL03

Menzies Flitwick Manor

British, European

Fine dining in classic country house

☎ 01525 712242 Church Rd MK45 1AE

MENU GUIDE Tuna ceviche with pan-fried scallops • Loin of Woburn venison, oxtail faggot • Valrhona pur-caraibe chocolate fondant

WINE GUIDE ♀ J Moreau et Fils Chablis £36 • ♀ La Campagne Merlot £19 • 60 bottles over £20, 4 bottles under £20 • 15 by the glass (£4-£7)

PRICE GUIDE Fixed L £25 • Fixed D £45 • min/water £3 • Service optional

PLACE: A grand 17th-century Georgian manor house retaining many of its original features and furnished throughout with

continued

England

continued

England

FLITWICK *continued* MAP 11 TL03

antiques and fine art. The dining room, with lovely views across the lawns and terraces, has a wonderfully romantic candle-lit country house atmosphere. Professional waiting staff expertly deliver dishes based in modern British style with European twists.
FOOD: The finest local suppliers provide the fresh produce on the carte which, though not extensive, is carefully thought out to present a good choice of ingredients and flavours. The global wine list offers plenty of affordable options.
OUR TIP: Perfect for a meal à deux
Chef: Richard Walker **Owners:** Menzies Hotels plc **Times:** 12-2.30/7-9.30 **Notes:** Tasting menu 6 courses £60, coffee incl, Vegetarian available, Dress Restrictions, Jacket preferred, no jeans, Civ Wed 50 **Seats:** 50, Pr/dining room 16 **Smoking:** N/Sm in restaurant **Children:** Min 7 yrs **Rooms:** 17 (17 en suite) ★★★ **Directions:** M1 junct 12, follow Flitwick after 1m turn left into Church Rd. Manor 200 yds on left. **Parking:** 30
e-mail: Flitwick@menzies-hotels.co.uk **web:** www.menzies-hotels.co.uk

MILTON ERNEST MAP 11 TL05
⬤⬤ The Strawberry Tree
British, Mediterranean
Quintessentially English cottage restaurant
☎ 01234 823633 3 Radwell Rd MK44 1RY
MENU GUIDE Mackerel, haricot beans, orange & beetroot • Loin of venison, red wine & bitter chocolate sauce • Caramelised apple tart
WINE GUIDE ⚲ A Cailbourdin Pouilly Fumé £28.90 • ⚲ Château Fanin Cabernet Sauvignon Merlot £18.80 • 21 bottles over £20, 9 bottles under £20 • 3 by the glass (£4.20)
PRICE GUIDE Fixed D £41.50 • starter £5-£8 • main £13-£20 • dessert £7.50 • coffee £3.50 • min/water £2.95 • Service optional • Group min 6 service 12.5%
PLACE: Initially a successful tea room, this 17th-century thatched cottage has been developed into a restaurant since the owners' sons have joined the business. There's a cool, relaxed feel to the interior - paintings with a food theme set against white walls, dark-stained beams, inglenook fireplaces and flagstone floors. A small private dining room is also available.
FOOD: A short, clear carte menu offers unfussy, British food with a hint of the continent. Suppliers are listed in the menu and obvious pride is taken in sourcing fine ingredients, locally where possible.
OUR TIP: Home-made jams, marmalades and chutneys on sale
Chef: Jason & Andrew Bona **Owners:** John & Wendy Bona **Times:** 12-1.45/7-9, Closed 2 wks Jan & Sep, Sun-Tue, closed L Sat
Notes: Vegetarian available **Seats:** 22, Pr/dining room 8 **Smoking:** N/Sm in restaurant **Children:** Portions **Directions:** M1 junct 13. 4m N of Bedford on A6. **Parking:** 8
e-mail: strawberrytree_restaurant@yahoo.co.uk

WOBURN MAP 11 SP93
⬤ The Inn at Woburn
British, Mediterranean
Modern dining in historic village inn
☎ 01525 292292 290441 George St MK17 9PX
MENU GUIDE Duck wonton, ginger & plum sauce • Sea bass & red pepper butter, saffron risotto, wilted spinach • Apple & banana toffee crumble, clotted cream
WINE GUIDE ⚲ San Elias Chardonnay 2003 £13 • ⚲ Montana Wine Estate Timara Cabernet Merlot 2002 £16.75 • 22 bottles over £20, 23 bottles under £20 • 17 by the glass (£2.35-£4.45)
PRICE GUIDE Fixed L £10.50 • starter £3.75-£6.75 • main £9.95-£14.75 • dessert £3.95-£6.75 • coffee £1.50 • min/water £2.50 • Service optional

The Inn at Woburn

PLACE: Originally built in 1724 to serve the coaches of the Royal Mail, extensive refurbishment has brought this superb, upmarket inn bang up to date. Olivier's (named after the head chef) is the hotel's elegant, relaxed, bistro-style restaurant, decked out in subtle shades and contemporary woods.
FOOD: The kitchen takes an appropriately modern British line, with an appealing, crowd-pleasing repertoire, which also offers a menu of lighter meals adapted from main-course dishes for smaller appetites.
OUR TIP: Afternoon teas served from 3pm to 5pm; and there's plenty of parking
Chef: Olivier Bertho **Owners:** Bedford Estates **Times:** 12-2.30/6-10.15 **Notes:** Vegetarian available **Seats:** 40, Pr/dining room 90 **Smoking:** N/Sm in restaurant, Air con **Children:** Menu, Portions **Rooms:** 57 (57 en suite) ★★★ **Directions:** 5mins from junct 13 of M1. Follow signs to Woburn. Inn is in middle of town at crossroads - car parking to rear via Parm St **Parking:** 80
e-mail: enquiries@theinnatwoburn.com **web:** www.theinnatwoburn.com

⬤⬤ Paris House Restaurant
French
Classic French food in an English park setting
☎ 01525 290692 Woburn Park MK17 9QP
MENU GUIDE Confit of crispy duck • Venison medallions, port & cranberry sauce • Hot raspberry soufflé
WINE GUIDE ⚲ Jean et Michel Nault Sancerre Sauvignon £29 • ⚲ De la Bouroniere Beaujolous Fleurie £29.50 • 40 bottles over £20, 12 bottles under £20 • 6 by the glass (£4.50-£9)
PRICE GUIDE Fixed L £22-£35 • Fixed D £55 • min/water £3.75 • Service optional
PLACE: Built in 1878 for the Paris Exhibition, and used as a hospital in World War I, Paris House was dismantled and brought to England by the 9th Duke of Bedford and reassembled on the Woburn Estate. It is a black and white timbered construction, Tudor in style, approached via tree-lined avenues and set among fields of deer.

continued

Paris House Restaurant

FOOD: Cooking, under the personal direction of Peter Chandler (apprenticed to the Roux Brothers at Le Gavroche in the 1970s), is classical French with some modern twists, offered from a choice of fixed-price menus.

OUR TIP: Soufflés are a house speciality

Chef: Peter Chandler **Owners:** Mr P Chandler **Times:** 12-2/7-9.45, Closed Feb, Mon, closed D Sun **Notes:** ALC £55 (all incl), Fixed D 5 courses £60, Vegetarian available **Seats:** 48, Pr/dining room 16 **Smoking:** N/Sm in restaurant **Children:** Menu, Portions **Directions:** M1 junct 13. From Woburn take A4012 Hockliffe, 1.75m out of Woburn village on left **Parking:** 24 **e-mail:** gailbaker@parishouse.co.uk **web:** www.parishouse.co.uk

BERKSHIRE

ASCOT MAP 06 SU96

The Berystede
British, International NEW

Smart dining room and accurate seasonal cooking

☎ 01344 623311 Bagshot Rd, Sunninghill SL5 9JH

MENU GUIDE Ham hock terrine • Seared sea bass, champagne butter sauce • Pear & cinnamon Tatin

WINE GUIDE ♀ Katherine Hills Colombard Chardonnay £17.50 • ♀ Robert Skalli Merlot £18.95 • 40 bottles over £20, 40 bottles under £20 • 12 by the glass (£4-£5.75)

PRICE GUIDE Food prices not confirmed for 2006. Please telephone for details

PLACE: A traditional hotel dining room with a relaxed feel, and gorgeous views over the manicured gardens. The Hyperion Restaurant is named after a famous racehorse, and is often frequented by racegoers.

FOOD: The set menu offers ample choice along modern lines, with the likes of tian of crab and prawns, and balsamic glazed lamb chump delivering clean flavours. Traditional lambs' liver and

continued

bacon also makes an appearance.

OUR TIP: Stay overnight on a hotel special deal

Chef: Gordon Inglis **Owners:** Macdonalds Hotels **Times:** 12.30-2/7-9.45, closed L Sat **Notes:** Vegetarian available, Smart Dress, Civ Wed 340 **Seats:** 120, Pr/dining room 150 **Smoking:** N/Sm in restaurant, Air con **Children:** Menu, Portions **Rooms:** 90 (90 en suite) ★★★★ **Directions:** Join A30 from M3 junct 3, A322 then left onto B3020 to Ascot or M25 - junct 13, follow signs for Bagshot. At Sunningdale turn right onto A330 **Parking:** 120 **e-mail:** mathew.turvey@macdonalds.co.uk **web:** www.berystede.com

BRACKNELL MAP 05 SU86

Coppid Beech
British, Pacific Rim

Enjoyable dining in Alpine-style hotel

☎ 01344 303333 John Nike Way RG12 8TF

MENU GUIDE Marinated mackerel, soused vegetables • Seared rump of lamb, roast root vegetables, rosemary jus • Bread & butter pudding

WINE GUIDE ♀ Cabernet Sauvignon • 76 bottles over £20, 12 bottles under £20 • 16 by the glass (£3.75-£9.50)

PRICE GUIDE Fixed L £17.95 • Fixed D £24.95 • starter £4.95-£9.75 • main £11.95-£22.75 • dessert £6.95-£7.95 • min/water £3.50 • Service optional

PLACE: The building looks like a huge ski chalet from the outside, and the alpine theme extends to include a ski slope, ice rink, 'Apres' nightclub and the hotel's very own Bier Keller. Rowans Restaurant takes a slightly different tack, providing a fresh modern setting with crystal chandeliers and partitioning created from natural farmed timbers.

FOOD: Best of British food with a hint of Pacific Rim and good vegetarian choices. Accurate cooking showing ingredients to their best advantage. Traditional English puddings feature in the hot dessert of the day slot, and there's a good selection of cheeses from the trolley.

OUR TIP: Have a ski or a skate before lunch

Chef: Neil Thrift, Paul Zolik **Owners:** Nike Group Hotels Ltd **Times:** 12-2.15/7-10 **Notes:** coffee included, Vegetarian available, Smart Dress, Civ Wed 150 **Seats:** 120, Pr/dining room 20 **Smoking:** N/Sm in restaurant, Air con **Children:** Menu, Portions **Rooms:** 205 (205 en suite) ★★★★ **Directions:** From M4 junct 10 follow A329(M) (Bracknell/Wokingham) to 1st exit. At rdbt take 1st exit to Binfield (B3408); hotel 200yds on right **Parking:** 350 **e-mail:** welcome@coppid-beech-hotel.co.uk **web:** www.coppidbeech.com

Sultan Balti House 7 Great Hollands Square, Great Hollands RG12 8UX ☎ 01344 303330 Step from a shopping arcade into a verdant Indian orange grove. Wide menu specialises in Balti, and dishes exhibit freshness and quality.

The Best Use of Seafood sponsored by Seafish In conjunction with Seafish, the Sea Fish Industry Authority, we have sought out restaurants that make the most of seafood on their menus. In addition to the four country award winners (see page 9), look out for the seafish symbol throughout the book; this denotes restaurants serving a good range of fish and shellfish dishes, where the accent is firmly on freshness.

BRAY MAP 06 SU97

The Fat Duck

Modern British *The epitome of contemporary dining experiences*
☎ 01628 580333 High St SL6 2AQ
web: www.fatduck.co.uk

PLACE: Who would have thought the tiny, well-groomed, Thames-side village of Bray would be home to two of Britain's most prestigious restaurants; the French classicalism of the Roux's Waterside (see entry) and the cutting-edge gastronomy of Heston Blumenthal's Fat Duck. But there's a new kid on the block here too. With Blumenthal taking over the Hinds Head Hotel (see entry) and purveying fine English pub food, Bray now has a trio of cuisine choices. But it's the Fat Duck that proves the real centre of epicurean pilgrimage and adventure, the unlikely international destination of the molecular gastronomy movement. Two small cottages on the main village road seems an unassuming location, but they conceal a restaurant that exudes quality and modern, understated elegance. Oak beams and low ceilings are complemented by contemporary art, glass partitions and iron sculpture that add contrast and chic to the Tudor building. White-clothed tables, comfortable chairs; and faultless service (a real part of the Fat Duck experience) is professional, but unstuffy and knowledgeable.

FOOD: Blumenthal is a true culinary pioneer and the leading exponent of the scientific approach to cuisine, which sees him work with the scientific community. He researches aspects like the molecular compounds of ingredients to enable greater understanding of the way we register taste and flavour and how the mind records taste through memory. This drive to improve flavour and texture and maximise sensory effect has evolved into a unique dining-out art form. And, whilst there's nothing bizarre about the ingredients, it is the combinations of flavours that sometimes raise eyebrows, take snail porridge with jabugo ham, or dessert of smoked bacon and egg ice cream with pain perdu and tea jelly, for instance, and he also cleverly fools visual expectation. But it's the exciting combinations that are a hallmark of this stunning experience, while clarity of flavour, balance, seasonality, seasoning and technical execution all excel. So sit back and be wowed by the gastronomic journey.

MENU GUIDE Cauliflower risotto, cauliflower carpaccio, chocolate jelly • Pot roast best end pork, gratin of truffled macaroni • Chocolate délice, chocolate sorbet, cumin caramel

WINE GUIDE ♀ P Thomas Sancerre Terres Blanches £30 • ♀ C Jogue Chinon La Cure Cabernet Franc £30.50 • 850 bottles over £20 • 28 by the glass (£7-£17)

PRICE GUIDE Fixed L £37.50 • Fixed D £67.50 • coffee £4.75 • min/water £4.50 • Service added but optional 12.5%

OUR TIP: Be brave and adventurous in your choice

Chef: Heston Blumenthal **Owners:** Fat Duck Ltd **Times:** 12-1.45/7-9.45, Closed 2 wks at Xmas, Mon, closed D Sun
Notes: Tasting menu £97.50, Vegetarian available **Seats:** 46
Smoking: N/Sm in restaurant, Air con **Children:** Portions
Directions: M4 junct 8/9 (Maidenhead) take A308 towards Windsor, turn left into Bray. Restaurant in centre of village on right
Parking: Two village car parks

◉◉ Hinds Head Hotel

Traditional British **NEW**

Welcoming pub meets top-notch traditional British cooking

☎ 01628 626151 High St SL6 2AB

MENU GUIDE Soused herrings, beetroot & horseradish • Old Spot pork chop, pease pudding • Sherry trifle

WINE GUIDE ⚲ Kanu Stellenbosch Chenin Blanc £17.95 • ❢ Falesco Vitiano Cabernet Merlot £20.75 • 49 bottles over £20, 13 bottles under £20 • 12 by the glass (£4.65-£10.50)

PRICE GUIDE Starter £4.95-£9 • main £9.50-£16.50 • dessert £4.50-£5 • coffee £1.50 • min/water £3 • Service added but optional 12.5%

PLACE: Cheek by jowl with its big brother, The Fat Duck (see entry), the Hinds Head probes the delights of British tavern food. The Tudor village inn boasts a celebrated past, with former patrons that include the current Royal Family, alongside its celebrated new owner, Heston Blumenthal. Oak panelling and beams, leather chairs and real fires provide a warm, intimate and informal atmosphere.

FOOD: Traditional pub dishes, served without fuss or unnecessary garnish and clear, defined flavours is the product of the accomplished kitchen. Expect favourites like Lancashire hotpot or treacle tart and look out for the introduction of the likes of quaking pudding.

OUR TIP: Don't miss the treacle tart

Chef: Heston Blumenthal **Owners:** The Hindhead Ltd **Times:** 12-2.30/6.30-9.30, Closed 25-26 Dec, closed D Sun **Seats:** 90, Pr/dining room 22 **Smoking:** No pipes, No cigars, Air con **Children:** Portions **Parking:** Car park across road

◉ Monkey Island Hotel

French

Modern cooking with river views

☎ 01628 623400 Old Mill Ln SL6 2EE

MENU GUIDE Chicken liver pâté, honey pickled vegetables • Beef fillet, mushroom crust beetroot dauphinois, vichy glazed carrots • White chocolate cheesecake, Bailey's Anglaise

WINE GUIDE ⚲ Domaine Perrin Viognier Marsanne £24.50 • ❢ Les Jalets Crozes Hermitage £30 • 87 bottles over £20, 1 bottle under £20 • 8 by the glass (£4.40-£7.50)

PRICE GUIDE Fixed L £25 • Fixed D £30 • starter £6.25-£7.50 • main £19.50-£28.50 • coffee £3.50 • min/water £3.50 • Service added but optional 10%

PLACE: This hotel is really on its own private island. Reached by footbridge or boat, the willow-lined grounds provide a haven for wildlife. The smart Pavilion Restaurant (in a separate building

from the hotel) has plenty of glass ensuring excellent Thames-side views.

FOOD: Dishes reflect modern, classical and cosmopolitan influences on appealing, monthly changing fixed-price menus and seasonal carte.

OUR TIP: Exclusive tables on the terrace; and make time for a walk around the island

Chef: James Larkins **Owners:** Metropolitan Hotels International **Times:** 12.30-2.30/7-10 **Notes:** Vegetarian available, Dress Restrictions, Smart casual, no trainers, Civ Wed 120 **Seats:** 100, Pr/dining room 120 **Smoking:** N/Sm in restaurant **Children:** Menu, Portions **Rooms:** 26 (26 en suite) ★★★★ **Directions:** M4 junct 8/9, A308 towards Windsor, before flyover turn left towards Bray Village, then follow signs. **Parking:** 100 **e-mail:** sales@monkeyisland.co.uk **web:** www.monkeyisland.co.uk

◉◉ The Riverside Brasserie

French

Brasserie dining beside Thames-side marina

☎ 01628 780553 Bray Marina SL6 2EB

MENU GUIDE Chicken liver & foie gras parfait • Pork belly, chorizo & black pudding • Lavender pannacotta

WINE GUIDE 39 bottles over £20, 6 bottles under £20 • 10 by the glass (£4.50-£8)

PRICE GUIDE Starter £5.50-£7.70 • main £13.95-£14.95 • dessert £5.50 • coffee £2.50 • min/water £3.50 • Service added but optional 12.5%

PLACE: Hidden in the marina complex in a small café-like building that also houses the boatyard facilities, the brasserie comes into its own in the summer, with a decked area beside the Thames. Inside has a contemporary, no-frills, minimalist edge, with wooden floors and veneered walls, open kitchen, glass doors opening up to the terrace and a relaxed atmosphere.

FOOD: The straightforward yet accomplished brasserie fare focuses on quality ingredients and clean, light presentation. Expect classics alongside dishes with a Mediterranean twist perhaps, or signatures like rib-eye with triple-cooked chips and bone marrow sauce.

OUR TIP: Go in the summer and book an outside table on the terrace

Chef: Garrey Dylan Dawson **Owners:** Garrey Dylan Dawson, Lee Dixon, Alfie Hitchcock **Times:** 12-3/6.30-10, Closed Xmas & New Year, Mon (Oct-Mar), closed D Sun (Winter) **Notes:** Vegetarian available **Seats:** 60 **Smoking:** No pipes, No cigars **Children:** Menu, Portions **Directions:** Off A308, signed Bray Marina. **e-mail:** grrydws@aol.com **web:** www.riversidebrasserie.co.uk

continued

England

BRAY MAP 06 SU97

Waterside Inn

French *A gastronomic Thames-side legend delivering classic French cuisine*

☎ 01628 620691 **Ferry Rd SL6 2AT**

e-mail: reservations@waterside-inn.co.uk

web: www.waterside-inn.co.uk

PLACE: What else could it be called? Nestling right beside the Thames at the end of a small lane in the pretty village of Bray, the endearing Waterside and the Roux family - a name synonymous with fine food - have been offering the perfect combination of classical French cuisine and quintessential English setting here for more than 30 years. While most tables have a river view, the tiered terrace outside is a magical location for aperitifs and canapés on a warm summer's day, sat beneath a weeping willow and watching Thames life pass by. Those with a boat could arrive at the smart, whitewashed converted inn by water and tie up at the restaurant's own moorings, while car drivers are equally pampered with valet parking. On winter days, drinks are taken in small, comfortable lounge areas to build anticipation and, as one might expect from a haven of French excellence, the restaurant decor, like the cuisine, is classical too; white linen, fine silverware and formal service from an attentive, professional team, but with a balance of friendliness and courtesy that puts everyone at ease.

FOOD: After an apprenticeship in France as a pâtissier and many years behind the stove, Alain Roux joined his father Michel here in 1992, and since 2001 has assumed the mantle of chef-patron. The food still remains firmly entrenched in the traditional taste of the classics, so expect impeccable ingredients, plentiful luxury items, clear flavours and highly accomplished technique rather than high fashion. The approach is via a repertoire of fixed-price Menu Gastronomique and tasting Menu Exceptionnel, plus a lengthy and appealing carte, which might deliver warm oysters with truffles, caviar and a champagne sauce to open, perhaps grilled rabbit fillets served on a celeriac fondant with Armagnac sauce and glazed chestnuts to follow, and a finale of warm golden plum soufflé.

MENU GUIDE Traditional pike quenelle, langoustine tails • Cocotte of oxtail & beef cheek braised in Beaujolais wine, button onions, mushrooms & smoked bacon • Pistachio crème brûlée, vanilla ice cream

WINE GUIDE ♀ Etienne Defaix Chablis £37 • ♀ Geraud Gauby La Soula Syrah/Cabernet Sauvignon £48 • 790 bottles over £20 • 4 by the glass (£7-£12)

PRICE GUIDE Fixed L £40-£56 • starter £22-£38.70 • main £36-£49 • dessert £19-£30 • coffee £8.50 • Service added but optional 12.5%

OUR TIP: Take advantage of the delightful riverside terrace

Chef: Michel Roux, Alain Roux **Owners:** Michel Roux & Alain Roux **Times:** 12-2/7-10, Closed 26 Dec for 5 wks, Mon, closed L Tue, D Tue ex Jun-Aug **Notes:** Set price D 5 courses £87.50, Fixed L Sun only, Vegetarian available, No jeans/trainers, Civ Wed 70 **Seats:** 75, Pr/dining room 8 **Smoking:** No pipes, No cigars **Children:** Min 12 yrs, Menu **Directions:** M4 junct 8/9, A308(Windsor) then B3028 to Bray. Restaurant clearly signed **Parking:** 20

CHIEVELEY MAP 05 SU47

The Crab at Chieveley
Fish, Modern

Excellent seafood in stunning hilltop location

☎ 01635 247550 Wantage Rd RG20 8UE

MENU GUIDE Hot & sour shellfish broth, Asian greens, crab dumplings • Skate wing, beurre noisette, caper mash • Lemon posset, lime granite

WINE GUIDE 130 bottles over £20, 15 bottles under £20 • 16 by the glass (£3.75-£6.50)

PRICE GUIDE Fixed L £15 • starter £6.50-£13.50 • main £10.50-£37.50 • dessert £6 • coffee £3 • min/water £3 • Service optional

PLACE: This stylish country seafood restaurant is divided into three areas - a cosy bar, modern brasserie and a main dining room. Sitting on the terrace for pre-dinner drinks on a summer evening is a delight. If staying over, you'll find the accommodation is beautifully designed with each bedroom themed with an exotic location in mind.

FOOD: Although situated in the heart of landlocked Berkshire, seafood is paramount with deliveries from Brixham and Newlyn markets. The flavours shine through in contemporary dishes, with exciting global influences appearing throughout the menu. Meat eaters aren't forgotten, but fish lovers are totally spoilt for choice.

OUR TIP: Booking ahead is essential especially for Fridays and weekends

Chef: David Moss **Owners:** David and Jackie Barnard **Times:** 12-11 **Notes:** Vegetarian available, Civ Wed 100 **Seats:** 100, Pr/dining room 20 **Smoking:** N/Sm in restaurant **Children:** Menu, Portions **Rooms:** 10 (10 en suite) 🏡 **Directions:** M4 junct 13 to Chieveley, School Rd to B4494, turn right to Wantage **Parking:** 80 **e-mail:** info@crabatchieveley.com **web:** www.crabatchieveley.com

COOKHAM MAP 06 SU88

Malik's
Indian, Bangladesh

Real Indian cuisine in very English surroundings

☎ 01628 520085 High St SL6 9SF

MENU GUIDE Alkrashma (Sliced egg & spicy minced lamb) • Methi saag gosth (Lamb with spinach, fenugreek & herbs) • Kulfi (Pistachio or Indian ice cream)

WINE GUIDE 🍷 Jacobs Creek Chardonnay £14 • 🍷 Jacobs Creek Shiraz £14 • 25 bottles over £20, 7 bottles under £20 2 by the glass (£3.95)

PRICE GUIDE Fixed D £18.95 • starter £3.95-£7.95 • main £7.25-£15.95 • dessert £3.50-£6.95 • coffee £2.50 • min/water £3.95 • Service optional

PLACE: This ivy clad former coaching inn, at the heart of Stanley Spencer's Cookham on the River Thames, is an unlikely setting

continued

Malik's

for an Indian restaurant. The dining area is cosy and intimate and serves authentic Indian cuisine. The staff are both friendly and knowledgeable and happy to recommend dishes to suit your palate.

FOOD: The large choice menu offers traditional favourites such as chicken tikka masala plus many more specialities from the Bengali chef including comprehensive seafood and vegetarian sections. Caters for every taste from very mild through to fiery hot, all prepared and cooked with great care and a lightness of touch.

OUR TIP: Reservations are strongly recommended as popular with locals

Chef: Malik Ahmed, Shapon Miah **Owners:** Malik Ahmed **Times:** 12-2.30/6-11.00, Closed 25-26 Dec, closed L Eid festival **Notes:** Sunday lunch buffet £9.95, Vegetarian available, Smart **Seats:** 70, Pr/dining room 30 **Smoking:** N/Sm area, No pipes, No cigars **Children:** Portions **Directions:** M4 junct 7, take A4 towards Maidenhead, 2 m **Parking:** 26 **web:** www.maliks.co.uk

COOKHAM DEAN MAP 05 SU88

The Inn on The Green
British, French

Stylish inn dedicated to serious cooking

☎ 01628 482638 The Old Cricket Common SL6 9NZ

MENU GUIDE Venison carpaccio • Sautéed calves' liver, pancetta bacon • Chocolate & banana fondant

PRICE GUIDE Food prices not confirmed for 2006. Please telephone for details

PLACE: A traditional country inn with a glamorous restaurant and stylish bedrooms for those who don't want to drive home. The three inter-connecting rooms include a spacious conservatory and a burgundy-backed area with rustic wooden panelling and open brickwork.

FOOD: The ambitious kitchen handles fresh seasonal produce with imagination, introducing luxury foods (lobster, foie gras) onto the carte and daily menus; alongside the international flavours of sea scallop and miso broth, and roast cod with clam chowder and Alsace bacon.

OUR TIP: Good selection of dessert wines and ports

Times: 12-2.30/7-10, Mon, closed D Sun **Rooms:** 9 (9 en suite) 🏡 **e-mail:** reception@theinnonthegreen.com **web:** www.theinnonthegreen.com

The AA Wine Awards recognise the finest wine lists in England, Scotland and Wales. For full details, see pages 14-15

For information on Service Charge, see p21.

HURST MAP 05 SU77

 Castle Brasserie

British, Pacific Rim

Enjoyable dining in former village inn

☎ 0118 934 0034 Church Hill RG10 0SJ

MENU GUIDE Wild mushroom soup, truffle oil • Navarin of lamb • Iced banana parfait

WINE GUIDE ♀ La Huerta Sauvignon Blanc £13.25 • ♥ La Huerta Cabernet Sauvignon £13.25 • 22 bottles over £20, 16 bottles under £20 • 5 by the glass (£3.50-£4.50)

PRICE GUIDE Fixed L £12.95 • starter £5.25-£8.95 • main £13.95-£19.95 • dessert £4.95-£6.95 • coffee £1.95 • min/water £3 • Service added but optional 10%

PLACE: This 500-year-old inn with its whitewashed frontage and restored brickwork now houses three simply furnished dining rooms - one smoking - replete with original features like open fires, a baker's oven and wattle and daub showcase. Located in the middle of the village opposite the church, it overlooks the second oldest bowls green in the country. Service is friendly, helpful and efficient.
FOOD: The cheerful, single page menu includes modern British dishes like deep-fried oated mackerel and venison in red wine as well as some brasserie classics.
OUR TIP: Take a stroll around this attractive village before dinner
Chef: Mark Speirs **Owners:** Amanda Hill **Times:** 12-2.30/7-10, Closed 26-30 Dec, Occasionally Mon, closed D Sun **Notes:** Service included lunchtime, Vegetarian available **Seats:** 80, Pr/dining room 40
Smoking: N/Sm area **Children:** Portions **Directions:** M4 junct 10, A329(M) towards Reading (E). Take first exit to Winnersh/Wokingham. Continue for 1m and at Sainsburys turn left into Robin Hood Lane. Continue for 1.5m and go straight when approaching sharp left bend towards St Nicholas Church **Parking:** 43
e-mail: info@castlerestaurant.co.uk **web:** www.castlerestaurant.co.uk

---

LAMBOURN MAP 05 SU37

⊛ The Hare Restaurant @ The Hare & Hounds

British, European   **NEW**

Interesting menus in comfortable surroundings

☎ 01488 71386 RG17 7SD

MENU GUIDE Braised rabbit leg • Poached turbot, oyster ravioli • Banana tarte Tatin

WINE GUIDE ♀ Crusan Colombard Sauvignon £15 • ♥ D'istinto, Sagiovese -Merlot £15 • 42 bottles over £20, 14 bottles under £20 • 8 by the glass (£3.75-£5)

PRICE GUIDE Food prices not confirmed for 2006. Please telephone for details

PLACE: The horse racing village of Lambourn houses this stylish restaurant in a converted pub. Inside it's all geared up for relaxation, with squashy sofas, leather chairs and a bright modern decor.
FOOD: Top class ingredients appear in interesting combinations on the menu, and the pretty presentations are almost too perfect to eat. The short menus are well balanced between fish, meat and game in season.
OUR TIP: Charming terrace for summer dining
Chef: Tristan Lee Mason **Owners:** Paul Whitsford, Helen Windridge **Times:** 12-2/7-9.30, Closed Xmas-30 Dec, 1 Jan, Mon, closed D Sun **Notes:** Vegetarian available, Smart Dress **Seats:** 40, Pr/dining room 20 **Smoking:** N/Sm in restaurant **Directions:** Please ring for directions **Parking:** 30 **e-mail:** cuisine@theharerestaurant.co.uk **web:** www.theharerestaurant.co.uk

---

MAIDENHEAD MAP 06 SU88

⊛⊛⊛ Fredrick's Hotel Restaurant Spa *see page 39*

⊛ The Royal Oak

International   **NEW**

Village gastro-pub with celebrity connections

☎ 01628 620541 Paley St, Littlefield Green SL6 3JN

MENU GUIDE Wild mushroom risotto • Fillet steak on horseradish mash with morel jus • Apple & cinnamon cheesecake

WINE GUIDE ♀ Coast Line Chenin Blanc £15 • ♥ Boschendal Cabernet Sauvignon /Merlot £15 • 40 bottles over £20, 19 bottles under £20 • 5 by the glass (£3.60-£5)

PRICE GUIDE Fixed L £16.50 • starter £4.50-£10 • main £12.50-£19 • dessert £5-£6 • coffee £2.50 • min/water £3.50 • Service optional

PLACE: White-washed pub in the pretty village of Paley Street owned by Nick Parkinson, son of veteran TV presenter Michael Parkinson. The L-shaped pub boasts many original features, as well as a gallery of framed pictures from Parky's star-studded career.
FOOD: Honest, bold and simple cooking with an eye on seasonality and careful ingredient sourcing. Well-priced snack lunch menu also available.
OUR TIP: Check out the jazz nights
Chef: Luke Stockley **Owners:** Nick Parkinson **Times:** 11-3/6-12, Closed 27 Dec-1 Jan, closed D Sun **Notes:** Vegetarian available **Seats:** 40 **Smoking:** N/Sm in restaurant **Children:** Portions **Directions:** M4 junct 8/9. Take A308 towards Maidenhead Central. Take A330 to Ascot, continue for about 2m and then take right onto B3024 to Twyford. The Royal Oak is second pub on left **Parking:** 50 **web:** www.theroyaloakpaleystreet.com

---

MARSH BENHAM MAP 05 SU46

⊛ Red House

European, International

Country restaurant with friendly and unobtrusive service

☎ 01635 582017 RG20 8LY

MENU GUIDE Roast quail stuffed with wild rice • Braised lamb & savoy cabbage pie • Vanilla crème brûlée

WINE GUIDE ♀ Valle Dorado Sauvignon Blanc £13.50 • ♥ Domaine des 2 Soleils Merlot £13.50 • 36 bottles over £20, 26 bottles under £20 • 8 by the glass (£3.25-£4.50)

PRICE GUIDE Fixed L £13.95 • Fixed D £16.95 • starter £6.95-£8.95 • main £15.25-£18.95 • dessert £5.25 • coffee £2.25 • min/water £2.95 • Service added but optional 10% • Group min 6 service 10%

continued on page 40

England

MAIDENHEAD MAP 06 SU88

Fredrick's Hotel Restaurant Spa

British, French *Country-style retreat with polished German hospitality*

☎ 01628 581000 Shoppenhangers Rd SL6 2PZ

e-mail: eat@fredricks-hotel.co.uk

web: www.fredricks-hotel.co.uk

PLACE: Fredrick's - named after its proprietor, Fredrick Lösel - has a bright, elegant, traditionally styled dining room richly decorated in blues and golds. Crisp white-linen dressed tables enjoy a backdrop of striking artwork, including oil paintings and sculptures from the Lösel's personal collection, combined with views over the terrace, patio and gardens. The club-style bar, decked out in leather tub chairs and bar stalls, is the place for aperitifs, while in summer, the patio comes into its own for fair-weather dining and cocktails beneath the shade of colonial-style parasols. Just minutes from the M4, Fredrick's proves a calm oasis with a swanky spa and courteous, attentive and slick service.

FOOD: Classically based but with a contemporary outlook, the kitchen pays due respect to well-sourced, high quality, seasonal ingredients in assured, accomplished dishes. The approach is via appealing fixed-price lunch and dinner jour and carte, which deliver the likes of a noisette of wild venison with red cabbage strudel and thyme gnocchi. The traditional three-course options are bolstered by a separate selection of Fredrick's Classics, perhaps Dover sole grilled or meunière, or Cornish lobster aux choix.

MENU GUIDE Pan-fried oxtail in brioche, scallops, seasonal salads • Supreme of halibut, potatoes, shellfish ragoût • Sushi of pineapple, coconut water ice

WINE GUIDE ♀ Buiten Ver Wachting Sauvignon Blanc £31.50 • ♟ Bodegas Fundadas Vina Ardanza Reserva Tempranillo/Grenache £35.50 • all bottles over £20 5 by the glass (£4.80-£5.20)

PRICE GUIDE Fixed L £21.50 • Fixed D £39.50 • starter £13.50-£15.50 • main £22.50-£32.50 • dessert £10.50 • coffee £4.50 • min/water £4.50 • Service optional

OUR TIP: Be sure to check out the amazing spa

Chef: Brian Cutler **Owners:** F W Lösel **Times:** 12-2.30/7-10, Closed 25 Dec, 1 Jan, closed L Sat **Notes:** Vegetarian available, Dress Restrictions, Smart casual, Civ Wed 120 **Seats:** 60, Pr/dining room 130 **Smoking:** N/Sm in restaurant, Air con **Children:** Portions **Rooms:** 37 (37 en suite) ★★★★ **Directions:** From M4 junct 8/9 take A404(M), then turning (junct 9A) for Cox Green/White Waltham. Left on to Shoppenhangers Rd, restaurant 400 mtrs on right **Parking:** 90

MARSH BENHAM MAP 05 SU46

PLACE: An 18th-century thatched pub tucked away in a hamlet, offering a bar/bistro and a more formal restaurant. Filled bookcases line the room and tables are nicely spaced, but the formal looks are balanced by relaxed and friendly service.
FOOD: A mix of modern British with classic European twists. Savoury dishes demonstrate well balanced flavours in tried and tested combinations, while desserts are more simple but just as effective.
OUR TIP: Excellent value bistro menu
Chef: Yves Girard **Owners:** Tricrane Ltd **Times:** 12-2.15/7-10, Closed Xmas, New Year, closed D Sun **Notes:** Vegetarian available **Seats:** 60, Pr/dining room 30 **Smoking:** N/Sm in restaurant **Children:** Min 6 yrs, Menu, Portions **Directions:** 400yds off A4, 3m from Newbury, 5m from Hungerford. **Parking:** 60 **web:** www.theredhousepub.com

NEWBURY MAP 05 SU46

⊚⊚ Donnington Valley Hotel

British, International

Impressive cuisine in modern golfing hotel
☎ 01635 551199 Old Oxford Rd, Donnington
RG14 3AG

MENU GUIDE Poached pear filled with stilton • Calves' liver, bacon, mash, spinach, black pudding • Warm chocolate mousse
WINE GUIDE ♀ Tierra Arina Sauvignon Blanc £12 • ♀ Opal Ridge Shiraz £12 • 300 bottles over £20, 20 bottles under £20 • 30 by the glass (£2.50-£11)
PRICE GUIDE Fixed L £18 • Fixed D £23 • coffee £2.95 • min/water £3.25 • Service optional
PLACE: Smart modern hotel in the Berkshire countryside that boasts its own 18-hole golf course. You can dine at the clubhouse, but the real draw is the WinePress restaurant, an airy split-level affair where the food just seems to get better and better.
FOOD: Donnington delivers accomplished and imaginative renditions of classic favourites, its dishes notable for their clear, well-balanced combinations of flavour. Lighter portions are available if you just fancy a snack, and there's an award-winning wine list with a comprehensive selection on offer by the glass.
OUR TIP: Only 5 minutes from the M4
Chef: Kelvin Johnson **Owners:** Sir Peter Michael **Times:** 12-2/7-10 **Notes:** Sun L 1 course £11, 2 courses £15, 3 courses £18, Vegetarian available, Smart casual, Civ Wed 85 **Seats:** 120, Pr/dining room 130 **Smoking:** N/Sm in restaurant **Children:** Menu, Portions **Rooms:** 58 (58 en suite) ★★★★ **Directions:** M4 junct 13, A34 towards Newbury. Take immediate left signposted Donnington Hotels. At rdbt take right, at third rdbt take left and follow road for 2m. Hotel on right **Parking:** 100
e-mail: general@donningtonvalley.co.uk
web: www.donningtonvalley.co.uk

⊚ Regency Park Hotel

British

Bold, modern hotel brasserie with winning menus
☎ 01635 871555 Bowling Green Rd, Thatcham
RG18 3RP

MENU GUIDE Tiger prawn tempura • Baked cod, pea & chorizo mash • English apple plate
WINE GUIDE ♀ Richmond Ridge Colombard Chardonnay £13.95 • ♀ Richmond Ridge Shiraz/Merlot/Cabernet Sauvignon £13.95 • 19 bottles over £20, 22 bottles under £20 • 12 by the glass (£3.25-£4.30)
PRICE GUIDE Fixed L £16.50 • Fixed D £19.50 • starter £8.50 • main £18 • dessert £6 • coffee £3 • min/water £3.05 • Service optional
PLACE: This hotel has undergone extensive refurbishment and now boasts first class leisure facilities as well as a large, bright, modern restaurant complete with rock and metal waterfall, contemporary art and well-spaced tables. Knowledgeable service.
FOOD: Modern British dishes, brasserie classics and the occasional Mediterranean accent such as the chive and Parmesan risotto with roasted garlic and olive sablé.
OUR TIP: Within easy reach of Newbury racecourse
Chef: Paul Green **Owners:** Pedersen Caterers **Times:** 12.30-2/7-10, closed L Sat **Notes:** Vegetarian available, Smart Dress, Civ Wed 100 **Seats:** 100, Pr/dining room 140 **Smoking:** N/Sm in restaurant **Children:** Menu, Portions **Rooms:** 109 (109 en suite) ★★★★ **Directions:** M4 junct 13, follow A339 to Newbury for 2m, then take the A4 (Reading) and the hotel is signposted. **Parking:** 210
web: www.regencyparkhotel.co.uk

⊚⊚⊚⊚ Vineyard at Stockcross see page 41

PANGBOURNE MAP 05 SU67

⊚⊚ Copper Inn

Modern European

Accomplished dining in peaceful rural setting
☎ 0118 984 2244 RG8 7AR
MENU GUIDE Terrine of Gressingham duck legs, aged balsamic vinegar • Fillets of red mullet with rosemary & vine cherry tomatoes • Dark chocolate marquise
WINE GUIDE 10 bottles over £20, 12 bottles under £20 • 6 by the glass (£3.50-£4.25)
PRICE GUIDE Fixed L £14.50-£16.50 • Fixed D £21.50-£24.95 • starter £5-£10 • main £15-£19 • dessert £4.95-£6 • coffee £2.50 • min/water £3.50 • Service optional

continued on page 42

England

Vineyard at Stockcross

British, International
Fine wines and innovative cooking in elegant hideaway
☎ 01635 528770 Stockcross RG20 8JU
e-mail: general@the-vineyard.co.uk
web: www.the-vineyard.co.uk

PLACE: Nestling in the Berkshire countryside close to Newbury and the A34, the Vineyard takes its name and inspiration from proprietor Sir Peter Michael's winery in the mountainous landscape of northern California. Once an old hunting lodge, it has been fashioned into a luxury hotel; a haven of style and individuality, blending the contemporary with the traditional country house. First impressions count, and the 'Fire and Water' entrance sculpture makes a dramatic impact, especially at night, with its flaming torches set on a large pond. Opulence reigns, though it's not over the top, with calming colours and a sense of space. Art and sculpture are an integral part of the Vineyard experience, with the fine collection providing an intriguing backdrop to comfortable lounges (one with quintessentially English furnishings, the other a more modish conservatory) and inspired cooking. The stylish, split-level dining room embodies the hotel name and theme, its dramatic steel grapevine balustrade wrapping its way round the bright room, with precise table settings, views over the pond sculpture and slick, professional but warm and friendly service.
FOOD: The premier-league cuisine more than lives up to the setting, with the Vineyard conceding ultimate pride of place to chef John Campbell's poise and inspired cooking, with its serious menu for serious food lovers. His style is very much 'modern' British, based on the innovative scientific approach and exciting blend of textures, flavours and ingredients, with the menu's crisply scripted, understated dish descriptions (take roast Anjou squab, black treacle, celeriac or turbot, braised oxtail) delivering a big impact on the plate. The approach is exacting and precise, the performance strong, with plenty of skill, flair and luxury ingredients on show. And, as becomes the Vineyard name, expect to be dazzled by two stunning wine lists; one tome magnificently devoted to California, the other volume takes in the rest of the world.

MENU GUIDE Diver scallop, pea purée, smoked bacon jus • John Dory, smoked confit pork belly, garlic soubise, jerez sauce • Blackberry financier, yogurt sherbet

WINE GUIDE ♀ Miner Chardonnay £9.50 • ♀ Rosenblum Cellars Cabernet Sauvignon/Merlot £10 • 2000 bottles over £20, 50 bottles under £20 • 10 by the glass (£4.50-£10)

PRICE GUIDE Fixed L £19 • Fixed D £55 • coffee £3.95 • min/water £3.95 • Service optional

OUR TIP: Be brave with your choice of food and adventurous with your choice of wine

Chef: John Campbell **Owners:** Sir Peter Michael **Times:** 12-2/7-9.45 **Notes:** Tasting menu 8 courses £65, Vegetarian available, Civ Wed 60 **Seats:** 70, Pr/dining room 60 **Smoking:** N/Sm in restaurant, Air con **Children:** Menu, Portions **Rooms:** 49 (49 en suite) ★★★★★ **Directions:** M4 junct 13 join A34 Newbury by-pass southbound, take 3rd exit signed for Hungerford/Bath road interchange. Take 2nd exit at first and second rdbt signed for Stockcross, 0.6 mile on right. **Parking:** 100

PANGBOURNE continued MAP 05 SU67

PLACE: This 19th-century coaching inn is in the heart of a quaint Berkshire village. Beamed ceilings, tapestries and copper pans hanging from the walls of its attractive restaurant provide plenty of character. Diners can also enjoy views of the landscaped gardens.

FOOD: The modern menus reflect the technical skills of the chef. Dishes could include smooth chicken liver parfait with pear chutney for starters, followed by roast rump of lamb glazed with herb crust and redcurrant and ginger jus, and finished with prune and Armagnac crème brûlée, tarragon shortbread.

OUR TIP: Good value for money

Owners: Mr F Phillips **Times:** 12-2.30/7-9.30, closed D Sun, BH Mons **Notes:** Vegetarian available, Civ Wed 80 **Seats:** 60, Pr/dining room 40 **Smoking:** N/Sm in restaurant **Children:** Portions **Rooms:** 22 (22 en suite) ★★★ **Directions:** 5m from M4 junct 12, at junct of A329 Reading/Oxford & A340; next to church **Parking:** 20 **e-mail:** manager@copper-inn.co.uk **web:** www.copper-inn.co.uk

READING MAP 05 SU77

◉◉ Millennium Madejski Hotel Reading

French

Luxury dining in large hotel complex

☎ 0118 925 3500 Madejski Stadium RG2 0FL

MENU GUIDE Salad of roasted pigeon with fried quail egg • Bresse chicken with truffle, foie gras with roast langoustines • Warm banana bread, clotted cream

WINE GUIDE ♀ Crusan Colombard/Sauvignon Blanc £14.95 • ♀ Crusan Grenache/Merlot £14.95 • 57 bottles over £20, 37 bottles under £20 • 13 by the glass (£3.50-£8.95)

PRICE GUIDE Fixed D £45-£47.50 • coffee £3.50 • min/water £3.95 • Service optional

PLACE: With striking contemporary decor and aubergine walls,

the smart and stylish Cilantro hotel restaurant has plate glass windows along the entire length of the external wall. Banquette seating, crisp linen napery and precision lighting make this a sophisticated venue. Service is reassuringly professional. (The hotel is part of the Madejski stadium complex.)

FOOD: Accomplished chefs produce refined, technically complex dishes with slick modern presentation, utilising quality produce with luxuries that pepper the menu. The 7-course gourmande menu demonstrates their skills.

OUR TIP: Great seafood straight from Scottish lochs

Chef: John O'Reilly **Owners:** Madejski Hotel Co **Times:** 7-10, Closed 25 Dec, 1 Jan, BHs, Sun, closed L Mon-Sun **Notes:** Tasting menu £49.50, Vegetarian available, Smart Dress **Seats:** 55 **Smoking:** N/Sm area, Air con **Children:** Min 12yrs, Portions **Rooms:** 140 (140 en suite) ★★★★ **Directions:** 1m N from M4 junct 11. 2m S from Reading town centre. **Parking:** 100 **e-mail:** sales.reading@mill-cop.com **web:** www.millennium-hotels.com

⑪ **Loch Fyne Restaurant** The Maltings, Bear Wharf, Fobney St RG1 6BT ☎ 0118 918 5850 Quality seafood chain.

⑪ **LSQ2 Bar and Brasserie** Lime Square, 220 South Oak Way, Green Park RG2 6UP ☎ 0118 9873702 Modern British fare in business park location.

⑪ **Pepe Sale** 3 Queens Walk RG1 7QF ☎ 0118 959 7700 Buzzing Italian/Sardinian.

SHINFIELD MAP 05 SU76

◉◉◉ L'Ortolan see page 43

SONNING MAP 05 SU77

◉◉ The French Horn

British, French

Formal dining room in riverside setting

☎ 0118 969 2204 RG4 6TN

MENU GUIDE Tian de crabe • Canard rôti à l'Anglaise • Chocolat fondant

WINE GUIDE 600 bottles over £20 • 12 by the glass (£6-£16.50)

PRICE GUIDE Fixed L £24-£42 • Fixed D £40 • starter £11.50-£85 • main £25.50-£35 • dessert £11.50 • coffee £4.50 • min/water £3.70 • Service included

PLACE: Privately owned and carefully maintained, the French Horn sits on a bend of the River Thames. The cosy bar has spit-roasted duck, the house speciality, turning in the fireplace in the evening. Most restaurant tables have river views, with dining on the terrace on summer days.

FOOD: Traditional French and British fare, with the Gallic language dominating throughout the menus, offer many choices for each course. The lunchtime fixed-price menu represents best value, otherwise things can be a bit on the pricey side.

OUR TIP: Stunning views for a romantic evening

Chef: G Company **Owners:** Mr Emmanuel **Times:** 12-1.45/7-9.15, Closed 26-30 Dec **Notes:** Vegetarian available, Dress Restrictions, No shorts **Seats:** 70, Pr/dining room 24 **Smoking:** No pipes, No cigars **Children:** Portions **Rooms:** 21 (21 en suite) ★★★ **Directions:** A4 into Sonning. Follow B478 through village over bridge, hotel on right, car park on left **Parking:** 40 **e-mail:** thefrenchhorn@compuserve.com **web:** www.thefrenchhorn.co.uk

continued

L'Ortolan

French, British *Serious fine dining in quiet setting minutes from M4*

☎ 0118 988 8500 Church Ln RG2 9BY

e-mail: info@lortolan.com

web: www.lortolan.com

PLACE: The mature grounds and historic exterior of this Grade II listed, red-brick 17th-century former vicarage (which received critical acclaim firstly under Nico Ladenis and then under John Burton-Race, of recent TV fame and now at the New Angel, Dartmouth), belies the design-focused, modern interior. Sophisticated and uncluttered, the long dining room is bolstered by a conservatory and small luxurious bar for pre-meal drinks. Two recently completed private dining rooms on the first floor are extremely stylish. Service is professional, friendly and confident.

FOOD: Alan Murchison (who has worked with the likes of Burton-Race and Raymond Blanc and returns to L'Ortolan from a short stint at Chewton Glen, New Milton) shows his accomplished pedigree via a modern French approach, based on a serious classical foundation. High-quality seasonal ingredients (including bags of luxury items), excellent technique and clean, clear and refined flavours hit the spot on a repertoire of enticing carte and fixed-price lunch jour, gourmand (including vegetarian version), speciality menu and truffle tasting option. Expect corn-fed pigeon with choucroute, pan-fried foie gras, truffle and Madeira jus, or John Dory fillet with feuillatine of smoked bacon, cep and onion, and a thyme and cep sauce.

MENU GUIDE Black truffle & artichoke risotto, roasted cep, truffle cream • Duck tasting plate, truffled chicory, pear, Sauternes & honey jus • White chocolate pavé, griottine cherries

WINE GUIDE ♀ Domaine Chatelain Pouilly Fumé les Chailloux Sauvignon £32 • ♀ Castello di Brolio Chianti Sangiovese/Cab Sauv £26 • 350 bottles over £20 17 by the glass (£5.50-£15)

PRICE GUIDE Fixed L £18 • starter £13-£17 • main £25-£31 • dessert £9-£22 • coffee £4 • min/water £3.50 • Service added but optional

OUR TIP: Ask for a look at the private dining rooms

Chef: Alan Murchison **Owners:** Newfee Ltd **Times:** 11.45-2/7-10, Closed Xmas & New Year, Mon/Sun **Notes:** Tasting menu 5 courses £48, 7 courses £55, 9 courses £99, Vegetarian available, Civ Wed 50 **Seats:** 64, Pr/dining room 20 **Smoking:** N/Sm in restaurant **Children:** Menu, Portions **Directions:** From M4 junct 11 take A33 towards Basingstoke. At 1st rdbt turn left, after garage turn left, 1m turn right at Six Bells pub. Restaurant 1st left (follow English Tourist Board Signs) **Parking:** 45

England

STREATLEY MAP 05 SU58
The Swan at Streatley
British, International
Accomplished cooking in Thames-side setting
☎ 01491 878800 High St RG8 9HR

MENU GUIDE Carpaccio of marinated beef rib, aubergines & parmesan • Salmon steak roasted with rosemary & thyme • Citrus fruit tart, vanilla cream

WINE GUIDE ♀ Whitehaven Sauvignon Blanc £18 • ♂ Graham Beck Cabernet Sauvignon £24.50 • 64 bottles over £20, 20 bottles under £20 • 10 by the glass (£3.70-£10.50)

PRICE GUIDE Fixed L £22.50-£22.50 • Fixed D £29.50-£29.50 • Service optional

PLACE: The Swan, formerly the ferry operator's inn, is in a lovely location by the Thames. Cygnetures, the airy restaurant, has views downriver to the nearby bridge. The atmosphere is friendly and relaxed, perfect for a quiet chat and peaceful enough for a single diner to read a book.
FOOD: Top quality ingredients are treated with the utmost respect and technical execution of dishes is strong. Superb, clean and simple presentation is exemplified in a starter of hand-dived scallops, beautifully caramelised and served with crisp pancetta.
OUR TIP: Try a light summer lunch on the Riverside Terrace
Chef: Gavin Russell **Owners:** John Nike Group **Times:** 12.30-2/7-10
Notes: Vegetarian available, Dress Restrictions, Smart casual, Civ Wed 150
Seats: 70, Pr/dining room 130 **Smoking:** N/Sm in restaurant
Children: Menu, Portions **Rooms:** 46 (46 en suite) ★★★★
Directions: Follow A329 from Pangbourne, on entering Streatley turn right at lights. Hotel on left before bridge. **Parking:** 120
e-mail: sales@swan-at-streatley.co.uk **web:** www.swanatstreatley.co.uk

WINDSOR MAP 06 SU97
⚜⚜ Castle Hotel
International
Fine dining in centrally located hotel with castle views
☎ 0870 4008300 01753 851011 High St SL4 1LJ

MENU GUIDE Pressing of rabbit foie gras, endive salad • Pan-fried fillet of sea bass, langoustine risotto • Hazelnut parfait & tuile

WINE GUIDE ♀ Chardonnay £17.50 • ♂ Shiraz £17.50 • 24 bottles over £20, 12 bottles under £20 • 12 by the glass (£4-£6.50)

PRICE GUIDE Fixed D fr £25 • starter £3.50-£7.50 • main £12-£28 • dessert £3.50-£7.50 • coffee £2.95 • min/water £4.75 • Service added but optional 12.5%

PLACE: A former coaching inn, dating from the 16th century, the hotel is prominently located opposite Sir Christopher Wren's Guildhall with views of Windsor Castle. The elegant restaurant, with high backed chairs and white linen cloths, divides quite naturally into three areas, which helps to create an intimate atmosphere.
FOOD: An intelligent cooking style focusing on tried and tested combinations, but allowing imagination to play its part with beautiful presentation and some innovation. The international menu is priced for two or three courses.
OUR TIP: Indulge yourself with afternoon tea in the lounge
Chef: Cyril Strub **Owners:** Macdonald Hotels **Times:** 12.30-2.30/6-9.45, Closed Mon, closed L Tues-Sat **Notes:** Vegetarian available, Dress Restrictions, Smart casual, Civ Wed 100 **Seats:** 50, Pr/dining room 300 **Smoking:** N/Sm in restaurant, Air con **Children:** Menu, Portions **Rooms:** 111 (111 en suite) ★★★ **Directions:** In town centre opposite Guildhall **Parking:** 112 **e-mail:** castle@macdonald-hotels.co.uk **web:** www.macdonald-hotels.co.uk

⚜⚜ Sir Christopher Wren's House Hotel & Spa
British, European
Relaxed fine dining accompanied by unbeatable views
☎ 01753 861354 Thames St SL4 1PX

MENU GUIDE Venison carpaccio • Brill, confit celeriac, smoked chive dressing • Orange & hazelnut brûlée, dark chocolate sorbet

WINE GUIDE ♀ Colle Sori Pinot Grigio £17.50 • ♂ Lazo Cabernet Sauvignon £17.50 • 60 bottles over £20, 20 bottles under £20 • 8 by the glass (£3.50)

PRICE GUIDE Fixed L £18 • Fixed D £24 • starter £7.50-£10.50 • main £15.50-£18.50 • dessert £6.50 • coffee £3 • min/water £3.50 • Service added but optional 12.5%

PLACE: Watch the swans glide by and the sun set over the Thames from the smart, sophisticated restaurant at this historical landmark beside Eton Bridge. The modern and contemporary blend well with the opulence of the Art Deco style of decor. The mansion was originally home to celebrated architect Sir Christopher Wren.
FOOD: Classical dishes are intertwined with more adventurous combinations, including a six-course tasting menu. Cooking is imaginative and ingredients are carefully sourced. The brasserie-style bar menu offers lighter options.
OUR TIP: Dine on the terrace in summer
Chef: Stephen Boucher **Owners:** The Wrens Hotel Group **Times:** 12.30-2.30/6.30-10 **Notes:** Tasting menu 6 courses £37.50, 3 course Jazz sun £24.95, Vegetarian available, Dress Restrictions, Smart casual preferred, Civ Wed 90 **Seats:** 60, Pr/dining room 90 **Smoking:** N/Sm in restaurant, Air con **Children:** Menu, Portions **Rooms:** 90 (90 en suite) ★★★★
Directions: Telephone for directions **Parking:** 14
e-mail: wrens@wrensgroup.com **web:** www.sirchristopherwren.co.uk

WOOLHAMPTON MAP 05 SU56
The Angel
Modern British
Informal gastro-pub with striking interior decor
☎ 0118 971 3307 Bath Rd RG7 5RT

PLACE: 'Expect the unexpected' is The Angel's slogan and the interior of this large, creeper-clad pub certainly doesn't disappoint. Vibrant Mediterranean-coloured walls laden with pictures, dark-polished floors, palm trees, cacti and jars of colourful pulses and olive oils catch the eye, while the bar's ceiling comes lined with wine bottles. Add candlesticks and tall lilies to dark-wood tables and you have a relaxed but flamboyant ambience.

continued

England

FOOD: The accomplished modern brasserie fare suits the mood and wallet. Expect slow-braised belly of pork with creamed potato and baby spinach, raspberry crème brûlée, and attentive service too.
OUR TIP: Try the novel selection of home-made ice creams
Times: 12-2/6-9.30, Closed D Sun **e-mail:** mail@a4angel.com
web: www.a4angel.com

YATTENDON MAP 05 SU57

 ### Royal Oak Hotel
British, European
Stylish, up to the minute cooking in an old English country inn
☎ 01635 201325 The Square RG18 0UG
MENU GUIDE Duck & foie gras terrine, Cumberland jelly • Sea bass, clams & mussel cream • Baked vanilla cheesecake, stem ginger ice cream
WINE GUIDE ♀ Kanu Chenin Blanc £15 • ♀ Réunie La Place Merlot £15 • 55 bottles over £20, 15 bottles under £20 • 6 by the glass (£3.50-£4.75)
PRICE GUIDE Fixed L £14-£19.50 • starter £5.50-£11.75 • main £12.75-£18.75 • dessert £5.75-£5.95 • coffee £2 • min/water £2.95 • Service added but optional 10%
PLACE: Overlooking the village square, this is the archetypal English country inn, covered in wisteria and featuring open log fires and a chequered quarry-tile floor in the popular beamed bar. The adjoining brasserie has a relaxed atmosphere, while the separate, more formal restaurant is ideal for special occasions. Lovely walled garden for summer dining.
FOOD: Expect an interesting blend of modern British cuisine with international influences on seasonal brasserie-style menus that serves both the bar and restaurant. Cooking is simple yet innovative and use of quality local produce is to be commended.
OUR TIP: Work up an appetite with a beautiful Berkshire walk
Chef: Jamie Mould **Owners:** William Boyal **Times:** 12-2/7-10, Closed 1 Jan **Notes:** Vegetarian available, Dress Restrictions, Smart casual preferred **Seats:** 60, Pr/dining room 10 **Smoking:** N/Sm in restaurant **Children:** Portions **Rooms:** 5 (5 en suite) ★★ **Directions:** M4 junct 12, follow signs to Pangbourne, left to Yattendon. **Parking:** 25
e-mail: oakyattendon@aol.com **web:** www.royaloakyattendon.com

BRISTOL

BRISTOL MAP 04 ST57

Arno's Manor Hotel
British, Mediterranean
Comfortable hotel with a good range
☎ 0117 971 1461 470 Bath Rd, Arno's Vale BS4 3HQ
MENU GUIDE Duck confit salad, beetroot dressing • Venison, Brussels sprout purée, port & pancetta sauce • Tiramisù, light coffee sauce
WINE GUIDE ♀ Stowells Pinot Grigio £12 • ♀ Bolla Valpolicella £12 • all bottles under £20 • 6 by the glass (£3.25-£3.50)
PRICE GUIDE Fixed D £22 • starter £4.50 • main £13 • dessert £4.50 • coffee £2.95 • min/water £2.95 • Service optional
PLACE: This comfortable hotel was once the home of a wealthy merchant and retains many original 18th-century features despite the many changes years have brought. Its former chapel is now a cosy lounge, while a glass-domed roof turns an internal courtyard into an atmospheric, conservatory style restaurant.

continued

FOOD: A lengthy menu features crowd-pleasers (steak with a brandy and wild mushroom jus), alongside more accomplished modern British fare, such as pan-fried shark with lobster cream.
OUR TIP: Ample parking
Chef: Dylan Taylor **Owners:** Forestdale Hotels **Times:** 7-10 **Notes:** Sun L £12.95, Vegetarian available, Civ Wed 60 **Seats:** 65, Pr/dining room 16 **Smoking:** N/Sm in restaurant, Air con **Children:** Menu, Portions **Rooms:** 73 (73 en suite) ★★★ **Parking:** 200
e-mail: arnos.manor@forestdale.com **web:** www.forestdale.com

Bells Diner
British, European
Exciting cuisine in fashionable Montpellier
☎ 0117 924 0357 1-3 York Rd, Montpellier BS6 5QB

MENU GUIDE Potage of shellfish • Whole partridge 'vapeur' • Orange pannacotta, orange sorbet
WINE GUIDE ♀ Jurancon Sec Domaine de Lahargue • ♀ Bourgogne Rouge Pinot Noir £19.50 • 116 bottles over £20, 19 bottles under £20 • 11 by the glass (£3.50-£6)
PRICE GUIDE Starter £6-£13 • main £14.50-£18.50 • dessert £6.50-£12 • coffee £2.20 • Service added but optional 10%
PLACE: Bristol's gentrified Montpellier area houses this former grocery shop, where the grocer's paraphernalia shares space on the wall shelves with wine bottles. To add to the cheerful atmosphere, large windows flood the blue/grey colour scheme with natural light.
FOOD: Strong local support for the exciting European cooking is fully justified, with the kitchen taking pains to produce dishes with accurate, vibrant flavours. Presentation of food is a strength, whether the choice is from the evening tasting menu or the modern carte, which is available at lunch and dinnertime.
OUR TIP: Don't forgo the sensational breads
Chef: Christopher Wicks **Owners:** Christopher Wicks **Times:** 12-2.30/7-10.30, Closed 24-30 Dec, Sun, closed L Mon & Sat **Notes:** 8 course tasting menu £45, Vegetarian available, Dress Restrictions **Seats:** 60
Smoking: N/Sm in restaurant **Children:** Portions
Directions: Telephone for further details **Parking:** On street
e-mail: info@bellsdiner.com **web:** www.bellsdiner.com

City Café
European
Bustling contemporary hotel eaterie
☎ 0117 925 1001 City Inn Bristol, Temple Way BS1 6BF
MENU GUIDE Crab & crayfish risotto • Duck, fennel & orange compote, caraway jus • Raspberry Charlotte, gooseberries, crème Chantilly
WINE GUIDE ♀ Concha Y Toro Chardonnay £13.15 • ♀ Concha Y Toro Merlot £13.15 • 8 bottles over £20, 16 bottles under £20 • 16 by the glass (£3.50-£6.50)

continued

England

BRISTOL *continued* MAP 04 ST57

PRICE GUIDE Fixed L £12.50 • Fixed D £17.50-£20 • starter £5.50-
£9 • main £8-£21 • dessert £5.95-£7 • coffee £2.50 • min/water
£3.95 • Service optional • Group min 8 service 10%

PLACE: Smart city hotel handily located within walking distance
of the railway station and centre of town. Its bustling eaterie is a
popular haunt for local businesses, and has a terrace for alfresco
dining in the summer.

FOOD: The City Café aims to please offering an extensive
selection of modern British dishes, such as chicken with a root
vegetable and apple gratin and cider sauce, or lamb with a pesto
crust and parsley potatoes. Vegetarian menu available.

OUR TIP: Tea and coffee served all day in the adjacent bar

Chef: Peter Quinion **Owners:** City Inn Ltd **Times:** 12-2.30/7-10, closed
L Sat **Notes:** Vegetarian available **Seats:** 70, Pr/dining room 30
Smoking: N/Sm in restaurant, Air con **Children:** Portions **Rooms:** 167
(167 en suite) ★★★ **Parking:** 50 **e-mail:** reservations@cityinn.com
web: www.cityinn.com

⚫ Conrad at Jamesons

British, European

Modern bistro with great choice of menus

☎ 0117 927 6565 Upper Maudlin St BS2 8BJ

MENU GUIDE Steamed mussels • Oven-roasted rack of
lamb • Glazed sweet chestnut tart

WINE GUIDE ⚲ Mezza Corona Pinot Grigio £14.95 • ⚑ Mezza
Corona Merlot £14.95 • 31 bottles over £20, 30 bottles under
£20 • 6 by the glass (£3.95-£5.75)

PRICE GUIDE Starter £3.95-£7.95 • main £9.95-£34.75 • dessert
£4.25-£7.50 • coffee £2.75 • min/water £2.95 • Service
optional • Group min 10 service 10%

PLACE: Full length windows and high ceilings lend a spacious
feel to this friendly restaurant, where the split-level seating is
suitable for both chattering groups and intimate couples.

FOOD: Fresh fish brought daily from the Cornish ports is a
notable feature of the modern bistro-style menu, and a rotisserie
produces seared scallops, and slow-roasted pork belly. Of similar
interest are crispy veal sweetbreads, and fillet of beef Rossini
from the appealing carte.

OUR TIP: Express daytime menu offers terrific value

Chef: C Lynton-Jenkins, Paul Salmon, C Cowpe **Owners:** Conrad &
Simon Lynton-Jenkins **Times:** noon-mdnt **Notes:** Vegetarian available,
Smart Dress **Seats:** 95, Pr/dining room 24 **Smoking:** N/Sm area, No
pipes, No cigars **Children:** Portions **Directions:** Opposite childrens
hospital and BRI **Parking:** NCP & on street
e-mail: info@conradatjamesons.co.uk
web: www.conradatjamesons.co.uk

⚫⚫ Culinaria

British, European   NEW

A Mediterranean foodie heaven

☎ 0117 973 7999 1 Chandos Rd, Redland BS6 6PG

MENU GUIDE Provençale fish soup • Duck, purple sprouting
broccoli, pomegranate & balsamic dressing • Pannacotta with
passionfruit

WINE GUIDE ⚲ Tariquet Chardonnay £13.50 • ⚑ Domaine St
Bernard Merlot £12.25 • 12 bottles over £20, 24 bottles under
£20 • 4 by the glass (£2.50-£2.75)

PRICE GUIDE Starter £5.75-£6.50 • main £11.50-£14 • dessert
£5.50-£5.95 • coffee £2 • min/water £2.65 • Service optional

PLACE: This low-key eaterie has a relaxed neighbourhood
atmosphere and is increasingly popular, so book ahead. It's a
pleasant, airy room with pale beechwood tables and a bistro feel.

continued

FOOD: Culinaria brings the Mediterranean to Bristol, offering a
concise but accomplished menu, specialising in simple dishes
notable for high quality ingredients and divine flavour
combinations. Mains might include a butternut squash and
radicchio risotto, or boeuf bourguignon with mash and red
cabbage, and there's an extensive take-away selection of simpler
dishes if dinner wins you over.

OUR TIP: The 'Culinaria at home' range includes breads and ice
creams as well as full meals

Chef: Stephen Markwick **Owners:** Stephen & Judy Markwick **Times:** 12-
2/6.30-9.30, Closed Xmas, New Year, BHs, Sun-Tue, closed L Wed-Thur
Notes: Vegetarian available **Seats:** 30 **Smoking:** N/Sm in restaurant
Children: Portions **Parking:** on street **web:** www.culinariabristol.co.uk

⚫ Glass Boat Restaurant

British, International

Accurate cooking in novel river surroundings

☎ 0117 929 0704 Welsh Back BS1 4SB

MENU GUIDE Provençal fish soup • Ricotta & pinenut
ravioli • Chocolate tart, Morello cherry compôte

WINE GUIDE ⚲ Norte Chico Sauvignon Blanc £12.75 • ⚑ Norte
Chico Cabernet Sauvignon £12.75 • 100 bottles over £20,
40 bottles under £20 • 8 by the glass (£3-£5.50)

PRICE GUIDE Fixed L £10.90-£20 • Fixed D £23.50 • starter £4-
£8 • main £8-£20 • dessert £4-£6 • coffee £1.85 • min/water
£2.95 • Service added but optional 10%

PLACE: Once a lumber barge on the Avon, now a floating
restaurant moored alongside the historic harbour. The light and
airy decks offer exciting views of dockyard life.

FOOD: The cooking is honest and enjoyable, with plenty of
interest coming from the European influences, apparent in chilli
and garlic marinated calamari salad, and red mullet with
piperade and tapenade vinaigrette.

OUR TIP: Ask for river-facing table

Chef: Andrew Green **Owners:** Arne Ringer **Times:** 12-2.30/6-11, Closed
24-26 Dec, 1 Jan, Sun, closed L Sat **Notes:** Vegetarian available, Civ Wed
100 **Seats:** 120, Pr/dining room 40 **Smoking:** Air con
Directions: Moored below Bristol Bridge in the old centre of Bristol
Parking: NCP **e-mail:** bookings@glassboat.co.uk
web: www.glassboat.co.uk

What makes a Restaurant of the Year?
In selecting a Restaurant of the Year, we
look for somewhere that is exceptional in its
chosen area of the market. Whilst the
Rosette awards are based on the quality of
the food alone, Restaurant of the Year takes
into account all aspects of the operation.
For full details see pages 6-7.

England

Michael Caines at The Bristol Marriott Royal

Modern European

A truly impressive dining room and food to match

☎ 0117 925 5100 College Green BS1 5TA

MENU GUIDE Cannelonne of langoustines • Roasted pheasant & boudin noir • Rum savarin

PRICE GUIDE Fixed L fr £17.50 • starter £7.95-£14.50 • main £18.50-£26.50 • dessert £8.50

PLACE: Michael Caines' latest venture got off to a great start a couple of years ago, and continues to shine brightly in Bristol's luxury city centre hotel. The wow factor is apparent long before the food is served, conjured by the spectacular proportions of the restaurant involving lofty ceilings, a stunning stained glass wall, balconies and classical statues. The accoutrements of crisp white table linen, silver cutlery and sparkling glassware are reassuringly traditional, and a friendly team dispenses service with style and a precise formality.

FOOD: In such a setting much is expected of the food, and it does not disappoint. The cooking is accomplished and accurate, with the use of luxury ingredients (foie gras, truffles etc) injecting a suitably sophisticated element into the formal dinner and tasting menus. Flavours are clear cut and focused, with freshness and seasonality much in evidence in creations like partridge with endive, turnips, apples, onions and liquorice sauce. The wine list is presented by grape variety rather than country of origin and there's a good selection by the glass.

OUR TIP: Visit the Moët Vintage Champagne Bar

Chef: Shane Goodway **Times:** 12-2.30/7-10, Closed Sun, closed L Mon

Notes: 11-course Tasting Menu, Dress Restrictions, Smart casual

Seats: 60, Pr/dining room 12 **Smoking:** N/Sm in restaurant

Children: Min 12yrs **Rooms:** 242 (242 en suite) ★★★★

Directions: next to cathedral by College Green **Parking:** 200

e-mail: bristol.royal@marriotthotels.co.uk

web: www.marriott.com/marriott/brsry

⊛ Hotel du Vin & Bistro

British, Mediterranean

Effective bistro with buzz in hotel setting

☎ 0117 925 5577 The Sugar House, Narrow Lewins Mead BS1 2NU

MENU GUIDE Pan-fried scallops, rocket, aïoli • Rump of lamb, ratatouille, olive mash • Crème brûlée

WINE GUIDE ♀ Sieur d'Arques Chardonnay £13.50 • ♀ Sieur d'Arques Merlot £13.50 • 700 bottles over £20, 10 bottles under £20 • 11 by the glass (£3.80-£6.80)

PRICE GUIDE Starter £6.75-£7 • main £14-£14.50 • dessert £6.75 • coffee £2.50 • min/water £3.50 • Service optional • Group min 12 service 10%

PLACE: This fabulously conversion of an 18th-century former sugar warehouse presses all the right style buttons. As you'd expect from the name, decoration is wine inspired, the buzzy, popular bistro informally decked out with wooden floors, faded cream walls and varnished, upholstered chairs.

FOOD: Expect simply constructed, light, clean-cut brasserie-style dishes on a modern repertoire that also comes with a helping of simple classics like bouillabaise or coq au vin.

OUR TIP: The two-course Menu Rapide includes coffee and offers good value for those on the move

Chef: Marcus Lang **Owners:** Hotel du Vin Ltd **Times:** 12-2/6-10

Notes: Vegetarian available **Seats:** 85, Pr/dining room 72

Smoking: N/Sm in restaurant, Air con **Children:** Menu, Portions

Rooms: 40 (40 en suite) ★★★★ **Directions:** From M4 junct 19, M32 into Bristol. With Bentalls on left take right lane at next lights. Turn right onto opposite side of carriageway. Hotel 200yds in side road.

Parking: 20 **e-mail:** info@bristol.hotelduvin.com

web: www.hotelduvin.com

⊛ Howards Restaurant

British, French

Lively restaurant, with an easy flair

☎ 0117 926 2921 1a-2a Avon Crescent, Hotwells BS1 6XQ

MENU GUIDE Crab & smoked haddock tartlet • Braised lamb shank, parsnip mash • Iced Drambuie parfait

WINE GUIDE 25 bottles over £20, 40 bottles under £20 • 8 by the glass (£3.75-£4.25)

PRICE GUIDE Fixed L £12.50 • Fixed D £15.95 • starter £3.95-£7.50 • main £9.95-£17.95 • dessert £4.25-£6 • coffee £2.50 min/water £2.95 • Service optional • Group min 8 service 10%

PLACE: A character restaurant in a row of converted cottages near the docks and SS Great Britain. A series of cosy rooms is augmented by more space upstairs, with an established following keeping the place busy.

FOOD: Interesting flavours and combinations create their own excitement, with substantial portions to satisfy hearty appetites. A well-priced bistro menu supplements the carte, where meat dishes predominate.

OUR TIP: Visit nearby SS Great Britain

Chef: D Short, P Salmon, C Lynton-Jenkins **Owners:** C & S Lynton-Jenkins **Times:** 12-4/5.30-11.30 **Notes:** Vegetarian available **Seats:** 85, Pr/dining room 27 **Smoking:** N/Sm area, No pipes, No cigars

Children: Portions **Directions:** 5 mins from city centre following signs for M5/Avonmouth. On dockside over small bridge **Parking:** On street; free council car park **e-mail:** info@howardsrestaurant.co.uk

web: www.howardsrestaurant.co.uk

⊛⊛⊛ Michael Caines at The Bristol Marriott Royal *see above*

England

BRISTOL *continued* MAP 04 ST57

🍽 riverstation
British, European
Modern cooking in chic riverside restaurant
☎ 0117 914 4434 The Grove BS1 4RB

MENU GUIDE Chicken liver & foie gras parfait, red onion jam • Pork, butternut squash, greens, rhubarb pickle • Hot chocolate fondant

WINE GUIDE ♀ Jeannot Pouilly Fumé £23.45 • ♥ Conde de Valdertiar Rioja Reserva £22.40 • 45 bottles over £20, 17 bottles under £20 • 10 by the glass (£3-£10)

PRICE GUIDE Fixed L fr £11.50 • starter £5-£10 • main £12-£18 • dessert £5-£6.50 • coffee £1.70 • min/water £2 • Service optional • Group min 8 service 10%

PLACE: On the water's edge, this chic eaterie is decked out in contemporary style with lots of glass, wood and steel. Downstairs is a popular café cum deli for light meals and snacks, while upstairs an airy restaurant caters to a smarter business crowd.
FOOD: A modern European menu with some bold flavour combinations; kick off with langoustine bisque perhaps, before tucking into swordfish with a plantain fritter and pickled papaya, or duck with honey-roast vegetables.
OUR TIP: Book for a balcony table if the weather's good
Chef: Peter Taylor, Ross Wills **Owners:** J Payne, P Taylor **Times:** 12-2.30/6-10.30, Closed Xmas, 1 Jan **Notes:** 3 course Sun L £17.50, Vegetarian available **Seats:** 120 **Smoking:** N/Sm in restaurant **Children:** Menu, Portions **Directions:** On the dock side in central Bristol **Parking:** Pay & display, meter parking opposite
e-mail: relax@riverstation.co.uk **web:** www.riverstation.co.uk

🍺 The Boars Head The Main Rd, Aust BS35 4AX
☎ 01454 632278 Cosy candlelit pub with delightful ambience serving very good fresh fish dishes and excellent Sunday lunch.

🍽 Severnshed The Grove, Harbourside BS1 4SE
☎ 0117 925 1212 Riverside open-plan setup with mainly organic brasserie style menu.

🍽 Wagamama 63 Queens St, Clifton BS8 1QL
☎ 0117 922 1188 Relaxed, Japanese noodle-based eaterie.

BUCKINGHAMSHIRE

AMERSHAM MAP 06 SU99

🍽 The Artichoke
French 🔴 **NEW**
Stylish restaurant in historic old town
☎ 01494 726611 9 Market Square, Old Amersham HP7 0DF

MENU GUIDE Watercress soup, spinach-wrapped mushroom beignet • Spiced confit of duck • Rhubarb cheesecake

WINE GUIDE ♀ Morton Estate Sauvignon Blanc £20.50 • ♥ Domaine Vieille Julienne Côtes du Rhone Cabernet Sauvignon £22.50 • 25 bottles over £20, 14 bottles under £20 6 by the glass (£4-£6)

PRICE GUIDE Fixed L £23.50 • Fixed D £32.50 • starter £8-£10.50 • main £17-£21 • dessert £6.50 • coffee £3 • min/water £2.75 • Service added but optional 12.5%

PLACE: Look out for the frosted logo of a globe artichoke in the window of this intimate restaurant, situated in a Grade 11 listed building. The muted colour scheme inside is complemented by contemporary designs, and the clever modern lighting achieves a warm glow.
FOOD: Simple modern French and British food with pronounced flavours is presented elegantly, with lots of seasonal produce in evidence. Desserts like pear frangipane with lemon tart are clear winners.
OUR TIP: Try the value-for-money set lunch menu
Chef: Laurie Gear **Owners:** Laurie Gear, Jacquline Dare **Times:** 12-2/6.45-10, Closed 1 wk Xmas, 2 wks Aug BH, 1 wk Apr, Sun, Mon **Notes:** Tasting menu available, ALC available at lunch only, Vegetarian available, Smart Dress, Smart casual **Seats:** 25 **Smoking:** N/Sm in restaurant **Children:** Portions **Directions:** M40 junct 2. 1m from Amersham New Town. **Parking:** On street, nearby car park
e-mail: info@theartichokerestaurant.co.uk
web: www.theartichokerestaurant.co.uk

AYLESBURY MAP 11 SP81

🍽🍽🍽 Hartwell House Hotel Restaurant & Spa *see page 49*

BLETCHLEY MAP 11 SP83

🍽 The Crooked Billet
British, French 🍷🍽
Popular gastro-pub
☎ 01908 373936 2 Westbrook End, Newton Longville MK17 0DF

MENU GUIDE Beef fillet carpaccio, celeriac remoulade • Duck cassoulet • Blackberry & almond tart

WINE GUIDE ♀ Durban Viognier £14 • ♥ Tempranillo £14 320 bottles over £20, 80 bottles under £20 • 400 by the glass (£2.85-£150)

continued

continued

AYLESBURY MAP 11 SP81

Hartwell House Hotel Restaurant & Spa

British, International
Unfussy modern cooking meets historic, country-house hotel

☎ 01296 747444 Oxford Rd HP17 8NL

MENU GUIDE Shellfish linguine, langoustine sauce • Lamb noisettes, rosemary creamed potatoes, confit onion, mushrooms • Lemon soufflé, raspberry sorbet

WINE GUIDE ♀ J Mellot Sancerre Sauvignon Blanc £27
♀ P Guillemot Savigny les Beaunes Pinot Noir £35 • 285 bottles over £20, 7 bottles under £20 • 13 by the glass (£4.75-£7.50)

PRICE GUIDE Fixed L £22 • Fixed D £46 • min/water £2.50 • Service included

PLACE: This magnificent, sumptuously restored, palatial mansion, set in 90 acres of landscaped parkland, still feels stately enough for a king - its most famous resident, the exiled Louis XVIII and his French court, took refuge here for five years from 1809. Decorative ceilings and panelling, fine paintings and antique furniture grace the opulent interior thus, it comes without

too much surprise, that it's jackets for gentlemen in the formal but pleasant dining room. Graceful and high-ceilinged, with yellow walls and crisp white linen, it is appropriately and discreetly overseen by attentive, knowledgeable and polite staff.
FOOD: In this setting, comes seasonal, fixed-price, modern menus that combine British and classical influences without over-elaboration or confusion. Simple, intelligent combinations, top-quality ingredients and clear flavours are delivered in assured, accomplished dishes without contemporary fuss.
OUR TIP: Do look over the public rooms, the main staircase and grounds - they're quite wonderful
Chef: Daniel Richardson **Owners:** Historic House Hotels **Times:** 12.30-1.45/7.30-9.45 **Notes:** Vegetarian available, Dress Restrictions, No jeans or trainers; jacket at dinner, Civ Wed 60 **Seats:** 56, Pr/dining room 30
Smoking: N/Sm in restaurant **Children:** Min 8yrs, Portions **Rooms:** 46 (46 en suite) ★★★★ **Directions:** 2m SW of Aylesbury on A418 (Oxford road) **Parking:** 50 **e-mail:** info@hartwell-house.com
web: www.hartwell-house.com

BLETCHLEY *continued* MAP 11 SP83

PRICE GUIDE Starter £4.25-£9 • main £9.25-£20 • dessert £4.25-£9 • coffee £1.95 • min/water £2.60 • Service optional
PLACE: A dream of a village local complete with thatched roof, oak beams and log fires. The candlelit dining areas in this 17th-century coaching inn are packed with atmosphere.
FOOD: Gutsy, modern British and French cooking is delivered from this busy kitchen, with choices from beef and beer sausages with mash and wilted spinach to rack of lamb with a mustard and parsley crust aptly showing the range. Excellent local produce and seasonal ingredients keenly sourced with suppliers listed on the menu.
OUR TIP: Over 500 wines, all available by the glass, and a magnificent cheeseboard
Chef: Emma Gilchrist **Owners:** John & Emma Gilchrist **Times:** 12.30-2.30/7-10.30, Closed 25, 26 Dec, 1st wk Jan, closed L Mon-Sat, closed D Sun **Notes:** Tasting Menu 8 courses £50, with wine £70, Vegetarian available **Seats:** 50 **Smoking:** N/Sm in restaurant **Children:** Min 5 yrs, Portions **Directions:** M1 junct 14 follow A421 towards Buckingham. Turn left at Bottledump rdbt to Newton Longville. Restaurant on right as you enter the village **Parking:** 30 **e-mail:** john@thebillet.co.uk
web: www.thebillet.co.uk

NEW
denotes a restaurant which is new to the guide this year.

🍾 denotes a restaurant with a particularly good wine list.

BUCKINGHAM MAP 11 SP63
🌹🌹 *Villiers Hotel, Henry's Restaurant*
Modern British
Simple enjoyable food in popular coaching inn
☎ 01280 822444 3 Castle St MK18 1BS

MENU GUIDE Garden pea & ham knuckle soup • Lobster, scallop & asparagus risotto • Hot pistachio soufflé

PRICE GUIDE Food prices not confirmed for 2006. Please telephone for details

PLACE: Steeped in history and dating back several centuries, this coaching inn is benefiting from a smart refurbishment. The restaurant look is still classical, but with comfortable contemporary overtones.
FOOD: Bold flavours and superb saucing stand out on the

continued

England

BUCKINGHAM continued MAP 11 SP63

Villiers Hotel, Henry's Restaurant

inventive menu, that aims to feature the cream of the local crop. Quality produce and strong technical skills aside, the chef's fresh ideas and uncomplicated approach to cooking marks this place out as a rising star in the locality.
OUR TIP: Enquire about the dining clubs
Times: 12.30-2/7-10, closed L Mon-Sat **Rooms:** 46 (46 en suite)
★★★★ **Directions:** Town centre - Castle Street is to the R of Town Hall near main square. **e-mail:** buckingham@villiershotels.com
web: www.villiershotels.com/buckinghamshire

DINTON MAP 05 SP71
 La Chouette
Belgian
Authentic Belgian cuisine in peaceful village setting
☎ 01296 747422 Westlington Green HP17 8UW
MENU GUIDE Salad of wild pigeon breast • Beef, green pepper sauce • Glazed winter fruits, sabayon
WINE GUIDE ♀ Pouilly Fumé £25.50 • 85% bottles over £20 2 by the glass (£3)
PRICE GUIDE Fixed L £13.50 • Fixed D £29.50 • starter £9-£16 • main £13.50-£17 • dessert £4.85-£7 • coffee £2 • min/water £4 • Service added but optional 12.5%
PLACE: Set on the green in the delightful village of Dinton, this former pub is now a Belgian restaurant full of character. Original 16th-century features have been preserved, including stone walls, wooden beams and a hearty inglenook fireplace.
FOOD: Carefully crafted classical cuisine. Dishes are simple in style and rely on high quality produce for impact; expect a lengthy menu with idiosyncratic notes from the owner to indicate dishes conjured from completely Belgian produce.
OUR TIP: Excellent wine list
Chef: Frederic Desmette **Owners:** M F Desmette **Times:** 12-2/7-9, Closed Sun, closed L Sat **Notes:** Fixed D 5 courses £39.50, Vegetarian by request only **Seats:** 35 **Smoking:** N/Sm in restaurant
Children: Portions **Directions:** On A418 at Dinton **Parking:** 20

GREAT MISSENDEN MAP 06 SP80
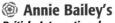 **Annie Bailey's**
British, International
Lively Mediterranean-themed restaurant
☎ 01494 865625 Chesham Rd, Hyde End HP16 0QT
MENU GUIDE Grilled black pudding, braised red cabbage Beer-battered haddock fillet • Chocolate bread & butter pudding
WINE GUIDE ♀ Pecile Pinot Grigio £15 • ♀ Rioja Vega £17.50 • 10 bottles over £20, 16 bottles under £20 • 12 by the glass (£2.75-£7.50)

continued

PRICE GUIDE Fixed L £12.50-£22 • Fixed D £16.50-£28.50 • starter £4.50-£7.50 • main £8.50-£17.50 • dessert £4-£6 • coffee £2 • min/water £2.25 • Service optional
PLACE: A former roadside pub just outside Great Missenden, named after a previous landlady. A warming Mediterranean colour scheme is backed up by a crackling fire in winter.
FOOD: The Mediterranean theme extends to the food, with a brasserie-style menu dispensing generous portions of versatile dishes. Starters double as light bites, with mains like pot roast partridge with juniper berries yielding a feast of flavours.
OUR TIP: Remember the daily specials section
Chef: Nelson Linhares **Owners:** Open All Hours (UK) Ltd **Times:** 12-2.30/7-9.30, Closed D Sun **Notes:** Speciality menus, 2 courses £15, 3 courses £19, Vegetarian available **Seats:** 65 **Smoking:** N/Sm area, No pipes, No cigars **Children:** Portions **Directions:** Off A413 at Great Missenden. On B485 towards Chesham **Parking:** 40
e-mail: stephanie@anniebaileys.com **web:** www.anniebaileys.com

HADDENHAM MAP 05 SP70
◎◎ **Green Dragon**
British
Quality food in a relaxed pub atmosphere
☎ 01844 291403 8 Churchway HP17 8AA

MENU GUIDE Avocado & crab tian • Sautéed calves' liver & bacon, caramelised baby onion sauce • Sticky toffee & date pudding
WINE GUIDE ♀ Mount Marble Chenin £12.75 • ♀ Mount Marble Pinotage £16 • 23 bottles over £20, 29 bottles under £20 • 14 by the glass (£3.10-£6.50)
PRICE GUIDE Starter £3.95-£8.50 • main £8.95-£18.50 • dessert £5.50 • min/water £3.50 • Service added but optional 10%
PLACE: Converted into a gastro venture a few years ago, this pretty 17th-century pub has appeared in several television programmes due to its picturesque village location, close to the duck pond and church. One large room is dominated by a bar accessible on three sides. Contemporary lighting contrasts with an eclectic mix of artefacts, prints and pottery.

continued

England

FOOD: Friendly pub favourites alongside more contemporary dishes, provide a diversity of choice appropriate for the range of clientele, from walkers in for snack to those celebrating a special occasion. **OUR TIP:** Try the specials lunch menu - great value! **Chef:** Paul Berry **Owners:** Mr & Mrs Moffat, Paul Berry **Times:** 12-2/6.30-9.30, Closed 25 Dec & 1 Jan, closed D Sun **Notes:** Fixed D Tue & Thu only. Sun L £18.95, Vegetarian available, Dress Restrictions, No cut off jeans **Seats:** 60, Pr/dining room 14 **Smoking:** N/Sm in restaurant **Children:** Min 7 yrs, Portions **Directions:** From M40 take A329 towards Thame, then A418. Turn 1st right after entering Haddenham **Parking:** 18 **e-mail:** paul@eatatthedragon.co.uk **web:** www.eatatthedragon.co.uk

HIGH WYCOMBE MAP 05 SU89

🎖 Fusions Restaurant & Bar
British, International **NEW**

Contemporary dining in smart conservatory

☎ 01494 430378 Ambassador Court Hotel, 145 West Wycombe Rd HP12 3AB

MENU GUIDE Pan-fried scallops • Salmon fillet, vegetable risotto • Carrot & ginger pudding

WINE GUIDE ♀ Domaine de la Pauliere Petit Chablis £18.50 • ♀ Marques de Caceres Rioja Crianza £16.50 • 9 bottles over £20, 20 bottles under £20 • 7 by the glass (£2.95-£4.20)

PRICE GUIDE Fixed D £25-£35 • starter £5.25-£8.95 • main £12.50-£17.50 • dessert £5.50-£7.50 • coffee £2.95 • min/water £1.50 • Service added but optional 12.5%

PLACE: A bright and airy conservatory with cherry wood flooring and beech furniture houses this hotel restaurant. Funky cutlery, square plates and oddly-shaped saucers are a delightfully quirky feature. **FOOD:** Named Fusions after its Eastern-influenced cooking, the food is also a mixture of modern and classical styles, with chicken liver parfait and loin of venison sharing the menu with tomato and lemongrass broth, and butternut and goats' cheese mille-feuille. **OUR TIP:** Good wines by the glass **Chef:** Bernard Gerretsen **Owners:** Shafiq Ahmed **Times:** 6.30-9, Closed Sun-Mon, closed L Mon-Sun **Notes:** Vegetarian available, Smart Dress **Seats:** 32 **Smoking:** N/Sm in restaurant **Children:** Min 12 yrs, Menu **Rooms:** 18 (18 en suite) ★★★ **Directions:** M40 junct 4. A404 towards High Wycombe. Down hill , at rdbts, follow A40 Aylesbury. Restaurant on left, next to BP garage. **Parking:** 18 **e-mail:** dine@fusionsrestaurant.com **web:** www.fusionsrestaurant.com

🍴 The Red Lion Missenden Rd, Great Kingshill HP15 6EB
☎ 01494 711262 & 713173 Rustic value-for-money dining

IVINGHOE MAP 11 SP91

🎖 The King's Head
British, French 🚜

Formal dining with old-fashioned style

☎ 01296 668264 & 668388 LU7 9EB

MENU GUIDE Chicken liver parfait, port jelly • Poached fillet of turbot, vermouth & carrot jus • Chocolate marquise

WINE GUIDE 80 bottles over £20, 2 bottles under £20 • 2 by the glass (£4.50)

PRICE GUIDE Fixed L £17.50 • coffee £3.95 • min/water £3.95 • Service added but optional 12.5%

PLACE: Delightful old coaching inn, where old-fashioned values hold sway among the beams, flagstone floors and crackling log fires. The proprietor leads his team of immaculately dressed staff with understated professionalism. The heavily timbered dining
continued

The King's Head

room is decorated in rich colours with tables dressed in crisp white napery. **FOOD:** Modern British with French accents and concessions to tradition, such as carving and flambé at the table and desserts from the trolley. Separate vegetarian menu. **OUR TIP:** Banqueting suite for private functions. **Chef:** Jonathan O'Keeffe **Owners:** G.A.P.J Ltd **Times:** 12-3/7-10, Closed 27-30 Dec, closed D Sun **Notes:** ALC 3 courses £32.50-£42.50 incl coffee, Vegetarian available, No jeans, trainers or shorts **Seats:** 55, Pr/dining room 40 **Smoking:** N/Sm in restaurant, Air con **Children:** Portions **Directions:** From M25 junct 20 take A41 past Tring. Turn right on to B488 (Ivinghoe), hotel at junction with B489 **Parking:** 20 **e-mail:** info@kingsheadivinghoe.co.uk **web:** www.kingsheadivinghoe.co.uk

LONG CRENDON MAP 05 SP60

🎖 The Angel Restaurant
European, Pacific Rim 🐟

Attractive, busy gastro-pub

☎ 01844 208268 47 Bicester Rd HP18 9EE

MENU GUIDE Duck and bacon salad, hoi sin dressing • Chargrilled Highland beef, stilton rarebit • Espresso crème brûlée

continued

England

LONG CRENDON *continued* MAP 05 SP60

WINE GUIDE 11 by the glass (£3.75-£6.50)

PRICE GUIDE Fixed L fr £14.95 • Fixed D £29.50-£32.50 • starter £3.75-£7.50 • main £15.95-£23.50 • dessert £4.50-£4.95 • coffee £2.95 • min/water £3.50 • Service optional

PLACE: An old coaching inn whose cared-for white façade hides an appealing interior of exposed wood, flagged floors and contemporary use of natural materials. Deep cosy sofas face wood fires opposite the bar; four separate dining areas include an air-conditioned conservatory.

FOOD: Classic, mainly European treatments of simply cooked dishes, where the flavour, texture and presentation maximise the quality of ingredients used. Fish is a speciality, with daily arrivals listed on the blackboard.

OUR TIP: Ideal for informal small parties

Chef: Trevor Bosch, Donald Joyce **Owners:** Trevor Bosch, Annie Bosch **Times:** 12-2.30/7-9.30, Closed D Sun **Notes:** Vegetarian available, Smart Dress **Seats:** 75, Pr/dining room 14 **Smoking:** N/Sm area, Air con **Children:** Portions **Directions:** Beside B4011, 2m NW of Thame **Parking:** 30 **e-mail:** angelrestaurant@aol.com **web:** www.angelrestaurant.co.uk

---

MARLOW MAP 05 SU88

⊛⊛⊛ The Compleat Angler *see page 53*

⊛⊛ Danesfield House Hotel & Spa
British, French
Refined country house dining with a view
☎ 01628 891010 Henley Rd SL7 2EY

MENU GUIDE Roast sea scallops with ginger • Rack of English lamb with rosemary • Malmsbury berry flan, vanilla anglaise

WINE GUIDE ♀ Bellefontaine Chardonnay £21 • ♀ Bellefontaine Grenache £21 • 4 by the glass (£4.95-£5.50)

continued

PRICE GUIDE Fixed D £43 • coffee £4.50 • Service added but optional 12.5%

PLACE: Set high above the Thames with magnificent views, this stunning white stone country house is set in 65 acres. There is a cavenous great hall with high rafters and an elegant Oak Room restaurant with oak panelling from floor to ceiling.

FOOD: The modern British menu with French influences offers both simple and elaborate dishes, all carried off with excellent presentation and quality. The extensive wine list is well worth a look. Service is formal yet friendly and unobtrusive.

OUR TIP: Enjoy alfresco dining on the terrace

Chef: Steven Morris **Owners:** Danesfield House Hotel Ltd **Times:** 12-2/7-10 **Notes:** Vegetarian available, Dress Restrictions, Jacket & tie, Civ Wed 100 **Seats:** 45, Pr/dining room 100 **Smoking:** N/Sm in restaurant **Children:** Min 4yrs, Menu, Portions **Rooms:** 87 (87 en suite) ★★★★ **Directions:** M4 junct 8/9 to Marlow. 2m from Marlow on A4155 **Parking:** 100 **e-mail:** sales@danesfieldhouse.co.uk **web:** www.danesfieldhouse.co.uk

⊛⊛ The Vanilla Pod
British, French
Creative cooking in relaxed environment
☎ 01628 898101 31 West St SL7 2LS

MENU GUIDE Lemon risotto, smoked salmon, tiger prawns • Pot-roast pork, mushroom fricassée, prunes • Praline crème brûlée, rice pudding

WINE GUIDE ♀ Jean Rax Roger Sancerre Sauvignon Blanc £28.50 • ♀ Château Laplagnotte-Bellevue Merlot/Cabernet Sauvignon £35 • 45 bottles over £20, 5 bottles under £20 • 4 by the glass (£3.50)

PRICE GUIDE Fixed L £17.50 • Fixed D £40 • coffee £3 • min/water £3 • Service optional

PLACE: This cosy cottage restaurant in the centre of Marlow has a warm and welcoming ambience thanks to a bright Mediterranean colour scheme and bold paintings. It draws a mix of suits and day-trippers, and is handily located opposite a public car park.

FOOD: Imagination and a light touch lift the Vanilla Pod's modern British menu with French influences out of the ordinary. Well-judged combinations might include corn-fed chicken with apple mash, or rib of beef with beans wrapped in Parma ham and boulangère potatoes. Vegetarian and seven-course tasting menus available.

OUR TIP: TS Eliot once lived here

Chef: Michael Macdonald **Owners:** Michael & Stephanie Macdonald **Times:** 12-2.30/7-11, Closed 23 Dec-3 Jan, 22 Aug-6 Sep, Mon-Sun **Notes:** Tasting menu 7 courses £45, Vegetarian available, Dress Restrictions, Smart casual **Seats:** 34, Pr/dining room 8 **Smoking:** N/Sm in restaurant **Children:** Portions **Directions:** From M4 junct 8/9 or M40 junct 4 take A404, A4155 to Marlow. From Henley take A4155 **Parking:** On West Street **e-mail:** info@thevanillapod.co.uk **web:** www.thevanillapod.co.uk

MARLOW MAP 05 SU88

The Compleat Angler

International
Assured cooking in formal restaurant overlooking the Thames
☎ 0870 4008100 Marlow Bridge SL7 1RG
e-mail: compleatangler@macdonald-hotels.co.uk
web: www.compleatangler-hotel.co.uk

PLACE: A fabulous setting on the banks of the River Thames, overlooking the rushing waters at Marlow Weir, ensures the popularity of this well-established Georgian hotel named after Izaak Walton's famous book on angling. The formal Riverside Restaurant, with its high-backed chairs and crisp white linen, offers those Thameside views through windows dotted with the occasional pane of stained glass, while other walls feature friezes of the town and countryside in times gone by. The relaxed atmosphere is enhanced by candlelight, a roaring fire in winter and a warm approach from friendly staff.

FOOD: Imaginative menus show sound judgement and execution from breads through to petits fours, with dish construction kept intelligently simple. High-quality ingredients, clean flavours, good presentation and technical skill - based around classical themes - feature on crisply scripted, fixed-price menus (with a few supplements thrown in). Think crab tortellini with cep mushroom ice cream, followed by wild sea bass fillet served on fennel with langoustine, and a rhubarb soufflé and ginger ice cream finale.

MENU GUIDE Truffle & celery risotto, sautéed brill • Roast suckling pig, apple purée, pak choi • Honey sponge, rich chocolate & honey sorbet

WINE GUIDE ♀ Katherine Hills Colombard Chardonnay £19.50 • ♂ Katherine Hills Shiraz Cabernet £19.50 • 100 bottles over £20, 4 bottles under £20 • 8 by the glass (£4.25-£6.75)

PRICE GUIDE Fixed L £22-£32 • Fixed D £37.50-£48.50 • coffee £3.50 • min/water £4.75 • Service added but optional 12.5%

OUR TIP: Be sure to enjoy a drink outside on the terrace in fine weather

Chef: Dean Timpson **Owners:** Macdonald Hotels **Times:** 12.30-2/7-10 **Notes:** Vegetarian available, Dress Restrictions, Smart casual, no jeans or trainers, Civ Wed 100 **Seats:** 80, Pr/dining room 110 **Smoking:** N/Sm in restaurant **Children:** Portions **Rooms:** 64 (64 en suite) ★★★★ **Directions:** From M4 junct8/9, A404 to rdbt, take Bisham exit, 1m to Marlow Bridge, hotel on right. **Parking:** 60

England

TAPLOW MAP 06 SU98

⊚⊚ Cliveden, The Terrace Dining Room
French
Grand dining at grand prices
☎ 01628 668561 Cliveden Estate SL6 0JF

MENU GUIDE Chilled avocado & cucumber soup • Angus beef fillet with stuffed braised lettuce • Cliveden sherry trifle

WINE GUIDE ♀ Domaine Jean Pierre Grossot Chablis Chardonnay £49 • ♥ Château Branaire Ducru Blend £59 520 bottles over £20 • 8 by the glass (£6-£44)

PRICE GUIDE Fixed L £29.50 • Fixed D £49.50 • Service optional

PLACE: The three-storey Italianate mansion is famous for having been home to Lady Nancy Astor, whose hospitality was legendary - keeping the likes of Winston Churchill and Charlie Chaplin entertained. The interiors are truly lavish; this is reflected in the Terrace Dining Room, with its high ceilings, chandeliers and classic views over the parterre down to the River Thames. The opulence is balanced with excellent service by smartly uniformed staff.

FOOD: Fixed-price seasonal French menus have a traditional feel with some more modern touches. The wine list is exceptional - and enormous - have it sent to your room to study before dinner!

OUR TIP: Enjoy the wonderful National Trust gardens
Chef: Daniel Galmiche **Owners:** Von Essen Hotels **Times:** 12-2.30/7-9.30 **Notes:** Vegetarian available, Dress Restrictions, Jacket or tie, Civ Wed 120 **Seats:** 80, Pr/dining room 60 **Smoking:** N/Sm in restaurant **Children:** Menu, Portions **Directions:** M40 junct 2 A355 into Burnham Rd/Littleworth Rd. Follow signs for Wooburn/Taplow, then for Cliveden. **Parking:** 60 **e-mail:** reservations@clivedenhouse.co.uk
web: www.clivedenhouse.co.uk

⊚⊚ Taplow House Hotel
Modern French **NEW**
Skilful cooking in elegant Georgian manor
☎ 01628 670056 Berry Hill SL6 0DA
MENU GUIDE Salmon tartare, caviar • Rabbit, braised leg tortellini, Madeira cream • Hot chocolate fondant, prune & Armagnac ice cream

PRICE GUIDE Food prices not confirmed for 2006. Please telephone for details

PLACE: Restored with care, this appealing Georgian manor sits in beautiful gardens not far from Cliveden. Period pictures and a pastel green colour scheme give its restaurant an elegant, traditional feel, with tables well-spaced for privacy and presided over by attentive staff.

FOOD: Tried and tested combinations are the foundation for a tempting modern French menu, but there's the odd touch of innovation too and no shortage of skill. Choose from the carte, or treat yourself to the tasting menu.

OUR TIP: Terrace and bar for lighter options or alfresco dining
Times: 12-2/7-9.30 **e-mail:** taplow@wrensgroup.com
web: www.taplowhouse.com

⊚⊚⊚ Waldo's Restaurant, Cliveden see page 55

WOOBURN COMMON MAP 06 SU98

⊚ Chequers Inn
British, French
Quintessential English coaching inn
☎ 01628 529575 Kiln Ln HP10 0JQ
MENU GUIDE Pan-fried baby octopus salad • Asian-spiced red mullet fillets • Toffee & banana crumble

PRICE GUIDE Fixed L £13.95 • starter £6-£9 • main £14.50-£22 • dessert fr £6 • coffee £2.75 • min/water £3.95 • Service optional

PLACE: Lots of character will be found in this delightful inn, where open fires, exposed beams and flagstone floors attest to its age. Away from the bar's hustle and bustle is the conservatory restaurant, not unlike the pub in style and with a similarly cosy atmosphere.

FOOD: The innovative British and French menu with global influences benefits from superb quality ingredients, with breast of duck glazed in redcurrant jelly likely to melt in the mouth.

OUR TIP: Try the bar menu in the comfy new lounge
Chef: Alex Turner **Owners:** PJ Roehrig **Times:** 12-2.30/7-9.30 **Notes:** Vegetarian available, Smart Dress **Seats:** 60, Pr/dining room 60 **Smoking:** No pipes, No cigars **Children:** Portions **Rooms:** 17 (17 en suite) ★★ **Directions:** Telephone for directions **Parking:** 50 **e-mail:** info@chequers-inn.com
web: thechequersatwooburncommon.co.uk

> **Three Rosettes** Outstanding restaurants that demand recognition well beyond their local area. Timing, seasoning and the judgement of flavour combinations will be consistently excellent, supported by other elements such as intelligent service and a well-chosen wine list. Around 10% of restaurants with Rosettes have been awarded three.

England

TAPLOW MAP 06 SU98

Waldo's Restaurant, Cliveden

French *Discreet, luxurious, with exceptional cooking and service*
☎ 01628 668561   Cliveden Estate SL6 0JF
e-mail: reservations@clivedenhouse.co.uk
web: www.clivedenhouse.co.uk

PLACE: One of the country's finest stately homes, set at the top of a magnificent gravel drive and brimful of fabulous art, Cliveden oozes a sense of history and class. The views from the terrace over the formal parterre to the Thames beyond are quite breathtaking. The intimate and plush Waldo's is the hotel's flagship restaurant, with luxurious carpet, wood panelling and large round tables, where orchids and shimmering silverware are the norm. Walls are lined with a fascinating collection of paintings, including a pastel portrait by Stephen Ward of his friend Christine Keeler, who together brought controversy to Cliveden via the Profumo scandal.
FOOD: Chef Daniel Galmiche's (ex L'Ortolan, Shinfield and one-time Harveys, Bristol) pedigree is assured, his well-considered, modern approach - underpinned by classical themes - lets knock-out quality ingredients shine, with clean, clear flavours and a lightness of touch. Expect the likes of langoustines sautéed with smooth caramelised cauliflower purée, essence of crustacés and a thin seaweed cracker, perhaps followed by monkfish, roasted on the bone, with braised pork, sautéed salsify and caramelised pancetta to grace the fixed-price dinner or seasonal-changing tasting menus.

MENU GUIDE Scallops, new potatoes, truffle & parmesan salad • Beef fillet, truffle potato purée, duck liver salad • Bitter chocolate delice, basil & yogurt sorbet

WINE GUIDE ♀ Domaine Grossot Chablis Chardonnay £49 • ♀ Château Troqlong Rondof Merlot/Cabernet Sauvignon £91 • 520 bottles over £20 • 8 by the glass (£5-£44)

PRICE GUIDE Fixed D £65 • min/water £4.50 • Service optional

OUR TIP: You do need to book well in advance for this small restaurant

Chef: Daniel Galmiche **Owners:** Von Essen Hotels **Times:** 7-9.30, Closed Sun & Mon, closed L all week **Notes:** Vegetarian available, Dress Restrictions, Jacket, Civ Wed 120 **Seats:** 28, Pr/dining room 12 **Smoking:** N/Sm in restaurant, Air con **Children:** Min 12yrs **Rooms:** 39 (39 en suite) ★★★★★ **Directions:** M40 junct 2 onto A355, right into Burnham Rd/Littleworth Rd. Follow signs for Wooburn/Taplow, then for Cliveden. **Parking:** 60

England

CAMBRIDGESHIRE

BRAMPTON MAP 12 TL27

The Grange Hotel

British, European

Quality cooking in a relaxed village setting

☎ 01480 459516 115 High St PE28 4RA

MENU GUIDE Seared scallops, fennel, crispy black pudding • Braised lamb shank, mashed winter vegetables • Tarte Tatin, Calvados sorbet

WINE GUIDE ♀ Avio Pinot Grigio £15 • ♂ Robertson Cabernet £14 • 12 by the glass (£2.10-£4.50)

PRICE GUIDE Starter £4.50-£8 • main £8.50-£18 • dessert £4.75-£6 • coffee £2 • min/water £3 • Service optional

PLACE: Historic building on the village high street, which has in its time been the HQ of the American Eighth Airforce and a girls' school. The restaurant is airy, comfortable and traditionally decorated.
FOOD: The same modern British menu with French influences is offered throughout the hotel including some quite simple dishes, but there is no doubting the skill in the kitchen. The monthly selection reflects the seasons and highlights creative combinations, such as gazpacho sorbet, and quality seasonal ingredients, with sausages, bacon, pork and venison sourced from the Denham Estate.
OUR TIP: Additional blackboard menu in the bar
Chef: Nick Steiger **Owners:** Susanna & Nick Steiger **Times:** 12-2/6.30-9.30, Closed 1st wk Jan, BHs, closed D Sun **Notes:** Sun lunch 2 courses £12.50, 3 courses £15, coffee incl, Vegetarian available, Dress Restrictions, No shorts or bare feet, Civ Wed 40 **Seats:** 32, Pr/dining room 16 **Smoking:** N/Sm in restaurant **Children:** Portions **Rooms:** 7 (7 en suite) ★★ **Directions:** 0.5m E from A1/A14 junct 21 on B1514. Close to Brampton racecourse, 1.5m W from Huntingdon **Parking:** 25
e-mail: info@grangehotelbrampton.com
web: www.grangehotelbrampton.com

CAMBRIDGE MAP 12 TL45

Cambridge Quy Mill Hotel

British

Enjoyable dining in converted former watermill

☎ 01223 293383 Newmarket Rd, Stow Cum Quy CB5 9AG

MENU GUIDE Turbot & king prawn terrine • Duck breast with sesame & honey • Coffee & Tia Maria roulade

WINE GUIDE ♀ Chardonnay £15.75 • ♂ Shiraz £15.75 9 bottles over £20, 21 bottles under £20 • 13 by the glass (£2.95-£4.75)

Cambridge Quy Mill Hotel

PRICE GUIDE Starter £5-£7.95 • main £12.95-£19.75 • dessert £5-£6.95 • coffee £2.75 • min/water £3.75 • Service optional • Group min 8 service 10%

PLACE: This 19th-century former watermill and miller's house is conveniently located for Cambridge. The huge original water wheel can be viewed behind glass in the private dining room.
FOOD: Good use of quality ingredients is in evidence in the cooking. The menus features fairly traditional dishes that have been given a modern interpretation, like fillet of cod Viennoise with warm tomato chutney and thyme roasted new potatoes.
OUR TIP: Spacious and comfortable lounge areas
Chef: Nathan Carriage **Owners:** David Munro **Times:** 12-2.30/7-9.45, Closed 27-31 Dec, closed D 24-26 Dec **Notes:** Vegetarian available, Dress Restrictions, No shorts (men), Civ Wed 80 **Seats:** 48, Pr/dining room 70 **Smoking:** N/Sm area, No pipes, No cigars **Children:** Menu, Portions **Rooms:** 41 (41 en suite) ★★★ **Directions:** Turn off A14 at junction 35 E of Cambridge onto B1102 for 50yds, hotel entrance opposite church **Parking:** 90 **e-mail:** cambridgequy@bestwestern.co.uk

Graffiti at Hotel Felix

Mediterranean

Enjoyable brasserie dining in stylish hotel

☎ 01223 277977 Whitehouse Ln CB3 0LX

continued

continued on page 58

CAMBRIDGE MAP 12 TL45

Midsummer House

French *The city's finest restaurant*
☎ 01223 369299 Midsummer Common CB4 1HA
e-mail: reservations@midsummerhouse.co.uk
web: www.midsummerhouse.co.uk

PLACE: Even when the sun doesn't shine into the airy double conservatory that dominates this restaurant housed in a handsome Victorian villa on the appealingly named Midsummer Common, a bright interior and some vivacious, imaginative cooking mean you won't miss out. Backing onto the river and opening onto a pretty, secluded walled garden of fragrant herbs and mature trees, with views of the common and river boathouses, the dining room incorporates white-clothed, well-spaced tables and burgundy and gold high-back chairs. Service is discreet and welcoming, slick and well informed from Jean Bertraud and the sommelier.
FOOD: This is seriously accomplished cooking, Daniel Clifford's inventive style has a strong classic French grounding with modern focus, delivering plenty of vibrant colours and clear, fresh flavours in unusual combinations, backed by impeccable workmanship and care over sauces and garnishes. Take poached and grilled Anjou squab pigeon, for instance, served with a pastilla of cherries, sweet potato purée, spinach and pistachios, chocolate jelly and sauce Valrhona, or a classic apple tart Tatin, paired with garlic and bay leaf foam and vanilla ice cream.

MENU GUIDE Foie gras ballotine, apricots & rocket • Monkfish, sauté chanterelles, parsnip purée, spinach, essence of bacon • Caramel & lime soufflé, ginger & lemongrass ice cream

PRICE GUIDE Fixed L £20 • Fixed D £48.50 • coffee £4 • min/water £3.95 • Group min 7 service 12.5%

OUR TIP: Take time for a walk along the river

Chef: Daniel Clifford **Owners:** Midsummer House Ltd.
Times: 12-2/7-9.30, Closed 18 Dec-3 Jan, 20-29 Mar, 14-30 Aug, Sun-Mon, closed L Tues-Thurs **Notes:** Tasting menu £65, Vegetarian available, Civ Wed 50 **Seats:** 50, Pr/dining room 20 **Smoking:** N/Sm in restaurant **Children:** Menu, Portions **Directions:** Park in Pretoria Rd, then walk across footbridge. Restaurant on left **Parking:** On street

England

CAMBRIDGE continued MAP 12 TL45

MENU GUIDE Girolle & smoked garlic risotto • Lamb noisettes, pumpkin & oregano fondant • Cassis soufflé

WINE GUIDE ♀ Hoopenburg Sauvignon Blanc £16.50 • ♀ Christa Rolf Shiraz Grenache £23.50 • 39 bottles over £20, 14 bottles under £20 • 13 by the glass (£3.50-£4)

PRICE GUIDE Fixed L £12.50 • starter £5.75-£11.95 • main £12.95-£23.95 • dessert £6.50-£6.75 • coffee £2.50 • min/water £3 • Service optional • Group min 10 service 10%

PLACE: Based on a Victorian mansion dating from 1852, this modern stylish hotel has three acres of landscaped gardens. The interior is unabashedly modern. Pastel tones predominate. Yet for all the clean lines and dark hardwood flooring, most original features have been retained. The bistro-style Graffiti restaurant overlooks the garden and has a terrace for alfresco dining.
FOOD: In keeping with the decor, cooking is modern with Mediterranean influences with starters like merguez sausage and haricot blanc cappuccino, and main courses such as monkfish with spinach, squid ink and elderflower and grappa jelly.
OUR TIP: Great base for touring Cambridge
Chef: Stuart Conibear **Owners:** Jeremy Cassel **Times:** 12-2/6.30-10.30
Notes: Vegetarian available, Smart Dress, Civ Wed 75 **Seats:** 45, Pr/dining room 60 **Smoking:** N/Sm in restaurant **Children:** Portions **Rooms:** 52 (52 en suite) ★★★★ **Directions:** From A1 N take A14 turning onto A1307. At City of Cambridge sign turn left into Whitehouse Lane. M11 junct 12 **Parking:** 90 **e-mail:** help@hotelfelix.co.uk **web:** www.hotelfelix.co.uk

⊛⊛⊛ Midsummer House see page 57

see page 57

⊛ 22 Chesterton Road

British, European

Good food and reasonable prices in relaxed setting

☎ 01223 351880 22 Chesterton Rd CB4 3AX

MENU GUIDE Spiced marinated squid, rocket • Duck breast, rhubarb Tatin, Calvados jus • Grand Marnier parfait, orange salad, biscotti

WINE GUIDE ♀ Domaine Pouilly Fumé Pablot Sauvignon £19.95 • ♀ Montes Pinot Noir £18.95 • 45 bottles over £20, 27 bottles under £20 • 4 by the glass (£3.50-£3.75)

PRICE GUIDE Fixed D £24.50 • coffee £2.25 • min/water £2.75 • Service optional

PLACE: This Victorian townhouse has been converted to provide a candlelit dining area with an intimate and comfortable ambience. Service is friendly and informal but never too relaxed. A private dining room is also available, seating 12 people.
FOOD: Modern British with some French dishes. There's an emphasis on good quality, fresh local ingredients. Skilled preparation and traditional combinations create comforting menus.
OUR TIP: Wine evening events are a feature
Chef: Martin Cullum/Seb Mansfield **Owners:** Mr D Carter **Times:** 7-9.45, Closed 25 Dec & New Year, Sun-Mon, closed L all week
Notes: Vegetarian available **Seats:** 26, Pr/dining room 12
Smoking: N/Sm in restaurant, Air con **Children:** Min 10yrs, Portions **Directions:** Telephone for directions **Parking:** on street
e-mail: davidcarter@restaurant22.co.uk **web:** www.restaurant22.co.uk

⊛ **Anatolies** Bridge St CB2 1UJ ☎ 01223 312412 This Turkish restaurant is set in the basement of the building and has a charcoal grill and live entertainment.

⊛ **Loch Fyne Restaurant & Oyster Bar** The Little Rose, 37 Trumpington St CB2 1QY ☎ 01223 362433 Quality seafood chain.

⊛ **The Venue** 1st Floor, Cambridge Art Theatre Building CB2 3PJ ☎ 01223 367333 A contemporary, leather and chrome style restaurant with contemporary fusion cooking and live piano.

DUXFORD MAP 12 TL44

⊛⊛ Duxford Lodge Hotel

Modern European

Elegant dining in country house restaurant

☎ 01223 836444 Ickleton Rd CB2 4RT

MENU GUIDE Rabbit & foie gras terrine, beetroot dressing • Pan-fried duck, juniper berry jus • Pear & blueberry tart

PRICE GUIDE Food prices not confirmed for 2006. Please telephone for details

PLACE: A secluded village centre setting, close proximity to the M11 (J10) and historic connections with the Duxford Imperial War Museum: this neat, red-brick hotel has much going for it. Birds of paradise wall coverings decorate the light and airy Le Paradis dining room. Polished formal service from welcoming staff.
FOOD: Bold, modern European-style menu combining a healthy dose of imagination with technical ability.
OUR TIP: Good value fixed-price menu
Times: 12-3/7-10 **Rooms:** 15 (15 en suite) ★★★ **Directions:** M11 J10, take A505 E, then 1st R at roundabout to Duxford; take R fork at T-junction, entrance 70 yds on L
e-mail: admin@duxfordlodgehotel.co.uk
web: www.duxfordlodgehotel.co.uk

ELY MAP 12 TL58

🏵 The Anchor Inn
British, International

Simple fresh food in cosy waterside inn

☎ 01353 778537 Sutton Gault, Sutton CB6 2BD

MENU GUIDE Red mullet, vanilla cream sauce • Confit shoulder of pork • Date, fig & carrot pudding

WINE GUIDE ♀ Domaine Les Escasses Ugni Blanc, Colombard £13.25 • ♀ Rioja Tinto Livor £14.50 • 19 bottles over £20, 22 bottles under £20 • 11 by the glass (£3.25-£5.80)

PRICE GUIDE Fixed L £10 • Fixed D £18-£21 • starter £4.50-£6.50 • main £10-£19 • dessert £4.50-£6.50 • coffee £2.35 • min/water £3.20 • Service optional • Group min 10 service 10%

PLACE: Superbly located beside the New Bedford River deep in Fen country, this typically English inn was built in 1650 to accommodate the workers draining the Fens. It retains much of its original rustic charm, with original beams, undulating floors, roaring log fires, scrubbed pine tables and gas lighting. Relaxed service from friendly staff.
FOOD: Reliance on quality local produce is evident on daily menus and the resulting clear flavours from simple, confident cooking.
OUR TIP: Busy in summer so best to book
Chef: Barbara Jordan **Owners:** Robin & Heather Moore **Times:** 12-3.30/7-11, Closed 26 Dec **Notes:** Sun L 2 course £17, 3 course £21, Vegetarian available **Seats:** 70 **Smoking:** N/Sm area, No pipes **Children:** Menu, Portions **Rooms:** 2 (2 en suite) ♦♦♦♦
Directions: Signed off B1381 in Sutton village, 7m W of Ely via A142 **Parking:** 16 **e-mail:** AnchorInnSG@aol.com
web: www.anchor-inn-restaurant.co.uk

HUNTINGDON MAP 12 TL27

🏵🏵 Old Bridge Hotel
British, Mediterranean

18th-century hotel and inn stamped throughout with quality

☎ 01480 424300 PE29 3TQ

MENU GUIDE Tuna carpaccio • Roast Bleesdale pheasant breast, braised red cabbage • Fig tart, Earl Grey ice cream

WINE GUIDE ♀ Maoridge Sauvignon Blanc £14.75 • ♀ The Beak Rolf Binder Shiraz Grenache £16.75 • 250 bottles over £20, 40 bottles under £20 • 16 by the glass (£3.25-£9.50)

PRICE GUIDE Fixed L £12.50 • starter £4.95-£9.95 • main £9.95-£22.50 • dessert £4.95-£7.95 • coffee £2.50 • min/water £3 • Service optional

PLACE: Guarding the old bridge into town is this delightful ivy-clad hotel, where the traditional values of warm hospitality and fine food and wines continue to exert a timeless appeal. A stylish modern makeover in the restaurant provides further confirmation of high standards.
FOOD: The uncompromising quality of the building also defines the menus, where seasonal flavours are captured and dispatched to diners with consistent skill. A fixed-price menu brings the same elegant cooking into range for a lower budget.
OUR TIP: Award-winning wine list deserves careful consideration
Chef: Martin Lee **Owners:** J Hoskins, Martin Lee, Jayne Lee **Times:** 12-2.30/6.30-9.30 **Notes:** Vegetarian available, Civ Wed 80 **Seats:** 100, Pr/dining room 20 **Smoking:** N/Sm in restaurant, Air con **Children:** Menu, Portions **Rooms:** 24 (24 en suite) ★★★
Directions: Off A1 near junction with A1/M1 link and A604/M11 **Parking:** 60 **e-mail:** oldbridge@huntsbridge.co.uk
web: www.huntsbridge.com

KEYSTON MAP 11 TL07

🏵 Pheasant Inn
British, European

Gastro-pub in a rural village

☎ 01832 710241 Village Loop Rd PE28 0RE

MENU GUIDE Salt beef, baby beet, potato, gherkin & chive salad • Calves' liver, Puy lentil casserole, pancetta • Hot chocolate fondant

WINE GUIDE ♀ Hellfire Bay Chardonnay £15.95 • ♀ The Beak Rolf Binder Shiraz-Grenache £14.50 • 100 bottles over £20, 50 bottles under £20 • 16 by the glass (£3.25-£9.50)

PRICE GUIDE Starter £4.75-£8.95 • main £9.75-£19.50 • dessert £4.50-£6.95 • coffee £1.90 • min/water £2.95 • Service optional

PLACE: This thatched inn turned gastro-pub has kept its old-fashioned charm and is prettily set by a green in a rural village. Dine in the smart restaurant or the more informal bar.
FOOD: Modern fare, with a monthly menu complemented by daily blackboard specials. Mains include fresh fish from Cornwall and steaks, as well as more complex contemporary dishes such as corn-fed chicken with purple sprouting broccoli, and celeriac and potato purée.
OUR TIP: Children's menu available
Chef: James Claydon **Owners:** John Hoskins **Times:** 12-2.15/6.30-9.30 **Notes:** Vegetarian available **Seats:** 100, Pr/dining room 30 **Smoking:** N/Sm in restaurant **Children:** Menu, Portions **Directions:** 0.5m off A14, clearly signposted. **Parking:** 40 **e-mail:** pheasant.keyston@btopenworld.com
web: www.huntsbridge.com

MADINGLEY MAP 12 TL36

🏵 Three Horseshoes Restaurant
Italian, Mediterranean

Relaxed Italian dining in East Anglian countryside

☎ 01954 210221 High St CB3 8AB

MENU GUIDE Portland crab salad • Fillet steak marinated in Chianti, purple sprouting broccoli, salsa rosa • Caramelised lemon tart

WINE GUIDE ♀ Sangoma Chenin Blanc £12.75 • ♀ Leonardo Sangiovese Chianti £14.50 • 75 bottles over £20, 43 bottles under £20 • 16 by the glass (£3.25-£7.50)

PRICE GUIDE Starter £6.75-£10 • main £15.50-£23 • dessert £6-£8 • coffee £2.10 • min/water £3 • Service optional • Group min 10 service 10%

PLACE: Picturesque thatched gastro-pub in a village setting, with a garden stretching down to the cricket pitch. The lively bar is popular with all age groups, and the conservatory restaurant has a pale, fresh look, with contemporary art and a polished wooden floor.
continued

England

MELBOURN MAP 12 TL34

Pink Geranium

International
Quintessential English charm
☎ 01763 260215 Station Rd SG8 6DX

 MENU GUIDE Pea & mint soup, truffle oil • Beef fillet, roast beetroot, wild mushroom jus • Toffee banana soufflé

PRICE GUIDE Fixed L £16.50 • Fixed D £27.50 • starter £7-£10.50 • main £19.50-£26.50 • dessert £7.95

PLACE: This delightful 16th-century thatched cottage in the village centre is all that a country restaurant should be. Approached through a well-tended garden, the restaurant is pink-washed from the outside, while inside low oak beams, blazing log fires and cosy lounges filled with plush sofas create an intimate rustic charm. Dining room decor is no longer pink, walls are now cream, and the chintzy, floral theme has been replaced with brown and gold carpeting and gold curtains. Champagne is served in the beautiful garden on warm summer evenings.
FOOD: Care characterises every aspect of this restaurant, not least the precise, interesting cooking that never loses sight of its classical French roots, typified by a starter of marinated foie gras and duck confit terrine. A well thought out wine list uses fine suppliers and contains a good range of exciting half bottles.
OUR TIP: Prince Charles was a regular customer while at Cambridge University
Chef: Gordon Campbell **Owners:** Mr L Champion **Times:** 12-2/7-late, Closed BHs, Mon, closed D Sun **Notes:** Smart **Seats:** 60, Pr/dining room 16 **Smoking:** N/Sm in restaurant **Children:** Portions
Directions: On A10 between Royston & Cambridge. In village centre, opposite church **Parking:** 20 **e-mail:** lawrence@pinkgeranium.co.uk
web: www.pinkgeranium.co.uk

MADINGLEY continued MAP 12 TL36

FOOD: Simple modern Italian/Mediterranean dishes offered from a comprehensive daily carte. This variety is reflected in the good list of wine by the glass.
OUR TIP: Accomplished wine list chosen by the talented young owner
Chef: Richard Stokes **Owners:** Huntsbridge **Times:** 12-2/6.30-9.30, Closed 31 Dec-1 Jan, closed D Sun **Notes:** Vegetarian available
Seats: 65 **Smoking:** N/Sm in restaurant **Children:** Portions
Directions: M11 junct 13, take left, then next right and continue to end of road, and at mini-rdbt turn right **Parking:** 50
e-mail: 3hs@btconnect.co.uk **web:** www.huntsbridge.com

MELBOURN MAP 12 TL34

Pink Geranium *see above*

Sheene Mill
British, International
Picturesque foodie haven
☎ 01763 261393 Station Rd SG8 6DX

MENU GUIDE Crispy crab in a banana leaf, chilli & coriander dip • Pork belly, apples, cider & mash • Tropical fruit crème brûlée

WINE GUIDE ♀ Vanel Sauvignon Blanc £13.50 • ♀ Vanel Merlot £13.50 • 56 bottles over £20, 21 bottles under £20 • 12 by the glass (£4-£9.50)

PRICE GUIDE Fixed L £18-£25 • starter £5.50-£9 • main £13-£27 • dessert £6.50-£9.50 • coffee £2 • min/water £2.85 • Service added but optional 10%

Sheene Mill

PLACE: The word 'restaurant' hardly does justice here. Alongside a chic contemporary dining room, this 16th-century watermill houses a smart champagne bar, an airy conservatory for all day snacks and coffees, as well as offering alfresco dining beside a picturesque pond.
FOOD: Modern British dishes win out at lunchtime, while dinner is a more cosmopolitan affair with inspiration drawn from around the globe. Expect good quality produce treated sympathetically: pot-roast pheasant with griottine cherries perhaps, or aromatic duckling with yellow bean juices and Chinese noodles.
OUR TIP: Jazz piano nightly in the restaurant
Chef: Steven Saunders, Adrian Doughty **Owners:** Mr & Mrs S Saunders
Times: 12-2.30/7-10.30, Closed 26 Dec, 1 Jan, closed D Sun
Notes: Vegetarian available, Civ Wed 125 **Seats:** 110 **Smoking:** N/Sm in restaurant, Air con **Children:** Portions **Directions:** Take 2nd exit from A10 Melbourn by-pass signed Melbourn. Sheene Mill is 300yds down Station Road on right **Parking:** 50 **e-mail:** info@sheenemill.co.uk
web: www.sheenemill.co.uk

continued

England

PETERBOROUGH MAP 12 TL19

🌸 Best Western Orton Hall Hotel
British
Historic old building serving modern cuisine
☎ 01733 391111 Orton Longueville PE2 7DN

MENU GUIDE Trio of salmon with aioli • Baked lamb rump, spicy black pudding • Orange & strawberry terrine
WINE GUIDE ♀ Penfolds Koonunga Hill Chardonnay £12.50 • ♀ Valle Andino Merlot £13.45 • 21 bottles over £20, 34 bottles under £20 • 3 by the glass (£2.90)
PRICE GUIDE Fixed L £15.95 • Fixed D £26-£27 • starter £5.25-£6.95 • main £15.95-£22.95 • dessert £4.95-£5.95 • coffee £3.50 • min/water £3.50 • Service optional
PLACE: A pleasant pastoral scene surrounds this historic 17th-century country hotel next to the parish churchyard. In the calm and restful restaurant, old panelling and beautiful stained glass windows keep the past attractively alive.
FOOD: The food is firmly rooted in the present, and well paced with the seasons the kitchen opting for a tried-and-tested approach. A well-balanced menu might end with decent English cheeses.
OUR TIP: Ask for a window seat
Chef: Kevin Wood **Owners:** Abacus Hotels **Times:** 12.30-2/7-9.30, Closed 25 Dec, closed L Mon-Sat **Notes:** Vegetarian available, Smart Dress, Civ Wed 90 **Seats:** 34, Pr/dining room 40 **Smoking:** N/Sm in restaurant **Rooms:** 65 (65 en suite) ★★★ **Directions:** Telephone for directions **Parking:** 200 **e-mail:** reception@ortonhall.co.uk **web:** www.abacushotels.co.uk

🍷 Gaston Café Bar & Restaurant 44 Broadway
PE1 1RS ☎ 01733 3 346837 An open plan, modern informal dining room. Watch the pizzas being made.

🍴 Loch Fyne Restaurant & Oyster Bar The
Old Dairy, Elton PE8 6SH ☎ 01832 280298 Quality seafood chain.

ST IVES MAP 12 TL37

🌸 Olivers Lodge Hotel
International   NEW
Uplifting surroundings and exciting modern cooking
☎ 01480 463252 Needingworth Rd PE27 5JP
MENU GUIDE Mozzarella & fig salad, strawberry dressing • Roast venison fillet, braised red cabbage • Spiced pineapple, coconut ice cream
WINE GUIDE ♀ One Tree Hill Chardonnay £11.95 • 4 bottles over £20, 35 bottles under £20 • 8 by the glass (£3.50-£4.25)
continued

PRICE GUIDE Fixed L £14-£16 • Fixed D £17-£19 • starter £3.75-£4.75 • main £9.95-£18.75 • dessert £3-£4.75 • coffee £2.25 • min/water £3 • Service optional
PLACE: A light and spacious conservatory restaurant looking out over the secluded garden cheers the spirits even on the dullest day. Although a friendly, relaxed atmosphere pervades, crisp linen and attentive service indicate a serious approach to dining.
FOOD: The chef's technical skills and exciting use of good ingredients is the reason for the appreciative buzz from diners, making this a restaurant to watch. Starters like brochette of scampi on a tomato bisque set a high standard.
OUR TIP: Try the local asparagus in May
Chef: Manoj Kmanickan **Owners:** Shiren Patel **Times:** 12-2.30/6.30-9.30 **Notes:** Smart Dress, Civ Wed 85 **Seats:** 20 **Smoking:** N/Sm in restaurant **Children:** Menu, Portions **Rooms:** 17 (17 en suite) ★★★ **Parking:** 30

SIX MILE BOTTOM MAP 12 TL55

🌸 Swynford Paddocks
British, European
Imaginative cooking in historic country-house hotel
☎ 01638 570234 CB8 0UE
MENU GUIDE Seared scallops, wilted spinach, herb butter sauce • Beef fillet, thyme mash & Burgundy jus • Mascarpone cheesecake, vanilla nage
WINE GUIDE ♀ Santa Rita Sauvignon Blanc £14.95 • ♀ Angelo Sangiovese £14.50 • 70% bottles over £20, 30% bottles under £20 • 8 by the glass (£3.50-£6)
PRICE GUIDE Food prices not confirmed for 2006. Please telephone for details
PLACE: A small country-house hotel set in 64 acres of parkland. The elegant Byron Restaurant, named after Lord Byron, who was a frequent visitor, serves both lunch and dinner but the Silks conservatory is open all day. Service is helpful and attentive.
FOOD: Good quality ingredients are sourced locally and further afield. The style is modern English with old favourites like gravad lax, here with honey and mustard dressing, alongside a warm Roquefort tartlet with candied walnuts as starter choices.
OUR TIP: Excellently placed for a day at Newmarket races
Chef: Patrick Collins **Owners:** Paul & Lucie Smith **Times:** 12-2/7-10, Closed Sat (if sole occupancy wedding) **Notes:** Vegetarian available, Dress Restrictions, No jeans/trainers at dinner, Civ Wed 95 **Seats:** 25, Pr/dining room 40 **Smoking:** N/Sm in restaurant **Children:** Portions **Rooms:** 15 (15 en suite) ★★★ **Directions:** On A1304, 6m SW of Newmarket. Pass Green Man pub on right, restaurant on left after 200 yds **Parking:** 100 **e-mail:** info@swynfordpaddocks.com **web:** www.swynfordpaddocks.com

STILTON MAP 12 TL18

🌸 Bell Inn Hotel
British, French
Accomplished cooking in historic inn
☎ 01733 241066 Great North Rd PE7 3RA
MENU GUIDE Seared scallops, black pudding • Lamb, dauphinoise potatoes, haricot verte, rosemary jus • Lemon tart, raspberry sorbet
WINE GUIDE ♀ Highcliff Chardonnay £11.95 • ♀ Highcliff Shiraz £11.95 • 29 bottles over £20, 33 bottles under £20 • 8 by the glass (£2.95)
PRICE GUIDE Fixed L £10.95 • Fixed D £25.95 • coffee £1.35 • min/water £2.50 • Service included
continued

England

STILTON *continued* MAP 12 TL18

Bell Inn Hotel

PLACE: In the town where Stilton cheese originated, this character inn dates back to the 16th century. It offers a choice of dining options with lighter meals available in the bar and the bistro, and more formal fare served upstairs in an elegantly beamed restaurant. There's also a courtyard and garden for alfresco eating if the weather's fine.
FOOD: The restaurant delivers a well-balanced range of tempting well-executed dishes, many distinguished by thoughtful and adventurous flavour combinations.
OUR TIP: If staying over, consider a four-poster deluxe room
Chef: Stuart Johnson **Owners:** Mr L A McGivern **Times:** 12-2/7-9.30, Closed 25 Dec, closed L Sat, closed D Sun **Notes:** Sun L 3 courses £15.95, Vegetarian available, Smart Dress, Civ Wed 90 **Seats:** 60, Pr/dining room 20 **Smoking:** N/Sm in restaurant **Children:** Min 5yrs **Rooms:** 19 (19 en suite) ★★★ **Directions:** 1m N A1(M) junct 16 follow signs to Stilton. Hotel on High Street in centre of village **Parking:** 30 **e-mail:** reception@thebellstilton.co.uk **web:** www.thebellstilton.co.uk

CHESHIRE

ALDERLEY EDGE MAP 16 SJ87

 Alderley Edge Hotel
British, International
Country-house conservatory dining
☎ 01625 583033 Macclesfield Rd SK9 7BJ

MENU GUIDE Seared smoked salmon, haddock pannacotta, leek vinaigrette • Sautéed calves' liver, ox tongue fritter • Passionfruit soufflé
WINE GUIDE ⚲ Brown Brothers Sauvignon Blanc £24.50 • ⚑ Villa Rosa Merlot £14.50 • 220 bottles over £20, 45 bottles under £20 • 12 by the glass (£2.75-£6.95)

continued

PRICE GUIDE Fixed L £12.95 • Fixed D £29.50 • starter £6.50-£9.95 • main £22.50-£24.50 • dessert £5.50 • coffee £2.50 • min/water £2.90 • Service optional
PLACE: Built as a textile merchant's house, the hotel has been modernised and extended in recent times but retains its classic design. Key elements are comfort and quality, no less so in the airy, split-level conservatory restaurant with its earthy colour scheme, high backed leather chairs and exquisitely appointed tables.
FOOD: Cooking is imaginative, taking full advantage of good local ingredients, with liberal use of luxury items. The modern European menus change with the seasons and flavour is the first priority.
OUR TIP: Interesting choice of hand-made cheeses
Chef: Chris Holland **Owners:** J W Lees (Brewers) Ltd **Times:** 12-2/7-10 Closed 1 Jan, closed L 31 Dec, closed D 25-26 Dec **Notes:** Vegetarian available, Smart Dress, Civ Wed 100 **Seats:** 65, Pr/dining room 100 **Smoking:** N/Sm in restaurant, Air con **Children:** Portions **Rooms:** 52 (52 en suite) ★★★ **Directions:** A538 to Alderley Edge, then B5087 Macclesfield Rd **Parking:** 82 **e-mail:** sales@alderlyedgehotel.com **web:** www.alderleyedgehotel.com

BURWARDSLEY MAP 15 SJ55

 The Pheasant Inn
Modern British
Historic hostelry to suit all tastes
☎ 01829 770434 Higher Burwardsley CH3 9PF
MENU GUIDE Monkfish, tiger prawns, sweet chilli jam • Lambs' liver, smoked bacon, mash, onion gravy • Pavlova, berry compote
PRICE GUIDE Starter £1.25-£8.25 • main £5.95-£12.95 • dessert £3.95-£5.95 • coffee £1.40 • Service added but optional
PLACE: This upmarket gastro-pub does a brisk trade catering for muddy walkers and serious diners alike, and is particularly busy at lunchtimes. Mellow stone walls, slate floors and open fires show its historic roots, while the Cheshire countryside provides a stunning backdrop.
FOOD: A lengthy menu with something for everyone. Hearty pub basics such as steak and ale pie, and fish and chips jostle for attention alongside classier modern British dishes such as pot-roast pheasant, and there's also a good selection of vegetarian options and snackier fare such as sandwiches and wraps.
OUR TIP: The same menu is served in the bar and more formal restaurant
Chef: Mark Brooks, Adam Shave **Owners:** Sue and Harold Nelson **Times:** 12-2.30/6.30-9.30 **Notes:** Vegetarian available, Smart Dress **Seats:** 40, Pr/dining room 20 **Smoking:** N/Sm in restaurant **Children:** Menu, Portions **Rooms:** 10 (10 en suite) ★★ **Directions:** A41 from Chester towards Whitchurch. After 6m turn left for Tattenhall. In village signs for Burwardsley. Top of hill left at PO **Parking:** 70 **e-mail:** info@thepheasantinn.co.uk **web:** www.thepheasantinn.co.uk

CHESTER MAP 15 SJ46

 The Arkle *see page 63*

Prices quoted in the guide are for guidance only and are subject to change without notice.

England

The Arkle

French *Gastronomic odyssey in a renowned hotel*
☎ 01244 324024 Chester Grosvenor & Spa, Eastgate CH1 1LT
e-mail: hotel@chestergrosvenor.co.uk
web: www.chestergrosvenor.co.uk

PLACE: Located beside the old Roman wall, this grand city-centre hotel is the essence of Englishness. The elegant, fine-dining Arkle restaurant is named after the famous steeplechase racehorse. An elegant, contemporary space, lit by a beautiful, ornate skylight, it is decorated in black and gold, the racing colours of the horse's owner, the late Anne, Duchess of Westminster. Tailored modern furniture, pale carpet, black lacquered pillars and horsey paintings offer a sophisticated winning recipe, backed by appropriately formal, but friendly, attentive service. The cosy Library offers the perfect place to unwind over aperitifs.
FOOD: Simon Radley's sophisticated, upbeat, seasonal-changing, fixed-price menus make the very best use of high-quality, fresh produce. His imaginative, complex and often daring repertoire is steeped in the contemporary French idiom, brimful of interest, flair and excitement, with innovative combinations, clear flavours and balance all finding their place in assured, accomplished dishes such as potato foie gras velouté with ham hock boudin, cushion of veal sweetbread with carved fillet and roasted langoustine, and tranche of monkfish, cured ham and sauce bisque.

MENU GUIDE French pigeon, seasonal mushrooms, smoked bacon • Beef fillet, sticky short rib, ox & truffle pudding • Apple pastry, Calvados, bourbon vanilla
WINE GUIDE ⚲ 2003 Kotare Sauvignon Blanc, Marlborough NZ £26 • ⚲ 1998 Château Les Hauts De Pontet, Pavillac £37.50 • 550 bottles over £20, 50 bottles under £20 • 20 by the glass (£5-£25)
PRICE GUIDE Main £55 • coffee £4 • min/water £4 • Service added but optional 12.5% • Group service 12.5%

OUR TIP: Massive wine list of over 600 bins

Chef: Simon Radley **Owners:** Grosvenor - Duke of Westminster **Times:** 7-9.30, Closed 1st 3wks Jan, 1 wk Aug, Sun, Mon, closed L all week **Notes:** Tasting menu £65, Vegetarian available, Dress Restrictions, Jacket & tie in The Arkle, Civ Wed 120 **Seats:** 45 **Smoking:** N/Sm in restaurant, Air con **Children:** Min 12yrs **Rooms:** 80 (80 en suite) ★★★★★ **Directions:** Chester city centre adjacent to the Eastgate Clock and Roman walls **Parking:** 600

England

CHESTER *continued* MAP 15 SJ46

La Brasserie at the Chester Grosvenor & Spa
Modern French **NEW**
Bustling hotel brasserie
☎ 01244 324024 Chester Grosvenor & Spa, Eastgate CH1 1LT

MENU GUIDE Mediterranean fish soup • Calves' liver with cured tomato tart • Amaretto parfait with poached plums

WINE GUIDE ♀ Touraine Valley Loire Sauvignon Blanc £15.50 • ♀ Stonefish Shiraz £16.50 • 60% bottles over £20, 40% bottles under £20 • 10 by the glass (£3.25-£4.50)

PRICE GUIDE Starter £5.50-£11.95 • main £10.50-£19.95 • dessert £4.50-£5.95 • coffee £3.50 • min/water £3.50 • Service optional • Group min 8 service 12.5%

PLACE: Situated in this well known hotel - the area's only five-star operation - this Parisian-style brasserie complements the hotel's three-rosette Arkle fine dining restaurant. Art deco in style, with black leather banquettes, mirrors and marble-topped tables, there's also a large bar for snacks, coffees and pre-dinner drinks.
FOOD: The menu is studded with confident, well-presented modern French dishes, done simply: salads, grills, meats and poultry, fish and seafood.
OUR TIP: Take time to visit the impressive spa facilities
Chef: Simon Radley Owners: Grosvenor - Duke of Westminster
Times: 12-10.30, Closed 25-26 Dec Notes: Vegetarian available, Civ Wed 120 Seats: 80 Smoking: N/Sm in restaurant, Air con Children: Menu, Portions Directions: 2m from M53, located in city centre Parking: 600
e-mail: hotel@chestergrosvenor.co.uk web: www.chestergrosvenor.co.uk

The Chester Crabwall Manor Hotel
British, French
Complex cooking in historic manor
☎ 01244 851666 Parkgate Rd, Mollington CH1 6NE

MENU GUIDE Seared scallops, orange butter sauce • Duck, Pithivier of apple & confit duck, sage gnocchi, vanilla & thyme jus • Lemon tart

WINE GUIDE ♀ Hardy's Semillion Chardonnay £16.25 • ♀ Hardy's Shiraz-Cabernet £16.25 • 134 bottles over £20, 32 bottles under £20 • 14 by the glass (£4.10-£8.95)

PRICE GUIDE Fixed D £25 • starter £10.95-£13.75 • main £28.75-£33.50 • dessert £5.95 • coffee £3.95 • min/water £3.75

PLACE: Layer upon layer of history marks this site, which was recorded as a dwelling place in the Domesday Book. The current hotel occupies a 17th-century manor, and has a wide range of facilities including a leisure club and pool, as well as comfortable lounges and a conservatory restaurant with woodland views.
FOOD: Elaborate fare from the kitchen, especially the signature menu. Expect modern British and French dishes with the odd imaginative twist: beef with a ragout of veal sweetbreads perhaps, served with morel mushrooms and a truffle sauce.
OUR TIP: Vegetarian menu available
Chef: Paul Baxter Owners: Marston Hotels Times: 12-2/7-9.30, Closed L Sat Notes: Sun L 3 courses incl. coffee £18.95, Vegetarian available, Smart casual, Civ Wed 90 Seats: 80, Pr/dining room 80
Smoking: N/Sm in restaurant, Air con Children: Menu, Portions
Rooms: 48 (48 en suite) ★★★★ Directions: From A55 take A5117 then A540. Hotel set back from A540, N of Chester Parking: 120
e-mail: crabwallmanor@marstonhotels.com
web: www.marstonhotels.com

Mollington Banastre Hotel
Modern European **NEW**
Good, simple food in traditional, stylish hotel
☎ 01244 851471 Parkgate Rd CH1 6NN

MENU GUIDE Confit duck & leek terrine • Monkfish, Parma ham, soy sauce • Sticky toffee pudding

WINE GUIDE ♀ La Serre Sauvignon Blanc £14.95 • ♀ La Serre Merlot Vin de Pays d'Oc £14.95 • 34 bottles over £20, 15 bottles under £20 • 10 by the glass (£3.50-£7)

PRICE GUIDE Fixed L £9.95 • Fixed D £26 • min/water £2.95 • Service optional

PLACE: Extended Victorian mansion with up-to-date conference and leisure facilities, conveniently located between the city and the M6. The conservatory-style Garden Room Restaurant is attractively furnished and overlooks the grounds.
FOOD: Simply described menus list an interesting choice of modern European dishes. Quality ingredients are carefully cooked and the dishes have a good depth of flavour.
OUR TIP: Music entertainment on Friday and Saturday evenings
Chef: Ian Fellowes Owners: Handpicked Hotels Times: 12.30-2/7-10, Sat Notes: Coffee incl, Vegetarian available, Smart Dress Seats: 65, Pr/dining room 150 Smoking: N/Sm in restaurant, Air con
Children: Menu, Portions Rooms: 63 (63 en suite) ★★★★
Parking: 250 e-mail: info@mollingtonbanastre.com
web: www.mollingtonbanastrehotel.com

Rowton Hall Country House Hotel
British, European
Understated luxury in Georgian manor
☎ 01244 335262 Whitchurch Rd, Rowton CH3 6AD

MENU GUIDE White crab & dill ravioli • Cannon of lamb, tarragon cream • White chocolate cheesecake

PRICE GUIDE Food prices not confirmed for 2006. Please telephone for details

PLACE: Refurbished Georgian manor house hotel set in mature grounds and retaining many original features, notably a superbly carved staircase. There's a lovely atmosphere in the dining room which is decorated in contemporary style.
FOOD: An accomplished kitchen works hard to produce a good choice of imaginative, often adventurous, dishes that rely on fresh home-grown and local produce. Extensive menus are complemented by a very individual selection of wines.
OUR TIP: Serious wine list (150 bins)
Times: 12-2/7-9.30 Rooms: 38 (38 en suite) ★★★ Directions: M56 J12 take A56 to Chester. At rdbt turn L on A41 to Whitchurch. Approx 1m and follow signs for hotel e-mail: rowtonhall@rowtonhall.co.uk
web: www.rowtonhallhotel.co.uk

England

CREWE MAP 15 SJ75

Crewe Hall

British

Modern cuisine in the grandest of settings

☎ 01270 253333 Weston Rd CW1 6UZ

MENU GUIDE Scallops in pancetta, pea purée, lime dressing • Lamb, minted mousse, garlic, lentils, bacon • Dark chocolate cheesecake

WINE GUIDE ♀ J Moreau Chablis/Chardonnay £25.50 • ♀ Verramonte Maule Valley Merlot £24.25 • 117 bottles over £20, 3 bottles under £20 • 8 by the glass (£4.80-£8.50)

PRICE GUIDE Fixed L £17.50 • starter £7.25-£12.50 • main £18.50-£27.95 • dessert £6.50-£8 • coffee £3.75 • min/water £3.50 • Service optional

PLACE: Once owned by the Queen, this stateliest of stately piles still drips grandeur, its Jacobean interior reconstructed as a fantasia of ornate panelling and plasterwork by the Victorians. Outside is a similarly grand affair and, with 500 acres of mature grounds to explore, there's no excuse for not working up an appetite.
FOOD: An experienced kitchen delivers a contemporary menu that belies the setting, with dishes along the lines of smoked salmon with lemon blinis, or Scotch beef and horseradish dumpling. If you're celebrating, there's a range of over 30 champagnes to enjoy with dinner.
OUR TIP: Afternoon tea in the lounge
Chef: D Edwards, A Hollinshead & L Collis **Owners:** Marston Hotels
Times: 12-2/7-9.30, Closed L Sat, closed D Sun **Notes:** Sun lunch 3 courses £22.95, Vegetarian available, No jeans/T-shirts, Civ Wed 170
Seats: 60, Pr/dining room 30 **Smoking:** N/Sm in restaurant
Children: Portions **Rooms:** 65 (65 en suite) ★★★★
Directions: From M6 junct 16 take A500 towards Crewe. At 1st rdbt take last exit, at next rdbt take 1st exit, then right into drive after 0.5m
Parking: 180 **e-mail:** reservationsch@marstonhotels.com
web: www.marstonhotels.com

Hunters Lodge Hotel

British, French

Satisfying dining in 18th-century farmhouse hotel

☎ 01270 583440 Sydney Rd, Sydney CW1 5LU

MENU GUIDE Roast langoustines, sweetcorn froth • Beef medallions, asparagus tempura • Pink champagne jelly

WINE GUIDE ♀ Domaine Verger Alain Geoffroy Chablis £20.50 • ♀ Bodega Estraunza Rioja Gran Reserva £27.95 20 bottles over £20, 19 bottles under £20 • 5 by the glass (£2.95-£4.50)

PRICE GUIDE Fixed D £27.50-£34 • min/water £3.20

PLACE: Dating back to the 18th century, this family-run hotel has been expanded to include a spacious, beamed restaurant and well-equipped bedrooms. There's also a popular bar for less formal dining.
FOOD: Constantly changing menus include traditional British items like roast Haslington lamb and international dishes such as spring roll of duck with foie gras, all carefully prepared from locally sourced, fresh seasonal produce. Service is reasonably formal but friendly and helpful.
OUR TIP: Take a drink in the courtyard on summer evenings
Chef: David Wall **Owners:** Mr A Panayi **Times:** 12-2/7-9.30, Closed BHs, closed D Sun **Notes:** Vegetarian available, Smart Dress, Civ Wed 130
Seats: 60, Pr/dining room 30 **Smoking:** N/Sm in restaurant
Children: Menu, Portions **Rooms:** 57 (57 en suite) ★★★
Directions: 1m from station, follow signs to Leighton Hospital
Parking: 200 **e-mail:** info@hunterslodge.co.uk
web: www.hunterslodge.co.uk

KNUTSFORD MAP 15 SJ77

Mere Court Hotel

Modern British

Enjoyable dining in attractive hotel with extensive gardens

☎ 01565 831000 Warrington Rd, Mere WA16 0RW

MENU GUIDE Ham hock & parsley terrine, home-made piccalilli • Seared salmon, provençale vegetables • Lemon tart

PRICE GUIDE Food prices not confirmed for 2006. Please telephone for details

PLACE: Take a window seat in the sophisticated Arboretum restaurant to view the ornamental lake and lush gardens of this attractive Edwardian country house hotel. The restaurant is decorated in traditional, elegant style.
FOOD: British classics are successfully influenced by the cuisine of the Mediterranean on the fixed-price lunch and dinner menus.
OUR TIP: Conference facilities are impressive
Times: 12-2/7-9.30, Closed L Sat **Rooms:** 34 (34 en suite) ★★★★
Directions: M6 J19 and follow signs for A50
e-mail: sales@merecourt.co.uk **web:** www.merecourt.co.uk

NANTWICH MAP 15 SJ65

 Rookery Hall

French

Candlelit fine dining in historic atmosphere

☎ 01270 610016 Main Rd, Worleston CW5 6DQ

MENU GUIDE Scallops, pancetta, sweet & sour sauce • Roast sea bass, pistou sauce • Hazelnut parfait, pear compote

PRICE GUIDE Food prices not confirmed for 2006. Please telephone for details

PLACE: An imposing Victorian château-style country house set in 200 acres of parkland, Rookery Hall oozes charm and comfort. With views over the garden and countryside beyond, the striking, mahogany panelled dining room features a roaring log fire, attractive paintings and soft evening candlelight. Relaxed and friendly service from a professional team.
FOOD: Classic French cuisine with some imaginative combinations, a few unusual twists and influences from across the globe. The kitchen displays sound culinary skills and flair and there's a strong emphasis on using quality ingredients.
OUR TIP: Cigar friendly bar
Times: 12-2/7-9.30, Closed L Sat **Rooms:** 46 (46 en suite) ★★★★
Directions: On B5074 N of Nantwich, 1.5m on R towards Worleston
e-mail: rookeryhall@handpicked.co.uk
web: www.handpicked.co.uk/rookery

Two Rosettes The best local restaurants, which aim for and achieve higher standards, better consistency and where a greater precision is apparent in the cooking. There will be obvious attention to the selection of quality ingredients. About 40% of restaurants in the guide have two Rosettes.

PRESTBURY MAP 16 SJ87

⊛⊛ White House Restaurant

British, International

Slick village restaurant

☎ 01625 829376 SK10 4DG

MENU GUIDE Pan-seared scallops, oriental tomato fondue, courgette fritters • Grilled Dover sole, dill & pink peppercorn butter • Treacle tart, vanilla ice cream

WINE GUIDE ♀ Los Vilos Chardonnay/Sauuvignon Blanc £14.25 • ♥ Los Vilos Cabernet Sauvignon £14.25 • 25 bottles over £20, 35 bottles under £20 • 10 by the glass (£3.75-£5)

PRICE GUIDE Fixed L £16.95-£20.70 • Fixed D £18.95-£20.95 • starter £4.25-£10.50 • main £11.95-£19.95 • dessert £4.95-£6.95 • coffee £2.75 • min/water £3

PLACE: A stylish modern relaxed, bistro-style restaurant housed in a former 18th-century farmhouse, brings a contemporary twist to proceedings. Vibrant, bright colours, designer glass screens and sculptures, suede chairs and crisp linen, rub shoulders with mullioned, leaded windows, grand stone fireplaces and limed oak beams. Outdoor seating offers alfresco summer dining.

FOOD: Creative and assured modern British cooking, with an international spin, hits all the right notes. Some luxury seasonal produce, a good focus on vegetarian options and value for money round off a confident act.

OUR TIP: Romantic venue

Chef: Ryland Wakeham, Richard Clark **Owners:** Ryland & Judith Wakeham **Times:** 12-2/7-10, Closed 25 Dec, closed L Mon, closed D Sun **Notes:** Vegetarian available **Seats:** 70, Pr/dining room 40 **Smoking:** No pipes, No cigars **Children:** Portions **Directions:** Village centre on A538 N of Macclesfield **Parking:** 11 **e-mail:** info@thewhitehouse.uk.com **web:** www.thewhitehouse.uk.com

PUDDINGTON MAP 15 SJ37

⊛ Craxton Wood

European

Classy hotel and friendly service

☎ 0151 347 4000 Parkgate Rd, Ledsham, Nr Chester CH66 9PB

MENU GUIDE Quail egg & pancetta salad • Beef tournedos • Assiette of raspberry

WINE GUIDE ♀ Burgundy £26.50 • ♥ Katherine Hills Shiraz £17.95 • 45 bottles over £20, 25 bottles under £20 • 12 by the glass (£4.25-£6.35)

PRICE GUIDE Starter £4.50-£7.50 • main £13.95-£28.95 • dessert £5.50-£7.95 • coffee £3.95 • min/water £3.50 • Service included

PLACE: A reassuringly smart hotel with superior leisure facilities. The dining room is divided into three for more intimate spacing,

with a conservatory adding a bright dimension.

FOOD: The broad menu allows the adventurous a chance to experiment whilst also catering for a more conservative palate. Oven-baked chicken breast is uplifted with the addition of tomato linguine, and pork fillet pairs up with mustard pomme purée.

OUR TIP: Leave room for the excellent variety of home-made breads

Chef: Matthew Lloyd **Owners:** MacDonalds Hotels Plc **Times:** 12.30-2/7-9.30, Closed L Sat **Notes:** Sun L £18.50, Vegetarian available, Dress Restrictions, No jeans, Civ Wed 300 **Seats:** 56, Pr/dining room 40 **Smoking:** N/Sm in restaurant, Air con **Children:** Menu, Portions **Rooms:** 72 (72 en suite) ★★★★ **Directions:** From end of M56 take A5117 Queensferry, right at 1st rdbt onto A540 (Hoylake). Hotel 200yds after next traffic lights **Parking:** 200 **e-mail:** info@craxton.macdonald-hotels.co.uk **web:** www.macdonaldhotels.co.uk

WILMSLOW MAP 16 SJ88

⊛⊛ Stanneylands Hotel

British, European

Modern and classical cuisine in country-house hotel

☎ 01625 525225 Stanneylands Rd SK9 4EY

MENU GUIDE Grilled nugget of sea bass • Sautéed venison loin, black olives & courgettes • Glazed rice pudding, raspberry coulis

WINE GUIDE ♀ Berri Estates Chardonnay £15.45 • ♥ Berri Estates Shiraz £15.45 • 86 bottles over £20, 44 bottles under £20 • 6 by the glass (£3.75-£9.25)

PRICE GUIDE Fixed L £13.50 • Fixed D £25.50 • starter £8.05-£11.25 • main £18.95-£24 • dessert £6 • coffee £2.50 • min/water £3.50 • Service optional

PLACE: An oak-panelled restaurant with soft lighting, warm colours and well-dressed tables is the centrepiece of this smart country-house hotel. The bright, modern lounges are perfect for a pre-dinner drink or coffee afterwards.

FOOD: You can sample traditional favourites like Goosnargh duck supreme (with crisp Parma ham and blueberries) as well as more imaginative contemporary dishes like seared pheasant breast with Puy lentils and parsnip purée. The carte and set price menu show some exciting touches, and an amuse of wild mushroom soup with truffle oil and lavender is in a class of its own.

OUR TIP: Take a walk through the lovely grounds

Chef: Colin Harding-Jones **Owners:** Mr L Walshe **Times:** 12.30-2.30/7-9.30, closed D Sun **Notes:** Vegetarian available, Civ Wed 80 **Seats:** 60, Pr/dining room 120 **Smoking:** No pipes **Children:** Portions **Rooms:** 31 (31 en suite) ★★★★ **Directions:** From M56 junct 5 follow signs for Cheadle. At traffic lights turn right, through Styal, left at Handforth sign, follow into Stanneylands Rd **Parking:** 80 **e-mail:** enquiries@stanneylandshotel.co.uk **web:** www.stanneylandshotel.co.uk.

One Rosette Excellent local restaurants serving food prepared with care, understanding and skill, using good quality ingredients. These restaurants stand out in their local area. Of the total number of establishments with Rosettes around 50% have one Rosette.

continued

CORNWALL & ISLES OF SCILLY

England

BODMIN MAP 02 SX06

Trehellas House Hotel & Restaurant

British, International

Romantic candlelit restaurant in lovely Cornish location

☎ 01208 72700   Washaway PL30 3AD

MENU GUIDE Avocado & smoked salmon tower • Sea bass with mango, chilli & lime salad • Chocolate & pear bread & butter pudding

WINE GUIDE ♀ Lurton Sauvignon Blanc £12.50 • ♀ Norte Chico Merlot £12.50 • 7 bottles over £20, 27 bottles under £20 • 4 by the glass (£3.50)

PRICE GUIDE Fixed D £17.50-£25.50 • coffee £2 • min/water £3 • Service optional • Group min 10 service 10%

PLACE: An 18th-century coaching inn/courthouse with a wealth of old beams and flagstones. The restaurant is in a listed part of the building and has beautiful Delabole slate floors. Original paintings by Cornish artists are displayed, and there are crisp white tablecloths and fresh flowers on each table.

FOOD: High quality ingredients from local suppliers are used in an eclectic mix of modern Cornish dishes, with occasional South East Asian influences.

OUR TIP: Located close to the Camel Trail

Chef: Garth Borrowdale **Owners:** Alan & Chris Street **Times:** 7-8.30, Closed 25 Dec, Sun (non-res), closed L all week **Notes:** Chefs weekly special menu £17.50, Vegetarian available **Seats:** 40, Pr/dining room 8 **Smoking:** N/Sm in restaurant **Children:** Portions **Rooms:** 11 (11 en suite) ★★ **Directions:** 4m from Bodmin on A389 to Wadebridge, adjacent to Pencarrow **Parking:** 15

e-mail: enquiries@trehellashouse.co.uk **web:** www.trehellashouse.co.uk

BOSCASTLE MAP 02 SX09

The Bottreaux Hotel and Restaurant

Modern British ➤NEW

Fine dining by the sea

☎ 01840 250231   PL35 0BG

MENU GUIDE Pan-seared Mevagissey scallops • Wild Cornish sea bass & steamed Cornish mussels • Garden rhubarb & strawberry crumble

WINE GUIDE ♀ Chilean Sauvignon Blanc £13 • ♀ Italian Corvina £13 • 25 bottles over £20, 25 bottles under £20 • 6 by the glass (£3.50)

PRICE GUIDE Food prices not confirmed for 2006. Please telephone for details

PLACE: Set in an elevated position at the top of the village, this smart, white-painted hotel is just a short walk from the harbour. Interiors are stylish, from the wooden flooring and classical-style sofas of the lounge to cosy bar and pleasant dining room, replete with brown leather chairs and white linen.

FOOD: Contemporary-style dishes with a simple format allow fresh, local Cornish produce to shine, perhaps a fillet of Boscastle Red Ruby beef with a béarnaise sauce.

continued

OUR TIP: Excellent Italian wines

Chef: Alan Cooper **Owners:** Alan & Carlotta Cooper **Times:** 6-11, Closed 2 weeks in low season, Mon **Notes:** Dress Restrictions **Seats:** 24 **Smoking:** N/Sm area, Air con **Children:** Min 10 **Rooms:** 9 (9 en suite) ★★ **Directions:** From A30, take A39 towards North Cornwall, and follow signs to Boscastle/Tintagel. **Parking:** 9

e-mail: info@boscastlecornwall.co.uk **web:** www.boscastlecornwall.co.uk

BRYHER MAP 02 SV81

Hell Bay

British, International

Idyllic island retreat with great contemporary art and food

☎ 01720 422947   TR23 0PR

MENU GUIDE Roast duck terrine • Smoked haddock, bubble & squeak, poached egg, hollandaise • Cherry & frangipane tart, clotted cream

WINE GUIDE ♀ Villa Sandi Pinot Grigio £14.50 • ♀ Finca Carbonell Tempranillo £14 • 32 bottles over £20, 41 bottles under £20 • 10 by the glass (£3.50-£4.25)

PRICE GUIDE Fixed D £35-£37.50 • starter £4-£8 • main £7.50-£18 • dessert £5 • coffee £2 • min/water £2 • Service included

PLACE: The only hotel on Bryher, the smallest community in the Scillies, the Hell Bay stands overlooking the Atlantic Ocean. Large metal sculptures adorn the decked areas in the courtyard, and walls are hung with huge works of art by local artists. Lloyd Loom chairs meet chunky tables in the bar and restaurant, and big sofas are set around the open fire.

FOOD: All that's best in Scillion produce: fresh fish and local vegetables. Tables too are set with local flowers. Standards as a whole are high, achieving consistently good quality.

OUR TIP: Don't be put off by the journey

Chef: Graham Shone **Owners:** Tresco Estate **Times:** 12-3/6.30-9.30, Closed Jan-Feb **Notes:** Vegetarian available, Smart Dress, No jeans, T-shirts in eve **Seats:** 75, Pr/dining room 20 **Smoking:** N/Sm in restaurant **Children:** Menu, Portions **Rooms:** 23 (23 en suite) ★★★ **Directions:** Helicopter from Penzance to Tresco, St Mary's. Plane from Southampton, Bristol, Exeter, Newquay or Lands End

e-mail: contactus@hellbay.co.uk **web:** www.hellbay.co.uk

CALLINGTON MAP 03 SX36

Langmans Restaurant

British

A foodie haven

☎ 01579 384933   3 Church St PL17 7RE

MENU GUIDE Sea bass fillet, fennel, saffron risotto • Beef fillet, bay leaf sauce, rösti potato, spinach, salsify, oyster mushrooms • Trio of puddings

WINE GUIDE ♀ Hunters Sauvignon Blanc £18.95 • ♀ Bethany Grenache £19.95 • 27 bottles over £20, 57 bottles under £20 10 by the glass (£3.50)

PRICE GUIDE Fixed D £29.95 • coffee £2.50 • min/water £2.75 • Service optional

PLACE: Set in a listed 16th-century building, Langmans is a friendly, relaxed and popular little place tucked away from the main street. Inside the decor has a stylish modern feel, with a colourful bar decked out in leather sofas and an intimate, candlelit dining room with attractively appointed tables.

FOOD: Chef-patron Anton Buttery's modern British approach (wife Gail runs front of house) is an unhurried, fixed-price, six-course tasting affair, with the menu changing every four weeks. A skillful chef (one-man band), careful timings and fresh

continued

England

CALLINGTON *continued* MAP 03 SX36

ingredients provide an assured platform for impressive cuisine.
OUR TIP: Booking is essential at this small, dinner-only affair
Chef: Anton Buttery **Owners:** Anton & Gail Buttery **Times:** 7.30-8.30,
Closed 25 Dec, Sun-Tue, closed L all week **Notes:** Fixed D 6 courses
£29.95, Vegetarian by request only, Dress Restrictions, Smart casual
preferred **Seats:** 20 **Smoking:** N/Sm in restaurant **Children:** Min
12 yrs **Directions:** From the direction of Plymouth into Callington town
centre, left at lights and right into Church St **Parking:** Town centre car
park **e-mail:** dine@langmansrestaurant.co.uk
web: www.langmansrestaurant.co.uk

CONSTANTINE MAP 02 SW72
Trengilly Wartha Inn
British

Relaxed and friendly restaurant, showcase for local ingredients
☎ 01326 340332 Nancenoy TR11 5RP

MENU GUIDE Scallops & Jerusalem artichoke purée • Fillet
steak, celeriac rösti, baked apple, burnt orange sauce • Baked
Fingals' cheese

WINE GUIDE ♀ Sanderson Sauvignon Blanc £14 • ♀ Finca La
Estacada Tempranillo £12.50 • 69 bottles over £20, 112 bottles
under £20 • 18 by the glass (£2.10-£4.90)

PRICE GUIDE Fixed D £29 • coffee £1.90 • min/water
£2.80 • Service included

PLACE: A traditional inn with comfortable rooms in a charming
location by the River Helford. Popular with local diners and
visitors alike for its excellent wine list, real ales and generous
selection of single malts.
FOOD: Modern British cuisine with European influences served in
the bar and restaurant using high quality, locally produced beef
and lamb and locally caught seafood such as Cornish crab, sea
bass and John Dory.
OUR TIP: Try the local Helford oysters in season
Chef: Mike Maguire, Nick Tyler **Owners:** Mr & Mrs Logan, Mr & Mrs
Maguire **Times:** 7.30-9.30, Closed 25 Dec, 31 Dec, closed L all week
Notes: Vegetarian available **Seats:** 28 **Smoking:** N/Sm in restaurant
Children: Menu, Portions **Rooms:** 8 (8 en suite) ★★ **Directions:** In
Constantine village turn left at top of hill, follow signs for Gweek, 1m out
of village turn left, follow hotel signs **Parking:** 40
e-mail: reception@trengilly.co.uk **web:** www.trengilly.co.uk

CONSTANTINE BAY MAP 02 SW87
Treglos Hotel
British

Seaside veteran with a pleasing mix of traditional and modern
☎ 01841 520727 PL28 8JH

MENU GUIDE Seared scallops, watercress mayonnaise • Roast
beef, roast parsnips, claret jus • Dark chocolate brûlée, brandied
prunes

WINE GUIDE 60 bottles over £20, 12 bottles under £20 • 3 by
the glass (£3.75)

PRICE GUIDE Fixed D £26 • min/water £3 • Service optional

PLACE: Set on the spectacular north Cornwall coast, this seaside
hotel has been run by the same family for over 30 years and is
something of an institution. Dinner is served in a spacious
restaurant with a conservatory extension, and there's a comfy
lounge for drinks.
FOOD: An accessible menu of classy fare, with an emphasis on

continued

seasonal local produce. Mains are straightforward in style: lemon
sole with a lime salad perhaps, or guinea fowl with pancetta and
glazed apples.
OUR TIP: 20 minutes drive from The Eden Project
Chef: Paul Becker **Owners:** Mr & Mrs J Barlow **Times:** 12.15-2.15/7.30-
9.15, Closed mid Nov-Mar **Seats:** 100, Pr/dining room 20
Smoking: N/Sm in restaurant, Air con **Rooms:** 42 (42 en suite) ★★★
Directions: Take B3276 (Constantine Bay). At village stores turn right,
hotel 50yds on left. **e-mail:** stay@treglos hotel.com
web: www.tregloshotel.com

FALMOUTH MAP 02 SW83
Harbourside Restaurant
Modern British

Spectacular harbour views from a smart maritime restaurant
☎ 01326 312440 Greenbank Hotel, Harbourside
TR11 2SR

MENU GUIDE Lobster ravioli on celeriac • Grilled beef fillet, wild
mushroom risotto • Dark chocolate fondant

WINE GUIDE ♀ Louis Chatel Sauvignon Blanc £12 • ♀ Los Vilos
Cabernet Sauvignon £13 • 18 bottles over £20, 44 bottles under
£20 • 9 by the glass (£3-£3.50)

PRICE GUIDE Fixed L £10.75 • Fixed D £29.50 • Service optional

PLACE: You might be on a cruise ship, so close to the water is
this bright, open restaurant with huge picture windows. Colonial-
style chairs, smart table dressings and light wooden floors add a
classy touch.
FOOD: Dinner is in a different league from lunch, though local
seafood features strongly in both. Chartreuse of asparagus and
courgette, and chicken breast stuffed with crab and dill mousse
bring more sophistication to the evenings.
OUR TIP: Dine on the waterside terrace in summer
Chef: David Waplington **Owners:** Greenbank Hotel (Falmouth) Ltd
Times: 12-2/7-9.30, Closed L Sat **Notes:** Coffee, mineral water and petits
fours incl., Vegetarian available, Dress Restrictions, Smart Casual, Civ Wed

continued

100 **Seats:** 60, Pr/dining room 16 **Smoking:** N/Sm in restaurant
Children: Portions **Rooms:** 60 (60 en suite) ★★★
Directions: Approaching Falmouth from Penryn, take left along North
Parade. Follow sign to Falmouth Marina and Greenbank Hotel.
Parking: 60 **e-mail:** sales@greenbank-hotel.com
web: www.greenbank-hotel.com

 ## Royal Duchy Hotel
British, International
Modern hotel dining with sea views
☎ 01326 313042 Cliff Rd TR11 4NX

MENU GUIDE Smoked chicken & artichoke salad • Baked local
cod with Bombay potatoes • Summer fruit iced soufflé
WINE GUIDE ♀ Macon Blanc Villages Chardonnay
£14.95 • ♀ Piers 42 Shiraz £13.95 • 62 bottles over £20,
58 bottles under £20 • 12 by the glass (£2.80-£6)
PRICE GUIDE Fixed L £14.95 • Fixed D £28 • coffee
£2.25 • min/water £2.95 • Service optional
PLACE: Looking out over the sea towards Pendennis Castle, the
Royal Duchy is a well-maintained, spacious and hospitable hotel.
A microcosm of these qualities is found in the dining room,
where comfortable seating, good quality table settings and those
wonderful sea views set guests at their ease. Smart/casual dress
code.
FOOD: Lots of seafood here, naturally, but also good Cornish
beef, with accurate cooking and the modern touch allowing an
intriguing but not too complex mix of flavours. An attentive
sommelier is on hand to help with the ample wine list.
OUR TIP: Dining with cabaret is a nice option
Chef: Des Turland **Owners:** Brend Hotel Group **Times:** 12.30-2/7-9,
Closed L Mon-Sat **Notes:** Vegetarian available, Dress Restrictions, Jacket &
tie, Civ Wed 150 **Seats:** 100, Pr/dining room 24 **Smoking:** No pipes, Air
con **Children:** Menu, Portions **Rooms:** 43 (43 en suite) ★★★★
Directions: At Pendennis Castle end of Promenade **Parking:** 40
e-mail: info@royalduchy.co.uk **web:** www.brend-hotels.co.uk

 ## St Michael's of Falmouth
British **NEW**
Fine dining in chic Cornish hotel
☎ 01326 312707 Gyllyngvase Beach, Seafront
TR11 4NB
MENU GUIDE Scallops, pancetta, rocket • Red wine braised
lamb shank, basil crushed potatoes • Black forest pudding,
lemon ice cream
PLACE: The past few years have seen the steady transformation
of this friendly hotel into a chic contemporary venue to rival any
in Cornwall. Giant sails billow outside reception, while the Oyster
Bay restaurant continues the aquatic theme with a large inset fish
tank.

continued

FOOD: Simple unfussy food from an ambitious new chef with his
sights set on greater things. Choose from the carte or try the
seven-course tasting menu.
OUR TIP: Lighter bistro fare available at St Michael's second
restaurant, The Flying Fish
Times: 7.30-9.30am/7-9 **e-mail:** info@stmichaelshotel.co.uk
web: www.stmichaels.com

FOWEY MAP 02 SX15
 ## Fowey Hall
British, International
*Accomplished cuisine in grand hotel at the top of
the popular port*
☎ 01726 833866 Hanson Dr PL23 1ET

MENU GUIDE Chicken liver & foie gras parfait • Brill, mussel &
leek broth, sweet potato crisps • Glazed orange tart, bramble
sorbet
WINE GUIDE ♀ Hawkes Bay Sauvignon Blanc
£23 • ♀ Mezzacorona Teroldego £15.50 • 63 bottles over £20,
23 bottles under £20 • 4 by the glass (£4-£5.50)
PRICE GUIDE Fixed L £11-£16 • Fixed D £35 • coffee
£2.50 • min/water £3.50 • Service optional
PLACE: Family friendly hotel with original walled gardens
overlooking the estuary and out to sea. Dine amid the grandeur
of the Victorian restaurant, complete with parquet flooring, oak
panelling, swags and tails, fine art, sumptuous table settings and
deep leather dining chairs. (You can almost hear the bells jingling
in the servant's quarters.)
FOOD: Excellent use is made of local produce, with an emphasis
on seafood. The dazzling seasonal menu is studded with luxury
items. Lobsters come from the hotel's own tank, and oysters and
mussels from the nearby oyster farm.
OUR TIP: Informal eating in the Palm Court
Chef: Tony Duce **Owners:** Mr N Dickinson & Mr N Chapman
Times: 12-2.15/7-10 **Notes:** Vegetarian available, Civ Wed 50 **Seats:** 60,
Pr/dining room 20 **Smoking:** N/Sm in restaurant **Children:** Menu,
Portions **Rooms:** 24 (24 en suite) ★★★ **Directions:** Into town centre,
pass school on right, 400yds turn right onto Hanson Dr **Parking:** 35
e-mail: info@foweyhall.com **web:** www.luxuryfamilyhotels.com

AA's Chefs' Chef is the annual poll of all the
chefs included in The Restaurant Guide.
Around 1800 of the country's top chefs are
asked to vote to recognise the achievements
of one of their peers.
This year's winner is featured on page 19.

England

FOWEY continued MAP 02 SX15

⑧⑧ Fowey Hotel

European

Imaginative cooking in Victorian hotel with superb views

☎ 01726 832551 The Esplanade PL23 1HX

MENU GUIDE Dressed crab, mango salsa • Slow-braised lamb shank • Warm chocolate orange fondant
WINE GUIDE ♀ Valle Andino Sauvignon Blanc £14.75 • ♀ Valle Andino Cabernet Sauvignon £14.75 • 15 bottles over £20, 38 bottles under £20 • 6 by the glass (£3.25-£4.90)
PRICE GUIDE Fixed D £32.50 • coffee £1.95 • min/water £3.50 • Service optional

PLACE: Standing above the estuary, and with stunning views out across the water, this hotel restaurant is popular all year round. The relaxed atmosphere is helped by pleasant, willing staff.
FOOD: Specific dining times for each table keep the food last-minute fresh, and there is much to impress on the simple carte at both lunch and dinner. Grilled roulade of sole with lobster sauce and pea purée shows a good balance of flavours and textures, and assiette of chocolate brings the right meeting of sweet and bitter.
OUR TIP: Parking shortages locally, ask at reception
Chef: Mark Griffiths **Owners:** Keith Richardson **Times:** 12-2/6.30-9
Notes: Fixed price 4 course dinner £32.50, Vegetarian available, Dress Restrictions, No jeans, trainers or shorts **Seats:** 60 **Smoking:** N/Sm in restaurant **Children:** Menu, Portions **Rooms:** 37 (37 en suite) ★★★
Directions: From A390 take B3269 for approx 5m, follow signs for Fowey continue along Pavillion Rd for 0.75m, 2nd right **Parking:** 13
e-mail: info@thefoweyhotel.co.uk **web:** www.richardsonhotels.co.uk

⑧⑧ Marina Hotel

Modern French

Chic riverside restaurant specialising in seafood

☎ 01726 833315 Esplanade PL23 1HY
MENU GUIDE Pumpkin soup • Halibut, cauliflower purée, pancetta, cabbage, red wine • Clotted cream crème brûlée, blueberry crumble
WINE GUIDE ♀ Teddy Hall Kanu Wooded Chenin Blanc £19.50 • ♀ Domaine Jean Descombes Gamay £19 • 41 bottles over £20, 19 bottles under £20 • 11 by the glass (£4.25-£5.50)
PRICE GUIDE Fixed L £16.95-£18.95 • Fixed D £38-£42.50 • starter £5.95-£9.95 • main £16.95-£20.95 • dessert £6.95-£8.95 • coffee £2.25 • min/water £1.95 • Service optional

PLACE: Take your seat in this smart contemporary restaurant and enjoy its stunning views over the busy river and harbour. There's always a ship or sailboat to watch, and you can dine alfresco on the terrace when weather permits.

FOOD: Plenty of promise here, from a strong kitchen team set on taking the Waterside Restaurant from good to great. Fish is the speciality but it's a balanced menu, so you can take your pick from the likes of sea bass with a champagne and oyster velouté, or venison with roast foie gras.
OUR TIP: Allow time to chill out on the terrace to watch the world go by
Chef: Chris Eden **Owners:** Mr S Westwell **Times:** 12-2/6.30-9.15
Notes: Sun L from £12.95, Vegetarian available, Smart Dress, Smart casual, Civ Wed 65 **Seats:** 40 **Smoking:** N/Sm in restaurant
Children: Menu, Portions **Rooms:** 13 (13 en suite) ★★ **Parking:** 16
e-mail: marina.hotel@dial.pipex.com **web:** www.themarinahotel.co.uk

⑨ Food for Thought The Quay PL23 1AT
☎ 01726 832221 Modern European menu in smart modern eaterie.

HELSTON MAP 02 SW62

⑧⑧ New Yard Restaurant

Modern British   **NEW**

Exciting food in an informal country atmosphere

☎ 01326 221595 Trelowarren, Mawgan TR12 6AF
MENU GUIDE Smoked trout salad • Sautéed pigeon breasts, truffle-scented parsnip purée • Apple & blackberry crème fraîche
WINE GUIDE ♀ Château Tour des Gendres 2002 £16.50 • ♀ Domaine de Mignaberry 1999 £19.50 • 18 bottles over £20, 32 bottles under £20 • 8 by the glass (£3.75-£5.50)
PRICE GUIDE Food prices not confirmed for 2006. Please telephone for details

PLACE: The converted carriage house on this extensive private estate makes for a smartly minimalist restaurant. The tables are hewn from fallen timber, artwork lines the simple white walls, and rolled sacking curtains make a surprisingly tasteful window covering.
FOOD: This is one of Cornwall's 'in' places to eat, with a growing reputation for memorable cooking. Fish, naturally, has its place on the dinner menu, but it shares it with much of the best meats and vegetables that the county produces. Game terrine with elderberry jelly encapsulates the wow factor.
OUR TIP: Persist with the long forest drive - you'll get there!
Chef: Greg Laskey **Owners:** Sir Ferrers Vyvyan **Times:** 12-2.15/7-9.30, Closed all Jan, Mon, closed D Sun **Notes:** Vegetarian available, Smart Dress **Seats:** 45 **Smoking:** N/Sm area **Children:** Portions
Directions: 5m from Helston **Parking:** 20
e-mail: info@trelowarren.com **web:** www.trelowarren.co.uk

LISKEARD MAP 02 SX26

⑧⑧⑧ Well House Hotel see page 71

LIZARD, THE MAP 02 SW71

⑧ Housel Bay Hotel

English, French

Stunning views and assured cooking

☎ 01326 290417 Housel Cove TR12 7PG
MENU GUIDE Cappuccino of wild mushrooms • Plaice fillets on baby spinach with mussels, white wine & cream • Egg custard tart
PRICE GUIDE Food prices not confirmed for 2006. Please telephone for details

PLACE: England's most southerly mainland hotel, with stunning views of Housel Bay from the bar and lounge.

continued

continued

LISKEARD MAP 02 SX26

Well House Hotel

British, International

Top quality cooking in Cornish culinary hideaway

☎ 01579 342001 St Keyne PL14 4RN

MENU GUIDE Confit of salmon, citrus couscous • Guinea fowl, buttered Savoy cabbage, fondant potatoes • Pear Tatin, vanilla ice cream

WINE GUIDE ♀ Villa Rosa Chardonnay £12.50 • ♀ Villa Rosa Merlot £12.50 • 96 bottles over £20, 48 bottles under £20 • 4 by the glass (£2.75)

PRICE GUIDE Fixed L £18.50 • Fixed D £32.50 coffee £3 • Service optional

PLACE: Built at the turn of the century by a Victorian tea planter, this enchanting country house is peacefully set along a country lane in the beautiful Cornish valley of Looe. It's an intimate affair with only nine bedrooms, but the well-tended gardens reveal impressive facilities including tennis courts, a swimming pool and croquet lawn. The restaurant is decorated in simple contemporary style, with dark leather chairs and quality tableware, and there's a comfortable lounge and bar for pre- or post-dinner drinks.

FOOD: Uncluttered by superfluous ingredients, dishes at the Well House are prepared with a mature simplicity by Glenn Gatland that enhances rather than masks the flavour of top quality local produce. Fish is a speciality, brought fresh from the famous market at Looe and turned into treats such as Cornish crab risotto, or pan-roast monkfish with braised fennel and dauphine potatoes, while meat dishes see some contemporary twists on English classics, such as beef with braised oxtail and horseradish mash. The menu changes daily.

OUR TIP: A 30-minute drive from the Eden Project

Chef: Glenn Gatland **Owners:** Mr N Wainford, Mrs Ione Nurdin **Times:** 12.30-1.30/7-8.30, Closed 1 wk Jan **Notes:** Vegetarian available, Dress Restrictions, Smart casual **Seats:** 36 **Smoking:** N/Sm in restaurant **Children:** Min 8yrs D, Portions **Rooms:** 9 (9 en suite) ★★ **Directions:** From Liskeard take B3254 to St Keyne 3m. In village take left fork at church signed St Keyne. Hotel 0.5m on left **Parking:** 30 **e-mail:** enquiries@wellhouse.co.uk **web:** www.wellhouse.co.uk

---

FOOD: Modern ideas combine with classic techniques on a menu that's full of interest and always seasonal. There is a clear commitment to Cornish produce, especially fresh fish. Skilful cooking and quality ingredients are to the fore. Lunch and dinner are available in the bistro, but the restaurant opens for dinner only.

OUR TIP: Particularly good vegetarian and fish choices

Times: 12-2/7-9, closed D Sun **Rooms:** 20 (20 en suite) ★★★ **e-mail:** info@housebay.com **web:** www.housebay.com

LOSTWITHIEL MAP 02 SX15

Muffins 32 Fore St PL22 0BN ☎ 01208 872278

Winner of The Tea Guild Award of Excellence 2005.

MARAZION MAP 02 SW53

Mount Haven Hotel

British

Enjoyable dining accompanied by stunning views

☎ 01736 710249 Turnpike Rd TR17 0DQ

MENU GUIDE Scallops, leek mash, pickled cucumber • Lamb, rosemary & mushroom duxelle, redcurrant & port sauce • Chilled lemon soufflé

WINE GUIDE ♀ Selaks Marlborough Sauvignon Blanc £19.50 • ♀ Weinert Pedro del Castillo Malbec £13.50 • 4 bottles over £20, 39 bottles under £20 • 6 by the glass (£2.75-£3.75)

PRICE GUIDE Starter £4.95-£7.50 • main £12.95-£16.95 • dessert £4.50-£5.50 • coffee £2 • min/water £2.25 • Service optional

PLACE: Sunset is a good time to visit this tranquil hotel, which boasts unparalleled views of St Michael's Mount. The interior is

Mount Haven Hotel

architecturally designed to emphasise light and space, and features beautiful art and antique Jaipur tapestries.

FOOD: Fresh seafood and the best of local produce is treated with thoughtful simplicity to create modern British dishes such as beef with a gratin of wild mushrooms and parmesan, or roast cod with garlic pomme purée.

OUR TIP: Try lunch on the terrace

Chef: Julie Manley **Owners:** Orange & Mike Trevillion **Times:** 12-2.30/6.45-8.45, Closed last wk Dec-end Jan **Notes:** Vegetarian available, Dress Restrictions, Smart casual **Seats:** 50 **Smoking:** N/Sm in restaurant **Children:** Portions **Rooms:** 19 (19 en suite) ★★ **Directions:** Through village to end of built up area **Parking:** 30 **e-mail:** reception@mounthaven.co.uk **web:** www.mounthaven.co.uk

continued

England

MAWGAN PORTH

⊕ Bedruthan Steps Hotel

Modern British 🖙NEW

Atlantic views and full flavoured food with visual impact

☎ 01637 860555   TR8 4BU

MENU GUIDE Scallops in mango & Madeira jelly, beetroot purée • South Devon Cross beef fillet, potato fondant, farci & cep jus • Baked Alaska, rhubarb sauce

WINE GUIDE ♀ Cloudy Bay Chardonnay £17.50 • ♀ Marques du Murrieta Rioja £25 • 45 bottles over £20, 53 bottles under £20 • 9 by the glass (£2.50-£4.50)

PRICE GUIDE Fixed L fr £29.50 • Fixed D £25.50 • coffee £3.95 • min/water £2 • Service included

PLACE: The hotel is situated between Newquay and Padstow overlooking the clear Atlantic waters and is currently being refurbished at an impressive pace. Grassed terraces are accessed directly from the lounge and bar areas - perfect for a drink before dinner. The Indigo Bay restaurant is cool, contemporary and comfortable, with white walls, white linen, candles and orchids.
FOOD: Accomplished cooking, adventurous menus and fabulous presentation. The short dinner menu, using fresh local ingredients, is priced for two or three courses.
OUR TIP: A great place to stay and take the children
Chef: Mr P Ray **Owners:** Mrs Stratton & Mrs Wakefield **Times:** 12-2/7.30-9.30, Closed Xmas **Notes:** Set price ALC, Dress Restrictions, No jeans, T-shirts, beach wear **Seats:** 200, Pr/dining room 150
Children: Min 7 yrs, Menu, Portions **e-mail:** office@bedruthan.com
web: www.bedruthan.com

MAWNAN SMITH MAP 02 SW72

⊕ Budock Vean - The Hotel on the River

British, Seafood 🖙🐟

Good food in a comfortable, relaxing hotel

☎ 01326 252100 & 250230   TR11 5LG

MENU GUIDE Pan-fried Falmouth Bay scallops, melted Cornish brie • Roast lamb, parmesan polenta • Sticky toffee pudding, caramel sauce

WINE GUIDE ♀ Vendange Chardonnay £13.95 • ♀ Valle Andino Cabernet Sauvignon £13.40 • 41 bottles over £20, 31 bottles under £20 • 3 by the glass (£2.90)

PRICE GUIDE Fixed L £15.50 • starter £7-£18 • main £12.50-£32.50 • dessert £5 • coffee £2.70 • min/water £3 • Service optional

PLACE: A classically elegant dining room, with minstrels' gallery where musicians still play. Crisp linen, sparkling glasses, silverware and candlelight make for a wonderful atmosphere.
FOOD: Meats are reared on Cornish farms, and most fish is locally caught. Ice creams and sorbets, as well as seasonal fruit and vegetables, are also supplied from within the county boundary. This commitment is carried through to careful preparation of simply flavoured dishes.
OUR TIP: Stroll in the grounds, with or without a golf trolley
Chef: Darren Kelly **Owners:** Barlow family **Times:** 12.30-2.30/7.30-9, Closed 3 wks Jan, closed L Mon-Sat **Notes:** Fixed D 5 courses £29.50, Vegetarian available, Dress Restrictions, Jacket & tie, Civ Wed 60
Seats: 100, Pr/dining room 40 **Smoking:** N/Sm in restaurant, Air con
Children: Min 7yrs, Menu, Portions **Rooms:** 57 (57 en suite) ★★★★
Directions: Telephone for directions **Parking:** 100
e-mail: relax@budockvean.co.uk **web:** www.budockvean.co.uk

⊕ Meudon Hotel

British NEW

Traditional-style dining in country house with magnificent gardens

☎ 01326 250541   TR11 5HT

MENU GUIDE Cauliflower & stilton soup • Seared lamb loin, Madeira & lentil jus • Spotted dick

PRICE GUIDE Food prices not confirmed for 2006. Please telephone for details

PLACE: Owned by the Pilgrim family since 1966, this charming Victorian mansion stands in eight acres of impressive sub-tropical gardens, which lead down to a private beach. A relaxing place to stay and you can dine beneath a fruiting vine in the traditional conservatory restaurant.
FOOD: Sound country-house style cooking reliant on quality locally sourced ingredients.
OUR TIP: Notable Cornish cheeseboard
Times: 12.30-2/7.30-9 **Rooms:** 29 (29 en suite) ★★★
e-mail: wecare@meudon.co.uk **web:** www.meudon.co.uk

⊕ Trelawne Hotel

Modern British

Family-run hotel restaurant with a strong local following

☎ 01326 250226   TR11 5HS

MENU GUIDE Salmon & chive ravioli, shellfish velouté • Pot roasted partridge, kale, glazed chestnuts • Poached pear, Calvados sabayon

PRICE GUIDE Food prices not confirmed for 2006. Please telephone for details

PLACE: Small hotel with pleasant sea views surrounded by attractive lawns and gardens. The restaurant is traditional in style with good linen, crockery and glassware.
FOOD: Dinner only is served from a concise carte with some additional daily specials. Local produce features strongly and there are some modern touches with dishes such as gilled sea bass with fennel and leek court bouillon.
OUR TIP: Quiet location, ideal for visiting many local gardens
Times: 7-9, Closed 17 Dec-10 Feb, closed L all week **Rooms:** 14 (14 en suite) ★★★ **Directions:** From Truro take A39 towards Falmouth. R at Hillhead rdbt, take exit signed Maenporth. After 3m, past Maenporth Beach, hotel at top of hill **e-mail:** info@trelawnehotel.co.uk
web: www.trelawnehotel.co.uk

MOUSEHOLE MAP 02 SW42

The Cornish Range Restaurant with Rooms

European, Seafood

Good seafood dining in picturesque location

☎ 01736 731488 6 Chapel St TR19 6BD

MENU GUIDE Mediterranean fish soup, aioli • Pan-fried gurnard, crayfish velouté • Trio of miniature brûlées
WINE GUIDE ♀ Pinot Grigio £13.95 • ♀ Rioja £18.95 • 6 bottles over £20, 6 bottles under £20 • 1 by the glass
PRICE GUIDE Starter £4.75-£8.95 • main £12.95-£19.50 • dessert £4.95-£6.50 • coffee £1.95 • min/water £3.95 • Service optional

PLACE: This charming restaurant with rooms, complete with hand-made Cornish furniture, used to be a pilchard processing factory. The shop-fronted restaurant and the bedrooms are turned out to a high standard with soft terracotta surfaces, wooden tables and chairs and paintings by local artists.
FOOD: No surprise that well-prepared dishes on the daily-changing menu make the most, not just of Newlyn and Mousehole landed seafood, but also Cornwall's abundant seasonal fruit and vegetables. There's a list of lethal-sounding cocktails.
OUR TIP: Try the Sunday Brunch
Chef: Simon Prest **Owners:** Richard O'Shea & Chad James **Times:** 6-10, Closed L all week, closed D Sun-Tue (Nov-Mar) **Notes:** Vegetarian available **Seats:** 60 **Smoking:** N/Sm area, No pipes, No cigars
Rooms: 3 (3 en suite) 🏠 **Directions:** Mousehole is 3m S from Penzance, via Newlyn **Parking:** Harbour car park
e-mail: info@cornishrange.co.uk **web:** www.cornishrange.co.uk

Old Coastguard Inn

Modern British

Fresh, interesting cuisine with magnificent coastal views

☎ 01736 731222 The Parade TR19 6PR

MENU GUIDE Roasted parsnip, celeriac & ginger soup • Mixed grilled fish, lemon crushed potatoes, spinach, caper & olive tapenade • Dark chocolate & rum torte
WINE GUIDE ♀ Casa do Lago Fernao Pires £13 • ♀ Domaine Jonction Syrah £13 • 22 bottles over £20, 15 bottles under £20 • 7 by the glass (£2.50-£3)
PRICE GUIDE Starter £4.50-£7 • main £10-£18 • dessert £3.50-£5 • coffee £1.50 • min/water £3.20 • Service optional

PLACE: As its name suggests, this one-time coastguard station - perched above the fishing village - has commanding views over its sub-tropical gardens to Mount's Bay. The relaxed restaurant is contemporarily styled with clean lines, wooden floors, wicker chairs and bright artwork. There's also a garden terrace for alfresco summer dining.
FOOD: Fresh local produce, especially the fruits of the sea, are confidently delivered with contemporary spin.
OUR TIP: Worth staying the night, most rooms have spectacular sea views and some have balconies
Chef: K Terry, S Coyne, A Gilbert **Owners:** A W Treloar **Times:** 12-2.30/6-10, Closed 25 Dec (reservations only), closed D 31 Dec (reservations only) **Notes:** Vegetarian available, Dress Restrictions, Smart casual preferred **Seats:** 80 **Smoking:** N/Sm in restaurant
Children: Menu, Portions **Rooms:** 21 (21 en suite) ★★
Directions: A30 to Penzance. From Penzance take coast road through Newlyn to Mousehole. Inn 1st large building on left on entering village, after car park **Parking:** 15 **e-mail:** bookings@oldcoastguardhotel.co.uk
web: www.oldcoastguardhotel.co.uk

England

NEWQUAY MAP 02 SW86

Corisande Manor Hotel
British
Good food and wine in beautiful setting
☎ 01637 872042 Riverside Av, Pentire TR7 1PL
MENU GUIDE Newquay mussels with herb butter • Pork fillet in cider sauce • Sticky toffee pudding
WINE GUIDE 250 bottles over £20, 50 bottles under £20 • 3 by the glass (£2.50)
PRICE GUIDE Fixed D £25.50-£25.50 • min/water £2 • Service included
PLACE: Commanding superb views, this imposing 19th-century Germanic-style manor house sits in a delightful location on an estuary. The restaurant, once the billiard room of the house, has impressive high ceilings and exposed beams.
FOOD: Menu choices, though limited, are changed daily and focus on fresh produce locally supplied. Everything is home made, from soups to sauces and puddings to ice creams. The owner's serious interest in wine is reflected on the wine list.
OUR TIP: Allow time to read the wine list
Chef: Chris Grant **Owners:** Mr & Mrs D Grant **Times:** 8, Closed Nov-March, closed L Mon-Sun **Notes:** Coffee included, Dinner 4 courses, Vegetarian available **Seats:** 20 **Smoking:** N/Sm in restaurant **Children:** Portions **Rooms:** 12 (12 en suite) ◆◆◆◆◆
Directions: Main road to Pentire headland, left at Newquay Nursing Home on to Pentire Crescent, then right on to Riverside Av **Parking:** 10
e-mail: relax@corisande.com **web:** www.corisande.com

Finn's
Modern British **NEW**
Funky fish restaurant with direct beach access
☎ 01637 874062 & 854367 The Old Boat House, South Quay Hill TR7 1HR
MENU GUIDE Black pudding & pancetta salad • Spiced Cornish monkfish, saffron celeriac • Chocolate fudge torte
WINE GUIDE ♀ Pouille Fumé £22.50 • ♀ French Organic Rouge £11.50 • 11 bottles over £20, 15 bottles under £20 • 5 by the glass (£2.50-£3.50)
PRICE GUIDE Starter £3.95-£12.95 • main £9.95-£36 • dessert £3.50-£6 • coffee £1.80 • min/water £3.50 • Service optional
PLACE: Relaxed and trendy harbourside restaurant much loved by surfers but frequented by all types, as the 'wetsuits and waistcoats' dress code suggests. The brightly coloured and stylish main area is supported by a summer terrace and a barbecue shack.
FOOD: The freshest imaginable fish is treated seriously, with exciting results. Called 'sexy fish and chips', the food is more sophisticated than that, as the interesting short menus show.
OUR TIP: Try the organic wines
Chef: Luke Finne **Owners:** Roger Spurrell **Times:** 12-4/6.30-11, Closed 25-26 Dec (also winter opening times) **Notes:** Vegetarian available
Seats: 150 **Smoking:** N/Sm area, Air con **Children:** Menu, Portions
Directions: Newquay town centre, by harbour off Fore St
Parking: Public car park **e-mail:** info@finnscafe.com
web: www.finnscafe.com

Headland Hotel
French, British NEW
Elegant dining on the outskirts of Newquay
☎ 01637 872211 Fistral Beach TR7 1EW
MENU GUIDE Cod fritters, mango, papaya, chilli salsa • Beef, Lyonnaise potatoes, leeks, thyme jus • Orange tart, lemon butter sauce
PLACE: Set on a peaceful headland away from the noise and bustle of Newquay, this comfortable four-star hotel has an ornate Edwardian dining room, with well-spaced tables and long windows that overlook surfers braving the waves on Fistral beach.
FOOD: Quality ingredients are the mainstay of this tempting menu; start with smoked duck breast with apple marmalade perhaps, and then move on to sea bass with a chive hollandaise, or chicken with a Madeira sauce.
OUR TIP: Lighter meals available in the Conservatory restaurant, open for lunch and dinner.
Times: 7-10.30am/7-9.45, Closed Xmas
e-mail: office@headlandhotel.co.uk **web:** www.headlandhotel.co.uk

Trenance Cottage Tea Room & Gardens Trenance Ln TR7 2HX ☎ 01637 872034
Winner of The Tea Guild Award of Excellence 2005.

PADSTOW MAP 02 SW97

Margot's
British
Accurate cooking in bistro a short stroll from the harbour
☎ 01841 533441 11 Duke St PL28 8AB
MENU GUIDE Grilled goats' cheese with roasted peppers • Grilled fillet of brill with chive butter sauce • Sticky toffee pudding, butterscotch sauce
WINE GUIDE ♀ Concha y Toro Sauvignon Blanc £10.50 • ♀ Concha y Toro Merlot £10.50 • 9 bottles over £20, 16 bottles under £20 • 5 by the glass (£3.25-£5.95)
PRICE GUIDE Fixed D fr £26.50 • starter £3.95-£5.95 • main £12.50-£15.50 • dessert fr £3.95 • coffee £2.25 • min/water £2.25 • Service optional
PLACE: A welcoming, colourful frontage and an informal feel, with just nine tables the relaxed and genial chef-proprietor efficiently combines service and cooking. White linen-clothed tables contrast well with the locally-produced art on the walls.
FOOD: Accomplished skills, great raw ingredients and an uncomplicated style make this a popular place. The fish is great, perfectly fresh and accurately cooked, and the short wine list is mainly French.
OUR TIP: Best to book ahead
Chef: Adrian Oliver, Philip Cortis **Owners:** Adrian & Julie Oliver
Times: 12.30-2/7-9, Closed Nov, Jan, restricted opening Dec, Sun-Mon, closed L Tue **Notes:** Vegetarian available **Seats:** 20 **Smoking:** N/Sm in restaurant **Children:** Portions **Directions:** Telephone for directions.
e-mail: enquiries@margots.co.uk **web:** www.margots.co.uk

PADSTOW MAP 02 SW97

England

The Seafood Restaurant

Seafood

Rick Stein's famous seafood restaurant with rooms

☎ 01841 532700 Riverside PL28 8BY

MENU GUIDE Fish & shellfish soup, rouille, parmesan • Roast tronçon of turbot, hollandaise sauce • Chilled black rice pudding, coconut cream, mango sorbet

WINE GUIDE ♀ Haut Poitou Sauvignon £18 • ♀ Rick Steins Tower Estate Shiraz £20.50 • 200 bottles over £20, 15 bottles under £20 • 11 by the glass (£3.55-£4.50)

PRICE GUIDE Fixed L £50 • Fixed D £50 • starter £8-£15.50 • main £17.50-£39.50 • dessert £8.50 • coffee £3.10 • min/water £2.25 • Service optional

PLACE: In a town now synonymous with Rick Stein, The Seafood Restaurant is still firmly charting its course as the flagship of a blossoming empire, which now includes the St Petroc's Hotel and Bistro (see entry), a café, deli, pâtisserie, fish 'n' chip shop and seafood cookery school. The spacious conservatory at the front of the restaurant makes the most of the quayside location, overlooking estuary and fishing boats, and is the place for pre-

and post-meal drinks and coffees. The light and airy, parquet-floored and white-walled dining room is enlivened with colourful paintings and mirrors. Crisp, white linen tablecloths and civilized but relaxed service build on the unpretentious atmosphere.
FOOD: Wonderful fish and more fish! Superbly fresh and simply prepared with well chosen combinations; the repertoire following the Stein fresh-is-best ethos and commitment to using the finest local produce. The style is a crowd-pleasing mix of the classic (Dover sole meunière) and modern, dotted with global influences (monkfish vindaloo), the approach via lengthy, daily-changing carte and six-course tasting option. Notable wine list.
OUR TIP: Tasting menu offers surprisingly good value; there are delightful bedrooms above
Chef: R Brett, S Delourme **Owners:** R & J Stein **Times:** 12-2.30/7-10, Closed 25-27 Dec, 1 May **Notes:** Tasting menu available L/D every day, Vegetarian available **Seats:** 104 **Smoking:** Air con **Children:** Min 3yrs+, Portions **Rooms:** 32 (32 en suite) 👪 **Directions:** Follow signs for town centre. Restaurant on riverside **Parking:** Directly opposite restaurant (pay & display) **e-mail:** reservations@rickstein.com
web: www.rickstein.com

⊚ The Metropole
British

Victorian grandeur in the famously foodie town

☎ 01841 532486 Station Rd PL28 8DB

MENU GUIDE Crab & langoustine brûlée • Sea bass, cep risotto, sautéed salsify, vanilla cream • Pineapple tarte Tatin, coconut ice cream

WINE GUIDE ♀ Norte Chico Sauvignon Blanc £14.95 • ♀ Norte Chico Merlot £15.95 • 15 bottles over £20, 28 bottles under £20 • 8 by the glass (£3.25-£6.95)

PRICE GUIDE Fixed D £27.95-£33.95 • min/water £3.50 • Service added but optional 12.50%

PLACE: This grand hotel overlooks the fishing village of Padstow and retains the sophistication of a bygone era. The spacious dining room has picture windows, making the most of the harbour views.
FOOD: Seasonally changing menu with creative flair inspired by high quality local produce. Fresh fish and shellfish, of course, make a significant showing, along with Cornish beef and West Country cheeses.
OUR TIP: Take a stroll round town before dining
Chef: Jon Guest **Owners:** Richardson Hotels Ltd **Times:** 6.30-9.00, closed L Mon-Sat **Notes:** Coffee included, Vegetarian available, No jeans, shorts, swimwear, trainers **Seats:** 70 **Smoking:** N/Sm in restaurant **Children:** Menu, Portions **Rooms:** 50 (50 en suite) ★★★
Directions: M5/A30 pass Launceston, follow signs for Wadebridge and N Cornwall. THen take A39 and follow signs for Padstow **Parking:** 40
e-mail: info@the-metropole.co.uk **web:** www.the-metropole.com

---

⊚ Old Custom House Inn, Pescadou Restaurant
Mediterranean

Fresh fish in great location at the harbourside

☎ 01841 532359 South Quay PL28 8BL

MENU GUIDE Smoked pollack & risotto cake, pesto • Shank of lamb, lentils & vegetables • Chocolate torte

PRICE GUIDE Food prices not confirmed for 2006. Please telephone for details

PLACE: Proudly set on the quayside with picturesque views across the bustling harbour, this charming inn began life as the Customs and Excise building in the 1800s. The lively bar is popular with locals and visitors and serves real ales and good bar meals. Pescadou's restaurant provides a stylish and convivial dining venue.
FOOD: The open kitchen produces some imaginative dishes that place the emphasis on locally caught fish and seafood.
OUR TIP: It's the fashionable face of Padstow
Times: 12-3/7-9.30, Closed Xmas, 1 May **Rooms:** 24 (24 en suite)
★★★ **Directions:** From Wadebridge take A389 (Padstow). Take 2nd R after Padstow School, round sharp bend at bottom of hill. Inn is opposite entrance to harbour car park
e-mail: oldcustomhouse@smallandfriendly.co.uk
web: www.smallandfriendly.co.uk

England

PADSTOW *continued* MAP 02 SW97

⊚⊚ St Ervan Manor
Modern British   **NEW**
Peaceful foodie haven
☎ 01841 540255   St Ervan PL27 7TA
MENU GUIDE Celeriac soup, roast scallop • Lamb, white bean & apricot purée, shallots, thyme • Chocolate fondant, pistachio ice cream
PLACE: With just eight tables, this former vicarage is a culinary hideaway, an intimate place to dine, the restaurant comprising two pretty rooms hung with contemporary art and decorated in delicate French blue. A cosy, magazine-strewed lounge completes the picture.
FOOD: St Ervan takes its cooking seriously, offering a choice of seasonal tasting menus based around fresh local produce. Flavours are precise and combinations thoughtful, with dishes complemented by an impressive wine list featuring a good range of sherries and digestifs.
OUR TIP: Book ahead
Times: Telephone for details   **e-mail:** info@stervanmanor.co.uk
web: www.stervanmanor.co.uk

⊚ St Petroc's Bistro
French
Cheerful bistro with distinctly French flavours
☎ 01841 532700   4 New St PL28 8EA
MENU GUIDE Moules marinière • Fillet of gurnard with shrimps & mushrooms • Sticky toffee pudding
WINE GUIDE ♀ Haut Poitou Sauvignon £16.50 • ♀ Rick Steins Tower Estate Shiraz £20.50 • 17 bottles over £20, 20 bottles under £20 • 8 by the glass (£3.75-£4.25)
PRICE GUIDE Starter £6.50-£7.50 • main £14.50-£16.50 • dessert £6 • coffee £2.65 • min/water £2.25 • Service optional
PLACE: A beautiful old house, reputedly one of Padstow's oldest, is the lively setting for this French-orientated bistro. Part of the Rick Stein stable, its plain walls are enlivened by modern art.
FOOD: As you would expect, the freshest of fish appears on the daily-changing carte along with decent meat choices - perhaps coq au vin - all with a distinctly Gallic flavour. The cooking is straightforward and effective.
OUR TIP: Enjoy an alfresco meal
Chef: Roy Brett, Alistair Clive   **Owners:** R & J Stein   **Times:** 12-2/7-10, Closed 1 May, 24-26 Dec   **Notes:** Vegetarian available   **Seats:** 54   **Smoking:** N/Sm in restaurant, Air con   **Children:** Portions   **Rooms:** 10 (10 en suite) ♦♦♦♦   **Directions:** Follow one-way around harbour, 1st L, situated on R   **Parking:** 10   **e-mail:** reservations@rickstein.com
web: www.rickstein.com

⊚⊚⊚ The Seafood Restaurant
see page 75

🍴 Rick Stein's Café 10 Middle St PL28 8AP
☎ 01841 532700   Fish in the Stein style, mostly deliciously simple, sometimes bold and striking. No lunch bookings taken, so arrive early.

🍴 Stein's Fish & Chip Shop South Quay PL28 8BY
☎ 01841 532700   Traditional fish and chips on the quayside where you can watch the fish being landed.

PENZANCE MAP 02 SW43

⊚⊚ The Abbey Restaurant
International
Modern restaurant with harbour views offering unfussy, modern cuisine
☎ 01736 330680 366906   Abbey St TR18 4AR
MENU GUIDE Grilled mackerel, pickled cucumber • Roast monkfish, broad bean & dill risotto, rocket pesto • Hot marmalade soufflé, vanilla ice cream
WINE GUIDE 41 bottles over £20, 38 bottles under £20 • 1 by the glass (£3.95)
PRICE GUIDE Fixed L £15 • Fixed D £32 • starter £5-£9.50 • main £14-£22 • dessert £5-£6 • coffee £3 • min/water £3.20 • Service optional
PLACE: Adjoining the bright blue and very individual Abbey Hotel in a narrow street that leads down to the sea, this modern eaterie comes in two distinct halves. Funky red and purple walls, tubs seats and sofas recall the cellar bar's days as a night club in the 1960s, while upstairs the light and airy restaurant offers pleasant harbour views and a more refined ambience.
FOOD: Dishes are simply described and the unfussy approach to modern British cooking results in notable precision and robust flavours. Huge emphasis on using top quality, local, seasonal produce.
OUR TIP: Wise to book ahead
Chef: Ben Tunnicliffe   **Owners:** B & K Tunnicliffe   **Times:** 12-2/7-10.30, Closed Winter closure (annual holiday), Sun-Mon, closed L Tue-Thu, closed D Winter-9 pm   **Notes:** Fixed D hotel only, Vegetarian available   **Seats:** 26, Pr/dining room 20   **Smoking:** N/Sm in restaurant, Air con   **Children:** Min 10 years, Portions   **Directions:** In centre of Penzance turn into Chapel Street opposite Lloyds TSB Bank, 500 yds & turn left at Admiral Benon public house, onto Abbey St   **Parking:** On street   **e-mail:** kinga@theabbeyonline.com   **web:** www.theabbeyonline.com

⊚⊚ The Bay Restaurant
British, Pacific Rim
Accomplished cooking by the coast
☎ 01736 366890   Mount Prospect Hotel, Britons Hill TR18 3AE
MENU GUIDE Walnut & thyme soufflé • Beef, cannellini beans, herb & pistachio crust, port wine jus • Banana Tatin, cardamom ice cream
WINE GUIDE ♀ Les Bateaux Cabernet Sauvignon £12.95 • 3 by the glass (£3.75-£4.80)
PRICE GUIDE Starter £4.75-£8 • main £12.95-£18.50 • dessert £5.50-£7 • coffee £2.50 • min/water £2.50 • Service optional • Group min 8 service 10%
PLACE: This contemporary restaurant doubles as an art gallery, displaying a changing monthly selection of work by local painters. Polished granite tables, stripped floors, white walls with huge windows which offer mesmerising views along the Penzance coast.
FOOD: The food goes from strength to strength, demonstrating the kitchen's skill, precision and commitment to the use of fresh local produce. Lighter meals and salads are available at lunchtimes and between 6 and 7.30pm.
OUR TIP: Terrace for summer dining
Chef: Ben Reeve, Katie Semmens   **Owners:** Yvonne & Stephen Hill   **Times:** 11-2/6.15-9.15, Closed L Oct-Apr   **Notes:** Vegetarian available, Dress Restrictions, Smart casual, no shorts   **Seats:** 60, Pr/dining room 12   **Smoking:** N/Sm in restaurant, Air con   **Children:** Menu, Portions   **Rooms:** 24 (24 en suite) ★★★   **Directions:** Approaching Penzance from A30, at 'Tesco' rdbt take first exit towards town centre. Britons Hill is third turning on right   **Parking:** 13   **e-mail:** table@bay-penzance.co.uk   **web:** www.bay-penzance.co.uk

Harris's Restaurant

English, French

Classic cooking close to the harbour

☎ 01736 364408 46 New St TR18 2LZ

MENU GUIDE Crab Florentine • Roast monkfish, wild mushroom risotto • Chocolate torte, amaretto cream

WINE GUIDE ♀ A & J James Saint Hilaire Chardonnay £12.95 • ♣ Browns Brothers Cabernet Sauvignon/Shiraz/Malbec £12.95 • 25 bottles over £20, 30 bottles under £20 • 6 by the glass (£3.50-£4.50)

PRICE GUIDE Starter £6.50-£9.50 • main £15.95-£23.95 • dessert £6.95-£8.50 • Service added but optional 10%

PLACE: Well known locally and popular with summer visitors, Harris's brings a classical touch to Penzance from its quiet off-High Street location. The well-dressed tables and charming owners are as reassuring as the menu.
FOOD: Fish is the real attraction here, with unfussy cooking bringing out the natural flavours of local lobster, crab, scallops and John Dory among others. You'll find meat too: noisettes of Cornish lamb, and grilled fillet steak perhaps.
OUR TIP: Ideal for a quick bite at lunchtime
Chef: Roger Harris **Owners:** Roger & Anne Harris **Times:** 12-2/7-9.30, Closed 3 wks winter, 25-26 Dec, 1 Jan, Sun, closed L Mon
Notes: Vegetarian by request only **Seats:** 40, Pr/dining room 20
Smoking: N/Sm in restaurant **Children:** Min 5yrs **Directions:** Located down narrow cobbled street opposite Lloyds TSB **Parking:** On street, local car park **e-mail:** contact@harrissrestaurant.co.uk
web: www.harissrestaurant.co.uk

The Navy Inn

British, European **NEW**

Contemporary gastro-pub with nautical theme

☎ 01736 333232 Lower Queen St TR18 4DE

MENU GUIDE Fresh tower of Newlyn crab • Hake poached in saffron sauce • Raspberry brûlée

WINE GUIDE ♀ Garganega Pinot Grigio £10.50 • ♣ San Antonia Primitivo Puglia £13.50 • 12 bottles under £20 • 8 by the glass (£2-£4)

PRICE GUIDE Starter £2.50-£6.50 • main £7.50-£9.95 • dessert £3.25-£3.95 • coffee £1.50 • min/water £1.85 • Service optional

PLACE: The name's nautical connotation is manifested in pulleys and ropes, telescopes and portholes, and the transformation of traditional inn into contemporary gastro-pub is proving a big hit locally.
FOOD: Up to the minute culinary ideas are confidently delivered, with quality local produce including freshly-caught fish making an impact. Classics like omelette Arnold Bennett appear alongside gâteau of Rosary goats' cheese, and it's open from 10am to 10pm.
OUR TIP: Very child friendly
Chef: Keir Meikle **Owners:** Keir Meikle **Times:** 12-10, Closed 25 Dec
Notes: Brunch avail. from 10-12, Vegetarian available **Seats:** 54
Smoking: N/Sm area **Children:** Menu, Portions **Directions:** In town centre, follow Chapel St for 50yds turn right into Queen St and follow to the bottom of road. **Parking:** free parking on promenade
e-mail: keir@navyinn.co.uk

The Summerhouse

Mediterranean

Top-notch cooking in delightful little restaurant with rooms

☎ 01736 363744 Cornwall Ter TR18 4HL

MENU GUIDE Seared scallops, rocket purée • Brill, champagne & sorrel sauce • Warm apple tart, crème chantilly

The Summerhouse

WINE GUIDE 26 bottles over £20, 15 bottles under £20 • 2 by the glass (£3.50)

PRICE GUIDE Fixed D £26 • coffee £1.50 • min/water £3 • Service added 10%

PLACE: Once home to one of Cornwall's leading artists, this listed Regency house is now a delightful restaurant with rooms. It's an intimate warren of squashy sofas and intriguing art, decorated in cheerful colours and set just 50 metres from the sea. Dine in the pretty walled garden if weather permits - it's just the spot to while away a lazy afternoon.
FOOD: Innovative Mediterranean cooking built around the best of each morning's market fare. A concise menu offers three choices at each course, and features plenty of fresh local fish.
OUR TIP: Indulge in a culinary weekend break
Chef: Ciro Zaino **Owners:** Ciro & Linda Zaino **Times:** 7-9.30, Closed Dec-Feb, Mon-Wed, closed L Mon-Sun **Notes:** Vegetarian available
Seats: 22 **Smoking:** N/Sm in restaurant **Children:** Min 8yrs **Rooms:** 5 (5 en suite) ♦♦♦♦♦ **Directions:** Into Penzance on A30. Along harbour past open air bathing pool & the Promenade to Queens Hotel. Turn right immediately after hotel & restaurant 30mtrs on left **Parking:** 5
e-mail: reception@summerhouse-cornwall.com
web: www.summerhouse-cornwall.com

PORTLOE MAP 02 SW93

The Lugger Hotel

British, European

Sound cooking in chic seaside hotel

☎ 01872 501322 TR2 5RD

MENU GUIDE Tuna spring roll, ginger & lemon dip • Pork au croûte, apple cider chutney • Dark chocolate torte

WINE GUIDE ♀ Malon Prisse Chardonnay £18.50 • ♣ Casa Silva Merlot £17.50 • 105 bottles over £20, 11 bottles under £20 • 9 by the glass (£4.50-£5.50)

PRICE GUIDE Fixed L £16.50 • Fixed D £37.50 • coffee £3 • min/water £3 • Service optional

continued

PORTSCATHO MAP 02 SW83

Driftwood

European
Chic dining with sea views
☎ 01872 580644 Rosevine TR2 5EW
MENU GUIDE Skate tian, crab, tomato & avocado • Pork rack, belly ravioli, chilli & apple • Rum Baba
WINE GUIDE ♀ San Esteban Sauvignon Blanc £13.50 • ♥ Antunuu Mapa Merlot £13.50 • 40 bottles over £20, 13 bottles under £20 • 7 by the glass (£3.50-£5)
PRICE GUIDE Fixed D £36-£50 • coffee £2 • min/water £2.25 • Service optional
PLACE: Overlooking Garrans Bay, Driftwood is one of the new generation of chic Cornish hotels filled with contemporary furniture and decoration, and possessing a relaxed atmosphere. The dining room has good sea views and simple, high quality settings. Friendly and efficient service.
FOOD: The kitchen is the heart of this hotel and short menus of well-conceived dishes emphasise local, seasonal and organic produce. Suppliers are listed. Short menus also allow the kitchen to concentrate on producing dishes with innovative and

interesting combinations such as chicken baked in hay, celery soup and coco beans. Preparation and presentation show that flair and imagination are no strangers to this kitchen. Expect tempting main courses like pig's trotter ballotine, butter beans and morels or sea bass with dill purée, smoked eel and a lobster vinaigrette.
OUR TIP: Book the Cabin to be even closer to the sea
Chef: Rory Duncan **Owners:** Robinsons **Times:** 7-10, Closed Xmas, Jan, closed L all week **Notes:** Lobster and Fruits de la Mer-order in advance, Vegetarian available, Smart Dress **Seats:** 40 **Smoking:** N/Sm in restaurant **Rooms:** 11 (11 en suite) ★★ **Directions:** 5m from St Mawes off the A3078, signposted Rosevine **Parking:** 30
e-mail: info@driftwoodhotel.co.uk **web:** www.driftwood.co.uk

PORTLOE *continued* MAP 02 SW93

PLACE: It doesn't get much more Cornish than the coastal setting of this chic hotel. Watch the gulls at work in the rock pools from the smartly appointed restaurant, before a cliff-top constitutional or a stroll along the pretty streets of Portloe.
FOOD: Fish comes straight from the boat to the kitchen and is hard to beat, but meat dishes hold their own. West Country lamb with a chive crust is a typical main.
OUR TIP: Indulge yourself with a visit to the hotel's luxurious spa
Chef: Franz Hornegger **Owners:** Richard & Sheryl Young **Times:** 12-2/7-9 **Notes:** Sun L 3 courses £19.50, Vegetarian available, Smart casual **Seats:** 44 **Smoking:** N/Sm in restaurant **Children:** Min 12 years **Rooms:** 21 (21 en suite) ★★★ **Directions:** Turn off A390 St Austell to Truro road onto the B3287 to Tregony. Then A3078 St Mawes road in 2m fork left for Veryan/Portloe, turn left at T-junct for Portloe. **Parking:** 21
e-mail: office@luggerhotel.com **web:** www.luggerhotel.com

PORTREATH MAP 02 SW64

🌹 Tabb's Restaurant
British, Mediterranean
Popular village restaurant
☎ 01209 842488 Railway Ter TR16 4LD
MENU GUIDE Shredded chicken soup • Seared monkfish with red pepper oil • Mandarin sorbet, kiwi purée
WINE GUIDE ♀ Laroche Chablis £20.50 • ♥ San Antonio Primitivo £12.95 • 10 bottles over £20, 21 bottles under £20 4 by the glass (£2.95)
PRICE GUIDE Fixed L £15 • Fixed D £19.50 • starter £5.95-£7.75 • main £11.50-£19.75 • dessert £5.25 • coffee £2.50 • min/water £2.65 • Service optional

PLACE: This old blacksmith's shop has been reinvented as a smart eaterie, with its stout stone walls concealing prettily dressed tables. A separate area furnished in cane serves as the bar lounge.
FOOD: Nigel Tabb's reputation in the kitchen is what brings people here, with everything made on the premises. Expect plenty of fish amongst the meat, with grilled mackerel and steamed Dover sole fillet showing what fresh seafood should taste like.
OUR TIP: Don't miss the home-made chocolates
Chef: Nigel Tabb **Owners:** Nigel & Melanie Tabb **Times:** 12.15-2.15/7-9.30, Closed 2 wks Jan & Nov, Tue, closed L Mon-Sat **Notes:** Vegetarian available **Seats:** 35 **Smoking:** N/Sm in restaurant **Children:** Portions **Directions:** 3m from Redruth, on left half way through Portreath, across the stream **Parking:** 4

PORTSCATHO MAP 02 SW83

🌹 Driftwood *see above*

🌹 Rosevine Hotel
European
Accomplished cooking in Georgian elegance on the Cornish coast
☎ 01872 580206 TR2 5EW
MENU GUIDE Wild mushroom soup • John Dory, celery and fennel stir fry, Pernod cream sauce • Chocolate crunch torte, pistachio and coffee anglaise
WINE GUIDE ♀ Chablis St Martin £29 • ♥ Château Segonzac £27.70 • 50 bottles over £20, 6 bottles under £20 • 20 by the glass (£4.20-£9)

continued

PRICE GUIDE Fixed L £25 • Fixed D £38 • min/water £2.90 • Service optional

PLACE: Set in secluded splendour with views over sub-tropical, palm filled gardens towards the sea, this Georgian country house has its own beach at the head of the spectacular Roseland peninsula. A pianist plays throughout dinner in the elegant, spacious Didiers Restaurant, contributing to the relaxed atmosphere. Service is attentive and friendly.

FOOD: The best of Cornish produce, in particular fresh fish and shellfish, play a vital role on the fixed-price menu, which offers a good choice at each course. The style is modern English with a Gallic twist.

OUR TIP: Good vegetarian and children's menu

Chef: Didier Bienaime, Rafael Maxia **Owners:** The Makepeace Family **Times:** 12-3/7.15-9.30, Closed Nov-Feb **Notes:** Fixed L 3 courses, fixed D 4 courses, Coffee included, Vegetarian available, Dress Restrictions, Smart casual **Seats:** 50 **Smoking:** N/Sm in restaurant **Children:** Menu, Portions **Rooms:** 17 (17 en suite) ★★★ **Directions:** Off A3078, hotel signed on right, 2m after Ruan High Lanes **Parking:** 40 **e-mail:** info@rosevine.co.uk **web:** www.rosevine.co.uk

ROCK MAP 02 SW97

 Black Pig Restaurant

British

A foodie gem in rural Cornwall

☎ 01208 862622 Rock Rd PL27 6JS

MENU GUIDE Lobster risotto • Rabbit, lemon & onion marmalade tart, mustard & sage sauce • Rhubarb sponge & sorbet, lavender sugar

WINE GUIDE ♀ Waipara Hills Sauvignon Blanc £23 • ♥ Château du Pavillon Merlot £24.50 • 46 bottles over £20, 11 bottles under £20 • 4 by the glass (£3.75-£4.20)

PRICE GUIDE Fixed L £17.50 • starter £10.25-£13.50 • main £21.50-£22.50 • dessert £7.50-£9.50 • coffee £3.50 • min/water £3 • Service optional

PLACE: Set in the small village of Rock on the north Cornwall coast, this friendly restaurant is a good alternative to the better known eateries of nearby Padstow. It's an intimate and special venue, decked with contemporary art and stylishly fitted with black leather chairs and elegantly laid tables.

FOOD: A commitment to the best of local produce and a thoughtful approach to seasonality lift the Black Pig's cooking out of the ordinary and suggest even better things are to come. Vegetarian dishes available on request.

OUR TIP: Small garden for alfresco dining in summer

Chef: Nathan Outlaw **Owners:** N Tigwell, C Morris, N Outlaw **Times:** 12-3/7-9.30, Closed 2-3 days at Xmas, 2 wks end Jan, 2 wks end Nov, Sun(all yr), Mon(winter only) **Notes:** 6 course tasting menu £60, Vegetarian available, Smart Dress **Seats:** 36 **Smoking:** N/Sm in restaurant **Children:** Min 12yrs **Directions:** From Wadebridge follow signs to Rock, pass petrol station. Restaurant in 300yds. **Parking:** 10 **e-mail:** reservations@blackpigrestaurant.co.uk **web:** www.blackpigrestaurant.co.uk

The St Enodoc Hotel Restaurant

Mediterranean, European

Contemporary cooking in bright modern hotel

☎ 01208 863394 The St Enodoc Hotel PL27 6LA

MENU GUIDE Thai fish cakes • Guinea fowl supreme, confit potato, mushroom & cream sauce • Dark chocolate & star anise terrine, plums

PRICE GUIDE Starter £5.25-£8.95 • main £9.25-£19.95 • dessert £5.75-£6.95 • coffee £2 • min/water £2.50 • Service added but optional 10%

continued

The St Enodoc Hotel Restaurant

PLACE: Chic hotel on Cornwall's rugged north coast with its own championship golf course. The airy split-level restaurant features an eclectic collection of local art, and has a panoramic terrace for pre-dinner drinks or alfresco dining in the summer.

FOOD: A contemporary menu to suit most tastes, with locally landed fish a speciality. Lighter meals available at lunch.

OUR TIP: A small ferry runs to and fro from Padstow

Chef: Rupert Brown **Owners:** Linedegree Ltd **Times:** 12.30-2.30/7-10, Closed 2 mths (late Dec, Jan, early Feb) **Notes:** Sun L 3 courses £24.95, Vegetarian available **Seats:** 55, Pr/dining room 30 **Smoking:** N/Sm in restaurant, Air con **Children:** Menu, Portions **Parking:** 60 **e-mail:** enodochotel@aol.com **web:** www.enodoc-hotel.co.uk

ST AUSTELL MAP 02 SX05

Carlyon Bay Hotel

British

Delightful coastal hotel serving accomplished food

☎ 01726 812304 Sea Rd, Carlyon Bay PL25 3RD

MENU GUIDE Pan-fried scallops, tomato & truffle butter • Roasted guinea fowl breast • Sticky toffee pudding

PRICE GUIDE Food prices not confirmed for 2006. Please telephone for details

PLACE: An imposing cliff top hotel with sweeping views over Carlyon Bay, and a restaurant with a large curved window designed to make the most of the outlook. Tables are well spaced and smart.

FOOD: A new look menu focuses on classic fish specialities as well as traditional favourites like prawn cocktail and steaks, rack of lamb, pan-fried calves' liver, and roast breast of chicken.

OUR TIP: Great for a golfing break

Times: 12.30-2/7-9.30 **Rooms:** 87 (87 en suite) ★★★★ **Directions:** A390 towards St Austell; from town follow Charlestown then Carlyon Bay/Crinnis. Hotel at end of Sea Road near Cornwall Coliseum. Hotel at end of Sea Road. **e-mail:** info@carlyonbay.co.uk **web:** www.carlyonbay.com

Revival

Modern British   **NEW**

Fresh, exciting cooking in historic Charlestown

☎ 01726 879053 Charleston Harbour PL25 3NJ

MENU GUIDE Crab gâteau • Roast guinea fowl, buttered pears • Hot chocolate fondant

WINE GUIDE ♀ Pinot Grigio (Tommasi) £18.50 • ♥ Vina Alberdi Rioja (La Rioja Alta) £25.75 • 22 bottles over £20, 20 bottles under £20 • 6 by the glass (£3.25-£4.75)

PRICE GUIDE Food prices not confirmed for 2006. Please telephone for details

continued

ST AUSTELL continued MAP 02 SX05

PLACE: A former cooperage in the historic harbour, with fresh white walls, colourful burgundy seating and striking artwork and artefacts. Service is relaxed but attentive.

FOOD: A fast-growing reputation owes much to the accurate cooking of fresh fish, and interesting handling of local meat and game, with attractive presentations adding high scores to starters like hot buttered mushroom with wilted rocket, smoked mackerel and fried quail's egg.

OUR TIP: Take time to look at the square rigged ships nearby

Chef: Tommy Garrett **Owners:** Ashley Waller, Angela Husband, Tommy Garrett **Times:** 10-14.45/6.30-10, Closed Mon, closed D Sun **Notes:** Vegetarian available, Dress Restrictions, Smart Casual **Seats:** 40 **Smoking:** N/Sm in restaurant **Directions:** Follow signs for Charlestown from St Austell bypass, restaurant on R **Parking:** Pay & display nearby **web:** www.cornwall-revival.co.uk

ST IVES MAP 02 SW54

Alba Restaurant

European

Modern cuisine in contemporary harbourside eaterie

☎ 01736 797222 Old Lifeboat House, Wharf Rd TR26 1LF

MENU GUIDE Scallops, black pudding sautéed apple, Calvados jus • Line caught sea bass, crab & spinach ravioli • Grappa pannacotta, stewed plums

WINE GUIDE ♀ Inheritance Redvale Colombard/Chardonnay £11.95 • ♀ Inheritance Redvale Cabernet /Shiraz £11.95 22 bottles over £20, 38 bottles under £20 • 31 by the glass (£3-£8.15)

PRICE GUIDE Fixed L £18.50 • starter £4.95-£7.95 • main £13.95-£19.95 • dessert £4.95-£6.95 • coffee £2.75 • min/water £2.95 • Service optional • Group min 6 service 10%

PLACE: An old lifeboat house with views that maximise its enviable harbourside location. Now occupying two floors, the restaurant is a popular place for a relaxed lunch, and in the evening the dining rooms are dressed more formally with linen cloths and designer cutlery.

FOOD: Fresh fish is naturally the order of the day, sometimes cooked with flavours of the East but always allowing the natural ingredients to shine. A dedicated vegetarian menu offers both starters and main courses. Tasting menu available.

OUR TIP: Book ahead for a window seat

Chef: Grant Nethercott **Owners:** Harbour Kitchen Co Ltd **Times:** 12-2/6-9.45, Closed 25-26 Dec **Notes:** Tasting menu 6 courses £40 (incl. coffee), Vegetarian available **Seats:** 60 **Smoking:** N/Sm in restaurant, Air con **Children:** Menu, Portions **Directions:** First building onto St Ives harbour front, opposite the new Lifeboat House **e-mail:** nantarro@aol.com **web:** www.alba-restaurant.co.uk

Carbis Bay Hotel

Modern British

Classic setting, sea views and modern menu

☎ 01736 795311 Carbis Bay TR26 2NP

PLACE: A peaceful location with access to its own white sand beach. Public areas include a smart bar and lounge, and a conservatory overlooking the sea. The restaurant also has sea views and is decorated in classic style with ornate plasterwork and French flock wallpaper.

FOOD: Fresh fish is to the fore on this interesting menu with international influences.

OUR TIP: Breakfast is a strength.

Times: 6-8.30, Closed Mid Dec-31 Jan **Directions:** Telephone for directions **e-mail:** carisbayhotel@talk21.com **web:** www.carbisbayhotel.co.uk

Garrack Hotel & Restaurant

Modern British

Quiet venue for impressive fresh fish

☎ 01736 796199 Burthallan Ln, Higher Ayr TR26 3AA

MENU GUIDE Pan-fried south coast scallops • Oven-roasted Cornish sea bass • Garrack's fresh fruit salad platter

WINE GUIDE ♀ Sancerre • ♀ Clancys Shiraz/Merlot • 20 bottles over £20, 74 bottles under £20 • 6 by the glass (£1.70-£4)

PRICE GUIDE Fixed D £21 • starter £3.50-£6.75 • main £8.95-£32 • dessert £4-£4.50 • coffee £1.30 • min/water £1.35 • Service optional

PLACE: Set above the bustling town of St Ives, The Garrack is a pleasantly quiet hotel with tranquil gardens and open fires in the lounge. Harbour views can be enjoyed from one of the dining rooms.

FOOD: Fresh fish is served in adventurous and occasionally surprising ways, or choose a classic lobster dish. Excellent quality meat from named sources includes local Penwith lamb.

OUR TIP: Come here to escape the town centre crowds

Chef: Phil Thomas **Owners:** Kilby family **Times:** 7-9.30, Closed L Mon-Sun **Notes:** Vegetarian available, Dress Restrictions, Smart casual **Seats:** 40 **Smoking:** N/Sm in restaurant **Children:** Menu, Portions **Rooms:** 18 (18 en suite) ★★★ **Directions:** From Tate Gallery & Porthmeor Beach car park follow road uphill to top. Burthallan Lane & Garrack Rd signs on right **Parking:** 36 **e-mail:** aarest@garrack.com **web:** www.garrack.com

Porthminster Beach Restaurant
Mediterranean, Pacific Rim
Confident modern cuisine by the sea
☎ 01736 795352 Porthminster TR26 2EB

MENU GUIDE Cornish scallops, foie gras, shaved truffle • John Dory, black olive potatoes, salsa verde, asparagus • Double chocolate tart

WINE GUIDE ♀ Oyster Bay Sauvignon Blanc £16.50 • ♥ Yellow Tail Shiraz £14.95 • 5 bottles over £20, 22 bottles under £20 9 by the glass (£2.65-£3.95)

PRICE GUIDE Starter £3.95-£7.95 • main £6.95-£17.95 • dessert £4.95-£5.95 • coffee £1.40 • min/water £1.95 • Service optional

PLACE: A sedate tearoom back in the 1930s, this beachside eaterie now majors in tongue-in-cheek chic, offering its guests sandcastle buckets for discarded shells. It's a classy affair none the less with stunning views across St Ives Bay.
FOOD: Confident cooking with a Mediterranean slant. A distinctly ish and shellfish menu makes the most of local seafood, but also offers alternative fare, such as a West Country beef fillet with thyme and Parma ham.
OUR TIP: Book ahead
Chef: M Smith **Owners:** Jim Woolcock, David Fox, Roger Symons, Tim Symons **Times:** 12-3.30/6, Closed from end Autumn half term to Apr **Notes:** Vegetarian available, Smart Dress **Seats:** 60
Smoking: N/Sm in restaurant **Children:** Portions **Directions:** On Porthminster Beach, beneath the St Ives Railway Station
Parking: 300yds (railway station) **e-mail:** pminster@btconnect.com
web: www.porthminstercafe.co.uk

The Wave Restaurant
Modern, Mediterranean 🍴NEW
Modern dining in a picturesque Cornish location
☎ 01736 796661 17 St Andrews St TR26 1AH
MENU GUIDE Seared squid, chorizo & salsa • Cornish beef, goats' cheese rösti, caramelised onion • Chocolate pannacotta & raspberries

WINE GUIDE ♀ Vignoble du Sud Sauvignon Blanc £10.95 • ♥ Boulders Ridge Shiraz Cabernet Chouses £10.95 2 bottles over £20, 18 bottles under £20 • 6 by the glass (£3.50-£4.25)

PRICE GUIDE Starter £3.95-£7.50 • main £10.95-£16.95 • dessert £4.95 • coffee £1.20 • min/water £3.50 • Service included

PLACE: This stylish restaurant relies on clean lines and skilful use of the fabled St Ives light to create an enticing space, where work by local artists becomes a focal point.
FOOD: The distinctly Mediterranean influence is freshened up with judicious use of local flavours. Look out for saffron, a Cornish favourite, and plenty of locally-caught seafood.

OUR TIP: Keep an eye on street scenes from the window tables
Chef: S M Pellow **Owners:** Mr&Mrs Cowling, Mr&Mrs Pellow
Times: 12-2/6.30-9.30, Closed End Nov-Beg Mar, Sun, closed L Sun, closed D Sun **Notes:** No children under 3yrs at dinner, Vegetarian available, Smart casual, no swim wear or bare chests **Seats:** 50
Smoking: N/Sm in restaurant **Children:** Menu, Portions
Directions: located just off the town centre, 100yards from the Parish Church **Parking:** Station car park

🍴 **Onshore** Wharf Rd TR26 ☎ 01736 796000 Quality, wood-baked pizza.

ST MARTIN'S MAP 02 SV91
🏵🏵🏵 **St Martin's on the Isle**
see page 82

ST MAWES MAP 02 SW83
🏵🏵 **Hotel Tresanton**
British, Mediterranean
Re-inventing seaside dining
☎ 01326 270055 Lower Castle Rd TR2 5DR

MENU GUIDE Foie gras & ham hock terrine, toasted brioche • Herb-crusted pan-fried brill, mashed potatoes & mussels • Glazed lemon tart, raspberry sorbet

PRICE GUIDE Fixed L £20 • Fixed D £36 • coffee £2.50 • min/water £3 • Service optional

PLACE: The magical view from the terrace - over a dazzling Cornish sea to the Roseland Peninsula and St Anthony's Lighthouse - is a draw in itself at fashionable Tresanton, but add Olga Polizzi's much-admired, stylish, urban-retro design and you have real appeal and a stunning original gem. The dining room has a calm, cool Mediterranean air, with fine mosaic floor and a terrace on two sides.
FOOD: The simple approach is the kitchen's ethos, via compact, fixed-price menus that allow quality produce centre stage, with the fruits of the sea an obvious strength.
OUR TIP: Aperitifs on the terrace are a highlight
Chef: Paul Wadham **Owners:** Tresanton Restaurant **Times:** 12-2.30/7-9.30 **Notes:** Vegetarian available, Civ Wed 50 **Seats:** 50, Pr/dining room 40 **Smoking:** No pipes, No cigars **Children:** Min 6 yrs, Menu
Directions: On the waterfront in town centre **Parking:** 30
e-mail: info@tresanton.com **web:** www.tresanton.com

continued

England

ST MARTIN'S MAP 02 SV91

St Martin's on the Isle

French, Mediterranean
Hotel dining on the beach in a peaceful island paradise
☎ 01720 422092 Lower Town TR25 0QW

e-mail: stay@stmartinshotel.co.uk
web: www.stmartinshotel.co.uk

PLACE: A splendid get-away-from-it-all waterfront hotel, idyllically perched on the edge of the Scillies, St Martin's has its own sandy beach and breathtaking views out to the islands of Tean and Tresco. Its aptly named Tean Restaurant is light and airy and set on the first floor to make the best of the panorama, with huge floor-to-ceiling windows and a bright blue-and-yellow colour scheme that echoes the surroundings. Table appointments are suitably stylish and service friendly, enthusiastic and professional.

FOOD: From an accomplished kitchen team, the cooking more than lives up to the views, with enticing daily-changing menus making full use of the first rate local ingredients, with the fruits of the sea finding pride of place, its quality and freshness assured. So expect elaborate, light, clear-flavoured dishes that allow key components to shine, perhaps Cornish monkfish served with a cauliflower and parmesan risotto, roasted scallops and a red wine sauce.

MENU GUIDE John Dory & shellfish potage, tarragon foam • Fillet of Cornish beef, roasted shallots, braised oxtail sauce • Assiette of apple

WINE GUIDE ♀ Van Zylshof Chenin Blanc £21.50 • ♀ Château Los Boldas Merlot • 50 bottles over £20, 25 bottles under £20 • 10 by the glass (£2.25-£4.95)

PRICE GUIDE Fixed D £44.50 • min/water £1 • Service included

OUR TIP: The seafood quality is outstanding, and the separate vegetarian menu enticing

Chef: John Mijatovic **Owners:** Peter Sykes **Times:** 7-10, Closed Nov-Feb, closed L Mon-Sun **Notes:** coffee incl., Vegetarian available, No jeans, T-shirts or shorts, Civ Wed 100 **Seats:** 60 **Smoking:** N/Sm in restaurant **Children:** Min 9yrs, Menu, Portions **Rooms:** 30 (30 en suite) ★ ★ ★ **Directions:** By helicopter or boat from Penzance to St Mary's. Flights from Bristol, Exeter, Southampton, Newquay or Land's End. Then 20-min launch transfer to St Martin's

ST MAWES *continued* MAP 02 SW83

 Idle Rocks Hotel

Modern, French

Careful cooking at water's edge location

☎ 01326 270771 Harbour Side TR2 5AN

MENU GUIDE Lobster ravioli, scallops, ginger & cucumber • Turbot, lentils & bacon, onion purée • Chocolate coulant, java ice cream

WINE GUIDE ♀ Yalumba Chardonnay £16.95 • ♀ Santa Rita Merlot £16.95 • 32 bottles over £20, 34 bottles under £20 27 by the glass (£4.25-£5.95)

PRICE GUIDE Fixed D £34.95 • min/water £3.65 • Service optional

PLACE: Literally on the water's edge in the lovely Roseland peninsula, the spick-and-span Idle Rocks enjoys a glorious setting, overlooking St Mawes harbour to distant Falmouth. Decorated in shades of blue, gold and sand, with a light wood floor and floor-to-ceiling windows, the romantic, split-level restaurant makes the most of the location, with all tables enjoying the stunning view.
FOOD: The sensibly short fixed-price menu changes daily and features fresh, locally sourced produce cooked in modern style, with some innovative twists to classic dishes. Fish is a highlight. Brasserie menu available in the bar.
OUR TIP: Try and stay, the setting and views are delightful
Chef: Damian Broom **Owners:** E K Richardson **Times:** 12-3/6.30-9
Notes: Coffee incl. Vegetarian by request only, Dress Restrictions, No jeans; Smart casual **Seats:** 52 **Smoking:** N/Sm in restaurant
Children: Portions **Rooms:** 33 (33 en suite) ★★★
Directions: Telephone for directions **Parking:** 5
e-mail: reception@idlerocks.co.uk **web:** www.idlerocks.co.uk

⊕ Rising Sun Hotel

British

Smart harbourside hotel specialising in seafood

☎ 01326 270233 TR2 5DJ

MENU GUIDE Seared scallops, black pudding & salad • Grilled sea bass, redcurrant dressing • Mini clotted cream & praline cheesecake

WINE GUIDE 22 bottles over £20, 22 bottles under £20 • 11 by the glass (£2.80)

PRICE GUIDE Food prices not confirmed for 2006. Please telephone for details

PLACE: Stylish and immaculately presented hotel situated at the water's edge overlooking St Mawes harbour towards the Fal Estuary. The restaurant extends into an attractive conservatory taking full advantage of the glorious views, and outside there is a terrace for pre-dinner drinks in summer.

continued

FOOD: The sensibly sized, daily fixed-price menu is planned around top quality seafood and other local produce.
OUR TIP: Casual dining available in the brasserie and bar
Chef: Ann Long **Owners:** Mr R J Milan **Times:** 12-2/7-9, Closed L Mon-Sat **Notes:** Vegetarian available, Smart Dress **Seats:** 50
Smoking: N/Sm in restaurant **Children:** Min 6yrs, Portions **Rooms:** 8 (8 en suite) ★★ **Directions:** On harbour front **Parking:** 8
e-mail: info@risingsunstmawes.co.uk **web:** www.risingsunstmawes.com

ST MERRYN MAP 02 SW87

⊚⊚ Ripley's

British, French

Simple yet innovative cooking in a Cornish cottage with style

☎ 01841 520179 PL28 8NQ

MENU GUIDE Herbed ham hock & lentil salad • Rump pavé, Café de Paris butter • Warm walnut tart

WINE GUIDE ♀ Klein Constantia Sauvignon Blanc £21 • ♀ Vina Albali Gran Reserva Rioja £27.50 • 20 bottles over £20, 18 bottles under £20 • 6 by the glass (£3-£3.50)

PRICE GUIDE Starter £7-£8.50 • main £13.50-£17.50 • dessert £6.50 • coffee £3 • min/water £2.55 • Service optional

PLACE: A simple but effective design has lent this place an unpretentious feel, with its bare wooden tables, white walls and artwork. Two neat areas, one small with slate flooring and the other larger with wooden boards, are enhanced by an attractive garden for summer aperitifs.
FOOD: Fish is a great strength of a menu that offers no gimmicks but rather relies on sound technique and top notch ingredients. The honest cooking embraces meat too, though roast monkfish with leek fondue and a cockle and mussel casserole might be hard to beat.
OUR TIP: Make sure you book!
Chef: Paul Ripley **Owners:** Paul Ripley **Times:** 12-2/7-9.30, Closed 2 wks Xmas, BHs, Sun-Mon, Limited lunch opening, phone for details
Notes: Smart Dress **Seats:** 32 **Children:** Portions **Parking:** on street

SUMMERCOURT MAP 02 SW85

⊚ *Viners Bar & Restaurant*

British   NEW

Chic gastro-pub serving hearty fare

☎ 01872 510544 Carvynick TR8 5AF

PLACE: After developing a number of different and rosette-winning restaurants over the years, well established and popular chef, Kevin Viner, has set up a new dining business in Summercourt. An impressive manor house has been tastefully transformed into a chic gastro dining pub, the original architecture blending well with marble topped tables, wooden floors and comfy leather chairs.
FOOD: The accomplished cooking has a relaxed, family-friendly style, delivering hearty pub portions while paying attention to stylish presentation. Plenty of fresh Cornish fish, plus shoulder of lamb, filled chicken breast, and chargrilled steak.
OUR TIP: Children welcome
Times: Telephone for details

TALLAND BAY MAP 02 SX25

⊚⊚⊚ Terrace Restaurant at Talland Bay Hotel *see page 84*

England

TALLAND BAY MAP 02 SX25

Terrace Restaurant at Talland Bay Hotel

British

Interesting combinations in peaceful family-run hotel

☎ 01503 272667 PL13 2JB

MENU GUIDE Terrine of ham hock & foie gras • Line-caught John Dory, shellfish cassoulet, braised lettuce • Caramel pear, lemon pannacotta

WINE GUIDE 52 bottles over £20, 19 bottles under £20 • 11 by the glass (£3.25-£4.75)

PRICE GUIDE Fixed L £23.50-£28.50 • Fixed D £32.50-£37.50 coffee £2.50 • min/water £2.50 • Service optional

PLACE: With gardens running down almost to the cliff edge at Talland Bay, this delightfully remote small hotel enjoys an enviably tranquil situation. The wood panelled restaurant is traditional and comfortable, and tables are nicely set with starched cloths and pretty flower arrangements.
FOOD: Behind the quiet exterior, there's a lot of hard work being done in the kitchen. Modern British dishes are prepared with a high level of intricacy and finesse. Local seafood is naturally a major element. The fixed-price three- or four-course dinner menu offers four choices at each course, including the West Country cheese board. Expect exciting combinations in main courses, such as saddle of lamb with spring greens, almonds, cauliflower tempura and goats' cheese purée.
OUR TIP: The breakfast menu gives the day's weather forecast
Chef: Shay Cooper **Owners:** Mr & Mrs G Granville **Times:** 12.30-2/7-9
Notes: Tasting menu available, Vegetarian available **Seats:** 40
Smoking: N/Sm in restaurant **Children:** Menu **Rooms:** 23 (23 en suite) ★★★ **Directions:** Signed from x-rds on A387 between Looe and Polperro **Parking:** 20 **e-mail:** reception@tallandbayhotel.co.uk
web: www.tallandbayhotel.co.uk

TRESCO MAP 02 SV81

Island Hotel
British, International

A wonderful romantic island escape

☎ 01720 422883 TR24 0PU

MENU GUIDE Shellfish risotto, shellfish bisque • Cornish lamb, Savoy cabbage, rosemary jus • Chocolate trio

WINE GUIDE ♀ Brampton Sauvignon Blanc £20 • ♀ Merlot £16 • 80 bottles over £20, 6 bottles under £20 • 12 by the glass (£3.50-£9)

PRICE GUIDE Fixed L fr £18 • Fixed D £37.50-£39.50 • starter fr £4.50 • main £7.50-£17.50 • dessert fr £5.50 • coffee £3 • min/water £3 • Service optional

PLACE: Run by Tresco Estate, this spacious, colonial-style hotel has sweeping sea and island views. The interior is simply decorated with cream walls and huge, bold prints. Service is professional in the two dining rooms.
FOOD: Fresh fish is the speciality of this restaurant but all ingredients, often grown on the island, are of excellent quality. Expect well-flavoured, simply presented starters of Bryher crab and avocado and main courses of sea bass with aubergine caviar and a pea velouté.
OUR TIP: Dine informally in the bar and enjoy the view
Chef: Peter Hingston **Owners:** Robert Dorrien-Smith **Times:** 12-2/6.30-9.15, Closed 5 Nov-1 Mar, closed L all week **Notes:** Vegetarian available, Dress Restrictions, No jeans, t-shirts **Seats:** 150, Pr/dining room 25
Smoking: N/Sm in restaurant **Children:** Menu, Portions **Rooms:** 48 (48 en suite) ★★★ **Directions:** 20 minutes from Penzance by helicopter **e-mail:** islandhotel@tresco.co.uk
web: www.tresco.co.uk/holidays/island_hotel.asp

New Inn
International

Friendly seaside inn with wide-ranging menu

☎ 01720 422844 TR24 0QQ

MENU GUIDE Pear & walnut salad, blue cheese dressing • Mussels in coconut cream, crispy egg noodles • Lemon meringue pie

WINE GUIDE ♀ San Andres Sauvignon blanc £13.50 • ♀ San Andres Merlot £13.50 • 14 bottles over £20, 24 bottles under £20 • 8 by the glass (£2.50-£5.50)

PRICE GUIDE Fixed D £29 • min/water £3 • Service optional

PLACE: Set just back from the beach, this hospitable pub has stunning views, and gives its diners a choice of eating alfresco in the garden, at the bar, or in an airy conservatory-style pavilion.
FOOD: As the only pub on the island, the New Inn caters to all-comers, offering a lengthy carte plus daily-changing, fixed-price selection. Make the most of the friendly staff who are knowledgeable and happy to help.
OUR TIP: Lighter bar menu available
Chef: Christian Gott & Stephanie Clark **Owners:** Mr R Dorien-Smith
Times: 7-9, Closed L Mon-Sun **Notes:** Dinner only served in restaurant (coffee inc), Vegetarian available **Seats:** 40 **Smoking:** N/Sm in restaurant **Children:** Menu, Portions **Rooms:** 16 (16 en suite) ★★
Directions: 250yds from harbour (private island, contact hotel for details)
e-mail: newinn@tresco.co.uk
web: www.tresco.co.uk/holidays/new_inn.asp

TRURO MAP 02 SW84

 Alverton Manor

British

Former convent with exciting food

☎ 01872 276633 Tregolls Rd TR1 1ZQ

MENU GUIDE Mussels & cockles, tomato broth • Bitter poached turbot • Carrageen & berry compote

WINE GUIDE 64 bottles over £20, 139 bottles under £20 • 10 by the glass (£3-£5.25)

PRICE GUIDE Fixed L £9.50 • Fixed D £27.50 • starter £5 • main £17 • dessert £5.50 • coffee £2 • min/water £3 • Service optional

PLACE: This 19th-century former convent has been extensively refurbished. It stands in six acres of grounds and is within easy walking distance of Truro city centre. Decoration is in the country house style with lots of antiques in public areas and deep leather sofas in the bar and lounge.

FOOD: This is exciting cooking using high quality ingredients gathered from far and wide - although there is a growing emphasis on local produce such as St Ives mussels and Cornish brill. Strong clear flavours and generous portions characterise dishes here.

OUR TIP: Impressive sherry and Madeira list in the bar

Chef: Keith Brooksbank **Owners:** Mr M Sagin **Times:** 11.45-1.45/7-9.15, Closed L Sat **Notes:** Sun L 3 courses £14.95, Vegetarian available, Smart Dress, Civ Wed 80 **Seats:** 30, Pr/dining room 80 **Smoking:** N/Sm in restaurant **Children:** Min 12yrs, Menu, Portions **Rooms:** 32 (32 en suite) ★★★ **Directions:** From Truro bypass take A39 to St Austell. Just past the church on left **Parking:** 80

e-mail: reception@alvertonmanor.co.uk **web:** www.connexions.co.uk

 Probus Lamplighter Restaurant

International, Pacific Rim

Tempting cuisine with a hint of South Africa in smart restaurant

☎ 01726 882453 Fore St, Probus TR2 4JL

MENU GUIDE Carpaccio of beef • Seared monkfish 'Mama Africa', salsa mango & saffron risotto • Passionfruit brûlée, exotic fruit sorbet

PLACE: An unassuming shop front hides this smartly presented restaurant just off the A390. Fresh yellow flowers, white walls, dark beams, blue carpets, and crisp linen set the tone for a warm welcoming chef owner who can be seen frequently circulating among the diners.

FOOD: Food has a certain South African touch, thanks to award-winning chef/owner Sidney Bond's South African roots. The cuisine is international offering skilful, accomplished dishes, such as pot-roasted guinea fowl, hog's pudding, sarriette potato rosti with wild bullace and crab apple jelly. The chef's wife makes the desserts every morning.

OUR TIP: Don't miss the desserts

Times: 6.30-11, Closed Sun-Mon

☕ **Charlotte's Tea House** Coinage Hall, 1 Boscawen St TR1 2QU ☎ 01872 263706
Winner of The Tea Guild Award of Excellence 2005.

TYWARDREATH MAP 02 SX05

Trenython Manor

Modern European

Fine dining in Palladian setting

☎ 01726 814797 Castle Dore Rd PL24 2TS

MENU GUIDE Mussel & prawn cassoulet, curry sabayon • Rack of lamb, herb crust, red wine reduction • Assiette of chocolate

PRICE GUIDE Food prices not confirmed for 2006. Please telephone for details

PLACE: Dating from the 1800s, there is something distinctly different about Trenython, a classic English manor house designed by an Italian architect. The impressive, oak-panelled dining room looks out across the gardens towards St Austell Bay and is the venue for contemporary cuisine. Service is friendly and attentive.

FOOD: Modern eclectic cooking reveals a good level of technical skill and excellent sourcing of luxury and humbler ingredients. Separate bistro menu.

OUR TIP: Take a stroll around the grounds before dinner

Times: 12-2.30/7-9.30, Closed L Mon-Sat

★★★ **Directions:** From Exeter join A30 towards Cornwall, then B3269 to Lostwithiel. Take A390 St Austell/Fowey, follow Fowey signs for approx 4 miles. The hotel is then signed. **e-mail:** reception@miconsortium.com **web:** www.trenython.co.uk

---

VERYAN MAP 02 SW93

Nare Hotel

Traditional British

Traditional dining in seaside hotel with great views

☎ 01872 501279 Carne Beach TR2 5PF

MENU GUIDE Grilled sardines with ratatouille • Flambéed steak au poivre • Strawberries & clotted cream

WINE GUIDE ⚲ Nare Hotel Dry White £14 • ⚲ Nare Hotel Full Red £14 • 100 bottles over £20, 61 bottles under £20

PRICE GUIDE Starter £5.50-£13.50 • main £16.50-£25 • dessert £4.40-£5.05 • coffee £2.10 • Service optional

PLACE: With delightful views of Veryan Bay, this family-run clifftop hotel is comfortable and staff are friendly. Service in the Dining Room is formal, and the hors d'oeuvres and flambé trolleys are still popular. The nautical-themed Quarterdeck restaurant offers a more contemporary, less formal dining experience.

FOOD: Traditional dishes are given a contemporary twist and there's a heavy reliance on fresh seafood and shellfish.

OUR TIP: Order the local lobster

Chef: Malcolm Sparks **Owners:** Mrs T N Gray **Times:** 12.30-2.30/7.30, Closed L Mon-Sat **Notes:** Fixed D £38 (5 courses), Vegetarian available, Dress Restrictions, Jacket and tie **Seats:** 75 **Smoking:** N/Sm in restaurant **Children:** Min 7, Menu, Portions **Rooms:** 38 (38 en suite) ★★★★ **Directions:** Through village passing New Inn on left, continue 1 mile to the sea **Parking:** 70 **e-mail:** office@narehotel.co.uk **web:** www.narehotel.co.uk

---

WADEBRIDGE MAP 02 SW97

☕ **The Tea Shop** 6 Polmorla Rd PL27 7ND
☎ 01208 813331
Winner of The Tea Guild Award of Excellence 2005.

England

CUMBRIA

ALSTON MAP 18 NY74

Lovelady Shield House
British, European

Country-house cuisine in friendly family-run hotel in the Pennines

☎ 01434 381203   CA9 3LF

Drunken Duck Inn

MENU GUIDE Smoked trout, cucumber & dill mousse • Roast loin of venison, port & juniper jus • Chocolate fondant, pineapple & kiwi

PRICE GUIDE Food prices not confirmed for 2006. Please telephone for details

PLACE: Country house hotel with three acres of grounds in a valley setting close to Alston, the highest market town in England. The dining room is elegant but informal, with stylish decor, antiques and fine paintings. Tables are laid with cloths, fresh flowers and candles.

FOOD: Good quality fresh local ingredients are a feature of the country house dinner party-style cooking, with tasty, traditional English dishes offered from a fixed-price menu.

OUR TIP: Try the local and locally sourced cheeses

Times: 12-2/7-8.30, Closed L Mon-Sat **Rooms:** 10 (10 en suite) ★★
Directions: 2m E of Alston, signed off A689 at jnct with B6294
e-mail: enquiries@lovelady.co.uk **web:** www.lovelady.co.uk

AMBLESIDE MAP 18 NY30

Drunken Duck Inn
Modern British

Thriving country inn with refined cooking

☎ 015394 36347 Barngates LA22 0NG

MENU GUIDE Smoked haddock & pea risotto, truffle oil, pancetta • Rib eye, mushrooms, chips, chive hollandaise • Crème caramel, tropical fruit salsa, hazelnut tuile

WINE GUIDE ♀ Domaine de la Perriére Sancerre £24.50 • ♀ Biurko Gorri Rioja £16.95 • 31 bottles over £20, 26 bottles under £20 • 20 by the glass (£2.95-£9.50)

PRICE GUIDE Starter £6.25-£11.50 • main £13.95-£22.95 • dessert £5.95-£6.95 • coffee £2 • min/water £2.50 • Service optional

PLACE: A charismatic, 400-year-old, traditional country inn stylishly upgraded and modernized but retaining bags of atmosphere - log fires, low ceilings and wooden beams. The restaurant's two rooms are a fresh, harmonious mix of traditional and contemporary, framed by oodles of prints.

FOOD: The extensive, crowd-pleasing, imaginative, modern menus hit the spot and showcase fresh local produce - suppliers are listed on the back of the menu. Good choice of English cheeses, and fine beers from the on-site micro-brewery.
OUR TIP: Booking essential to avoid disappointment
Chef: Nick Foster **Owners:** Stephanie Barton **Times:** 12-2.30/6-9, Closed 25 Dec **Notes:** Vegetarian available **Seats:** 42 **Smoking:** N/Sm in restaurant **Children:** Portions **Rooms:** 11 (11 en suite) ♦♦♦♦
Directions: Take A592 from Kendal, follow signs for Hawkshead(from Ambleside), in 2.5m sign for inn on right. 1m up hill **Parking:** 40
e-mail: info@drunkenduckinn.co.uk
web: www.drunkenduckinn.co.uk

Regent Hotel
British

Contemporary restaurant with upbeat menus

☎ 015394 32254 Waterhead Bay LA22 0ES

MENU GUIDE Wok-fried prawns, sweet chilli sauce • Slow-braised lamb shank • Rich chocolate truffle torte, summer berries

WINE GUIDE ♀ Chardonnay £14.50 • ♀ Grant Burge Shiraz £15.50 • 6 bottles over £20, 20 bottles under £20 • 12 by the glass (£3.25-£5.50)

PRICE GUIDE Fixed L £15-£15 • starter £4.95-£6.95 • main £13.50-£18.50 • dessert £4.95 • coffee £2.50 • min/water £2.95

PLACE: A contemporary restaurant overlooking a pretty Italianate courtyard. Interesting modern art bedecks the walls, and stylish white plates and bright brasserie-style menus show the new upbeat mood.

FOOD: The food has taken a contemporary turn too, with a more accessible range still taking strict account of local and seasonal produce. Posh home-made burgers, and duck breast with damsons and wild mushrooms mingle with risottos, pasta and vegetarian.
OUR TIP: Enjoy a stroll by the lake
Chef: Nick Martin **Owners:** Vogue Leisure Ltd. **Times:** 12-2/7-9, Closed Xmas wk **Notes:** Vegetarian available **Seats:** 60 **Smoking:** N/Sm in

continued

continued

restaurant **Children:** Menu, Portions **Rooms:** 30 (30 en suite) ★★★ **Directions:** 1m S of Ambleside at Waterhead Bay **Parking:** 35 **e-mail:** info@regentlakes.co.uk **web:** www.regentlakes.co.uk

Rothay Manor

British

Classic country-house setting for simple dishes delivered with style

☎ 015394 33605 Rothay Bridge LA22 0EH

MENU GUIDE Spiced Morecambe Bay shrimps • Cartmel Valley roast pheasant • Sticky toffee pudding

WINE GUIDE ♀ Withers Sauvignon Blanc £20 • ♀ Kano Merlot £21 • 90 bottles over £20, 62 bottles under £20 • 5 by the glass (£3.25)

PRICE GUIDE Fixed L £8.70-£19.50 • Fixed D £33 • starter £3.50-£4.50 • main £10 • dessert £4 • coffee £1.70 • min/water £2.70 • Service optional

PLACE: An attractive hotel with a listed Regency façade set in landscaped gardens close to Ambleside and Lake Windermere. The dining room is elegant, with unclothed wooden tables set with fine china, silver and crystal. In winter there'll be a fire in one of the lounges.

FOOD: Accurate cooking with clear flavours using quality Cumbrian ingredients. Presentation is superb, with dinner dishes as picturesque as the views outside.

OUR TIP: Choice of three or four five-courses at dinner **Chef:** Jane Binns **Owners:** Nigel and Stephen Nixon **Times:** 12.30-1.45/7.15-9, Closed 3-27 Jan **Notes:** Alc L only, Vegetarian available, Dress Restrictions, Smart casual **Seats:** 65, Pr/dining room 34 **Smoking:** N/Sm in restaurant, Air con **Children:** Min 7yrs D, Menu, Portions **Rooms:** 19 (19 en suite) ★★★ **Directions:** From Ambleside, follow signs for Coniston (A593). Establishment is 0.25 mile SW from the centre of Ambleside opposite the rugby club **Parking:** 35 **e-mail:** hotel@rothaymanor.co.uk **web:** www.rothaymanor.co.uk

The Log House Restaurant Lake Rd LA22 0DN
☎ 015394 31077 Cosy restaurant and wine bar with rooms.

APPLEBY-IN-WESTMORLAND MAP 18 NY62

Appleby Manor Country House Hotel

Modern British

Modern cuisine in comfortable Westmorland hotel

☎ 017683 51571 Roman Rd CA16 6JB

MENU GUIDE Thai lobster & crab ravioli • Calves' liver, parsnip mash, Cumberland ham, red wine jus • Sticky toffee pudding

WINE GUIDE ♀ Santa Digna Sauvignon Blanc £14.25 • ♀ Best's Shiraz £16.50 • 15 bottles over £20, 55 bottles under £20 • 6 by the glass (£3.50)

PRICE GUIDE Starter £3.95-£9.50 • main £13.95-£17.95 • dessert £5.50 • coffee £2.50 • min/water £2.95 • Service included

PLACE: Built from local sandstone, this imposing Victorian manor is set in the rolling countryside of the Northern Pennines. Two rooms make up the restaurant - The Oak, a wood-panelled affair with original features, and The Chandelier, an airy conservatory extension.

FOOD: Interesting modern English and French cuisine making use of quality local produce wherever possible. Well-presented dishes can be on the hearty side, so come with an appetite.

OUR TIP: Save room for cheese - the superb selection changes daily

Chef: Sue Sampson **Owners:** Dunbobbin family **Times:** 12-2/7-9, Closed 24-26 Dec **Notes:** Sun lunch 3 courses £14.50, Vegetarian available, Smart Dress, Smart casual **Seats:** 96, Pr/dining room 20 **Smoking:** N/Sm in restaurant **Children:** Menu, Portions **Rooms:** 30 (30 en suite) ★★★ **Directions:** M6 junct 40 take A66 for Scotch Corner. (12m) Take turn for Appleby. Manor 1.5m on right **Parking:** 60 **e-mail:** reception@applebymanor.co.uk **web:** www.applebymanor.co.uk

BARROW-IN-FURNESS MAP 18 SD26

Clarence House Country Hotel & Restaurant

Modern British · **NEW**

Conservatory dining with garden and country views

☎ 01229 462508 Skelgate LA15 8BQ

PLACE: Country-house style Victorian hotel, much extended, set amid its own ornamental grounds on the edge of the town. It is popular with business people midweek and for weddings, in a delightful barn conversion, at weekends. Meals are served in the spacious conservatory restaurant as well as in the original house.

FOOD: Sound British cooking offered from a choice of menus, including a carte, fixed-price menu and a set five-course speciality selection.

OUR TIP: Window tables are in high demand in summer **Times:** 12-2/7-9 Closed Sun D **e-mail:** info@clarencehouse-hotel.co.uk **web:** www.clarencehouse-hotel.co.uk

BASSENTHWAITE MAP 18 NY23

Lake View Restaurant at Armathwaite Hall

British, International

Fine dining in mansion with lake views

☎ 017687 76551 Armathwaite Hall CA12 4RE

MENU GUIDE Halibut goujons, remoulade • Roast of the day, trimmings • Sticky toffee pudding

PRICE GUIDE Fixed L £19.95 • Fixed D £39.95 • min/water £3 • Service optional

PLACE: Outside, there are good views over Bassenthwaite Lake and 400 acres of deer park, inside, there's rich wood panelling, the smell of wood smoke, deep sofas and hunting trophies as well as comfortable, well-equipped bedrooms.

continued

continued

BASSENTHWAITE continued MAP 18 NY23

Lake View Restaurant at Armathwaite Hall

FOOD: Cooking in the Lake View Restaurant is traditional with French and International influences. There's a six-course tasting menu that makes full use of local Cumbrian produce. Formal service includes some dishes being carved at table and a great choice of wines.
OUR TIP: Impressive list of well-organised outdoor activities
Chef: Kevin Dowling **Owners:** Graves Family **Times:** 12.30-1.45/7.30-9.15 **Notes:** Fixed L 4 courses £19.95, D 6 courses £39.95, Coffee incl, Vegetarian available, Dress Restrictions, Smart casual, no jeans/T-shirts/trainers, Civ Wed 80 **Seats:** 80, Pr/dining room 25 **Children:** Portions **Rooms:** 43 (43 en suite) ★★★★ **Directions:** From M6 junct 40/A66 to Keswick then A591 towards Carlisle. Continue for 7m and turn left at Castle Inn **Parking:** 100
e-mail: reservations@armathwaite-hall.com
web: www.armathwaite-hall.com

The Pheasant
French, British
Traditional lakeside inn with well-presented food
☎ 01768 776234   CA13 9YE

continued

MENU GUIDE Chicken liver & brandy pâté • Seared chicken breast, grilled black pudding • Grand Marnier crème brûlée
WINE GUIDE ♀ Chablis Chardonnay £28.95 • ♀ Fleurie Gamay £25.95 • 39 bottles over £20, 21 bottles under £20 • 10 by the glass (£3.25-£8.95)
PRICE GUIDE Fixed L £18.50 • Fixed D £29.95 • coffee £1.95 • min/water £2.25 • Service optional • Group min 8 service 10%
PLACE: Sprawling old inn with a history dating back to the 16th century, and plenty of evidence to prove it. Inside are oak panelling and log fires, while outside benefits from beautiful gardens and the proximity of Bassenthwaite Lake.
FOOD: A sound menu of modern dishes with some good marriages of tastes and ingredients. Old Spot pork escalope with sautéed wild mushrooms and a soft green peppercorn, brandy and shallot sauce successfully pairs distinctive flavours.
OUR TIP: Enjoy the garden in summer
Chef: Malcolm Ennis **Owners:** Trustees of Lord Inglewood **Times:** 12-2/7-9, Closed 25 Dec **Notes:** Vegetarian available, Samrt casual, no jeans, T-shirts, trainers **Seats:** 45, Pr/dining room 12 **Smoking:** N/Sm in restaurant **Children:** Min 8yrs D **Rooms:** 15 (15 en suite) ★★★ **Directions:** M6 junct 40, take A66 (Keswick and North Lakes). Continue past Keswick and head for Cockermouth. Signposted from A66 **Parking:** 40 **e-mail:** info@the-pheasant.co.uk
web: www.the-pheasant.co.uk

BORROWDALE MAP 18 NY21
Borrowdale Gates Country House Hotel
British, French
Modern country-house cuisine in welcoming hotel with dramatic views
☎ 017687 77204   CA12 5UQ
MENU GUIDE Grilled marinated sardine escabeche, herb tagliatelle • Duo of Lune Valley lamb • Bread & butter pudding
WINE GUIDE ♀ Chablis Domaine Emile Petit, Jean Marc Brocard £23 • ♀ Coun Bourisset £14.50 • 54 bottles over £20, 25 bottles under £20 • 7 by the glass (£3-£4.50)
PRICE GUIDE Fixed D £34.50-£44.50 • coffee £3.15 • min/water £3.25 • Service optional
PLACE: Country house hotel in an idyllic location, set in two acres of wooded gardens with a backdrop of rugged fells. Large windows afford panoramic views of the gorgeous scenery. It is very much a residential hotel with no public bar.
FOOD: Modern country house in style, artistically presented with plenty of flavours and textures on the plate. The fixed-price menu includes vegetarian options.
OUR TIP: Ideal hideaway for a special weekend
Owners: Mr Roland Ayling **Times:** 12.15-1.30/7-8.45 **Notes:** Set 5 course D £34.50-£44.50, Vegetarian available, Dress Restrictions, Jacket & tie preferred, no jeans **Seats:** 55 **Smoking:** N/Sm in restaurant **Children:** Min 12yrs, Portions **Rooms:** 29 (29 en suite) ★★★ **Directions:** B5289 from Keswick, after 4m turn right over bridge to Grange. Hotel 400yds on right **Parking:** 30
e-mail: hotel@borrowdale-gates.com **web:** www.borrowdale-gates.com

Hazel Bank Country House
British, European
Victorian house with sweeping views
☎ 017687 77248 Rosthwaite CA12 5XB
MENU GUIDE Smoked salmon, mango, avocado & lime salsa • Herbed chicken breast ham wrapped, tomato sauce, roasted potatoes • Raspberry crème brûlée

continued

Hazel Bank Country House

WINE GUIDE ♀ Miguel Torres Chardonnay £12.50 • ♥ Miguel Torres Merlot £12.50 • 6 bottles over £20, 43 bottles under £20 • 5 by the glass (£4.90)

PRICE GUIDE Fixed D £29.50 • min/water 90p • Service optional

PLACE: Set in an elevated position against a backdrop of mountain peaks and surrounded by sweeping lawns and woodland, this Victorian residence offers tranquility and magnificent views over the Borrowdale valley. The traditional-styled restaurant is decorated in rich, warm burgundy and beige hues, bathed in candlelight over dinner.
FOOD: The approach is via set, fixed-price four-course dinner, executed with skill and showcasing quality local produce. Service is attentive, hospitality warm.
OUR TIP: Enjoy the marvellous views
Chef: Brenda Davies **Owners:** Glen & Brenda Davies **Times:** from 7, Closed 25-26 Dec, closed L Mon-Sun **Notes:** Coffee included, Smart Dress **Seats:** 22 **Smoking:** N/Sm in restaurant **Children:** Min 12 yrs **Rooms:** 8 (8 en suite) ♦♦♦♦ **Directions:** From M6 junct 40, leave the A66 and take the B5289 to Borrowdale. Just before Rosthwaite turn left over humped back bridge **Parking:** 12
e-mail: enquiries@hazelbankhotel.co.uk
web: www.hazelbankhotel.co.uk

⚜ *Leathes Head Hotel*
Modern British   NEW
Peaceful location with lovely views and great cooking
☎ 017687 77247   CA12 5UY
MENU GUIDE Peppered smoked mackerel fillet • Pan-fried beef escalope • Poached pear, champagne sorbet
PRICE GUIDE Food prices not confirmed for 2006. Please telephone for details

PLACE: Is Borrowdale the most beautiful valley in England? The locals think so, and the view from this elegant restaurant is as pretty as they come.
FOOD: Fresh ingredients are handled with a refreshing lack of artifice, and the interesting combination of flavours has a broad appeal. From the set four-course dinner expect decently cooked grilled Ullswater lamb cutlets with a sharp redcurrant sauce, and a rich chocolate truffle cake.
OUR TIP: An ideal base for fell walking
Times: 7.30-8.15, Closed Mid Nov-Mid Feb **Rooms:** 12 (12 en suite) ★★★ **e-mail:** enq@leatheshead.co.uk **web:** www.leatheshead.co.uk

BRAITHWAITE MAP 18 NY22
⚜ **The Cottage in the Wood**
British, European   NEW
Good honest food in charming hotel
☎ 017687 78409   Whinlatter Pass CA12 5TW
MENU GUIDE Spiced William pear with blue Wensleydale strudel • Seared Loch Duart salmon on spinach creamy mash, etuvée of peas & spring onions • Caramelised pineapple, crème renversee, tropical salsa
WINE GUIDE ♀ Cloudy Bay Sauvignon Blanc £24 • ♥ Brown Brothers Shiraz £18.50 • 12 bottles over £20, 12 bottles under £20 • 6 by the glass (£3.25-£4.50)
PRICE GUIDE Fixed D £20.50 • min/water £2.50 • Service optional

PLACE: A cottage-style hotel within Whinlatter Forest, in one of the most dramatic and unspoilt areas of the Lake District. The former 17th-century coaching inn run by a friendly husband and wife team has classic country house decor and separate cosy bar.
FOOD: The modern British set dinner with French influences offers choice only at dessert, but the menu changes every day and the quality of cooking with fresh local produce will satisfy every appetite.
OUR TIP: Great walking country
Chef: Liam Berney **Owners:** Liam & Kath Berney **Times:** 7-9.30, Closed Jan, Mon, closed L all week **Notes:** Coffee incl, Fixed D 3 courses Sun-Thu,4 courses Fri-Sat £25, Vegetarian available **Seats:** 26
Smoking: N/Sm in restaurant **Children:** Min 7yrs **Rooms:** 10 (10 en suite) ★★ **Parking:** 10 **e-mail:** info@thecottageinthewood.co.uk **web:** www.thecottageinthewood.co.uk

BRAMPTON MAP 21 NY56
⚜⚜ **Farlam Hall Hotel**
British
Stunningly peaceful and friendly hotel with contemporary cuisine
☎ 016977 46234   Hallbankgate CA8 2NG

MENU GUIDE Warm herb croûton • Medallion of beef fillet • Honey & lemon mousse
WINE GUIDE ♀ Grove Mill Sauvignon Blanc £19.95 • ♥ Trentham Estate Merlot £19.95 • 30 bottles over £20, 17 bottles under £20 • 6 by the glass (£4.95)
PRICE GUIDE Fixed D £36 • min/water £2.50 • Service optional
PLACE: Outstanding hospitality is an exemplary feature of this lovely old hotel, where 15th-century origins have been painstakingly restored to bring style and comfort to modern guests. The restaurant is just one of several rooms geared towards relaxation.

continued

BRAMPTON continued MAP 21 NY56

FOOD: The dinner menu offers a straightforward choice of well-executed dishes, using top notch ingredients that yield the expected superb flavours. Good saucing raises this cooking to a higher plateau, with a fine pink peppercorn sauce getting the most from a medallion of beef.
OUR TIP: Take a stroll in the beautifully landscaped Victorian gardens
Chef: Barry Quinion **Owners:** Quinion & Stevenson families **Times:** 8-8.30, Closed 25-30 Dec, closed L Mon-Sun **Notes:** Coffee included, Vegetarian by request only, No jeans **Seats:** 40, Pr/dining room 20 **Smoking:** N/Sm in restaurant **Children:** Min 5 yrs, Portions **Rooms:** 12 (12 en suite) ★★★ **Directions:** On A689, 2.5m SE of Brampton. (Not in Farlam Village) **Parking:** 25 **e-mail:** farlam@relaischateaux.com **web:** www.farlamhall.co.uk

CARTMEL MAP 18 SD37

⬡ Aynsome Manor Hotel
British ⚑NEW
Country-house cooking in elegant Lakeland setting
☎ 01539 536653 LA11 6HH
MENU GUIDE Sun-dried tomato & asparagus risotto • Cumbrian pork, mustard pomme purée, cider cream sauce • Chocolate tart
WINE GUIDE ♀ Matua Valley Sauvignon Blanc £14.75 • ♀ De Bortoli Shiraz £14 • 40 bottles over £20, 50 bottles under £20 7 by the glass (£2.50)
PRICE GUIDE Fixed L £14.75-£15 • Fixed D £21-£22 • coffee £2.50 • min/water £2 • Service optional
PLACE: Dating back to the 16th century, this charming country house offers a view unchanged by time across peaceful meadowland to a Norman priory. Enjoy a drink in the cosy bar, and then move through to the traditional elegance of the candlelit Georgian dining room.
FOOD: Wholesome British cooking rooted in classical techniques with the odd modern twist. Ingredients are locally sourced, with game from a nearby estate a speciality.
OUR TIP: A good base for the Lake District
Chef: Gordon Topp **Owners:** P A Varley **Times:** 1/7, Closed 2-28 Jan, closed L Mon-Sat, closed D Sun (ex residents) **Notes:** Fixed L 4 courses £14.75-£15, Sun D 5 course Buffet, Vegetarian available, Dress Restrictions, Jacket & Tie preferred **Seats:** 28 **Smoking:** N/Sm in restaurant **Children:** Min 5yrs, Menu, Portions **Rooms:** 12 (12 en suite) ★★ **Directions:** Leave A590 signed Cartmel. Hotel is 0.5m N of Cartmel village on right. Opposite Pig & Whistle pub **Parking:** 20 **e-mail:** info@aynsomemanorhotel.co.uk **web:** www.aynsomemanorhotel.co.uk

 ⬡⬡⬡⬡ **L'Enclume** *see page 91*

⬡⬡ Uplands Hotel
British
Accomplished cooking in peaceful Lakeland setting
☎ 015395 36248 Haggs Ln LA11 6HD
MENU GUIDE Hot sole soufflé stuffed with mushroom pâté, watercress soup • Venison, blackcurrant & juniper sauce, French beans • Chocolate Grand Marnier mousse
WINE GUIDE ♀ Macon Chardonnay £16.50 • ♀ Brown Brothers Shiraz £16.90 • 9 bottles over £20, 33 bottles under £20 • 6 by the glass (£3.70)
PRICE GUIDE Fixed L £17.50 • Fixed D £32.50 • min/water £1.90 • Service optional
continued

Uplands Hotel

PLACE: Just a few miles from the head of Lake Windermere, this genteel hotel is sheltered from the tourist hoards by its peaceful location in a relatively undiscovered valley. It's a warm and unpretentious haunt, run by a husband and wife team who formerly worked with John Tovey at Miller Howe.
FOOD: A skilful and experienced chef makes the most of high quality ingredients, delivering a concise four course menu of traditional dishes with flair such as halibut with cucumber, lemon and dill sauce, or salt marsh lamb with redcurrant and caper sauce.
OUR TIP: A tranquil base for the Lakes
Chef: Tom Peter **Owners:** Tom & Diana Peter **Times:** 12.30/7.30, Closed Jan-Feb, Mon, closed L Mon-Sat, closed D Mon **Notes:** Coffee incl Fixed dinner 4 courses, Vegetarian available **Seats:** 28 **Smoking:** N/Sm in restaurant **Children:** Min 8yrs **Rooms:** 5 (5 en suite) ♦♦♦♦ **Directions:** M6 junct 36 signs to Grange-over-Sands. In Grange, pass station on left. Straight on at x-roads into Grange Fell Rd. At T-junction turn right. Hotel on right. **Parking:** 18 **e-mail:** enquiries@uplandshotel.co.uk **web:** www.uplands.uk.com

COCKERMOUTH MAP 18 NY13

⬡ The Trout Hotel
British, European
Formal dining in riverside hotel
☎ 01900 823591 Crown St CA13 0EJ
MENU GUIDE Moules marinière • Dover sole with rock salt • Trio of crème brûlée
WINE GUIDE ♀ Opal Ridge Semillion Chardonnay £11.95 • ♀ Opal Ridge Shiraz Cabernet £11.95 • 10 bottles over £20, 24 bottles under £20 • 20 by the glass (£3-£7.15)
PRICE GUIDE Fixed L £11.95 • Fixed D £25.95 • starter £5.95-£9.45 • main £14.50-£23.95 • dessert £5.50 • coffee £1.75 • min/water £3 • Service optional
PLACE: A popular riverside hotel with all-day food served in the new Terrace bar and bistro, and a more traditional dining room with smart ornate features.
FOOD: The food makes a strong visual impact with its emphasis on design and appearance, and decent flavours and interesting combinations like pigeon and pheasant ragout with scallion mash are a hit with resident diners.
OUR TIP: Watch out for special offers
Chef: Michael Cork **Owners:** Mr N Mills **Times:** 12-2/7-9.30, Closed L Mon-Sat **Notes:** Fixed dinner 4 courses, Vegetarian available, Civ Wed 60 **Seats:** 60, Pr/dining room 15 **Smoking:** N/Sm in restaurant **Children:** Menu, Portions **Rooms:** 43 (43 en suite) ★★★ **Directions:** M6 junct 40, follow A66 to Cockermouth, Hotel situated next to Wordsworth House **Parking:** 40 **e-mail:** enquiries@trouthotel.co.uk **web:** www.trouthotel.co.uk

⑪ **Quince & Medlar** 13 Castlegate CA13 9EU
☎ 01900 823579 Imaginative and very good value vegetarian cooking in the centre of town.

CARTMEL MAP 18 SD37

L'Enclume

French *Exhilarating, innovative cuisine to stir a quiet Lakeland village*
☎ 015395 36362 Cavendish St LA11 6PZ
e-mail: info@lenclume.co.uk
web: www.lenclume.co.uk

PLACE: This former village blacksmiths (*enclume* translating as anvil), which dates back to the 13th century, has been converted into a smart restaurant-with-rooms. The decor is slick, light and understated while retaining original features and a relaxed atmosphere. Think uneven whitewashed walls, dark exposed ceiling beams and flagstone floor, offset by dramatic modern artwork, clothed tables, good glassware and simple but striking flower arrangements. Enjoy aperitif and coffees in the conservatory at the back, where you can gaze up at the priory and out over the riverside garden. Service is professional, yet friendly and necessarily informed.
FOOD: L'Enclume is home to chef-patron Simon Rogan's bold and inventive modern cuisine. It's sophisticated and complex, oozes ambition and has a highly individual and original 'voice'. His approach is via an enticing array of menu options, and though these encompass a fixed-price lunch and carte offering, his unique trademark is reflected in the Taste and Texture menus; three fixed-price set options that range from an 8-course Introduction, through 14-course Intermediate to the 20-course Gourmand menu. Stunning flavours, temperatures and textures arrive in well-judged sequence and leave the diner stimulated but not overwhelmed. Innovative and unusual combinations (the use of many wild ingredients for instance; herbs, flowers, roots, saps, etc), technique and presentation stretch the senses and ooze artistry, precision and restraint. Contrasts, depth of flavour and balance all hit top notes. So expect the likes of a carte threesome (these also find their way onto the Taste and Texture repertoire): Cubism of foie gras (two cold, one hot, cantaloupe, fragrant myrrh, almond cake); Mr Little's beef fillet, with Waberthwaite air-dried ham, apple and juniper berry juices; hazelnut praline 'sandwich' with mandarin filling and sage infusion. So sit back and enjoy a stunning gastronomic journey with a skilled innovator at the controls.

MENU GUIDE Flaky crab, curried avocado, parmesan yogurt sorbet • John Dory, bergamot aromas, bitter caramel • Melting fig fondant, cassia bark, icy fennel, spice

WINE GUIDE ♀ Morande Pinot Noir £34 • ♀ Georges Gardet Pinot Meunier £41 • 400 bottles over £20 11 by the glass (£3.50-£6.50)

PRICE GUIDE Fixed L £25 • Fixed D £50, £75 or £95 starter £10-£16 • main £21-£27 • dessert £8 • coffee £4 • min/water £3 • Service optional

OUR TIP: Do try one of the Taste and Texture menus for the real L'Enclume experience.

Chef: Simon Rogan **Owners:** Simon Rogan, Penny Tapsell **Times:** 12-1.45/7-9.30, Closed 1st 2 wks Jan, Mon, closed D Sun **Notes:** Tasting menu 8 courses £50, 14 courses £75, 20 courses £95 **Seats:** 35 **Smoking:** N/Sm in restaurant **Children:** Min 10yrs **Directions:** 10m from M6 junct 36 **Parking:** 7

England

GRANGE-OVER-SANDS MAP 18 SD47
Clare House
British, French

Elegant dining room serving wholesome cooking

☎ 015395 33026 34253 Park Rd LA11 7HQ

MENU GUIDE Deep-fried stilton fritters • Pan-fried fillet of sea bass • Sticky toffee pudding

WINE GUIDE ♀ Simon Hackett Chardonnay £14.50 • ♀ Casa Silva Merlot £12 • 8 bottles over £20, 30 bottles under £20 4 by the glass (£3.50)

PRICE GUIDE Fixed D £30

PLACE: This smart Victorian house, overlooking Morecambe Bay, stands in well-tended gardens. The tables are fairly close, and there are two cosy lounges for pre-dinner drinks and coffee with petits fours.

FOOD: Quality ingredients are simply prepared and honestly cooked, giving the short fixed price menu a reassuring appeal that its local following appreciates.

OUR TIP: Dinner served promptly at 6.45pm

Chef: Andrew Read, Mark Johnston **Owners:** Mr & Mrs D S Read
Times: 6.45-7.15, Closed Dec-Apr, closed L Mon-Sun **Notes:** Fixed D 6 courses £30, Vegetarian available **Seats:** 32 **Smoking:** N/Sm in restaurant **Children:** Menu, Portions **Rooms:** 19 (18 en suite) ★
Directions: From M6 take A590 then B5277 to Grange-over-Sands Park Road follows the shore line. Hotel on left next to swimming pool
Parking: 16 **e-mail:** info@clarehousehotel.co.uk
web: www.clarehousehotel.co.uk

🍵 Hazlemere Café and Bakery
1 Yewbarrow Ter LA11 6ED ☎ 01539 532972 Winner of The Tea Guild Award of Excellence 2005.

GRASMERE MAP 18 NY30
 Grasmere Hotel
Traditional European ✦NEW

Traditional country-house dining in lovely waterside setting

☎ 015394 35277 Broadgate LA22 9TA

MENU GUIDE Salmon & tuna fishcakes, red pepper coulis • Demerara glazed Barbary duck, orange & Cointreau jus • Individual sticky toffee pudding

WINE GUIDE ♀ Tappery Nook Chenin Blanc £12 • ♀ Tappery Nook Ruby Cabernet £12 • 8 bottles over £20, 45 bottles under £20 • 8 by the glass (£3-£4)

PRICE GUIDE Fixed D £13.75-£27.50 • min/water £3 • Service optional

PLACE: This Victorian mansion, now a family-run hotel, is nestled in pretty gardens on the banks of the River Rothay. The dining room is elegantly set and overlooks the gardens, fells and river.

FOOD: Country house cooking, with an emphasis on the use of the best of local produce. The daily changing menu might include a well-timed individual rack of Herdwick lamb with port and red wine reduction.

OUR TIP: Ideally located for exploring the Lakes

Chef: Paul Hetherington & Steve Pettigrew **Owners:** Andrew Pilkington & Sara Mackay **Times:** 7, Closed Jan-early Feb, closed L all week
Notes: Vegetarian available, Dress Restrictions, No jeans or shorts
Seats: 30 **Smoking:** N/Sm in restaurant **Children:** Min 9yrs, Portions
Rooms: 13 (13 en suite) ★★ **Directions:** Off A591 close to village centre **Parking:** 13 **e-mail:** enquiries@grasmerehotel.co.uk
web: www.grasmerehotel.co.uk

⊚⊚ Rothay Garden Hotel
British, International

Fine dining in candlelit conservatory

☎ 015394 35334 Broadgate LA22 9RJ

MENU GUIDE Lambs' liver, black pudding, whisky & thyme jus • Roast pork, red onion jam, apple & crotin Charlotte • Lemon posset

WINE GUIDE ♀ Matua Valley Sauvignon Blanc £15.25 • ♀ Palo Alto Merlot £15.25 • 90 bottles over £20, 48 bottles under £20 • 60 by the glass (£4.25-£7.50)

PRICE GUIDE Fixed L £14.50 • Fixed D £29.95 • coffee £2.30 • min/water £2.95 • Service optional

PLACE: Not far from the centre of Grasmere, this delightful Lakeland hotel offers fine dining in an airy conservatory overlooking pretty riverside gardens. Tables are well spaced and candlelit at night.

FOOD: A seasonal menu features a mix of modern and traditional dishes, and is complemented by a range of daily specials. Expect complex combinations - chicken supreme perhaps, served with a chicken and prawn spring roll, anise risotto, and sweet and sour chilli sauce - as well as simpler fare, such as Lakeland lamb with rosemary jus.

OUR TIP: Vegetarian menu available on request

Chef: Andrew Burton **Owners:** Chris Carss **Times:** 12-1.45/7.30-9, Closed L 24, 25, 31 Dec, 1 Jan **Notes:** Fixed dinner 4 courses, Vegetarian available, Dress Restrictions, Smart casual, no jeans or T-shirts **Seats:** 60
Smoking: N/Sm in restaurant **Children:** Min 5 yrs **Rooms:** 25 (25 en suite) ★★★ **Directions:** From N M6 junct 40, A66 to Keswick, then S on A591 to Grasmere. From S M6 junct 36 take A591 through Windermere/Ambleside to Grasmere. At N end of village adjacent to park **Parking:** 35 **e-mail:** stay@rothay-garden.com
web: www.rothay-garden.com

⊚ White Moss House
British

Perfect Cumbrian retreat offering fixed menu dining

☎ 015394 35295 Rydal Water LA22 9SE

MENU GUIDE Fennel soup • Guinea fowl braised in cider & tarragon • Strawberry shortbread

WINE GUIDE ♀ Yalum Bay Chardonnay £14.95 • ♀ Fonty's Pool Pinot Noir £16.95 • 109 bottles over £20, 67 bottles under £20 • 7 by the glass (£2.75-£6.75)

PRICE GUIDE Fixed D £35.50 • min/water £2.75 • Service optional

PLACE: This lakeside house hotel, largely unchanged since Wordsworth bought it for his son, has a beautiful garden. The dining room and lounge are furnished in country house style with deep sofas, comfortable armchairs and open fires.

continued

FOOD: The no-choice (apart from pudding) dinner menu is a balanced feast of traditional Cumbrian flavours and refined cooking skills. Be warned - bring a healthy appetite.
OUR TIP: Stay over in one of the charming cottage-style bedrooms
Chef: Peter Dixon & Ian Armstrong **Owners:** Peter & Sue Dixon **Times:** 8, Closed Dec-Jan, Sun, closed L all week **Notes:** Fixed D 5 courses £35.50 (coffee incl.), Vegetarian available **Seats:** 18 **Smoking:** N/Sm in restaurant **Children:** Portions **Rooms:** 7 (7 en suite) ★ **Directions:** On A591 between Grasmere and Ambleside opposite Rydal Water. **Parking:** 10 **e-mail:** sue@whitemoss.com **web:** www.whitemoss.com

◎◎ Wordsworth Hotel

British, French

Impressive culinary display in the heart of Lakeland

☎ 015394 35592   LA22 9SW

MENU GUIDE Ham shank, chervil & pea risotto • Slow roast partridge, chive gnocchi, apple fondant • Ginger & cardamom soup
WINE GUIDE ♀ House £14.75 • ♥ House £14.75 • 153 bottles over £20, 37 bottles under £20 • 12 by the glass (£3.75-£10.50)
PRICE GUIDE Fixed L £14.95-£24.50 • Fixed D £37.50 • coffee £2.50 • min/water £3.95 • Service optional
PLACE: A very traditional Lake District hotel surrounded by well-tended gardens and the impressive Fells, and named after the famous poet buried in the adjoining graveyard. There's an easy pace here - a real retreat from hectic modern life.
FOOD: Diners have a choice of either the popular pub bar or the more formal Prelude Restaurant where the menu is classical in influence but each dish is produced with care and flair. When local ingredients are not used, high quality alternatives are found elsewhere in the UK. Little touches of luxury such as lobster and delightful roast quail do not go amiss. Good, competent preparation and exact timing.

continued

OUR TIP: Good robust pub fare also available
Chef: Simon Kelly **Owners:** Mr Gifford **Times:** 12.30-2/7-9.30
Notes: Vegetarian available, Dress Restrictions, Formal, Civ Wed 110
Seats: 65, Pr/dining room 26 **Smoking:** N/Sm in restaurant, Air con
Children: Min 8 yrs, Menu, Portions **Rooms:** 37 (37 en suite) ★★★★
Directions: From Ambleside follow A591 N to Grasmere. Hotel in town centre next to church. **Parking:** 50
e-mail: enquiry@wordsworth-grasmere.co.uk
web: www.grasmere-hotels.co.uk

HAWKSHEAD MAP 18 SD39

◎ Queen's Head Hotel

British, Mediterranean

Old world inn serving honest fare

☎ 015394 36271   Main St LA22 0NS

MENU GUIDE Quenelle of chicken liver parfait, Cumbrian air-dried ham • Rack of lamb, black pudding mousse • Bread & butter pudding
WINE GUIDE ♀ Sauvignon Blanc £13 • ♥ McGuigans Cabernet Sauvignon £13 • 7 bottles over £20, 39 bottles under £20 • 8 by the glass (£2.10-£3)
PRICE GUIDE Starter £3.95-£7.50 • main £11.75-£17.50 • dessert £4.95 • coffee £1.40 • min/water £2.50 • Service optional
PLACE: Charming 16th-century inn at the centre of a picturesque Lakeland village, with original flagstone floors, wood panelling and low oak-beamed ceilings.
FOOD: Robust food with more than the normal range of dishes, served in generous portions. Quality ingredients are locally sourced and carefully cooked to deliver good flavours. An interesting choice of seafood dishes is offered and local lamb features.
OUR TIP: Check out the range of cask ales
Chef: Jamie Connolly **Owners:** Anthony Merrick **Times:** 12-2.30/6.15-9.15 **Notes:** Vegetarian available **Seats:** 38, Pr/dining room 20 **Smoking:** N/Sm in restaurant, Air con **Children:** Menu, Portions
Rooms: 14 (12 en suite) ★★ **Directions:** village centre **Parking:** NCP-permits issued **e-mail:** enquiries@queensheadhotel.co.uk
web: www.queensheadhotel.co.uk

England

HAWKSHEAD *continued* MAP 18 SD39

🏵 West Vale Country House
British, French

Country-house cooking in Lake District retreat

☎ 01539 442817 Far Sawrey LA22 0LQ

MENU GUIDE Welsh rarebit brochette, crispy pancetta • Rack of Cumbrian lamb, minted mash, sherry jus • Tiramisù

WINE GUIDE ♀ Angles Creek Cabernet Franc £17.50 • 15 bottles over £20, 13 bottles under £20 • 2 by the glass (£3.75-£5.75)

PRICE GUIDE Fixed D £32 • coffee £3.75 • min/water £2.75 • Service optional

PLACE: Set near the beautiful village of Far Sawrey, this peaceful country retreat was built in the 19th century as a gentleman's residence and is decked out appropriately with antique prints and furniture. A pretty garden offers views across to the Old Man of Coniston.

FOOD: Sound country-house cooking that's modern in style but rooted in classical techniques. Sauces are a particular strength, and flavours are clear and honest.

OUR TIP: Book in advance

Chef: Glynn Pennington **Owners:** Dee & Glynn Pennington **Times:** 6.30-8, Closed 25 Dec, closed L Mon-Sun **Notes:** Fixed D 5 courses, £32, Vegetarian available, Smart casual **Seats:** 16 **Smoking:** N/Sm in restaurant **Children:** Min 12 years, Menu, Portions **Rooms:** 8 (6 en suite) ♦♦♦♦♦ **Parking:** 10 **e-mail:** enquiries@westvalecountryhouse.co.uk **web:** www.westvalecountryhouse.co.uk

HOWTOWN MAP 18 NY41

🏵🏵 Sharrow Bay Country House Hotel
British, French

Elegant lakeside classic country house dining with stunning views

☎ 017684 86301 Sharrow Bay CA10 2LZ

MENU GUIDE Duck foie gras, buttered spinach • Best end of Lakeland lamb, herb crust • Berries in Cassis jelly

WINE GUIDE ♀ Cloudy Bay Sauvignon Blanc £33 • ♀ Cousino-Macul Cabernet Sauvignon £19 • 600 bottles over £20, 40 bottles under £20 • 17 by the glass (£4.95-£8.75)

PRICE GUIDE Fixed L £30 • Fixed D £49.75 • min/water £2.50 • Service optional

PLACE: This hotel brings a touch of the Italian Lakes to Cumbria with its Italianate façade. The interior is typically country house in style with antiques, soft furnishings and fresh flowers. Views from most rooms are second to none looking out across Ullswater. The elegant restaurant attracts a loyal and well-dressed clientele. Attentive, friendly service.

FOOD: Traditional and modern British dishes sit comfortably side-by-side on this menu that makes good use of local, high quality produce. Clever combinations of flavours and simple concepts work well. Excellent wine list.

OUR TIP: Take a pre-dinner stroll around the well-tended gardens

Chef: Juan Martin, Colin Akrigg **Owners:** Sparrow Bay Hotels Ltd **Times:** 1/8 **Notes:** Fixed L 5 courses £38.75, Fixed D 6 courses £49.75, Vegetarian available, Civ Wed 35 **Seats:** 55, Pr/dining room 40 **Smoking:** N/Sm in restaurant, Air con **Children:** Min 13yrs **Rooms:** 23 (23 en suite) ★★★ **Directions:** M6 junct 40. From Pooley Bridge fork right by church towards Howtown. At x-rds turn right and follow lakeside road for 2m. **Parking:** 30 **e-mail:** info@sharrowbay.co.uk **web:** www.sharrowbay.co.uk

KENDAL MAP 18 SD59SEE

🏵🏵 The Castle Green Hotel in Kendal
British

Good value dining with great views

☎ 01539 734000 Castle Green Ln LA9 6BH

MENU GUIDE Roast scallops, Parma ham • Roast Grizedale partridge, creamed caraway cabbage • Lemon tarte brûlée, raspberry sorbet

WINE GUIDE ♀ Eagles Point Semillion Chardonnay £14.75 • ♀ Porta Del Alto Merlot Reserva £18.75 • 14 bottles over £20, 22 bottles under £20 • 8 by the glass (£3.30-£6.90)

PRICE GUIDE Fixed D £24.95 • min/water £2.95 • Service included

PLACE: This smart, modern hotel is actually based around a Victorian building and enjoys lovely views over the town and the castle to the fells beyond. A major refurbishment was imminent at the time of the last inspection.

FOOD: The modern British menu in the Greenhouse Restaurant has hints of the Mediterranean about it, as in grilled goats'

continued

continued

cheese with figs, basil and mint, and fillet of sea bass with fennel and aubergine.

OUR TIP: The daily specials are well worth trying
Chef: Justin Woods **Owners:** James & Catherine Alexander **Times:** 12-2/6-10 **Notes:** Vegetarian available, Dress Restrictions, Smart casual, Civ Wed 100 **Seats:** 80 **Smoking:** N/Sm in restaurant, Air con
Children: Menu, Portions **Rooms:** 100 (100 en suite) ★★★
Directions: 9m from M6 junct 36 **Parking:** 200
e-mail: reception@castlegreen.co.uk **web:** www.castlegreen.co.uk

KESWICK MAP 18 NY22

⊛⊛ Dale Head Hall

Modern British

Delightful lakeside hotel restaurant

☎ 017687 72478 Lake Thirlmere CA12 4TN

MENU GUIDE Trio of smoked salmon, home-cured gravadlax & Flookburgh crab • Monkfish fillet, parsley mash, pot-roasted carrots & celery, curry oil • Crème brûlée

WINE GUIDE ♀ Cullen Chardonnay £27 • ♀ Manrinborough Pinot Noir £26.50 • 55 bottles over £20, 17 bottles under £20 8 by the glass (£4)

PRICE GUIDE Fixed D £37.50 • min/water £3 • Service included

PLACE: A spectacular lakeside setting and well-tended gardens is the stage for this charming Elizabethan house, once the summer residence of the rather lucky Mayor of Manchester. The atmospheric, beamed restaurant makes the best of the views and comes lily by oil lamps in the evening.
FOOD: Modern country-house cooking is the unexpected partner to the traditional setting, with interesting combinations and creative presentation delivered via imaginative dinner menus. Expect quality local produce and a couple of choices per course.
OUR TIP: Great area for walking
Chef: Fred Salvini, Jose Lopez **Owners:** Mr & Mrs A Lowe **Times:** 7.30-8, Closed Jan **Notes:** Fixed dinner 4 courses, Vegetarian by request only, Dress Restrictions, No jeans or casual wear **Seats:** 28, Pr/dining room 12
Smoking: N/Sm in restaurant **Children:** Min 10yrs, Portions **Rooms:** 12 (12 en suite) ★★★ **Directions:** 5m from Keswick on A591
Parking: 16 **e-mail:** onthelakeside@daleheadhall.co.uk
web: www.daleheadhall.co.uk

One Rosette Excellent local restaurants serving food prepared with care, understanding and skill, using good quality ingredients. These restaurants stand out in their local area. Of the total number of establishments with Rosettes around 50% have one Rosette.

⊛⊛ Highfield Hotel

British, European

Ambitious cooking in friendly Lakeland hotel

☎ 017687 72508 THe Heads CA12 5ER

MENU GUIDE Crab cakes, candied lemon, sweet chilli dressing • Venison loin, châteaux potatoes, blackberry jus • Iced Amaretto parfait

WINE GUIDE ♀ Domaine Caude Val Sauvignon Blanc £11.95 • ♀ Opal Ridge Shiraz/Cabernet Sauvignon £11.95 11 bottles over £20, 60 bottles under £20 • 6 by the glass (£3.50-£4.75)

PRICE GUIDE Fixed D £32.50-£37 • min/water £1.80 • Service optional

PLACE: There's an informal country house feel to this lovely Victorian hotel on the edge of pretty Keswick. The recently refurbished restaurant is classical in style and offers views over parkland to Derwentwater and the fells.
FOOD: The setting may be traditional, but the food's anything but - expect ambitious modern British cooking with the odd twist. Mains might include a dish of corn-fed chicken wrapped in Parma ham and sage, with a wild mushroom sauce, or chump of lamb with spring onion mash and lavender jus.
OUR TIP: Get a window table and enjoy the views
Chef: Gus Cleghorn **Owners:** Howard & Caroline Speck **Times:** 6.30-8.30, Closed Late Nov-Early Feb **Notes:** Vegetarian available, Smart casual
Seats: 40 **Smoking:** N/Sm in restaurant **Children:** Min 8yrs, Menu, Portions **Rooms:** 20 (20 en suite) ★★ **Directions:** M6 junct 40, follow signs for Keswick. On approaching Keswick, ignore first sign. Continue on A66, at Peach rdbt turn left. At next t-junction turn left, and continue to mini rdbt and take right exit and take third right onto the Heads.
Parking: 20 **e-mail:** info@highfieldkeswick.co.uk
web: www.highfieldkeswick.co.uk

⊛⊛ Swinside Lodge

British, European

Luxurious country house with dinner party atmosphere

☎ 017687 72948 Grange Rd, Newlands CA12 5UE

MENU GUIDE Pan-fried red mullet, provençal vegetables • Roast cannon of Cumbrian lamb, rosemary rösti • Tuscan orange polenta cake

WINE GUIDE ♀ Malborough Villa Maria Sauvignon Blanc £17.50 • ♀ Concha y Toro Merlot £14.95 • 13 bottles over £20, 15 bottles under £20 • 4 by the glass (£2-£3)

PRICE GUIDE Fixed D £35 • Service optional

PLACE: Close to Derwentwater, this charming 18th-century country house is a haven of good food and wonderful, cosseting service. The dining room is classically opulent, and guests are welcomed like old friends.
FOOD: The fixed four-course dinner menu, with choice of dessert, is preceded by aperitifs and canapés, giving a real feeling of being part of a country house dinner party. Elaborate and carefully crafted presentation demonstrate the kitchen's skills - creating dishes that not only taste good but look wonderful. Coffee and petits fours are served afterwards in the sitting rooms.
OUR TIP: Stay for a few days to fully appreciate the place
Chef: Clive Imber **Owners:** Eric & Irene Fell **Times:** 7-10.30, Closed 25 Dec, closed L Mon-Sun **Notes:** Coffee incl, Vegetarian available
Seats: 18 **Smoking:** N/Sm in restaurant **Children:** Min 12yrs, Portions
Rooms: 7 (7 en suite) ★ **Directions:** M1 junct 40 take A66 to Cockermouth, ignore exits to Keswick, next left to Portinscale. Follow country road for 2m (do not take this road). Hotel on right **Parking:** 12
e-mail: info@swinsidelodge-hotel.co.uk
web: www.swinsidelodge-hotel.co.uk

England

England

KESWICK continued MAP 18 NY22

⊚⊚ Underscar Manor
British, French
Formal country house dining with magnificent views
☎ 017687 75000 Applethwaite CA12 4PH

MENU GUIDE Duck liver & foie gras, apricot chutney • Saddle of venison, lentil & game hotpot, game sauce • Banana & butterscotch tart

PRICE GUIDE Food prices not confirmed for 2006. Please telephone for details

PLACE: The impressive house is Italianate in design and sits in 40 acres in the foothills of Skiddaw. Indeed, from the lavishly chintzy conservatory-style restaurant there are sweeping views over Keswick and Derwentwater and the surrounding fells. Service is in the formal style and men are requested to wear jackets.
FOOD: The classic setting is matched by some ambitious classic cooking. Modern, fashionable twists often merge unexpected elements, and presentation on the plate is impressive.
OUR TIP: Special occasion dining
Times: 12-1/7-8.30 **Directions:** Exit M6 at J36 on to Keswick, follow for 17 miles (don't turn off in to Keswick). At rdbt take 3rd exit and turn immediately right at sign for Underscar Manor.

⑨ **Morrel's** 34 Lake Rd CA12 5DQ ☎ 017687 72666
Non-smoking restaurant, handy for the theatre.

KIRKBY LONSDALE MAP 18 SD67

⊚ The Whoop Hall
British   **NEW**
Welcoming hotel that caters to all
☎ 015242 71284 Burrow with Burrow LA6 2HP
PLACE: This welcoming inn has been extended over the years and now offers all the facilities of a hotel, including a well-equipped leisure complex. Dine in the restaurant, a bright modern space on two floors, or in the more relaxed bar.
FOOD: Quality and quantity is on offer here; expect generous portions of British cooking designed to suit a wide-ranging clientele. The carte changes monthly and stretches from light snacks to classier fine-dining fare.
OUR TIP: Good vegetarian choice
Times: 12-10 **e-mail:** info@whoophall.co.uk
web: www.whoophall.co.uk

NEAR SAWREY MAP 18 SD39

⊚ Sawrey House Country Hotel
British
Ambitious cooking in Lakeland retreat
☎ 015394 36387 LA22 0LF

MENU GUIDE Salmon & asparagus terrine • Lamb, rosemary & garlic dauphinoise, red wine & white truffle reduction • Raspberry mousse

PRICE GUIDE Fixed D £35-£45 • coffee £2.50 • min/water £3.75 • Service included

PLACE: Set in mature gardens next door to Beatrix Potter's one-time home, this Victorian country house offers stunning views across Esthwaite Water from its spacious restaurant. Take a pre-dinner drink on a sofa by the fire in winter, or outside when weather permits.
FOOD: A concise menu of modern British fare offers three choices at each course. Dishes are elaborate; a cod main shows the style, served with sautéed courgettes, a feta and olive spring roll, and basil pesto. Dinner only.
OUR TIP: A pianist plays in the restaurant every evening.
Chef: Bryan Parsons **Owners:** Mr C Whiteside **Times:** 7.30-8, Closed Jan, closed L Mon-Sun **Notes:** Fixed dinner 4 courses, Vegetarian by request only, Smart casual **Seats:** 30 **Smoking:** N/Sm in restaurant, Air con **Children:** Min 10yrs **Rooms:** 12 (12 en suite) ♦♦♦♦
Directions: From Ambleside A593 S. left at Clappersgate onto B5286 towards Hawkshead then take B5285 towards Sawrey/Ferry. Hotel 1.5m on right **Parking:** 25 **e-mail:** enquiries@sawreyhouse.com
web: www.sawrey-house.com

NEW
denotes a restaurant which is new
to the guide this year.

For information on Service Charge, see p21.

NETHER WASDALE MAP 18 NY10

Low Wood Hall Hotel
British
Reliable cooking in scenic splendour
☎ 019467 26100 CA20 1ET

MENU GUIDE Ham & beetroot salad • Pork chop, cider sauce • Scottish strawberry shortcake

WINE GUIDE ♀ Casa Silva £14.50 • ♀ Baronne de Coussergues £9.95 • 6 bottles over £20, 21 bottles under £20 • 4 by the glass (£3.50)

PRICE GUIDE Fixed D £22.50 • coffee £1.75 • min/water £1.50 • Service optional

PLACE: Hidden away in a remote valley on Lakeland's wilder side, this Victorian hotel sits in a pocket of beautiful gardens. The conservatory restaurant, candlelit at night, surveys the glorious views.
FOOD: The pick of the local produce, including home-grown herbs, is handled deftly and without fuss to create an effective fixed-price menu: expect modern classics like Caesar's salad, roast rib of organic beef with Yorkshire pudding, and bread and butter pudding.
OUR TIP: Visit England's deepest lake
Chef: Paul Neill **Owners:** Glenn & Gwen Spalding **Times:** 7-9, Closed L all wk **Notes:** Vegetarian available **Seats:** 30, Pr/dining room 8
Smoking: N/Sm in restaurant **Children:** Min 12yrs, Menu **Rooms:** 12 (11 en suite) ★★ **Directions:** Exit A595 at Gosforth & bear left for Wasdale, after 3 miles turn right for Nether Wasdale **Parking:** 15
e-mail: enquiries@lowwoodhall.co.uk **web:** www.lowwoodhall.co.uk

NEWBY BRIDGE MAP 18 SD38

Lakeside Hotel
British, European
Fine dining in picturesque Lakeland shore setting
☎ 015395 30001 Lakeside, Lake Windermere LA12 8AT

MENU GUIDE Crab & tomato risotto • Chicken breast, confit garlic mousse • Lemon posset, lemon sherbet

WINE GUIDE ♀ Domaine des Valery Chardonnay £26 • ♀ Lonsdale Ridge Cabernet/Shiraz £19 • 150 bottles over £20, 20 bottles under £20 • 12 by the glass (£4.50-£11)

PRICE GUIDE Fixed L £20-£22 • Fixed D £29-£35 • coffee £2.95 • min/water £3.50 • Service optional

PLACE: This popular, family-run hotel on the southern shore of Lake Windermere has picturesque gardens reaching to the water's edge. There's the John Ruskin brasserie or the more formal, oak-panelled Lakeview Restaurant with it fresh flowers, floor-length tablecloths and sparkling glassware. Service is friendly and efficient.
continued

FOOD: Traditional British and European dishes - some carved at table - with classical influences are prepared and presented with expertise and imagination. Good use of local ingredients such as Herdwick lamb and Cumbrian beef and from further afield such as West Coast fish.
OUR TIP: Relax in the luxury spa
Chef: Duncan Collinge **Owners:** Mr N Talbot **Times:** 12.30-2.30/7-9.30
Notes: Fixed D 6 courses £42-45, Vegetarian available, Smart casual, Civ Wed 180 **Seats:** 70, Pr/dining room 30 **Smoking:** N/Sm in restaurant, Air con **Children:** Menu, Portions **Rooms:** 80 (80 en suite) ★★★★
Directions: M6 junct 36 follow A590 to Newby Bridge, straight over rdbt, right over bridge, Hotel within 1m **Parking:** 100
e-mail: sales@lakesidehotel.co.uk **web:** www.lakesidehotel.co.uk

Swan Hotel
British
Sound cooking in peaceful river setting
☎ 015395 31681 LA12 8NB

MENU GUIDE Chilled cucumber & mint soup • Pan-fried calves' liver, honey roast onions, apple & Calvados gravy • Summer pudding, ginger marmalade

WINE GUIDE ♀ Wattleglen Chardonnay £14.25 • ♀ Wattleglen Shiraz/Cabernet Sauvignon £14.50 • 38 bottles over £20, 49 bottles under £20 • 4 by the glass (£1.75-£3.50)

PRICE GUIDE Fixed D £31 • starter £3.25-£4.60 • main £8.25-£17 • dessert £3.95-£4.65 • coffee £2.25 • min/water £3.50 • Service optional

PLACE: Nestling peacefully in a curve of the quiet River Leven in 14 acres of gardens, this 17th-century coaching inn offers a welcome to boaters and land-lovers alike. Head upstairs to Revell's restaurant (there's also a brasserie and traditional bar), decorated in traditional style with cast-iron chandeliers and farming bric-a-brac.
FOOD: Revell's ambitious, fixed-price British menu delivers sound, well-crafted dishes, based around familiar and more modern themes.
OUR TIP: Mooring for 80 boats and ample parking
Chef: Andrew Turner **Owners:** Roland Bardsley Ltd **Times:** 12-2/7-9.30, Closed L Mon-Sat **Notes:** Sunday lunch £14.50, Vegetarian available, Dress Restrictions, No jeans, Civ Wed 140 **Seats:** 70, Pr/dining room 120
Smoking: N/Sm in restaurant, Air con **Children:** Menu, Portions
Rooms: 55 (55 en suite) ★★★★ **Directions:** A59, at Newby Bridge take right over 5 arch bridge, Hotel is immediately opposite **Parking:** 80
e-mail: enquiries@swanhotel.com **web:** www.swanhotel.com

PENRITH MAP 18 NY53

Edenhall Country Hotel
British
Formal dining in friendly village hotel
☎ 01768 881454 Edenhall CA11 8SX

MENU GUIDE King scallops, fennel & apple salsa • Lakeland lamb, gratin dauphinoise potatoes, port wine jus • Bread & butter pudding

WINE GUIDE ♀ Moondarra Chardonnay £11.95 • ♀ Wolf Blass President's Select £21.95 • 5 by the glass (£2.95-£3.50)

PRICE GUIDE Starter £3.95-£8.95 • main £8.95-£18.95 • dessert £3.95-£4.95 • coffee £1.75 • min/water £3.50 • Service optional

PLACE: This ivy-clad hotel is set in a pretty village on the northern edge of the Lake District. Light meals are served in the homely bar, while the restaurant is a more formal venue with well-spaced tables and views over the gardens.
FOOD: Edenhall strives to source the best of local produce, and treats it simply without too much fuss. The affordable traditional
continued

PENRITH continued MAP 18 NY53

British menu with French influences features dishes such as pan-roast pork with a sultana and cider jus.

OUR TIP: Great value weekend packages available in winter **Chef:** Colin Sim **Owners:** Clare Simmons/Tony Simpson **Times:** 6.30-9.30 **Notes:** Vegetarian available, Smart Dress, Civ Wed 60 **Seats:** 60, Pr/dining room 25 **Smoking:** N/Sm in restaurant **Children:** Menu, Portions **Rooms:** 25 (25 en suite) ★★ **Directions:** M6 junct 40, take A66 towards Scotch Corner. At rdbt follow signs to Alston (A686). Edenhall is 3m on right. **Parking:** 60 **e-mail:** reception@edenhallhotel.co.uk **web:** www.edenhallhotel.co.uk

☕ New Village Tea Rooms

Orton CA10 3RH ☎ 01539 624886 Winner of The Tea Guild Award of Excellence 2005.

SEASCALE MAP 18 NY00

◉ Cumbrian Lodge Hotel

British, International   NEW

Swiss, Asian and British influences in friendly stylish setting

☎ 019467 27309 Gosforth Rd CA20 1JG

MENU GUIDE Moules marinière • Baked lamb, onion & caper sauce • Strawberry Eton Mess

WINE GUIDE ♀ Mountbridge Chardonnay £13.95 • ♥ Mountbridge Shiraz £13.95 • 3 bottles over £20, 16 bottles under £20 • 11 by the glass (£3.25-£4.75)

PRICE GUIDE Starter £3.95-£5.45 • main £9.95-£15.95 • dessert £3.95-£5.95 • coffee £1.90 • min/water £3 • Service included

PLACE: Simple white walls adorned with modern art set the tone in this small, privately owned village hotel. There's a clear commitment to quality throughout, from chinaware to furniture. Always popular with the locals, the bar and restaurant have a friendly, relaxed atmosphere enhanced by great service, led by the proprietor.

FOOD: Choose from the carte or the daily blackboard selection. The style is modern British with Swiss and Asian influences. Expect mains like Geschnetzeltes Schweinefleisch - thinly sliced pork sautéed in butter, with mushrooms, onion, paprika white wine and cream.

OUR TIP: Booking is advised

Chef: Richard Hickson, Andrea Carnall **Owners:** David J Morgan **Times:** 12-2/6.30-9.30, Closed Xmas, L Mon, D Sun **Notes:** Vegetarian available **Seats:** 30 **Smoking:** N/Sm in restaurant **Directions:** From A595 onto B5344, hotel on left after 2m **Parking:** 17 **e-mail:** cumbrianlodge@btconnect.com **web:** www.cumbrianlodge.com

TEMPLE SOWERBY MAP 18 NY62

◉◉ Temple Sowerby House Hotel

British

Ambitious cooking in country house hotel

☎ 017683 61578 CA10 1RZ

MENU GUIDE Pork rillette, Bramley apple sauce • Chicken, leek & walnut tart, Tio Pepe scented jus • Chocolate pudding, banana ice cream

WINE GUIDE ♀ Cave de Ribeauville Pinot Blanc £15.85 • ♥ Merlot £15.85 • 20 bottles over £20, 25 bottles under £20 • 4 by the glass (£2.85-£4.95)

PRICE GUIDE Starter £4.95-£6.25 • main £15.50-£18.75 • dessert £5.25-£7.50 • coffee £2.85 • min/water £2.70 • Service optional

continued

PLACE: Dating back to the 16th century, this country house hotel was once the principle building in the village and is still an impressive destination. It's located in the heart of the Eden valley and is handily placed for both the Pennines and Lake District.

FOOD: An ambitious kitchen team shows imagination with monthly changing menus that reflect the seasons. A range of tempting modern dishes are featured, distinguished by clear flavours and intriguing combinations.

OUR TIP: Delightful walled garden for summer drinks **Chef:** Ashley Whittaker **Owners:** Paul & Julie Evans **Times:** 7-9, Closed 5 days Xmas, closed L Mon-Sun **Notes:** Vegetarian available, Dress Restrictions, Smart casual preferred, Civ Wed 40 **Seats:** 24, Pr/dining room 24 **Smoking:** N/Sm in restaurant **Children:** Min depends **Rooms:** 12 (12 en suite) ★★★ **Directions:** On A66, 7m E of Penrith in village centre **Parking:** 20 **e-mail:** stay@temple-sowerby.com **web:** www.temple-sowerby.com

WATERMILLOCK MAP 18 NY42

◉ Leeming House

British, French   NEW

Country house with a view

☎ 0870 4008131 CA11 0JJ

MENU GUIDE Smoked salmon ravioli • Sautéed calves' liver, grilled bacon • French lemon tart

WINE GUIDE 79 bottles over £20, 28 bottles under £20 • 12 by the glass (£4.25-£5.25)

PRICE GUIDE Fixed L £9.95-£18.50 • Fixed D £20-£33.50 • coffee £2.35 • min/water £4.55 • Service added but optional 12.5%

PLACE: Superbly set hotel with the Ullswater providing a striking backdrop for the several acres of its formal gardens. A traditional dining room makes the most of the views.

FOOD: A mixed menu veers between safe classics and some exciting and imaginative modern creations. There's no doubting the kitchen's flair, nor the quality of the local produce.

OUR TIP: Try the lovely home-made breads

Chef: Adam Marks **Owners:** Macdonalds Hotels **Times:** 12-2/7-9 **Notes:** Vegetarian available, Dress Restrictions, Smart casual; no jeans or T-shirts, Civ Wed 30 **Seats:** 60, Pr/dining room 24 **Smoking:** N/Sm in restaurant **Children:** Menu, Portions **Rooms:** 41 (41 en suite) ★★★★ **Directions:** A592 towards Ullswater, at t-junct turn right, hotel 3m on left **Parking:** 50 **e-mail:** leeminghouse@macdonald-hotels.co.uk **web:** www.macdonald-hotels.co.uk

◉◉◉ Rampsbeck Country House Hotel *see page 99*

WATERMILLOCK MAP 18 NY42

England

Rampsbeck Country House Hotel

British, French

Innovative modern cooking in lakeside hotel

☎ 017684 86442 CA11 0LP

MENU GUIDE Foie gras, Balsamico dressing • Deep-fried monkfish, spaghetti carbonara, shellfish dressing • Raspberry soufflé, Artic roll

WINE GUIDE ♀ Simon Hackett Chardonnay £16.95 • ♀ Miguel Torres Merlot £12.95 • 39 bottles over £20, 60 bottles under £20 • 6 by the glass (£2.40-£3.40)

PRICE GUIDE Fixed L £28-£38 • Fixed D £44.50 • min/water £3.50 • Service optional

PLACE: The gardens of this comfortable country-house hotel run down to the shores of Lake Ullswater, making a beautiful setting for some first-rate cooking. Large windows ensure the colourful restaurant gets the best of the views; it's a pretty room that's candlelit by night, with well-spaced tables and fine antiques. A choice of three different lounges, including an elegant drawing room, is available for a pre-dinner drink or nightcap.
FOOD: This is cooking to get the taste buds racing; innovative British and French cuisine created from the finest ingredients by a kitchen that knows its stuff. Interesting tastes and textures are brought together in well-judged combinations, with complex and accomplished dishes on offer such as veal with a bacon rösti,

wild mushroom boudin and St Emilion wine sauce, or halibut with a smoked salmon spring roll and lemongrass velouté.
OUR TIP: Afternoon tea on the terrace
Chef: Andrew McGeorge **Owners:** Mr & Mrs T Gibb **Times:** 12-1.30/7-9, Closed 5 Jan-9 Feb, L booking only **Notes:** Coffee included, Vegetarian available, Dress Restrictions, No jeans or shorts **Seats:** 40, Pr/dining room 15 **Smoking:** N/Sm in restaurant **Children:** Min 7 yrs, Portions
Rooms: 19 (19 en suite) ★★★ **Directions:** M6 junct 40, A592 to Ullswater, T-junct turn right at lake's edge. Hotel 1.25m **Parking:** 30
e-mail: enquiries@rampsbeck.fsnet.co.uk
web: www.rampsbeck.fsnet.co.uk

WINDERMERE MAP 18 SD49

⚜⚜ Beech Hill Hotel
British, French

Eye-opening cuisine in lakeside setting

☎ 015394 42137 Newby Bridge Rd LA23 3LR

MENU GUIDE Crab & fennel risotto • Monkfish, leek & mussel meunière • White chocolate & raspberry mousse

WINE GUIDE ♀ Richmond Ridge Chardonnay £14.95 • ♀ Richmond Ridge Merlot Shiraz £14.95 • 7 bottles over £20, 30 bottles under £20 • 3 by the glass (£3.60)

PRICE GUIDE Fixed D £29.95-£36.95 • min/water £3.50 • Service optional

PLACE: A stylish hotel set on high ground with a series of terraced extensions and grounds leading down to Lake Windermere and its own waterside jetty. Make the most of the magical views over the lake to Coniston's Old Man beyond from the oak-panelled dining room as you tuck into a four-course set dinner.
FOOD: Daily dinner menus are innovative and make excellent use of top-notch Cumbrian produce. Cooking is bold and bang up-to-date.
OUR TIP: Magnificent views at sunset
Chef: Christopher Davies **Owners:** Mr & Mrs E K Richardson **Times:** 7-9, Closed L all wk **Notes:** Coffee incl., Vegetarian available, Dress Restrictions, No denim or trainers, Civ Wed 130 **Seats:** 130, Pr/dining room 90 **Smoking:** N/Sm in restaurant **Children:** Menu, Portions
Rooms: 58 (58 en suite) ★★★ **Directions:** M6 junct 36, take A591 to Windermere, left onto A592 to Newby Bridge, hotel 4m on right **Parking:** 60 **e-mail:** reservations@beechhillhotel.co.uk
web: www.beechhillhotel.co.uk

⚜ Burn How Garden House Hotel
British, French   **NEW**

Formal dining overlooking pretty gardens

☎ 015394 46226 Back Belsfield Rd, Bowness LA23 3HH

MENU GUIDE Burn How fishcakes • Chargrilled tuna loin, mussel & crab in samphire, white crab chowder • Rich dark chocolate truffle tart

PRICE GUIDE Fixed D £18, £22, £25 • min/water £2.50 • Service optional

PLACE: A traditional Victorian country house in its own grounds. The restaurant is intimate and relaxing, with interesting art on the walls and lovely garden views.
FOOD: Influences from Europe and beyond mark the cooking style here. There are plenty of popular dishes from locally sourced ingredients to choose from in the two-, three- or four-course set dinner menu.
OUR TIP: Try the bedrooms in modern buildings around the grounds
Chef: Joe Hargreaves **Owners:** Michael Robinson **Times:** 6.30-8.30, Closed Xmas, closed L all wk **Notes:** Coffee incl., Vegetarian available, Smart dress **Seats:** 40 **Smoking:** N/Sm in restaurant **Children:** Min 5 yrs, Menu, Portions **Rooms:** 28 (28 en suite) ★★★ **Directions:** 7m from M6. Follow A590 to A591 (Windermere to Bowness) **Parking:** 28
e-mail: info@burnhow.co.uk **web:** ww.burnhow.co.uk

England

WINDERMERE *continued* MAP 18 SD49

⊛⊛ Fayrer Garden Hotel
British, European

Reliable cooking in elegant country house hotel
☎ 015394 88195 Lyth Valley Rd, Bowness on
Windermere LA23 3JP

MENU GUIDE Tempura chicken, honey & chilli sauce • Kentmere
beef fillet, celeriac purée • Chocolate tart

WINE GUIDE ♀ Miguel Torres Sauvignon Blanc £13.95
♀ Concha y Toro Cabernet Sauvignon £13.95 • 42 bottles over
£20, 62 bottles under £20 • 6 by the glass (£2.95-£3.95)

PRICE GUIDE Fixed D £35 • min/water £1.50 • Service optional

PLACE: This elegant, traditional country-house hotel is set high
up on a hill overlooking Lake Windermere. The two lounges and
the conservatory dining room have wonderful views and there's
a terrace for outside dining, too. Young, helpful staff.
FOOD: The five-course menus change daily and include
traditional dishes which sit comfortably with this environment.
Expect well-executed cooking based on local produce such
Cartmel Valley game terrine with home-made chutneys and
brioche or Pooley Bridge chicken supreme stuffed with wild
mushrooms and a risotto.
OUR TIP: Non-residents need to book
Chef: Edward Wilkinson **Owners:** Mr & Mrs Wildsmith **Times:** 7-8.30,
Closed L Mon-Sun **Notes:** Coffee incl, Vegetarian available, No jean or
T-shirts, Civ Wed 50 **Seats:** 60, Pr/dining room 20 **Smoking:** N/Sm in
restaurant, Air con **Children:** Min 5yrs, Portions **Rooms:** 24 (24 en
suite) ★★★ **Directions:** M6 junct 36, onto A591. Past Kendal, at rdbt
turn left onto B5284 (signposted Crook Bowness & Ferry) and continue for
8m, then turn left onto B5074 for 400yds **Parking:** 40
e-mail: lakescene@fayrergarden.com **web:** www.fayrergarden.com

⊛⊛⊛ Gilpin Lodge Country
House Hotel & Restaurant *see page 101*

⊛⊛⊛ Holbeck Ghyll Country
House Hotel *see page 102*

⊛ Jambo
Modern British

*Quality British cooking in African-themed dining
room*
☎ 015394 43429 7 Victoria St LA23 1AE
MENU GUIDE Linguine of crab, chilli & garlic • Slow confit leg of
local lamb, herb mash • Apple & Calvados rice crème brûlée

continued

WINE GUIDE ♀ Aotea Sauvignon Blanc £15.50 • ♀ Klippenkop
Pinotage £14.95 • 10 bottles over £20, 20 bottles under £20
7 by the glass (£2.95-£4.50)

PRICE GUIDE Starter £4.50-£6.95 • main £12.50-£16.95 • dessert
£4.50-£5.50 • coffee £3.25 • min/water £3.50 • Service optional

PLACE: A short walk from the town centre, this small, cosy
restaurant offers much more than its modest shop-front window
first suggests. High-backed chairs, wooden floors and fresh
flowers add to the modern feel of the relaxed dining room, which
has a subtle African influence.
FOOD: Modern British cooking with occasional Mediterranean
twists, all conjured from well-sourced ingredients supplied by
local producers, many of whom are listed on the menu.
OUR TIP: Only open for dinner
Chef: Kevin & Andrea Wyper **Owners:** Kevin & Andrea Wyper
Times: 6.30-10.30, Closed 1st 2 wks in Jan, Thurs, closed L Mon-Sun,
closed D Thurs **Notes:** Vegetarian available, Smart dress **Seats:** 28
Smoking: N/Sm in restaurant **Children:** Min 12 **Directions:** M6 junct
36, towards Windermere A591, turn left into village. Restaurant 100yds on
left, past the tourist info. **Parking:** On Victoria Street
e-mail: kevatjambo@aol.com **web:** www.jamborestaurant.co.uk

⊛⊛ Jerichos
British, Mediterranean

Creative cooking in Windermere
☎ 015394 42522 Birch St LA23 1EG
MENU GUIDE Confit of poussin, mustard sauce • Skate wing,
parsley mash, Dijon butter • Lemon tart, raspberry coulis

WINE GUIDE ♀ Paul Mas Sauvignon Blanc £13 • ♀ Opal Ridge
Cabernet Sauvignon/Shiraz £13 • 10 by the glass (£3.50-£6.50)

PRICE GUIDE Starter £3.95-£8 • main £13.95-£17.50 • dessert
£5.50-£6 • coffee £2.50 • min/water £2.50 • Service optional

PLACE: Look for the red canopy in the sleepy side street off
Windermere's main road to locate this intimate and atmospheric
little restaurant. Subtle spotlighting, piped jazz, simply dressed
tables, a warm, rich decor, and an open-to-view kitchen exuding
enticing aromas set the scene at this thoroughly modern eatery.
Service is relaxed and friendly.
FOOD: Local foodies beat a path to the door for innovative and
accomplished dishes prepared by a kitchen team keen to share
their passion for food. Good use of quality seasonal ingredients
and expect some striking combinations.
OUR TIP: Book early to ensure a table
Chef: Chris Blaydes, Tim Dalzell **Owners:** Mr & Mrs C Blaydes
Times: 6.45, Closed 2 wk end Nov-1st wk Dec, Xmas, 1 Jan, Mon, Sun
(Jan-Mar), closed L Tue-Sun **Notes:** Vegetarian available **Seats:** 36,
Pr/dining room 24 **Smoking:** N/Sm in restaurant **Children:** Min 12 yrs
Directions: M6 junct 36, then A591. In town centre.
e-mail: enquiries@jerichos.co.uk **web:** www.jerichos.co.uk

⊛ Langdale Chase Hotel
European

Dining with a view in stunning lakeside setting
☎ 015394 32201 Langdale Chase LA23 1LW
MENU GUIDE Confit duck leg, braised red cabbage, crisp
parsnip • Roast pork loin, Puy lentils, garlic confit, star anis
jus • White & dark chocolate quenelles, raspberry coulis

WINE GUIDE ♀ Coopers Creek Chardonnay • ♀ Best's Great
Western Shiraz £18 • 9 by the glass (£4.25)

PRICE GUIDE Fixed L £16.95 • Fixed D £34 • min/water
£3.50 • Service optional

PLACE: Picture windows in the restaurant of this imposing
country house offer stunning views over Lake Windermere, while
continued on page 102

WINDERMERE MAP 18 SD49

Gilpin Lodge Country House Hotel & Restaurant

British *Vibrant cuisine in elegant dining rooms*
☎ 015394 88818 Crook Rd LA23 3NE
e-mail: hotel@gilpinlodge.com
web: www.gilpinlodge.com

PLACE: Four dining rooms - all smart, intimate, tasteful and typically country house (though each has its own individual style) - share the hallmark of warm hospitality, subtle colours, antique furnishings, white damask napery, and, most importantly, the same repertoire of enticing, skillfully prepared food. Gilpin is set amid delightful gardens, a whitewashed, turn-of-the-century Lakeland hotel situated high up in the fells, delivering lovely scenic views and an atmosphere of relaxation and tranquility.

FOOD: A classically based repertoire, though with a lighter, modern-focus, delivers skilfully prepared dishes using locally sourced produce, simply cooked with precision and passion. The freshness of ingredients and clear, clean flavours might be showcased in a best end of local Herdwick lamb with fondant potato and confit vegetables, or perhaps a starter of lobster tortellini with wilted baby spinach, sea lettuce and a lemon-grass infusion that might almost taste of the sea. The appealing repertoire of fixed-price menus is backed up by discreet, friendly and professional service.

MENU GUIDE Pan-fried scallops, fennel purée, ginger cream • Pan-fried sea bass, aubergine caviar, beurre noisette provençale • Tarte Tatin, vanilla bean ice cream

WINE GUIDE ♀ Aotea Nelson NZ Sauvignon Blanc £19.50 • ♀ Jordan Estate Stellenbosch Cabernet Sauvignon £25.50 • 238 bottles over £20 • 62 bottles under £20 • 9 by the glass (£4.50-£5.25)

PRICE GUIDE Fixed L £20-25 • D £42.50 • Service optional

OUR TIP: All meals here are special, including afternoon teas and breakfasts

Chef: Chris Meredith **Owners:** John & Christine Cunliffe
Times: 12-2/6.45-9 **Notes:** Vegetarian available, Dress Restrictions, Smart Casual **Seats:** 60, Pr/dining room 20
Smoking: N/Sm in restaurant **Children:** Min 7yrs **Rooms:** 14 (14 en suite) ★★★ **Directions:** M6 J36 & A590, then B5284 for 5m **Parking:** 40

England

Holbeck Ghyll Country House Hotel

British, French

Classical cuisine in former hunting lodge

☎ 015394 32375 Holbeck Ln LA23 1LU

MENU GUIDE Ravioli of veal sweetbreads, asparagus, morels • Loin of venison, celeriac, juniper • Date pudding, caramel sauce

WINE GUIDE ♀ Drouhin Chardonnay £18.50 • ♀ Domaine des Beaumont Pinot Noir £22 • 162 bottles over £20, 10 under £20

PRICE GUIDE Fixed L £25-£30 • Fixed D £49.50-£55 • coffee £3.50 • min/water £3.95 • Service optional

PLACE: Set in pretty gardens on a hillside above Lake Windermere, this Victorian hunting lodge offers magnificent views of the National Park in all its seasonal glory. It's decorated in luxurious country house style with deep sofas and antiques, and boasts a range of facilities including a spa, a jogging trail and gym. Dinner is served in two elegant rooms that take full advantage of the scenery, and there's also a terrace for alfresco lunches or early evening meals.

FOOD: Accomplished and memorable cuisine distinguished by clear flavours and quality ingredients. The menu is concise but well balanced, and leans towards classical rather than more modern fare: beef with truffle pomme purée and wild mushrooms for example, or best end of lamb with aubergine and a tapenade jus. An extensive wine list completes the picture and features a good range of half bottles.

OUR TIP: An aperitif on the terrace

Chef: David McLaughlin **Owners:** David & Patricia Nicholson **Times:** 12.30-2/7-9.30 **Notes:** Fixed dinner 4 courses, Vegetarian available, Civ Wed 65 **Seats:** 50, Pr/dining room 20 **Smoking:** N/Sm in restaurant **Children:** Min 8yrs, Portions **Rooms:** 20 (20 en suite) ★★★ **Directions:** 3m N of Windermere on A591. Past Brockhole Visitor Centre. Turn right into Holbeck Lane. Hotel is 0.5 mile on left **Parking:** 25 **e-mail:** stay@holbeckghyll.com **web:** www.holbeckghyll.com

the terrace garden leads down to the shoreline. The atmospheric interior includes carved fireplaces, oak panelling and a galleried staircase, while the restaurant is bathed in intimate candlelight in the evenings.

FOOD: The cooking is traditional with interesting contemporary, cosmopolitan touches, using local organic produce where possible. Daily-changing menus and attentive but unobtrusive service.

OUR TIP: Good value wines by the glass

Chef: Daniel Hopkins **Owners:** Mr TG Noblett **Times:** 12-2/6-9 **Notes:** Vegetarian available, Dress Restrictions, Smart casual, Civ Wed 120 **Seats:** 80, Pr/dining room 36 **Smoking:** N/Sm in restaurant, Air con **Children:** Menu, Portions **Rooms:** 27 (27 en suite) ★★★ **Directions:** 2m S of Ambleside & 3m N of Windermere **Parking:** 60 **e-mail:** sales@langdalechase.co.uk **web:** www.langdalechase.co.uk

🌸 Lindeth Fell Country House Hotel

British

Country-house hotel offering traditional and modern cuisine in superb setting

☎ 015394 43286 & 44287 Lyth Valley Rd, Bowness-on-Windermere LA23 3JP

MENU GUIDE Salmon terrine • Breast of guinea fowl, honey, rosemary glaze • Sticky toffee pudding

PRICE GUIDE Prices not confirmed for 2006. Please telephone for details

PLACE: Lakeland hotel with wonderful views of Windermere and the fells. It is an Edwardian property with a strong Arts and Crafts

influence and landscaped gardens designed by Thomas Mawson. Three dining rooms, all with starched white linen napery, are romantically candlelit by night.

FOOD: The short fixed-price menu makes good use of quality local farm produce in modern British dishes. There's always a vegetarian option and one hot pudding.

OUR TIP: Excellent hospitality and very relaxing lounges

Chef: Philip Taylor **Owners:** Pat & Diana Kennedy **Times:** 12.30-1.45/7.30-9.00, Closed 3 wks in Jan **Notes:** Vegetarian available, Dress Restrictions, Smart casual preferred **Seats:** 50, Pr/dining room 30 **Smoking:** N/Sm in restaurant **Children:** Min 7yrs D, Menu, Portions **Rooms:** 14 (14 en suite) ★★ **Directions:** 1m S of Bowness-on-Windermere on A5074 **Parking:** 20 **e-mail:** kennedy@lindethfell.co.uk **web:** www.lindethfell.co.uk

🌸 Lindeth Howe Country House Hotel

British, European

Hearty fare in Lakeland home of Beatrix Potter

☎ 015394 45759 Lindeth Dr, Longtail Hill LA23 3JF

MENU GUIDE Confit duck & cranberry terrine • Goosnargh chicken breast, wild mushroom ravioli & chargrilled Thai asparagus • Lyth Valley damson clafoutis

WINE GUIDE ♀ Sauvignon £15 • ♀ Shiraz £15 • 40 bottles over £20, 40 bottles under £20 • 8 by the glass (£3.75-£6.95)

PRICE GUIDE Food prices not confirmed for 2006. Please telephone for details

PLACE: Cast an eye over the old photographs on display at Lindeth Howe; they commemorate the fact that the country house was once the family home of Beatrix Potter. Dinner is served in

continued

continued

Lindeth Howe Country House Hotel

the airy conservatory restaurant overlooking the gardens.
FOOD: You'll need to work up an appetite fell-walking to do justice to Lindeth Howe's daily changing four course menu - using fresh local produce.
OUR TIP: Potter illustrated Timmy Tiptoes here in 1911
Chef: Paul White **Owners:** Lakeinvest Ltd **Times:** 7, Closed L Mon-Sun
Notes: Vegetarian available, Dress Restrictions, No frayed jeans, or men's sleeveless T-shirts **Seats:** 70, Pr/dining room 20 **Smoking:** N/Sm in restaurant **Children:** Min 7 yrs, Menu, Portions **Rooms:** 36 (36 en suite) ★★★ **Directions:** 1m S of Bowness onto B5284, signed Kendal and Lancaster. Hotel last driveway on left. **Parking:** 50
e-mail: hotel@lindeth-howe.co.uk **web:** www.lindeth-howe.co.uk

⑩⑩ Linthwaite House Hotel
British

Accomplished cooking and stunning views
☎ 015394 88600 Crook Rd LA23 3JA

MENU GUIDE Monkfish tail with vanilla, crisp pancetta lardons • Prime fillet of Cumbrian beef, braised rib ravioli • Warm hazelnut & honey cake
WINE GUIDE ♀ Cloudy Bay New Zealand Sauvignon Blanc £35 • ♀ Trilogy Warwick Estate Blend £30 • 110 bottles over £20, 14 bottles under £20 • 6 by the glass (£3.25-£5.50)

continued

PRICE GUIDE Fixed L £10-£15 • Fixed D £44 • starter £3.50-£10 • main £9.95-£20 • dessert £3.95-£10 • coffee £3.50 • min/water £3.25 • Service optional
PLACE: Set in 14 acres of hilltop grounds, Linthwaite House is in the heart of the Lake District enjoying stunning views over Lake Windermere. Pre-dinner drinks and canapés are served in the cosy bar or the conservatory. The restaurant itself comprises two interconnecting rooms with contrasting decor, one being opulent rich reds and the other more contemporary neutral tones.
FOOD: The modern British menu uses quality local ingredients. Presentation is immaculate and there are intermediary courses which make this a fine dining experience. Sunday lunch and weekday set lunch menu represent good value.
OUR TIP: Enjoy a walk around the tarn after lunch
Chef: Simon Bolsover **Owners:** Mike Bevans **Times:** 12.30-2/7-9.30
Notes: Vegetarian available, Dress Restrictions, Smart casual, Civ Wed 52 **Seats:** 60, Pr/dining room 16 **Smoking:** N/Sm in restaurant
Children: Min 7yrs D, Menu, Portions **Rooms:** 26 (26 en suite) ★★★ **Directions:** Take 1st left off A591 at rdbt NW of Kendal (B5284). Follow for 6m, hotel is 1m after Windermere Golf Club on left **Parking:** 30
e-mail: admin@linthwaite.com **web:** www.linthwaite.com

⑩⑩ Miller Howe Hotel
British, French

Imaginative cooking in opulent Lakeside setting
☎ 015394 42536 Rayrigg Rd LA23 1EY

MENU GUIDE Roast quail, buttered lentils, beans • Slow cooked beef fillet, ox cheek • Praline soufflé
WINE GUIDE ♀ Sancerre Fontaine Audon Sauvignon Blanc £22 • ♀ Château de Roques-St Emilion Merlot £22 • 154 bottles over £20, 5 bottles under £20 • 8 by the glass (£4-£6)
PRICE GUIDE Fixed L £19.50 • Fixed D £42.50 • starter £9.50 • main £18.50 • dessert £7 • coffee £3 • min/water £3 • Service added but optional 10%
PLACE: This enduringly popular lakeside hotel is luxuriously furnished with real fires in all public rooms. Italian-style, light-coloured decor and furniture provide a comfortable setting to enjoy the stunning views across the gardens, Lake Windermere and the mountains.
FOOD: There's a sense of theatre about dining here and the set dinner time means that everyone sits down together. Imaginative menus of traditional British dishes make full use of fresh, local produce and Sunday lunch proves very popular and great value too.
OUR TIP: Traditional afternoon tea is a must
Chef: Paul Webster **Owners:** Charles Garside **Times:** 12.30-1.45/6.45-8.45 **Notes:** Fixed D 6 course £42.50/ Sun L £21.50 D Sat one sitting only, Vegetarian available, Smart Casual, Civ Wed 64 **Seats:** 64, Pr/dining room 30 **Smoking:** N/Sm in restaurant, Air con **Rooms:** 15 (15 en suite) ★★ **Directions:** M6 junct 36. Follow the A591 bypass for Kendal. Enter Windemere and continue to a mini rdbt, take left onto A592. Miller Howe is 1/4m on right. **Parking:** 40 **e-mail:** lakeview@millerhowe.com **web:** www.millerhowe.com

England

WINDERMERE continued MAP 18 SD49

The Samling *Rosettes not confirmed at time of going to press*

British

Lakeside hotel dining in magnificent grounds

☎ 01539 431922 Ambleside Rd LA23 1LR

PLACE: Hiding behind a traditional stone exterior, this chic little 17th-century hotel on the shores of Lake Windermere has a contemporary decor. Enjoy the estate's 70 acres of woodland, fields and landscaped gardens, and then take your place for dinner in the fashionably minimalist restaurant, with its crisp napery and exotic flower displays.

FOOD: New chef Nigel Mendham has just taken over the reins at The Samling as we go to press. With a fine pedigree in some of the best kitchens in the country, it looks as if The Samling's reputation for high quality cuisine will be maintained.

Chef: Nigel Mendham **Owners:** Tom Maxfield **Times:** 12.30-2/7-10, Closed L Mon-Sun (ex bookings) **Notes:** Vegetarian available, Civ Wed 20 **Seats:** 22 **Smoking:** N/Sm in restaurant **Children:** Min 12 years, Menu, Portions **Rooms:** 11 (11 en suite) ★★★ **Directions:** On A591 towards Ambleside. 1st on right after Low Wood Hotel. 2m from Windermere. **Parking:** 15 **e-mail:** info@thesamling.com **web:** www.thesamling.com

◉◉ Storrs Hall Hotel

British, French

Fine dining in sumptuously furnished hotel overlooking Lake Windermere

☎ 015394 47111 Storrs Park LA23 3LG

MENU GUIDE Warm quail salad • Local pork fillet, black pudding, belly & brawn • Fine apple tart

WINE GUIDE 85 bottles over £20, 46 bottles under £20 • 8 by the glass (£3.75-£4.50)

PRICE GUIDE Fixed L £17.50-£19.75 • Fixed D £37.50 • min/water £3.25 • Service optional

PLACE: This stately Georgian property is set in 17 acres of landscaped grounds on the shores of Lake Windermere. Classic period decor, fine art and antique pieces are ubiquitous. The spacious restaurant - with views over the lake to the fells beyond - is tastefully decorated with beautiful china and crisp white table linen. Courteous and attentive staff.

FOOD: Locally sourced ingredients are the basis for a range of modern English/French dishes. Local touches like the risotto of Morecambe Bay shrimps and the Cumbrian bread & butter pudding work well.

OUR TIP: A stroll along this historic lakeside to the Temple of Heroes

Chef: Craig Sherrington **Owners:** English Lakes Hotels **Times:** 12/19

continued

Notes: Coffee incl., Vegetarian available, Dress Restrictions, Smart casual, Civ Wed 64 **Seats:** 64, Pr/dining room 30 **Smoking:** N/Sm in restaurant **Children:** Min 10 years, Portions **Rooms:** 29 (29 en suite) ★★★ **Directions:** On A592, 2 miles S of Bowness on the Newby Bridge Road. **Parking:** 50 **e-mail:** storrshall@elhmail.co.uk **web:** www.elh.co.uk

WORKINGTON MAP 18 NY02

◉ Washington Central Hotel

British, European

Skilful modern cooking in popular town centre hotel

☎ 01900 65772 Washington St CA14 3JF

MENU GUIDE Ham hock & wood pigeon terrine • Lamb, black pudding hot pot, pan-fried kidneys, rosemary jus • Chocolate & Drambuie truffle

WINE GUIDE ♀ Angoves Chardonnay £14.95 • ♀ Lindemans Cabernet Sauvignon £15.95 • 13 bottles over £20, 41 bottles under £20 • 10 by the glass (£2.60-£4.95)

PRICE GUIDE Fixed L £15.50 • Fixed D £24 • starter £5.25-£7.25 • main £16.50-£20.50 • dessert £4.95 • coffee £2 • min/water £3.95 • Service optional

PLACE: Unassuming town centre hotel that's a favourite with locals in search of quality cuisine. A friendly coffee shop offers snacks and pastries, but the intimate Carlton restaurant is the real draw.

FOOD: Interesting combinations appear on the modern British and European menu, as in chargrilled mackerel with sweet red cabbage and Cape gooseberry piccalilli. The four course set menu is very good value.

OUR TIP: Book the tiny clock tower dining room for a special occasion

Chef: Michael Buckley, Lee Poland **Owners:** William Dobie **Times:** 12-2/7-9.30, Closed 25 Dec, BH's **Notes:** Fixed L 4 courses £18, Sun L 3 courses £9.95, Vegetarian available, Dress Restrictions, No jeans or training shoes, no mobile phones, Civ Wed 350 **Seats:** 45, Pr/dining room 40 **Smoking:** N/Sm in restaurant **Children:** Menu, Portions **Rooms:** 46 (46 en suite) ★★★ **Directions:** M6 junct 40, follow A66 to Workington **Parking:** 10 **e-mail:** kawildwchotel@aol.com **web:** www.washingtoncentralhotelworkington.com

Give us your views! All the rosetted restaurants in this guide have been visited by one of the AA's team of professional inspectors, but we want to hear from you! Use the report forms in the back of the guide or email us at lifestyleguides@theaa.com with your comments on any establishments featured or on the restaurants that you feel are worthy of an entry. We would also be pleased to receive your views on the guide itself and suggestions for information you would like to see included.

Prices quoted in the guide are for guidance only and are subject to change without notice.

DERBYSHIRE

ASHBOURNE MAP 10 SK14

Bramhall's

British, International

Informal dining in historic market town

☎ 01335 346158 6 Buxton Rd DE6 1EX

MENU GUIDE Red Thai black tiger prawns, pak choi noodles • Steamed sea bass fillet, ginger & saffron rice • Bakewell tart, crème anglaise

WINE GUIDE ♀ La Roncière Sauvignon Blanc £11.95 • ♥ La Roncière Merlot £11.95 • 8 bottles over £20, 28 bottles under £20 • 6 by the glass (£2.75-£3.95)

PRICE GUIDE Fixed L £9.95 • starter £3.50-£6.95 • main £8.95-£14.95 • dessert £3.95-£4.95 • coffee £1.95 • min/water £2.25 • Service included

PLACE: Increasingly popular restaurant with rooms housed in a sympathetic conversion of two former cottages and a period town house in the heart of historic Ashbourne. The draw is the imaginative food, the warm welcome and the attentive service.

FOOD: Modern brasserie fare simply prepared from fresh local produce is the order of the day. The modern menu is served in four dining areas.

OUR TIP: Book well ahead!

Chef: Mark Hadfield **Owners:** Timothy Bramhall, Tracey Bramhall **Times:** 12-3/6.30-9.30, Closed 25-26 Dec, 1 Jan **Notes:** Vegetarian available **Seats:** 60 **Smoking:** N/Sm area, No pipes **Children:** Menu, Portions **Rooms:** 10 (8 en suite) ♦♦♦ **Directions:** From Ashbourne Market Square take Buxton road N. Restaurant 30yds on left **Parking:** 5 **e-mail:** info@bramhalls.co.uk **web:** www.bramhalls.co.uk

⊛⊛ Callow Hall

British, European

Luxury dining in Grade II listed building

☎ 01335 300900 Mappleton Rd DE6 2AA

MENU GUIDE Hebredian home-cured salmon • Welsh lamb en croute, mint pesto • Dark chocolate fondant , raspberries, choc chip ice cream

WINE GUIDE ♀ Domaine Jean Paul Balland Sauvignon Blanc Sancerre £22.50 • ♥ Château Segonnes Blend Bordeaux £32.95 • 115 bottles over £20, 39 bottles under £20 • 8 by the glass (£5-£6)

PRICE GUIDE Starter £6.25-£9.25 • main £16.50-£19.25 • dessert £7.50 • coffee £3.50 • min/water £3.25 • Service optional

PLACE: Full of character, this creeper-clad early Victorian mansion is set in a 44-acre estate and enjoys views over Bentley Brook and

Callow Hall

the Dove Valley. Period features abound, and one of the dining rooms features warm deep red decor - 'pure William Morris'.

FOOD: The proprietor and his son work together in the kitchen to unfailing high standards. Fish is a speciality, and only the freshest will do. Beef is hung in the larder for at least three weeks, which could explain why Sunday lunch here is such a popular family outing.

OUR TIP: Perfect for a special occasion

Chef: David & Anthony Spencer **Owners:** David, Dorothy, Anthony & Emma Spencer **Times:** 12.30-1.30/7.30-9, Closed 25-26 Dec, closed L Mon-Sat, closed D Sun (ex residents) **Notes:** Fixed L 4 courses £23.50 , Fixed D 5 courses £39.50, Vegetarian available, Dress Restrictions, Smart casual **Seats:** 70, Pr/dining room 40 **Smoking:** N/Sm in restaurant **Children:** Portions **Rooms:** 16 (16 en suite) ★★★ **Directions:** A515 through Ashbourne in Buxton direction, left at Bowling Green Pub, 1st right Mappleton Rd. **Parking:** 30 **e-mail:** reservations@callowhall.co.uk **web:** www.callowhall.co.uk

⊛⊛ Dining Room

British, International

Food cooked and served with a passion in intimate surroundings

☎ 01335 300666 33 St John St DE6 1GP

the dining room
@ 33 st john street
telephone
01335 300666

continued

continued

ASHBOURNE continued MAP 10 SK14

Dining Room

MENU GUIDE Pressed terrine of ham hock & foie gras • Confit pork, buttered brown shrimps • American-style cherry pancakes

WINE GUIDE ♀ Vergelegen Sauvignon Blanc £18.95 • ♥ Garry Crittenden Shiraz £18.95 • 25 bottles over £20, 18 bottles under £20 • 2 by the glass (£4.25-£7)

PRICE GUIDE Fixed L £22 • starter £10 • main £20 • dessert £6 • coffee £2.20 • min/water £3.50 • Service optional

PLACE: A tiny restaurant with just six tables, where old world beams and wooden floorboards are brightened by its tasteful pastel green walls. It may be small, but its reputation for fine dining is rapidly expanding.

FOOD: An evident passion for good food shows itself in the meticulous selection of quality ingredients and a pleasing artistic presentation on the plate. The chef's tasting menu is a work of art in itself, and the short but perfectly balanced evening carte is matched by a versatile lunch menu and a set seasonal list.

OUR TIP: Try the daily fish dish

Chef: Peter Dale **Owners:** Peter & Laura Dale **Times:** 12-1.30/7-8.30, Closed 2 wks fr 26 Dec, 1 wk Sep, 1 wk fr 6-15 Mar, BH Mons, Sun-Mon **Notes:** Tasting menu 7-10 courses £40, Vegetarian by request only, Smart casual **Seats:** 18 **Smoking:** N/Sm in restaurant **Children:** Min 12yrs, Portions **Directions:** On A52 Derby to Leek road. **Parking:** Opposite restaurant (evening) **web:** www.thediningroomashbourne.co.uk

ASHFORD-IN-THE-WATER MAP 16 SK16

⚜⚜ Riverside House Hotel

British, French

Classic country house dining on the Wye

☎ 01629 814275 Fennel St DE45 1QF

MENU GUIDE Pan-fried scallops, apple & ginger mousse • Chargrilled beef fillet, salsify & shallot confit • Espresso pannacotta

WINE GUIDE ♀ Highfield Estates Marlborough Chardonnay

£31.95 • ♥ Conde de Valdemar Crianza Rioja Tempranillo £21.95 • 139 bottles over £20, 54 bottles under £20 • 12 by the glass (£3.40-£4)

PRICE GUIDE Fixed L £18.95-£28.95 • Fixed D £44.95 • coffee £3 • min/water £2.95 • Service optional

PLACE: Georgian property in the heart of the Peak District, near the town of Bakewell. It is set in its own grounds on the banks of the River Wye in the charming village of Ashford-in-the-Water. The dining room is luxurious, intimate and richly furnished, with wood panelling, polished tables, sparkling glassware and quality place settings.

FOOD: The cooking style is essentially classical, but takes sound ideas and adds a flourish. The dishes are always interesting and well presented, and make good use of local produce.

OUR TIP: Notable wine list

Chef: John Whelan **Owners:** Penelope Thornton **Times:** 12-2.30/7-9.30 **Notes:** Sun L menu £28.95, Vegetarian available, Civ Wed 30 **Seats:** 40, Pr/dining room 30 **Smoking:** N/Sm in restaurant **Children:** Min 16 yrs **Rooms:** 15 (15 en suite) ★★★ **Directions:** M1 junct 29 take A619 and continue to Bakewell.2m from the centre of Bakewell on A6 towards Buxton. In Ashford village located on Fennel St. **Parking:** 25 **e-mail:** riversidehouse@enta.net **web:** www.riversidehousehotel.co.uk

BAKEWELL MAP 16 SK26

⚜ The Prospect   NEW

Modern British

Good value fine dining in stylish surroundings

☎ 01629 810077 Unit 6, Theme Court, Bridge St DE45 1DS

MENU GUIDE Crab & crayfish cheesecake, mango & coriander • Beef fillet en croute, Madeira gravy • Bread & butter pudding

WINE GUIDE ♀ Gordons Crossing Semillion Chardonnay £13 • ♥ Carlos Serres Crianza Rioja Tempranillo £17 • 6 bottles over £20, 16 bottles under £20 • 3 by the glass (£2.75-£3.75)

PRICE GUIDE Starter £4.50-£6.75 • main £13.50-£16.50 • dessert £4.50-£5 • coffee £2 • min/water £2.75 • Service optional

PLACE: Clad in reclaimed oak panelling from Hassop Hall and with original timber beams, the structure of the dining room offers a welcoming atmosphere to diners. The contemporary chairs, tables and settings subvert the effect to achieve a chic cosmopolitan look.

FOOD: Like the decor, the menu is inspired by all that is traditionally British, but the dishes have an engaging twist that is entirely modern and full of interest.

OUR TIP: Value-for-money light bite lunch menu

Chef: Darren Goodwin **Owners:** Darren Williams **Times:** 12-2.30/6.30-12, Closed 25-26 Dec, 1 Jan, Easter Sun & Mon, Mon, closed D Sun, Tue **Notes:** Vegetarian available **Seats:** 40 **Smoking:** N/Sm in restaurant, Air con **Children:** Portions **Directions:** From A6 (Matlock to Buxton road), follow signs for Baslow. Theme Court is opposite Castle Pub **Parking:** across road **e-mail:** theprospect@btinternet.com

⚜ Renaissance Restaurant

French

Beautifully appointed French restaurant in the town centre

☎ 01629 812687 Bath St DE45 1BX

MENU GUIDE Oxtail soup, herb dumpling • Dover sole dieppoise, mussels, mushrooms, prawn sauce • Tarte au citron, orange sorbet

continued

continued

WINE GUIDE ♀ Gerard Tremblay £19.99 • ♀ Zeven Nacht £18.95 • 25 bottles over £20, 30 bottles under £20 • 3 by the glass (£1.99)

PRICE GUIDE D £27.95 • coffee £2.10 • min/water £2.75 Service included

PLACE: Long established and popular with locals, this chic French-style eaterie is housed in a stone-built town house in the centre of Bakewell. You can take your pick from the dining room or less formal brasserie with a family garden.

FOOD: French classics cooked with skill, including imaginative gallic dishes and some good daily specials, like salmon wrapped in sole with chive sauce.

OUR TIP: Don't miss the fresh fish or crêpes Suzette **Chef:** E Piedaniel, J. Gibbard **Owners:** E Piedaniel **Times:** 12-2/7-10, Closed Xmas & New Year, 2wks Jan, 2wks Aug, Mon, closed D Sun **Notes:** ALC 3 courses £27.95, Gourmet night £45, Sun L £17.95, Vegetarian available **Seats:** 50, Pr/dining room 25 **Smoking:** N/Sm in restaurant **Children:** Portions **Directions:** From Bakewell rdbt in town centre take A6 Buxton exit. 1st right into Bath St (one-way) **Parking:** Town Centre **web:** www.renaissance-restaurant.com

Rutland Arms Hotel

British

Enjoyable dining in welcoming traditional hotel

☎ 01629 812812 The Square DE45 1BT

MENU GUIDE Venison carpaccio, baby beetroot, horseradish • Pan-fried chicken breast, potato dauphinoise, asparagus • Banana tarte Tatin

PRICE GUIDE Food prices not confirmed for 2006. Please telephone for details

PLACE: This striking 19th-century stone-built hotel is in the centre of Bakewell and offers not just comfortable bedrooms but also the candlelit Four Seasons restaurant with its elegant, classical decor.

FOOD: Good quality Peak District ingredients are handled skilfully in the kitchen that apparently invented the Bakewell tart. There are good choices on both the fixed-price and carte menus plus vegetarian options.

OUR TIP: Visit nearby Chatsworth House and Gardens **Chef:** Bryan Moran **Owners:** David Doneoan **Times:** 12/7 **Notes:** Vegetarian available **Seats:** 80, Pr/dining room 32 **Smoking:** N/Sm in restaurant **Children:** Menu, Portions **Rooms:** 35 (35 en suite) ★★★ **Directions:** On A6 in Bakewell centre opposite war memorial. Parking opposite side entrance **Parking:** 30 **e-mail:** rutland@bakewell.demon.co.uk **web:** www.bakewell.demon.co.uk

BASLOW MAP 16 SK27

⊛ Cavendish Hotel

British, International ⚔**NEW**

Imaginative food in sumptuous surroundings

☎ 01246 582311 Church Ln DE45 1SP

MENU GUIDE Wild mushroom ravioli • Warm tartlet of langoustine & quail eggs • Tarte Tatin

WINE GUIDE ♀ Vina Mont Gras De Gras Sauvignon Blanc £13.75 • ♀ Vina Mont Gras De Gras Merlot £13.75 • 34 bottles over £20, 24 bottles under £20 • 4 by the glass (£3.95)

PRICE GUIDE Starter £6.25-£9.95 • main £13.50-£19.50 • dessert £5.75-£6.75 • coffee £3.50 • min/water £3.95 • Service added 5%

PLACE: Glorious views over the Chatsworth Estate can be enjoyed from this Georgian country house, and the fine artwork lining the restaurant walls provides another charming distraction. Lighter meals are served in the informal conservatory.

FOOD: Fresh ingredients and imaginative concepts have been successfully harnessed to produce satisfying results, and even the odd unexpected twist. The menu delivers what it promises from a team that is definitely going places.

OUR TIP: Try a Chilean wine by the glass **Chef:** Chris Allison, Ben Handley **Owners:** Eric Marsh **Times:** 12.30-2.30/6.30-10 **Notes:** Vegetarian available, Dress Restrictions, No trainers, T-shirts, Civ Wed 50 **Seats:** 50, Pr/dining room 16 **Smoking:** N/Sm in restaurant **Children:** Portions **Rooms:** 24 (24 en suite) ★★★ **Directions:** M1 junct 29 follow signs for Chesterfield. From Chesterfield take A 619 to Bakewell, Chatsworth & Baslow. **Parking:** 40 **e-mail:** info@cavendish-hotel.net **web:** www.cavendish-hotel.net

⊛⊛⊛ Fischer's Baslow Hall

see page 108

BREADSALL MAP 11 SK33

⊛ Marriott Breadsall Priory

European

Popular fine dining in a priory setting

☎ 01332 832235 Moor Rd DE7 6DL

MENU GUIDE Red mullet, tomato risotto, herb salad • Supreme of duck, cassoulet, pumpkin pancake • Pear Linzertorte, almond sabayon

WINE GUIDE ♀ Pinot Grigio £14.85 • ♀ Galope Merlot £14.75 • 31 bottles over £20, 36 bottles under £20 • 18 by the glass (£4.65-£7.10)

PRICE GUIDE Fixed L £16.50 • Fixed D £30 • coffee £1.95 • min/water £3.95 • Service optional

PLACE: The restaurant is the priory's former wine cellar and the decor complements the period building, parts of which date from 1260. Tables are well spaced, and the staff focused and friendly.

FOOD: Popular food simply presented, using seasonal local produce. Ingredients are first class and combinations work well - some innovative, some classical. The fixed-price British menu with French overtones has some supplemented dishes and a number of grills.

OUR TIP: The hotel stands in 400 acres **Chef:** Mark Astbury **Owners:** Whitbread Hotel Company **Times:** 1-3/7-10.15, Closed L Mon-Sat (conference only) **Notes:** Sun carvery lunch, Vegetarian available, Dress Restrictions, Shirt with collar, no trainers, no jeans, Civ Wed 100 **Seats:** 110 **Smoking:** N/Sm in restaurant, Air con **Children:** Min 14yrs **Rooms:** 112 (112 en suite) ★★★★ **Directions:** M1 junct 28 take A38 towards Derby. Signposted from rdbt. Approx 4m from Derby City centre **Parking:** 300 **web:** www.marriott.co.uk/emags

BASLOW MAP 16 SK27

England

Fischer's Baslow Hall

European *Sophisticated cuisine in memorable setting*
☎ 01246 583259 Calver Rd DE45 1RR
e-mail: m.s@fischers-baslowhall.co.uk
web: www.fischers-baslowhall.co.uk

PLACE: Bordering the Chatsworth Estate at the end of a chestnut tree-lined drive in five acres of well-tended gardens (including a potager), Baslow Hall is a charming place that appears much older than its 99 years. Inside, the lavish use of fabrics, antiques and pictures reflect the Fischer's (Baslow's owners) individual taste, and there's plenty of cosseting in the form of log fires, comfortable sofas and friendly, attentive service, while the elegant dining room is the calm and reflective focus of the house.

FOOD: The cosseting extends to the crisply scripted menus, where classic French techniques (layered duck and foie gras terrine glazed with sauternes jelly and toasted sourdough, or perhaps prune and Armagnac soufflé) are teamed with a modern focus (perhaps roasted saddle of French farmed rabbit with pan-fried scallop, sauté of sweet potatoes and a spring herb salad) into sophisticated, well-executed, elegant dishes. Aided by the Hall's kitchen garden, the sourcing of top quality ingredients is taken seriously, with traceable produce (local where possible) delivered in style on the plate.

MENU GUIDE Crab & salmon tortellini in ginger crab bisque • Pigeon pie, layered with butternut squash in pastry shell • Chocolate soufflé tart, pistachio ice cream, chocolate mousse

WINE GUIDE ♀ Lecumn Estate Sauvignon Blanc £30 • ♀ Maranges Premier Cru Pinot £31

PRICE GUIDE Fixed L £20 • Fixed ALC £65 min/water £3.75 • Service optional

OUR TIP: Good value lunch

Chef: Max Fischer/Rupert Rowley **Owners:** Mr M & Mrs M Fischer **Times:** 12-2/7-10, Closed 25 -26 Dec, closed L Mon, closed D Sun (ex residents) **Notes:** Menu de Jour £30-35, Fixed ALC £65, Prestige menu £60, Vegetarian available, Dress Restrictions, No jeans, sweatshirts or trainers, Civ Wed 40 **Seats:** 40, Pr/dining room 16 **Smoking:** N/Sm in restaurant **Children:** Min 12yrs, Portions **Rooms:** 11 (11 en suite) ★★ **Directions:** From Baslow on A623 towards Calver. Hotel on R **Parking:** 40

BUXTON MAP 16 SK07

Best Western Lee Wood Hotel

British, European

Fine hotel with elegant conservatory dining

☎ 01298 23002 The Park SK17 6TQ

MENU GUIDE Wild mushroom consommé • Pork fillet & belly, Parma ham, apple jus • Apple & raisin crumble

WINE GUIDE ♀ S Africa Semillion Chardonnay £13.95 • ♀ S Africa Cabernet Merlot £13.95 • 15 bottles over £20, 20 bottles under £20 • 4 by the glass (£3.50-£6)

PRICE GUIDE Fixed L £14-£19 • Fixed D £25.50-£29.50 • starter £4.95-£7.50 • main £14.95-£21 • dessert £5.25-£7 • coffee £2.50 • min/water £2.95 • Service added but optional 10%

PLACE: Originally built by the Duke of Devonshire, the Lee Wood Hotel opened its doors for business in 1860 and is now Buxton's longest established hotel. It's family-run and sports a large, bright conservatory restaurant that is the closest you can get to alfresco dining indoors. Many tables have great views across the mature gardens.

FOOD: Cooking here is modern in style and flamboyant in presentation with weekly changing menus which make good use of local produce such as pigeon and venison. A good selection of cheeses rivals the desserts menu.

OUR TIP: Visit Chatsworth or Buxton Opera House

Chef: Dale Edwards **Owners:** Mr J C Millican **Times:** 12-2.15/7.15-9.30 **Notes:** Vegetarian available, Dress Restrictions, Smart casual preferred, Civ Wed 120 **Seats:** 80, Pr/dining room 120 **Smoking:** N/Sm in restaurant **Children:** Portions **Rooms:** 40 (40 en suite) ★★★ **Directions:** M1 Junct 24, A50 towards Ashbourne, A515 to Buxton. From Buxton town centre follow A5004 Long Hill to Whaley Bridge. Hotel approx 200mtrs beyond University of Derby Campus **Parking:** 50

e-mail: leewoodhotel@btinternet.com **web:** www.leewoodhotel.co.uk

CHESTERFIELD MAP 16 SK37
Old Post Restaurant

British, European   **NEW**

Converted shop with bold cuisine

☎ 01246 279479 43 Holywell St S41 7SH

MENU GUIDE Pork & chicken rillettes • Lamb & borlotti bean pot au feu • Lemon posset

WINE GUIDE ♀ Domaine Aucherre Sancerre £18.50 • ♀ Costa Brava Rigau Ros G.Reserva £17.50 • 5 bottles over £20, 24 bottles under £20 • 4 by the glass (£2.95)

PRICE GUIDE Fixed L £11.25 • Fixed D £23.50 • starter £5-£6.75 • main £13.50-£19.50 • dessert £5.50-£6.35 • coffee £2 • min/water £3.50 • Service optional

continued

PLACE: In former times it has housed a butcher's, a laundry and later a post office, but now this fusion of 15th- and 18th-century character buildings has settled comfortably into its current role. The beamed, split-level restaurant is relaxed and informal.

FOOD: An adventurous kitchen produces bold flavours and beguiling presentations, with everything from bread to petits fours made on the premises.

OUR TIP: Look out for the 'taste of' dishes

Chef: Hugh Cocker **Owners:** Hugh & Mary Cocker **Times:** 12-2/7-9.30, Closed 1 wk Jan, 1wk Apr, Mon, closed L Sat, closed D Sun **Notes:** Sun lunch, Vegetarian available **Seats:** 24 **Smoking:** N/Sm in restaurant **Directions:** M1 junct 29, follow signs for town centre and central parking. Pass Crooked Spire on left and use Holywell Cross Car Park. Restaurant opposite. **Parking:** Car park opposite

e-mail: theoldpostrestaurant@btopenworld.com

☕ Northern Tea Merchants

193 Chatsworth Rd S40 2BA ☎ 01246 233243 Winner of The Tea Guild Award of Excellence 2005.

DARLEY ABBEY MAP 11 SK33

Darleys Restaurant

British, European

Interesting cuisine delivered in a former cotton mill

☎ 01332 364987 Darley Abbey Mill DE22 1DZ

MENU GUIDE Butternut squash velouté, herb dumplings • Smoked beef fillet, carrot purée • Apple rice pudding, caramel syrup, red berry parfait

WINE GUIDE ♀ Selaks New Zealand Sauvignon Blanc £18 • ♀ Vina Real Tempranillo £18.50 • 32 bottles over £20, 58 bottles under £20 • 14 by the glass (£3.50-£5.50)

PRICE GUIDE Fixed L £13.50 • starter £6-£9 • main £16-£22 dessert £5.50-£8 • coffee £2.20 • min/water £3.50 • Service optional

PLACE: Smack on the banks of the River Derwent, this former cotton mill provides the fabric for a relaxed, contemporary styled

continued

DARLEY ABBEY continued MAP 11 SK33

dining room in sophisticated neutral tones of leather, suede and silk. There's also a decked terrace for fair-weather dining.
FOOD: Far from run-of-the-mill, the sensibly compact, appealing modern British menus befit the decor and friendly, informal service. A skilled kitchen and intelligent handling of fresh local ingredients deliver slick, well-presented dishes.
OUR TIP: Check out the good-value lunches
Chef: Kevin Stone, Jonathan Hobson **Owners:** Jonathan & Kathryn Hobson **Times:** 12-2.30/7-10.30, Closed BHs, closed D Sun **Notes:** Sun L 2 courses £13.50, 3 courses £15.50, Vegetarian available **Seats:** 70 **Smoking:** N/Sm in restaurant, Air con **Children:** Portions
Directions: A6 N from Derby. (Duffield Rd). After 1m turn right into Mileash Lane, down to Old Lane, turn right and follow road over bridge. Restaurant on right **Parking:** 12 **e-mail:** info@darleys.com
web: www.darleys.com

DERBY MAP 11 SK33
Menzies Mickleover Court Hotel
European
Informal modern hotel brasserie
☎ 01332 521234 Etwall Rd, Mickleover DE3 0XX
MENU GUIDE Wok-fried shellfish linguini • Roast rump of lamb, bubble & squeak • Pannacotta, pineapple carpaccio, balsamic reduction
WINE GUIDE ♀ La Campagne Marsanne Chardonnay £13.40 • ♀ La Campagne Merlot £13.40 • 25 bottles over £20, 21 bottles under £20 • 10 by the glass (£4.20-£7.75)
PRICE GUIDE Fixed L £13.25-£14 • Fixed D £26.50 • starter £4.85-£8 • main £11.50-£22 • dessert £5.95 • coffee £2.95 • min/water £3.95 • Service optional
PLACE: A bright, contemporary brasserie within this modern hotel, with informal table settings and a bright and cheerful decor. Ideal for a quick lunch or a relaxed, well-served dinner.
FOOD: The European cooking has a wide appeal, with a 'menu rapide' doing good lunchtime business. Pan-fried calves' liver, medallions of beef fillet and seared salmon are among the simply-presented dishes.
OUR TIP: Just off a link road into Derby
Chef: Simon Johnston **Owners:** Menzies Hotels Plc **Times:** 12.30-2.30/7-10 **Notes:** Vegetarian available, Civ Wed 140 **Seats:** 130, Pr/dining room 150 **Smoking:** N/Sm area, No pipes, Air con **Children:** Menu, Portions **Rooms:** 99 (99 en suite) ★★★★
Directions: From Mickleover take A516 (Uttoxeter) Hotel is left of 1st rdbt. **Parking:** 224 **e-mail:** info@menzies-hotels.co.uk
web: www.bookmenzies.com

FROGGATT MAP 16 SK27
The Chequers Inn
British, European
Busy roadside inn
☎ 01433 630231 S32 3ZJ
MENU GUIDE Seared scallops, pancetta, basil pesto • Beef medallions, creamed spinach, white bean jus • Cappuccino mousse
WINE GUIDE ♀ Badgers Creek Semillon £12.50 • ♀ Badgers Creek Shiraz £12.50 • 9 bottles over £20, 27 bottles under £20 • 8 by the glass (£2.70-£4.30)
PRICE GUIDE Starter £3.95-£5.95 • main £7.75-£15.95 • dessert £4.50 • coffee £1.50 • min/water £3.50 • Service optional
PLACE: Originally four stone-built 16th-century cottages, this popular roadside inn stands on the steep banks of Froggatt Edge,
continued

with open views across rolling hills. The smart interior has a bistro feel, with rag-washed yellow walls, bare board floors and comfortable furnishings.
FOOD: Impressive, modern gastro-pub fare that utilises quality local produce. Expect blackboard menus, consistent and accurate cooking, and value for money.
OUR TIP: Try the Bakewell pudding, it's an absolute delight
Chef: Marcus Jefford **Owners:** Jonathan & Joanne Tindall **Times:** 12-2/6-9.30, Closed 25 Dec **Notes:** Vegetarian available **Seats:** 90 **Smoking:** N/Sm in restaurant **Rooms:** 5 (5 en suite) ♦♦♦♦
Directions: On the A635 in Froggatt, 0.75m from Calver **Parking:** 50 **e-mail:** info@chequers-froggatt.com **web:** www.chequers-froggatt.com

HATHERSAGE MAP 16 SK28
The George at Hathersage
British, International
Peak district pub with history and quality food
☎ 01433 650436 Main Rd S32 1BB
MENU GUIDE Goats' cheese ravioli, slow-roast tomatoes, pesto • Sweet & sticky pork salad with cashews • Plum strudel, ginger ice cream
WINE GUIDE ♀ De Gras Sauvignon Blanc £14.95 • ♀ De Gras Cabernet Sauvignon £14.95 • 14 bottles over £20, 19 bottles under £20 • 8 by the glass (£3.95-£5.35)
PRICE GUIDE Starter £5.50-£7.95 • main £11-£18 • dessert £5.50 £6.25 • coffee £2.95 • min/water £2.95 • Service included
PLACE: With hundreds of years under its belt, the George has a rich history with which to woo its guests. Originally a turnpike inn, it also played home to Charlotte Brontë during the writing of *Jane Eyre*. Nowadays it's a cosy mix of old and new, with a traditional beamed bar and light, modern restaurant.
FOOD: A modern menu notable for its emphasis on the finest regional produce. Expect accomplished and imaginative cooking, with dishes along the lines of pheasant with black pudding and shallot tarte Tatin.
OUR TIP: Indulgent afternoon teas served from noon until 6pm
Chef: Ben Handley **Owners:** Eric Marsh **Times:** 12-2.30/7-10 **Notes:** Separate lunch menu, Vegetarian available, Smart Dress, Civ Wed 45 **Seats:** 45, Pr/dining room 80 **Smoking:** N/Sm in restaurant **Children:** Portions **Rooms:** 19 (19 en suite) ★★★ **Directions:** In village centre on junction of A625/B6001. **Parking:** 45
e-mail: info@george-hotel.net **web:** www.george-hotel.net

The Plough Inn
British, European
Popular destination dining in picturesque surroundings
☎ 01433 650319 Leadmill Bridge S32 1BA
MENU GUIDE Lamb sweetbreads & pancetta • Poached beef fillet, horseradish rösti • Profiteroles, chocolate sauce
WINE GUIDE ♀ Comte Tolosan Sauvignon £12.75 • ♀ Sandford Khate Shiraz £13.75 • 15 bottles over £20, 26 bottles under £20 • 15 by the glass (£3.50-£5.25)
PRICE GUIDE Starter £5.95-£7.95 • main £8.95-£16.95 • dessert £3.95-£4.50 • coffee £1.20 • min/water £3 • Service optional
PLACE: A mixed past has seen this inn go from corn mill to lead smelter to locals' drinking house, though it's as an idyllically located restaurant that it now receives praise, and many visitors.
FOOD: The food is gastro-pub style, with prime local ingredients making up the modern British and European choice. An extensive menu embraces both the popular (braised lamb
continued

shank) and the inspired (seared scallops on a red onion and tomato Tatin).
OUR TIP: Good pub atmosphere & real ales on tap
Chef: Robert Navarro **Owners:** Robert Emery **Times:** 11.30-2.30/6.30-9.30, Closed 25 Dec **Notes:** Vegetarian available, Smart Casual
Seats: 40, Pr/dining room 24 **Smoking:** N/Sm in restaurant, Air con
Children: Portions **Rooms:** 5 (5 en suite) ♦♦♦♦ **Directions:** 1m from Hathersage village on B6001, 12m from Sheffield city centre via A625
Parking: 40 **e-mail:** theploughinn@leadmillbridge.fsnet.co.uk
web: www.theploughinn-hathersage.co.uk

LONG EATON MAP 11 SK43

🍵 Lock House Tea Rooms
Trent Lock, Lock Ln NG10 2FY ☎ 0115 972 2288 Winner of The Tea Guild Award of Excellence 2005.

MARSTON MONTGOMERY MAP 10 SK13

🌹 Bramhalls at the Crown Inn
British, International
Good modern flavours in an old inn
☎ 01889 590541 Rigg Ln DE6 2FF
MENU GUIDE Wok steamed mussels • Roasted rack of

lamb • Strawberry & rosemary brûlée
WINE GUIDE 🍷 La Roncière Sauvignon Blanc £11.95 • 🍷 La Roncière Cabernet Sauvignon £11.95 • 10 bottles over £20, 25 bottles under £20 • 6 by the glass (£2.75-£3.95)
PRICE GUIDE Fixed L £10.95-£11.95 • starter £3.50-£6.95 • main £8.95-£14.95 • dessert £3.50-£4.95 • coffee £1.95 • min/water £2.25 • Service optional
PLACE: There's an unexpectedly modern style to this relaxed old country inn despite the presence of exposed beams and flagstone floors. Light contemporary furniture and richly coloured walls strike an engaging note.
FOOD: Cooking in keeping with the building's adventurous modern makeover puts this place on the local foodie map. The brasserie-style menu favours up-to-date starters like ham hock and black pudding terrine.
OUR TIP: Relax and enjoy good friendly service
Chef: Jaz Singh **Owners:** Timothy & Tracey Bramhall **Times:** 12-3/7-9.30, Closed 25 Dec, 1 Jan, closed D Sun **Notes:** Vegetarian available
Seats: 40 **Smoking:** N/Sm in restaurant **Children:** Menu, Portions
Rooms: 7 (7 en suite) ♦♦♦♦ **Directions:** From Ashbourne take A515 towards Litchfield, after 5m turn right at Cubley crossroads then follow signs to Marston Montgomery for 1m, take left into Marston Montgomery. The Crown Inn is in centre of village **Parking:** 16
e-mail: info@bramhalls.co.uk **web:** www.bramhalls.co.uk

MATLOCK MAP 16 SK35

🍷🍷 Riber Hall
British, French
Impressive cooking in a manor house setting
☎ 01629 582795 DE4 5JU

MENU GUIDE Smoked haddock, rice cake, curried egg • Braised oxtail, Derbyshire beef fillet • Chocolate tart, marmalade ice cream
WINE GUIDE 🍷 Montes Sauvignon Blanc £17.25 • 🍷 Montes Merlot £17.25 • 88 bottles over £20, 22 bottles under £20 • 3 by the glass (£4.45)
PRICE GUIDE Fixed L £19 • Fixed D £37 • coffee £3.75 • min/water £2.75 • Service optional
PLACE: Built in the grounds of a ruined castle, this Elizabethan manor house provides a rural retreat in the foothills of the Pennines. Open fires and antique furniture make for comfortable grandeur, while the pretty walled garden offers magnificent views across Matlock.
FOOD: Riber Hall is known for its consistent delivery of well executed dishes. A good choice of local produce is included on the menu. The lamb is notable and there is some fine fresh fish. The set-price dinner menu is fairly expensive, but you won't be disappointed.
OUR TIP: Separate vegetarian menu and notable wine list
Chef: Mark Walsh **Owners:** Alex Biggin **Times:** 12-2/7-10, Closed 25 Dec **Notes:** Vegetarian available, Civ Wed 70 **Seats:** 60, Pr/dining room 30 **Smoking:** N/Sm in restaurant **Children:** Portions **Rooms:** 14 (14 en suite) ★★★ **Directions:** Off A615 at Tansley, 1m up Alders Lane & Carr Lane **Parking:** 50 **e-mail:** info@riber-hall.co.uk
web: www.riber-hall.co.uk

England

MELBOURNE MAP 11 SK32
🏵 The Bay Tree
Modern British
Imaginative cuisine in contemporary village setting
☎ 01332 863358   4 Potter St DE73 8HW

MENU GUIDE Smoked haddock & vodka risotto • Mignons of prime English beef au poivre

PRICE GUIDE Food prices not confirmed for 2006. Please telephone for details

PLACE: Smartly decorated in warm yellow with timber floors, this friendly restaurant is set just off the main square. A small bar leads to a more spacious, informal dining room, where chatter between tables is actively encouraged.
FOOD: Robust modern brasserie-style cuisine, with a definite eye to the aesthetics of presentation. Intriguing dishes from further afield include 'ants climbing trees', a Chinese minced pork and pasta dish.
OUR TIP: Sample the champagne breakfast
Times: 10.30-3/6.30-10.30 **Directions:** Telephone for further details
e-mail: enquirie@baytreerestaurant.co.uk
web: www.baytreerestaurant.co.uk

RIDGEWAY MAP 16 SK48
🏵🏵🏵 The Old Vicarage see page 113

ROWSLEY MAP 16 SK26
🏵 East Lodge Hotel
Modern British
Delightful hotel dining in romantic setting
☎ 01629 734474   DE4 2EF

MENU GUIDE Goats' cheese ravioli, wilted pak choi • Seared sea bass, artichoke & potato fricassée • Iced blackberry parfait, apple fritters
PRICE GUIDE Fixed D £30-£35 • coffee £2.50 • min/water £2.75 • Service optional
PLACE: Climb the driveway to this hilltop hotel and you'll be rewarded with exquisite views over the ten acres of landscaped gardens in the beautiful Peak District. There is a warm and friendly ambience in the elegant and stylish restaurant.
FOOD: Classic country house cuisine with modern influences interspersed with some innovative dishes. Local produce is well used and there is an excellent vegetarian selection, including wild mushroom and aubergine gâteau with chive butter.
OUR TIP: Famed for its Finnan haddock fishcakes
Chef: Marcus Hall **Owners:** Elyzian Hospitality Ltd **Times:** 12-2/7-9.30
Notes: Sun lunch £21.95, Vegetarian available, Dress Restrictions, No jeans or trainers, Civ Wed 66 **Seats:** 50, Pr/dining room 36 **Smoking:** N/Sm in restaurant, Air con **Children:** Min 12yrs, Menu, Portions **Rooms:** 14 (14 en suite) ★★★ **Directions:** On A6, 5m from Matlock & 3m from Bakewell, at junct with B6012 **Parking:** 40 **e-mail:** info@eastlodge.com
web: www.eastlodge.com

🏵 Peacock Hotel
British
Fine dining in wonderful riverside setting
☎ 01629 733518   Bakewell Rd, Rowsley DE4 2EB

MENU GUIDE Confit duck, bok choi, sweet potato • Lamb shank, redcurrant sauce • Lemon tart, raspberry sauce
WINE GUIDE ♀ Georges Duboeuf Chardonnay/Grenache £12.95 • ♀ Georges Duboeuf Gamay £12.95 • 20 bottles over £20, 14 bottles under £20 • 8 by the glass (£3.25-£4.50)
PRICE GUIDE Fixed L £19.50-£22.50 • starter £6.50-£15.50 • main £19.95-£27.50 • dessert £5.75-£7.95 • coffee £2.95 • min/water £3.95 • Service optional
PLACE: Once the dower house of Haddon Hall, this hotel has been given a contemporary makeover. Cool interiors are enriched with original 17th-century features and period furniture. Ten miles of the River Wye maintain the hotel's popularity with fly fishermen.
FOOD: A peaceful dining room with Mouseman furniture and garden views is a great setting for modern British dishes using good quality, local ingredients in some simple but effective preparations.
OUR TIP: Visit nearby Chatsworth House
Chef: Mathew Rushton **Owners:** Rutland Hotels **Times:** 12-2.30/7-9.30
Notes: Sun D £22.50, Vegetarian available, Smart casual, Civ Wed 20
Seats: 40, Pr/dining room 20 **Smoking:** N/Sm in restaurant
Children: Menu, Portions **Rooms:** 16 (16 en suite) ★★★
Directions: M1 junct 29 (Chesterfield), 20 mins to Rowsley **Parking:** 25
e-mail: reception@thepeacockatrowsley.com
web: www.thepeacockatrowsley.com

continued

RIDGEWAY MAP 16 SK48

England

The Old Vicarage

Modern British

Memorable dining in striking house and gardens

☎ 0114 2475814 Ridgeway Moor S12 3XW

e-mail: eat@theoldvicarage.co.uk

web: www.theoldvicarage.co.uk

PLACE: Close to the village and set back from the road, the Old Vicarage is a grand Victorian house surrounded by rolling lawns and hidden copses of mature specimen trees, laid out by a celebrated Victorian horticulturist. The welcome is warm and friendly and the decor is pleasingly unfussy in country-house style with cosy lounges with open fires, and where pre-dinner drinks and canapés are served. The main dining room, candlelit at night, is decorated in soft pastel shades offset by contemporary paintings, including two specially commissioned watercolours that show off the lovely grounds. It is a bright and sunny room in summer and warm and cosy in winter thanks to the log fires. The conservatory dining area leads out to the terrace and serene views. Comfortable rather than grand service is attentive and well informed.

FOOD: Top quality local, seasonal ingredients are precisely cooked in modern British style, with influences from the Mediterranean and further afield. Although the emphasis is on traditional, simple, tried-and-tested concepts, food combinations and accomplished cooking results in clear, vivid flavours at each course.

MENU GUIDE Crayfish & scallop casserole • Lime & ginger roasted guinea fowl, saffron braised fennel • Baked chocolate pudding

WINE GUIDE ♀ Professor Black Sauvignon Blanc £33 • ♀ Jeff Cohn Syrah £39 • 250 bottles over £20, 24 bottles under £20 • 24 by the glass (£4.50-£5.25)

PRICE GUIDE Fixed L £25-£49 • Fixed D fr £38 coffee £2.50 • min/water £3 • Service optional

OUR TIP: Cosy and warm in winter, but the terrace is ideal for warm summer evening dining

Chef: T Bramley, N Smith **Owners:** Tessa Bramley
Times: 12.30/6.30, Closed 26 & 31 Dec, 1 Jan, BH Mons, Sun & Mon, closed L Sat **Notes:** Fixed L incl glass of wine, Tasting menu available for 6+, Vegetarian available, Smart Dress, Civ Wed 50
Seats: 50, Pr/dining room 24 **Smoking:** N/Sm in restaurant
Children: Portions **Directions:** Telephone for further details
Parking: 30

THORPE MAP 16 SK15

Izaak Walton Hotel

Traditional British **NEW**

Sound cooking in heady location

☎ 01335 350555 Dovedale DE6 2AY

MENU GUIDE Chicken liver parfait • Honey roasted Gressingham duck breast • Tiramisù

WINE GUIDE ♀ Pouilly Fuisse £19.95 • ♀ Shiraz Cabernet £14.50 • 20 bottles over £20, 24 bottles under £20 • 4 by the glass (£3.95-£4)

PRICE GUIDE Fixed D £28 • starter £4.25-£8.95 • main £11.25-£17.95 • dessert £3.95-£5.25 • coffee £3 • min/water £3.10 • Service optional

PLACE: A long dining room with windows all down its length takes in the beautiful gardens and the breathtaking views beyond. This elegant room is in keeping with the rest of the country house.

FOOD: Sound cooking skills match the fine ingredients used to produce the fixed-price dinner menu, where the likes of caramelised king scallops with beetroot purée and truffle oil make an impressive start to a meal.

OUR TIP: Bar meals are also available

Chef: Dean Sweeting **Owners:** Mrs & Mr JW Day **Times:** 12-2.30/7-9.30

Notes: Vegetarian available, Dress Restrictions, No jeans, Civ Wed 80

Seats: 80, Pr/dining room 30 **Smoking:** N/Sm in restaurant

Children: Menu, Portions **Rooms:** 37 (37 en suite) ★★★

Directions: Telephone for directions **Parking:** 60

e-mail: reception@izaakwaltonhotel.com

web: www.izaakwalton-hotel.com

DEVON

ASHBURTON MAP 03 SX77

 Agaric

European, International

Popular Dartmoor eaterie for flavoursome cooking

☎ 01364 654478 30 North St TQ13 7QD

MENU GUIDE Crab & prawn bisque • Grilled brill steak, fennel & Seville orange hollandaise • Apple tarte Tatin

WINE GUIDE ♀ Libertad Chenin Chardonnay £13 • ♀ Libertad Malbec/Bonarda £13 • 10 bottles over £20, 15 bottles under £20 • 2 by the glass (£3.10)

PRICE GUIDE Fixed L £11.50-£13.95 • Fixed D £32.50-£35 • starter £5.95-£8.95 • main £14.95-£17.50 • dessert £4.95-£6.95 • coffee £1.60 • min/water £3 • Service optional

PLACE: Exposed granite walls, oak beams and fireplace with a wood-burning stove, sets the scene at this engagingly relaxed, friendly and welcoming restaurant in the heart of town. Informally decked out with wooden tables and floors, complemented by a beige and terracotta colour scheme, the mood is rustic, mellow and unpretentious.

FOOD: Nick Coiley's modern approach is based around quality local ingredients, with earthy flavours to the fore in well balanced dishes that display a minimum of fuss. A fine selection of local cheeses, good breads and friendly, informed service complete the picture.

OUR TIP: Many of the chutneys, pickles and preserves used in the kitchen are available to purchase

continued

Chef: Nick Coiley **Owners:** Mr N Coiley & Mrs S Coiley **Times:** 12-2.30/7-9.30, Closed 2 wks Aug, Xmas, 1wk Jan, Mon-Tue, closed L Sat, closed D Sun **Notes:** Vegetarian available **Seats:** 30 **Smoking:** N/Sm in restaurant **Children:** Portions **Directions:** opposite town hall. Ashburton off A38 between Exeter & Plymouth **Parking:** Car park opposite **e-mail:** eat@agaricrestaurant.co.uk **web:** www.agaricrestaurant.co.uk

Holne Chase Hotel

British

Romantic and secluded Dartmoor retreat

☎ 01364 631471 Two Bridges Rd TQ13 7NS

MENU GUIDE Sea trout fillet, cherry tomato dressing • Roast Dartmoor venison saddle • Home-made ice creams

WINE GUIDE ♀ Louis Latour Macon Lugny 2000 £16 • ♀ Berrys Brothers Good Ordinary Claret £14 • 90 bottles over £20, 36 bottles under £20 • 5 by the glass (£4-£4.50)

PRICE GUIDE Fixed L £20-£25 • Fixed D £34.50-£45 • coffee £2 • Service optional

PLACE: This old hunting lodge dates back to the Domesday Book and, up to the 1930s, so did the plumbing apparently! Occupying a secluded position on the edge of Dartmoor, this comfortable and well-equipped hotel has sweeping lawns leading to the river, a walled garden and panoramic views of the moor. A perfect country hotel in which to relax.

FOOD: Good quality local produce prepared in classical English style. The daily changing menu comprises simply presented dishes with good, clear flavours. Good selection of West Country cheeses.

OUR TIP: Fishing on the Dart, riding and shooting on the moor

Chef: Brendan Carroll **Owners:** Sebastian & P Hughes West Country Hotels Ltd. **Times:** 12-2/7-8.45 **Notes:** Dress Restrictions, Smart casual, no jeans or trainers, Civ Wed 60 **Seats:** 80, Pr/dining room 12 **Smoking:** N/Sm in restaurant **Children:** Min 12 yrs D, Menu, Portions **Rooms:** 17 (17 en suite) ★★★ **Directions:** Travelling N & E, take 2nd Ashburton turn off A38. 2m to Holne Bridge, hotel is 0.25m on right. From Plymouth take 1st Ashburton turn. **Parking:** 40 **e-mail:** info@holne-chase.co.uk **web:** www.holne-chase.co.uk

ASHWATER MAP 03 SX39

Blagdon Manor

British, Mediterranean

Honest cooking in intimate Devon hideaway with extensive gardens

☎ 01409 211224 EX21 5DF

MENU GUIDE Tian of West Country crab, tempura • Roast pork hogs pudding, cider cream sauce • Pithiviers of apple, Drambuie ice cream

continued

Chef: Arnauld Le Calloch, Joel Turner **Owners:** Christian & Sarah Leydet
Times: 12-2/7-9, Closed 2 wks after Xmas, closed L Sun
Notes: Vegetarian available, Smart Dress **Seats:** 50, Pr/dining room 12
Smoking: N/Sm in restaurant **Children:** Min 8yrs, Portions **Rooms:** 21
(21 en suite) ★★★ **Directions:** Turn off B3165 Crewkerne to Lyme
Regis road, hotel signed from Hawkchurch **Parking:** 40
e-mail: info@fairwaterheadhotel.co.uk
web: www.fairwaterheadhotel.co.uk

BARNSTAPLE MAP 03 SS53

 Halmpstone Manor

British

Blagdon Manor

A weekend haven with fine dining

☎ 01271 830321 Bishop's Tawton EX32 0EA

MENU GUIDE Asparagus soup • Medallions of roe deer, Worcester and cream • Tarte Tatin

WINE GUIDE ♀ Les Anastis Colombard £12.35 • ♀ Montes Estate Merlot £15.95 • 11 bottles over £20, 22 bottles under £20 • 5 by the glass (£3-£3.45)

PRICE GUIDE Food prices not confirmed for 2006. Please telephone for details

PRICE GUIDE Fixed L £15 • Fixed D £32 • coffee £2.75 • min/water £2.20 • Service optional

PLACE: Friendly, owner-run hotel on the Devon/Cornwall border, parts of which date back to the 16th century. Original features are still evident throughout the building, and the richly decorated dining room extends into a conservatory, which effectively doubles the size of the room and affords views across to Dartmoor.

FOOD: High quality fish, meat, game and vegetables come from local suppliers credited in the menu, as are the loyal staff. Good, honest modern British dishes with clear, strong flavours make up the daily changing menus, with some oriental and Mediterranean influences.

OUR TIP: Ask for a conservatory table to enjoy the view

Chef: Stephen Morey **Owners:** Stephen & Liz Morey **Times:** 12-2/7-9, closed 2 wks Nov, 2 wks Feb, Mon (ex residents), closed L Tue, closed D Sun (ex residents) **Notes:** Sun L £21.50, Vegetarian by request only, Dress Restrictions, Smart casual **Seats:** 24, Pr/dining room 16
Smoking: N/Sm in restaurant **Children:** Min 12 yrs **Rooms:** 7 (7 en suite) ★★ **Directions:** From A388 towards Holsworthy, 2m N of Chapmans Well take 2nd right towards Ashwater. Next right turn by Blagdon Lodge. Hotel drive 2nd on right **Parking:** 12
e-mail: stay@blagdon.com **web:** www.blagdon.com

AXMINSTER MAP 04 SY29

☺☺ **Fairwater Head Hotel**

British, French

Confident cooking in secluded country house with stunning views

☎ 01297 678349 Hawkchurch EX13 5TX

MENU GUIDE King scallops, black pudding & apple • Ballotine of corn-fed chicken, fondant potato, asparagus, cheddar chips • Lemon tart

WINE GUIDE ♀ Château Haut Rian £15.50 • ♀ Château la Passonne £14.50 • 32 bottles over £20, 38 bottles under £20 • 9 by the glass (£2.40-£6)

PRICE GUIDE Fixed L £9.50-£11.50 • Fixed D £25-£31.50 • coffee £2.75 • min/water £4 • Service optional • Group min 15 service 10%

PLACE: Tucked away along leafy lanes, this Edwardian country house makes a peaceful dinner destination and offers stunning views over the Axe Valley, particularly at sunset.

FOOD: The ambitious kitchen creates plenty to enjoy with a five-course gastronomic menu to choose from, plus the fixed-price selection. You might tuck into blade of beef with creamed potato and Parma ham, or cod with spinach and rocket cannelloni.

OUR TIP: Pianist on Saturday nights

PLACE: Popular as a weekend break venue, this Queen Anne manor house dates back in part to the 13th century and offers panoramic views towards Dartmoor. A spacious lounge comes complete with deep sofas and a crackling fire, while dinner is served in an elegantly understated restaurant.

FOOD: A daily changing menu makes good use of local produce from the surrounding Devonshire countryside, featuring dishes such as a lamb main course, served with a herb and brioche crust and a port sauce.

OUR TIP: Prepare to be spoiled

Times: 7-9, Closed Xmas,N Yr,Feb (Closed non-residents fr 2005), closed L Mon-Sun ex by arrangement **Rooms:** 5 (5 en suite) ◆◆◆◆◆
Directions: From Barnstaple take A377 to Bishop's Tawton. At end of village turn L for Cobbaton; sign on R after 2m
e-mail: jane@halmpstonemanor.co.uk
web: www.halmpstonemanor.co.uk

BIDEFORD MAP 03 SS42

☺ **Yeoldon Country House Hotel**

British

Modern cooking in country house setting

☎ 01237 474400 Durrant Ln, Northam EX39 2RL

MENU GUIDE Fresh crab, horseradish & chive dressing • Chump of lamb, rosemary & redcurrant jus • Bramley apple & cinnamon cheesecake

WINE GUIDE ♀ Pere Patriarche Blend £12.25 • ♀ Pere Patriarche Blend £12.25 • 5 bottles over £20, 31 bottles under £20 • 3 by the glass (£3.15)

PRICE GUIDE Fixed D £25 • starter £4.75-£6.75 • main £15.75-£21.75 • dessert £4.75-£5.75 • coffee £2.50 • min/water £3.50 • Service optional

PLACE: Owned and run by husband and wife team Brian and Jennifer Steele, this Victorian country house is set in attractive grounds overlooking the River Torridge. Public rooms are full of character with lots of interesting artefacts, and the restaurant, Soyer's, is named after the renowned Victorian chef Alexis Soyer. Brian, the chef, has a vast collection of antiquarian books on food and wine, with works by Soyer among them.

FOOD: A daily changing menu of imaginative dishes is offered at dinner, making good use of fresh local produce.

OUR TIP: Try the fish from Clovelly

continued

continued

England

BIDEFORD *continued* MAP 03 SS42

Chef: Brian Steele **Owners:** Brian & Jennifer Steele **Times:** 7-8, Closed Xmas, Sun, closed L Mon-Sat **Notes:** Vegetarian available **Seats:** 30 **Smoking:** N/Sm in restaurant **Children:** Portions **Rooms:** 10 (10 en suite) ★★ **Directions:** A361 to Bideford. Go over Torridge Bridge and at rdbt turn right. Take 3rd right into Durrant Lane. Hotel 0.25m. **Parking:** 30 **e-mail:** yeoldonhouse@aol.com **web:** www.yeoldonhousehotel.co.uk

BRANSCOMBE MAP 04 SY18

 The Masons Arms

British

14th-century inn with a separate modern restaurant
☎ 01297 680300 EX12 3DJ
MENU GUIDE Escabeche of red mullet, saffron vegetable salad • Medallions of beef, brandy & peppercorn jus • Berry & frangipane tart
PRICE GUIDE Fixed D fr £25 • coffee £1.50 • min/water £3 • Service optional

PLACE: The Waterfall restaurant is located on the other side of the car park from the 14th-century inn. It has a contemporary feel to it with striking orange walls and a polished wooden floor. Some of the cooking is done in view of the diners.
FOOD: Modern dishes with some good bold flavours are offered from an achievable menu of six starters and main courses priced for two or three courses.
OUR TIP: Look out for local specialities
Chef: R Roodaway, S Garland **Owners:** Mr & Mrs C Slaney **Times:** 12-2/7-9, Closed L all **Notes:** Vegetarian available, Dress Restrictions, No shorts or jeans **Seats:** 50, Pr/dining room 20 **Smoking:** N/Sm in restaurant, Air con **Children:** Min 14yrs **Rooms:** 22 (20 en suite) ★★ **Parking:** 45 **e-mail:** reception@masonsarms.co.uk **web:** www.masonsarms.co.uk

BROADHEMBURY MAP 03 ST10

Drewe Arms

European

Classic seafood dining pub
☎ 01404 841267 EX14 0NF
MENU GUIDE Smoked haddock, stilton rarebit • Brill fillet, remoulade • Lemon posset
WINE GUIDE ♀ Les Vignerons de Rivesalites Rouissillon £12.85 • ♀ Les Vignerons de Rivesalites Rouissillon Macebeo/Maluoisie £12.85 • 20 bottles over £20, 19 bottles under £20 • 8 by the glass (£3-£5.50)
PRICE GUIDE Starter £6.50 • main £17.50 • dessert £5 • coffee £2 • min/water £3 • Group min 10

PLACE: This 13th-century, Grade II listed inn has lots of appealing features, not least its large garden and attractive thatched village setting. Inside, there are oak beams, open fires and a warm and welcoming atmosphere. Service is personable and efficient.
FOOD: There's a heavy emphasis on fish here and the occasional Scandinavian influence as well. Blackboards include offerings like crab thermidor, Dover sole and the occasional surprise such as rhubarb soup.
OUR TIP: Very popular eaterie so booking essential
Chef: Andrew Burge **Owners:** Nigel & Kerstin Burge **Times:** 12-2/7-9, Closed D Sun **Seats:** **Smoking:** N/Sm in restaurant **Directions:** M5 junct 28, take A373 Cullompton to Honiton. Follow signs for 5.2m **Parking:** 40

BURRINGTON MAP 03 SS61

⑩⑩ Northcote Manor

British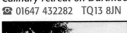

Classic cooking in historic country house
☎ 01769 560501 EX37 9LZ
MENU GUIDE Plum tomato & basil soup • Local grouse, mushroom & bacon casserole • Citrus soufflé, Grand Marnier ice cappucino
WINE GUIDE ♀ Montes Sauvignon Blanc £15.25 • ♀ Cornellana Cabernet Merlot £13.95 • 63 bottles over £20, 18 bottles under £20 • 8 by the glass (£3.65-£6.50)
PRICE GUIDE Fixed L £18.50 • Fixed D £35 • coffee £3 • min/water £3 • Service optional

PLACE: Bright murals in Northcote's sunny yellow dining room tell a colourful history, dating back to the house's origins as a Benedictine monastery. A secluded country setting, in 20 acres of grounds with views over the Taw Valley, ensures it still has a peaceful, cloistered air today.
FOOD: Classic British dishes with an emphasis on seasonal local produce. Tuck into Exmoor game with a Madeira jelly to start, and then follow up with grilled Dover sole with a lemon butter sauce perhaps, or beef tournedos with rösti potatoes, seared foie gras and cep sauce.
OUR TIP: Vegetarian menu available
Chef: Richie Herkes **Owners:** J Pierre Mifsud **Times:** 12/7 **Notes:** Seasonal Gourmet menu (evening) £40, Vegetarian available, Dress Restrictions, Smart casual preferred, Civ Wed 50 **Seats:** 34, Pr/dining room 14 **Smoking:** N/Sm in restaurant **Children:** Portions **Rooms:** 11 (11 en suite) ★★★ **Directions:** M5 junct 27 towards Barnstaple. left at rdbt to South Molton. Do not enter Burrington village. Follow A377. Right at T-junction to Barnstaple . Entrance after 3m, opp Portsmouth Arms railway station and pub. **Parking:** 30 **e-mail:** rest@northcotemanor.co.uk **web:** www.northcote-manor.com

CHAGFORD MAP 03 SX78

⑩⑩⑩⑩ Gidleigh Park *see page 117*

⑩⑩ Mill End

British, French

Culinary retreat on Dartmoor
☎ 01647 432282 TQ13 8JN

MENU GUIDE Chicken liver parfait, roast figs • Venison, beetroot fondant, glazed baby vegetables • Raspberry soufflé, chocolate sauce
WINE GUIDE ♀ Pinot Grigio • ♀ Côtes du Rhône £20 • 65 bottles over £20, 34 bottles under £20 • 8 by the glass (£4.50)
PRICE GUIDE Fixed D £35-£35 • coffee £3 • min/water £3 • Service optional • Group min 8 service 10%

continued on page 11

CHAGFORD MAP 03 SX78

Gidleigh Park

Modern British *Fine dining in magical country house hotel*
☎ 01647 432367   TQ13 8HH
e-mail: gidleighpark@gidleigh.co.uk
web: www.gidleigh.com

PLACE: Dining at Gidleigh Park is one of life's not-to-be-missed experiences. From the moment you arrive at this globally acclaimed, black-and-white mock Tudor Dartmoor retreat - connected to everyday life by a tricky, one-and-a-half-mile twisting single-track lane from Chagford village - you'll realise you've arrived at a very special place indeed. A pre- or post-meal stroll in the 45 acres of grounds among manicured lawns, delightful terraced gardens and beech woods is an absolute must. Inside, the feeling is almost more country home than luxury country-house hotel, with welcoming, unpretentious service led by efficient hostess Catherine Endicott. The style is classic country house, refined yet relaxed, sprinkled with a hint of romance. Oak panelling, chintzy lounges with sumptuous sofas (just the place for aperitifs, excellent canapés, coffees and petits fours), plus a pair of equally traditional dining rooms, all offer stunning views over the gardens to the moorland hills.
FOOD: Despite his expanding restaurant business (see Michael Caines at the Royal Clarence, Exeter and the Bristol Marriott Royal Hotel), culinary icon and local celebrity chef Michael Caines continues to deliver exquisite, modern, classically inspired cuisine at Gidleigh. The imaginative cooking showcases superb quality, fresh local produce on a fixed-priced repertoire of lunch, carte and tasting menu options dotted with luxury items. The wine list is appropriately superb and the perfect partner to Caines's cooking, with particular strengths in the USA, France and a reasonable pricing policy.

MENU GUIDE Frog's legs, wild mushroom risotto, herb purée • Roast sea bass, fennel purée, fennel cream, red wine sauce • Hot apple tart, vanilla ice cream

WINE GUIDE ♀ Au Bon Climat Chardonnay £30 • ♀ Château Grand Puy Lacoste Cabernet Sauvignon/Merlot £45 • 400 bottles over £20 • 9 by the glass (£5-£13)

PRICE GUIDE Fixed L £27-£35 • Fixed ALC £75 min/water £2.50 • Service included

OUR TIP: Perfect for a romantic break to soak up the complete Gidleigh 'experience'

Chef: Michael Caines **Owners:** The Bath Priory Ltd **Times:** 12.30-2/7-9 **Notes:** Fixed ALC £75, Tasting menu 7 courses £80, coffee incl at D, Vegetarian by request only, Smart Dress **Seats:** 35, Pr/dining room 22 **Smoking:** N/Sm in restaurant **Children:** Min 7yrs **Rooms:** 15 (15 en suite) ★★★ **Directions:** From Chagford Sq turn right at Lloyds Bank into Mill St, after 150yds right fork, across x-rds into Holy St. Restaurant 1.5m **Parking:** 20

CHAGFORD *continued* MAP 03 SX78

PLACE: Boasting a stunning Dartmoor location, this working water mill doubles as a comfortable country house hotel, with guests treated as returning friends by its amiable staff. Quality fabrics abound in the recently refurbished restaurant, but it's still a homely and convivial venue for delicious food.

FOOD: Confident and innovative cooking that's never marred by ostentation. Flavours are fresh and vibrant, with dishes based around the finest West Country produce: beef with an oxtail ravioli and bourguignon garnish, for example, or Barbary duckling cassoulet.

OUR TIP: Enjoy a cream tea on the lawn

Chef: Barnaby Mason **Owners:** Keith Green **Times:** 12-2/7-9, Closed L by appoint. only - open Sun **Notes:** Sun L £20, Vegetarian available, Dress Restrictions, No jeans/training shoes **Seats:** 42 **Smoking:** N/Sm in restaurant **Children:** Min 12 yrs, Menu, Portions **Rooms:** 15 (15 en suite) ★★ **Directions:** From A30 turn on to A382. Establishment on right before Chagford turning **Parking:** 20
e-mail: millendhotel@talk21.com **web:** www.millendhotel.com

22 Mill Street *see page 119*

COLYFORD MAP 04 SY29

Swallows Eaves
British

Flavoursome cooking in welcoming hotel
☎ 01297 553184 Swan Hill Rd EX24 6QJ

MENU GUIDE Grilled goats' cheese, spinach • Chicken, sun-dried tomatoes, camembert, tarragon & orange sauce • Chocolate roulade, berry coulis

WINE GUIDE ♀ Brown Brothers Chenin Blanc £12.50 • ♀ Dalwood Cabernet Shiraz £12.50 • 2 bottles over £20, 24 bottles under £20 • 11 by the glass (£3.50)

PRICE GUIDE Fixed D £26 • min/water £1 • Service included

PLACE: This Edwardian gentleman's residence turned delightful little hotel is prettily set in Devonshire countryside not far from the coast. Ample parking.

FOOD: Expect a concise selection of straightforward fare, with fresh local produce to the fore. The menu changes daily, and might feature tempting desserts such as warm banana pudding with vanilla ice cream or char-grilled sabayon with strawberries.

OUR TIP: Take a stroll along the nearby Heritage Coastal Path

Chef: Jane Beck **Owners:** Mr & Mrs J Beck **Times:** 7-8, Closed Nov-Feb, closed L Mon-Sun **Notes:** Vegetarian by request only **Seats:** 16 **Smoking:** N/Sm in restaurant **Children:** Min 14 yrs **Rooms:** 8 (8 en suite) ★★ **Directions:** In village centre on A3052 opposite village shop. **Parking:** 10 **e-mail:** swallows_eaves@hotmail.com **web:** www.lymeregis.com/swallowseaveshotel

DARTMOUTH MAP 03 SX85

The New Angel *see page 119*

Cafe Alf Resco Lower St TQ6 ☎ 01803 835880
Terrific breakfasts, a great atmosphere, an attractive courtyard and staff with character.

EXETER MAP 03 SX99

Barton Cross Hotel
British, French
Quality cooking in engaging 17th-century thatched property
☎ 01392 841245 Huxham, Stoke Canon EX5 4EJ

MENU GUIDE Sea bass & ginger fishcakes, coriander, lime & chilli butter • Beef Wellington • Maple & walnut pudding, crème anglaise

WINE GUIDE ♀ Brown Brothers Chardonnay £16.25 • ♀ Stellenbosch Pinotage £14 • 54 bottles over £20, 48 bottles under £20 • 8 by the glass (£2.75-£3.85)

PRICE GUIDE Fixed D £22.50-£27.50 • starter £4.50-£8 • main £12.50-£18 • dessert £4.50-£6.50 • coffee £2.50 • min/water £2.95 • Service optional

PLACE: Just five miles from the city centre, Barton Cross is a converted 17th-century thatched longhouse in a pretty rural setting. Expect a traditional cottage feel with deep cob walls and low beams, and an impressive, galleried candlelit restaurant replete with huge inglenook fireplace.

FOOD: Fixed dinner menus make good use of local produce, notably fish from Brixham. Ingredients are sensibly combined and classic British dishes are given a modern twist.

OUR TIP: Romantic tables on the upper gallery level

Chef: Paul Bending **Owners:** Brian Hamilton **Times:** 6.30-11, Closed Sun, closed L Mon **Notes:** Vegetarian available **Seats:** 50, Pr/dining room 15 **Smoking:** N/Sm in restaurant **Children:** Menu, Portions **Rooms:** 9 (9 en suite) ★★★ **Directions:** 0.5 mile off A396 at Stoke Canon, 3m N of Exeter **Parking:** 50 **e-mail:** bartonxhuxham@aol.com

CHAGFORD MAP 03 SX78

22 Mill Street

European

Modern cooking with strong flavours in village setting

☎ 01647 432244 22 Mill St TQ13 8AW

MENU GUIDE Roast wood pigeon breast, ceps, parmesan, gnocchi • Roast sea bass fillet, warm cucumber salad, oysters • Plate of passionfruit

WINE GUIDE ♀ Hawks Cabernet Sauvignon £19.95 • ♀ Pienno L T C £19.90 • 30 bottles over £20, 32 bottles under £20 • 10 by the glass (£4.40-£6.75)

PRICE GUIDE Fixed L £21 • Fixed D £34 • coffee £2.75 • min/water £2.50 • Service included

PLACE: Just a few paces from the centre of this pretty Dartmoor village, nestling behind an unassuming terraced shop front on a street of attractive old townhouses, Duncan Walker's 22 Mill Street is a small, unassuming but inviting affair. Inside is a charming mix of leather chesterfields, wicker seating and brightly painted walls that combine with some beguiling cooking and a

friendly, relaxed atmosphere to draw a devoted following.
FOOD: Chef-patron Walker intelligently and seamlessly combines accomplished classical cooking with a lighter, more modern approach. Dishes are highly technically adept, with superb, clear flavours and top-notch ingredients to the fore. His approach is via an appealing fixed-price repertoire (lunch, a six-course no-choice set menu with coffee and petits fours, and three-course carte - all at reasonable prices) that might deliver an inviting lasagne of crab with basil and pickled ginger and roasted shellfish velouté among impressive starters, or perhaps an equally seductive dish of Pithiviers of roast calves' sweetbreads and Jerusalem artichoke with a Madeira sauce as mains.
OUR TIP: Great value fixed-price lunch
Chef: Duncan Walker, Dexter Fuller, Raphael Rabien **Owners:** Duncan Walker **Times:** 12.30-1.45/7.30-9, Closed Jan, Sun, closed L Sun-Tue
Notes: Fixed D 7 courses £38, Vegetarian by request only **Seats:** 22
Smoking: N/Sm in restaurant **Directions:** Telephone for further details
Parking: On street

DARTMOUTH MAP 03 SX85

The New Angel

British, French

A Restaurant of the Year for England

☎ 01803 839425 2 South Embankment TQ6 9BH

MENU GUIDE Dorset crab salad • Fillet of Blackawton lamb, tartlet of sweetbread, fondant potatoes, port sauce • Hot chocolate fondant, pistachio ice cream

WINE GUIDE ♀ Domaine Feliner-Jourdan £20 • ♀ Château Auzias Grenache Merlot Cabernet £17.50 • 120 bottles over £20, 28 bottles under £20 • 13 by the glass (£3-£8.90)

PRICE GUIDE Fixed L £19-£33.50 • Fixed D £30-£45 • starter £7.50-£12.50 • main £16-£25 • dessert £7.50 • coffee £2.50 • min/water £3 • Service optional • Group min 8 service 10%

PLACE: This venerable two-floored restaurant, one-time domain of the renowned Joyce Molyneux, has been brought back to life with a change of name (formerly the Carved Angel) by celebrated chef-patron John Burton-Race, the episode serialized on television's Return of the Chef. The wonderful, half-timbered Tudor exterior catches the eye on Dartmouth's waterfront, while menus at the entrance attract passer-by interest. The interior is simple yet stylish, with pale grey painted floorboards, dark-wood

tables, comfortable wicker chairs and antique chandeliers. The theatre of the open-to-view kitchen certainly adds drama to the lively ground floor, while upstairs provides a quieter option, with both rooms offering fabulous views over the busy river Dart estuary, from where the restaurant's sparkling fresh fish and seafood are landed.
FOOD: French-orientated cooking in the impeccable hands of John Burton-Race and head chefs Robin Zavou and Nigel Mariage show polished strength and skill, with great deference and intelligence given to the simple treatment of the very best and freshest ingredients (perhaps Umberleigh snails, Blackawton lamb and, of course, the fruits of the sea). Tiptop flavours and balance are bolstered by menu flexibility, with specials supporting lunch, backed by an appealing carte.
OUR TIP: Booking essential, with downstairs offering the sights, sounds and aromas of the kitchen
Chef: J Burton-Race, N Mariage, R Zavou **Owners:** Kim & John Burton-Race **Times:** 12-2.30/6.30-10.30, Closed Jan, Mon, closed D Sun
Seats: 70, Pr/dining room 50 **Smoking:** N/Sm area, Air con
Children: Menu, Portions **Directions:** Dartmouth centre, on the water's edge. **Parking:** Mayor's Avenue, centre of Dartmouth
e-mail: reservations@thenewangel.co.uk **web:** www.thenewangel.co.uk

EXETER *continued* MAP 03 SX99

Brazz

Modern British

Stylish brasserie putting fun into eating out

☎ 01392 252525 10-12 Palace Gate EX1 1JA

MENU GUIDE Chicken liver parfait, toasted brioche • Home-made salmon fishcakes • Cathedral pudding

WINE GUIDE 14 bottles over £20, 24 bottles under £20 • 15 by the glass (£2.10-£8.50)

PRICE GUIDE Starter £4.50-£7.50 • main £6.50-£16.95 • dessert £4.50-£5.50 • Service added but optional 10%

PLACE: A converted convent school, now a fun brasserie on two floors. A theatrical star-lit dome, a huge cylindrical aquarium and a magnificent staircase add to the busy, buzzy ambience. Comfort food with friendly service does not come much better than this.

FOOD: The menu is built for all ages and appetites; graze on olives and garlic bread as you choose one course or five. Identified bread, meat and cheese suppliers nonetheless reflect a serious approach to good food.

OUR TIP: Order small grazing portions or large

Chef: Mark Pulman **Owners:** Brazz Plc **Times:** 12-3/6-10.30, Closed 25 Dec **Notes:** Vegetarian available **Seats:** 150 **Smoking:** N/Sm in restaurant, Air con **Children:** Portions **Directions:** Exit M5 junct 30, follow Topsham Rd then first right off South St. **Parking:** 6

e-mail: exeter@brazz.co.uk **web:** www.brazz.co.uk

Carved Angel

European

Quality bistro with stunning views of Exeter Cathedral

☎ 01392 210303 21A Cathedral Yard EX1 1HB

MENU GUIDE Thai prawn, coconut & noodle soup • Fillet steak, creamy mashed potato, crispy onions & mushrooms • Vanilla crème brûlée

WINE GUIDE ♀ Porto Italica Pinot Grigio • ♀ Los Espinos Merlot £14.25 • 7 bottles over £20, 7 bottles under £20 • 6 by the glass (£3.10-£5.10)

PRICE GUIDE Starter £4.50-£8.25 • main £10.25-£14.95 • dessert £4.50-£4.95 • coffee £1.40 • min/water £3 • Service optional • Group min 10 service 10%

PLACE: Simply decorated bistro on the ground floor and basement of a property in a prime location opposite the cathedral. It offers daytime snacks and in the evening a full à la carte and good-value fixed-price menu. Service is relaxed and friendly.

FOOD: An interesting range of well presented dishes is offered, based on local produce. Vibrant Mediterranean, Middle Eastern and Pacific flavours and combinations appear throughout.

OUR TIP: Daily specials and extra vegetarian options available every day

Chef: Patrick Sanders **Owners:** Peter Gorton & Paul Roston **Times:** 12-4/7-10, Closed 25-26 Dec, 1 Jan, closed D Sun **Notes:** Vegetarian available **Seats:** 50, Pr/dining room 25 **Smoking:** N/Sm in restaurant, Air con **Children:** Menu, Portions **Directions:** Opposite Exeter Cathedral, just off the High Street **Parking:** City centre

e-mail: enquiries@thecarvedangel.com

web: www.thecarvedangel.com

The Conservatory

Modern British ⚟NEW

Imaginative cooking in city centre conservatory restaurant

☎ 01392 273858 18 North St EX4 3QS

continued

MENU GUIDE Tiger prawns in coconut milk, chilli, coriander • Calves' liver, sage, bacon, pommes Anna • Burnt lemon cream, strawberries

WINE GUIDE ♀ Perito Semillon Sauvignon £11.95 • ♀ Rocheburg Shiraz £12.95 • 12 bottles over £20, 35 bottles under £20 • 8 by the glass (£3.30-£4.70)

PRICE GUIDE Fixed L £8.95 • starter £4.25-£7.95 • main £13.95-£19.95 • dessert £5.50 • coffee £1.75 • Service optional • Group min 7 service 10%

PLACE: A blend of laid-back brasserie and quality restaurant, this spacious eaterie is popular, so book ahead. Shabby chic best describes the decor; the walls are hung with mirrors and tapestries while white painted tables are simply set with quality tableware.

FOOD: Tried and tested modern British/French combinations with the odd twist. Favoured dishes include line caught sea bass with sauce vierge, or West country steak with smoked oysters, and pink peppercorn and lemon butter.

OUR TIP: Great value early bird menu available before 6.45pm

Chef: Alan Loman **Owners:** S W A Simmons **Times:** 12-2.30/5.30-11, Closed 24 Dec-3 Jan, Sun-Mon **Notes:** Vegetarian available **Seats:** 45, Pr/dining room 12 **Smoking:** N/Sm in restaurant **Directions:** 100yds from the cathedral **Parking:** NCP attached

e-mail: alanreeve@onetel.com

Galley Fish & Seafood Restaurant with Rooms

Fish, Seafood

Eclectic dining at the water's edge

☎ 0845 602 6862 41 Fore St, Topsham EX3 0HU

MENU GUIDE Szechwan spice marinated squid • Mille feuille of scallops, turbot & sea trout • Brioche bread & butter pudding

WINE GUIDE ♀ Sancerre £19.95 • ♀ Novas Carnernevere £14.95 • 7 bottles over £20, 26 bottles under £20 • 10 by the glass (£3.95-£5.95)

PRICE GUIDE Fixed L £27.50 • starter £7.50-£9.95 • main £16.95-£22.95 • dessert £6.95 • coffee £2.95 • min/water £3.95 • Service optional • Group min 7 service 10%

PLACE: A waterside location with views across the estuary. The interior is quite 'Old Curiosity Shop' with low ceilings and a cosy approach to table spacing. It is popular with locals so booking is advised.

FOOD: An exotically phrased menu adds to the eclectic style of cooking which includes some unheard of but often highly effective combinations of flavour. Massive choice of starters which can be ordered as tapas plus good bread and dips.

OUR TIP: Parking tricky so be prepared for short walk

Chef: P Da-Costa Greaves/F Roseler/R Hunter/A Lester/D Smith **Owners:** Mark Wright/Paul Da-Costa Greaves **Times:** 12-1.30/7-9.30, Closed L Sun **Notes:** Vegetarian available **Seats:** 48 **Smoking:** N/Sm restaurant **Children:** Min 12yrs **Rooms:** 4 (4 en suite) ◆◆◆◆

continued

Directions: M5 junct 30, follow signs for Topsham. Come through High St see Globe Hotel on left, continue for 250yds. **Parking:** 3
e-mail: fish@galleyrestaurant.co.uk **web:** www.galleyrestaurant.co.uk

Hotel Barcelona
British, Mediterranean
Light, bright, enjoyable conservatory dining
☎ 01392 281010 Magdalen St EX2 4HY

MENU GUIDE Duck foie gras parfait • Roast lamb rump, chick pea salsa • Summer berry crème brûlée

WINE GUIDE ♀ Le Vigne Vigneto Contralle Pinot Grigio £16.50 • ♀ Andrew Hurley Shiraz Cabernet Sauvignon £13.50 • 31 bottles over £20, 27 bottles under £20 • 13 by the glass (£2.95-£4.25)

PRICE GUIDE Starter £2.95-£7.50 • main £7.95-£16.95 • dessert £4.50-£5.50 • coffee £2.50 • min/water £2.50 • Service optional • Group min 10 service 10%

PLACE: A 'circus top' style conservatory attached to the stylish Hotel Barcelona provides the vibrant venue for the Café Paradiso. A glass wall provides good views over the terrace and gardens. Service is relaxed and friendly.
FOOD: Lots of fresh, local supplies used here to produce simply conceived but well executed modern Mediterranean dishes such as wood-roasted sea bass with shallots, lemon and white wine.
OUR TIP: Dine alfresco on the garden terrace
Chef: Chris Archambault **Owners:** Alias Hotels plc **Times:** 12-2/7-10, closed 25 Dec (evening) **Notes:** Jazz L first Sun of every month, Vegetarian available **Seats:** 72, Pr/dining room 22 **Smoking:** N/Sm in restaurant, Air con **Children:** Menu, Portions **Rooms:** 46 (46 en suite) ★★★★ **Directions:** From M5 junct 30 take A379 to Exeter. At Countess Wear rdbt take 3rd exit to city centre and follow Topsham Rd for 2m. At main jnct follow into right lane into Magdalen St. Hotel on right **Parking:** 45 **e-mail:** info@aliasbarcelona.com **web:** www.aliasbarcelona.com

Lord Haldon Hotel
British, European
Picturesque country house setting for skilful cooking
☎ 01392 832483 Dunchideock EX6 7YF

MENU GUIDE Smoked chicken, duck & ham hock terrine • Herb roasted chump of lamb, crushed sweet potatoes • Chocolate fondant

PRICE GUIDE Food prices not confirmed for 2006. Please telephone for details

PLACE: Nestled in the lush hills between Exeter and the coast, this traditional country-house hotel maintains high standards under the long-standing owners. The deep carpets, linen cloths and gold chandeliers are in keeping with the historic nature of the building, which was the stable block of this 1737-built house. The restaurant overlooks a terrace with a delightful fountain.
FOOD: The modern British style of the cooking has European flourishes, with the daily-changing set menus offering a good choice and an impressively consistent use of good quality local ingredients.
OUR TIP: Great crème brûlée here
Chef: Andrew Shortman **Owners:** Mr M & S Preece **Times:** 12-2.30/7-9.30, Closed L Mon-Sat **Notes:** Vegetarian available, Civ Wed 120 **Seats:** 60, Pr/dining room 25 **Smoking:** N/Sm in restaurant **Children:** Menu, Portions **Rooms:** 19 (19 en suite) ★★★ **Directions:** From M5 junct 31 or A30 follow signs to Ide, continue through village for 2.5m. left after red phone box . 0.5m, pass under stone bridge, left. **Parking:** 120 **e-mail:** enquiries@lordhaldonhotel.co.uk **web:** www.lordhaldonhotel.co.uk

Michael Caines at the Royal Clarence
French, European
A welcome touch of glamour in city centre
☎ 01392 310031 Cathedral Yard EX1 1HD

continued

EXETER continued MAP 03 SX99

Michael Caines at the Royal Clarence

MENU GUIDE Pan-fried scallops, parsnip & vanilla purée • Venison saddle, red cabbage, roasted root vegetables • Prune & Armagnac soufflé

WINE GUIDE ♀ Vigne Lourac Sauvignon Blanc £16 • ♥ Domaine la Galiniere Merlot £16 • 58 bottles over £20, 11 bottles under £20 • 7 by the glass (£2.85-£3.95)

PRICE GUIDE Fixed L £18 • starter £8-£14.50 • main £18.50-£26 • dessert £9 • coffee £2.50 • min/water £3.50 • Service optional • Group min 10 service 12.5%

PLACE: Set in pride of place overlooking the cathedral on the ground floor of the venerable Royal Clarence Hotel, local celebrity chef and industry icon Michael Caines has firmly established this restaurant and champagne bar as a city-centre landmark. The popular dining room has a stylish, relaxed and contemporary, cosmopolitan air, with wooden floors, muted tones, striking artwork and views over the cathedral.

FOOD: Simon Dow heads up the kitchen to deliver the Caines inspired, modern repertoire, underpinned by a classical theme, which admirably befits the decor and utilizes the very best of local, seasonal produce in well-balanced, clear flavoured, well-presented dishes. The classy food certainly hits the restaurant vision of 'Service with Style'. A value, fixed-price lunch menu bolsters the appealing carte.

OUR TIP: Book ahead if you want to dine at the weekend
Chef: Simon Dow **Owners:** Michael Caines & Andrew Brownsword **Times:** 12.30-2.30/7-10, Closed Sun, closed D Xmas **Notes:** Tasting menu 7 courses £60, Vegetarian available, Dress Restrictions, Smart casual, Civ Wed 50 **Seats:** 70, Pr/dining room 80 **Smoking:** N/Sm in restaurant, Air con **Children:** Menu, Portions **Rooms:** 55 (55 en suite) ★★★ **Directions:** Town centre, opposite Cathedral. **Parking:** 7
e-mail: tables@michaelcaines.com
web: www.michaelcaines.com

The Olive Tree at Queens Court Hotel
British, French
Contemporary cooking in secluded city hotel
☎ 01392 272709 Bystock Ter EX4 4HY

MENU GUIDE Crab bisque • Devon lamb, creamy Calvados sauce, new potatoes • Dark Belgian chocolate & cherry cheesecake

WINE GUIDE ♀ De Gras Sauvignon £12 • ♥ De Gras Merlot £12 • 42 bottles over £20, 35 bottles under £20 • 6 by the glass (£3-£3.50)

PRICE GUIDE Fixed L £8.95-£15 • Fixed D £15-£30 • starter £3.95-£6.95 • main £8.95-£16.45 • dessert £4.95 • coffee £1.50 • min/water £2.75 • Service optional • Group min 10 service 10%

continued

PLACE: Quietly located in a leafy square, this Georgian townhouse has been tastefully refurbished in contemporary style. Well-spaced tables ensure privacy in the tranquil Olive Tree restaurant, with its pale cream and olive green decor.

FOOD: A good selection of modern dishes distinguished by the use of high quality local produce and organic ingredients where possible. Your choice might include monkfish in Parma ham, or Devonshire beef with pommes Anna and a port wine sauce.

OUR TIP: Within walking distance of the city centre
Chef: Chris Billingsley **Owners:** Mr & Mrs Sharpes **Times:** 12-2/7-9.30, Closed 25-30 Dec, closed L Sun **Notes:** Vegetarian available **Seats:** 42, Pr/dining room 80 **Smoking:** N/Sm in restaurant **Children:** Portions **Rooms:** 18 (18 en suite) ★★★ **Directions:** 5 miles from M5, town centre near to clocktower rdbt. **Parking:** Public car park
e-mail: enquiries@queenscourt-hotel.co.uk
web: www.queenscourt-hotel.co.uk

The Puffing Billy
British, French
Creative pub fare
☎ 01392 877888 Station Rd, Exton EX3 0PR

MENU GUIDE Crab crostini, warm salsa • Braised belly pork, toffee apple sauce • Toffee & date pudding, Armagnac ice cream

WINE GUIDE ♀ Vin de Pays des Côtes de Thau Chardonnay £12 • ♥ Lonsdale Ridge Shiraz/Cabernet Sauvignon £12 • 14 bottles over £20, 27 bottles under £20 • 12 by the glass (£2-£4)

PRICE GUIDE Starter £7-£8 • main £14-£21 • dessert £5 • coffee £2.25 • min/water £3 • Service optional

PLACE: A modern makeover has given The Puffing Billy a chic contemporary feel with polished wooden tables and open viewing access to the kitchen. Photographs of local culinary suppliers are a feature.

FOOD: With a reputation for modern, spacious and relaxed dining, the menu of modern dishes with French influences will suit most tastes, offering dishes such as crispy sea bass with a

continued

warm potato salad, or a dish of duckling with orange fondant potato and asparagus. A selection of sandwiches filled with the likes of beef and caramelised onion, or fresh Salcombe crab is available at lunchtime.
OUR TIP: Good value lunch menu
Chef: Spencer Jones **Owners:** Martin & Jenny Humphries **Times:** 11-2.30/6.30-9.30, Closed Xmas break, closed D Sun **Notes:** Sun roast £9, Vegetarian available, Dress Restrictions, Smart casual **Seats:** 60 **Smoking:** N/Sm in restaurant, Air con **Children:** Portions
Directions: 3m from M5 junct 30 take A376 signposted Exmouth, pass through Ebford and follow signs for The Puffing Billy. **Parking:** 30
e-mail: food@thepuffingbilly.com
web: www.thepuffingbilly.com

 ## St Olaves Hotel & Restaurant
British, European
Adventurous British cooking in gracious Georgian surroundings
☎ 01392 217736 Mary Arches St EX4 3AZ

MENU GUIDE Tempura of squid, black ink lemon mayonnaise • Lamb rump, flageolet beans & root vegetables, spiced jus • Chocolate brioche bread-and-butter pudding
WINE GUIDE ♀ Down St Mary £13.95 • ♟ Willow Glen Shiraz £13.95 • 21 bottles over £20, 19 bottles under £20 • 5 by the glass (£2.95-£5)
PRICE GUIDE Fixed L £12.95-£15.95 • Fixed D £29.50 • starter £4.95-£7.95 • main £9.95-£14.95 • dessert £3.95-£6.95 • coffee £2.50 • Service added but optional 5% • Group min 6 service 10%
PLACE: Built in 1827 by a wealthy merchant, this attractive Georgian townhouse is a comfortable and secluded private hotel, situated in its own walled garden and close to the cathedral. A country house feel prevails throughout, although decor and furnishings in the intimate Golsworthy Restaurant are modern and contemporary.
FOOD: Daily-changing European menus are traditional in style

continued

but display some interesting modern touches. Presentation is imaginative and use of quality local produce is to be commended.
OUR TIP: 400 yards from Exeter Cathedral
Chef: Simeon Baber **Owners:** Carol A Livingston **Times:** 12-2.30/7-9.30, Closed Mon,3 days between Xmas and New Year, closed D Sun
Notes: Mineral water incl., Vegetarian available, Dress Restrictions, Smart Casual, Civ Wed 100 **Seats:** 50, Pr/dining room 10 **Smoking:** N/Sm in restaurant **Children:** Menu, Portions **Rooms:** 15 (15 en suite) ★★★
Directions: M5 junct 30. Follow signs to city centre, then 'Mary Arches car park'; hotel entrance directly opp car park **Parking:** 15
e-mail: info@olaves.co.uk **web:** www.olaves.co.uk

GULWORTHY MAP 03 SX47
 ## Horn of Plenty *see page 124*

HAYTOR VALE MAP 03 SX77
 ## Rock Inn
British, French
Imaginative cooking in 18th-century coaching inn
☎ 01364 661305 TQ13 9XP
MENU GUIDE Game terrine, cranberry compote • Rabbit loin stuffed with prunes • Cranberry & orange brûlée
WINE GUIDE ♀ Laroche Chablis £26.95 • ♟ McGuigan Shiraz £16.95 • 40 bottles over £20, 35 bottles under £20 • 10 by the glass (£2.95-£4.95)
PRICE GUIDE Fixed D £24.95 • starter £3.95-£5.95 • main £9.95-£15.95 • dessert £4.95-£5.95 • coffee £2.25 • min/water £3.50 • Service optional
PLACE: Old coaching inn in a quiet Dartmoor hamlet, with loads of character thanks to the old beams and flagstones in the public areas. Hospitality and service are a pleasure to experience.
FOOD: The cooking shows generous helpings of care and attention, by chefs who shop from the best local markets. The sensible menu is strong on uncomplicated flavours, with pan-fried duck breast with a honey and green peppercorn sauce typical of the choice.
OUR TIP: Try the good locally-made breads
Chef: Sue Beaumont Graves **Owners:** Mr C Graves **Times:** 12-2.15/6.30-9, Closed 25-26 Dec **Notes:** Vegetarian available, Dress Restrictions, No jeans **Seats:** 75 **Smoking:** N/Sm in restaurant **Children:** Menu, Portions **Rooms:** 9 (9 en suite) ★★
Directions: From A38 at Drum Bridges, join the A382 to Bovey Tracey. After 2m join B3387 towards Haytor and continue for 3.5m, follow brown signs **Parking:** 25 **e-mail:** reservations@rockinn.co.uk
web: www.rock-inn.co.uk

Four Rosettes Amongst the very best restaurants in the British Isles, where the cooking demands national recognition. These restaurants will exhibit intense ambition, a passion for excellence, superb technical skills and remarkable consistency. They will combine appreciation of culinary traditions with a passionate desire for further exploration and improvement. Around twenty restaurants have four Rosettes.

England

GULWORTHY MAP 03 SX47

Horn of Plenty

British, International
Well established, accomplished cooking in country retreat
☎ 01822 832528   PL19 8JD
e-mail: enquiries@thehornofplenty.co.uk
web: www.thehornofplenty.co.uk

PLACE: Set in five acres of pretty gardens and orchards, this intimate country house is the quintessential retreat. Comfy chairs and quiet nooks abound, a roaring fire warms the lounge and windows offer stunning views of the Tamar Valley. The restaurant is simply decorated with an array of bright local artwork, and romantically lit at night by quaint table lanterns. Well trained staff are attentive and caring and encourage a leisurely mood.

FOOD: This accomplished kitchen team has worked together for over a decade now and knows its stuff, delivering a tempting modern British menu that combines the best of local produce with the odd nod to more exotic culinary climes. Dishes are straightforward in style, but skilfully done; your choice might include sea bass with a saffron chive sauce perhaps, or beef with truffle gnocchi, wild mushrooms and roasted vegetables.

MENU GUIDE Scallops, mushroom ravioli, watercress sauce • Partridge, potato & parsnip rösti, port sauce • Lime & ginger crème brûlée

WINE GUIDE ♀ Conca de Barbera Viura/Chardonnay £13.50 • ♀ Casa Rivas Cabernet Sauvignon £14.75 • 96 bottles over £20, 29 bottles under £20 10 by the glass (£3.50-£4.75)

PRICE GUIDE Fixed L £25 • Fixed D £42 • coffee £2.75 • min/water £3.50 • Service included • Group min 10 service 10%

OUR TIP: Dine at sunset to make the most of the views

Chef: Peter Gorton **Owners:** Mr & Mrs P Roston, Peter Gorton **Times:** 12/7, Closed 24-26 Dec, closed L Mon **Notes:** Fixed L 3 courses, Vegetarian available, Dress Restrictions, Smart casual, Civ Wed 150 **Seats:** 60, Pr/dining room 20 **Smoking:** N/Sm in restaurant **Children:** Menu, Portions **Rooms:** 10 (10 en suite) ★★★ **Directions:** 3m from Tavistock on A390. Turn right at Gulworthy cross, follow signpost. **Parking:** 20

HOLBETON MAP 03 SX65

The Dartmoor Union Inn

International   **NEW**

Smart village inn with contemporary restaurant

☎ 01752 830288 Fore St PL8 1NE

MENU GUIDE Boned confit duck leg • Potato wrapped turbot, petit ratatouille • Coffee bread & butter pudding

PRICE GUIDE Food prices not confirmed for 2006. Please telephone for details

PLACE: A cool contemporary style helped by big leather sofas in the bar area and smart new furniture in the restaurant has put this 'new look' pub/restaurant firmly on the map after a lengthy renovation.

FOOD: The menu has been restyled too, with good value dishes offering bold flavours and heaps of imagination from a pick and mix choice of specials, set lunches and carte.

OUR TIP: Try the in-house brewed ale

Times: 12-2.30/5.30-11 **e-mail:** sue.constantine@dartmoorunion.co.uk

HONITON MAP 04 ST10

Combe House Hotel and Restaurant, Gittisham

Modern British

Stunning country hotel delivering a class act

☎ 01404 540400 Gittisham EX14 3AD

MENU GUIDE Roast boneless quail, wild mushroom mousse • Pot-roasted poussin • White chocolate bavarois

WINE GUIDE ⚲ Lofthouse Marlborough Sauvignon Blanc £22 • ♥ Domaine Chantal Lescure Côte de Beaune de Topes Bizot £25 • 148 bottles over £20, 12 bottles under £20 • 6 by the glass (£3.60-£5)

PRICE GUIDE Fixed L £19 • Fixed D £38 • coffee £3.50

continued

Combe House Hotel and Restaurant, Gittisham

PLACE: Think romantic Elizabethan manor set on an extensive private estate, with stately public rooms and a glamorous restaurant featuring hand-painted murals of country scenes, and you'll begin to get the flavour of Combe House. Very traditional, very country house, exceedingly appealing.

FOOD: A skilled kitchen brigade garners top class local and home-grown produce, with the menus paying a clear respect for the seasons. A creative approach with good technical skills produces sea bream with provençale couscous, and Earl Grey tea mousse with chocolate ice cream.

OUR TIP: Excellent wine list

Chef: Philip Leach **Owners:** Ken & Ruth Hunt **Times:** 12-2/7-9.30, Closed 4-20 Jan **Notes:** Tasting menu 5 courses £49, Sun L 3 courses £27.50, Vegetarian available, Smart casual, Civ Wed 100 **Seats:** 60, Pr/dining room 48 **Smoking:** N/Sm in restaurant **Children:** Menu, Portions **Rooms:** 15 (15 en suite) ★★★ **Directions:** A373 to Honiton. Right in High Street and follow signs for Sidmouth A375, then brown tourist signs for Combe. **Parking:** 35 **e-mail:** stay@thishotel.com **web:** www.thishotel.com

HORNS CROSS MAP 03 SS32

The Hoops Inn & Country Hotel

British, European   **NEW**

Honest cooking in 13th-century inn

☎ 01237 451222 EX39 5DL

MENU GUIDE Steamed langoustines with tomato & herb oil • Crediton duck with cider & apple sauce • Banoffee pie

WINE GUIDE ⚲ Montagne Noir Marsanne £12.50 • ♥ Montagne Noir Grenache £12.50 • 67 bottles over £20, 108 bottles under £20 • 14 by the glass (£2.30-£6.50)

PRICE GUIDE Starter £3.90-£8.50 • main £7.90-£18.50 • dessert £4.50 • coffee £1.50 • min/water £3 • Service optional

PLACE: A Grade II listed thatched inn with all the trimmings - lots of beams, huge inglenook fireplaces and a friendly welcome.

FOOD: Locally sourced produce is the backbone of the operation, some done to earth honest, down to earth cooking with no unnecessary fuss. The smooth chicken liver parfait is pleasing with well balanced flavours. Follow that with roasted best end of lamb, served very pink with beautifully crisp fatty edges, a hint of thyme and thin port jus - simple, but very effective.

OUR TIP: More informal dining takes place in the bar

Chef: Mark Somerville, Peter Richardson **Owners:** Gerry & Dee Goodwin **Times:** 12-3.30/6-9.30 **Notes:** Dress Restrictions, Smart casual **Seats:** 90, Pr/dining room 14 **Smoking:** N/Sm in restaurant **Children:** Menu, Portions **Directions:** Follow A39 from Bideford towards Clovelly/Bude, through Fairy Cross and Horns Cross, restaurant on the right. **Parking:** 100 **e-mail:** sales@hoopsinn.co.uk **web:** www.hoopsinn.co.uk

ILSINGTON MAP 03 SX77

⊚⊚ The Ilsington Country Hotel

British, French

Country-house hotel with stunning views

☎ 01364 661452 Ilsington Village TQ13 9RR

MENU GUIDE Seared sea scallops • Saddle of venison, wild mushrooms, juniper & thyme jus • Chocolate marquise

WINE GUIDE 25 bottles over £20, 35 bottles under £20 • 11 by the glass (£2.65)

PRICE GUIDE Fixed L £15.95-£16.50 • Fixed D £28.50-£28.95 • starter £5-£8 • main £10-£17 • dessert £6-£7 • coffee £2.25 • min/water £2.90 • Service included

PLACE: Occupying an elevated position on the southern slopes of Dartmoor, this friendly, family-owned hotel is a peacefully situated hideaway with far-reaching views. The smart dining room is homely and traditional. For the more energetic visitors, the swimming pool and gym are also popular.

FOOD: Classic Anglo-French cookery with an emphasis on locally sourced produce, which is reflected in the innovative daily-changing menus featuring local fish, meat and game. Dishes are well presented and flavours are bold and vibrant.

OUR TIP: Relax in the garden with its scenic views

Chef: Mike O'Donnell **Owners:** Tim & Maura Hassell **Times:** 12-2/6.30-9 **Notes:** Vegetarian available, Dress Restrictions, Shirt with a collar (smart casual) **Seats:** 40, Pr/dining room 32 **Smoking:** N/Sm in restaurant **Children:** Portions **Rooms:** 25 (25 en suite) ★★★ **Directions:** A38 to Plymouth, exit at Bovey Tracey turn, then 3rd exit from rdbt to Ilsington, then 1st right and hotel 5m after Post Office. **Parking:** 60 **e-mail:** hotel@ilsington.co.uk **web:** www.ilsington.co.uk

INSTOW MAP 03 SS43

⊚ Decks Restaurant

Modern British

Simple modern cooking in maritime setting

☎ 01271 860671 Hatton Croft House, Marine Pde EX39 4JJ

MENU GUIDE Smoked haddock, leek & potato chowder • Beef, potato rösti, spinach, chestnut mushrooms, red wine jus • Crêpes Suzette

WINE GUIDE ⚲ Frazers Bay Chenin Blanc £11.50 • ⚑ McGuigan Shiraz £13.40 • 33 bottles over £20, 30 bottles under £20 • 8 by the glass (£3.10-£3.55)

PRICE GUIDE Fixed D £24.50 • coffee £1.80 • min/water £2.50 • Service optional

PLACE: Built around a ship's mast, this vibrant eatery, with extensive murals by a local artist, takes its maritime theme seriously and boasts stunning coastal views. Dine outside if weather permits.

FOOD: Simple modern British dishes - roast cod perhaps, with spring onion and garlic, or Gressingham duck with confit leg and a pommery mustard jus.

OUR TIP: Try and book a window seat

Chef: Lee Timmins **Owners:** Lee Timmins **Times:** 12-2.30/7-9.30, Closed 25-26 Dec, 1 Jan, 1st 2 wks of Nov, Sun-Mon **Notes:** Lunch specials; starter £3.50-6, main £6-13, dessert £3.50-5, Vegetarian available **Seats:** 50 **Smoking:** N/Sm area, Air con **Children:** Portions **Directions:** From Barnstaple follow A38 to Bideford. Following signs for Instow, restaurant situated at far end of sea front **Parking:** On street; beach car park **e-mail:** decks@instow.net **web:** www.decksrestaurant.co.uk

KINGSBRIDGE MAP 03 SX74

⊚⊚ Buckland-Tout-Saints

British, French

Sound cooking in imposing country house

☎ 01548 853055 Goveton TQ7 2DS

MENU GUIDE Confit of duck, baby leek, and foie gras terrine • Devonshire steak, herb mash, wild mushroom sauce • Iced pear parfait

WINE GUIDE ⚲ Domaine Montmarrin Chardonnay £13 • ⚑ Hellfire Bay Shiraz/Grenache £16 • 61 bottles over £20, 28 bottles under £20 • 6 by the glass (£4.50-£7)

PRICE GUIDE Fixed L £15 • Fixed D £37.50 • coffee £2.50 • min/water £4 • Service optional

PLACE: A rural retreat in the lush Devon countryside, this delightful Queen Anne manor is decorated in suitably restrained style with comfy sofas, antiques and wood-panelling.

FOOD: Expect British cuisine with French influences from a kitchen team that know their stuff. A concise menu offers four choices at each course: dive in with pan-fried Salcombe scallops perhaps, or sweet pear and parsnip soup, before moving on to roast rump of Devonshire lamb with a red wine sauce, and a warm dark chocolate tart to finish.

OUR TIP: A popular wedding venue

Chef: Jean-Philippe Bidar **Owners:** Capt Mark Trumble **Times:** 12-1.30/7-9, Closed 3 wks end Jan **Notes:** Sun L £19, Vegetarian by request only, Dress Restrictions, Smart casual, no shorts, Civ Wed 100 **Seats:** 40, Pr/dining room 18 **Smoking:** N/Sm in restaurant **Children:** Menu, Portions **Rooms:** 12 (12 en suite) ★★★ **Directions:** 3m NE of Kingsbridge off A381. Through hamlet to Goveton, 500 yds past church. **Parking:** 40 **e-mail:** buckland@tout-saints.co.uk **web:** www.tout-saints.co.uk

LEWDOWN MAP 03 SX48

⊚⊚⊚ Lewtrenchard Manor

see page 127

continued

LEWDOWN MAP 03 SX48

Lewtrenchard Manor

British

Fine food in Jacobean splendour in a secret valley

☎ 01566 783222   EX20 4PN

MENU GUIDE Tiger prawns, sweet chilli pickled vegetables • Pan-fried monkfish, mushroom risotto, fish velouté • Glazed lemon tart, raspberry purée, raspberry ice cream

WINE GUIDE ♀ Domaine Chatelain Chablis Chardonnay £25 • ♀ St Emilion Château Lassegue £35 • 145 bottles over £20, 82 bottles under £20 • 6 by the glass (£3-£3.75)

PRICE GUIDE Fixed L £12 • Fixed D £37 • coffee £2.50 • min/water £3 • Service optional

PLACE: This magnificent, Jacobean manor lives up to the promise of its beautiful exterior and idyllic country garden and parkland setting on the fringe of Dartmoor. It exudes understated charm with oak panelling, ornate ceilings, leaded windows, large fireplaces and period furnishings, while the panelled, candlelit dining room is relatively intimate and overlooks a pretty courtyard.

FOOD: Top-notch local produce from West Country suppliers, and herbs and most of the vegetables from Lewtrenchard's own walled garden, are key to Jason Hornbuckle's appealing, fixed-price modern menu's success. Skilful, cooking displays flair and imagination, with interesting flavour combinations and a light touch that allows the main ingredient to shine – sautéed loin of lamb with twice-cooked breast, pea purée and thyme infused jus.

OUR TIP: Book one of the luxurious bedrooms

Chef: Jason Hornbuckle **Owners:** Von Essen Hotels **Times:** 12-1.30/7-9, closed L Mon **Notes:** Vegetarian available, Dress Restrictions, Smart Casual, no jeans, Civ Wed 100 **Seats:** 35, Pr/dining room 16 **Smoking:** N/Sm in restaurant **Children:** Min 8 yrs, Portions **Rooms:** 14 (14 en suite) ★★★ **Directions:** Take A30 Okehampton from M5 junct 31. Continue for 25m, exit at Sourton Cross. Follow signs to Lewdown, then Lewtrenchard **Parking:** 40 **e-mail:** info@lewtrenchard.co.uk **web:** www.lewtrenchard.co.uk

LIFTON MAP 03 SX38

⚜⚜ Arundell Arms

Modern British

Character hotel for country pursuits and fine food

☎ 01566 784666   PL16 0AA

MENU GUIDE Sea bass fillet, saffron, ginger & green onion • Beef tournedos, parsley tartlet, red wine & thyme sauce • Quince pannacotta

WINE GUIDE ♀ Madfish Chardonnay £16.50 • ♀ Brown Brothers Shiraz £16.50 • 41 bottles over £20, 34 bottles under £20 • 6 by the glass (£3.50-£4.50)

PRICE GUIDE Fixed L £21 • Fixed D £40 • min/water £2.50 • Service optional

PLACE: A former coaching inn, full of character, the hotel makes the most of it proximity to the River Tamar, and is popular for fishing trips and other country pursuits. Flagstone floors, low ceilings, a cosy bar and lounge set the scene and lead to a large restaurant decorated predominantly in yellow.

FOOD: Carefully sourced West Country ingredients are the key to the food's success, with suppliers proudly acknowledged in the menu. Menus are priced for two or three courses, plus there's a daily set five-course alternative, including coffee and chocolates.

OUR TIP: Bring a fishing rod

Chef: Nick Shopland, Steven Pidgeon **Owners:** Anne Voss-Bark **Times:** 12.30-2.30/7.30-10, Closed 24 Dec, closed D 25-26 Dec **Notes:** Menu of the day £35, Vegetarian available, Smart casual, Civ Wed 80 **Seats:** 70, Pr/dining room 24 **Smoking:** N/Sm in restaurant **Children:** Menu, Portions **Rooms:** 27 (27 en suite) ★★★ **Directions:** Just off A30 in village of Lifton, 3m E of Launceston **Parking:** 70 **e-mail:** reservations@arundellarms.com **web:** www.arundellarms.com

Arundell Arms

continued

England

LIFTON *continued* MAP 03 SX38

⊛ Tinhay Mill Guest House and Restaurant

British, French

Traditional cooking close to Devon and Cornwall border

☎ 01566 784201 Tinhay PL16 0AJ

MENU GUIDE Creamy chicken liver crêpes • Roast breast of duckling, port & black cherry sauce • Apple & almond creams

WINE GUIDE ♀ Bordeaux £12 • ♀ French Merlot £13 • 11 bottles over £20, 17 bottles under £20 • 4 by the glass (£2.90-£4)

PRICE GUIDE Fixed D £21.75-£27.50 • starter £4.50-£7.50 • main £12.95-£19 • dessert £4.25-£7 • coffee £2.50 • min/water £1.20 • Service optional

PLACE: Housed in former 15th-century mill cottages, this unpretentious, friendly restaurant has bags of character and rustic charm.

FOOD: A strong French influence runs through the English menu, with plenty of local produce cropping up in dishes such as rillette of salmon flavoured with Cornish smoked bacon and capers. Try the selection of West Country cheeses, including Devon Blue.

OUR TIP: Only open for dinner

Chef: Margaret Wilson **Owners:** Mr P & Mrs M Wilson **Times:** 7-9.30, Closed 2 wks Nov, 2 wks Apr, Sun & Mon (ex residents), closed L all week, closed D Sun-Mon **Notes:** Vegetarian available, Dress Restrictions, No jeans **Seats:** 24, Pr/dining room 24 **Smoking:** N/Sm in restaurant **Children:** Min 12yrs **Rooms:** 3 (3 en suite) ⏹ **Directions:** From M5 take A30 towards Okehampton/Launceston. Lifton off A30 on left. Follow brown tourist signs. Restaurant at bottom of village near river **Parking:** 20 **e-mail:** tinhay.mill@talk21.com **web:** www.tinhaymillrestaurant.co.uk

---

LYDFORD MAP 03 SX58

⊛⊛ *Dartmoor Inn*

Modern British

Stylish rural gastro-pub

☎ 01822 820221 EX20 4AY

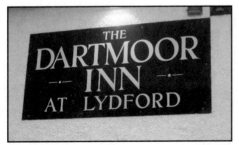

MENU GUIDE Chicken liver pâté, peppered toast • Turbot cutlet, herbs & lemon • Orange & passionfruit tart, clotted cream

PRICE GUIDE Food prices not confirmed for 2006. Please telephone for details

PLACE: There's a cosy, rustic feel to this 16th-century coaching inn, which combines smart contemporary style without sacrificing any old-fashioned charm. Log fires and patchwork add to the feel, while dashing colour schemes and striking flowers bring the ambience up to date.

FOOD: A simple approach allows the quality of ingredients to speak for themselves. Such is the commitment to local produce that the name of the herd providing the day's beef is chalked on the blackboard. The modern British brasserie-style dishes demonstrate considerable skill and accuracy, such as crisp sea fish fritters with a punchy green mayonnaise.

OUR TIP: Booking vital at weekends

Times: 12-2.15/6.30-9.30, Closed Bank holidays, Mon, closed D Sun **Directions:** On A386, Tavistock to Okehampton road. **e-mail:** info@dartmoorinn.co.uk **web:** www.dartmoorinn.co.uk

---

LYNMOUTH MAP 03 SS74

⊛⊛ *Rising Sun Hotel*

British, French

Innovative cooking in former smugglers' inn

☎ 01598 753223 Harbourside EX35 6EG

PLACE: A classic thatched English inn, the Rising Sun dates from the 14th century and overlooks the delightful harbour. RD Blackmore stayed while writing *Lorna Doone*, and it's believed that Shelley honeymooned here. Once frequented by smugglers, it is now rather more respectable, and as full of character inside as out.

FOOD: Great use of quality produce, cooked with real care and attention to detail. The balance of flavours is clear and dishes well constructed. Local Exmoor game and Lynmouth Bay lobster may feature. Good amuse bouche and petits fours.

OUR TIP: They smoke their own scallops

Times: 12-4/7-9 **Rooms:** 16 (16 en suite) ★★ **e-mail:** risingsunlynmouth@easynet.co.uk **web:** www.risingsunlynmouth.co.uk

continued

England

LYNTON MAP 03 SS74

⊚ Chough's Nest Hotel

English **NEW**

Carefully cooked food accompanied by great views across the Bristol Channel

☎ 01598 753315 North Walk EX35 6HJ

MENU GUIDE Cream of white onion soup • Baked breast of Gressingham duck, pak choi, honey glaze • Mille-feuille of chocolate & mango

PRICE GUIDE Food prices not confirmed for 2006. Please telephone for details

PLACE: Truly spectacular views can be expected at this friendly hotel on the coastal path. Hands-on owners are friendly and enthusiastic. The intimate dining room also takes advantage of the glorious setting.

FOOD: Good use of local produce, carefully prepared with no unnecessary frills to detract from the promised flavours.

OUR TIP: A window table is a must

Times: 6.30-8 **e-mail:** relax@choughsnesthotel.co.uk

web: www.choughsnesthotel.co.uk

⊚ Lynton Cottage Hotel

British, Mediterranean

Stunning food to match the stunning view

☎ 01598 752342 North Walk EX35 6ED

MENU GUIDE Smoked salmon, crab, pink grapefruit • Red beef fillet, truffle mash, Exmoor ale sauce • Lemon & Exmoor honey cheesecake

WINE GUIDE ♀ Mansion House Bay Sauvignon Blanc £16.95 • ♀ Degras 2003 Merlot £15.95 • 14 bottles over £20, 36 bottles under £20 • 6 by the glass (£3.50-£6)

PRICE GUIDE Fixed L £15 • Fixed D £28 • starter £6-£10 • main £16-£22 • dessert £5-£8 • coffee £3.50 • min/water £3 • Service optional

PLACE: Lynton Cottage is a country house hotel in an amazing location, perched 500 feet above the sea overlooking Lynmouth Bay. There are fabulous views of the bay and Lyn Valley from both the intimate restaurant and the cosy Victorian bar.

FOOD: Imaginative modern cooking features locally sourced produce, including freshly caught seafood, cheeses, Exmoor venison and farm reared Devon meat. Desserts are particularly eye-catching with their dramatic presentation.

OUR TIP: Stay over in recently upgraded bedrooms

Chef: Allan Earl **Owners:** Grace Jeferyes **Times:** 12-2.30/7-9.30, Closed Dec & Jan **Notes:** Vegetarian available, Smart casual **Seats:** 40 **Smoking:** N/Sm in restaurant **Children:** Menu, Portions **Rooms:** 15 (15 en suite) ★★★ **Directions:** M5 junct 27, follow A361 towards Barnstaple. Follow signs to Lynton A39. In Lynton Turn right at church. Hotel on right **Parking:** 18 **e-mail:** enquiries@lynton-cottage.co.uk **web:** www.lynton-cottage.co.uk

MARTINHOE MAP 03 SS64

⊚ The Old Rectory

Modern British

Local produce at delightful country hideaway

☎ 01598 763368 EX31 4QT

MENU GUIDE Goats' cheese & thyme soufflé • Garlic & ginger sticky beef • Chocolate mousse, lavender ice cream

WINE GUIDE ♀ Castillo de Mont Blanc Viura Chardonnay

£11.50 • ♀ Montes Cabernet Sauvignon £13 • 5 bottles over £20, 18 bottles under £20 • 2 by the glass (£3.50-£4)

PRICE GUIDE Fixed D £32 • Service optional

PLACE: Built in the 1800s and the village rectory until 1955, this peaceful country hotel is set in three acres of well tended gardens, just 500 yards from the coastal footpath. The spacious, Georgian-style dining room is tastefully furnished with antique furniture.

FOOD: Modern British dishes on the short fixed-price menu are prepared with imagination and care, with most of the ingredients being free range and organic sourced locally.

OUR TIP: The glorious, peaceful gardens include a cascading brook and duck pond

Chef: Enid Richmond **Owners:** Christopher & Enid Richmond **Times:** 7.30, Closed Nov-Feb, Sun-Thu (Mar), closed L Mon-Sun **Notes:** Fixed D 5 courses £32, Vegetarian by request only, Dress Restrictions, smart casual **Seats:** 18 **Smoking:** N/Sm in restaurant **Children:** Min 14yrs **Rooms:** 9 (9 en suite) ★★ **Directions:** M5 junct 27/A361, right onto A399 Blackmoor Gate, right onto A39 Parracombe. At Martinhoe Cross, take unclass road to Martinhoe. **Parking:** 9 **e-mail:** reception@oldrectoryhotel.co.uk **web:** www.oldrectoryhotel.co.uk

MORETONHAMPSTEAD MAP 03 SX78

⊚ Bovey Castle

French, English **NEW**

Art deco dining in Jacobean-style mansion

☎ 01647 445000 TQ13 8RE

MENU GUIDE Pressed ham hock & foie gras terrine • Assiette of Brixham seafood, caviar bisque • Rice pudding, champagne rhubarb compote

PRICE GUIDE Food prices not confirmed for 2006. Please telephone for details

PLACE: An extensive refurbishment has seen this Jacobean-style mansion, set above Dartmoor in magnificent grounds, returned to its former glory. The unusual art deco dining room has recaptured all its elegance, complete with mirrored pillars, painted wallpapers, orchids and palms.

FOOD: Simple, classic dishes are skilfully prepared, with the freshest local produce sourced whenever possible. The menu might include tarte Tatin of Vulscombe goats' cheese with pear purée, or organic Red Ruby beef with creamed vegetables, rosti potato and brouilly sauce.

OUR TIP: Bring your children

Times: 12-2/7-9.30 **Rooms:** 65 (65 en suite) ★★★★★ **Directions:** 2miles from Moretonhamstead towards Princetown on B3212 **e-mail:** pnh@boveycastle.com **web:** www.boveycastle.com

NEWTON ABBOT MAP 03 SX87

⊚ Sampsons Hotel & Restaurant

British

Former farmhouse serving fine local produce

☎ 01626 354913 Preston TQ12 3PP

MENU GUIDE Pan-fried scallops, tomato & chilli jam • Fillet of venison, roast celeriac, juniper jus • Belgian apple cake, clotted cream

PRICE GUIDE Fixed D £20-£33 • coffee £2.95 • min/water £1.95

PLACE: Atmospheric restaurant converted from a 16th-century Devon longhouse with low ceilings, beams, open fireplaces and stone floors. The space is divided into intimate dining areas with subdued lighting and classical music.

continued

continued

England

NEWTON ABBOT continued MAP 03 SX87

FOOD: Food scores on freshness, local produce and the accuracy of the cooking. The carte menu is supplemented by daily blackboard specials and seafood is a speciality.
OUR TIP: Accommodation in the main house and converted stables
Chef: Colin John Bell **Owners:** Nigel Bell **Times:** 7, Closed 25-26 Dec, closed L Mon-Sun, closed D Sun (Winter) **Notes:** Vegetarian available, Dress Restrictions, No jeans **Seats:** 36, Pr/dining room 20 **Smoking:** N/Sm in restaurant **Children:** Menu, Portions **Rooms:** 11 (8 en suite) ◆◆◆◆ **Directions:** M5/A380/B3195 signed Kingsteignton. Pass Ten Tors Inn on left & take 2nd rd signed B3193 to Chudleigh. At rdbt 3rd exit, left after 1m. **Parking:** 20 **e-mail:** info@sampsonsfarm.com **web:** www.sampsonsfarm.com

PARKHAM MAP 03 SS32

Penhaven Country Hotel

British
Country house cooking in conservatory restaurant
☎ 01237 451711 Rectory Ln EX39 5PL
MENU GUIDE Asparagus & Parma ham, rocket, pesto dressing • Venison haunch, grain mustard & mushroom sauce • Treacle & almond tart
WINE GUIDE ♀ Chilean Sauvignon Blanc £14.95 • ♀ Chilean Merlot £14.95 • 10 bottles over £20, 25 bottles under £20 • 3 by the glass (£2.60)
PRICE GUIDE Fixed L £13.50 • Fixed D £21 • starter £6-£9 • main £16-£20 • dessert £5 • Service optional
PLACE: Privately owned for many years by a couple previously in the recording industry, this former rectory is located on the edge of the village. The Orangery Restaurant overlooks the garden, with distant views of Exmoor (a great place for badger watching).
FOOD: Imaginative cooking using fresh local produce. Vegetarian food is a speciality, with dishes such as korma cutlets, or stuffed peppers with couscous and smoked cheese.
OUR TIP: Vegetarian owners ensure interesting vegetarian choices
Chef: Richard Copp **Owners:** Mr & Mrs Wade **Times:** 12.15-1.30/7.15-9.00, Closed L Mon-Sat **Notes:** Coffee incl, Vegetarian available, Dress Restrictions, Smart casual, no jeans **Seats:** 45 **Smoking:** N/Sm in restaurant **Children:** Min 10yrs **Rooms:** 12 (12 en suite) ★★★ **Directions:** From Bideford A39 to Horns Cross, left opposite pub, follow signs to Parkham; turn 2nd left with church on right. **Parking:** 50 **e-mail:** reception@penhaven.co.uk **web:** www.penhaven.co.uk

PLYMOUTH MAP 03 SX45

Artillery Tower Restaurant

British
Interesting old building on the seafront offering skilful cooking
☎ 01752 257610 Firestone Bay PL1 3QR
MENU GUIDE Mediterranean fish soup • Skate & caper butter sauce • Chocolate fondant sponge pudding, pear sorbet
WINE GUIDE ♀ Meridian Chardonnay £12.50 • ♀ Meridian Cabernet Sauvignon £12.50 • 20 bottles under £20 • 3 by the glass (£3.50-£6.50)
PRICE GUIDE Fixed L £15.50-£23 • Fixed D £31-£39 • starter £4.50-£9.50 • main £11-£24 • dessert £5-£6.50 • coffee £2.50 • min/water £3
PLACE: There are no cold and draughty gun ports at this old artillery tower, but a welcoming atmosphere helped in winter by a blazing fire. An open-air terrace upstairs provides great views.

continued

FOOD: A serious approach to sourcing fresh local produce, shown by the list of suppliers, is partnered by accomplished cooking skills and attractive presentation. A straightforward set dinner menu follows along modern British lines.
OUR TIP: Mind your head on the way in!
Chef: Peter Constable **Owners:** Peter Constable **Times:** 12-2.15/7-9.30, Closed Xmas & New Year, Sun-Mon, closed L Sat **Notes:** Vegetarian available **Seats:** 40, Pr/dining room 16 **Children:** Portions **Directions:** 1 mile from city centre and train station. **Parking:** 20 **web:** www.artillerytower.co.uk

Duke of Cornwall Hotel

British, European
City hotel and Plymouth landmark
☎ 01752 275850 Millbay Rd PL1 3LG
MENU GUIDE Duck liver & morel terrine • Seared loin of lamb, leek & bacon mash, redcurrant sauce • White chocolate & pistachio delice
PRICE GUIDE Starter £5-£9 • main £9-£20 • dessert £4-£6 • coffee £2 • min/water £2.95
PLACE: Grade II listed hotel which has seen much change and investment and now has a smart contemporary feel. The impressive restaurant has a domed ceiling and marble pillars rise 25 feet to a sublime crystal chandelier, part of its Victorian heritage.
FOOD: The restaurant has a good local reputation, with modern British food, and there is a strong resident dining clientele. Dinner only, offered from a monthly carte.
OUR TIP: Conveniently located in the city centre
Chef: Darren Kester **Owners:** L Smith, W Combstock, J Morcom **Times:** 7-10, Closed L all week **Notes:** Vegetarian available, Civ Wed 300 **Seats:** 80, Pr/dining room 30 **Smoking:** N/Sm in restaurant **Children:** Portions **Rooms:** 71 (71 en suite) ★★★ **Directions:** City centre, follow signs 'Pavilions', hotel road is opposite **Parking:** 40 **e-mail:** info@thedukeofcornwallhotel.com **web:** www.thedukeofcornwallhotel.com

Langdon Court Hotel

British, European
Brasserie-style food in Tudor grandeur
☎ 01752 862358 Down Thomas PL9 0DY

MENU GUIDE Warm scallop salad, bacon & balsamic • Roast venison, wild mushroom risotto, port sauce • Lemon & lime posset, cinnamon biscuits
WINE GUIDE ♀ Geisen Sauvignon £13.75 • ♀ Ronchi Montepulcian £13.75 • 35 bottles over £20, 65 bottles under £20 • 10 by the glass (£3-£4.50)
PRICE GUIDE Starter £4.50-£7.50 • main £12.50-£16.50 • dessert £4.95 • coffee £1.95 • min/water £3.75 • Service optional
PLACE: Stylishly updated Tudor manor house set in seven acres

continued

of lush countryside close to Wembury beach and the coast path. The interior is surprisingly chic and contemporary, with casual dining in the bar and a touch more formality in the brasserie-style restaurant.

FOOD: Rustic, modern British cooking with dedicated attention to quality and freshness, and incorporating local produce, notably excellent seafood.

OUR TIP: Ideal wedding venue
Chef: Mark Jones **Owners:** Mark and Ruth Jones **Times:** 12-2.30/6.30-9.30, Closed 25-26 Dec **Notes:** Vegetarian available, Civ Wed 80
Seats: 60, Pr/dining room 60 **Smoking:** N/Sm in restaurant
Children: Portions **Rooms:** 18 (18 en suite) ★★ **Directions:** From A379 at Elburton, follow brown tourist signs. **Parking:** 80
e-mail: enquiries@langdoncourt.com
web: www.langdoncourt.com

Seawings The Restaurant *Rosettes not confirmed at time of going to press*

British, International   NEW
Contemporary restaurant on Plymouth Sound
☎ 01752 402233 Breakwater House, Lawrence Rd, Mountbatten PL9 9SJ

PLACE: This chic contemporary eaterie is a short drive from town, but well worth the journey as a growing local following attests. Surrounded on three sides by Plymouth Sound, it offers stunning views to the Cornish coast, as well as the atmospheric sight of the harbour traffic going to and fro.
FOOD: At the time of going to press, we are awaiting the results of the next inspection.
OUR TIP: Terrace for alfresco dining
Times: 11-2.30/7-9.30 **Directions:** Accessible by road on the Mountbatten peninsula or via a short water taxi ride from the Barbican
e-mail: bookit@theseawings.co.uk **web:** www.the seawings.co.uk

⑩⑩ Tanners Restaurant

European
Contemporary cooking, historic setting
☎ 01752 252001 Prysten House, Finewell St PL1 2AE

MENU GUIDE Devon crab crostini • Monkfish in prosciutto, squid ink risotto, red wine sauce • Chocolate tart, mint choc chip ice cream
WINE GUIDE ♀ Sauvignon Blanc £12.95 • ♀ Merlot £12.95
15 bottles over £20, 26 bottles under £20 • 7 by the glass (£3.50-£6)
PRICE GUIDE Fixed L £12.50 • Fixed D £30 • coffee £2.50 • min/water £2.95 • Service optional

PLACE: This renowned West Country eaterie makes the most of ts listed 15th-century setting, offering alfresco dining in the summer in a pretty medieval courtyard. It's a popular venue,

Tanners Restaurant

particularly at lunchtime, so book ahead.
FOOD: The modern European menu changes fortnightly and features plenty of local produce. Lunch is particularly good value, when your choice of dishes might include honey-glazed pork belly with celeriac and apple mash, or lemon sole in tapenade and basil.
OUR TIP: The Pilgrim Fathers ate their final meal here before leaving for America
Chef: Christopher & James Tanner **Owners:** Christopher & James Tanner **Times:** 12-2.30/7-9.30, Closed 25, 31 Dec, 1st wk Jan, Sun
Notes: Vegetarian available, Dress Restrictions, Smart casual preferred
Seats: 45, Pr/dining room 26 **Smoking:** N/Sm in restaurant
Children: Portions **Directions:** Town centre. Behind St Andrews Church on Royal Parade. **Parking:** On street, Car parks
e-mail: tannerbros@aol.com **web:** www.tannersrestaurant.co.uk

ROCKBEARE MAP 03 SY09

⑩⑩ The Jack In The Green
British, International
Perennially popular dining pub
☎ 01404 822240 EX5 2EE

MENU GUIDE Salcombe crab with gazpacho • Loin of Exmoor venison with chestnuts • Ginger & strawberry mousse
WINE GUIDE ♀ Montes Sauvignon Blanc £13.50 • ♀ Cornellana Estate Cabernet Sauvignon/Merlot £13.50 • 22 bottles over £20, 70 bottles under £20 • 12 by the glass (£2.85-£3.35)
PRICE GUIDE Fixed L £17.95 • starter £3.95-£8.50 • main £9.50-£18.50 • dessert £5.25 • coffee £1.50 • min/water £2.50

PLACE: As popular as ever and having undergone a makeover, this dining pub oozes charm, and draws equal interest from locals in the know to those making a special trip. Set just off the old A30, it is smart, friendly and several cuts above the norm.

continued   *continued*

ROCKBEARE continued MAP 03 SY09

FOOD: Central to the kitchen's philosophy is an emphasis on fresh local produce, a consistent approach and an attention to detail evident in the strong fixed-price menu and interesting bar choices (braised Tatalon belly pork, black pudding and mustard mash). Cornish sea bass with Chinese spices has an enjoyable modern edge.

OUR TIP: Go for the local produce

Chef: Matthew Mason **Owners:** Paul Parnell **Times:** 11-2/5.30-9.30, Closed 25 Dec-6 Jan **Notes:** Vegetarian available, Dress Restrictions, Smart Casual **Seats:** 60, Pr/dining room 80 **Smoking:** N/Sm in restaurant, Air con **Children:** Menu, Portions **Directions:** 3m E of M5 junct 29 on old A30. **Parking:** 120 **e-mail:** info@jackinthegreen.uk.com **web:** www.jackinthegreen.uk.com

ROUSDON MAP 04 SY29

Dower House Hotel

Modern British

Imaginative cuisine in country house

☎ 01297 21047 Rousdon DT7 3RB

MENU GUIDE Black pudding pannacotta, Waldorf salad • Slow-cooked beef, oxtail, tarragon, morels • Champagne rhubarb

WINE GUIDE ♀ Jean D'Alibert Sauvignon £12.50 • ♀ Jean D'Alibert Merlot £12.50 • 21 bottles over £20, 29 bottles under £20 • 4 by the glass (£3)

PRICE GUIDE Fixed D fr £27.50 • starter £4-£5.50 • main £7.50-£15 • dessert £3.50-£5.50 • coffee £2.50 • min/water £2.95 • Service optional

PLACE: Three miles west of Lyme Regis, this late Victorian country house offers a choice of two eateries: a relaxed, modern bistro, or a more traditional fine dining restaurant hung with pictures painted by local artists.

FOOD: The setting may be traditional, but the food is anything but; Peeks restaurant majors in ambitious and complex dishes designed to wow. High quality ingredients are in evidence in imaginative dishes such as Musbury duck with pear, parsnip, vanilla and star anise.

OUR TIP: A good base for Devon's heritage coastline

Chef: Ian Webber **Owners:** Tim Chew **Times:** 12-2/7-9 **Notes:** Set D 6 course, Vegetarian available, Dress Restrictions, No shorts or vests, Civ Wed 35 **Seats:** 24, Pr/dining room 20 **Smoking:** N/Sm in restaurant **Children:** Menu **Rooms:** 10 (10 en suite) ★★ **Directions:** 3m W of Lyme Regis on A3052 coast road **Parking:** 35 **e-mail:** info@dhhotel.com **web:** www.dhhotel.com

SALCOMBE MAP 03 SX73

Restaurant 42

Modern International   **NEW**

Classy cooking in idyllic setting

☎ 01548 843408 Fore St TQ8 8JG

MENU GUIDE Pea & mint risotto • Braised shoulder of Devon lamb • Blackberry bavarois

WINE GUIDE ♀ Sauvignon Blanc Selaks New Zealand £22.50 • ♀ Crianza Rioja Marques de Caceres £18.20 • 26 bottles over £20, 14 bottles under £20 • 6 by the glass (£3.50-£7)

PRICE GUIDE Food prices not confirmed for 2006. Please telephone for details

PLACE: The sublime Salcombe setting is fully taken advantage of, with tables arranged for the sea views, and a water's edge terrace for pre-dinner drinks. The simple, elegant style is not overly minimalist, and the atmosphere is good natured and convivial.

continued

FOOD: Carefully chosen combinations make optimum use of the local larder, and flavours are clear and pronounced. A confident cooking style results in eloquent dishes arranged without need for elaborate frills, with grilled John Dory fillets, black truffle potatoes and sautéed chorizo showing a marked pedigree.

OUR TIP: Try the never-fresher Salcombe crab

Chef: Mike Reid, Julie Clark **Owners:** Jane & Neil Storkey **Times:** 7-12, Closed 6 weeks Jan, Sun, (Mon Sep-Apr) **Notes:** Vegetarian available **Seats:** 42 **Directions:** 15m from A38 Exeter to Plymouth

Soar Mill Cove Hotel

British, Mediterranean

Classic hotel cooking in stunning coastal setting

☎ 01548 561566 Soar Mill Cove, Marlborough TQ7 3DS

MENU GUIDE Pineapple carpaccio, lime sorbet • Beef, celeriac purée, shallot & Madeira sauce • Raspberry bavarois, strawberry coulis

WINE GUIDE ♀ Macon Lugny Chardonnay £27 • ♀ Murphys Shiraz £22 • 60 bottles over £20, 4 bottles under £20 • 4 by the glass (£4.50)

PRICE GUIDE Fixed L £29 • Fixed D £39 • min/water £2.90 • Service optional

PLACE: Hidden away from the crowds along a series of winding roads, this family-run hotel overlooks a beautiful sandy bay and boasts activities galore, including cookery courses, an adventure playground, tennis courts and two pools. Its spacious restaurant caters predominantly to residents and has floor-to-ceiling windows to make the most of the views.

FOOD: Soar Mill leans towards classic combinations rather than edgier modern fare; dishes might include sea bass with a Mediterranean ratatouille, or calves' liver with garlic mash, bacon and a red wine jus. Generous portions.

OUR TIP: Treat yourself to a cream tea

Chef: I Macdonald **Owners:** Mr & Mrs K Makepeace & family **Times:** 12-3/7.15-10, Closed Jan **Notes:** Coffee included, Tasting menu

continued

£54 Fixed dinner 4 courses, Vegetarian available **Seats:** 60
Smoking: N/Sm in restaurant **Children:** Menu, Portions **Rooms:** 22
(22 en suite) ★★★★ **Directions:** A381 to Salcombe, through village
follow signs to sea. **Parking:** 25 **e-mail:** info@soarmillcove.co.uk
web: www.soarmillcove.co.uk

Tides Reach Hotel

British, European

Holiday hotel dining in splendid beach location
☎ 01548 843466 South Sands TQ8 8LJ

MENU GUIDE Salcombe scallops & Caesar salad • Venison
medallions, blackberry jus • Blueberry frangipane tart

WINE GUIDE ♀ Chereau-Carre Melon de Bourgogne
£14.95 • ♀ Excelsior Cabernet Sauvignon £15.95 • 76 bottles
over £20, 15 bottles under £20 • 6 by the glass (£3.70)

PRICE GUIDE Fixed D £34-£36 • min/water £3.20 • Service
included

PLACE: This family-run, traditional holiday hotel enjoys a
wonderful location on South Sands beach with splendid views
across Salcombe Estuary. Competition for the well-presented
window tables is brisk. The Aquarium Bar includes a large fish
tank built into the wall, stocked with local reef life.
FOOD: The unfussy set-price menu changes daily. Dishes are
modern British in style and simply presented. Good use is made
of local beef, game and especially seafood.
OUR TIP: Try and get a window seat
Chef: Finn Ibsen **Owners:** Edwards Family **Times:** 7-9, Closed Dec-Jan,
closed L all week **Notes:** Coffee incl, Vegetarian available, Dress
Restrictions, Smart casual. No jeans or T-shirts **Seats:** 80
Smoking: N/Sm in restaurant **Children:** Min 8yrs **Rooms:** 35 (35 en
suite) ★★★ **Directions:** Take cliff road towards sea and Bolt Head
Parking: 80 **e-mail:** enquire@tidesreach.com
web: www.tidesreach.com

SAUNTON MAP 03 SS43

Saunton Sands Hotel

Classical, Modern **NEW**

Seaside hotel with a good range
☎ 01271 890212 EX33 1LQ

MENU GUIDE Terrine of duck, foie gras, black truffle • Chicken,
leek & cheese fondue, Madeira sauce • Chocolate & toffee
fondant

WINE GUIDE ♀ Penfolds Shiraz £14.95 • 110 bottles over £20,
30 bottles under £20 • 20 by the glass (£3-£9.25)

PRICE GUIDE Fixed L fr £16.95 • Fixed D £30 • starter £3.80-
£6 • main £9-£11.50 • dessert £9.50 • min/water £3.95 • Service
optional

PLACE: Smart art deco hotel overlooking the sandy lengths of
Saunton Beach. Dine in the restaurant, an airy room with
stunning views, or at the new café/bar on the shore, which serves
light lunches and imaginative evening meals.
FOOD: A skilful kitchen tackles fresh local produce with care,
delivering a daily changing fixed-price selection, plus an extensive
carte. Choose something straightforward from the grill or seafood
menu, or a more complex modern dish.
OUR TIP: Vegetarian menu available
Chef: Mr David Keer **Owners:** Brend Hotels **Times:** 12.30-2/7.30-9.30
Notes: Vegetarian available, Dress Restrictions, Jacket and tie, Civ Wed
200 **Seats:** 250, Pr/dining room 100 **Smoking:** N/Sm in restaurant, Air
con **Children:** Menu, Portions **Directions:** M5 junct 27 onto A361
towards Braunton, left onto B3231 Sauntons rd. **Parking:** 10
e-mail: reservations@sauntonsands.com
web: www.sauntonsands.com

SIDMOUTH MAP 03 SY18

Riviera Hotel

British, French

Fine Regency hotel dining with sea views
☎ 01395 515201 The Esplanade EX10 8AY

MENU GUIDE Confit duck rillette • Pan-fried guinea fowl with
Savoy cabbage • Hot chocolate fondant with cherry compote

WINE GUIDE ♀ Brown Brothers Sauvignon Blanc
£17.13 • ♀ Château Latour de By 1999 £26.21 • 36 bottles over
£20, 38 bottles under £20 • 4 by the glass

PRICE GUIDE Starter £8.50-£12 • main £20.50-£28 • dessert £6-
£6.95 • coffee £2.15 • min/water £3.70

PLACE: An elegant, white Regency building overlooking Lyme
Bay, with a chintzy dining room and a lovely terrace that's tailor-
made for summer dining. Staff are well-drilled and customer-
focused, and the restaurant is run by a dedicated team – front of
house and in the kitchen.
FOOD: The modern British menu changes daily according to the
market, and there is a good use of local ingredients: John Dory is
served with creamed leeks and spinach with a crab risotto, and a
selection of West Country truckles dominates the cheeseboard.
OUR TIP: Sunny terrace great for alfresco lunches
Chef: Matthew Weaver **Owners:** Peter Wharton **Times:** 12.30-2/7-9
Notes: Fixed L 5 courses £22, Fixed D 6 courses £34, Vegetarian
available, Smart casual **Seats:** 85, Pr/dining room 65 **Smoking:** N/Sm in
restaurant, Air con **Children:** Menu, Portions **Rooms:** 27 (27 en suite)
★★★★ **Directions:** From M5 junct 30 take A3052 to Sidmouth.
Situated in centre of Esplanade **Parking:** 26
e-mail: enquiries@hotelriviera.co.uk **web:** www.hotelriviera.co.uk

The Salty Monk

British, Mediterranean

*Enjoyable modern cooking in historic
surroundings*
☎ 01395 513174 Church St, Sidford EX10 9QP

continued

England

England

SIDMOUTH continued MAP 03 SY18

MENU GUIDE Foie gras terrine, Melba toast • Griddled beef, braised brisket, creamed potatoes • Honey & vanilla pannacotta

WINE GUIDE ♀ Montes Sauvignon Blanc £15.75 • ♀ Dalwood Cabernet Shiraz £11.50 • 17 bottles over £20, 31 bottles under £20 • 7 by the glass (£3.55)

PRICE GUIDE Fixed L £16.50 • Fixed D £30 • Service optional

PLACE: This delightful restaurant with rooms was originally used as a salt house by the Benedictine monks who traded salt at nearby Exeter Cathedral. Dinner is served in a tasteful extension to the 16th-century building, or alfresco in a pretty courtyard.
FOOD: The hotel's owners double as chefs, delivering a straightforward menu of enjoyable modern British dishes, such as maize-fed chicken with a cherry tomato dressing, or duck with a chickpea and chorizo cassoulet.
OUR TIP: Cream tea in the courtyard
Chef: Annette & Andy Witheridge **Owners:** Annette & Andy Witheridge **Times:** 12-1.30/7-9, Closed 2 wks Jan, 2 wks Nov **Notes:** Mineral water & coffee incl., Vegetarian available, Dress Restrictions, Smart casual **Seats:** 55, Pr/dining room 14 **Smoking:** N/Sm in restaurant **Children:** Portions **Rooms:** 5 (5 en suite) ◆◆◆◆ **Directions:** From M5 junct 30 take A3052 to Sidmouth, or from Honiton take A375 to Sidmouth, left at lights in Sidford, 200yds on right **Parking:** 18 **e-mail:** saltymonk@btconnect.com **web:** www.saltymonk.co.uk

Victoria Hotel
Traditional
British seaside hotel dining at its best
☎ 01395 512651 The Esplanade EX10 8RY
PLACE: Imposing Victorian building, with manicured grounds overlooking Sidmouth town and the sea beyond.
FOOD: Professional and friendly staff attend to diners in the refined atmosphere of the restaurant, where you can sample classically based cooking, with a daily changing set menu and carte supplement.
OUR TIP: The elegant lounges overlook the sea and town
Times: 7-9 **Rooms:** 61 (61 en suite) ★★★★ **Directions:** At the western end of The Esplanade **e-mail:** info@victoriahotel.co.uk **web:** www.victoriahotel.co.uk

SOUTH BRENT MAP 03 SX66
Glazebrook House Hotel & Restaurant
British ⚔NEW
Intimate dining in relaxing Dartmoor hotel
☎ 01364 73322 TQ10 9JE
MENU GUIDE Thai crab cakes, sweet chilli sauce • Chargrilled turbot, tomato & basil dressing • Caramelised citrus tart, soft fruit coulis

WINE GUIDE ♀ Sharpham Phoenix and Kernling, Madeleine Angevine £11 • ♀ Ngatarawa Merlot Cabernet £15.95 • 3 bottles over £20, 30 bottles under £20 • 8 by the glass (£3)

PRICE GUIDE Fixed D £19.50 • starter £4.50-£6.50 • main £16.50-£20.50 • dessert £4.50 • coffee £1.95 • min/water £2 • Service optional

PLACE: A delightful 18th-century former gentleman's residence set in beautiful gardens on the southern flanks of Dartmoor. The elegant, candlelit restaurant is intimate and relaxing, and the service is friendly and informal.
FOOD: The menu uses the best of local produce to create imaginative and well-balanced dishes. Cooking is unfussy but accurate and presentation is straightforward.

continued

OUR TIP: Perfect for getting away from it all
Chef: David Merriman **Owners:** Mr & Mrs Davey **Times:** 12-2/7-9, Closed 1 wk Jan, 1 wk Aug, Sun **Notes:** Vegetarian available, Smart Dress, Civ Wed 80 **Seats:** 60, Pr/dining room 12 **Smoking:** N/Sm in restaurant **Children:** Portions **Rooms:** 10 (10 en suite) ★★ **Directions:** From A38, between Ivybridge and Buckfastleigh, follow 'Hotel' signs to South Brent. **Parking:** 30 **e-mail:** enquiries@glazebrookhouse.com **web:** www.glazebrookhouse.com

SOUTH MOLTON MAP 03 SS72
 The Corn Dolly 115a East St EX36 3DB
☎ 01769 574249 Winner of The Tea Guild Award of Excellence 2005.

STAVERTON MAP 03 SX76
Sea Trout Inn
British
Ever popular Dart Valley inn
☎ 01803 762274 TQ9 6PA
MENU GUIDE Chicken, saffron & baby leek terrine • Poached fillet of halibut, fresh samphire • Milk chocolate tartlet, mint clotted cream

PRICE GUIDE Food prices not confirmed for 2006. Please telephone for details

PLACE: A charming 15th-century country inn, very popular with locals and visitors alike. Restaurant menu is available in the conservatory Friday and Saturday nights only, with a simpler menu in the bar.
FOOD: Ambitious kitchen striving to impress, with competent use of good quality local produce. Unfussy combinations with an emphasis on flavour, this is neat cooking with no unnecessary flamboyance.
OUR TIP: Great for fishing on the River Dart
Times: 12-2.30/7-9, Closed L Mon-Sat **Rooms:** 10 (10 en suite) ★★ **Directions:** From A38 follow A384 at Buckfastleigh (Dart Bridge) and proceed to Staverton. **e-mail:** enquiries@seatroutinn.com **web:** www.seatroutinn.com

TEIGNMOUTH MAP 03 SX97
Ness House Hotel
European
Seafront hotel with stunning views and fresh local fare
☎ 01626 873480 Ness Dr, Shaldon TQ14 0HP

MENU GUIDE Sauté rabbit, passionfruit dressing • Pan-fried turbot, parsnip crust, watercress sauce • Chocolate soufflé, white chocolate sorbet

continued

WINE GUIDE ♀ Moreau Chardonnay £12.50 • ♥ Concha y Toro Merlot £12.50 • 15 bottles over £20, 40 bottles under £20 • 12 by the glass (£3.15-£3.95)

PRICE GUIDE Fixed L £27.50 • Fixed D £27.50 • coffee £1.55 • min/water £2.50 • Group min 10

PLACE: Colonial-style Georgian mansion, built for Lord Clifford of Chudleigh in the village of Shaldon, overlooking the Teign Estuary. There are memorable sea views from the elegant Terrace Restaurant, where a gentle but formal atmosphere is maintained. **FOOD:** Well-sourced ingredients, accurate cooking and seasonality add up to appealing dishes with plenty of interest. Full advantage is taken of Teign seafood and quality West Country produce.

OUR TIP: Beautiful secluded beach to relax on **Chef:** Dirk Doose **Owners:** P Reynolds **Times:** 12-2.15/6-10, Closed 24-25 Dec **Notes:** Vegetarian available, Smart Dress **Seats:** 40 **Smoking:** N/Sm in restaurant **Children:** Menu, Portions **Rooms:** 12 (12 en suite) ★★★ **Directions:** M5/A380 onto A381 to Teignmouth, cross bridge to Shaldon and turn left, follow hotel signs **Parking:** 20 **e-mail:** nesshouse@talk21.com **web:** www.nesshouse.co.uk

THURLESTONE MAP 03 SX64

⊙ Thurlestone Hotel

British, European

Straightforward fare in well-established seaside hotel

☎ 01548 560382   TQ7 3NN

MENU GUIDE Sea bass, watercress & red chilli pesto • Steak, bordelaise potatoes, thyme scented gravy • Iced orange & grapefruit parfait, honeyed figs

WINE GUIDE ♀ Excelsior Sauvignon Blanc £15.95 • ♥ Curnellana Merlot £16.50 • 110 bottles over £20, 38 bottles under £20 • 9 by the glass (£3-£5)

PRICE GUIDE Fixed L £18 • Fixed D £32 • coffee £2.30 • min/water £3.50 • Service optional

PLACE: Owned by the same family since 1896, this veteran seaside hotel has acquired an extensive range of leisure facilities over the years, including indoor and outdoor pools, a beauty salon and golf course. Its elegant restaurant has long picture windows that take full advantage of the beautiful coastal scenery. **FOOD:** The menu changes daily, featuring traditional offerings in keeping with the setting. A lighter lunch selection is available on the terrace.

OUR TIP: Poolside barbecues in season **Chef:** David Bunn **Owners:** Grose family **Times:** 12.30-2.30/7.30-9, closed L Mon-Sat **Notes:** Sun L £18, Vegetarian available, Dress restrictions, Jacket, Civ Wed 150 **Seats:** 150, Pr/dining room 150 **Smoking:** N/Sm in restaurant, Air con **Children:** Menu, Portions **Rooms:** 64 (64 en suite) ★★★★ **Directions:** At Buckfastleigh on A38, take A384 into Totnes and then A381 (Kingsbridge). Continue for 10m then turn right at mini rdbt onto A379 towards Churchstow, turn left at rdbt onto B3197, then turn right into lane signposted Thurlestone. **Parking:** 120 **e-mail:** enquiries@thurlestone.co.uk **web:** www.thurlestone.co.uk

---

One Rosette Excellent local restaurants serving food prepared with care, understanding and skill, using good quality ingredients. These restaurants stand out in their local area. Of the total number of establishments with Rosettes around 50% have one Rosette.

TORQUAY MAP 03 SX96

◉◉ Corbyn Head Hotel & Orchid Restaurant

British, French

Superb views combined with superlative cooking

☎ 01803 296366 Sea Front TQ2 6RH

MENU GUIDE Salmon, beetroot sorbet, horseradish cream • Beef fillet, oxtail bourguignon, cep foam • Lemongrass crème brûlée

WINE GUIDE ♀ Errazuriz Sauvignon Blanc £14.85 • ♥ Oxford Landing Shiraz £14.85 • 39 bottles over £20, 54 bottles under £20 • 12 by the glass (£3.50-£4.95)

PRICE GUIDE Fixed L £19.95-£34.90 • Fixed D £25-£37.95 • starter £5.95-£11.95 • main £17.95-£22.95 • dessert £6.95-£8.75 • coffee £3.50 • min/water £3.50 • Service optional

PLACE: Now refurbished in contemporary style, this smart modern restaurant offers stunning views over Torbay. It's the more formal of two restaurants at the Corbyn, with lighter fare on offer in the Harbour View dining room. **FOOD:** Uncomplicated modern cuisine, created from quality organic produce where possible. Kick off with curried cauliflower soup, or foie gras ballotine, before tucking into unusual mains such as turbot with cured belly pork, a langoustine beignet and red wine vinaigrette.

OUR TIP: Bar overlooking the bay ideal for pre-dinner drinks and canapés **Chef:** Daniel Kay/Marc Evans **Owners:** Rew Hotels Ltd **Times:** 12.30-2.30/7-9.30, Closed 2 wks Jan, 2 wks Nov, Sun-Mon **Notes:** Vegetarian available, Dress Restrictions, Formal dress. No trainers **Seats:** 24 **Smoking:** N/Sm in restaurant, Air con **Children:** Min 6yrs, Portions **Rooms:** 44 (44 en suite) ★★★ **Directions:** Follow signs to Torquay seafront, turn R, hotel on R on the edge of Cockington Valley **Parking:** 50 **e-mail:** dine@orchidrestaurant.net **web:** www.orchidrestaurant.net

The Elephant Bar & Restaurant

Modern British, European   NEW

One to watch

☎ 01803 200044 3/4 Beacon Ter TQ1 2BH

MENU GUIDE Warm salad of skate & smoked pigeon • Sea bass, truffled Savoy cabbage, scampi tortellini • Wild berry & champagne jelly

WINE GUIDE ♀ Montes Currico Valley Sauvignon Blanc £13.50 • ♀ Salisbury Shiraz £13.50 • 16 bottles over £20, 24 bottles under £20 • 26 by the glass (£3.50-£9.50)

PRICE GUIDE Fixed L fr £12.50 • starter £7-£9 • main £12-£20 • dessert £4.50-£6 • coffee £1.60 • min/water £2.25 • Service optional • Group min 8 service 10%

PLACE: Smart contemporary restaurant with an upbeat atmosphere and growing reputation for great food. Carved elephants nestle among the potted palms of the ground floor restaurant, with its smartly clothed tables and blue leather chairs, while upstairs, deep sofas beckon, offering views of the bustling harbour.

FOOD: The Elephant has a chef with a strong pedigree at the helm and is aiming for greater things. This is confident and accomplished cooking, the menu offering such contemporary concoctions as pork with a langoustine and squid risotto, or beef with a honey and onion compote and smoked garlic purée.

OUR TIP: Eat upstairs in the bar for a more informal setting

Chef: Simon Hulstone **Owners:** Peter Morgan, Rose & Mark Ashton, Frederike Etessami **Times:** 11.30/6.30-9.30 **Seats:** 65, Pr/dining room 25 **Smoking:** N/Sm in restaurant, Air con **Children:** Portions **Parking:** Opposite **e-mail:** elephant@orestone.co.uk **web:** www.elephantrestaurant.co.uk

Grand Hotel

British, International

Enjoyable dining with wonderful coastal views

☎ 01803 296677 Sea Front TQ2 6NT

MENU GUIDE Lobster & crab tian, saffron mayonnaise • Tournedos Rossini, spinach • Strawberry & champagne trio

WINE GUIDE ♀ Houghton Chardonnay £18.95 • ♀ Houghton Shiraz £18.95 • 21 bottles over £20, 32 bottles under £20 • 6 by the glass (£4.95-£6.65)

PRICE GUIDE Fixed L £7.50-£12.50 • Fixed D £27.95-£37.95 • starter £4.95-£8 • main £6.95-£10 • min/water £3.50 • Service included

PLACE: Within easy walking distance of the town, this large Edwardian hotel overlooks the bay. There are also good views from the Boaters' Bar; a less formal alternative to the recently grandly refurbished Gainsborough Restaurant.

FOOD: Modern and traditional dishes share this menu. There's an emphasis on local Devon ingredients as well as local fish. Dishes are prepared with skill.

OUR TIP: Try the Compass Lounge for afternoon tea

Chef: Wayne Maddern **Owners:** Richardson Hotels **Times:** 12.30-2/7-9.30, Closed L Mon-Sat **Notes:** Coffee included, Vegetarian available, Smart casual, no jeans or trainers, Civ Wed 300 **Seats:** 180, Pr/dining room 200 **Smoking:** N/Sm in restaurant **Children:** Menu, Portions **Rooms:** 114 (114 en suite) ★★★★ **Directions:** A380 to Torquay sea front, hotel immediately on right. **Parking:** 20 **e-mail:** info@grandtorquay.co.uk **web:** www.richardsonhotels.co.uk

Orestone Manor Hotel & Restaurant

Modern British

Modern cooking in a colonial atmosphere

☎ 01803 328098 Rockhouse Ln, Maidencombe TQ1 4SX

WINE GUIDE 112 bottles over £20, 23 bottles under £20 • 8 by the glass (£3.25-£4.25)

PRICE GUIDE Fixed L £14.95 • starter £6.95-£12.50 • main £16.50-£24 • dessert £7.95 • coffee £1.60 • min/water £2.25 • Service optional • Group min 8 service 10%

PLACE: This privately-owned country house hotel is tucked away in well-tended gardens on the fringes of Torbay, overlooking Lyme Bay. The restaurant recalls colonial days with its green palms, loom chairs and wooden floors. The Georgian house also has connections with Victorian engineer Isambard Kingdom Brunel, who held parties here in the mid 19th century.

FOOD: As the guide goes to press, Darren Button and his team have just taken responsibility for the kitchen here. This happened too late to reflect the changes but we are excited about the future.

OUR TIP: Non-residents should book in advance

Chef: Darren Button **Owners:** Peter Morgan, Rose & Mark Ashton, Frederike Etessami **Times:** 12-2.30/7-9 **Notes:** Vegetarian available, Dress Restrictions, No jeans **Seats:** 65, Pr/dining room 18 **Smoking:** N/Sm in restaurant **Children:** Min 7yrs, Menu, Portions **Rooms:** 12 (12 en suite) ★★★ **Directions:** From Teignmouth take A379, through Shaldon towards Torquay. 3m take sharp L into Rockhouse Lane. Hotel signed **Parking:** 40 **e-mail:** enquiries@orestone.co.uk **web:** www.orestone.co.uk

Hanburys Princes St, Babbacombe TQ1 3LW
☎ 01803 314616 Popular fish restaurant.

No 7 Fish Bistro Beacon Ter, Inner Harbour TQ1 2BH ☎ 01803 295055 Deliciously simple treatment of local fish in family-run bistro near the harbour.

Restaurant 2-18 135 Babbacombe Rd, Babbacombe TQ1 3SR ☎ 01803 322664 An intimate and relaxed atmosphere with a serious approach to traditional dishes.

TOTNES MAP 03 SX86

Effings
Modern International
Simple modern cooking at a friendly deli
☎ 01803 863435 50 Fore St TQ9 5RP
MENU GUIDE Mushroom & mascarpone pancakes • Salmon salad, potato, apple, poached quail egg, fennel dressing • Soufflé crêpes, orange & Grand Marnier sauce
WINE GUIDE ♀ Château L'Etoile 2002 Semillion/Sauvignon Blanc £13.75 • ♀ Salento Tenute San Marco Primitivo £13.75 3 bottles over £20, 8 bottles under £20 • 2 by the glass (£3.75)
PRICE GUIDE Starter £5.25-£7.95 • main £10.95-£24.50 • dessert £5.25-£7.50 • coffee £1.25 • min/water £2.50 • Service optional
PLACE: There's a real passion for food at this chirpy little deli, which offers lunch at a handful of wooden tables at the back of the shop. Take a seat beneath the hanging panettone and enjoy the show.
FOOD: Giving the setting an emphasis on simple antipasto dishes is no surprise, but there's also a concise menu of more complex options, such as a duck breast salad with orange and pickled ginger. The style is unfussy and robust, and there are home-made meals to go if lunch leaves you wanting more.
OUR TIP: Stock up at the deli on the way out
Chef: Karl Rasmussen, Karen Miller **Owners:** Michael Kann, Jacqueline Williams **Times:** 9.30-5, Closed BHs, Sun, closed D Mon-Sat
Notes: Vegetarian available **Seats:** 14 **Smoking:** N/Sm in restaurant, Air con **Children:** Portions **Directions:** From A38 (Exeter to Plymouth) follow signs for Totnes, then for town centre and car parks. Restaurant located approx 100mtrs below Eastgate Arch. **Parking:** on street
e-mail: info@effings.co.uk

TWO BRIDGES MAP 03 SX67

Prince Hall Hotel
British, Mediterranean
Quality cooking in comfortable Dartmoor hotel
☎ 01822 890403 PL20 6SA

MENU GUIDE Pigeon, sloe gin & juniper jus • Pan-fried steak, Devon blue cheese & bacon sauce • Crème brûlée, raspberry coulis
WINE GUIDE ♀ Domaine Serge Laporte Sancerre £23 • ♀ Domaine St George Côtes du Rhône £17.25 • 27 bottles over £20, 30 bottles under £20 • 4 by the glass (£3.75-£4.50)
PRICE GUIDE Fixed D £40 • coffee £2.75 • min/water £3 Service optional

PLACE: Set in the heart of Dartmoor, this country house hotel is a cosy place to relax after a day's walking. Fresh flowers and bold artwork liven up the intimate, stonewalled restaurant.
FOOD: A concise menu offers three choices at each course, plus a daily special. It's the quality of the ingredients that impress, with dishes along the lines of roast guinea fowl with a wild berry and port wine sauce. Dinner only.
OUR TIP: Find time for a walk - the hotel can arrange guides
Chef: Les Pratt, Anne Grove **Owners:** John & Anne Grove **Times:** 7-9, Closed Jan-early Feb, closed L Mon-Sun **Notes:** Fixed D 5 courses £40, Vegetarian available, Dress Restrictions, Smart casual preferred **Seats:** 24 **Smoking:** N/Sm in restaurant **Children:** Min 10 yrs **Rooms:** 8 (8 en suite) ★★ **Directions:** Located on B3357 (Ashburton to Tavistock road), 1m E of Two Bridges junction with B3212 **Parking:** 12
e-mail: info@princehall.co.uk **web:** www.princehall.co.uk

WINKLEIGH MAP 03 SS60

Pophams
British
The ultimate in intimate dining experiences
☎ 01837 83767 Castle St EX19 8HQ
PLACE: Red-tiled floors, walls lined with photos of old film stars and just enough space for three dining tables - how is that for a snug restaurant? Pophams is run as a two-hand act, finely honed over 18 years. Service is chatty, friendly and relaxed, with meals served at a leisurely pace. No wonder, eating here always feels like a special occasion. Limited opening hours.
FOOD: The menu is simple and very short - however the great care and attention with which everything is prepared, using mostly local produce, more than makes up for it.
OUR TIP: Bring your own wine - it is encouraged
Times: 11.30-3.00, Closed D Mon-Sun, Sat-Wed, Feb

WOODBURY MAP 03 SY08

Woodbury Park Hotel & Golf Country Club
British   **NEW**
Careful cooking in golfers' paradise
☎ 01395 233382 Woodbury Castle EX5 1JJ
PLACE: Impressive modern hotel with two golf courses and stunning views across 500 acres of unspoilt countryside. The Atrium restaurant has a high glass roof, marble floors and well spaced tables with very comfortable chairs. Service is fairly formal.
FOOD: A modern approach makes great use of high quality, local produce. Presentation is simple, with no unnecessary frills. For example, the duck liver parfait is smooth and intensely flavoured, with a good contrast provided by red onion marmalade. Or new season roasted lamb rack, beautifully tender and served with a rosemary and redcurrant sauce.
OUR TIP: More casual eating is available in the Clubhouse
Times: 12-3.30/6.30-9.30 **Rooms:** 57 (57 en suite) ★★★★
e-mail: enquiries@woodburypark.co.uk **web:** www.woodburypark.co.uk

continued

England

WOOLACOMBE MAP 03 SS44
◉ Watersmeet Hotel
European
Modern cooking in welcoming hotel overlooking the sea
☎ 01271 870333 Mortehoe EX34 7EB

MENU GUIDE Seared scallops, lemon butter sauce, asparagus • Lamb, minted Madeira sauce, dauphinoise potato • Lemon soufflé, red berries

PRICE GUIDE Fixed L £12.95 • Fixed D £33 • min/water £3

PLACE: This popular hotel offers splendid views across Woolacombe Bay to Lundy Island from its elegant split-level restaurant.

FOOD: An imaginative range of modern dishes that stretches from lighter mains along the lines of John Dory with a green pea velouté, to more innovative fare such as sugar-roast duckling with couscous and blackberry sauce.

OUR TIP: Book a window table

Chef: John Prince **Owners:** Mr & Mrs James **Times:** 12-2.15/7-8.30, closed L all week **Notes:** Vegetarian available, Dress Restrictions, Jacket & tie preferred **Seats:** 50 **Smoking:** N/Sm in restaurant **Children:** Min 8 yrs, Portions **Rooms:** 25 (25 en suite) ★★★ **Directions:** M5 junct 27. Follow A361 to Woolacombe, right at beach car park, 300yds on right. **Parking:** 40 **e-mail:** info@watersmeethotel.co.uk **web:** www.watersmeethotel.co.uk

 denotes restaurants that place particular emphasis on making the most of local ingredients.

NEW
denotes a restaurant which is new to the guide this year.

DORSET

BEAMINSTER MAP 04 ST40
◉◉ Bridge House Hotel
British
Country cooking in historic setting
☎ 01308 862200 3 Prout Bridge DT8 3AY

MENU GUIDE Spicy smoked haddock & saffron soup • Beef Wellington, winter vegetables, red wine jus • Plum frangipane

WINE GUIDE ♀ Pasqua Pinot Grigio £12.50 • ♀ Neblina Merlot £12.50 • 25 bottles over £20, 41 bottles under £20 • 10 by the glass (£2.90-£3.50)

PRICE GUIDE Fixed L £12.75 • Fixed D £31.50 • starter £6.50-£9.25 • main £20-£24 • dessert £6.50-£8.50 • coffee £2.50 • Service optional • Group min 10 service 10%

PLACE: Dating back to the 13th century, this Beaminster landmark is heavy on historic charm, boasting inglenook fireplaces and mullioned windows, as well as a walled garden and hidden priest's hole.

FOOD: No fuss, no pretension - just honest country cooking created from quality ingredients. Typical mains might include beef in a Chianti wine sauce with white Tuscan beans, or venison with red cabbage and a potato and apple gratin.

OUR TIP: Good value three-course lunch menu

Chef: Mrs Linda Paget **Owners:** Mark and Joanna Donovan **Times:** 12-2/7-9, Closed 30-31 Dec, closed L Mon-Tue **Notes:** Sun roast available, Vegetarian available, Smart Dress **Seats:** 36, Pr/dining room 30 **Smoking:** N/Sm in restaurant **Children:** Portions **Rooms:** 14 (14 en suite) ★★★ **Directions:** From A303 take A356 towards Dorchester. Turn right onto A3066, 200mtrs down hill from town centre **Parking:** 20 **e-mail:** enquiries@bridge-house.co.uk **web:** www.bridge-house.co.uk

BLANDFORD FORUM MAP 04 ST80
◉ Castleman Hotel
Modern British
Pleasant country hotel with good value food
☎ 01258 830096 Chettle DT11 8DB

MENU GUIDE Crab, prawn & lobster bisque • Medallions of venison haunch with bacon, mushrooms, port & cream • Pear frangipane tart

PRICE GUIDE Food prices not confirmed for 2006. Please telephone for details

PLACE: The long airy dining room of this country house hotel, a period property on the edge of a large estate, has soft yellow walls, indigo curtains and crisp white table linen. The large windows have pleasant views of the gardens and the fields beyond.

continue

FOOD: Modern touches have been given to classic British dishes. The seasonal menu features food which is based on local produce wherever possible.
OUR TIP: Perfect for a weekend break
Times: 12/7, Closed Feb, closed L Mon-Sat **Directions:** 1 mile from A354. Hotel is signposted in village **e-mail:** chettle@globalnet.co.uk
web: www.castlemanhotel.co.uk

BOURNEMOUTH MAP 05 SZ09

Bistro on the Beach
Modern British
Popular seaside bistro
☎ 01202 431473 Solent Promenade, Southbourne Coast Rd, Southbourne BH6 4BE

MENU GUIDE Scallops & tiger prawns, lemongrass, ginger butter • Veal, pancetta, emmental, red wine jus • Rum & raisin crème brûlée

WINE GUIDE ♀ Neblina Sauvignon Blanc £13.50 • ♂ Neblina Merlot £13.50 • 13 bottles over £20, 22 bottles under £20 • 6 by the glass (£3-£3.35)

PRICE GUIDE Fixed D £18.95 • starter £4.25-£8.95 • main £9.95-£18.95 • dessert £4.50-£6.25 • coffee £1.30 • min/water £2.75 • Service optional

PLACE: Just a short paddle from the water's edge, this beach-side café has a long glass frontage that makes the most of the stunning views. It's popular with all ages, particularly in summer.
FOOD: Lots of fresh fish, as you'd expect, but a well-balanced modern menu offers plenty of choice, from Dover sole with lemon and parsley butter to wild mushroom risotto. A range of steaks should keep the carnivores happy too.
OUR TIP: Book ahead for a window table
Chef: Matt Dean **Owners:** Sheila Ryan **Times:** 6.30-12, Closed L Mon-Sun, closed D Sun-Mon **Notes:** Vegetarian available, Smart casual **Seats:** 67 **Smoking:** N/Sm in restaurant, Air con **Children:** Menu, Portions **Directions:** From Bournemouth take coast road to East Cliff, at lights right, then right again. Join overcliff. 1m to mini rdbt, take 2nd turn. 400yds to car park. **Parking:** Public car park nearby, on street **e-mail:** bistroonthebeach@tiscali.co.uk **web:** www.bistroonthebeach.co.uk

Chine Hotel
International
Seaside hotel with views and a range of flavours
☎ 01202 396234 Boscombe Spa Rd BH5 1AX
MENU GUIDE Ham hock terrine • Grilled fillet of red mullet • Dark chocolate tart

WINE GUIDE ♀ Crusan Blanc £13.50 • ♂ Crusan Rouge £13.50 • 31 bottles over £20, 36 bottles under £20 • 6 by the glass (£3.60-£6)

Chine Hotel

PRICE GUIDE Fixed L £12.50 • Fixed D £24.95-£34.95 • coffee £1.80 • min/water £3 • Service optional
PLACE: Huge windows allow the breathtaking sea and garden views to be enjoyed throughout this large restaurant, and friendly staff understand the true essence of hospitality.
FOOD: Influences ranging from classical French cuisine to the spices of Thailand are responsible for the eclectic appearance of the menu, including tournedos of beef with a peppercorn sauce, and Barbary duck breast with stir-fried vegetables and plum sauce. Competent cooking pulls it all off safely.
OUR TIP: Beautiful gardens for summer months
Chef: Chris Wyburn-Risdale **Owners:** Brownsea Haven Properties Ltd **Times:** 12.30-2/7-9, Closed L Sat **Notes:** Seasonal supplements available in addition to menu, Vegetarian available, Dress Restrictions, No jeans, T-shirts or trainers at D, Civ Wed 130 **Seats:** 160, Pr/dining room 130 **Smoking:** N/Sm in restaurant **Children:** Menu, Portions **Rooms:** 87 (87 en suite) ★★★ **Directions:** From M27, A31 and A338 follow signs to Boscombe Pier, Boscombe Spa Rd is off Christchurch Rd near Boscombe Gardens **Parking:** 67 **e-mail:** reservations@chinehotel.co.uk **web:** www.chinehotel.co.uk

Langtry Restaurant
British
Edwardian romance and contemporary cooking
☎ 01202 553887 Langtry Manor, 26 Derby Rd, East Cliff BH1 3QB
MENU GUIDE Dorset crab chowder • Confit sea bass, vanilla bean risotto, sauce vièrge • Orange & lemon soufflé

PRICE GUIDE Food prices not confirmed for 2006. Please telephone for details

PLACE: Brimming with history and original features, this property was originally built in 1877 by Edward VII for his mistress Lillie Langtry. The magnificent dining hall features a minstrel's gallery, stained glass windows and large tapestries. Charming service by staff in period costume.

continued   *continued*

BOURNEMOUTH *continued* MAP 05 SZ09

FOOD: Daily fixed-price menus offer plenty of choice and interest. Promising cooking from a chef who understands that a simple approach to quality ingredients will enhance rather than detract from the dish.
OUR TIP: Edwardian banquet on Saturday evenings
Times: 7, Closed 1st 2 wks Jan, closed L Mon-Sun **Rooms:** 20
(20 en suite) ★★★ **Directions:** On the East Cliff, at corner of Derby & Knyveton Roads **e-mail:** lillie@langtrymanor.com
web: www.langtrymanor.com

'Oscars' at the De Vere Royal Bath Hotel

British, French
Elegant dining in luxurious seaside hotel
☎ 01202 555555 Bath Rd BH1 2EW

MENU GUIDE Goats' cheese croustade, chilli butter • Monkfish, thyme mash, haddock tartar • Hot chocolate fondant pudding, banana & muscovado ice cream
WINE GUIDE ♀ Concha y Torro Sauvignon Blanc £18 • ♀ Concha y Torro Merlot £18 • 19 bottles under £20
PRICE GUIDE Fixed L fr £13.50 • Fixed D fr £32.50 • coffee £3 • min/water £3.50 • Service optional

PLACE: Bournemouth's first hotel, this seaside grandee was a regular haunt of Oscar Wilde, from whom the fine dining restaurant takes its name. It sits in beautifully kept gardens, not far from the conference centre, and boasts extensive indoor leisure facilities.
FOOD: Expect a menu of simple contemporary dishes: duck with red cabbage, broad bean and cider cream for example, or lemon sole with a chive and tomato butter. Good value fixed price lunch menus available.
OUR TIP: A good base for Bournemouth
Chef: Jonathan Wood **Owners:** De Vere Hotels **Times:** 12.30-2/7.30-9.30, Closed Mon, closed D Sun **Notes:** Vegetarian available, Dress Restrictions, Strictly no denim or sportswear, Civ Wed 200 **Seats:** 40
Smoking: N/Sm in restaurant, Air con **Children:** Min 16yrs, Portions
Rooms: 140 (140 en suite) ★★★★ **Directions:** Follow signs for Bournemouth Pier and beaches **Parking:** 95
e-mail: royal.bath@devere-hotels.com
web: www.devereroyalbath.co.uk

 denotes a restaurant with a particularly good wine list.

The AA Wine Awards recognise the finest wine lists in England, Scotland and Wales. For full details, see pages 14-15

Saint Michel

British, French
Stylish hotel brasserie
☎ 01202 315716 Bournemouth Highcliff Marriott, Saint Michael's Rd BH2 5DU

MENU GUIDE Crab with mango, coriander & lime salsa • Crispy duck • Steamed ginger pudding
WINE GUIDE ♀ Valle Andino Sauvignon Blanc £12.50 • ♀ La Diva Cabernet Merlot £12.50 • 34 bottles over £20, 15 bottles under £20 • 6 by the glass (£3-£4.50)
PRICE GUIDE Fixed L £14 • Fixed D £17.50 • starter £5.50-£8.50 • main £14.50-£16.50 • dessert £4.95-£5.95 • coffee £1.50 • min/water £2.50 • Service optional

PLACE: Part of the Highcliff Marriott Hotel, a brasserie-style restaurant with distinctive ceiling fans and large potted plants. Very subdued evening lighting dictates an intimate atmosphere.
FOOD: Fresh fish features prominently on the menu along with other carefully prepared and enjoyable dishes. Presentation is attractively colourful, with the carte and fixed-price menus offering plenty of variety.
OUR TIP: Enjoy a clifftop walk after your meal
Chef: Mark Hasell **Owners:** Mr Kralj **Times:** 12-2/6-9.30, Closed L Sat, closed D Sun **Notes:** Vegetarian available **Seats:** 70, Pr/dining room 30
Smoking: N/Sm in restaurant **Children:** Menu, Portions
Directions: Travel towards Bournemouth Pier, turn left at mini-rdbt. Up Poole Hill then take second left and Saint Michel is situated directly behind Highcliff Marriott Hotel at end of St Michael's Rd. **Parking:** 10

West Beach

British, French
AA Seafood Restaurant of the Year for England
☎ 01202 587785 Pier Approach BH2 5AA

MENU GUIDE Spinach, roquefort, quail salad • Baked cod, Savoy cabbage, chorizo • Baked figs, pecan nuts, honey

continued

England

West Beach

WINE GUIDE ♀ Oveja Negra Chardonnay/Viognier 2004 £16.95 ♀ Michel Laroche Unoaked Grenache 2003 £16.95 40 bottles over £20, 22 bottles under £20 • 8 by the glass (£2.95-£6)

PRICE GUIDE Starter £5-£12 • main £10.95-£75 • dessert £3.50-£7 • coffee £1.75 • min/water £3 • Service optional • Group min 16 service 10%

PLACE: Buzzy, beachfront restaurant with great bay and pier views. Big glass frontage, smart wooden flooring and furniture give a contemporary ambience. The kitchen is open plan so diners can watch the food being freshly prepared.
FOOD: The daily changing menu focuses around high quality fish and seafood (Scottish rope-grown mussels, line caught Mudeford sea bass) which is delivered on a daily basis from Newlyn, Brixham and Billingsgate markets. Regular dishes on the menu include classics such as Moules marinières and rock oysters, with favourite dishes like West Beach fish soup, chargrilled tuna and salmon fishcakes.
OUR TIP: Enjoy alfresco dining on the decking on the beach
Chef: Greg Etheridge **Owners:** Andrew Price **Times:** 12-6/6-10, Closed 25 Dec, closed D 26 Dec-1 Jan **Notes:** Vegetarian available **Seats:** 90 **Smoking:** N/Sm area, Air con **Children:** Menu, Portions
Directions: 100yds W of the pier **Parking:** Restaurant parking evening only; NCP 2mins **web:** www.west-beach.co.uk

BRIDPORT MAP 04 SY49
⊛ Riverside Restaurant
Seafood
Good seafood dining in relaxed island setting
☎ 01308 422011 West Bay DT6 4EZ

MENU GUIDE Seared scallops, pea purée • Poached turbot fillet, mustard & lemon butter sauce • Chocolate fondant
WINE GUIDE ♀ Vartan Sancerre £21.75 • 20 bottles over £20, 55 bottles under £20 • 6 by the glass (£2.50-£4)
PRICE GUIDE Fixed L £13 • starter £4.25-£8.95 • main £10.50-£27.50 • dessert £4-£5.50 • coffee £1.50 • min/water £2.75 • Service optional • Group min 6 service 10%

continued

PLACE: This restaurant is in an unusual island setting. Originally a café and shops, it was redesigned by Piers Gough as a modern dining venue with wooden floors, scrubbed tables and a friendly, informal atmosphere.
FOOD: Local and seasonal are the important words here. Fresh seafood from the harbour is simply cooked and sauced in dishes such as grilled fillets of lemon sole with langoustine sauce. There are also vegetarian and meat dishes. Accurate, effective cooking and beautifully presented desserts.
OUR TIP: Great location for spotting water birds
Chef: Nic Larcombe, George Marsh **Owners:** Mr & Mrs A Watson **Times:** 12-2.30/6.30-9.00, Closed 1 Dec-mid Feb/Valentines Day, Mon (ex BHs), closed D Sun **Notes:** Vegetarian available **Seats:** 80, Pr/dining room 20 **Smoking:** N/Sm in restaurant **Children:** Menu, Portions
Directions: A35 Bridport ring road, turn to West Bay at Crown rdbt **Parking:** Public car park **e-mail:** artwatfish@hotmail.com **web:** thefishrestaurant-westbay.co.uk

CHIDEOCK MAP 04 SY49
⊛ Chideock House Hotel & Restaurant
British, French
Country house cooking in relaxed, rustic setting
☎ 01297 489242 Main St DT6 6JN

MENU GUIDE Spinach & cheddar soufflé • Pork fillet stuffed with prunes, port reduction • Fresh figues tarte fine
WINE GUIDE ♀ Bois d'Yever Chardonnay £23.95 • ♀ Masson Blondet Pinot Noir £24.95 • 22 bottles over £20, 26 bottles under £20 • 5 by the glass (£2.50-£3)
PRICE GUIDE Fixed L £14.95 • starter £3.95-£7.95 • main £13.50-£17.95 • dessert £4.50-£6.75 • coffee £2 • min/water £2 • Service optional

PLACE: Part-thatched and dating from the 15th century, this is the oldest building in the village and just a short walk from the sea. Original features abound in the cosy candlelit restaurant with its low oak beams and inglenook fireplace. Expect a friendly and relaxed atmosphere and attentive service.
FOOD: Unpretentious country-house cooking with French influences at its best; interesting dishes simply prepared using quality ingredients, and tasting wonderful.
OUR TIP: Magnificent Adam fireplace
Chef: Anna Dunn **Owners:** Anna Dunn **Times:** 12-2.30/7-9, Closed Jan, closed L Mon, closed D Sun, (ex residents) **Notes:** Sun L 3 courses £12.95, Vegetarian available, Smart Dress **Seats:** 32, Pr/dining room 16 **Smoking:** N/Sm in restaurant **Rooms:** 9 (8 en suite) ★★
Directions: 3m W of Bridport, on A35 in centre of village **Parking:** 20 **e-mail:** aa@chideockhousehotel.com **web:** www.chideockhousehotel.com

CHRISTCHURCH MAP 05 SZ19

The Avonmouth NEW

Inventive cuisine in quayside hotel restaurant

☎ 01202 483434 95 Mudeford BH23 3NT

MENU GUIDE Duck liver parfait, kumquat relish • Pan-roasted quail, fava beans, candied apples, white bean purée, Calvados sauce • Crème brûlée

PLACE: Built in the 1830s as a gentleman's residence, this elegant hotel offers picturesque views of Mudeford Quay and Christchurch harbour. Its Quays Restaurant is tastefully decorated in muted shades of green and blue.

FOOD: Expect an interesting mix of traditional options and more complex modern fare. An extensive selection features dishes such as salmon with a sorrel sauce, or lamb with a ratatouille mousse.

OUR TIP: Exclusive South African wines available from the hotel's vineyard in Stellenbosch

Times: 12-2.15/6.30-9.30 **e-mail:** info@avonmouth-hotel.co.uk
web: www.avonmouth-hotel.co.uk

Splinters Restaurant

International

Family-run restaurant in listed building

☎ 01202 483454 12 Church St BH23 1BW

MENU GUIDE Crab, avocado, salad, crab dressing • Roast lamb rump, rosemary & lemon marinade, herb jus • Raspberry brûlée, shortbread

WINE GUIDE ♀ Thomas Sancerre Sauvignon Blanc £25.95 • ♀ Daroze Fleurie Gamay £20.95 • 66 bottles over £20, 40 bottles under £20 • 4 by the glass (£3.40-£3.70)

PRICE GUIDE Fixed L £9.95 • Fixed D £24.95-£35.95 • coffee £2.95 • min/water £2.95 • Service included

PLACE: Run as a restaurant for 40 years, Splinters is part of Christchurch history. The building is 200 years old, tucked away in a cobbled street near the priory church. A reception area with raised tables for a bar meal or aperitif leads into two small rooms, one intimate with wooden booths and dimmed lighting, and the other open and contemporary.

FOOD: The modern menu presents a balanced choice, constructed with an eye for visual appeal. The cooking is assured, with some classic desserts on the value-for-money set menus.

OUR TIP: Individual rooms available for private dining
Chef: Paul Putt **Owners:** Paul and Agnes Putt **Times:** 11-2/7-10.00, Closed 26 Dec, 1 Jan, Sun-Mon **Notes:** Alc £28.95 (2 courses), £35.95 (3 courses), Vegetarian available **Seats:** 42, Pr/dining room 26 **Smoking:** N/Sm in restaurant **Children:** Portions **Directions:** Directly in front of Priory gates **e-mail:** eating@splinters.uk.com
web: www.splinters.uk.com

Waterford Lodge Hotel

British, French

Well-established seaside hotel serving inspirational dishes

☎ 01425 272948 87 Bure Ln, Friars Cliff, Mudeford BH23 4DN

MENU GUIDE Thai crab cakes • Fillet of beef, pesto-flavoured sauté potatoes • Glazed lemon tart, mascarpone cheese, fresh fruit

WINE GUIDE ♀ La Diva Chardonnay £12.50 • ♀ Penfolds Shiraz Cabernet £12.50 • 16 bottles over £20, 28 bottles under £20 3 by the glass (£2.75-£3.50)

PRICE GUIDE Fixed L £12.50-£15.50 • Fixed D £27.50-£29.50 coffee £1.75 • min/water £2.90 • Service optional

PLACE: Intimate, friendly and comfortable restaurant, with deep sofas and chairs and warm decor, located in what was once the lodge to Highcliffe Castle. The building has been extended and modernised to accommodate a hotel and restaurant, which attracts a loyal clientele.

FOOD: The modern British cooking is inspired by some good ideas, producing imaginative dishes that are always beautifully presented. Local produce sourced whenever possible.

OUR TIP: Leave room for the home-made bread and petits fours
Chef: Cedric Kerdranvat **Owners:** Michael & Vicki Harrison **Times:** 12-1.30/7-9 **Notes:** Vegetarian available, Dress Restrictions, No jeans, trainers or T-shirts **Seats:** 40, Pr/dining room 70 **Smoking:** N/Sm in restaurant **Children:** Min 7yrs, Menu, Portions **Rooms:** 18 (18 en suite) ★★★ **Directions:** A35 through Lyndhurst to Christchurch. Turn left onto A337. Follow signs to rdbt to Hotel. **Parking:** 36
e-mail: waterford@bestwestern.co.uk **web:** www.waterfordlodge.com

❦ The Ship in Distress 68 Stanpit BH23 3NA

☎ 01202 485123 Offers a varied and imaginative selection of fresh fish dishes.

CORFE CASTLE MAP 04 SY98

Mortons House Hotel

British, European

Notable dining in glorious Elizabethan surroundings

☎ 01929 480988 East St BH20 5EE

MENU GUIDE Feta & fig salad • Duck confit, verdina lentils, gingery greens • Walnut tart, crème anglaise

WINE GUIDE ♀ Andes Peak Sauvignon Blanc £16 • ♀ Andes Peak Merlot £16 • 68 bottles over £20, 11 bottles under £20 6 by the glass (£3.20-£3.80)

PRICE GUIDE Starter £5-£8 • main £15-£26.50 • dessert £4-£6 • coffee £2.50 • min/water £2.80 • Service optional • Group min 20 service 10%

PLACE: Overlooking the ruins of Corfe Castle and the nearby village, this impressive Tudor house was built in an E shape to honour Queen Elizabeth I. Beautifully updated and stylishly furnished, it retains traditional features like oak-panelling and open fireplaces. The dining room is well appointed with a serene ambience.

FOOD: Classical in style, the cooking here is technically assured with skilful handling of best quality local ingredients. Flavours are clear and strong, such as the lamb and basil terrine or the tuna with cod brandade, olives and sauce vièrge.

OUR TIP: Convenient for the Purbeck coastline
Chef: Derek Woods **Owners:** Mr & Mrs Hageman, Mr & Mrs Clayton **Times:** 12-2/7-9.30 **Notes:** Sun L £19.50, Vegetarian available, Dress Restrictions, Smart casual preferred, no denim, no shorts, Civ Wed 60

continued

England

FOOD: Owner Mac La Fosse (with wife Sue) is an accomplished chef with a host of international influences to his repertoire. His handwritten menus list some elaborate choices, like supreme of salmon with almond crust and champagne sauce.
OUR TIP: Look out for the excellent value meal deals
Chef: Mac La Fosse **Owners:** MJ & S La Fosse **Times:** 12-2/7-9.30, Closed Mon-Tue, Closed D Sun **Notes:** Sun Lunch 2 courses £15.50, Vegetarian available, Dress Restrictions, No shorts, T-shirts **Seats:** 30 **Smoking:** N/Sm in restaurant **Children:** Portions **Rooms:** 3 (3 en suite) ◆◆◆◆ **Directions:** M3, M27 W to A31 to Ringwood. Turn left to B3081 to Verwood then Cranborne (5 m) **Parking:** In square
e-mail: mac@la-fosse.com **web:** www.la-fosse.com

DORCHESTER MAP 04 SY69

◉◉ Sienna
British
Intimate dining, Dorchester-style
☎ 01305 250022 36 High West St DT1 1UP
MENU GUIDE Scallops, chorizo & cauliflower ragoût • Monkfish, rösti potato, bourguignonne sauce • Pineapple tarte Tatin, coconut ice cream
WINE GUIDE ♀ Boland Chenin Blanc £14.95 • ♀ Chuscian Syrah/Grenache £15.75 • 20 bottles over £20, 15 bottles under £20 • 6 by the glass (£3.75-£6.25)
PRICE GUIDE Fixed L £14.50 • Fixed D £31 • coffee £2.50 • min/water £2.50 • Service optional
PLACE: A converted town-centre shop fashioned into a small but well-planned, well-presented dining room of just 15 seats, provides a homely backdrop to an intimate experience. The high-ceilinged room of muted, warm natural colours, bright spotlights, modern artwork and colourful floral arrangements has a contemporary edge, backed up by friendly, precise and knowledgeable service.
FOOD: The sensibly compact modern British menus make good use of fresh, seasonal, regional produce in well-presented, clear-flavoured dishes that underline the kitchen's high technical skill.
OUR TIP: Great value lunches
Chef: Russell Brown **Owners:** Russell & Elena Brown **Times:** 12-2/7-9.30, Closed 2 wks Feb/Mar, 2 wks Sep/Oct, Sun-Mon **Notes:** Vegetarian available **Seats:** 15 **Smoking:** N/Sm in restaurant, Air con **Children:** Min 10 **Directions:** Near top of town rdbt in Dorchester **Parking:** Top of town car park, on street
e-mail: browns@siennarestaurant.co.uk
web: www.siennarestaurant.co.uk

◉◉ *Yalbury Cottage*
British
Rural haven for foodies
☎ 01305 262382 Lower Bockhampton DT2 8PZ

Mortons House Hotel

Seats: 60, Pr/dining room 22 **Smoking:** N/Sm in restaurant
Children: Min 5yrs, Portions **Rooms:** 19 (19 en suite) ★★★
Directions: In centre of village on A351 **Parking:** 45
e-mail: stay@mortonshouse.co.uk **web:** www.mortonshouse.co.uk

CRANBORNE MAP 05 SU01

◉ La Fosse at Cranborne
British, International
Accurate cooking in a sleepy village
☎ 01725 517604 London House, The Square BH21 5PR
MENU GUIDE Indonesian seafood laksa • Roasted duckling breast, plum sauce • Steamed lemon sponge pudding

WINE GUIDE ♀ Vina San Pedro Sauvignon £12.95 • ♀ Vina San Pedro Cabernet Sauvignon £12.95 • 26 bottles over £20, 51 bottles under £20 • 12 by the glass (£3.50)
PRICE GUIDE Fixed L £6-£11.95 • Fixed D £15.45-£24.45 • coffee £2.25 • min/water £3.25 • Service optional
PLACE: Chintzy greens and pinks bring a homely feel to this country restaurant, where a large inglenook fireplace testifies to a long history. The measured peak time service is compensated by friendly staff.

continued

continued

DORCHESTER continued MAP 04 SY69

MENU GUIDE White asparagus, hollandaise • Lamb, gratin potatoes, aubergine purée, coriander jus • Banana & white chocolate parfait

PRICE GUIDE Food prices not confirmed for 2006. Please telephone for details

PLACE: Set in a pretty Dorset village, this quintessential English country cottage is a rural haven, complete with thatched roof, low beamed ceilings and an inglenook fireplace. Book ahead for a table in the intimate restaurant, a relaxed setting attended by friendly and unpretentious staff.

FOOD: Plenty of skill and imagination here; expect straightforward modern cooking with some intriguing twists. The menu changes daily and pays pleasing attention to seasonal produce.

OUR TIP: Not open for lunch except for large parties by prior arrangement

Times: 7-9, Closed L Mon-Sun **Rooms:** 8 (8 en suite) ♦♦♦♦
Directions: Two miles east of Dorchester, off A35.
e-mail: yalburycottage@aol.com **web:** www.yalburycottage.com

EVERSHOT MAP 04 ST50

🌸 The Acorn Inn

British, Mediterranean

Accomplished cooking in historic coaching inn

☎ 01935 83228 DT2 0JW

MENU GUIDE Carrot & coconut soup • Rainbow trout stuffed with crab & asparagus, lemon sauce • Steamed pudding with toffee sauce

continued

WINE GUIDE ♀ D O Maule Valley Chile Chardonnay/Sauvignon Blanc £11.95 • ♀ Vina Santa Monica Chile Merlot £14.95 16 bottles over £20, 15 bottles under £20 • 7 by the glass (£3-£9.50)

PRICE GUIDE Starter £4.25-£7.95 • main £11.25-£16.95 • dessert £4.50-£5.95 • coffee £1.50 • min/water £2.25 • Service optional

PLACE: Set in the heart of a quintessential English village, this 16th-century inn is popular with locals and tourists alike, and boasts a range of pretty bedrooms. Relax with a drink or light bite in the bar, or opt for more formal fare in the cosy restaurant.

FOOD: A skilful kitchen handles local produce with care to deliver a range of dishes, such as pork schnitzel with a wild mushroom, cognac and mustard sauce, or rack of Dorset lamb with rosemary new potatoes.

OUR TIP: Features in Thomas Hardy's *Tess of the d'Urbevilles*
Chef: Justin Mackenzie **Owners:** Red Carnation Hotels **Times:** 12-2/6.45-9.30 **Notes:** Sun L 1 course £8.95, 2 courses £11.95, 3 courses £14.95, Vegetarian available, Dress Restrictions, Smart casual **Seats:** 45, Pr/dining room 65 **Smoking:** N/Sm in restaurant **Children:** Portions **Rooms:** 9 (9 en suite) ♦♦♦♦ **Directions:** 2m off A37, between Dorchester and Yeovil. In village centre. **Parking:** 40
e-mail: stay@acorn-inn.co.uk **web:** www.acorn-inn.co.uk

🌸🌸🌸 Summer Lodge Country House Hotel, Restaurant & Spa

see below

EVERSHOT MAP 04 ST50

Summer Lodge Country House Hotel, Restaurant & Spa

British

Idyllic, intimate retreat meets refined cooking and wine list

☎ 01935 482030 DT2 0JR

MENU GUIDE Terrine & pan-fried foie gras, Sauternes jelly, toasted brioche & pomegranate • Halibut & scallop strudel, steamed leeks, confit tomato & champagne • Assiette of desserts

WINE GUIDE ♀ Alta Vista Terrentes £26 • ♀ Bouchard Finlayson Sangiovese £34 • 60 bottles over £20, 15 bottles under £20 • 8 by the glass (£8-£15)

PRICE GUIDE Fixed L £22-£26 • Fixed D £32-£48 • coffee £4 • min/water £3.50 • Service included • Group min 12 service 12.5%

PLACE: Blessed with a picture-postcard village setting, this former dower house turned country-house hotel is a true hideaway, set in the heart of the Dorset countryside. Since new owners took over, it has undergone a complete refurbishment with impressive results; retaining a classic, chintzy country-house feel but with an air of luxury and high quality. Full-length windows - with extensive views over the gardens - grace the traditional, split-level dining room, while the rose and honeysuckle-covered gazebo offers an enchanting summer alfresco option. Service is predictably formal but appropriately friendly, and the sommelier brings serious expertise. Literature loving diners will be thrilled that local architect and celebrated chronicler, Thomas Hardy, designed part of the property.

FOOD: Steven Titman's classically based, refined cooking - with modern focus and presentation - showcases first-rate local ingredients through clean, clear flavours and accurate technical skill and execution. His approach, via appealing fixed price, carte and nine-course tasting option, delivers the likes of seared sea scallops with cauliflower purée and a truffle and port wine jus to open, and perhaps roast loin of Dorset lamb, served with sage and onion purée, gratin potato and crisp sweetbreads to follow.

OUR TIP: First-class wine list and award-wining sommelier
Chef: Steven Titman **Owners:** Beatrice Tollman **Times:** 12-2.30/7-9.30
Notes: Tasting menu £60 (8 courses), Sun L £30 (4 courses), Vegetarian available, Dress Restrictions, No shorts, T-shirts or sandals, Civ Wed 30 **Seats:** 48, Pr/dining room 12 **Smoking:** N/Sm in restaurant, Air con **Children:** Min 7 yrs D, Menu, Portions **Rooms:** 24 (24 en suite) ★★★★ **Directions:** 1.5m off A37 between Yeovil and Dorchester **Parking:** 60 **e-mail:** summer@relaischateaux.com
web: www.summerlodgehotel.com

GILLINGHAM MAP 04 ST82

Stock Hill Country House Hotel

European, Austrian
Classic cuisine in elegant country house
☎ 01747 823626 Stock Hill SP8 5NR
MENU GUIDE Quail, goose liver balantine, crabapple jelly
Lamb, sautéed kidneys in puff pastry • Trio of créme brûlée
WINE GUIDE ♀ Château de Loché Louis Jadot Chardonnay
£32.80 • ♥ St Laurent 2003 Ernst Triebaumer £27.90 • 87 bottles
over £20, 7 bottles under £20 • 7 by the glass (£3.80-£4.60)
PRICE GUIDE Fixed L £25-£28 • Fixed D £35.50-£38.50
PLACE: Set at the end of a beech-lined driveway, this elegant
country house hotel is sumptuously decorated and stands in
acres of pretty gardens that are home to a wide variety of
wildlife. The elegant dining room offers views of the manicured
lawns from white clothed tables decked with sparkling glassware.
FOOD: Quality ingredients are at the heart of Stock Hill's daily
hanging menu; fish comes fresh from Brixham, while meat is
sourced from surrounding Dorset towns, and fruit and vegetables
are grown organically in the hotel's Victorian walled kitchen
garden. Dishes are rooted in classical French cuisine, but also
owe a nod to the chef's native land of Austria, with specials such
as zweibel röstbraten - sirloin steak cooked with onions and

cream, with a Bohemian bread dumpling. There is an extensive
vegetarian selection.
OUR TIP: Try the special Austrian dishes
Chef: Peter Hauser, Lorna Connor **Owners:** Peter & Nita Hauser
Times: 12.30-1.45/7.30-8.45, Closed L Sat & Mon **Notes:** Vegetarian
available, Dress Restrictions, No jeans or t-shirts **Seats:** 24, Pr/dining
room 12 **Smoking:** N/Sm in restaurant **Children:** Min 7 yrs, Portions
Rooms: 9 (9 en suite) ★★★ **Directions:** 3m E on B3081, off A303
Parking: 20 **e-mail:** reception@stockhillhouse.co.uk
web: www.stockhillhouse.co.uk

FARNHAM MAP 04 ST91
The Museum Inn
Modern, European
Great gastro-pub with some famous regulars
☎ 01725 516261 DT11 8DE
PLACE: A traditional inn in the best sense of the phrase, the
building has been sympathetically renovated, retaining the
original flagged floors and fireplaces and adding stylish
furnishings. Very popular at lunchtimes.
FOOD: Meat is fully traceable and comes guaranteed to have
been traditionally reared, and many other ingredients are
organic. Local and seasonal produce make a strong show on the
modern British menu and all this contributes to the fine food on
offer here. Tender crispy belly pork comes with sticky red wine
sauce and soft creamy mash - well balanced flavours and neat
presentation.
OUR TIP: Best to book, even at lunch
Times: 12/7, Closed Mon-Thu, 25 Dec, closed D 26 Dec, & 31 Dec

FONTMELL MAGNA MAP 04 ST81
The Crown Inn
Traditional British   **NEW**
Well prepared food in cosy country inn
☎ 01747 811441 SP1 0PA
MENU GUIDE Dorset Blue Vinney soufflé • Roast belly of pork
stuffed with apricots & basil • Baileys & dark chocolate mousse
WINE GUIDE 13 bottles over £20, 25 bottles under £20 • 8 by
the glass (£2.99-£3.65)

PRICE GUIDE Starter £4.25-£9.95 • main £6.95-£36 • dessert
£4.25-£9.95 • coffee £1.50 • min/water £2 • Service optional
PLACE: This traditional Georgian, farmhouse-style village inn has
a relaxed and friendly ambience with a cosy bar and a busy
restaurant area with linen table cloths and heavy cutlery.
FOOD: There's something for everyone on the menus. This is
simply prepared, honest food created from good quality
ingredients, including local meat and fish from Poole Bay.
OUR TIP: Book at weekends
Chef: Robin Davies, Paul Firmin **Owners:** Mrs & Mr AJ Neilson
Times: 12-2.45/6.45-9, Closed Xmas Day **Notes:** Vegetarian available
Seats: 35 **Smoking:** N/Sm in restaurant, Air con **Children:** Min 9,
Portions **Rooms:** 3 (1 en suite) ◆◆◆ **Directions:** On A350 towards
Blanford S, pass through Cann & Compton Abbas villages - restaurant on
X-rds centre of Fontmell Magna on right **Parking:** 17
e-mail: crowninnfm@hotmail.com **web:** www.crowninn.me.uk

GILLINGHAM MAP 04 ST82
Stock Hill Country House Hotel *see above*

LYME REGIS MAP 04 SY39
Alexandra Hotel
British, International
Elegant dining overlooking Lyme Regis
☎ 01297 442010 Pound St DT7 3HZ
MENU GUIDE Asparagus, lemon & dill butter • Red snapper,
couscous crust, green pea risotto • Sticky toffee pudding,
butterscotch sauce

continued
continued

LYME REGIS continued MAP 04 SY39

Alexandra Hotel

WINE GUIDE ♀ Berry Brothers & Rudd Aged Chardonnay £12.50 • ♀ Berry Brothers & Rudd Cabernet Sauvignon £12.50 • 25 bottles over £20, 31 bottles under £20 • 3 by the glass (£2.20-£4.40)

PRICE GUIDE Fixed L £15.95 • Fixed D £25 • coffee £1.60 • min/water £2.50 • Service optional

PLACE: Set in pretty gardens, this family-run Grade II listed hotel is just a short walk from the beach at Lyme Bay, and offers stunning views across the Cobb. The elegant restaurant is newly refurbished in traditional country house style.

FOOD: Expect classical cuisine with the odd international touch: a starter of carpaccio of Lyme Bay scallops with lemon and roasted fennel perhaps, followed by char-grilled sirloin with brandy cream, or veal with colcannon potatoes.

OUR TIP: Afternoon tea in the conservatory or garden **Chef:** David Percivial **Owners:** Mr & Mrs D J Haskins **Times:** 12.30-1.30/7-9, Closed last weekend before Xmas-end Jan **Notes:** Vegetarian available, Dress Restrictions, No shorts, T-shirts **Seats:** 60 **Smoking:** N/Sm in restaurant, Air con **Children:** Min 10yrs, Portions **Rooms:** 26 (26 en suite) ★★★ **Directions:** Off A303 at Chard, head for Axminster, then Lyme Regis **Parking:** 17 **e-mail:** enquiries@hotelalexandra.co.uk **web:** www.lymeregis.co.uk

⊚ Mariners Hotel

British, Mediterranean

Eclectic cuisine in character hotel with sea and cliff views

☎ 01297 442753 Silver St DT7 3HS

MENU GUIDE Asparagus soup • Breast of duck with prunes & brandy • Passionfruit pannacotta

WINE GUIDE 3 bottles over £20, 25 bottles under £20 • 3 by the glass (£2.50-£5)

PRICE GUIDE Fixed D £20.50 • coffee £1.50 • min/water £3 • Service optional

PLACE: The hotel is a conversion from a 17th-century coaching inn, full of period charm and original features, located in the heart of the town. Beatrix Potter, who holidayed in Lyme Regis as a child, immortalised the hotel in her *Tale of Little Pig Robinson*. From the garden there are views of Lyme Bay and the surrounding countryside.

FOOD: The spacious restaurant is the setting for an eclectic selection of dishes using local ingredients, particularly seafood.

OUR TIP: Summer afternoon teas in the garden **Chef:** Nick & Claire Larby **Owners:** Nick & Claire Larby **Times:** 12-2/7-9, Closed 27 Dec-28 Jan, closed L Mon-Sat, closed D Sun **Notes:** Vegetarian available **Seats:** 40 **Smoking:** N/Sm in restaurant **Children:** Min 7yrs **Rooms:** 12 (12 en suite) ★★ **Directions:** Telephone for directions **Parking:** 20 **e-mail:** marinershotel@btopenworld.com **web:** hotellymeregis.co.uk

MAIDEN NEWTON MAP 04 SY59

⊚ Le Petit Canard

British, French

Atmospheric village restaurant

☎ 01300 320536 Dorchester Rd DT2 0BE

MENU GUIDE Seared scallops, mustard & shallot sauce • Venison loin, red wine & redcurrant sauce • Iced chocolate & raspberry parfait

WINE GUIDE ♀ Serge Laporte Sancerre Sauvignon Blanc £22.95 • ♀ Fernand Verpoix Fleurie Gamay £21 • 12 bottles over £20, 21 bottles under £20 • 6 by the glass (£3.50-£4.50)

PRICE GUIDE Fixed L £19.50 • Fixed D £28-£30.50 • coffee £2.25 • min/water £3 • Service optional

PLACE: Friendly and attentive service, soothing classical music, soft candlelight and seascape prints create a relaxed atmosphere at this pretty, 350-year-old building in the village centre.

FOOD: Ambitious fixed-price menus are well balanced and modern English and French in style, with the occasional foray to the Orient for inspiration. Good use of local produce includes fish, scallops and crab from West Bay.

OUR TIP: Try the sticky toffee pudding **Chef:** Gerry Craig **Owners:** Mr & Mrs G Craig **Times:** 12-2.15/7-9.30, Closed Mon, closed L all week (ex 1st & 3rd Sun in month), closed D Sun **Notes:** Vegetarian available, Dress Restrictions, Smart casual preferred **Seats:** 28 **Smoking:** N/Sm in restaurant **Children:** Min 12yrs **Directions:** In centre of Maiden Newton, 8m W of Dorchester. **Parking:** On street/village car park **e-mail:** craigs@le-petit-canard.co.uk **web:** www.le-petit-canard.co.uk

POOLE MAP 04 SZ09

⊚⊚ Harbour Heights Hotel

Modern English **NEW**

Contemporary brasserie commanding the best views across Poole Harbour

☎ 01202 707272 73 Haven Rd, Sandbanks BH13 7PS

continue

Harbour Heights Hotel

Haven Hotel

MENU GUIDE Poole Bay crab, lime, chilli & mint dressing • Trout, sautéed clams, fennel & vermouth • Chocolate fondant

WINE GUIDE ♀ Errazuriz Sauvignon £14.50 • ♀ Errazuriz Cabernet Merlot £14.50 • 96 bottles over £20, 24 bottles under £20 • 12 by the glass (£3.95-£15)

PRICE GUIDE Fixed D £21 • starter £6.80-£17.50 • main £13.90-£19.95 • dessert £5.75 • coffee £2.25 • min/water £3.50 • Service optional

PLACE: Re-opened in 2003 following extensive refurbishment, the unassuming appearance of this chic seaside hotel belies a wealth of innovation, quality and style. Throughout the smart public areas, which include the contemporary HarBar brasserie, picture windows accentuate panoramic views across Poole Harbour. Dine on the fabulous sun terrace in summer. Knowledgeable service is professional, efficient and friendly.
FOOD: Cooking is skilful, thoughtful and inventive without compromising flavour and quality. The kitchen produces some interesting dishes based on classical ideas and presentation is elegant and simple with no unnecessary embellishments.
OUR TIP: Arrive before the sun sets to enjoy the harbour views
Chef: Glen Elie **Owners:** FJB Hotels **Times:** 12-2.30/7-9.30
Notes: Dress Restrictions, Smart casual, Civ Wed 120 **Seats:** 90, Pr/dining room 120 **Smoking:** N/Sm in restaurant, Air con **Children:** Menu, Portions **Directions:** From A338 follow signs to Sandbanks, restaurant on left past Candford Cliffs **Parking:** 80
e-mail: enquiries@harbourheights.net **web:** www.fjbhotels.co.uk

⚜⚜ Haven Hotel
International

Fine dining at the water's edge
☎ 01202 707333 Banks Rd, Sandbanks BH13 7QL

MENU GUIDE Lobster & sweetcorn bisque • Braised beef, pumpkin & Dunsyere Blue risotto • Cornish cream pannacotta, raspberry sablé

continued

WINE GUIDE ♀ Les Collinettes Sancerre Sauvignon £23.50 • ♀ Moulin de la Grange Cabernet Sauvignon/Syrah £13.50

PRICE GUIDE Fixed L £16 • starter £6.75-£13 • main £12.95-£23 • dessert £5.95-£8 • coffee £2.95 • min/water £3.50 • Service optional

PLACE: Overlooking the broad sweep of Poole Bay, this luxurious hotel offers an array of eating options, including a terrace for alfresco dining in summer, and a choice of relaxed or formal restaurants. La Roche, the fine dining option, is the main draw, with a water's edge setting that provides stunning views.
FOOD: A seasonal menu with an emphasis on local produce. Seafood predominates, but meat-eaters aren't forgotten; mains might include Dorset lamb with truffle pan juices or monkfish saltimbocca. A concise vegetarian menu is also available.
OUR TIP: The hotel was used by Marconi for his early radio experiments
Chef: Peter Whittingham, Carl France **Owners:** Mr J Butterworth
Times: 12-2/7-9, Closed Xmas, Mon (winter), closed D Sun (winter)
Notes: Vegetarian available, Dress Restrictions, No shorts or beach wear, Civ Wed 180 **Seats:** 59, Pr/dining room 160 **Smoking:** N/Sm in restaurant, Air con **Children:** Menu, Portions **Rooms:** 78 (78 en suite)
★★★★ **Directions:** Follow signs to Sandbanks Peninsula; hotel next to Swanage ferry departure point. **Parking:** 90
e-mail: reservations@havenhotel.co.uk **web:** www.havenhotel.co.uk

⚜⚜ Mansion House Hotel
Modern British

A sophisticated Georgian setting for accomplished cuisine
☎ 01202 685666 Thames St BH15 1JN

MENU GUIDE Ham hock terrine, beetroot chutney • Scallops, pumpkin risotto, chorizo • Vanilla & pistachio parfait, chocolate ice cream

WINE GUIDE ♀ Joseph Meuot Sancerre Sauvignon Blanc £22.50 • ♀ Zenato Ripassa Valpolicella £22.50 • 95 bottles over £20, 40 bottles under £20 • 8 by the glass (£3.25-£5.50)

continued

POOLE continued MAP 04 SZ09

PRICE GUIDE Fixed L £15.50-£17.50 • Fixed D £24.95-£27.45 coffee £2 • min/water £2.80 • Service optional

PLACE: Set in a splendidly restored Georgian townhouse in a quiet mews just off Poole's quayside, this hotel restaurant has a sophisticated clubby feel. Cherrywood panels line the walls, while crisp white linen and quality appointments deck the tables.
FOOD: Simple in conception, the food here is a testament to what can be achieved with top-notch ingredients and a light touch. There's nothing showy, just enjoyable and accomplished cuisine, with main dishes along the lines of beef in pancetta with a mushroom ragout, or whole Dover sole with herb butter.
OUR TIP: More informal fare available at the hotel bistro
Chef: Gerry Godden **Owners:** Jackie & Gerry Godden **Times:** 12-2/7-9.30, Closed L Sat, closed D Sun (ex BHs) **Notes:** Vegetarian available, Dress Restrictions, Smart casual, Civ Wed 35 **Seats:** 85, Pr/dining room 36 **Smoking:** N/Sm in restaurant, Air con **Children:** Menu, Portions **Rooms:** 32 (32 en suite) ★★★ **Directions:** A350 into town centre follow signs to Channel Ferry/Poole Quay, left at bridge, 1st left is Thames St **Parking:** 46 **e-mail:** enquiries@themansionhouse.co.uk
web: www.themansionhouse.co.uk

Sandbanks Hotel

European

Seafront conservatory-style brasserie

☎ 01202 707377/709884 15 Banks Rd, Sandbanks BH13 7PS

MENU GUIDE Tian of crab & French caviar • Dorset milk fed lamb • Dark Cuban chocolate fondant, raspberry ice cream cream

WINE GUIDE ♀ Errezurit Sauvignon Blanc £14.50 • ♀ Errezurit Cabernet Sauvignon £14.50 • 33 bottles over £20, 27 bottles under £20 • 6 by the glass (£3.60-£4.95)

PRICE GUIDE Fixed L £14.50 • Fixed D £18.50 • starter £5.95-£8.50 • main £12.90-£18.75 • dessert £5.50-£6.90 • coffee £2.10 • min/water £3.50 • Service optional

PLACE: A conservatory set right on the beach is the memorable setting for this brasserie, with views of Poole Bay and the sea beyond to be soaked up.
FOOD: Fish and shellfish head the brasserie style menu and also feature at lunchtime, with meat and game choices available. The accurate cooking is modern in style and presentation, with popular dishes included, all using the freshest local produce.
OUR TIP: New beachside terrace for alfresco dining
Chef: Stephan Jouan **Owners:** Mr J Butterworth **Times:** 12-3/6-10, closed D Sun-Tue **Notes:** Vegetarian available, Dress Restrictions, No jeans, smart casual, Civ Wed 40 **Seats:** 65, Pr/dining room 40 **Smoking:** N/Sm in restaurant, Air con **Children:** Menu, Portions **Rooms:** 110 (110 en suite) ★★★ **Directions:** From Poole or Bournemouth, follow signs to Sandbanks Peninsula. Hotel on left. **Parking:** 130 **e-mail:** reservations@sandbankshotel.co.uk **web:** www.sandbankshotel.co.uk

PORTLAND MAP 04 SY67

⊛ Blue Fish Café

Modern   **NEW**

Breakfast, lunch and fine dining next to Chesil Beach

☎ 01305 822991 15-17a Chiswell DT5 1AN

MENU GUIDE Dill & cauliflower pannacotta, pickled vegetables, parmesan shortbread • Roasted partridge, quince confit • Tarte Tatin

WINE GUIDE 2 bottles over £20, 15 bottles under £20 • 6 by the glass (£2.75-£5.50)

PRICE GUIDE Food prices not confirmed for 2006. Please telephone for details

PLACE: Appealingly unpretentious pair of connected dining rooms, with exposed stone walls and bare wooden floorboards. The furniture is an eclectic collection, but there are also crisp white table cloths and linen napkins, under twinkling lights.
FOOD: Breakfasts and popular dishes during the day give way to more serious evening dining, the whole backed up by fresh organic and locally-produced ingredients. Expect anything from field mushroom burger to braised veal shin with risotto milanaise
OUR TIP: Wide choice of breakfast dishes
Chef: Luciano Da Silva **Owners:** Jo & Luciano Da Silva **Times:** 12-3/6.30-10, closed L Times seasonal, closed D Times seasonal **Notes:** Vegetarian available, Dress Restrictions, Smart casual **Seats:** 35 **Smoking:** N/Sm in restaurant **Directions:** Take A354 by Chesil Bank, off Victoria Square in Portland, over rdbt towards Chesil Beach **Parking:** 36 hr free car park, on street **e-mail:** the bluefish@clara.co.uk **web:** www.thebluefishcafe.co.uk

SHAFTESBURY MAP 04 ST82

⊛ La Fleur de Lys Restaurant with Rooms

British, French

Smart restaurant with rooms to suit all tastes

☎ 01747 853717 Bleke St SP7 8AW

MENU GUIDE Hot lobster mousse, caviar • Venison, fig & pear chutney, Armagnac sauce • Lemon crème brûlée

WINE GUIDE 10 by the glass (£3.25-£5.75)

PRICE GUIDE Fixed L £21.50 • Fixed D £26.50 • starter £5.50-£10.50 • main £16.50-£21.50 • dessert £5-£6.75 • coffee £2.50 • min/water £2.50 • Service optional

PLACE: Housed in a former girls' boarding house, this spacious restaurant with rooms has a comfortable lounge for pre-dinner drinks, and an elegant dining room with conservatory extension

continued

continued

England

FOOD: An accommodating menu designed to intrigue culinary adventurers as well as those with more traditional tastes. Fish features strongly, as do interesting modern interpretations of classic French dishes.

OUR TIP: Stay over in one of the comfortable bedrooms
Chef: D Shepherd & M Preston **Owners:** D Shepherd, M Preston & M Griffin **Times:** 12-3/7-10.30, Closed L Mon & Tue, closed D Sun **Notes:** Vegetarian available, Dress Restrictions, No T-shirts or dirty clothes **Seats:** 45, Pr/dining room 12 **Smoking:** N/Sm in restaurant **Children:** Portions **Rooms:** 7 (7 en suite) 🏨 **Directions:** Junct A350/A30 **Parking:** 10 **e-mail:** info@fleurdelys.co.uk **web:** www.lafleurdelys.co.uk

⊛ Royal Chase Hotel
Modern British

Intimate hotel dining room close to Gold Hill

☎ 01747 853358 Royal Chase Roundabout SP7 8DB

MENU GUIDE Oak smoked venison, artichoke salad • Freshwater carp steamed in white wine, coriander pilaff rice • Warm Dorset apple cake

PRICE GUIDE Fixed alc £28.50 • coffee £2 • min/water £3

PLACE: Popular white-painted roadside hotel set in its own gardens close to historic Shaftesbury, in the heart of Thomas Hardy country. Byzant, the hotel's restaurant, is named after a token used in an ancient water ceremony.

FOOD: The fixed-price, three-course menu reads well, offering an interesting choice of dishes using the best local ingredients, plus complimentary appetiser.

OUR TIP: You can also eat informally in the bar
Chef: Stuart Robbins **Owners:** Travel West Inns **Times:** 12-2/7-9.30 **Notes:** ALC £28.50, Vegetarian available, Civ Wed 78 **Seats:** 65, Pr/dining room 120 **Smoking:** N/Sm in restaurant **Children:** Menu, Portions **Rooms:** 33 (33 en suite) ★★★ **Directions:** On rdbt at A350 & A30 junction (avoid town centre) **Parking:** 100 **e-mail:** royalchasehotel@btinternet.com **web:** www.theroyalchasehotel.co.uk

⊛⊛ Wayfarers Restaurant
French, European

Contemporary inn with intriguing tastes

☎ 01747 852821 Sherborne Causeway SP7 9PX

MENU GUIDE Tuna loin, lemon grass & chilli dressing • Sika deer, garlic roasted beetroot, prunes & fondant potato • Hot pear tarte Tatin

WINE GUIDE ♀ La Joya Chardonnay • ♥ Fleurie Domaine de Prion Gamay £18 • 20 bottles over £20, 35 bottles under £20 • by the glass (£2.75-£3.85)

PRICE GUIDE Fixed L £18.50 • Fixed D £18.50 • starter £7-£8.50 • main £16.75-£18.50 • dessert £7-£7.25 • coffee £2.60 • min/water £2.75 • Service optional

continued

PLACE: With its stone walls, beamed ceiling and inglenook fireplace, this 18th-century cottage makes a cosy setting for a contemporary restaurant. It's located in the Vale of Blackmore and is a good base for exploring rural Dorset.

FOOD: French and Mediterranean flavours predominate at the Wayfarers, where the ambitious kitchen likes to tease guests with unexpected combinations. A quail dish shows the style, served in ham with a thyme, mushroom and apricot mousse, while a cheese course marries French brie with an orange-walnut salad and warm prune, walnut and molasses bread.

OUR TIP: Booking for lunch essential
Chef: Mark Newton **Owners:** Clare & Mark Newton **Times:** 12-1.30/7-9, Closed 3 wks after 25 Dec, 2 wks Jun/Jul, Mon, closed L Sat, Tue, closed D Sun **Notes:** Bistro menu Tue-Fri 4 courses £21, Sun L 4 courses £22.50, Vegetarian available, Dress Restrictions, Smart casual, no sportswear **Seats:** 34 **Smoking:** N/Sm in restaurant **Children:** Min 8yrs **Rooms:** 1 (1 en suite) ♦♦♦♦ **Directions:** 2m W of Shaftesbury on A30 to Sherborne & Yeovil **Parking:** 30

SHERBORNE MAP 04 ST61

⊛⊛ Eastbury Hotel
British, European

Modern British cuisine in elegant Georgian house

☎ 01935 813131 Long St DT9 3BY

MENU GUIDE Tiger prawn spring roll, sweet chilli relish • Lamb, black pudding, mash, Parisienne vegetables • Cherry crème brûlée

WINE GUIDE ♀ Santa Rita Sauvignon Blanc £13.90 • ♥ Santa Rita Merlot £13.90 • 28 bottles over £20, 37 bottles under £20 • 6 by the glass (£2.60-£5.40)

PRICE GUIDE Fixed L £13.50-£15.95 • starter £4-£8 • main £12-£20 • dessert £4.50-£8 • coffee £1.95 • min/water £3 • Service optional

PLACE: Five minutes stroll from Sherborne's historic abbey, this family-run Georgian town house serves food in an airy conservatory overlooking a walled garden. Two bars and a lounge are available for coffee or pre-dinner drinks, and there's a terrace for alfresco dining in summer.

FOOD: Expect generous portions of modern British cuisine, created from local Dorset produce where possible. Start with a ham hock and vegetable terrine perhaps, and then move onto a main such as stilton stuffed beef with fondant potato and Marsala jus.

OUR TIP: Visit Sherborne's historic abbey
Chef: Brett Sutton **Owners:** Mr & Mrs P King **Times:** 12-2/7-9.30 **Notes:** Vegetarian available, Civ Wed 80 **Seats:** 40, Pr/dining room 12 **Smoking:** N/Sm in restaurant **Children:** Menu, Portions **Rooms:** 23 (23 en suite) ★★★ **Directions:** 5m E of Yeovil, follow brown signs for The Eastbury Hotel **Parking:** 20 **e-mail:** enquiries@theeastburyhotel.com **web:** www.theeastburyhotel.co.uk

England

SHERBORNE continued MAP 04 ST61

⊛⊛ The Green   NEW
Modern British
Innovative food in a period setting
☎ 01935 813821 3 The Green DT9 3HY

MENU GUIDE Goats' cheese soufflé, red wine pears • Pan-fried brill fillet & shrimps • Dark chocolate & Grand Marnier terrine

WINE GUIDE ♀ Cepage Sauvignon Haut Poitou £16.95 • ♀ Montes de Ciria Rioja Reserva £19.50 • 10 bottles over £20, 37 bottles under £20 • 15 by the glass (£3.50-£5.25)

PRICE GUIDE Fixed L £13.95-£18.95 • Fixed D £27.95 • coffee £1.70 • min/water £2.40 • Service optional

PLACE: The smart green-painted woodwork makes this attractive old stone property easy to spot. Inside it's just as tasteful, with the exposed beams and antique tables looking romantic by candlelight.
FOOD: Appetising menus let you eat as much or as little as you like, with their one, two or three course options. An innovative style that insists on the best local produce is hard to resist, though, with starters like warm salad of rabbit loin, and such artistic desserts as apple and almond tart with butterscotch sauce, restraint is nigh on impossible.
OUR TIP: Private dining room for parties
Chef: Michael Rust **Owners:** Michael & Judith Rust **Times:** 12-2/7-9, Closed 2 wks Jan, 1 wk Jun, 1 wk Sept, BHs, Xmas, Sun-Mon
Notes: Vegetarian available **Seats:** 40, Pr/dining room 25
Smoking: N/Sm in restaurant **Parking:** on street, car park
web: thegreensherborne.co.uk

STURMINSTER NEWTON MAP 04 ST71

⊛ Plumber Manor
British, French
Manor house of charm and character
☎ 01258 472507 Hazelbury Bryan Rd DT10 2AF

MENU GUIDE Chicken liver pâté, onion marmalade • Loin of pork with prunes & brandy • Lemon roulade

WINE GUIDE ♀ Chardonnay • ♀ Grenache £10 • 94 bottles over £20, 58 bottles under £20 • 5 by the glass (£3-£4)

PRICE GUIDE Fixed L £21 • Fixed D £26 • coffee £2 • min/water £2 • Service optional

PLACE: Old fashioned values are preserved at this delightful Jacobean manor set in lovingly tended grounds, where the owner's family have been in residence since the 17th century. At its hub, the restaurant is fittingly traditional, furnished with antiques, crisply-starched table linen and quality silverware.
FOOD: There's no pandering to fads or fashion here, but appropriately features fresh, local produce delivered in classic country-house style, the approach via set-priced menus with carte supplements.
continued

OUR TIP: Breakfasts provide a particularly good start to the day
Chef: Brian Prideaux-Brune **Owners:** R Prideaux-Brune **Times:** 12-2/7.30-9.15, Closed Feb, closed L Mon-Sat **Notes:** Vegetarian available, Dress Restrictions, Smart casual **Seats:** 60, Pr/dining room 40
Smoking: N/Sm in restaurant **Children:** Portions **Rooms:** 16 (16 en suite) ★★★ **Directions:** In Sturminster Newton cross packhorse bridge, right to Stalbridge (A537). 1st left to Hazelbury Bryan. Marked by brown tourist sign. **Parking:** 30 **e-mail:** book@plumbermanor.com
web: www.plumbermanor.com

WAREHAM MAP 04 SY98

⊛ Kemps Country House Hotel
British
Flavourful menus in country house setting
☎ 01929 462563 East Stoke BH20 6AL

MENU GUIDE Sautéed scallops with rocket • Lamb trilogy • Pancake with chocolate & coconut sauce

WINE GUIDE ♀ Eagle Point Chardonnay/Semillion £12 • ♀ Eagle Point Merlot/Cabernet Sauvignon £12 • 17 bottles over £20, 50 bottles under £20 • 7 by the glass (£3.50-£4.25)

PRICE GUIDE Fixed D £26-£30 • starter £3.50-£6 • main £8-£18 dessert £4-£5 • coffee £1.75 • min/water £2.75 • Service optional

PLACE: Dating from 1874, this Victorian house in the Frome Valley was formerly a rectory and is set in its own grounds, with views of the Purbeck Hills and surrounding countryside. The country house style restaurant has a conservatory overlooking the garden and across the valley.
FOOD: Modern English cooking with French undertones using top quality fresh Dorset ingredients, including a wealth of locally caught seafood.
OUR TIP: Bar meals available at lunchtime
Chef: Anton Goodwin **Owners:** Mary & Graham Craddock **Times:** 12-2/7-9.30, Closed L Sat **Notes:** ALC L only, Fixed D 5 courses £30-34, Coffee incl at D, Vegetarian available, Smart casual **Seats:** 66, Pr/dining room 100 **Smoking:** N/Sm in restaurant **Children:** L only, Portions
Rooms: 15 (14 en suite) ★★ **Directions:** On A352 midway between Wareham and Wool. **Parking:** 50 **e-mail:** stay@kempshotel.com
web: www.kempshotel.com

WEYMOUTH MAP 04 SY67

⊛ Glenburn Hotel
European, Pacific Rim
Friendly and relaxed seaside hotel dining
☎ 01305 832353 42 Preston Rd DT3 6PZ

MENU GUIDE Mushroom croustade • Baked plaice Veronique • Bread & butter pudding, chocolate sauce

WINE GUIDE ♀ La Huerta Sauvignon Blanc £12.95 • ♀ La Huerta Cabernet Sauvignon £12.95 • 2 bottles over £20, 15 bottles under £20 • 4 by the glass (£2.95-£3.95)

continue

England

PRICE GUIDE Fixed L £12-£14.95 • Fixed D £14.95-£17.95 • starter £3.95-£5.50 • main £11.95-£17.95 • dessert £5.50 • coffee £1.95 • min/water £2.95 • Service optional

PLACE: A comfortable family-run hotel located close to the seafront. There's ample parking and attractive gardens including a hot tub for the more adventurous. The dining room has a relaxed modern feel and good views. Efficient, unhurried service.
FOOD: The daily-changing menu is European in style, offering simply prepared dishes using good quality local produce. With food cooked to order, skilful handling and accuracy of cooking ensure good flavours.
OUR TIP: Handy for beaches and town centre
Chef: Tim Way, Leonard Ngapo **Owners:** Leonard & Anne Ngapo **Times:** 6.30-9.30, Closed Xmas, 31 Dec, Sun (ex residents), closed L Mon-Sun (ex functions) **Notes:** Vegetarian available, Dress Restrictions, Shirts must be worn **Seats:** 60, Pr/dining room 8 **Smoking:** N/Sm in restaurant **Children:** Menu, Portions **Rooms:** 13 (13 en suite) ★★
Directions: 1m from town centre on A353. From town follow beach road by sea wall, hotel 500yds on right **Parking:** 20
e-mail: info@glenburnhotel.com **web:** www.glenburnhotel.com

Moonfleet Manor
British, French
Imaginative cooking in country hideaway by the sea
☎ 01305 786948 Fleet DT3 4ED

MENU GUIDE Crab cake, saffron vinaigrette • Confit duck leg, olive mash, Kirsch & griottine cherry sauce • Sticky toffee pudding
PRICE GUIDE Food prices not confirmed for 2006. Please telephone for details
PLACE: Hidden away at the end of a winding two-mile lane in Fleet village, this enchanting Georgian house overlooks Chesil Beach and the sea. These fabulous views are best enjoyed from the stylish restaurant, where well-spaced tables and subtle lighting make for intimate dining.
FOOD: Choose from the well-balanced carte (three courses) or the daily menu of specials and expect modern British and French cuisine with a nod towards the Mediterranean. Cooking is careful and consistent and draws on quality seasonal produce, especially local fish and seafood.
OUR TIP: Eat alfresco on warm summer days
Times: 12.30-2.00/7-9.30 **Rooms:** 39 (39 en suite) ★★★
Directions: A354 from Dorchester, R into Weymouth at Manor Rdbt. R at next rdbt, L at next rdbt, up hill (B3157) then L, 2m towards sea.
e-mail: info@moonfleetmanor.com **web:** www.moonfleetmanor.com

Perry's Restaurant
British
Harbourside restaurant with locally landed seafood
☎ 01305 785799 4 Trinity Rd, The Old Harbour DT4 8TJ

MENU GUIDE Steamed mussels, garlic & cream • Baked haddock, crab, cheese & Chablis sauce • Apple Bakewell tart, praline ice cream
WINE GUIDE ♀ House £10.95 • ♂ House £10.95 • 14 bottles over £20, 26 bottles under £20 • 2 by the glass (£2.50)
PRICE GUIDE Starter £4.50-£7.95 • main £10.95-£16.95 • dessert £4.95 • coffee £1.50 • min/water £2.50 • Service optional
PLACE: Popular for many years and serving a loyal local clientele, this family owned and run restaurant is right on the waterside in the older part of town. It occupies two floors of a 19th-century merchant's house and also has a small garden area which accommodates smokers.
FOOD: The modern British menu is based around freshly available produce, with local seafood predominating. This could be along the lines of pan-fried scallops with creamed leeks and coarse grain mustard or grilled whole lemon or Dover sole with shrimp butter.
OUR TIP: Ask for a table by the window
Chef: Andy Pike **Owners:** A, V & R Hodder **Times:** 12-2/7-9.30, Closed 25-27 Dec,1 Jan, closed L Mon & Sat, closed D Sun (winter)
Notes: Lunch main courses £7.95-£10.95 **Seats:** 60, Pr/dining room 30 **Smoking:** N/Sm in restaurant **Children:** Portions **Directions:** On western side of old harbour - follow signs for Brewers Quay **Parking:** On street or Brewers Quay car park (200 yds)
e-mail: enquiries@perrysrestaurant.co.uk **web:** www.perrysrestaurant.co.uk

---

WIMBORNE MINSTER MAP 05 SZ09
Les Bouviers
French
Elegant and cosy restaurant serving skilful cooking
☎ 01202 889555 Arrowsmith Road, Canford Magna BH21 3BD

continued

WIMBORNE MINSTER continued MAP 05 SZ09

Les Bouviers

MENU GUIDE Seared duck foie gras • Partridge, game, rosemary & chorizo • Hot raspberry soufflé

WINE GUIDE ♀ Sancerre £21.95 • ♥ Penfolds Bin 28 Shiraz £19.85 • 309 bottles over £20, 91 bottles under £20 • 20 by the glass (£3.25-£6.95)

PRICE GUIDE Fixed L £15.95-£16.95 • Fixed D £22.95-£25.50 coffee £3.25 • min/water £3.25 • Service optional • Group min 8 service 10%

PLACE: Les Bouviers is a cosy and intimate restaurant in a converted private house, with a restful decor and subdued lighting. The mainly French staff look after their business and leisure diners with friendly expertise.

FOOD: The cooking is French too, inspired by a classical and traditional style that produces a menu gourmand alongside the carte and 'menu surprise'. Regular speciality evenings encourage local interest in fine food, though dishes like pan-fried escalope of wild hake with ginger and Chinese noodles are a perennial temptation.

OUR TIP: Check out the extensive and mainly French wine list

Chef: James Coward **Owners:** James & Kate Coward **Times:** 12-2.15/7-10.00, Closed 26 Dec, 1st wk Jan, Mon, closed L Sat, closed D Sun **Notes:** Alc £31 (2 courses), £37 (3 courses), Vegetarian available, Dress Restrictions, No jeans, shorts **Seats:** 50, Pr/dining room 30 **Smoking:** N/Sm area, Air con **Children:** Portions **Directions:** 1.5m S of Wimborne on A349, turn left on A341, turn right after 1m **Parking:** 15 **e-mail:** info@lesbouviers.co.uk **web:** www.lesbouviers.co.uk

CO DURHAM

BARNARD CASTLE MAP 19 NZ01

Gilroys

British, International   ☆NEW

Traditional cooking in historic coaching inn

☎ 01833 627232 The Morritt Arms Hotel, Greta Bridge DL12 9SE

MENU GUIDE Roast pear & goats' cheese salad • Local beef, truffle mash, Madeira sauce • French apple tart, clotted cream ice cream

WINE GUIDE ♀ Trulli Pinot Grigio • ♥ Moondara Shiraz £12.50 • 51 bottles over £20, 73 bottles under £20 • 11 by the glass (£2.50-£7.95)

PRICE GUIDE Fixed L £15 • Fixed D £25-£30 • starter £3.75-£6.25 • main £8.95-£15 • dessert £4-£5.75 • coffee £2 • min/water £3.75 • Service included

continued

PLACE: Once an overnight stop for the London to Carlisle coach, this 17th-century inn still offers a warm welcome, albeit in more contemporary style. Its tasteful wood-panelled dining room is a charming place to dine, with fresh flowers, crystal and subtle lighting.

FOOD: A traditional menu with international flavours offers plenty to tempt: lamb with a red onion crust perhaps, or duck with sautéed pancetta and a honey and peppercorn jus. Food also available in the bar.

OUR TIP: The hotel is built on the ruins of a large Roman settlement

Chef: Robert Bennett **Owners:** B A Johnson & P J Phillips **Times:** 12-2.30/7-9.30 **Notes:** Vegetarian available, No jeans or trainers, Civ Wed 200 **Seats:** 50, Pr/dining room 20 **Smoking:** N/Sm in restaurant **Children:** Menu, Portions **Rooms:** 23 (23 en suite) ★★★ **Directions:** 3m S of Barnard Castle off A66. 9m W of Scotch Corner from A1 (Darlington) **Parking:** 50 **e-mail:** relax@themorritt.co.uk **web:** www.themorritt.co.uk

BEAMISH MAP 19 NZ25

⊚⊚ Beamish Park Hotel

Mediterranean, European

A global slant in jazz-themed setting

☎ 01207 230666 Beamish Burn Rd NE16 5EG

MENU GUIDE Fresh crab cake with pineapple salsa • Peppered loin of Beamish venison with fondant potato • Caramelised lemon tart with winter berries

WINE GUIDE ♀ Pierre Javert Sauvignon/Colombard £12.95 • ♥ Pierre Javert Merlot/Syrah £12.50 • 9 bottles over £20, 24 bottles under £20 • 10 by the glass (£2.30-£5.40)

PRICE GUIDE Fixed L £9.95 • starter £3.50-£6.50 • main £11.25-£16.25 • dessert £4.50-£4.95 • coffee £1.60 • min/water £3.95 • Service optional

PLACE: The split-level Conservatory Bistro, is modern, chic and has a distinct jazz theme set by jazz figurines and jazz-themed photographs. Use of imaginative lighting, unusual fabrics and warm Mediterranean colours give it a relaxed feel, perfect for a business drink with colleagues or for an evening out with friends and family.

FOOD: The constantly changing menus reflect the best of currently available local produce. An eclectic mix of dishes include Mediterranean, European, local specialities, and several 'favourites'. Examples include Asian-spiced pork belly on Chines greens, sweet potato purée, and confit of duckling on saffron mash, Toulouse sausage.

OUR TIP: Best to book ahead

Chef: Christopher Walker **Owners:** William Walker **Times:** 12-2.30/7-10.30 **Notes:** Vegetarian available, Dress Restrictions, Smart casual preferred **Seats:** 70, Pr/dining room 80 **Smoking:** N/Sm area, Air con **Children:** Portions **Rooms:** 47 (47 en suite) ★★★ **Directions:** A1(M) turn off onto A692 and continue for 2m into Sunniside. At traffic lights take A6076 signposted Beamish Museum & Tanfield Museum. Hotel is situated behind Causey Arch Inn **Parking:** 100 **e-mail:** reception@beamish-park-hotel.co.uk **web:** www.beamish-park-hotel.co.uk

---

What makes a Restaurant of the Year?
In selecting a Restaurant of the Year, we look for somewhere that is exceptional in its chosen area of the market. Whilst the Rosette awards are based on the quality of the food alone, Restaurant of the Year takes into account all aspects of the operation. For full details see pages 6-7.

DARLINGTON MAP 19 NZ21

🏵 *Hall Garth Hotel*

Modern British

16th-century manor with short modern menu

☎ 01325 300400 Coatham Mundeville DL1 3LU

PLACE: Just a few minutes from the motorway yet peacefully situated, this attractive hotel includes a golf course, extensive leisure facilities, a pub and Hugo's, an intimate candlelit restaurant. The building dates from the 16th-century and its romantic atmosphere is enhanced by soft music and an open fire.
FOOD: The short menu focuses on British fare, but also includes some European influences.
OUR TIP: Peaceful yet handy for the motorway
Times: 12.30-2/7-9.30, Closed L Mon-Sat **Rooms:** 51 (51 en suite)
★★★ **Directions:** A1(M) J 59 (A167) (Darlington), top of hill turn L signed Brafferton, hotel 200yds on R **e-mail:** hallgarth@corushotels.com **web:** www.corushotels.co.uk

🏵 Headlam Hall Hotel

British, French

Ambitious cooking in historic hall

☎ 01325 730238 Headlam, Gainford DL2 3HA

MENU GUIDE Poached oysters, watercress sauce • Slow-roast pork belly, garlic mash, leek fondue, thyme jus • Raspberry crème brûlée

WINE GUIDE ♀ Santa Rita Sauvignon Blanc £14 • ♀ Georges Duboeuf Grand Cuvée £12 • 60 bottles over £20, 14 bottles under £20 • 6 by the glass (£3.50-£7.50)

PRICE GUIDE Fixed L £10-£15 • starter £4.50-£7.50 • main £11.50-£18.50 • dessert £5-£7 • coffee £2.50 • min/water £3.50 • Service included

PLACE: Set in pretty grounds, this impressive Jacobean hall offers a choice of dining rooms designed to reflect the different eras of its history. They're all intimate and welcoming, from the rich splendour of the panelled room, to the airy greenery of the conservatory.
FOOD: This ambitious kitchen consistently delivers and deserves its excellent local reputation. Choices on the modern British and French menu might include sea bass with red pepper couscous, or beef with horseradish mash.
OUR TIP: The hotel has its own 9-hole golf course
Chef: Austen Shaw **Owners:** JH Robinson **Times:** 12-2.30/7-9.30, Closed 25-26 Dec **Notes:** Vegetarian available, Dress Restrictions, No sportswear, shorts, Civ Wed 150 **Seats:** 70, Pr/dining room 30
Smoking: N/Sm in restaurant **Children:** Menu, Portions **Rooms:** 36 (36 en suite) ★★★ **Directions:** 8m W of Darlington off A67
Parking: 70 **e-mail:** admin@headlamhall.co.uk
web: www.headlamhall.co.uk

DURHAM MAP 19 NZ24

🏵 Bistro 21

British, European

French country bistro in the heart of County Durham

☎ 0191 384 4354 Aykley Heads House, Aykley Heads DH1 5TS

MENU GUIDE Roast quail, walnut salad • Glazed pork knuckle • Ginger tiramisù

WINE GUIDE ♀ Georges Duboeuf £12.50 • ♀ Georges Duboeuf £12.50 • 20 bottles over £20, 20 bottles under £20 • 6 by the glass (£3.20-£5)

Bistro 21

PRICE GUIDE Fixed L £13 • starter £4.50-£9.50 • main £11-£19.50 • dessert £4.50-£6.50 • coffee £1.80 • min/water £2.50 • Service optional • Group min 11 service 10%

PLACE: The rustic chic of this converted country-house kitchen has all the appeal of a rural French bistro. The clean lines, dictated by wooden and stone floors, and high windows contribute to the easy-going mood.
FOOD: The no-fuss menus live up to their promise, yielding simple, well executed dishes that move from classical French towards a refreshing modern bistro interpretation. Grilled calves' liver and confit duck get the best out of quality ingredients.
OUR TIP: Summer dining in the chic courtyard
Chef: Paul O'Hara **Owners:** Terence Laybourne **Times:** 12-2/7-10.25, Closed 25 Dec, 1Jan, BHs, Sun **Notes:** Vegetarian available **Seats:** 55, Pr/dining room 20 **Smoking:** N/Sm in restaurant **Children:** Portions **Directions:** Off B6532 from Durham centre, pass County Hall on right and Dryburn Hospital on left. Turn right at double rdbt into Aykley Heads **Parking:** 11

🏵 Durham Marriott Hotel, Royal County

European

Artistic food in classical restaurant

☎ 0191 386 6821 Old Elvet DH1 3JN

MENU GUIDE Black pudding & poached egg • Roast pork loin, apple risotto • Marbled chocolate truffle

WINE GUIDE ♀ Rosemount Shiraz £19.55 • ♀ Rosemount Chardonnay £19.55 • 36 bottles over £20, 30 bottles under £20 • 20 by the glass (£5.10-£7.85)

PRICE GUIDE Fixed D £29.95 • starter £3.95-£11.95 • main £15.95-£24.95 • dessert £5-£6.50 • min/water £3.50 • Service optional

PLACE: Plush leather armchairs and smart table dressings in the restaurant suggest a classical elegance which this long-established hotel lives up to comfortably.
FOOD: Artistic presentation scores highly here, with the beautiful modern cooking arranged on square white plates. Seafood panache with grilled peppers and lemon cream is an exemplary main dish from a talented kitchen's repertoire.
OUR TIP: Handy city centre location
Chef: James Marron **Owners:** Whitbread **Times:** 12.30-2.30/7-10, Closed L Mon-Sat **Notes:** Sun lunch 3 courses, Vegetarian available, Dress Restrictions, Smart casual, Civ Wed 60 **Seats:** 90, Pr/dining room 120 **Smoking:** N/Sm in restaurant, Air con **Children:** Menu, Portions **Rooms:** 150 (150 en suite) ★★★★ **Directions:** From A1(M) onto A690. Follow City Centre signs, over 1st rdbt, left at 2nd, over bridge, left at lights, hotel on left. **Parking:** 70
e-mail: durhamroyal.marriott@whitbread.com
web: www.marriotthotels.com/xvudm

continued

REDWORTH MAP 19 NZ22

⚛⚛ Redworth Hall Hotel

Traditional British

Imposing country house dining

☎ 01388 770600 DL5 6NL

MENU GUIDE Poached salmon ballotine • Turbot fillet, brioche crumb • Chocolate tart, Horlicks ice cream

WINE GUIDE ⚲ Mavida Chardonnay £16.50 • ⚲ Mavida Merlot £16.50 • 20 bottles over £20, 8 bottles under £20 • 28 by the glass (£4.50-£9)

PRICE GUIDE Fixed D £18.50-£30 • starter £4.75-£12 • main £12-£25 • dessert £7-£12 • coffee £2.50 • min/water £3.75 • Service optional

PLACE: Driving up a winding woodland path leads to this magnificent Jacobean country house hotel set in 25 acres of gardens. There's the Conservatory Restaurant for bistro dining or the 1744 restaurant for fine dining with its comfortable furniture, large fireplace, formal table settings and relaxed, friendly service.

FOOD: Traditional British and French dishes populate the menu. Starters can include ravioli of scallops or asparagus and almond soup while main courses revert to old favourites such as tournedos of beef and suckling pig. Good choice of Northumberland cheeses.

OUR TIP: Visit the nearby Beamish Open Air Museum
Chef: Chris Delaney **Owners:** Paramount Group of Hotels
Times: 11.30-2.30/7-10, Closed Sat before Xmas-1st Sat New Year, Sun-Mon **Notes:** Vegetarian available, Smart Dress, Smart casual, Civ Wed 300 **Seats:** 145, Pr/dining room 30 **Smoking:** N/Sm in restaurant, Air con **Rooms:** 100 (100 en suite) ★★★★ **Directions:** From A1(M) J58 take A68 towards Corbridge. At 1st rdbt take A6072 towards Bishop Auckland. At next rdbt take 2nd exit (A6072). Hotel on L **Parking:** 350
e-mail: redworthhall@paramount-hotels.co.uk
web: www.paramount-hotels.co.uk

ROMALDKIRK MAP 19 NY92

⚛⚛ Rose & Crown Hotel

British

Cosy country inn in picture postcard village green setting

☎ 01833 650213 DL12 9EB

MENU GUIDE Seared king scallops, leek risotto, parsley pesto • Roast Teesdale Fell lamb with kidney casserole • Warm lemon tart

WINE GUIDE ⚲ Schinus Gary Crittendon Sauvignon Blanc £16.50 • ⚲ Iron Stone Shiraz £16.50 • 30 bottles over £20, 24 bottles under £20 • 10 by the glass (£3-£4.95)

PRICE GUIDE Fixed L £16.50 • Fixed D £26-£29 • coffee £1.95 • min/water £3 • Service optional

PLACE: This unpretentious 18th-century coaching inn is next to the Saxon church in this quintessentially English village. Eat in the buzzy bar, with its old prints and crackling fire, or in the oak-panelled restaurant with its crisp white linen cloths, fine china and evening candlelight.

FOOD: Classic British and modern dishes with strong regional influence are well executed and provide clean, bold flavours from local ingredients: baked cheese soufflé uses local Cotherstone cheese, and a main course of roasted monkfish tails arrives wrapped in Cumberland ham.

OUR TIP: The bedrooms are away from the hustle and bustle
Chef: Chris Davy, Andrew Lee **Times:** 12-1.30/7.30-9, Closed Xmas, closed L Mon-Sat **Notes:** Vegetarian available **Seats:** 24 **Smoking:** N/Sm in restaurant **Children:** Min 6yrs, Portions **Rooms:** 12 (12 en suite) ★★ **Directions:** 6m NW of Barnard Castle on B6277 **Parking:** 24 **e-mail:** hotel@rose-and-crown.co.uk
web: www.rose-and-crown.co.uk

SEAHAM MAP 19 NZ44

⚛⚛⚛ Seaham Hall Hotel

see page 155

STOCKTON-ON-TEES MAP 19 NZ41

⚛ Parkmore Hotel

International

Heady cooking in a stylish hotel restaurant

☎ 01642 786815 636 Yarm Rd, Eaglescliffe TS16 0DH

MENU GUIDE Pan-fried Toulouse sausage • Roast rack of lamb • Raspberry torte, blackberry compote

WINE GUIDE ⚲ Moondarra Semillon Chardonnay £14.95 • ⚲ Moondarra Shiraz £14.95 • 25 bottles over £20, 80 bottles under £20 • 15 by the glass (£2.50-£3.50)

PRICE GUIDE Fixed L £9.95-£12.95 • Fixed D £18.25-£21 • starter £5.95-£7.50 • main £14-£22 • dessert £4.50 • coffee £1.50 • min/water £3.50

PLACE: Extensive leisure and conference facilities offer their own incentives to business visitors, but the classical appeal of the modern restaurant provides another serious reason for visiting this smart Victorian hotel.

FOOD: The kitchen gets the best flavours out of their ingredients, with the odd tendency towards spontaneity generally paying off. Simple lunch dishes are taken up a few gears in the evening.

OUR TIP: Very good fixed-price menu
Chef: Marc Lake **Owners:** Brian Reed **Times:** 12-2/6.45-9.30, Closed 25 Dec (eve) **Notes:** Vegetarian available, Civ Wed 100 **Seats:** 60, Pr/dining room 30 **Smoking:** N/Sm in restaurant **Children:** Menu, Portions **Rooms:** 55 (55 en suite) ★★★ **Directions:** On A135 between Yarm & Stockton-on-Tees, almost opposite Eaglescliffe Golf Course **Parking:** 108
e-mail: enquiries@parkmorehotel.co.uk
web: www.parkmorehotel.co.uk

Prices quoted in the guide are for guidance only and are subject to change without notice.

For information on Service Charge, see p21.

continued

SEAHAM MAP 19 NZ44

Seaham Hall Hotel

French, European

Stylish hotel serving accomplish cuisine with style

☎ 0191 5161400 Lord Byron's Walk SR7 7AG

MENU GUIDE Roast sea scallops, celeriac & truffle • Braised pig's trotter, white pudding mousseline, morels & sage • Tonka bean crème brûlée, rhubarb

WINE GUIDE ♀ Chablis Servin Chardonnay £30.50 • ♀ Solar Samaniego Rioja Crianza £24.50 • 250 bottles over £20, 4 bottles under £20 • 8 by the glass (£4.50-£12)

PRICE GUIDE Fixed L £19.50 • starter £9-£19 • main £17.50-£29 • dessert £7-£12.50 • coffee £3.50 • Service optional

PLACE: Set in 64 acres of landscaped gardens and perched on the edge of the North Sea, this striking hotel was the scene of Lord Byron's wedding and honeymoon in 1815. Decor throughout is chic, tasteful and extremely stylish, mixing comfort with the latest in hi-tech. The aptly named White Room restaurant continues the theme, with wooden floor, limestone fireplace and larger-than-average tables set with white linen and classically simple glassware. Centre stage is given to the food, wine and exceptional service from a team who will offer the finest detail on sourcing, flavours or wine combinations.
FOOD: New chef Stephen Smith's style is up-to-the-minute but underpinned by a classical theme. Expect simplicity, high quality fresh

ingredients and vibrant, bold flavours to illustrate accomplished technical skills. The approach is via an appealing range of menus, from value fixed-price lunch, lunch and dinner cartes and a gourmand option.
OUR TIP: Visit the Spa and Ozone restaurant
Chef: Stephen Smith **Owners:** Tom & Jocelyn Maxfield **Times:** 12-2.30/7-10 **Notes:** Menu Gourmand £65, Sun L £27.50, Vegetarian available, Civ Wed 112 **Seats:** 55, Pr/dining room 20 **Smoking:** N/Sm in restaurant, Air con **Children:** Portions **Rooms:** 19 (19 en suite) ★★★★
Directions: A19/B1404, follow signs to Seaham Hall **Parking:** 150
e-mail: reservations@seaham-hall.com **web:** www.seaham-hall.com

ESSEX

BRENTWOOD MAP 06 TQ59

Marygreen Manor

International

Exciting dining in striking Tudor surroundings

☎ 01277 225252 London Rd CM14 4NR

MENU GUIDE Tempura prawn, plum & red pepper coulis • Roast lamb loin, artichoke & duxelle • Caramelised apples

WINE GUIDE ♀ Los Vascos Baron de Rothschild Chardonnay £20.70 • ♀ Los Vascos Baron de Rothschild Cabernet Sauvignon £20.70 • 98 bottles over £20, 32 bottles under £20 • 7 by the glass (£3.10-£4)

PRICE GUIDE Fixed L £19.50 • Fixed D £35 • starter £7-£12.50 • main £19.50-£27.50 • dessert £6.95 • coffee £3 • min/water £3.50 • Service included *continued*

PLACE: This 16th-century manor house - now a hotel - makes an impressive setting for a restaurant. The baronial dining room of the Tudors Restaurant has smart, formal settings and service and a wealth of beams, carvings and panelling.
FOOD: A good choice of contemporary dishes with an emphasis on local produce. The menu features some exciting combinations such as sea bass with courgette and pepper couscous, roasted banana and chilli and coconut cappuccino. Notable wine list.
OUR TIP: Plenty of choice if you're a fish lover
Chef: Lee Brooker **Owners:** Mr S Bhattessa **Times:** 12.30-2.30/7.15-10.15 **Notes:** Sun L £22.50, Vegetarian available, Dress Restrictions, No jeans or trainers, Civ Wed 60 **Seats:** 80, Pr/dining room 85
Smoking: N/Sm in restaurant, Air con **Children:** Portions **Rooms:** 44 (44 en suite) ★★★★ **Directions:** 1m from Brentwood town centre, 0.5m from M25 junct 28 **Parking:** 100
e-mail: info@marygreenmanor.co.uk
web: www.marygreenmanor.co.uk

CHELMSFORD MAP 06 TL70

Atlantic Hotel

Modern European 🐟NEW

Good brasserie dining in Essex town centre

☎ 01245 268168 & 268179 New St CM1 1PP

MENU GUIDE Wild mushroom salad, poached egg • Roast beef sirloin, Anna potatoes, Madeira jus • Zabaglione

WINE GUIDE ♀ Madfish Chardonnay £22 • ♀ The Paddock Shiraz £14 • 32 bottles over £20, 27 bottles under £20 • 10 by the glass (£3.50-£8.75)

PRICE GUIDE Fixed L £15-£25 • Fixed D £20-£35 • starter £4-£9.95 • main £11-£22 • dessert £4.50-£6.50 • coffee £1.95 • min/water £3 • Service optional *continued*

CHELMSFORD *continued* MAP 06 TL70

PLACE: A modern, purpose-built hotel situated close to the town centre. Its open, airy public areas include a lounge bar and brasserie as well as a conservatory. Uniformed staff, friendly service and good quality settings make for a pleasant dining venue.
FOOD: There's a good choice of dishes on the brasserie style menu with meat, fish and vegetarian items. Good quality produce is carefully prepared here and accompaniments are well chosen.
OUR TIP: There is a fish counter for daily seafood specialities
Chef: Jon Tindle **Owners:** Shahrohh Bagherzadeh **Times:** 12-3/6-10.30, Closed 27-30 Dec, closed L Sat-Sun **Notes:** Vegetarian available
Seats: 100, Pr/dining room 25 **Smoking:** N/Sm in restaurant, Air con
Children: Portions **Parking:** 70 **e-mail:** info@atlantichotel.co.uk
web: www.atlantichotel.co.uk

Russells

British, French
Classic cuisine in old converted barn
☎ 01245 478484 Bell St, Great Baddow CM2 7JF

MENU GUIDE Scallops wrapped in Parma ham • Baked fillet of cod, crispy pancetta • Caramelised banana parfait, Malibu & coconut sauce

WINE GUIDE ♀ Le Grys Malborough Sauvignon Blanc £21.95 • ♀ Valle Andino Merlot £14.50 • 42 bottles over £20, 27 bottles under £20 • 7 by the glass (£2.95-£3.95)

PRICE GUIDE Fixed L £9.95 • Fixed D £21.95 • starter £5.50-£11.95 • main £12.95-£24.95 • dessert £4.95-£7.95 • coffee £2.45 • min/water £3.50 • Service optional • Group min 10 service 15%

PLACE: In the pretty village of Great Baddow a few miles outside Chelmsford, this converted barn has beams that can be dated back to 1372. A smart reception/bar area is furnished with comfortable Victorian sofas and chairs. Gaze down on neatly clothed tables from the upstairs gallery.
FOOD: Extensive fixed price and carte menus of classic English and French dishes with some modern touches. Expect mains like chicken supreme with sun-dried tomato and pear stuffing, set on spinach with timbale of wild rice and sherry cream velouté.
OUR TIP: Take a walk in the village before dinner
Chef: Kris Sadler **Owners:** Mr BJ Warren-Watson **Times:** 12-2.30/7-11.30, Closed 2 wks from 2 Jan, Mon, closed L Sat, closed D Sun
Notes: Sun L 3 courses £15.95, Vegetarian available, Dress Restrictions, No jeans **Seats:** 70, Pr/dining room 36 **Smoking:** N/Sm in restaurant, Air con **Children:** Portions **Directions:** Telephone for directions
Parking: 40 **e-mail:** russellsrestaurant@hotmail.com
web: www.russellsrest.co.uk

COGGESHALL MAP 07 TL82

Baumann's Brasserie

British, French
Bright and friendly brasserie in town centre
☎ 01376 561453 4-6 Stoneham St CO6 1TT

MENU GUIDE Barbecue duck potato cake, pickled soba noodles • Sea bass, curried peach chutney, champagne cream sauce • Cappuccino brûlée

WINE GUIDE ♀ Mansion House Bay Sauvignon Blanc £18.50 • ♀ Yalumba Shiraz £14.95 • 14 bottles over £20, 21 bottles under £20 • 8 by the glass (£2.95-£5.95)

PRICE GUIDE Fixed L £10.95 • Fixed D £21 • starter £5.50-£8.95 • main £15.95-£19.50 • dessert £6.50 • coffee £1.40 • min/water £2.75 • Service optional

PLACE: This busy, eponymous brasserie, set in a 16th-century building at the heart of town, is smart yet informal. The decor fits the bill, matching stripped floors with whitewashed walls and colourful prints, and linen-dressed tables alongside an array of antique chairs.
FOOD: Mark Baumann's menus deliver an eclectic mix of interesting, well-executed dishes, the approach via carte, set-priced three-course lunch, plus informal, express-style lunch offerings like Baumann's paninis.
OUR TIP: Good value lunch
Chef: Mark Baumann, C Jeanneau **Owners:** Baumanns Brasserie Ltd
Times: 12-2/7-9.30, Closed 2 wks Jan, Mon-Tue **Notes:** Sun L £21 (incl coffee, petit fours), Vegetarian available, Smart Dress **Seats:** 80
Smoking: N/Sm in restaurant **Children:** Portions **Directions:** A12 from Chelmsford, turn off at Kelvedon **Parking:** Opposite
e-mail: food@baumannsbrasserie.co.uk
web: www.baumannsbrasserie.co.uk

COLCHESTER MAP 13 TL92

The Rose & Crown Hotel

Indian, French
15th-century coaching inn serving colourful dishes of fusion food
☎ 01206 866677 East St CO1 2TZ

MENU GUIDE Exotic smoked salmon, onion & cucumber yoghurt • Lucknowi lamb, sweet potato, roasted nut sauce • Nougatine crème caramel

WINE GUIDE ♀ Yalumba "Y" Series Chardonnay £19.75 • ♀ Lodge Hill Shiraz £27.50 • 16 bottles over £20, 16 bottles under £20 • 7 by the glass (£3.35-£4.65)

PRICE GUIDE Fixed L £13.95 • Fixed D £19.95 • starter £4.95-£7.25 • main £14.95-£18.95 • dessert £5.25 • coffee £2.20 • min/water £3.25 • Service included • Group min 5 service 10%

continued

PLACE: A traditional black and white building, reputedly the oldest hotel in the oldest recorded town in England. Situated close to the shops, it has retained all its period charm thanks to careful and loving restoration. Exposed beams, panelled walls and log fires naturally feature, especially in the Tudor Bar and Oak Room restaurant.
FOOD: The classically trained chef fuses Indian and French flavours to create menus of unique style. The kitchen's aim is to present dishes that are visually dramatic, as in the starter of spiced smoked salmon, lamb rolls and crab cakes.
OUR TIP: A popular venue for civil weddings
Chef: Uday Shankar **Owners:** Karim Chaouch **Times:** 12-2/7-9.45, Closed 27-30 Dec, closed D Sun **Notes:** Sun L £15.95, Vegetarian available, Smart Dress, Civ Wed 150 **Seats:** 80, Pr/dining room 50 **Smoking:** N/Sm in restaurant **Children:** Menu, Portions **Rooms:** 31 (31 en suite) ★★★ **Directions:** From A12 take exit to Colchester North onto the A1232 **Parking:** 90 **e-mail:** info@rose-and-crown.com **web:** www.rose-and-crown.com

DANBURY MAP 07 TL70

🍵 Tea on the Green 3 Eves Corner CM3 4QF
☎ 01245 226616 Winner of The Tea Guild Award of Excellence 2005.

DEDHAM MAP 13 TM03

◎◎ Le Talbooth Restaurant
British
Serious cuisine in beautiful setting
☎ 01206 323150   CO7 6HP

MENU GUIDE Lobster Pithiviers • Venison, white bean & garlic purée, potato & haggis beignet, redcurrant jus • Plum & almond pudding
WINE GUIDE ♀ Billaud Simon Chardonnay £25.50 • ♀ Château Côtes des Trois Moulins Grand Cru St Emilion Merlot £33 • 200 bottles over £20, 34 bottles under £20 • 10 by the glass (£4)

continued

PRICE GUIDE Fixed L £21 • starter £6.50-£17 • main £17.50-£27 dessert £9.25 • coffee £3.75 • min/water £4 • Service added 10%
PLACE: Once painted by Constable, this magnificent timber-framed house has a picture-perfect setting by an ivy-clad bridge on the banks of the River Stour. It's been a weaver's cottage, toll booth, and humble tearoom in its time, but is now an acclaimed hotel, with a beamed restaurant.
FOOD: A lengthy modern British menu of serious fare to suit all tastes if not pockets. Mains range from simple fish dishes (grilled Dover sole with herb butter) to heartier options such as veal steak and kidney suet pudding with clapshot and champ, or rump of lamb with redcurrant juices. Excellent wine list.
OUR TIP: Very busy at weekends, so book ahead
Chef: Terry Barber, Ian Rhodes **Owners:** Paul Milsom **Times:** 12-2/7-9, Closed D Sun (Oct-Apr) **Notes:** Sun L 3 courses £30, Vegetarian available, Dress Restrictions, Smart casual, No jeans, Civ Wed 50 **Seats:** 75, Pr/dining room 34 **Smoking:** No pipes, No cigars **Children:** Portions **Directions:** 6m from Colchester: follow signs from A12 to Stratford St Mary, restaurant on left before village **Parking:** 50 **e-mail:** talbooth@milsomhotels.com **web:** www.milsomhotels.com

◎ milsoms
International
Popular local restaurant with wide-ranging menu
☎ 01206 322795   Stratford Rd CO7 6HN

MENU GUIDE Haloumi, meats, stuffed vine leaves, sardines • Lamb on flageolet bean purée, balsamic dressing • Raspberry & sherry trifle
WINE GUIDE ♀ Moa Ridge Sauvignon Blanc £17.75 • ♀ Tin Hat Shiraz/Cabernet Sauvignon £15.25 • 52 bottles over £20, 19 bottles under £20 • 12 by the glass (£3.20-£5.35)
PRICE GUIDE Starter £3.50-£6.95 • main £8.50-£19.95 • dessert £5.25 • coffee £2 • min/water £4 • Service optional
PLACE: This ever popular restaurant and bar in the beautiful Vale of Dedham has become a huge hit with the locals, thanks to its crowd-pleasing menu and informal, contemporary style, which sees guests write out their own orders. No bookings taken.

continued

DEDHAM continued MAP 13 TM03

FOOD: A lengthy and flexible international menu of simple dishes served in a rustic style. Mains range from old favourites (shepherd's pie, calves' liver and bacon) to lighter Mediterranean and Asian fare.

OUR TIP: Terraced gardens for alfresco dining in the summer

Chef: Stas Anastasiades **Owners:** Paul Milsom **Times:** 12-2.15/6-9.30 **Notes:** Vegetarian available **Seats:** 80, Pr/dining room 16 **Smoking:** N/Sm area, Air con **Children:** Menu, Portions **Rooms:** 14 (14 en suite) ★★★ **Directions:** 7m N of Colchester, just off A12 **Parking:** 60 **e-mail:** milsoms@milsomhotels.com **web:** www.milsomhotels.com

EARLS COLNE MAP 13 TL82

The Carved Angel

British, Mediterranean

Popular gastro-pub

☎ 01787 222330 Upper Holt St CO6 2PG

MENU GUIDE Seafood risotto • Braised lamb shank, celeriac purée & port jus • Custard tart with mascarpone

WINE GUIDE ♀ Nagaryese Pinot Grigio £10.25 • ♀ Moulin de Laval Merlot £10.25 • 21 bottles over £20, 28 bottles under £20 • 14 by the glass (£1.90-£3.50)

PRICE GUIDE Fixed L £9.95 • starter £3.95-£5.75 • main £7.95-£14.95 • dessert £4.50 • coffee £1.95 • min/water £2.95 • Service optional • Group min 10 service 10%

PLACE: This 15th-century coaching inn has been transformed into a modern gastro-pub with clean lines and contemporary fittings, and a large conservatory for non-smokers. Food is ordered at the bar, but brought to the table by waiting staff.

FOOD: The European menu is eclectic: pan-fried fillets of sea bass appearing with braised fennel, bok choi and a soy and ginger glaze.

OUR TIP: Alfresco eating in the summer

Chef: Dan Hibble **Owners:** Melissa & Michael Deckers **Times:** 11.30-3.30/6.30-11, Closed 26 Dec & 1 Jan **Notes:** Sun roast £7.95, Vegetarian

available **Seats:** 71 **Smoking:** N/Sm area **Children:** Portions **Directions:** A120 to Coggeshall, take B1024 to Earl Colne. At mini rdbt with A1124 turn right. From Colchester on A1124 (signed to Halstead). Village 7m and restaurant on sharp bend **Parking:** 50 **e-mail:** info@carvedangel.com **web:** www.carvedangel.com

de Vere Arms

Traditional, Modern

Rural venue with striking decor in traditional setting

☎ 01787 223353 53 High St CO6 2PB

MENU GUIDE Roast scallops, glazed salsify, blood orange sauce • Beef fillet, crispy veal sweetbread • Assiette of chocolate desserts

WINE GUIDE ♀ Norte Chico Chardonnay £13.90 • ♀ Château Pitray Côtes de Castillon £13.90 • 53 bottles over £20, 15 bottles under £20 • 11 by the glass (£2.50-£6.50)

PRICE GUIDE Fixed D £35 • coffee £2.25 • min/water £3 • Service included

PLACE: Beautifully crafted transformation of a former inn on the village high street, with its own unique style. This has involved the work of local artists and artisans, and personally imported antiques and artefacts. Rich colours and old beams offset tables laid with contemporary linens, glassware and crockery.

FOOD: The food is both traditional and modern in character, skilfully executed and tending towards the elaborate. The seasonal fixed-price menu changes regularly and alternatives are available for vegetarians.

OUR TIP: Lovely location in the Colne Valley

Chef: Chris Standhaven **Owners:** Michael & Melissa Deckers **Times:** 12-2/7-9.30, Closed L Sat **Notes:** Vegetarian available, Dress Restrictions, Smart Casual **Seats:** 52 **Smoking:** N/Sm in restaurant **Children:** Portions **Rooms:** 9 (9 en suite) ★★★ **Directions:** B1024 towards Earls Colne, left at mini-rdbt onto High St, hotel on right. **Parking:** 15 **e-mail:** dining@deverearms.com **web:** www.deverearms.com

continued

FELSTED MAP 06 TL62

🏵 *Reeves Restaurant*
Modern British

Intimate cottage restaurant with imaginative cooking

☎ 01371 820996 Rumbles Cottage, Braintree Rd CM6 3DJ

PLACE: A cottage restaurant housed in a 16th-century building in the heart of a bustling village. The decor and furnishing are cosily traditional, with paintings by local artists on the walls.
FOOD: The eclectic, interesting menu combines modern British (braised lamb shank with baby vegetables) with international influences (Cajun tuna steak with oriental vegetables). Dishes are well executed and in tune with the seasons.
OUR TIP: The fixed price lunch menu is good value
Times: 12-2/From 7, Closed Mon
e-mail: info@reeves-restaurant.co.uk **web:** www.reeves-restaurant.co.uk

GREAT CHESTERFORD MAP 12 TL54

🏵 The Crown House
British

Simple and enjoyable dining in historic coaching inn

☎ 01799 530515 CB10 1NY

MENU GUIDE Chicken & duck liver parfait • Scotch beef sirloin • Steamed syrup pudding

WINE GUIDE 20 bottles over £20, 32 bottles under £20 • 4 by the glass (£2.50)

PRICE GUIDE Fixed L £15.95 • starter £4.25-£5.25 • main £13.95-£16.95 • dessert £4.95-£6.25 • coffee £1.95 • min/water £2.50 • Service optional

PLACE: This listed coaching inn is situated in a quiet village location. It has been extensively and sympathetically restored, retaining many of its original features. There's a warm and welcoming lounge bar, a conservatory and an oak-panelled dining room.
FOOD: A refreshingly simple style of cooking with nicely presented dishes and good, clear flavours.
OUR TIP: Terrace dining overlooking walled garden in summer
Chef: John Kichenbrand **Owners:** F D Ebdon **Times:** 12-2/7-9.15
Notes: Sun lunch 2 courses £12.95, 3 courses £14.95, Vegetarian available, Smart Dress, Civ Wed 50 **Seats:** 60, Pr/dining room 28 **Smoking:** N/Sm in restaurant **Children:** Portions **Rooms:** 18 (18 en suite) ★★★
Parking: 30 **e-mail:** dine@thecrownhouse.com
web: www.thecrownhouse.com

GREAT DUNMOW MAP 06 TL62

🏵🏵 Starr Restaurant
British, French

Ancient inn with a strong local following

☎ 01371 874321 Market Place CM6 1AX

MENU GUIDE Scallops, pea purée, pancetta, mint relish • Beef with mustard rarebit crust, rösti potato, truffle jus • Chocolate marquis

WINE GUIDE ♀ Pouilly Fumé Pabiot Freres Sauvignon Blanc £29.50 • ♀ Allan Scott Pinot Noir £34.50 • 125 bottles over £20, 28 bottles under £20 • 7 by the glass (£4.50-£5.95)

PRICE GUIDE Fixed L £15.50-£27.50 • Fixed D £32.50-£42.50 coffee £3 • min/water £3.50 • Service optional • Group min 6 service 10%

continued

continued

GREAT DUNMOW *continued* MAP 06 TL62

PLACE: Dating back to the 15th century, this former coaching inn sits in the heart of a pretty Essex village and has an established local reputation. Lunch and dinner are served in the heavily beamed dining room and adjacent conservatory.

FOOD: A daily changing carte is predominantly British in style, with the odd French and international touch, so your choice of mains might include calves' liver with a shallot and herb croquette, or duck with jasmine rice and roast mangoes. Good value lunch menu.

OUR TIP: Eight rooms available if you're too full to move

Chef: Mark Pearson **Owners:** Terence & Louise George **Times:** 12-1.30/7-9.30, Closed 4 days between Xmas & New Year, closed D Sun

Notes: Vegetarian available, Dress Restrictions, No jeans, trainers or shorts

Seats: 70, Pr/dining room 36 **Smoking:** N/Sm in restaurant

Children: Portions **Rooms:** 8 (8 en suite) 🏨 **Directions:** M11 junct 8, A120 7m E towards Colchester. In town centre **Parking:** 16

e-mail: starrrestaurant@btinternet.com **web:** www.the-starr.co.uk

---

GREAT YELDHAM MAP 13 TL73

🏵 White Hart

Modern British

15th-century country pub with a serious local following

☎ 01787 237250   CO9 4HJ

MENU GUIDE Seared scallops, black pudding • Roasted partridge, colcannon, cranberry chutney, roasted vegetables • Neapolitan parfait

WINE GUIDE ♀ Froncalieu Montagne Noir Marsanne £12.50 • ♀ Froncalieu Montagne Noir Merlot £12.50 • 48 bottles over £20, 30 bottles under £20 • 12 by the glass (£3.25-£5.50)

PRICE GUIDE Fixed L £10.50 • starter £5.75-£8.95 • main £11.95-£17.25 • dessert £5.25-£7.50 • coffee £1.75 • min/water £2.95 • Service optional

PLACE: The distinctive black and white beamed frontage make this Tudor pub/restaurant easy to find, especially when lit at night. The bar, garden room and formal dining room are all charming eating venues.

FOOD: Modern British ideas bring vitality to the menu, where chorizo and red pepper risotto, and pear and stilton tartlet might lead to similarly vibrant main dishes: rump of lamb with sweet potato mash, perhaps, or beef medallions on horseradish rösti.

OUR TIP: Excellent wine list.

Chef: John Dicken **Owners:** John Dicken **Times:** 12-2/6.30-9.30, Closed D 25-26 Dec **Notes:** Sun lunch 2 courses £16.95, 3 courses £22.95, Vegetarian available, Civ Wed 75 **Seats:** 60, Pr/dining room 36

Smoking: N/Sm in restaurant **Children:** Portions **Directions:** On A1017, between Halstead and Haverhill. **Parking:** 40

e-mail: reservations@whitehartyeldham.co.uk

web: www.whitehartyeldham.co.uk

HARWICH MAP 13 TM23

🏵🏵 The Pier at Harwich

British, European

Modish seafood restaurant on the quayside

☎ 01255 241212   The Quay CO12 3HH

MENU GUIDE New England clam chowder • Seared salmon, wilted spinach, asparagus, lemon sauce • Strawberry bavarois, vanilla pod sauce

WINE GUIDE ♀ Randall Bridge Chardonnay £14.50 • ♀ Bradgate Cabernet Sauvignon/Merlot £14.50 10 bottles over £20, 45 bottles under £20 • 6 by the glass (£3.30-£3.70)

continued

The Pier at Harwich

PRICE GUIDE Fixed L £18 • starter £6-£12 • main £12.95-£32 • dessert £6.50 • coffee £2.95 • min/water £3.25 • Service added 10%

PLACE: Set on the quay overlooking Harwich and Felixstowe, this small hotel offers fantastic views from its recently refurbished Harbour Restaurant. It's an informal brasserie style venue, with a classy new champagne and oyster bar for pre-dinner drinks or a snack.

FOOD: With a working harbour on its doorstep, it's no surprise that seafood is the draw. Ingredients are handled sympathetically and with skill to allow flavours to come through; your choice might include Dover sole with nut brown butter and lemon, or poached turbot with creamed spinach and hollandaise.

OUR TIP: The hotel bistro offers a less formal menu

Chef: Chris Oakley **Owners:** P Milsom **Times:** 12-2/6.30-9.30, Closed 25 Dec evening **Notes:** Sun L £22.50, Vegetarian available, Dress Restrictions, Smart casual, Civ Wed 50 **Seats:** 80, Pr/dining room 16 **Smoking:** N/Sm in restaurant, Air con **Children:** Menu, Portions **Rooms:** 14 (14 en suite) ★★★ **Directions:** A12 to Colchester then A120 to Harwich harbour front **Parking:** 20

e-mail: pier@milsomhotels.com **web:** www.milsomhotels.co.uk

---

MANNINGTREE MAP 13 TM13

🏵 Stour Bay Café

Modern International

Good value food in welcoming rustic setting

☎ 01206 396687   39-43 High St CO11 1AH

MENU GUIDE Polynesian style crab spring roll • Roast beef, potato rösti, Madeira sauce • Raspberry crème brûlée

PRICE GUIDE Food prices not confirmed for 2006. Please telephone for details

PLACE: A relaxed, friendly restaurant whose cheery interior combines original beams and fireplaces, stripped wooden floors and bright orange walls.

continued

Stour Bay Café

OOD: A thoroughly modern menu that caters for most tastes, /ith dishes ranging from the traditional (slow cooked lamb, bubble nd squeak, root vegetables) to the international (peppered seared una steak with tomato, chilli and butter bean stew).
UR TIP: Ask about their live music evenings
imes: 12-2/7-9.30, Closed 1st wk in Jan, Mon-Tue **Directions:** Town entre (A317 from Colchester to Ipswich) - large green building in High reet **e-mail:** jaynewarner@btconnect.com
eb: www.stourbaycafe.com

OUTHEND-ON-SEA MAP 07 TQ88

Fleur de Provence
1odern French

hic modern French restaurant ideal for special ccasions
☎ 01702 352987 52-54 Alexander St SS1 1BJ
MENU GUIDE Wild mushroom terrine, truffle coulis • Fillet of amb Fleur de Provence • Hot chocolate fondant, pistachio ice ream
WINE GUIDE 45 bottles over £20, 18 bottles under £20 • 8 by he glass (£3.25-£4.50)
PRICE GUIDE Fixed L £15 • Fixed D £15 • starter £7.95-£12.95 • main £15.95-£17.95 • dessert £6.95-£7.95 • coffee 2.50 • min/water £3.50 • Service optional • Group min 6 ervice 10%
LACE: Outside, a frosted glass, high street frontage; inside, an timate and romantic atmosphere created with soft colours and mpathetic lighting. There is a separate bar area, and tables in e dining room are set with white linen and stylish glassware. ench staff are attentive and discreet.
OOD: Dishes are modern French in style and the menus are ritten in French with full English translations.
UR TIP: Perfect lunchtime retreat from the busy High Street
hef: Marcel Bouchenga **Owners:** Marcel Bouchenga **Times:** 12-2/7-10, osed 1st 2 wks Jan, BHs, Sun, closed L Sat **Notes:** Vegetarian available, ess Restrictions, Smart casual **Seats:** 45, Pr/dining room 20
noking: N/Sm area, No pipes, Air con **Children:** Portions
arking: Street parking, public car parks
mail: mancel@fleurdeprovence.co.uk
eb: fleurdeprovence.co.uk

AA's Chefs' Chef is the annual poll of all the chefs included in The Restaurant Guide. Around 1800 of the country's top chefs are asked to vote to recognise the achievements of one of their peers.
This year's winner is featured on page 19.

STOCK MAP 06 TQ69
Bear Restaurant & Bar
European   **NEW**
Historic inn serving innovative food
☎ 01277 829100 The Square CM4 9LH

MENU GUIDE Thai crab spring roll • Rack of lamb & braised lentils • Apple tarte Tatin
WINE GUIDE ♀ Los Vascos Rothchild Chardonnay £26.95 • ♀ Louis Latour Pinot Noir £25.95 • 41 bottles over £20, 19 bottles under £20 • 17 by the glass (£3.25-£6.65)
PRICE GUIDE Fixed L £16 • Fixed D £24 • coffee £2.50 • min/water £3.50 • Service optional
PLACE: This former inn sits a short drive from the A12, in the pretty little village of Stock. Inside there is an informal bar area, a bistro and a fine dining restaurant. A wealth of oak beams, raspberry-coloured walls, contemporary style leather dining chairs and clothed tables with crisp napkins complete the picture.
FOOD: The eclectic cooking style has global influences. A wide choice of meals using good quality produce, displaying clear flavours, are available - from the bar menu to a full five courses in the restaurant.
OUR TIP: Check out the stories about the Inn's past.
Chef: Phil Utz, Scott Hiskett **Owners:** Lee & Kathryn Anderson-Frogley **Times:** 12-3/5-11, Closed New Year, Mon, closed D Sun eve **Notes:** ALC 5 courses £37.50 (inc. coffee), Vegetarian available **Seats:** 90, Pr/dining room 10 **Smoking:** N/Sm in restaurant **Children:** Portions
Directions: M25 junct 28, onto A12, turn off for Billericay **Parking:** 30
e-mail: info@thebearinn.biz **web:** www.thebearinn.biz

TOLLESHUNT KNIGHTS MAP 07 TL91
Five Lakes Resort
Modern British, European
Resort hotel with restaurant fit for a king
☎ 01621 868888 Colchester Rd CM9 8HX

continued

England

TOLLESHUNT KNIGHTS *continued* MAP 07 TL91

MENU GUIDE Natural Black Water oysters • Roast rack of lamb, herb crust, rosemary & redcurrant jus • Chocolate fondant, nutmeg brûlée

WINE GUIDE ♀ Eugenio Collavini Villa di Canlungo Pinot Grigio £25.50 • ♀ Domaine Pradelle Crozes Hermitage Syrah £24.75 • 87 bottles over £20, 38 bottles under £20 • 6 by the glass (£3.95-£4.95)

PRICE GUIDE Fixed D £24 • starter £4.50-£8 • main £16.50-£21 • dessert £4.50-£6 • coffee £1.90 • min/water £3.75 • Service optional

PLACE: Imposing, purpose-built resort hotel set amid 320 acres of open countryside, complete with two 18-hole golf courses, a country club, and extensive sport, health and beauty facilities. The split-level Camelot Restaurant and Cocktail Bar is themed on the medieval story of King Arthur and, despite its size, achieves a sophisticated and understated intimacy.

FOOD: Two menus are offered, a fixed-price daily indulgence selection, with canapés and champagne, and the regular carte. Dishes reflect seasonal variations, using fresh produce from the local area.

OUR TIP: Everything you need for a weekend leisure break

Chef: Sean Melville **Owners:** Mr A Bejerano **Times:** 7-10, Closed 26, 31 Dec, 1 Jan, Mon-Sun **Notes:** Vegetarian available, Dress Restrictions, Smart casual, No trainers/T-shirts/ jeans, Civ Wed 300 **Seats:** 80 **Smoking:** N/Sm in restaurant, Air con **Children:** Menu, Portions **Rooms:** 194 (194 en suite) ★★★★ **Directions:** M25 junct 28, then on A12. At Kelvedon take B1024 then B1023 to Tolleshunt Knights, clearly marked by brown tourist signs. **Parking:** 550 **e-mail:** enquiries@fivelakes.co.uk **web:** www.fivelakes.co.uk

GLOUCESTERSHIRE

ALMONDSBURY MAP 04 ST68

🌸 Aztec Hotel

British, European 🐟🍴 **NEW**

Good regional dining in modern Nordic interior

☎ 01454 201090 Aztec West Business Park BS32 4TS

MENU GUIDE Tomato tart, Blue Vinney cheese • Pan-fried calves' liver • Treacle tart, vanilla bean ice cream

WINE GUIDE ♀ Chardonnay £23.45 • ♀ Pays D'Oc Merlot £14.95 • 48 bottles over £20, 24 bottles under £20 • 8 by the glass (£4.95-£7.25)

PRICE GUIDE Fixed L £15.95-£24.95 • starter £5.50-£8.50 • main £15.95-£24.95 • dessert £2-£5.85 • coffee £3.50 • min/water £3.60 • Service optional

PLACE: Located to the north of Bristol, this stylish hotel has comfortable, well-equipped rooms decorated in the Nordic style. Public areas boast log fires and vaulted ceilings. The Quarterjacks Restaurant has a relaxed and comfortable atmosphere.

FOOD: Simply prepared, regional dishes prepared from best quality ingredients. There are daily specials including Brixham fish of the day. Expect Welsh salt marsh lamb and Scottish beef with chunky chips.

OUR TIP: Popular base for shopping at nearby Cribbs Causeway **Chef:** Mike Riordan **Owners:** Shire Hotels **Times:** 12.30-2/7-10, Closed 26 Dec, closed L Sat & Sun **Notes:** Smart Dress **Seats:** 80, Pr/dining room 40 **Smoking:** N/Sm in restaurant **Children:** Menu, Portions **Parking:** 200 **e-mail:** aztec@shirehotels.co.uk **web:** www.shirehotels.co.uk

AMBERLEY

🌸 The Amberley Inn

British

Traditional inn with innovative food

☎ 01453 872565 Culver Hill GL5 5AF

MENU GUIDE Duck liver pâté, toasted brioche • Seared beef fillet, mushroom risotto, cauliflower velouté • Poached pear tart Tatin

PRICE GUIDE Food prices not confirmed for 2006. Please telephone for details

PLACE: Charming Cotswold inn set on a hillside with views over the Woodchester Valley. A warm welcome awaits visitors and locals alike.

FOOD: There's real ambition in this kitchen, with complex dishes using local produce whenever possible, especially rare breed meats. The modern British approach may include mains like pigeon en croûte with foie gras, Savoy cabbage, parsnip and truffle mousse.

OUR TIP: Leave room for dessert

Times: 12-2/7-9 **Rooms:** 14 (14 en suite) ★★ **Directions:** Telephone for directions **e-mail:** theamberley@zoom.co.uk **web:** www.theamberley.co.uk

ARLINGHAM MAP 04 SO71

🌸🌸 The Old Passage Inn 🐟

Seafood

Delicious seafood by the Severn

☎ 01452 740547 Passage Rd GL2 7JR

MENU GUIDE Pan-fried scallops, black pudding • Line caught sea bass, wild mushrooms • Pistachio crème brûlée

WINE GUIDE 36 bottles over £20, 30 bottles under £20 • 6 by the glass (£3.20-£5)

PRICE GUIDE Starter £4.50-£12.50 • main £11.50-£24 • dessert £4.50-£6 • coffee £2.60 • min/water £2.50 • Service optional

PLACE: The restaurant is fresh, vibrant and relaxed, and has a fabulous location on the banks of the River Severn, where the inn marks the site of an ancient crossing.

FOOD: The menu is virtually all fish, carefully sourced and sauced. Quality is a key factor, with the freshest possible catch, accurately cooked and served in simple dishes. The perfect example is a memorable halibut with butter emulsion.

OUR TIP: Take a stroll on the riverbank and enjoy the tranquility **Chef:** P Le Mesurier, Raoul Moore **Owners:** The Moore Family **Times:** 12.00-2/6.30-9, Closed 24-30 Dec, Mon, closed D Sun **Notes:** Vegetarian available **Seats:** 60, Pr/dining room 14 **Smoking:** N/Sm in restaurant, Air con **Children:** Portions **Rooms:** 3 (3 en suite) ♦♦♦ **Directions:** Telephone for directions **Parking:** 40 **e-mail:** oldpassage@ukonline.co.uk **web:** www.fishattheoldpassageinn.co.uk

BARNSLEY MAP 05 SP00

🌸 The Village Pub

Modern European

An inn for all seasons

☎ 01285 740421 GL7 5EF

MENU GUIDE Coln Valley smoked salmon, horseradish cream • Braised lamb shank, creamed cabbage & leek • Sticky toffee pudding

PRICE GUIDE Food prices not confirmed for 2006. Please telephone for details

continue

LACE: Log fires, flagged floors, eclectic furnishings and a
ontemporary decor create a warm and relaxed atmosphere at
is revamped Cotswold stone pub.
OOD: Light years away from being the average 'village' local,
ort daily menus list simply constructed dishes that range from
aditional English to classic French and some Mediterranean.
xpect confident cooking using local seasonal produce.
UR TIP: Allow enough time to enjoy the relaxing atmosphere
imes: 11-3/7-11 Directions: 4m from Cirencester
mail: info@thevillagepub.co.uk web: www.thevillagepub.co.uk

BIBURY MAP 05 SP10

Bibury Court Hotel
ritish, European
omfortable and relaxing formal dining in Tudor
anor
☎ 01285 740337 & 740324 GL7 5NT

MENU GUIDE Seafood assiette, citrus fruit & chive
dressing • Sea bass, crayfish tail & saffron cream • Passionfruit
art, clotted cream

WINE GUIDE ♀ Casa la Joya Sauvignon Blanc £17.25 • ♀ Valle
Andino Merlot £16.75 • 24 bottles over £20, 16 bottles under
£20 • 6 by the glass (£3.50-£3.95)

PRICE GUIDE Fixed D £32.50 • starter £5.50-£6.95 • main
£10.95-£14.95 • dessert £5.95 • coffee £2.95 • min/water
£3 • Service optional

LACE: An oasis of calm on the outskirts of a beautiful Cotswold
llage, this elegant country mansion dates back to Tudor times.
he intimate dining room is in part of the original building dating
om 1633, has lovely views over the grounds and a tangible
nse of history. The traditional, wood-panelled drawing room,
ith log fire and comfy sofas, is ideal for aperitifs.
OOD: The cooking follows the philosophy that makes the hotel
o appealing; unfussy, unpretentious and understated, backed by
ndeniable quality. Fine ingredients, seasonality and simple, well-
onceived combinations illustrate a confident kitchen.
UR TIP: Arrive early for a walk around the grounds
hef: Tom Bridgeman Owners: Mr & Mrs Johnston, Miss Collier
mes: 12-2/7-9 Notes: Vegetarian available, Civ Wed 32 Seats: 65,
/dining room 30 Smoking: N/Sm in restaurant Children: Menu,
ortions Rooms: 18 (18 en suite) ★★★ Directions: On B4425
etween Cirencester & Burford; hotel behind church Parking: 100
mail: info@biburycourt.com web: www.biburycourt.com

Swan Hotel
nternational
lodern 17th-century hotel serving lively flavours
☎ 01285 740695 GL7 5NW
LACE: Originally a coaching inn, the 17th-century Swan Hotel is
t in beautiful riverside surroundings next to an old stone
idge. Well-equipped and smartly presented, this creeper-clad
untry hotel is a tranquil and picturesque dining destination.
he restaurant makes the most of the stunning views over the
ver and pretty garden, and is elegantly styled with Regency
ripes, heavy gold drapes and dazzling chandeliers.
OOD: Quality produce and vibrant flavours are the key to
oking here. The menu is brief and reflects seasonality. Local
h, especially Bibury trout, features regularly. Expect quality
shes such as confit duck roulade and pickled kim chee, and
n-fried Bibury trout fillet, braised baby fennel, spring onion
ashed potato and star anise beurre blanc.

continued

OUR TIP: Hotel has its own spring for mineral water and an
excellent spa
Times: 7-9, Closed L Mon-Sun Rooms: 20 (20 en suite) ★★★
Directions: On B4425 between Cirencester (7 miles) and Burford (9
miles). Beside bridge in centre of Bibury. e-mail: info@swanhotel.co.uk
web: www.swanhotel.co.uk

BOURTON-ON-THE-WATER MAP 10 SP12
Dial House Hotel
British
Stunning food by romantic candlelight
☎ 01451 822244 The Chestnuts, High St GL54 2AN

MENU GUIDE Haggis, pigeon sausage, deep-fried quail
eggs • Assiette of local lamb • Plum brandy mousse, plum &
blackberry milkshake

WINE GUIDE ♀ Ladera Verde Sauvignon Blanc £13.95 • ♀ Los
Villos Cabernet Sauvignon £13.95 • 35 bottles over £20,
11 bottles under £20 • 6 by the glass (£3.50-£5.95)

PRICE GUIDE Fixed L £22 • starter £8-£9.50 • main £16-
£19 • dessert £8.50 • coffee £2.50 • min/water £3 • Service
added but optional 10%

PLACE: Dating back to the 17th century, this Cotswold stone
hotel is the epitome of country house chic, blending period
features with modern comfort and taste. Fresh flowers and
candlelight make for romance in the restaurant.
FOOD: There's a polish and consistency to the cooking here that
suggests the Dial House's new seven-course tasting menu could
be worth a flutter. Plenty of choice and creativity on the carte too:
you might start with sautéed foie gras with a rillette of local rabbit,
before tucking into wild Balmoral venison with a juniper jus.
OUR TIP: A drink by the fire in the cosy lounge
Chef: Daniel Bunce Owners: Jane & Adrian Campbell-Howard
Times: 12-3/6.30-10 Notes: Tasting menu £55, Sun L Fixed menu £15-18,
Vegetarian available, Dress Restrictions, Smart casual preferred Seats: 28,
Pr/dining room 18 Smoking: N/Sm in restaurant Children: Min 10 yrs,
Portions Rooms: 13 (13 en suite) ★★ Directions: Off A40 onto A429,
follow signs to Stow, village is 4m from Stow. A436 from Cheltenham,
A40-A424 from Oxford. Parking: 15 e-mail: info@dialhousehotel.com
web: www.dialhousehotel.com

NEW
denotes a restaurant which is new
to the guide this year.

The AA Wine Awards recognise the finest
wine lists in England, Scotland and Wales. For
full details, see pages 14-15

England

BUCKLAND MAP 10 SP03

Buckland Manor

British, French *Contemporary cooking in medieval manor*
☎ 01386 852626   WR12 7LY
e-mail: enquire@bucklandmanor.com
web: www.bucklandmanor.com

PLACE: On a hill next to the church with sweeping views and set in immaculate 10-acre grounds of ponds, fountains, running streams and manicured lawns (perfect for a pre- or post-meal stroll), this grand, 13th-century mellow-stone Cotswold manor house hotel creates an impression of something quintessentially English. Inside, the feeling is almost more traditional country home than luxury country house hotel, with roaring fires, tapestries and comfortable sitting rooms, while the equally traditional (jacket and tie required for dinner and Sunday lunch please gentlemen) oak-panelled dining room boasts an inglenook fireplace and warm atmosphere, buoyed by candlelight in the evenings and backed by professional and efficient formal service.

FOOD: The style is modern British, but with European influences, showcasing quality local produce from the fertile Vale of Evesham in addition to fresh herbs from the hotel's own garden. Ingredients are intelligently simply prepared and allowed to shine. The highly accomplished cooking displays plenty of skill and panache; take pan-roasted saddle of local venison with braised red cabbage, butternut squash and a blueberry and pepper jus, or warm pear and cinnamon soufflé with vanilla ice cream and chocolate sauce. Excellent wine list.

MENU GUIDE Crab assiette, spiced mango salsa • Turbot fillet, fennel, crisp potato, white wine caviar beurre blanc • Tiramisù in chocolate cup, biscotti & coffee sauce

WINE GUIDE ♀ Montes Sauvignon Blanc £26.50 ♀ Crozes-Hermitage £26.50 • 700 bottles over £20 2 by the glass (£6.45)

PRICE GUIDE Fixed L £19.50 • starter £7.95-£13.50 • main £25.50-£29.50 • dessert £8.75-£12.50 • coffee £3.25 • min/water £3.95 • Service optional

OUR TIP: Luxurious romantic retreat, especially if you stay over in the manor

Chef: Adrian Jarrad **Owners:** Von Essen **Times:** 12.30-1.45/7.30-9 **Notes:** Sun L 3 courses £24.50, Vegetarian available, Dress Restrictions, Jacket & tie **Seats:** 40 **Smoking:** N/Sm in restaurant
Children: Min 8yrs **Rooms:** 13 (13 en suite) ★★★
Directions: 2m SW of Broadway. Take B4632 signed Cheltenham, then take turn for Buckland. Hotel through village on right.
Parking: 30

UCKLAND MAP 10 SP03

 Buckland Manor

see opposite page

HELTENHAM MAP 10 SO92

 **Le Champignon Sauvage**

see page 166

George Hotel

eafood

onfident cooking, and balance of refinement and
relaxation

☎ 01242 235751 St Georges Rd GL50 3DZ

continued

England

MENU GUIDE Beetroot salmon gravadlax • Sea bass, mushroom risotto, crayfish tails • Peach parfait, toasted praline marshmallow

WINE GUIDE ♀ Corte Vigne Pinot Grigio £13.50 • ♀ Casa La Joya Merlot £16.50 • 36 bottles over £20, 21 bottles under £20 • 10 by the glass (£2.80-£5.85)

PRICE GUIDE Starter £6-£10 • main £14-£21 • dessert £5-£7.50 • coffee £2.25 • min/water £3 • Group min 10 service 10%

PLACE: This long-established, stylishly modernised Cheltenham hotel is set in an elegant Regency terrace. Monty's Seafood restaurant is contemporary and overseen by hospitable staff, while pre-meal drinks can be taken in the lively Monty's brasserie.

FOOD: Confident, innovative and elegant modern cooking befits the venue, where a lightness of touch, strength of flavour and texture contrasts all have their place on the seafood-based repertoire. (The brasserie has a separate menu.)

OUR TIP: Just off the Promenade, close to fashionable Montpellier

Chef: Kevin Harris & James Lovatt **Owners:** Jeremy Shaw **Times:** 7-10, Closed Xmas, Sun-Mon, closed L Mon-Sun **Notes:** Vegetarian available
Seats: 26, Pr/dining room 26 **Smoking:** N/Sm in restaurant
Children: Menu **Rooms:** 38 (38 en suite) ★★★ **Parking:** 30
e-mail: hotel@stayatthegeorge.co.uk **web:** www.stayatthegeorge.co.uk

HELTENHAM MAP 10 SO92

The Greenway

ritish, European

ick modern cooking in Elizabethan manor

☎ 01242 862352 Shurdington GL51 4UG

MENU GUIDE Sea bass, braised oxtail, creamed celeriac, salsify morels • Salmon, lobster & fennel risotto, confit beetroot, eeks & red wine • Chocolate fondant, orange & raspberry salad

WINE GUIDE ♀ Daniel Dampt Chablis £25.50 • ♀ McGuigans Merlot £25.50 • 160 bottles over £20 • 6 by the glass (£6)

PRICE GUIDE Fixed L £15.50 • Fixed D £45 • coffee 3.75 • min/water £3.50 • Service optional

PLACE: This charming, mellow, Elizabethan manor house, set in rmal gardens and dating back to 1584, provides a tranquil retreat close to Cheltenham. There's a cosy, country-house ambience, with wellies by the door, deep sofas in the lounge and a warm, intimate, friendly atmosphere. The elegant, sunny dining room is furnished in appropriate style, with swagged and tailed rtains, richly dressed tables and views over the sunken garden nd lily pond.

FOOD: Kenny Atkinson's menus certainly set the pulse racing,

the range includes a ten-course gourmand and six-course tasting option backing up the appealing carte, all at fixed prices. Dotted with luxury items, the modern approach sees exceptional seasonality vying with eye-catching organic produce and precise, high quality, bold cooking that delivers plenty of wow factor. Excellent presentation, fresh, clear flavours, balance and poise are all to the fore. It's flawless cooking at this level. Formal service from a dedicated, attentive team adds the final touch.

OUR TIP: Top-notch canapés and petits fours

Chef: Kenny Atkinson **Owners:** Von Essen Hotels **Times:** 12-2/7-9.30
Notes: Sun L 3 courses £25 (incl coffee), Fixed D 6 courses £55, Vegetarian available, Dress Restrictions, No jeans or trainers, Civ Wed 45
Seats: 50, Pr/dining room 30 **Smoking:** N/Sm in restaurant
Children: Portions **Rooms:** 21 (21 en suite) ★★★ **Directions:** 3m S of Cheltenham on A46 (Stroud), pass through the village of Shurdington
Parking: 50 **e-mail:** info@thegreenway.co.uk
web: www.the-greenway.co.uk

England

Le Champignon Sauvage

French *Serious French cooking, attentive service and modern, stylish environment*

☎ 01242 573449 24 Suffolk Rd GL50 2AQ

e-mail: mail@lechampignonsauvage.co.uk

web: www.lechampignonsauvage.com

PLACE: The unassuming, easy-to-miss exterior of this tiny, smart French restaurant provides few clues to its enduring charm or culinary excellence, tucked away in a terrace of shops on a busy main road in the quieter Montpellier district of town. Inside Everitt-Matthias's Le Champignon Sauvage, there's immediate warmth and vitality, and a surprisingly personal touch for a culinary premier leaguer, its handful of much-in-demand, well-spaced and smartly attired tables is the province of wife Helen at front of house, while David is to be found at the stove. Colourful, striking modern artworks adorn sunny pale yellow walls, while the small lounge-bar offers space for pre-meal drinks and time to study the appealing menus. Service is attentive and delivered in a friendly manner, with helpful and informed menu explanations on offer.

FOOD: There's no shortage of flair and imagination from David's tiny kitchen, the style highly accomplished, classic French with the occasional modern twist and unusual combination. Take a risotto of snails and pig trotter to accompany a fillet of cod, for instance, or local lamb, onion roasted with liquorice. The small ancillaries, like amuse bouche (foie gras topped with sweetcorn cream, for instance) or balanced selection of petits fours are another strength. A peerless reputation for hard work and dedication to his craft, David concentrates on allowing the full flavour of top-notch ingredients to shine. So expect supreme technical skill and some complex, intelligent cooking and flavour combinations on an enticing repertoire of fixed-price menus (Tuesday to Friday lunch and dinner offers great value), while the carte (with its set prices for two, three or four courses) might deliver duck foie gras with roasted quince and walnuts and maury syrup to start, or braised belly of old spot pork, pig's cheek and Chinese spices to follow.

MENU GUIDE Sheltand scallops, pea purée, lettuce, roasted onion sauce • Roasted monkfish tail, pumpkin purée, toasted barley jus • Hot fig tart, browned butter ice cream

WINE GUIDE 91 bottles over £20, 44 bottles under £20 • 6 by the glass (£2.75-£3.75)

PRICE GUIDE Fixed L £20-£36 • Fixed D £25-£44 coffee £3.50 • min/water £2.50 • Service optional

OUR TIP: Excellent value lunch

Chef: David Everitt-Matthias **Owners:** Mr & Mrs D Everitt-Matthias **Times:** 12.30-1.30/7.30-9, Closed 10 days Xmas, 3 wks Jun, Sun-Mon **Notes:** Vegetarian by request only **Seats:** 28 **Smoking:** No pipes, No cigars **Directions:** S of the town centre, on A40, near Cheltenham College **Parking:** Public car park (Bath Rd)

Hotel Kandinsky, Café Paradiso

Mediterranean

Pleasant food amid an appealingly eccentric hotel

☎ 01242 527788 Bayshill Rd, Montpellier GL50 3AS

MENU GUIDE Oven baked sardines, salsa verde • Chargrilled rib of beef, thick chips, onion jus • Dark chocolate cone, lavender mousse

WINE GUIDE ♀ George Kinross Chardonnay £12.75 • ♀ George Kinross Merlot/Shiraz £12.75 • 41 bottles over £20, 24 bottles under £20 • 10 by the glass (£3.35-£6.50)

PRICE GUIDE Fixed D £16.50-£18.50 • starter £4.50-£7.25 • main £10-£14.25 • dessert £4.50-£5.50 • coffee £2.50 • min/water £3.50 • Service optional

PLACE: There is a quirky decorative style at this large white Regency villa, with a 'shabby chic' lounge bar, super sunny conservatory, and a 1950's-style cocktail bar hidden away in the cellars. Café Paradiso, the buzzy brasserie-style restaurant, has a traditional Napolitan pizza oven as its focal point.

FOOD: Very much in the Italian mould, with a few touches of modern European and an emphasis on locally sourced fresh ingredients.

OUR TIP: Pronto Paradiso quick lunch menu Mon-Sat

Chef: Andrew Gotting **Owners:** Nigel Chapman, Nicholas Dickinson **Times:** 12-2/6.30-10 **Notes:** Vegetarian available **Seats:** 40, Pr/dining room 16 **Smoking:** N/Sm in restaurant **Children:** Menu, Portions **Rooms:** 48 (48 en suite) ★★★★ **Directions:** From M5 junct 11 follow A40 towards town centre. right at rdbt, 2nd exit at next rdbt into Bayshill Rd. **Parking:** 25 **e-mail:** kandinsky@aliashotels.com **web:** www.aliashotels.com

NEW
denotes a restaurant which is new to the guide this year.

⊛⊛ Lumière

Modern International

One of Cheltenham's best-kept secrets

☎ 01242 222200 Clarence Pde GL50 3PA

MENU GUIDE Parma ham, foie gras, balsamic & quince jelly • Seared sea bass, chilli tiger prawns, coriander rice • stilton cheesecake

WINE GUIDE ♀ Domaine des Gerbeaux Pouilly Fuissé £29 • ♀ Ancient Vine Zinfandel Cline £28 • 42 bottles over £20, 6 bottles under £20 • 4 by the glass (£3.50-£5)

PRICE GUIDE Fixed D £35 • coffee £1.50 • min/water £1.50 • Service optional

PLACE: Lumière is located in a small Regency terrace in the centre of Cheltenham. The decor is contemporary: clean lines with deep chocolatey grape and pale creamy grey walls, moody lighting and three large abstract canvases. Tables are set white on white, with Riedel glassware, fine white china, mirror finish cutlery and a simple opalescent candle chimney as a centrepiece.

FOOD: The proprietors are Canadian, which explains the Pacific north west influences. Bold, clearly defined flavours are key to the kitchen's approach, along with light sauces and great soups.

OUR TIP: Excellent wine list

Chef: Geoff Chapman **Owners:** Lin & Geoff Chapman **Times:** 7-8.30, Closed 2 wks Jan, 2 wks summer, Sun-Mon, closed L Tues-Sat **Notes:** Vegetarian by request only **Seats:** 30 **Smoking:** N/Sm in restaurant, Air con **Children:** Min 8 yrs **Directions:** Town centre, near bus station **Parking:** On street, nearby car parks **e-mail:** dinner@lumiere.cc **web:** www.lumiere.cc

⊛⊛ Parkers

Modern International **NEW**

Elegant townhouse with adventurous brasserie menu

☎ 01242 518898 The Hotel on the Park, 38 Evesham Rd GL52 2AH

MENU GUIDE Snapper, lemon rice, crème fraîche • Pork belly, Parmentier potatoes, beetroot, lentil jus • Rum parfait, raisin bavarois

WINE GUIDE ♀ Brampton Stellenbosch Sauvignon Blanc £18.45 • ♀ Duboeuf Fleurie Gamay £23.95 • 21 bottles over £20, 17 bottles under £20 • 4 by the glass

PRICE GUIDE Fixed L £9.95-£14.95 • starter £5.50-£7.95 • main £10.50-£15.25 • dessert £5.95-£7.25 • coffee £2.50 • min/water £3.25 • Service optional • Group min 8 service 10%

PLACE: Just a short walk from the shops and town centre, this elegant Regency townhouse is peacefully set overlooking one of Cheltenham's attractive parks. Opulence with a touch of fun captures the decor, although the informal brasserie is a more minimalist affair with dark wooden tables and a timber floor.

FOOD: Expect a modern menu with a hint of fusion and some bold flavours - swordfish with curried coconut and ginger perhaps, or asparagus ice cream with orange blossom - as well as safer options such as sausages and mash.

OUR TIP: Light bite selection available

Chef: Freek Peters **Owners:** Peter Dann **Times:** 12-2/6.30-9.30, Closed D 25 Dec **Notes:** Vegetarian available, Dress Restrictions, Smart casual **Seats:** 42, Pr/dining room 16 **Smoking:** N/Sm in restaurant **Children:** Min 12 yrs, Portions **Rooms:** 12 (12 en suite) ★★★ **Directions:** 4m off M5 junct 10. 0.75m from Cheltenham racecourse. **Parking:** 8 **e-mail:** stay@hotelonthepark.co.uk **web:** www.hotelonthepark.com

England

CHIPPING CAMPDEN MAP 10 SP13

 Cotswold House

British, European

Vibrant and stylish cooking to match the new restaurant design

☎ 01386 840330 The Square GL55 6AN

MENU GUIDE Roasted Anjou pigeon breast • Pork loin marinated in spices & tea leaves • Honey Madeleines

WINE GUIDE ♀ Kim Crawford Sauvignon Blanc £24.50 • ♀ White Haven Pinot Noir £24.50 • 25 bottles over £20, 40 bottles under £20 • 10 by the glass (£3.50-£5.95)

PRICE GUIDE Fixed L £12.50-£17 • Fixed D £40-£45 • starter £8-£10 • main £14-£24 • dessert £6-£10 • coffee £4.50 • min/water £3.50 • Service optional • Group min 8 service 10%

PLACE: A few surprises await beyond the mellow Cotswold stone walls of this former wool merchant's house: the traditional decor has gone, replaced by a bold decorative style that brings a bright colour scheme to the restaurant. Hospitality and service are exemplary.

FOOD: The forward-looking kitchen more than matches the new modern design, bringing skill and imagination to bear on the prime ingredients. Flavours are often simply superb - try the roasted fillet of brill with lobster and fennel risotto for proof, or tuck into a tiramisù based on dark chocolate for a worthy finale. Notable wine list.

OUR TIP: Picturesque town centre location

Chef: Jamie Forman **Owners:** Christa & Ian Taylor **Times:** 12-2.30/7-10, Closed L Mon-Sat **Notes:** Vegetarian available, Civ Wed 80 **Seats:** 40, Pr/dining room 80 **Smoking:** N/Sm in restaurant, Air con **Children:** Portions **Rooms:** 20 (20 en suite) ★★★ **Directions:** 1m N of A44 between Moreton-in-Marsh & Broadway on B4081. **Parking:** 25 **e-mail:** reception@cotswoldhouse.com **web:** www.cotswoldhouse.com

The Kings Arms Hotel

British, European

Buzzy dining venue in attractive Cotswold town setting

☎ 01386 840256 The Square GL55 6AW

MENU GUIDE Cornish crab cake, spinach & mustard velouté • Confit duck leg, chorizo mash • Pistachio crème brûlée

WINE GUIDE 25 bottles under £20 • 14 by the glass (£3.85-£7.50)

PRICE GUIDE Starter £3.75-£7 • main £9.50-£18 • dessert £4.95-£5.95 • coffee £2.15 • min/water £3.50 • Service optional • Group min 8 service 10%

PLACE: This 17th-century inn offers a bar, brasserie, snug & restaurant with private dining room as well some chic bedrooms. Cotswold stone floors, harlequin furniture and candles give the place an intimate yet lively ambience.

FOOD: Eclectic menu uses lots of local ingredients. Thai curries jostle for attention with brasserie classics like skate wings with parsley beurre blanc.

OUR TIP: A pre-dinner drink in the snug

Chef: Ellery Powell **Owners:** Mike Thorne **Times:** 12-2.30/6.30-9.30 **Notes:** Vegetarian available **Seats:** Pr/dining room **Children:** Menu, Portions **Rooms:** 13 (13 en suite) ♦♦♦ **Directions:** 10m from Stratford **Parking:** 8 **e-mail:** info@thekingsarmshotel.com **web:** www.thekingsarmshotel.com

Three Ways House

British

Traditional Cotswold hotel restaurant specialising in puddings

☎ 01386 438429 Mickleton GL55 6SB

MENU GUIDE Bubble & squeak cakes • Roast duck breast, beetroot risotto • Tiramisù, coffee bean sauce

WINE GUIDE ♀ Hugues de Beauvignac Sauvignon Blanc £14 • ♀ Whistling Duck Shiraz/Cabernet £16 • 18 bottles over £20, 30 bottles under £20 • 8 by the glass (£3.25-£4)

PRICE GUIDE Fixed D £30-£35 • min/water £3 • Service option

PLACE: The famous Pudding Club, founded to promote traditional English puds, is run from this pretty Cotswold hotel. Another attraction is the elegant restaurant, a picture in blue an white.

FOOD: Tried and tested recipes dominate the menu in deferenc to the loyal local following, though a suggestion of Asia can sometimes be tasted. Flavours are generally well defined and accurate.

OUR TIP: Ask about the Pudding Club events

Chef: Mark Rowlandson **Owners:** Simon Coombe & Peter Henderson **Times:** 12-2.30/7-9.30, Closed L Mon-Sat **Notes:** Coffee included, Vegetarian available, Civ Wed 80 **Seats:** 80, Pr/dining room 70 **Smoking:** N/Sm in restaurant, Air con **Children:** Menu, Portions **Rooms:** 48 (48 en suite) ★★★ **Directions:** On B4632, in village cen **Parking:** 37 **e-mail:** threeways@puddingclub.com **web:** www.puddingclub.com

CLEARWELL MAP 04 SO50

 Tudor Farmhouse Hotel

British

Romantic setting in the Forest of Dean

☎ 01594 833046 GL16 8JS

continu

MENU GUIDE Bruschetta of thyme foccacia • Pistachio stuffed breast & roasted leg of guinea fowl • Honeycomb & banana parfait

WINE GUIDE ♀ Cabernet Sauvignon £9.95 • 4 bottles over £20, 40 bottles under £20 • 3 by the glass (£2.50-£3.65)

PRICE GUIDE Fixed L £10-£11.50 • starter £3.95-£6.50 • main £11.95-£18.25 • dessert £4.95 • coffee £2.25 • min/water £1.95 • Service optional

PLACE: Charming 13th-century former farmhouse, Grade II listed, with exposed stone walls, inglenook fireplaces, wooden circular stairs, heavy oak beams and low ceilings. Many guests will recognise the proprietors (previously the focus of a documentary), who have invested much and put their hearts into is now successful venture.

FOOD: Dishes from the lengthy carte are selected for seasonality and prepared from locally sourced produce. Suggestions for appropriate wines are also listed. The main menu is supplemented by simple options from the grill - steaks with a choice of sauces.

OUR TIP: Perfect for an intimate candlelit dinner **Chef:** Peter Teague **Owners:** Owen & Eirwen Evans **Times:** 12-5.30/7-9, closed 24-27 Dec **Notes:** Vegetarian available **Seats:** 30, Pr/dining room **Smoking:** N/Sm in restaurant **Children:** Menu, Portions **Rooms:** 22 (22 en suite) ★★ **Directions:** Leave Monmouth to Chepstow road at Redbrook, follow signs Clearwell, turn left at village cross. Hotel on left **Parking:** 24 **e-mail:** info@tudorfarmhousehotel.co.uk **web:** www.tudorfarmhousehotel.co.uk

The Wyndham Arms Hotel

British
NEW

Ancient hostelry that always impresses

☎ 01594 833666 GL16 8JT

MENU GUIDE Pan-fried scallops with chorizo sausage • Pan-fried rack of lamb, fondant potato, rosemary jus • Chocolate & walnut brownie, mascarpone cream

PLACE: Dating back over 600 years, this ancient hostelry sits in the heart of a picturesque village and combines gastro-pub charm with all the facilities of a hotel. Its restaurant has a traditional feel, with dark beams, comfy upholstered chairs and linen-clothed tables.

FOOD: A capable and enthusiastic young chef consistently impresses, delivering hearty portions of enjoyable modern cuisine. Bar menu also available.

OUR TIP: Explore one of the many local walks
Times: 12-2/7-9.30 **e-mail:** nigel@thewyndhamhotel.co.uk **web:** www.thewyndhamhotel.co.uk

COLN ST ALDWYNS MAP 05 SP10

The New Inn At Coln

British, French

Quintessential Cotswold inn

☎ 01285 750651 GL7 5AN

MENU GUIDE Seafood chowder • Roasted duck breast with celeriac purée • Griottine cherry and kirsch crème brûlée

WINE GUIDE ♀ Paarl Heights Chenin Blanc £13.50 • ♀ Vina Gracia Merlot £16.50 • 26 bottles over £20, 28 bottles under £20 • 8 by the glass (£3-£3.80)

PRICE GUIDE Food prices not confirmed for 2006. Please telephone for details

PLACE: Set in the heart of the Coln Valley, this attractive Cotswold-stone village inn dates back to the 16th century. With its

exposed beams, flagstone floors, real fires and creaky floorboards, the dining areas are intimate, and there are several letting rooms available.

FOOD: An Anglo-French selection of dishes is well presented and somewhat decorative. More traditional dishes include a terrine of confit rabbit, foie gras and wild mushrooms, or a main course of baked fillet of salmon with crushed new potatoes, asparagus and lobster bisque sauce.

OUR TIP: Stay over in one of the cosy bedrooms
Chef: Matthew Haines **Owners:** Mr & Mrs R Kimmet **Times:** 12-2/7-9 **Notes:** Vegetarian available **Seats:** 32, Pr/dining room 20 **Smoking:** N/Sm in restaurant **Children:** Min 10yrs **Rooms:** 14 (14 en suite) ★★ **Directions:** 8m E of Cirencester, between Bibury and Fairford. **Parking:** 22 **e-mail:** stay@new-inn.co.uk **web:** www.new-inn.co.uk

CORSE LAWN MAP 10 SO83

◎◎ Corse Lawn House Hotel

British, French

Simple classics in elegant village setting

☎ 01452 780771 GL19 4LZ

MENU GUIDE Game terrine, cranberry relish • Calves' liver, pancetta, olive butter, champ • Lemon tart, lemon ice cream

WINE GUIDE ♀ Muscadet £12.50 • ♀ Barreda Vino de la Tierra de Castilla Tempranillo £12.50 • 300 bottles over £20, 60 bottles under £20 • 6 by the glass (£3.40-£4.50)

PRICE GUIDE Fixed L £19.50 • Fixed D £29.50 • starter £3.95-£9.95 • main £12.95-£28.50 • dessert £3.95-£6.95 • coffee £2.30 • min/water £2 • Service optional

PLACE: Quaintly located on the village green behind an ornamental pond, this red brick Queen Anne hotel has a cosy country house ambience. Log fires and comfy sofas abound, while outside there are pretty gardens to explore. The intimate restaurant is popular, so book ahead.

FOOD: You won't go hungry here - the portions are hearty and the cooking accomplished. Expect simple dishes that rely on the freshest ingredients and deft handling: pork with grilled apple and curly kale perhaps, or chargrilled salmon with crushed peas and chive beurre blanc. Notable wine list.

OUR TIP: Endangered fish species are banned from the menu
Chef: Baba Hine, Andrew Poole **Owners:** Hine Family **Times:** 12-2/7-9.30, Closed 24-26 Dec **Notes:** Vegetarian available, Dress Restrictions, No jeans and T-shirts, Civ Wed 80 **Seats:** 34, Pr/dining room 28 **Smoking:** N/Sm in restaurant **Children:** Portions **Rooms:** 19 (19 en suite) ★★★ **Directions:** 5m SW of Tewkesbury on B4211, in village centre **Parking:** 60 **e-mail:** enquiries@corselawn.com **web:** www.corselawnhousehotel.com

FRAMPTON MANSELL MAP 04 SO90

◎ White Horse

Modern British

Colourful foodie pub

☎ 01285 760960 Cirencester Rd GL6 8HZ

MENU GUIDE Moules marinière • Duck leg cassoulet with chorizo & pancetta • Dark chocolate & pistachio crème brûlée

WINE GUIDE ♀ George Kinross Chenin Blanc £11.75 • ♀ Andrew Hurley Shiraz Cabernet Merlot £13.75 12 bottles over £20, 31 bottles under £20 • 7 by the glass (£2.95-£3.95)

PRICE GUIDE Starter £3.95-£9.50 • main £8.95-£15.25 • dessert £3.50-£4.75 • coffee £1.50 • min/water £2.50 • Service optional

continued

continued

England

FRAMPTON MANSELL *continued* MAP 04 SO90

PLACE: Unassuming roadside pub with a stylish modern interior. Pop in for a drink in the cosy bar, or a meal in the brightly coloured restaurant with its ever-changing art display. A well-tended garden makes a pretty venue for alfresco dining in the summer.
FOOD: An eclectic mix of punchy, flavourful dishes, such as veal osso buco or calves' liver with bacon and onion gravy. Fish comes fresh from Cornwall daily, or the pub's new lobster tank.
OUR TIP: Lighter snacks are also available at lunchtime
Chef: Howard Matthews **Owners:** Emma & Shaun Davis **Times:** 11-3/6-11, Closed 24-26 Dec, 1 Jan, closed D Sun **Notes:** Sun L one course £10.50, Vegetarian available **Seats:** 45 **Smoking:** N/Sm in restaurant **Children:** Portions **Directions:** 6m from Cirencester on the A419 towards Stroud. **Parking:** 30 **web:** www.cotswoldwhitehorse.com

LOWER SLAUGHTER MAP 10 SP12

⊛⊛ Lower Slaughter Manor
British, French
Reliable dining in historic country house
☎ 01451 820456   GL54 2HP

MENU GUIDE Scallops, pea & smoked bacon fricassée • Venison saddle, root purée, game jus • Rhubarb & custard
WINE GUIDE ♀ Pouilly Fumé £32 • ♀ Hartlands Shiraz £24 • 272 bottles over £20, 9 bottles under £20 • 12 by the glass (£6-£10)
PRICE GUIDE Fixed L £15 • Fixed D £34.99-£45 • coffee £3.50 • min/water £3.75 • Service optional

PLACE: Dating from the 17th century, this historic Grade II listed manor house is located on the edge of this charming Cotswold village. Interiors are very traditional with classic country house chintz and deep sofas. The hotel's new dining room is elegant with French windows opening onto a pleasant patio with pristine gardens beyond. Knowledgeable, helpful staff look after well-heeled diners.
FOOD: Modern British dishes with the occasional French accent predominate here although the quintessential English setting makes any meal here a very British affair.
OUR TIP: Great place for a weekend retreat
Chef: David Kelman **Owners:** Von Essen Collection **Times:** 12-2.30/7-9.30 **Notes:** Vegetarian available, Dress Restrictions, Smart, no jeans or trainers, Civ Wed 60 **Seats:** 34, Pr/dining room 20 **Smoking:** N/Sm in restaurant **Children:** Min 12yrs **Rooms:** 16 (16 en suite) ★★★
Directions: Off A429, signposted The Slaughters. 0.5m into village on right **Parking:** 30 **e-mail:** info@lowerslaughter.co.uk
web: www.lowerslaughter.co.uk

⊛⊛ Washbourne Court Hotel
British, French
Cotswold hotel on the River Eye with fine dining
☎ 01451 822143   GL54 2HS

MENU GUIDE French onion soup • Magret duck, Bigarade sau⏐ Hot chocolate fondant
WINE GUIDE ♀ Hippolyte Reverdy Sancerre £25.75 • ♀ Santa⏐ Rita Cabernet Sauvignon £16.90 • 42 bottles over £20, 18 bottl⏐ under £20 • 10 by the glass (£3.95-£8.50)
PRICE GUIDE Fixed L £15.95 • Fixed D £30-£40 • starter £4.50-⏐ £9.50 • main £16.95-£28 • dessert £6-£7.50 • coffee £3.95⏐ min/water £3.50 • Service optional • Group min 10 service 10⏐

PLACE: Beamed ceilings, log fires and flagstone floors reinforc⏐ the 17th-century character of this stone-built hotel. The four ac⏐ of riverbank gardens and beautiful Cotswold village setting add⏐ the allure. There's an elegant dining room as well as a terrace.
FOOD: Modern British cooking with distinct French overtones based on good, local, seasonal ingredients. Good clear flavours⏐ and freshness characterise dishes like the lasagne of scallops a⏐ tiger prawns, and corn-fed chicken wrapped in Parma ham wit⏐ truffled baby leeks.
OUR TIP: Garden terrace for drinks and light lunches
Chef: Matt Pashley **Owners:** Von Essen Hotels **Times:** 12.30-3/7-9,⏐ Closed L Mon-Sat **Notes:** Vegetarian available, Dress Restrictions, Sma⏐ casual, Civ Wed 60 **Seats:** 60, Pr/dining room 16 **Smoking:** N/Sm in restaurant **Children:** Min 8 yrs, Menu, Portions **Rooms:** 28 (28 en suite) ★★★ **Directions:** Off A429, village centre by river **Parking:** 4⏐ **e-mail:** info@washbournecourt.co.uk
web: www.washbournecourt.co.uk

MORETON-IN-MARSH MAP 10 SP23

⊛⊛ Mulberry Restaurant
British, French
Accomplished cuisine in stylish manor house
☎ 01608 650501   Manor House Hotel, High St GL56 ⊂

contin⏐

MENU GUIDE Roasted vine tomato & rocket soup, rosemary oil • Brill, vanilla vinaigrette • Turkish Delight pannacotta, sesame & poppy seed snaps

WINE GUIDE ♀ Peter Lehman Chardonnay £14.95 • ♥ Montes Estate Cabernet Sauvignon £14.75 • 35 bottles over £20, 25 bottles under £20 • 8 by the glass (£3.75-£7.50)

PRICE GUIDE Fixed L £12.50 • Fixed D £29.95 • coffee £3.25 • min/water £4 • Service optional

PLACE: Parts of this Cotswold stone manor house set in lush gardens date back to 1545 but recent extensions and the refurbished decor has injected contemporary chic into the period charm. The bar and brasserie sport leather sofas, bold colours and modern art, while the Mulberry Restaurant, decorated in warm sunny colours with comfortable, upholstered chairs, opens on to the superb terrace and gardens.

FOOD: Good use of seasonal and local produce on a set menu that offers an extensive and well-balanced choice at each course.

OUR TIP: Enjoy a drink in the Mulberry champagne and cocktail bar

Chef: Jonathon Harvey-Barnes, Andy Troughton **Owners:** Michael & Pamela Horton **Times:** 12-2.30/7-9.30 **Notes:** Vegetarian available, Dress Restrictions, Smart casual, no jeans, Civ Wed 120 **Seats:** 76, Pr/dining room 96 **Smoking:** N/Sm in restaurant **Children:** Min 8yrs, Portions **Rooms:** 38 (38 en suite) ★★★ **Directions:** Off A429 at south end of town **Parking:** 32 **e-mail:** bookings@cotswold-inns-hotels.co.uk **web:** www.cotswold-inns-hotel.co.uk

🍵 The Marshmallow High St GL56 0AT
☎ 01608 651536 Winner of The Tea Guild Award of Excellence 2005.

NAILSWORTH MAP 04 ST89
🍽 Egypt Mill Hotel
British

Creative cooking in delightful old watermill
☎ 01453 833449 GL6 0AE

MENU GUIDE Seafood chowder risotto • Rack of lamb, Provençal vegetables, sweet balsamic jus • Chocolate pyramid

WINE GUIDE ♀ Sauvignon Blanc/Pinot Grigio £14.95 • ♥ Merlot/Shiraz £12.95 • 4 bottles over £20, 18 bottles under £20 • 8 by the glass (£2.75-£6)

PRICE GUIDE Starter £2.95-£7 • main £8.95-£15.95 • dessert £4.50 • coffee £1.75 • min/water £2.50 • Service optional

PLACE: The setting for this luxurious hotel and restaurant is a 16th-century watermill. The oak-beamed dining rooms are quirky and romantic, with views over rushing water, while in the bar you can enjoy cocktails whilst admiring the skilfully renovated mill workings from behind glass.

FOOD: The modern menu ranges between simple, vibrant dishes such as home-smoked chicken salad, to more elaborate and complex affairs, including roast venison with chocolate and raspberry jus.

OUR TIP: Book early for a riverside table

Chef: Dan Copcatt **Owners:** Mrs S Webb **Times:** 12-2/6.30-9.30 **Notes:** Vegetarian available **Seats:** 80, Pr/dining room 120 **Smoking:** N/Sm in restaurant **Children:** Menu, Portions **Rooms:** 18 (18 en suite) ★★ **Directions:** Centre of Nailsworth, on A46 **Parking:** 80 **e-mail:** reception@egyptmill.com **web:** www.egyptmill.com

🍽 The Mad Hatters Restaurant
British, French

Organic food & wine in Cotswold town centre
☎ 01453 832615 3 Cossack Square GL6 0DB

MENU GUIDE Soupe au pistou • Salt marsh lamb noisettes, rosemary & garlic jus • Pistachio meringue, fruits & cream

continued

WINE GUIDE ♀ Montalbano Pinot Grigio £11.50 • ♥ Alvaro Espinosa Carmenere Cabernet Sauvignon £11.50 • 6 bottles over £20, 19 bottles under £20 • 3 by the glass (£3.50-£4)

PRICE GUIDE Fixed L £12.50-£15.50 • Fixed D £26.50-£30 • starter £4.60-£5.90 • main £16.50-£19.50 • dessert £5.50 • coffee £1.50 • min/water £2.50 • Service optional

PLACE: This charming 200-year-old ironmonger's building is situated in the heart of this delightful old Cotswold town. The dining room has large oak-framed bow windows, wooden floors and beams. The welcome is warm and the service both relaxed and attentive.

FOOD: The menu offers skilfully executed rustic French dishes. 'Slow cooking' with a heavy emphasis on organic, local and seasonal produce. Everything is produced from scratch including bread, pastries and ice creams.

OUR TIP: Popular venue so booking advisable

Chef: Michael Findlay & Emma Edwards **Owners:** Michael Findlay & Carolyn Findlay **Times:** 12.30-2/7.30-9, Closed end Jan-1st wk Feb, 1st wk Jun, 1st 2wk Aug, Mon-Tue, closed D Sun-Tue **Notes:** Sun L 3 courses £15 (prebooked), Vegetarian available **Seats:** 45 **Smoking:** N/Sm in restaurant **Rooms:** 3 (1 en suite) ♦♦♦ **Directions:** M5 junct 13. A419 to Stroud then A46 to Nailsworth. Take a right at rdbt and then an immediate left, restaurant is located opposite Britannia Pub **Parking:** NCP, parking on street **e-mail:** mafindlay@waitrose.com

NEWENT MAP 10 SO72
✿ Three Choirs Vineyards
British

Tuscan-style vineyard views and summer terrace dining
☎ 01531 890223 GL18 1LS

MENU GUIDE Home pickled scallop & red mullet • Pan-fried organic lamb, honey roast parsnip purée • Sticky pear & ginger pudding

WINE GUIDE ♀ Three Choirs Bacchus £16 • ♥ Three Choirs Rondo/Regent £14.50

PRICE GUIDE Service optional • Group min 10 service 10%

PLACE: A wine-lover's heaven, with floor-to-ceiling views across acres of vineyards and surrounding hills. Well-spaced tables, a pleasant and relaxing atmosphere, and a cosy lounge with open fire provide the comforts.

FOOD: The modern British repertoire - with a classical bent - doesn't overcomplicate, showing due respect for well-sourced, quality ingredients and careful presentation.

OUR TIP: Try the home-produced wine

Chef: Darren Leonard **Owners:** Three Choirs Vineyards Ltd **Times:** 12-2/7-9, Closed 24 Dec-3 Jan, closed L Mon **Notes:** Vegetarian available, Smart casual, Civ Wed 20 **Seats:** 50, Pr/dining room 20 **Smoking:** N/Sm in restaurant **Children:** Menu, Portions **Rooms:** 8 (8 en suite) 🏠 **Directions:** 2m N of Newent on B4215, follow brown tourist signs **Parking:** 50 **e-mail:** ts@threechoirs.com **web:** www.threechoirs.com

England

NORTHLEACH MAP 10 SP11

The Puesdown Inn
Modern British   **NEW**
Traditional Cotswold inn with a
contemporary twist
☎ 01451 860262 Compton Abdale GL54 4DN

MENU GUIDE Seared scallops , red pesto dressing • Monkfish & crispy Serrano ham • Lemon tart

WINE GUIDE ♀ Santiago Morena Sauvignon Blanc £10.95 • ♀ Valentin Merlot £9.95 • 7 bottles over £20, 21 bottles under £20 • 12 by the glass (£2.70-£4.50)

PRICE GUIDE Fixed L £10-£15.50 • Fixed D £17.95-£23.50 • starter £3.95-£8.50 • main £12.95-£18.95 • dessert £4.75 • coffee £1.60 • min/water £2.20 • Service optional • Group min 6 service 10%

PLACE: The relaxed atmosphere makes it easy to while away the hours here without noticing, with log fires and lots of comfy sofas conspiring against an early departure. This stylishly reconstructed inn epitomises the ideals of good hospitality.

FOOD: Much more than just a foodie pub, with assured cooking from a chef dedicated to transforming quality local produce. Accurate flavours are evident in the likes of salmon and roast cod with mushy peas.

OUR TIP: Regular jazz evenings and alfresco dining

Chef: John Armstrong **Owners:** John & Maggie Armstrong **Times:** 12-3/7-11 **Notes:** Wine tasting D 4 courses £30, jazz menu 3 courses £17.95, Vegetarian available, Smart Dress **Seats:** 45, Pr/dining room 26 **Smoking:** N/Sm in restaurant **Children:** Portions **Rooms:** 3 (3 en suite) ♦♦♦♦ **Directions:** On A40 (Cheltenham-Oxford), 7m from Cheltenham, 3m from Northleach **Parking:** 80 **e-mail:** inn4food@btopenworld.com **web:** www.puesdown.cotswoldinns.com

PAINSWICK MAP 04 SO80

Painswick Hotel
British, French
Relaxed approach, understated professionalism
☎ 01452 812160 Kemps Ln GL6 6YB

MENU GUIDE Home-made venison & fig sausage • John Dory, parsley & cockle risotto • Rhubarb pannacotta, shortbread soldier

WINE GUIDE ♀ Fontcharres Vin Pays d'Oc Sauvignon Blanc £16.50 • ♀ Fontcharres Vin de Pays d'Oc Merlot £16.50 • 122 bottles over £20, 12 bottles under £20 • 10 by the glass (£3.75-£6.25)

PRICE GUIDE Fixed L £14 • Fixed D £35 • starter £7.50-£11.50 • main £22-£24.50 • dessert £6-£7.25 • coffee £3 • min/water £3 • Service included

PLACE: With a history as far back as 1790, this former rectory with Palladian features is situated in an enchanting Cotswold village. The comfortably relaxed hotel offers genuine hospitality; its oak-panelled dining room with sumptuous curtains has formal tables dressed with stiff white napery, and warm and friendly serving staff in attendance.

FOOD: With a commitment to using local produce, Cotswold lamb and venison from nearby estates appear on the menus, augmented by deliveries of fresh Cornish fish and prime Aberdeen Angus beef. The cheeseboard mixes the West Country Gloucestershire and France.

OUR TIP: Snuggle up next to the fire to choose from the extensive wine list

Chef: Kevin Barron **Owners:** Max Sabatini, Bob & Pauline Young **Times:** 12-2/7-9.30 **Notes:** Sun D £19.50, Tasting Menu £50-£80, Vegetarian available, Civ Wed 50 **Seats:** 36, Pr/dining room 16 **Smoking:** N/Sm in restaurant **Children:** Portions **Rooms:** 19 (19 en suite) ★★★ **Directions:** From A46 turn by church in Painswick, right at The March Hare. Hotel 200yds on right. **Parking:** 22 **e-mail:** reservations@painswickhotel.com **web:** www.painswickhotel.com

PAXFORD MAP 10 SP13

Churchill Arms
British, European
Confident cooking in friendly Cotswold pub
☎ 01386 594000 GL55 6XH

MENU GUIDE Hot cheese soufflé • Cod, grain mustard mash, beetroot vinaigrette • Black coffee jelly, cream, walnuts, butterscotch sauce

WINE GUIDE ♀ Taiac Montravel Sauvignon £11.75 • ♀ Pillor Box Tree Merlot £13.25 • 7 bottles over £20, 18 bottles under £20 • 10 by the glass (£2.70-£5)

PRICE GUIDE Starter £4-£8.50 • main £8-£16 • dessert £3.50-£5 • coffee £1.50 • min/water £2 • Service optional

PLACE: If you're looking for good food in an unpretentious atmosphere, this is the place - a Cotswold stone inn with a loyal local following thanks to its consistent ability to impress.

FOOD: It looks easy, but the Churchill's simple menu depends on high quality ingredients and confident technique. This is assured and classy cooking, with mains along the lines of quail with a saffron risotto, or black bream with sweet potato purée and a lime butter sauce.

OUR TIP: No table bookings taken so arrive early

Chef: David Toon, Sonya Brooke-Little **Owners:** Sonya & Leo Brooke-Little **Times:** 12-2/7-9, Closed 25 Dec **Notes:** Vegetarian available **Seats:** 60 **Smoking:** N/Sm area, Air con **Children:** Portions **Directions:** Situated 2m E of Chipping Campden **Parking:** On street **e-mail:** mail@thechurchillarms.com **web:** www.thechurchillarms.com

STOW-ON-THE-WOLD MAP 11 SP12

The Conservatory Restaurant
British, French

Fine dining under trailing vines

☎ 01451 830344 Grapevine Hotel, Sheep St GL54 1AU

MENU GUIDE Smoked duck & fig salad • Roast monkfish with confit cabbage & wild mushrooms • Raspberry Pavlova

WINE GUIDE ♀ Mezza Corona Pinot Grigio £14.75 • ♀ Santa Rita Merlot £14.75 • 23 bottles over £20, 17 bottles under £20 8 by the glass (£3.40-£4.95)

PRICE GUIDE Fixed L £12.50 • Fixed D £28 • starter £6 • main £17 • dessert £5 • coffee £1.75 • min/water £3 • Service optional • Group min 6 service 10%

PLACE: With its much talked about canopy of century-old Black Hamburg grapes, the candlelit conservatory of this 17th-century hotel is a romantic place to enjoy a formal, fine dining experience.
FOOD: A modern interpretation of French classics, there are Mediterranean twists to the cooking, where smoked salmon is paired with fromage blanc, baby capers and rocket, and seared tuna steak turns up with wilted spinach and plum tomato sauce.
OUR TIP: Good selection of British cheeses
Chef: Mark Jenkins **Owners:** Mark & Janine Vance **Times:** 12-2.30/7-30 **Notes:** Vegetarian available, Smart Dress, Civ Wed 60 **Seats:** 50, /dining room 25 **Smoking:** N/Sm in restaurant **Children:** Menu, Portions **Rooms:** 22 (22 en suite) ★★★ **Directions:** Take A436 towards Chipping Norton; 150yds on right facing green **Parking:** 30
e-mail: enquiries@vines.co.uk **web:** www.vines.co.uk

Fosse Manor
Modern British   NEW

Classic and modern successfully blended in cooking and decor

☎ 01451 830354 GL54 1JX

MENU GUIDE Parfait of chicken livers • Grilled seafood medley • Warm apple tart

PRICE GUIDE Food prices not confirmed for 2006. Please telephone for details

PLACE: A stylish and comfortable country house hotel with a nicely balanced marriage of contemporary and traditional decor. Choose from the informal bistro style dining area or the more formal dining room with wooden flooring and high backed leather chairs.
FOOD: Classic English dishes such as calves' liver, steak and mushroom pie, beer battered cod and roast free range chicken are lovingly recreated with a modern twist. There is nothing overly elaborate, but the dishes are all the more successful because of this.
continued

OUR TIP: Lunch is good value
Times: 6-9.30 **Rooms:** 21 (21 en suite) ★★★
e-mail: enquiries@fossemanor.co.uk **web:** www.fossemanor.co.uk

Hamilton's Brasserie
Modern International

Innovative cuisine in Cotswold town restaurant

☎ 01451 831700 Park St GL54 1AQ

PLACE: A shop-front restaurant with stone flooring, unclothed wooden tables and linen napkins. A successful fusion of contemporary and traditional cuisine, just right for this popular and pretty town. Staff are smiling and unobtrusive.
FOOD: Carefully constructed but unfussy dishes with punchy, lively flavours. The menu changes monthly and features interesting combinations and innovative ideas, plus there are some great breakfast ideas. Everything is home made.
OUR TIP: Sit outside in warm weather or book a window seat indoors
Times: 12-2.30/6-9.30, Closed D Sun, 25-26 Dec
web: www.hamiltons.br.com

The Kings Arms
Modern British   NEW

Bustling, atmospheric 500-year-old coaching inn

☎ 01451 830364 Market Square GL54 1AF

MENU GUIDE Grilled quail, French beans, yoghurt & cumin • Roast monkfish, fennel, spinach & peperonata • Pannacotta with raspberries

PRICE GUIDE Food prices not confirmed for 2006. Please telephone for details

PLACE: A tangible sense of history oozes from this atmospheric old coaching inn. All the details, including wooden floors, beams and roaring fires, are intact, and a buzzy crowd simply brings the place to life.
FOOD: Simple, eloquent dishes deliver punchy flavour with little in the way of unnecessary embellishment. There's a hint of rural Italy to the daily changing menus, and the experienced chef is an expert at sourcing the freshest of produce.
OUR TIP: Excellent fish comes daily from Cornwall
Times: 12-2.30/6-9.30 **web:** www.kingsarms.stowonthewold.co.uk

947AD at the Royalist
British

Assured cooking in historic hostelry

☎ 01451 830670 Digbeth St GL54 1BN

MENU GUIDE Scallops, tomato sorbet, ratatouille • Duck, vanilla mash, prune jus • Apple parfait, toffee & vanilla ice

PLACE: Renowned as the oldest hotel in Britain, this charming inn is a dinner venue with character and combines period features with contemporary style. The 947AD restaurant is always busy, particularly at weekends, so book ahead.
FOOD: Accomplished cooking distinguished by the freshest of ingredients and well-judged flavour combinations. Desserts are a highlight; your choice might include warm chocolate fondant with cinnamon ice cream, or iced pineapple parfait.
OUR TIP: Six-course tasting menu available
Times: 12-2.30/7-9.30, Closed Sun-Mon **Rooms:** 8 (8 en suite) ★★★
e-mail: info@theroyalisthotel.co.uk **web:** www.theroyalisthotel.co.uk

England

STOW-ON-THE-WOLD *continued* MAP 11 SP12

◎◎ Wyck Hill House Hotel
British

Contemporary cooking in elegant Cotswold house

☎ 01451 831936 Burford Rd GL54 1HY

MENU GUIDE Smoked duck, oriental salad, plum jam, beetroot crisps • Lamb chump, tomato & basil jus • Pecan tart, prune & date ice cream

WINE GUIDE ♀ Concha y Toro Sauvignon Blanc £19.50 • ♀ McGuigan Shiraz £19.50 • 30 bottles over £20, 14 bottles under £20 • 4 by the glass (£4.50)

PRICE GUIDE Fixed L £14.50 • Fixed D £36.50 coffee £2.95 • min/water £3.50

PLACE: Adjoining the original restaurant of this charming 18th-century county house is a pretty, Victorian-style conservatory that revels in the fine views over the sprawling grounds and Windrush Valley. Wood panelling, high ceilings and log fires ooze character and lend an air of grandeur, yet the service is relaxed and friendly and contributes to the warm atmosphere.

FOOD: The kitchen moves with the times, the modern British menu delivering a fashionable nod to the Mediterranean and beyond, via contemporary flavours and light, imaginative, uncluttered dishes that utilize local, seasonal produce. Good range of cheeses.

OUR TIP: Wonderful views from the conservatory-style dining room

Chef: Mathew Dare **Owners:** Niche Hotels **Times:** 12.30-2/7.30-9.30 **Notes:** Vegetarian available, Dress Restrictions, No denim or trainers, Civ Wed 80 **Seats:** 60, Pr/dining room 80 **Smoking:** N/Sm in restaurant, Air con **Children:** Menu, Portions **Rooms:** 32 (32 en suite) ★★★★ **Directions:** Take Oxford turning off A429. Hotel is 1m on right **Parking:** 60 **e-mail:** enquiries@wyckhillhouse.com **web:** www.wyckhillhouse.com

STROUD MAP 04 SO80

◎ The Bear of Rodborough
British

Historic surroundings for some serious food

☎ 01453 878522 Rodborough Common GL5 5DE

MENU GUIDE White bean cappuccino, morels, truffle oil • Seafood navarin, smoked morteau sausage, espume of liquorice • Chocolate fetish

WINE GUIDE ♀ Montes Sauvignon Blanc £14.75 • ♀ Montes Cabernet Sauvignon £14.75 • 75% bottles over £20, 25% bottles under £20 • 8 by the glass (£2.75-£3.65)

PRICE GUIDE Fixed L £12.95 • Fixed D £28.95 • starter £5.95-£8.95 • main £15.95-£26.95 • dessert £5.95-£7.95 • coffee £2.95 • min/water £3.45 • Service optional

PLACE: Popular inn retaining all its 17th-century atmosphere and charm, set in National Trust parkland overlooking Stroud. The lounge, cocktail bar and elegant restaurant all have plenty of character. The restaurant is traditional in style, with starched linen and quality appointments, and service (with a smile) is fairly formal.

FOOD: Dishes, produced from local ingredients, tend towards the elaborate with modern combinations, as in poached duck breast, crispy duck crackling, velouté of wild mushroom, roasted leeks, confit duck leg hash brown, and port and raisin jus.

OUR TIP: Less complicated blackboard menu in the bar

Chef: Andy Troughton **Owners:** Cotswold Inns & Hotels Ltd **Times:** 12-2.30/7-9.30, Closed L Mon & Sat **Notes:** Vegetarian available, Smart

Dress, Civ Wed 70 **Seats:** 70, Pr/dining room 50 **Smoking:** N/Sm in restaurant **Children:** Menu, Portions **Rooms:** 46 (46 en suite) ★★★ **Directions:** 2.5m S from Stroud **Parking:** 100 **e-mail:** info@bearofrodborough.info **web:** www.cotswold-inns-hotels.co.uk

◎ Burleigh Court Hotel
British, Mediterranean

Country-house hotel with glorious views and accurate cooking

☎ 01453 883804 Burleigh, Minchinhampton GL5 2PF

MENU GUIDE Foie gras terrine & ham hock • Sautéed venison, rich red wine sauce • Trio of chocolate puddings

WINE GUIDE ♀ Macon Village £15.50 • ♀ Merlot £15.50 30 bottles over £20, 30 bottles under £20 • 6 by the glass (£3.50)

PRICE GUIDE Fixed L £16.95 • Fixed D £29.50 • coffee £2 min/water £3

PLACE: Country house comforts can be enjoyed at this elegant period property set high above the Slad Valley. Sweeping garden and tasteful public rooms contribute to the pleasures of a visit.

FOOD: Well-tried combinations bring a traditional flavour to the formal restaurant, with the short dinner menu offering a quality tasting experience: medallions of pork, for example, pair well with an apple and cider sauce.

OUR TIP: Enjoy the tempting petits fours served with coffee

Chef: Steven Woodcock **Owners:** Louise Noble **Times:** 12-2/7-9, Closed 24-26 Dec **Notes:** Vegetarian available, Civ Wed 50 **Seats:** 34, Pr/dining room 18 **Smoking:** N/Sm in restaurant **Children:** Min 10yrs, Menu, Portions **Rooms:** 18 (18 en suite) ★★★ **Directions:** Telephon for directions **Parking:** 28 **e-mail:** info@burleighcourthotel.co.uk **web:** www.burleighcourthotel.co.uk

continued

ETBURY MAP 04 ST89

Calcot Manor
British, Mediterranean

Contemporary dining in country surroundings

☎ 01666 890391 Calcot GL8 8YJ

MENU GUIDE Scallops in shell, fennel butter sauce • Lamb cannon, aubergine gâteau, polenta, anchovy butter & basil purée • Chocolate fondant, rosemary ice cream

WINE GUIDE ♀ Louis Latour Macon Lugny Genievres Chardonnay • ♀ Capmartin Château Lestrille Bordeaux superieur £18 • 150 bottles over £20, 9 bottles under £20 12 by the glass (£4-£8.30)

PRICE GUIDE Starter £6.50-£12 • main £14-£19.50 • dessert £6-7.25 • coffee £2.50 • Service included

PLACE: This charming English farmhouse, set around a flowered courtyard of ancient barns and stables, was built in the 14th century by Cistercian monks and is now a stylish, relax and renowned hotel set in over 200 acres of countryside. The elegant, contemporary-styled Conservatory Restaurant has views of the kitchen, wood-fired oven and gardens, while service is suitably professional and unstuffy. The hotel's Gumstool Inn provides a less formal dining option. **Winner of the AA Hotel of the Year Award for England 2005-2006.**

FOOD: Predominantly Mediterranean in influence, the light, modern, sophisticated cuisine feels surprisingly appropriate to the setting, and makes the best of quality local produce.

OUR TIP: Make a day, or night of it, and enjoy a treatment in the spa and leisure centre

Chef: Michael Croft **Owners:** Richard Ball (MD) **Times:** 12-2/7-9.30 **Notes:** Sun L 2 courses £22.50, 3 courses £25, Vegetarian available, Smart dress, Civ Wed 90 **Seats:** 100, Pr/dining room 100 **Smoking:** N/Sm in restaurant, Air con **Children:** Menu, Portions **Rooms:** 30 (30 en suite) ★★ **Directions:** M4 junct 18, take A46 towards Stroud and at x-roads with A4135 turn right and then 1st left **Parking:** 100 **e-mail:** reception@calcotmanor.co.uk **web:** www.calcotmanor.co.uk

---

The Trouble House
British, French

Tasty cooking in relaxed pub

☎ 01666 502206 Cirencester Rd GL8 8SG

MENU GUIDE Hot rabbit confit, mustard lentils • Duck & ham hock cassoulet • Sticky toffee pudding

WINE GUIDE ♀ Villa Rosa Sauvignon Blanc £12.50 • ♀ Rocheburg Shiraz £12.95 • 22 bottles over £20, 36 bottles under £20 • 13 by the glass (£2.80-£8.95)

PRICE GUIDE Starter £7-£12 • main £14-£18 • dessert £6-£8 • coffee £2 • min/water £3 • Service optional • Group min 8 service 10%

PLACE: Former coaching inn with an unpretentious feel thanks to stone walls, wooden floors and bare polished tables. It's all very rustic and relaxed, with friendly staff on hand to help, and alfresco dining in the garden in summer.

FOOD: Simple but imaginative British and French cooking is the Trouble House's strong suit with an emphasis on good ingredients and clear flavours. That's worth celebrating in itself, and there's a very reasonably priced wine list on offer if you feel like doing it in style.

OUR TIP: Interesting selection of cheeses

Chef: Michael Bedford **Owners:** Michael & Sarah Bedford **Times:** 12-2/7-9.30, Closed Xmas to New Year & BHs, Mon, closed D Sun **Notes:** Vegetarian available **Seats:** 50 **Smoking:** N/Sm area **Children:** Min 10yrs D, Portions **Directions:** Telephone for directions **Parking:** 25 **e-mail:** enquiries@troublehouse.co.uk **web:** www.troublehouse.co.uk

---

THORNBURY MAP 04 ST69

Thornbury Castle
British, Mediterranean

Modern cuisine in a fairytale setting

☎ 01454 281182 Castle St BS35 1HH

MENU GUIDE Shellfish nage, crab & coriander tortellini • Scotch beef fillet, oxtail Pithivier, roasted ceps • Banana soufflé, dark chocolate ice cream

WINE GUIDE ♀ Thornbury Castle Mullar Thurgau £18 • ♀ Adelaide Plains Ceravolo 2001 Merlot £36 • 20 bottles under £20 • 8 by the glass (£5-£7)

PRICE GUIDE Fixed L £22.50 • Fixed D £42.50 • coffee £3.50 • min/water £3 • Service optional

PLACE: It's not everyday you get chance to eat in such a magnificent setting as this historic Tudor castle, once used by Henry VIII and Mary Tudor. The great hall is imposing, while the experience continues in the formal wood-panelled dining rooms, filled with grand portraits, tapestries and flickering log fire and candlelight. Service comes appropriately professional, attentive and friendly.

continued on page 177

England

UPPER SLAUGHTER MAP 10 SP12

Lords of the Manor

Modern European
Relaxed and welcoming country house dining

☎ 01451 820243 GL54 2JD

MENU GUIDE Tuna Sumac, iced fennel • Pork belly, smoked mash, scallop • Roast fig, honeycomb, port ice cream

WINE GUIDE ♀ Huia Sauvignon Blanc £36 • ♀ Bolla Sangiovese di Romagna £26 • 125 bottles over £20, 35 bottles under £20 9 by the glass (£5-£9)

PRICE GUIDE Fixed L fr £17.95 • Fixed D fr £49 • coffee £3.50 • min/water £3.50 • Service added but optional 10%

PLACE: This welcoming stone rectory dates from 1650 and sits in eight acres of gardens and parkland surrounded by Cotswold countryside. Victorian additions add space and light to a traditional interior decorated in true country house style with log fires, deep sofas and period pieces in profusion. The smart and inviting restaurant has built up a reputation for its food down the years and its establishment credentials are reinforced by the restrained formality of the dining room which, thanks to the attentive, approachable staff, always remains a perfect dining experience.

FOOD: An intelligent, classical approach to cooking, using local quality ingredients wherever possible, produces some memorable dishes. Consistency and attention to details characterise a meal here. The menu is never complacent and the tried and trusted share the page with the unusual and innovative such as Gressingham duck, choucroute and bok choi, and pan-fried foie gras, tamarind ice cream and aged balsamic, respectively.

OUR TIP: A perfect romantic weekend Cotswold retreat

Chef: Les Rennie **Owners:** Empire Ventures **Times:** 12-2/7.00-9.30, Closed L Mon **Notes:** Tasting menu £59, Vegetarian available, Dress Restrictions, Smart casual, no jeans or trainers, Civ Wed 50 **Seats:** 55, Pr/dining room 30 **Smoking:** N/Sm in restaurant **Children:** Menu, Portions **Rooms:** 27 (27 en suite) ★★★ **Directions:** Follow signs towards The Slaughters 2m W of A429. Hotel on right in centre of Upper Slaughter **Parking:** 40 **e-mail:** enquiries@lordsofthemanor.com **web:** www.lordsofthemanor.com

---

WINCHCOMBE MAP 10 SP02

5 North Street

British, French
Unpretentious, stunning cooking in Cotswolds

☎ 01242 604566 5 North St GL54 5LH

MENU GUIDE Onion & sage tartlet • Beef, ox tongue mash, wild mushrooms, Madeira sauce • Fig & honey pastry, honey ice cream

WINE GUIDE ♀ Vinha d'or Sauvignon Blanc £13.50 • ♀ Vinha d'or Merlot £13.50 • 48 bottles over £20, 12 bottles under £20 • 4 by the glass (£3.50-£4)

PRICE GUIDE Fixed L £17.50 • Fixed D £25-£35 • starter £8-£12 • main £12-£17 • dessert £5-£8 • coffee £3

PLACE: This delightful mellow stone restaurant in the pretty Cotswold village of Winchcombe has a number of intimate dining areas, each simply set with plain wooden tables.

FOOD: North Street majors in refreshingly straightforward cooking that demonstrates both the quality of ingredients and abilities of the chef. Expect a modern menu distinguished by wonderful flavours and a lack of pretension: duck with celeriac fondant and burnt orange sauce perhaps, or local game served with its own jus and choucroute.

OUR TIP: Try the ten-course tasting menu

Chef: Marcus Ashenford **Owners:** Marcus & Kate Ashenford **Times:** 1 2/7-9, Closed First 2 wks Jan, 1st wk Aug, Mon, closed L Tue, closed D S **Notes:** Tasting menu 10 courses £48.50, Sun L 4 courses £25, Vegetaria available **Seats:** 26 **Smoking:** N/Sm in restaurant **Children:** Menu, Portions **Directions:** 7m from Cheltenham **Parking:** On street, pay & display **e-mail:** marcusashenford@yahoo.co.uk

THORNBURY *continued* MAP 04 ST69

FOOD: Feast like a king on the sensibly compact, fixed-price modern-focused menus, underpinned by a classical theme, where thoughtful presentation and the treatment of quality ingredients show off the kitchen's pedigree.

OUR TIP: Try the Thornbury White Wine, with grapes grown in the castle grounds

Chef: Steve Rimmer **Owners:** Von Essen **Times:** 12-2/7-9.30 **Notes:** Vegetarian available, Dress Restrictions, Smart casual, Civ Wed 50 **Seats:** 72, Pr/dining room 22 **Smoking:** N/Sm in restaurant **Children:** Menu, Portions **Rooms:** 25 (25 en suite) ★★★ **Directions:** M5 junct 16. N on A38. Continue for 4m to lights and turn rt. Following brown Historic Castle signs **Parking:** 50 **e-mail:** info@thornburycastle.co.uk **web:** www.thornburycastle.co.uk

---

UPPER SLAUGHTER MAP 10 SP12

 ### Lords of the Manor

see page 176

WINCHCOMBE MAP 10 SP02

 ### 5 North Street *see page 176*

 ### Wesley House
European
Period flower-filled setting for modern cuisine
☎ 01242 602366 High St GL54 5LJ

 Noilly Prat steamed Fowey mussels • Braised lamb shank • Praline soufflé, chocolate sauce, praline ice cream
WINE GUIDE ♀ Mount Riley Sauvignon £21 • ♥ Fox Wood Marignan • 65 bottles over £20, 19 bottles under £20 • 11 by the glass (£3.75-£9.50)

continued

PRICE GUIDE Fixed L £12.50 • Fixed D £35 • coffee £2.50 • min/water £3 • Service optional

PLACE: A 15th-century half-timbered property named after the founder of the Methodist church who stayed here while preaching in the town. In a complete redecoration, a glass atrium was added to cover the outside terrace. Unique modern lighting can change colour to suit the atmosphere required, and highlight creations by a world renowned, gold medal-winning flower arranger.

FOOD: Accomplished cooking from a chef delivering good clean flavours, light on seasoning, from top quality produce. A good value lunch carte is followed by a fixed-price dinner menu with a broader range of dishes.

OUR TIP: Available for exclusive private parties

Chef: Martin Dunn **Owners:** Matthew Brown **Times:** 12-2/7-9, Closed Xmas, closed D Sun **Notes:** Vegetarian available **Seats:** 70, Pr/dining room 24 **Smoking:** N/Sm in restaurant, Air con **Children:** Portions **Rooms:** 6 (6 en suite) **Directions:** In centre of Winchcombe **e-mail:** enquiries@wesleyhouse.co.uk **web:** www.wesleyhouse.co.uk

GREATER MANCHESTER

ALTRINCHAM MAP 15 SJ78

 ### Juniper *see page 178*

HORWICH MAP 15 SD61

De Vere Whites
British, French
Fine dining for footballing foodies
☎ 01204 667788 De Havilland Way BL6 6SF
MENU GUIDE Terrine of rabbit, chicken & foie gras • Venison, dauphinoise potatoes, salsify, wild mushrooms • Pear & apple Tatin

WINE GUIDE ♀ Spy Valley Sauvignon Blanc £22 • ♥ Palena Merlot £20.50 • 40 bottles over £20, 2 bottles under £20 • 2 by the glass (£3.70-£4.50)

PRICE GUIDE Starter £5.25-£8.75 • main £16.95-£22 • dessert £4.95-£6 • coffee £2 • min/water £3.50 • Service optional

PLACE: This classy pitch-side restaurant is part of the Reebok stadium, home to the Bolton Wanderers, and offers fine dining at well-spaced and elegantly dressed tables. Lighter meals are available at the stadium's brasserie.

FOOD: Reflections restaurant delivers a modern menu of accomplished British dishes with French influences. Kick off with scallop and lobster tortelloni, and then try veal belly with polenta and winter vegetables, or sea bass with a bouillabaisse sauce. Open for evening meals only, Wednesday to Saturday.

OUR TIP: Match day window booths run at a premium

Chef: Paul Hoad **Owners:** Reflections - De Vere Hotels **Times:** 7-10, Closed 25 Dec, Sun, Mon & Tues, closed L all week **Notes:** Fixed D 5 courses £50, £75 (with wine), Vegetarian available, Dress Restrictions, Smart casual, no jeans or trainers, Civ Wed 60 **Seats:** 65 **Smoking:** N/Sm in restaurant, Air con **Children:** Min 14yrs, Portions **Rooms:** 125 (125 en suite) ★★★★ **Directions:** Off M61 junct 6 **Parking:** 2500 **e-mail:** whites@devere-hotels.com **web:** www.devereonline.co.uk

England

Juniper

French, Unique *Dazzling culinary fun in popular neighbourhood restaurant*
☎ 0161 929 4008 21 The Downs WA14 2QD

PLACE: For one of the country's most renowned and talked about restaurants, Juniper is not what, or located where, you would expect it to be. Set in a parade of ordinary shops, bustling pubs and late-night Indian venues, it looks like any other mild-mannered suburban restaurant rather than a culinary playground, but then there's not too much about Juniper that is conventional. The interior, on two levels, is equally discreet and unpretentious, but cool, with a basement bar downstairs being the place to kick off the Juniper experience while perusing the flamboyant menu over cocktails. Upstairs, the dining room is decorated in shades of green, with quirky artwork, subdued lighting and a large tree occupying one corner providing character, and with the stamp of quality shining through from highly polished glassware, cutlery and crisp white linen. Staff are very relaxed and friendly, but extremely attentive, informative and professional, and this in itself, helps make the evening go with a swing.

FOOD: There's little that can prepare you for your first encounter with Paul Kitching's highly individual cooking, its playful way with ingredients has helped redefine the boundaries of fine dining. The man himself describes his style as "from the heart, sensitive and open", and it's certainly idiosyncratic, adventurous and breathtaking. Ambition, boundless creative energy and improvisation combine with masterful technical skills to pull off some daring culinary coups and combinations. His unique approach to menus, food and presentation, sees everything delivered in small portions on small plates with immaculate and, in many cases, quirky presentation; take smoked salmon mayonnaise presented on a small square plate, piped in the shape of a fish, while an amuse bouche might be delivered on an array of 15 miniature plates and a grande assiette of French cheese, making more than 20 individual portions. Menus read more like a list of ingredients, some with amusing names (think 'when a rabbit met a scallop', for instance) than is the norm on lunch and carte offerings, while gourmet surprise menus deliver an impromptu take on Paul's cooking philosophy, where one simply sits back and enjoys the ride.

MENU GUIDE Olive oil baked scallops • Venison, assiette of meats • Assiette of six miniature desserts

WINE GUIDE ♀ Cape Mentelle Semillion/Sauvignon Blanc £29 • ♀ Cape Mentelle Shiraz £37

PRICE GUIDE Fixed L £17.50 • starter £8-£12 • main £18-£24 • dessert £7-£12 • coffee £3.75 • min/water £3 • Service included

OUR TIP: Don't miss the lemon tart

Chef: Paul Kitching **Owners:** P & D Keeling, P Kitching, K O'Brien **Times:** 12-2/7-10, Closed 1 wk Jan, 2 wks summer, Sun - Mon, closed L Sat **Notes:** 12 courses £65 **Seats:** 36 **Smoking:** N/Sm in restaurant, Air con **Directions:** A556, Chester-Manchester road. Altrincham town centre
e-mail: reservations@juniper-restaurant.co.uk
web: www.juniper-restaurant.co.uk

MANCHESTER MAP 16 SJ89
Alias Hotel Rossetti

Mediterranean

Brasserie style cooking in easy going atmosphere

☎ 0161 247 7744 107 Piccadilly M1 2DB

MENU GUIDE Grilled oysters with courgette & pancetta • Veal saltimbocca with roast artichokes • Strawberry parfait & strawberry & mint salsa

WINE GUIDE ♀ Andrew Hurley Semillion Chardonnay £12.95 • ♀ Pleno Tempranillo £12.95 • 20 bottles over £20, 35 bottles under £20 • 10 by the glass (£3.50-£9.95)

PRICE GUIDE Starter £3.50-£5 • main £8.50-£13 • dessert £4.75 • coffee £2.50 • min/water £3 • Service included

PLACE: Situated in a converted warehouse, the Café Paradiso decor is funky and the staff wear black T-shirts and jeans. Easy listening background music is played and the atmosphere is laid back.

FOOD: Upmarket brasserie style food with some good value set menu choices, the food is principally Mediterranean with a Italian bias. There are open wood burning pizza ovens and a good choice of toppings.

OUR TIP: Large wine list plus full bar and cocktail list
Chef: David Gale **Owners:** John Migel **Times:** 12-5.30/5.30-10
Notes: Vegetarian available **Seats:** 92, Pr/dining room 24
Smoking: N/Sm in restaurant **Children:** Menu, Portions **Rooms:** 61 (61 en suite) ★★★★ **Directions:** Located in city centre close to Piccadilly station **Parking:** Opposite hotel **e-mail:** info@aliasrossetti.com
web: www.aliashotels.com

The AA Wine Awards recognise the finest wine lists in England, Scotland and Wales. For full details, see pages 14-15

Copthorne Hotel Manchester

International

Metropolitan hotel with quayside views

☎ 0161 873 7321 Clippers Quay, Salford Quays M50 3SN

MENU GUIDE Crab & langoustine spring roll, soy & sweet chilli dressing • Saddle of venison, fennel & caraway seed mousse, blackcurrant gravy • Cherry & rum bread & butter pudding

WINE GUIDE ♀ Colombard Sauvignon £14.95 • ♀ Grenache Merlot £14.95 • 14 bottles over £20, 30 bottles under £20 • 10 by the glass (£3.50-£7)

PRICE GUIDE Fixed L £24.95 • Fixed D £33.50 • starter £3.95-£7.95 • main £8.95-£18.95 • dessert £3.95-£5.95 • coffee £2.75 • min/water £3.60 • Service included

PLACE: Standing next to the quays in the redeveloped Salford Docks, close to Old Trafford and the Lowry Centre, is this smart, modern, red-brick hotel. The unusual crescent-shaped Chandlers Restaurant makes the most of the stunning setting with views of the magnificent waterfront.

FOOD: Expect an extensive modern British menu infused with international ingredients. The seasonal menus are prepared with the finest fresh local produce.

OUR TIP: Try the chef's daily fish special
Chef: Paul Wilde **Owners:** Millennium & Copthorne Hotels plc
Times: 7-10, Closed Xmas, 1 Jan, Sun, closed L Mon-Sat
Notes: Vegetarian available, Smart Dress **Seats:** 40, Pr/dining room 130
Smoking: No pipes **Children:** Menu, Portions **Rooms:** 166 (166 en suite) ★★★★ **Directions:** From M602 follow signs to Salford Quays/Trafford Park. Hotel is 0.75m along A5063 (Trafford Rd)
Parking: 120 **e-mail:** roomsales.manchester@mill-cop.com
web: www.millenniumhotels.com

The Establishment

British, French   **NEW**

New kid on the block produces stylish food in grand surroundings

☎ 0161 839 6300 43-45 Spring Gardens M2 2BG

MENU GUIDE Seared yellow fin tuna, tomato & mushroom relish, shellfish mayonnaise • Roast & confit guinea fowl, peppered apricots, white bean purée, burgundy jus • Quartet of desserts - sticky toffee pudding, lemon tart, bread & butter pudding, egg custard

PRICE GUIDE Food prices not confirmed for 2006. Please telephone for details

PLACE: Bang in the city centre, this was originally a bank, and more recently a pub, converted to this stylish, spacious restaurant in 2004. It has a smart, contemporary feel, with some original features retained, including the double domed glass atrium, marble columns and an ornate plaster ceiling. Light polished wood tables, and chairs upholstered in caramel leather and light gold. Service is friendly and goes the extra mile.

FOOD: Carefully thought out dishes, executed to a high standard using great ingredients. Menu descriptions may sound flamboyant, but there's a refreshing simplicity to the food on the plate. They take the wine seriously, too. (The restaurant has its own wine club.) Start with excellent seared scallops on wild mushroom risotto, creamy and full flavoured, with a wonderful purée of Jerusalem artichoke. After that, how about pan-fried turbot with fantastic oxtail shredded and served around the plate and a slightly sweet tomato relish. One to watch.

OUR TIP: Great value lunch
Times: 12-2.30/7-10 Closed 25 Dec & BHs, Sun & Mon, closed L Sat
Directions: Manchester City centre at top of King St
e-mail: peggy@establishmentrestaurant.com
web: www.establishmentrestaurant.com

MANCHESTER continued MAP 16 SJ89

🏵 Greens NEW
Modern Vegetarian
Well established venue for vegetarians
☎ 0161 434 4259 43 Lapwing Ln, Didsbury M20 2NT
MENU GUIDE Thai spiced potato cake, Asian coleslaw • Filo strudel, leeks, mushrooms, tomato, cream cheese • Sherry trifle
WINE GUIDE ♀ Pasqua Pinot Grigio £13.50 • ♀ Sospiro Malbec £12 • 2 bottles over £20, 12 bottles under £20 • 4 by the glass (£2.95-£3.95)
PRICE GUIDE Fixed D £14.95 • starter £3.25-£5.25 • main £10.50 • dessert £4.25 • coffee £1.25 • min/water £3.25 • Service optional • Group min 6 service 10%

PLACE: Located in a row of shops this unpretentious, contemporary vegetarian restaurant has friendly, relaxed staff and is very popular with locals.
FOOD: Simple and eclectic vegetarian dishes that stem from international, meat-inspired recipes, such as a version of Lancashire hot pot containing parsnips, pumpkin, onion, spiced gravy and a crispy potato top.
OUR TIP: Great value set menu at restricted times
Chef: Simon Connolly & Simon Rimmer **Owners:** Simon Connolly & Simon Rimmer **Times:** 12-2/5.30-10.30, Closed BHs, closed L Mon-Sat **Notes:** Vegetarian available **Seats:** 48 **Smoking:** N/Sm in restaurant **Children:** Menu **Parking:** On street **e-mail:** greensrestaurant@tiscali.co.uk

🏵 Harvey Nichols 2nd Floor Restaurant
European, Pacific Rim
Eclectic food in designer surroundings
☎ 0161 828 8898 21 New Cathedral St M1 1AD

MENU GUIDE Crisp calamari with lemon oil & capers • Slow roast belly of pork, apple & Madeira jus • Classic banana split

continued

WINE GUIDE ♀ Harvey Nichols Sauvignon Blanc • ♀ Harvey Nichols Rouge Merlot • 150 bottles over £20, 50 bottles under £20 • 16 by the glass (£3.65-£7.40)
PRICE GUIDE Fixed D £13.50-£21.50 • starter £4.50-£8.50 • main £8.50-£20 • dessert £6-£7.50 • coffee £2 • min/water £3 • Service added but optional 10%

PLACE: As you'd expect at 'Harvey Nicks' both the restaurant and brasserie are stylish and contemporary. The floor to ceiling windows give great views over the city and state-of-the-art lighting provides ever-changing colour to reflect both season and time of day.
FOOD: Modern European with a touch of Pacific Rim. There are classics like French onion soup sitting alongside some interesting and exotic combinations such as cauliflower pannacotta.
OUR TIP: Great city centre eaterie for sophisticated shoppers
Chef: Robert Craggs **Owners:** Harvey Nichols **Times:** 10-3/6-10.30, Closed 25-26 Dec, 1 Jan, Easter Sun, closed D Sun-Mon **Notes:** Vegetarian available **Seats:** 50 **Smoking:** N/Sm in restaurant, Air con **Directions:** Just off Deansgate, town centre. 5 min walk from Victoria Station **Parking:** Under store, across road **e-mail:** secondfloor.reservations@harveynichols.com **web:** www.harveynichols.com

🏵 Lowry Hotel, River Room, Marco Pierre White
British, European
Modern British brasserie in luxury hotel
☎ 0161 827 4000 50 Dearmans Place, Chapel Wharf, Salford M3 5LH
MENU GUIDE Risotto of langoustine • Lamb cutlet with Garstang blue cheese • Traditional tiramisù
WINE GUIDE ♀ Craggy Range Sauvignon Blanc £29 • ♀ Monte Real Tempranillo £28 • 130 bottles over £20, 10 bottles under £20 • 17 by the glass (£4.75-£6.50)
PRICE GUIDE Fixed L £18.50 • Fixed D £20.50 • starter £8.95-£9.95 • main £17.95-£30 • dessert £6.95 • coffee £3.25 • min/water £4 • Service added but optional 10%

PLACE: The Lowry is a five-star hotel in the Rocco Forte Collection, on the edge of Salford's centre. The large dining room, overlooking the River Irwell, has a contemporary feel with bronze, cream and brown decor. Leather banquette seating around the walls surrounds cream leather chairs at the elegantly appointed tables in the centre.
FOOD: A new head chef appointment is due at the time of writing; it is understood that the modern and unpretentious menu will continue offering a combination of international influences, classic cuisine and clean, contemporary flavours.
OUR TIP: Book a window seat
Owners: Sir Rocco Forte & family **Times:** 12-2.30/6-10.30 **Notes:** Vegetarian available, Dress Restrictions, Smart casual prefered, Civ Wed 120 **Seats:** 120, Pr/dining room 20 **Smoking:** N/Sm area, Air con **Children:** Menu, Portions **Rooms:** 165 (165 en suite) ★★★★★ **Directions:** Manchester Piccadilly main exit. Along Market St, left into Deansgate, right into King St West onto footbridge. Lowry Hotel straight ahead **Parking:** 100 **e-mail:** enquiries@thelowryhotel.com **web:** www.roccofortehotels.com

🏵 Marriott Worsley Park Hotel & Country Club
International
Elegant, modern setting serving British based food
☎ 0161 975 2000 Worsley Park, Worsley M28 2QT

continued

England

PLACE: Impressive grounds, including a championship golf course, surround this smart, modern hotel. Public areas include extensive leisure and conference facilities, an all-day bistro and the elegant split level restaurant.
FOOD: Though underpinned by tried and tested British dishes, global cuisine also influences the cooking.
OUR TIP: Ideal for golfers
Times: 7-10 Rooms: 158 (158 en suite) ★★★★ Directions: Just off M60 J13, take A575. Hotel on left.
e-mail: salesadmin.worsleypark@marriotthotels.co.uk
web: www.marriott.com

Midland Hotel

British, French 🐟➔NEW
Opulent Edwardian hotel offering fine French cuisine
☎ 0161 236 3333 Peter St M60 2DS
MENU GUIDE Seared scallops, vanilla dauphinoise, mint dressing • Fillet of beef, tortellini of shin • Chocolate assiette gourmande
WINE GUIDE 1 bottle under £20 • 5 by the glass (£6.95)
PRICE GUIDE Fixed D £29 • starter £7.50-£14.95 • main £23.95-£59.95 • dessert £7.50 • coffee £3.95 • min/water £3.95
PLACE: Originally a railway hotel, this grand Grade I listed property has been at the centre of city life since 1903. Since a new company acquisitioned in 2004, it has benefited from a £12 million upgrade. The Trafford is the main restaurant but the fine dining option is The French, with its impressive period decor.
FOOD: A good range of ingredients is used in what is essentially French classical cooking, skilfully produced with a modern slant that hits the mark. The luxurious surroundings are reflected in the prices.
OUR TIP: Piano music in the Octagon Terrace & Bar before dinner
Chef: David Kirkpatrick, Andre Matter Owners: Quintessential Hotels
Times: 7-11, Closed BHs, Sun, closed L all week Notes: Civ Wed 500
Seats: 55 Smoking: N/Sm in restaurant, Air con Children: Menu, Portions Rooms: 303 (303 en suite) ★★★★ Parking: Behind hotel
web: www.themidland.co.uk

Le Mont @ Urbis

Modern French NEW
Dazzling modern venue, fantastic views of the city, creative fine dining
☎ 0161 605 8282 Levels 5 & 6 Cathedral Gardens M4 3BG

MENU GUIDE Terrine of confit duck & foie gras • Belly pork, Calvados, apple & tomato sauce • Orange tart, Grand Marnier & mandarin sorbet
PRICE GUIDE Food prices not confirmed for 2006. Please telephone for details
PLACE: Situated on the 5th and 6th floor of the dazzling, futuristic, steel-and-glass Urbis Centre, this ultra-modern, split-level restaurant provides outstanding views over Manchester's skyline. An inspiring sense of elevated freedom and openness is created by plate glass walls and, although very minimalist in style, table appointments are classical with crisp linen and Wedgwood cutlery.
FOOD: Cooking is richly French in style, yet restraint and discipline in handling complex ingredients results in wholesome, simply presented dishes that are full of flavour. The classical French carte makes good use of British produce and luxury ingredients.
OUR TIP: Every table is a window seat
Times: 12-2.30/7-10.30 e-mail: le-mont@urbis.org.uk
web: www.urbis.org.uk

Moss Nook

British, French 🐟➔
Classical food in a sumptuous setting
☎ 0161 437 4778 Ringway Rd, Moss Nook M22 5WD
MENU GUIDE Pan-seared scallops, vegetable tagliatelle • Grilled loin of venison, redcurrant jus • Medley of chocolate desserts & sauces
WINE GUIDE ♀ Domaine de Fussiacus Macon Fuissé Chardonnay £19.50 • ♥ Baron de Rothschild Lafite Los Vascos Cabernet Sauvignon £18.50 • 26 bottles under £20 • 3 by the glass (£3.50-£7.50)
PRICE GUIDE Fixed D £32-£44.25 • starter £8-£14 • main £19.50-£23 • dessert £4.50-£7.25 • coffee £3 • min/water £2.50 • Service included
PLACE: Detached property with a pretty patio garden and the benefit of its own car park. The spacious open-plan restaurant has been refurbished in modern classic style. Diners are comfortably seated on padded and buttoned chairs at well-spaced tables laid with crisp linen and quality tableware.
FOOD: Very much classical French with correct cloche service. The goal here is consistency - just what the clientele values in an area of fashionable eateries. Daily specials in addition to the main menus include fresh fish and there's a five-course tasting menu.
OUR TIP: Aperitifs and plane spotting on the terrace
Chef: Kevin Lofthouse Owners: P & D Harrison Times: 12-1.30/7-10, Closed 2 wks Xmas, Sun & Mon, closed L Sat Notes: Fixed L 5 courses £19.50, Vegetarian available, Dress Restrictions, No jeans, trainers Seats: 65
Smoking: No pipes, Air con Children: Min 12yrs Directions: 1m from airport at junction of Ringway with B5166 Parking: 30

Le Petit Blanc

French NEW
Modern, regional French brasserie cooking in smart setting
☎ 0161 832 1000 55 Kings St M2 4LQ
MENU GUIDE Morteau sausage & potato salad • Hot smoked Duart salmon, soused beetroot • Bourbon vanilla crème brûlée
WINE GUIDE ♀ Bourgogne Blanc £18.95 • ♥ Côtes du Rhône Blend £18.95 • 21 bottles over £20, 16 bottles under £20 • 13 by the glass (£3.25-£5.75)
PRICE GUIDE Fixed L £12 • Fixed D £14.50 • starter £4.50-£8.50 • main £9.50-£17.95 • dessert £4.95-£6.50 • coffee £1.75 • min/water £3 • Service added but optional 10% • Group min 6 service 10%
PLACE: Chic but simple, Raymond Blanc's Manchester outlet is a cosmopolitan brasserie in the heart of the city centre. Elevated window seats with views and comfy banquettes encourage diners to linger and enjoy the experience.
FOOD: Expect modern, authentic French brasserie-style cooking, succinctly described and slickly presented. The informality is equally suited to quickie lunches and relaxed dining, and the natural flavours of honest, wholesome ingredients defines the traditional dishes.
OUR TIP: Enjoy a drink in the new cocktail bar
Chef: Simon Stanley Owners: Raymond Blanc, Loch Fyne Restaurants
Times: 12, Closed 25, 26 Dec, 1 Jan Notes: Vegetarian available
Seats: 100, Pr/dining room 40 Smoking: N/Sm in restaurant, Air con
Children: Menu, Portions Directions: King St, City centre
Parking: Nearby car parks e-mail: manchester@lepetitblanc.co.uk
web: www.lepetitblanc.co.uk

MANCHESTER *continued* MAP 16 SJ89

🌸 Simply Heathcotes
British 🐟💷
Stylish metropolitan dining venue with extensive menu
☎ 0161 835 3536 Jacksons Row, Deansgate M2 5WD

MENU GUIDE Spiced lamb terrine, toasted almonds • Baked cod, grain mustard mash • Iced vanilla parfait

WINE GUIDE ♀ Dream Bay Sauvignon Blanc £27.50 • ♀ Bodegas Sierra Cantabria Rioja Tempranillo £19.50 • 47 bottles over £20, 13 bottles under £20 • 10 by the glass (£3.85-£5.25)

PRICE GUIDE Fixed L £14 • Fixed D £30-£40 • starter £2.75-£7.50 • main £11.50-£18.50 • dessert £5.50 • coffee £1.80 • min/water £1.25 • Service optional • Group service 10%

PLACE: Hidden away down a side street between the Town Hall and Deansgate, this old registry office building now has a minimalist, designer interior with natural surfaces, high ceilings and Philippe Starck bucket chairs.
FOOD: With the menu changing seasonally, the modern British and brasserie classics are cooked with care and attention to detail. With efficient service, the restaurant is popular with shopping and business clientele.
OUR TIP: Great value set lunch
Chef: Olivia Casson **Owners:** Mr P Heathcote **Times:** 12-2.30/5.30-10, Closed 25-26 Dec, 1-3 Jan, BHs **Notes:** Sun menu 2 courses £14.50, 3 courses £17 (open 12-9), Vegetarian available, Civ Wed 60 **Seats:** 170, Pr/dining room 60 **Smoking:** N/Sm in restaurant, Air con **Children:** Menu, Portions **Directions:** M62 junct 17. Restaurant at top end of Deansgate **Parking:** On street
e-mail: manchester@simplyheathcotes.co.uk
web: www.heathcotes.co.uk

🌸🌸 Viego
Mediterranean **NEW**
Modern food in modern setting
☎ 0161 873 8899 Golden Tulip, Waters Reach, Trafford Park M17 1WS

MENU GUIDE Calves' liver with home-made haggis • Honey & lavender pannacotta, spiced figs

WINE GUIDE ♀ Jaques Vertier Sauvignon Blanc £12.95 • ♀ Salisbury Shiraz £16.50 • 7 bottles over £20, 24 bottles under £20 • 6 by the glass (£3.50-£5.50)

PRICE GUIDE Fixed L £12.95 • Fixed D £14.95 • starter £3.95-£6.95 • main £8.60-£17 • dessert £4.50-£5.95 • coffee £2.20 • min/water £3 • Service added but optional 10%

PLACE: In the shadow of Old Trafford (you can see the stadium from the bar and the restaurant) this is the official Manchester

United hotel. The stylish Viego restaurant is very modern, with simple and uncluttered design - wooden floors and plain walls.
FOOD: Fresh and modern British cooking with Mediterranean influences. Interesting and successful combinations might include oxtail terrine, full of depth of flavour, moist and studded with finely diced vegetables and served with home-made piccalilli, or pan-fried black bream on a lightly tangy roasted vine tomato sauce.
OUR TIP: Don't miss the treacle tart
Chef: Michael Wilson **Owners:** Golden Tulip UK **Times:** 12-2.30/6-10, Closed L Sat-Sun **Seats:** 86, Pr/dining room 160 **Smoking:** N/Sm in restaurant, Air con **Children:** Menu, Portions **Rooms:** 160 (160 en suite) ★★★ **Directions:** Telephone for directions. **Parking:** 180
e-mail: info@goldentulipmanchester.co.uk
web: www.goldentulipmanchester.co.uk

🌸 Yang Sing Restaurant
Chinese, Cantonese
Pioneering Chinese restaurant
☎ 0161 236 2200 34 Princess St M1 4JY

MENU GUIDE Shark fin soup with chicken meat • Chile fried crispy beef, chow yung fried rice

WINE GUIDE ♀ Sierra Cantabria Tempranillo £14.90 • ♀ Vina Rucahue Cabernet Sauvignon £13.90 • 90 bottles over £20, 30 bottles under £20 • 5 by the glass (£3.95)

PRICE GUIDE Starter £2.20-£8.80 • main £7.90-£15.50 • coffee £1.50 • min/water £2.95 • Service included

PLACE: This ever busy Chinese eaterie occupies four floors of a former Victorian warehouse and is decorated with a blend of contemporary European style and oriental art work. Fish tanks and a theatre kitchen complete the ensemble.
FOOD: The undisputed pioneer of the Chinese restaurant scene in Britain, Yang Sing continues to delight and educate the public with ever higher levels of authenticity. Asian cooking at its imaginative best.
OUR TIP: Vegetarian menu also available
Chef: Harry Yeung **Owners:** Harry & Gerry Yeung **Times:** 12, Closed 25 Dec, 25 Dec **Notes:** Vegetarian available **Seats:** 260, Pr/dining room 360 **Smoking:** Air con **Directions:** Located in city centre on Princes St, which runs from Albert Square **Parking:** Public car park adjacent
e-mail: info@yang-sing.com **web:** www.yang-sing.com

🌸 Market Restaurant 104 High St, Northern Quarter M4 1HQ ☎ 0161 834 3743 Quirky, well-established restaurant focusing on freshly-prepared dishes and organic ingredients.

🌸 Restaurant Bar and Grill 14 John Dalton St M2 6JR ☎ 0161 839 1999 Trendy, fusion oriented bar and restaurant.

continued

Royal Naz 16-18 Wilmslow Rd, Rusholme M14 5TQ
☎ 0161 256 1060 Pakistani and Indian dishes with top-quality spices.

Shere Khan 52 Wilmslow Rd, Rusholme M14 5TQ
☎ 0161 256 2624 Something of a local legend, justly popular and a haunt of celebrities.

Wagamama 1 The Printworks, Corporation St M4 4DG
☎ 0161 839 5916 Informal noodle bar with no booking.

Zinc Bar and Grill The Triangle, Hanging Ditch M4 3ES ☎ 0161 827 4200 Contemporary Conran-owned eaterie.

MANCHESTER AIRPORT MAP 15 SJ88

Etrop Grange Hotel
British, French

Creative cooking in elegant Georgian setting
☎ 0161 499 0500 Thorley Ln M90 4EG

MENU GUIDE Crayfish bisque, chicken & crab wonton • Beef, celeriac rösti, port wine & shallot jus • Apricot parfait, honey-roast figs

WINE GUIDE ♀ One Tree Hill £13.95 • ♀ One Tree Hill £13.95 • 38 bottles over £20, 19 bottles under £20 • 1 by the glass (£3.50)

PRICE GUIDE Fixed L £14.95 • Fixed D £31.95 • starter £4.25-£8.95 • main £11.95-£14.95 • dessert £3.95-£4.50 • coffee £2.95 • min/water £3.50 • Service optional

PLACE: Gracious Georgian manor with a range of elegant public spaces including the softly-lit Coach House restaurant, a formal dining room decorated in burgundy and gold.
FOOD: Traditional British combinations rub shoulders with more modish fare, with dishes along the lines of guinea fowl with a whisky and peppercorn sauce, or chicken with goats' cheese, prosciutto and basil polenta. Tempting cheese selection.
OUR TIP: Handy for Manchester Airport
Chef: Andrew Firth **Owners:** Corus & Regal Hotels **Times:** 12-2/7-10, Closed L Sat **Notes:** Vegetarian available, Dress Restrictions, No Jeans, Civ Wed 30 **Seats:** 50, Pr/dining room 90 **Smoking:** N/Sm in restaurant **Children:** Portions **Rooms:** 64 (64 en suite) ★★★ **Directions:** Off M56 junct 5. Follow signs to Terminal 2, take 1st left (Thornley Ln), 200yds on right. **Parking:** 80 **e-mail:** etropgrange@corushotels.com **web:** www.corushotels.com/etropgrange

Radisson SAS Hotel Manchester Airport
British, International

Sophisticated pre-flight dining
☎ 0161 490 5000 Chicago Av M90 3RA

MENU GUIDE Carpaccio of beef, spiced guacamole • Sea bass, herb crab cake, beurre rouge • Hot chocolate pudding

PRICE GUIDE Starter £8-£12 • main £17.50-£23 • dessert £6 • coffee £2.50 • min/water £3.50 • Service optional

PLACE: This strikingly designed, ultra-modern hotel, with a central atrium, is connected by an elevated passenger walkway to the airport's terminals. The restaurant is named after the fictional traveller Phileas Fogg and floor-to-ceiling windows afford great views over the runways. The views are matched with an impressive decor and an international menu. Friendly, knowledgeable staff.

Radisson SAS Hotel Manchester Airport

FOOD: Cooking is modern British in style using international techniques and flavours. Expect snappy menu descriptions and exciting combinations of ingredients.
OUR TIP: Perfect for plane spotting
Chef: R Faulkener-Walford **Owners:** Radisson SAS **Times:** 12-2.30/7-10.30, Closed L Sat-Sun **Notes:** Vegetarian available, Civ Wed 80 **Seats:** 180 **Smoking:** N/Sm area, Air con **Children:** Menu, Portions **Rooms:** 360 (360 en suite) ★★★★ **Directions:** M56 junct 5, follow signs for Terminal 2, take 1st exit at rdbt for railway station, hotel opposite station **Parking:** 220
e-mail: sales.airport.manchester@radissonsas.com
web: www.radissonsas.com

OLDHAM MAP 16 SD90

White Hart Inn
British, European

Bold modern cooking in welcoming coaching inn
☎ 01457 872566 51 Stockport Rd, Lydgate OL4 4JJ

MENU GUIDE Chicken liver parfait, tomato jam • Beef fillet, chicken oxtail sausage, celeriac purée • Assiette of chocolate

WINE GUIDE ♀ Calitera Sauvignon Blanc £14.50 • ♀ Calitera Merlot £14.50 • 108 bottles over £20, 51 bottles under £20 11 by the glass (£2.75-£3.45)

PRICE GUIDE Fixed L £13.50-£14.50 • Fixed D £20-£37.50 • starter £4.75-£8 • main £12-£18 • dessert £4.95-£7 • coffee £1.60 • min/water £3.25 • Service optional

PLACE: A 200-year-old inn restored to traditional standards high up on the rugged moors above Oldham overlooking the Pennines; as it has expanded and become more contemporary, so the food has simply become better and better. Take your pick between the smart restaurant and the cosy brasserie with the pub feel and open fires.
FOOD: Bold, imaginative modern British cooking with international influences makes good use of high quality, seasonal ingredients and brings classic flavour combinations together with a modern twist. Good value fixed-price lunch.
OUR TIP: Home-made sausages are a speciality
Chef: John Rudden **Owners:** Mr C Brierley & J Rudden **Times:** 1-3.30/6-9.30, Closed Mon (brasserie open Mon-Sun), closed L Tue-Sat, closed D Sun **Notes:** Tasting menu available, Sun L £19, Vegetarian available, Smart Dress, Civ Wed 85 **Seats:** 50, Pr/dining room 38 **Smoking:** N/Sm in restaurant, Air con **Children:** Portions **Directions:** M62 junct 20, take A627 and continue to the end of bypass, then take the A669 to Saddleworth. Enter Lydgate turn right onto Stockport road, White Hart In is 50yds on left **Parking:** 75
e-mail: bookings@thewhitehart.co.uk
web: www.thewhitehart.co.uk

continued

England

ROCHDALE MAP 16 SD81

⊛⊛ Nutters

British, International

One of the most popular restaurants in the North of England

☎ 01706 650167 Edenfield Rd (A680), Norden OL12 7TT

MENU GUIDE Lobster, mango & asparagus salad • Roast cod, sea bass fish fingers, Thai reduction • Gypsy tart with lucky lavender syrup

WINE GUIDE ♀ Lincoln Heritage Marlborough Sauvignon Blanc £21.50 • ♥ Château de Fleurie Gamay £21 • 76 bottles over £20, 30 bottles under £20 • 8 by the glass (£3.40-£4.20)

PRICE GUIDE Fixed L £12.95-£15.95 • starter £4.80-£8.50 • main £15.95-£18.90 • dessert £3.95-£5.80 • coffee £1.40 • min/water £2.80 • Service optional • Group min 10 service 10%

PLACE: Celebrated locally for having a celebrity chef in the kitchen, this well established restaurant has moved to larger premises. It now occupies a Victorian Gothic manor house with plush fittings, surrounded by six and a half acres of landscaped grounds, including a terrace for summer dining.
FOOD: TV chef Andrew Nutter uses the best local and regional produce to produce vibrant contemporary food. He has a strong and skilful brigade taking great pride in the standards they achieve. Presentation, although pretty and appealing, is not fussy.
OUR TIP: Lunch is both a bargain and a feast
Chef: Andrew Nutter **Owners:** Mr A Nutter, Mr R Nutter, Mrs K J Nutter **Times:** 12-2/6.30-10, Closed 1-2 days after Xmas and New Year, Mon **Notes:** Fixed L/D 6 courses £34, Sun L £22, Vegetarian available, Dress Restrictions, Smart casual, Civ Wed 70 **Seats:** 154, Pr/dining room 120 **Smoking:** N/Sm in restaurant, Air con **Children:** Portions **Directions:** From Rochdale take A680 signposted for Blackburn. Nutters is situated on Edenfield Rd and is on right when leaving Norden **Parking:** 100

SALE MAP 15 SJ79

⊛⊛ Belmore Hotel

British, International

Refined country house dining

☎ 0161 973 2538 143 Brooklands Rd M33 3QN

MENU GUIDE Foie gras terrine, apple chutney • Canon of lamb, roasted garlic jus • Date & walnut pudding

WINE GUIDE ♀ Touraine Sauvignon Blanc £13.50 • ♥ Rucahue Merlot £13.50 • 139 bottles over £20, 50 bottles under £20 8 by the glass (£3.50-£5)

PRICE GUIDE Fixed L £11.50 • Fixed D £26.95-£29.95 • starter £5.55-£9.15 • main £17.95-£22.50 • dessert £6.25-£7.50 • coffee £2.95 • min/water £3 • Service optional

PLACE: With a balustraded terrace and mature Victorian gardens surrounding it, this stylishly refurbished hotel reflects the elegant ambience of bygone days. It was built in 1875 as a wedding present for a coal merchant's daughter and has the feel of an English country manor in a suburban setting. Marble fireplaces, stained glass windows, high ceilings and decorative chandeliers remain intact in the quintessentially Victorian dining room.
FOOD: Imaginative, modern cuisine with classic French influences is prepared with skill to a consistently high standard using locally sourced produce. Desserts are elaborately presented. Silver service is friendly and formal.
OUR TIP: Take the sommelier's recommendations for wines
Chef: Romain Camos **Owners:** Carol Deaville **Times:** 12-2/7-10, Closed L Sat **Notes:** Sun D £15.50, Vegetarian available, Civ Wed 40 **Seats:** 36, Pr/dining room 12 **Smoking:** N/Sm in restaurant **Children:** Portions **Rooms:** 23 (23 en suite) ★★★★ **Directions:** M56 junct 3A, follow signs towards Altrincham. At large rdbt take 4th exit (Brooklands Rd). Continue for 1m and take right into Norris Rd. **Parking:** 40
e-mail: belmore_hotel@hotmail.com **web:** www.belmorehotel.co.uk

WIGAN

Simply Heathcotes Wrightington see Late Entries

HAMPSHIRE

ALTON MAP 05 SU73

⊛⊛ Alton Grange Hotel

British, French

Country house offering good quality food

☎ 01420 86565 London Rd GU34 4EG

MENU GUIDE Rabbit loin, smoked bacon, cassoulet • Brocks Farm rib-eye, roasted root vegetables, horseradish • Caramelised pineapple tart

continued

WINE GUIDE ♀ Louis Latour Macon-Villages Chardonnay £18.50 • ♀ Vicar S.A. Tolva Merlot £15.95 • 104 bottles over £20, 39 bottles under £20 • 16 by the glass (£2.75-£5.75)

PRICE GUIDE Starter £6.50-£9.50 • main £15.50-£19.50 • dessert £7.50 • coffee £2.95 • min/water £3.50 • Service added but optional 10%

PLACE: Popular hotel with hands-on proprietors, David and Andrea Levene, who have been here 20 years. Mrs Levene has a passion for Tiffany-style lamps, which are featured throughout the hotel, and create an intimate atmosphere in the restaurant alongside the exotic plants. The patio can be converted into an extension of the restaurant, making it a popular venue for weddings.
FOOD: The kitchen uses as much local produce available, offering a good choice of dishes from the carte, fixed-price gourmet menu and an Atkins-style low carbohydrate selection.
OUR TIP: Take a stroll in the lovely grounds
Chef: David Heath **Owners:** Andrea & David Levene **Times:** 12-2.30/7-9.30, Closed 24 Dec-3 Jan, ex 31 Dec **Notes:** 7 course Gourmet menu £42.50, Sun lunch £16.95, Vegetarian available, Dress Restrictions, No shorts or jeans, Civ Wed 100 **Seats:** 45, Pr/dining room 18
Smoking: N/Sm in restaurant **Children:** Min 5yrs, Portions **Rooms:** 30 (30 en suite) ★★★ **Directions:** 300yds from A31 on A339
Parking: 40 **e-mail:** info@altongrange.co.uk
web: www.altongrange.co.uk

ANDOVER MAP 05 SU34

⊚⊚ Esseborne Manor
British, French
Old-fashioned hospitality and fine dining
☎ 01264 736444 Hurstbourne Tarrant SP11 0ER

MENU GUIDE Smoked goose breast, confit leg, citrus dressing • Shooter's pie, local mushrooms • Raspberry & tonka bean crème brûlée

WINE GUIDE ♀ Thorne Hill Semillion/Chardonnay £13.50 • ♀ Thorne Hill Shiraz £13.50 • 54 bottles over £20, 46 bottles under £20 • 8 by the glass (£3-£4)

PRICE GUIDE Fixed L £13 • Fixed D £22 • starter £5-£9 • main £12-£28 • dessert £5-£8 • coffee £2 • min/water £2.50 • Service optional

PLACE: Located near the lovely Bourne Valley, this invitingly snug 19th-century manor house hotel is set in pretty gardens. It retains the feel of a family home with friendly staff, fresh flowers and comfortable lounges. The coral red dining room has an open log fire, fabric-lined walls and floor-to-ceiling curtains.
FOOD: Traditional dishes with the occasional modern twist make extensive use of local and home-grown seasonal produce, and ingredients from elsewhere are high quality such as Scottish fillet mignon. The accurate timing results in good, clear flavours.
OUR TIP: Good value menu du vin
Chef: David Morris **Owners:** Ian Hamilton **Times:** 12-2/7-9.30
Notes: Menu with wine, add £2 per course, Vegetarian available, Civ Wed 100 **Seats:** 35, Pr/dining room 70 **Smoking:** N/Sm in restaurant
Children: Portions **Rooms:** 15 (15 en suite) ★★★ **Directions:** On A343, halfway between Andover and Newbury **Parking:** 40
e-mail: info@esseborne-manor.co.uk **web:** www.esseborne-manor.co.uk

BARTON-ON-SEA MAP 05 SZ29

⊚ Pebble Beach
French, Mediterranean
Lively modern restaurant with great sea views
☎ 01425 627777 Marine Dr BH25 7DZ

MENU GUIDE Asian marinated duck, shredded vegetables, noodles • Chargrilled tuna tournedos, port sauce • Iced raspberry soufflé

WINE GUIDE ♀ Villa Romanti Pinot Grigio £13.95 • ♀ McGuigan Shiraz £13.95 • 25 bottles over £20, 20 bottles under £20 • 9 by the glass (£2.95-£4.95)

PRICE GUIDE Starter £3.95-£12.50 • main £8.95-£21.50 • dessert £5.50-£6.50 • coffee £1.80 • min/water £3.75 • Service optional

PLACE: Cliff top establishment with an open-plan design in summery colours overlooking Christchurch Bay, offering fabulous views from the restaurant/bar and terrace. At the oyster counter you can watch chefs work in the open kitchen, and the atmosphere is fun, friendly and relaxed.
FOOD: The emphasis is on carefully cooked fresh produce, with influences from around the world in a varied menu including good vegetarian choices.
OUR TIP: Fresh fish is a speciality here
Chef: Pierre Chevillard **Owners:** Mike Caddy **Times:** 11-2.30/6-10, Closed D 25 Dec & 1 Jan **Notes:** Vegetarian available, Smart casual, no beach wear **Seats:** 70 **Smoking:** N/Sm in restaurant, Air con
Children: Portions **Directions:** Follow A35 from Southampton on to A337 to New Milton, turn L down Barton Court Av to cliff top
Parking: 20 **e-mail:** mail@pebblebeach-uk.com
web: www.pebblebeach-uk.com

BASINGSTOKE MAP 05 SU65

⊚ Apollo Hotel
British
Formal dining in contemporary corporate hotel
☎ 01256 796700 Aldermaston Roundabout RG24 9NU

MENU GUIDE Wild mushroom tortellini, porcini mushroom cream • Sea bass fillet, noodle & spring onion rösti, coriander pesto • Banana crème brûlée

WINE GUIDE 6 bottles over £20, 12 bottles under £20 • 6 by the glass (£4.50-£7.50)

PRICE GUIDE Starter £4.50-£7.50 • main £13-£20 • dessert £4-£6 • min/water £4 • Service included

continued

continued

BASINGSTOKE continued MAP 05 SU65

PLACE: Leisure and business guests are drawn to this modern hotel by the ring road. Although windowless, the fine-dining Vespers restaurant offers plenty of space and style, where diners are treated to formal, skilled but friendly service.

FOOD: Vespers modern repertoire places presentation to the fore; menus arrive on glass plates in great style, while the wine list gets a similar treatment with wood-bound covers. Intricate combinations deliver appealing, balanced dishes.

OUR TIP: Weekend breaks and leisure club available

Chef: John Griffiths **Owners:** Huggler Hotel **Times:** 12/7, Closed Xmas, New Year, Sun, closed L Sat **Notes:** Vegetarian available, Civ Wed 200 **Seats:** 28, Pr/dining room 200 **Smoking:** N/Sm in restaurant, Air con **Children:** Portions **Rooms:** 125 (125 en suite) ★★★★
Directions: From M3 junct 6 follow ring road N & signs for Aldermaston/Newbury. Follow signs for A340 (Aldermaston) & on rdbt take 5th exit onto Popley Way. Hotel entrance 1st left **Parking:** 120 **e-mail:** admin@apollo-hotels.co.uk **web:** www.apollohotels.com

🇬🇧 Ciao Baby Cucina Festival Place RG21 7BB
☎ 01256 477299 Honest cooking in relaxed modern surroundings.

BEAULIEU MAP 05 SU30

🏵 *Beaulieu Hotel*
British   **NEW**
Charming New Forest country house dining
☎ 023 8029 3344 Beaulieu Rd SO42 7YQ
MENU GUIDE Smoked salmon fishcakes, sweet chilli sauce • Pork tenderloin, caramelised apple • Calypso crème brûlée, Turkish delight
PRICE GUIDE Food prices not confirmed for 2006. Please telephone for details
PLACE: Pale green walls in the dining room set a relaxing note at this small country-house hotel, as well as acting as a backdrop for a range of artwork celebrating horses.
FOOD: Expect traditional country house cooking, well in keeping with the surrounds and justifiably popular with visitors and locals alike. Oven baked salmon with hollandaise sauce, followed by honey and whisky cheesecake shows the style.
OUR TIP: Great value Sunday lunches
Times: 7-9, Closed L all week **Rooms:** 18 (18 en suite) ★★★
Directions: On B3056 between Lyndhurst & Beaulieu. Near Beaulieu Rd railway station **e-mail:** beaulieu@newforesthotels.co.uk
web: www.newforesthotels.co.uk

🏵🏵 *Montagu Arms Hotel*
Modern British
Old world charm with modern cuisine
☎ 01590 612324 Palace Ln SO42 7ZL
MENU GUIDE Pigeon consommé, pigeon croquettes • Pork tenderloin, Parma ham, prune sauce • White chocolate pannacotta
PRICE GUIDE Food prices not confirmed for 2006. Please telephone for details
PLACE: The glorious scenery of the New Forest and the Beaulieu River surrounds this lovely old hotel that nestles at the foot of the tiny High Street. Dining is in the stylish Terrace Restaurant with its views over the lovely gardens, or the informal Monty's bar and brasserie.
FOOD: Italian undertones are detectable in the modern British cooking, with a simple, unfussy approach making the best use of

continued

Montagu Arms Hotel

the largely seasonal, local ingredients. A varied choice comes from the carte and a fixed-price menu. Shaun Hill (ex Merchant House, Ludlow, Shropshire) has joined the hotel as consultant chef.

OUR TIP: Take the scenic walk to Buckler's Hard
Times: 12-2.30/7-9.30 **Rooms:** 23 (23 en suite) ★★★
Directions: From M27 J2 take A326 & B3054 for Beaulieu.
e-mail: reservations@montaguarmshotel.co.uk
web: www.montaguarmshotel.co.uk

BROCKENHURST MAP 05 SU30

🏵🏵 Balmer Lawn Hotel
British, European
Global flavours at this imposing country house
☎ 01590 623116 Lyndhurst Rd SO42 7ZB
MENU GUIDE King scallop ceviche, cucumber jelly, herring caviar • Supreme of guinea fowl, ballotine of leg • Amaretti & vanilla parfait
WINE GUIDE ♀ Carta Vieja Sauvignon Blanc £15.50 • ♀ Carta Vieja Merlot £15.50 • 18 bottles over £20, 17 bottles under £20 • 7 by the glass (£3.75-£5.75)
PRICE GUIDE Fixed L £13.95 • starter £4.75-£9.75 • main £13.75-£22.50 • dessert £5.50-£8.95 • coffee £4.50 • min/water £3.50 • Service optional
PLACE: The Balmer Lawn is a country house hotel set against a woodland backdrop on the outskirts of Brockenhurst village. Now refurbished, the richly decorated restaurant is adorned with modern art and combines contemporary style with traditional elegance.
FOOD: Food is fresh and appealing, incorporating many world cuisines with flair and imagination. The lunch menu is cheaper, offering less choice and lighter, less complicated dishes. Dinner is more adventurous, providing a more fitting showcase for the kitchen's evident skills.
OUR TIP: The New Forest, Britain's newest National Park, is on the doorstep
Chef: Moray Cameron **Owners:** Mr C Wilson **Times:** 12.30-2.30/6.30-9.30 **Notes:** Sun L £15.95, Vegetarian available, Dress Restrictions, Smart casual. No jeans or trainers, Civ Wed 120 **Seats:** 90, Pr/dining room 100 **Smoking:** N/Sm in restaurant, Air con **Children:** Menu, Portions **Rooms:** 55 (55 en suite) ★★★ **Directions:** Take A337 towards Brockenhurst, hotel on left after 'Welcome to Brockenhurst' sign **Parking:** 100 **e-mail:** info@balmerlawnhotel.com **web:** www.balmerlawnhotel.com

 denotes restaurants that place particular emphasis on making the most of local ingredients.

⚜⚜ Carey's Manor Hotel

British, European

Great local produce in a manor house setting

☎ 08707 512305   SO42 7RH

MENU GUIDE Seared Lulworth scallops, spinach risotto • Local venison, parsnip mash, mushroom confit, juniper sauce • Pear tarte Tatin

WINE GUIDE ♀ Domaine la Cailbouron Pouilly Fumé Sauvignon Blanc £29.50 • ♥ Ferngrove Estate Merlot £19.95 • 232 bottles over £20, 58 bottles under £20 • 10 by the glass (£3.95-£6)

PRICE GUIDE Fixed L £16.95 • Fixed D £29.50 • starter £8.50-£10.50 • main £13.50-£18.50 • dessert £5.50-£7 • coffee £3.50 • min/water £3.50 • Service optional

PLACE: Victorian property on the edge of the New Forest, where the delightful restaurant has a country house feel, with well spaced tables and quality tableware. The atmosphere is light and unpretentious, while the service is attentive.

FOOD: The menu is strong on comfort food using quality produce: local, organic and free range wherever possible. Dishes are both natural to the season and well judged, including an interesting vegetarian selection. Flavours are clear and defined and the execution is spot on.

OUR TIP: Organic, fair trade and vegetarian friendly

Chef: David Ryan **Owners:** Greenclose Ltd **Times:** 12-2/7-10, Closed L Mon-Sat **Notes:** Vegetarian available, Dress Restrictions, No jeans, T-shirts or trainers, Civ Wed 100 **Seats:** 80, Pr/dining room 100 **Smoking:** N/Sm in restaurant **Children:** Min 7yrs, Portions **Rooms:** 80 (80 en suite) ★★★ **Directions:** M27 junct 1, follow signs for Lyndhurst and Lymington A337. Railway station 5 mins from hotel **Parking:** 100 **e-mail:** stay@careysmanor.com **web:** www.careysmanor.com

⚜⚜ New Park Manor

British, European

Intimate dining in former royal hunting lodge

☎ 01590 623467   Lyndhurst Rd SO42 7QH

MENU GUIDE Parma ham & warm fig salad • Beef, truffle scented mash, celeriac fondant, oxtail jus • Lemon tart, lemon sorbet

WINE GUIDE ♀ Marquis de Touron Côtes du Duras Sauvignon Blanc 2002 £16.50 • ♥ Delas Frere Côtes du Ventoux Rhône Valley 2002 £16.50 • 80 bottles over £20, 14 bottles under £20 • 2 by the glass (£3-£3.50)

PRICE GUIDE Fixed L £15 • Fixed D £35 • coffee £3 • min/water £2.40

PLACE: Once Charles II's favourite hunting lodge, New Park wears its classy pedigree lightly, its public rooms a winning mix of the cosy and contemporary, decked out with leather armchairs, deep sofas and log fires in winter. Dinner is served amid oak panelling and oils in a decorous room that overlooks the croquet lawn.

continued

FOOD: A modern British menu assembled from quality ingredients including local game. Dishes might include stuffed haunch of rabbit with smoked bacon or pork belly with mustard mash, while lighter meals are available in the Polo Bar.

OUR TIP: The hotel has its own equestrian centre

Chef: Mark Davidson **Owners:** Von Essen Hotels **Times:** 12-2/7-9 **Notes:** Breakfast served, Vegetarian available, Dress Restrictions, Smart casual, no jeans or trainers, Civ Wed 50 **Seats:** 40, Pr/dining room 12 **Smoking:** N/Sm in restaurant **Children:** Menu, Portions **Rooms:** 24 (24 en suite) ★★★ **Directions:** On A337, 8m S of M27 J1 **Parking:** 35 **e-mail:** enquiries@newparkmanorhotel.co.uk **web:** www.vonessenhotels.com

⚜⚜⚜ Le Poussin@Whitley Ridge Country House Hotel *see page 188*

⚜⚜ Rhinefield House

British, European

Country pile with plenty of wow factor

☎ 01590 622922   Rhinefield Rd SO42 7QB

MENU GUIDE Scallops, caramelised chicory, kumquat & coriander • Guinea fowl supreme, celery mousse, morels, Puy lentils • Lemon tart

WINE GUIDE ♀ Laroche Chardonnay £19 • ♥ Laroche Merlot/Grenache £20 • 100 bottles over £20, 6 bottles under £20 • 8 by the glass (£4.25-£7.80)

PRICE GUIDE Fixed L £19.95 • Fixed D £34.95 • coffee £2.95 • min/water £4 • Service optional

PLACE: Impressive stone-built country mansion with all the trimmings: oak panelling, ornate chandeliers and sumptuous soft furnishings. The hotel is located in the middle of the New Forest with 40 acres of grounds, including ornamental gardens, Italianate ponds and fabulous rhododendrons in spring. The restaurant fireplace features a carving of the Armada worked from a solid block of oak, four-foot thick, which took nine years to complete.

FOOD: Local produce and fresh flavours are highlighted in a menu with definite leanings towards France and beyond. Expect interesting combinations and many twists on classic dishes.

OUR TIP: Stunningly embellished Alhambra room for private dinners

Chef: Kevin Hartley **Owners:** Hand Picked Hotels Ltd **Times:** 12.30-2/7-9.30 **Notes:** Vegetarian available, Dress Restrictions, Smart casual preferred, Civ Wed 125 **Seats:** 58, Pr/dining room 28 **Smoking:** N/Sm in restaurant **Children:** Portions **Rooms:** 34 (34 en suite) ★★★★ **Directions:** From M27 junct 1 take A337 to Lyndhurst, follow A35 W towards Christchurch. 3.5m from Lyndhurst, turn left into the Forest at sign for Rhinefield House. Hotel 1.5m on right **Parking:** 150 **e-mail:** info@rhinefieldhousehotel.co.uk **web:** www.rhinefieldhousehotel.co.uk

⚜⚜ *Simply Poussin*

Modern British

Popular brasserie in lovely Hampshire village

☎ 01590 623063   The Courtyard, Brookley Rd SO42 7RB

MENU GUIDE Twice baked cheese soufflé • Fillet of beef on creamy beans, wild mushroom sauce • Rhubarb cheesecake, rhubarb jelly & sorbet

PRICE GUIDE Food prices not confirmed for 2006. Please telephone for details

continued

England

BROCKENHURST MAP 05 SU30

Le Poussin
@Whitley Ridge Country House Hotel

British, French

Fine dining in classic country house in heart of the New Forest

☎ 01590 622354 Beaulieu Rd SO42 7QL

MENU GUIDE Warborne Farm Pork belly with prawns, lime syrup • Quail pie, foie gras & morels • Vanilla rice pudding

WINE GUIDE ♀ Les Setilles Leflaive Chardonnay £25 • ♥ La Fortuna Malbec £17.50 • 200 bottles over £20, 40 bottles under £20 • 12 by the glass (£5-£15)

PRICE GUIDE Fixed L £15-£20 • Fixed D £35 • coffee £3.50 min/water £3.50 • Service added but optional 10%

PLACE: This Georgian, former royal hunting lodge is set in stunning, secluded grounds extending over five acres and now makes for a very comfortable New Forest hotel hideaway. As well as comfortable lounges, the restaurant is understated in style, with heather-coloured carpets, sage-coloured seating, crisp linen and striking flower displays. The dining room, which is candlelit by night, has large bay windows that overlook the terrace to the woodland beyond. The polished service is classical and attentive.

FOOD: Although the cooking here has classical influences, more modern twists can be spotted on the carte menu, with bresaola of beef appearing with fig, parmesan and rocket salad and truffle dressing. Ingredients are of a very high quality and the composition of dishes clearly highlights the skill and professionalism of the kitchen. This is illustrated in dishes such as the casserole of veal sweetbreads, served with a tortellini of pea and ham hock and reduced chicken sauce.

OUR TIP: Lunch is a bargain

Chef: Alex Aitken, Shane Hughes **Owners:** Alex & Caroline Aitken **Times:** 12.30-2/6.30-9.30 **Rooms:** 18 (18 en suite) **Directions:** From Brockenhurst, 1m along Beaulieu Rd **e-mail:** sales@le pouissin.co.uk **web:** www.lepoussin.co.uk

---

BROCKENHURST *continued* MAP 05 SU30

Simply Poussin

PLACE: Located in the pretty village of Brockenhurst, this homely restaurant may take a little finding but it's undoubtedly worth the effort. Cheerful background chatter in the intimate dining room comes courtesy of locals who clearly treasure the place. The warm welcome and excellence of ingredients are just two reasons why.

FOOD: The eponymous bird is the signature dish of a menu that unites French bistro style with English classics. European ingredients are skilfully handled, as in terrine of roasted poussin and foie gras, and many ingredients are locally sourced like wild mushrooms from the forest.

OUR TIP: Book ahead

Times: 12-2/7-9.30, Closed 25-26 Dec, Sun-Mon **Directions:** Village centre through an archway between two shops.

e-mail: sales@simplypoussin.co.uk **web:** www.simplypoussin.co.uk

BROOK MAP 05 SU21

🌸 Bell Inn

British, International

Fine dining in well-known golfing hotel

☎ 023 8081 2214 SO43 7HE

MENU GUIDE Trout & spinach roll • Smoked lamb chump • Dark chocolate terrine

WINE GUIDE ♀ Eaglehawk Chardonnay £14.50 • ♥ L'Emage Merlot £12.50 • 22 bottles over £20, 25 bottles under £20 • 5 by the glass (£3.50-£4.50)

PRICE GUIDE Fixed L £16.50-£22.50 • Fixed D £31-£37 • coffee £2 • min/water £3.50 • Service included

PLACE: A popular golfing hotel with a welcoming bar and more formal but still comfortable restaurant. Non golfers and those visiting the New Forest are equally at home amidst the rich warm colours and exposed beams.

FOOD: The short menu focuses on an unpretentious market while not sacrificing anything in the way of quality. The simple and the classical - particularly desserts - are equally appealing.

OUR TIP: Try the popular golfing menu

Chef: Richard Jones **Owners:** Crosthwaite Eyre Family **Times:** 12-2.30/7.30-9.30 **Notes:** Vegetarian available, Dress Restrictions, No jeans, T-shirts, trainers or shorts **Seats:** 50, Pr/dining room 40 **Smoking:** N/Sm in restaurant **Children:** Menu, Portions **Rooms:** 25 (25 en suite) ★★★ **Directions:** M27 junct 1 (Cadnam) 3rd exit onto B3079, signed Brook, follow for 1m on right. **Parking:** 40 **e-mail:** bell@bramshaw.co.uk **web:** www.bramshaw.co.uk

BUCKLERS HARD MAP 05 SU40

⊚⊚ Master Builders House Hotel

European

Contemporary cooking in historic maritime setting

☎ 01590 616253   SO42 7XB

MENU GUIDE Crab ravioli, red pepper sauce • Breast of duck with duck cassoulet • Ginger & honey nougat glacé

WINE GUIDE 33 bottles over £20, 13 bottles under £20 • 13 by the glass (£3.95)

PRICE GUIDE Fixed L £16.50 • Fixed D £29.50 • starter £4.95-£9.25 • main £12.95-£17.95 • dessert £6.25 • coffee £2.50 • min/water £3.50 • Service included

PLACE: Once the home of master ship builder Henry Adam, circa 750, the hotel is steeped in maritime history. It is located in the ship-building village of Bucklers Hard, where many of Nelson's craft were constructed. The brasserie-style Riverside Restaurant, with its wooden floor, contemporary photography and artworks, looks out over the Beaulieu River.

FOOD: Excellent ingredients and innovative ideas are combined with classical cooking styles to produce a light modern menu with European influences. Cooking is skilful and honest, and presentation clean and simple.

OUR TIP: Charter the hotel's boat for a scenic cruise
Chef: Denis Rhoden **Owners:** Jeremy Willcock, John Illsley **Times:** 12-/7-11 **Notes:** Sun L 3 courses £22.50, Vegetarian available, Civ Wed 60 **Seats:** 80, Pr/dining room 40 **Smoking:** No pipes, No cigars **Children:** Menu, Portions **Rooms:** 25 (25 en suite) ★★★ **Directions:** From M27 junct 2 follow signs to Beaulieu. Turn left onto 3056. 1st left. Hotel in 2m **Parking:** 60
e-mail: res@themasterbuilders.co.uk **web:** www.themasterbuilders.co.uk

BURLEY MAP 05 SU20

⊚ Moorhill House

Modern British

Popular dishes from local produce in New Forest hotel

☎ 01425 403285   BH24 4AG

MENU GUIDE Ham hock terrine • Pan-fried duck breast, lemon couscous • Baked cheesecake, caramel sauce

PRICE GUIDE Food prices not confirmed for 2006. Please telephone for details

PLACE: Built as a gentleman's residence, this grand house with extensive grounds is deep in the New Forest. Staff are friendly and attentive.

FOOD: A short modern British menu with some European influences focuses on local produce. Wood pigeon with lentil casserole is a tender, gamey dish with delicate yet full flavoured saucing.

OUR TIP: Work up an appetite by strolling in the grounds
Times: 7-9/12-2, closed L Mon-Sat **Rooms:** 31 (31 en suite) ★★★
e-mail: moorhill@newforesthotels.co.uk
web: www.newforesthotels.co.uk

CADNAM MAP 05 SZ21

⊚ Bartley Lodge

British   **NEW**

Accomplished cooking in New Forest former hunting lodge

☎ 023 8081 2248 Lyndhurst Rd SO40 2NR

continued

MENU GUIDE Terrine of naturally smoked haddock, leeks & lentils • Grilled salmon, asparagus & prawn Pithiviers • Chocolate fondant

PRICE GUIDE Food prices not confirmed for 2006. Please telephone for details

PLACE: Set on the edge of New Forest is this 18th-century former hunting lodge. Inside there is a grand entrance hall, a selection of small lounge areas, cosy bar and the Chrystal dining room.

FOOD: Good cooking skills with some innovative ideas are on show on the concise modern British menu with French influences. Excellent use is made of local and seasonal produce.

OUR TIP: Great for visiting New Forest
Times: 7-9, Closed L all week **Rooms:** 31 (31 en suite) ★★★
Directions: M27 J1, A337 and follow signs for Lyndhurst. Hotel on L
e-mail: reservations@newforesthotels.co.uk
web: www.newforesthotels.co.uk

DENMEAD MAP 05 SU61

⊚ Barnard's Restaurant

British, Mediterranean

Adventurous cooking in friendly neighbourhood restaurant

☎ 023 9225 7788 Hambledon Rd PO7 6NU

MENU GUIDE Garlic, almond & coconut soup • Duck breast, spiced kumquats, honey glaze • Espresso coffee parfait, home-made macaroons

WINE GUIDE ♀ Domaine de Fussiagos Chardonnay £14.50 • ♀ McGuigans Black Label Merlot £15.45 • 6 bottles over £20, 28 bottles under £20 • 6 by the glass (£3-£4.50)

PRICE GUIDE Fixed L fr £14.50 • Fixed D fr £16.95 • starter £5-£7.50 • main £12-£17.95 • dessert £4.60-£6.95 • coffee £2.20 • min/water £2.60 • Service optional

PLACE: In a row of shops, with exposed brick walls and a warm yellow decor, this small, family-run country restaurant offers a cosy setting and upbeat atmosphere. Young staff provide friendly and unobtrusive service.

FOOD: The modern European menu may hold few surprises, but it uses fresh local produce, flavours are distinct and dishes are well presented.

OUR TIP: Good value fixed-price meals
Chef: David Barnard & Paul Thompson **Owners:** Mr & Mrs D Barnard, Mrs S Barnard **Times:** 12-1.30/7-9.30, Closed 25-26 Dec, New Year, Sun-Mon, closed L Sat **Notes:** Vegetarian available **Seats:** 40, Pr/dining room 34 **Smoking:** N/Sm in restaurant **Children:** Portions **Directions:** A3M junct 3, B1250 into Denmead. Opposite church. **Parking:** 3
web: www.barnardsrestaurant.co.uk

England

EAST TYTHERLEY MAP 05 SU22

🏵🏵 Star Inn
British, European
Traditional village pub cooking to high standards
☎ 01794 340225   SO51 0LW

MENU GUIDE Warm tart of ceps, caramelised shallots, linguini • Pork medallions, sage mash • Apple & blackberry crumble, clotted cream

WINE GUIDE ♀ Pinot Grigio £13.50 • ♥ French Merlot £13.50 • 10 bottles over £20, 20 bottles under £20 • 10 by the glass (£3.50)

PRICE GUIDE Fixed L £10 • Fixed D £15 • starter £3.25-£8.50 • main £8.95-£20 • dessert £4.25-£6.40 • coffee £1.60 • min/water £3 • Service optional

PLACE: Dating from the 16th-century, this charming former coaching inn has a loyal following of both locals and visitors. Inside the atmosphere is cosy with warm deep colours, bare wood tables, leather sofas and crackling open fires in winter.
FOOD: The kitchen produces classic British food with some more adventurous dishes, all prepared with well chosen ingredients of consistent quality and confidently presented by a friendly team. An approachable international wine list provides plenty of affordable, easy drinking options.
OUR TIP: Perfect place for a super meal or just a nice quiet drink
Chef: Paul Bingham   **Owners:** Paul & Sarah Bingham   **Times:** 12-2/7-9, Closed D 25, 26 Dec, Mon, closed D Sun   **Notes:** Vegetarian available
Seats: 80, Pr/dining room 45   **Smoking:** N/Sm in restaurant
Children: Menu, Portions   **Rooms:** 3 (3 en suite) ♦♦♦♦
Directions: 5m N of Romsey A3057, take B3084 for Awbridge & Lockerley, follow road through Lockerley for 1m   **Parking:** 50
e-mail: info@starinn-uk.com   **web:** www.starinn-uk.com

EMSWORTH MAP 05 SU70

🏵 Fat Olives
British, Mediterrranean
Imaginative food in a delightful historic setting
☎ 01243 377914   30 South St PO10 7EH

MENU GUIDE Gurnard, red pepper & onion tart • Brill, chorizo, cavolo nero & beurre blanc • Apple crumble

WINE GUIDE ♀ Concha y Toro Chardonnay £11.95 • ♥ Concha y Toro Cabernet Sauvignon £11.95 • 26 bottles over £20, 16 bottles under £20 • 5 by the glass (£2.95-£3.50)

PRICE GUIDE Fixed L £14.50 • starter £4.75-£7.50 • main £11.95-£18.50 • dessert £5.25-£5.50 • coffee £2.10 • min/water £2.95 • Service optional • Group min 10 service 10%

PLACE: Situated in the conservation of Emsworth, this restaurant was originally a fisherman's cottage dating back to 1670. By contrast, the interior is modern and minimalist in style with wooden floors, tables and chairs.
FOOD: Offering modern British cuisine with Mediterranean influences, nearly half the menu is dedicated to locally sourced, fresh fish but there are also enticing game and meat dishes. Skilful preparation produces clear, strong flavours. Service is friendly and attentive.
OUR TIP: Build up your appetite with a harbourside walk
Chef: Lawrence Murphy   **Owners:** Lawrence & Julia Murphy   **Times:** 12-2.15/7-10.15, Closed 2 wks Xmas - Jan, 1 wk Oct, Sun-Mon & Tue after a BH   **Notes:** Vegetarian available   **Seats:** 28   **Smoking:** N/Sm in restaurant   **Children:** Min 8yrs   **Directions:** In town centre, 1st right after Emsworth Square, 100yds towards the Quay. Restaurant on left with public car park opposite.   **Parking:** Opposite restaurant
e-mail: info@fatolives.co.uk   **web:** www.fatolives.co.uk

🏵 Spencers Restaurant & Brasserie
British, European
Skilled cosmopolitan cooking and welcoming atmosphere
☎ 01243 372744 379017   36 North St PO10 7DG

MENU GUIDE Fresh crab salad • Roast confit of duck, braised red cabbage • Warm honey poached pear

WINE GUIDE ♀ Allan Scott Sauvignon Blanc £20.25 • ♥ Cune Rioja £20.60 • 11 bottles over £20, 19 bottles under £20 • 5 by the glass (£2.40-£3)

PRICE GUIDE Fixed L £9.25 • starter £3.25-£5.95 • main £11.50-£16.50 • dessert £4.95 • coffee £1.30 • min/water £2.65 • Service optional

PLACE: Two different levels and two different styles - both welcoming and comfortable with efficient service. The simpler brasserie is downstairs, while a creaking staircase leads up to the cosy, intimate restaurant with tables in separate booths, and some in a hidden alcove.
FOOD: Menus are seasonal, offering fresh local meat and fish, and some main course dishes are adventurously matched with classy sauces.
OUR TIP: Special lunch and early-diner bargains
Chef: Denis Spencer   **Owners:** Denis & Lesley Spencer   **Times:** 12-2/6-10, Closed 25-26 Dec, BHs, Sun, closed L Sun/Mon, closed D Mon (Brasserie Mon-Sat 12-2, 6-10)   **Seats:** Vegetarian available   **Seats:** 64, Pr/dining room 8   **Smoking:** N/Sm in restaurant, Air con
Children: Portions   **Directions:** Off A259, in town centre
web: www.spencersrestaurant.co.uk

🏵🏵🏵 36 on the Quay see page 191

EVERSLEY MAP 05 SU76

🏵 New Mill
British, European
Waterside dining in old mill setting
☎ 0118 973 2277   New Mill Rd RG27 0RA

MENU GUIDE Wild trout & salmon tartare, monkfish carpaccio • Griddled scallops, shredded duck confit, Bordelaise sauce • Lemon sponge, lemon cream

WINE GUIDE ♀ Val d'Orbieu Vin de Pays d'Oc £14.50 • ♥ Val d'Orbieu Vin de Pays d'Oc £14.50 • 200 bottles over £20, 52 bottles under £20 • 14 by the glass (£3-£8.25)

PRICE GUIDE Fixed L £13.50 • Fixed D £24 • starter £4.95-£12.50 • main £17.50-£25 • dessert £5.95-£8.80 • coffee £3.50 • min/water £3 • Service optional

PLACE: This black and white listed mill stands on the River Blackwater and can trace its history back to the days of William

continue

EMSWORTH MAP 05 SU70

36 on the Quay

British, European

Established waterside restaurant with loyal following

☎ 01243 375592 47 South St PO10 7EG

MENU GUIDE Scallop & pork belly, warm vanilla dressing • Brill, leek velouté, crab & lime beignet • Rhubarb soufflé

WINE GUIDE 200+ bottles over £20, 15 bottles under £20 • 6 by the glass (£4-£5)

PRICE GUIDE Fixed L £17.95 • Fixed D £42.95 • coffee £3.50 • min/water £3 • Service optional

PLACE: At high tide, you feel the sea is practically lapping your feet as this pristine 17th-century house stands beside the quay, with lovely views over tidal Chichester Harbour. The marine setting is enhanced by the mass of white sails skimming across the horizon on race days, and by the salty sea breezes. Within, the elegant restaurant occupies centre stage with a peaceful pastel green decor, local art on the walls and crisp clothed tables, together with glimpses of the bustling harbour outside. It may be smart and intimate but dinner is a relaxed affair and service is fluent and well judged. The 'Quay' operates as a successful restaurant-with-rooms and the contemporary rooms ooze style and comfort.

FOOD: The impressive carte offers a good choice at each course, a blend of intricate and simple dishes, but if you can't choose, opt for the tasting version which offers smaller portions of house specialities over ten courses. The kitchen expresses passion alongside considerable skill and expertise to bring out the individual flavours of each dish. Combinations are well judged and quality ingredients well sourced, with good use of local fish and game. The global wine list includes some rare finds, especially from the US.

OUR TIP: Stay the night

Chef: Ramon Farthing, James Dugan **Owners:** Ramon & Karen Farthing **Times:** 12-2/7-9.30, Closed 23-30 Oct, 1-22 Jan, Sun, Mon **Notes:** Tasting menu 10 courses £55, Vegetarian by request only, Dress Restrictions, No shorts, smart casual **Seats:** 43, Pr/dining room 10 **Smoking:** N/Sm in restaurant **Children:** Portions **Rooms:** 4 (4 en suite) 🛏 **Parking:** 6 **web:** www.36onthequay.co.uk

---

The original mill was destroyed by fire, hence the word 'new' attached to its name today. There's a mill wheel, open fires and lots of beams.

FOOD: Dine in the Grill Room or more formal River Room. Menu includes both traditional and innovative dishes using many seasonal ingredients that are grown on site. A wide choice of fish and game dishes appear including venison from the New Forest.

OUR TIP: Exceptional wine list

Chef: Colin Robson-Wright **Owners:** Judith & Nick Scade **Times:** 12-2/7-10, Closed 26-29 Dec, 1 Jan, closed L Sat **Notes:** Sun L 3 courses £17, Vegetarian available, smart casual, Civ Wed 180 **Seats:** 80, Pr/dining room 40 **Smoking:** N/Sm area, No pipes, No cigars, Air con **Children:** Portions **Directions:** Off A327 2m S of Arborfield Cross. N of village and follow brown signs. Approach from New Mill Rd **Parking:** 40 **e-mail:** info@thenewmill.co.uk **web:** www.thenewmill.co.uk

FAREHAM MAP 05 SU50

🌹 Lysses House Hotel

British, French

Imaginative cuisine in impressively presented listed property in the town centre

☎ 01329 822622 51 High St PO16 7BQ

MENU GUIDE King prawns, vanilla oil • Grilled beef fillet, celeriac purée, morel sauce • Chocolate sponge with Grand Marnier

WINE GUIDE ♀ Concha y Toro Sauvignon Blanc £12.25 • ♟ Concha y Toro Merlot £12.25 • 7 bottles over £20, 27 bottles under £20 • 3 by the glass (£2.20-£4.50)

PRICE GUIDE Fixed L £13 • Fixed D £20.50 • starter £4.25-£6.25 • main £12.50-£16.75 • dessert £5.50 • coffee £1.90 • min/water £2.70 • Service optional

PLACE: Elegant Georgian building close to the High Street with attractive public rooms, including a bar, lounge and the Richmond Restaurant. The restaurant tables are clothed with pastel linens and adorned with fresh flowers.

FOOD: Extensive use is made of fresh ingredients in both the fixed-price and carte menus. Imaginative modern dishes with classic and European influences are cooked with skill and enthusiasm, and there is also a choice of items from the grill.

OUR TIP: Private dining room to seat up to 14 people

Chef: Clive Wright **Owners:** Dr Colin Mercer **Times:** 12-1.45/7.30-9.45, Closed 24 Dec-2 Jan, BHs, Sun, closed L Sat **Notes:** Vegetarian available, Smart Dress, Civ Wed 95 **Seats:** 60, Pr/dining room 10 **Smoking:** N/Sm in restaurant, Air con **Children:** Portions **Rooms:** 21 (21 en suite) ★★★ **Directions:** M27 junct 11, follow signs for Fareham. Stay in left lane to rdbt, 3rd exit into East St - road veers to right onto High St. Hotel on left opposite junction with Civic Way. **Parking:** 30 **e-mail:** lysses@lysses.co.uk **web:** www.lysses.co.uk

🌹 Solent Hotel

International

Modern cuisine in traditional setting

☎ 01489 880000 Rookery Av, Whiteley PO15 7AJ

MENU GUIDE Oysters Kilpatrick • Rack of lamb • Chocolate tasting plate

WINE GUIDE ♀ Marco Felluga Pinot Grigio £21.95 • ♟ Palandri Estate Cabernet Sauvignon £21.95 • 38 bottles over £20, 23 bottles under £20 • 12 by the glass (£4.95-£7.95)

PRICE GUIDE Starter £6-£8 • main £13.50-£19.50 • dessert £6.50 • coffee £3.50 • min/water £3.50

continued

continued

England

FAREHAM *continued* MAP 05 SU50

PLACE: Smart hotel in a quiet location close to the M27, set in its own landscaped gardens surrounded by meadowland. There's a country pub on site, and traditional features include a beamed ceiling, tiled floor, rugs and an open fire. A live pianist plays on a Friday and Saturday night. The hotel also has a well equipped leisure centre and spa.
FOOD: An eclectic range of simple and well executed dishes with an emphasis on regional produce.
OUR TIP: Relax over coffee on a comfy sofa by an open fire
Chef: Peter Williams **Owners:** Shire Hotels Ltd **Times:** 12.15-2/7-9.30, Closed Xmas, New Year, Easter (residents only), closed L Sat-Sun **Notes:** Dress Restrictions, No jeans, T-shirts, Civ Wed 160 **Seats:** 130, Pr/dining room 40 **Smoking:** N/Sm in restaurant, Air con **Children:** Min Pre 8.30, Menu, Portions **Rooms:** 111 (111 en suite) ★★★★
Directions: From M27 junct 9 follow signs to Solent Business Park & Whiteley. At rdbt take 1st left, then right at mini rdbt **Parking:** 200
e-mail: solent@shirehotels.co.uk
web: www.shirehotels.co.uk

FLEET MAP 05 SU85
 The Gurkha Square
Nepalese
Subtle and delicate Nepalese specialities
☎ 01252 810286 & 811588 327 Fleet Rd GU51 3BU
MENU GUIDE Sandheko khasi • Gurkha chicken • Kulfi - mango & pistachio
WINE GUIDE ♀ Sierre Grande Sauvignon Blanc £10.50 • ♀ Sierre Grande Merlot £10.50 • all bottles over £20, all bottles under £20 • 2 by the glass (£3.10)
PRICE GUIDE Fixed L £15-£20 • Fixed D £16-£25 • starter £3.25-£9 • main £6.25-£10.90 • dessert £1.95-£3.95 • coffee £1.50 • min/water £3.75

PLACE: Striking Nepalese photographs, carved wall ornaments and straw awnings set the scene for an authentic Himalayan experience at this homely restaurant set in a parade of shops conveniently opposite public parking.
FOOD: Authentic Nepalese cooking using fresh ingredients. The delicately flavoured and highly fragrant cuisine includes sizzling dishes, clay oven cooking and chef's specialities. The friendly waiters are happy to advise.
OUR TIP: Dishes graded according to spiciness
Chef: Pradip Basnet, Indra Guruna **Owners:** Bishnu Ghale & Imansingh Ghale **Times:** 12-2.30/6-11, Closed 25-26 Dec, Nepalese festivals **Notes:** Vegetarian available, Smart Dress **Seats:** 44 **Smoking:** No pipes, No cigars, Air con **Directions:** Telephone for directions.
Parking: Gurkha Square public car park
e-mail: gurkhasquare@hotmail.com

FORDINGBRIDGE MAP 05 SU11
Ashburn Hotel
British, French
Country house hotel dining
☎ 01425 652060 Station Rd SP6 1JP
MENU GUIDE Avocado & crayfish tian • Duck supreme, Thai noodles, hoi sin sauce • Lemon tart, strawberry sauce
WINE GUIDE ♀ Moondara Semillon Chardonnay £11 • ♀ Moondara Shiraz £11 • 4 bottles over £20, 24 bottles under £20 • 3 by the glass (£2.70-£3.60)
PRICE GUIDE Fixed L £11.50 • Fixed D £19.50 • coffee £1.50 • min/water £2.50 • Service added but optional 10%

PLACE: This red-brick Victorian country house is set amid pretty gardens on the edge of the New Forest. There is a cosy bar for pre-dinner drinks.
FOOD: Old favourites and traditional British dishes predominate, with mains along the lines of mushroom stroganoff, or beef Wellington. The menu often introduces a contemporary international twist in dishes such as supreme of duck on Thai style noodles.
OUR TIP: Take a walk in the beautifully landscaped garden before dinner
Chef: Simon Charles **Owners:** Mr & Mrs Robson **Times:** 12-2/7-9, Closed 24 Dec, 26-29 Dec, 1-6 Jan, closed L Mon-Sat **Notes:** Vegetarian available, Dress Restrictions, Smart casual, Civ Wed 180 **Seats:** 50, Pr/dining room 120 **Smoking:** N/Sm in restaurant **Children:** Menu, Portions **Rooms:** 20 (20 en suite) ★★ **Directions:** M27(W) junct 1 follow B3079/8 to Fordingbridge. In town turn left at mini-rdbt and continue for 0.5m, hotel is located at top of hill on left **Parking:** 60
e-mail: ashburn@mistral.co.uk **web:** www.ashburn.mistral.co.uk

Hour Glass
British, French
Sophisticated dining close to New Forest
☎ 01425 652348 Burgate SP6 1LX

MENU GUIDE Salt cod cakes, pepper compote, saffron rouille • Roast lamb rump, potato croquette, provençale garnish • Poached pear, raspberry sorbet
WINE GUIDE ♀ 2003 Domaine Joel Delaunay Touraine Sauvignon Blanc £14.75 • ♀ Vina Carmen Chile Cabernet Sauvignon £12.95 • 19 bottles over £20, 26 bottles under £20 7 by the glass (£3-£4.95)
PRICE GUIDE Fixed L £14.50 • starter £3.90-£7.90 • main £8.90-£16.50 • dessert £4-£5 • coffee £1.75 • min/water £3 • Service optional • Group min 6 service 10%

PLACE: The 16th-century rustic exterior hides a surprisingly modern, understated interior complete with brick-built bar and huge inglenook fireplace. With low beamed ceilings, open beams divide the dining area to create an intimate country style.
FOOD: Menus are modern British with a French twist. Simple and unpretentious, they making good use of local game and other ingredients from the nearby New Forest. Preparation is skilful and service is friendly.
OUR TIP: Take an aperitif in the adjoining wine bar area
Chef: Jon Snodgrass, Mark Williams **Owners:** Hannah & Charlotte Wiggins **Times:** 12-2/7-10, Closed 1st 2 wks Jan, BH Mon, Mon, closed D Sun **Notes:** Sun Fixed L only, Vegetarian available **Seats:** 45, Pr/dining room 30 **Smoking:** N/Sm in restaurant **Children:** Portions **Directions:** 1m from Fordingbridge on A338 towards Salisbury **Parking:** 30 **e-mail:** hglassrestaurant@aol.com **web:** www.thehourglassrestaurant.com

continued

IPHOOK MAP 05 SU83

⊚⊚ Nippon-Kan
ritish, International

*uthentic Japanese, country club style, on a
00-acre estate*

☎ 01428 724555 Old Thorns Hotel, Griggs Green
U30 7PE

MENU GUIDE Sushi (raw fish) • Sliced beef & vegetables with
ukiyaki sauce • Maccha green tea ice cream

PRICE GUIDE Food prices not confirmed for 2006. Please
elephone for details

LACE: Old Thorns Hotel, Golf & Country Club has a choice of
ning venues: the elegant but informal Greenview and this
uthentic Japanese restaurant. The understated decor focuses
tention on the open griddle at your table, where an
complished chef will conjure dinner.

OOD: There's lots of choice from the set menus or lengthy
rte, including sushi or teppan yaki - the traditional griddle
oking. Teppan yaki sittings are at 7, 8.30 and 9pm, and there's
popular oriental Sunday buffet lunch 12-3.30pm.

UR TIP: Booking essential for Sunday buffet, and
commended for teppan yaki

ef: Mr T Suzuki **Times:** 12/6.30, Mon **Notes:** Vegetarian available, Civ
ed 75 **Seats:** 40 **Smoking:** N/Sm in restaurant **Children:** Portions
oms: 33 (32 en suite) ★★★ **Directions:** Telephone for directions
rking: 120 **e-mail:** info@oldthorns.com **web:** www.oldthorns.com

---

MINGTON MAP 05 SZ39

⊚ The Mill at Gordleton
ritish, French

*elaxed riverside dining in converted
atermill*

☎ 01590 682219 Silver St, Hordle SO41 6DJ

MENU GUIDE Tian of prawns (prawn cocktail twist) • Sea bass
llet, chorizo mash, red wine sauce • Lemon posset, home-
nade shortbread

WINE GUIDE ⵌ Terre del Mole Pinot £13.95 • ⵌ Bodena
Morton Merlot £13.95 • 23 bottles over £20, 30 bottles under
20 • 15 by the glass (£3-£8.95)

PRICE GUIDE Fixed L £10.50-£22.50 • starter £4.50-£9 • main
13.50-£21 • dessert £5.25-£8.50 • coffee £2 • min/water
3.50 • Service optional

LACE: A 17th-century watermill, in the New Forest near
mington, with the river meandering through the grounds. In
mmer, lunch and dinner are served on the terrace and patio.
side, there's a restaurant and two bars, with lots of wood,
ipes and checks, and not a hint of chintz.

OOD: Generous portions and a robust style of cooking but with
telligent flavour combinations and accuracy.

UR TIP: Terrace dining in fine weather overlooking the millrace

ef: David Baker and Carl Wiggins **Owners:** Liz Cottingham
nes: 12-2.15/7-9.15, Closed 25 Dec, closed D Sun **Notes:** Sun lunch
courses £16.75, 3 courses £19.95, Vegetarian available, Smart Dress
ats: 65 **Smoking:** N/Sm in restaurant, Air con **Children:** Portions
oms: 9 (9 en suite) ★★ **Directions:** M27 junct 1 towards Lyndhurst.
ke A337 through Brockenhurst to Lymington under railway bridge.
aight over mini rdbt, take right before Tollhouse pub. 1.5m on right
rking: 70 **e-mail:** gordletonmill@aol.com
eb: www.gordletonmill.co.uk

⊚ Stanwell House
British, European

Sumptuous comforts and enjoyable cuisine

☎ 01590 677123 High St SO41 9AA

MENU GUIDE Sea urchin tempura • Veal schnitzel • Sloe gin
jelly

WINE GUIDE 68 bottles over £20, 33 bottles under £20 • 12 by
the glass (£3.50-£4.25)

PRICE GUIDE Fixed L £7.50 • starter £3.95-£6.95 • main £11.95-
£16.95 • dessert £4.95 • coffee £2.25 • min/water £4 • Service
included

PLACE: Oozing history from its well-trodden stone staircase and
flagged floors, this hotel restaurant is furnished and decorated in
sumptuous fabrics and rich colour schemes. Candlelight adds an
atmospheric evening touch.

FOOD: The carte brings a balanced style varying from robust old
favourites like braised chump of Welsh lamb, and pot roasted
pheasant with root vegetables, to a well-prepared modern sea
bass with saffron and lime risotto, and tempura-style red mullet
fillets.

OUR TIP: Enjoy an afternoon tea

Chef: Colin Nash **Owners:** Mrs J McIntyre **Times:** 12-2/7-9.30
Notes: Vegetarian available, Civ Wed 60 **Seats:** 60, Pr/dining room 40
Smoking: N/Sm in restaurant **Children:** Portions **Rooms:** 29 (29 en
suite) ★★★ **Directions:** M 27 junct 1, follow signs for
Lyndhurst/Brockenhurst, A337 and Lymington. Head into the main high
street for hotel **Parking:** Public car park or on street
e-mail: sales@stanwellhousehotel.co.uk
web: www.stanwellhousehotel.co.uk

Give us your views! All the rosetted
restaurants in this guide have been visited
by one of the AA's team of professional
inspectors, but we want to hear from you!
Use the report forms in the back of the
guide or email us at
lifestyleguides@theaa.com with your
comments on any establishments featured
or on the restaurants that you feel are
worthy of an entry. We would also be
pleased to receive your views on the guide
itself and suggestions for information you
would like to see included.

England

England

MILFORD ON SEA MAP 05 SZ29

Rouille Restaurant
Modern British
Popular bistro by the sea
☎ 01590 642340 69-71 High St SO41 0QG

PLACE: In the heart of this beautiful village is the Rouille restaurant, a hospitable little establishment where guests are welcomed into the bar for aperitifs and canapés before moving into the restaurant. Subtle lighting, candles and music contribute to the cosy ambience.
FOOD: The modern British menu offers generous meals, with lots of fresh vegetables, and traditional home-made desserts like sticky toffee pudding. Cooking is wholesome and hearty with a simple approach using good local produce. The carte is offered additionally to the good value fixed-price lunch and exclusively in the evening.
OUR TIP: Space is limited so book ahead
Times: 12-2.30/7, Closed 2 wks Jan, Mon, closed D Sun
Directions: From A337 take B3058 to Milford, 150yds on L in village centre **e-mail:** rouille2003@aol.com

South Lawn Hotel
British
Traditional cooking in friendly hotel
☎ 01590 643911 Lymington Rd SO41 0RF

MENU GUIDE Warm leek & asparagus tart • Pan-fried monkfish fillet • Apple & sultana pie

WINE GUIDE ♀ Villa Maria Sauvignon Blanc £17.25 • ♀ Barossa Valley Shiraz £16.25 • 6 bottles over £20, 26 bottles under £20 • 5 by the glass (£2-£3)

PRICE GUIDE Fixed L £12.50-£15.50 • Fixed D £15-£19.50 • starter £3.50-£4.95 • main £11.50-£14.95 • dessert £4.50 • coffee £1.95 • min/water £3.25 • Service optional • Group min 20 service 10%

PLACE: This former dower house is situated close to the sea, and set in delightful gardens. Arches divide the restaurant up into intimate areas, with smartly set tables on a deep red carpet.
FOOD: Traditional menus are delivered with flair and accuracy, from a carte devoted to tried and tested favourites like pan-fried calves' liver, and grilled sea bass fillets, and a short list of daily chef's specials.
OUR TIP: Ideal for short or longer breaks
Chef: Gilles Rehal **Owners:** Mr & Mrs D Edwards **Times:** 12-1.45/7-8.45, Closed 20 Dec-19 Jan, closed L Mon **Notes:** Smart casual, no jeans or T-shirts, Civ Wed 120 **Seats:** 80 **Smoking:** N/Sm in restaurant
Children: Min 7yrs, Portions **Directions:** M27 junct 1, take A337 to Lyndhurst then onto Lymington and Christchurch. Follow signs for A3058 Milford-on-Sea. Hotel is 0.5m on left **Parking:** 60
e-mail: enquiries@southlawn.co.uk **web:** www.southlawn.co.uk

---

Westover Hall
French
Stunning Victorian mansion with breathtaking sea views
☎ 01590 643044 Park Ln SO41 0PT

WINE GUIDE ♀ Louis Latour Chardonnay £18.50 • ♀ Vera Monte Merlot £18.50 • 51 bottles over £20, 11 bottles under £20 • 11 by the glass (£4.50-£5)

PRICE GUIDE Fixed L £19.50 • Fixed D £38.50-£41.50 • coffee £2.50 • min/water £3.75 • Service optional

PLACE: A Grade II listed Victorian mansion with uninterrupted views of Christchurch Bay, the Needles and the Isle of Wight. The interior is a riot of oak panelling, wooden floors, stained glass and decorative ceilings. Service is excellent with great attention detail.
FOOD: Head chef, Jimmy Desrivières has gained extensive experience in France (Hotel Meurice, Georges Blanc) and the food reflects his classical background with modern presentation Expect top quality ingredients, much of it locally sourced, and precise cooking, in dishes such as langoustine and organic salmon raviolis with cep emulsion.
OUR TIP: Visit the national Motor Museum at Beaulieu
Chef: Jimmy Desrivières **Owners:** N Musetti & S Mechem **Times:** 12-1.45/7-8.45 **Notes:** Tasting menu 6 courses £50, Vegetarian available, Civ Wed 50 **Seats:** 40, Pr/dining room 10 **Smoking:** N/Sm in restaurant
Children: Min 12yrs, Portions **Rooms:** 12 (12 en suite) ★★★
Directions: From M27 junct 1 take A337 then B3058. Hotel just outside centre of Milford, towards clifftop **Parking:** 60
e-mail: info@westoverhallhotel.com **web:** www.westoverhallhotel.com

---

Two Rosettes The best local restaurants, which aim for and achieve higher standards, better consistency and where a greater precision is apparent in the cooking. There will be obvious attention to the selection of quality ingredients. About 40% of restaurants in the guide have two Rosettes.

NEW MILTON MAP 05 SZ29

Chewton Glen Hotel

British, French

Fine dining in impeccable Palladian-style hotel

☎ 01425 275341 Christchurch Rd BH25 6QS

e-mail: reservations@chewtonglen.com

web: www.chewtonglen.com

PLACE: Martin and Brigitte Skan's renowned country-house hotel has lived in a land of superlatives for nearly forty years. Once you drive through the wrought-iron entrance gates you are cosseted in a world of luxury; log fires, afternoon teas, a sweeping croquet lawn, impeccable service and country-house furnishings are all part of the tradition. But Chewton Glen has kept up to the minute too; its fabulous new spa and leisure facilities are among the best in the country. The appropriately stylish restaurant occupies a chic conservatory with a tented ceiling and, like the lounges and clubbier bar, has lovely views over the immaculate grounds. An equally perfect, more formal dining room may also be used.

FOOD: Classical dishes form the backbone of Luke Matthews' menus. Carefully sourced, top-quality ingredients - with plenty of luxury items - are key to its success, with suppliers admirably listed at the back of the menu. Expect clear flavours, well-conceived dishes and accomplished culinary skills on a repertoire that also includes a tasting gourmand menu, while the dazzling, appropriately classically led wine list has over 500 bins.

MENU GUIDE Lobster avocado tartar, lemon caviar dressing • Beef tournedos, mushroom crust, asparagus & Madeira jus • Fig & almond tart, strawberry ice cream

WINE GUIDE ♀ Spy Valley Sauvignon Blanc • ♟ Domaine Carneros Avant Garde Pinot Noir • 560 bottles over £20, 5 bottles under £20 • 20 by the glass (£6-£14)

PRICE GUIDE Fixed L £22.50 • Fixed D £59.50 starter £10 • main £20 • dessert £8.50 Service included

OUR TIP: Don't miss the fabulous afternoon teas

Chef: Luke Matthews **Owners:** Martin & Brigitte Skan
Times: 12.30-1.45/7.30-9.30 **Notes:** Vegetarian available, Dress Restrictions, Jackets preferred, no denim, Civ Wed 60 **Seats:** 120, Pr/dining room 120 **Smoking:** N/Sm in restaurant, Air con
Children: Min 5 yrs, Menu, Portions **Rooms:** 58 (58 en suite)
★★★★★ **Directions:** Off A35 (Lyndhurst) turn right through Walkford, 2nd left into Chewton Farm Road **Parking:** 150

England

OLD BURGHCLERE MAP 05 SU45

🌸 The Dew Pond Restaurant

British

Historic setting for traditional cooking

☎ 01635 278408   RG20 9LH

MENU GUIDE Leek & roquefort tart • Calves' liver, mash, melted onions, bacon, red wine sauce • Raspberry vacherin, passionfruit cream, strawberry purée

WINE GUIDE ♀ Macon Charnay Chardonnay £16.50 • ♀ Andrew Hurley Shiraz Cabernet £13.50

PRICE GUIDE Fixed D £28-£35 • coffee £2.75 • min/water £2.50 • Service optional

PLACE: Oak beams and open fires are a feature of this 16th-century country house, which has two cosy lounges for pre-dinner drinks. The candlelit dining room is decorated in traditional style with linen tablecloths and fresh flowers.

FOOD: A traditional menu with modern twists offers a well-balanced range of tempting dishes such as beef with caramelised shallots, rösti and a port wine sauce, or lemon sole with a Vermouth cream and spinach.

OUR TIP: Outdoor decking area for summer drinks

Chef: Keith Marshall **Owners:** Keith Marshall **Times:** 7-12, Closed Xmas, 2 wks Aug, Sun-Mon **Seats:** 45, Pr/dining room 30 **Smoking:** N/Sm in restaurant **Children:** Portions **Directions:** Telephone for further details **Parking:** 20 **web:** www.dewpond.co.uk

PETERSFIELD MAP 05 SU72

 JSW *see below*

🌸 Langrish House

Modern British   **NEW**

Accomplished cooking in picturesque surroundings

☎ 01730 266941 Langrish GU32 1RN

PLACE: A quiet country-house setting amid well-tended grounds. Frederick's Restaurant is comfortable with attractive paintings adorning the walls.

FOOD: Modern and traditional British fare with a short but sound menu including chicken and mango roulade with pickled plums and grilled fillet of pink bream, olive oil mash and baby spinach.

OUR TIP: Comfortable lounge for a pre-dinner drink

Times: 12-2/7-9.30 **Rooms:** 13 (13 en suite) ★★

e-mail: frontdesk@langrishhouse.co.uk

web: www.langrishhouse.co.uk

PETERSFIELD MAP 05 SU72

British, French

Small-town restaurant of distinct quality

☎ 01730 262030 1 Heath Rd GU31 4JE

MENU GUIDE Sea bass, ratatouille, garlic velouté • Veal loin, truffled mash, wild mushrooms • Salted caramel mousse, hazelnut praline

WINE GUIDE ♀ Villa Maria Private Bin Sauvignon Blanc £25.50 • ♀ Château de Parenchere Merlot/Cabernet Sauvignon £28.50 • 627 bottles over £20, 17 bottles under £20 • 7 by the glass (£3.75-£4.75)

PRICE GUIDE Fixed L £19.50 • Fixed D £35.50 • coffee £2.50 min/water £3 • Service optional • Group min 10 service 10%

PLACE: JSW is the kind of stylish, understated neighbourhood restaurant that, in a perfect world, would be found in small towns throughout the land. Small and appealing, the single, frosted-window-lined room has a neutral pastel beige decor, bold life drawings, simple wicker chairs and impeccable linen-dressed tables. The atmosphere is warm, friendly and comfortable.

FOOD: Chef-proprietor Jake Watkins opened the doors to JSW, his first solo venture, in 2001 and it has been on the rise ever since. Discerning foodies are beating a path to the door for bold and precise modern British cooking. Jake delivers immediately appealing, compact set-price menus of infinite style and quality, with balanced, well-presented and proportioned dishes that display a depth and richness of flavour. Materials are well sourced, from luxurious foie gras and ceps to local and seasonal produce, and the impressive breads, like the pasta and ice creams, are made in-house. The classy wine list offers great detail, weight and interest to wine lovers.

OUR TIP: Study the wine list - and be daring!

Chef: Jake Watkins **Owners:** Jake Watkins **Times:** 12-1.30/7-9.30, Closed 2 wks Jan, 2 wks Aug, Sun-Mon **Notes:** Tasting menu 6 courses L£29.50, D£39.50, Vegetarian available **Seats:** 22 **Smoking:** N/Sm in restaurant **Children:** Min 6yrs **Directions:** A3 to Petersfield town centr follow signs to Festival Hall car park. Restaurant 80yds from car park **Parking:** 80yds from restaurant

ROMSEY MAP 05 SU32

Bertie's

British, Mediterranean

ively converted inn with French atmosphere

☎ 01794 830708 80 The Hundred SO51 8BX

MENU GUIDE Confit duck terrine, prune & apple compote • Roast rump of lamb, beetroot confit • Treacle tart, crème fraîche sorbet

WINE GUIDE ♀ Marlborough Tasman Bay Sauvignon £24 • ♀ Madeba Estate Railroad Shiraz £17.95 • 15 bottles over £20, 35 bottles under £20 • 12 by the glass (£3-£4.50)

PRICE GUIDE Fixed L £12.95 • Fixed D £15.95 • starter £4.95-£7.95 • main £11.95-£18.95 • dessert £5.75 • coffee £2.50 min/water £2.75 • Service optional • Group min service 10%

PLACE: Francophiles will find much to enjoy in this former oaching inn, which combines rustic quaintness with distinctly continental style. Ceilings are low and beamed, food-related murals adorn the walls, and French staff add authenticity to proceedings.

FOOD: The food is fresh and honest, with clear, well flavoured combinations. Modern dishes drawing inspiration from the Mediterranean include double-baked goats' cheese soufflé with roasted tomato, and fillet of salmon with pea and prawn risotto.

OUR TIP: Good value lunch and fixed-price menus
Chef: David Heyward **Owners:** David Birmingham **Times:** 12-2/7-10, closed 26-30 Dec, Sun **Notes:** Vegetarian available **Seats:** 34, Pr/dining room 36 **Smoking:** N/Sm area, No pipes **Children:** Portions **Directions:** 200yds from Broadlands' gate in town centre **Parking:** 10 e-mail: sales@berties.co.uk **web:** www.berties.co.uk

The Three Tuns 58 Middlebridge St SO51 8HL

☎ 01704 512639 Smart modern character pub serving quality food.

ROTHERWICK MAP 05 SU75

Tylney Hall

British, French

Innovative cooking approach in imposing country house hotel

☎ 01256 764881 RG27 9AZ

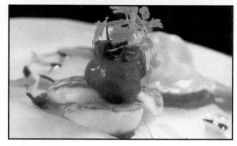

MENU GUIDE Crab cake, crème fraîche, cucumber • Duck, spinach, wild mushroom risotto • Vanilla pannacotta, poached peaches

WINE GUIDE ♀ Rizzardi Pinot Grigio £21.50 • ♀ Bodegas Trapiche Syrah £21.75 • 260 bottles over £20, 22 bottles under £20 • 10 by the glass (£5.20-£6.25)

PRICE GUIDE Fixed L £16.50 • Fixed D £35-£46 • coffee £2.95 • min/water £3 • Service included

PLACE: Set in beautiful Hampshire parkland, this grand Victorian manor has a number of gracious lounges and a terrace for cocktails or a cool glass of champagne. Dinner is served in the airy, glass domed Oak Room, which combines rich wood-panelling and smartly appointed tables with leafy views of the garden.

FOOD: A modern menu which retains all the qualities of classical cuisine and drips with luxury ingredients; start with duck and foie gras terrine perhaps, and then move on to lamb with roast Mediterranean vegetables, or venison with spätzle and shallot confit.

OUR TIP: Take a summer stroll around the hotel's beautiful water gardens
Chef: Stephen Hine **Owners:** Elite Hotels **Times:** 12.30-2/7-10 **Notes:** Sun lunch £27.50, Vegetarian available, Dress Restrictions, jacket & tie at D, Civ Wed 100 **Seats:** 80, Pr/dining room 100 **Smoking:** N/Sm in restaurant **Children:** Menu, Portions **Rooms:** 112 (112 en suite) ★★★★ **Directions:** M3 junct 5 take A287 (Newnham). From M4 junct 11 take B3349 (Hook), at sharp bend left (Rotherwick), left again & left in village (Newnham), 1m on right **Parking:** 150 e-mail: sales@tylneyhall.com **web:** www.tylneyhall.com

England

SELBORNE MAP 05 SU73

☕ **Gilbert White's House** The Wakes GU34 3JH
☎ 01420 511275 Winner of The Tea Guild Award of Excellence 2005.

SOUTHAMPTON MAP 05 SU41

⊚⊚ Botleigh Grange
British
Formal dining in a country house
☎ 01489 787700 Hedge End, Grange Rd SO30 2GA

MENU GUIDE Ricotta & spinach tart • Noisette, faggot & roulade of lamb • Glazed lemon tart

WINE GUIDE ♀ Woodbridge Sauvignon Blanc £18.50 • ♥ Woodbridge Merlot £18.50 • 22 bottles over £20, 25 bottles under £20 • 7 by the glass (£3.50-£6)

PRICE GUIDE Fixed L £19.50 • Fixed D £24.95 • starter £5.75-£7 • main £15.95-£19 • dessert £5-£6 • coffee £2.35 • min/water £3.95 • Service optional

PLACE: The beautiful grounds and lake set the tone for this impressive country mansion, handily located for the M27 but effectively in another world. Polished staff man the formal dining room, as well as the terrace beyond on warm days.
FOOD: The cooking has moved up a notch in recent months to general acclaim, and kitchen creativity matches the advanced culinary skills. Ingredients have a good quality provenance with flavours to match, and presentation is pleasing without being too fussy.
OUR TIP: Take a pre-dinner drink in the cocktail lounge
Chef: Nick Funnell **Owners:** David K Plumpton **Times:** 12.30-2.30/7-9.45, closed L Sat **Notes:** Vegetarian available, Dress Restrictions, No jeans, Civ Wed 200 **Seats:** 80, Pr/dining room 180 **Smoking:** N/Sm in restaurant **Children:** Menu, Portions **Rooms:** 56 (56 en suite) ★★★★
Directions: On A334, 1m from M27 junct 7 **Parking:** 300
e-mail: enquiries@botleighgrangehotel.co.uk
web: www.botleighgrangehotel.co.uk

⊚⊚ De Vere Grand Harbour Hotel
Modern Eclectic **NEW**
Striking waterfront hotel with eclectic fine dining
☎ 023 8063 3033 West Quay Rd SO15 1AG
PLACE: An elegant modern restaurant whose large windows overlook Southampton's fortified walls. In the evening, the atmosphere in Allertons Restaurant is enhanced by candlelight.
FOOD: A modern, eclectic approach to fine dining popular with leisure and business customers alike. A meal could take in marinated yellow fin tuna with soused baby vegetables and pink grapefruit dressing followed by slow braised lamb with roasted loin and lamb sauce. Optional extras include a choice of cooked-at-table 'Gueridon' dishes. More simple hotel dining is available in Restaurant No 5.
OUR TIP: Ideal for exploring Southampton's waterfront
Times: 12.30-1.45/7-9.45 **e-mail:** grandharbour@devere-hotels.com
web: www.devereonline.co.uk

⊚ Woodlands Lodge Hotel
British
Well-executed dishes in fine Georgian mansion
☎ 023 8029 2257 Bartley Rd, Woodlands SO40 7GN
MENU GUIDE Pancetta, black pudding & Hampshire herb sausage • Confit duck leg • Chocolate tart

WINE GUIDE ♀ Frontera Sauvignon Blanc £15.25 • ♥ Frontera Cabernet Sauvignon £15.25 • 12 bottles over £20, 13 bottles under £20 • 3 by the glass (£3.75)

PRICE GUIDE Fixed L £16.95 • Fixed D £33-£40 • coffee £2.10 • min/water £3.50 • Service optional

PLACE: A Victorian music room in a former royal hunting lodge makes a serene setting for this hotel restaurant. Outside, the garden is a delightful distraction.
FOOD: You'll find plenty of local game in season, and New Forest reared meat at all times, cooked to a no-frills formula that leaves robust flavours intact. Modern English recipes define the fixed-price three or four course menu.
OUR TIP: Overnight guests are welcome to bring their pets
Chef: Simon Torr **Owners:** David & Jenny Norbury **Times:** 12-1.45/7-9, Closed L Mon-Sat **Notes:** Lunch Sun only, Vegetarian available, Dress Restrictions, Jacket & tie, no jeans, Civ Wed 60 **Seats:** 30, Pr/dining room 20 **Smoking:** N/Sm in restaurant **Children:** Portions **Rooms:** 16 (16 suite) ★★★ **Directions:** M27 junct 1 **Parking:** 45
e-mail: reception@woodlands-lodge.co.uk
web: www.woodlands-lodge.co.uk

STOCKBRIDGE MAP 05 SU33

⊚⊚ The Greyhound
British, French
Gastro-pub grub by the river
☎ 01264 810833 High St SO20 6EY
MENU GUIDE Foie gras, lentils, bacon • Sea bass, mussel & clam fondue, basil linguini • Apple & Calvados bavarois, rhubarb compote

WINE GUIDE ♀ Vincent Delaporte Sancerre Sauvignon Blanc £28 • ♥ Barth Ehsteen Shiraz £15 • 120 bottles over £20, 30 bottles under £20 • 8 by the glass (£4.50)

PRICE GUIDE Starter £5-£8.50 • main £14-£21 • dessert £6 • coffee £2 • min/water £2.95 • Service added but optional 10%

continue

England

PLACE: This smart gastro-pub blends rustic charm with modern chic, and sits in pretty gardens that lead down to the River Test. Old beams and inglenook fires lend character, while wooden tables are left bare and teamed with comfortable leather chairs. Alfresco dining in summer.
FOOD: Expect a straightforward modern menu to match the setting. Dishes are classically based and conjured from high quality local produce; your choice might include turbot with a white bean and chorizo cassoulet, or Scotch beef with foie gras and a cep sauce.
OUR TIP: Try your hand at trout fishing in the river garden
Chef: Helene Schoeman **Times:** 12-2.30/7-9.30, Closed 25-26 Dec, 1 Jan, closed D Sun **Notes:** Vegetarian available **Seats:** 52 **Smoking:** N/Sm area, No pipes, No cigars **Children:** Portions **Directions:** 9m NW from Winchester, 8m S from Andover **Parking:** 20
web: www.thegreyhoundstockbridge.com

TITCHFIELD MAP 05 SU50
The Radcliffe Dining Rooms
Modern French
Fine dining in rural Hampshire
☎ 01329 845981 Whiteley Ln PO15 6RQ
PLACE: A modern members' club/restaurant conjured from a Hampshire farmhouse. Oak or flagstone floors, an inglenook fireplace and exposed beams remain, giving a comfortable, eclectic feel. On the ground floor the Champagne bar has a choice of lounges, while upstairs is the dining room and a balcony for sunny days.
FOOD: Described as 'contemporary French' this is serious, accomplished cooking which makes excellent use of great ingredients. Classical favourites sit well with more innovative ideas, and the style is simple, unfussy and precise.
OUR TIP: Lively bar
Times: 12-2.30/7-11, Closed D Sun, Mon
e-mail: enquiries@theradcliffe.co.uk **web:** www.theradcliffe.co.uk

WHITCHURCH MAP 05 SU44
Red House Inn
Modern European
Enjoyable dining with relaxing ambience in historical setting
☎ 01256 895558 London St RG28 7LH
MENU GUIDE Hand-made tortellini of crab, spinach & mascarpone • Seared skate wing, gazpacho sauce • Chocolate pie, wild berry coulis
PRICE GUIDE Food prices not confirmed for 2006. Please telephone for details
PLACE: This old inn has retained its character as a village local while also offering some seriously good food. It has beams, big fireplaces and the added allure of floor-to-ceiling mirrors. Staff are friendly and bright.
FOOD: The approach is honest and rustic with a sensibly short menu of satisfying dishes focusing on good fresh fish, high quality meats and game.
OUR TIP: Light meals are also available.
Chef: Shannon Wells & Pete Nash **Owners:** Shannon & Caroline Wells **Times:** 12-3/6.30-9.30 **Notes:** Vegetarian available **Seats:** 28 **Smoking:** N/Sm in restaurant **Children:** Min 10yrs, Menu **Directions:** Between Andover and Basingstoke, off the A34 **Parking:** 25

WICKHAM MAP 05 SU51
Old House Hotel & Restaurant
International
Georgian townhouse with a menu to suit most tastes
☎ 01329 833049 The Square PO17 5JG

MENU GUIDE Red mullet, potato, artichoke & shallot salad • Honey glazed duck • Chocolate & toffee fondant, vanilla ice cream
WINE GUIDE ♀ Bailley Reuerdy Sauvignon Blanc £22.95 • ♀ Urbina Res 96 Rioja £25.50 • 34 bottles over £20, 31 bottles under £20 • 11 by the glass (£4-£6.50)
PRICE GUIDE Starter £4.95-£7.50 • main £10.50-£21.50 • dessert £5.95-£7.95 • coffee £2.50 • min/water £3 • Group min 8 service 10%
PLACE: Prettily set in an ancient market square, the restaurant of this creeper-clad Georgian house ranges through three separate rooms and an airy conservatory. The atmosphere is relaxed and informal, with roaring log fires when it's cold, and alfresco dining in the summer.
FOOD: Drawing on the local area for quality ingredients, The Old House delivers a lengthy selection of old favourites and imaginative modern cuisine. Dishes are distinguished by understated simplicity, and might include calves' liver and onions, or halibut with bacon and chive mash.
OUR TIP: Simpler menu available at lunchtime
Chef: James Fairchild-Dickson **Owners:** Mr & Mrs P Scott **Times:** 12-2.30/7-9.30, Closed 26-30 Dec, closed D Sun **Notes:** Vegetarian available, Civ Wed 70 **Seats:** 85, Pr/dining room 45 **Smoking:** N/Sm in restaurant **Children:** Portions **Rooms:** 12 (12 en suite) ★★ **Directions:** In centre of Wickham, 2m N of Fareham at junct of A32 & B2177 **Parking:** 12
e-mail: oldhousehotel@aol.com **web:** www.oldhousehotel.co.uk

WINCHESTER MAP 05 SU42
The Chesil Rectory
British, French
Honest cooking in charming historic setting
☎ 01962 851555 1 Chesil St SO23 0HU
MENU GUIDE Foie gras, seared scallop galette • Sea bass, parsnip purée, oyster sauce, caviar • Saffron cheesecake, mixed berry jelly
WINE GUIDE ♀ Château de Tracy Sauvignon Blanc £35 • ♀ Evans and Tate Shiraz £24 • 74 bottles over £20, 6 bottles under £20 • 16 by the glass (£4-£10)
PRICE GUIDE Fixed L £20 • Fixed D £45 • coffee £4 min/water £4 • Service optional • Group min 7 service 12.5%

continued

England

The Chesil Rectory

PLACE: The oldest house in the historic City of Winchester, the Chesil Rectory dates from 1427, though most of the building you see today is 16th century. The restaurant has all the atmospheric period features you'd expect: low ceilings, beams and an inglenook fireplace, set off by simple modern decor.
FOOD: The four-course dinner menu includes an appetiser and refresher course of the chef's choice - mussel and saffron soup and raspberry sorbet for example. The quality of the ingredients is superb. Local produce is important, notably south coast seafood and New Forest mushrooms.
OUR TIP: Good range of coffees, teas and herbal infusions
Chef: Mr R Quehan **Owners:** Mr & Mrs Carl Reeve **Times:** 12-1.30/7-9.30, Closed 2 wks Xmas-New Year, 2 wks Aug, Sun-Mon
Notes: Vegetarian available, Smart Dress **Seats:** 42, Pr/dining room 15
Smoking: N/Sm area **Directions:** S from King Alfred's statue at bottom of The Broadway, cross small bridge, turn right, restaurant on left, just off mini rdbt **Parking:** 600 **web:** www.chesilrectory.co.uk

◉◉ Hotel du Vin & Bistro
British, Mediterranean
Busy bistro in popular, city centre, boutique-chain hotel
☎ 01962 841414 14 Southgate St SO23 9EF
MENU GUIDE Chicken liver & foie gras parfait, spicy pear chutney • Cod, wild mushroom & Jerusalem artichoke risotto • Crème brûlée
PRICE GUIDE Starter £6.75 • main £14.50 • dessert £6.75 • coffee £2.50 • min/water £3 • Service optional • Group service 10%

PLACE: The original in a successful boutique hotel chain, with bustling, informal, French-style bistro and bar at its heart, donning an appropriate wine-themed decor and charmingly unpretentious atmosphere that spills out onto the courtyard garden in summer. Relaxed, friendly and knowledgeable staff apply Gallic commitment, while the wine list is a delight, with excellent prices and high quality.
FOOD: Expect simple, light, clean cut, well presented classics with imaginative twists on the modern menu, with its easy-going set prices for starters, mains and puddings. French bread, knife and breadboard hits the table no sooner than you're seated.
OUR TIP: Booking essential, while the wine list commands respect
Chef: Andy Clark **Owners:** Hotel Du Vin Ltd. **Times:** 12-1.45/7-9.45
Notes: Sun L £24.50, Vegetarian available, Civ Wed 60 **Seats:** 65, Pr/dining room 48 **Smoking:** N/Sm in restaurant **Children:** Menu, Portions **Rooms:** 23 (23 en suite) ★★★★ **Directions:** M3 junct 11, follow signs to Winchester town centre. **Parking:** 40
e-mail: info@winchester.hotelduvin.co.uk **web:** www.hotelduvin.com

◉◉ Lainston House Hotel
British, International
Distinguished setting for bold, imaginative cooking
☎ 01962 863588 Sparsholt SO21 2LT

MENU GUIDE Foie gras parfait, Sauternes jelly • Sea bass, courgette spaghetti, watercress purée, tomato pistou • Tasting o Agen prunes
WINE GUIDE ♀ Chablis Chardonnay £40 • ♀ Chilean Cabernet Sauvignon Merlot £24 • 150 bottles over £20, 2 bottles under £20 • 12 by the glass (£4-£18)
PRICE GUIDE Fixed L £15.50 • Fixed D £33 • starter £9.60-£14 • main £15-£25 • dessert £8.90 • coffee £4.50 • min/water £4.50

PLACE: The stunning avenue of lime trees that sweeps up to this charming William and Mary period country house is easily matched by its sumptuous furnishings and courteous service. Roaring fires, heavy drapes, wood panelling, grand chandeliers and countless antique portraits grace the interior. The two inter-connecting dining rooms are a study in traditional luxury, with burgundy high-back leather chairs, crisp linen and views over th grounds.
FOOD: The modern focused British menus are underpinned by classical French theme with International influences and based around quality produce. Balanced flavours, imagination and hig skill levels shine.
OUR TIP: A lovely romantic setting, plus good-value fixed-price lunch option
Chef: Andrew Mackenzie **Owners:** Exclusive Hotels **Times:** 12.30-2.30/7-10 **Notes:** Tasting menu (Fri-Sat) £50, Sun L 3 courses £25, Vegetarian available, Dress Restrictions, No jeans or trainers; Smart casual Civ Wed 90 **Seats:** 55, Pr/dining room 18 **Smoking:** N/Sm in restaurar **Children:** Menu, Portions **Rooms:** 50 (50 en suite) ★★★★
Directions: Off A272, road to Stockbridge, signposted. **Parking:** 200
e-mail: enquiries@lainstonhouse.com **web:** www.exclusivehotels.co.uk

Ⓨ Loch Fyne Restaurant & Oyster Bar
18 Jewry St SO23 8RZ ☎ 01962 872930 Quality seafood chain

HEREFORDSHIRE

HEREFORD MAP 10 SO53

The Ancient Camp Inn

British, Mediterranean

Rustic inn with unrivalled views and classy food

☎ 01981 250449   HR2 9QX

MENU GUIDE Lady Llanover's salt duck, pickled damsons • Roast belly pork, cider sauce • Amaretto spumoni

WINE GUIDE ♀ Norte Chico Sauvignon Blanc £12.50 • ♀ Norte Chico Merlot £12.50 • 8 bottles over £20, 19 bottles under £20 • 4 by the glass (£3.50-£4.50)

PRICE GUIDE Starter £4.95-£9.50 • main £12.50-£17.50 • dessert £5-£6 • coffee £2.75 • min/water £3.50 • Service optional

PLACE: So named because the site was an Iron Age fort, this engaging old inn stands atop an escarpment with stunning views over the meandering River Wye. Inside, flagstone floors, beams, crackling log fires and scrubbed wooden tables set the rustic scene.

FOOD: Having lived and trained in France, the chef understands the power of simplicity and the use of excellent seasonal produce. Menus are short and punchy and the British and Mediterranean cooking impressive and assured.

OUR TIP: Family run with son as chef

Chef: Harry Mackintosh **Owners:** Kathryn Mackintosh **Times:** 12-3/7-11, Closed 3 wks Feb, Mon, Tues, closed D Sun **Notes:** Sun lunch 2 courses £15, 3 courses £18, Vegetarian available **Seats:** 30 **Smoking:** N/Sm in restaurant **Rooms:** 5 (5 en suite) **Directions:** From Hereford take A465 towards Abergavenny. Turn right to Ruckhall & after 2m follow inn signs **Parking:** 30

e-mail: reservations@theancientcampinn.co.uk

web: www.theancientcampinn.co.uk

◉◉◉ Castle House *see page 202*

see page 202

Three Rosettes Outstanding restaurants that demand recognition well beyond their local area. Timing, seasoning and the judgement of flavour combinations will be consistently excellent, supported by other elements such as intelligent service and a well-chosen wine list. Around 10% of restaurants with Rosettes have been awarded three.

KINGTON MAP 09 SO25

◉◉ The Stagg Inn and Restaurant

British

Friendly, quality-driven gastro-pub

☎ 01544 230221 Titley HR5 3RL

MENU GUIDE Seared scallops, celeriac purée & cumin • Wild sea bass fillet, crab risotto • Lemon tart, cassis sorbet

WINE GUIDE ♀ Norte Chico Sauvignon Blanc £12.90 • ♀ Norte Chico Merlot £12.90 • 32 bottles over £20, 32 bottles under £20 • 8 by the glass (£2.20-£7.50)

PRICE GUIDE Starter £3.70-£7.90 • main £12.90-£17 • dessert £4.90 • coffee £2.50 • min/water £2.40 • Service included

PLACE: A traditional country pub that's earthy and reassuring. With real fires and the relaxed, convivial character of a local, its bar still frequented by locals. The down-to-earth mood is reflected in the rustic decor, with original features and chunky farmhouse tables. The three dining rooms are on different levels, the largest in a medieval barn.

FOOD: The setting may be informal, but the cuisine is a classy, assured act, with top-notch, seasonal local produce playing a lead role. Precise and unfussy dishes are well conceived, intelligently playing due reverence to ingredients.

OUR TIP: Excellent range of regional cheeses

Chef: S Reynolds, G Powell, M Handley **Owners:** Steve Reynolds & Nicola Reynolds **Times:** 12-3/6.30-10, Closed 1st 2 wk Nov, 25-26 Dec,1 Jan, May Day, Mon (Tue after a BH), closed D Sun **Notes:** Vegetarian available **Seats:** 70, Pr/dining room 30 **Smoking:** N/Sm in restaurant **Children:** Portions **Directions:** Between Kington and Presteigne on B4335. **Parking:** 22

e-mail: reservations@thestagg.co.uk

web: www.thestagg.co.uk

LEDBURY MAP 10 SO73

◉ Feathers Hotel

British

Modern cuisine in Elizabethan coaching inn

☎ 01531 635266 High St HR8 1DS

MENU GUIDE Feathers local game terrine • Tournedos of Herefordshire beef fillet with foie gras parfait • Sharp lemon posset

WINE GUIDE 30 bottles over £20, 70 bottles under £20 • 18 by the glass (£3.50-£6)

PRICE GUIDE Starter £4-£7 • main £10-£17 • dessert £5 • coffee £1.30 • min/water £2.50 • Service added but optional 10%

PLACE: Since Elizabethan times, this famous black and white coaching inn has dominated historic Ledbury's main street. Oozing charm and character, Feathers Hotel combines all the characteristics of a town centre hostelry with the comforts of a modern hotel.

FOOD: Dinner is served in the elegant Quills Restaurant and the bustling Fuggles Brasserie with adjoining bar. The modern British cooking is simple with local produce used whenever possible. Excellent fish and vegetarian choices offered daily.

OUR TIP: Excellent leisure spa with heated swimming pool

Chef: John Capaldi **Owners:** David Elliston **Times:** 12-2/7-9.30 **Notes:** Vegetarian available, Civ Wed 100 **Seats:** 55, Pr/dining room 60 **Smoking:** N/Sm area, No pipes, No cigars, Air con **Children:** Menu **Rooms:** 19 (19 en suite) ★★★ **Directions:** M50 junct 2 Ledbury is on A449/A438/A417, and the hotel is on the main street **Parking:** 30

e-mail: mary@feathers-ledbury.co.uk

web: www.feathers-ledbury.co.uk

England

Castle House

Classic with modern twist
Adventurous cooking in contemporary luxury
☎ 01432 356321 Castle St HR1 2NW
e-mail: info@castlehse.co.uk
web: www.castlehse.co.uk

PLACE: Set slightly away from the centre of the town, this magnificent Georgian town house hotel overlooks the ancient castle moat and is just a short stroll from the cathedral. Elegant and sophisticated, and with a surprisingly tranquil setting, there is also a terrace and garden, perfect for fair-weather drinks and dining. The light and airy La Rive restaurant has floor to ceiling windows, piano music in the background and formally dressed tables. A wonderful venue to celebrate a special occasion or impress a business client over lunch.

FOOD: Expect some very finely tuned cooking here, with classical roots and fresh, contemporary interpretations. The dishes enable the kitchen to fully put their skills to the test and with the use of such excellent ingredients, expectations are always met, and often exceeded in dishes such as halibut married with creamed cabbage, an oyster beignet and cassis jus. Intricate cooking skills also show up in desserts like blackberry crumble soufflé with blackberry ripple and crème fraîche.

MENU GUIDE Pan-fried king scallops, shellfish risotto • Loin of venison, smoked garlic fondant • Dark chocolate & orange parfait

PRICE GUIDE Fixed L £21.95 • starter £5.95-£11.95 • main £13.95-£22.95 • dessert £6.95-£8.95

OUR TIP: Stay for the weekend

Chef: Claire Nicholls **Owners:** Dr & Mrs A Heijn **Times:** 12.30-1.30/7-9.30 **Notes:** 7 course Menu Surprise £44.95, Set price L - Sun only, Dress Restrictions, No jeans, T-shirts or trainers **Seats:** 30 **Smoking:** N/Sm in restaurant **Rooms:** 15 (15 en suite) ★★★ **Directions:** City centre, near cathedral **Parking:** 12 **e-mail:** info@castlehse.co.uk **web:** www.castlehse.co.uk

LEDBURY continued MAP 10 SO73

🌟 The Verzon Bar, Brasserie & Hotel

British, European

Brasserie dining with loyal local following

☎ 01531 670381 Hereford Rd, Trumpet HR8 2PZ

MENU GUIDE Goats' cheese fondant, roast vegetables • Pan-fried monkfish, curried mussels • Pear financier

WINE GUIDE ♀ Privilege de Drouet Sauvignon Blanc £11 • ♥ Privilege de Drouet Merlot £11 • 10 bottles over £20, 36 bottles under £20 • 6 by the glass (£2.85-£3.65)

PRICE GUIDE Fixed L £15.50-£22.50 • Fixed D £25-£42.50 • starter £4.50-£8.50 • main £10-£17.50 • dessert £5.25 • coffee £2.50 • min/water £2.85 • Service optional

PLACE: This stunning three-storey Georgian country house in an elevated position just outside Ledbury has been completely upgraded. The interior is a successful mix of the modern and traditional giving the dining room a pleasant, lively ambience. Service is helpful and unobtrusive.

FOOD: Classic brasserie dishes like confit duck leg with scallions share the menu with traditional British items like the beer battered cod, chunky chips and mushy peas.

OUR TIP: Enjoy the four acres of grounds

Chef: Matthew Warburton **Owners:** David & Gillian Pinchbeck **Times:** 12-2/7-9.30 **Notes:** Vegetarian available **Seats:** 50, Pr/dining room 70 **Smoking:** N/Sm in restaurant **Children:** Menu, Portions **Rooms:** 8 (8 en suite) ★★ **Directions:** M5 junct 8, M50 junct 2 (signposted Ledbury A417). Follow signs for Hereford (A438) **Parking:** 80 **e-mail:** info@theverzon.co.uk **web:** www.theverzon.co.uk

LEOMINSTER MAP 10 SO45

🌟 Royal Oak Hotel

British   **NEW**

Modern cuisine in traditional coaching inn

☎ 01568 612610 South St HR6 8JA

MENU GUIDE Omelette Arnold Bennett, pancetta & mustard dressing • Supreme of salmon with basil pesto • Apple tart Tatin

WINE GUIDE ♀ Paarl Heights Sauvignon Blanc £11 • ♥ Paarl Heights Cinsault Shiraz £13 • 17 bottles over £20, 34 bottles under £20 • 4 by the glass (£2.25-£3.75)

PRICE GUIDE Fixed L £10.50-£15 • starter £4.50-£7.50 • main £9.95-£15.95 • dessert £4.50-£6.95 • coffee £1.50 • min/water £3.50

PLACE: This traditional coaching inn has bags of character and history, including an original minstrels' gallery. As well as a welcoming bar with a good range of home-made bar food, the modern Déjà Vu restaurant has a relaxed Mediterranean feel with friendly, efficient service.

FOOD: Carefully sourced ingredients, cooked and presented simply, are key here: roasted local black pudding being accompanied by poached hen's egg, pancetta and wild mushroom sauce.

OUR TIP: Don't miss the treacle tart

Chef: John Badley **Owners:** I M Hotels Ltd **Times:** 12-2.30/7-9.30, Closed L Mon-Fri **Notes:** Dress Restrictions, Smart casual **Seats:** 40, Pr/dining room 12 **Smoking:** N/Sm in restaurant **Children:** Portions **Directions:** (A49/A44 junct, follow signs for Leominster Railway Station, pass station, follow road to left, hotel on right before junct) **Parking:** 20 **e-mail:** reservations@theroyaloakhotel.net **web:** www.theroyaloakhotel.net

ROSS-ON-WYE MAP 10 SO52

🌟 The Bridge House

British   ⭐NEW

Riverside hotel with tempting modern menu

☎ 01989 562655 Wilton HR9 6AA

MENU GUIDE Duck salad, ginger, lime & coriander dressing • Beef, dauphinoise potatoes, beetroot tempura, morel jus • Sticky toffee pudding

WINE GUIDE ♀ Mezzacorona Pinot Grigio £16.50 • ♥ Baron de Ley Rioja £19 • 6 bottles over £20, 20 bottles under £20 • 4 by the glass (£3.50-£5)

PRICE GUIDE Fixed D £30 • starter £5-£10 • main £15-£20 • dessert £5-£10 • coffee £2.50 • min/water £2.50 • Service optional

PLACE: Just a short stroll outside Ross-on-Wye, this elegant Georgian house sits in pretty gardens which run right down to the river. Take an aperitif outside in the summer, before moving into the light, airy dining room for dinner.

FOOD: Accomplished modern British cooking with European influences that shows a commitment to local produce. Mains range from light to heavier fare: smoked salmon on a warm tomato and asparagus salad perhaps, or venison in pancetta with apple rösti.

OUR TIP: Leave time to explore Ross-on-Wye

Chef: Aaron Simms **Owners:** Mike & Jane Pritchard **Times:** 12-2/7-9 **Notes:** Dress Restrictions, Smart casual **Seats:** 30, Pr/dining room 18 **Smoking:** N/Sm in restaurant **Children:** Min 14yrs **Rooms:** 9 (9 en suite) ◆◆◆ **Directions:** A49 3rd rdbt and left into Ross. 150yds on left before river bridge. **Parking:** 40 **e-mail:** info@bridge-house-hotel.com **web:** www.bridge-house-hotel.com

ROSS-ON-WYE *continued* MAP 10 SO52

Glewstone Court

British, French

Fine dining in elegant Regency manor

☎ 01989 770367 Glewstone HR9 6AW

MENU GUIDE Chargrilled asparagus, hollandaise • Welsh lamb loin, celeriac rösti, rosemary jus • Bread-and-butter pudding

WINE GUIDE ♀ Tanners Sauvignon Blanc £12 • ♀ Tanners Claret £12 • 4 bottles over £20, 20 bottles under £20 • 5 by the glass (£2.85-£3.75)

PRICE GUIDE Starter £3.95-£7.95 • main £9.95-£15.95 • dessert £3.95-£4.95 • coffee £1.50 • min/water £3 • Service optional • Group min 8 service 10%

PLACE: Charming Georgian house set in well-tended gardens with peaceful views over the Wye Valley. Period features abound throughout. The recently refurbished, elegant dining room is filled with eclectic antiques, curios and prints and enjoys views over the grounds. Although quite formal, service is relaxed and enthusiastic.

FOOD: Fresh local produce influences extensive menus, with individual suppliers mentioned by name. Cooking is straightforward and unfussy yet good clear flavours shine through at each course.

OUR TIP: After dinner, enjoy coffee beside the blazing log fire **Chef:** C Reeve-Tucker, P Meek, M Price **Owners:** C & W Reeve-Tucker **Times:** 12-2/7-10, Closed 25-27 Dec **Notes:** Vegetarian available, Dress Restrictions, No baseball caps or mobile phones **Seats:** 36, Pr/dining room 36 **Smoking:** N/Sm in restaurant **Children:** Menu, Portions **Rooms:** 8 (8 en suite) ★★ **Directions:** From Ross Market Place take A40/A49 (Monmouth/Hereford) over Wilton Bridge. At rdbt left onto A40 (Monmouth/S Wales), after 1m turn right for Glewstone. Hotel 0.5m on left **Parking:** 28 **e-mail:** glewstone@aol.com **web:** www.glewstonecourt.com

Harry's

British **NEW**

Ambitious cuisine in Georgian hotel

☎ 01989 760644 Chase Hotel, Gloucester Rd HR9 5LH

MENU GUIDE Game faggots, bubble & squeak, onion marmalade • Beef, oxtail dumpling, baby onions, smoked bacon • Apple, cider & honey pie

WINE GUIDE ♀ Hardy's Riddle Semillion Chardonnay £13.50 • ♀ Hardy's Riddle Cabernet Sauvignon £13.50 • 18 bottles over £20, 23 bottles under £20 • 11 by the glass (£2.95-£7.50)

PRICE GUIDE Fixed L £15.50 • Fixed D £25 • starter £4.50-£7.95 • main £8.95-£19.95 • dessert £5.50-£6.95 • coffee £2.95 • min/water £3

PLACE: Elegant Georgian country house hotel with a refurbished modern restaurant, located on the outskirts of the market town of Ross-on-Wye.

FOOD: Complex and elaborate modern British cooking with European and Far Eastern influences from an ambitious kitchen. The extensive menu features creative mains such as honey roast ham hock with mustard seed crumble, or pork with a Granny Smith fondant.

OUR TIP: Hot air balloon flights from the grounds in summer **Chef:** Martin Lovell **Owners:** The Porter Family **Times:** 12-2/7-10, Closed 24-30 Dec **Notes:** Vegetarian available, Civ Wed 300 **Seats:** 70, Pr/dining room 60 **Smoking:** N/Sm in restaurant **Children:** Portions **Rooms:** 36 (36 en suite) ★★★ **Directions:** M50 junct 4 A449, A440 towards Ross-on-Wye. **Parking:** 150 **e-mail:** res@chasehotel.co.uk **web:** www.chasehotel.co.uk

The Lough Pool Inn

European

Down-to-earth cooking at traditional country inn

☎ 01989 730236 Sellack HR9 6LX

MENU GUIDE Brixham crab cakes • 8-hour roast lamb with white bean, chorizo & saffron stew • Sticky toffee pudding

WINE GUIDE ♀ A Marcadet Touraine Sauvignon Blanc £14.75 • ♀ Aresti Merlot £12.50 • 9 bottles over £20, 38 bottles under £20 • 10 by the glass (£2.95-£3.50)

PRICE GUIDE Starter £3.50-£8.50 • main £9.50-£17 • dessert £5.25 • coffee £1.25 • min/water £2.50 • Service optional • Group min 12 service 5%

PLACE: Tucked away in rural Herefordshire, this quaint 16th-century inn is a friendly, rustic affair boasting flagstones, beams and own-brewed beer. Dine outside if weather permits.

FOOD: The food is as unpretentious as the setting with attentive service. A daily changing modern European menu offers quality produce handled simply, plus the occasional surprise such as deep-fried haggis fritters with beetroot relish.

OUR TIP: Just the place to while away a summer evening

continue

Chef: Chris Leeton **Owners:** Stephen Bull **Times:** 12-2.30/6.30-11, Closed 25 Dec, Mon Oct-Mar, closed D 26 Dec, Sun **Notes:** Vegetarian available **Seats:** 40 **Smoking:** N/Sm in restaurant **Children:** Portions **Directions:** 2.5m N of Ross-on-Wye, on Hoarwithy Rd **Parking:** 50

Wilton Court Hotel
European
Traditional cooking in riverside retreat
☎ 01989 562569 Wilton Ln HR9 6AQ

MENU GUIDE Chicken liver parfait, red onion marmalade • Beef, wild mushrooms, herb mustard sauce • Sticky toffee pudding, butterscotch

WINE GUIDE ♀ Gloire de Chablis J Moreau et Fils Chardonnay £19.95 • ♥ Casa La Joya Signature Merlot £17.50 • 6 bottles over £20, 19 bottles under £20 • 5 by the glass (£2.80-£4)

PRICE GUIDE Starter £4.25-£7.25 • main £8.95-£18.50 • dessert £4.75 • min/water £3.50 • Service optional

PLACE: Peacefully set on the banks of the Wye, this rambling 16th-century house offers guests the choice of dining in a cosy wood-panelled room, or in a bright conservatory overlooking the garden. FOOD: The menu name-checks a lengthy list of local suppliers so there's no doubt about the pedigree of ingredients. Expect traditional British dishes - Gloucester Old Spot pork with peaches, or steak and ale pie - plus lighter fish options. OUR TIP: Take a pre-dinner stroll along the river Chef: Mark Gaukroger **Owners:** Roger and Helen Wynn **Times:** 12-2.30/7-9.30, Closed L Mon-Sat, Closed D Sun **Notes:** Set Sun lunch 14.50, Vegetarian available, Dress Restrictions, Smart casual preferred **Seats:** 40, Pr/dining room 12 **Smoking:** N/Sm in restaurant **Children:** Portions **Rooms:** 10 (10 en suite) ★★ **Directions:** M50 junct 4 follow signs to Ross, turn into Ross at rdbt at junct of A40 and A49. Take 1st right after 100yds, hotel opposite river **Parking:** 25 e-mail: info@wiltoncourthotel.com **web:** www.wiltoncourthotel.com

ULLINGSWICK MAP 10 SO54

Three Crowns Inn
British, French
Bustling inn with new restaurant extension
☎ 01432 820279 HR1 3JQ

MENU GUIDE Fish soup, croutons & rouille • Pork loin, home-made black pudding, apple compote • Lemon tart

WINE GUIDE ♀ Picpoul de Pinet £14 • ♥ Santa Rita Merlot £14.50 • 14 bottles over £20, 15 bottles under £20 • 10 by the glass (£3.75-£7.50)

PRICE GUIDE Starter £6 • main £14.25 • dessert £4.50 • coffee £2.25 • min/water £2.50 • Service optional

PLACE: The inn is a converted 16th-century farmhouse, which was for many years a cider house producing its own cider. The interior is homely and rustic, but the latest development is a new

continued

Three Crowns Inn

restaurant extension with a contemporary classical design. FOOD: Good accurate cooking with a confident approach and excellent timing. The style is modern with Mediterranean leanings, using familiar combinations and top quality ingredients to provide clear, distinct flavours. There is good textural awareness and the lightness of touch is a strength. OUR TIP: Great value menu at lunchtime Chef: Brent Castle **Owners:** Brent Castle & Rachel Baker **Times:** 12-3/7-10, Closed 2 wks from 24 Dec, Mon **Notes:** Vegetarian available **Seats:** 75, Pr/dining room 36 **Smoking:** N/Sm in restaurant **Children:** Portions **Directions:** Telephone for directions **Parking:** 30 e-mail: info@threecrownsinn.com **web:** www.threecrownsinn.com

HERTFORDSHIRE

BISHOP'S STORTFORD MAP 06 TL42

Ibbetson's Restaurant
European
Fine dining in imposing country house hotel
☎ 01279 731441 Down Hall Country House Hotel, Hatfield Heath CM22 7AS

continued

England

BISHOP'S STORTFORD *continued* MAP 06 TL42

MENU GUIDE Pan-seared scallops, endive and ruby chard salad • Roast breast of guinea fowl, buttered spinach • Pistachio & chocolate soufflé

WINE GUIDE 12 by the glass (£4.50-£11)

PRICE GUIDE Fixed L £16.50 • starter £7.50-£14.50 • main £17-£24.50 • dessert £6.25-£7.50 • coffee £2.20 • min/water £3.75 • Service added but optional 10%

PLACE: Located in Down Hall, an imposing country house hotel whose decor includes antiques, chandeliers and tapestries. Ibbetson's is traditional and elegant, with a relaxed atmosphere. The dress code is smart casual.

FOOD: Ibbetson's is the hotel's fine dining option. The modern European menu is shaped by the availability of local ingredients, especially fish. There's a clear emphasis on seasonality in dishes such as Royal Dornoch rack of lamb with rosemary dauphinoise potatoes.

OUR TIP: Explore the extensive grounds
Chef: Chris Wheeldon **Owners:** Mr Gulhati, Down Hall **Times:** 12-1.45/7-9.45, Closed Sun-Mon, closed L Sat **Notes:** Vegetarian available, Dress Restrictions, No denim or trainers, Civ Wed 120 **Seats:** 36 **Smoking:** N/Sm in restaurant, Air con **Children:** Min 12yrs **Directions:** Take A414 towards Harlow. At 4th rdbt follow B183 towards Hatfield Heath, keep left and follow hotel sign. **Parking:** 150 **e-mail:** Ibbetsons@downhall.co.uk **web:** www.downhall.co.uk

---

ELSTREE MAP 06 TQ19

Corus hotel Elstree

British

Simple enjoyable food in stately surroundings

☎ 020 8953 8227 Barnet Ln WD6 3RE

MENU GUIDE Smoked chicken & ginger salad • Grilled fillets of red mullet, caper dressing • Steamed syrup sponge

WINE GUIDE ♀ One Tree Hill Semillion £15.50 • ♥ One Tree Hill Cabernet/Shiraz £15.50 • 11 bottles over £20, 15 bottles under £20 • 6 by the glass (£2.95-£6)

PRICE GUIDE Fixed L £18.95 • Fixed D £22.95 • starter £5.95-£8.95 • main £10.95-£17.95 • dessert £4.95-£6.95 • coffee £2.95 • min/water £4.20 • Service optional

PLACE: A grand black and white Tudor-style manor set in an elevated position, with views over landscaped gardens and beyond - the twinkling lights of London can be seen on a clear night. Dinner is served in the Cavendish restaurant, where oak panelling, beautifully laid long tables and ornate chandeliers create an opulent atmosphere.

FOOD: A set dinner menu with five choices at each course. Dishes are well balanced and beautifully presented.

OUR TIP: Stay over - some great offers available
Chef: Andy Bowden **Owners:** Corus Hotels **Times:** 12.30-2.15/7-9.30, Closed L Sat **Notes:** Vegetarian available, Civ Wed 100 **Seats:** 60, Pr/dining room 40 **Smoking:** N/Sm in restaurant **Children:** Menu, Portions **Rooms:** 47 (47 en suite) ★★★ **Directions:** From A1 take A411 from Stirling Corner **Parking:** 100 **e-mail:** edgwarebury@corushotels.com **web:** www.corushotels.com/edgwarebury

---

Prices quoted in the guide are for guidance only and are subject to change without notice.

HATFIELD MAP 06 TL20

⊛⊛ Bush Hall

British, European

Sound country house cuisine in comfortable surroundings

☎ 01707 271251 Mill Green AL9 5NT

MENU GUIDE Pressed ham terrine, home-made piccalilli • Poached lemon & thyme chicken breast • Warm chocolate fondant, coffee ice cream

WINE GUIDE ♀ Berri Estate Unoaked Chardonnay £13.95 • ♥ Berri Estate Shiraz £13.95 • 86 bottles over £20, 43 bottles under £20 • 8 by the glass (£3.50-£4)

PRICE GUIDE Starter £4.95-£9 • main £8.85-£17.50 • dessert £5.95-£9.95 • coffee £3.75 • min/water £3.50 • Service added but optional

PLACE: Country house hotel set in 25 acres of parkland, 25 miles north of London. On-site activities include go-karting and clay pigeon shooting, but dinner is a more sedate affair. Kiplings, the split-level restaurant, is part oak panelled and decorated in gold and green. Pre-meal drinks are taken in the lounge bar and coffee and sweetmeats in the drawing room, with a selection of ports, brandies and liqueurs.

FOOD: An extensive carte is offered at lunch and dinner, changing fairly regularly. Cooking is reliable and quality ingredients are evident throughout the meal.

OUR TIP: Five centuries of history are represented at Bush Hall
Chef: Steve Moore, Jamie Celnik **Owners:** Kiplings **Times:** 12-2/7-10, Closed D 25 Dec-early Jan, closed L Sat-Sun **Notes:** Vegetarian available, Dress Restrictions, Smart casual, Civ Wed 150 **Seats:** 38, Pr/dining room 22 **Smoking:** No pipes, No cigars, Air con **Children:** Min 8yrs, Portions **Rooms:** 25 (25 en suite) ★★★ **Directions:** From A1 (M) follow signs for A414 (Hereford/Welwyn Garden City). Take slip rd onto A1000 (signs for Hatfield Hse). left at lights, immediately left into hotel drive **Parking:** 100 **e-mail:** enquiries@bush-hall.com **web:** www.bush-hall.com

England

HITCHIN MAP 12 TL12

Redcoats Farmhouse Hotel
International

Popular farmhouse conversion surrounded by open countryside

☎ 01438 729500 Redcoats Green SG4 7JR

MENU GUIDE Indian spiced salmon & cod cakes • Gressingham duck breast au poivre, Puy lentils, diced vegetables • Pistachio crème brûlée

PRICE GUIDE Food prices not confirmed for 2006. Please telephone for details

PLACE: Delightful 15th-century property with a Victorian frontage set in four acres of gardens. Exposed brickwork, oak beams and open fireplaces are features of the original building. In recent years the place has expanded to include a large conservatory restaurant as well as an array of intimate dining rooms.
FOOD: A busy place where everything is pretty much made on the premises. Dishes are fairly simple and served complete with the appropriate accompaniments.
OUR TIP: It's advisable to book, particularly at weekends
Chef: John Ruffel **Owners:** Mr P Butterfield & Mrs J Gainsford **Times:** 12/6.30, Closed 1 wk after Xmas, BH Mons, closed L Sat, closed D Sun **Notes:** Vegetarian available, Dress Restrictions, Smart casual, No jeans, T-shirts, Civ Wed 70 **Seats:** 70, Pr/dining room 24 **Smoking:** N/Sm in restaurant **Children:** Portions **Rooms:** 14 (12 en suite) ◆◆◆ **Directions:** Telephone for directions **Parking:** 30 **e-mail:** sales@redcoats.co.uk **web:** www.redcoats.co.uk

RICKMANSWORTH MAP 06 TQ09

The Grove *see below*

ROYSTON MAP 12 TL34

The Cabinet at Reed
British, French   NEW

Gastro-pub run by TV chef

☎ 01763 848366 High St, Reed SG8 8AH

MENU GUIDE Baked French onion soup • Roast pheasant breast, onion tart Tatin, braised cabbage • Valrhona chocolate soufflé

WINE GUIDE ♀ La Serre Sauvignon Blanc £16 • ♀ Firefly Shiraz, Night Harvest £18.50 • 50 bottles over £20, 50 bottles under £20 • 30 by the glass (£3-£5.50)

PRICE GUIDE Fixed L £15.95 • starter £5-£10 • main £12-£25 • dessert £5-£7 • coffee £2 • min/water £3.50 • Service added 10%

PLACE: Secluded 16th-century inn with low-beamed ceilings, stripped wooden floors, open fire and fresh flowers. White linen tablecloths and attentive service hints that this TV chef-run operation is a serious gastro-pub.
FOOD: A modern menu reveals modern French, British and American inspiration, with quality produce used to create dishes such as fillet of 21-day dry aged sirloin of beef with blue cheese, corn and potato cake with a caramelised shallot sauce.
OUR TIP: Check directions for this tucked away place
Chef: Paul Bloxham **Owners:** The Cabinet Rooms Ltd **Times:** 12-3/6-11.30, Closed 25 Dec, 1 Jan, Mon, closed D Sun **Notes:** Coffee with petit fours £5, Vegetarian available, Dress Restrictions, Smart casual, Civ Wed 60 **Seats:** 70, Pr/dining room 14 **Smoking:** N/Sm in restaurant **Children:** Portions **Directions:** Just off A10 between Buntingford and Royston **Parking:** 40 **e-mail:** thecabinet@btopenworld.com **web:** www.thecabinetinn.co.uk

RICKMANSWORTH MAP 06 TQ09

The Grove

French, British

Fine dining in smart, contemporary, relaxed setting of 'London's country estate'

☎ 01923 296015 Chandler's Cross WD3 4TG

MENU GUIDE Roasted veal sweetbreads, artichoke risotto & truffle • Pan-fried Dover sole, cockles & clams, linguini, herb juice • Raspberry soufflé, crème fraîche, vanilla mousse

WINE GUIDE ♀ Jean Marc Boillot Montagny Chardonnay £37 • ♀ Château Sénejac Cabernet/Merlot £50 • 350 bottles over £20 • 10 by the glass (£7-£16)

PRICE GUIDE Fixed L £40 • starter £12.50-£18.50 • main £25-£32 • dessert £8-£11 • Service optional

PLACE: Colette's is the fine-dining operation at The Grove, the former stately home of the Earls of Clarendon. Today though, it's part of a world-class contemporary hotel development set in 300 acres of rolling grounds, much of which is a championship golf course, and there's a fabulous spa and two more dining options among its treasures. It's certainly at the cutting-edge of style and as modern, sophisticated and stylish as everything else here,

Colette's offers beautiful views over the Charlotte's Vale and the manor's formal gardens. There's a bar and lounge to review the extensive wine list and menus, and a terrace for fine-weather aperitifs. Service is relaxed, friendly and attentive.
FOOD: The kitchen delivers an ambitious, classically based repertoire with modern focus that's dotted with flavours from around the world, showcasing clarity of flavour and successful combinations that excite rather than shock. The approach, via dinner carte and tasting option, plus Sunday lunch jour and carte, comes liberally sprinkled with luxury items. Think white crab meat with sevruga caviar, coriander-cured tuna and lemon confit dressing, followed by spit-roast suckling pig with truffle macaroni.
OUR TIP: Great place to stay for the weekend
Chef: Chris Harrod **Owners:** Ralph Trustees Ltd **Times:** 12.30-3/7-10.30, Closed L Mon-Sat, closed D Sun **Notes:** Tasting menu 7 courses £65, Vegetarian available, Civ Wed 40 **Seats:** 40 **Smoking:** N/Sm in restaurant, Air con **Children:** Min 12yrs **Rooms:** 227 (227 en suite) ★★★★★ **Directions:** M25 junct 19, follow signs to Watford. At fist large rdbt take 3rd exit. Continue on 0.5m entrance on right **Parking:** 500 **e-mail:** restaurants@thegrove.co.uk **web:** www.thegrove.co.uk

England

ST ALBANS MAP 06 TL10
⊛⊛ St Michael's Manor
British, European
Accomplished country house cooking
☎ 01727 864444 Fishpool St AL3 4RY

MENU GUIDE Cornish crab, lime aioli, tomato crostini • Duck, caramelised plum, five spice jus • Lavender crème brûlée, pecan shortbread

WINE GUIDE ♀ Les Fumées Sauvignon £16.90 • ♀ McGuigan Merlot £16.90 • 30 bottles over £20, 35 bottles under £20 20 by the glass (£4.75-£6.50)

PRICE GUIDE Starter £6-£11.90 • main £11.50-£21.90 • dessert £5-£6.50 • coffee £3.25 • min/water £2.95 • Service added but optional 10%

PLACE: Luxurious country house hotel set by a lake in beautifully landscaped gardens. The airy dining room with its conservatory extension is elegantly understated, and simply decorated with fresh flowers, mirrors and sparkling glassware.

FOOD: A lengthy menu of accomplished modern British cuisine underpinned by considerable technical skill. Combinations are simple but imaginative, such as sea bass with a lemongrass and ginger risotto, or guinea fowl with a Madeira and grape sauce.

OUR TIP: A glass of champagne on the sun terrace

Chef: Barry MacMillan **Owners:** David & Sheila Newling-Ward **Times:** 12-2.30/7-10, Closed L 31 Dec **Notes:** Set Sun L £28.50, Smart Dress, Civ Wed 100 **Seats:** 95, Pr/dining room 22 **Smoking:** N/Sm in restaurant, Air con **Children:** Menu, Portions **Rooms:** 22 (22 en suite) ★★★ **Directions:** At the Tudor Tavern in High St turn into George St. After abbey & school on left, rd continues onto Fishpool St. Hotel is 1m on left **Parking:** 75 **e-mail:** reservations@stmichaelsmanor.com **web:** www.stmichaelsmanor.com

⊛⊛ Sopwell House
British, European
Sophisticated dining in a glamorous setting
☎ 01727 864477 Cottonmill Ln, Sopwell AL1 2HQ

MENU GUIDE Baby leeks, quails' eggs, hollandaise • John Dory, aubergine caviar • Poached pear in port

WINE GUIDE ♀ Eugenio Collavini Villa di Canlungo Pinot Grigio £25.50 • ♀ E Loron et Fils Fleurie Domaine de Prion Gamay £29.75 • 75 bottles over £20, 24 bottles under £20 • 8 by the glass (£3.90-£6.40)

PRICE GUIDE Fixed L £17.95 • Fixed D £25.95 • starter £5.75-£12.85 • main £15.95-£21.50 • dessert £5.25-£6.70 • coffee £2.95 • min/water £3.75 • Service included

PLACE: Replete with modern leisure facilities including indoor swimming pool, this modernised Georgian country house used to be home to Lord Mountbatten. The highlight of any visit here is a meal in the glass-ceilinged Magnolia Restaurant designed around a living magnolia tree.

FOOD: The menu offers modern British dishes with classical European influence. High quality, fresh ingredients including local game and imported luxury items are handled with care to produce clear flavours, as in perfectly timed lamb fillets or pigeon breast tartlets.

OUR TIP: Convenient for visiting St Albans' historic sites

Chef: Alastair Bancroft **Owners:** Abraham Bejerano **Times:** 12-14.30/7-10.30, Closed L Sat, Mon **Notes:** Sun L set 3 course menu £22.50, Vegetarian available, Dress Restrictions, No jeans or trainers, Civ Wed 250 **Seats:** 100, Pr/dining room 12 **Smoking:** N/Sm in restaurant, Air con **Children:** Menu, Portions **Rooms:** 129 (129 en suite) ★★★★ **Directions:** On London Road from St Albans follow signs to Sopwell, over mini-rdbt, hotel on L. M1 junct 7, M25 junct 22 **Parking:** 350 **e-mail:** enquiries@sopwellhouse.co.uk **web:** www.sopwellhouse.co.uk

🏢 Carluccio's Caffè Christopher Place AL3 5DQ
☎ 01727 837681 Quality Italian chain.

⊚ Sukiyaki 6 Spencer St AL3 5EG ☎ 01727 865009 Neat and authentic Japanese offering a range of good value dishes.

⊚ Wagamama Unit 6, Christopher Place AL3 5DQ
☎ 01727 865 122 Informal noodle bar with no booking.

🍷 denotes a restaurant with a particularly good wine list.

NEW denotes a restaurant which is new to the guide this year.

TRING MAP 06 SP91

Pendley Manor

British, French

Ambitious menu in an elegant setting

☎ 01442 891891 Cow Ln HP23 5QY

MENU GUIDE Timbale of chicken • Poppy seed crusted monkfish, chorizo mash & beetroot jus • Chocolate & lavender parfait

WINE GUIDE ♀ Côte de Roussillon Semillion Chardonnay £14 • ♀ Côte de Roussillon Shiraz Cabernet £14 • 31 bottles over £20, 19 bottles under £20 • 2 by the glass (£2.70)

PRICE GUIDE Fixed L £22.50 • Fixed D £31 • coffee £2.50 • min/water £3.50 • Service optional

PLACE: This traditional country manor house sits in extensive and mature landscaped gardens, complete with strutting peacocks. A cosy bar and conservatory lounge are ideal for pre-dinner drinks. The oak panelled restaurant with festoons of drapery, linen napery and chandeliers aims for a formal, fine dining experience.

FOOD: The Oak Room promises a gourmet's delight and the menu reads encouragingly. Classic ingredients and occasional international flavours.

OUR TIP: Wines represent good value for money

Chef: Simon Green **Owners:** Craydawn Pendley Manor **Times:** 12.30-30/7-9.30 **Notes:** Sun lunch £22.50, Vegetarian available, Smart casual, Civ Wed 225 **Seats:** 60, Pr/dining room 200 **Smoking:** N/Sm in restaurant **Children:** Portions **Rooms:** 74 (74 en suite) ★★★★ **Directions:** M25 junct 20. Take A41 and Tring exit, follow signs for Berkhamsted. 1st left, right after rugby club **Parking:** 250 **e-mail:** info@pendley-manor.co.uk **web:** www.pendley-manor.co.uk

WARE MAP 06 TL31

Marriott Hanbury Manor Hotel

International

Classy dining from a well regarded chain

☎ 01920 487722 SG12 0SD

MENU GUIDE Truffle sandwich & lobster burger with tuna sushi • Seared scallops on a wild mushroom mousse with cayenne-raisin sauce • The Hanbury indulgence

WINE GUIDE ♀ Billaud-Simon Chablis £48 • ♀ Marques de Grinon Rioja £49 • 163 bottles over £20

PRICE GUIDE Fixed L £20 • starter £8.50-£18.95 • main £24.50-£32.50 • dessert £8.95-£10.75 • coffee £2.50 • min/water £4.50 • Service optional

PLACE: Set in 200 acres of well-tended grounds, incorporating a championship golf course, this Jacobean-style mansion is elegant with a stunning decor. The Zodiac restaurant, its formal dining room, is beautifully appointed with pale colours, ornate ceilings and formal portraits; and its terrace overlooks the golf course. The tables are traditionally set with crisp white napery, sparkling glassware and silver cutlery.

FOOD: The menu features finest European cuisine with an Asian twist. Dishes can range from classically simple to opulently elaborate. Plenty of luxury ingredients like truffles, lobster and foie gras in evidence.

OUR TIP: Superb leisure facilities

Chef: Andreas Mahl **Owners:** Whitbread Hotels **Times:** 12-2/7.30-9.30, Closed BHs, 1-9 Jan, Mon, closed L Sat, closed D Sun **Notes:** Taste of Hanbury 7 courses £65, Vegetarian available, Dress Restrictions, Smart casual, Jacket preferred for men, Civ Wed 120 **Seats:** 50, Pr/dining room 20 **Smoking:** N/Sm in restaurant **Children:** Min 12yrs, Portions **Rooms:** 161 (161 en suite) ★★★★★ **Directions:** From M25 junct 25, take A10 towards Cambridge. Follow A10 for 12m. Leave A10 Wadesmill/Thundridge/Ware. Right at roundabout, hotel on left **Parking:** 200 **e-mail:** gisele.clark@marriotthotels.co.uk **web:** www.hanbury-manor.com

WELWYN MAP 06 TL21

⚫⚫ Novelli at Auberge du Lac

Modern French

Exclusive restaurant in fabulous location

☎ 01707 368888 Brocket Hall AL8 7XG

MENU GUIDE Foie gras & truffle terrine • Roast leg of Pyrenees milk-fed lamb • Chocolate passionfruit layer cake

PRICE GUIDE Food prices not confirmed for 2006. Please telephone for details

PLACE: Celebrated chef of television's *Hell's Kitchen* fame, Jean-Christophe Novelli has a superbly located restaurant on the edge of a lake in the grounds of stately Brocket Hall, which also includes woodland, parkland, Nick Faldo's Golf Academy and two 18-hole golf courses. The elegant dining room is very French, as are the attentive, formal staff.

FOOD: Imaginative, accurate modern French cooking that centres on excellent produce. The good value lunch is especially popular, as are the more serious tasting menus. Dishes might include mosaic of Garennes rabbit with sweet Dutch carrot marmalade, or acacia honey-glazed breast of local duck with caramelised baby turnips and soft figs.

OUR TIP: Go in summer and dine on the terrace

Chef: Jean Christophe Novelli, Phil Thompson **Owners:** CCA International **Times:** 12-2.30/7-10, Closed Mon, closed D Sun **Notes:** Coffee included (£150 Tasting Menu inc wine), Vegetarian available, Dress Restrictions, Smart casual preferred, Civ Wed 70 **Seats:** 70, Pr/dining room 16 **Smoking:** No pipes, No cigars, Air con **Children:** Menu, Portions **Directions:** Telephone for directions or see website **Parking:** 50 **e-mail:** auberge@brocket-hall.co.uk **web:** www.brocket-hall.co.uk

---

What makes a Restaurant of the Year?
In selecting a Restaurant of the Year, we look for somewhere that is exceptional in its chosen area of the market. Whilst the Rosette awards are based on the quality of the food alone, Restaurant of the Year takes into account all aspects of the operation. For full details see pages 6-7.

continued

England

KENT

ASHFORD MAP 07 TR04

☺☺ Eastwell Manor
British, French
Grand country-house hotel with fine food
☎ 01233 213000 Eastwell Park, Boughton Lees TN25 4HR

MENU GUIDE Pan-fried scallops, vierge dressing • Assiette of Sussex Red beef • Tart Tatin of caramelised pear

WINE GUIDE ♀ Château de Maligny Petit Chablis £28 • ♀ Domaine de la Bournniere Fleurie £31 • 206 bottles over £20, 21 bottles under £20 • 10 by the glass (£4-£6)

PRICE GUIDE Fixed L £10 • Fixed D £37.50 • starter £8.50-£65 • main £24.50-£53 • dessert £8 • coffee £3.25 • min/water £4 • Service optional

PLACE: Set in 62 acres of landscaped grounds, this historic hotel dates back to the Norman Conquest and boasts carved wood-panelled rooms and huge baronial stone fireplaces. The traditional feel to the place is balanced by modern decor and contemporary edges.

FOOD: Classical cooking with modern influences and an emphasis on local produce is perfectly illustrated by a substantial main course of breast of Gressingham duck with cider fondant potato on a mead jus. Technical skill is impressive and presentation is refined.

OUR TIP: Allow time to visit the stunning spa
Chef: Neil Wiggins **Owners:** Turrloo Parrett **Times:** 12-2.30/7-10 **Notes:** Vegetarian available, Dress Restrictions, Jacket and tie at D, no Jeans, Civ Wed 250 **Seats:** 80, Pr/dining room 80 **Smoking:** N/Sm in restaurant **Children:** Menu, Portions **Rooms:** 62 (62 en suite) ★★★★ **Directions:** From M20 junct 9 take 1st left (Trinity Rd). Through 4 rdbts to lights. Take left filter onto A251 signed Faversham. 1.5m to sign for Boughton Aluph, then 200yds to hotel **Parking:** 120
e-mail: enquiries@eastwellmanor.co.uk **web:** www.eastwellmanor.co.uk

BEARSTED MAP 07 TQ85

☺☺ Soufflé Restaurant
Mediterranean, European
Understated village dining
☎ 01622 737065 31 The Green ME14 4DN

MENU GUIDE Terrine of wild mushrooms in herb pancake • Pavé of salmon, confit tomatoes • Pear Tatin, vanilla ice cream

WINE GUIDE ♀ Louis Latour Chablis £24 • ♀ Louis Latour Morgan £22 • 30 bottles over £20, 28 bottles under £20 • 2 by the glass (£3)

PRICE GUIDE Fixed L £13.50 • Fixed D £22.50 • starter £7-£10 • main £16.50-£18 • dessert £7.50-£8.50 • coffee £2.50 • min/water £4 • Service added but optional 10%

PLACE: This charming 16th-century cottage, once the village bakery, overlooks the green. Comfortable upholstered chairs and gentle lighting combine well with crisp white linen and crystal for a cosy ambience, and the terrace is perfect on a beautiful summer's day. The dress code is smart/casual.

FOOD: Fixed-price menus are available at lunch and dinner, as well as the creative carte. Lamb, beef and fish are all sourced locally; such quality ingredients are key to the imaginative and modern cooking style, which nonetheless avoids slavishly following fashion.

OUR TIP: Good selection of champagnes
Chef: Nick Evenden **Owners:** Nick & Karen Evenden **Times:** 12-2.30/7-10, Closed Mon, closed L Sat, closed D Sun **Notes:** Vegetarian available **Seats:** 40, Pr/dining room 23 **Smoking:** N/Sm in restaurant **Children:** Portions **Directions:** Telephone for directions **Parking:** 15

BIDDENDEN MAP 07 TQ83

☺☺ *The West House*
Modern European   **NEW**
Family-run restaurant in picturesque village setting
☎ 01580 291341 28 High St TN27 8AH

PLACE: Ancient building with beams as big as trees, low ceilings and a pot bellied stove set in a huge inglenook fireplace. Chunky tables are lightly dressed with buxom wine glasses and place mats. Staff, often family, are casually dressed, pleasant, warm and refreshing, and really know their stuff.

FOOD: Local ingredients cooked skilfully by a chef patron who has spent many a year in London cooking for others. There is a set three-course dinner menu, offering dishes like samphire and lobster hollandaise

OUR TIP: Take a stroll around the village before dinner
Times: 12-2/7-9.30, Closed 25 Dec-1 Jan, Mon, closed L Sat, D Sun
e-mail: westhouse@fsmail.net

Claris's 1-3 High St TN27 8AL
☎ 01580 291025 Winner of The Tea Guild Award of Excellence 005.

RANDS HATCH MAP 06 TQ56

ⓓ⓪ Brandshatch Place

European

Accomplished cuisine near the race track
☎ 01474 875000 Brands Hatch Rd, Fawkham DA3 8NQ

MENU GUIDE Ham hock terrine, celeriac remoulade • Blade of beef, garlic potato purée, parsnips, blade jus • Warm chocolate fondant

WINE GUIDE ♀ La Serre Sauvignon Blanc £17 • ♀ La Serre Merlot £17 • 52 bottles over £20, 8 bottles under £20 • 8 by the glass (£4.50-£8)

PRICE GUIDE Fixed L £19.95-£28.50 • Fixed D £28.50-£38.50 coffee £3.50 • min/water £4.50 • Service optional

PLACE: With its elegant range of public rooms, this charming country-house hotel is a peaceful place to unwind after a day at the track. Dinner is served in the refurbished restaurant, a tasteful concoction of mirrors and objets d'art.
FOOD: Top-notch ingredients and accomplished skills make for a tempting range of modern British dishes, such as pork belly with apple rösti and caramelised button onions, or grilled Dover sole with hollandaise sauce. The friendly staff are happy to help.
OUR TIP: The hotel also has a leisure club with crèche facilities
Chef: Paul Sage **Owners:** Handpicked Hotels **Times:** 12-2/7-9.30, closed L Sat **Notes:** Vegetarian available, Smart Dress, Civ Wed 80 **Seats:** 60, Pr/dining room 35 **Smoking:** N/Sm in restaurant, Air con **Children:** Menu, Portions **Rooms:** 38 (38 en suite) ★★★★
Directions: From M25/M20 follow signs for Brands Hatch Circuit onto 20. Follow signs to Paddock entrance, hotel is located on Brands Hatch d. **Parking:** 50 **e-mail:** brandshatchplace@handpicked.co.uk **Web:** www.handpicked.co.uk/brandshatchplace

---

ANTERBURY MAP 07 TR15

ⓓ Augustine's Restaurant

British, European

Fine dining in elegant Georgian setting
☎ 01227 453063 1 & 2 Longport CT1 1PE

MENU GUIDE Smoked eel, creamed horseradish • Brill, gnocchi, saffron ratatouille • Rhubarb & orange compote

WINE GUIDE ♀ Chat Pavillion de Brie Semillion Sauvignon £14 ♀ Big Rivers Shiraz/Cabernet Sauvignon £13.95 • 12 bottles over £20, 16 bottles under £20 • 4 by the glass (£2.95-£3.50)

PRICE GUIDE Fixed L £12.95-£13.95 • starter £4.50-£8.50 • main £12.50-£16.95 • dessert £4.50-£5 • coffee £2.50 • min/water £3 • Service optional

PLACE: Named after St Augustine's monastery, this elegantly presented, family-run restaurant is located in this city centre Georgian townhouse. Original features include an ornamental staircase in the entrance hall and exposed beams, and an open fire in the ancient bar. Friendly and efficient service.
FOOD: The accomplished cooking draws on both British and French traditions. Locally sourced, fresh produce provides the basis for imaginative and satisfying dishes like Romney Marsh lamb and cassoulet.
OUR TIP: See Canterbury's ancient sites before dining
Chef: Robert Grimer **Owners:** Mr R & Mr T Grimer **Times:** 12-1.30/6.30-9, Closed 2 wks Jan, Mon, Sun **Notes:** Vegetarian available **Seats:** 30 **Smoking:** N/Sm in restaurant **Directions:** Follow signs to St Augustine's Abbey **Parking:** On street

ⓓ The Dove Inn

European

Country pub serving local fish and classic combinations
☎ 01227 751360 Plumpudding Ln, Dargate ME13 9HB

MENU GUIDE Avocado, bacon & rocket salad • Whole pan-fried Dover sole with caper shallot & herb butter • Chocolate sponge pudding

PRICE GUIDE Food prices not confirmed for 2006. Please telephone for details

PLACE: Bare stripped tables and paper napkins, candle bottles covered in wax, and friendly staff characterise this cosy country pub, tucked away but within easy reach of Canterbury and the coast.
FOOD: Mainly British and traditional French dishes which suit the local clientele very well. Nothing is over-complicated and good ingredients are used in hearty plates of food. Innovative snacks and baguette on offer for smaller appetites.
OUR TIP: Book ahead to avoid disappointment
Times: 12-2/7-9, Closed Mon, closed D Sun, Tue **Directions:** 5m NW of Canterbury. Telephone for directions
e-mail: nigel@thedoveinn.fsnet.co.uk

ⓓ The White Horse Inn

British, French

Charming inn with smart restaurant
☎ 01227 830249 High St, Bridge CT4 5LA

MENU GUIDE Pan-fried scallops, black pudding, apple compote • Sea bass, spinach, salsify, smoked haddock velouté, dill crème fraîche • Coffee caramel soufflé

WINE GUIDE ♀ Todd Vintners Pinot Grigio £12.50 • ♀ Concha y Toro Merlot £12.50 • 17 bottles over £20, 43 bottles under £20 • 11 by the glass (£3-£4.50)

PRICE GUIDE Fixed L £11.95 • Fixed D £24.50 • starter £6-£9.50 • main £13.50-£21 • dessert £5.50-£7.50 • coffee £2.75 • min/water £3.75 • Service optional

PLACE: Still very much an inn, this upmarket gastro-pub has a village location on the outskirts of town. Its smart restaurant is in a Georgian extension (with bar and lounge), decked out with quality furniture, coordinated fabrics, clothed tables and trendy glass crockery. The atmosphere's suitably relaxed and service professional.
FOOD: The well presented modern cooking admirably showcases fresh, seasonal local produce, listing suppliers on the menu's reverse. Impressive range of locally produced wines too.

continued

continued

England

CANTERBURY *continued* MAP 07 TR15

OUR TIP: Good local farm produce and wines are a hallmark; the fixed-price lunch offers value
Chef: B Walton, Ryan Tasker, Paul Rogers **Owners:** Alan Walton
Times: 12-3/7-11, Closed 25 Dec, 1 Jan, Mon, closed D Sun
Notes: Vegetarian available **Seats:** 30 **Smoking:** N/Sm in restaurant
Children: Menu, Portions **Directions:** 3m S of Canterbury on the Dover rd. A2 signposted for Bridge **Parking:** 20
e-mail: thewaltons_thewhitehorse@hotmail.com
web: www.whitehorsebridge.co.uk

CHATHAM MAP 07 TQ76

Bridgewood Manor

British, International
Modern, purpose-built hotel with informal or fine dining
☎ 01634 201333 Bridgewood Roundabout, Walderslade Woods ME5 9AX

MENU GUIDE Open lobster ravioli, cream sauce • Monkfish, Parma ham • Hot chocolate fondant, vanilla ice cream

PRICE GUIDE Fixed L £20.50 • Fixed D £32.50 • starter £8.95-£9.95 • main £18.95-£24.95 • dessert £7-£9.50 • coffee £2.90 • min/water £3.75 • Service optional

PLACE: Situated on the outskirts of historic Rochester, this modern, purpose-built hotel offers a choice of dining. There's the informal Terrace Bistro or the more formal Squires restaurant. Service is both attentive and friendly.

continued

FOOD: Well-executed and enjoyable modern British dishes such as foie gras and duck pâté served with cucumber ribbons and cherry balsamic dressing, or Dover sole fillet with crayfish, Avruga caviar, scallop cream and lobster oil. Simpler combinations work well too.

OUR TIP: Try the excellent leisure facilities
Chef: Nigel Stringer **Owners:** Marston Hotels **Times:** 12.30-2.30/7-9.45
Closed 24-27 Dec (ex residents), closed L Sat **Notes:** Vegetarian available
Dress Restrictions, Smart casual, no denim or trainers, Civ Wed 150
Seats: 120, Pr/dining room 30 **Smoking:** N/Sm in restaurant, Air con
Children: Menu, Portions **Rooms:** 100 (100 en suite) ★★★★
Directions: From M2 junct 3 or M20 junct 6 follow A229 towards Chatham. At Bridgewood rdbt take 3rd exit (Walderslade). Hotel 50yds on left **Parking:** 170 **e-mail:** bridgewoodmanor@marstonhotels.com
web: www.marstonhotels.com

CRANBROOK MAP 07 TQ73

 Apicius *see below*

The George Hotel

Modern British **NEW**
Charming inn with great local reputation
☎ 01580 713348 Stone St TN17 3HE

MENU GUIDE Foie gras & apple terrine, black grape chutney • Pan-fried rib of beef, horseradish mash, roasted onions • Roasted plums, mascarpone, brandy & ginger syrup

WINE GUIDE ♀ Sauvignon Blanc Semillon £14 • ♀ Azabache Rioja £18 • 6 bottles over £20, 11 bottles under £20 • 7 by the glass (£3-£4.50)

continue

CRANBROOK MAP 07 TQ73

Apicius

European **NEW**
Serious cuisine in pretty town setting
☎ 01580 714666 23 Stone St TN17 3HF

MENU GUIDE Salt cod croquettes, aioli • Fennel-roasted monkfish, lobster vinaigrette • Chocolate marquise

WINE GUIDE ♀ Colefield Sauvignon Blanc £16 • ♀ Columbia Crest Cabernet Sauvignon £17 • 10 bottles over £20, 10 bottles under £20 • 4 by the glass (£3-£5)

PRICE GUIDE Fixed L £15.50 • Fixed D £23.50 • Service optional

PLACE: New owners have given a new feel to this attractive and intimate little restaurant tucked away in a narrow street in this pretty Kent town. Once used by Flemish weavers to ply their trade, this timber-clad building dates from 1530 and retains much its rustic charm with lots of beams and a glass frontage with slatted shutters. White clothed tables are well spaced with high-backed electric blue upholstered chairs. The name comes from the famous Roman gastronome of the first century AD.
FOOD: Short menus and never more than three flavours on the plate. A modern European style of cooking firmly founded on classical foundations allows the fresh, seasonal ingredients to

speak for themselves. To start, expect dishes like ballotine of foie gras, toasted pain d'epice and pickled girolles. To follow, there's boned osso bucco with deep-fried marrow.
OUR TIP: Excellent value lunchtime menu
Chef: Timothy Johnson **Owners:** Timothy Johnson, Faith Hawkins
Times: 12-2/7.45-9, Closed 2 wks Jan, Mon, L Tues, D Sun
Notes: Vegetarian available **Seats:** 24 **Smoking:** N/Sm in restaurant
Children: Min 8 yrs **Directions:** Opposite Barclays Bank
Parking: Public car park at rear

PRICE GUIDE Fixed L £12-£17 • Fixed D £25-£30 • starter £5-£7 • main £11-£17 • dessert £5-£7 • coffee £2 • min/water £4 • Service optional

PLACE: This centuries-old former coaching inn is right in the heart of the bustling town centre. The main feature of the heavily beamed restaurant is the striking 16th-century inglenook fireplace, and the room is furnished in plainly finished contemporary oak with comfortable leather chairs. Staff are relaxed but professional.

FOOD: Sound, locally sourced produce, accurately cooked and full of flavour. The modern English menu offers great combinations and simple presentation in dishes like confit duck leg with seasonal leaves and thyme jus. There's also a wine bar serving snacks.

OUR TIP: Handy free car park just down the road

Chef: Ben Miell **Owners:** Mark & Sara Colley **Times:** 12-3/7-9.30, closed D Sun-Mon **Notes:** Vegetarian available, Smart Dress **Seats:** 40 **Smoking:** N/Sm in restaurant **Children:** Menu, Portions **Rooms:** 8 (8 en suite) ★★ **Parking:** 12
e-mail: reservations@thegeorgehotelkent.co.uk
web: www.thegeorgehotelkent.co.uk

DARTFORD MAP 06 TQ57

Rowhill Grange

British, French

Quality cooking with a modern theme

☎ 01322 615136   DA2 7QH

MENU GUIDE Croquette of cod brandade • Slow-roast belly of pork, pan-fried foie gras, cream cabbage & caramelised apple purée • Warm apple & almond cream latte

WINE GUIDE ♀ Villa Maria Private Bin Sauvignon Blanc £26 • ♀ Casa La Joya Signature Merlot £28 • 60 bottles over £20, 10 bottles under £20 • 4 by the glass (£4.25)

PRICE GUIDE Fixed L £18-£22 • Fixed D £33-£40 • starter £8-£9.50 • main £17-£22.50 • dessert £8 • coffee £2.95 • min/water £3.50 • Service added but optional 12.50%

PLACE: This classy, country house hotel is set in 9 acres of mature woodland, including a walled Victorian garden. Arty silver and gold pictures, high-backed black leather chairs and polite service from French staff create an upmarket and slightly formal mood in the conservatory dining room.

FOOD: The separate brasserie has its own short menu but the more sophisticated offering in the Truffles dining room is the primary attraction. The ambitious, elaborate style shows a bold approach to matching flavours – ham hock risotto with Italian pea and white truffle foam, or blackened organic salmon, miso egg drop soup and seaweed dumplings.

OUR TIP: Spa facilities are very popular

Chef: Richard Cameron **Owners:** Utopia Leisure **Times:** 12-2.30/7-9.30, closed L Sat **Notes:** Vegetarian available, Dress Restrictions, No shorts,

continued

T-shirts, trainers, Civ Wed 120 **Seats:** 100, Pr/dining room 150 **Smoking:** N/Sm in restaurant **Children:** Menu, Portions **Rooms:** 38 (38 en suite) ★★★★ **Directions:** M25 junct 3, take B2173 towards Swanley, then B258 towards Hextable. Straight on at 3 rdbts. Hotel 1.5m on left **Parking:** 200 **e-mail:** admin@rowhillgrange.com **web:** www.rowhillgrange.com

---

DEAL MAP 07 TR35

ⓖⓖ Dunkerleys Hotel

Modern British

Accomplished seaside cuisine

☎ 01304 375016   19 Beach St CT14 7AH

MENU GUIDE Crab bisque • Wild Atlantic halibut casseroled with ceps, shallots, garlic • Plum & apple crumble, crème anglaise

WINE GUIDE ♀ Côte du Roussillon Syrah £11.50 • ♀ Côte du Roussillon Maccabeu Grenache Blanc £11.50 • 20 bottles over £20, 35 bottles under £20 • 8 by the glass (£2.75-£5.50)

PRICE GUIDE Fixed L £10.95 • Fixed D £21.95-£25 • starter £5.50-£9.95 • main £14.50-£24.95 • dessert £4.95-£7.95 • coffee £1.95 • min/water £3.25 • Service optional

PLACE: Top notch seafood restaurant housed in a smartly presented Edwardian house set opposite Deal's historic pier. Sink into a comfy leather sofa for a pre-dinner drink in the bar and then move through to the brightly-coloured restaurant decorated with local art.

FOOD: Top quality fresh fish, perfectly cooked and complemented by accomplished sauces. Mains might include sea bass with mash and asparagus, as well as meatier fare: duck with a red wine jus perhaps, or pork belly on cider soaked red cabbage. Good choice of wines by the glass and bottle.

OUR TIP: Pianist plays every evening except Saturday

Chef: Ian Dunkerley **Owners:** Ian Dunkerley & Linda Dunkerley **Times:** 12-2.30/7-9.30, Closed L Mon **Notes:** Sun L 2 courses £10.95, 3 courses £13.95, Vegetarian available, Dress Restrictions, Smart casual preferred **Seats:** 50 **Smoking:** N/Sm in restaurant, Air con **Children:** Portions **Rooms:** 16 (16 en suite) ★★★ **Directions:** Turn off A2 onto A258 to Deal - situated 100yds before Deal Pier **Parking:** Public car park **e-mail:** dunkerleysofdeal@btinternet.com **web:** www.dunkerleys.co.uk

---

DOVER MAP 07 TR34

ⓖⓖ Wallet's Court

British

Historic manor not far from the White Cliffs

☎ 01304 852424   West Cliffe, St Margarets-at-Cliffe CT15 6EW

MENU GUIDE Wood pigeon Tatin • Cod, tempura vegetables • Blackcurrant tart, blackcurrant coulis

continued

DOVER *continued* MAP 07 TR34

WINE GUIDE ♀ E Guigal Côtes du Rhone £14.95 • ♦ Torres Sauvignon Blanc £14.95 • 40 bottles over £20, 40 bottles under £20 • 16 by the glass (£4.25-£7.50)

PRICE GUIDE Fixed L £17.50 • Fixed D £35 • coffee £2.50 min/water £3 • Service optional • Group min 8 service 10%

PLACE: Based around a lovely Jacobean manor, this family run, country-house hotel set in pretty gardens, has a homely feel and plenty of charm and character. At its heart, the oak-beamed dining room features pillars that date back to 1627. Original art hangs on the walls, tables are clothed in white linen and, in the evenings, there's subtle candlelight and the glow of an open fire.
FOOD: The modern British cooking is fashionably influenced by global trends and based around locally sourced and organic raw materials on appealing, seasonal-changing, fixed-price menus.
OUR TIP: Good-value set lunch, and good choice of wines by glass **Chef:** Stephen Harvey **Owners:** Gavin Oakley **Times:** 12-2/7-9, Closed 25-26 Dec, closed L Mon **Notes:** Vegetarian available, **Seats:** 60, Pr/dining room 40 **Smoking:** N/Sm in restaurant **Children:** Menu, Portions **Rooms:** 16 (16 en suite) ★★★ **Directions:** M2/A2 or M20/A20, follow signs for Deal (A258), 1st right for St Margaret's at Cliffe. Restaurant 1m on right **Parking:** 50 **e-mail:** dine@wallettscourt.com **web:** www.wallettscourt.com

EDENBRIDGE MAP 06 TQ44

⑧ Haxted Mill & Riverside Brasserie
British, Mediterranean 🐟
Riverside brasserie in the Eden Valley
☎ 01732 862914 Haxted Rd TN8 6PU

MENU GUIDE Crab cakes, coriander & red chilli sauce • Roast saddle of hare, rich game sauce • Hazelnut parfait, blackcurrant compote

PRICE GUIDE Food prices not confirmed for 2006, Please telephone for details

PLACE: The restaurant is located in converted stables next to the old watermill, which is still in working order. Enter through the ground floor bar to the beamed, first floor restaurant. The terrace overlooking the millpond is popular for summer use.
FOOD: Using fresh, seasonal ingredients, an evolving list of dishes is offered from the carte, with European influences, and an emphasis on fresh fish, seafood and game.
OUR TIP: Regular live jazz events
Chef: David Peek, Olivier Bontnemeux **Owners:** David & Linda Peek
Times: 12-2/7-9, Closed 23 Dec-6 Jan, Mon-Tue, closed D Sun
Notes: Vegetarian by request only, Smart Dress **Seats:** 42
Smoking: N/Sm in restaurant **Directions:** M25 junct 6, A22 towards East Grinstead. Through Blindley Heath and after Texaco garage left at lights. 1m take 1st left after Red Barn PH. 2m to Haxted Mill **Parking:** 100
e-mail: david@haxtedmill.co.uk **web:** www.haxtedmill.co.uk

FAVERSHAM MAP 07 TR06

  Read's Restaurant *see page 215*

FOLKESTONE MAP 07 TR23

⑧ Sandgate Hotel
International, British 🐟▷**NEW**
Confident cooking in a contemporary seaside setting
☎ 01303 220444 The Esplanade, Sandgate CT20 3D▼

MENU GUIDE Ravioli of Dungeness crab • Knuckle of slow-cooked lamb • Orange & Grand Marnier pancakes

WINE GUIDE ♀ Laroche Petit Chablis £25 • ♦ Castillo Clavijo Rioja Reserva £22 • 13 bottles over £20, 12 bottles under £20 6 by the glass (£11-£48)

PRICE GUIDE Fixed L fr £15 • starter £3-£7.50 • main £12-£15.50 • dessert £6 • coffee £1.30 • min/water £3 • Service optional • Group min 20 service 10%

PLACE: An understated contemporary feel in the dining room comes from the tan suede chairs, beech tables, beige carpet and light fawn walls; though this smart beachside hotel dates from Victorian times. In summer, doors open onto the terrace.
FOOD: Quality produce is simply cooked, and gently spiced up with full-flavoured sauces. Honest menu descriptions are delivered without unwanted surprises or embellishments.
OUR TIP: Lovely for alfresco dining on hot days
Chef: Stephen Piddock **Owners:** Lois & Peter Hamilton-Slade
Times: 12-3/6-10, Closed Xmas, Boxing Day, New Year's Day
Notes: Vegetarian available, Smart Dress, Civ Wed 50 **Seats:** 32
Children: Portions **Directions:** 2m from junct 12 on M20 to London
Parking: 3 **e-mail:** info@sandgatehotel.com
web: www.sandgatehotel.com

HYTHE MAP 07 TR13

⑧ The Hythe Imperial Hotel
British, European
Elegant Victorian hotel with a smart restaurant
☎ 01303 267441 The Mews, Prince's Pde CT21 6AQ

MENU GUIDE Mosaic of game terrine, peach schnapps chutney • Fondants of venison loin, sauce Grand Veneur • Hazelnut Bavarois

WINE GUIDE ♀ Hardys Chardonnay Semillon £16.25 • ♦ Hardys Shiraz Cabernet £16.25 • 65 bottles over £20 35 bottles under £20 • 12 by the glass (£4.10-£7.85)

PRICE GUIDE Fixed L £17.50 • Fixed D £30 • starter £8-£12.95 • main £21-£29 • dessert £6-£8.50 • coffee £2.95 • min/water £3.50 • Service included

PLACE: Surrounded by fifty acres of golf course, there's much to recommend at this smart seaside hotel: superb indoor and outdoor leisure facilities, treatment rooms, a hairdressers and, not least, a plush restaurant with views over the Channel.
FOOD: The sense of luxury extends to the menu, where seared tranche of goose foie gras starter might be followed by an inventive cannon of lamb and braised shoulder with Venezuelan chocolate ju▼
OUR TIP: Food is served in the bars and lounges too
Chef: Richard Yearnshire **Owners:** Marston Hotels **Times:** 12.30-2/7-9.30, Closed L Sat (ex Bistro) **Notes:** Vegetarian available, Smart casual, no jeans, no sport shoes, Civ Wed 100 **Seats:** 200, Pr/dining room 60
Smoking: N/Sm in restaurant, Air con **Children:** Menu, Portions
Rooms: 100 (100 en suite) ★★★★ **Directions:** M20 junct 11/A261 to Hythe signs to Folkestone, right into the Twiss Road to hotel
Parking: 200 **e-mail:** hytheimperial@marstonhotels.com
web: www.marstonhotels.com

AVERSHAM MAP 07 TR06

Read's Restaurant

British

Classical cuisine in immaculate setting

☎ 01795 535344 Macknade Manor, Canterbury Rd
E13 8XE

MENU GUIDE Crab & smoked salmon roulade, horseradish cream • Lamb, hot-pot potatoes, braised onions, rosemary jus • Calvados pannacotta

WINE GUIDE ♀ Louis Latour Chardonnay £16 • ♀ Georges Duboeuf Beaujolais Fleurie £22 • 220 bottles over £20, 60 bottles under £20 • 8 by the glass (£4-£8)

PRICE GUIDE Fixed L £21 • Fixed D £45 • coffee £2.50 • min/water £3 • Service optional

PLACE: This rather grand Georgian manor is set in beautiful grounds on the outskirts of Faversham. Immaculate inside and out, it's a haven of taste with six individually designed bedrooms furnished in period style. Take a seat in the elegant drawing room to read the menu and enjoy a pre-dinner drink and nibbles, and then move through to the restaurant, a grand and spacious room with well-spaced and elegantly clothed tables.

FOOD: Eschewing adventure in favour of tradition, Read's delivers classical cuisine of the highest order with modern interpretations, drawing its first-rate ingredients from the local area and the hotel's own walled kitchen gardens. Dinner is a more elaborate affair than lunch and features a seven-course tasting menu in addition to the carte: you might start with a hot cheddar soufflé on a bed of smoked haddock, before trying oxtail braised in Madeira wine, or roast chicken served with spinach and wild mushrooms.

OUR TIP: Handy for the A2 and local motorway connections
Chef: David Pitchford **Owners:** David & Rona Pitchford **Times:** 12-2.30/7-10, Closed BHs, Sun, Mon **Notes:** Tasting menu (Tue-Sat) £45, Vegetarian available, Dress Restrictions, Smart casual, Civ Wed 60 **Seats:** 40, Pr/dining room 30 **Smoking:** No pipes, No cigars **Children:** Portions **Directions:** From M2 junct 6 follow A251 towards Faversham. At T-junct with A2 (Canterbury road) turn right. Hotel 0.5m on right **Parking:** 30 **e-mail:** enquiries@reads.com **web:** www.reads.com

---

LENHAM MAP 07 TQ85

⊚⊚ Chilston Park Hotel

British, French

Stylish British cooking in romantic country house setting

☎ 01622 859803 Sandway ME17 2BE

MENU GUIDE Scallops, cauliflower purée, curry sauce • Lamb, dauphinoise potatoes, rosemary jus • White chocolate soufflé, lime sorbet

WINE GUIDE ♀ Laroche Chardonnay £19.50 • ♀ Laroche Cabernet Sauvignon £29.50 • 8 by the glass (£4.95-£8)

PRICE GUIDE Fixed L £10-£17.50 • Fixed D £38 • coffee £3.50 • min/water £4.25 • Service optional

PLACE: Chilston Park is a romantic place to dine: an elegant country house dating back to 1100, with a sunken, Venetian-style restaurant. Chandeliers and opulent drapes add a touch of luxury to the dining room, while elsewhere paintings and antiques abound.

FOOD: Stylish modern British cuisine with the odd French twist. Cooking is precise and not overly complicated, with dishes distinguished by flavourful combinations of quality seasonal produce. The menu changes every few days and is complemented by an informative drinks list that notes which styles of wine suit which dish.

OUR TIP: Take a stroll around the elegant gardens
Chef: Paul Sage **Owners:** Hand Picked hotels **Times:** 12-1.30/7-9.30, Closed L Sat **Notes:** Fixed D 2 courses, Vegetarian available, Civ Wed 90 **Seats:** 35, Pr/dining room 22 **Smoking:** N/Sm in restaurant **Children:** Menu, Portions **Rooms:** 53 (53 en suite) ★★★★ **Directions:** Telephone for directions. **Parking:** 100 **e-mail:** chilstonpark@handpicked.co.uk **web:** www.handpicked.co.uk/chilstonpark

---

MAIDSTONE MAP 07 TQ75

⊚ Marriott Tudor Park Hotel & Country Club

British

Country hotel with formal or brasserie dining

☎ 01622 734334 Ashford Rd, Bearsted ME14 4NQ

MENU GUIDE Smoked venison, plum compote • Grilled calves' liver, crisp bacon • Rice pudding, pineapple compote

WINE GUIDE ♀ Corte Vigna Pinot Grigio £16.35 • ♀ Côte du Rhone £16.25 • 35 bottles over £20, 30 bottles under £20 • 17 by the glass (£5.10-£7.35)

continued

continued

MAIDSTONE *continued* MAP 07 TQ75

PRICE GUIDE Fixed L £15.95-£19.95 • Fixed D £25 • starter £5.50-£7.50 • main £15.50-£18 • dessert £5.50-£6.50 • coffee £2.20 • min/water £2.95 • Service optional

PLACE: This fine country hotel offers a choice of settings for dining. The Fairviews Restaurant has impressive views over the championship golf course and traditional table service. The Long Weekend brasserie is less formal venue providing coffee and meals throughout the day.

FOOD: Modern British with the occasional continental accent. Menus include a good choice of meat, fish and seasonal game dishes as well as some tempting vegetarian options.

OUR TIP: Make use of the lavish leisure facilities

Chef: Mark Jordan **Owners:** Marriott Group/Whitbread Hotels Ltd **Times:** 12.30-2/7-9.30, Closed 1st 2 wks Jan, closed L Sat **Notes:** Vegetarian available, Smart Dress **Seats:** 90, Pr/dining room 170 **Smoking:** N/Sm in restaurant **Children:** Menu, Portions **Rooms:** 120 (120 en suite) ★★★★ **Directions:** Telephone for directions **Parking:** 400 **e-mail:** salesadmin.tudorpark@marriotthotels.co.uk **web:** www.marriotthotels.co.uk

SEVENOAKS MAP 06 TQ55

⑯⑯ Greggs Restaurant

Modern European   NEW

Popular high street restaurant with charming hands-on owners

☎ 01732 456373 28-30 High St TN13 1HX

MENU GUIDE Guinea fowl & ham terrine, prunes, sourdough bread • Baked sea bream, carrot purée, risotto cake • Nougat & pistachio parfait

WINE GUIDE ♀ Macon Lugny Latour £19 • ♥ Step Road Shiraz £22 • 15 bottles over £20, 10 bottles under £20 • 4 by the glass (£3-£6.50)

PRICE GUIDE Fixed L £9.95-£11.95 • Fixed D £19.95-£25 • starter £4.50-£9 • main £13.50-£17 • dessert £5-£6 • coffee £1.50 • min/water £3.50 • Service added but optional 12%

continued

PLACE: Grade II listed building at the top of the High Street with a triple bay window frontage. Built in 1650 as a gracious residence and previously converted to a coffee house, it makes a fine restaurant with a clean modern interior including a small bar area. The atmosphere is relaxed and informal with service admirably led by the patron.

FOOD: Cooking is straightforward, sticking mainly to tried and tested combinations, with European overtones to some of the dishes. Presentation is simple and honest.

OUR TIP: The lunch menu offers great value

Chef: Gavin Gregg, Sebastian Gougeon **Owners:** Gavin & Lucinda Gregg **Times:** 12-2.30/6.30-9.30, Closed 25-26 Dec, 1st week Jan, Mon, closed Sun **Notes:** Tasting menu £35-£45, Vegetarian available, Smart Dress **Seats:** 50, Pr/dining room 28 **Smoking:** N/Sm in restaurant, Air con **Children:** Portions **Directions:** 1m from Sevenoaks train station. 500yd from top of town centre towards Tonbridge on left. **Parking:** Town cent **web:** www.greggsrestaurant.com

SISSINGHURST MAP 07 TQ73

⑯ Rankins

British, Mediterranean

Bistro-style dining in a comfortable setting with a friendly atmosphere

☎ 01580 713964 The Street TN17 2JH

MENU GUIDE Leek & onion soup with chorizo • Lamb noisettes, thyme & orange sauce • Lemon, cinnamon & ginger tart

WINE GUIDE ♀ Pabiot Pouilly Fumé Sauvignon Blanc £23.50 • ♥ Sichel Château la Nauve St Emilion Cabernet Sauvignon £21 10 bottles over £20, 14 bottles under £20 • 2 by the glass (£4)

PRICE GUIDE Fixed L £21 • Fixed D £29.50 • coffee £2.75 • min/water £2.60 • Service optional

PLACE: This charming weatherboarded building has an attractive dining room with a cosy, homely feel. The exposed wooden beams and interesting collection of artworks add character. Mrs Rankin is a friendly hostess.

FOOD: Quality ingredients carefully cooked in an elaborate but unpretentious style with a contemporary twist, as in hot gratin of monkfish, sea bass and crab.

OUR TIP: Handy for Sissinghurst Castle Gardens

Chef: Hugh Rankin **Owners:** Hugh & Leonora Rankin **Times:** 12.30-2/7.30-9, Closed BHs, Mon, Tue, closed L Wed-Sat, closed D Sun **Notes:** Vegetarian available **Seats:** 25 **Smoking:** N/Sm in restaurant **Children:** Portions **Directions:** Village centre, on A262 **Parking:** On street **web:** www.rankinsrestaurant.com

SITTINGBOURNE MAP 07 TQ96

⑯ Lakes Restaurant

British, French

Elegant Victorian indulgence

☎ 01795 428020 Hempstead House Country Hotel, London Rd, Bapchild ME9 9PP

MENU GUIDE Sauté of scallop & king prawns • Roast fillet of beef in bacon, wild mushroom Madeira sauce • Lime & ginger mousse on a lemon biscuit

WINE GUIDE ♀ Jaques Cap de Moklin Château Roudier Merlot £24 • ♥ William Fevre Chablis Chardonnay £20 • 22 bottles over £20, 44 bottles under £20 • 3 by the glass (£2.95-£3.95)

PRICE GUIDE Fixed L £10-£15 • Fixed D £24.50 • starter £5.95-£8.50 • main £16.95-£22.50 • dessert £6.50 • coffee £3 • min/water £3 • Service included

continue

England

Lakes Restaurant

PLACE: This charming Victorian mansion, built in 1850, makes an elegant destination for an evening meal with its beautifully furnished lounges, classical decor, Gothic columns, drapes and crystal chandeliers.
FOOD: Accomplished British and French fare is presented in contemporary style using seasonal and locally sourced ingredients whenever possible. Extensive wine list, with a reasonable choice by the glass.
OUR TIP: There's a fully trained wine waiter
Chef: Matthew Levett **Owners:** Mr & Mrs A J Holdstock **Times:** 12-2.30/7-10.00 **Notes:** Sun L £16.50, Vegetarian available, Dress Restrictions, Smart casual, Civ Wed 150 **Seats:** 70, Pr/dining room 50 **Smoking:** N/Sm in restaurant **Children:** Portions **Rooms:** 27 (27 en suite) ★★★ **Directions:** On A2 1.5m E of Sittingbourne **Parking:** 100 **e-mail:** lakes@hempsteadhouse.co.uk
web: www.hempsteadhouse.co.uk/lakes

TUNBRIDGE WELLS (ROYAL) MAP 06 TQ53
 Hotel du Vin & Bistro
British, Mediterranean
Elegant bistro in stylish town house
☎ 01892 526455 Crescent Rd TN1 2LY
MENU GUIDE Foie gras & chicken liver parfait • Loin of venison, choucroûte & red wine jus • Lemon & raspberry posset
PRICE GUIDE Starter £4.50-£8 • main £13.50-£16.50 • dessert £6.75 • coffee £2.75 • min/water £3 • Service optional • Group min 14 service 10%
PLACE: This impressive Grade II listed building dates from 1762 and lists past guests as grand as Queen Victoria, who often stayed here. Now a contemporary boutique hotel close to the centre of town, the tastefully designed bar and bistro is a destination dining venue in its own right.
FOOD: Well-honed, contemporary cooking brings together a tantalising balance between modern dishes and simple classics: seared duck foie gras, pear Tatin with limoncello sauce, perhaps, followed by Châteaubriand for two with sauce béarnaise and pommes frites.

continued

OUR TIP: Exceptional wine list
Chef: Matt Green Armytage **Owners:** Hotel du Vin Ltd **Times:** 12-1.45/7-9.45, Closed L 31 Dec **Notes:** Sun L £24.50, Vegetarian available **Seats:** 80, Pr/dining room 80 **Smoking:** N/Sm in restaurant **Children:** Menu, Portions **Rooms:** 35 (35 en suite) ★★★★ **Directions:** Telephone for directions **Parking:** 30 **e-mail:** info@tunbridgewells.hotelduvin.com
web: www.hotelduvin.com

⊛⊛ Right on the Green
British
Intimate dining in a warm, friendly atmosphere
☎ 01892 513161 15A Church Rd, Southborough TN4 0RX
MENU GUIDE Twice baked goats' cheese soufflé • Fillet of sea bass, green tomato Tatin • Marinated clementines, mandarin sorbet
WINE GUIDE ♀ Maison Auvigue Macon Villages Chardonnay £22 • ♀ Louis Latour Domaine Valmoisine Pinot Noir £24 12 bottles over £20, 5 bottles under £20 • 6 by the glass (£4.50-£6.50)
PRICE GUIDE Fixed L £12.50 • starter £5.50-£9.50 • main £16-£19 • dessert £5-£6.50 • coffee £3 • min/water £3 • Service optional
PLACE: With its soft jazz and candlelight, this light and airy restaurant makes a great romantic dinner destination. Formal table service is provided by relaxed and attentive staff.
FOOD: Expect a seasonal modern British menu with the emphasis on quality local ingredients and simplicity of style, as in dishes of baked cod with tomato, chorizo and onion, or shepherd's pie and mashed neeps.
OUR TIP: Pretty views across the green
Chef: Adrian Martin **Owners:** Adrian & Erica Martin **Times:** 12-2/7-11, Closed 25-26 Dec, 1 Jan, Mon, closed L Mon & Sat, closed D Sun **Notes:** Sun lunch, 2courses £15, 3 courses £17.50, Vegetarian available **Seats:** 32, Pr/dining room 16 **Smoking:** N/Sm in restaurant **Directions:** A26 towards Tunbridge Wells next to Henry Baines antique shop. **e-mail:** info@rightonthegreen.co.uk
web: www.rightonthegreen.co.uk

⊛ The Spa Hotel
British
An imposing setting for fine dining
☎ 01892 520331 Mount Ephraim TN4 8XJ

MENU GUIDE Goose liver terrine, Sauternes jelly, toasted fig & raisin bread • Dover sole with lemon butter • Sticky toffee pudding

continued

TUNBRIDGE WELLS (ROYAL) *continued* MAP 06 TQ53

WINE GUIDE ♀ Louis Latour Chardonnay £14.75 • ♥ Baron Philippe De Rothschild Merlot £12.75 • 70 bottles over £20, 40 bottles under £20 • 18 by the glass (£2.75-£9)

PRICE GUIDE Fixed L £15-£19.50 • Fixed D £29-£34 • starter £6.75-£12.25 • main £15.50-£19.75 • dessert £5-£6 • coffee £2 • min/water £3 • Service included

PLACE: Just the place for a special celebration, the restaurant of this Georgian country house is a spacious, elegant affair decked out with sparkling chandeliers, fresh cut flowers and quality tableware.

FOOD: A broad selection rooted in classical French and traditional British cuisines. Offerings range from chargrilled steaks and simple fish dishes, to more complex fare: locally shot wild mallard perhaps, or crispy pork belly with black pudding and bubble and squeak.

OUR TIP: Excellent leisure facilities

Chef: Steve Cole **Owners:** Richard Goring **Times:** 12.30-2/7-9.30, Closed L Sat **Notes:** Sun L £21.95, Vegetarian available, Dress Restrictions, No jeans or T-shirts, Civ Wed 200 **Seats:** 80, Pr/dining room 250
Smoking: N/Sm in restaurant **Children:** Menu, Portions **Rooms:** 69 (69 en suite) ★★★★ **Directions:** On A264 leaving Tunbridge Wells towards East Grinstead **Parking:** 140
e-mail: info@spahotel.co.uk
web: www.spahotel.co.uk

 **Thackeray's** *see below*

WEST MALLING MAP 06 TQ65

❁❁ The Swan

British

Brasserie cooking in ancient yet modern setting

☎ 01732 521910 35 Swan St ME19 6JU

MENU GUIDE Spinach & Slipscote cheese tart • Pork Wellington celeriac mash • Roast nectarines, lemon mousse

WINE GUIDE 40 bottles over £20, 30 bottles under £20 • 12 by the glass (£3.25-£6.50)

PRICE GUIDE Starter £5-£6 • main £10-£14 • dessert £5 • coffee £2 • min/water £3.75 • Service added but optional 12.5%

PLACE: Soft, neutral colours, bare wooden floors, tables and beams provide a contemporary yet appropriate setting for dining at this inn which dates back to 15th century. Cushioned banquette seating, low lighting and candles create an intimate ambience made more enjoyable by enthusiastic staff. Alfresco dining is an option under canopies and terrace heaters.

FOOD: British brasserie dishes with French influences are produced with care and an attention to detail which makes crab linguine with sorrel sauce, confit Gressingham duck with potato rissoles and Hawkhurst Bramley apple crumble with custard all the more enjoyable.

OUR TIP: Explore this picturesque and historic village

Chef: P Denham, C Reeves **Owners:** Fishbone Ltd **Times:** 12-3.15/6-11.15, Closed 26 Dec, 1 Jan **Notes:** Sun 2 courses £16, 3 courses £18, Vegetarian available, Smart Dress, Civ Wed 100 **Seats:** 90, Pr/dining room 20 **Smoking:** N/Sm in restaurant, Air con **Children:** Menu, Portions
Directions: M20 junct 4 follow signs for West Malling **Parking:** Long-stay car park **e-mail:** fishboneltd@aol.com
web: www.theswanwestmalling.co.uk

TUNBRIDGE WELLS (ROYAL) MAP 06 TQ53

Thackeray's

Modern French 🐟

Inventive, contemporary cuisine in chic eaterie

☎ 01892 511921 TN1 1EA

MENU GUIDE Foie gras trio, fig chutney, brioche • Marinated pork 'three ways', pomme fondant, apple & sage purée, red wine jus • Raspberry soufflé, raspberry sorbet

WINE GUIDE ♀ Domaine Marie Berangere Chablis £26.95 • ♥ Château la Nauve St Emilion £24 • 160 bottles over £20, 16 bottles under £20 • 20 by the glass (£3.75-£21.20)

PRICE GUIDE Fixed L £12.95 • starter £8.95-£13.95 • main £15.95-£24.50 • dessert £8.95 • coffee £3.75 • min/water £3.50 • Service added but optional 12.5%

PLACE: Chocolate suede banquettes, cream tub chairs, warm neutral tones, wooden floors, glass and mirror panels and modern artwork offer that stylish, minimal edge; erstwhile owner, novelist William Makepeace Thackeray, would never recognize the place. The handsome building dates back to 1660.

FOOD: In tune with the sleek surroundings, the cooking is modern and imaginative, the kitchen classically schooled and producing exciting, and complexly presented dishes that utilize quality ingredients with assured attention to detail.

OUR TIP: Japanese terrace garden for alfresco dining

Chef: Richard Phillips **Owners:** Richard Phillips **Times:** 12-2.30/6.30-10.30, Closed Mon, D Sun **Notes:** Tasting Menu 7 courses £55, Sun lunc £24.50, Vegetarian available, Smart Dress **Seats:** 54, Pr/dining room 16
Smoking: N/Sm, Air con **Directions:** A21/A26, Southborough towards Tunbridge. On left 500yds after hospital **Parking:** NCP, on st in eve
e-mail: reservations@thackeraysrestaurant.co.uk
web: www.thackerays-restaurant.co.uk

WHITSTABLE MAP 07 TR16

Crab & Winkle Seafood Restaurant

Seafood ⌦NEW

Enjoyable fish dining straight from the harbour

☎ 01227 779377 South Quay, The Harbour CT5 1AB

MENU GUIDE Half dozen Whitstable Bay rock oysters, Merlot shallot vinegar • Natural smoked haddock on a cheese potato cake, baby leeks, poached egg, wholegrain mustard cream • Vanilla crème brulee with raspberry coulis

WINE GUIDE ⚲ House Cuvée Select £10.95 • ♀ House Cuvée Select £10.95 • 19 bottles over £20, 28 bottles under £20 • 6 by the glass (£2.95-£5.95)

PRICE GUIDE Starter £4.95-£9.95 • main £9.95-£33 • dessert £4.50-£6.50 • coffee £1.50 • min/water £2.95 • Service optional • Group min 8 service 10%

PLACE: Situated above Whitstable's fish market on the quay overlooking the harbour, this restaurant has a light and airy modern feel, with jazzy music and a casual, buzzy atmosphere. Informal but professional service from a young team.

FOOD: In a location like this, naturally it's an almost entirely fish based menu. There are well executed simple fish dishes interspersed with some more complex modern ideas, all with an emphasis on fresh local produce. The menu changes according to what's been landed that day. You can see for yourself where the fish has come from, and buy some if you want to. (Diners get a 10% discount!)

OUR TIP: Get a seat on the balcony in warm weather
Chef: Joanne Montier & Paul Weaver **Owners:** Andrew & Victoria Bennett **Times:** 11.30-6/6-9, Closed D Sun (Nov-Jan) **Notes:** Vegetarian available **Seats:** 72 **Smoking:** N/Sm in restaurant, Air con **Children:** Menu, Portions **Parking:** Gorrel Tank Car Park **e-mail:** www.seafood-restaurant-uk.com/contact-us.html **web:** www.seafood-restaurant-uk.com

The Sportsman

Modern British **NEW**

Rustic gastro-pub serving superb fresh fish

☎ 01227 273370 Faversham Rd CT5 4BP

MENU GUIDE Oysters with hot chorizo • Braised brill fillet, wine & morels • Chocolate tart, orange ice cream

PRICE GUIDE Food prices not confirmed for 2006. Please telephone for details

PLACE: Stripped floors, scrubbed pine tables and cream painted tongue and groove panelling add up to a cosily rustic interior for this unpretentious gastro-pub with glorious views over the surrounding marshes.

FOOD: Fresh fish is the name of the game, from home-smoked eel with soda bread, to baked cod with mussel tartare and Savoy cabbage.

OUR TIP: Booking is advised, especially in summer
Times: 12-3/6-11

WYE MAP 07 TR04

Wife of Bath Restaurant

British, French 🚜

Notable village restaurant

☎ 01233 812540 4 Upper Bridge St TN25 5AF

MENU GUIDE Pumpkin & pine nut risotto • Roast lamb loin, provençale vegetables • Brown bread ice cream

WINE GUIDE ⚲ Chablis Domaine J P Ellevin £27 • ♀ Chorey Les Beaunes Domaine Maillard £31 • 68 bottles over £20, 16 bottles under £20 • 2 by the glass (£3.50)

PRICE GUIDE Fixed L £15 • Fixed D £24.50 • starter £6-£13.50 • main £19.50-£23.50 • dessert £7-£8 • coffee £2.80 • min/water £3 • Group min 8 service 10%

PLACE: A traditional restaurant with understated and modest decor, with neutral hues and flagstone floors. Once the local doctor's house, this 18th-century, timber-framed building occupies a prominent position on the town's main street.

FOOD: Cooking is in the modern French style with good use of local, fresh ingredients. Consistently high standards of food have attracted a good local following. Expect well-prepared dishes of game in season such as partridge as well as flavoursome, matured Charolais beef.

OUR TIP: Look out for trout in the nearby River Stour
Chef: Robert Hymers **Owners:** Andrew & Nicola Fraser **Times:** 12-1.30/7-9.30, Closed 2 wks from 25 Dec, 2 wks from mid August, Sun & Mon **Notes:** Vegetarian available **Seats:** 50 **Smoking:** N/Sm in restaurant **Directions:** Just off A28 Ashford to Canterbury Rd **Parking:** 18 **e-mail:** reservations@wifeofbath.com **web:** www.wifeofbath.com

Give us your views! All the rosetted restaurants in this guide have been visited by one of the AA's team of professional inspectors, but we want to hear from you! Use the report forms in the back of the guide or email us at lifestyleguides@theaa.com with your comments on any establishments featured or on the restaurants that you feel are worthy of an entry. We would also be pleased to receive your views on the guide itself and suggestions for information you would like to see included.

England

LANCASHIRE

BLACKBURN MAP 18 SD62

🏵 Clarion Hotel & Suites Foxfields

British

Contemporary hotel dining

☎ 01254 822556 Whalley Rd, Billington BB7 9HY

MENU GUIDE Chicken liver parfait • Pan-fried chicken breast with stilton and grapes • Chocolate torte

PRICE GUIDE Fixed L £9.95-£12.95 • Fixed D £19.95-£22.95 • starter £3.85-£5.95 • main £13.45-£18.95 • dessert £3.95-£4.95 • coffee £1.95 • min/water £3.50 • Service included

PLACE: Located in the heart of the Ribble Valley, this modern hotel and leisure club boasts a dining room with patio or balcony overlooking the spectacular Pendle Hill.

FOOD: The assured kitchen team isn't afraid of straying from its British roots, with deep-fried Cajun salmon sitting happily alongside fillet of beef stroganoff on the varied, well-balanced menus.

OUR TIP: Good leisure facilities

Chef: Gary Simm **Owners:** Choice Hotels Europe **Times:** 12/7, Closed L BHs (ex 25-26 Dec, 1 Jan) **Notes:** Vegetarian available, Smart Dress, Civ Wed 150 **Seats:** **Smoking:** N/Sm in restaurant **Children:** Menu, Portions **Rooms:** 44 (44 en suite) ★★★★ **Directions:** M6 junct 31, follow A59. Hotel is situated on A666 signposted Whalley **Parking:** 200 **e-mail:** enquiries@hotels-blackburn.com **web:** www.gb65.u-net.com

🏵🏵 The Millstone at Mellor

British

Enjoyable dining in rural village inn

☎ 01254 813333 Church Ln, Mellor BB2 7JR

MENU GUIDE Pressed chicken & black pudding terrine • Pendle lamb, bubble & squeak • Glazed lemon tart

WINE GUIDE ♀ Marco Felluga Pinot Grigio £21.95 • ♀ Domaine Berrod Fleurie Gamay £21.45 • 32 bottles over £20, 18 bottles under £20 • 21 by the glass (£2.55-£7.95)

PRICE GUIDE Fixed L £16.95 • Fixed D £25.95 • coffee £1.95 • min/water £3.40

PLACE: A classic coaching inn in a serene village setting. The robust stone-built exterior gives way to a warm and welcoming interior characterised by cosy fires in winter and period furniture including grandfather clocks. The busy restaurant has rich oak panelling and a relaxed and cheerful atmosphere along with helpful and friendly staff.

FOOD: Modern British dishes populate the menu where fresh, seasonal, local produce is used whenever possible, including the local delicacy, black pudding. Preparation is skilful and dishes are full of clear, strong flavours; pan-fried sea bass with spring onion champ and vermouth cream sauce being a good example.

OUR TIP: Good selection of English cheeses

Chef: Anson Bolton **Owners:** Shire Hotels Ltd **Times:** 12-2.15/6.30-9.15 **Notes:** Vegetarian available, Smart Dress, Civ Wed 60 **Seats:** 62, Pr/dining room 20 **Smoking:** N/Sm in restaurant **Children:** Menu, Portions **Rooms:** 23 (23 en suite) ★★ **Directions:** 4m from M6 junct 31 follow signs for Blackburn. Mellor is on right 1m after 1st set of traffic lights **Parking:** 45 **e-mail:** millstone@shireinns.co.uk **web:** www.shireinns.co.uk

BLACKPOOL MAP 18 SD33

🏵 Kwizeen

European

Contemporary oasis in the heart of Blackpool

☎ 01253 290045 47-49 Kings St FY1 3EJ

MENU GUIDE Sweet chilli beef bake • Pheasant breast, roasted root vegetables • Banana & toffee crumble, Drambuie ice cream

PRICE GUIDE Fixed L £5.95 • starter £4.75-£7.95 • main £11-£19.95 • dessert £3.95 • coffee £2 • min/water £3.50 • Service included

PLACE: Amidst the kitsch of Blackpool, this minimalist restaurant stands out. The pale wood and stainless steel interior maximises light, creating a clean, modern feel.

FOOD: Lots of effort and great ingredients in the bistro-style modern European menu result in some unusual and skilled dishes. Look out for the chef who is often seen mingling with the local foodies in the restaurant.

OUR TIP: Book one of the special gourmet nights

Chef: Marco Calle-Calatayud **Owners:** Marco Calle-Calatayud, Antony Beswick **Times:** 12-1.45/6, Closed 21 Feb-10 Mar, last wk Aug, Sun, close L Sat **Seats:** 40 **Smoking:** No pipes, No cigars **Directions:** From front of Blackpool Winter Gardens, 100yds to King St, and as road forks restaurant 30yds on left **Parking:** On street **e-mail:** info@kwizeen.co.uk **web:** www.kwizeen.co.uk

One Rosette Excellent local restaurants serving food prepared with care, understanding and skill, using good quality ingredients. These restaurants stand out in their local area. Of the total number of establishments with Rosettes around 50% have one Rosette.

ANCASTER MAP 18 SD46

Lancaster House Hotel

British 🍴

imple modern cooking accompanied by wonderful views

☎ 01524 844822 Green Ln, Ellel LA1 4GJ

MENU GUIDE Morecambe Bay potted shrimps • Pork, sage & pancetta mash, glazed apple, thyme reduction • Kahlua crème brûlée

WINE GUIDE ♀ Tyrrells Chardonnay £15.95 • ♀ Brown Bros Shiraz £17.50 • 15 bottles over £20, 38 bottles under £20 • 11 by the glass (£3.65-£6.30)

PRICE GUIDE Fixed L £15.95 • Fixed D £24.95 • coffee £2.25 • min/water £2.95 • Service included

PLACE: Excellent business and leisure facilities make this smart modern hotel a popular conference venue. It's peacefully set in rural surroundings close to the university, and has a bright contemporary restaurant.

FOOD: Simple and effective cooking with a pleasing emphasis on local ingredients; tuck into salmon with a dill sauce perhaps, or chicken with a cassoulet of wild mushrooms, and save room for top-notch puds such as white chocolate and orange blossom cheesecake.

OUR TIP: Lighter bar menu available

Chef: Mick Heaton **Owners:** English Lakes Hotels **Times:** 12.30-2/7-30 **Notes:** Sun L 3 courses (incl. coffee) £14.95, Vegetarian available, ♀ Wed 100 **Seats:** 82, Pr/dining room 160 **Smoking:** N/Sm in restaurant, Air con **Children:** Menu **Rooms:** 80 (80 en suite) ★★★★ **Directions:** 3m from Lancaster city centre. From S M6 junct 33, head towards Lancaster. Continue through Galgate village, and turn left up Green Ln just before Lancaster University **Parking:** 140 **e-mail:** lancaster@elhmail.co.uk **web:** www.elh.co.uk/hotels/lancaster

ANGHO MAP 18 SD73

Northcote Manor see page 222

ONGRIDGE MAP 18 SD63

The Longridge Restaurant

see page 223

Two Rosettes The best local restaurants, which aim for and achieve higher standards, better consistency and where a greater precision is apparent in the cooking. There will be obvious attention to the selection of quality ingredients. About 40% of restaurants in the guide have two Rosettes.

Three Rosettes Outstanding restaurants that demand recognition well beyond their local area. Timing, seasoning and the judgement of flavour combinations will be consistently excellent, supported by other elements such as intelligent service and a well-chosen wine list. Around 10% of restaurants with Rosettes have been awarded three.

LYTHAM ST ANNES MAP 18 SD32

Chicory

Modern European 🍴

Vibrant restaurant and cocktail bar

☎ 01253 737111 5 Henry St FY8 5LE

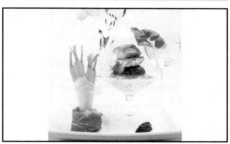

MENU GUIDE Thai seafood casserole • Chargrilled venison medallions, brie & mushroom parcel, mulled wine sauce • Glazed lemon tart

WINE GUIDE ♀ Valle Andino Chardonnay £11.95 • ♀ Stonefish Shiraz £14.95 • 29 bottles over £20, 28 bottles under £20 • 19 by the glass (£2.65-£7.95)

PRICE GUIDE Fixed D fr £17.95 • starter £4.15-£8.95 • main £14.95-£22.95 • dessert fr £4.95 • coffee £1.65 • min/water £2.95 • Service optional

PLACE: Rich Mediterranean colours - terracotta, yellow and burnt orange - give this lively restaurant a continental feel. The large room is divided by banquette seating to create intimate areas, and it's a fun place with loud music and plenty of atmosphere.

FOOD: Chicory is owned by four partners, three cooking and one out front. The modern European cooking is ambitious and imaginative, offering plenty of choice and good value for money.

OUR TIP: Visit nearby Sweet Chicory for chocolates and deli foods

Chef: G Cartwright, F Santoni, R Martin **Owners:** B Middleton, G Cartwright, F Santoni & R Martin **Times:** 12-2/6-9.30, Closed 25 Dec, 1 Jan **Notes:** Sun L (3 courses) £17.95, Vegetarian available, Dress Restrictions, Smart Casual **Seats:** 70 **Smoking:** N/Sm area, No pipes, No cigars, Air con **Children:** Menu, Portions **Directions:** In Lytham town centre, behind Clifton Arms Hotel **Parking:** On street

LANGHO MAP 18 SD73

Northcote Manor

Modern British *A powerhouse of regional British gastronomy*
☎ 01254 240555 Northcote Rd BB6 8BE
e-mail: sales@northcotemanor.com
web: www.northcotemanor.com

PLACE: Northcote's modern, minimalistic, softly lit dining room and striking display of local contemporary art, contras sharply with the Edwardian wood panelling of the rest of the house. The room is spacious, light and airy with a conservatory front that allows splendid views over the organic garden, from where many of the herbs, salads and vegetables are used in season. Crisp white linen, fine wines (some 450 bins) and formal, professional service all hit th mark. (The exciting refurbishment of the hotel is scheduled for completed by mid 2006.)
FOOD: Chef-patron Nigel Haworth creates an exciting menu that has its roots firmly in Lancashire, making the most o the fabulous produce available in the North West. Cooking is intelligently simple and crisp, with clear emphasis on the freshness and quality of seasonal produce, and oozes skill and finesse. Stunning modern dishes deliver true Lancashir *terroir*; think braised shin of heather-fed Bowland lamb with pan-roast liver, purée potatoes and black cabbage, or melting ginger parkin with Simpson's iced double cream and caramel custard. Outstanding breads and superb petits fours hold form to the end.

MENU GUIDE Southport shrimp organic porridge, tomato relish • Monkfish fillet, cockles, salsify fritter, butter bean velouté • Eccles cake soufflé, orange peel & tea ice cream

WINE GUIDE ♀ Marsanne Domaine des Fontaines Vin Pays d'Oc £16.75 • ♀ Tempranillo, Bodegas, Sonsierra £17.50 • 271 bottles over £20, 30 bottles under £20 • 10 by the glass (£4.30-£9.75)

PRICE GUIDE Starter £8.25-£15.50 • main £21-£26.95 • dessert £7.50-£9.50 • coffee £2.50 • min/water £3.75 • Service optional

OUR TIP: Without doubt one of the best displays of British cooking in the North West
Chef: Nigel Haworth, Matt Harris **Owners:** Nigel Haworth, Craig Bancroft **Times:** 12-2/7-9.30, Closed 25 Dec, 1-2 Jan, BH Mon
Notes: Fixed D 5 courses £50, 8 courses £70, Sun L 3 courses, Vegetarian available, Dress Restrictions, No jeans, Civ Wed 40
Seats: 80, Pr/dining room 40 **Smoking:** N/Sm in restaurant
Children: Menu, Portions **Rooms:** 14 (14 en suite) 🛏
Directions: From M6 junct 31 take A59, follow signs for Clitheroe. left at 1st traffic light, onto Skipton/Clitheroe Rd for 9m. left into Northcote Rd, hotel on right **Parking:** 60

ONGRIDGE MAP 18 SD63

The Longridge Restaurant

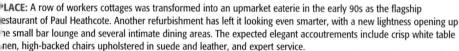

ritish *Strong cooking in stylish surroundings*

☎ 01772 784969   104-106 Higher Rd PR3 3SY

e-mail: longridge@heathcotes.co.uk

web: www.heathcotes.co.uk/longridge.htm

PLACE: A row of workers cottages was transformed into an upmarket eaterie in the early 90s as the flagship restaurant of Paul Heathcote. Another refurbishment has left it looking even smarter, with a new lightness opening up he small bar lounge and several intimate dining areas. The expected elegant accoutrements include crisp white table nen, high-backed chairs upholstered in suede and leather, and expert service.

OOD: The lengthy menu might suggest a rustic approach to cooking, but the food itself is quite sophisticated, and resentation is suitable attractive. The strong regional identity associated with Heathcote's restaurants is balanced by everal unchanging staples - black pudding (grilled with sautéed chestnuts, baby onions and mushrooms), Goosnargh oultry (ravioli of smoked chicken), and bread and butter pudding are all part of the trademark. The first class ngredients ensure that a meal here stands head and shoulders above many restaurants in the area.

MENU GUIDE Roast pumpkin soup, sage fritters • Braised shin of beef & oxtail • Rum baba

WINE GUIDE ♀ Brampton Sauvignon Blanc £21.50 • ♀ Sierra Cantabria Rioja £26.75 • 65 bottles over £20, 15 bottles under £20 • 13 by the glass (£3-£6.50)

PRICE GUIDE Fixed L £14 • Fixed D £25 • starter £4.50-£13.50 • main £13.50-£19 • dessert £6-£7 • coffee £1.80 • min/water £3.25 • Service optional

OUR TIP: Terrific value at lunchtime

Chef: Paul Heathcote, Leigh Myers **Owners:** Paul Heathcote **Times:** 12-2.30/6-10, Closed 1 Jan, Mon, closed L Sat **Notes:** 3 course set menu, incl 1/2 bottle of wine £25, Vegetarian available **Seats:** 70, Pr/dining room 18 **Smoking:** N/Sm area, No pipes **Children:** Portions **Directions:** Follow signs for Golf Club & Jeffrey Hill. Higher Rd is beside White Bull Pub in Longridge **Parking:** 10

England

LYTHAM ST ANNES *continued* MAP 18 SD32

⑤ Clifton Arms Hotel

British

Honest cooking in elegant hotel

☎ 01253 739898 West Beach, Lytham FY8 5QJ

MENU GUIDE Black pudding, scallops, hollandaise • Rack of lamb, minted mash, red wine sauce • Sticky toffee pudding, butterscotch sauce

WINE GUIDE ♀ Chablis Premier Cru Montmains £25 • ♀ Beelgara Cabernet Merlot Pinot Noir £14.50 • 34 bottles over £20, 26 bottles under £20 • 11 by the glass (£3.50-£6.50)

PRICE GUIDE Fixed D £25 • starter £3.50-£8.95 • main £9.50-£18 • dessert £4.50 • coffee £3.50 • min/water £3.50 • Service optional

PLACE: Blackpool's classy neighbour, Lytham is a picturesque setting for this renowned red brick hotel. Chandeliers and heavy fabrics ensure the spacious restaurant is suitably elegant, and there are views across the green to the coast.

FOOD: Straightforward modern cooking that makes the most of quality ingredients and doesn't break the bank. Roasts and familiar favourites provide the bulk of the menu, but there's more upmarket fare too - duckling with bitter orange sauce for example.

OUR TIP: Afternoon tea is a highlight

Chef: Paul Caddy **Owners:** Paul Caddy **Times:** 7-9.30, Closed L Mon-Sat **Notes:** Vegetarian available, Civ Wed 100 **Seats:** 60, Pr/dining room 140 **Smoking:** N/Sm in restaurant **Children:** Portions **Rooms:** 48 (48 en suite) ★★★★ **Directions:** M55 junct 4, take first left onto A583 (Preston), take the right hand lane. At traffic lights turn right onto Peel Rd. Turn right at t-junction into Ballam Rd. Continue onto Lytham town centre. Turn right and then left into Queen St. **Parking:** 50

e-mail: welcome@cliftonarms-lytham.com

web: www.cliftonarms-lytham.com

⑤ Greens Bistro

British, International

Peaceful seaside bistro

☎ 01253 789990 3-9 St Andrews Rd South, St Annes On Sea FY8 1SX

MENU GUIDE Crispy spring rolls of Goosnargh chicken • Slow cooked leg of Pendle lamb, creamed potatoes, rosemary jus • Amaretto crème brûlée

WINE GUIDE ♀ Rams Leap Semillion/Sauvignon £15 • ♀ Rams Leap Shiraz £15 • 13 bottles over £20, 16 bottles under £20 6 by the glass (£2.50-£2.95)

PRICE GUIDE Food prices not confirmed for 2006. Please telephone for details

PLACE: The rugged whitewashed walls of this seaside bistro conceal a cosy interior. Low ceilings and green walls create a calm rustic feel, with alcoves for more intimate dining.

FOOD: Good local and seasonal ingredients are treated with well-judged accurate cooking - the result being modern British food with International influences, flair and depth of flavour.

OUR TIP: Excellent value set menu on week nights

Chef: Paul Webster **Owners:** Paul Webster **Times:** 6-10, Closed 25 Dec, BHs, Sun-Mon, closed L all week **Notes:** Vegetarian available **Seats:** 38 **Children:** Portions **Directions:** Telephone for directions **Parking:** On street **e-mail:** info@greensbistro.co.uk

web: www.greensbistro.co.uk

PRESTON MAP 18 SD52

⑤⑤ The Park Restaurant Hotel

British

Good Northern dining in comfortable Edwardian surroundings

☎ 01772 726250 728096 209 Tulketh Rd, Ashton-on-Ribble PR2 1ES

MENU GUIDE Lancashire hot pot • Roast Goosnargh duck breast, parsnip tart • Strawberry crème brûlée

PRICE GUIDE Starter £4.45-£7.95 • main £12.95-£21.95 dessert £4.95-£7.95 • coffee £1.95 • min/water £3.25 • Service optional

PLACE: This Edwardian mansion house is situated close to Preston. The mosaic-tiled lobby floor gives the entrance a homely feel whilst stained-glass windows, high ceilings and tasteful, stylish decor in the public areas give a grander impression. There's a small, snug bar and a traditional dining room with quality settings and glassware. Notable, attentive service.

FOOD: Modern British dishes with Northern accents are prepared with flair and imagination. Presentation is contemporary, often with dramatic garnishes. High quality local ingredients are skilfully prepared to produce simple and clearly flavoured food.

OUR TIP: Stay over in one of the comfortable rooms

Chef: Derek Cheetham **Owners:** Nicola & Derek Cheetham **Times:** 6.30, Closed 25-28 Dec, Sun, closed L all, closed D Sun **Notes:** Vegetarian available **Seats:** 36 **Smoking:** N/Sm in restaurant **Children:** Min 12 **Rooms:** 14 (14 en suite) ♦♦♦♦ **Parking:** 14

e-mail: parkrestaurant@hotmail.com

web: www.theparkpreston.com

⑤ Pines Hotel

International

Imaginative cuisine in handsome hotel

☎ 01772 338551 570 Preston Rd, Clayton Le-Woods PR6 7ED

MENU GUIDE Wild mushroom fricassée • Pan-fried medallions of pork, apple & Calvados jus • Baked vanilla rice pudding

PRICE GUIDE Food prices not confirmed for 2006. Please telephone for details

PLACE: This unique and stylish hotel is set within four acres of mature grounds. The restaurant, Haworths, offers modern brasserie fare.

FOOD: An imaginative menu that should please most tastes. You might start with king scallops and Bury black pudding, before supreme of chicken filled with roasted Mediterranean vegetables.

OUR TIP: Extensive wine list

Times: 12-2.45/6-9.45, Closed 26 Dec **Rooms:** 37 (37 en suite) ★★★
e-mail: mail@thepineshotel.co.uk
web: www.thepineshotel.co.uk

What makes a Restaurant of the Year?
In selecting a Restaurant of the Year, we look for somewhere that is exceptional in its chosen area of the market. Whilst the Rosette awards are based on the quality of the food alone, Restaurant of the Year takes into account all aspects of the operation. For full details see pages 6-7.

England

Winckley Square Chop House and Bar

British

Busy city centre brasserie

☎ 01772 252732 23 Winckley Square PR1 3JJ

MENU GUIDE Potato, parsley & garlic pie • Goosnargh duck with cider & apples • Spiced poached pears

WINE GUIDE House Chardonnay £14.50 • House Cabernet Sauvignon £14.50 • 65 bottles over £20, 12 bottles under £20 • 10 by the glass (£3.85-£5.25)

PRICE GUIDE Fixed L £13-£15 • starter £3.95-£8 • main £8.50-£25 • dessert £5-£6 • coffee £2 • min/water £3.50 • Service included

PLACE: This former convent school turned airy modern eaterie has a handy city centre location, and is one of a chain of restaurants run by celebrity chef, Paul Heathcote.
FOOD: Using the freshest local and organic farmers' produce, this brasserie menu aims to please the crowds, with old favourites like fish and chips up for grabs alongside more sophisticated fare, such as char-grilled veal rump with sage and mushroom risotto.
OUR TIP: Enjoy a cocktail in the bar area
Chef: Paul Gray **Owners:** Paul Heathcote **Times:** 12-2.30/6-10, Closed 25-26 Dec, 1-3 Jan, BHs **Notes:** Vegetarian available, Dress Restrictions, Casual **Seats:** 90 **Smoking:** N/Sm in restaurant, Air con **Children:** Menu, Portions **Directions:** Town centre, just off Fishergate (main shopping street). **Parking:** On street
e-mail: preston@heathcotes.co.uk **web:** www.heathcotes.co.uk

THORNTON MAP 18 SD34

Twelve Restaurant

Modern British NEW

Modern food with a British twist in contemporary setting

☎ 01253 821212 Marsh Mill Village, Marsh Mill-in-Wyre FY5 4JZ

MENU GUIDE Ham & foie gras terrine, fig jam • Beef fillet, wild mushroom cappuccino • Bread-and-butter pudding

WINE GUIDE Thorne Hill Semillon/Chardonnay £14.50 • Thorne Hill Shiraz Cabernet £14.50 • 21 bottles over £20, 23 bottles under £20 • 4 by the glass (£3.05-£3.35)

PRICE GUIDE Fixed L £12.50 • Fixed D £16.95 • starter £4.75-£9.50 • main £13.95-£19.50 • dessert £4.95-£6.95 • coffee £1.50 • min/water £2.85 • Service optional

PLACE: Housed in a converted granary in the shadows of the sails of the beautifully restored Marsh Mill Windmill, Twelve has a contemporary, structural feel, with exposed brick, steel girders,

continued

wooden floors, glass screens, plain tables and trendy bucket seats. Service is friendly and professional and the atmosphere buzzy like a brasserie.
FOOD: Modern British food with an innovative twist to some classic dishes show the style. Expect well-sourced ingredients, good combinations and simple presentation.
OUR TIP: Take a window seat to view the working windmill
Chef: Paul Moss **Owners:** Paul Moss & Caroline Upton **Times:** 12-3/6.30-12, Closed 1st 2wks Jan, Mon, closed L Tues-Wed, Fri-Sun **Notes:** 3 course set D (Fri & Sat) £22.50, Vegetarian available **Seats:** 68 **Smoking:** N/Sm in restaurant **Children:** Portions **Directions:** A585 follow signs for Marsh Mill Complex. Turn right into Victoria Rd East, entrance 0.5m on left. **Parking:** 150
e-mail: info@twelve-restaurant.co.uk **web:** www.twelve-restaurant.co.uk

WRIGHTINGTON MAP 15 SD51

The Mulberry Tree

British, French

Ambitious gastro-pub fare

☎ 01257 451400 Wrightington Bar WN6 9SE

MENU GUIDE Ham & foie gras terrine, piccalilli • Duck, black pudding, mash, brandy & peppercorn jus • Treacle tart, whisky ice cream

WINE GUIDE Tuatara Bay Sauvignon Blanc £19.75 • Penny's Hill Shiraz/Cabernet/Merlot £26.25 30 bottles over £20, 40 bottles under £20 • 12 by the glass (£3.25-£3.75)

PRICE GUIDE Starter £4.50-£10.95 • main £12.50-£19.95 • dessert £5.50 • coffee £2.50 • min/water £4 • Service added but optional 10%

PLACE: This village landmark has played home to a wheelwright's, brewery and blacksmith since it was built in the early 19th century, and is now a cavernous gastro-pub, popular with local residents and businesses alike. Expect urban chic rather than olde world charm, and a bright modern interior divided into a bar area and more formal dining room.
FOOD: Contemporary cooking with quality ingredients and plenty of flare. You will be spoilt for choice with impressive dishes such as pork with rösti potato and three mustard sauce, or fresh lobster with a herb and champagne sauce.
OUR TIP: A similar menu is served in the bar at reduced prices
Chef: Mark Prescott **Owners:** Mr M Prescott & Mr J Moore **Times:** 12-2/6-9.30, Closed 26 Dec, 1 Jan **Notes:** Sun L 3 courses £21.50, Vegetarian available **Seats:** 60 **Smoking:** N/Sm in restaurant, Air con **Children:** Portions **Directions:** 4m from Wigan. From M6 junct 27 towards Parbold, right after motorway exit, by BP garage into Mossy Lea Rd. On right after 2m **Parking:** 80

LEICESTERSHIRE

CASTLE DONINGTON MAP 11 SK42

🍽️🍽️ *The Priest House on the River*

Modern British

Classical food and a riverside setting

☎ 01332 810649 Kings Mills DE74 2RR

MENU GUIDE Butternut squash soup • Rack of lamb, tapenade, Mediterranean vegetables • Lemon tart

PRICE GUIDE Food prices not confirmed for 2006. Please telephone for details

PLACE: Historic, former working mill tucked down a long lane in a picturesque riverside setting. Dining options include a brasserie - a casual, all-day affair - and a comfortable, contemporary-style restaurant overlooking the River Trent.
FOOD: Expect a modern approach to cooking British classics. Dishes are simple, well-gauged and not too elaborate in construction and presentation, yet show flair and imagination revealing good flavours.
OUR TIP: Handy for the airport
Times: 12-3/7-9, Closed L Mon-Sat **Rooms:** 42 (42 en suite) ★★★★
Directions: Northbound: M1 J23a to airport. After 1.5m turn R to Castle Donington. L at 1st lights, 2m. Southbound: M1 J24a onto A50. Take 1st sliproad signed Long Eaton/Castle Donington. Turn R at lights in Castle Donington **e-mail:** priesthouse@arcadianhotels.co.uk
web: www.thepriesthouse.co.uk

HINCKLEY MAP 11 SP49

🍽️🍽️ Sketchley Grange Hotel 🐟

British, European

Ambitious hotel fare

☎ 01455 251133 Sketchley Ln, Burbage LE10 3HU

MENU GUIDE Morel & truffle risotto, confit leeks • Venison, fondant potato, chocolate & orange oil • Rhubarb soufflé, ginger sorbet

WINE GUIDE ⚲ Chablis Simonnet Febure Chardonnay £22.50 • ⚲ Lindemans Shiraz £16.25 • 32 bottles over £20, 36 bottles under £20 • 4 by the glass (£4.50-£6.95)

PRICE GUIDE Starter £4.95-£9.25 • main £13.50-£19 • dessert £4.95-£5.95 • coffee £2.50 • min/water £3.95 • Service optional

PLACE: This old country farmhouse turned modern hotel has extensive facilities including a range of bars and dining options, as well as a leisure spa and crèche. Candlelit by night, the Willow

restaurant is an airy room overlooking pretty gardens, with generous, well-spaced tables.
FOOD: Expect ambitious modern cooking conjured from modish ingredients, sourced organically where possible. A lamb main shows the style, served pink and tender with aubergine mash, and a flavourful tomato and basil jus.
OUR TIP: Dinner only
Chef: Darren Curson **Owners:** Nigel Downes **Times:** 7-9.30, Closed Mon, closed L Mon-Sat, closed D Sun **Notes:** Vegetarian available, Dress Restrictions, Smart casual, Civ Wed 250 **Seats:** 80, Pr/dining room 40 **Smoking:** N/Sm in restaurant, Air con **Children:** Portions **Rooms:** 52 (52 en suite) ★★★★ **Directions:** From M69 junct 1 take B4109 (Hinckley). Straight on 1st rdbt, L at 2nd rdbt & immediately right into Sketchley Lane. Hotel at end of ln **Parking:** 200
e-mail: reservations@sketchleygrange.co.uk
web: www.sketchleygrange.co.uk

KEGWORTH MAP 11 SK42

🍽️ *Best Western Yew Lodge Hotel*

Modern European

Busy hotel restaurant offering quality cooking

☎ 01509 672518 Packington Hill DE74 2DF

MENU GUIDE Mozzarella filo parcel with spinach • Venison Bourguinon • Strawberry pannacotta

PRICE GUIDE Food prices not confirmed for 2006. Please telephone for details

PLACE: Large family-owned hotel, peacefully located despite its proximity to the motorway and airport. The smartly appointed restaurant does a brisk business trade during the week.
FOOD: Quality produce is matched by good attention to detail. Attractively presented dishes include braised lamb shank with sweet potatoes, and a meltingly light chocolate bread and butter pudding.
OUR TIP: Excellent new spa centre
Times: 12-2.30/6.30-10, closed L Sat **Rooms:** 98 (98 en suite) ★★★
Directions: M1 J24, follow signs Loughborough & Kegworth on A6. At bottom of hill take 1st R onto Packington Hill. Hotel 400yds on R **e-mail:** info@yewlodgehotel.co.uk **web:** www.yewlodgehotel.co.uk

---

AA's Chefs' Chef is the annual poll of all the chefs included in The Restaurant Guide. Around 1800 of the country's top chefs are asked to vote to recognise the achievements of one of their peers.
This year's winner is featured on page 19.

continued

LEICESTER MAP 11 SK50

🕸 Belmont House Hotel
British, European   **NEW**
Modern cooking at classy Victorian town house
☎ 0116 254 4773   De Montfort St LE1 7GR

MENU GUIDE Chicken liver & garlic pâté • Smoked haddock & prawn risotto with poached egg • White chocolate crème brûlée

WINE GUIDE ⚲ Macon Chardonnay £16.95 • 🍷 Merlot Reserva Merlot £15.50 • 39 bottles over £20, 51 bottles under £20 • 5 by the glass (£3.25-£4.25)

PRICE GUIDE Fixed L £11.95-£25 • Fixed D £22.95-£29.90 coffee £2.45 • min/water £3 • Service added but optional 10%

PLACE: Built in the 1850s as a girls' school, this popular townhouse offers an array of eateries including two bars and a bistro as well as the sophisticated Cherry restaurant.

FOOD: Cherry's offers a modern British mix of roasts and lighter fare, and puts a fashionable emphasis on local produce. Save room for dessert - alongside the likes of dark chocolate rum trifle and clotted cream cheesecake, there's also a sweet soufflé of the day.

OUR TIP: Close to Victoria Park for an after-lunch stroll
Chef: Stewart Westwater **Owners:** The Bowie Family **Times:** 12.30-2.30/7-10.00, Closed BHs Mondays, closed L Sat, closed D Sun **Notes:** Smart casual, Civ Wed 70 **Seats:** 65, Pr/dining room 30 **Smoking:** N/Sm in restaurant, Air con **Children:** Portions **Rooms:** 77 (77 en suite) ★★★ **Directions:** M1 junct 21/A6 S onto A6 rdbt follow signs for railway station **Parking:** 70 **e-mail:** info@belmonthotel.co.uk **web:** www.belmonthotel.co.uk

🕸 Entropy
Modern European   **NEW**
Modern cooking in minimalist designer setting
☎ 0116 254 8530   3 Dover St LE1 6PW

MENU GUIDE Truffled ballotine of foie gras • Loin of hare in puff pastry, wild mushrooms • Port roasted figs, cinnamon fritters & mascarpone

WINE GUIDE ⚲ Givery 1er Cru £19 • 🍷 Merloblu £15 14 bottles over £20, 16 bottles under £20 • 6 by the glass £3.25-£5)

PRICE GUIDE Fixed L £12.95 • starter £5.50-£10.95 • main £17.50-£24 • dessert £5.50-£7.95 • coffee £1.50 • min/water £3.75 • Service optional

PLACE: Constructed in the late 1970s, this concrete building was previously a joiners' workshop. An open staircase leads to a reception bar and lounge on a mezzanine floor, then the restaurant on the first floor. Decor in shades of white and large abstract murals is the setting for designer tables and chairs. Floor to ceiling windows make the room airy and light.

continued

FOOD: Concise menus using fresh ingredients avoid pretension. Cooking influences are primarily French, with the emphasis on a perfect-looking finished dish.
OUR TIP: Fixed price lunch and pre-theatre dinner menus available
Chef: Tom Cockerill, Elliot Moss **Owners:** Tom & Cassandra Cockerill **Times:** 12-2.30/6-10, Closed BHs, 24 Dec-4 Jan, Sun **Notes:** Vegetarian available **Seats:** 60, Pr/dining room 20 **Smoking:** N/Sm in restaurant, Air con **Directions:** Located in Leicester city centre, 2 min walk from station. From Train Station on A6 take Granby St into city centre, Dover St is second on left. Restaurant is located opposite Dover St car park **Parking:** On street, NCP **e-mail:** mail@entropylife.com **web:** www.entropylife.com

🕸 Watsons Restaurant & Bar
Mediterranean, British
Contemporary cooking in converted cotton mill
☎ 0116 222 7770   5-9 Upper Brown St LE1 5TE

MENU GUIDE Fish soup with gruyère • Roasted monkfish with Parma ham & fennel confit • Chocolate malt parfait

WINE GUIDE ⚲ De Gras Sauvignon Blanc £12.95 • 🍷 De Gras Merlot £12.95 • 15 bottles over £20, 25 bottles under £20 • 6 by the glass (£2.95-£5.50)

PRICE GUIDE Fixed L £9.50 • Fixed D £15 • starter £5-£6.95 • main £9.95-£17 • dessert £5 • coffee £1.50 • min/water £3 • Service added but optional 10%

PLACE: Conveniently and centrally located next to the Phoenix Theatre, Watsons is a stylishly converted former sock mill saved from dereliction to become a modern brasserie.
FOOD: Diners have a choice between a reasonably priced set menu and the carte, with daily specials on the blackboard. Food is brasserie style - simple classics with a modern twist such as pheasant with pomegranate and Marsala.
OUR TIP: Look out for the fish dish of the day
Chef: Graeme Watson, **Owners:** Graeme Watson **Times:** 12-2.30/7-10.30, Closed BHs, 10 days at Xmas, Sun **Notes:** Vegetarian available, Casual **Seats:** 80 **Smoking:** N/Sm in restaurant, Air con **Children:** Portions **Directions:** City centre, next to Phoenix Arts Theatre **e-mail:** watsons.restaurant@virgin.net

⑨ Dinos Restaurant 13 Garrick Walk LE1 3YL
☎ 0116 262 8208   Mediterranean style with a contemporary feel, situated next to the Haymarket Theatre.

▮▮ San Carlo Granby St LE1 1DE ☎ 0116 251 9332
Extremely busy Italian with open kitchen and wood-burning oven.

MEDBOURNE MAP 11 SP89

🕸🕸 The Horse & Trumpet
Modern British
A rising star in traditional village setting
☎ 01858 565000   Old Green LE16 8DX

MENU GUIDE Young carrots, iced Granny Smith, cardamom, coconut foam • Lamb saddle, sweetbreads, cumin, peas, poached leek, caper jus • Chocolate fondant, iced double cream, pistachio, toffee

WINE GUIDE ⚲ Jean Marc Brocard Les Manants Chablis £21.95 • 🍷 Paul Jaboulet Vacqueyras £22.95 • 70 bottles over £20, 8 bottles under £20 • 10 by the glass (£3.10-£3.80)

PRICE GUIDE Fixed L £16-£18 • starter £7-£9.75 • main £16-£25 • dessert £7-£8 • coffee £2 • min/water £1 • Service optional • Group min 16 service 10%

continued

MEDBOURNE continued MAP 11 SP89

PLACE: Tucked away behind the village bowling green and across from the church, this three-storey, thatched former farmhouse and one-time inn has been impressively and sympathetically restored into a stylish fine dining restaurant with rooms. The enclosed rear courtyard provides a secluded spot for summer dining or aperitifs, while inside the restaurant is spread across three intimate rooms around a central lounge with an inglenook fireplace. Beamed ceilings and antiques reflect the building's age, while crisp white linen and stylish appointments add an elegant, upmarket touch.

FOOD: Chef David Lennox (ex Inverlochy Castle Hotel, Fort William) shows his pedigree and ambition via an imaginative modern British repertoire. Quality produce, skilled preparation and excellent presentation are paired with a sophisticated blend of fresh flavours and assured, accurate cooking. Take slow-cooked fillet of beef with cauliflower, apple, foie gras ganache, baby morels and a Madeira jus, and perhaps a lemon rice pudding finale, served with a lemon sorbet, lemon jelly and gingerbread.

OUR TIP: Choose the tasting menu

Chef: D Lennox, G Magnani, L Goodwill **Owners:** Horse & Trumpet Ltd **Times:** 12-2/7-9.30, Closed 1st Week Jan, Mon, closed D Sun **Notes:** Tasting Menu £50, Sun L £25, Vegetarian available, Dress Restrictions, Smart casual, no trainers or baseball caps **Seats:** 50, Pr/dining room 32 **Smoking:** N/Sm area **Children:** Min 12yrs **Rooms:** 4 (4 en suite) 🏨 **Directions:** Between Market Harborough and Uppingham on B664 **Parking:** 4 **e-mail:** info@horseandtrumpet.com **web:** www.horseandtrumpet.com

MELTON MOWBRAY MAP 11 SK71

◉◉ Stapleford Park
Classical British

Accomplished cuisine in sumptuous surroundings
☎ 01572 787522 Stapleford LE14 2EF

MENU GUIDE Poached foie gras, Puy lentils, Sauternes jus • Turbot, baby leeks, langoustine tempura, miso broth Plum tart

WINE GUIDE ⚲ La Roche Petit Chablis £30 • ⚑ Marques de Riscal Tempranillo £42 • 99 bottles over £20 • 6 by the glass (£8.60)

PRICE GUIDE Fixed D £44-£49 • coffee £3.95 • min/water £3.95 • Service optional • Group service 5%

PLACE: Set in 500 acres of parkland designed by 'Capability' Brown, this imposing stately home dates back to the 14th century and is decorated in sumptuous style. Shooting, fishing, tennis and golf are among extensive facilities, as well as a comfortable library for pre-dinner drinks.

FOOD: Classically based cuisine made from high quality luxury ingredients and presented with contemporary flair. Start with roast scallops with caviar and a cauliflower purée, and then try sea bream with a garlic and mussel broth, or veal with a casserole of white beans and red wine jus.

OUR TIP: Unwind and detox in the wonderful hotel spa

Chef: Wayne Vickerage **Owners:** Shuif Hussain **Times:** 12-2.30/7.30-9.30 **Notes:** Vegetarian available, Dress Restrictions, Jacket required, tie optional, Civ Wed 200 **Seats:** 60, Pr/dining room 190 **Smoking:** N/Sm in restaurant **Children:** Min 9 yrs, Menu **Rooms:** 52 (52 en suite) ★★★★ **Directions:** Follow Melton ring road A607 (Grantham) onto B676, 4m turn right signed Stapleford **Parking:** 200 **e-mail:** reservations@stapleford.co.uk **web:** www.staplefordpark.com

NORTH KILWORTH MAP 11 SP68

◉◉ Kilworth House Hotel
Modern British

Sumptuous setting for modern and classical cooking
☎ 01858 880058 Lutterworth Rd LE17 6JE

MENU GUIDE Lobster & rocket tart • Beef poached in red wine, parsnip mash, sautéed wild mushrooms • Pineapple tarte Tatin, coconut ice cream

WINE GUIDE ⚲ Robertson Chenin Blanc £13.50 • ⚑ Merlot Veneto £13.50 • 62 bottles over £20, 25 bottles under £20 • 9 by the glass (£3.25-£5.25)

PRICE GUIDE Fixed L £15.45-£24 • Fixed D £28.50 • starter £8.95-£14 • main £13.95-£24.50 • dessert £6.50-£7.95 • coffee £2.50 • min/water £3.50 • Service optional

PLACE: Rolling parkland and formal courtyard gardens surround this beautifully restored country house, which offers an enchanting blend of Victorian opulence and contemporary luxury. Dining options include informal eating in the large Orangery restaurant, with glorious views across the estate, and the more formal Wordsworth Restaurant, with its ornate ceiling, stained-glass windows and original artwork.

continued

continued

FOOD: There's a short daily fixed-price menu and an imaginative arte offering classic dishes with a modern British twist from a hi-ech kitchen.
OUR TIP: Lighter meals and afternoon teas in the superb ictorian Orangery
Chef: Carl Dovey **Owners:** Mr & Mrs Mackay **Times:** 12-3/7-9.30
Notes: Vegetarian available, Dress Restrictions, No jeans or trainers, Civ Wed 100 **Seats:** 70, Pr/dining room 36 **Smoking:** N/Sm in restaurant
Children: Menu, Portions **Rooms:** 41 (41 en suite) ★★★★
Directions: Located on A4304, 4m E of M1 junct 20 towards Market Harborough **Parking:** 140 **e-mail:** info@kilworthhouse.co.uk
web: www.kilworthhouse.co.uk

QUORN MAP 11 SK51

⚫⚫ Quorn Country Hotel
British, European

Enjoyable dining in well-run country hotel
☎ 01509 415050 Charnwood House, 66 Leicester Rd LE12 8BB

MENU GUIDE Roast salmon fishcakes • Tournedos steak, thyme rösti, green pepper sauce • Sticky toffee pudding

WINE GUIDE ♀ Hardys Riddle Chardonnay-Semillion £14.25 • ♀ Hardys Riddle Shiraz Cabaret £14.25 • 29 bottles over £20, 19 bottles under £20 • 5 by the glass (£3-£3.50)

PRICE GUIDE Fixed L £18-£19 • Fixed D £26-£27 • starter £5-£9 • main £17-£26.50 • dessert £5.50 • coffee £2.95 • min/water £4.25

PLACE: This 17th-century manor house has a choice of the airy conservatory bistro - The Orangery - or the more formal Shires restaurant with its intimate atmosphere, low-beamed ceilings and candlelit, alcoved tables.
FOOD: Predominantly classical dishes are lightened with the occasional modern touch. A dedicated local following ensures several dishes are always present such as the twice-roasted Fressingham duck and the Dover sole. There's a substantial wine list and formal silver service.
OUR TIP: A pre-dinner stroll around the beautiful riverside gardens
Chef: David Wilkinson **Owners:** Mr Walshe **Times:** 12-2.30/7-9.30, closed L Sat **Notes:** Sun eve pasta evenings, Smart Dress, Civ Wed 120 **Seats:** 112, Pr/dining room 240 **Children:** Menu, Portions **Rooms:** 30 (30 en suite) ★★★★ **Directions:** M1 junct 23/A6 wards Leicester, follow signs for Quorn. **Parking:** 120
e-mail: sales@quorncountryhotel.co.uk
web: www.quorncountryhotel.co.uk

⬛ Ferrari's Trattoria 4 High St LE12 8DT
☎ 01509 412191 Family-run Italian in an old cottage in the main street.

WATHERN MAP 11 SK73

⚫ Red Lion Inn
British, European

Sound cooking in a friendly village inn
☎ 01949 860868 Red Lion St LE14 4HS

MENU GUIDE Chicken liver parfait, chutney, toasted brioche Toulouse sausages, mash, onion gravy • Cherry crème brûlée

WINE GUIDE ♀ Noel Laudet Dom de Laballe Ugni Blanc £11.50 • ♀ Jean Luc Terrier Grenache £10.95 • 40 bottles over £20, 28 bottles under £20 • 8 by the glass (£2.75-£3.50)

PRICE GUIDE Fixed L £12.50 • starter £3.95-£7.50 • main £8.95-£16.50 • dessert £4.50-£6 • coffee £2 • min/water £3 • Service optional • Group min 12 service 10%
continued

PLACE: Surely the dream local: a 16th- century village inn that combines bags of character and charm with comfy sofas, real ales and quality pub grub.
FOOD: The Red Lion takes its food seriously, sourcing ingredients from around the area and listing suppliers on the back of the menu. An extensive selection includes hearty crowd-pleasers plus some classier dishes: venison with a mulled wine sauce perhaps, or smoked haddock and spring onion mash. **Winner of AA Pub of The Year for England 2005-2006**
OUR TIP: Short set menu available at lunchtime
Chef: Phillip Lowe **Owners:** Ben Jones, Marcus Welford, Sean Hope **Times:** 12-2/7-9.30, Closed D 25 Dec & 1 Jan, closed D Sun **Notes:** Vegetarian available **Seats:** 50 **Smoking:** N/Sm in restaurant **Children:** Menu, Portions **Parking:** 20
e-mail: info@theredlioninn.co.uk
web: www.theredlioninn.co.uk

LINCOLNSHIRE

CLEETHORPES MAP 17 TA30

⚫ Kingsway Hotel
British, International

Traditional dining by the sea
☎ 01472 601122 Kingsway DN35 0AE

MENU GUIDE Deep-fried sesame tiger prawns, sweet & sour dip • Lambs' liver, bacon, onion balsamic gravy • Sweet trolley

WINE GUIDE ♀ Borgo Selene Catarratto Inzolia £12.95 • ♀ Lande Tree Cabernet Shiraz £12.95 • 30 bottles over £20, 41 bottles under £20 • 4 by the glass (£3.20)

PRICE GUIDE Fixed L £14.50 • Fixed D £22.95 • starter £4.50-£7.95 • main £13.95-£18.95 • dessert £5.25 • coffee £2 • min/water £3 • Service optional

PLACE: Overlooking the Humber estuary, the restaurant of this seaside hotel is decorated in traditional style with wood panelling and smartly appointed tables.
FOOD: An extensive menu of traditional British fare with the odd international twist. Among a tempting range of mains you might find favourites like pork with a sage and onion stuffing, or a more exotic dish of scampi provençale.
OUR TIP: The hotel has been run by the same family for four generations
Chef: Guy Stevens **Owners:** Mr J Harris **Times:** 12.30-1.45/7-9, Closed 26 Dec **Notes:** Vegetarian available **Seats:** 85, Pr/dining room 24 **Smoking:** N/Sm in restaurant **Children:** Min 5yrs, Portions **Rooms:** 49 (49 en suite) ★★★ **Directions:** At junction of A1098 and seafront **Parking:** 50 **e-mail:** reception@kingsway-hotel.com
web: www.kingsway-hotel.com

GRANTHAM MAP 11 SK93

⚫ Angel & Royal Hotel
British, Mediterranean

Choice of bistro and fine dining in coaching inn
☎ 01476 565816 High St NG31 6PN

MENU GUIDE Stuffed field mushrooms • Pan-fried calves' liver • Treacle tart, toffee & honey

WINE GUIDE 3 bottles over £20, 16 bottles under £20 • 4 by the glass (£2.75-£3.75)

PRICE GUIDE Fixed L £11.95 • Fixed D £25.95 • starter £3.95-£7.50 • main £6.95-£14.95 • dessert £3.95-£4.95 • coffee £1.95 • Service optional
continued

England

GRANTHAM continued MAP 11 SK93

PLACE: Purportedly one of the oldest coaching inns in the country, with original features intact. The modern all-day bistro is augmented at the weekend by fine dining in the King's Room.

FOOD: The relaxed bistro menu delivers a reliable modern choice, plus a daily blackboard specials listing. Salmon fillet with a lemon and dill sauce, and chocolate and orange mousse, may be amongst the dishes on offer.

OUR TIP: Try the daily roast joint

Chef: Michael Savill **Owners:** Angel & Royal Hotel Limited **Times:** 12-2/7-9.30, Closed L Mon-Sat, closed D Sun-Thur **Notes:** Fixed L Sun only, Fixed D ALC, Vegetarian available, Dress Restrictions, Smart casual
Seats: 55, Pr/dining room 16 **Smoking:** N/Sm in restaurant, Air con
Children: Menu, Portions **Rooms:** 26 (26 en suite) ★★★
Directions: Grantham exit off A1 and follow signs to the town centre
Parking: 55 **e-mail:** enquiries@angelandroyal.co.uk
web: www.angelandroyal.co uk

 **Harry's Place** *see below*

GRIMSBY MAP 17 TA21

 **Beeches Hotel**

French, European

Hotel brasserie offering a quiet oasis in a busy suburb

☎ 01472 278830 42 Waltham Rd, Scartho DN33 2LX

continued

MENU GUIDE Thai-style haddock fishcakes, herb mayonnaise • Pan-fried halibut fillet, shellfish sauce • Lemon tart

PRICE GUIDE Fixed L £16.50 • starter £4-£6.95 • main £14.50-£22 • dessert £4.50-£6 • coffee £1.20 • min/water £2 • Service optional

PLACE: This minimalist boutique hotel offers comfort and style in a convenient location. Low leather sofas and soft tapestry decor lends an Eastern vibe to the lounge bar, while light and sanded pine add an informal air to the brasserie.

FOOD: Careful cooking with an eye on seasonality and local produce are key to the menu's success; with up-to-date but, sensibly, not too complex dishes.

OUR TIP: When in Grimsby you must try the fish

Chef: David Ramackers **Owners:** Ramsden Family **Times:** 12-2/7-9, Closed Xmas & New Year, closed L Mon-Thurs **Notes:** Fixed L Sun, 3 courses, £11.99, Vegetarian available **Seats:** 50 **Smoking:** N/Sm in restaurant **Children:** Portions **Rooms:** 18 (18 en suite) ★★★
Directions: On A1203, off A16 from Louth **Parking:** 30
e-mail: joeramsden@freeuk.com **web:** www.thebeecheshotel.com

LINCOLN MAP 17 SK97

 **Branston Hall Hotel**

Eclectic

Contemporary food in country house splendour

☎ 01522 793305 Branston Park, Branston LN4 1PD

MENU GUIDE Scallops, confit pork belly • Braised guinea fowl, truffled gnocchi • Lemongrass parfait, pineapple salsa, pomegranate syrup

continued

GRANTHAM MAP 11 SK93

Harry's Place

British, French

The finest local food prepared with great skill and enthusiasm

☎ 01476 561780 17 High St, Great Gonerby NG31 8JS

MENU GUIDE Fresh tomato soup • Lincolnshire Grey partridge, white wine sauce • Caramel mousse brûlée

WINE GUIDE ♀ Luis Canas Rioja Viura/Malvasia £20 • ♀ Tempranillo Graciano Campo Viejo Gran Reserva Rioja £39 • all bottles over £20 • 4 by the glass (£4.50-£5)

PRICE GUIDE Starter £8.50-£17.50 • main £32 • dessert £7 • coffee £2 • Service optional

PLACE: Just three highly polished tables fit into the tiny dining room in this former farmhouse, ensuring that the limited number of nightly guests feel as welcome and comfortable as honoured friends. The blue-painted frontage stands out in the main street, as does the highly individual service inside. Delicate pieces of antique china adorn the tables, and family memorabilia fills the rich red walls.

FOOD: This is a place for serious lovers of good food, and Harry Hallam's reputation is spread far and wide. The beautifully hand-written French menu lists two starters, two mains and two desserts, plus a mouthwatering selection of home and Continental cheeses. Harry's much-praised repertoire is devoted to producing simple food with flavours that are at once complex and pure. The range may be necessarily small, but the quality of ingredients and skill of the chef are truly superb.

OUR TIP: Book reasonably far in advance to avoid any disappointment

Chef: Harry Hallam **Owners:** Harry & Caroline Hallam **Times:** 12.30-2.30/7-9.30, Closed 25-26 Dec, BHs, Sun & Mon **Notes:** min/water free of charge, Vegetarian by request only **Seats:** 10 **Smoking:** N/Sm in restaurant **Children:** Min 5 yrs, Portions **Directions:** 1.5m NW of Grantham on B1174 **Parking:** 4

Branston Hall Hotel

WINE GUIDE ♀ Badgers Creek Semillion/Chardonnay 11.95 • ♥ Badgers Creek Cabernet/Shiraz £11.95 • 12 bottles ver £20, 40 bottles under £20 • 8 by the glass (£2.95-£6)

PRICE GUIDE Fixed L £14.95 • Fixed D £21.50 • starter £4.95-8.50 • main £12.95-£20 • dessert £3.95-£4.75 • coffee 1.50 • min/water £2.50 • Service optional

PLACE: A fine county house close to the city of Lincoln, set in 88 res of beautiful grounds complete with a lake. The elegant staurant retains many original features and is adorned with andeliers, paintings and Italianate furniture.

FOOD: Ambitious carte and fixed-price menus of modern British shes with flavours and influences from around the world. A od choice of vegetarian and vegan dishes is also available.

OUR TIP: Take a walk in the grounds

Chef: Miles Collins **Owners:** Southsprings Ltd **Times:** 12-2/7-9.30, osed 1 Jan **Notes:** Tasting menu 6 courses £37.50, Vegetarian available, ess Restrictions, Smart casual - no sportswear, Civ Wed 120 **Seats:** 75, dining room 28 **Smoking:** N/Sm in restaurant **Children:** Min 12 yrs, tions **Rooms:** 50 (50 en suite) ★★★ **Directions:** On B1188, 3m S Lincoln. In village, hotel drive opposite village hall **Parking:** 75 mail: info@branstonhall.com b: www.branstonhall.com

⊕ The Restaurant in the Jew's ouse

ritish, French

odern cooking in unique historic setting

☎ 01522 524851 15 The Strait LN2 1JD

MENU GUIDE Rabbit pâté, onion jam, brioche • Lamb, garlic & arsala jus, fondant potatoes • Raspberry crème brûlée

WINE GUIDE 30 bottles over £20, 20 bottles under £20 • 6 by e glass (£2.20-£5.50)

PRICE GUIDE Fixed L £11.95 • Fixed D £26.95 • coffee 1.50 • min/water £2

PLACE: Tucked away along a small passageway near Lincoln stle, this 12th-century stone house is one of few surviving ildings of its type in the world. Inside has a quietly classical el with wide windows that overlook cobbled streets low.

FOOD: A reverential approach to food finds expression in a nge of tempting modern dishes, such as chicken in pancetta h tarragon and asparagus. The menu changes monthly.

OUR TIP: Ask about the house's fascinating history

Chef: Fabian Hombourger **Owners:** Robert Wilkinson **Times:** 12-0/6-10, Closed Xmas, Mon **Notes:** Vegetarian available, Smart dress, jeans **Seats:** 46, Pr/dining room 14 **Smoking:** N/Sm in restaurant ildren: Portions **Directions:** At bottom of Steep Hill from cathedral rking: Parking 50yds away

⊛ Wig & Mitre

British, International

Honest cooking in traditional inn

☎ 01522 535190 30/32 Steep Hill LN2 1TL

MENU GUIDE Cheese soufflé & leeks • Salmon escalope, cream & chive sauce • Bread & butter pudding

WINE GUIDE ♀ Prince Labouré Cuvée Blanc £12.45 • ♥ Prince Labouré Cuvée Rouge £12.45 • 27 bottles over £20, 32 bottles under £20 • 23 by the glass (£3.20-£12.80)

PRICE GUIDE Fixed L £11.50-£12.50 • starter £4.50-£19.50 • main £10.50-£18.50 • dessert £4.95-£5.95 • coffee 80p • min/water £2.70 • Service optional

PLACE: An ancient inn at the top of Steep Hill, with winding stairways and cosy nooks and crannies. The atmosphere is intimate and informal, fostered by casual, friendly staff.

FOOD: The ever-growing reputation for food is well deserved, with a refreshing lack of fuss and an honest focus on quality ingredients marking it as special. Caviar is a feature of the menu, with beef stroganoff or halibut with saffron, perhaps, to follow.

OUR TIP: Aim for simple dishes with the freshest flavours

Chef: Valérie Hope **Owners:** Hope family **Times:** 8am-11pm **Notes:** Vegetarian available **Seats:** 65, Pr/dining room 20 **Smoking:** N/Sm in restaurant **Children:** Portions **Directions:** At the top of Steep Hill, adjacent to Lincoln Cathedral and Lincoln Castle car parks **Parking:** Public car park adjacent

e-mail: email@wigandmitre.com **web:** www.wigandmitre.com

SCUNTHORPE MAP 17 SE81

⊛ Forest Pines Hotel

European, British

Classical food in elegant setting

☎ 01652 650770 Ermine St, Broughton DN20 0AQ

MENU GUIDE Spinach tagliatelle, sauté monkfish • Pan-fried pork medallions, sweet potato, caramelised apple • Crème brûlée, plum compote

WINE GUIDE ♀ Cape Promise Sauvignon Blanc £14.85 • ♥ Moondarra Shiraz £12.65 • 31 bottles over £20, 26 bottles under £20 • 7 by the glass (£2.70-£4.95)

PRICE GUIDE Fixed L £15-£32 • Fixed D £25-£35 • coffee £2.50 • min/water £3.25 • Service optional

PLACE: One of three places to eat in this smart modern hotel and golf complex, the Beech Tree Restaurant is air-conditioned and offers high levels of comfort. The decor is fresh and modern, and the well spaced tables are set with crisp linen and sparkling glassware.

FOOD: A modern menu with European influences, priced for two or three courses. Dishes are based on good quality ingredients and are generally simply cooked.

OUR TIP: Work up an appetite for the generous portions

Chef: Arve Refvik **Owners:** Mr D & Mr A Middleton **Times:** 12-2/7-9.45, Closed L Sat **Notes:** Vegetarian available, Dress Restrictions, Smart, no jeans, Civ Wed 300 **Seats:** 132, Pr/dining room 40 **Smoking:** N/Sm in restaurant, Air con **Children:** Menu, Portions **Rooms:** 114 (114 en suite) ★★★★ **Directions:** From M180 junct 4, travel towards Scunthorpe on A18. Continue straight over rdbt, hotel is situated on left **Parking:** 300 **e-mail:** enquiries@forestpines.co.uk **web:** www.forestpines.co.uk

England

SPALDING MAP 12 TF22

⊛ Cley Hall Hotel

British, International

Bistro-style food in manor house setting

☎ 01775 725157 22 High St PE11 1TX

MENU GUIDE Crab & lettuce spring roll, pineapple sauce • Grilled poussin, spinach, ricotta & herb stuffing • Prune & Armagnac tart

WINE GUIDE ♀ Boland Sauvignon Blanc £16.50 • ♥ Dolman de Fees Merlot £12 • 50% bottles over £20, 50% bottles under £20 • 10 by the glass (£2.60-£3.95)

PRICE GUIDE Fixed L £8.95 • starter £3.95-£9 • main £10.95-£17 • dessert £5-£6.50 • coffee £1.95 • min/water £2.50 • Service optional

PLACE: Fine Georgian property overlooking the River Welland; derelict in the 1960s, saved from demolition by a preservation order, and now Grade II listed. There are three dining areas with different atmospheres but the same menu: the marquee-style Terrace Restaurant, the Garden Restaurant and the Down Below Restaurant in the cellars beneath the hotel.

FOOD: A modern British menu plus some International influences, with mostly simply presented dishes dependent on quality ingredients.

OUR TIP: Sip an aperitif in the adjoining bar

Chef: Mark Tomeo **Owners:** Mr & Mrs Mowat **Times:** 12-2.00/6.30-9.30, Closed D 25-26 Dec **Notes:** Vegetarian available, Civ Wed 30 **Seats:** 60, Pr/dining room 30 **Smoking:** N/Sm in restaurant **Children:** Portions **Rooms:** 12 (12 en suite) ★★ **Directions:** Telephone for directions **Parking:** 20 **e-mail:** cleyhall@enterprise.net **web:** www.cleyhallhotel.com

STAMFORD MAP 11 TF00

⊛ George of Stamford Hotel

British, International

Formal dining in historic coaching inn

☎ 01780 750750 71 St Martins PE9 2LB

MENU GUIDE Pan-fried scallops, stir-fry vegetables, Thai green curry • English sirloin, Yorkshire pudding, horseradish sauce • Crème caramel

WINE GUIDE ♀ Roussane-Sauvignon Maison des Pourthie Vin Pays d'Oc £12.95 • ♥ 2001 Domaine de Lavabre Coteaux du Languedoc £13.75 • 82 bottles over £20, 75 bottles under £20 • 15 by the glass (£3.95-£6)

PRICE GUIDE Fixed L £17.50 • starter £5.50-£13.95 • main £15.95-£28 • dessert £5.55 • coffee £3.25 • min/water £2.85 • Service optional

PLACE: There are two restaurants at this 16th-century coaching inn, the main oak-panelled dining room and the less formal Garden Room with its ivy-clad courtyard.

FOOD: Customers delight in the old favourite dishes and the traditional trolley service of meats, sweets and cheeses, though modern tastes and ingredients are also accommodated incorporating international overtones. Cooking is careful and accurate from good fresh produce.

OUR TIP: Try freshly carved beef from the carving trolley

Chef: Chris Pitman, Paul Reseigh **Owners:** Lawrence Hoskins **Times:** 12.30-2.30/7.30-10.30 **Notes:** Vegetarian available, Dress Restrictions, Jacket & tie, Civ Wed 50 **Seats:** 90, Pr/dining room 40 **Smoking:** No pipes, No cigars **Children:** Min 10yrs **Rooms:** 47 (47 en suite) ★★★ **Directions:** From A1(Peterborough) take rdbt signed B1081. Follow road to 1st set of lights, hotel on left **Parking:** 120 **e-mail:** reservations@georgehotelofstamford.com **web:** www.georgehotelofstamford.com/

■ Fratelli's PE9 2DP ☎ 01780 754333 Very popular Italian serving a good selection of reliable dishes.

SUTTON ON SEA MAP 17 TF58

⊛ Grange & Links Hotel

British, French

Good food between the fields and the sea

☎ 01507 441334 Sea Ln, Sandilands LN12 2RA

MENU GUIDE Carrot & coriander soup • Beef fillet, rosemary mash, red wine sauce • Pear & almond tart

PRICE GUIDE Starter £3-£7 • main £9.50-£15 • dessert £3-£3.80 • coffee £2 • min/water £3.50 • Service optional

PLACE: Close to the beach and boasting its own 18-hole golf course, this friendly, family-run hotel stands in five acres of grounds. The restaurant is traditionally furnished and quite formal in style. Service, however, is friendly and relaxed.

FOOD: Cooking is simple and unpretentious, utilising quality local produce, including North Sea fish and lobster in season. Good clean flavours shine in uncomplicated dishes.

OUR TIP: Ideal getaway for keen golfers

Chef: Tina Harrison **Owners:** Ann Askew **Times:** 7-10, Closed L Mon-Sun **Notes:** Vegetarian available, Dress Restrictions, Jacket & tie, Civ Wed 150 **Seats:** Menu, Portions **Rooms:** 23 (23 en suite) ★★★ **Parking:** 60 **e-mail:** grangeandlinkshotel@btconnect.com **web:** www.thegrangeandlinkshotel.co.uk

WINTERINGHAM MAP 17 SE92

⊛⊛⊛⊛⊛ Winteringham Fields

see page 2

WOOLSTHORPE MAP 11 SK83

⊛ The Chequers Inn

British, European   **⚑NEW**

Classic country cooking in delightful gastro-pub

☎ 01476 870701 Main St NG32 1LU

MENU GUIDE Beef fillet carpaccio • Loin of lamb, truffle polenta, braised pork belly • Eton mess

WINE GUIDE ♀ Short Mile Bay Sauvignon Blanc £12.50 • ♥ Short Mile Bay Shiraz £13 • 70 bottles over £20, 45 bottles under £20 • 29 by the glass (£3-£12)

PRICE GUIDE Fixed L £9.50 • Fixed D £13.95 • starter £4.25-£8.95 • main £9.95-£18.95 • dessert £4.70-£5.20 • coffee £1.75 • min/water £3 • Service optional

PLACE: A delightful coaching inn close to Belvoir Castle and the village cricket pitch. Roaring log fires in winter, and a casual, contemporary atmosphere, combined with exposed brickwork and an original bakery oven, contribute to its appeal.

FOOD: Plenty of natural talent is evident in a classic asparagus with hollandaise and soft-poached egg. The modern gastro menu yields similar quality with pan-fried pork fillet, honey-roasted carrots and classic dauphinoise potatoes.

OUR TIP: Try any of the seasonal local produce

Chef: John Melican **Owners:** Justin & Joanne Chad **Times:** 12-3/5.30-11, closed D 25-26 Dec **Notes:** Sun L 2 courses £10.95, Vegetarian available **Seats:** 70, Pr/dining room 14 **Smoking:** N/Sm in restaurant **Children:** Menu, Portions **Rooms:** 4 (4 en suite) ♦♦♦♦ **Directions:** From A1 exit A607 towards Melton Mowbray follow heritage signs for Belvoir Castle. **Parking:** 35 **e-mail:** justinnabar@yahoo.co.u **web:** www.chequers-inn.net

WINTERINGHAM MAP 17 SE92

Winteringham Fields

British, French *A lifetime of dedicated craft*

☎ 01724 733096   DN15 9PF

e-mail: wintfields@aol.com

web: www.winteringhamfields.com

PLACE: A lifetime of dedication and a labour of love, ensures that the Schwab's restaurant with rooms offers the crème de la crème of dining experiences, even if it is hidden away in an unassuming village in the Lincolnshire outback. Their 16th-century former manor house has original beams, log fires, sloping floors and period features, while Victoriana rules with chintz, antiques, fabulous pictures and collectables that charmingly reflect the era. It's a serious destination for diners, with peerless cooking at its heart, and it stands among the best in the country, though displaying an appealing warm, inviting and relaxed atmosphere. A choice of comfortable sitting rooms and a conservatory offer plenty of seating for aperitifs, while in summer, the rose garden comes into play. Service, with Annie overseeing out front, is friendly, not at all stuffy, but highly professional, knowledgeable and attentive; staff are dedicated and really care about the product as if it were their own.

FOOD: Germain Schwab has been behind the stoves for some 18 years honing his craft, and his brigade of eleven, headed up by protégé Robert Thompson, ensures consistency and attention to detail. The kitchen uses only the finest quality ingredients, local where possible (fish arrives daily from Grimsby, game in season from local shoots and vegetables, fruit and herbs come from Winteringham's own potager when available), while the cooking style is provincial, classical French with modern influences. Precision, clean, distinct flavours, freshness, seasoning and timings all deliver spot on, with peripherals like amuse bouche, pre-dessert and petits fours (a choice of ten) hitting the top notes too, while superb cheeses (a restaurant signature) hold form with aplomb. Absolute dedication from Germain and his youthful team ensure sheer perfection throughout, and show a real, passionate love of food, which comes across on every plate. Germain is AA Chef's Chef 2005-2006 (see page 19).

MENU GUIDE Brill fillet glazed with mulled wine, pumpkin fondant • Cod fillet, belly pork cassoulet, sorrel sauce • Vanilla crème brûlée, red fruit compôte, brandy snaps

WINE GUIDE ♀ Marlborough Waipara Hills Sauvignon Blanc £30 • ♀ Langhorne Creek Trig Point Shiraz £22 • all bottles over £20 • 16 by the glass (£4.50–£12.60)

PRICE GUIDE Fixed L £31-£33 • Fixed D £40 • starter £23-£24.50 • main £32-£33 • dessert £10-£20 • coffee £4.50 • min/water £2.90 • Service included

OUR TIP: Everyone should visit this magical place at least once

Chef: Germain Schwab, Robert Thompson **Owners:** Mr & Mrs Schwab **Times:** 12-2/7-10, Closed 2 wks Xmas, 1st wk Aug, last wk Mar, Sun-Mon **Notes:** Tasting menu 6 courses £72, Vegetarian available **Seats:** 42, Pr/dining room 10 **Smoking:** N/Sm in restaurant **Rooms:** 10 (10 en suite) 🕮 **Directions:** Village centre, off A1077, 4m S of Humber Bridge **Parking:** 20

London
Restaurant of the Year for London
Le Cercle, SW1
(see page 278)

Index of London Restaurants

This index shows restaurants in London in alphabetical order, followed by their postcodes. Page numbers precede each entry.

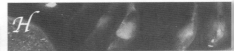

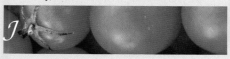

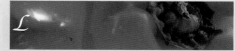

London Plan 1

6

Totteridge
Highwood Hill
Mill Hill
Bushey Heath
Grim's Dyke Hotel
Stanmore
Edgware
Harrow Weald
Church End
Belmont
Burnt Oak
Queensbury
Northwood
Hatch End
Northwood

0   1   2 miles
0   1   2   3 kilometres

Pinner Friends Restaurant
Wealdstone
Kenton
Kingsbury
Colindale
West Hendon
Hendon

5
Eastcote Village
North Harrow
HARROW
Golders Green
Ruislip Barn Hotel
Rayners Lane
Harrow on the Hill
North Wembley
Cricklewood
Ickenham
South Harrow
Sudbury
Neasden
Willesden
Northolt Aerodrome
North Hillingdon
WEMBLEY
Sabras Restaurant
Willesden Green
Kilburn
Hillingdon
Northolt
Alperton
Stonebridge
Harlesden
Kensal Green

4
Hayes End
Yeading
Greenford
Perivale
Park Royal
North Acton
North Kensington
Lonso
Wood End
Momo
E & O
Notting Hill Brasserie
Notti
Hayes
Southall
Hanwell
EALING
East Acton
Acton
Hill
Edera
Simply Nico
Norwood Green
KENSIN
Chez Kristof
Cotto
Cibc
Anglesea Arms
Snows-on-the-Green

3
Radisson Edwardian Heathrow
Heston Services
Heston
Fish Hoek
The Brackenbury
Sagar
La Trompette
Chiswick
HAMMERSMITH
OSTERLEY PARK
Devonshire House
The Gate
The River Café
Brentford
KEW
Ma Cuisine
Kew
Sonny's Restaurant
FULHAM
HEATHROW AIRPORT
Cranford
The Glasshouse
GARDENS
Barnes
Hounslow
Isleworth
The Depot
Mortlake
Waterfront Brasserie
MVH
Enoteca Turi
Hatton
Redmond's
East Sheen
Talad Thai
Putney

2
East Bedfont
Whitton
Ma Cuisine
Brula
Crowthers Restaurant
The Victoria
Feltham
McClements Restaurant
La Buvette
Bingham Hotel
Richmond Gate Hotel
Roehampton
Lower Feltham
Restaurant at the Petersham
Twickenham
RICHMOND
Felthamhill
Hanworth
Petersham
PARK
WIMBLEDON COMMON
WIMBLED
Hampton Hill
Monsieur Max
Teddington
Ham
ford

1
Charlton
BUSHY PARK
Hampton Wick
The Light House Restaurant
Sunbury
Ayudhya Thai Restaurant
Frere Jacques
West Molesey
Hampton
KINGSTON UPON THAMES
Norbiton
New Malden
Raynes Park
Central London
Congestion Charging Zone
East Molesey
HAMPTON COURT PARK
The French Table
Berrylands
Motspur Park
Mo
Littleton
Queen Elizabeth II Reservoir
Thames Ditton
Surbiton
Old Malden
pperton
Walton-on-Thames
Long Ditton
Tolworth

A   **B**   **C**   **D**

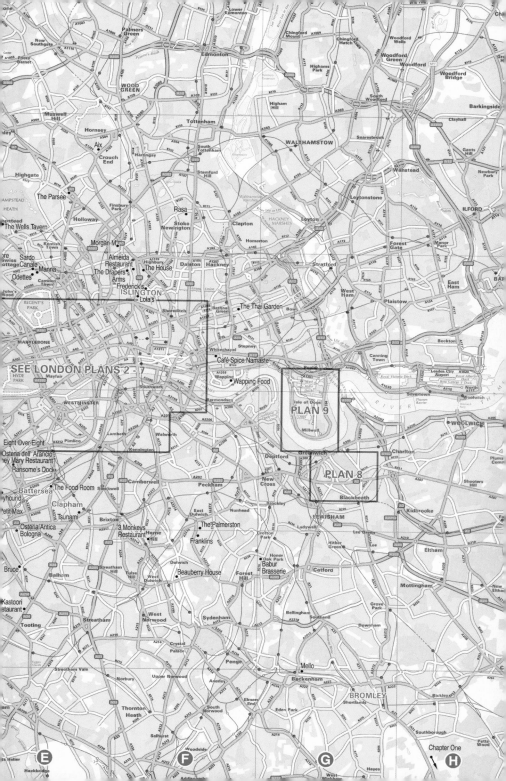

London Plan 6

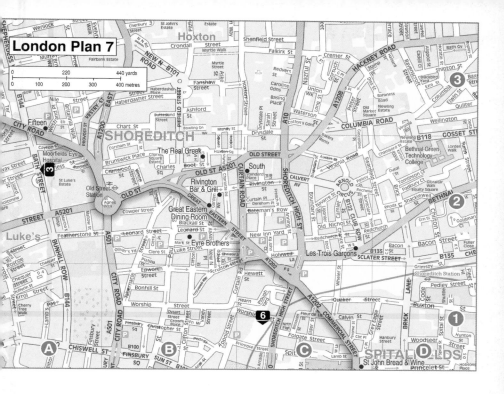

London Plan 7

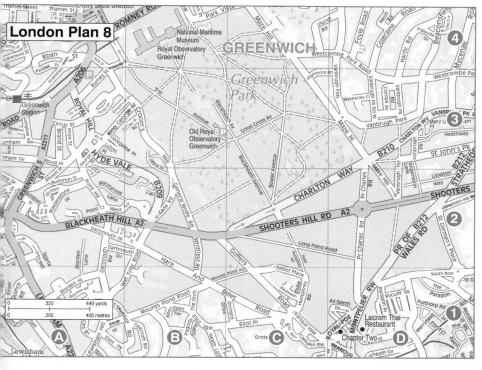

London Plan 8

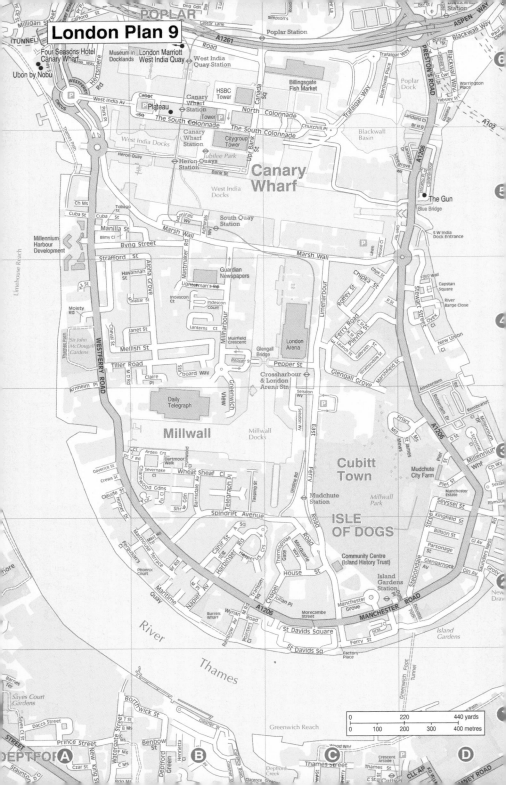

LONDON, CENTRAL

Greater London Plans 1-9, pages 240-252. (Small scale maps 6 & 7 at back of guide.) Restaurants are listed below in postal district order, commencing East, then North, South and West, with a brief indication of the area covered. Detailed plans 2-9 show the locations of restaurants with AA Rosette Awards within the Central London postal districts. If you do not know the postal district of the restaurant you want, please refer to the index preceding the street plans for the entry and map pages. The plan reference for each restaurant also appears within its directory entry.

LONDON E1

Café Spice Namaste

Pan-Asian

Innovative Indian cuisine in The City

☎ 020 7488 9242 16 Prescot St E1 8AZ Plan 1-F4

MENU GUIDE Keema no puff pattice (Spicy lamb in pastry) • Vindalho de porco (Goan pork vindaloo) • Parsee apricot & toffee ice cream

WINE GUIDE ♀ Sancerre £24.95 • ♀ Bodegas Rioja Crianza 15 bottles over £20, 15 bottles under £20 • 6 by the glass (£3.95-£5.25)

PRICE GUIDE Fixed L £25 • Fixed D £30 • starter £4.25-£7.75 • main £9.75-£17.50 • dessert £3.25-£5.50 • coffee £1.50 • min/water £2.75 • Service added but optional 12.5%

PLACE: Located in a former courthouse, this destination Indian restaurant has built a loyal following in recent years being just minutes from the City. Dining rooms are bright and airy and decorated with swags of colourful fabric.

FOOD: Extensive menus may include the famous and not so famous dishes of the subcontinent but all are prepared with refinement and dexterity. Indian classical culinary skills meet fresh British produce.

OUR TIP: Hone your appetite with a walk across nearby Tower Bridge

Chef: Cyrus Todiwala **Owners:** Cafe Spice Ltd **Times:** 12-3/6.15-10.30, Closed Xmas, BHs, Sun, closed L Sat **Notes:** Vegetarian available, Dress Restrictions, Smart casual **Seats:** 120 **Smoking:** Air con **Children:** Portions **Parking:** On street; NCP **e-mail:** binay@cafespice.co.uk **web:** www.cafespice.co.uk

Lanes Restaurant & Bar

European

Fashionable venue with modern European cuisine

☎ 020 7247 5050 109-117 Middlesex St E1 7JF Plan 6-C5

MENU GUIDE Smoked swordfish, lemon risotto, pickled fennel • Mussel & clam stuffed brill • Lanes quince crumble

WINE GUIDE ♀ Buitenverwachting Sauvignon Blanc £24.95 • ♀ Madfish Pinot Noir £25 • 45 bottles over £20, 8 bottles under £20 • 14 by the glass (£3.50-£5.95)

Lanes Restaurant & Bar

PRICE GUIDE Fixed D £21.50 • starter £7.50-£12.95 • main £10.50-£19.50 • dessert £6.50 • coffee £2.50 • min/water £3.25 • Service added but optional 12.5%

PLACE: Wind down with a glass of champagne in the inviting bar of this smart but informal basement restaurant. Modern prints adorn the walls and the dining room sports high-backed linen chairs, leather banquette seating and wooden floors.

FOOD: Accomplished cooking with quality ingredients and an imaginative choice of modern brasserie dishes, with some Italian and classical elements, make the food worth making the trip for. Dishes are packed with flavours and presentation is crisp and clean.

OUR TIP: The bright modern art is for sale

Chef: Hayden Smith **Owners:** James Robertson & Hamish Smith **Times:** 12-3/5.30-10, Closed BHs, 25 Dec, 1 Jan, Sun, closed L Sat **Notes:** Vegetarian available **Seats:** 70, Pr/dining room 28 **Smoking:** Air con **Children:** Min 7yrs L, Portions **Parking:** On street after 6.30 pm **e-mail:** info@lanesrestaurant.co.uk **web:** www.lanesrestaurant.co.uk

St John Bread & Wine

British

Modern dining in old Clerkenwell

☎ 020 7247 8724 94-96 Commercial St E1 6LZ Plan 6-D6

MENU GUIDE Brown shrimp, white cabbage & chervil • Roast goose & quince • Pear sorbet & pear vodka

WINE GUIDE ♀ Côtes de Gascogne Domaine de Millet Colombard £15 • ♀ VDP Coteaux du Libron Domaine la Colombette Grenache £17.50 • 43 bottles over £20, 14 bottles under £20 • 17 by the glass (£3.40-£5.80)

PRICE GUIDE Starter £5.80-£10 • main £11-£19 • dessert £5.40-£6.10 • coffee £1.75 • min/water £3 • Service optional • Group min 6 service 12.5%

PLACE: Younger sibling to St. John just around the corner, this old bank building now houses a busy, modern restaurant which doubles as an excellent bread shop. Whitewashed brickwork, parquet flooring and utilitarian settings offer little distraction from the food.

FOOD: British - and proud of it - the emphasis is on the quality of ingredients. The daily-changing menu is a wide-ranging affair with offal, smoked fish, pork chops, razor clams and chestnuts all vying for attention.

OUR TIP: Buy some of the great sourdough bread

Chef: Karl Goward **Owners:** Trevor Gulliver & Fergus Henderson **Times:** 9am-11pm, Closed 24 Dec-2 Jan, BHs, closed D Sun **Notes:** Tasting menus available for parties larger than 10, Vegetarian available **Seats:** 60 **Smoking:** Air con **Parking:** on street **e-mail:** reservations@stjohnbreadandwine.com **web:** www.stjohnbreadandwine.com

continued

England

LONDON E1 *continued*

🌐 Les Trois Garçons

French

Playful, warm and atmospheric French restaurant

☎ 020 7613 1924   1 Club Row E1 6JX   Plan 7-C2

MENU GUIDE Sautéed prawns in red wine butter, fennel broth • Lamb rack, carrot-beetroot galette, crispy bacon, red berry jus • Mixed berry crème brûlée, tuile biscuit

WINE GUIDE ⚲ La Roche Blanche Pouilly Fumé £29 • ⚲ Château Bouquoyran £25 • 7 by the glass (£5.50-£7.50)

PRICE GUIDE Fixed D £26-£45 • starter £8.50-£14 • main £15-£26 • dessert £6-£7.50 • coffee £3.50 • min/water £3.75 • Service added but optional 12.5%

PLACE: Outside this looks like any other one-time Victorian corner pub, but the interior is brilliantly playful, glitzy and jaw dropping. Surreally packed with a menagerie of bejewelled stuffed animals and all manner of objets d'art from dangling chandeliers to ladies' handbags. There's French music, white tablecloths and a welcoming atmosphere too.

FOOD: The generous, rich, well-presented classic French cooking comes dotted with luxury items (foie gras, caviar, truffles, etc) that suits the mood and friendly, attentive service.

OUR TIP: Don't miss the theatre of the Calvados flambéed apple tart Tatin to finish

Chef: Eddie Ademola **Owners:** Stefan Karlson, Hussan Abdullah, Michel Lasserre **Times:** 12-4/7-12, Closed Sun, closed L all week (open Xmas only) **Notes:** Vegetarian available **Seats:** 80, Pr/dining room 12 **Smoking:** Air con **Children:** Min 12yrs **Directions:** Nearest station: Liverpool Street 10mins walk from station, at the end of Brick Ln **Parking:** On street after 7pm **e-mail:** info@lestroisgarcons.com **web:** www.lestroisgarcons.com

🌐 Wapping Food

British, European

Interesting food in industrial surroundings at the Wapping Project

☎ 020 7680 2080   Wapping Hydraulic Power Station, Wapping Wall E1W 3ST   Plan 1-F4

MENU GUIDE Steamed shellfish, ginger, chilli & lemongrass • Roast deer haunch, wild mushrooms, foie gras pâté • Quince & almond tart

WINE GUIDE ⚲ Echo Point Semillon £16 • ⚲ Echo Point Pinot Noir £16 • 57 bottles over £20, 10 bottles under £20 • 10 by the glass (£4.25-£9)

PRICE GUIDE Fixed D £40 • starter £6-£9 • main £9-£18 • dessert £4.50-£7 • coffee £1.50 • min/water £2.90 • Service added but optional 12.5%

PLACE: Once a hydraulic power station, this idiosyncratic restaurant--cultural centre for theatre, music and visual art, has an architecture and design-led clientele thanks to its widely praised conversion. It is sensational to look at and there's plenty going on.

FOOD: Daily-changing menu of British and European dishes with an emphasis on Italian cooking, plus an 'eating together' menu for 9-24 people at £40 a head. Home-made bread sold Saturdays.

OUR TIP: Snacks and drinks all day and brunch at weekends

Chef: James Robson **Owners:** Womens Playhouse Trust **Times:** 12-3/6.30-11, Closed 24 Dec-3 Jan, closed D Sun **Notes:** Vegetarian available **Seats:** 100 **Smoking:** No pipes, No cigars **Children:** Portions **Directions:** Nearest station: Wapping Turn right from tube, walk east & parallel to the river (approx 4 mins) **Parking:** 20 **e-mail:** info@wapping-wpt.com **web:** www.thewappingproject.com

🌐 **Café Naz** 46-48 Brick Ln E1 6RF ☎ 020 7247 0234 Smart Bangladeshi with a touch of sophistication.

🎏 **One Blossom Street** 1 Blossom St E1 6BX ☎ 020 7247 6532 Stylish restaurant with simple but effective Italian food and a good wine list.

LONDON E2

🌐 The Thai Garden

Thai

Authentic Thai with neighbourhood feel

☎ 020 8981 5748   249 Globe Rd E2 0JD   Plan 1-F4

MENU GUIDE Hot & sour mushroom soup • Stir-fried prawns, basil leaves, hot chilli • Thai custard

WINE GUIDE ⚲ House White £8.50 • ⚲ House Red £8.50 • all bottles under £20 • 2 by the glass (£2.25)

PRICE GUIDE Fixed D £16-£20 • starter £3.50-£5.50 • main £4.50-£7 • dessert £3-£3 • coffee £1 • min/water £2.50 • Service added but optional 10%

PLACE: Tucked away down a quiet side street in Bethnal Green, this intimate Thai bustles with a regular crowd of young locals. Service comes with a smile from waiting staff dressed in traditional costume. Book ahead.

FOOD: The kitchen prides itself on delivering authentic Thai, which means a lengthy range of vegetarian and seafood dishes, but no meat. All the staples dishes make an appearance, plus some more unusual options.

OUR TIP: The use of both MSG and GM products is avoided

Chef: Napathorn Duff **Owners:** S & J Hufton **Times:** 12-2.30/6-11, Closed BHs, closed L Sat & Sun **Notes:** Vegetarian available **Seats:** 32, Pr/dining room 12 **Smoking:** N/Sm area **Children:** Portions **Directions:** Nearest station: Bethnal Green 2nd left off Roman Road (one-way street). Near London Buddhist Centre **Parking:** on street **e-mail:** thaigarden@hotmail.com **web:** www.thethaigarden.co.uk

LONDON E14

🌐 Four Seasons Hotel Canary Wharf

Italian

Sophisticated Italian at Canary Wharf

☎ 020 7510 1999   Westferry Circus, Canary Wharf E14 8RS   Plan 9-A6

MENU GUIDE Duck foie gras, red onion compote • Veal osso buco, sautéed vegetables, saffron risotto timbale • Tiramisù

continued

continue

England

WINE GUIDE Borgo del Tiglio Tocai/Malvasia £44 • Fattori a Felsina Berardenga Chianti Sangiovese £45 • 150 bottles over £20 • 28 by the glass (£6.50-£14.50)

PRICE GUIDE Fixed L £30 • starter £10-£15.50 • main £14-£28.50 • dessert £9.50 • coffee £4.50 • min/water £4 • Service optional • Group min 8 service 12.5%

PLACE: Designed by Philip Starcke, this five star hotel sits on a bend of the Thames at Canary Wharf, and offers stunning views of the London skyline from many of its bedrooms. The Quadrato restaurant is a sleek contemporary setting of deep reds and browns, with a theatre kitchen and friendly staff who are passionate about both food and wine.

FOOD: A predominantly northern Italian menu is complemented by a range of specials themed around a different region each week. Ingredients are good quality and brought together in simple and tasty combinations.

OUR TIP: 20 minutes from the West End on the Jubilee Line
Chef: Sebastiano Spriveri **Owners:** Four Seasons Hotels **Times:** 12-3/6-10.30 **Notes:** Sun brunch £36 (incl. glass of sparkling wine), Vegetarian available, Dress Restrictions, Smart casual preferred, Civ Wed 200
Seats: 90 **Smoking:** N/Sm area, No pipes, No cigars, Air con
Children: Menu, Portions **Rooms:** 142 (142 en suite) ★★★★★
Directions: Nearest station: Canary Wharf Jubilee Line Just off Westbury Circus rdbt. **Parking:** 26 **web:** www.fourseasons.com/canarywharf

The Gun

English, French   **NEW**

Smart Docklands gastro-pub serving modern British food

☎ 020 7515 5222   27 Coldharbour, Docklands E14 9NS   Plan 9-D5

MENU GUIDE Black truffle omelette • Pot au feu guinea fowl • Rum & raisin parfait

PRICE GUIDE Food prices not confirmed for 2006. Please telephone for details

PLACE: Classy waterside pub in a listed building with great views of the Millenium Dome from the terrace. Beautifully restored with oak timber floors and Georgian-style fireplaces, one side is devoted to upmarket dining and the other to an inviting bar.
FOOD: Versatile menus feature rustic choices alongside more sophisticated offerings: from braised monkfish osso buco with risotto milanaise to boiled beef and carrots with thyme dumplings, and plenty in between.
OUR TIP: Great spot for Sunday brunch
Times: 12-3/6-11 **e-mail:** info@thegundocklands.com
web: www.thegundocklands.com

London Marriott West India Quay

Contemporary American   **NEW**

Accomplished cooking in impressive Docklands hotel

☎ 020 7093 1000   22 Hertsmere Rd, Canary Wharf E14 4ED   Plan 9-B6

MENU GUIDE Crab cakes & chilli aioli • Halibut with peppers, shrimps & mustard sauce • Key lime pie & fruit sorbet

PRICE GUIDE Food prices not confirmed for 2006. Please telephone for details

PLACE: This spectacular skyscraper hotel, with its curved glass façade, is located in the heart of the Docklands, adjacent to Canary Wharf and overlooking the water of West India Quay.
FOOD: American-influenced cooking is of a high quality and consistency.
OUR TIP: Stay in one of the bedrooms with quay views
Times: 12-2.30/5-10.30 **Rooms:** 301 (301 en suite) ★★★★★
e-mail: remus.boydon@marriotthotel.com **web:** www.marriott.com

Plateau

French

Sleek modern dining at Canary Wharf

☎ 020 7715 7100   Canada Place, Canada Square, Canary Wharf E14 4QS   Plan 9-B6

MENU GUIDE Prawn salad, champagne vinaigrette • Lamb, belly confit, choucroute • Tarte Tatin, green apple Calvados sorbet

WINE GUIDE Louis Michel Chablis 1er Cru les Vaillons £36 • Jean Pierre Mouiex St Emilion £27 • 180 bottles over £20, 17 bottles under £20 • 14 by the glass (£4-£7.50)

PRICE GUIDE Fixed D £24.75 • starter £8-£14.75 • main £14.50-£27 • dessert £6.50 • coffee £3 • min/water £3.45 • Service added but optional 12.5%

PLACE: Buzzy, modern restaurant with a grown-up decor of designer chairs and marble topped tables. A floor to ceiling glass frontage completes the sleek, urban feel and offers stunning views of Canary Wharf.
FOOD: Straightforward modern fare that's full of flavour, with mains such as baked monkfish with chestnuts and baby leeks, or beef with wild mushrooms and salsify boulangère. A simpler, cheaper bar menu is also available. Notable wine list.
OUR TIP: Two terraces for alfresco drinking or dining in the summer
Chef: Tim Tolley **Owners:** Bertrand Pierson **Times:** 12-3/6-11, Closed 25-26 Dec, 1 Jan, Sun, closed L Sat **Notes:** Tasting menu £48, Vegetarian available **Seats:** 124, Pr/dining room 24 **Children:** Menu, Portions
Directions: Nearest station: Canary Wharf Facing Canary Wharf Tower
e-mail: plateau@conran-restaurants.co.uk
web: www.conran.com

Ubon by Nobu see page 256

Carluccios Caffè 2 Nash Court, Canary Wharf E14 5AG ☎ 020 7719 1749 Quality Italian chain.

Corney & Barrow at Canary Wharf 9 Cabot Square E14 4QF ☎ 020 7512 0397 City wine bar chain offering contemporary dishes.

LONDON EC1

The Bleeding Heart

Modern French

Discreet and hospitable French restaurant in Hatton Garden

☎ 020 7242 2056   19 Greville St, Bleeding Heart Yard EC1N 8SQ   Plan 3-F4

MENU GUIDE Green pea velouté, Avruga caviar crème • Roasted monkfish fillet, broad beans, saffron potatoes • Warm chocolate pudding, pistachio ice cream

WINE GUIDE Trinity Hill Hawkes Bay Sauvignon Blanc £16.45 • Trinity Hill Hawkes Bay Cabernet Sauvignon/Merlot £19.95 • 550 bottles over £20, 17 bottles under £20 • 20 by the glass (£4.15-£12.50)

continued

continued

England

LONDON E14

Ubon by Nobu

Japanese, American

Westernised Japanese food in stunning panoramic setting

☎ 020 7719 7800 34 Westferry Circus, Canary Wharf E14 8RR Plan 9-A6

MENU GUIDE Sashimi salad, Matshihisa dressing • Black cod with miso • Mango soufflé, passionfruit sauce

WINE GUIDE ♀ Sancerre Grande Cuvée £55 • ♀ Château de Pez £55 • 7 by the glass (£6-£8.50)

PRICE GUIDE Starter £5-£23.50 • main £5.50-£29.50 • dessert £5.50-£9.50 • coffee £1.75 • min/water £4.50 • Service added but optional 15%

PLACE: Dining at Ubon, the sibling restaurant of Nobu in Mayfair, is as much a visual treat as it is a culinary one. The location is hard to beat, on the top floor of an eccentrically styled building in Canary Wharf, with glass windows stretching from floor to ceiling allowing awesome views of the Thames and city beyond – a sanctuary of light, airy simplicity high above London's hustle and bustle. This sophisticated, modern venue is decked out with wooden floors, and a cream and brown decor, and a theatrical, open-plan sushi area with strategically placed mirrors. Having marvelled at the view, attention turns to Ubon's huge and equally mind-boggling menu. Don't fret though, well-informed, friendly staff are keen to help and explain the pleasures of Japanese food to the uninitiated.

FOOD: Food is funky modern Japanese and very fashionable. Expect a great variety of dishes and styles on offer, from sushi and sashimi to Ubon specials, tempura and noodles. Simple, fresh, high quality ingredients are beyond reproach and the food is innovative and accomplished with clear flavours and accurately balanced dishes.

OUR TIP: First-timers should try a bento box which includes a range of signature dishes

Chef: Youcef Khelil, Mark Edwards **Owners:** Nobu Matsuhisa, B S Ong **Times:** 12-2.15/6-10.15, Closed Xmas, all BHs, Sun, closed L Sat **Notes:** Omakase menu L£50, D £70, Vegetarian available **Seats:** 120 **Smoking:** N/Sm in restaurant, Air con **Directions:** Nearest station: Westferry, Canary Wharf. Follow signs to Canary Riverside Restaurant behind Four Seasons Hotel. **Parking:** Riverside car park **e-mail:** ubon@noburestaurants.com **web:** www.noburestaurants.com

---

LONDON EC1 *continued*

PRICE GUIDE Fixed L £29.95 • starter £6.45-£12.50 • main £11.95-£21.50 • dessert £5.95-£6.95 • coffee £2.50 • min/water £3 • Service added but optional 12.5%

PLACE: Hidden away in the corner of a historic, cobbled courtyard behind the tavern, and beneath the bistro of the same name, this atmospheric basement dining room oozes character, with its wooden floors, beams, charming French service and dark, romantic, if somewhat clubby, atmosphere.

FOOD: Sophisticated French food is the approach, with classics like an evening special Châteaubriand with sauce béarnaise and pommes frites alongside more modern options like warm seared foie gras on sweet potatoes and tamarind.

OUR TIP: Sample the award-winning wine list

Chef: Pascal Even **Owners:** Robert & Robyn Wilson **Times:** 12-3.15/6-11, Closed Xmas & New Year (10 days), Sat-Sun **Notes:** Fixed D £24.95 for groups of 8+, Vegetarian available, Smart Dress **Seats:** 110, Pr/dining room 40 **Smoking:** No pipes, Air con **Children:** Min 7yrs **Directions:** Nearest station: Farringdon Turn right out of Farringdon Station onto Cowcross St, continue down Greville St for 50mtrs. Turn left into Bleeding Heart Yard. **Parking:** 20 evening only, NCP nearby **e-mail:** bookings@bleedingheart.co.uk **web:** www.bleedingheart.co.uk

⚜ Le Café du Marché

French

Provincial France in London

☎ 020 7608 1609 Charterhouse Mews, Charterhouse Square EC1M 6AH Plan 3-G4

MENU GUIDE Terrine of foie gras, quince jelly • Tronçon of turbot, sauce hollandaise • Cherry tart

continued

PRICE GUIDE Fixed D £27.95 • coffee £2 • min/water £1.75 • Service added but optional 15%

PLACE: This aptly named brasserie, hidden away in a quiet, cobbled mews a stone's throw from Smithfield Market, is a engaging slice of London that's forever France. Bare-brick walls, floorboards, exposed rafters and cane chairs with striped cushions characterise the charmingly unpretentious interior. Attentive Gallic staff add to the colourful, lively atmosphere.

FOOD: The French-language, fixed-price menu changes monthly and bristles with generous, unfussy and accomplished provincial French cooking that precisely fits the mood.

OUR TIP: Good if pricey French wines

Chef: Simon Cottard **Owners:** Anna Graham-Wood **Times:** 12-2.30/6-10, Closed Xmas, New Year, Easter, BHs, Sun, closed L Sat **Notes:** Vegetarian available **Seats:** 120, Pr/dining room 65 **Smoking:** Air con **Children:** Portions **Directions:** Nearest station: Barbican Telephone for directions **Parking:** Next door, free after 6pm

⚜ Café Lazeez

Indian   **NEW**

Slick modern Indian with traditional and contemporary cuisine

☎ 020 7253 2224 88 St John St, Clerkenwell EC1M 4EH Plan 3-G4

PLACE: Bare wooden flooring, dimmed lighting, an open kitchen and a conservatory-style dining room set the tone for this unusual upmarket Indian restaurant in Clerkenwell

FOOD: Individual dishes are given well-judged accurate treatment, and the overall quality of the ingredients is very high. The menu main courses are divided into the well-known Lazeez

continue

formula of evolved and traditional. The evolved side including modern dishes such as cumin-crusted sea bass with saffron mash; and the traditional featuring well-executed familiars such as Kashmiri rogan josh.

OUR TIP: Don't miss out on the delicious mango Peshawari naan
Times: 11/mdnt **e-mail:** sh@cafelazeez.com **web:** www.cafelazeez.com

Clerkenwell Dining Room

European

Affordable European food in sophisticated surroundings

☎ 020 7253 9000 69-73 St. John St EC1 4AN
Plan 3-G4

MENU GUIDE Braised oxtail, black pudding, parsnip purée • Wild sea bass fillet, mussel tagliolini • Chocolate fondant, coconut sorbet

WINE GUIDE ♀ Seresin Sauvignon Blanc £20.50 • ♀ Duckbill Pinot Noir £17.50 • 62 bottles over £20, 13 bottles under £20 7 by the glass (£4.50-£7)

PRICE GUIDE Fixed L £15 • starter £8.50-£12.50 • main £13.50-£19.50 • dessert £7 • coffee £2.50 • min/water £3 • Service added but optional 12.5%

PLACE: There's an intimate feel to this discreetly set restaurant and bar. Modern artwork is hung against dark wood and warm tones of Oxford blue and mushroom. Service is relatively friendly, formally structured and attentive.

FOOD: Cooking is rooted in the classics featuring veloutés, terrines and raviolis in a menu that is more European than solely French, with modern presentation.

continued

OUR TIP: Good value lunch menu
Chef: Andrew Thompson & Nelson Reposo **Owners:** Zak Jones & Andrew Thompson **Times:** 12-2.30/6-11.15, Closed 24, 26, 31 Dec & 1 Jan, closed L Sat, closed D Sun **Notes:** Sun L 2 courses £15.50, 3 courses £19.50, Vegetarian available **Seats:** 70, Pr/dining room 40 **Smoking:** N/Sm area, No pipes, Air con **Children:** Portions **Parking:** On street **e-mail:** zak@theclerkenwell.com **web:** www.theclerkenwell.com

Club Gascon *see below*

Malmaison Charterhouse Square

Traditional French

French-style brasserie in trendy hotel

☎ 020 7012 3700 18-21 Charterhouse Square, Clerkenwell EC1M 6AH Plan 3-G4

MENU GUIDE Chicken liver & foie gras parfait • Monkfish cutlet au poivre, pommes parmentier • Creamed rice pudding, Armagnac Agen prunes

PRICE GUIDE Food prices not confirmed for 2006. Please telephone for details

PLACE: The hotel's brasserie-style restaurant is located in the basement of Charterhouse Chambers, running around a spiral staircase. Tables are set on two levels, some in brick backed alcoves, with luxurious cushions and stunning metalwork light fittings. Others are perched on the mezzanine, where you might enjoy a game of chess and a pint of Guinness.

continued

Club Gascon

French

Specialising in gastronomy of south west France

☎ 020 7796 0600 57 West Smithfield EC1A 9DS
Plan 3-G3

MENU GUIDE Marinated foie gras, black figs, walnuts • Fricassée of turbot, parsley pulp • 'Burnt' milk parfait, roasted figs & maple

WINE GUIDE 162 bottles over £20, 7 bottles under £20 • 9 by the glass (£4.50-£7.50)

PRICE GUIDE Fixed L £25 • starter £6.50-£38 • main £9.50-£19 • dessert £6.50-£7.50 • coffee £2.50 • min/water £3 • Service added but optional 12.5%

PLACE: Located just across from Smithfield Market, this listed building - formerly a Lyons teahouse - is now an intimate, elegant restaurant drawing an adoring crowd. Owned by much-lauded chef-patron Pascal Aussignac (and Vincent Labeyrie), who are slowly building a little empire, with a wine bar next door, a deli opposite and a new restaurant, Le Cercle, just off Sloane Square.

The decor is themed on browns, enhanced by huge floral displays. There's lots of glass, marble and leather, tables are closely packed, staff predominantly Gallic, the atmosphere French chic with a casual, unpretentious vibe.

FOOD: A little different from your average French restaurant, Pascal Aussignac's approach is a variation on the grazing concept, allowing diners to try a number of small dishes from the menu's seven sections. Excellent ingredients, with the accent on Pascal's native Gascony, are delivered in daring combinations with depth of flavour and presentation a high point. Foie gras in all its glory features heavily. Notable wine list.

OUR TIP: Tasting menu offers excellent value, and be sure to visit the deli

Chef: Pascal Aussignac **Owners:** P Aussignac & V Labeyrie **Times:** 12-2/7-10, Closed Xmas, New Year, BHs, Sun, closed L Sat **Notes:** Fixed L 5 courses (£38-£60), Fixed D 5 courses (£38-£60), Vegetarian available **Seats:** 45 **Smoking:** No pipes, Air con **Children:** Portions **Parking:** NCP opposite restaurant

England

LONDON EC1 *continued*

FOOD: Simple and tasty - the menu is predominantly French with some British and Italian influences.
OUR TIP: Take an alcove seat for an intimate occasion
Times: 12-2.30/6-10.30 **Rooms:** 97 (97 en suite) ★★★
e-mail: london@malmaison.com
web: www.malmaison.com

Moro

Mediterranean, N African
Cosmopolitan cooking in Clerkenwell
☎ 020 7833 8336 34/36 Exmouth Market EC1R 4QE
Plan 3-F5

MENU GUIDE Quail & flat bread, pistachio sauce • Wood-roasted pork, garlic aioli, mushrooms migas • Rosewater & cardamom ice cream

WINE GUIDE 36 bottles over £20, 11 bottles under £20 • 11 by the glass (£3-£7.80)

PRICE GUIDE Starter £5.50-£8.50 • main £13-£17 • dessert £5 • coffee £1.50 • min/water £2.75 • Group min 6 service 12.5%

PLACE: This cosmopolitan culinary venture draws a well-heeled city crowd thanks to its fashionable Clerkenwell location. It's an expansive, though understated, restaurant, with unclothed, rustic tables, a long zinc-topped bar, and a bustling theatre kitchen that's not just for show.
FOOD: Moro majors in a fusion of influences from Spain, Turkey, Greece and North Africa, offering a menu of intriguing combinations as well as more classical fare. Flavours are strong and portions generous, with produce organic where possible and cooked traditionally in a wood-fired oven. Good vegetarian selection.
OUR TIP: Try the popular tapas menu if you're in a hurry
Chef: Samuel & Samantha Clark **Owners:** Mr & Mrs S Clark & Mark Sainsbury **Times:** 12.30-2.30/7-10.30, Closed Xmas, New Year, BHs, Sun, closed L Sat **Notes:** Vegetarian available **Seats:** 90, Pr/dining room 14 **Smoking:** No pipes, No cigars, Air con **Children:** Portions
Directions: Nearest station: Farringdon or Angel 5 mins walk from Sadlers Wells theatre, between Farringdon Road and Rosebery Ave
e-mail: info@moro.co.uk **web:** www.moro.co.uk

St John

British
The best of British nose-to-tail cooking
☎ 020 7251 0848 26 St John St EC1M 4AY
Plan 3-G4

MENU GUIDE Snails, sausages & horseradish • Smoked Gloucestershire Old Spot chop & prunes • Apple cake & Jersey cream

PRICE GUIDE Starter £5.20-£8.50 • main £13.50-£26 • dessert £5.80-£6 • coffee £2 • min/water £3 • Service optional • Group min 6 service 12.5%

PLACE: This no frills, converted Smithfield smokehouse is a champion of robust British cooking. The unassuming entrance leads into the informal bar and bakery, while steps lead up to the spacious dining room, with its whitewashed brick walls, high ceilings and worn wooden floors. Tables have paper top cloths and basic wooden chairs, staff wear branded chef jackets and offer relaxed, friendly service.
FOOD: Fergus Henderson's book is entitled *Nose to Tail Eating*, and fairly summarises the unfussy, flavour-driven, traditional cookery here, which makes use of the whole animal. Expect thrifty menu descriptions and some dishes using wonderfully earthy ingredients.
OUR TIP: Perfect for meat lovers, and a bar popular for after-work drinks
Chef: Christopher Gillard **Owners:** T Gulliver & F Henderson **Times:** 12-3/6-11, Closed Xmas, New Year, Easter BH, Sun, closed L Sat **Seats:** 100, Pr/dining room 18 **Smoking:** Air con **Directions:** Nearest station: Farringdon 100yds from Smithfield Market, northside **Parking:** Meters in street **e-mail:** reservations@stjohnrestaurant.com **web:** www.stjohnrestaurant.com

Smiths of Smithfield

British
Quality food in stylish warehouse conversion
☎ 020 7251 7950 (Top Floor), 67-77 Charterhouse S EC1M 6HJ Plan 3-F4

MENU GUIDE Dorset crab on toast • Roast chicken, swede mash, leek & black pudding • Banana parfait, caramel sauce

WINE GUIDE 30 bottles over £20, 15 bottles under £20 • 20 by the glass (£3.50-£7)

PRICE GUIDE Starter £4.75-£5.75 • main £10.50-£11.50 • dessert £4.50-£5.50 • coffee £2 • min/water £2.50 • Service added but optional 12.5%

PLACE: A converted warehouse with industrial-style decor and an open kitchen is never going to be an intimate place to dine. The general hubbub gives it a happening feel which appeals to the largely city clientele, and the staff are well versed and slick.
FOOD: As well as rare breed and organic steaks to choose from, you can go for Irish rock oysters or cottage pie, roast halibut with lobster mash or fish and chips with tartare sauce. Sophisticated or earthy, the ingredients are top class and the flavours can be stunning.
OUR TIP: The top floor is more serene with great views
Chef: Tony Moyse, Ashley Shergold **Owners:** John Torode **Times:** 12-3.30/6.30-12, Closed 25-26 Dec, 1 Jan, closed L Sat **Notes:** Vegetarian available **Seats:** 80, Pr/dining room 30 **Smoking:** Air con **Children:** Portions **Directions:** Nearest station: Farringdon, Barbican, Chancery Lane Opposite Smithfield Meat Market **Parking:** NCP: Snowhi **e-mail:** reservations@smithsofsmithfield.co.uk **web:** www.smithsofsmithfield.co.uk

England

Alba 107 Whitecross St EC1Y 8JD ☎ 020 7588 1798
Contemporary Italian within a short walk of the Barbican. The generous carte is supplemented by daily specials.

Carluccio's Caffè 12 West Smithfield EC1A 9JR
☎ 020 7329 5904 Quality Italian chain.

Strada 8-10 Exmouth Market EC1R 4QA
☎ 020 7278 0800 Superior pizza from quality ingredients cooked in wood-fired ovens.

Yo! Sushi 95 Farringdon Road EC1R 3BT
☎ 020 7841 0785 Sushi, Sashimi, noodles and more delivered by conveyor belt and priced according to colour coded plates.

LONDON EC2

 Aurora at Great Eastern Hotel *see below*

Boisdale of Bishopsgate
Scottish   **NEW**
Scottish cuisine in relaxed setting
☎ 020 7283 1763 Swedeland Court, 202 Bishopsgate EC2M 4NR Plan 7-C5

MENU GUIDE Potted spiced pheasant • Halibut with mashed potato, mussels, leek & white wine cream sauce • Scottish tart

PRICE GUIDE Food prices not confirmed for 2006. Please telephone for details

continued

PLACE: So tucked away that you may even need to ask directions at the end of the passageway where it's located, this Scottish-influenced bar and restaurant also has a large reputation for its live jazz.

FOOD: The assured, accomplished cooking here majors on using the very best quality Scottish produce, including marinated Orkney herrings, 28-day matured Scottish beef and Scottish raspberries.

OUR TIP: Book for lunch
Times: 11.30am-11pm **e-mail:** katie@boisdale-city.co.uk
web: www.boisdale.co.uk

 Bonds
French
Contemporary cuisine in a boldly beautiful former City bank
☎ 020 7657 8080 Threadneedles, 5 Threadneedle St EC2R 8AY Plan 6-B4

MENU GUIDE Sauté of foie gras, pain d'epice, mango confit • Roast duck, red onion & sweet potato tarte Tatin • Tuscan chocolate fondant

WINE GUIDE ♀ Domaine Billaud Simon Chablis Chardonnay £30 • ♀ Domaine Guyot Hermitage le Millepertius £30 133 bottles over £20, 8 bottles under £20 • 11 by the glass (£5.50-£8.50)

PRICE GUIDE Fixed L £23.50 • starter £10.50-£18.50 • main £19.50-£27.50 • dessert £8.50 • coffee £3.95 • min/water £5 • Service added but optional 12.5%

continued

LONDON EC2

Aurora at Great Eastern Hotel

Modern European
Flavourful modern cooking in a dramatic setting
☎ 020 7618 7000 Liverpool St EC2M 7QN Plan 6-C5

MENU GUIDE Foie gras, Agen prunes, Sauternes jelly • Saddle of lamb, parmesan gnocchi, rosemary bouillon • Almond fondant with vanilla ice cream

WINE GUIDE ♀ Fiano di Avellino £35 • ♀ Crozes-Hermitage £34 • 450 bottles over £20, 20 bottles under £20 • 13 by the glass (£3.75-£13.50)

PRICE GUIDE Fixed L £28.50 • Fixed D £50-£70 • starter £9.50-£15 • main £16.50-£24 • dessert £7.50-£9 • coffee £3.50 • min/water £3.50 • Service added but optional 12.5%

PLACE: One of several eating options on offer at this designer hotel in the city, Aurora is set in a palatial Victorian dining room with ceilings of a lofty, cathedral height and a stunning stained glass dome. Billowing voiles in deep red and grey keep things contemporary, along with striking modern chandeliers and a brushed steel bar that runs along one side of the room that serves a tempting range of cocktails. Busy, so book ahead, particularly for lunch.

FOOD: The monthly-changing carte offers a lengthy range of modern European dishes, and is complemented by a carving trolley of imposing dimensions serving more traditional roasts. Flavours are bold and intense - daube of beef combined with parsley mash for example, or pork belly with a sauté of snails and salsify - and fish a particular highlight; a monkfish main shows the style, wrapped in prosciutto and artfully teamed with braised oxtail and a morel jus. A seven-course dégustation menu completes the picture.

OUR TIP: The Great Eastern also has a café, champagne bar and gastro-pub

Chef: Allan Pickett **Owners:** Great Eastern Hotel **Times:** 12-2.30/6.45-10, Closed Xmas, New Year, BHs, Sat-Sun **Notes:** Fixed D 4 courses £50-£70, Vegetarian available, Civ Wed 160 **Seats:** 100 **Smoking:** Air con
Rooms: 267 (267 en suite) ★★★★★ **Directions:** Nearest station: Liverpool Street Telephone for directions
e-mail: restaurantres@great-eastern-hotel.co.uk
web: www.aurora-restaurant.co.uk

England

LONDON EC2 *continued*

PLACE: Giant room with plenty of evidence of the building's former function as a banking hall. Subtle lighting softens the effect of the restaurant's lofty proportions, and the decor is chic and contemporary.
FOOD: Dishes are skilfully prepared in the London fine dining style, where cappuccinos and confits punctuate the menu and luxurious ingredients and modern techniques abound. Enjoy a tian of Cornish crab, pink grapefruit jelly, pea and pistachio bavarois to start, then noisettes of Elwy Valley Welsh lamb with polenta and grilled Provençale vegetables, and Garigette strawberry trifle to finish.
OUR TIP: The bar is a great meeting place early evening
Chef: Barry Tonks **Owners:** The Eton Group **Times:** 12-2.30/6-10, Closed 2 wks Xmas, 4 days Etr & BHs, Sat, Sun **Notes:** Tasting menu £55, Vegetarian available, Dress Restrictions, Smart casual **Seats:** 80, Pr/dining room 16 **Smoking:** N/Sm in restaurant, Air con
e-mail: bonds@theetongroup.com **web:** www.bonds-restaurant.com

🍴🍴 *Eyre Brothers*
Iberian
Bustling, contemporary Shoreditch chic
☎ 020 7613 5346 70 Leonard St EC2A 4BP
Plan 7-B2
MENU GUIDE Scallops, fried artichokes, grilled jambon serrano • Duck confit, cabbage with chestnut, celeriac & parsley purée • Crème brûlée
PRICE GUIDE Food prices not confirmed for 2006. Please telephone for details

PLACE: Full-length windows, mahogany-panelled ceiling and floors, American black walnut and leather for chairs and banquettes, a long bar, glimpses of the kitchen and loud jazz music dominate this lively, trendy, metropolitan, urban-chic restaurant and bar. Four booth-style areas break up the large dining space, while lighting is subdued and black-clad staff friendly and attentive.
FOOD: The Iberian-influenced cooking, which catches the mood perfectly, is driven by top quality ingredients and is strong on flavour and simplicity, with colour and texture variation providing additional interest. A place for the young at heart.
OUR TIP: Don't miss the delicious marinated olives
Times: 12-3/6.30-11, Closed Xmas-New Year, BHs, closed L Sat
e-mail: eyrebros@btconnect.com **web:** www.eyrebrothers.co.uk

🍴🍴 Fishmarket
Fish and Seafood
Sharp, yet intimate fish restaurant
☎ 020 7618 7200 Great Eastern Hotel, Liverpool St EC2M 7QN Plan 6-C5
MENU GUIDE Glazed rock oysters • Seared scallops • Tarte Tatin
WINE GUIDE ♀ Spy Valley Sauvignon Blanc • ♀ Painters Bridge Zinfandel/Shiraz • 128 bottles over £20, 1 bottles under £20 18 by the glass (£3.50-£11.50)
PRICE GUIDE Fixed D £21.50-£41.50 • starter £5.40-£9.50 • main £10.50-£26 • dessert £5-£6 • coffee £2.50 • min/water £3.50 • Service added but optional 12.5%

PLACE: Situated in the heart of the Grade II listed Great Eastern Hotel, the interior of the Fishmarket – one of four eateries in the hotel – has elegant high ceilings and acres of white marble. The adjacent Champagne bar has a trendy mosaic tiled horseshoe bar. Service by a young, enthusiastic and knowledgeable team.
FOOD: The restaurant, as its name suggests, specialises in fish

and seafood with a mix of classic and modern dishes featuring o the menu. Well sourced ingredients and some excellent sauces show the skill of the kitchen.
OUR TIP: Good place for children
Chef: Stuart Lyall **Owners:** Great Eastern Hotel **Times:** 12-2.30/6-10.30, Closed Xmas,New Year, BHs, Sat-Sun **Notes:** Vegetarian available **Seats:** 96 **Smoking:** Air con **Directions:** Nearest station: Liverpool Street Telephone for directions
e-mail: restaurantres@great-eastern-hotel.co.uk **web:** www.fish-market.co.u

🍴 Great Eastern Dining Room
Pan Asian
Fashionable Eastern eaterie and bar
☎ 020 7613 4545 54 Great Eastern St EC2A 3QR
Plan 7-B2
MENU GUIDE Scallop siu mai • Whole fried sea bass, three flavoured sauce • Chocolate pudding, coconut & caramel ice cream
WINE GUIDE 24 bottles over £20, 8 bottles under £20 • 6 by th glass (£4.80-£7)
PRICE GUIDE Starter £4-£7 • main £8-£14 • dessert £4-£6 • coffee £1.50 • min/water £3 • Service included

PLACE: A buzzy, trendy, contemporary bar/restaurant in the gritty, up-and-coming City extremities. Dark-wood walls and floors, leather seating, funky chandeliers and high decibels reign The dining room continues the minimalist theme and has small, closely-packed tables, low lights and black-clad staff.
FOOD: The Eastern grazing concept menu raids Japan, Thailand Malaysia and China, dividing into divisions for dim sum, maki rolls/sashimi, tempura, salads, curries, house dishes and dessert and is perfect for eating with company.
OUR TIP: Useful glossary of Asian food on reverse of menu
Chef: Mark Adler **Owners:** Will Ricker **Times:** 12-3.30/6-10, Closed Xmas & Etr, Sun, closed L Sat **Notes:** Vegetarian available **Seats:** 70 **Smoking:** No pipes, No cigars, Air con **Parking:** Car Park opposite hote
e-mail: sherren@thediningrooms.com
web: www.greateasterndining.co.uk

🍴 Mehek
Indian
Modern-style, upmarket Indian to woo the city suit
☎ 020 7588 5043 & 7588 5044 45 London Wall, Moorgate EC2M 5TE Plan 7-B5
MENU GUIDE Bengal king prawn special • Chicken jalfezi • Shahi pineapple
WINE GUIDE ♀ Chablis la Colombe £23 • ♀ Bilimoria Shiraz Pinotage £12.90
PRICE GUIDE Fixed L £11.95-£16.50 • starter £2.95-£5 • main £7.90-£11 • dessert £2.50-£3.80 • min/water £3.70 • Service added but optional 10%

PLACE: Tucked away in an arcade of City shops - blink and you miss the name, so watch for the clipped topiary outside. The L-shaped room has modern styling, featuring a long bar, yellow and terracotta, authentic artefacts and banquettes, chairs and white tablecloths.
FOOD: The modern Indian cuisine has a classic ring, delivering lengthy repertoire of assured, well-chosen and well-presented dishes that shape up well alongside the decor, high-standard fundamentals (rice and nans) and attentive, relaxed service.
OUR TIP: Great naans and, if you go for dessert, try the gulab jamun**Chef:** A Motlib **Owners:** Salim B Rashid **Times:** 11.30-3/6-11, Closed Xmas, New Year, BHs, Sat-Sun **Notes:** Vegetarian available, Sma casual **Seats:** 120 **Smoking:** N/Sm area, Air con **Parking:** on street, NCP **e-mail:** info@mehek.co.uk **web:** www.mehek.co.uk

continued

England

Rhodes Twentyfour

British

Signature Rhodes overlooking the City

☎ 020 7877 7703 Tower 42, Old Broad St EC2N 1HQ
Plan 6-C5

MENU GUIDE Pork faggot, caramelised apple, gravy • Pan-fried haddock, cockle & potato casserole, steamed spinach • Jam roly-poly, custard, hot jam sauce

WINE GUIDE ♀ Paul Cluver Sauvignon Blanc £25 • ♀ Klem Bustrouw Cabernet Merlot £37 • 100+ bottles over £20, bottles under £20 • 10 by the glass (£5.50-£9.50)

PRICE GUIDE Starter £7.80-£16 • main £11.60-£23 • dessert £7.50 • coffee £2.50 • min/water £3.50 • Service added but optional

PLACE: This culinary eyrie perches on the 24th floor of the tallest building in the Square Mile and offers stunning views of London by day or night. It's a romantic venue, and also a popular business haunt for the well-heeled city types who work nearby.
FOOD: A straightforward menu distinguished by Gary Rhodes' flair for updating traditional British favourites. Start with hot smoked eel with piccalilli perhaps, and then tuck into Irish stew, faggot pudding, or poached sea trout with caramelised shallots, lemon and fried anchovies. Excellent wine list.
OUR TIP: Take a vertiginous trip to the Champagne bar at the top of the tower
Chef: Gary Rhodes, Adam Gray **Owners:** Restaurant Associates
Times: 12-2.30/6-9.00, Closed BHs, Xmas, Sat-Sun **Notes:** Vegetarian available, Dress Restrictions, No ripped jeans or dirty trainers **Seats:** 75
Smoking: No pipes, No cigars, Air con **Children:** Portions **Directions:** Nearest station: Bank, Liverpool Street Telephone for directions
Parking: On street **web:** www.rhodes24.co.uk

Rivington Bar & Grill

British

Seasonal British favourites in fashionable area

☎ 020 7729 7053 28-30 Rivington St EC2A 3DZ
Plan 7-B2

MENU GUIDE Salt beef & green bean salad • Roast suckling pig, greens, Bramley apple sauce • Plum crumble, custard

WINE GUIDE ♀ J & F Lurton les Fumées Blanches Sauvignon £15.15 • ♀ Berrys Ordinary Claret Cabernet Sauvignon £17 • 40 bottles over £20, 10 bottles under £20 • 9 by the glass (£3.75-£6)

PRICE GUIDE Fixed L £22.50 • starter £5.50-£14.50 • main £9.50-£22.50 • dessert £5.50-£6.50 • coffee £2 • min/water £2.25 • Service added but optional 12.5%

PLACE: Tucked away down a narrow Hoxton side street, this buzzy eaterie is a restaurant, bar and deli all in one. Wooden floors and white walls make for a predictably minimalist decor.
FOOD: No frills, just quality seasonal produce put to work in straightforward modern British dishes. With plenty of old favourites, you may not tuck into Shetland mussels to start, before moving on to bangers and mash, or lamb chops with bubble & squeak, and whisky and walnut tart. Relaxed but professional table service.
OUR TIP: Shorter blackboard bar menu also available
Chef: Sami Talberg **Times:** 12-3/6.30-11, Closed L Sat **Notes:** Vegetarian available **Seats:** 85, Pr/dining room 25 **Smoking:** Air con **Parking:** on street **e-mail:** office@rivingtongrill.co.uk **web:** www.rivingtongrill.co.uk

South

French

Simple French cooking in trendy location

☎ 020 7729 4452 128 Curtain Rd EC2A 3AQ
Plan 7-B2

MENU GUIDE Goats' cheese fritters, hazelnut & green salad • Baby octopus & red mullet fillets, niçoise bouillon • Tarte au citron

WINE GUIDE ♀ Domaine de l'Hortus Viognier Sauvignon £23.50 • ♀ Château la Dournie St Chinian Syrah £19.50 13 bottles over £20, 12 bottles under £20 • 6 by the glass (£3.40-£4.50)

PRICE GUIDE Fixed L £12.95 • Fixed D £12.95 • starter £4.50-£8.50 • main £9.50-£17.90 • dessert £5 • coffee £2.10 • min/water £2.70 • Service added but optional 12.5%

PLACE: South delivers an endearing taste of France to up-and-coming Hoxton. The pale blue exterior gives way to a small, light, modern room of plain cream walls, blond-wood floorboards and contemporary chairs that's as unpretentious as the cooking. An open kitchen adds atmosphere alongside attentive, relaxed service.
FOOD: A focus on quality produce, simplicity and accurate cooking, coupled with light, colourful and balanced combinations, deliver authentic, sunny flavours of southern France at reasonable prices.
OUR TIP: Fixed-price, no-choice, good-value menu available lunchtime and until 7.30pm
Chef: Barry Atkins **Owners:** Catherine Bolton **Times:** 12-3/6-10.30, Closed 1 week xmas, BH's, Sun **Notes:** Vegetarian available **Seats:** 49
Smoking: N/Sm area **Children:** Portions **Directions:** Nearest station: Old Street/Liverpool Street At junct of Rivington St and Curtain Rd
Parking: NCP **e-mail:** southrestaurant@aol.com

Tatsuso Restaurant

Japanese

Authentic City Japanese delivers high quality

☎ 020 7638 5863 32 Broadgate Circle EC2M 2QS
Plan 6-C5

PLACE: Brimming with corporate City suits at lunchtime, on the lower level of Broadgate Circle, this bustling, two-tier Japanese restaurant is well kitted out in pastel shades, light wood furniture and screens. Service is slick and professional from waitresses in traditional costume.
FOOD: Authentic full range of classic Japanese dishes. Raw materials are of high quality and the breadth of the menu offers a bewildering choice backed up by set options.
OUR TIP: Soak up the atmosphere at the teppan-yaki tables upstairs
Times: 11.30-2.30/6-9.45, Closed Xmas, New Year, BHs, Sat-Sun
Directions: Nearest station: Liverpool Street. Ground floor of Broadgate Circle

♀ Corney & Barrow at Broadgate Circle

19 Broadgate Circle EC2M 2QS ☎ 020 7628 1251 Wine bar offshoot from famous wine merchants.

♀ Corney & Barrow at Citypoint

1 Ropemaker St EC2Y 9AW ☎ 020 7382 0606 Wine bar offshoot from famous wine merchants.

♀ Corney & Barrow at Exchange Square

5 Exchange Square EC2A 2EH ☎ 020 7728 4367 Wine bar offshoot from famous wine merchants.

England

LONDON EC2 *continued*

♀ Corney & Barrow at Mason's Avenue
12 Mason's Av EC2V 5BT ☎ 020 7726 6030 City wine bar chain offering contemporary dishes.

♀ Corney & Barrow at Old Broad Street
111 Old Broad St EC2N 1AP ☎ 020 7638 9308 Wine bar offshoot from famous wine merchants.

🕥 The Fox Dining Room 28 Paul St EC2A 4LB
☎ 020 7729 5708 Rustic, unfussy food in a restaurant designed to create the impression of a 1950s municipal library.

🍜 Wagamama 1a Ropemaker St EC2V 9AW
☎ 020 7588 2688 Informal noodle bar with no booking.

🍜 Wagamama 22 Old Broad St EC2N 1HQ
☎ 020 7256 9992 Informal noodle bar with no booking.

LONDON EC3
🌸🌸 *Chamberlains Restaurant*
Classy seafood eatery in
Leadenhall Market 🐟▷ **NEW**
☎ 020 7648 8693 23/25 Leadenhall Market
EC3V 0LR Plan 6-C4

MENU GUIDE Sardines, aubergine caviar, tomato & parsley salad • Sea bass, confit leeks, girolles, champagne froth • Chocolate fondant

PLACE: Tucked away in the City amid the Victorian splendour of Leadenhall Market, this three-storey eatery offers a choice of dining areas including a relaxed basement bar. The ground floor restaurant is light and airy, while upstairs things are more formal though just as chic.
FOOD: Chamberlains' owner supplies fish to Billingsgate Market, so it's no surprise that high quality seafood is the order of the day. Choose from an extensive carte, or plump for the tasting menu; prices are in keeping with the city setting with most mains over £20.
OUR TIP: Open Monday to Friday only
Times: 12-3/5.30-9.30, Closed Sat, Sun, BHs, Xmas, New Year
Directions: Nearest station: Bank and Monument
e-mail: info@chamberlains.org **web:** www.chamberlains.org

🌸🌸 1 Lombard Street - Fine Dining Restaurant
French, International
Fine dining in a former bank
☎ 020 7929 6611 1 Lombard St EC3V 9AA
Plan 6-B4

MENU GUIDE Duck consommé • Roast turbot, Pinot Noir jus • Roast figs, Camargue rice pudding

WINE GUIDE ♀ Domaine Pico Race Chablis 1'er Cru Chardonnay £38.50 • ♀ St Laurent de Medoc Château Belgrave 5 eme cru Merlot £59.50 • 200 bottles over £20, 11 bottles under £20 • 10 by the glass (£4.75-£9.75)

PRICE GUIDE Fixed L £34 • starter £14.50-£19.50 • main £28.50-£29.50 • dessert £9-£9.50 • coffee £3 • min/water £3.75 • Service added but optional 12.5% • Group min 10 service 15%

PLACE: A classical background - Titian's *Rape of Europa* sets the stage for the decor and furniture - sits well inside this former banking hall turned gastronomic destination. Private conversations between diners are discreetly accommodated by well-spaced tables.
FOOD: The food is unashamedly expensive, but the luxury ingredients and ambitious cooking go some way towards justifying the cost. Presentation of dishes makes an impact: grilled scallops with Sauternes, lime and lobster emulsion served in a shell on a bed of sea salt is a feast for the eyes as well as the stomach.
OUR TIP: Remember your credit card
Chef: Herbet Berger **Owners:** Jessen & Co **Times:** 12-2.30/6-10, Closed Xmas, New Year, BHs, Sat-Sun, closed D 24 Dec **Notes:** Fixed D 6 courses £34, Vegetarian available **Seats:** 40, Pr/dining room 40 **Smoking:** No pipes, Air con **Directions:** Nearest station: Bank Opposite Bank of England **Parking:** NCP Cannon Street
e-mail: hb@1lombardstreet.com **web:** www.1lombardstreet.com

🌸🌸 *Prism*
City restaurant offering classical
cuisine **NEW**
☎ 020 7256 3888 147 Leadenhall St EC3V 4QT
Plan 6-C4

MENU GUIDE Beef carpaccio, artichoke & pickled girolles • Roasted pave of salmon, salmon confit, spring vegetable salsa • Passion fruit crème caramel, mango

PLACE: Set in the heart of the City, this was the bank of New York in another life. Today, imposing white pillars, high ceilings and luxury marble flooring dominate the huge dining room. A long contemporary bar stretches down one side of the room, and tables are clothed in white linen, which contrasts with red leather chrome framed chairs.
FOOD: The menu takes a straightforward, simple approach with an overall classical style. The cooking takes its cue from that and clear flavours are allowed to come through the dishes without unnecessary saucing.
OUR TIP: Perfect for a business lunch
Times: 12-12.30/6-10, Closed Sat, Sun **Directions:** Nearest station: Bank and Monument **e-mail:** prism@harveynichols.com
web: www.harveynichols.com

♀ Corney & Barrow at Jewry Street 37A Jewry
St EC3N 2EX ☎ 020 7680 8550 City wine bar chain offering contemporary dishes.

♀ Corney & Barrow at Lloyds of London
Lloyds of London, 1 Leadenhall Place EC3M 7DX
☎ 020 7261 9201 City wine bar chain offering contemporary dishes.

♀ Corney & Barrow at Monument
2B Eastcheap EC3M 1AB ☎ 020 7929 3220 Wine bar offshoot from famous wine merchants.

♀ Corney & Barrrow at Royal Exchange
16 Royal Exchange EC3V 3LP ☎ 020 7929 3131 Wine bar offshoot from famous wine merchants.

🍽 Matab's 76 Aldgate High St EC3N 1BD
☎ 020 7481 4010 High quality Bangladeshi cuisine in stylish surroundings.

continued

LONDON EC4

The Chancery

British/European NEW

Urbane City restaurant with intimate atmosphere

☎ 020 7831 4000 9 Cursitor St EC4A 1LL Plan 3-E3

MENU GUIDE Beignet of tiger prawns, spring onions, hot & sour dressing. Seared red mullet, lemon confit, bulgar wheat. Jellied fruits, elderflower ice cream, blackberry coulis

WINE GUIDE ♀ Steenberg Sauvignon Blanc £27 • ♀ Duckbill Shiraz £18 • 20 bottles over £20, 5 bottles under £20 • 6 by the glass (£4.50-£7.50)

PRICE GUIDE Food prices not confirmed for 2006. Please telephone for details

PLACE: Tucked away between Lincoln's Inn and Chancery Lane, this is slap bang in the middle of London's law courts and legal offices. This is a historic area with narrow streets and some old timbered buildings still remain. The Chancery has floor to ceiling windows, dark flooring and leather chairs, complemented by white linen and expensive glassware. Staff are skilful and knowlegeable.

FOOD: This is a sister restaurant of the Clerkenwell Dining Room (see page 257) and offers an interesting, French-influenced menu making good use of luxury ingredients. Technical cooking skills are clearly apparent in dishes such as ravioli of crab with tarragon and tomato, and trio of pork with cauliflower purée and calvados apples. The short wine list is mainly French with a sprinkling of New World and Italian bottles.

OUR TIP: The all-inclusive menu is good value

Chef: Andrew Thompson **Owners:** Zak Jones & Andrew Thompson **Times:** 12-2.30/6-10.30, Closed Xmas/New Yr (2 wks), Sat-Sun **Seats:** 50 **Smoking:** N/Sm area, No pipes, No cigars, Air con **Children:** Menu, Portions **Directions:** Nearest station: Chancery Lane Situated between High Holborn and Fleet St **Parking:** On street **e-mail:** reservations@thechancery.co.uk **web:** www.thechancery.co.uk

Novelli in the City

French, Mediterranean

Stylish city club offering fine French cuisine

☎ 020 7717 0088 The London Capital Club, Abchurch Ln EC4N 7BW Plan 7-B4

MENU GUIDE Roasted scallops with boudin noir • Liquorice beef daube, creamed Brussels sprouts, truffle mash • Chocolate fondant with pistachio parfait

WINE GUIDE ♀ Sancerre £25 • ♀ Fleurie £22 • 31 bottles over £20, 5 bottles under £20 • 28 by the glass (£4.50-£9.75)

PRICE GUIDE Fixed L £16.25 • Fixed D £18.50 • starter £6-£10 • main £15-£20 • dessert £5 • coffee £3.25 • min/water £3.50 • Service included

PLACE: Occupying the lower ground floor of the London Capital Club, a private members' club - although non-members can make dinner reservations. The square dining room is hung with mirrors, and covered with caricatures of club members. Service is prompt, attentive and discreet, and the restaurant is largely frequented by suits.

FOOD: A very French style of menu, as one would expect in a Novelli establishment, although some English and European influences do creep in. Good quality ingredients are given a skilled and accurate treatment by the chef.

OUR TIP: Watch out for the Jean-Christophe special of the day

Chef: Jean-Christophe Novelli **Owners:** CCA International **Times:** 12-5.30-9, Closed Xmas, New Year, BHs, Sat-Sun, closed L Lunch not served to non-members **Notes:** Vegetarian by request only, Dress Restrictions, Smart casual **Seats:** 50 **Smoking:** No pipes, No cigars, Air con **Children:** Min 8 yrs **Parking:** NCP **web:** www.londoncapitalclub.com

Refettorio

Italian

Authentic Italian food eaten as it's meant to be

☎ 020 7438 8052 Crowne Plaza Hotel, 19 New Bridge St EC4V 6DB Plan 3-F2

MENU GUIDE Pan-fried quail & beetroot salad • Osso bucco, crispy saffron risotto • Sicilian chestnut cannoli

WINE GUIDE ♀ Di Lenardo Pinot Grigio £23.50 • ♀ Fattoria Mancini Sangiovese £26 • 60 bottles over £20 • 8 by the glass (£4.50-£8)

PRICE GUIDE Fixed D £35-£60 • starter £7-£11.50 • main £11.85-£21.50 • dessert £4-£6 • coffee £3.75 • min/water £3.50 • Service added but optional 12.5%

PLACE: The fresh meats and cheeses on display release an aroma that leaves no doubt about this Italian restaurant's authenticity. Housed inside the stylish new hotel at Blackfriars Bridge, the Refettorio (the name means refectory) offers a buzzy communal space where couples can also dine privately.

FOOD: Proper Italian food sourced from small suppliers throughout Italy is showcased on a succinct menu that includes lots of grazing dishes and selections for sharing. Also an unusual range of pastas and risottos, with mouthwatering sauces and fillings like pear and Italian sausage.

OUR TIP: Try some of the 30 cheeses

Chef: Pasquale Amico **Owners:** Parallel/Crown Plaza **Times:** 12-2.30/6.30-10.30, Closed Xmas, New Year & BHs, Sun, closed L Sat **Notes:** Vegetarian available, Smart Casual **Seats:** Pr/dining room 30 **Directions:** Nearest station: Blackfriars Situated on New Bridge St. Opposite Blackfriars underground **e-mail:** info@tableinthecity.com **web:** www.tableinthecity.com

The White Swan Pub & Dining Room

British, European

Busy gastro-pub with smart first-floor dining room

☎ 020 7242 9696 108 Fetter Ln EC4A 1ES Plan 3-F3

MENU GUIDE Rabbit rillette, onion confit • Monkfish fricassée, fennel, chervil & truffle oil • Chocolate fondant, cardamom ice cream

WINE GUIDE ♀ Palena Sauvignon Blanc £17 • ♀ El Coto Rioja £18.50 • 74 bottles over £20, 17 bottles under £20 • 17 by the glass (£3.50-£6.25)

PRICE GUIDE Fixed L £20 • Fixed D fr £28 • coffee £2.50 • min/water £3.25 • Service added but optional 12.5%

PLACE: Traditional real ale city pub downstairs plus mezzanine and stylish dining room upstairs, with cream walls, beige leather seating, reclaimed wooden flooring and a mirrored ceiling. All this in a 1960s building tucked away behind the inns of court, with formal service from French staff.

FOOD: Upmarket gastro-pub cooking using first rate ingredients. Traditional ideas are given a modern twist on the regularly changing menu - corn fed chicken with wild mushroom risotto and cep foam.

OUR TIP: Try the first rate British and Irish cheeses

Chef: Jason Scrimshaw **Owners:** Tom & Ed Martin **Times:** 12-3/6-10, Closed 25 Dec, 1 Jan and Bank Holidays, Sat-Sun except private parties, closed D Mon **Notes:** Vegetarian available **Seats:** 44, Pr/dining room 44 **Smoking:** Air con **Children:** Portions **Directions:** Nearest station: Chancery Lane Tube Station Fetter Lane runs parallel with Chancery Lane in the City of London and it joins Fleet St with Holborn **Parking:** On Street and NCP (Hatton Garden) **e-mail:** info@thewhiteswanlondon.com **web:** www.thewhiteswanlondon.com

England

England

LONDON EC4 *continued*

🍷 Corney & Barrow at Fleet Place 3 Fleet Place
EC4M 7RD ☎ 020 7329 3141   City wine bar chain offering
contemporary dishes.

🕮 The Don The Courtyard, 20 St Swithins Ln EC4 8AD
☎ 020 7626 2606   Modern European menu, in vibrant city
restaurant.

LONDON N1

🕮🕮 Almeida Restaurant
French

Conran style meets rustic French cuisine
☎ 020 7354 4777   30 Almeida St, Islington N1 1TD
Plan 1-F4

MENU GUIDE Terrine de foie gras • Filet de boeuf au
poivre • Pot au chocolat

WINE GUIDE ♀ Domaine Cauhapé Jurançon Sec Chant des
Vignes £28.50 • ♀ Domaine des Roches Neuves Saumur-
Champigny, Terres Chaudes £29.50 • 323 bottles over £20,
17 bottles under £20 • 19 by the glass (£3.50-£6.95)

PRICE GUIDE Fixed L fr £14.50 • Fixed D fr £17.50 • starter
£5.50-£12.50 • main £12.50-£19.50 • dessert £4.50-£6 • coffee
£2.25 • min/water £2.95 • Service added but optional 12.5%

PLACE: All-French dishes on an all-French menu, but the interior
of Conran's Islington outpost is very much trademark designer
style rather than rustic French brasserie. It's smart, cosy and
contemporary, with warm pastel colours, clean lines, subtle
lighting, and an open-to-view kitchen.
FOOD: A devoted Gallic affair from start to finish. The authentic
brasserie-style menu is a roll call of rustic regional French
classics, which extends to charcuterie and tarts being presented
on parading trolleys. Dishes burst with flavours due to the simple
presentation and cooking style of quality produce.
OUR TIP: Good value lunches
Chef: Ian Wood **Owners:** Sir Terence Conran **Times:** 12-2.30/5.30-11,
Closed 25-26 Dec, 1 Jan, Good Fri **Notes:** Vegetarian available
Seats: 100, Pr/dining room 20 **Smoking:** N/Sm area, No pipes, Air con
Children: Portions **Directions:** Nearest station:
Angel/Islington/Highbury Turn right from station, along Upper St, past
church **Parking:** Parking around building
e-mail: almeida-reservations@conran-restaurants.co.uk
web: www.almeida-restaurants.co.uk

🕮 The Drapers Arms
International

Delightful, convivial gastro-pub
☎ 020 7619 0348   44 Barnsbury St N1 1ER   Plan 1-F4

MENU GUIDE Fish soup, rouille, gruyère & croûtons • Italian
sausage on garlic mash • Lemon tart, crème fraîche

WINE GUIDE ♀ Domaine Bertrand Viognier £14 • ♀ Casa Azul
Cabernet Sauvignon £13.50 • 39 bottles over £20, 22 bottles
under £20 • 18 by the glass (£3.60-£5.50)

PRICE GUIDE Starter £4.75-£8.50 • main £10.50-£15 • dessert
£5.50 • coffee £1.50 • min/water £2.50 • Service added but
optional 12.5%

PLACE: A stylishly converted traditional pub in smart Georgian
Islington, with wooden floors, squashy sofas and beautiful flower
arrangements. The upstairs restaurant is a large bright space with
tall ceilings and windows.
FOOD: You can eat wherever you like, and the interesting
repertoire encompasses a range of modern dishes with a
distinctly European nod towards Asia. Flavours are strikingly
compatible, as in roast bream with Thai green salad and sweet
and sour sauce.
OUR TIP: Eat in the garden on warm days
Chef: Mark Emberton **Owners:** Paul McElhinney & Mark Emberton
Times: 12-3/7-10.30, Closed 24-27 Dec, 1-2 Jan, closed L Mon-Sat, closed
D Sun **Notes:** Vegetarian available **Seats:** 50 **Smoking:** N/Sm in
restaurant **Children:** Menu, Portions **Directions:** Nearest tube:
Highbury & Islington **e-mail:** info@thedrapersarms.co.uk
web: www.thedrapersarms.co.uk

🕮🕮 Fifteen
Italian, Mediterranean

Celebrity chef's successful venture
☎ 0871 330 1515   13 Westland Place N1 7LP
Plan 3-H6

MENU GUIDE Blue fin tuna crudo • Loin of lamb, roast
Jerusalem artichoke, cavolo nero, black olive
sauce • Caramelised figs, mascarpone, shortbread

WINE GUIDE ♀ 2004 Kim Crawford Sauvignon Blanc
£31 • ♀ Poggerino Chianti Classico 2002 Sangiovese £33
all bottles over £20 • 15 by the glass (£5-£12)

PRICE GUIDE Fixed L £22 • starter £9.50-£14 • main £19.50-
£26 • dessert £7.50-£8 • coffee £2 • min/water £3.25 • Service
added but optional 12.5%

PLACE: Several years on, Jamie Oliver's much hyped culinary
experiment is still one of London's most talked about restaurants.
And deservedly so - it's a buzzy and innovative venue,
comprising a laid-back trattoria for snacks and drinks, and a
more formal downstairs dining room with a bustling open
kitchen.
FOOD: It's a rare thing to see the culinary crusader at the stove
these days, but the food still delights - expect convivial modern
Italian food with a strong Mediterranean influence. A six-course
tasting menu is available if you want to do the place justice.
Excellent wine list.
OUR TIP: Grab a snack in the ground floor bar if you can't get a
table downstairs
Chef: Jamie Oliver **Owners:** Jamie Oliver **Times:** 12-2.45/6.30-9.30,
Closed BHs, closed D Sun **Notes:** Tasting menu 7 courses £60, vegetaria
£50, ALC L only, Vegetarian available **Seats:** 70 **Smoking:** N/Sm in
restaurant, Air con **Children:** Portions **Directions:** Nearest station: Old
Street Exit 1 from Old St tube station, walk up City road, opposite
Moorfields Eye Hospital **Parking:** On street & NCP
web: www.fifteenrestaurant.com

England

Frederick's Restaurant

European

Fashionable food in a smart conservatory

☎ 020 7359 2888 Camden Passage, Islington N1 8EG Plan 1-F4

MENU GUIDE Spicy salt cod & crayfish crepe • Smoked haddock, bubble & squeak • Hot Bakewell tart, clotted cream

WINE GUIDE 150 bottles over £20, 10 bottles under £20 • 10 by the glass (£4-£7)

PRICE GUIDE Fixed L £12.50 • Fixed D £12.50 • starter £6-£12.50 • main £13-£20 • dessert £5.50 • coffee £1.75 • min/water £3 • Service added but optional 12.5%

PLACE: The Tardis effect takes you from a small frontage to a very spacious conservatory where contemporary styling and a friendly young team create a good metropolitan vibe.
FOOD: The fashionable menus range around Europe for inspiration, coming up with the signature lamb kleftico, beef Bourguignon, and tomato, leek and talegio tart along with Dover sole meunière, grilled veal chop, and roast skate with brown shrimps.
OUR TIP: Check out the good value Pre-Theatre menu
Chef: Andrew Jeffs **Owners:** Louis Segal **Times:** 12-2.30/5.45-11.30, Closed Xmas, New Year, BHs, Sun (ex functions) **Notes:** Vegetarian available, Civ Wed 200 **Seats:** 150, Pr/dining room 30 **Smoking:** N/Sm area, Air con **Children:** Menu, Portions **Directions:** Nearest station: Angel From underground 2 mins walk to Camden Passage. Restaurant among the antique shops **e-mail:** eat@fredericks.co.uk
web: www.fredericks.co.uk

The House

British, French

Contemporary gastro-pub with a good neighbourhood following

☎ 020 7704 7410 63-69 Canonbury Rd N1 2DG Plan 1-F4

MENU GUIDE Game terrine, spiced pear chutney • Veal escalope, pomme fondant, confit tomato & field mushroom • Hot chocolate pudding

WINE GUIDE ♀ Puiattino Pinot Grigio £18.75 • ♀ Budegas Norton Barbera £14.50 • 37 bottles over £20, 17 bottles under £20 • 8 by the glass (£3.05-£6.50)

PRICE GUIDE Fixed L £12.95 • starter £5.50-£10.50 • main £9.50-£22.50 • dessert £5-£6 • coffee £1.70 • min/water £3 • Service added but optional 12.5%

PLACE: Popular gastro-pub easily distinguished by its 1930's red-brick exterior, maroon awning and delightful patio. Natural daylight floods the wooden floors and whitewashed walls of the interior, where there are large sofas and comfy seating in the bar and well spaced tables in the dining area.
FOOD: The carte menu offers a combination of hearty British food and classical French favourites. The approach is simple and the quality of the produce good. Daily specials are offered and a good value, no choice lunch.
OUR TIP: Great alfresco dining in the summer
Chef: Jeremy Hollingsworth **Owners:** Barnaby & Grace Meredith/Jeremy Hollingsworth **Times:** 12-2.30/6-10.30, Closed 24-26 Dec, closed L Mon **Notes:** Vegetarian available **Seats:** 60 **Smoking:** N/Sm in restaurant **Children:** Menu, Portions **Directions:** Nearest station: Highbury & Islington tube Behind town hall on Upper St Islington. Between Highbury Corner and Essex Rd **Parking:** Meter parking on street
e-mail: info@inthehouse.biz **web:** www.inthehouse.biz

Lola's

European

Creative eaterie in antique hunters' heaven

☎ 020 7359 1932 359 Upper St, Islington N1 0PD Plan 1-F4

MENU GUIDE Seared tuna, pak choi, crispy noodles • Roast pigeon, polenta cake, braised cabbage • Seville orange tart

WINE GUIDE 50 bottles over £20, 50 bottles under £20 • 14 by the glass (£3.75-£8.50)

PRICE GUIDE Fixed L £12.75 • Fixed D £18.75 • starter £5.75-£9.50 • main £12.50-£22 • dessert £6.75 • min/water £3 • Service optional • Group min 6 service 12.5%

PLACE: Converted from a former tram shed, Lola's certainly takes this listed building on a new journey, occupying the first floor above Islington's antiques market. It's a bright, calming room, decked out with parquet flooring and decorated in relaxing shades of aubergine and creamy beige. The pitched glass roof is hung with black wooden blinds and an arched window at one end provides a focal point to watch the world go past below.
FOOD: Sensibly compact, appealing, fashionable modern European-style menus suit the ambience, with presentation intelligently simple and elegant, delivering high quality produce and notable flavours and aromas.
OUR TIP: Value fixed-price lunch menu (with matching wines at extra cost)
Chef: Brian Sparks **Owners:** Morfudd Richards **Times:** 12-2.30/6-11, Closed 25-26 Dec, 1 Jan, Easter Mon, BHs **Notes:** Set menu incl. matching wines, Vegetarian available **Seats:** 80, Pr/dining room 16 **Smoking:** Air con **Children:** Menu, Portions **Directions:** Nearest station: Angel From station exit turn R, pass The York pub. Restaurant ahead in building named The Mall **e-mail:** lolas@lolas.co.uk
web: www.lolas.co.uk

The Real Greek

Greek

Earthy and authentic Hoxton Greek experience

☎ 020 7739 8212 15 Hoxton Market N1 6HG Plan 7-B2

MENU GUIDE Crevettes in batter with skordalia • Ismir-style dumplings with trahana • Baklava with honey & cardamom ice cream

WINE GUIDE ♀ Creta Olympias Vin de Crete £12.50 • ♀ Creta Olympias Mirambello £13.50 • 16 bottles over £20, 29 bottles under £20

PRICE GUIDE Starter £3.20-£8.95 • main £8.10-£18.90 • dessert £1.40-£5 • coffee £1.75 • min/water £2.80 • Service added but optional 12.5%

PLACE: Urban trendy Greek restaurant on the market square with a relaxed vibe and youthful service. Originally the Hoxton Christian Mission Hall, catering for the poorer children of the area, it has dark polished floorboards, tightly packed linen-clad tables and an open kitchen. Entrance is via the adjoining sister venture Mezedopolio, a wine and mezedes bar.
FOOD: The lively repertoire draws on the bountiful Greek larder to produce robust, regional Greek cooking, full of colour and texture, using top quality ingredients.
OUR TIP: Try the tantalising platefuls of 'medezes' (appetisers)
Chef: Alasdair Fraser **Owners:** Theodore Kyriakou & Paloma Campbell **Times:** 12-3/5.30-10.30, Closed 23-27 Dec, BHs, Sun **Notes:** Vegetarian available **Seats:** 76, Pr/dining room 24 **Smoking:** No pipes, No cigars **Directions:** Nearest station: Old Street Situated in square behind Holiday Inn on Old St. From tube station walk down Old St past Fire Station then 1st left 1st right to the back of inn **Parking:** Meter parking available
e-mail: admin@therealgreek.demon.co.uk **web:** www.therealgreek.co.uk

England

LONDON N1 *continued*

⑪ **Cru** 2-4 Rufus St, Hoxton N1 6PE ☎ 020 7729 5252
European dishes with some global additions, served in a relaxed friendly environment.

⑪ **Masala Zones** 80 Upper St N1 0NP
☎ 020 7359 3399 Modern Indian with a balanced approach.

▮▮ **Strada** 105-106 Upper St N1 1QN ☎ 020 7226 9742
Superior pizza from quality ingredients cooked in wood-fired ovens.

⑨ **Wagamama** The N1 Centre, Parkfield St, Islington N1
☎ 020 7226 2664 Informal noodle bar with no booking.

LONDON N7
ⓖⓖ **Morgan M**
French

Confident French cooking in stylish surroundings
☎ 020 7609 3560 489 Liverpool Rd, Islington
N7 8NS Plan 1-F5

MENU GUIDE Game & foie gras terrine, confit, fig caviar & chutney • Sea bass, crayfish ravioli, saffron & pastis velouté • Pineapple soufflè, coconut sorbet

WINE GUIDE ♀ Gerard Tremblay Chardonnay £32 • ♟ Henri de Villamont Pinot Noir £24 • 80 bottles over £20, 6 bottles under £20 • 11 by the glass (£4.50-£9.50)

PRICE GUIDE Fixed L £19.50 • Fixed D £30 • coffee £3 min/water £3.50 • Service added • Service added but optional

PLACE: A frosted glass frontage, bare wooden floors and pastel walls hung with modern artwork set the contemporary scene at this intimate Islington restaurant. A tranquil foodie haven with a restrained elegance and where service is both professional and attentive.

FOOD: An accomplished kitchen skilfully prepares classical French dishes with the odd modern twist. Flavours shine through and dishes closely live up to their menu description.

OUR TIP: The 'Garden' menu offers a good choice for vegetarians
Chef: Morgan Meunier, Sylvain Soulard **Owners:** Morgan Meunier
Times: 12-2.30/7-10.30, Closed 24 Dec-30 Dec, Mon, closed L Tues, Sat, closed D Sun **Notes:** Tasting menu £39, Vegetarian available **Seats:** 48, Pr/dining room 12 **Smoking:** N/Sm in restaurant, Air con
Children: Portions **Directions:** Nearest station: Highbury and Islington **Parking:** On Liverpool Rd

LONDON N8
ⓖ **Aix**
French

Classic bistro with an infectious buzz
☎ 020 8340 6346 54 Topsfield Pde, Tottenham Ln, Crouch End N8 8PT Plan 1-E5

MENU GUIDE Batter fried squid, tartare sauce • Fillet of beef Rossini, seared foie gras, bordelaise sauce • Tarte au citron

WINE GUIDE ♀ Cantina Valdadige Pinot Grigio £15 • ♟ Jean Orliac Berberie de l'Hortus Syrah/Grenache £20 • 23 bottles over £20, 14 bottles under £20 • 2 by the glass (£3.50)

PRICE GUIDE Fixed L £11.50-£13.50 • Fixed D £15 • starter £4.50-£10.50 • main £9.95-£17.95 • dessert £3.95-£7.95 • coffee £2 • min/water £3 • Service added 12.5%

PLACE: The simply presented dining room of this essentially French bistro has wonderful rustic charm and a relaxed and friendly atmosphere. Small linen-clothed tables and low lighting add a note of intimacy. *continued*

FOOD: A wide choice of bistro dishes ranges from the likes of steak frites, or indeed cod and chips, to a choucroute platter with braised ham hock, pork belly and Morteau sausages with juniper spiced sauerkraut.

OUR TIP: A couple of good vegetarian options
Chef: Lynne Sanders **Owners:** Lynne Sanders, Andrew Schatt
Times: 12-3/6.30-12, Mon **Notes:** Vegetarian available **Seats:** 70, Pr/dining room 26 **Smoking:** No pipes, No cigars, Air con
Children: Portions **Directions:** Nearest station: Highgate Situated on Topsfield Parade, near corner of Tottenham Ln and Rosebury Gardens, central Crouch End **Parking:** On-street **e-mail:** gwenquiel@yahoo.fr
web: www.bistroaix.co.uk

LONDON N16
ⓖ **Rasa**
Vegetarian Indian

One of London's best Indian vegetarian restaurants
☎ 020 7249 0344 55 Stoke Newington Church St
N16 0AR Plan 1-F5

MENU GUIDE Idli (Black lentil cakes, vegetable masala, coconut chutney) • Nadan Paripu (Curry of mung beans, split yellow lentils, tomato, chillies, garlic) • Banana dosa

WINE GUIDE ♀ Hazy View Chenin Blanc £10.95 • ♟ Bodegas Ondarre Rioja £10.95 • all bottles under £20 • 1 by the glass (£2.50)

PRICE GUIDE Fixed D £16 • starter £2.75-£3 • main £5-£10 • dessert £2-£3 • coffee £1 • min/water £2.75 • Service added but optional 12.5%

PLACE: Glorious in shocking pink, this original Rasa (spawning several siblings) has an avid following and buzzy atmosphere. The exterior and interior - including table over-cloths - are awash with hallmark bright pink, but thankfully the floor is tiled and walls punctuated by photos of herbs and Keralan artefacts. (The back room extension is painted white).

FOOD: Traditional home-style Keralan vegetarian cooking, with skilful and subtle combinations of herbs and spices, is the kitchen's stock in trade.

OUR TIP: Don't miss out on the pre-starter snacks and home-made pickles
Chef: Rajan Karattil **Owners:** Mr S Sreedharan **Times:** 12-3/6-11.30, Closed 24-26 Dec, 1 Jan, closed L Mon-Fri **Notes:** Vegetarian available
Seats: 64, Pr/dining room 26 **Smoking:** N/Sm in restaurant, Air con
Directions: Nearest station: Angel or Finsbury Park Telephone for directions **Parking:** On street **e-mail:** dasrasa@hotmail.com
web: www. rasarestaurants.com

LONDON N19
ⓖ **The Parsee**
Indian, Parsee

Authentic Parsee cooking in a modern setting
☎ 020 7272 9091 34 Highgate Hill N19 5NL
Plan 1-E5

MENU GUIDE Black tiger prawns in red masala • Dhansak • Rose kulfi

WINE GUIDE ♀ General Billimoria Shiraz Pinotage £12.90 • ♟ General Billimoria Colombard Chardonnay £12.90 • 3 bottles over £20, 18 bottles under £20 • 9 by the glass (£3.25-£4.50)

PRICE GUIDE Fixed D £25-£35 • starter £3.50-£6.75 • main £9.75-£12.95 • dessert £3.25-£3.75 • coffee £1 • min/water £2.75 • Service added but optional 10%

continued

PLACE: With its deep blue walls, bamboo chairs and bare tables, The Parsee is a low-key modern setting for some unusual and authentic cooking.

FOOD: Parsee cuisine (a blend of Persian and Indian traditions) is relatively rare outside Bombay, so this is a chance to try something a little different. A wide-ranging menu includes lengthy notes to help you get your bearings, while the dishes themselves are simply presented and notable for good quality ingredients.

OUR TIP: The mixed platters are a good way to sample the cuisine **Chef:** Cyrus Todiwala, Chef Angelo, Chef Chuttan **Owners:** Arif Choudhury **Times:** 6-10.45, Closed Xmas, 1 Jan, BHs, Sun, closed L Mon-Sat **Notes:** Vegetarian available **Seats:** 50, Pr/dining room 40 **Smoking:** N/Sm area, No pipes, Air con **Children:** Portions **Directions:** Nearest station: Archway Opposite Whittington Hospital **Parking:** On street **e-mail:** dining@theparsee.co.uk **web:** www.theparsee.co.uk

LONDON NW1

 **Novotel London Euston**

Modern European

Modern hotel brasserie

☎ 020 7666 9000 100-110 Euston Rd NW1 2AJ Plan 3-C5

MENU GUIDE Slow roast Parma ham, mozzarella, salad • Roast Gressingham duck breast, Cumberland ring • Valrhona chocolate eggs, orange ganache

WINE GUIDE ♀ De Neuville - Sauvignon Blanc £16 • ♥ De Neuville - Cabernet Sauvignon £16 • 15 bottles over £20, 10 bottles under £20 • 13 by the glass (£3.95-£7.50)

PRICE GUIDE Fixed L £14.95 • starter £5.25-£8.95 • main £12.50-£17.95 • dessert £5 • coffee £2.85 • min/water £3.50 • Service added but optional 10%

PLACE: Spacious open plan room overlooking the street, with a bar area, lounges and a restaurant called Mirrors. Full length windows enhance the impression of light and space, and the look is clean and uncluttered, with unclothed tables and banquette seating in rows.

FOOD: The Perceptions menu promises understanding and insight into new flavours, with global influences, while the carte is slightly more traditional.

OUR TIP: Beef fillet is not to be missed **Chef:** Denzil Newton **Owners:** Accor UK Business & Leisure **Times:** 12-2.30/6-10.30, Closed L Sat, Sun, BHs **Notes:** Buffet Lunch £14.50, dinner £19.50, Vegetarian available, Smart Dress **Seats:** 84, Pr/dining room 20 **Smoking:** N/Sm area, Air con **Children:** Menu, Portions **Rooms:** 312, 312 en suite) ★★★★ **Directions:** Nearest station: King's Cross or Euston 5 mins walk between King's Cross and Euston Station, opposite British Library. 1m from Regents Park **Parking:** Car park by Euston Station **e-mail:** h5309-fb@accor.com **web:** www.novotel.com

 Odettes

French, European

Intimate neighbourhood restaurant with loyal following

☎ 020 7586 5486 130 Regents Park Rd NW1 8XL Plan 1-E4

MENU GUIDE Morel mushroom & gruyère cheese tartlet, pea shoot & broad bean salad • Fillet of turbot, tartare sauce, deep-fried parsley • Crème brûlée

WINE GUIDE ♀ Western Cape Sauvignon Blanc £24 • ♥ Caves des Papes Côtes du Rhône £19.23 • 37 bottles over £20, 6 bottles under £20 • 6 by the glass (£6-£8)

continued

PRICE GUIDE Fixed L £16.50 • starter £5-£12 • main £12-£28 • dessert £5-£6.50 • coffee £3.50 • min/water £5.50 • Service added but optional 12.5%

PLACE: An ever-popular Primrose Hill institution, its green awning and exterior paint work still pull in an adoring crowd. Gilt-framed mirrors cram every inch of wall space in the front, green-themed dining room, while out back there's a further conservatory-style room and downstairs a small bar. Atmospheric and intimate at night with tables bathed in candlelight.

FOOD: The modern European carte is a lengthy affair and comes sprinkled with luxury items and some unfamiliar combinations. Take a warm salad of marinated salmon with organic Old Spot pork, native lobster and celery, and a vanilla, apple and cider dressing. Colourful, creative presentation is a strength.

OUR TIP: Try for a table in the front dining room - great for couples **Chef:** Simon Bradley **Owners:** S Bradley **Times:** 12.30-2.30/7-11, Closed BHs, closed L Sat, closed D Sun **Notes:** Vegetarian available **Seats:** 65, Pr/dining room 30 **Smoking:** No pipes, No cigars **Children:** Portions **Directions:** Nearest station: Chalk Farm. By Primrose Hill. Telephone for directions

 **Sardo Canale**

Italian, Sardinian   **NEW**

Authentic Sardinian restaurant on the canal

☎ 020 7722 2800 42 Gloucester Av NW1 8JD Plan 1-E4

MENU GUIDE Grilled baby squid stuffed with aromatic herbs • Grilled veal escalope, Sardinian blue cheese sauce • Ravioli fritti

WINE GUIDE ♀ Cantina Trexenta Vermentino £14 • ♥ Cantina del Mandrolisai Cannonav £22 • 48 bottles over £20, 22 bottles under £20 • 10 by the glass (£3.75-£5.25)

PRICE GUIDE Fixed L £13 • Fixed D £28-£35 • starter £5.90-£8.90 • main £12-£18 • dessert £5.50-£6.50 • coffee £2.50 • min/water £2.90 • Service added but optional 12.5%

PLACE: Located in a stylish residential area of Primrose Hill, by the canal, the restaurant occupies an L-shaped room with floor to ceiling plate glass windows opening onto a delightful patio with tables set around an olive tree.

FOOD: Some of the best Sardinian cooking outside Sardinia, fairly simple in style, focusing on good clear flavours and excellent raw ingredients. Expect real Sardinian specialities such as fregola (large grain risotto), salsiccia Sarda (Sardinian sausages), and spaghetti alla bottarga (with a sauce made from dried mullet roe).

OUR TIP: Ask for a table outside, weather permitting **Chef:** Roberto Mudu **Owners:** Romolo & Bianca Mudu **Times:** 12-3/6-11, Closed 25-26 Dec, BHs, closed L Mon **Notes:** Vegetarian available **Seats:** 100, Pr/dining room 40 **Smoking:** N/Sm area, No pipes, No cigars, Air con **Children:** Portions **Parking:** on street **e-mail:** info@sardocanale.com **web:** www.sardocanale.com

The Winter Garden

International

Luxurious hotel with an engaging atmosphere

☎ 020 7631 8000 The Landmark London, 222 Marylebone Rd NW1 6JQ Plan 2-F4

MENU GUIDE Seared scallops, artichoke purée, trumpet mushroom sauce • Herb crusted rack of lamb, rosemary sauce • Sticky toffee pudding

WINE GUIDE ♀ Pinot Grigio Pinot Gris £23 • ♥ Merlot del Veneto £23 • 33 bottles over £20 • 15 by the glass (£7-£8)

PRICE GUIDE Fixed L £22.75 • starter £6.95-£14.50 • main £19.95-£34.50 • dessert £7.50-£8.50 • coffee £4.75 • min/water £5.25 • Service optional

continued

England

LONDON NW1 *continued*

PLACE: The Landmark is one of the last truly grand railway hotels, with a stunning naturally lit central atrium. There is a good choice of eating and drinking options, with the Winter Garden restaurant taking centre stage, ideal for a business lunch, afternoon tea or a romantic dinner.
FOOD: The kitchen delivers seasonal menus offering a good range of dishes to match the diversity of diners in the restaurant, with traditional favourites alongside contemporary offerings.
OUR TIP: Great place to watch the world go by
Chef: Gary Klaner **Owners:** Jatuporn Sihanatkathakul **Times:** 11.30-3/5-11.30 **Notes:** Afternoon tea £22.50 (+ Champagne £29.50), Sun Champagne Brunch £59.50, Vegetarian available, Civ Wed 100 **Seats:** 80, Pr/dining room 36 **Smoking:** Air con **Children:** Menu, Portions
Rooms: 299 (299 en suite) ★ ★ ★ ★ ★ **Directions:** Nearest station: Marylebone. M25 turn on to the A40 and continue 16m following signs for West End. Continue along Marylbone Rd for 300 mtrs. Restaurant on left.
Parking: 75 **e-mail:** dining@thelandmark.co.uk
web: www.landmarklondon.co.uk

(¶¶) **Belgo** 72 Chalk Farm Rd NW1 8AN ☎ 020 7267 0718
Belgian style, with strong beer, good seafood (mussels of course) and staff in habits.

(⌾) **Wagamama** 11 Jamestown Rd, Camden NW1 7BW
☎ 020 7428 0800 Informal noodle bar with no booking.

LONDON NW3

(⊚) **Manna**
Vegetarian
Simple and earthy
☎ 020 7722 8028 4 Erskine Rd, Primrose Hill NW3 3AJ Plan 1-E4
MENU GUIDE Sweet potato & coriander roulade with jalapeno cream cheese, black bean salsa • Smoked mozzarella & chilli tamale • Organic chocolate & pecan brownie, vanilla ice cream
WINE GUIDE ⚲ Piave Pinot Grigio £12.75 • ⚑ Piave Merlot £12.75 • 6 bottles over £20, 21 bottles under £20 • 4 by the glass (£2.95-£3.75)
PRICE GUIDE Starter £4.75-£6.95 • main £9.25-£12.50 • dessert £3.50-£6.95 • coffee £1.40 • min/water £2.95 • Service optional • Group min 6 service 12.5%
PLACE: Twinkling fairy lights and heavy wooden tables set the scene in this small, shop front restaurant. The staff are charming, relaxed and very knowledgeable, and the buzzy atmosphere makes for fun, informal dining.
FOOD: Urban farmhouse style cooking would be one way to describe the food here. Menus are simple, with lots of organic ingredients and plenty of dishes for vegans. Cooking is competent and presentation unfussy - and be warned, the portions (especially of main courses and salads) are large.
OUR TIP: Wine list includes some organic wines
Chef: Matthew Kay **Owners:** S.Hague, R.Swallow, M.Kay **Times:** 12.30-3/6.30-11, Closed 25 Dec-1 Jan, closed L Mon-Sat **Notes:** Vegetarian available **Seats:** 50 **Smoking:** N/Sm in restaurant, Air con
Children: Portions **Directions:** Nearest station: Chalk Farm Telephone for directions. **Parking:** On street **e-mail:** yourhost@manna-veg.com
web: www.manna-veg.com

(⊚) **The Wells Tavern**
British, European
Cosy gastro-pub in literary Hampstead
☎ 020 7794 3785 30 Well Walk NW3 1BX Plan 1-G5
continued

MENU GUIDE Pheasant & foie gras terrine, thyme toast • Roast mallard, butternut squash purèe, chestnuts • Bitter chocolate mousse
WINE GUIDE ⚲ Cloudy Bay Sauvignon Blanc £45 • ⚑ Anubis Malbec £20 • 45 bottles over £20, 9 bottles under £20 • 10 by the glass (£3.50-£5.50)
PRICE GUIDE Fixed L £20 • Fixed D £31 • coffee £2.50 • min/water £2.90 • Service added but optional 12.5%
PLACE: Poised between the designer shops of Hampstead village and the tamed wilds of the heath, this award-winning gastro-pub is split over two floors. Downstairs is a laid-back bar with comfy leather sofas, open fires and board games galore, while the first floor restaurant is comprised of three intimate dining rooms. Book ahead, and leave time for parking.
FOOD: Seasonal British cooking with the odd French twist. Expect straightforward modern fare based around quality ingredients: venison with braised red cabbage and tagliatelle for example, or sea bass with olive oil mash.
OUR TIP: Bring some change for the parking meters
Chef: Andrew Gale **Owners:** Beth Coventry **Times:** 12.30-3/7-10.30, Closed 25-26 Dec, 1 Jan, closed D 24-25 Dec **Notes:** Vegetarian available **Seats:** 50, Pr/dining room 12 **Smoking:** N/Sm area, No pipes, No cigars, Air con **Children:** Portions **Directions:** Nearest station: Hampstead Left out of station, 1st left through Flask Walk. 5 mins from Hampstead Heath **Parking:** on street pay & display **e-mail:** info@thewellshampstead.co.uk
web: www.thewellshampstead.co.uk

(❚❚) **Artigiano** 12a Belsize Ter NW3 4AX ☎ 020 7794 4288
Mix of contemporary Italian cuisine.

(⌾) **Yo! Sushi** 02 Centre, 255 Finchley Rd NW3 6LH
☎ 020 7431 4499 Sushi, Sashimi, noodles and more delivered by conveyor belt and priced according to colour coded plates.

LONDON NW6

(⊚) **Singapore Garden Restaurant**
Singaporean, Malaysian
Well established Oriental with a mixture of Chinese and Singaporean dishes
☎ 020 7328 5314 & 7624 8233 83-83a Fairfax Rd, West Hampstead NW6 4DY Plan 1-E4
MENU GUIDE Spring rolls with plum sauce dip • Squid balchan with crispy mange-tout • Coconut Chendol
WINE GUIDE ⚲ Sancerre Sauvignon Blanc £28 • ⚑ Montes Cabernet Sauvignon £19 • 29 bottles over £20, 12 bottles under £20
PRICE GUIDE Fixed L £7.50 • Fixed D £22 • starter £5.20-£10 • main £6-£32.50 • dessert £4.50-£6.50 • coffee £2.20 • min/water £3.20 • Service added but optional 12.5%
PLACE: An unobtrusive entrance marks this oriental restaurant, located amongst a row of upmarket shops just off the Finchley Road. Cream walls, green hues and plants dominate the two-room dining area, with waitresses dressed in traditional Singaporean batik uniforms.
FOOD: Well executed Chinese standard dishes mix with fiery Singaporean Straits specials encompassing a number of curries and noodle dishes. There is a fine selection of good value fixed-price menus to choose from.
OUR TIP: Good place for a family night out.
Chef: Siam Kiang Lim **Owners:** Lim family **Times:** 12-2.45/6-10.45, Closed 4 days at Xmas **Notes:** Vegetarian available **Seats:** 100, Pr/dining room 6 **Smoking:** No pipes, No cigars, Air con **Directions:** Nearest station: Swiss Cottage, Finchley Road Off Finchley Rd, on right before Belsize Rd rdbt **Parking:** Meters on street

Gourmet Burger Kitchen 331 West End Ln, West Hampstead NW6 1RS ☎ 020 7794 5455 New Zealand inspired burger joint using top notch beef.

Mario's 155 Broadhurst Gardens, West Hampstead NW6 3AU ☎ 020 7625 5827 Good value, bustling Greek.

LONDON NW10
Sabras Restaurant
Indian

Family-run popular Indian vegetarian
☎ 020 8459 0340 263 High Rd, Willesden Green NW10 2RX Plan 1-D4

PLACE: Owned and run by the same family for 30 years, this is a busy bistro-style restaurant with a simple interior of pastel shades, perched among shops along high street.
FOOD: South Indian regional fare: some dishes are family recipes, along with traditional mainstays, but all are vegetarian.
OUR TIP: Booking is essential
Times: 6.30-10.30pm, Closed Mon, closed L all week

LONDON SE1
The Anchor & Hope
British, European

Lively gastro-pub with attitude
☎ 020 7928 9898 36 The Cut SE1 8LP Plan 5-F5
MENU GUIDE Beetroot & horseradish salad • Rabbit, chorizo & snails • Pecan pie

WINE GUIDE ♀ Marcel Martin Muscadet £13.20 • ♀ Domaine des Moulines Cabernet Sauvignon £12.50 • 11 bottles over £20, 24 bottles under £20 • 12 by the glass (£1.80-£2.85)

PRICE GUIDE Starter £4.80-£8 • main £10.80-£21.80 • dessert £4.40-£5 • coffee £1 • min/water £2.50 • Service optional
PLACE: This place is packed as soon as the doors open, the resulting buzz exaggerated by wooden floors and furniture, bare walls and an open kitchen. Its 'happening' feel attracts a well-heeled, youngish crowd who relish the crowded, tightly-packed atmosphere.
FOOD: The ever-changing menu shows a daringly outrageous chutzpah (this is South London after all!) with its earthy bottled rabbit, pig's head glossed over in the Italian word 'cotechino', snails and 'Stinking Bishop' pie. Lamb cooked two ways is breathakingly tasty, and cuttlefish risotto a skilfully understated success. Service is warm and willing.
OUR TIP: The Tate Modern is just around the corner
Chef: Jonathan Jones, Harry Lester **Owners:** Robert Shaw, Mike Belben, Jonathan Jones, Harry Lester **Times:** 12-2.30/6-10.30, Closed BHs, 25 Dec-1 Jan, Sun, closed L Mon **Notes:** Vegetarian available **Seats:** 58 **Smoking:** No pipes, No cigars **e-mail:** anchorandhope@btconnect.com

Baltic
Eastern European

East European restaurant with modern, hearty food
☎ 020 7928 1111 74 Blackfriars Rd SE1 8HA Plan 5-F5
MENU GUIDE Beetroot soup, sour cream • Salt beef, horseradish dumplings, pickles • White chocolate cheesecake
WINE GUIDE ♀ Domaine de la Cessane Marsanne Viognier £15.50 • ♀ Lavabre Domaine Pic Stain Loup £17 • 20 bottles over £20, 10 bottles under £20 • 4 by the glass (£3.50-£5.75)

PRICE GUIDE Fixed L £11.90 • starter £4-£9 • main £9.50-£15 • dessert £4-£6 • coffee £1.75 • min/water £2.50 • Service added but optional 12.5%
PLACE: Step through the velvet curtains at the entrance to this Southwark eatery and you'll find an understated modern dining room with a buzzy, convivial feel.
FOOD: A lengthy eastern European menu deserves to be dithered over given the kitchen's accomplished skills and use of quality ingredients. Main dishes are hearty affairs such as schabowy (breaded pork with garlic mushrooms) or braised rabbit with cider, bacon and sauerkraut.
OUR TIP: Good value pre-theatre menu
Chef: Peter Resinski **Owners:** Jan Woroniecki **Times:** 12-3.30/6-11, Closed Xmas, 1 Jan, BHs **Notes:** Vegetarian available, Civ Wed 300 **Seats:** 100, Pr/dining room 35 **Smoking:** No pipes, Air con **Children:** Menu, Portions **Directions:** Nearest station: Southwark Opposite Southwark Station, 5 mins walk from Waterloo **Parking:** Meters on 'The Cut' **e-mail:** info@balticrestaurant.co.uk **web:** www.balticrestaurant.co.uk

Blueprint Café
European

Stunning Thames-side views and simple, honest cooking
☎ 020 7378 7031 The Design Museum, 28 Shad Thames SE1 2YD Plan 6-D2
MENU GUIDE Baked sardines & parsley crust • Sweetbreads, almonds, peas & mint • Peach & almond tart
WINE GUIDE ♀ Domaine St Bernard Chardonnay £15 • ♀ Domaine St Bernard Merlot £15 • 50 bottles over £20, 20 bottles under £20 • 6 by the glass (£4-£6)

PRICE GUIDE Starter £5-£7.50 • main £12.50-£19.50 • dessert £5.50-£7 • coffee £2 • min/water £3.30 • Service added but optional 12.5%
PLACE: Tower Bridge and the Thames hover magnificently beyond this minimalist restaurant, where the full length glass frontage pays suitable homage to the view. Inside it's all spot lighting, light wooden floors and well-spaced tables.
FOOD: The uncomplicated, almost terse, menu offers a modern romp through Europe, stopping off at Venice for fegato (chopped calves' liver) and Spain for salchichon and olives (salami). Service is charming and accurate.
OUR TIP: First-comers secure the window tables
Chef: Jeremy Lee **Owners:** Conran Restaurants **Times:** 12-3/6-11, Closed 25-28 Dec, 1 Jan, closed D Sun **Notes:** Vegetarian available **Seats:** 120 **Children:** Portions **Directions:** Nearest station: Tower Hill or London Bridge SE of Tower Bridge on riverside. 1st floor of Design Museum **Parking:** Nearby car parks, NCP Gainsford Street **e-mail:** blueprintcafe@conran-restaurants.co.uk **web:** www.conran.com

Butlers Wharf Chop House
British

Traditional fare in a lively riverside eaterie
☎ 020 7403 3403 The Butlers Wharf Building, 36e Shad Thames SE1 2YE Plan 6-D2
MENU GUIDE Leek & potato soup • Fish & chips, mushy peas • Chocolate & chestnut log
WINE GUIDE ♀ Saint Bernard Chardonnay £14.95 • ♀ Saint Bernard Merlot £14.95 • 120 bottles over £20, 16 bottles under £20 • 12 by the glass (£3.95-£6.25)
PRICE GUIDE Fixed L £19.75 • starter £6-£13.50 • main £13.50-£26 • dessert £4.50-£6.50 • coffee £2.50 • min/water £3.50 • Service added but optional 12.5%

continued

continued

England

England

LONDON SE1 *continued*

PLACE: A high-volume eaterie overlooking Tower Bridge in the rejuvenated Butlers Wharf area, busy with City types and well-heeled young locals. Efficient staff match the hectic pace.
FOOD: The food is traditional British along the lines of charcoal-grilled Barnsley chop, roast rib of beef, steak and kidney pudding, and fish pie with potato crust, matched with old-school puds like queen of puddings, bread and butter pudding, and baked apple.
OUR TIP: Try for a window table, or terrace in summer
Owners: Conran Restaurants **Times:** 12-3/6-11, Closed Good Friday
Notes: Vegetarian available **Seats:** 110 **Children:** Portions
Directions: Nearest station: Tower Hill, London Bridge On river front, SE side of Tower Bridge **Parking:** NCP, on street, multi-storey
e-mail: bwchophouse@conran-restaurants.co.uk
web: www.conran.com

Cantina del Ponte
Italian
Fun Thameside restaurant with views of Tower Bridge
☎ 020 7403 5403 The Butlers Wharf Building, 36c Shad Thames SE1 2YE Plan 6-D2

MENU GUIDE Grilled sardines, sun-dried tomatoes, chilli • Roast suckling pig, fennel seeds, rosemary, garlic • Figs, cardamom ice cream

WINE GUIDE ♀ Garganega Chardonnay £14.50 • ♀ Corvina Merlot £14.75 • 22 bottles over £20, 10 bottles under £20 • 7 by the glass (£3.95-£6)

PRICE GUIDE Starter £7 • main £9.50-£14.50 • dessert £5.50 • coffee £2.25 • min/water £3.25 • Service added but optional 12.5%

PLACE: One of the Conran stable, this converted riverside warehouse is simple in style with rustic furniture, a terracotta floor and a large mural of an Italian marketplace running the length of the restaurant. In summer you can eat outside.
FOOD: A reasonably authentic approach to regional Italian cooking, robust rather than refined, with pasta and pizzas (cooked in a wood stove) complementing the more formal dishes.
OUR TIP: Pizzas now available to take away
Chef: Justin West **Owners:** Conran Restaurants **Times:** 12-3/6-11, Closed 24-26 Dec **Notes:** Vegetarian available **Seats:** 95 **Smoking:** No pipes **Children:** Menu, Portions **Directions:** Nearest station: Tower Hill, London Bridge.SE side of Tower Bridge, on riverfront **Parking:** NCP Gainsford St **e-mail:** cantina@conran-restaurants.co.uk
web: www.conran.com/eat

Cantina Vinopolis
Mediterranean, European
Bustling restaurant and wine business
☎ 020 7940 8333 & 7089 9339 1 Bankside SE1 9BU
Plan 6-A3

MENU GUIDE Tian of avocado & dressed crab • Halibut fillet & wild mushrooms • Pear & almond tart

WINE GUIDE ♀ Boland Cellar Chenin Blanc £17.50 • ♀ Rioja Ontanon Tempranillo £22.50 • 170 bottles over £20, 31 bottles under £20 • 45 by the glass (£4.25-£11.50)

PRICE GUIDE Fixed L £12.50-£19.50 • Fixed D £15.50-£29.50 • starter £4.95-£7.95 • main £9.50-£15.95 • dessert £4.50-£5.95 • coffee £1.75 • min/water £3.50 • Service added but optional 12.5%

PLACE: A cool and airy restaurant under massive Victorian railway arches, with a cavernous feel engendered by vaulted ceilings exposed brickwork and tiled flooring. There's plenty of bustle, and a café and a small bar serving snacks also do well.
FOOD: Expect unfussy modern cooking prepared with care and accuracy. The modern European menu might run to Spanish black pudding, chorizo and deep fried potatoes, or Barbary duck breast with bok choy, honeyed root vegetables and black cherry sauce. A fantastic wine list from the Vinopolis wine operation.
OUR TIP: Visit the wine museum
Chef: Moges A Wolde **Owners:** T Gulliver & C Pulze **Times:** 12-3/6-10.30, Closed 24 Dec-3 Jan, closed D Sun **Notes:** Tasting menu available, Vegetarian available, Dress Restrictions, No trainers or jeans (Smart casual) **Seats:** 160, Pr/dining room 160 **Smoking:** N/Sm area, No pipes, No cigars, Air con **Children:** Portions **Directions:** Nearest station: London Bridge Telephone for directions **Parking:** Street parking (free after 6.30pm) **e-mail:** cantina@vinopolis.co.uk
web: www.cantinavinopolis.com

Champor Champor
Asian
South East Asian compilation cooking in cosy ethnic setting
☎ 020 7403 4600 62-64 Weston St SE1 3QJ
Plan 6-B2

MENU GUIDE Sardine curry puff, lime yogurt • Baked catfish, watercress fried rice • Burnt sugar steam cake, pickled cherry sorbet

WINE GUIDE 10 bottles over £20, 25 bottles under £20 • 4 by the glass (£3.80)

PRICE GUIDE Fixed L £21.50-£25 • Fixed D £25.50-£28 • coffee £1.90 • min/water £2.20 • Service added but optional 12.5%

PLACE: Tribal artefacts and Buddhist statues mingle easily with modern art and well-dressed tables to create an authentic Asian experience, with dozens of candles and floating oil lamps adding a magical appeal.
FOOD: Creative cooking using ideas and flavours from all over South East Asia bring an innovative touch to the short fixed price menu. Fresh, seasonal produce predominates - ask for help choosing.
OUR TIP: Book the secret mezzanine table
Chef: Adu Amran Hassan **Owners:** Charles Tyler, Adu Amran Hassan
Times: 6.15-10.15, Closed Xmas-N Year (14 days), Etr (7 days), BHs, Sun, closed L Times may vary - please check **Notes:** Vegetarian available **Seats:** 38, Pr/dining room 8 **Smoking:** No pipes, No cigars, Air con **Directions:** Nearest station: London Bridge Joiner St exit. Follow Saint Thomas St & 1st right into Weston St. Restaurant 100yds on left **Parking:** Snowsfields multi-storey **e-mail:** mail@champor-champor.com
web: www.champor-champor.com

continued

Fire Station

Modern European

Buzzing, functional pub-restaurant

☎ 020 7620 2226 150 Waterloo Rd SE1 8SB Plan 5-E5

MENU GUIDE Onion tartelette • Parsley-crusted calves' liver • Crème brûlée

PRICE GUIDE Food prices not confirmed for 2006. Please telephone for details.

PLACE: A cavernous pub and restaurant that is often packed with enthusiasts, therefore can be noisy. Expect plenty of evidence of its former life as a fire station, with no frills to soften the experience.

FOOD: A truly European menu (fixed-price specials at value-conscious prices), taking in chicken satay, grilled lamb brochette with couscous, and pan-fried ostrich steak with sweet potato pancake.

OUR TIP: Handy for Waterloo Station

Chef: Bam Gabamien **Owners:** Wizard Inns **Times:** 12-3/5.30-11 **Notes:** Vegetarian available **Seats:** 100, Pr/dining room 90 **Smoking:** No pipes, No cigars, Air con **Children:** Menu, Portions **Directions:** Nearest station: Waterloo Adjacent to Waterloo station **e-mail:** info@pathfinderpubs.co.uk **web:** www.pathfinderpubs.co.uk

The Oxo Tower Restaurant

European

Great venue, great food, great views

☎ 020 7803 3888 8th Floor, Oxo Tower Wharf, Barge House St SE1 9PH Plan 3-F1

MENU GUIDE Lobster tempura, daikon & wasabi • Roast partridge, quince purée, foie gras terrine • Mascarpone parfait, espresso sauce

WINE GUIDE ♀ Sancerre La Guiberte Sauvignon Blanc £28 ♂ Chateau Teyssier, St Emilion Grand Cru Merlot £33 • 350 bottles over £20, 10 bottles under £20 • 20 by the glass (£4.50-£9)

continued

The Oxo Tower Restaurant

PRICE GUIDE Fixed L £29.50 • starter £9-£18 • main £18-£31 • dessert £7.75 • coffee £2.50 • min/water £3.50 • Service added but optional 12.5%

PLACE: Stylish modern restaurant on the glass fronted 8th floor of the restored Oxo Tower, a riverside landmark since the late 1920s. There are fabulous views over the Thames and the London skyline from the restaurant, bar and brasserie.

FOOD: Interesting and inventive modern European menus at lunch and dinner, delivering a consistently high standard of cooking. Clean flavours come through and there are some imaginative combinations. A good value two or three-course set menu is available at lunchtime Monday to Friday and until 7pm Monday to Saturday.

OUR TIP: A good selection of breads

Chef: Jeremy Bloor **Owners:** Harvey Nichols & Co Ltd **Times:** 12-3/6-11.30, Closed 25-26 Dec **Notes:** ALC Sat and Sun only, Vegetarian available, Smart casual, Civ Wed 100 **Seats:** 130 **Smoking:** No pipes, Air con **Children:** Menu, Portions **Directions:** Nearest station: Blackfriars. Between Blackfriars & Waterloo Bridge **Parking:** NCP **e-mail:** oxo.reservations@harveynichols.co.uk **web:** www.harveynichols.co.uk

Ozu

Japanese **NEW**

Traditional Japanese cuisine in contemporary setting

☎ 020 7928 7766 County Hall Riverside Building, Westminster Bridge Rd SE1 7PB Plan 5-D5

MENU GUIDE Dobin-mushi shirumono (Steamed clear soup) Buta shoga yaki (Pork with ginger) • Green tea ice cream

WINE GUIDE ♀ Tolenda Gavi di Gavi £28.50 • ♂ Parker Coonawarra Estate £34.85 • 40 bottles over £20, 3 bottles under £20 • 6 by the glass (£4-£6)

PRICE GUIDE Fixed L £7-£14 • starter £4-£12 • main £8-£16 • dessert £2-£4.70 • coffee £2.45 • min/water £2.50 • Service added but optional 12.5%

PLACE: Situated inside County Hall, this Japanese restaurant's kitchens are visible through the floor-to-ceiling glass wall by the entrance. The spacious L-shaped dining room is decorated in the contemporary style with plain white walls and darkwood furniture.

FOOD: Good choice of traditional Japanese dishes in bento box and carte menus including some unusual items like the marinated squid (ika natto) or kamado gohan with quails' eggs. Short sake list.

OUR TIP: Convenient for The London Eye

Chef: Jong Dea Jeong **Owners:** Ozu (London) Ltd. **Times:** 12-3/5.30-10.30 **Notes:** Tasting menu £17-£34, Vegetarian available, Smart Dress **Seats:** 65 **Smoking:** N/Sm area, No pipes, No cigars **Directions:** Nearest station: Waterloo/Westminster Part of County Hall, building next to London Eye **Parking:** Waterloo Station **e-mail:** info@ozulondon.com

England

LONDON SE1 *continued*

⊕⊕ Le Pont de la Tour
French
Stylish, elegant Conran restaurant and bar
☎ 020 7403 8403 The Butlers Wharf Building, 36d Shad Thames SE1 2YE Plan 6-D2

MENU GUIDE Foie gras terrine, confit de vin • Venison tenderloin, celeriac purée, chocolate & cinnamon • Lemon tart, lime syrup

WINE GUIDE ♀ Mauzac Sauvignon Blanc £16 • ♥ Duras Cabernet Sauvignon £16 • 900 bottles over £20, 20 bottles under £20 • 16 by the glass (£4.50-£15)

PRICE GUIDE Fixed L £29.50 • starter £7-£15 • main £12-£35.50 • dessert £8.50 • coffee £2.75 • min/water £3.50 • Service added but optional 12.5%

PLACE: Smack on the waterfront wharf, this popular, attractive South Bank Conran offers stunning floodlit views of Tower Bridge by night, and there's a promenade terrace for alfresco summer dining that's great for Thameside people and riverboat watching. In tune with the location, the cruise liner-influenced interior is light and cosmopolitan, while smartly turned-out staff provide efficient, formal service.
FOOD: The well-established, modern French cooking is consistently fresh, slick, straightforward and well presented, with the appealing menus dotted with some tried-and-tested favourites and cracking seafood.
OUR TIP: Luxury produce peppers the menu
Chef: James Walker **Owners:** Conran Restaurants **Times:** 12-3/6-11.30, Closed 25-26 Dec, closed L Sat **Notes:** Vegetarian available, Smart casual **Seats:** 105, Pr/dining room 20 **Smoking:** No pipes **Children:** Menu, Portions **Directions:** Nearest station: Tower Hill, London Bridge SE of Tower Bridge **Parking:** NCP Gainsford St
web: www.conran.com

⊕ RSJ, The Restaurant on the South Bank
Modern British
Handy for South Bank theatres
☎ 020 7928 4554 33 Coin St SE1 9NR Plan 5-F6
MENU GUIDE Wild mushroom soup, truffle salsa • Venison loin, chocolate & chilli sauce • Steamed blueberry pudding, orange custard

PRICE GUIDE Food prices not confirmed for 2006. Please telephone for details

PLACE: A plain and simple first floor restaurant, popular with the media folk and theatre/concert goers from the adjacent South Bank. Friendly staff keep things moving efficiently with an eye on performance times.
FOOD: Modern flavours offer much of interest from a repertoire based around the seasons. Some stock French classics like lamb shank and confit duck leg share the menu with lighter contemporary options, and saucing is a strength.
OUR TIP: Try some of the Loire Valley wines
Times: 12-2/5.30-11, Closed Xmas, 1 Jan, Sun, closed L Sat
Directions: Nearest station: Waterloo Telephone for directions
e-mail: sally.webber@rsj.uk.com **web:** www.rsj.uk.com

⊕ **Yo! Sushi** County Hall, Belvedere Rd SE1 7GP
☎ 020 7928 8871 Sushi, Sashimi, noodles and more delivered by conveyor belt and priced according to colour coded plates.

LONDON SE3

⊕⊕⊕ Chapter Two see page 273

⊕ Laicram Thai Restaurant
Thai
Authentic Thai
☎ 020 8852 4710 1 Blackheath Grove, Blackheath SE3 0DD Plan 8-D1
MENU GUIDE Popia Soht (crab & pork rice pancake) • Phat Thai (prawns & noodles) • Deep-fried banana with honey & cream

WINE GUIDE ♀ Sancerre £16.95 • ♥ Saint Emilion £17.50 2 bottles over £20, 21 bottles under £20 • 1 by the glass (£2.20-£3)

PRICE GUIDE Starter £3-£6.50 • main £5.80-£13.90 • dessert £2.50-£4.50 • coffee £2.50 • min/water £3.50

PLACE: This cosy side street restaurant is close to Blackheath Station. Carved wooden panels and Thai trinkets set the mood; the staff are authentically dressed.
FOOD: Traditional Thai cuisine, at its aromatic and fragrant best. The menu is lengthy with plenty of vegetarian and lighter choices. Don't forget to try the Thai beer.
OUR TIP: Weekends are busy - book in advance
Chef: Mrs S Dhirabutra **Owners:** Mr D Dhirabutra **Times:** 12-2.30/6-11, Closed BHs, Mon **Seats:** 50 **Smoking:** Air con **Directions:** Nearest station: Blackheath Off main shopping street, in a side road near the Post Office. Opposite station, near library.

ONDON SE3

Chapter Two

uropean

rominent restaurant with imaginative cuisine

☎ 020 8333 2666 43-45 Montpelier Vale, Blackheath Village SE3 0TJ

Ian 8-D1

Web: www.chapterrestaurants.co.uk

LACE: A spiral staircase connects the small ground floor dining area with the larger basement space, while splashes bold colours - blues, reds and dark browns - bring a thematic harmony to the two parts. The open heath setting is aceful yet accessible on foot from the town centre, and the clever use of mirrors inside along with light wooden ors and smartly-set tables results in a feeling of lightness and space. Service is similarly informal.

OOD: This is imaginative cooking which shows its pedigree without the need for unnecessary flourishes or empty avado. The expected technical know-how is evident from the start, and dishes deliver exactly what the stimulating enu promises. The clean flavours of marinated salmon with beetroot tortellini are given an almost effervescent boost a horseradish foam, and earthy items like confit brisket of beef with pearl barley are cleverly elevated to the same fty heights as more luxurious ingredients.

MENU GUIDE Mackerel rillette, prawn tempura • Slow roast pork belly, pomme mousseline • Coconut parfait, mango assiette

WINE GUIDE ♀ Baron Philippe De Rothschild Sauvignon Blanc £17.50 • ♀ Baron Philippe de Rothschild Merlot £17.50 • 43 bottles over £20, 16 bottles under £20 • 7 by the glass (£3.65-£3.95)

PRICE GUIDE Fixed L £14.50-£21 • Fixed D £19.95 min/water £2.95 • Service added but optional 12.5%

OUR TIP: Booking absolutely essential at weekends

Chef: Trevor Tobin **Owners:** Selective Restaurants Group
Times: 12-3/6.30-11, Closed 2-4 Jan **Notes:** Sun L 2 courses £14.50, 3 courses £16.50, Vegetarian available, Dress Restrictions, No shorts or trainers **Seats:** 70 **Smoking:** N/Sm in restaurant, Air con **Children:** Portions **Parking:** Car park by station

LONDON SE22

Franklins
Modern British
Adventurous gastro-pub fare
☎ 020 8299 9598 157 Lordship Ln SE22 8HX
Plan 1-F2

MENU GUIDE Salt beef hash, fried egg • Smoked haddock, mussels, sprouting broccoli • Bread & butter pudding

WINE GUIDE ♀ Criadores Viura £11 • ♀ Palena Merlot £13.50 • 24 bottles over £20, 15 bottles under £20 • 11 by the glass (£2.75-£6.50)

PRICE GUIDE Fixed L £9 • starter £5-£8 • main £10-£17.50 • dessert £4.75 • coffee £2 • min/water £2.20 • Service optional • Group min 6 service 10%

PLACE: The intimate dining room at the back of a South London gastro-pub has a dozen simply clothed tables are decorated with single flowers. Bold art lends colour to the exposed brickwork.
FOOD: A daily changing menu of accomplished, seasonal British cooking features dishes such as saddle back pork with snails and black pudding, or chicken with butter beans and chorizo. Great value weekday lunch selection.
OUR TIP: Very busy at weekends
Chef: Tim Sheehan **Owners:** Tim Sheehan & Rodney Franklin
Times: 12, Closed 25-26, 31 Dec, 1 Jan **Notes:** Fixed D £28.50 for larger parties, Vegetarian available **Seats:** 42, Pr/dining room 20
Smoking: N/Sm area, No pipes **Children:** Portions **Parking:** Bawdale Road **e-mail:** franklins@madasafish.com

The Palmerston
Modern British   NEW
Smart pub serving good modern food
☎ 020 8693 1629 91 Lordship Ln, East Dulwich
SE22 8EP Plan 1-F3

MENU GUIDE Salad of brown shrimps • Grilled calves' liver, béarnaise sauce • Vanilla rice pudding with plums

PRICE GUIDE Food prices not confirmed for 2006. Please telephone for details

PLACE: On the corner of trendy Lordship Lane and run by chef/patron Jamie Younger, a traditional old pub whose authenticity survives intact despite a stylish makeover. Wooden floors and light wooden panelling enhance the non-smoking rear restaurant and front dining and drinking areas.
FOOD: Well-sourced ingredients and accurate modern British cooking mark this kitchen as one to watch. The short menu inspires with a textbook chicken liver parfait, rump of lamb with spinach pûrée, and pink grapefruit and champagne jelly.
OUR TIP: Be sure to book at weekends
Times: 12, Closed BHs, closed L Mon, closed D Sun **Directions:** Nearest station: East Dulwich Bridge 2m from Clapham, 1/2m from Dulwich Village
e-mail: thepalmerston@tiscali.co.uk **web:** www.thepalmerston.co.uk

---

What makes a Restaurant of the Year?
In selecting a Restaurant of the Year, we look for somewhere that is exceptional in its chosen area of the market. Whilst the Rosette awards are based on the quality of the food alone, Restaurant of the Year takes into account all aspects of the operation. For full details see pages 6-7.

LONDON SE23

Babur Brasserie
Indian
Stylish setting for Indian specialities
☎ 020 8291 2400 & 8291 4881 119 Brockley Rise, Forest Hill SE23 1JP Plan 1-G2

MENU GUIDE Ros tos crab, cooked with spice, wine & cheese topping • Beef salan (cashew and yogurt purée) • Chocolate & coconut samosas

WINE GUIDE ♀ Mastri Vernacoli Pinot Grigio £12.50 • ♀ Windowrie The Mill Shiraz £14.95 • 9 bottles over £20, 26 bottles under £20 • 7 by the glass (£2.95-£4.55)

PRICE GUIDE Starter £3.75-£5.95 • main £7.95-£12.75 • dessert £3.95-£4.95 • coffee £1.75 • min/water £2.95

PLACE: You can tell by the full-size Bengal tiger prowling on the roof that this is no ordinary Indian restaurant. Cool colours and fresh flowers make for an attractive and relaxing interior, with a choice of seating from banqueting tables to cosy nooks for two.
FOOD: Regional Indian cooking with menus developed from years of research and regular food festivals. Fish dishes are particularly popular, including a classic Madras John Dory, and there are good vegetarian choices. Spicing is subtle with few roaring hot dishes (highlighted with one or two tiger heads).
OUR TIP: Extensive takeaway service available
Chef: Enam Rahman **Owners:** Babur 1998 Ltd **Times:** 12.30-2.30/6-11.30, Closed 25-26 Dec, closed L Fri **Notes:** Sun buffet L £9.25, Vegetarian available **Seats:** 56 **Smoking:** N/Sm area, Air con
Directions: Nearest station: Honor Oak 5 mins walk from Honor Oak Station, where parking is available **Parking:** On street
e-mail: enquiries@babur-brasserie.com
web: www.babur-brasserie.com

England

LONDON SE24

 ## 3 Monkeys Restaurant

Indian

Vintage Indian cuisine in converted bank

☎ 020 7738 5500 136-140 Herne Hill SE24 9QH
Plan 1-F2

MENU GUIDE Calamari varuval (Seared scallops on squid curls) • Murgh tikka makhanwala (Grilled chicken tikka with tomato & cream) • Aam ki phirni (Rice pudding with mango)

WINE GUIDE ♀ Vina Albina Virura Rioja £19 • ♀ Santa Isabel Malbec £16.50 • 25 bottles over £20, 8 bottles under £20 • 3 by the glass (£3.50-£4.50)

PRICE GUIDE Fixed L £7.95 • Fixed D £18.95 • starter £3.45-£7.25 • main £6.95-£22.95 • dessert £4.25-£4.50 • coffee £1.95 • min/water £2.75 • Service added but optional 12.5%

PLACE: The ambience is lively and interesting, with a state-of-the-art open grill being the centre of attraction. The restaurant's location on a busy south-east London road is soon forgotten as you sit down to enjoy the dramatic glass bridges, circular bar, exotic lighting and the menu.

FOOD: Indian cuisine at its authentic best, with dishes from every part of the sub-continent - tandoori specialities from the north-west, seafood curries from the west and vegetarian options from the south all compete for selection.

OUR TIP: Deli next door for take-home ingredients

Chef: Raminder Malhotra **Owners:** Kuldeep Singh, Raminder Malhotra **Times:** 12-2.30/6-11, Closed L Sat **Notes:** Vegetarian available **Seats:** 90 **Smoking:** N/Sm area, Air con **Children:** Menu, Portions **Directions:** Nearest station: Herne Hill, Brixton Adjacent to Herne Hill station **e-mail:** info@3monkeysrestaurant.com **web:** www.3monkeysrestaurant.com

LONDON SW1

 ## Al Duca

Italian

Rustic Italian cooking in Piccadilly

☎ 020 7839 3090 4-5 Duke of York St SW1Y 6LA
Plan 5-B6

MENU GUIDE Poached egg, parmesan, bacon, potatoes, mushrooms • Braised beef, mash, Barolo sauce • Dark chocolate marquise, caramel

WINE GUIDE ♀ Abbazia di Novacello Kerner £28 • ♀ Capestrano Montepulciano D'Abruzzo £21 • 100 bottles over £20, 10 bottles under £20 • 15 by the glass (£4-£14)

PRICE GUIDE Fixed L fr £17.50 • Fixed D fr £24 • coffee £2.50 • min/water £3 • Service added but optional 12.5%

PLACE: In a quiet side street near Piccadilly, this chic Italian draws a crowd of appreciative regulars with its friendly ambience and authentic cuisine. It's candlelit by night, with a warm terracotta colour scheme, smartly dressed tables and beige leather banquettes.

FOOD: Enjoyable and unpretentious cooking that draws inspiration from all the regions of Italy. Mains might include crab and mascarpone tortello with a saffron sauce, or sea bass with zucchini.

OUR TIP: Pre- and post-theatre menus also available

Chef: Frank Martinez **Owners:** Cuisine Collection **Times:** 12-2.30/6-11, Closed Christmas, New Year, BHs, Sun **Notes:** Vegetarian available, Dress restrictions, Smart casual. No shorts **Seats:** 56 **Smoking:** No pipes, No cigars, Air con **Children:** Portions **Directions:** Nearest station: Piccadilly 5mins walk from station towards Piccadilly. Right into St James, left into Jermyn St. Duke of York St, halfway along on right **e-mail:** info@alduca-restaurant.co.uk **web:** www.alduca-restaurant.co.uk

 ## Allium

Modern European

Accomplished modern cooking in contemporary nautical-themed resturant

☎ 020 7798 6888 Dolphin Square Hotel, Chichester St SW1V 3LX Plan 5-B1

MENU GUIDE Seared scallops, carrot/cardamom purée • Roast loin of veal, pan-fried sweetbread, truffle potato purée • Chocolate soufflé

PRICE GUIDE Fixed L £17.50 • Fixed D £33.50 • starter £7.40-£14 • main £16.50-£24.10 • dessert fr £7.20 • coffee £3.25 • min/water £3.50 • Service added but optional 12.5%

PLACE: An independent restaurant at the Dolphin Square Hotel - part of a major complex close to Victoria and the river. Allium has a nautical theme in dark blue with chrome stair rails and portholes. Contemporary artworks feature, including a sculpture of an allium flower by Ruth Mouiette. Entry is via a raised area with a crescent shaped bar. Service is slick, attentive and friendly.

FOOD: Light contemporary European style with a heavy French influence and liberal use of luxury ingredients. Skilled cooking with accurate timing and excellent balance of flavours.

OUR TIP: Good value lunch and pre-theatre menus

Chef: Anton Edelmann, Peter Woods **Owners:** Sodexho **Times:** 12.30-2.30/6-10.30, Closed 1 Jan, Mon, closed L Sat, closed D Sun **Notes:** Tasting menu £39.50, Vegetarian available, Dress Restrictions, Smart casual **Seats:** 82, Pr/dining room 90 **Smoking:** Air con **Children:** Portions **Rooms:** 148 (148 en suite) ★★★★ **Parking:** 18 **e-mail:** info@allium.co.uk **web:** www.allium.co.uk

Amaya

Indian **NEW**

Chic modern Indian with theatrical open kitchen

☎ 020 7823 1166 Halkin Arcade, 19 Motcomb St SW1X 8JT Plan 4-G4

MENU GUIDE Mussels peri peri • Dover sole, coconut, coriander & mint crust • Lime & mint tart, Kaffir lime jelly, blueberry compote

WINE GUIDE 65 bottles over £20, 3 bottles under £20 • 26 by the glass (£4.45-£9.85)

PRICE GUIDE Starter £3.50-£24 • main £12.50-£16.50 • dessert fr £6.50 • coffee £2.50 • min/water £3.90 • Service included • Service added but optional 12.5%

PLACE: Modern Indian grill and bar deep in the Sloane belt and styled accordingly with a sophisticated and elegant interior. A glass atrium allows natural daylight to pour through onto the open-plan kitchen where chefs cook against a backdrop of glass-fronted chillers, greenery and backlit flagons of oil. Comfy leather seating, modern glass plates and delicious cooking aromas complete the picture.

FOOD: Grazing-style restaurant where you are encouraged to order a succession of grilled meats and fish cooked Tandoori, Sigri (barbecue) or Tawa (hot plate) style. Food is competently cooked and decoratively presented.

OUR TIP: Desserts are a must-have here

Chef: Karunesh Khanna **Owners:** R Mathrani, C Panjabi, N Panjabi **Times:** 12-2.30/6.30-11.15, Closed D Xmas **Notes:** Tasting menu **Seats:** 90, Pr/dining room 14 **Smoking:** N/Sm in restaurant, Air con **Parking:** NCP **e-mail:** amaya@realindianfood.com **web:** www.realindianfood.com

England

LONDON SW1 *continued*

🏵 The Avenue

British

Buzzing contemporary restaurant with reliable cooking

☎ 020 7321 2111 7-9 St James's St SW1A 1EE
Plan 5-B5

MENU GUIDE Hot smoked mackerel, potato & horseradish sauce • Salt beef, bubble & squeak • Rhubarb crumble

PRICE GUIDE Fixed L £17.95 • Fixed D £19.95 • starter £6.50-£10.50 • main £16-£19 • dessert £6.50 • Service added but optional 12.5%

PLACE: Plain white walls, white polished limestone tiled floors and high white ceilings create a lively ambience. Apart from recessed spotlights and a few mirrors, the only colour comes from a blue suede banquette along one wall and the grey and white chairs.

FOOD: Long and varied regularly changing menus include modern and traditional dishes. Offering fresh, seasonal ingredients simply prepared and cooked, careful presentation and accurate cooking is always apparent.

OUR TIP: Lunch here after shopping or site-seeing in St James
Chef: Lawrence Keogh **Owners:** Image Restaurants **Times:** 12-3/5.45-12, Closed 25-26 Dec, 1 Jan **Notes:** Vegetarian available, Smart Dress, Civ Wed 150 **Seats:** 180 **Smoking:** Air con **Children:** Portions
Directions: Nearest station: Green Park Turn R past The Ritz, 2nd turning into St James's St. Telephone for further details **Parking:** Parking meters on streets **e-mail:** avenue@egami.co.uk **web:** www.egami.co.uk

🏵 Boisdale of Belgravia

British

Traditional, clubby but fun Scottish restaurant

☎ 020 7730 6922 15 Eccleston St SW1W 9LX
Plan 4-H3

MENU GUIDE Tobermory cheddar & sweet onion soufflé • Roasted halibut with mixed pepper, warm cherry tomato, roast garlic & rosemary salad • Lemon tart

WINE GUIDE ♀ St Cair New Zealand Sauvignon Blanc £26 • ♀ Bonhomme France Merlot £13.95 • 172 bottles over £20, 28 bottles under £20 • 14 by the glass (£3.50-£7.20)

PRICE GUIDE Fixed L £14 • starter £7.50-£15 • main £13.50-£25 • dessert £6.50 • coffee £3.50 • min/water £3.75 • Service added but optional 12.5%

PLACE: Buzzy, tardis-like Scottish restaurant draws a well-heeled Belgravia crowd to the labyrinth of dining areas and bars. With its clubby atmosphere and evening live jazz, the deep reds and greens, tartan, dark floorboards and picture-laden walls deliver a resolutely Scottish experience. There are one hundred and fifty malts and a hundred cigars on offer.

FOOD: The Anglo-Caledonian menu features quality Scottish produce from Macsween haggis to Dunkeld oak-smoked salmon and Aberdeen Angus steaks.

OUR TIP: Try the quieter front restaurant
Chef: Nick Bell **Owners:** Mr R Macdonald **Times:** 12-2.15/7-1am, Closed Xmas, New Year, Easter, BHs, Sun, closed L Sat **Notes:** Vegetarian available **Seats:** 100, Pr/dining room 22 **Smoking:** Air con
Directions: Nearest station: Victoria Turn left along Buckingham Palace Rd heading W, Eccleston Street is 1st on right
e-mail: info@boisdale.co.uk **web:** www.boisdale.co.uk

🏵🏵 Boxwood Café

British, American

Upmarket brasserie in high class hotel

☎ 020 7235 1010 The Berkeley Hotel, Wilton Place, Knightsbridge SW1X 7RL Plan 4-G4

MENU GUIDE Pickled Arctic herrings, new potatoes, crème fraîche • Veal & foie gras burger, chips • Warm doughnuts, espresso sorbet

WINE GUIDE ♀ Marlborough Gravitas Sauvignon Blanc £34 • ♀ Lopez de Heredia Rioja ina Cubillo 1999 £34 90 bottles over £20, 3 bottles under £20 • 11 by the glass (£4.75-£8.50)

PRICE GUIDE Fixed L £18.50-£21 • starter £7-£12.50 • main £8.50-£25 • dessert £6-£7 • coffee £4 • min/water £3.50 • Service optional • Group min 12 service 12.5%

PLACE: Part of Gordon Ramsay's culinary empire, this upmarke New York style café is always bustling with a relaxed crowd of a ages. The elegant dining room is a split-level affair, decorated i a mix of glitzy golds and earthy tones, while staff are young, friendly and know their stuff. Book ahead.

FOOD: An accomplished kitchen delivers an eclectic mix of upmarket brasserie fare, handling high quality ingredients with deft simplicity. A lengthy list of mains might include a brill, salmon and lobster pie, or suckling pig with mash and a grain mustard sauce.

OUR TIP: Private dining room available
Chef: Stuart Gillies **Owners:** Gordon Ramsay Holdings Ltd **Times:** 12 3/6.00-11 **Notes:** Weekend lunch menu £21, Vegetarian available
Seats: 140, Pr/dining room 16 **Smoking:** N/Sm in restaurant, Air con
Children: Menu, Portions **Parking:** Street parking available
e-mail: boxwoodcafe@gordonramsay.com
web: www.gordonramsay.com

🏵🏵 Brasserie Roux

French

Popular brasserie serving rustic French cuisine

☎ 020 7968 2900 Sofitel St James London, 6 Waterloo Place SW1Y 4AN Plan 5-B6

MENU GUIDE Lobster bisque • Braised lamb shank with olives orange peel • Coffee crème brûlée

WINE GUIDE ♀ R and F Crochet Sancerre le Chene Marchand Sauvignon Blanc £32.50 • ♀ Domaine St Antonin Coteaux du Languedoc Faugeres Grenache £22 • 236 bottles over £20, 17 bottles under £20 • 18 by the glass (£4.50-£12)

PRICE GUIDE Fixed L £15-£20 • Fixed D £15-£20 • starter £6-£12.50 • main £7-£14.50 • dessert £5-£8 • coffee £3 • min/wat £4 • Service added but optional 17.5%

continu

England

ACE: A touch of Paris just round the corner from Buckingham
ace. Bright red leather chairs, pale yellow walls and bare
od tables comprise the chic but low-key decor of this vibrant
sserie, whose friendly waiters really know their stuff.
OD: Come hungry - this is hearty French cuisine at its unfussy,
tic best. Expect flavourful classics conjured from good quality
duce, such as cassoulet, braised beef cheek à l'ancienne, or
louse sausage and mash.
R TIP: Snacks available in the hotel bar
ef: Richard Tonks Owners: Accor UK Times: 12-3/5.30-11.30
tes: Sun Jazz Brunch, Vegetarian available, Civ Wed 150 Seats: 100,
lining room 12 Smoking: N/Sm area, Air con Children: Menu,
tions Rooms: 186 (186 en suite) ★★★★★ Directions: Nearest
on: Piccadilly Circus Telephone for directions Parking: NCP at
adilly e-mail: brasserieroux@sofitelstjames.com
b: www.sofitelstjames.com

The Cadogan Hotel

ternational, Pacific Rim

ntemporary dining in opulent surroundings
020 7235 7141 75 Sloane St SW1X 9SG Plan 4-F3

ENU GUIDE Trio of salmon, gin sorbet • Rack of lamb,
semary polenta, beetroot confit, thyme jus • Chocolate
ndant, milk mousse

INE GUIDE ♀ Chablis Domaine Long Depaquit Chardonnay
0 • ♥ Bourgogne Vielles Vignes Albert Biochot Pinot Noir £32
bottles over £20, 9 bottles under £20 • 11 by the glass (£6-£8)

ICE GUIDE Fixed L £15-£18 • Fixed D £15-£18 • starter £5-
1 • main £13.50-£21 • dessert £6-£9 • coffee £3.50 • min/water
.75 • Service added but optional 12.5%

ACE: The Cadogan, a grand hotel with a fascinating history
celebrated association with Lillie Langtry and Oscar Wilde,
changed ownership and undergone a major refurbishment.
s'anges, the new restaurant is a complete change of direction,
h modern art, sand suede walls and trompe d'oeil columns.
OD: Modern International carte and smaller set menu with a
nber of vegetarian options and innovative combinations, such
blueberry marinated venison.
R TIP: Refreshments all day in the lounge
ef: Judith Marra Owners: GLA Hotels Times: 12-2.30/7-10.30
tes: Vegetarian available, Dress Restrictions, Smart casual, no jeans or
irts, Civ Wed 38 Seats: 45, Pr/dining room 32 Smoking: N/Sm in
aurant, Air con Children: Menu Rooms: 65 (65 en suite) ★★★★
ections: Nearest station: Knightsbridge, Sloane Square Telephone for
ctions Parking: NCP opposite e-mail: info@cadogan.com
b: www.cadogan.com

Le Caprice Restaurant

odern European

lebrity haunt with superb food
020 7629 2239 Arlington House, Arlington St
/1A 1RT Plan 5-A6

ENU GUIDE Eggs Benedict • Pan-fried calves' liver, champ,
icon • Whiskey & walnut tart, clotted cream

INE GUIDE 68 bottles over £20, 10 bottles under £20 • 12 by
e glass (£4.75-£9.75)

ICE GUIDE Starter £6.25-£15.75 • main £12.50-
4.75 • dessert £5.75-£8.50 • coffee £2.75 • min/water
.50 • Service optional

ACE: Starry veteran of the London restaurant scene that still
ws its share of the rich and famous. The decor is low-key -
ck and white with lots of glass and mirrors, and a set of David
ley portraits on the walls. Watch the celebs come and go.

continued

FOOD: No airs or graces here. Le Caprice treats all its guests with
the same even-handed respect, and there's a similar lack of
pretension about the food. The wide-ranging menu offers a range
of simple classics to suit most tastes and a vegetarian selection is
also available.
OUR TIP: Book ahead
Chef: Kevin Gratton Owners: Signature Group Plc Times: 12-3/5.30-12,
Closed 25-26 Dec, 1 Jan, Aug BH, closed L 27 Dec, closed D 24 Dec
Notes: Sun brunch available, Vegetarian available Seats: 80
Smoking: No pipes, Air con Children: Portions Directions: Nearest
station: Green Park Arlington St runs beside The Ritz. Restaurant is at end
Parking: NCP, On street

Caraffini

Italian

Busy traditional Italian
☎ 020 7259 0235 61-63 Lower Sloane St
SW1W 8DH Plan 4-G2

MENU GUIDE Carpaccio with parmesan & baby
spinach • Monkfish wrapped in Parma ham with pesto &
seafood coulis • Cassata

WINE GUIDE ♀ Santa Margherita Pinot Grigio 2003
£20.50 • ♥ Villa Antinori IGT 2001 Sangiovese/Merlot/Syrah
£25.50 • 34 bottles over £20, 14 bottles under £20 • 4 by the
glass (£3.95-£5.75)

PRICE GUIDE Starter £4.25-£9.50 • main £10-£18.50 • dessert
£3.95-£4.50 • coffee £1.95 • min/water £3.15 • Service
optional • Group min 6 service 12.5%

PLACE: A smartly old-fashioned restaurant with a lively
atmosphere and a clientele of well-heeled locals. Service is
capably handled by a legion of effusive Italian gentlemen.
FOOD: The long menu is a comprehensive run through the
fundamentals of traditional regional Italian cuisine, offering a range
of classic dishes enhanced with one or two more modern ideas.
OUR TIP: A great lunch stop from shopping in Sloane Street
Chef: John Patino, S Ramalhoto Owners: F Di Rienzo & Paolo Caraffini
Times: 12.15-2.30/6.30-11.30, Closed BHs, Xmas, Sun Notes: Vegetarian
available Seats: 70 Smoking: No pipes, Air con Directions: Nearest
station: Sloane Square Telephone for directions Parking: Meters on street
e-mail: info@caraffini.co.uk web: www.caraffini.co.uk

For information on Service Charge, see p21.

The AA Wine Awards recognise the finest
wine lists in England, Scotland and Wales. For
full details, see pages 14-15

LONDON SW1 *continued*

ⓐⓐ Le Cercle

Modern French   **NEW**

Winner of AA Restaurant of the Year for London

☎ 020 7901 9999 1 Wilbraham Place SW1X 9AE Plan 4-F3

MENU GUIDE Crispy black pudding pie & apple • Veal sweetbreads, cep confit • Chocolate & mint igloo

WINE GUIDE ♀ H Pelle Menetou Salon £25 • ♀ A Graulot Crozes Hermitage £28.50 • 200 bottles over £20, 20 bottles under £20 • 16 by the glass (£3.80-£8.50)

PRICE GUIDE Fixed L £15-£19.50 • starter £3.25-£35 • dessert £3-£4.50 • coffee £2.25 • min/water £3.75 • Service added 12.5%

PLACE: You could be forgiven for walking past the discreet entrance to Club Gascon's little sister, sandwiched as it is between smart residential properties. Polished wooden tables and lots of leather suggest a modern/retro mood, with a separate 'chill out' area for drinks.

FOOD: Superb little dishes stamped with quality and presented impeccably are the hallmark of this inspired French cooking. The innovative style fuses starters and mains, separating them instead by type: vegetarian, seafood, meat, rural *terroirs* (like braised pig's cheek) and luxury items, with some daring flavour and textural combinations.

OUR TIP: Afternoon tea also served

Chef: Thierry Beyris **Owners:** Vincent Labeyrie & Pascal Aussignac **Times:** 12-3/6-11, Closed Sun, Mon **Notes:** Vegetarian available **Seats:** 60 **Smoking:** N/Sm in restaurant, Air con **Directions:** Nearest station: Sloane Square Just off Sloane Street **Parking:** Outside after 6, NCP in Cadogan Sq **e-mail:** info@lecercle.co.uk

ⓐⓐ The Cinnamon Club

Indian   🍴NEW

Fashionable Indian in hallowed Westminster

☎ 020 7222 2555 The Old Westminster Library, Great Smith St SW1P 3BU Plan 5-C4

MENU GUIDE Tandori Anjou squab pigeon breast • Smoked lamb rack, Rajasthani corn sauce, pilau rice • Banana & ginger sticky toffee pudding

WINE GUIDE ♀ Shaw & Smith Sauvignon Blanc £32 • ♀ Plantagenet Pinot Noir £31 • 150 bottles over £20, 6 bottles under £20 • 12 by the glass (£3.60-£10)

PRICE GUIDE Fixed L £19 • Fixed D £60 • coffee £3.50 min/water £3.50 • Service included

PLACE: The former Westminster Library makes an unusual but highly original setting for a contemporary Indian. Polished

parquet floors, dark wood, high ceilings, domed skylights and a gallery of books retain the building's heritage and old English charm, while crisp white linen, high-backed suede banquettes, professional service and a clubby bar cultivate a civilised, sophisticated mood.

FOOD: Traditional Indian cooking - elegantly and colourfully presented in European style - is the formula, built around top quality ingredients and well-judged spicing. Chefs from differen parts of India offer a balanced variety of dishes, plus two European options.

OUR TIP: Excellent wine list

Chef: Vivek Singh **Owners:** Iqbal Wahhab **Times:** 12-3/6-11, Closed Xmas, Easter, BH's, Sun, closed L Sat **Notes:** Gastronomic menu, 5 courses £60 (£95 with wine), Vegetarian available, Smart casual preferre Civ Wed 150 **Seats:** 180, Pr/dining room 50 **Smoking:** Air con **Directions:** Nearest station: Westminster Take exit 6, across Parliament Sq, then pass Westminster Abbey on left. Take 1st left into Great Smith **Parking:** Little Smith Street **e-mail:** info@cinnamonclub.com **web:** www.cinnamonclub.com

ⓐⓐ Il Convivio

Modern Italian   🐟

Stylish, exclusive neighbourhood Italian

☎ 020 7730 4099 143 Ebury St SW1W 9QN Plan 4-H2

MENU GUIDE Crab risotto, mustard leaves • Veal fillet, glazed shallots, peas, wild mushrooms • Chocolate trilogy

WINE GUIDE ♀ Ca Dei Frati Brolettino 2002 Trebbiano £33 • ♀ Vigneti Massa Assolo 1997 Barbera £28 • 130 bottles over £20, 15 bottles under £20 • 10 by the glass (£3.80-£12.50)

PRICE GUIDE Fixed L £15.50 • Fixed D £32.50 • starter £5-£13 • main £7.50-£18 • dessert £5-£9 • coffee £2 • min/water £3.50 • Service added but optional 12.5%

PLACE: The black iron railings and understated exterior of this converted Georgian terraced house marks this stylish, contemporary Italian out from the Belgravia crowd. And, true to i name, it's a thoroughly congenial place. Dante quotes are inscrib on scarlet and cream walls, there's an atrium-like glass roof at th rear, polished light wood floors and fashionable, modern seating

FOOD: The cooking is as modern as the decor and as Italian as the professional service and wine list. Expect black spaghetti wit lobster and spring onions, and pan-fried cod with a citrus and liquorice sauce on a generous length menu.

OUR TIP: Poilane bakery shop just across the road

Chef: Lukas Pfaff **Owners:** Piero & Enzo Quaradeghini **Times:** 12-2.45/7-10.45, Closed Xmas, New Year, BHs, Sun **Notes:** Vegetarian available **Seats:** 65, Pr/dining room 14 **Smoking:** Air con **Children:** Portions **Directions:** Nearest station: Victoria 7 min walk fro Victoria Station - corner of Ebury St and Elizabeth St. **Parking:** on stree **e-mail:** comments@etruscarestaurants.com **web:** www.etruscarestaurants.com

continued

England

🕭🕮 Drones of Pont Street

French, British

classy restaurant from Marco Pierre White's empire

☎ 020 7235 9555 1 Pont St SW1X 9EJ Plan 4-G3

MENU GUIDE Kipper pâté with whiskey • Grilled calves' liver, bacon, fried onion • Drones rice pudding, red fruit compote

WINE GUIDE ♀ Domaine J M Brocard Chablis £31 • ♀ Domaine Grand Romane Gigondas £44 • 40 bottles over £20, 2 bottles under £20 • 8 by the glass (£4.75-£8)

PRICE GUIDE Fixed L £14.95 • starter £7.50-£12.50 • main £9.50-£24.50 • dessert £6.50 • coffee £3 • min/water £3.50 • Service added but optional 12.5% • Group service 15%

PLACE: This London veteran is a classy affair, with generous, well-spaced tables and a slick serving team. Black and white photos deck the walls, while crystal decanters catch the light behind the large bar.

FOOD: Quality ingredients, simply prepared and presented - that's the recipe for Drones's success and the badge of its membership to Marco Pierre White's culinary empire. The lengthy menu features a spread of French and English dishes, from light seafood options such as smoked haddock with cannon to heartier fare - boiled beef with dumplings perhaps, or rib-eye steak with béarnaise sauce.

OUR TIP: Great value fixed price lunch
Chef: Joseph Croan **Owners:** White Star Line Restaurant Ltd.
Times: 12-2/6-11, Closed 26 Dec-1 Jan, closed L Sat, closed D Sun
Notes: Sun L 3 courses £19.50, Vegetarian available **Seats:** 96, Pr/dining room 40 **Smoking:** No pipes, Air con **Children:** Portions **Parking:** On street, NCP **e-mail:** sales@whitestarline.org.uk
web: www.whitestarline.org.uk

🕮🕮 Ebury

European, International 🐟

Fashionable bar and restaurant

☎ 020 7730 6784 11 Pimlico Rd SW1W 8NA Plan 4-G2

MENU GUIDE Cracked crab, ratte potatoes, rocket, aïoli • Crispy confit pork belly, creamed onion • Roast pineapple, lychee parfait

WINE GUIDE ♀ Isonzo Borgo di Vassalli Pinot Grigio £22 • ♀ Rioja Navajas Tempranillo £18 • 130 bottles over £20, 20 bottles under £20 • 11 by the glass (£3.50-£8.50)

PRICE GUIDE Starter £6-£8.50 • main £9.75-£22 • dessert £5.50 coffee £1.50 • min/water £2.95 • Service added but optional 12.5%

PLACE: A 250-year-old building, with a Grade II listed staircase, now providing a thoroughly modern dining environment. There is a lively bar downstairs and a first floor dining room with hardwood floors, brown leather seats, clothed tables, chandeliers and light jazz music. Chef can be seen and heard preparing food in a large service area. Staff are friendly and attentive providing professional service.

FOOD: With international cuisine, classically French based, the technical skill stands the kitchen in good stead, and there's a pleasing emphasis on simplicity and flavour.

OUR TIP: Lighter options available in the downstairs bar
Chef: Andrew Donovan **Owners:** Tom Etridge **Times:** 12-3.30/6-10.30, Closed 24-30 Dec **Notes:** Vegetarian available, Smart Dress **Seats:** 60
Smoking: No pipes, No cigars, Air con **Directions:** Nearest station: Sloane Sq or Victoria From Sloane Sq Tube left into Holbein Place, then left at intersection with Pimlico Rd. The Ebury is on right on corner of Pimlico Rd & Ranelagh Grove. From Victoria, left down Buckingham Palace Rd, then right onto Pimlico Rd **Parking:** NCP
e-mail: info@theebury.co.uk **web:** www.theebury.co.uk

🕮🕮 The Fifth Floor Restaurant

French, Mediterranean

Simple modern cooking at Harvey Nichols

☎ 020 7235 5250 Harvey Nichols, 109-125 Knightsbridge SW1X 7RJ Plan 4-F4

continued

England

LONDON SW1 continued

MENU GUIDE Crab, chilli, rocket linguine • Poulet au vin, pomme puree • Praline tart, almond ice cream

WINE GUIDE ♀ Domaine Geoffry Chablis Beauroy Chardonnay £31.50 • ♥ Vina Ardanza La Rioja Alta Tempranillo £38.50 • 400 bottles over £20, 12 bottles under £20 • 34 by the glass (£4-£14)

PRICE GUIDE Fixed L £26-£33 • Fixed D £24 • starter £8.50-£16.50 • main £15.50-£28 • dessert £6.50-£12 • coffee £2.50 • min/water £3.50 • Service added but optional 12.5%

PLACE: Achingly fashionable haunt in Harvey Nichols department store, which shares the fifth floor with an impressive food hall and wine shop. White leather chairs and napery sit beneath an arched ceiling of frosted glass, the only touch of colour coming courtesy of cut flowers.

FOOD: Quality ingredients are no surprise given the culinary setting; they're handled with accurate simplicity and put to work in modern British dishes such as roast rack of lamb with a thyme jus, or steamed salmon with a soy and ginger broth.

OUR TIP: A spot of shopping in the food hall after lunch

Chef: Simon Shaw **Owners:** Harvey Nichols & Co Ltd **Times:** 12-3/6-11, Closed 25-26 Dec, Easter Sunday, closed D Sun **Notes:** Vegetarian available **Seats:** 114 **Smoking:** N/Sm area, Air con **Children:** Menu, Portions **Directions:** Nearest station: Knightsbridge, Hyde Park Corner Entrance on Sloane Street **Parking:** NCP opposite, on street **web:** www.harveynichols.com

 Goring Hotel
British
Luxury dining in distinguished hotel

☎ 020 7396 9000 Beeston Place SW1W 0JW Plan 4-H4

MENU GUIDE Deep-fried whitebait, tartare sauce • Calves' liver, Suffolk bacon, onion gravy • Lemon tart

WINE GUIDE ♀ Louis Latour Chardonnnay £23 • ♥ Baron Philippe Rothschild Merlot £23 • 400 bottles over £20 • 9 by the glass (£5.25-£18.50)

PRICE GUIDE Fixed L £26 • Fixed D £40 • coffee £4.50 • min/water £3.50 • Service added 12.5%

PLACE: This privately owned hotel has been run by the same family for three generations and is a by-word for quiet good taste. Its stately dining room has played host to politicians, celebrities and even royalty over the years, but staff don't let it go to their heads, offering friendly and attentive service to all-comers.

FOOD: The Goring offers safe but accomplished cooking; a mix of traditional English dishes and French classics made from the finest ingredients. Fish is a speciality. Excellent wine list.

OUR TIP: Take afternoon tea or evening cocktails in the garden bar or drawing room

Chef: Derek Quelch **Owners:** Mr G E Goring **Times:** 12.30-2.30/6-10, Closed L Sat **Notes:** Vegetarian available, Civ Wed 50 **Seats:** 70, pr/dining room 50 **Smoking:** No pipes, Air con **Children:** Portions **Rooms:** 73 (73 en suite) ★★★★★ **Directions:** Nearest station: Victoria From Victoria St turn left into Grosvenor Gdns, cross Buckingham Palace Rd, 75yds turn right into Beeston Place. **Parking:** 5 **e-mail:** reception@goringhotel.co.uk **web:** www.goringhotel.co.uk

Inn the Park
Modern British   NEW
All day eaterie in park setting

☎ 020 7451 9999 St James's Park SW1A 1AA Plan 5-C5

MENU GUIDE Poached organic salmon • Roast suckling pig, champ & apple sauce • mixed berry meringue

WINE GUIDE ♀ Boland Chenin Blanc £16 • ♥ Venoimia Herencia Remondo Rioja £19 • 8 bottles over £20, 18 bottles under £20 • 9 by the glass (£3.20-£5)

PRICE GUIDE Food prices not confirmed for 2006. Please telephone for details

PLACE: Set in St James' Park, a long Scandinavian-style building opening on to a decked area. Somewhere between a restaurant and a café, with a counter for quick snacks and a separate, more formal area beyond a series of marble booths.

FOOD: Simple food is the prevailing flavour here, with good quality produce leading to brasserie-style dishes like smoked Gressingham duck breast, and grilled calves' liver with crispy bacon.

OUR TIP: Perfect for summer alfresco dining

Chef: Mark Bradbury **Owners:** Oliver Deyton **Times:** 12-3/6-10.45 **Notes:** Vegetarian available **Seats:** 134 **Smoking:** N/Sm in restaurant, Air con **Children:** Portions **Directions:** Nearest station: St James, Charing Cross 200 metres down The Mall towards Buckingham Palace **Parking:** On street **e-mail:** info@innthepark.co.uk **web:** www.innthepark.co.uk

⑳ Just St James
British
Highly ornate setting with a fashionable, upmarket vibe

☎ 020 7976 2222 12 St James St SW1A 1ER Plan 5-B

MENU GUIDE Seared peppered tuna, basil niçoise & balsamic • Monkfish tail, seafood & samphire broth • Lemon cheesecake, raspberry sauce

WINE GUIDE ♀ Kanu Chenin £16.80 • ♥ Château la Baronne Corbiéres £14 • 70 bottles over £20, 14 bottles under £20 22 by the glass (£4-£7.50)

PRICE GUIDE Fixed L fr £16.50 • Fixed D fr £16.50 • starter £6.75-£13.50 • main £12.50-£19.50 • dessert £6.50-£7.50 • coffee £2.75 • min/water £3.25 • Service added but optional 12.5%

PLACE: Wall-to-wall marble, huge arched windows, lofty decorative ceiling and a modern glass lift to a mezzanine gallery, all add up to a striking first impression at this airy, classical Edwardian former banking hall. Suede banquettes, white-clothed tables, glass-fronted kitchen, modern paintings and a glass-topped bar and lounge flush with leather seating offers a stylish, contemporary edge.

FOOD: The modern carte fits the bill, delivering straightforward, clean-cut, well presented and accomplished dishes. Take roasted halibut with a pea purée and glazed baby vegetables, or Gressingham duck breast with foie gras, summer truffle and spinach. Expect professional service and St James's prices.

OUR TIP: There is a more relaxed oriental bar and brasserie downstairs

Chef: Peter Gladwin **Owners:** Peter Gladwin **Times:** 12-3/6-11, Closed 25-26 Dec, 1 Jan, Sun, closed L Sat **Notes:** Vegetarian available **Seats:** 120, Pr/dining room 140 **Smoking:** No pipes, No cigars, Air con **Children:** Menu, Portions **Directions:** Nearest station: Green Park Turn right on Piccadilly towards Piccadilly Circus, then right into St James St. Restaurant on corner of St James St & King St. **Parking:** St James Square - meters **e-mail:** bookings@juststjames.com **web:** www.juststjames.co

⑳ Ken Lo's Memories of China
Chinese
Stylish, contemporary Chinese

☎ 020 7730 7734 65-69 Ebury St SW1W 0NZ Plan 4-H3

MENU GUIDE Crispy soft-shell crab • Cantonese ginger & spring onion lobster • Chilled lotus nut soup

continued

continued

WINE GUIDE ♀ Chablis 1er Cru Fourchame Chardonnay £39 ♀ Ninquen Mont Gras Cabernet Sauvignon £44 • 115 bottles over £20, 6 bottles under £20 • 6 by the glass (£3.50-£6.50)

PRICE GUIDE Fixed L £18.50-£21.50 • Fixed D £30-£48 • starter £4.80-£12.50 • main £2.75-£28.50 • dessert £4.50-£7 • coffee £2.50 • min/water £3.50 • Service added but optional 12.5%

PLACE: This upmarket Pimlico Chinese restaurant has a stylish feel and its attention to detail means that china, glasses and even chopsticks are of the highest quality.

FOOD: A lengthy menu offers the canon of Oriental classics (Sichuan aromatic and crispy duck), plus more interesting specials such as sautéed spicy salt and pepper lobster. Large parties and families are well served with a number of set menus, and the intriguing, Italian-biased wine list is extensive, with the fine cellar located in the centre of the restaurant.

OUR TIP: Try the chef's specials

Chef: Mr But **Owners:** A-Z Groups **Times:** 12-3/7-12, Closed 24-25 Dec, meals, closed L Sun **Notes:** Vegetarian available **Seats:** 120, Pr/dining room 26 **Smoking:** No pipes, No cigars, Air con **Directions:** Nearest station: Sloane Square, Victoria At junction of Ebury Street & Eccleston St. near Victoria station **Parking:** On street **e-mail:** moc.hotmail.com

The Lanesborough
International ♣ ⚒

Engaging and atmospheric, with sound cooking

☎ 020 7259 5599 Hyde Park Corner SW1X 7TA
Plan 4-G5

MENU GUIDE Crab spring roll, pickled ginger • Baked cod with shellfish • Fruit terrine

WINE GUIDE ♀ Chablis £64 ♀ Châteauneuf du Pape £56 • 120 bottles over £20 • 10 by the glass (£6-£12.50)

PRICE GUIDE Fixed L fr £24 • Fixed D £38-£48 • starter £12.50-£19.50 • main £12.50-£38.50 • dessert £8.50 • coffee £4.90 • min/water £4.50 • Service included

PLACE: The perfect setting for an Agatha Christie thriller, with its giant bamboos and palm trees, and the sound of running water. The ageless charm and unstuffy atmosphere of this conservatory restaurant make it a hit with a discerning clientele.

FOOD: The robust cooking produces punchy flavours and generous servings, with international influences found in seared tuna and white bean chorizo, and tortellini of samfina and feta with harissa salsa. Many precious gems can be discovered in the wine list, aided by a master sommelier.

OUR TIP: Excellent vegetarian menu

Chef: Paul Gayler **Owners:** Lanesborough Management **Times:** 12-10/6.30-11.30 **Notes:** Vegetarian available, Dress Restrictions, No shorts, Wed Wed **Seats:** 120, Pr/dining room 100 **Smoking:** Air con **Children:** Menu, Portions **Rooms:** 95 (95 en suite) ★★★★★ **Directions:** Nearest station: Hyde Park Corner On Hyde Park corner **Parking:** 50 **e-mail:** info@lanesborough.co.uk **web:** www.lanesborough.com

Mandarin Oriental Hyde Park *see page 282*

Mint Leaf
Indian

Trendy, slick contemporary Indian

☎ 020 7930 9020 Suffolk Place SW1Y 4HX Plan 5-C3

MENU GUIDE Sakht Seekh (Tandoori lamb stuffed with cheese & mint) • Chatpata Seena (Duck breast, tamarind sauce, pea pilao) • Chocolate fondant, mint ice cream

WINE GUIDE ♀ La Moynerie Chardonnay £30 • ♀ Wakefield Estate Shiraz £26 • 112 bottles over £20, 8 bottles under £20 10 by the glass (£4.75-£11.50)

PRICE GUIDE Fixed L £25-£50 • starter £6.50-£9 • main £10-£28 • dessert £5-£7 • coffee £2.75 • min/water £4 • Service added but optional 12.5%

PLACE: With a striking cocktail bar and large dining room, divided into intimate areas by trendy wire-mesh screens and dark-wood slates that resemble giant Venetian blinds, Mint Leaf cuts an immediate up-to-the-minute edge. Add central raised catwalks, dark wood, leather and atmospheric lighting and you have sleek, designer-led modern Indian styling.

FOOD: Relatively simple contemporary Indian cooking, using quality produce, vibrant spicing and colourful modern presentation to match the buzzy atmosphere and decor.

OUR TIP: Try one of the extensive range of cocktails

Chef: K K Anand **Owners:** Out of Africa Investments **Times:** 12-3/5.30-11, Closed 25 & 26 Dec, Good Fri, Etr Sun & Mon, Sun, closed L Sat **Notes:** Vegetarian available, Dress Restrictions, No ripped jeans, no scruffy trainers, Civ Wed 450 **Seats:** 140, Pr/dining room 60 **Smoking:** Air con **Directions:** Nearest station: Piccadilly/Charing Cross At end of Haymarket **Parking:** NCP, on street **e-mail:** reservations@mintleafrestaurant.com **web:** www.mintleafrestaurant.co.uk

Mitsukoshi
Japanese

Established Japanese restaurant popular with the Japanese

☎ 020 7930 0317 Dorland House, 14-20 Lower Regent St SW1Y 4PH Plan 3-B1

MENU GUIDE Assorted sashimi • Shabu Shabu • Anmitsu

WINE GUIDE ♀ Chablis £23 • ♀ Pinot Noir £19 • 6 bottles over £20, 5 bottles under £20 • 2 by the glass (£2.50)

PRICE GUIDE Fixed L £12-£20 • Fixed D £28-£48 • starter £2-£15 • main £8-£23 • dessert £3-£6 • coffee £2 • min/water £4 • Service added 15%

PLACE: Located in the basement of the Japanese department store of the same name near Piccadilly, this restaurant has light, neutral decor in traditional Japanese style. There is a separate sushi bar and a couple of private dining rooms.

FOOD: Authentic Japanese cuisine, with a monthly changing menu. Excellent ingredients are in evidence, particularly the fish, and clear flavours are prominent at all stages of the meal.

OUR TIP: The place for sushi - watch the chefs as they make it

Chef: Yoshihiro Motohashi **Owners:** Mitsukoshi (UK) Ltd. **Times:** 12-2/6-10, Closed 25, 26 Dec, 1 Jan **Notes:** Vegetarian available **Seats:** 56, Pr/dining room 28 **Smoking:** N/Sm area, No pipes, No cigars, Air con **Children:** Menu, Portions **e-mail:** lonrest@mitsukoshi.co.jp **web:** www.mitsukoshi-restaurant.co.uk

continued

LONDON SW1

Mandarin Oriental Hyde Park

Modern European *One of the capital's best bargains*
☎ 020 72352000 66 Knightsbridge SW1X 7LA Plan 4-F4
e-mail: molon-reservations@mohg.com
web: www.mandarinoriental.com/london

PLACE: The aptly named Foliage restaurant is contemporary, chic and stylish, conceived by internationally renowned designer Adam Tihany to 'bring the park into the restaurant'. Giant glass wall panels enclose thousands of white silk leaves that come alive with lighting and change colour to echo the seasons, while a split-level floor ensures all have a view of park life. Clean lines, soft lighting, huge flower arrangements and luxury fabrics and furnishings add to the sophisticated, fine-dining experience at this luxury, landmark Edwardian hotel in the heart of Knightsbridge, grandly set between Hyde Park and Harvey Nichols, and playground of the highfliers, the young and fashionable. Liveried doorman, smiling greeting staff, a sumptuous marble foyer, fashionable bar and eye-catching, glass-fronted wine-store entrance to Foliage, all ooze class.

FOOD: High-quality, luxury ingredients are the mainstay of the intricate cooking that shows off the kitchen's high-level technique. Balance of flavour and texture and interesting combinations shine in assured, well-constructed and well-presented dishes that befit the chic setting. Head Chef Chris Staines' approach is via an appealing medley of fixed-price menus that take in an excellent-value *jour* (something of a bargain, and taken either exclusive or inclusive of wine), tantalising carte and five-course tasting dinner option. So expect an intricate, labour-intensive threesome the likes of: roast sweetbread mille-feuille with onion compote, garlic caramel and potato gnocchi; pan-fried fillet of gilt-head bream with a risotto of Jerusalem artichokes and smoked bacon, scallop and sesame brochette, and garlic cream; and hot chocolate fondant with amaretto parfait and pearl barley sorbet.

MENU GUIDE Foie gras duo, caramelised endive tart Tatin, vinaigrette of leeks • Roast & pot-roast turbot ravioli, pork, langoustine, horseradish cream • Bitter orange parfait & salad, basil, carmelised hazelnuts

WINE GUIDE ♀ Remi Jobard Chardonnay £55 • ♀ Pichou Bavou Cabernet Sauvignon £80 590 bottles over £20, 65 bottles under £20 • 12 by the glass (£5.70-£18)

PRICE GUIDE Fixed L £25-£47.50 • Fixed D £50 coffee £3.50 • min/water £5 • Service added but optional 12.5%

OUR TIP: Great value lunch

Chef: David Nicholls, Chris Staines **Owners:** Mandarin Oriental Hyde Park Hotel **Times:** 12-2.30/7-10 **Notes:** Tasting menu 5 courses £70, Vegetarian available, Smart casual, Civ Wed 220 **Seats:** 46, Pr/dining room 250 **Smoking:** No pipes, No cigars, Air con **Rooms:** 200 (200 en suite) ★★★★★
Directions: Nearest station: Knightsbridge With Harrods on right, hotel is 0.5m on left, opposite Harvey Nichols **Parking:** Valet parking

ONDON SW1

Mju at Millennium Knightsbridge

rench, Asian

tense cooking to really dress up for

☎ 020 7201 6330 17 Sloane St, Knightsbridge SW1X
NU Plan 4-F4

MENU GUIDE Scallops, caramelised cauliflower, raisin
auce • Black Angus beef, horseradish, pepper
inaigrette • Crème brûlée

WINE GUIDE ♀ Domaine Wachau Gruener Veltliner
:36 • ♀ Bajoz Toro Crianza £30 • 219 bottles over £20 • 10 by
he glass (£6.50-£9)

PRICE GUIDE Fixed L £17.50-£19.50 • starter £11-£20 • main £23-
:29 • dessert £6-£11 • coffee £3.50 • min/water £5 • Service
dded but optional 12.5%

LACE: The chic shopping district of ever-fashionable
nightsbridge is the enviable location for this elegant hotel,
hich blends in well with its smart, modern and contemporary
el. Take the winding staircase from the popular lobby lounge to
d the much-acclaimed Mju Restaurant and Bar on the first
or. The magnificent atrium dining room has an exclusive feel,

with rich olive green wall-coverings and deep maroon upholstery,
and a wealth of dark wood. The atmosphere is warm and
inviting, enhanced by subtle lighting and contemporary music.
Service is highly professional from a slick team, and includes a
great sommelier.

FOOD: Cooking is modern, innovative and hugely creative,
resulting in exciting, challenging and well executed dish
combinations. This accomplished cuisine has its roots in the
French classics but draws on influences from Asia, as seen in
sashimi - tuna and sea bass with citrus soy and wasabi - and
oysters with ginger and mirin dressing. Ingredients are first class
and wonderfully fresh flavours abound.

OUR TIP: Try one of the tasting menus

Chef: Tom Thomsen **Owners:** Millennium & Copthorne Hotels
Times: 12-2.30/6-10.30, Closed Sun, closed L Sat **Notes:** Chefs menu
£60-65, Vegetarian available **Seats:** 110, Pr/dining room 50
Smoking: N/Sm in restaurant **Children:** Portions **Rooms:** 222 (222 en
suite) ★★★★ **Directions:** Knightsbridge tube/Victoria
200yds from Knightsbridge Stn/near Harrods **Parking:** 8
e-mail: mju@mill-cop.com
web: www.millenniumhotels.com/knightsbridge

ONDON SW1

One-O-One

eafood

rst-rate seafood restaurant

☎ 020 7290 7101 Sheraton Park Tower,
1 Knightsbridge SW1X 7RN Plan 4-F4

MENU GUIDE Seaweed steamed langoustines, aioli • Sea bass,
bugo ham, artichoke fricassée, hazelnut
appuccino • Passionfruit tart

WINE GUIDE 101 bottles over £20 • 15 by the glass (£6.50-£13)

PRICE GUIDE Fixed L £21 • starter £13-£28 • main £22-
28 • dessert £8 • coffee £4 • min/water £4.80 • Service optional

ACE: One of the country's finest seafood restaurants, this
phisticated hotel eaterie draws a well-heeled crowd in keeping
th its classy Knightsbridge setting. A simple blue and white
lour scheme prevails, while frosted windows let in the light in a
screet fashion that ensures privacy. Service comes from a
ung and friendly team who do their stuff brilliantly.

OD: One-O-One brings together fresh, high quality ingredients
classic combinations, producing dishes distinguished by clear

flavours and the odd innovation. An extensive carte is on offer,
plus - for those who want to do full justice to Pascal Proyart's fine
cuisine - a five or nine course tasting option; if you're really
hooked, book on one of the regular 'cook & eat' evenings to meet
the chef and discover his secrets. Each course features a few sops
to meat-eaters, such as slow-braised lamb shank with red onion
compote, but vegetarians are less well served.

OUR TIP: Well-placed for the fashionable stores of Knightsbridge

Chef: Pascal Proyart **Owners:** Starwood Hotels & Resorts **Times:** 12-
2.30/7-10.15 **Notes:** Tasting menu 5 courses £48, 9 courses £79,
Vegetarian available **Seats:** 60, Pr/dining room 10 **Smoking:** N/Sm area,
No pipes, No cigars, Air con **Children:** Portions **Rooms:** 280 (280 en
suite) ★★★★★ **Directions:** Nearest station: Knightsbridge E from
station, just after Harvey Nichols. **Parking:** 60
e-mail: franck.hardy@luxurycollection.com
web: www.luxurycollection.com/parktowerlondon

England

England

LONDON SW1 *continued*

⊕⊕⊕ Mju at Millennium Knightsbridge *see page 283*

⊕⊕⊕ Nahm *see page 285*

⊕⊕⊕ One-O-One *see page 283*

⊕⊕ L'Oranger

French

Sophisticated French dining

☎ 020 7839 3774 5 St James's St SW1A 1EF Plan 5-B5

MENU GUIDE Duck liver confit, celeriac purée, apple granité • Rack of lamb, aubergine caviar, feta • Poached pear, almond ice cream

WINE GUIDE ♀ Gérard Tremblay Chablis £45 • ♀ Jacques Mestre Châteauneuf du Pape £55 • 2 bottles under £20 • 10 by the glass (£5-£8)

PRICE GUIDE Fixed L £24-£28 • starter £13-£25 • main £22-£33 • dessert £6-£8 • coffee £3.50 • min/water £4 • Service added but optional 12.5%

PLACE: Just a short walk from St James's Park, this upmarket French restaurant is set in a pretty courtyard where you can dine alfresco in the summer. Inside is as elegant as you'd expect: a long, panelled room decorated with attractive flower displays and mirrors.
FOOD: Top-notch classical French cuisine with a few modern twists and Mediterranean touches. Seafood dominates, but there are plenty of alternatives - your choice might include Dover sole with a fumet dressing, or wild duck with braised red cabbage and roasted fig.
OUR TIP: Private dining room available
Chef: Laurent Michel **Times:** 12-2.30/6.30-10.45, Closed Xmas, BHs, Sun, closed L Sat **Notes:** Tasting menu £70, Vegetarian available, smart casual **Seats:** 55, Pr/dining room 30 **Smoking:** No pipes, No cigars, Air con **Children:** Min 6 yrs, Portions **Directions:** Nearest station: Green Park Access by car via Pall Mall. **Parking:** on street
e-mail: oranger.restaurant@fsmail.net

⊕⊕ *Pengelley's*

Asian   **NEW**

New Asian cuisine, fun setting in the heart of Knightsbridge

☎ 020 7750 5000 164 Sloane St SW1X 9SG Plan 4-F4

MENU GUIDE Clear soup with watercress and tofu • Halibut with black bean & chilli • Jasmine custard, tea poached pear

PRICE GUIDE Food prices not confirmed for 2006. Please telephone for details

PLACE: The heart of Knightsbridge is the unlikely setting for Ian Pengelley's new eaterie. The sleek, uncluttered dining room uses natural materials to good effect, with contrasting woods on the floor, walls and ceiling, and there's brown leather seating at well-paced tables, and richly coloured artwork on the walls.
FOOD: Food is New Asian cuisine, part sushi, part dim sum and part wok cooking, with no set sequence of dishes, just choose a number of dishes and share. Simple, effective and exciting cooking using stunning ingredients, resulting in 'knock-out' tastes and flavours.
OUR TIP: Good grazing for shopaholics
Times: 12-3/6-11 **e-mail:** reservations@pengelleys.com
web: www.pengelleys.com

⊕⊕⊕⊕⊕ Pétrus *see page 286*

⊕ Quaglino's

Modern European

Vast basement brasserie from the Conran stable

☎ 020 7930 6767 16 Bury St, St James's SW1Y 6AJ Plan 5-B6

MENU GUIDE Sautéed squid with chilli • Veal chop, anchovy butter • Coconut pannacotta, mango jelly

WINE GUIDE ♀ St Bernard Chardonnay £14.50 • ♀ St Bernard Merlot £14.50 • 108 bottles over £20, 20 bottles under £20 22 by the glass (£3.95-£7.50)

PRICE GUIDE Fixed L £17 • starter £5.50-£12 • main £11.50-£24 • dessert £5.50-£6.50 • coffee £2.50 • min/water £3.25 • Service added but optional 12.5%

PLACE: Discreetly set off St James's, this Parisien-style brasserie is anything but modest inside. A dramatic staircase sweeps down to the cavernous space supported by colourful columns, where glamour and theatre strut their extroverted stuff. Usually buzzy with animated conversation.
FOOD: The modern brasserie-style dishes are seasonal and simple, and there's a separate seafood counter. Perfect cod fish and chips with home-made tartare sauce is a perennial favourite
OUR TIP: Ideal for large parties
Chef: Julian O'Neill **Owners:** Conran Restaurants **Times:** 12-3/5.30-12, Closed 24-25 Dec, 1 Jan, closed L 26, 31 Dec, 2 Jan **Notes:** Vegetarian available, Dress Restrictions, Smart casual **Seats:** 267, Pr/dining room 44 **Smoking:** Air con **Children:** Menu, Portions **Directions:** Nearest station: Green Park/Piccadilly Circus Bury St is off Jermyn St
Parking: Arlington Street NCP **e-mail:** kateg@conran-restaurants.co.uk
web: www.conran.com

⊕⊕ Quirinale

Italian

Light, airy basement Italian

☎ 020 7222 7080 North Court, 1 Great Peter St SW1P 3LL Plan 5-C3

MENU GUIDE Radiccio & chicory salad with gorgonzola • Calve liver 'alla Veneziana' • Apple & pear crumble with vanilla ice cream

WINE GUIDE ♀ La Prendina Pinot Grigio £19 • ♀ Umani Ronchi Montephiciano £20 • 110 bottles over £20, 7 bottles under £20 • 8 by the glass (£4-£5.50)

PRICE GUIDE Starter £7.50-£10.50 • main £12-£16 • dessert £6 • coffee £2.50 • min/water £3.50 • Service added but option 12.5%

PLACE: A smart David Collins-designed basement restaurant, set in an attractive building on a pleasant street, light and airy by day, romantic and candle-lit for dinner. Just a few minutes from Parliament, it's popular with politicians, journalists and business people. Attractively dressed tables and central banquettes ensure discreet seating arrangements.
FOOD: Dishes are a mixture of classic and modern; pasta can be served as either starter or main, and many ingredients are specially imported from Italy. Cooking style is distinctly Italian, and presentation very up-to-date. An impressive selection of breads, cheeses and Italian wines.
OUR TIP: Close to the River Thames and Houses of Parliament
Chef: Stefano Savio **Owners:** Nadine Gourgey **Times:** 12-3/6-12, Closed Xmas & New Year, 2 wks Aug, Sat & Sun **Notes:** Vegetarian available **Seats:** 50 **Smoking:** Air con **Children:** Portions
Parking: Street parking available, NCP **e-mail:** info@quirnale.co.uk

ONDON SW1

England

Nahm

Thai *Top-notch Thai in chic hotel*

☎ 020 7333 1234 The Halkin Hotel, Halkin St, Belgravia SW1X 7DJ

Plan 4-G4

e-mail: res@halkin.como.bz

web: www.halkin.como.bz

PLACE: East meets west in both the food and decor of this chic Thai eaterie, located just a short stroll from Hyde Park and the designer shops of Knightsbridge at the achingly fashionable Halkin Hotel. Slatted wooden panelling creates intimate spaces within a large room, while gold and teak give an oriental feel to the minimalist furnishings.
FOOD: Nahm is the creation of celebrity chef David Thompson, well-known for his commitment to traditional Thai cuisine and research into near-forgotten cooking styles and recipes. The lengthy menu offers a tempting range of modern western interpretations of classic dishes, with high quality produce shipped direct from Thailand to ensure authenticity. To really sample the place, treat yourself to the eight-dish traditional menu: a set appetizer and starter followed by five dishes served at once, and a dessert.

MENU GUIDE Thai salad with tamarind, palm sugar, sesame seeds • Bream, three flavoured sauce • Black sticky rice, caramelised coconut

WINE GUIDE ♀ Cuvèe Caroline Shoffit Riesling £32 • ♥ Mornington Stonier Pinot Noir £35 • 200 bottles over £20 • 15 by the glass (£6.75-£9.50)

PRICE GUIDE Fixed L £26 • Fixed D £47 • starter £8.50-£12.50 • main £9.50-£16.50 • dessert £9.50 • coffee £4 • min/water £4 • Service added but optional 12.5%

OUR TIP: Make the most of the friendly and knowledgeable staff

Chef: David Thompson, Matthew Albert **Owners:** Halkin Hotel Ltd **Times:** 12-2.30/7-11, Closed L Sat-Sun **Notes:** Vegetarian available, Dress Restrictions, No Jeans **Seats:** 78, Pr/dining room 36 **Smoking:** No pipes, No cigars, Air con **Children:** Portions **Rooms:** 41 (41 en suite) ★★★★ **Directions:** Nearest station: Hyde Park Halkin Street just off Hyde Park Corner **Parking:** NCP

LONDON SW1

England

Pétrus

French *Benchmark for Britain's top cuisine in opulent Knightsbridge surroundings*

☎ 020 7235 1200 The Berkeley, Wilton Place, Knightsbridge SW1X 7RL
Plan 4-G4
e-mail: petrus@marcuswareing.com
web: www.marcuswareing.com

PLACE: Since its arrival at the Berkeley, Pétrus has become a mecca for food and wine lovers. Off the foyer and through a front lounge, Pétrus has a real air of sophistication and opulence. Rich and vivid, the interior is the work of design guru David Collins, the sensual claret colours and textures reflecting that of the wine which lends the restaurant its name. Stunning French blinds display a circle motif that appears in various guises throughout the dining room, while two giant abacuses replete with blown-glass beads act as a screen to the wine chiller. Chairs of soft burgundy leather, customised table appointments and stylish flower displays continue the theme. Staff are slick and attentive, though not at all stuffy, with maître'd Jean-Philippe (of TV's *Hell's Kitchen* fame), running front of house with humour and wit. There's a small lounge area for aperitifs out front and a much-sought-after chef's table in the kitchen. It's all bold and striking complement to the impeccable cooking.

FOOD: Marcus Wareing's cooking is classically based and, like the decor, has plenty of wow factor and integrity, and based around the very best raw ingredients. His elegant, richly detailed, modern French repertoire has few peers, with precision, balance and consummate technical skill of the highest level. The approach is via an appealing repertoire of fixed-price menus, from superb value lunch to tasting option and carte, with hallmark dishes delivering the likes of tournedos of poulet de Bresse, roasted and scented with garlic, rosemary and thyme, served with sautéed foie gras, tongue, a shallot purée and sherry vinegar cream. Theatre is the name of the game and the trolley certainly rules, with cheeses, liqueurs and, most importantly, the bonbon trolley - with its wonderful sweetmeats - circling the floor in great style. A seriously impressive wine list (with a good selection by the glass) naturally includes offerings from the namesake château.

MENU GUIDE Mushroom velouté, sautéed chestnuts, caramelized apple, foie gras • Sea bass fillet, dauphinoise, mussels, pesto broth • Apple tart Tatin

WINE GUIDE ♀ Montée de Tonerre Chablis 1er Cru 2002 Chardonnay £42 • ♀ Stellenbosch Meerlust Rubicon 2002 Cabernet Sauvignon £45 • 600 bottles over £20, 20 bottles under £20 • 10 by the glass (£5-£14.50)

PRICE GUIDE Fixed L £30-£80 • Fixed D £60 • coffee £5 • min/water £3.50 • Service optional • Group min 12 service 12.5%

OUR TIP: Book well in advance, and save room for the bonbon trolley

Chef: Marcus Wareing **Owners:** Marcus Wareing at the Berkeley Ltd **Times:** 12-2.30/6-11, Closed 1 week Xmas, Sun, closed L Sat **Notes:** Fixed D 6 courses £80, Vegetarian available, Dress Restrictions, Smart with jacket preferred **Seats:** 70, Pr/dining room 12 **Children:** Portions **Rooms:** 214 (214 en suite) ★★★★★ **Parking:** NCP and on street

ONDON SW1 *continued*

The Rib Room & Oyster Bar
ritish

obust British cooking in the heart of
nightsbridge

☎ 020 7858 7053 The Carlton Tower Hotel, Cadogan
ace SW1X 9PY Plan 4-F4

MENU GUIDE Chicken liver parfait, apple jelly • Aberdeen
Angus rib of beef, Yorkshire pudding • Marmalade brioche &
utter pudding

PRICE GUIDE Food prices not confirmed for 2006. Please
elephone for details

LACE: In keeping with its luxurious setting within the Carlton
ower Hotel, this true British restaurant is richly furnished with
ood panelling, wonderful floral displays and linen-clothed
bles. Seductive lighting creates a dark, moody club-like feel.
ntalising aromas of roasted beef fill the air and stimulate an
petite, while service gently balances formality and friendliness.
OOD: Presented in simple, unfussy style, with the occasional
sh of inspiration, dishes are robust and classically British with
casional American influences. The menu showcases the best of
itish meats, seafood and game, and oysters and caviar feature
rongly.
UR TIP: A lunch stop for Knightsbridge shoppers
mes: 12.30-2.45/7-10.45 Rooms: 220 (220 en suite) ★★★★★
mail: contact@carltontower.com web: www.carltontower.com

Roussillon
rench

ne French dining in chic intimate surroundings

☎ 020 7730 5550 16 St Barnabas St SW1W 8PB
an 4-G2

MENU GUIDE Jerusalem artichoke cream, lobster • Veal rack,
reamed spinach & polenta • Pineapple carpaccio

PRICE GUIDE Food prices not confirmed for 2006. Please
elephone for details

LACE: A cottage-like façade hides an airy and light interior in
e heart of Pimlico. Calming cream tones, low lighting and
mfortable furnishings make for an intimate dining venue. Well-
aced tables have good quality settings and dramatic orchids.
e large number of staff provides good professional service
ich compares with the best.
OD: Widely-sourced produce is transformed into dishes with
ong, regional French connections. The wow factor is provided
fish dishes which might include warm fondant of smoked eel
roast monkfish with larded salsify and red onion confit.
R TIP: Try the seven-course garden or tasting menu
mes: 12-2.30/6.30-11, Closed 24 Dec-5 Jan, Sun, closed L Sat, Mon,Tue
rections: Nearest station: Sloane Square Telephone for directions
mail: michael@roussillon.co.uk web: www.roussillon.co.uk

What makes a Restaurant of the Year?
In selecting a Restaurant of the Year, we
look for somewhere that is exceptional in its
chosen area of the market. Whilst the
Rosette awards are based on the quality of
the food alone, Restaurant of the Year takes
into account all aspects of the operation.
For full details see pages 6-7.

The Rubens at the Palace
British, French

Luxury dining near the Palace

☎ 020 7834 6600 39 Buckingham Palace Rd
SW1W 0PS Plan 5-A4

MENU GUIDE Porcini on polenta, truffle oil • Duck, caramelised
apple, fondant potatoes, peppercorn jus • Bitter orange
chocolate mousse

WINE GUIDE ♀ Bouchard Finlayson Sauvignon Blanc
£28 • ♀ Bouchard Finlayson Pinot Noir £36 • 46 bottles over
£20, 1 bottles under £20 • 10 by the glass (£4.50-£8.75)

PRICE GUIDE Fixed D £27.50 • starter £5.95-£9.50 • main
£15.25-£39.50 • dessert £5.95-£7.50 • coffee £3.50 • min/water
£3.95 • Service added but optional 12.5%

PLACE: The Library restaurant is just as classy as you'd expect
given its location in this upmarket hotel just across from
Buckingham Palace. It's decked out in richly embroidered fabrics
and warm browns and burgundies, while wing-backed armchairs
and bookcases lend a clubby feel.
FOOD: A wide-ranging modern British menu with classical roots.
Mains might include lamb with artichoke mash, or pot-roast
guinea fowl stuffed with prunes and leeks.
OUR TIP: The Rubens also has a carvery restaurant
Chef: Daniel Collins Owners: Red Carnation Hotels Times: 7.30-10,
Closed Xmas week, closed L all week Notes: Vegetarian available, Dress
Restrictions, No shorts or track suits Seats: 30, Pr/dining room 50
Smoking: N/Sm in restaurant, Air con Children: Menu Rooms: 173
(173 en suite) ★★★★ Directions: Nearest station: Victoria From
station head towards Buckingham Palace Parking: NCP at Victoria Coach
Station e-mail: bookrb@rchmail.com
web: www.redcarnationhotels.com

Salloos Restaurant
Pakistani

Knightsbridge stalwart offering fiery and authentic
curries

☎ 020 7235 4444 62-64 Kinnerton St SW1X 8ER
Plan 4-G4

MENU GUIDE Tandoori chops • Haleem akbari (lamb with
lentils) • Halwa gajar

WINE GUIDE ♀ Sancerre £25.50 • ♀ Châteauneuf du Pape
£32.50 • 20 bottles over £20, 6 bottles under £20 • 2 by the
glass (£3.50)

PRICE GUIDE Fixed L £16 • starter £4.50-£7.95 • main £10.90-
£13.90 • dessert £3.75 • coffee £2.50 • min/water £3.50 • Service
added but optional 12.5%

PLACE: Perched on a small side street just off the main
Knightsbridge thoroughfare, the entrance opens into the

continued

England

LONDON SW1 *continued*

restaurant's bar area. A staircase leads from the bar on to the main first floor dining room. Heavy carpeting, off-white walls with colourful paintings and impressive looking chandeliers add a sense of old fashioned luxury to the proceedings.

FOOD: Robust Pakistani and North Indian cuisine with mainly meat based cooking that offers strong spicing levels.

OUR TIP: Great bread and rice accompaniments

Chef: Abdul Aziz **Owners:** Mr & Mrs M Salahuddin **Times:** 12-3/7-11.45, Closed Xmas, BHs, Sun **Notes:** Vegetarian available **Seats:** 65 **Smoking:** No pipes, No cigars, Air con **Children:** Min 6 yrs **Directions:** Nearest station: Knightsbridge Kinnerton St is opposite Berkeley Hotel on Wilton Place **Parking:** Meters & car park Kinnerton St

Santini

Italian

Sophisticated family-run Italian restaurant

☎ 020 7730 4094 29 Ebury St SW1W 0NZ Plan 4-H3

MENU GUIDE Carciofo Santini (slow cooked globe artichokes) • Osso buco alla Milanese (stewed veal shin, saffron risotto) • Fruttini

WINE GUIDE 70 bottles over £20, 6 bottles under £20 • 10 by the glass (£4.50-£12)

PRICE GUIDE Fixed L £16.50 • starter £6.50-£17.50 • main £14.50-£27.50 • dessert £6.50-£7.50 • coffee £2.75 • min/water £3 • Service optional • Group min 10 service 12.5%

PLACE: Well established Italian restaurant in Belgravia. The interior is full of polished glass, slatted blinds and light marble floors, with softly coloured decor and furnishings. Service from mostly Italian staff is polished and friendly. This is one of the few London restaurants not to include a service charge on the bill.

FOOD: The menu offers a good choice of classical Italian dishes with a strong Venetian influence. Cooking delivers on all of its promises, with an emphasis on freshness, flavour and simplicity. There is also a limited but authentic Italian wine list.

OUR TIP: Private terrace for summer dining

Chef: Guiseppe Rosselli **Owners:** Mr G Santin **Times:** 12.30-2.30/6.30-11, Closed Xmas, 1 Jan, Easter Sun, closed L Sat **Notes:** Vegetarian available **Seats:** 65, Pr/dining room 30 **Smoking:** No pipes, Air con **Children:** Portions **Directions:** Nearest station: Victoria Take Lower Belgrave St off Buckingham Palace Rd. Restaurant on 1st corner on left opp Grosvenor Hotel **Parking:** Meters (no charge after 6.30pm)

e-mail: info@santini-restaurant.com **web:** www.santini-restaurant.com

 The Stafford

British, French

Romantic dining in the heart of St James's

☎ 020 7493 0111 16-18 St James's Place SW1A 1NJ Plan 5-A5

MENU GUIDE Goats' cheese tarte Tatin, salad • Rosettes of Welsh lamb, Anna potatoes • Raspberry soufflé, home-made vanilla ice cream

WINE GUIDE Many bottles over £20 • 5 by the glass (£6.50-£6.7?

PRICE GUIDE Fixed L £29.50 • starter £10.50-£22 • main £19.50 £30.50 • dessert £9.50 • coffee £4 • min/water £3.50 • Service included

PLACE: Boutique hotel, secluded in exclusive St James's, with cosy public areas reminiscent of an opulent family home. The American Bar sports an eccentric array of photos, caps and ties, while the split-level restaurant is classically presented with superbly laid up tables.

FOOD: The cooking style and presentation is classical British wi? French influences, suiting the club-like atmosphere of The Stafford. The menu is simpler at lunchtime with an additional daily special from the trolley, while the dinner selection is supplemented by 'Simple Classics' and dishes 'From the Stoves'.

OUR TIP: Check out the famous Stafford Dry Martini

Chef: Mark Budd **Owners:** Shire Hotels **Times:** 12.30-2.30/6.30-10, Closed L Sat **Notes:** Vegetarian available, Dress Restrictions, Jacket & tie in the evening, Civ Wed 44 **Seats:** 60, Pr/dining room 44 **Smoking:** N? pipes, No cigars, Air con **Rooms:** 81 (81 en suite) ★★★★ **Direction?** Nearest station: Green Park 5 mins St James' Palace **Parking:** NCP on Arlington Street **e-mail:** info@thestaffordhotel.co.uk **web:** www.thestaffordhotel.co.uk

The Best Use of Seafood sponsored by Seafish In conjunction with Seafish, the Sea Fish Industry Authority, we have sought out restaurants that make the most of seafood on their menus. In addition to the four country award winners (see page 9), look out for the seafish symbol throughout the book; this denotes restaurants serving a good range of fish and shellfish dishes, where the accent is firmly on freshness.

Wiltons

British

One of London's finest fish and game restaurants

☎ 020 7629 9955 55 Jermyn St SW1Y 6LX Plan 5-A6

MENU GUIDE Terrine of duck, pork & foie gras • Grilled turbot • Warm chocolate fondant

WINE GUIDE ♀ Portal del Alto Sauvignon Blanc £26 ♥ Groote Post Merlot £29 • All bottles over £20 • 12 by the glass £6-£15.50)

PRICE GUIDE Starter £7-£20 • main £17-£48 • dessert £6-£8 coffee £4 • min/water £4.90 • Service optional

PLACE: This St James's institution dates back to 1742 and is one of a dying breed. Very much in the tradition of a Gentleman's Club, jacket and tie are obligatory yet service is efficient and unstuffy. There is no music and seating is comfortable with an atmosphere of understated quality.

FOOD: Choose from seasonal, dégustation and classic menus, with prime seafood featuring on all of them. Many dishes are assembled à la minute such as oysters, smoked eel and foie gras. Vegetables from the market are priced separately. Notable wine list.

OUR TIP: Oysters and fresh fish will not disappoint

Chef: Jerome Ponchelle **Owners:** The Hambro Family **Times:** 12-30/6-10.45, Closed Xmas-New Year, BHs, Sat, Sun **Notes:** Vegetarian available, Dress Restrictions, Jackets Mon-Fri **Seats:** 100, Pr/dining room **Smoking:** No pipes, Air con **Directions:** Nearest station: Green Park/Piccadilly At the junction of Bury St. and Jermyn St., opposite Turnball Asser. **Parking:** NCP Arlington St. **e-mail:** wiltons@wiltons.co.uk **web:** www.wiltons.co.uk

W'Sens (by La Compagnie des Comptoirs)

French   **NEW**

Modern French food in stylish metropolitan surroundings

☎ 020 7484 1355 12 Waterloo Place, St James Plan 5-B6

MENU GUIDE Watercress soup, oysters • Sea bass, confit lemon vinaigrette • Chocolate & raspberry spring rolls

PRICE GUIDE Food prices not confirmed for 2006. Please telephone for details

PLACE: This former bank has been converted into a sophisticated restaurant and bar. The grand foyer area with its high ceilings houses the reception and modern oblong bar. Decor is beautifully designed with dark leather chairs (and tables) and neutral grey walls with floor to ceiling curtains.

FOOD: French dishes, ancient and modern, make up this menu although there are some Asian influences. High quality produce are prepared by a young and enthusiastic kitchen into a range of tempting offerings such as poached foie gras broth, ginger and enoki mushrooms.

OUR TIP: Great dinner venue after a day's sight-seeing in London

Times: 12-3.30/6.30-11, Closed 2 wks before Xmas

e-mail: reservation@wsens.co.uk **web:** www.wsens.co.uk

LONDON SW1

Zafferano

Italian

Chic Knightsbridge Italian

☎ 020 7235 5800 15 Lowndes St SW1X 9EY Plan 4-F4

MENU GUIDE Pan-fried scallops, saffron vinaigrette • Veal cutlet, mushrooms, rösti potato • Warm almond & cherry tart, amaretto cream

WINE GUIDE ♀ Planeta Chardonnay £43 • ♥ Morellino consono Sangiovese £26.50 • 420 bottles over £20, 12 bottles under £20 • 6 by the glass (£3.50-£6)

PRICE GUIDE Fixed L £25.50 • Fixed D £37.50 • coffee £2.50 • min/water £3.50

PLACE: Discreetly tucked away from the bustle of fashionable Knightsbridge and across the far end of Lowndes Square from Harvey Nichols, this intimate, friendly and deservedly popular Italian with closely packed tables and vibrant see-and-be-seen atmosphere, draws an adoring crowd. Lots of wood, exposed brick and tiled floors hint at Milanese styling, while service is

appropriately professional, attentive and friendly. The addition of a bar serving cocktails and offering antipasti-style food, plus a lounge and additional restaurant seating, will add to the package and comforts, while securing its enduring popularity.

FOOD: Accomplished, assured cooking, notable for its simply prepared dishes using the freshest, super-quality, seasonal ingredients and flawless execution, makes sure this Italian stands out from the crowd. Avoiding unnecessary complication, consistency and clean flavours feature on appealing, fixed-price lunch and dinner menus (dotted with a few supplements), while an authentic, well-constructed list of patriotic Italian wines rounds things off with due reverence to the cuisine.

OUR TIP: Book well in advance

Chef: Andrew Needham **Owners:** A-Z Restaurants **Times:** 12-2.30/7-11, Closed 1 wk Xmas & New Year, BHs **Notes:** Vegetarian available, Dress Restrictions, Smart casual **Seats:** 54 **Smoking:** No pipes, No cigars, Air con **Children:** No Children **Directions:** Nearest station: Knightsbridge Located off Sloane Street, behind Carlton Tower Hotel **Parking:** NCP behind Restaurant

England

LONDON SW1 *continued*

 Zafferano *see page 289*

Harvard Bar & Grill 101 Buckingham Palace Rd, Victoria SW1W 0SJ ☎ 020 7868 6249 Within walking distance of many London landmarks. Open early morning to late in the evening.

Wagamama 8 Norris St SW1Y 4RJ ☎ 020 7321 2755 Informal noodle bar with no booking.

Yo! Sushi 5th Floor, Harvey Nicholls Food Hall, 109-125 Knightsbridge SW1X 7RJ ☎ 020 7235 5000 Sushi, Sashimi, noodles and more delivered by conveyor belt and priced according to colour coded plates.

LONDON SW3
Bibendum
European
Classic and contemporary dishes with Conran style
☎ 020 7581 5817 Michelin House, 81 Fulham Rd SW3 6RD Plan 4-E3

MENU GUIDE Gratin of aubergine & goat's cheese • Roast quail with sage & white wine • Pithiviers au chocolat

WINE GUIDE L'Enclos Domeque Chardonnay £17.95 • Château Puyanché Cabernet Sauvignon £17.95 • 850 bottles over £20, 20 bottles under £20 • 8 by the glass (£4.75-£7.95)

PRICE GUIDE Fixed L £28.50 • starter £10-£22.50 • main £16.50-£29 • dessert £7-£9.50 • coffee £4 • min/water £3.50 • Service added but optional 12.5%

PLACE: A South Kensington landmark, this light, airy and elegant dining room has a sunny, atrium feel, occupying the first floor of the remarkable old Michelin building with its fabulous stained-glass windows portraying Bibendum, the Michelin man. Table settings and furnishings are comfortable, the atmosphere relaxed and unstuffy, and staff attentive and professional. The less formal Oyster Bar downstairs serves all manner of crustacea.
FOOD: A repertoire of French and British brasserie classics brought up to date is the Bibendum style - the intelligent, simple, clean-cut treatment of top quality ingredients makes it justifiably ever popular.
OUR TIP: Great for celebrity spotting, and there's a serious wine list to drool over
Chef: Matthew Harris **Owners:** Sir Terence Conran, Lord Hamlyn, S Hopkinson, G Williams **Times:** 12-2.30/7-11.30, Closed Dec 25-26, 1 Jan, closed D Dec 24 **Notes:** Vegetarian available **Seats:** 76 **Smoking:** No pipes, Air con **Children:** Portions **Parking:** On-street **e-mail:** manager@bibendum.co.uk **web:** www.bibendum.co.uk

Bluebird Dining Rooms
British
NEW
Classic British food in stylish setting
☎ 020 7559 1129 350 King's Rd SW3 5UU
Plan 4-D1
MENU GUIDE Warm potato drop scones, Cornish crab, land cress • Crumbed calves' sweetbreads, Morels, Jersey Royals, wild garlic leaf • Sticky date pudding, hot butterscotch, iced clotted cream

PRICE GUIDE Fixed L fr £19.50 • starter £5.50-£14.50 • main £12-£36 • dessert £5-£7 • coffee £3 • min/water £3.50 • Service added but optional 12.5%

PLACE: Above the food shop of the same name and part of the Conran empire, this large, airy restaurant boasts sleek art deco glamour, a glass atrium-style roof and a large lobster tank.
FOOD: Classic British cuisine at its most elegant. The menu prides itself on using top quality British produce in the right season. This makes for bold flavours in dishes such as roast rump of salt marsh lamb with Lancashire hotpot potatoes and pickled red cabbage, or Yorkshire rhubarb and pear crumble with stem ginger custard sauce.
OUR TIP: Jazz band on Friday evenings and Sunday lunch
Chef: Mark Broadbent **Owners:** Conran Ltd **Times:** 12-4/7-11, Closed Xmas, Easter Fri & Mon, closed L Mon-Sat, closed D Sun **Seats:** 80, Pr/dining room 20 **Smoking:** Air con **Children:** Portions **Parking:** The Vale **e-mail:** info@bluebirdclub.co.uk **web:** www.conran.com

 The Capital *see page 291*

 The Collection
International
Fashionable bar and dining room in Chelsea
☎ 020 7225 1212 264 Brompton Rd SW3 2AS
Plan 4-E3
MENU GUIDE Tempura oysters • Swordfish with spiced lentil salsa • Peach Melba

WINE GUIDE 14 by the glass (£4.75-£7.50)

PRICE GUIDE Fixed L £15 • Fixed D £40 • starter £4.50-£25 • main £13.50-£21 • dessert £5-£17 • coffee £2.50 • min/water £3 • Service added but optional 15%

PLACE: Enter through a glamorous, 80ft catwalk-like corridor lined with fashion photographs and into the open-plan former warehouse with its loud Latin jazz music. The dining room on the mezzanine floor overlooking the bar is perfect for people-watching as much as eating.
FOOD: The modern British cuisine has a fusion element to it, with innovative combinations that work surprisingly well: steamed sea bass with tomato sambal, spinach and mint raita, followed perhaps by blueberry and white chocolate samosas with Grand Marnier ice cream.
OUR TIP: Great value early evening menu
Chef: Warren Lee **Owners:** Scarporex **Times:** 6-11.30, Closed 25-26 Dec, 1 Jan, BH's, closed L Lunch Xmas period **Notes:** Vegetarian available, Dress Restrictions, No jeans, no trainers **Seats:** 165, Pr/dining room 50 **Smoking:** Air con **Children:** Min 18 **Directions:** Nearest station: South Kensington Pelham Street to traffic lights and turn left **Parking:** NCP, pay and display, on street after 6 pm **e-mail:** office@thecollection.co.uk **web:** www.the-collection.co.uk

England

LONDON SW3

The Capital

French

inspired cooking and impeccable service at Knightsbridge landmark

☎ 020 7589 5171   Basil St, Knightsbridge SW3 1AT   Plan 4-F4

e-mail: reservations@capitalhotel.co.uk   **web:** www.capitalhotel.co.uk

PLACE: Sporting a new-look bar, lounge and restaurant, this beautiful, family-owned-and-run luxury boutique hotel certainly lives up to its name. Its discreet townhouse location, hidden from the hubbub of Knightsbridge between Harrods and Harvey Nichols, oozes understated elegance, an impression confirmed by the liveried doorman, welcoming foyer fire and seamless service. The refurbished restaurant is light, airy and chic, with a suave but understated look inspired by the 1940s. Lightwood panelling, cool, pale blue upholstered chairs, matching drapes and crisp white napery set a sophisticated, clean-lined tone, while high ceilings house contemporarily styled chandeliers. Artwork by Dalí and sculptures by Henry Moore reinforce the aura of elegance and provide a fitting new backdrop to Eric Chavot's inspired cooking. The adjoining cocktail bar is equally stylish and service polished and attentive, while the superb wine list is very French and very sophisticated, which aptly matches the food.

FOOD: In these heady, contemporary surroundings, the food has to be very special indeed, and it is. Chef Eric Chavot, who has been at The Capital for some seven years, is fittingly renowned among his peers for producing consistently fine cuisine. His roots are firmly entrenched in the French classical style, but with a light, modern touch that includes some surprise elements that hold interest through to the end. There's no over-complication here, no molecular chemistry, just impressive, refined and imaginative cooking, utilising top-notch produce and a shopping list of luxury ingredients. Chavot's approach is via an enticing repertoire of fixed-price menus that include value lunch, dinner and six-course tasting dégustation (which includes the option of the sommelier's choice of accompanying wines). So expect deft dish combinations, clear, pronounced flavours and impeccable presentation, backed by stunning in-house breads and delicate amuse bouche that invite anticipation, and excellent petits fours that deliver a fitting finale.

MENU GUIDE Crab lasagne, langoustine cappuccino • Quail ballotine, foie gras boudin • Peach, chocolate & lavender trifle

WINE GUIDE ♀ Levin Sauvignon Blanc £31 • ♀ Cumienerge Geoffroy Pinot Noir £50 800 bottles over £20, 20 bottles under £20 • 10 by the glass (£6.50-£18.50)

PRICE GUIDE Fixed L £29.50 • Fixed D £55 • coffee £5 • min/water £3.95 • Service added but optional 12.5%

OUR TIP: Excellent value lunch menu

Chef: Eric Chavot **Owners:** Mr D Levin & Mr J Levin **Times:** 12-2.30/7-11, Closed 25 Dec D **Notes:** Dégustation menu 6 courses £68, Vegetarian available, Dress Restrictions, No jeans or trainers **Seats:** 35, Pr/dining room 24 **Smoking:** N/Sm in restaurant, Air con **Children:** Portions **Rooms:** 49 (49 en suite) ★★★★★ **Directions:** Nearest station: Knightsbridge Off Sloane St, beside Harrods **Parking:** 10

England

LONDON SW3 *continued*

Le Colombier
French   NEW
Popular French brasserie in the middle of Chelsea
☎ 020 7351 1155 145 Dovehouse St SW3 6LB
Plan 4-D2

MENU GUIDE Terrine de foie gras • Confit duck leg & lentils
Fine apple tart

PRICE GUIDE Food prices not confirmed for 2006. Please
telephone for details

PLACE: A Parisian-style brasserie in deepest Chelsea complete
with the buzz and bustle of a popular venue. Crisp white linen
and smartly dressed staff populate the more traditional dining
room and the terrace section at the front, which is perfect in
warmer weather.

FOOD: Good, traditional brasserie classics like steak with
béarnaise sauce and moules marinières prepared with care using
good quality ingredients. Also try the Dover sole or coquilles
Saint Jacques.

OUR TIP: Ideal retreat after a hard morning's shopping
Times: 12-3/6.30-10.30 **e-mail:** colombierparty@hotmail.com

Eight Over Eight
Pan Asian
Eclectic ethnic cuisine in fashionable Chelsea
☎ 020 7349 9934 392 King's Rd SW3 5UZ Plan 1-E3

MENU GUIDE Chilli salt squid • Chicken & physalis jungle
curry • Chocolate pudding, green tea ice cream

WINE GUIDE ♀ Mud House Sauvignon Blanc
£29 • ♥ Vergelegen Merlot £21 • 20 bottles over £20, 3 bottles
under £20 • 12 by the glass (£3.30-£11.30)

PRICE GUIDE Fixed L £15 • Fixed D £45 • starter £5-£7 • main
£10-£26 • dessert £5-£5.50 • min/water £3.50 • Service added
but optional 12.5%

PLACE: A modish joint to meet friends, this buzzy Kings Road
eaterie has a bar out front and laid-back restaurant behind.
Tables are simply set with a pot for chopsticks and cutlery, while
the decor's a fashionable mix of wood and suede.

FOOD: Good for sharing, the food continues the convivial theme,
with a lengthy menu to suit grazers as well as those looking for a
full meal. Inspiration comes from China, Thailand and Japan.

OUR TIP: Make the most of the friendly and knowledgeable staff
Chef: Andy Lassetier **Owners:** Will Ricker **Times:** 12-3/6-11, Closed 24-
29 Dec, closed L Sun **Notes:** Vegetarian available **Seats:** 95, Pr/dining
room 14 **Smoking:** No pipes, No cigars, Air con
e-mail: neil@eightovereight.nu **web:** www.eightovereight.nu

---

Three Rosettes Outstanding restaurants that
demand recognition well beyond their local
area. Timing, seasoning and the judgement of
flavour combinations will be consistently
excellent, supported by other elements such
as intelligent service and a well-chosen wine
list. Around 10% of restaurants with Rosettes
have been awarded three.

Frankie's Italian Bar & Grill
Italian   NEW
Clubby basement restaurant serving simple Italian
food
☎ 020 7590 9999 3 Yeoman's Row, Brompton Rd
SW3 2AL Plan 4-E3

MENU GUIDE Calamari fritti • Escalope of veal
milanese • Tiramisù

WINE GUIDE ♀ Formulae Sangiovese £23 • ♥ Planeta Segreta
Bianco £22 • 22 bottles over £20, 11 bottles under £20 • 8 by
the glass (£2.75-£5.20)

PRICE GUIDE Fixed L £11.75 • starter £5.50-£9.50 • main £9.50-
£22.50 • dessert £5.50 • coffee £2.50 • min/water £3 • Service
added but optional 12.5%

PLACE: Glitzy place in a tiny side street off Knightsbridge, owned
by Marco Pierre White and top jockey Frankie Dettori. The close-
packed tables are generally heaving and the atmosphere is
buzzing. Enter through a small bar area with red leather chairs,
and the restaurant beckons with its chequered ceramic floor tiles
and silver disco balls.

FOOD: Simple Italian food accurately cooked from good fresh
ingredients, with no fuss. Antipasta, pasta, pizza and grill pretty
well sorts the menu.

OUR TIP: Very child friendly, particularly at weekends
Chef: Callum Watson **Owners:** Marco Pierre White & Frankie Dettori
Times: 12-3/6-11 **Notes:** Vegetarian available **Seats:** 170 **Smoking:** Air
con **Children:** Menu, Portions **Directions:** Nearest station: South
Kensington/Knightsbridge Telephone for directions. **Parking:** South
Kensington/Knightsbridge

Manicomio
Italian
Bustling, stylish Italian eaterie in the heart of
Chelsea
☎ 020 7730 3366 85 Duke of York Square, Chelsea
SW3 4LY Plan 4-F2

MENU GUIDE Porcini pappardelle • Roast duck, chestnuts, lentil
& pancetta • Lemon tart, mandarin sorbet

WINE GUIDE ♀ Fozzaluzza Pinot Grigio £23.50 • ♥ Thaulero
Montepucciano £18.75 • 47 bottles over £20, 12 bottles under
£20 • 18 by the glass (£3.50-£9.25)

PRICE GUIDE Starter £6.25-£8.95 • main £11.75-£19.75 • dessert
£6-£7.50 • coffee £2 • min/water £3.50 • Service added but
optional 12.5%

PLACE: Manicomio comprises a delightful deli, buzzy coffee bar
and restaurant all set in an open-air shopping complex just off
Sloane Square. The frontage is all modern glass and steel with
planters and heaters for alfresco dining. Inside, there are wooden
floors and tables, brickwork, white walls and modern art. Staff
are friendly and service is helpful and well timed.

FOOD: Modern Italian food predominates here with lots of
imported Italian produce. Northern style dishes are simply
presented with an emphasis on clear flavours.

OUR TIP: Some pre-lunch shopping on the Kings Road
Chef: Bobby Cabral & Tom Salt **Owners:** Ninai & Andrew Zarach
Times: noon-3/6.30-10.30, Closed Xmas & New Year **Notes:** Tasting menu
3 starters £12.50, Vegetarian available **Seats:** 60, Pr/dining room 30
Smoking: N/Sm area, No pipes, No cigars, Air con **Children:** Portions
Parking: on street **e-mail:** manicomio@btconnect.com
web: www.manicomio.co.uk

England

Nathalie

Modern French   **NEW**

Innovative French cuisine in intimate surroundings

☎ 020 7581 2848 3 Milner St SW3 2QA Plan 4-F3

MENU GUIDE Tart of smoked haddock & leeks • Steamed fillet of sea bream with aubergine caviar • Chocolate délice with tea custard

WINE GUIDE ♀ Lafage Pays d'Oc Chardonnay £15 • ♀ Château Lezongars 1ere Côte de Bordeaux £15.50 • 101 bottles over £20, 11 bottles under £20 • 5 by the glass (£3.50-£7)

PRICE GUIDE Starter £6.75-£11.50 • main £14.50-£19.50 • dessert £6-£7 • coffee £2.50 • min/water £3.50 • Service added but optional 12.5%

PLACE: Tucked away in a quiet Chelsea street, this restaurant is housed in a pretty townhouse. A relaxed family-run establishment, it is named after the proprietor's first daughter. The atmosphere is cosily familiar, with the chef/patron and his wife both very hands-on. Decor is a simple affair of pewter flower-shaped chandeliers, black leather chairs and white linen tablecloths.

FOOD: Based on classical French cuisine, quality ingredients are cooked with a modern twist. Good simple cooking with good clean flavours.

OUR TIP: Quirky Bento Box lunch is excellent value

Chef: Eric Chatroux **Owners:** Eric Chatroux, Anne Jensen **Times:** 12-2.30/7-10.30, Closed Xmas, New Year, Easter, end of Aug, BHs, Sun & Mon **Notes:** Vegetarian available **Seats:** 35, Pr/dining room 14 **Smoking:** N/Sm in restaurant **Directions:** Parallel to Walton St. Between Fulham Rd and Kings Rd **Parking:** Pay at meter

e-mail: eric@nathalie-restaurant.co.uk
web: www.nathalie-restaurant.co.uk

Racine

French

Simple French brasserie cuisine

☎ 020 7584 4477 239 Brompton Rd SW3 2EP Plan 4-E3

MENU GUIDE Herring roes & sorrel on toast • Halibut fillet, cider vinegar sauce • Plum & almond compote

WINE GUIDE ♀ VDP d'Oc Chardonnay £13.75 • ♀ Château de Terrefort Bordeaux Cabernet Sauvignon £13.75 • 53 bottles over £20, 19 bottles under £20 • 13 by the glass (£3.65-£9.35)

PRICE GUIDE Fixed L £15.50 • Fixed D £17.50 • starter £5.25-£12.50 • main £12-£19.75 • dessert £4.50-£6.50 • coffee £2 • min/water £2.90

PLACE: A Parisian style restaurant conveniently set amidst that shoppers' paradise, the Brompton Road. The brown leather seating, smart white-clothed tables and attentive French staff are a comfort after the hustle and bustle outside.

FOOD: Straightforward French brasserie cooking is promised here, from traditional recipes served in a simple rustic style. A strong basis in classical techniques produces a competent carre d'agneau, served correctly pink with a rich béarnaise sauce. Other favourites might include confit de canard, and grilled rabbit with mustard sauce and smoked bacon.

OUR TIP: Ideal for Knightsbridge shoppers

Chef: Henry Harris, Chris Handley **Owners:** Eric Garnier, Henry Harris **Times:** 12-3.30/6-10.30, Closed 25 Dec **Notes:** Fixed D 6-7.30 only, Vegetarian available **Seats:** 75, Pr/dining room 18 **Smoking:** N/Sm area, No pipes, No cigars, Air con **Children:** Portions **Directions:** Nearest station: Knightsbridge, South Kensington Restaurant opposite Brompton Oratory

---

LONDON SW3

Rasoi Vineet Bhatia

Modern Indian   **NEW**

Elegant townhouse restaurant serving outstanding modern Indian cooking

☎ 020 7225 1881 10 Lincoln St SW3 2TS Plan 4-F2

MENU GUIDE Medley of samosas • Grilled spice marinated duck escalopes, hot tamarind chutney, crispy onion fritters • Mango rice kheer, spiced mango juice, lemongrass ice cream

WINE GUIDE ♀ Mittnacht Gewurztraminer £35 • ♀ Haute Cabriere Pinot Noir £35 • 130 bottles over £20, 2 bottles under £20 • 9 by the glass (£5-£10)

PRICE GUIDE Fixed L £19 • starter £9-£16 • main £18-£34 • dessert £8-£11 • coffee £4.50 • min/water £3.80 • Service added but optional 12.5%

PLACE: This 100-year-old Chelsea townhouse, cosily tucked away off the King's Road close to Sloane Square, has been adopted by the much-lauded Indian chef, Vineet Bhatia of Zaika fame (see under W8). Opened to much critical acclaim in the summer of 2004, Rasoi Vineet Bhatia (translating to Vineet Bhatia's Kitchen) is the personal venture of Vineet and wife, Rashima. The modern,

progressive attitude to Indian food is reflected in the decor, rich in vibrant Eastern styling, which sets the stage for a relaxed, intimate experience. The L-shaped area, with a conservatory roof at the rear and snug front room, is decorated in sandy beige and chocolate brown tones, replete with silk cushions and wall hangings.

FOOD: Bhatia's contemporary, evolved Indian cuisine delivers explosions of clear, vibrant flavours that would revitalize any jaded palate. Dishes are accurately cooked with great skill and panache, while clean, robust flavours are well balanced and don't overpower. Luxury ingredients and specially sourced crockery back an enticing carte, fixed-price and lunch offerings.

OUR TIP: Try the gourmand menu; there's private rooms upstairs too.

Chef: Vineet Bhatia **Owners:** Vineet & Rashima Bhatia **Times:** 12-2.30/6.30-10.30, Closed Xmas, New Year, BHs, Sun, closed L Sat **Notes:** Gourmand Menu 9 courses £65, Vegetarian available, Dress Restrictions, Smart casual **Seats:** 35, Pr/dining room 24 **Smoking:** N/Sm in restaurant, Air con **Directions:** Nearest station: Sloane Square Near Peter Jones and Duke of York Square **Parking:** on street

e-mail: rasoi.vineet@btconnect.com **web:** www.vineetbhatia.com

England

LONDON SW3

Restaurant Gordon Ramsay

French *London's finest*

☎ 020 7352 4441 68 Royal Hospital Rd SW3 4HP Plan 4-F1
e-mail: reservations@gordonramsay.com
web: www.gordonramsay.com

PLACE: Gordon Ramsay's hallmark purple discreetly marks out the entrance to his Chelsea temple of gastronomy, and is carried through in subtle touches to the beautifully understated and elegant dining room. Tranquil opaque glass panels, elegant cappuccino beige leather chairs and stunning sculptural pieces in Murano glass ooze class and provide a stylish, sophisticated and exclusive backdrop to some sublime cooking. It's surprisingly, though endearingly, intimate for the mothership of an ever-expanding restaurant empire, and for someone with such a huge reputation; Britain's most famous A-list chef and a household name following his various TV series. The burgeoning restaurant empire currently extends to the London institutions of Claridge's, The Connaught, and Pétrus and The Boxwood Café at the Berkeley (see entries) with rumours of Stateside openings. But back in upmarket Chelsea, neatly clothed, much-in-demand tables and polished, highly professional and attentive service is as good as it gets, charmingly orchestrated by maître d' Jean-Claude Breton. Explanations of dishes are offered with enthusiasm and increase anticipation, while there's plenty of help when it comes to navigating the fabulous wine list. So, sit back and enjoy a stunning experience from the master.

FOOD: Precision and innovation emerge from classical roots and, in a word, the results are very impressive. As you would expect, the skills on show are as good as you'll ever see; depth of flavour, texture, balance, impeccable ingredients and tremendous consistency hit the very pinnacle. Simplicity, integrity and a lightness of touch are hallmarks of the approach, which grace a repertoire of luxury-studded and enticing fixed-price menus that include a seven-course tasting option. So think roasted langoustine tails with braised pork belly, crushed white beans, mushrooms and creamed Cos lettuce, followed by fillet of wild sea bass with paysanne of vegetables, pasta, borlotto beans, pak choi and a cep velouté.

MENU GUIDE Sautéed foie gras, Braeburn apples three ways • Lamb cooked three ways, caviar aubergine, braised potatoes, thyme jus • Chocolate & hazelnut soufflé, vanilla ice cream

WINE GUIDE ♀ Louis Michel 2000 Chablis 1'er Cru Montmain Chardonnay £42 • ♀ Figeac 1999 Esquisse de la Tour £38 • 950 bottles over £20, 35 bottles under £20 • 8 by the glass (£5-£49)

PRICE GUIDE Fixed L £40-£90 • Fixed D £70 • coffee £5 • min/water £4 • Service optional

OUR TIP: Booking can be a nightmare, so be persistent (the book is only open on a month-by-month basis)

Chef: Gordon Ramsay **Owners:** Gordon Ramsay Holdings **Times:** 12-2.30/6.45-11, Closed 2 wks Xmas, BHs, Sat, Sun **Notes:** Fixed D 7 courses £90, Vegetarian available, Dress Restrictions, Jacket preferred, no jeans or trainers **Seats:** 44 **Smoking:** N/Sm in restaurant, Air con **Children:** Portions **Directions:** Nearest station: Sloane Square Near Royal Army Museum **Parking:** On street

LONDON SW3

Tom Aikens

French *Gastronomic big hitter of class and distinction*

☎ 020 7584 2003 43 Elystan St SW3 3NT Plan 4-E2

e-mail: info@tomaikens.co.uk
web: www.tomaikens.co.uk

PLACE: This eponymous, multi award-winning Chelsea haven to the serious foodie has put Tom Aikens up there with the Ramsays and Blumenthals. Tucked away in a quiet residential street, his smart, discreet restaurant (once a pub) has been transformed by Anouska Hempel's design into a dining room devoted to the theatre of fine dining. Clean, self confident lines, with lots of dark wood (floors and shutters), black leather chairs and white walls simply offset by modern artwork set the tone. Tables are well spaced, settings expensive and elegant, service well directed, professional, knowledgeable and attentive. And, as you would expect from this calibre of venue, there's a suitably extensive wine list, French dominated, with some heavyweights from Burgundy and Bordeaux.

FOOD: A successful mix of classical roots, top-notch ingredients and flamboyant presentation that make Tom Aiken's food very unique (dishes have a vibrant, almost Picasso-like delivery). French influences from this ex Pied-à-Terre chef combine with surprisingly generous portions. Adjectives like impressive, imaginative and ingenious, roll off the tongue, and it's no wonder this is the 'in' food destination and the talk of the town. Technical skill, balance, clear and pronounced flavours, great textures and timings all hit the mark. Attention to detail dominates every aspect, with peripherals hitting top form too; superb breads, cracking amuse bouche and pre-dessert, and excellent petits fours. So expect main menu dishes like a twosome of roasted scallops with crisp pork belly and pumpkin sauce, and a saddle of lamb with aubergine beignets, red onion purée and parmesan cassonde to wow the tastebuds.

MENU GUIDE Pheasant boudin, lentils with truffle, Sauternes foam • John Dory, celeriac & horseradish, foie gras boudin • Poached pineapple, crisp & sorbet

WINE GUIDE ♀ Alain Gras Saint Romain Chardonnay £45 • ♀ Maillard Chorey les Beaune Pinot Noir £45 • 450 bottles over £20, 5 bottles under £20 30 by the glass (£6-£20)

PRICE GUIDE Fixed L £29 • Fixed D £60 • min/water £4.50 • Service added but optional 12.5%

OUR TIP: Book well in advance; excellent value lunch menu

Chef: Tom Aikens **Owners:** T & L Ltd **Times:** 12-2.30/7-11, Closed 2 wks Xmas & N Year, lst 2wks Aug & BH's, Sat & Sun **Notes:** Tasting menu 7 courses £75, coffee incl., Smart Dress **Seats:** 60 **Smoking:** N/Sm in restaurant, Air con **Children:** Portions **Directions:** Nearest station: South Kensington Off Fulham Rd (Brompton Rd end) **Parking:** Parking meters outside

England

England

LONDON SW3 *continued*

⚜⚜⚜ Rasoi Vineet Bhatia

see page 293

⚜⚜⚜⚜ Restaurant Gordon Ramsay *see page 294*

⚜⚜⚜⚜ Tom Aikens *see page 295*

⑨ Brasserie St Quentin 243 Brompton Rd SW3 2EP
☎ 020 7589 8005 Simple classic dishes, with ingredients sourced from suppliers and farmers around the country.

▮▮ Riccardos 126 Fulham Rd SW3 6HU ☎ 020 7370 6656
Elegant Italian food with a modern twist.

▮▮ Spiga Chelsea 312 Kings Rd SW3 5UH
☎ 020 7351 0101 Contemporary but classic Italian with superior pasta and pizza. Sister of Spiga W1.

LONDON SW4

⚜ Tsunami

Japanese

Stylish, informal setting for a contemporary neighbourhood-style Japanese
☎ 020 7978 1610 5-7 Voltaire Rd SW4 6DQ Plan 1-E3
MENU GUIDE Black cod tempura • Chargrilled lamb with wasabi pepper sauce • Chocolate fondant
WINE GUIDE ♀ Framingham Estate Sauvignon £23.50 • ♀ Vieja Mendoza Sangiovesse £16 • 27 bottles over £20, 20 bottles under £20 • 9 by the glass (£3.75-£5.50)
PRICE GUIDE Starter £2.50-£9.95 • main £6.50-£16.50 • dessert £4.95-£5.95 • min/water £3 • Service added but optional 12.5%
PLACE: A big glass frontage, contemporary seating and lighting, dark wood, light walls, colourful flower displays, open-to-view kitchen and trendy black-clad staff cut a cool, trendy oasis in an unlikely location opposite Clapham Station.
FOOD: Modern Japanese with a hint of fusion is the style, from a foie gras and chive roll sushi with eel sauce to grilled scallops with smelt eggs and creamy spicy sauce, or black cod in sweet miso. Expect quality ingredients and imaginative presentation throughout.
OUR TIP: Try tempura selection to start or four mini dessert box to finish
Chef: Ken Sam **Owners:** Ken Sam **Times:** 12.30-11.30/6-11, Closed 25 Dec-4 Jan, Sun, closed L Mon-Fri, closed D Sun **Notes:** Vegetarian available **Seats:** 100 **Smoking:** N/Sm area, No pipes, No cigars, Air con **Children:** Portions **Directions:** Nearest station: Clapham North Telephone for directions **Parking:** On street
web: www.tsunamijapaneserestaurant.co.uk

▮▮ San Marco 126 Clapham High St SW4 7UH
☎ 020 7622 0452 Attractively simple pizza with checked tablecloths and house wine drunk out of tumblers.

▮▮ Strada 102-104 Clapham High St, Clapham SW4 7UL
☎ 020 7627 4847 Superior pizza from quality ingredients cooked in wood-fired ovens.

LONDON SW5

⚜ Cambio De Tercio

Modern Spanish
Complete Spanish experience - decor, service and cuisine
☎ 020 7244 8970 163 Old Brompton Rd SW5 0LJ Plan 4-C2
MENU GUIDE King prawns, garlic, baby chillies & lemon oil • Roasted wild rabbit, green beans, sherry • Milk and cinnamon bread pudding
PRICE GUIDE Food prices not confirmed for 2006. Please telephone for details
PLACE: Lively Spanish restaurant decorated in the bright red and yellow of the Spanish flag, with an impressive matador's cape displayed on the wall. Fast and friendly service provided by mainly Spanish staff to fairly closely set tables, adding to the buzz in the atmosphere.
FOOD: Authentic Spanish food from the different regions and cooking styles, notably fish with bright flavours and colours, and deep-fried Serrano ham croquettes for example.
OUR TIP: Tapas bar opposite - bring your own wine
Chef: Javier Jimenez **Owners:** Abel Lusa **Times:** 12-2.30/7-11.30, Closed Xmas, New Year **Notes:** Vegetarian available **Seats:** 45, Pr/dining room 22 **Smoking:** No pipes **Directions:** Nearest station: Gloucester Road Close to junction with Drayton Gardens
web: www.cambiodetercio.co.uk

⚜ London Marriott Kensington

Italian
Modern Italian glass-fronted restaurant
☎ 020 7973 1000 Cromwell Rd SW5 0TH Plan 4-B3
MENU GUIDE Ravioli alla Piemontese • Pan-fried sea bass, cherry tomatoes & thyme • Pannacotta al limoncello
WINE GUIDE ♀ Pinot Grigio £14.95 • ♀ Corte Vigna Merlot £14.95 • 29 bottles over £20, 19 bottles under £20 • 10 by the glass (£4.80-£8.50)
PRICE GUIDE Fixed L fr £12.50 • Fixed D fr £15 • starter £5-£8.50 • main £15-£22 • dessert £4.50-£7 • coffee £3 • min/water £3.50 • Service added but optional 12.5%
PLACE: Located off the amazing seven storey glass atrium of this glamorous hotel. The restaurant is stylish and contemporary, with a wooden floor, brown leather chairs and banquettes, and an open kitchen. Friendly, mainly Italian, staff are helpful and attentive.
FOOD: A good mix of traditional and modern Italian dishes on the extensive carte, including a good choice of antipasti, pasta/risotto, mains and pizzas. Shorter menus are available at lunch.
OUR TIP: Handy for Earl's Court and Kensington
Chef: David Britton **Owners:** Whitbread Hotel Co. **Times:** 12-2.30/5.30-11 **Notes:** Vegetarian available **Seats:** 93, Pr/dining room 18 **Smoking:** N/Sm in restaurant, Air con **Children:** Menu, Portions **Rooms:** 216 (216 en suite) ★★★★ **Parking:** 20
e-mail: event.kensington@marriotthotels.co.uk
web: www.marriotthotels.com/lonlm

▮▮ Strada 237 Earls Court Rd SW5 ☎ 020 7835 1180
Superior pizza from quality ingredients cooked in wood-fired ovens.

⑨ Tendido Cero 174 Old Brompton Rd SW5 0BA
☎ 020 7370 3685 Simpler sister of Cambio de Tercio with good tapas.

England

LONDON SW6

 ### *Darbar*
Modern Indian

Modern Indian in Chelsea

☎ 020 7348 7373 92-94 Waterford Rd, Fulham SW6 2HA Plan 1-D3

PLACE: Smart, contemporary looking Indian, with its extensive use of Indian imported granite as bar worktops and flooring, at the Fulham end of Chelsea and Kings Road. The dining room is airy and bright with some privacy in the alcoves.
FOOD: The extensive menu provides a good selection of starters and main dishes. With emphasis to the robust traditional North Indian Dum Pukht style of cooking; desserts, in particular, are given a modern twist.
OUR TIP: Good selection of starters and mains
Times: 12-3/6-12, Closed Sun
e-mail: darbar_restaurant@btinternet.com

 The Farm 18 Farm Ln SW16 1PP ☎ 020 7381 3331 Possibly the UK's first cash free restaurant. European food with a spicy ethnic twist.

 Loch Fyne Restaurant 676 Fulham Rd SW6 5SA ☎ 020 7610 8020 Quality seafood chain.

Strada 175 New Kings Rd, Parsons Green SW6 4SW ☎ 020 7731 6404 Superior pizza from quality ingredients cooked in wood-fired ovens.

LONDON SW7

The Bentley Kempinski Hotel *see page 298*

Brunello
Italian

An opulent setting for classy Italian cuisine

☎ 020 7368 5700 Baglioni Hotel, 60 Hyde Park Gate, Kensington Rd SW7 5BB Plan 4-C4

MENU GUIDE Beef carpaccio, wild mushrooms, parmesan, black truffle • Black ink cannelloni, broccoli, clams • Amaretto crème brûlée
WINE GUIDE ♀ Pojer & Sandri Chardonnay £35 • ♀ Teroldego Rotaliano Foradore £32 • 7 by the glass (£5-£20)
PRICE GUIDE Fixed L £20 • starter £11-£21 • main £11-£24 • dessert £10-£16 • coffee £3 • min/water £4.50 • Service added but optional 12.5%

PLACE: With its black Venetian glass chandeliers, candlelight and velvet, Brunello is the height of opulent chic and lives up to its boutique hotel setting in the heart of Kensington.
FOOD: Brunello takes its food as seriously as its decor, conjuring divine Italian dishes from superb ingredients and making innovative use of ethnic flavours and styles, such as ginger and chilli. Pasta is a highlight, although it's rivalled by a wide-ranging wine list designed to suit novices and experts alike.
OUR TIP: Just the place for an outrageously decadent weekend
Chef: Stefano Stecca **Owners:** Baglioni Hotels **Times:** 12-2.30/7-10.45
Notes: Vegetarian available, Smart Dress **Seats:** 70, Pr/dining room 60
Smoking: No pipes, Air con **Children:** Portions **Directions:** Nearest station: Kensington High Street. Hotel entrance on Hyde Park Gate facing park & Kensington Palace. **Parking:** NCP (Young St)
e-mail: l.virgilio@baglionihotels.com **web:** www.baglionihotels.com

 ### Café Lazeez
Indian
Modern Indian with traditional and contemporary cuisine

NEW

☎ 020 7581 9993 93-95 Old Brompton Rd SW7 5LD Plan 4-D2

MENU GUIDE Lazeez barbeque feast (for 2 or 3) • Saag gosht (Lamb cooked with spinach, fenugreek, dill & yoghurt) • Carrot halva
WINE GUIDE ♀ General Billimoria Colombard Chardonnay £10.75 • ♀ General Billimoria Shiraz/Pinotage £10.75 • 21 bottles over £20, 15 bottles under £20 • 9 by the glass (£3-£4.95)
PRICE GUIDE Fixed L fr £10 • starter £3.85-£10.95 • main £9-£16.25 • dessert £2.95-£4.45 • coffee £1.50 • min/water £3 • Service added 12.5%

PLACE: Shop-fronted restaurant, comfortable but not luxurious, with long opening hours. It's a local's destination, some just popping in for a drink at the bar. Staff are well informed and enthusiastic about the food.
FOOD: Plenty of choice from traditional and evolved Indian menus, with dishes designed to be light, healthy and full of flavour. Great presentation in dishes such as biryani served in a pot sealed with dough. Set meals also available.
OUR TIP: Take away service, home delivery and specialist catering
Chef: Avneet Bhutani **Owners:** Seasons Restaurant Ltd **Times:** 11-4/4-12 **Notes:** Vegetarian available, Smart Dress **Seats:** 130, Pr/dining room 50 **Smoking:** N/Sm area, Air con **Children:** Menu, Portions
Directions: Nearest station: South Kensington Please ring for directions
Parking: Pay & display nearby **e-mail:** southkensington@cafelazeez.com
web: www.cafelazeez.com

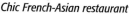 ### L'Etranger
French, Japanese

Chic French-Asian restaurant

☎ 020 7584 1118 36 Gloucester Rd SW7 4QT Plan 4-C4

MENU GUIDE Tuna spring roll, ginger & coriander • Caramelised black cod with miso • Mango soufflé
WINE GUIDE ♀ Lafon Mâcon-Milly Lamartine Chardonnay £32 • ♀ Esmonin Gevrey Chambertin clos Premier Pinot Noir £40 • 500 bottles over £20, 50 bottles under £20 • 24 by the glass (£4.50-£10)
PRICE GUIDE Fixed L £14.50 • Fixed D £16.50 • starter £7.50-£15.50 • main £15.50-£22 • dessert £7.50-£12.50 • coffee £2.50 • min/water £3.50 • Service added but optional 12.5%

PLACE: L'Etranger is part of a complex occupying two shop fronts with a basement cocktail bar and a wine shop. Slabs of rich colour and fresh orchids create a sophisticated setting, with the wine store open-plan to the restaurant.
FOOD: The strong French influence determines many of the primary elements of each dish - shoulder of lamb, pig's trotters and rabbit, alongside named breeds of beef, fresh oysters and a wide range of fish. However the dishes are given a twist with oriental spicing and cooking methods, and the results are exceptional.
OUR TIP: Come at lunchtime when it's not so busy
Chef: Jerome Tauvron **Owners:** Ibi Issolah **Times:** 12-3/6-11, Closed Sun, closed L Sat **Notes:** Vegetarian available **Seats:** 55, Pr/dining room 20 **Smoking:** No pipes, Air con **Children:** Portions **Parking:** NCP
e-mail: etranger@etranger.co.uk **web:** www.etranger.co.uk

England

LONDON SW7

The Bentley Kempinski Hotel

French, European

Grazing-menu concept in ornate restaurant

☎ 020 7244 5555 27-33 Harrington Gardens
SW7 4JX Plan 4-C2

MENU GUIDE Native lobster, anchovies, tomato & baby gem • Veal fillet, salsify, parsley ravioli, sauce charcutiere • Lemon tart, almond ice cream

WINE GUIDE ♀ Pouilly Fumé Sauvignon Blanc £35 • ♀ Crose Hermitage Shiraz £39 • 300 bottles over £20, 20 bottles under £20 • 150 by the glass (£5)

PRICE GUIDE Fixed L £20-£25 • starter £15-£20 • main £20-£30 • dessert £8-£15 • coffee £5 • min/water £5 • Service optional • Group min 10 service 12.5%

PLACE: The decadent Malachite Bar, with its jade-green marble counter and leopard-skin furnishings, is just the place for cocktails, here in one of London's newest hotels, discreetly tucked away in the heart of Kensington. Next door, also on the hotel's lower ground floor and accessed by the same sweeping circular staircase from the lobby, is the fine dining dinner-only

1880 restaurant (named after the date of the building). The palatial room offers a sense of occasion, with its elaborate ceiling, silk wall panels and richly coloured carpets and furniture. Well-spaced tables, professional and knowledgeable service.

FOOD: Dinner at the 1880 is notable for Andrew Turner's grazing-concept menus, with 7, 8, 9 and 10-course options, all miniature versions of dishes on the substantial and appealing fixed-price carte. There's also a surprise - sommelier's and pastry chef's menu. Clear and distinct flavours, balance and first class presentation of excellent ingredients (including many luxury items) abound in light, innovative combinations that amount to a notable, contemporary dining experience.

OUR TIP: Take a grazing menu for a gastronomic experience
Chef: Andrew Turner **Owners:** International Luxury Hotels **Times:** 6-10, Closed BHs, closed L all wk, closed D Sun **Notes:** Grazing menus 7-10 courses £40-£48, Vegetarian available, Dress Restrictions, Jacket/Shirt, Civ Wed 6 **Seats:** 45, Pr/dining room 12 **Smoking:** N/Sm in restaurant, Air con **Rooms:** 64 (64 en suite) ★★★★★ **Directions:** Nearest station: Gloucester Road Off A4 Cromwell Rd, opposite Gloucester Hotel **Parking:** on street & car park **e-mail:** hkoenig@thebentley-hotel.com **web:** www.thebentley-hotel.com

---

LONDON SW7 *continued*

🌹 Harrington Hall

British, European

Popular Kensington hotel with eclectic mix of dishes

☎ 020 7396 9696 5-25 Harrington Gardens
SW7 4JN Plan 4-C2

MENU GUIDE Roasted quail, celeriac mousseline • Barbary duck breast, wasabi potato cake • Mulled wine pudding

WINE GUIDE ♀ Louis Latour Ardeche Chardonnay £18.50 • ♀ Moondarra Shiraz £18.50 • 9 bottles over £20, 10 bottles under £20 • 10 by the glass (£4-£6.50)

PRICE GUIDE Fixed L £15.95 • Fixed D £17.95 • starter £5.55-£7.85 • main £9-£22.95 • dessert £5.50 • coffee £3 • min/water £3.50 • Service optional

PLACE: Large plants and shrubs soften the view between the grand columns, helped by muted coral and sand colours, and all the expected elegance associated with Kensington.

FOOD: The food appeals to different tastes, with a popular lunchtime carvery backed up by short set menu, and an evening carte listing adventurous choices based on excellent ingredients.

OUR TIP: Secure car parking across the road
Chef: Christoph Zetinnig **Owners:** Mr Cola **Times:** 12-2/5.30-10, Closed L Sat, Sun **Notes:** Mon-Fri lunch cavery £19.75, Vegetarian available, Smart **Seats:** 130, Pr/dining room 40 **Smoking:** N/Sm in restaurant, Air con **Children:** Portions **Rooms:** 200 (200 en suite) ★★★★
e-mail: sales@harringtonhall.co.uk **web:** www.harringtonhall.co.uk

---

🌹 Radisson Edwardian Vanderbilt Hotel

Modern British

Contemporary hotel serving stylishly simple food

☎ 020 7761 9000 68/86 Cromwell Rd SW7 5BT
Plan 4-C3

MENU GUIDE Venison & pistachio terrine • Roast wild duck • Chocolate sponge pudding & custard

PRICE GUIDE Food prices not confirmed for 2006. Please telephone for details

PLACE: A row of town houses makes up this smart hotel, and hides a contemporary interior well geared up to 21st-century expectations.

FOOD: Good use is made of fresh ingredients, and the presentation, like the orientation of the cooking, is appealingly modern. An ordinary-sounding roast breast of chicken with a prune, sage and onion stuffing is anything but run of the mill.

OUR TIP: Right opposite Gloucester Rd tube station
Times: 12.30-2.30/5.30-10, Closed L Sat-Sun **Rooms:** 215 (215 en suite) ★★★★ **Directions:** Telephone for directions
e-mail: 68/86cromwellroad@radisson.com **web:** www.radissonedwardian.com

England

⚙ Swag and Tails

International, Mediterranean

Upmarket Knightsbridge gastro-pub
☎ 020 7584 6926   10-11 Fairholt St SW7 1EG
Plan 4-E4

MENU GUIDE Caesar salad with chicken • Mushroom tortelloni, caramelised red onions, tarragon cream sauce • Rhubarb & vanilla crème brûlée
WINE GUIDE ♀ Domaine Alain Gautheron Chardonnay £21 • ♀ Laibach Merlot £19.95 • 11 bottles over £20, 22 bottles under £20 • 11 by the glass (£3.20-£10)
PRICE GUIDE Starter £5.25-£10.75 • main £10.25-£14.95 • dessert £5.25-£5.75 • coffee £2.25 • min/water £3.50 • Service added but optional 10%
PLACE: Discreetly hidden in a Knightsbridge mews, this smart gastro-pub presents well with its honeyed woods, cream walls covered in interesting prints, and closely-packed tables. In winter the open fire adds a cosy touch to the bistro atmosphere.
FOOD: The exuberant international cooking brings a riot of flavours, colours and textures. Each dish comprises several ingredients that create a talking point as much as they satisfy the palate.
OUR TIP: Ideal for a break from Knightsbridge shopping
Chef: Geoffrey Fisher **Owners:** Annemaria & Stuart Boomer-Davies
Times: 11am-11pm, Closed Xmas, New Year, BHs, Sat-Sun
Notes: Vegetarian available **Seats:** 34 **Smoking:** N/Sm area, No pipes, No cigars **Directions:** Nearest station: Knightsbridge Tube Station Close Harrods. **Parking:** On street **e-mail:** theswag@swagandtails.com
web: www.swagandtails.com

NEW
denotes a restaurant which is new
to the guide this year.

◎◎ Zuma

Modern Japanese

Glamorous, fashionable, contemporary Japanese
☎ 020 7584 1010   5 Raphael St SW7 1DL Plan 4-F4
MENU GUIDE Crispy fried squid, green chilli salt • Rib-eye steak, wafu sauce, garlic crisps • Dark chocolate pudding with passionfruit centre
WINE GUIDE 4 bottles under £20 • 8 by the glass (£5-£12)
PRICE GUIDE Fixed L £11.30 • starter £3.80-£22 • main £10.80-£60 • dessert £5.80-£12.80 • coffee £2.50 • min/water £4.50 • Service added but optional 12.5%
PLACE: Clean lines and cutting-edge modernity are delivered via blonde wood, granite, leather and open-to-view kitchens at buzzy, popular and highly fashionable Zuma.
FOOD: Impressive, contemporary Japanese cuisine is the format, so expect ultra-fresh produce, clear, vibrant flavours and imaginative presentation from an extensive but flexible range of small dishes designed for sharing and served as they are cooked. Choose from sashimi, sushi, maki rolls, tempura and so on, but perhaps try marinated monkfish with green chilli, soya shiso and yamagobo from the robata grill. Inspired desserts too.
OUR TIP: Staff are knowledgeable and very happy to guide the uninitiated through the menu
Chef: Colin Clague **Owners:** Rainer Becker **Times:** 12-2.30/6-10, Closed 25-26 Dec, 1 Jan, closed D 24 Dec **Notes:** Vegetarian available
Seats: 147, Pr/dining room 14 **Smoking:** N/Sm in restaurant, Air con
Children: Portions **Directions:** Nearest station: Knightsbridge Telephone for directions **Parking:** Street parking
e-mail: info@zumarestaurant.com **web:** www.zumarestaurant.com

---

LONDON SW8

◎◎ The Food Room

French, Mediterranean   **NEW**

Classy setting for fine French cuisine
☎ 020 7622 0555   123 Queenstown Rd SW8 3RH
Plan 1-E3
MENU GUIDE Mediterranean pistou soup • Pork fillet, pommes Anna, black pudding, red wine sauce • Assiette of chocolate
WINE GUIDE ♀ Casa Azul Chardonnay £14.75 • ♀ Gaillac Terret £15.50 • 45 bottles over £20, 20 bottles under £20 • 7 by the glass (£4-£4.95)
PRICE GUIDE Fixed L £13.50-£16.50 • starter £5.20-£9.80 • main £10.50-£15.20 • dessert £4.95-£5.50 • coffee £1.95 • min/water £2.95 • Service added but optional 12.5%
PLACE: Chic French eaterie in Battersea that is decorated in contemporary style with mirrors, metal and abstract art. It's a spacious and airy venue given warmth by friendly staff.
FOOD: French cooking at its imaginative best. A lengthy dinner menu offers plenty of choice, ranging from classic combinations to more imaginative fare, with dishes typically along the lines of venison with a pear and shallot Tatin, turnip purée and venison sauce. Lunch is simpler but no less impressive, and a wallet-friendly early bird menu is served evenings Tuesday to Friday.
OUR TIP: Excellent value lunch menu
Chef: Eric Guignard, Sebastian Mondoulet **Owners:** Eric & Sarah Guignard **Times:** 12-2.30/7-10.30, Closed 25-26 Dec, 1-8 Jan, Last 2 wks Aug, Sun & Mon, closed L Sat & Tue **Notes:** Vegetarian available, Smart casual **Seats:** 60 **Smoking:** N/Sm area, No pipes, No cigars, Air con
Children: Portions **Directions:** Nearest station: Queenstown Road 10 min from Clapham Junction **Parking:** on street
web: www.thefoodroom.com

LONDON SW10

@@@@ **Aubergine** *see page 301*

@@ Chutney Mary Restaurant

Indian

Contemporary and innovative Chelsea Indian
☎ 020 7351 3113 535 Kings Rd, Chelsea SW10 0SZ
Plan 1-E3

MENU GUIDE Lobster stir fry • Lamb chops with ginger & lime
WINE GUIDE ♀ La Puiattino Pinot Grigio £21.25 • ♀ Domaine de Triennes Vin Gris £21.25 • 90 bottles over £20, 9 bottles under £20 • 13 by the glass (£4.20-£10.30)
PRICE GUIDE Fixed L fr £16.50 • starter £6.25-£13.50 • main £13.50-£25.50 • dessert £5.50-£7.50 • coffee £2.50 • min/water £3.70 • Service added but optional 12.5%

PLACE: A contemporary ethnic style defines this classy Indian restaurant where the clever use of mirrors and subtle lighting makes the basement area feel more spacious than it is, and service is effortlessly efficient and friendly.
FOOD: The food is influenced but not restricted by traditional recipes, though the menu is usefully laid out in familiar style, tandoori, seafood, chicken etc. Quality Western produce impacts the Indian cuisine with innovative results, and flavours are deep, well-balanced and clean.
OUR TIP: Try the tasting platters or vegetarian choices
Chef: Nagarajan Rubinath **Owners:** Masala World, R Mathrani, N Panjabi **Times:** 12.30-3/6.30-11, Closed D Xmas **Notes:** Set price D 7 courses. Set price L applies to Sat & Sun, Vegetarian available **Seats:** 110, Pr/dining room 24 **Smoking:** N/Sm area, Air con **Directions:** Nearest station: Fulham Broadway On corner of King's Rd and Lots Rd; 2 mins from Chelsea Harbour. **Parking:** Parking meters outside
e-mail: chutneymary@realindianfood.com
web: www.realindianfood.com

@@ Osteria dell'Arancio

Italian ⚑NEW

Great Italian regional food and wine in lively Chelsea setting
☎ 020 7349 8111 383 King's Rd SW10 0LP
Plan 1-E3

MENU GUIDE Baked ricotta, broccoli & pancetta • Monkfish, potacchio sauce • Carrot cake, poached pear
WINE GUIDE ♀ Verdicchio le Vaglie Santa Barbara £25 • ♀ Barbera Ca di Pian La Spinetta £31 • 22 by the glass (£3.50-£35)
PRICE GUIDE Fixed L £14-£16 • coffee £1.50 • min/water £3 • Service included

continued

PLACE: This converted pub is now a vibrant little Italian osteria tucked away on the ever-fashionable King's Road. Bench seating, bright lighting, lots of mirrors and colourful artwork give this place a cheerful, sunny Mediterranean feel. Service is relaxed and friendly.
FOOD: Home cooking from the Marche region. Fixed prices and limited choices are no problem here. An excellent wine list adds to the attraction. But there is still balance to the menus for those wishing to avoid an expanding waistline.
OUR TIP: Great Chelsea lunch location
Chef: Massimo Garofoli **Owners:** Michele Alesiani **Times:** 12-3/7-11 **Notes:** Tasting menu £30-£35, Vegetarian available **Seats:** 70, Pr/dining room 30 **Smoking:** N/Sm area, No pipes, No cigars, Air con **Children:** Menu, Portions **Parking:** 5 min
e-mail: info@osteriadellarancio.co.uk **web:** www.osteriadellarancio.co.uk

@@ The Painted Heron

Modern Indian

Good value and unusual modern Indian cuisine
☎ 020 7351 5232 112 Cheyne Walk SW10 0DJ
Plan 1-E3

MENU GUIDE Tandoori lamb chops • Monkfish tail with green chillies & garlic • Indian bread & clarified butter pudding with saffron & nuts
WINE GUIDE ♀ Hugel Gewurztraminer £22 • ♀ Paul Conti Shiraz £23 • 25 bottles over £20, 14 bottles under £20 • 20 by the glass (£3-£7.50)
PRICE GUIDE Starter £5-£7.50 • main £11-£17 • dessert £3.50-£6 • coffee £3.50 • min/water £3 • Service added but optional 12.5%

PLACE: The blue awning and glass frontage, together with the name, do little to suggest the nationality of the cooking at this chic Chelsea Indian facing the Thames. Blond-wood floors, dark wood and leather chairs and dark wood slatted blinds lend a minimalist, contemporary edge, while coloured oil lamps on crisp white linen tables and modern art on walls - reflecting Chelsea's artisan past - add simple but elegant touches.
FOOD: High quality modern Indian cooking, with traditional dishes given contemporary spin and presentation. Focus is on fresh ingredients and subtle spicing.
OUR TIP: The small walled terrace at the rear is great for summer alfresco dining
Chef: Yogesh Datta **Owners:** Charles Hill **Times:** 12-3/6.30-11, Closed Xmas & Easter, closed L Sat **Notes:** Vegetarian available **Seats:** 70 **Smoking:** Air con **Children:** Portions **Directions:** Nearest station: South Kensington Telephone for directions **Parking:** On street
e-mail: thepaintedheron@btinternet.com
web: www.thepaintedheron.com

@@ Sticklebackpink

Indian

Stylish and friendly Chelsea Indian
☎ 020 7835 0874 168 Ifield Rd SW10 9AF Plan 4-B1
PLACE: A stylish venue in an equally fashionable part of town. Enter through the bright, welcoming and very well stocked bar then descend a spiral staircase into the restaurant, whose decor blends the ultra modern (lime green walls, shiny steel fish sculptures) with classic touches (rich smart, linen covered tables. Staff are knowledgeable and helpful, and the friendly chef is often seen front of house.
FOOD: New wave Indian cooking, blending Eastern and European techniques and ingredients. Spicing can be adjusted to suit the taste of individual diners.
OUR TIP: Good vegetarian choices
Times: 6.30-11.30, Closed L Tue-Sat, Mon, Xmas & New Year
e-mail: info@sticklebackrestaurant.com
web: www.stickleback-restaurant.com

CLOSED

LONDON SW10

England

Aubergine

French *Accomplished and refined cooking from eminent Chelsea eaterie*
☎ 020 7352 3449 11 Park Walk, Chelsea SW10 0AJ Plan 4-C1
e-mail: auberginerestaurant@yahoo.co.uk

PLACE: On a side street away from the Fulham Road's hustle and bustle, the tell-tail aubergine canopy and front door singles out this renowned, well-heeled Chelsea fixture. The theming continues inside at generous-sized, white-clothed tables (above chocolate silk underclothes), with aubergine cruets, dress plates and menus. Muted, subtle tones create a relaxed, understated, stylish mood, with comfortable high-backed chairs decked out in apricot, cream and dark red. Ragged-effect beige walls are hung with abstract paintings, floors are light wood, while a stunning floral display greets you at the entrance. There's also a small seating area to relax pre or post meal, while mainly French staff add a formal tone to proceedings, dispensing attentive and professional service.

FOOD: William Drabble's eminently refined, self confident modern French cooking, underpinned by a classical theme, is intelligently simple and stylish, unfussy and basking in clear flavours. The highest quality produce (including luxury items like foie gras, truffles and oysters) is beautifully and immaculately presented without unnecessary complication. The approach is via an appealing, fixed-price format of lunch (three courses with half bottle of wine, half bottle of still mineral water, coffee and petits fours) and generous and tantalising carte, backed by a seven-course gourmand offering (for the whole table). So expect to be wowed by an assured threesome, such as succulent seared scallops served on a vibrantly coloured and flavoured parsley purée with light, golden beignets of softened garlic; moist roasted pigeon (breast and leg) with soft and creamy turnip gratin and impressive Madeira jus; and a rich and indulgent guantaja mousse with hazelnut caramel and hazelnut ice cream.

MENU GUIDE Warm salad of quail, sweetbreads & foie gras • Baked John Dory, endive, bacon & red wine • Gratin of figs, red wine syrup, cinnamon ice cream

WINE GUIDE ♀ Rully Dury Chardonnay £30 • ♀ Château Labadie 2001 Cabernet Sauvignon/Merlot £30 • 450 bottles over £20, 6 bottles under £20 • 4 by the glass (£4-£6)

PRICE GUIDE Fixed L £34 • Fixed D £60 • coffee £5 • min/water £4 • Service added but optional 12.5%

OUR TIP: Three-course lunch is a bargain not to be missed

Chef: William Drabble **Times:** 12-2.30/7-11, Closed 2 wks Xmas, BHs, Easter, Sun, closed L Sat **Notes:** Tasting menu 7 courses £74, Vegetarian available, Dress Restrictions, Smart casual preferred **Seats:** 60 **Smoking:** No pipes, No cigars, Air con **Directions:** Nearest station: South Kensington, Fulham Broadway W along Fulham Rd, close to Chelsea and Westminster Hospital **Parking:** Local parking available

LONDON SW10 *continued*

⊛⊛ Vama
Indian
Rustic Punjabi cooking
☎ 020 565 8500 & 7565 8500 438 King's Rd
SW10 0LJ Plan 1-E3

MENU GUIDE Pudina aloo tikki • Crab kofta curry • Poached fruit
WINE GUIDE ♀ Napa Valley Beringer Fume Blanc
£28 • ♀ Belgravia Shiraz Reserve £32 • 14 bottles over £20,
8 bottles under £20 • 6 by the glass (£4.25-£7)
PRICE GUIDE Fixed L £10-£20 • starter £4.75-£14 • main £6.50-
£16 • dessert £4-£6 • coffee £3.50 • min/water £3.75 • Group
min 6 service 12.5%

PLACE: With its ochre coloured walls, crafted teak chairs, old oil
paintings and artefacts, and hand-made crockery from an ancient
pottery town, this place gives a realistic impression of India.
Friendly staff and a buzzy atmosphere do the rest.
FOOD: Dishes are from the North Indian Punjab region, where
marinades and clay oven cooking give them their authentic taste
of spices and charcoal. Some items are recognisable, like a silky
deep green sag paneer, and others are original, like matar methi
malai (spinach, peas and fenugreek leaves).The menu usefully
separates the vegetarian from the non-vegetarian.
OUR TIP: Outdoor dining in summer
Chef: Andy Varma **Owners:** Andy Varma, Arjun Varma **Times:** 12-
4/6.30-12, Closed 25-26 Dec, 1 Jan **Notes:** Brunch £14.95, Vegetarian
available **Seats:** 120, Pr/dining room 35 **Smoking:** Air con
Directions: Nearest station: Sloane Square About 20 mins walk down
King's Rd **Parking:** Edith Grove, NCP **e-mail:** enquiries@vama.co.uk
web: www.vama.co.uk

Friends 6 Hollywood Rd SW10 9HY ☎ 020 7376 3890
Rustic pizzeria.

LONDON SW11

⊛⊛ The Greyhound at Battersea
Modern European   **NEW**
Fashionable gastro-pub in up-and-coming area
☎ 020 7978 7021 136 Battersea High St SW11 3JR
Plan 1-D3
MENU GUIDE Loch Fyne scallop tartare • Herdwick mutton
loin • White chocolate & macadamia blondie
WINE GUIDE ♀ Veramont Sauvignon Blanc £18 • ♀ Kim
Crawford Pin Pinot Noir £20 • 350 bottles over £20, 100 bottles
under £20 • 16 by the glass (£1.85-£11)
PRICE GUIDE Fixed L £12 • Fixed D £29 • coffee
£1.30 • min/water £2.50 • Service added but optional
10% • Group min 10 service 12.5%

continued

PLACE: Battersea High Street is on the up, and among the Indian
grocers and art deco Italian coffee shops you'll find the very
popular Greyhound. The word 'pub' doesn't really do it justice -
the well spaced tables and comfortable leather seating take it in
another direction, and it's rapidly become extremely fashionable.
FOOD: The very short menu demonstrates the importance of
quality to the kitchen here. Stylish presentation on long plates
with precisely placed items. Golden Valley goat curd salad with
white beetroot mousse is a fascinating starter, a quenelle of
cheese looks almost identical to the mousse, but the flavours
couldn't be more different, the creamy cheese perfectly
complementing the sweet acidity of the beet. Really interesting,
innovative food - and they churn their own butter as well.
OUR TIP: Booking essential
Chef: Tomislav Martinovic **Owners:** Mark & Sharlyn Van der Goot
Times: 12-2.30/3-9.30, Closed 23-26 Dec, 31 Dec-3 Jan, Mon, closed L
Tues, closed D Sun **Notes:** Sun L £18.50 (3 courses), Dress Restrictions,
Smart casual **Seats:** 55 summer (37 winter), Pr/dining room 25
Smoking: N/Sm in restaurant **Children:** Min L only, Portions
Directions: Nearest station: Clapham Junct Located near Battersea Bridge
and Clapham Junction **Parking:** On street
e-mail: eat@thegreyhoundatbattersea.co.uk
web: www.thegreyhoundatbattersea.co.uk

⊛ Osteria Antica Bologna
Italian
Rustic Italian restaurant serving authentic food
☎ 020 7978 4771 23 Northcote Rd SW11 1NG Plan 1-E2

MENU GUIDE Sea bass & prawn ravioli, saffron
sauce • Pheasant stew, juniper sauce & spinach • Chocolate &
pear cake, vanilla ice cream
WINE GUIDE ♀ La Preudina Pinot Blanco £15 • ♀ La Preudina
Merlot £15 • 26 bottles over £20, 23 bottles under £20 • 8 by the
glass (£2.95-£5.25)
PRICE GUIDE Fixed L £9.50 • starter £3.75-£8.50 • main £5.90-
£16.90 • dessert £4.50 • coffee £1.20 • min/water £2.80 • Service
added but optional 12.5%

PLACE: Just a stroll from Clapham Junction, this typical Italian
osteria holds its own in a bustling neighbourhood of delis,
specialist shops and fashionable eateries. It's a cheerful place,
with rustic decor and a very friendly atmosphere.
FOOD: Genuine Italian cooking with an emphasis on fresh and
seasonal produce. The comprehensive carte changes every three
months and there's a good-value lunch menu.
OUR TIP: Dine alfresco when the weather permits
Chef: Massimo Peitinau **Owners:** Callegari/Cane **Times:** 12-3/6-11,
Closed 24-26 Dec, 31 Dec, 1 Jan **Notes:** Theme menu 5 courses £27.50,
Vegetarian available **Seats:** 75 **Smoking:** No pipes, No cigars, Air con
Children: Portions **Directions:** Nearest station: Clapham Junction Off
Battersea Rise, between Wandsworth & Clapham Commons.
Parking: On street **e-mail:** osteria@osteria.co.uk
web: www.osteria.co.uk

England

Le Petit Max
French

A little piece of France by the Thames

☎ 020 7223 0999 Riverside Plaza, Chatfield Rd, By Plantation Wharf SW11 3SE Plan 1-E3

MENU GUIDE Ballotine of foie gras maison, brioche • Chargrilled rib-eye steak, peppercorn sauce, pommes frites • Tarte Tatin, crème fraîche

WINE GUIDE ♀ Nelson Chairmans Sauvignon Blanc £20 • ♀ Casa d' la Ermita Jumilla £22.50 • 33 bottles over £20, 10 bottles under £20 • 10 by the glass (£3-£6)

PRICE GUIDE Fixed L £14.50 • Fixed D £18.50 • starter £4.50-£9.90 • main £9.50-£15.50 • dessert £5-£6 • coffee £2 • min/water £3 • Service added but optional 12.5%

PLACE: Tucked away in a plaza of modern Thames-side apartments, Petit Max's split-level interior is more left bank Parisian than South Bank Battersea. Dark oak floorboards, undressed tables, deep red and Provençal yellow walls set a relaxed, neighbourhood bistro vibe, with a 1930s bar, old framed menus and posters and colour-coordinated banquettes completing the endearing Gallic buzz.
FOOD: Cuisine Bourgeois; simple, uncluttered, authentic classic bistro fare using fresh quality ingredients delivered in style.
OUR TIP: Decked terrace for fair-weather dining and drinks
Chef: Simon Gale **Owners:** Patrick Jefferson **Times:** 12-2.30/7.00-10.30, closed Some BHs, Easter Mon, closed D Sun **Notes:** Monthly regional menu evenings available, Vegetarian available **Seats:** 80
Smoking: N/Sm in restaurant, Air con **Directions:** Nearest station: Clapham Junction From Wandsworth Bridge rdbt, take York Rd and then second left into Mendip Rd after petrol sation **Parking:** Chatfield Rd
Web: www.lepetitmax.co.uk

Ransome's Dock
British, European

Fine uncomplicated cooking in a waterside setting

☎ 020 7223 1611 & 7924 2462 Battersea SW11 4NP Plan 1-E3

MENU GUIDE Norfolk smoked eel fillets • Grilled loin of rabbit, creamed leeks & tarragon • Rhubarb fool

WINE GUIDE ♀ Cloudy Bay Sauvignon Blanc £25 • ♀ Domaine Charvin Côtes du Rhone Merlot £19 • 250 bottles over £20, 50 bottles under £20 • 8 by the glass (£3.50-£8.50)

PRICE GUIDE Fixed L £14.75 • starter £5-£11.50 • main £10-£20 • dessert £5-£7.50 • coffee £2.75 • min/water £2 • Service added but optional 12.5%

PLACE: You'll find this engaging waterside location close to Albert Bridge in a former ice cream factory. Snacks, coffee and juices are served in a popular bar area, and the friendly restaurant is a picture with its cornflower blue walls and modern artwork.
FOOD: One of the pioneers of using top quality, often organic, ingredients, and the philosophy of buying the best and cooking it simply remains. The carte evolves subtly through the seasons, with daily specials like Cornish turbot with pea and lemon risotto providing fresh appeal. Notable wine list.
OUR TIP: Eat outside in warm weather
Chef: Martin Lam, Vanessa Lam **Owners:** Mr & Mrs M Lam **Times:** 12/6-11, Closed Xmas, closed D Sun **Notes:** Vegetarian available **Seats:** 55 **Smoking:** N/Sm area, No pipes, Air con **Children:** Portions **Directions:** Nearest station: Sloane Square/Clapham Junction Between Albert Bridge & Battersea Bridge **Parking:** 20
e-mail: chef@ransomesdock.co.uk **web:** www.ransomesdock.co.uk

Gourmet Burger Kitchen 44 Northcote Rd
SW11 1NZ ☎ 020 7228 3309 New Zealand inspired burger joint using top notch beef.

Matilda 74/76 Battersea Bridge Rd SW11
☎ 020 7228 6482 Relaxed pub dining with emphasis on traditional and home-made recipes.

Strada 11-13 Battersea Rise SW11 1HG
☎ 020 7801 0794 Superior pizza from quality ingredients cooked in wood-fired ovens.

LONDON SW13

MVH
Classical

Choice of heaven or hell dining decor with divine cuisine

☎ 020 8392 1111 5 Whitehart Ln, Barnes SW13 0PX Plan 1-D3

MENU GUIDE Goose liver assiette, shallot jam • Cod fillet, sweet miso, beetroot purée • Ginger crème brûlée

PRICE GUIDE Food prices not confirmed for 2006. Please telephone for details

PLACE: Expect the unexpected at this rather eccentric eaterie hidden away in a residential area of Barnes. Decor on both floors is pure theatre, from the shocking deep reds, ethnic artefacts and chaotic furnishings of the den-like, 'Hell'-themed bar, to the serene, heavenly-themed dining room, replete with pale stone, white linen and Italian-style chandeliers. Service is quite informal but attentive.
FOOD: Cooking is innovative and eclectic, a real mix of styles that combine classical cuisine with the East and European influenced dishes.
OUR TIP: Take time to have a drink in the upstairs bar (and look at the loos!)
Times: 12-2.30/6-10.30, Closed L Mon, Tue, Wed

Sonny's Restaurant
British, French

Imaginative cooking in modern venue

☎ 020 8748 0393 94 Church Rd, Barnes SW13 0DQ Plan 1-D3

MENU GUIDE Salmon rillettes, endive & walnut salad • Plaice & lobster ballotine, herb risotto • Crispy apple & rice pudding parcel

WINE GUIDE ♀ Pommier Petit Chablis £22.50 • ♀ Plantagenate Omrah Shiraz £22.50 • 53 bottles over £20, 17 bottles under £20 • 14 by the glass (£3.50-£8.75)

PRICE GUIDE Fixed L £13.50 • Fixed D £17.50 • starter £4.50-£9 • main £11.50-£18 • dessert £5-£6 • coffee £2.25 • min/water £3 • Service added but optional 12.5%

PLACE: Hidden in a row of shops, the simple exterior hides a bustling restaurant, with its fresh interior, clean lines, modern furniture and artworks, and relaxed, friendly service. There's a café menu as well as a full restaurant menu on offer.
FOOD: Modern British in style with strong contemporary French influences, there's good use of high quality, seasonal ingredients here. Preparation is careful and dishes often include unusual items and combinations such as the veal loin with sheep's foot or duck and pistachio terrine with pickled cabbage, respectively.

continued

England

LONDON SW13 *continued*

OUR TIP: Remember to visit Sonny's food shop next door
Chef: Helena Puolakka **Owners:** Rebecca Mascarenhas, James Harris
Times: 12.30-2.30/7.30-11, Closed BHs, closed D Sun **Notes:** Vegetarian available **Seats:** 100, Pr/dining room 26 **Smoking:** No pipes, Air con
Children: Menu, Portions **Directions:** Nearest station: Barnes/Hammersmith. From Castelnau end of Church Rd on left by shops.
Parking: On street **e-mail:** barnes@sonnys.co.uk
web: www.sonnys.co.uk

Strada 375 Lonsdale Rd SW13 9PY ☎ 020 8392 9216
Superior pizza from quality ingredients cooked in wood-fired ovens.

LONDON SW14

Crowthers Restaurant

Modern British

Informal neighbourhood restaurant

☎ 020 8876 6372 481 Upper Richmond Rd West, East Sheen SW14 7PU Plan 1-C3

MENU GUIDE Roasted sweet potato & parsnip soup • Grilled calves' liver with sage & Madeira • Sticky toffee pudding, hot butterscotch sauce

PRICE GUIDE Fixed D £26.50 • coffee £2.75 • min/water £2.50 • Service optional

PLACE: A smart, intimate eaterie on the edge of Richmond Park. The informal and friendly atmosphere created by the husband-and-wife team keeps the locals coming back for more. Service is relaxed but professional.
FOOD: A short selection of classic and contemporary dishes on a good-value fixed-price menu. Expect mains like best end of lamb with Provencal herb crust, rosemary & redcurrant sauce.
OUR TIP: Catering services available
Chef: Philip Crowther **Owners:** Mr & Mrs P Crowther **Times:** 12-2.30/7-10.30, Closed 1 wk Xmas, 2 wks Aug, Sun-Mon, closed L all week (except for party bookings) **Notes:** Vegetarian available **Seats:** 30
Smoking: No pipes, No cigars, Air con **Children:** Portions
Directions: Nearest station: Richmond Between junction of Sheen Lane & Clifford Ave. **e-mail:** pacrowther@aol.com

The Depot Waterfront Brasserie

Modern British

Rustic riverside brasserie

☎ 020 8878 9462 Tideway Yard, Mortlake High St SW14 8SN Plan 1-D3

PLACE: Located in an old stable block on the river, this place has a rustic appearance that gives it both character and style. Simple bare tables, neutral shades and high ceilings add to the look.
FOOD: The menu consists of a good selection of dishes that are simple in construction. Typical modern British favourites are enhanced with Mediterranean ingredients in dishes such as chargrilled tuna with Jerusalem artichokes, spinach and red wine jus.
OUR TIP: Tables by the windows offer good views
Times: 12-3/6-10, Closed 24-26 Dec **Directions:** Nearest station: Barnes Bridge BR Between Barnes Bridge & Mortlake stations
e-mail: rupert@depotbrasserie.co.uk **web:** www.depotbrasserie.co.uk

 denotes restaurants that place particular emphasis on making the most of local ingredients.

Redmond's

European, British

Vibrant East Sheen favourite

☎ 020 8878 1922 170 Upper Richmond Rd West SW14 8AW Plan 1-D3

MENU GUIDE Foie gras, beetroot & ginger salad • Roasted cod, spicy Puy lentils • Petit chocolate fondant, rosemary & caramel ice cream

PRICE GUIDE Food prices not confirmed for 2006. Please telephone for details.

PLACE: A blue pavement awning and glass frontage picks out this ever-popular neighbourhood favourite. It's a modern, contemporary affair but with a relaxed, unpretentious vibe. Blond-wood floors, stylish chrome and leather chairs and plain, light walls decorated with striking abstract art cut an upbeat mood, that's backed by friendly, accomplished service.
FOOD: The cooking moves with the times too, playing to the gallery with light, colourful, contemporary dishes that display skilled simplicity and imagination. Take pan-fried calves' liver with lemon, a thyme and shallot potato cake and sherry jus, or pear and basil tarte Tatin with red pepper ice cream.
OUR TIP: Value set-priced menus
Chef: Redmond Hayward **Owners:** Mr R Hayward, Mrs P Hayward
Times: 12-2.30/7-10, Closed 4 days Xmas, BH Mon`s, closed L Mon-Sat, closed D Sun **Notes:** Vegetarian available **Seats:** 48 **Smoking:** N/Sm restaurant, Air con **Children:** Menu, Portions **Directions:** Nearest station: Mortlake Located half way between Putney and Richmond. On the South Circular Road at the Barnes end of Sheen **Parking:** Street parking after 7 pm **e-mail:** pippa@redmonds.org.uk
web: www.redmonds.org.uk

The Victoria

British, European

Friendly gastro-pub with seriously good food

☎ 020 8876 4238 10 West Temple Sheen SW14 7RT Plan 1-C2

MENU GUIDE Serrano ham, celeriac remoulade • Sea bass, couscous salad, pomegranate relish • Pecan pie, double cream & maple syrup

WINE GUIDE ♀ Valdadige Pinot Grigio £16.95 • ♀ Brampton RSA Old Vines Red Cabernet Blend £19.95 • 38 bottles over £20 • 19 bottles under £20 • 11 by the glass (£3.45-£4.95)

PRICE GUIDE Starter £3.95-£9.95 • main £7.95-£19.95 • dessert £3.95-£5.95 • coffee £1.60 • min/water £2.95 • Service added but optional 12.5%

PLACE: Quietly located in a residential area near the high street, this chic gastro-pub is well regarded by the locals, and has seven bedrooms for guests from further afield. A wood-burning stove keeps the conservatory cosy in winter, while a patio is available for alfresco dining on sunnier days.
FOOD: The Victoria keeps things simple, focusing on flavour rather than fuss, and delivering accomplished cuisine distinguished by quality seasonal ingredients. The modern European menu majors in British and Spanish dishes; you might kick off with a tapas selection, before moving onto calves' liver with bacon and mash.
OUR TIP: Children's play area in the garden
Chef: Darren Archer **Owners:** Mark Chester & Darren Archer
Times: 12-2.30/7-10, Closed 4 days Xmas **Notes:** Vegetarian available
Seats: 70, Pr/dining room 45 **Smoking:** N/Sm area, No pipes, No cigar
Children: Menu, Portions **Rooms:** 7 (7 en suite) ♦♦♦♦
Directions: Nearest station: Mortlake Between upper Richmond Road and Richmond Park, halfway between Putney and Richmond **Parking:**
e-mail: reservations@thevictoria.net **web:** www.thevictoria.net

England

LONDON SW15
Enoteca Turi
Italian **NEW**

Enjoyable Italian regional food in Putney

☎ 020 8785 4449 28 Putney High St SW15 1SQ
Plan 1-D3

MENU GUIDE Asparagus, deep-fried parmesan egg • Sea bass all'acqua pazza • Sorbetti

WINE GUIDE ♀ Pinot Bianco £16.50 • ♀ Barbera £19.50
285 bottles over £20, 27 bottles under £20 • 11 by the glass (£3.50-£7)

PRICE GUIDE Fixed L £13.50 • Fixed D £28 • starter £7.50-£9.50 • main £10.50-£16.50 • dessert £5.50-£5.75 • coffee £2 • min/water £3.25 • Service added but optional 12.5%

PLACE: Situated on the southern corner of Putney High Street, this friendly Italian restaurant has a modern dining room decorated in warm Tuscan colours, wooden floors, wine racks and modern art. It is best to book in the evening as it can get very busy. Service is formal and staff are smartly dressed.
FOOD: Food is exclusively Italian. Refreshingly simple regional dishes are prepared with flair from the best of seasonal produce. There is a good lunchtime menu.
OUR TIP: Staff will match your choice with a suitable glass of wine
Chef: Mr K Gnevry **Owners:** Mr G Turi **Times:** 12-2.30/7-11, Closed 25-26 Dec, 1 Jan, Sun **Notes:** ALC dinner only, Vegetarian available
Seats: 85, Pr/dining room 28 **Smoking:** N/Sm area, No pipes, No cigars, Air con **Children:** Portions **Directions:** Nearest station: Putney Opposite Odeon Cinema near bridge. **e-mail:** enoturi@aol.com

Talad Thai
Thai

Cheap and cheerful Thai offers hearty cooking

☎ 020 8789 8084 320 Upper Richmond Rd, Putney SW15 6TL Plan 1-D3

PLACE: This restaurant used to be part of Talad Thai supermarket, and is located on the quieter end of Upper Richmond Road. It is nonetheless an extremely popular fuel stop for cheap and cheerful Thai fare. Decor remains unfussy with plain wooden tables and chairs with sky blue walls and an open kitchen.
FOOD: Staple Thai dishes are the mainstay of the extensive menu with cooking which is competent and good value for money.
OUR TIP: Perfect for that quick stopover meal
Times: 11.30-3/5.30-11, Closed 25 Dec, 1 Jan **Directions:** Telephone for directions

Gourmet Burger Kitchen 333 Putney Bridge Rd, Putney SW15 2PG ☎ 020 8789 1199 New Zealand inspired burger joint using top notch beef.

LONDON SW17

 Chez Bruce see below

LONDON SW17

Chez Bruce

French, British

Skilful dining at great prices

☎ 020 8672 0114 2 Bellevue Rd, Wandsworth Common SW17 7EG Plan 1-E2

MENU GUIDE Tagliatelle of mussels, saffron & chives • Blanquette of pigs' cheeks, pork sausage, choucroute & chervil • Hot chocolate pudding, praline parfait

WINE GUIDE ♀ Matthias Roblin Sancerre 2002 Sauv Bl £34 • ♀ Domaine Charvin Côtes du Rhône Grenache £28
450 bottles over £20, 10 bottles under £20 • 28 by the glass (£4.50-£14)

PRICE GUIDE Fixed L £18.50-£23.50 • Fixed D £35 • coffee £3.25 • min/water £3.25 • Service added but optional 12.5%

PLACE: Wandsworth's hub of culinary distinction is a surprisingly discreet affair, located in a small arcade of shops in a popular residential area overlooking the common. Large maroon-coloured planters bursting with flowers make an attractive statement from outside, while the interior cuts contemporary style with wooden floors, restful beiges and caramels, soft lighting and a collection of framed prints. Space is at a premium, with no drinks area, so diners are shown direct to well-appointed tables dressed with crisp white linen and quality glass and tableware. The effect is simple but elegant and pleasing, and so suits the mood. Service is relaxed but attentive from a knowledgeable team that includes the sommelier.
FOOD: Bruce Poole's appealing, modern fixed-price menus reveal hints of classic France, but remain pleasingly unfussy and offer plenty of choice, his accomplished cuisine making the very best use of high quality ingredients. Flavours really stand out and make for a memorable experience, with dishes displaying impeccable skill, interesting textures and perfect harmony. An impressive wine list to study and enjoy.
OUR TIP: Try the Stornaway black pudding with hot foie gras, try the pigs' cheeks, in fact, try everything and go back again!
Chef: Bruce Poole, Matt Christmass **Owners:** Bruce Poole, Nigel Platts-Martin **Times:** 12-2/6.30-10.30, Closed 24-26 Dec,1 Jan, closed L 27,31 Dec & 2nd Jan **Notes:** Tasting menu £65, Vegetarian available **Seats:** 75, Pr/dining room 16 **Smoking:** N/Sm in restaurant, Air con
Children: Menu, Portions **Directions:** Nearest station: Wandsworth Common Near Wandsworth Common B.R. station **Parking:** On street, station car park **e-mail:** enquiries@chezbruce.co.uk
web: www.chezbruce.com

England

LONDON SW17 *continued*

⑧ Kastoori
Indian
Indian vegetarian with fresh and imaginative fare
☎ 020 8767 7027 188 Upper Tooting Rd SW17 7EJ
Plan 1-E2

MENU GUIDE Dahi puri • Special tomato curry • Shrikhand

WINE GUIDE ♀ Echeverria Sauvignon Blanc £12.95 • ♀ Opel Ridge Shiraz Cabernet Sauvignon £13.95 • 1 bottles over £20, 19 bottles under £20 • 2 by the glass (£2.25)

PRICE GUIDE Food prices not confirmed for 2006. Please telephone for details.

PLACE: In what used to be part of an old department store, this small, family-run restaurant is perched between a row of shops on Tooting High Street. The simple interior is bright in white, blue and yellow. Service is calm, friendly and down to earth.

FOOD: Cooking is vegetarian, mainly Kathiawadi (western part of Gujerat), with abundant use of tomatoes among a variety of ingredients. There are also Indo-African influences from Uganda.

OUR TIP: Full takeaway service available

Chef: Manoj Thanki **Owners:** Mr D Thanki **Times:** 12.30-2.30/6-10.30, Closed 25,26 Dec, closed L Mon & Tue **Notes:** Vegetarian available, Smart Dress **Seats:** 82 **Smoking:** Air con **Children:** Portions
Directions: Nearest station: Tooting Bec & Tooting Broadway. Situated between two stations. **Parking:** On street

▮▮ Pomino 35 Bellevue Rd, Wandsworth Common SW17
☎ 020 8672 5888 Food and wine of central Italy served in an open kitchen concept restaurant.

LONDON SW19

⑧⑧ The Light House Restaurant
International
Minimalist decor but maximum flavours
☎ 020 8944 6338 75-77 The Ridgeway, Wimbledon SW19 4ST Plan 1-D2

MENU GUIDE Tuna carpaccio, crunchy vegetables, yuku dressing • Lamb shank, spinach, tomato & chick pea stew • Pear frangipane tart, vanilla ice cream

WINE GUIDE ♀ Lugarara Gavi di Gavi Cortese £26 • ♀ Concejo Crianza Tempranillo £24.50 • 60 bottles over £20, 11 bottles under £20 • 12 by the glass (£3.25-£6.90)

PRICE GUIDE Fixed L £14 • starter £5-£8.50 • main £10-£21 • dessert £5.20 • coffee £2 • min/water £3 • Service added but optional 12.5%

PLACE: This smart, informal and relaxed neighbourhood restaurant lights the way in Wimbledon Village. The look is modern metropolitan, pale and minimalist, with muted natural woods, stainless steel and glass. Well-spaced tables allow plenty of privacy.

FOOD: Big flavours, Mediterranean and global influences and combinations, pepper the imaginative, eclectic and fashionable modern Italian-styled menu, laid out in traditional four-course format (antipasti, primi, secondi and so on). Be adventurous though, it's worth it.

OUR TIP: Arrive early on summer days for a terrace table

Chef: David Winton **Owners:** Mr Finch & Mr Taylor **Times:** 12-2.30/6.30-10.30, Closed 24-26 Dec, 1 Jan, Etr Sun & Mon, closed D Sun **Notes:** Vegetarian available **Seats:** 80 **Smoking:** N/Sm area, No pipes, No cigars **Children:** Menu, Portions **Directions:** Nearest station: Wimbledon Telephone for directions. **e-mail:** lightrest@aol.com

⑨ San Lorenzo Worple Rd Mews, Wimbledon SW19
☎ 020 8946 8463 Reliable neighbourhood restaurant.

▮▮ Strada 91 High St SW19 5EG ☎ 020 8946 4363 Superior pizza from quality ingredients cooked in wood-fired ovens.

LONDON W1

⑧ Alastair Little Restaurant
European, International
Harmonious flavours and vibrant colours in Soho
☎ 020 7734 5183 49 Frith St W1V 5TE Plan 3-B2

MENU GUIDE Lobster & avocado cocktail • Grilled lamb, hummus, broad bean, mint & feta salad • Affogato al caffe

WINE GUIDE ♀ Paul Tutton Waipara West Sauvignon Blanc £28.50 • ♀ Château la Claymore Lussac St Emilion Bordeaux £31 • 40 bottles over £20, 3 bottles under £20 • 4 by the glass (£5.50-£6.50)

PRICE GUIDE Fixed L £29 • Fixed D £38 • coffee £2 • min/water £3.75 • Service optional • Group min 8 service 12.5%

PLACE: A little gem amidst the hustle and bustle of Soho, and easy to miss if you're not looking carefully as it has no sign. Inside it's simple and modern, with a warm atmosphere and friendly service.

FOOD: There is nothing complicated about the unassuming International cooking, and the result is a refreshing choice of original dishes and vibrant flavours, with quality seasonal produce as their mainstay. Feast on smoked eel, carrot and pea shoot salad with potato cakes, and buffalo ricotta ravioli.

OUR TIP: Great for formal or informal dining

Chef: Sue Lewis **Owners:** K Pedersen, M Andre-Vega **Times:** 12-3/6-11.30, Closed Xmas, BHs, Sun, closed L Sat **Notes:** Vegetarian available **Seats:** 42, Pr/dining room 25 **Smoking:** No pipes, No cigars, Air con **Children:** Portions **Directions:** Nearest station: Tottenham Court Rd Near Ronnie Scott's Jazz Club. **Parking:** Brewer St, Poland St

⑧ Alloro
Italian
A taste of Italy in the heart of Mayfair
☎ 020 7495 4768 20 Dover St W1S 4LU Plan 3-A1

MENU GUIDE Gragnano spaghetti, fresh lobster, garlic & sweet chilli sauce • Milanese veal cutlet • Fig, chocolate & almond cake

WINE GUIDE ♀ Terre da Vino Gavi £25 • ♀ Rosso di Montalcino Sangiovese £32 • 180 bottles over £20, 50 bottles under £20 12 by the glass (£4-£14)

PRICE GUIDE Fixed L fr £25 • Fixed D fr £31 • min/water £3 • Service added but optional 12.5%

PLACE: Glass-fronted restaurant in a quiet street off Piccadilly. The interior comprises a part tiled and wooden floor, red and cream leather chairs, comfy banquettes, and traditionally laid tables with linen and silver. Clever use of mirrors creates a sense of space.

FOOD: Modern Italian cooking, honest and unfussy with rustic presentation. Tender squid stuffed with pine nuts and served with a vibrant sauce and crisp bruschetta is a good example.

OUR TIP: An enclosed area can be reserved for private parties

Chef: Marzo Zacchi **Owners:** New A2 Holdings **Times:** 12-2.30/7-10.30, Closed Xmas, 4 days Etr & BH's, Sun, closed L Sat **Notes:** Vegetarian available, Dress Restrictions, No trainers **Seats:** 60, Pr/dining room 18 **Smoking:** No pipes, No cigars, Air con **Children:** Portions

⌘⌘⌘ Angela Hartnett at The Connaught *see below*

⌘⌘ Archipelago

International, Fusion

Eclectic food in exotic surroundings

☎ 020 7383 3346 110 Whitfield St W1T 5ED
Plan 3-B3

MENU GUIDE Blue potato & cassava soup • Cambodian kangaroo, Nepalese potatoes • Italian rhubarb Alaska, chocolate honeycomb

WINE GUIDE ♀ Alana Estate Sauvignon Blanc £27.50 • ♀ Wollombi Brook Shiraz £22.50 • 38 bottles over £20, 5 bottles under £20 • 4 by the glass (£5) *continued*

PRICE GUIDE Fixed L £15.50 • starter £6.50-£10.50 • main £13.50-£19.50 • dessert £6-£7 • coffee £2.50 • min/water £3.50 • Service added but optional 12.5%

PLACE: Just round the corner from Goodge Street tube but on a different continent judging by the eclectic food and ethnic decor. A gated entrance reveals an interior packed with Asian exotica. Subdued lighting and soothing fabrics put customers at their ease.

FOOD: Adventurous and informative the menu (a antique rolled map) may be but dishes of crocodile, salads of love bugs and gold plated passionfruit bavarois make as much of an impact as the striking setting. Flavours are vivid and there's plenty of less eccentric choices.

OUR TIP: Excellent vegetarian dishes

Chef: Daniel Creedon **Owners:** Bruce Alexander **Times:** 12-2.30/6-11, Closed Xmas, BHs, Sun, closed L Sat **Notes:** Vegetarian available **Seats:** 38 **Smoking:** N/Sm area, No pipes, No cigars, Air con **Directions:** Nearest station: Warren Street From underground south along Tottenham Court Rd. 1st right into Grafton Way. 1st left into Whitfield St. **Parking:** NCP, street

AA's Chefs' Chef is the annual poll of all the chefs included in The Restaurant Guide. Around 1800 of the country's top chefs are asked to vote to recognise the achievements of one of their peers. This year's winner is featured on page 19.

England

LONDON W1

⌘⌘⌘

Angela Hartnett at The Connaught

Mediterranean, European ⚑

Mayfair opulence meets contemporary cooking

☎ 020 7592 1222 Carlos Place W1K 2AL Plan 2-G1

MENU GUIDE Grilled tranche of foie gras, warm chausson of apple & dates • Venison loin, pear purée, roasted salsify, venison sauce • Mille-feuille of quince & vanilla

WINE GUIDE ♀ 2002 Valet Freres Auxey-Duresses Chardonnay £49 • ♀ Icardi Piemonte 2000 Barbera d'Asti £50 • 852 bottles over £20, 12 bottles under £20 • 14 by the glass (£5-£16)

PRICE GUIDE Fixed L £30-£55 • Fixed D £55 • coffee £5 • min/water £3.50 • Service added but optional 12.5%

PLACE: Although much has changed at this Mayfair institution in the past few years - the arrival of Gordon Ramsay's protégée Angela Hartnett, a change from traditional cooking to refined contemporary cuisine, and the accompanying refurbishment and renaming of the dining room to the Menu - the high points of the old restaurant's decor have been retained. Designer Nina Campbell has integrated the Connaught's grandeur and

classicism with a feeling of light, warmth and intimacy; it's magnificent, rich and swish all rolled into one. Wood panelling, simple blinds, bold modern oil paintings and classic napery give a nod to the modern cooking, while service is prompt and well-informed. The wine list is a tome, Italian led, while an elegant terrace provides the opportunity for alfresco dining.

FOOD: Hartnett's Ramsay-influenced cooking is refined, well thought out and delivers much more wow than the average hotel restaurant. She draws on her Italian background as well as British and modern European influences to create winning combinations, presented without clutter on the plate. Strong technique, bold flavours, a reliance on quality produce and simplicity, and clear pricing all have their place.

OUR TIP: There is a chef's table located by the heart of the kitchen

Chef: Angela Hartnett **Owners:** Gordon Ramsay Holdings Ltd **Times:** 12-3/5.45-11 **Notes:** Fixed D 6 courses £70, Vegetarian available, Dress Restrictions, No jeans or trainers. Smart, jacket preferred **Seats:** 70, Pr/dining room 22 **Smoking:** N/Sm in restaurant, Air con **Children:** Menu, Portions **Rooms:** 92 (92 en suite) ★★★★★ **Directions:** Nearest station: Bond Street & Green Park. Telephone for directions **Parking:** Adams Row **e-mail:** reservations@angelahartnett.com **web:** www.angelahartnett.com

England

LONDON W1 continued

⊚ Athenaeum Hotel, Bullochs at 116

British, Mediterranean

Comtemporary dining in Mayfair

☎ 020 7499 3464 116 Piccadilly W1J 7BJ Plan 4-H5

MENU GUIDE Lobster & crab bisque • Braised shank of lamb, dauphinoise potatoes, rosemary jus • Sticky toffee pudding, clotted cream

WINE GUIDE ♀ Fumeés Blanches Sauvignon Blanc £20 • ♥ Cazalets Merlot £18 • 78 bottles over £20, 12 bottles under £20 • 8 by the glass (£6-£13)

PRICE GUIDE Fixed L £15 • Fixed D £21 • starter £8.50 • main £22.50 • dessert £7.50 • coffee £4.25 • min/water £4

PLACE: Heavy African fabrics and tiled floors set the scene at this eaterie, which has an informal brasserie atmosphere despite its Mayfair address. Slick service.

FOOD: An eclectic range of dishes based around British produce, with inspiration drawn from France and Italy as well as further afield. Mains are straightforward in style: Dover sole with béarnaise perhaps, or corn-fed chicken with roast baby onions and a light vanilla sauce.

OUR TIP: The hotel's bar has one of the largest selections of malts in London

Chef: David Marshall **Owners:** Ralph Trustees Ltd **Times:** 12.30-2.30/5.30-10.30, Closed L Sat & Sun **Notes:** Vegetarian available, Civ Wed 55 **Seats:** 46, Pr/dining room 44 **Smoking:** N/Sm in restaurant, Air con **Children:** Menu, Portions **Rooms:** 157 (157 en suite) ★★★★★ **Directions:** Nearest station: Hyde Park Corner, Green Park Telephone for directions **Parking:** Close car park **e-mail:** info@athenaeumhotel.com **web:** www.athenaeumhotel.com

⊚ Atlantic Bar & Grill

Modern British

Sophisticated venue with lively atmosphere & style

☎ 020 7734 4888 20 Glasshouse St W1R 5RQ Plan 3-B1

MENU GUIDE Crispy duck salad • Steamed chilli mussels, mash beer

WINE GUIDE ♀ Sprecogna Pinot Grigio £34 • ♥ Bodegas Urbina Rioja Tempranillo £25 • 132 bottles over £20, 8 bottles under £20 • 9 by the glass (£3.50-£6.75)

PRICE GUIDE Fixed D £14.50-£32 • starter £6-£23 • main £8-£22 • dessert fr £7.50 • coffee £2.20 • min/water £3 • Service added but optional 12.5%

PLACE: With the looks of an ocean liner in its vast spaces, lofty ceiling and huge bar in the middle of the floor, this place still feels glamorous. Lounge lizards hog the cocktail bar, and the separate restaurant is more formal than you might expect given the general joie de vivre.

FOOD: The brasserie-style menu reads well, with a modern choice ranging through carpaccio of octopus and pan-fried calves' liver.

OUR TIP: Sit in one of the open booths

Chef: Ben O'Donaghue **Owners:** Oliver Peyton **Times:** 12-3/6-12, Closed 25 Dec, New Year, BHs, Sun, closed L Sat **Notes:** Smart casual **Seats:** 200, Pr/dining room 70 **Smoking:** Air con **Directions:** Nearest station: Piccadilly Circus. Travelling S on Regent St, take left on Brewer St and first right onto Glasshouse St. **Parking:** Brewer St NCP **e-mail:** resception@atlantic-bar.com **web:** www.atlanticbarandgrill.com

⊚ Bam-Bou

French, Vietnamese

Lively restaurant inspired by Indochina

☎ 020 7323 9130 1 Percy St W1T 1DB Plan 3-B3

MENU GUIDE Fragrant chicken salad, sapu leaf, chilli & mint • Seared scallops, lacquered pork & choi shoots • Chocolate hazelnut sponge

WINE GUIDE ♀ J et F Lurton Sauvignon Blanc £17.50 • ♥ Margaret River W Australia Shiraz £25.75 • 45 bottles over £20, 13 bottles under £20 • 12 by the glass (£3.75-£8)

PRICE GUIDE Fixed L £12.50 • starter £3.75-£8.50 • main £9.75-£14.50 • dessert £3.75-£5.75 • coffee £1.95 • min/water £3.50 • Service added but optional 12.5%

PLACE: A discreet South East Asian restaurant complete with authentic artefacts, dark polished floor boards, candlelight and jazzy music, housed in a Georgian townhouse off Tottenham Court Road. The restaurant occupies two floors, accessed by the original spiral staircase, in what was once a retreat for Ezra Pound's art movement.

FOOD: A vibrant menu drawing on Thai, Vietnamese and Chinese cuisines with a pervading Western influence, bursting with fresh flavours and colours.

OUR TIP: Leave time to savour and enjoy the food

Chef: Gary Lee **Owners:** Signature Restaurants **Times:** 12-3/6-11, Closed 25-26 Dec, BH Mon's, Sun, closed L Sat **Notes:** Vegetarian available, Samrt casual **Seats:** 80, Pr/dining room 20 **Smoking:** No pipes, No cigars, Air con **Children:** Portions **Directions:** Nearest station: Tottenham Court Road One minute from Oxford Street **Parking:** Street parking **e-mail:** sthompson@bam-bou.co.uk **web:** www.bam-bou.co.uk

⊚ Bellamy's

French   **NEW**

Atmospheric French brasserie

☎ 020 7491 2727 18-18a Bruton Place W1J 6LY Plan 2-H2

MENU GUIDE Smoked Scottish salmon • Lamb cutlets, pommes boulangère • Tarte au citron

WINE GUIDE ♀ Berangere Chablis £23 • ♥ G Mouton Givry £28 • 42 bottles over £20, 4 bottles under £20 • 13 by the glass (£4.75-£18.50)

PRICE GUIDE Fixed D £25 • starter £6.50-£16 • main £14.50-£26 • dessert £6.50 • coffee £3.50 • min/water £3.50 • Service added but optional 12.5%

PLACE: Classic French brasserie located in a quiet London mews Art deco posters adorn yellow walls, and a noisy bustle rises from the close-set candlelit tables, which are worked by friendly and knowledgeable staff.

FOOD: Good quality, brasserie style French cooking. Begin with a dish of oysters perhaps, before moving on to sole with lemon oil, sautéed quail with haricots verts, or veal forestière.

OUR TIP: Stock up at the restaurant deli on the way out

Chef: Stephane Pacoud **Times:** 12-3/7-10.30, Closed BHs, 2 wks Aug, Sun, closed L Sat **Seats:** 70 **Smoking:** No pipes, Air con **Children:** Portions **Directions:** Nearest station: Green Park/Bond St Off Berkeley Sq, parallel with Bruton St **Parking:** On street, NCP **e-mail:** gavin@bellamysrestaurant.co.uk

The AA Wine Awards recognise the finest wine lists in England, Scotland and Wales. For full details, see pages 14-15

England

Benares

Indian

Fine dining Indian with top-notch cooking

☎ 020 7629 8886 12 Berkeley Square W1J 6BS
Plan 2-H1

MENU GUIDE Aloo tikki (potato cakes) • Nawabi Nalli Gosht (lamb shank speciality) • Gajjar Ka Halwa (ginger ice cream)

WINE GUIDE ♀ Chablis Emil Petit £34 • ♀ Luis Carias Rioja Crianza £28 • 130 bottles over £20 • 10 by the glass (£5.50-£7.50)

PRICE GUIDE Fixed L £14.95 • Fixed D £34.50-£39.50 • starter £6.50-£11 • main £11.50-£24 • dessert £6.50 • coffee £3 • min/water £4.25 • Service added but optional 12.5%

PLACE: Discreetly located restaurant on Berkeley Square with striking interior design and a staircase leading to a stand alone bar. The large dining room has closely set tables with dark brown leather banquette seating, limestone flooring and water features.
FOOD: Inspired by the holy city of Benares, chef Atul Kochhar prepares food with influences from every part of India, with subtle spicing and authentic flavours - all of it halaal. There is a comprehensive carte with upmarket prices, a five-course gourmet tasting menu and set price lunch and pre-theatre menus.
OUR TIP: Three rooms are available for private dining
Chef: Atul Kochhar **Owners:** Atul Kochhar **Times:** 12-3/5.30-11, Closed Jan, 25-26 Dec, closed L Sat-Sun **Notes:** Tasting menu £59, Vegetarian available, Smart Dress **Seats:** 85, Pr/dining room 24 **Smoking:** N/Sm in restaurant, Air con **Directions:** Nearest station: Green Park E along Piccadilly towards Regent St. Turn left into Berkeley St and continue straight to Berkeley Square **e-mail:** gavin@benaresrestaurant.com **web:** www.benaresrestaurant.com

Bentley's

British, Seafood

Traditional seafood restaurant

☎ 020 7734 4756 11/15 Swallow St W1B 4DG
Plan 3-B1

MENU GUIDE Crab risotto • Grilled Dover sole, meunière sauce • Chocolate fondant, chocolate ice cream, blood orange syrup

WINE GUIDE ♀ Blanchots Bois d'Yver Chablis Grand Cru Chardonnay £60 • ♀ Clos Rosseau Santenay 1er Cru Pinot Noir £54 • 84 bottles over £20, 4 bottles under £20 • 7 by the glass (£4.95-£6.20)

PRICE GUIDE Starter £7.50-£18.50 • main £12.50-£43 • dessert £8 • coffee £2.95 • min/water £4 • Service added but optional 12.5%

PLACE: There's a timeless air to this Piccadilly grandee as if it's barely changed since its opening early last century. Dark wood, comfy booths and oil paintings comprise the clubby decor at the downstairs oyster bar while upstairs there's an intimate dining room.
FOOD: Seafood is the draw here, though carnivores aren't neglected. Expect quality ingredients and classical simplicity from a kitchen that delivers a menu to match the setting.
OUR TIP: A lunchtime favourite
Chef: Kenny Warren **Owners:** Peter Batkin **Times:** 12, Closed 24-26 Dec, 1 Jan **Notes:** Vegetarian available **Seats:** 90, Pr/dining room 14 **Smoking:** No pipes, Air con **Children:** Portions **Directions:** Nearest station: Piccadilly Circus 2nd turning right after Piccadilly Circus **Parking:** 10 yds away **e-mail:** bentleyswest1@yahoo.co.uk

The Berkeley Square

see page 310

Blandford Street

British, European

Simple modern cooking in style

☎ 020 7486 9696 5-7 Blandford St, Marylebone W1U 3DB Plan 2-G3

MENU GUIDE Foie gras, toast, fig compote • Venison, bacon & venison faggot, red cabbage, red wine gravy • Valrhona chocolate mousse

WINE GUIDE ♀ Rossendale Sauvignon Blanc £28 • ♀ Château Lezongars Merlot/Cab Sauvignon £26 • 127 bottles over £20, 13 bottles under £20 • 8 by the glass (£4-£7.50)

PRICE GUIDE Fixed L £15 • starter £4.95-£12 • main £10-£24 • dessert £6-£8 • coffee £2 • min/water £3.25 • Service added but optional 12.5%

PLACE: On the brink of a major refurbishment, this sophisticated restaurant occupies an unassuming location just off swanky Marylebone High Street, and more than holds its own with the area's many eateries.
FOOD: The Blandford delivers simple yet imaginative cooking, notable for flavour and the freshest of ingredients. Seafood is a speciality, but doesn't dominate the modern European menu; so if you don't fancy the catch of the day, you might tuck into Scottish rib-eye with a gratin of Swiss chard, or chicken with parsley, garlic and poached leeks. Impressive wines.
OUR TIP: The Blandford Street mixed grill of fish with chips and tartare sauce
Chef: Martin Moore **Owners:** Nicholas & Emmaline Lambert **Times:** 12-3/6.30-11, Closed Xmas, New Year, Easter, BHs, closed L Mon, Sat, closed D Sun **Notes:** Vegetarian available **Seats:** 55, Pr/dining room 18 **Smoking:** N/Sm area, No pipes, Air con **Children:** Portions **Directions:** Nearest station: Bond Street Turn right out of Oxford St exit, cross road and down Marylebone Ln to Marylebone High St. Onto Blandford St, restaurant on left **Parking:** NCP: Weymouth Street **e-mail:** info@blandford-street.co.uk **web:** www.blandford-street.co.uk

continued

LONDON W1

The Berkeley Square

Modern, French

Mayfair fine dining without the pomp

☎ 020 7629 6993 7 Davies St, Berkeley Square
W1K 3DD Plan 2-H1

MENU GUIDE Morel mushroom risotto, Roasted loin of lamb, braised shoulder, basil dressing • Assiette of banana

WINE GUIDE ♀ Domaine Michel Vire Clessé 2001 Chardonnay £31.50 • ♀ Domaine Villemajou 2001 Syrah/Grenache £34 • 169 bottles over £20, 6 bottles under £20 • 12 by the glass (£5-£10)

PRICE GUIDE Fixed L £17.95 • Fixed D £21.95 • coffee £2 • min/water £3.50 • Service added but optional 12.5%

PLACE: A Mayfair shop front, with a blue canopy and little front terrace for fair weather dining, marks out this intimate restaurant. The interior design follows a stylish modern vogue.
FOOD: Chef-patron Steven Black has a fine pedigree and this shines through in classy dishes of confident simplicity. High quality ingredients, a light touch and elegant presentation hit the mark. Expect the likes of pan-fried fillets of John Dory served with baby spinach, a tomato fondue and tapénade dressing. Mrs Black is the epitome of charm at front of house. Impressive wine list.
OUR TIP: Vegetarian, children's and gourmet menus
Chef: Steven Black **Owners:** Vince Power, Steven Black **Times:** 12-2.30/6-10, Closed Xmas, BHs, last 2wk Aug, Sun, Sat **Notes:** Set ALC 2-3 course £38.50-£45, Suprise Menu 7-course £49.50, Vegetarian available, Smart Dress **Seats:** 70, Pr/dining room 14 **Smoking:** N/Sm area, Air co
Children: Menu, Portions **Directions:** Nearest station: Bond Street, Green Park **Parking:** On street **e-mail:** info@berkeleysquarecafe.com
web: www.berkeleysquarecafe.com

LONDON W1 *continued*

Brian Turner Mayfair

British

Back to basics British cooking in upmarket hotel

☎ 020 7596 3444 Millennium Hotel, 44 Grosvenor Square, Mayfair W1A 3AN Plan 2-G1

MENU GUIDE Beef sirloin, rocket, horseradish • Pork belly, cider gravy, celeriac & apple gratin • Victoria plum Bakewell, clotted cream

WINE GUIDE ♀ Springfield Estate Sauvignon Blanc £25 • ♀ Wynns Gonawarra Estate Shiraz £25 • 90 bottles over £20 • 12 by the glass (£5-£6.50)

PRICE GUIDE Fixed L £22.50 • starter £7.95-£9.50 • main £14-£28 • Service added

PLACE: One of several eateries in this swanky Mayfair hotel, Brian Turner's restaurant is an understated, contemporary affair decked out in fashionably neutral colours and natural materials.
FOOD: Brian Turner's stock in trade is traditional British comfort food which makes it mark on this menu. Bangers and mash, posh roasts and pie all make an appearance, alongside lighter fare such as Dover sole with lemon hollandaise. Save room for the nursery puds.
OUR TIP: Try a cocktail in the funky Turner's Bar
Chef: Brian Turner & Paul Bates **Owners:** Millennium Hotels
Times: 12.30-2.30/6-10.30, Closed BHs, Sun, closed L Sat
Notes: Vegetarian available, Smart Dress, Civ Wed 100 **Seats:** 86, Pr/dining room 50 **Smoking:** N/Sm area, Air con **Children:** Portions
Rooms: 348 (348 en suite) ★★★★ **Parking:** NCP next door
e-mail: annie.mckale@mill-cop.com
web: www.brianturneronline.co.uk

Butlers

British, International   **NEW**

Traditional dining in elegant Mayfair retreat

☎ 020 7491 2622 Chesterfield Mayfair Hotel, 35 Charles St, Mayfair W1J 5EB Plan 4-H6

MENU GUIDE Roast Portobello mushrooms • Truffled guinea fowl, red wine sauce • Butterscotch cheesecake

WINE GUIDE ♀ Bouchard Finlayson Walker Bay Sauvignon Blanc £28 • ♀ Bouchard Finlayson Gaplin Peak Pinot Noir £35 • 63 bottles over £20, 8 bottles under £20 • 11 by the glass (£4.50-£9.50)

PRICE GUIDE Fixed L £12.50-£19.95 • Fixed D £24.95 • starter £6-£14.50 • main £12.95-£27 • dessert £5.95 • coffee £3.75 • min/water £4.95 • Service added but optional 12.5%

PLACE: This elegant city hotel in the middle of Mayfair is richly and stylishly equipped and decorated. Attentive, friendly service

continue

England

is the highlight of any stay here. There's a choice of The Conservatory or the main traditional dining rooms with elegant red and gold decor with the hint of an African theme.

FOOD: This modern British menu offers a good range of dishes based on fine quality ingredients. There's still a traditional flavour to dining here with carving, salmon and wine trollies, and excellent service making a lasting impression.

OUR TIP: Good value, short lunch and pre-dinner menus
Chef: Stephen Henderson **Owners:** Red Carnation Hotels **Times:** 12-5.30/5.30-10.30 **Notes:** Sun roast £12.50, Vegetarian available, Smart Dress, Civ Wed 120 **Seats:** 85, Pr/dining room 100 **Smoking:** N/Sm area, No pipes, Air con **Children:** Menu, Portions **Rooms:** 110 (110 en suite) ★★★★ **Directions:** Nearest station: Green Park. From N side exit of Green Park tube station turn left and then first left into Berkeley St. Continue down to Berkeley Square and then left heading towards Charles St. **Parking:** NCP-5 minutes
e-mail: fandbch@rchmail.com
web: www.redcarnationhotels.com

Camerino

Italian

Buzzy Italian West End restaurant
☎ 020 7637 9900 16 Percy St W1T 1DT
Plan 3-B3

MENU GUIDE Goats' cheese & aubergine mousse • Baked sea bream, fennel gratin • Thin apple tart, vanilla ice cream

PRICE GUIDE Fixed L £17.50 • Fixed D £27.50 • coffee £2.50 • min/water £3 • Service added but optional 12.5%

PLACE: This smartly presented restaurant is down a side street, off Tottenham Court Road. The newly decorated interior is light and airy with wooden floors and cream and red walls. Candlelit tables with white tablecloths add to the cosy atmosphere. Friendly service.

FOOD: Good quality, simple Italian regional dishes with high quality ingredients. Expect pan-fried sardines, sea bass with artichoke as well as an excellent rabbit tortelli with asparagus and rosemary.

OUR TIP: Booking ahead is advised
Chef: Valerio Daros **Owners:** Paolo Boschi **Times:** 12-3.30/6-11.30, closed 1 wk Xmas, 1st Jan, Etr Day, most BHs, Sun, closed L Sat **Notes:** Vegetarian available, Dress Restrictions, Smart casual preferred **Seats:** 70 **Smoking:** No pipes, No cigars, Air con **Directions:** Nearest station: Tottenham Court Rd, Goodge St Telephone for directions **Parking:** Goodge St **e-mail:** info@camerinorestaurant.com **web:** www.camerinorestaurant.com

 denotes a restaurant with a particularly good wine list.

Cecconi's

Italian

Classy, popular Mayfair Italian
☎ 020 7434 1500 & 0171 434 1500 5a Burlington Gardens W1X 1LE Plan 3-A1

MENU GUIDE Chestnut tagliatelle, wild mushrooms • Braised neck of lamb, rosemary & Savoy cabbage • Lemon tart, lemon sorbet, mascarpone cream

PRICE GUIDE Food prices not confirmed for 2006. Please telephone for details

PLACE: This glass-fronted restaurant and bar looks out on to the back of the Royal Academy and sits nicely with its chic neighbours. Dark wood, glass, plain walls and striking artwork provide the backdrop for a stylish, contemporary interior, with burgundy leather chairs and elegant table settings providing the comforts. Service is attentive and professional but unstuffy. The atmosphere is buzzy and vibrant, driven by the popular bar up front.

FOOD: The well-presented Italian regional cooking uses authentic quality ingredients, with menus changing daily and providing a good balance between classic and more contemporary ideas.
OUR TIP: Excellent Italian wines and superb bread selection
Times: 12-3/6.30-11, Closed Xmas, New Year, closed L Sun
Directions: Nearest station: Piccadilly Circus, Oxford Circus. Burlington Gdns between New Bond St and Savile Row **web:** www.cecconis.co.uk

Cipriani

Italian   NEW

A dazzling piece of Venice in London
☎ 020 7399 0500 25 Davies St W1K 3DQ
Plan 2-H2

MENU GUIDE Risotto with seppe al Nero • Veal chop, butter & sage with mixed vegetables • Coffee cake

PRICE GUIDE Food prices not confirmed for 2006. Please telephone for details

PLACE: This is the well-known Arrigo Cipriani's first venture out of Venice and has been an instant hit with the glitterati. The glass-fronted fashionable exterior leads to a large airy room where art deco style is married with beautiful Murano chandeliers shipped in from Venice. Service is extremely slick, attentive and well-supervised.

FOOD: Classic, accurate, simple Italian food is created with lots of Cipriani touches (he founded the carpaccio, and pioneered risotto, Fegato all Veneziana and Bellini.) Chef is a long standing Cipriani protégée and prepares unfaltering Italian food that is fairly unique in London.

OUR TIP: The famed Cipriani pastries on the menu for afternoon tea
Times: 12-3/6-11.45 **e-mail:** cipriani.london@cipriani.com
web: www.cipriani.com

Cocoon

Asian   NEW

Funky pan-Asian restaurant
☎ 020 7494 7600 65 Regents St W1B 4EA Plan 3-B1

MENU GUIDE King prawn & minced pork in pastry • Sautéed red snapper with aubergines & spring onion • Fruit sorbet

PRICE GUIDE Food prices not confirmed for 2006. Please telephone for details

continued

England

LONDON W1 *continued*

PLACE: Once you have found its discreet entrance, climb a spiral staircase to this first floor restaurant with its six separate dining areas, each one bordered by opaque ceiling to floor curtains. Staff are young, friendly and dressed in black.
FOOD: Pan-Asian in style, the cooking has a strong Japanese, Chinese and Thai flavour, with sushi, sashimi, dim sum and numerous soups.
OUR TIP: Ideal place to share dishes
Times: 12-3.30/5.30-1am
e-mail: reservations@cocoon-restaurants.com
web: www.cocoon-restaurants.com

Crescent Restaurant at Montcalm Nikko Hotel

British, European
Modern cooking in classical surroundings
☎ 020 7402 4288 Great Cumberland Place W1A 2LF
Plan 2-F2

MENU GUIDE Scallops, black pudding, mushy peas, pancetta • Beef fillet, wild mushroom & black truffle ragout • Chocolate truffle tart, orange coulis
WINE GUIDE ♀ Don Christo Bag Chardonnay £20 • ♀ Casa Silva Dona Dominga Cabernet Sauvignon/Merlot £20 23 bottles over £20, 8 bottles under £20 • 23 by the glass (£3.90-£7.80)
PRICE GUIDE Fixed L £20 • Fixed D £27.50 • coffee £3.50 • min/water £3.50
PLACE: Occupying an attractive Georgian crescent close to Marble Arch, the hotel takes its name from the Marquis de Montcalm, an 18th-century general. The relaxed, club-like Crescent Restaurant has luxurious swags and tall windows, and the large English country-garden mural promotes a calm atmosphere at this popular hotel restaurant.
FOOD: The set-price menu of modern British cooking with European influences offers good value for money and the kitchen places a strong emphasis on quality ingredients.
OUR TIP: Wine included with dinner
Chef: Tristan Kenworthy **Owners:** Nikko Hotels(UK) Ltd **Times:** 12.30-2.30/6.30-10.30, Closed L Sat & Sun **Notes:** Vegetarian available, Dress Restrictions, Smart casual **Seats:** 70, Pr/dining room 60 **Smoking:** N/Sm area, No pipes, No cigars, Air con **Children:** Menu, Portions
Rooms: 120 (120 en suite) ★★★★ **Directions:** Nearest station: Marble Arch Telephone for directions **Parking:** NCP, Great Cumberland Place **e-mail:** montcalm@montcalm.co.uk
web: www.montcalm.co.uk

Criterion Grill

Classical French
London's only neo-Byzantine restaurant
☎ 020 7930 0488 224 Piccadilly W1J 9HP Plan 3-B1

MENU GUIDE Parfait of foie gras maison • Slow roast duck, sage & onion, apple sauce • Sticky toffee pudding, vanilla ice cream
WINE GUIDE ♀ Les Templiers Chardonnay £15 • ♀ Les Templiers Grenache/Merlot £15 • 84 bottles over £20, 5 bottles under £20 • 11 by the glass (£4-£7.50)
PRICE GUIDE Fixed L £14.95 • Fixed D fr £19.95 • starter £7.50-£18.50 • main £10.50-£22.50 • dessert fr £7.50 • coffee £2.50 • min/water £3.50 • Service added but optional 12.5%
PLACE: A breathtaking building outside and in, with a canopied entrance, marbled floor, pillared Byzantine arches and shimmering gold ceiling mosaics. Predominantly French waiters provide professional and unobtrusive service.
FOOD: A mix of French brasserie and classical British, with the likes of jambon de Bayonne, parfait of foie gras and crottin de chevre. On the British side, shrimp cocktail, Welsh rarebit and devilled whitebait take you right back.
OUR TIP: Popular pre- and post-theatre dinners
Chef: Roger Pizey **Owners:** Marco Pierre White & Jimmy Lahoud
Times: 12-2.30/5.30-11, Closed 24-26 Dec, Sun **Notes:** Vegetarian by request only **Seats:** 150 **Smoking:** No pipes, Air con
Children: Portions **Directions:** Nearest station: Piccadilly Circus Telephone for directions **Parking:** Chinatown NCP
e-mail: sales@whitestarline.org.uk **web:** www.whitestarline.org.uk

Embassy London

Modern European
Sophisticated Mayfair dining club
☎ 020 7851 0956 29 Old Burlington St W1S 3AN
Plan 3-A1
MENU GUIDE Cornish crab, gazpacho sauce • Calves' liver, Alsace bacon • Rhubarb financier
WINE GUIDE ♀ Angelo Rocca & Figli Pinot Grigio £23.50 • ♀ Maule Valley Tierra Alta Merlot £23.50 • 70 bottles over £20, 5 bottles under £20 • 7 by the glass (£4.50-£6.75)
PRICE GUIDE Fixed L £16.95 • Fixed D £19.95-£35 • starter £5.50-£16.50 • main £14.25-£26.50 • dessert £7.50 • coffee £2.50 • min/water £4.50 • Service added but optional 12.5%
PLACE: This stylish Mayfair brasserie occupies three levels set behind a glass frontage in the heart of the West End. There's a terrace for alfresco dining, a main dining level flooded with daylight by floor to ceiling windows and bar/restaurant below. The decor is unremittingly modern with lots of beige suede covered furniture, dark wood surfaces and modern artwork on the wall. Formal service and friendly staff.

continue

OD: Modern European dishes populate an imaginative menu ith the occasional retro touch. Preparation is skilful and cooking curate. Expect delicious carpaccio of beef, wild rocket, poached g and truffle dressing or steamed hake with chorizo and clams.
UR TIP: Perfect for lunch after shopping in Bond Street
ef: Garry Hollihead & Mark Grogan **Owners:** Mark Fuller & Garry ollihead **Times:** 12-3/6-11.30, Closed 25-26 Dec, 1 Jan, Good Fri, Sun-n, closed L Sat **Notes:** Vegetarian available, Smart Dress **Seats:** 120 oking: No pipes, Air con **Directions:** Nearest station: Green Park, cadilly Circus Just off Burlington Gardens, running between Bond and gent St **Parking:** NCP **e-mail:** embassy@embassylondon.com eb: www.embassylondon.com

L'Escargot - The Ground Floor estaurant

ench

shionable and popular Soho veteran
020 7439 7474 48 Greek St W1D 4EF Plan 3-C2

ENU GUIDE Ham hock & foie gras terrine, sauce ibiche • Daube of Aberdeen Angus bourguignonne, potato & rnip gratin • Lemon tart
INE GUIDE Jean-Marc Brocard Chablis £28.50 • Conde Valdemar Rioja £24.50 • 400 bottles over £20, 20 bottles nder £20 • 6 by the glass (£4-£7.95)
ICE GUIDE Fixed L £14.95 • Fixed D £17.95 • starter .50 • main £12.50-£14.95 • dessert £6.50 • coffee • min/water £3.50 • Service added but optional 12.5%
ACE: A Soho institution, L'Escargot brings a touch of class to stling Greek Street. Elegant and stylish art deco detailing and eathtaking modern art - including originals by Miro, Matisse, ckney and Warhol - catch the eye. Mirrors, wooden floors, rm colours and comfortable, sophisticated chairs and nquettes hit just the right note, while professional service and t jazz compliment a great atmosphere.
OD: The classy French cuisine comes full of delights - the carte inkled with old favourites like escargots bordelaise or omelette

continued

Arnold Bennett - and offers value given the quality ingredients, accomplished cooking and impressive finish.
OUR TIP: Lunch and pre-theatre menu are a bargain
Chef: Dominic Teague **Owners:** Jimmy Lahoud & Marco Pierre White **Times:** 12-2/6-11.30, Closed 25-26 Dec, 1 Jan, Sun, closed L Sat **Notes:** Vegetarian available, Smart casual **Seats:** 70, Pr/dining room 60 **Smoking:** No pipes, Air con **Children:** Portions **Directions:** Nearest station: Tottenham Court Rd, Leicester Square Telephone for directions **Parking:** NCP Chinatown, on street parking
e-mail: sales@whitestarline.org.uk
web: www.whitestarline.org.uk/LEscargot_Restaurant.htm

L'Escargot - The Picasso Room *see page 314*

Fino

Spanish

Fashionable tapas with an authentic range
020 7813 8010 33 Charlotte St W1T 1RR
Plan 3-B3
MENU GUIDE Crisp fried squid • Pa amb tomaquet/patatas bravas/marinated quail • White & dark chocolate shot
WINE GUIDE Pazo de Semorans Albarino £26 • Urbina Tempranillo £26 • 84 bottles over £20, 14 bottles under £20 8 by the glass (£4.75)
PRICE GUIDE Fixed L £14-£28 • Fixed D £17.95-£28 • starter £1.80-£15.50 • main £7.20-£15 • dessert £3.50-£11.50 • coffee £2 • min/water £4 • Service added but optional 12.5%

PLACE: Upmarket Spanish tapas restaurant and bar just off Charlotte Street that draws a fashionable crowd with its authentic food and contemporary blond wood and leather decor. A long eating bar with views of the kitchen runs along one wall for solo diners or those in a hurry.
FOOD: Fino is so committed to quality ingredients that its menus are printed twice daily to allow the chefs to introduce seasonal specials at the last moment. This is tapas at its most rustic, so make the most of the friendly Spanish staff who are knowledgeable and happy to help.
OUR TIP: Great for groups
Chef: Jean Phillipe Patruno **Owners:** Sam & Eddie Hart **Times:** 12-2.30/6-10.30, Closed Xmas & BH, Sun, closed L Sat **Notes:** Vegetarian available **Seats:** 80 **Smoking:** N/Sm area, No pipes, No cigars, Air con **Directions:** Nearest station: Goodge St/Tottenham Court Rd Entrance on Rathbone St **e-mail:** info@finorestaurant.com
web: www.finorestaurant.com

Floridita   NEW

Spanish/Cuban

Cuban inspired restaurant, bar and club
020 7314 4000 Mezzo Building, 100 Wardour St W1 Plan 3-B2
MENU GUIDE Stuffed piquillo peppers • Spice-blackened red snapper, fresh tomato, capers • Chilled vanilla rice pudding
PRICE GUIDE Food prices not confirmed for 2006. Please telephone for details

PLACE: Located in the basement of Mezzo, this cavernous restaurant is entered via a sweeping spiral staircase from above. The restaurant is furnished with an eclectic range of coloured seats and tables. There is live Cuban music every evening.

continued on page 315

England

LONDON W1

L'Escargot – The Picasso Room

French
Accomplished French cuisine in intimate dining room above L'Escargot
☎ 020 7439 7474 48 Greek St W1D 4EF Plan 3-C2
e-mail: sales@whitestarline.org.uk
web: www.whitestarline.org.uk

PLACE: Take the short flight of stairs from the buzz of the Ground Floor (see above) to the Picasso Room upstairs and you enter another world. Understandably popular, it has an instant feeling of comfort and quality, the understated elegance of the small dining room reflected in its name, with limited-edition Picasso sketches and original plates gracing its walls alongside a serious attitude to dining. Service is formal but discreet and relaxed, and an extensive wine list, dominated by the main French regions, echoes the quality of the food.

FOOD: The cooking style needs little introduction; pure French, classic and exact, with real emphasis placed on high quality produce, simply and skilfully prepared with carefully chosen flavours that let the main ingredient shine. Each mouthful on the fixed-price menus should be savoured, a superb dish of roast saddle of Balmoral venison comes with a simple accompaniment of creamed Savoy cabbage and jus of bitter chocolate that enhances rather than overpowers. The flawless culinary skills extend to the impressive selection of ancillaries; amuse-bouche (perhaps a stunning langoustine bisque), breads, pre-dessert and petits fours.

MENU GUIDE Dorset crab lasagne, wild mushroom velouté • Fillet of Aberdeen Angus, bouillon of young vegetables, sauce remoulade • Coconut crème brûlée

WINE GUIDE ♀ Jean-Marc Brocard Chablis £28.50 • ♟ Conde de Valdemar Rioja £24.50 • 400 bottles over £20, 20 bottles under £20 • 6 by the glass (£4-£7.95)

PRICE GUIDE Fixed L £19.50 • Fixed D £42 • coffee £4 • min/water £3.50 • Service added but optional 15%

OUR TIP: Ideal for romantic dinners

Chef: Jeff Galvin **Owners:** Jimmy Lahoud & Marco Pierre White
Times: 12-2/6-11, Closed 2 wks from 24 Dec & Aug, Sun-Mon, closed L Sat **Notes:** ALC 3 courses £42, Vegetarian available, Smart casual **Seats:** 30 **Smoking:** No pipes, Air con
Children: Min 8 yrs **Directions:** Nearest station: Tottenham Court Rd, Leicester Square Telephone for directions
Parking: NCP or street parking

LONDON W1 *continued*

FOOD: With influences from Spain and Latin America, Cuban cooking style even extends to using some Cuban and Argentinian ingredients.
OUR TIP: Try the famous cocktails
Chef: Andy Rose **Owners:** Sir Terrance Conran **Times:** 5.30-2am
e-mail: messzoreservations@conran-restaurants.co.uk
web: www.floridita.com

Four Seasons Hotel London
International

eclectic modern cooking in sophisticated Mayfair
☎ 020 7499 0888 Hamilton Place, Park Ln W1A 1AZ
Plan 4-G5
MENU GUIDE Curried duck hotpot, crispy dumplings • Loin of Welsh lamb with goats' cheese • Bitter sweet chocolate fondant, poached pear
WINE GUIDE ♀ Huid Vineyards Sauvignon Blanc £36 • ♀ The Footbolt d'Arenberg Shiraz £34 • all bottles over £20 • 14 by the glass (£6.60-£12)
PRICE GUIDE Fixed L £28 • Fixed D £35 • starter £9-£19 • main £22-£35 • dessert £9 • coffee £4.40 • min/water £3.50 • Service included
PLACE: A pianist playing in the nearby bar and floor-to-ceiling shelves filled with beautiful glassware add to the style of this well-known restaurant. Rich dark wood and individual spotlights create an atmosphere that sublimely suits the restaurant's upmarket clientele.

continued

FOOD: Asian influences reflect the Head Chef's long experience in the Far East, but overall the menu mixes cosmopolitan dishes with traditional British favourites. Notable wine list.
OUR TIP: Excellent afternoon tea
Chef: Bernhard Mayer **Owners:** Four Seasons Hotels & Resorts
Times: 12-3/6-11 **Notes:** Sun L £36 incl 1/2 bottle wine, Vegetarian available, Civ Wed 300 **Seats:** 90, Pr/dining room 300 **Smoking:** N/Sm area, No pipes, Air con **Children:** Menu, Portions **Rooms:** 220 (220 en suite) ★★★★★ **Directions:** Nearest station: Green Park/Hyde Park Corner Hamilton Place, just off Hyde Park corner end of Park Lane
Parking: 50 **e-mail:** fsh.london@fourseasons.com
web: www.fourseasons.com

 Le Gavroche Restaurant

see below

 Gordon Ramsay at Claridge's *see page 316*

 Greenhouse Restaurant

see page 316

The AA Wine Awards recognise the finest wine lists in England, Scotland and Wales. For full details, see pages 14-15

LONDON W1

Le Gavroche Restaurant

French

bastion of French tradition
☎ 020 7408 0881 & 7499 1826 43 Upper Brook St W1K 7QR Plan 2-G1
MENU GUIDE Soufflé Suissesse (cheese soufflé, double cream) • Roast rabbit saddle, crispy potatoes, parmesan • Omelette Rothschild (apricot & cointreau soufflé)
WINE GUIDE ♀ Domaine Gavoty Raule of Vermentino '30 • ♀ Château Vieux Sarpe Cabernet Sauvignon £55 • 2000 bottles over £20, 20 bottles under £20 • 4 by the glass (£4-£7)
PRICE GUIDE Fixed L £44 • starter £19.90-£43 • main £26.90-£42.60 • dessert £12.80-£30.20 • coffee £6.40 • min/water £4 • Service added but optional 12.5%
PLACE: The warm, cosseting opulence of this famous and unique Mayfair basement restaurant - with its rich green fabrics and polished bamboo trim, tables set with crisp linen, lavish crystal and silver, and immaculate, professional French service - has seen many a fashion go and come. The Roux brothers' first British venture, Le Gavroche may be almost 40 years old, but its

packed tables at any time of the week testify to its enduring appeal and popularity. So, just sit back and enjoy a truly faithful, classical French dining experience.
FOOD: Michel Roux Jr's superb, skilful, classic French cuisine, much like the decor, doesn't stint on the treats, with abundant luxury ingredients (lobster mousse with caviar and champagne butter sauce to start, for instance) dotting the repertoire of fixed-price lunch, tasting Menu Exceptionnel and the lengthy carte (where a minimum price of £60 per person applies). The patriotic, finely tuned, French-dominated wine list fits the bill perfectly, with some serious, heavyweight options.
OUR TIP: Excellent value lunch menu includes water and wine
Chef: Michel Roux Jr **Owners:** Le Gavroche Ltd **Times:** 12-2/6.30-11.00, Closed Xmas, New Year, BHs, Sun, closed L Sat **Notes:** Tasting Menu £86 (7 courses), Vegetarian available, Dress Restrictions, Jacket required. No jeans **Seats:** 60 **Smoking:** N/Sm in restaurant, Air con
Children: Portions **Directions:** Nearest station: Marble Arch From Park Lane into Upper Brook St, restaurant on right **Parking:** NCP - Park Lane
e-mail: bookings@le-gavroche.com
web: www.le-gavroche.co.uk, www.michelroux.co.uk

England

LONDON W1

Gordon Ramsay at Claridge's

British, European

Elegant dining and gastronomic flair

☎ 020 7499 0099 Brook St W1A 2JQ Plan 2-H2

MENU GUIDE Quail breasts, creamed celeriac, wild mushroom & Madeira reduction • Sea bass, sautéed potatoes, truffled broccoli & chervil velouté • Assiette of apple three ways

WINE GUIDE ♀ Tuvaoes Vermentino di Sardegna 2003 Giovanni Cherchi £32 • ♀ Morgenster Lourens River Valley 2000 Stellenbosch £39 • 660 bottles over £20, 10 bottles under £20 • 14 by the glass (£5-£20)

PRICE GUIDE Fixed L £30-£60 • Fixed D £60 • coffee £5 min/water £3.50 • Service optional • Group min 8 service 12.5%

PLACE: The marriage between Gordon Ramsay and this iconic Mayfair hotel, has fast become one of London's most popular dining venues. The high-ceilinged room has been restored to its former art deco glory by designer and architect Thierry Despont, the elegant room exuding 1930's sophistication and joie de vivre, from its dramatic three-tiered light shades to its delicate etched glass. There's a small bar lounge area, while the smartly dressed tables with their silver cutlery are attended by equally well-attired, highly professional and friendly staff.

FOOD: Mark Sargeant's accomplished modern French cooking has a strong classical grounding, as you would expect from a kitchen under the guidance of Gordon Ramsay. There's plentiful use of luxury items too, like roast duck foie gras with sautéed hand-dived scallops, forced Dutch rhubarb and Sauternes sauce to start, with an emphasis on freshness. There's a pleasing simplicity to some dishes and nothing outshines the main ingredient on a fixed-price repertoire of menus that offer plenty of choice and also includes a six-course tasting option. A galaxy of stars shine out from the wine list.

OUR TIP: Book early and be prepared to accept an earlier or later time

Chef: Mark Sargeant **Owners:** Gordon Ramsay Holdings Ltd **Times:** 12 3/5.45-11 **Notes:** Vegetarian available, Dress Restrictions, Smart, jacket preferred, no jeans/trainers **Seats:** 100, Pr/dining room 60 **Smoking:** N/Sm in restaurant, Air con **Children:** Portions **Rooms:** 203 (203 en suite) ★★★★★ **Directions:** Nearest station: Bond St the corner of Brook & Davies St. **Parking:** On street **e-mail:** gordonramsay@claridges.co.uk **web:** www.gordonramsay.com

LONDON W1

Greenhouse Restaurant

French, International

Fine dining at a discreet Mayfair address

☎ 020 7499 3331 27a Hay's Mews W1J 5NY

Plan 4-H6

MENU GUIDE Almond gazpacho, smoked paprika shrimp & tomato sorbet • Roasted Perigord duck breast • Pannacotta

WINE GUIDE ♀ Dog Point Sauvignon Blanc £40 • ♀ Dog Point Pinot Noir £45 • 2000 bottles over £20, 1 bottle under £20 20 by the glass (£6-£20)

PRICE GUIDE Fixed L £28 • Fixed D £60 • starter £5 • main £8 coffee £5 • min/water £5 • Service added but optional 12.5%

PLACE: A tasteful refurbishment has left The Greenhouse with a new cutting-edge. The entrance is via a smartly furnished terraced garden with decking between tables and pot plants. Inside it's softly-lit and calm, with neutral woods and sandstone.

FOOD: Bjorn van der Horst sets standards high. Copious quantities of creativity from all areas of the kitchen are blended smoothly with the necessary technical excellence to produce an exciting array of dishes - green tea steamed diver scallops with pork dim sum and samphire.

OUR TIP: Check out the serious wine list

Chef: Bjorn van der Horst **Owners:** Marlon Abela Restaurant Corporation **Times:** 12-2.45/6.45-11, Closed 25-26 Dec, 1 Jan, BHs, Sun, L Sat **Notes:** Tasting menu 7 courses £75, Vegetarian menu **Seats:** 65, Pr/dining room 10 **Directions:** Nearest station: Green Park, Behind Dorchester Hot just off Hill St. **Parking:** NCP, Meters **e-mail:** reservations@greenhouserestaurant.co.uk **web:** www.greenhousestaurant.co.uk

ONDON W1 *continued*

 The Grill (Dorchester Hotel)

ritish

ew chef and changes ahead at this renowned estaurant

☎ 020 7629 8888 The Dorchester, Park Ln W1A 2HJ
an 4-G6

the time of going to press French-born Olivier Couillard was
pointed head chef at The Grill. (He was previously head chef at
Trompette.) After establishing his kitchen brigade, a new menu
ll be introduced in late summer 2005. Classic dishes will
main, such as roast Aberdeen Angus beef, Dover sole and
me of the grills. From July 2005 expect to see Couillard's
linary mark, with a shorter menu of well balanced, earthy
shes, focusing on the best of British produce.
ef: Olivier Couillaud **Owners:** Dorchester Group **Times:** 12.30-
0/6-11 **Notes:** Dress Restrictions, No jeans, Civ Wed 450 **Seats:** 81
oking: No pipes, No cigars, Air con **Children:** Menu, Portions
rections: Nearest station: Hyde Park Corner/Oxford St(On Park Ln,
erlooking Hyde Park) **Parking:** South Audley St
ail: thegrillroom@dorchesterhotel.com
eb: www.dorchesterhotel.com

 Hakkasan *see below*

Kai Mayfair

Chinese

Upmarket Chinese with deliciously described dishes

☎ 020 7493 8988 65 South Audley St W1K 2QU
Plan 4-G6

MENU GUIDE Crispy smoked chicken, pickled
vegetables • Steamed sea bass, ginger & spring onions
WINE GUIDE ♀ Domaine de Ricaud Semillon/Sauvignon
£23 • ♀ Allozo Reserva Tempranillo £33 • 85 bottles over
£20 • 7 by the glass (£4.90-£8.10)
PRICE GUIDE Fixed L £25-£100 • Fixed D £40-£100 • starter £7-
£12 • main £13-£98 • dessert £6.50-£8 • coffee
£3.50 • min/water £6 • Service added but optional 3.5%

continued

ONDON W1

Hakkasan

hinese

:otic Chinese dining in Central London

☎ 020 7927 7000 No 8 Hanway Place W1T 9DH
an 3-B3

IENU GUIDE Wild venison satay roll • Braised whole abalone
andan soufflé
INE GUIDE ♀ Domaine de Sarry Sancerre Brock
29 • ♀ Selvapiana Chianti Rufina San Giovese £29 • 250 bottles
ver £20 • 14 by the glass (£6-£15)
RICE GUIDE Fixed L £30-£50 • Fixed D £50-£100 • starter
5.50-£42 • main £9.50-£68 • dessert £6-£10.50 • coffee
2 • min/water £4.50 • Service added but optional 13%

ACE: The discreet alley entrance just opposite Centrepoint
esn't prepare you for the dramatic basement interior of this
ndy Cantonese restaurant accessed via a spiral staircase.
unning orchid displays greet you, and black lacquer and red
ligraphy is everywhere. Designer Christian Liagre has brought
e dragon back in to Chinese restaurant interiors. Delicate

Balinese latticework divides up seating areas of green slate and
blue glass. There's a heady whiff of incense in the delicately
conditioned air. Staff are knowledgeable after intensive menu
training.
FOOD: The lengthy menu is built on a Cantonese foundation but
other regions are also well represented. Steamed, baked, fried
and wok-cooked delicacies appear from remote kitchens. Even
simple dim sum dishes are carefully garnished. Roast mango
duck is cooked to perfection with moist flesh, while lemon
chicken is served with a sauce of zesty freshness and Mabo tofu
is comforting with chicken, shitake and preserved cabbage. The
tea selection is especially impressive.
OUR TIP: A dim sum lunch after shopping in Oxford Street
Chef: C Tong Chee Hwee **Owners:** Alan Yau **Times:** 12-2.45/6-12.30,
Closed 25 Dec, closed L 26 Dec, 1 Jan, closed D 24 Dec **Notes:** Groups
of 9+ req to eat set menu, Vegetarian available, Dress Restrictions, No
jeans, shorts, trainers or caps **Seats:** 225 **Smoking:** Air con
Directions: Nearest station: Tottenham Court Rd Nearest tube:
Tottenham Court Road. From station take exit 2, then 1st left, 1st right,
restaurant straight ahead **Parking:** 50 **e-mail:** mail@hakkasan.com

England

England

LONDON W1 *continued*

PLACE: Comfortably opulent restaurant with rich dark reds, muted golds and silvers, and oriental accents to reflect the style of cooking. Staff are dressed in military-style cropped jackets with the restaurant's emblem in Chinese characters.

FOOD: Plenty of choice, including old favourites and innovative dishes adapting to non-traditional ingredients. Inventive titles include Buddha Jumps Over the Wall, a highly extravagant shark's fin soup requiring five days' notice.

OUR TIP: Aphrodisiac concoction called Celestial Thunder **Chef:** Alex Chow **Owners:** Bernard Yeoh **Times:** 12-2.15/6.30-11, Closed 25-26 Dec, New Year **Notes:** Tasting menu £85, Vegetarian available, Smart Dress **Seats:** 110, Pr/dining room 12 **Smoking:** Air con **Parking:** Directly outside **e-mail:** kai@kaimayfair.co.uk **web:** www.kaimayfair.co.uk

 Levant

Lebanese

Lebanese food in atmospheric setting
☎ 020 7224 1111 Jason Court, 76 Wigmore St W1H 9DQ Plan 2-G3

MENU GUIDE Squid coated in almonds • Chicken Shawarma • Chocolate and banana mousse

PRICE GUIDE Food prices not confirmed for 2006. Please telephone for details

PLACE: This atmospheric, candlelit basement restaurant with Arabic artefacts is reached by a stone staircase lined with candles.

FOOD: There's a freshness and lightness of touch with this authentic and carefully cooked Lebanese food. The tastes are clean, the use of colour is excellent and the combinations work well. Choose from mezze, salads, dips, breads, pastries, grilled meats and vegetable dishes. Eat straight from the dishes with your fingers for the full Lebanese experience. The food is backed by a strong wine list with a good balance between European and New World, including Lebanese.

continued

OUR TIP: Live music in the evening **Times:** 12/12-1, Closed Xmas, New Year **Directions:** Nearest station: Bond Street Cross into Oxford St, through St Christophers Place to Wigmore St. Jason Court is directly opposite. **e-mail:** reservations@leventrestaurant.co.uk **web:** www.leventrestaurant.co.uk

 Lindsay House Restaurant

see page 31

 Locanda Locatelli *see page 319*

Maze at London Marriott Hotel
Grosvenor Square *Rosettes not confirmed at time of going to press*

New Gordon Ramsay venture
☎ 020 7493 1232 Grosvenor Square W1K 6JP Plan 2-G2

As the guide went to press, a new restaurant and bar from Gordon Ramsay, called Maze, was due to open this summer. Cuisine will feature a grazing menu based on modern French cuisine with Asian spice influences from head chef Jason Atherton.

Chef: Jason Atherton **Rooms:** 221 (221 en suite) ★★★★ **Directions:** Nearest station: Bond Street Hotel entrance in on Duke St, off Oxford St **Parking:** 75 **e-mail:** businesscentre@londonmarriott.co.uk **web:** www.marriott.com/marriott/londt

The Best Use of Seafood sponsored by Seafish In conjunction with Seafish, the Sea Fish Industry Authority, we have sought out restaurants that make the most of seafood on their menus. In addition to the four country award winners (see page 9), look out for the seafish symbol throughout the book; this denotes restaurants serving a good range of fish and shellfish dishes, where the accent is firmly on freshness.

Give us your views! All the rosetted restaurants in this guide have been visited by one of the AA's team of professional inspectors, but we want to hear from you! Use the report forms in the back of the guide or email us at lifestyleguides@theaa.com with your comments on any establishments featured or on the restaurants that you feel are worthy of an entry. We would also be pleased to receive your views on the guide itself and suggestions for information you would like to see included.

LONDON W1

Lindsay House Restaurant

Modern British

Exciting cooking in Soho

☎ 020 7439 0450 21 Romilly St W1D 5AF Plan 3-C2

MENU GUIDE Tea-roasted sweetbread with aubergine • Poached veal rump, confit red onion & taleggio • Baked pear, prune & chocolate tart

WINE GUIDE ♀ Perchaud Chablis £35 • ♀ Roger Sabon Châteauneuf du Pape £45 • 10 by the glass (£6.50-£10)

PRICE GUIDE Fixed L £25 • Fixed D £48 • starter £14 • main £25 • dessert £8 • coffee £4.75 • min/water £4 • Service added but optional 12.5% • Group min 8 service 15%

PLACE: Amid Soho's glitz and glamour, this is a discreetly elegant Georgian town house with two graceful, intimate dining rooms. The aura of exclusivity is enhanced by the fact that you have to ring the doorbell to gain entry. Decor and mood is very traditional.

FOOD: Menus feature a preponderance of high quality, luxury ingredients, though dishes tend to be very simple, with rich, full flavours precise cooking bringing the best out of the materials. A vibrant salad of artichoke and crab may be followed by best end

of lamb with sweetbreads and kidneys, perfectly timed.

OUR TIP: The tasting menu is a must

Chef: Richard Corrigan **Owners:** Searcy Corrigan **Times:** 12-2.30/6-11, Closed 1 wk Xmas & Etr, Sun, L Sat-Sun, D Sun **Notes:** Tasting menu 7 courses £59, Vegetarian available, Smart casual **Seats:** 50, Pr/dining room 40 **Directions:** Nearest station: Leicester Sq. Off Shaftesbury Avenue & Dean St **Parking:** NCP **e-mail:** richardcorrigan@lindsayhouse.co.uk **web:** www.lindsayhouse.co.uk

LONDON W1

Locanda Locatelli

Italian

Inspired Italian cuisine in chic contemporary setting

☎ 020 7935 9088 8 Seymour St W1H 7JZ Plan 2-F2

PLACE: Seating around 100 guests, this celebrated Italian combines the buzz of a continental brasserie with the class of a formal restaurant. Parquet floors, grained wood walls and soft lighting comprise its sleek decor, while the clientele are a mixed crowd of suits, celebrities and special occasion parties. It's all presided over by quietly attentive staff who appear when needed, but are never pushy.

FOOD: Four courses are a must if you really want to do justice to Giorgio Locatelli's inspired cooking, so come hungry and ready to tackle the delights of antipasta, pasta, main and dessert. Rooted in northern Italian cuisine, the menu offers an extensive choice of dishes, which are generally characterised by a simple approach that lets quality ingredients speak for themselves. Enjoy a meal which begins with a simple salad of leaves, roast squash, beans and peas, followed by red onion ravioli with chianti sauce and

salted ricotta. Expect a meat course such as veal cutlet with saffron risotto, new season's garlic and calvo nero, with a grande finale of dégustation of chocolate Amedei. It's complemented by a lengthy and good value Italian wine list featuring a wide range of dessert wines and grappas.

OUR TIP: Busy, so book ahead

Chef: Giorgio Locatelli **Owners:** Plaxy & Giorgio Locatelli **Times:** 12-3/7-11, Closed Sun, Xmas, New Year, BHs **Rooms:** 445 (445 en suite) ★★★★★ **Directions:** Nearest station: Marble Arch Telephone for directions **e-mail:** info@locandalocatelli.com **web:** www.locandalocatelli.com

England

LONDON W1 *continued*

 Mirabelle
French
Chic and glamorous Mayfair dining
☎ 020 7499 4636 56 Curzon St W1J 8PA
Plan 4-H6

MENU GUIDE Ravioli of oxtail à la Bordelaise • Tuna escalope, aubergine caviar, sauce vierge au basilic • Pear tarte Tatin à la vanilla

WINE GUIDE ♀ J M Roger Sancerre Sauvignon £37 • ♀ Château Val Joanis Côtes du Luberon Syrah £32 • 267 bottles over £20, 2 bottles under £20 • 12 by the glass (£5-£10)

PRICE GUIDE Fixed L £17.50 • starter £10.50-£45 • main £15-£27 • dessert £8.50 • coffee £3.50 • min/water £3.50 • Service added but optional 12.50% • Group min 12 service 15%

PLACE: The Mirabelle has always been glamorous, and today's incarnation - part of the Marco Pierre White empire - captures the spirit of the times. Elegant, seductive and chic, it's every bit the part, with slinky bar, art deco mirrors, brown leather banquettes, trompe l'oeil wall paintings and displays of fragrant lilies.
FOOD: The classic Gallic menu fits the bill perfectly and offers extensive choice with plenty of Marco hallmarks. Impeccable ingredients are treated with intelligent simplicity, with balance and flavour to the fore. A fabulous wine list and slick service from a professional outfit round off proceedings.
OUR TIP: You can eat alfresco in the summer
Chef: Philip Cooper **Owners:** Marco Pierre White, Jimmy Lahoud
Times: 12-2.30/6-11.30, Closed 26 Dec, closed L 1 Jan, closed D 25 Dec
Notes: Dress Restrictions, No jeans and trainers **Seats:** 120, Pr/dining room 48 **Smoking:** No pipes, Air con **Children:** Portions
Directions: Nearest station: Green Park Telephone for directions
Parking: On street **e-mail:** sales@whitestarline.org.uk
web: www.whitestarline.org.uk

 Mosaico
Italian
Slick modern Italian in heart of Mayfair
☎ 020 7409 1011 13 Albermarle St W1S 4HJ
Plan 3-A1
MENU GUIDE Steamed courgette flowers filled with ricotta • Pan-fried calves' liver, red onions, black truffle & snails • Warm vanilla pannacotta, black cherry gelée
PRICE GUIDE Food prices not confirmed for 2006. Please telephone for details
PLACE: A stylish restaurant with an equally stylish location (beneath DKNY and opposite Brown's Hotel). Smart, predominantly Italian staff are skilled and attentive. It doesn't feel like a basement, with mirrors used cleverly to create a feeling of space, red leather banquettes and chairs, and lots of wood.
FOOD: There's a northern Italian slant to the food, which is fairly modern and includes some traditional dishes reinterpreted with a twist. Accurate cooking results in text book risotto and the quality of the ingredients is allowed to shine through. Pasta, bread, grissini and ice creams are all home made. A serious, all-Italian wine list.
OUR TIP: Great for lunch while Bond Street shopping
Times: 12-2.30/6.30-10.45, Closed Sunday, closed L Sat, Sun, Xmas, Easter, BHs **Directions:** Telephone for further details
e-mail: mosaico-restaurant.co.uk

 Deya
Indian
Modern Indian cooking in the heart of town
☎ 020 7224 0028 Mostyn Hotel, 34 Portman Square W1H 7BY
Plan 2-F2
MENU GUIDE Tandoori prawns in yoghurt & spices • Lamb rogan josh, saffron rice • Rosewater & vanilla crème brûlée
WINE GUIDE ♀ Casa Azul Sauvignon Blanc £14 • ♀ Mark & Elvelia Primitivo £16 • 418 bottles over £20, 24 bottles under £20 • 11 by the glass (£4.50-£6)
PRICE GUIDE Fixed L fr £14.50 • starter £6-£9.50 • main £9.50-£15 • dessert £4-£4.75 • coffee £2.50 • min/water £3 • Service added but optional 12.5%
PLACE: When you're fit to drop after a long day's shopping on Oxford Street, slope away to this elegant hotel near Marble Arch for some vibrant Indian cooking. The restaurant is a bright and airy room with high ceilings and colourful frescos throughout.
FOOD: Modern Indian cuisine in the style of Zaika, a well-established sister eaterie in Kensington. Choose from the carte or a range of set menus which include a vegetarian selection.
OUR TIP: Good value set price lunch
Chef: Virappan Muragappan **Owners:** Claudio Pulze/Raj Sharma/Sir Michael Caine **Times:** 12-2.45/6-11, Closed Xmas, New Yr, BHs, Sun, closed L Sat **Seats:** 80 **Smoking:** No pipes, No cigars, Air con
Children: Portions **Parking:** NCP Bryanston St
e-mail: info@deya-restaurant.co.uk **web:** www.deya-restaurant.co.uk

AA's Chefs' Chef is the annual poll of all the chefs included in The Restaurant Guide. Around 1800 of the country's top chefs are asked to vote to recognise the achievements of one of their peers. This year's winner is featured on page 19.

⊛ Nicole's

International

Contemporary dining for the chic and well-heeled

☎ 020 7499 8408   158 New Bond St W1Y 9PA
Plan 3-A1

MENU GUIDE Smoked haddock cake, leek & chive sauce • Pan-fried veal loin, pearl barley risotto • Warm fruit crumble, Jersey cream

PRICE GUIDE Starter £6-£11.50 • main £17.95-£23.50 dessert £7 • coffee £2.50 • min/water £3.95 • Service added but optional 15%

PLACE: A wide stone stairway leads down to the split-level dining room, with brown leather banquettes, polished-wood floor, white walls, linen-dressed tables with padded wooden chairs, and a leek bar. Below Nicole Farhi's flagship fashion store, Nicole's delivers a predictably contemporary edge to match that stylish label.

FOOD: Expect dishes with a nod to the Mediterranean and beyond, attentive service and Bond Street prices. The modern repertoire is based around seasonality, quality ingredients, and simplicity of cooking.

OUR TIP: A lunchtime venue for the must-be-seen
Chef: Annie Wayte   **Owners:** Stephen Marks   **Times:** 12-3.30/6.30-10.30, Closed BHs, Sun, closed D Sat   **Notes:** Vegetarian available   **Seats:** 65, Pr/dining room 80   **Smoking:** N/Sm area, No pipes, No cigars, Air con
Directions: Nearest station: Green Park, Bond St Between Hermes shop & Asprey   **e-mail:** nicoles@nicolefarhi.com   **web:** www.nicolefarhi.com

⊛⊛ Noble Rot

European

Wow-factor cooking meets fashionable venue

☎ 020 7629 8877   3-5 Mill St W1S 2AU   Plan 3-A2

MENU GUIDE Pan-fried foie gras, fig & liquorice gelée • Roast turbot, confit ceps & braised ox tail • Violet crème brûlée, coffee reduction

PRICE GUIDE Fixed L £19 • Fixed D £38-£69 • starter £7.95-£23 • main £18-£39 • dessert £6.50-£15 • coffee £2.75 • min/water £3.75 • Service added but optional 15%

PLACE: A smart Mayfair location, just off Conduit Street, draws crowds of admiring fans to this stylish, fashionable, contemporary venue. On the ground floor, huge windows are hung with wooden Venetian blinds, dark walls with photographs of star personalities, smartly dressed tables come accompanied by contemporary seating, and stone floors are softened with rugs. It's lively and buzzy, service is attentive and informed.
FOOD: The modern European cooking has classical roots, comes dotted with luxury items and some adventurous ideas, which mix clean flavours and textures with exquisite presentation.
OUR TIP: Fine selection of dessert wines
Chef: Julian Owen-Mold   **Owners:** Soren Jessen   **Times:** 12-4/6-12, Closed 25-26 Dec, New Year, BHs, Easter Hols, Sun, closed L Sat
Notes: Vegetarian available   **Seats:** 60, Pr/dining room 50   **Smoking:** Air con   **Children:** Portions   **Directions:** Nearest station: Oxford Circus 2 mins walk from Oxford Circus underground station, just off Conduit St
Parking: Metres Available   **e-mail:** reception@noblerot.com
web: www.noblerot.com

⊛⊛⊛ **Nobu** *see below*

LONDON W1

Japanese

Stylish, minimalist, upmarket Japanese restaurant with outstanding cuisine

☎ 020 7447 4747   Old Park Ln W1Y 4LB   Plan 4-G5

MENU GUIDE Yellowtail sashimi with jalapeno • King crab claw, butter ponzu sauce • Bento chocolate box

WINE GUIDE ♀ L'Arret Bufette Pouilly Fumé £34 • ♀ Casa Lapostolle Merlot £38 • 10 by the glass (£5.50-£12)

PRICE GUIDE Fixed L £24.50-£25 • starter £5-£14.50 • main £8.75-£29.50 • dessert £7.50-£9 • coffee £1.75 • min/water £5 • Service added but optional

PLACE: Situated on the first floor of the starkly minimalist and hip Metropolitan Hotel, Nobu - with its own Park Lane pavement entrance - woos a glamorous, fashion conscious clientele, and international celebrities, with some of the most imaginative and accomplished cuisine in town. Still one of London's trendiest dining rooms, this contemporary space is decked out in cool, neutral tones, while vast plate glass windows afford stunning views over Hyde Park and Park Lane. Beautiful, black-clad staff are well informed, friendly, and give sound advice to inexperienced guests, which is just as well, since it is not immediately clear how best to select dishes to make up a meal.
FOOD: The large and very flexible menu is clearly Japanese in style but is enlivened by South American flourishes, with a nod towards some Chilean and Peruvian influences. Fusion it may be, but it's the traditional Japanese that wins out in the end. Impeccable raw materials, sensitive handling, wonderful textures and flavours and impressive presentation all play their part to produce a unique dining experience.
OUR TIP: Book well in advance
Chef: Mark Edwards   **Owners:** Nobuyuki Matsuhisa, Robert de Niro, Drew Nieporent   **Times:** 12-2.15/6-10.15, Closed BHs   **Notes:** Vegetarian available   **Seats:** 150, Pr/dining room 40   **Smoking:** N/Sm area, No pipes, No cigars, Air con   **e-mail:** ecb@ecbpr.co.uk
web: www.noburestaurants.com

England

LONDON W1 *continued*

No 6
Modern, British
Food emporium

☎ 020 7935 1910 6 George St W1U 3QX Plan 2-G3

MENU GUIDE Grilled tiger prawns, basil & aïoli • Goats' cheese soufflé, globe artichokes, rocket • Plum & almond tart

WINE GUIDE ♀ Flagstone Cellar Hand The Spinnaker £15 • ♥ Forest Ville Vineyards Merlot £19 • 13 bottles over £20, 14 bottles under £20 • 2 by the glass (£3.50)

PRICE GUIDE Starter £5.95-£7.95 • main £10.50-£14.50 • dessert £4.95-£5.50 • coffee £2.95 • min/water £3.20 • Service optional

PLACE: This upmarket deli and restaurant just off the bottom end of Marylebone High Street draws an appreciative crowd. Beyond the shop are a few wooden tables, dark-wood chairs, floorboards and cream walls hung with foodie pictures, and there's a small atrium roof at the rear too.

FOOD: Emma Miller's light but accomplished cooking has a bright Mediterranean slant, focusing on simple, daily-changing menus and quality fresh produce. Everything's made in-house, where breakfasts and afternoon teas are also served.

OUR TIP: Always busy so make a booking (minimum spend of £14 noon - 3pm)

Chef: Emma Miller **Owners:** Emma Miller **Times:** 8, Closed 10 days in Aug, Xmas & New Year & BHs, Sat-Sun **Notes:** Vegetarian available **Seats:** 30 **Smoking:** N/Sm in restaurant, Air con **Children:** Portions **Directions:** Nearest station: Bond Street Just off Marylebone High St **Parking:** NCP, parking meters outside

 **Orrery** *see page 323*

Ozer
Turkish

Turkish delight a stone's throw from Oxford Circus

☎ 020 7323 0505 5 Langham Place W1N 7DD
Plan 3-A3

MENU GUIDE Mixed meze (9 dishes) • Shish Sofra (Marinated grilled lamb) • Su Muhallebisi (Milk dessert with fruit & nuts)

WINE GUIDE ♀ Yakut Sauvignon Blanc £12.50 • ♥ Cankaya £12.50 • 20 bottles over £20, 21 bottles under £20 • 5 by the glass (£3.85-£4.15)

PRICE GUIDE Fixed L £7.95-£9.95 • starter £3.25-£8.95 • main £6.95-£15.95 • dessert £3.45-£5.95 • coffee £1.75 • min/water £3 • Service added but optional 12.5%

PLACE: Enjoy drinks and nibbles in the bar area, which has an undulating dark red wall and curvy, comfy seating, or go straight into the main part of the restaurant, a high ceilinged room with a wall in copper and one in pale creamy marble. Staff are friendly and helpful, explaining dishes willingly and happy to make recommendations.

FOOD: Meze, arriving on rectangular glass plates, are light and full of fresh flavours, with great babagaresh, a smokey aubergine and tomato dish. Or try the seafood meze, including eel, fat kalamari and juicy prawns. Salmon stew with bulgar wheat risotto, a perfectly fresh, moist chunk of salmon on delicately spiced risotto, is an unusual main, and there is a wide vegetarian selection.

OUR TIP: The healthy eating meze meal - a tasting menu of 11 dishes for the calorie conscious

Chef: Seyhan Erdem **Owners:** Huseyin Ozer **Times:** noon-mdnt **Seats:** 115 **Smoking:** N/Sm area, Air con **Children:** Portions **Directions:** Nearest station: Oxford Circus 2 min walk towards Upper Regent Street. **Parking:** on street **web:** www.sofra.co.uk

Passione
Italian

Wonderful flavours from lively Italian

☎ 020 7636 2833 10 Charlotte St W1T 2LT Plan 3-B3

MENU GUIDE Risotto with wild sorrel • Rabbit with rosemary, sauté potatoes • Limoncello & wild strawberry ice cream

WINE GUIDE ♀ Tramin Pinot Grigio £23.50 • ♥ Villa Reale Montepulciano £22 • 32 bottles over £20, 3 bottles under £20 • 2 by the glass (£3.50)

PRICE GUIDE Starter £6-£11 • main £11.50-£22.50 • dessert £6 coffee £2.50 • min/water £3 • Service added but optional 12.5%

PLACE: The name says it all; summing up Gennaro Contaldo's love affair with great food, this intimate but big-hearted Italian has a lively, informal buzz. Herbs grow in little pots on tables and walls sport vibrant foodie prints.

FOOD: It's easy to see why Gennaro is a Jamie Oliver mentor, his rustic, traditional Italian cuisine delivering clean flavours via tip-top seasonal ingredients and sensitive handling. Breads, wine and staff are authentically Italian.

OUR TIP: Ideal for theatreland

Chef: Gennaro Contaldo **Owners:** G Contaldo, G D'Urso, Liz Przybylski **Times:** 12.30-2.15/7-10.15, Closed 1 wk Xmas, BHs, Sun, closed L Sat **Notes:** Vegetarian available **Seats:** 40, Pr/dining room 18 **Smoking:** No pipes, No cigars, Air con **Children:** Portions **Directions:** Nearest station: Goodge Street 5 mins walk from underground station **Parking:** Nearby pay & display **web:** www.passione.co.uk

Pattersons
British, French

Mayfair chic that tastes as good as it looks

☎ 020 7499 1308 4 Mill St, Mayfair W1S 2AX
Plan 3-A2

MENU GUIDE Crab lasagne, shellfish cappuccino • Scottish beef tournedos, cep pavé, caramelised baby carrots, sauce bordelaise • Apple Tatin, cinnamon ice cream

WINE GUIDE ♀ De la Croix Senaillet St Veran £24 • ♥ Jean Earnest des Combs Morgan £21 • 76 bottles over £20, 9 bottles under £20 • 6 by the glass (£3.50-£5.95)

PRICE GUIDE Fixed L £15 • starter £8-£12 • main £13-£17 • dessert £12 • coffee £3 • min/water £3.50 • Service added but optional 12.5%

PLACE: This stylish, eponymous Mayfair restaurant, discreetly tucked away off Conduit Street, sees chef-patron Raymond Patterson - former head chef at the Garrick Club - fronting a class act. Beyond its glass frontage and small bar, the dining room is spacious and modern with white-walled, oak floor, high-back leather chairs and formal white cloths covering generous-sized tables.

FOOD: The food is fittingly contemporary but without being a slave to fashion. Accomplished, sophisticated and underpinned by classical roots, it comes dotted with luxury items and high class ingredients. The appealing carte is also backed by worthy fixed-price options.

OUR TIP: Open from 5.30pm, perfect for an après shopping meal

Chef: Raymond & Thomas Patterson **Owners:** Raymond & Thomas Patterson **Times:** 12-3/5.30-11, Closed 25-26 Dec, 1 Jan, Good Fri & Etr Mon, Sun, closed L Sat **Notes:** Vegetarian available, Smart Dress **Seats:** 50, Pr/dining room 30 **Smoking:** N/Sm area, No pipes, Air con **Children:** Menu, Portions **Directions:** Nearest station: Oxford Circus Located off Conduit St opposite Saville Row entrance **Parking:** Saville Row **e-mail:** pattersonsmayfair@btconnect.com **web:** www.pattersonsrestaurant.com

LONDON W1

Orrery

French, European
Flagship Conran offering stunning food and service in equal measures
☎ 020 7616 8000 55-57 Marylebone High St W1M 3AE Plan 2-G4
e-mail: oliviere@conran-restaurants.co.uk
web: www.orrery.co.uk

PLACE: The first floor Orrery is a special place indeed - one of London's most prestigious dining venues - set in the heart of Marylebone village, undoubtedly the jewel in the crown of Conran eateries and once the site of Henry VIII's hunting lodge. Today, the mood is highly contemporary, typically understated trademark designer (perched above the Conran shop), with cool, clean lines of sophisticated simplicity, it exudes quality throughout. The long, thin, bright and airy room features striking circular windows and skylights, its two long rows of tables lined with chairs and banquette seating. Service is fluent and up with the best in town; totally professional and dispatched with flair and genuine hospitality. A small, intimate lounge bar for pre-meal drinks or after-dinner cigars tops off a premier-league act. **FOOD:** André Garrett's style is very focused on the modern, but with its roots in the classics. First rate, high quality ingredients (laced with luxury items), combine with highly accomplished technical skill, matched by an equal measure of creativity and innovation and backed by meticulous presentation. The approach is via an enticing repertoire of menus, from set-price jour and gourmand offering (with the option of recommended wines) to independent lunch and dinner cartes. So expect to be wowed by the likes of roasted veal sweetbreads with acidulated carrot salad, almonds and carrot jus, followed by Denham Estate venison (braised shoulder and roast saddle) served with spiced pears and sauce grand veneur, and to finish in style with a classic apple tart Tatin with apple sorbet. Superb ancillaries (canapés, breads, amuse bouche and pre-dessert) all keep up the pace, while the extensive wine list shows an equal eye for quality, delivered by first class, knowledgeable sommeliers.

MENU GUIDE White onion velouté, caramelised garlic purée & sautéed frogs' legs • Native lobster, hand-rolled macaroni 'carbonara' • Strawberries, sorbet, espuma & fraisier

WINE GUIDE ♀ Henry Pelle Menetou Salon Sauvignon Blanc £29 • ♀ Berthou Mieu Madiran Charles de Bate Tannat £29.50 • 900 bottles over £20, 12 bottles under £20 • 20 by the glass (£3.75-£18)

PRICE GUIDE Fixed L £25 • starter £11.50-£16.50 • main £17.50-£30 • dessert £6.50-£10 • coffee £3.50 • min/water £3.25 • Service added but optional 12.5%

OUR TIP: Visit the deli below

Chef: André Garrett **Owners:** Conran Restaurants **Times:** 12-3/7-11, Closed 25-26 Dec, New Year, Good Friday, closed D 24 Dec **Notes:** Tasting menu 7 courses £55, Sun D 3 courses £30, Vegetarian available **Seats:** 80 **Smoking:** N/Sm area, No pipes, Air con **Children:** Portions **Directions:** Nearest station: Baker St, Regents Park At north end of Marylebone High St **Parking:** NCP, 170 Marylebone Rd

England

LONDON W1

Pied à Terre

Modern French
Outstanding, highly refined modern cooking
☎ 020 7636 1178 34 Charlotte St W1P 1HJ Plan 3-B3
e-mail: p-a-t@dircon.co.uk **web:** www.pied.a.terre.co.uk

PLACE: Following a fire and subsequent rebuild and refurbishment, this discreet, unobtrusive and aptly named Pied à Terre is due to rise from the ashes and reopen at the beginning of September 2005. Modern, contemporary and bijoux as ever, the current plans are to reopen with a reduced number of covers (down from the previous 49 to just 40 seats) to allow diners more space and the feeling of greater luxury. There will also be a bar on the first floor and a private dining room on the second floor. Service will be as slick and professional as ever.

FOOD: Australian-born chef Shane Osborn's modern French cooking is individual, creative and stylish, and will continue to be as well mannered, sophisticated and refined as it comes, brimful of interest and oozing class. Shane, who has been at Pied à Terre for some five years or more, is the latest in an illustrious line of previous chefs that includes Tom Aikens - see entry - and Richard Neat. So expect superb technical skills, emphatic flavours and imaginative ideas to shine, without too much obvious modernism. Presentation is attractive without over indulgence, dishes complex but well conceived, and backed by masterful culinary judgement. Savoury items really shine, while peripherals like amuse bouche, pre-desserts and breads all hit high notes. Osborn's enticing fixed-price repertoire of lunch, carte, vegetarian and eight-course tasting menu promotes a genuine agony of choice and comes dotted with luxury items, while the tasting version can be taken with an optional seven-glass, or eight half-glass, wine selection. So think classic starter of seared and poached foie gras in sauternes consommé, followed by roasted sea bass with confit fennel, green olive and vanilla sauce, and for the finale, bitter-sweet chocolate tart with stout ice cream.

MENU GUIDE Teal breast, crispy salsify, choucroute, chanterelles, foie gras • Pork fillet, stuffed pigs' trotter, carrot & anis purée, cider sauce • Chocolate mousse, fig & butterscotch ice cream

WINE GUIDE ♀ Cloudy Bay Sauvignon £35 • ♀ Château Des Moines Cabernet Merlot £35 • 700 bottles over £20, 30 bottles under £20 12 by the glass (£3.50-£25)

PRICE GUIDE Fixed L £21.50-£45 • Fixed D £55 coffee £4.50 • min/water £4 • Service added but optional 12.5%

OUR TIP: Try the half-glass wine selection with the tasting menu

Chef: Shane Osborn **Owners:** David Moore & Shane Osborn
Times: 12-2.30/6.15-11, Closed 2 wks Xmas & New Year, Sun, closed L Sat **Notes:** Set D 10 course £70, Vegetarian available
Seats: 40, Pr/dining room 12 **Smoking:** N/Sm in restaurant, Air con **Directions:** Nearest station: Goodge Street S of BT Tower and Goodge St **Parking:** Cleveland St

LONDON W1 *continued*

@@@@ **Pied à Terre** *see page 324*

@ **La Porte des Indes**

Indian

Indian cuisine with a colonial twist

☎ 020 7224 0055 32 Bryanston St W1H 7EG
Plan 2-F2

MENU GUIDE Sole in banana leaves, mint & coriander chutney • Rogan josh • Yogurt chandernagone

WINE GUIDE ♀ Cuvée Royal Thai Gerwurztraminer £16 • ♀ Minervois Mouvedere/Grenache £15.50 • 110 bottles over £20, 5 bottles under £20 • 13 by the glass (£4.50-£8)

PRICE GUIDE Fixed L £19.90-£30 • Fixed D £30-£35 • starter £5-£9.50 • main £11.90-£28 • dessert £5-£6.50 • coffee £2.25 • min/water £4.50 • Service added but optional 12.5%

PLACE: Housed in a former Edwardian ballroom, this celebrated Indian eaterie is a unique and romantic dinner destination, despite its unassuming Marble Arch location. Take a drink downstairs if there's time; the bar is decked out in colonial style in homage to Raffles Hotel.

FOOD: An eclectic menu takes its inspiration from the former French colonies in India, and includes some exotic dishes as well as the old favourites. Good value weekday buffet lunch.

OUR TIP: Relax with a drink beside the restaurant's own 40-foot Moghul waterfall

Chef: Mehernosh Mody **Owners:** The Blue Elephant Group **Times:** 12-2.30/7-11.30, Closed 25-26 Dec, 1 Jan, closed L Sat **Notes:** Tasting menu 5 courses £35, Sun jazz brunch £22, Vegetarian available **Seats:** 300, Pr/dining room 14 **Smoking:** Air con **Children:** Portions **Directions:** Nearest station: Marble Arch Telephone for directions **Parking:** across road NCP **e-mail:** london@laportedesindes.com **web:** www.laportedesindes.com

@@ **The Providores**

Fusion

Manhattan deli meets fabulous ingredients for mouthwatering combinations

☎ 020 7935 6175 109 Marylebone High St W1U 4RX Plan 2-G3

MENU GUIDE Grilled scallops, plantain fritter, sweet chilli sauce, salted coconut milk • Pan-fried monkfish, braised morcilla & Puy lentils, cucumber, mange tout & rouille

WINE GUIDE ♀ Goldwater Sauvignon Blanc • ♀ Kim Crawford Pinot Noir • 55 bottles over £20, 11 bottles under £20 • 19 by the glass (£5.20-£7.90)

The Providores

PRICE GUIDE Starter £6-£14 • main £18-£24 • dessert £8 • coffee £1.60 • min/water £3 • Service added but optional 12.5%

PLACE: Set in the heart of Marylebone High Street, the bustling ground floor Drinks and Tapas Room looks somewhat like a coffee shop, with high tables set with bar stools. Upstairs is a little more refined, with chocolate leather banquettes, wooden floors and closely-set tables draped in heavy linen. Service is slick and staff necessarily knowledgeable.

FOOD: The lengthy menu makes intriguing reading; brimful of fusion-style combinations and unusual sounding, widely sourced ingredients. The produce has great provenance and is allowed pride of place, the kitchen skilled at keeping things simple. A brunch menu is served weekend lunchtimes.

OUR TIP: Book ahead to avoid disappointment

Chef: Peter Gordon, Anna Hansen **Owners:** P Gordon, A Hansen, M McGrath, J Leeming **Times:** 12-10.30, Closed 25-26, 31 Dec, 1 Jan **Notes:** Vegetarian available **Seats:** 38 **Smoking:** N/Sm in restaurant, Air con **Children:** Portions **Directions:** Nearest station: Bond St/Baker St/Regents Park From Bond St station cross Oxford St, down James St, into Thayer St then Marylebone High St **e-mail:** anyone@theprovidores.co.uk **web:** www.theprovidores.co.uk

@@ **Quo Vadis**

Italian

Classy Italian from the Marco Pierre White stable

☎ 020 7437 9585 26-29 Dean St W1D 3LL Plan 3-B2

MENU GUIDE Herb-crusted beef carpaccio • Barolo wine & Swiss chard risotto • Apple tart Tatin

WINE GUIDE ♀ Le Cuncare Monte Schiavo Verdicchio £37 • ♀ Cyenus Tasca Cabernet Sauvignon £36 • 81 bottles over £20, 4 bottles under £20 • 10 by the glass (£4.50-£9.50)

PRICE GUIDE Fixed L £14.95 • Fixed D £19.95 • starter £6.50-£12.50 • main £12.50-£18.50 • dessert £5 • coffee £1.75 • min/water £3.50 • Service added but optional 12.5%

continued

continued

England

LONDON W1 continued

Quo Vadis

PLACE: Well-established Soho restaurant distinguished by a black façade and frosted windows. Inside it remains chic with its range of elegant and outrageous artwork amidst plenty of mirrors, and a rarified gentleman's club atmosphere.

FOOD: The classic Italian cuisine with rustic leanings is reliably well cooked from top of the range produce, yielding the sort of clean yet vibrant flavours that come from simple handling. Cassoncelli with asparagus and goats' cheese ricotta, and chocolate fondant with basil yoghurt and balsamic dressing are typically inspired offerings.

OUR TIP: Good value early bird menu

Chef: Fernando Corradazzi **Owners:** Jimmy Lahoud, Marco Pierre White **Times:** 12-2.30/5.30-11.30, Closed 24-25 Dec, 1 Jan, Sun, closed L Sat **Notes:** Vegetarian available **Seats:** 80, Pr/dining room 90 **Smoking:** No pipes, Air con **Parking:** NCP or on street **e-mail:** sales@whitestarline.org.uk **web:** www.whitestarline.org.uk

Rasa Samudra

Indian

Authentical Keralan seafood and vegetarian restaurant

☎ 020 7637 0222 5 Charlotte St W1T 1RE Plan 3-B3

MENU GUIDE Chemmean Karumuru (Crunchy stirfry prawns) • Kappayum Meenum (Smoked tamarind king fish) • Banana pancakes

WINE GUIDE ♀ General Bilimoria Colombard Chardonnay £11.95 • ♀ General Bilimoria Shiraz Pinotage £11.95 • 5 bottles over £20, 7 bottles under £20 • 1 by the glass (£2.95)

PRICE GUIDE Fixed L £22.50-£30 • Fixed D £22.50-£30 • starter £4.95-£7.50 • main £6.25-£12.95 • dessert £2.50-£3.50 • coffee £2 • min/water £3.50 • Service added but optional

PLACE: The bold pink frontage gives way to a series of small individually decorated rooms creating an intimate atmosphere. Exotic ornaments adorn most walls. Staff are smartly dressed, courteous and attentive.

FOOD: Few of the authentic Keralan dishes have familiar names which makes the menu seem so much more exotic, as in Crab Varuthathu - a seafood stirfry with ginger, curry leaves and onions. Vegetarians might like to choose the Bagar Baingan - diced aubergines cooked in a spicy paste mixed with yoghurt and cashew nut sauce.

OUR TIP: Leave a little room for some lesser known Indian sweets

Chef: Prasad Mahadevan Nair **Owners:** Das Shreedharan **Times:** 12-3/6-11, Closed 2 wks Dec, closed L Sun **Notes:** Vegetarian available, Civ Wed 200 **Seats:** 100, Pr/dining room 70 **Smoking:** N/Sm in restaurant, Air con **e-mail:** dasrasa@hotmail.com **web:** www.rasarestaurants.com

Rasa W1

Indian

Impressive South Indian cuisine from Kerala

☎ 020 7629 1346 6 Dering St W1S 1AD Plan 2-H2

MENU GUIDE Rasam, a peppery lentil broth • Cheera Parippu (Curry of spinach & toor dal) • Kesari, halva with mango, cashews & raisins

WINE GUIDE ♀ Viognier £15.50 • ♀ Zinfandel £17.95 • 6 bottles over £20, 16 bottles under £20 • 1 by the glass (£2.95)

PRICE GUIDE Fixed L £13.50-£17.50 • Fixed D £16.50-£20.50 • starter £4.25-£7.50 • main £6.25-£12.95 • dessert £2.75-£3.50 • coffee £1.95 • min/water £3 • Service added but optional 12.5%

PLACE: A great find in an otherwise unremarkable location just off Oxford Street, this pleasant restaurant aims to bring a flavour of Kerala's traditions to W1. Enjoy a vibrant temple atmosphere with classical decor, compelling music and genuine friendliness.

FOOD: Authentic village-style cooking with a great choice of dishes, including pre-meal snacks and pickles. Vegetarian food is a speciality, but there are some more familiar lamb and chicken options if you prefer. Two tasting menus offer a real insight into the cuisine, available for as few as one guest.

OUR TIP: A popular takeaway service is provided

Chef: Sasidharan Nair **Owners:** Das Shreedharan **Times:** 12-3/6-11, Closed 24-30 Dec, 1 Jan, Sun **Notes:** Vegetarian available, Smart Dress, Casual **Seats:** 75 **Smoking:** N/Sm area, No pipes, No cigars, Air con **e-mail:** dasrasa@hotmail.com **web:** www.rasarestaurants.com

The Red Fort

Indian

Fine Mughal and Hyderabadi dishes in elegant surroundings

☎ 020 7437 2525 77 Dean St W1D 3SH Plan 3-B2

MENU GUIDE Seekh kebab • Shikaari teetar (Wild partridge) • Mango tart with ginger ice cream

WINE GUIDE ♀ Santo Stefano Pinot Grigio £24 • ♀ Yalumba Shiraz £25 • 58 bottles over £20, 4 bottles under £20 • 8 by the glass (£4.50-£6.25)

PRICE GUIDE Fixed L £12 • Fixed D £16 • starter £6-£8.95 • main £12-£29.50 • dessert £6-£7.50 • coffee £2.50 • min/water £4.95 • Service added but optional 12.5%

PLACE: This stalwart of London's sub-continental dining scene is back on excellent form. The discreet entrance leads to either the Akbar Bar for pre-dinner drinks or the dining room with its restrained, neutral walls and Indian artefacts. High back chairs, banquette seating and atmospheric lighting from the chandeliers give an intimate ambience.

FOOD: Most dishes are Mughal Court/North Western in style with a few regional specialities such as Dhum Phukt dishes from Hyderabad. High quality ingredients and skilful preparation make the Tandoori dishes especially effective.

OUR TIP: Excellent vegetarian menu available on request

Chef: Iqbal Ahamad **Owners:** Amin Ali **Times:** 12-2.15/5.45-11, Closed 24-26 Dec, closed L Sat & Sun **Notes:** Vegetarian available, Dress Restrictions, No shorts or sports clothes **Seats:** 84 **Smoking:** N/Sm area, No pipes, Air con **Directions:** Nearest station: Leicester Square Walk north on Charing Cross Rd. At Cambridge Circus turn left into Shaftesbury Ave. Dean St is 2nd road on right **e-mail:** info@redfort.co.uk **web:** www.redfort.co.uk

England

Restaurant 1837 at Brown's Hotel

Rosettes not confirmed at time of going to press

A classical retreat with fine dining   NEW

☎ 020 7408 1837 Albemarle St W1S 4BP Plan 3-A1

The oldest hotel restaurant in London. Now under the new ownership of Rocco Forte Hotels, the hotel has closed for complete refurbishment and is planning to re-open this autumn, 2005.

Rooms: 118 (118 en suite) **e-mail:** 1837brownshotel@rfhotels.com
Web: www.brownshotel.com

The Ritz

British, French

Traditional, grand and theatrical

☎ 020 7493 8181 150 Piccadilly W1J 9BR Plan 5-A6

MENU GUIDE Cornish lobster bisque with armagnac • Tournedos of Aberdeen Angus Rossini • Bitter chocolate dome, vanilla ice cream

WINE GUIDE ♀ Drouhin Chablis £30 • ♀ Fontana Fredda Barbera d'Alba £30 • all bottles over £20 • 20 by the glass (£9-£14)

PRICE GUIDE Fixed L £45 • Fixed D £45 • starter £12-£28 • main £19.50-£45 • dessert £12-£14 • coffee £5.10 • min/water £5 • Service included

PLACE: World-famous hotel that needs no introduction, immaculately restored to its original Louis XVI style. The famous dining room leaves an indelible impression; grand, stylish, ornate (the adjectives are many), with high ceilings, stunning chandeliers and heavy drapes that retain the opulence of a bygone age. The legendary service is formal and beautifully choreographed, with heavy silver clothed dishes uncovered in unison at the table.

FOOD: The cuisine blends the classical with more contemporary influences across a range of fixed-price menu options and carte, topped off with Ritz classics, specialities and a gourmet menu. Impressive wine list.

OUR TIP: Sit back and enjoy the experience
Chef: John T Williams **Owners:** Ritz Hotel (London) Ltd **Times:** 12.30-2.30/6-11 **Notes:** Sonata Tasting menu 5 courses £90, Vegetarian available, Dress Restrictions, Jacket & tie requested, no jeans or trainers, Civ Wed 50 **Seats:** 90, Pr/dining room 14 **Smoking:** Air con
Children: Menu, Portions **Rooms:** 133 (133 en suite) ★★★★★
Directions: Nearest station: Green Park 10-minute walk from Piccadilly Circus or Hyde Park Corner **Parking:** NCP on Arlington Street
e-mail: enquire@theritzlondon.com **web:** www.theritzlondon.com

⊛⊛ Roka

Japanese   NEW

Modern funky Japanese grill

☎ 020 7580 6464 37 Charlotte St W1T 1RR Plan 3-B3

MENU GUIDE Soft shell crab, chilli mayonnaise • Crispy rock shrimp, prickly ash & lime • Pomegranate jelly, lychee sorbet

WINE GUIDE 53 bottles over £20, 4 bottles under £20 • 5 by the glass (£4-£8)

PRICE GUIDE Starter £2.60-£6.60 • main £4.90-£15.60 • dessert £4.90-£8.90 • coffee £1.90 • min/water £3.50 • Service optional

PLACE: Roka has floor-to-ceiling windows overlooking Charlotte Street, and a basement bar where the full menu is also served. Decor throughout is a mix of wood, stainless steel and glass. The open-plan kitchen centres around the grill surrounded by bar-style seating, and tables simply laid with quality linen, chopsticks and soy sauce jug. Downstairs the basement has a more clubby feel, with occasional tables and comfortable sofas.

FOOD: Lunchtime set dishes include miso soup and home-made pickles. Carte choices are divided by type, including tempura and kushiage, sashimi and maki rolls, and roka dishes. Notable wine list.

OUR TIP: Friendly and knowledgeable staff can guide you through the menu
Chef: Rainer Becker, Nic Watt **Owners:** Rainer Becker, Arjun Waney
Times: 12-2.30/5.30-11, Closed Xmas, closed D Sun **Notes:** Tasting menu £50, Vegetarian available **Seats:** 90, Pr/dining room 30 **Smoking:** N/Sm in restaurant, Air con **Children:** Portions **Directions:** 5 min walk from Goodge St **Parking:** on street **e-mail:** info@rokarestaurant.com
web: www.rokarestaurant.com

⊛ Sherlock Holmes Hotel

European

Mesquite wood burning oven in boutique hotel restaurant

☎ 020 7486 6161 Sherlock Holmes Hotel, 108 Baker St W1U 6LJ Plan 2-F4

continued

LONDON W1 *continued*

MENU GUIDE Steamed asparagus, egg, smoked salmon & chive cream • Slowly braised lamb shank with cannelloni beans, shallots • Hot pancake with citrus sauce, Grand Marnier

WINE GUIDE ♀ Stellenbosch Sauvignon Blanc £22 • ♀ Vin Pays d'Oc Merlot £19.50 • 23 bottles over £20, 4 bottles under £20 8 by the glass (£4.90-£5.50)

PRICE GUIDE Fixed L £12.50 • starter £6.50-£10.50 • main £12.50-£26 • dessert £6-£7 • coffee £2.75 • min/water £4.75 • Service added 12.5%

PLACE: Baker Street and Sherlock Holmes are inextricably linked and Sherlock's Grill, in the boutique hotel, plays on this with its bronze casting and paintings. The chic, sand coloured decor is modern and unfussy.

FOOD: Interestingly, a mesquite wood burning oven and charcoal grill are the principle methods of cooking here, with an emphasis on quality ingredients, largely free range and organic. Grazing dishes available in the bar.

OUR TIP: Excellent pizzas straight from the oven

Chef: Rachid Hammoum **Owners:** Park Plaza Hotels **Times:** 12-2.30/6-10.30 **Notes:** Vegetarian available **Seats:** 50, Pr/dining room 50 **Smoking:** N/Sm in restaurant, Air con **Children:** Portions **Rooms:** 119 (119 en suite) ★★★★ **Directions:** Nearest station: Baker Street Located on Baker Street, close to the tube station **Parking:** Chiltern street **e-mail:** shh.fb@parkplazahotels.co.uk **web:** www.sherlockholmeshotel.com

Shogun, Millennium Hotel Mayfair

Japanese

Authentic Japanese cuisine in the heart of Mayfair

☎ 020 7629 9400 Grosvenor Square W1A 3AN Plan 2-G1

MENU GUIDE Soya bean paste soup with clams • Sliced pork fried with ginger • Fresh fruit

PRICE GUIDE Food prices not confirmed for 2006. Please telephone for details

PLACE: Well-established, traditional Japanese restaurant located in a lavishly decorated basement setting beneath the Millennium Hotel Mayfair, an impressive Georgian fronted building overlooking Grosvenor Square. Decor includes kyudo archery arrows, palm leaves and a large statue of a Samurai warrior. Discreet service from friendly staff dressed in traditional Japanese attire.

FOOD: The strength of its Japanese clientele is testimony to the success and authenticity of its cooking. Shogun produces some of the best Japanese food in the capital.

OUR TIP: Try one of the six set menus as they offer great value **Times:** 6.30-11, Closed Mon

Six-13

British, International

Eclectic, contemporary kosher food in elegant surroundings

☎ 020 7629 6133 19 Wigmore St W1H 9LA Plan 2-H3

MENU GUIDE Confit salmon, French bean salad • Cajun spiced lamb, ratatouille, roasted fennel • Baked chocolate & sour cherry pudding, vanilla anglaise

WINE GUIDE ♀ Efrat Samson Heights Chardonnay/Sauvignon £21 • ♀ Mt Tabor Cabernet Sauvignon £25 • 40 bottles over £20 7 bottles under £20 • 7 by the glass (£5-£5.95)

PRICE GUIDE Fixed L £20 • Fixed D £24 • starter £6.50-£17.50 • main £14.50-£26 • dessert £6.50-£8.50 • coffee £2.25 • min/water £3 • Service added but optional 12.5%

PLACE: Named after the 613 Jewish disciplines for living, this smart venue cuts a sophisticated modern edge on Wigmore Street. The elegant, art deco interior is chic and relaxing, with mahogany floor, suede banquettes and chairs, and sage-coloured walls all blending harmoniously, alongside closely packed white clothed tables. Popular with the Jewish community.

FOOD: The unusual kosher-fusion menu offers plenty of choice and takes influences from around the globe to deliver colourful, well-presented, innovative dishes that hit the mark.

OUR TIP: Lunch and early evening fixed-price menu, with plenty of Israeli bottles on the wine list

Chef: Michael Korzelius **Owners:** Jay Sinclair **Times:** 12-2.30/5.30-10.30, Closed 25 Dec, 1 Jan, Jewish Holidays, Fri-Sun **Notes:** Vegetarian available **Seats:** 65, Pr/dining room 22 **Smoking:** N/Sm area, Air con **Children:** Portions **Directions:** Nearest station: Oxford Circus or Bond Street Restaurant behind John Lewis store **Parking:** On street **e-mail:** inquiries@six13.com **web:** www.six13.com

Sketch (Lecture Room & Library) *see page 329*

Le Soufflé, InterContinental London

Modern French

Luxurious dining with a French theme

☎ 020 7409 3131 1 Hamilton Place, Hyde Park Corner W1J 7QY Plan 4-G5

MENU GUIDE Crab cake, lobster linguini, shellfish & red pepper coulis • John Dory, confit garlic, diable sauce • Soufflé Grand Marnier, chocolate truffle

PRICE GUIDE Food prices not confirmed for 2006. Please telephone for details

PLACE: Centrally located, overlooking Hyde Park and the London skyline, this much-loved landmark provides luxury facilities and high standard of service to an international clientele. Le Soufflé is an elegant, discreetly lit restaurant, decorated in pale, muted colours that engender a relaxed, sophisticated atmosphere.

FOOD: A modern French carte and set menu are offered, and the eponymous dish is recommended, alongside vegetarian and healthy options. Cooking is technically accomplished and full of interest.

At the time of going to press we were informed that the hotel was due to close in October 2005 for complete refurbishment.

OUR TIP: Try the chef's recommendation menu

Times: 12.30-3/7-10.30, Closed 1st wk Jan, BHs, Sun & Mon, closed L Sat **Rooms:** 458 (458 en suite) ★★★★★ **Directions:** Nearest station: Hyde Park Corner Telephone for directions

e-mail: london@interconti.com **web:** www.london.interconti.com

---

Two Rosettes The best local restaurants, which aim for and achieve higher standards, better consistency and where a greater precision is apparent in the cooking. There will be obvious attention to the selection of quality ingredients. About 40% of restaurants in the guide have two Rosettes.

continued

England

Sketch (Lecture Room & Library)

rench

echnical wizardry offers a unique experience

☎ 0870 777 4488   9 Conduit St W1S 2XG   Plan 3-A2

web: www.sketch.uk.com

ACE: This multi-level, food-based complex - the tantalising collaboration between Mourad Mazouz and Parisian super-chef erre Gagnaire - looks remarkably unassuming from outside on Conduit Street. Inside though, in the former HQ of Christian or, it's quite a different story. Upstairs, the fine-dining Lecture Room and Library (two adjoining rooms) are opulently corated but retain a warm, unostentatious atmosphere decked out in shades of orange with textured leather walls. Well- aced tables with crisp linen napery are paired with richly upholstered armchairs, while thick, brightly coloured carpet (that anages not to be too busy) and long hanging fabric lampshades cut a Middle Eastern vibe. Extremely attentive, professional ough not at all stuffy) staff are necessarily knowledgeable of the complex dish and menu compositions. (On the ground or, Sketch also boasts the more relaxed and vibrant Gallery brasserie, a bar and the Parlour pâtisserie, and throughout, ternational designers have created specially commissioned contemporary signature pieces - check out the jewel-encrusted lets for a start.)

OD: As you'd expect with French creative genius Pierre Gagnaire as consultant (and head chef and protégé Pascal Sanchez charge at the stove), the Lecture Room and Library cuisine is highly unique, breathtaking and technically brilliant. The borate cooking, with its wealth of interesting and intriguing combinations, is delivered with great technical artistry, while perb quality fresh produce and fantastic imagination and improvisation ensures there's a wow-factor at every turn. Clear, an flavours, texture contrast and harmony all hit the spot; think of a starter of langoustines that is delivered four ways, or e 'Pierre Gagnaire Grand Dessert' that may arrive as six dishes. The enticing carte is admirably backed by a fixed-price ting option (as well as an alternative vegetarian version) and lunch menu, and there are lots of extra courses too, so the h pricing does not seem excessive. So go and be wowed by this unique experience.

MENU GUIDE Scallops, black truffles & beef Limousin • Cumin-roasted milk-fed lamb, baby carrots, sweet onions, watercress • Quetsche, blackcurrant mousse, marzipan ravioli

WINE GUIDE ♀ Domaine Jeandeau Pouilly-Fuissé 'Tradition' 2002 Chardonnay £62.50 • ♀ Domaine Joblot Givry 1er Cru, Servoisine Pinot Noir £52.50 • 149 bottles over £20 • 15 by the glass (£5.50-£73.50)

PRICE GUIDE Fixed L £35 • starter £18-£52 • main £23-£58 • dessert £6-£12 • coffee £4 • min/water £4 • Service added but optional 12.5%

OUR TIP: Fabulous breads and pastries are available from the on-site pâtisserie (the Parlour; to take out too)

Chef: P Gagnaire, P Sanchez, G Sein **Owners:** Pierre Gagnaire, Mourad Mazouz **Times:** 12-2.30/7-10.30, Closed 25 Dec, Sun-Mon, closed L Sat **Notes:** Vegetarian available **Seats:** 50 **Smoking:** N/Sm area, Air con **Parking:** Cavendish Square

England

LONDON W1 *continued*

Spiga
Italian
Perennially reliable modern Italian in the West End
☎ 020 7734 3444 84/86 Wardour St W1V 3LF
Plan 3-B2
MENU GUIDE Mozzarella di bufala with aubergine caviar • Linguine all'Aragosta • Chocolate soufflé
WINE GUIDE ♀ Collenussi Pinot Grigio £20 • ♀ Mezzacorona Cabernet Sauvignon £17 • 36 bottles over £20, 15 bottles under £20 • 13 by the glass (£3.30-£6)
PRICE GUIDE Fixed D £27.50-£31 • starter £6-£7 • main £7.50-£14 • dessert £6 • coffee £1.80 • min/water £2.80 • Service added but optional 12.5%
PLACE: A family-friendly Italian restaurant in the best tradition, where the warm reception and great food ensure a busy atmosphere to which regulars of all ages keep coming back.
FOOD: Simple and natural Italian cuisine using excellent ingredients produces dishes of superbly cooked fresh pasta, delicious pizzas with vibrant toppings from a wood-fired oven, and char-grilled meat and fish.
OUR TIP: Book a booth for intimacy
Chef: Marzio Zacchi **Owners:** Giorgio Locatelli, A-Z Partnership
Times: 12-3/6-12, Closed Xmas, New Year, closed L Sun
Notes: Vegetarian available **Seats:** 120 **Smoking:** No pipes, No cigars, Air con **Directions:** Nearest station: Oxford Street At Shaftesbury Ave end of Wardour St **e-mail:** hellofred@hotmail.com
web: www.spigasoho.co.uk

Spoon at Sanderson
Modern European
Pick'n'mix in hip surroundings
☎ 020 7300 1444 50 Berners St W1T 3NG
Plan 3-B3
MENU GUIDE Spicy shrimp brochette • Chicken wings, Thai sauce • Chocolate tart
PRICE GUIDE Food prices not confirmed for 2006. Please telephone for details
PLACE: Straight out of the style magazines, an exclusive hotel with a restaurant to match. You can eat tapas at the bar, and dine outside in the lushly landscaped courtyard garden.
FOOD: A modern European selection of dishes is arranged so that guests can put together their own components, maybe having a selection of four main courses on one plate. Some high quality technical skills and creative concepts help things along.
OUR TIP: Eat outside if possible
Times: 12-3/6-11.30 **Directions:** Nearest station: Oxford Circus Restaurant on Berners St off Oxford St
e-mail: spoon@morganshotelgroup.com
web: www.morganshotelgroup.com

 The Square *see below*

Prices quoted in the guide are for guidance only and are subject to change without notice.

LONDON W1

The Square

French 🐟
A class culinary act in Mayfair
☎ 020 7495 7100 6-10 Bruton St W1J 6PU Plan 3-A1
MENU GUIDE Cornish crab lasagne, shellfish & basil cappuccino • Turbot, truffled potato ravioli, leek & chanterelles fondue • Assiette of chocolate
WINE GUIDE ♀ Puligny-Montrachet Chardonnay £62 • ♀ Segla Cabernet Sauvignon £49 • 1200 bottles over £20, 25 bottles under £20 • 13 by the glass (£4.95-£13)
PRICE GUIDE Fixed L £25-£55 • Fixed D £60 • coffee £5 • min/water £3.95 • Service added but optional 12.5%
PLACE: Behind its glass frontage, this corner restaurant is as chic, fashionable and discreet as its sophisticated Mayfair address just off Bond Street. Furnished in contemporary style, with parquet floors, neutral tones, vibrant abstract artworks and widely spaced tables draped in dark brown underclothes, topped-off with crisp white linen. Staff are young, mainly French, attentive and professional, while the well-heeled clientele give the place an upmarket buzz.

FOOD: The uncluttered dining room provides the perfect stage for Philip Howard's bright, intense cooking. His style is a progressive take on classic French, and comes dotted with premium ingredients (foie gras, black Périgord truffles etc) in cultured, well-judged, imaginative dishes with the emphasis clearly on flavour and balance. The approach is via a fixed-price repertoire of menus (with one or two supplements), including a tasting option (for the whole table). Expect admirable technical skill and fine visual presentation to beckon in an escalope of foie gras with port-glazed turnips, pain d'epice and toasted hazelnut or perhaps roast Bresse pigeon with wild mushroom ravioli, butternut squash, chestnuts and a Madeira sauce.
OUR TIP: Always busy, book well in advance
Chef: Philip Howard **Owners:** Mr N Platts-Martin & Philip Howard
Times: 12-3/6.30-10.45, Closed 24-26 Dec,1 Jan, closed L Sat & Sun, BH
Notes: Tasting menu £75, Vegetarian available, Smart Dress **Seats:** 70, Pr/dining room 18 **Smoking:** N/Sm in restaurant, Air con
Directions: Nearest station: Bond Street Telephone for directions
e-mail: info@squarerestaurant.com **web:** www.squarerestaurant.com

England

 ## Sumosan Restaurant

Modern Japanese   **NEW**

Contemporary Japanese with Western influence

☎ 020 7495 5999   26 Albermarle St, Mayfair W1S 4HY   Plan 3-A1

 MENU GUIDE Beef tataki • Honey mustard organic pork ribs • Green tea ice cream

PRICE GUIDE Food prices not confirmed for 2006. Please telephone for details

PLACE: Set in the middle of antiques and art dealer land, this upmarket Japanese restaurant has a minimalist decor with a curtain of what looks like glass eels at the window. There is a long sushi bar at one side, and a downstairs bar. Asian staff are extremely helpful.

FOOD: Comparable to Nobu, this is Japanese fusion food of a very high standard. The box lunch is a popular option and good value for money, and the carte menu has plenty to choose from, including traditional Japanese dishes.

OUR TIP: Try the lunch box special

Times: 12-12 **e-mail:** janina@sumosan.com

 ## Tajine

Moroccan

Popular, atmospheric Moroccan restaurant

☎ 020 7935 1545   7a Dorset St W1H 3FE   Plan 2-G3

PLACE: Off the beaten track at the quieter end of the Baker Street square mile, this slice of North Africa is decorated in earthy desert tones with Arabic inscriptions on the walls. Tiled floors, mosaic covered table tops and comfortable cushioned seating complete the picture.

FOOD: Very competent Moroccan cooking, with plenty of tried and tested favourites including couscous dishes and an excellent list of 14 different tagines.

OUR TIP: A single tagine dish makes a meal in itself

Times: 12-3/6-11, Closed L Sat, Sun **web:** www.originaltagines.com

Taman Gang

E. Asian

Vivacious basement venue with eclectic Asian menu, open late

☎ 020 7518 3160   141 Park Ln W1K 7AA   Plan 2-F2

MENU GUIDE Soft shell crab with Thai vinaigrette & crushed garlic • Marinated black cod in fresh hoba miso & black bean • Baked yoghurt fondant

PRICE GUIDE Food prices not confirmed for 2006. Please telephone for details

PLACE: Stone walls, sandalwood incense and low tables give an eastern feel, while a more contemporary atmosphere is created by resident DJs. Designer-clad staff are serene in black and sage green.

FOOD: Skilfully prepared and dressed to thrill, with fresh orchids and pansy petals used to good effect. Clean tasting, accurately judged eclectic Asian dishes demonstrate great ingredients and a confident kitchen. Many dishes are designed for sharing, so take a friend.

OUR TIP: Try the smoothie liquid lunches

Times: 12-2.30/6-10.30, Closed Sun, closed L Mon & Sat

e-mail: info@tamangang.com **web:** www.tamangang.com

Tamarind

Indian

Contemporary Indian in Mayfair

☎ 020 7629 3561   20 Queen St, Mayfair W1J 5PR Plan 4-H6

 MENU GUIDE Scallops & tiger prawns, sour grape & mint dressing • Murgh Makhni (tandoori chicken, creamed fresh tomatoes) • Fruit kebab

WINE GUIDE ♀ Maison Louis Moreau Chardonnay £28 • ♀ Paarl Heights Paarl Valley Cinsault £17 • 96 bottles over £20, 6 bottles under £20 • 12 by the glass (£4-£9)

PRICE GUIDE Fixed L £16.95 • Fixed D £65 • starter £6.50-£14 • main £12.95-£22 • dessert £4.50-£5 • coffee £1.95 • min/water £4.50 • Service added but optional 12.5%

PLACE: A sophisticated Indian restaurant done out in contemporary style with muted metallic colours, low lighting and a display kitchen to provide light entertainment if conversation lulls.

FOOD: Centring around the Tandoor oven, Tamarind's menu features a good mix of popular and innovative dishes from north west Indian cuisine. Typical mains include seafood moilee (scallops, squid, mussels and kingfish in a coconut sauce) and bhuna achari gosht (lamb cooked with onion, garlic, red chillies and pickling spices).

OUR TIP: Good value set lunch

Chef: Alfred Prasad **Owners:** Indian Cuisine Ltd. **Times:** 12-2.45/6-11, Closed 25-26 Dec,1 Jan, closed L Sat, BHs **Notes:** Vegetarian available, Dress Restrictions, no jeans, no shorts **Seats:** 90 **Smoking:** No pipes, No cigars, Air con **Children:** Min 10 yrs **Directions:** Nearest station: Green Park Towards Hyde Park, take 4th right into Half Moon St to end (Curzon St). Turn left. Queen St is 1st right. **Parking:** NCP

e-mail: tamarind.restaurant@virgin.net

web: www.tamarindrestaurant.com

Teca

Italian

Sophisticated Italian with a modern mindset

☎ 020 7495 4774   54 Brook's Mews W1K 4EG Plan 2-H2

MENU GUIDE Deep-fried calamari & courgette • Stewed wild boar, Barbaresco wine sauce • Chestnut mousse & three chocolates

WINE GUIDE ♀ Terreda Vino Gavi £30 • ♀ Fasilo Gino Amarone £85 • 350 bottles over £20, 1 bottles under £20 • 10 by the glass (£6-£12)

PRICE GUIDE Fixed D £31.50 • starter £7-£12 • main £12-£17 • dessert £7 • coffee £3 • min/water £3.50 • Service added but optional 12.5%

continued

England

LONDON W1 *continued*

PLACE: Tucked away behind Claridges in moneyed Mayfair is this smart Italian restaurant that more than fits its location's bill. The airy space benefits from its wide glass frontage and light wooden floors, with crisply clothed tables and classy glassware making their own quality statement.

FOOD: The lunch menu is priced individually and economically (dinner prices are set according to number of courses), but the upmarket modern Italian food is the same in both. The kitchen keeps it simple, and it's all the better for it.

OUR TIP: Great selection of home-made Italian breads
Chef: Luca Conti **Owners:** Teca Restaurant Ltd **Times:** 12-2.30/7-10.30, Closed Xmas, New Year, BHs, Sun, closed L Sat **Notes:** Vegetarian available, Civ Wed 70 **Seats:** 65 **Smoking:** No pipes, No cigars, Air con **Children:** Portions **Parking:** Brooks St
e-mail: teca@mayfair.freeserve.co.uk

The Terrace Restaurant & Bar
French, European
Airy dining in prime central London location
☎ 020 7851 3085 Le Meridien Piccadilly, 21 Piccadilly W1J 0BH Plan 3-B1

MENU GUIDE Carpaccio of veal • Roast rib of red deer • Blueberry & lime crème brûlée
WINE GUIDE ♀ Hardys Riddle Sauvignon £24.50 • ♀ Les Genets Merlot £24 • 58 bottles over £20 • 11 by the glass (£6-£7)
PRICE GUIDE Fixed L £18.50 • Fixed D £22.50 • starter £4-£7 • main £19 • dessert £4-£7 • coffee £4 • min/water £3.50 • Service added but optional 12.5%

PLACE: London's only completely glass-roofed restaurant is located in what was once Le Meridien hotel's open air swimming pool. Dine on the terrace for a pigeon's eye view of Piccadilly Circus, or if the weather is less favourable stay inside and enjoy the classical yet contemporary interior decor. The nine-floor landmark hotel provides a great location, bang in the centre of the West End.

FOOD: A crowd-pleasing contemporary menu with flavours from France and beyond. Cooking is simple and straightforward without any unnecessary frills.

OUR TIP: Handy for the theatres, shops and museums
Chef: Ryan Matheson **Owners:** Le Meridien **Times:** 12-2.30/6-10.30 **Notes:** Jazz Brunch Sun 12.30-3, Vegetarian available, Dress Restrictions, No Hats **Seats:** 120 **Smoking:** N/Sm area, Air con **Children:** Menu, Portions **Rooms:** 266 (266 en suite) ★★★★★ **Directions:** Nearest station: Piccadilly Circus Telephone for directions **Parking:** NCP, 5 min walk **e-mail:** nick.priestley@lemeridien.com
web: www.lemeridien.com

La Trouvaille
French
Buzzy, unpretentious, relaxed and authentically French
☎ 020 7287 8488 12a Newburgh St W1F 7RR Plan 3-A2

MENU GUIDE Pan-fried foie gras, Portobello mushroom, cocoa dressing • Braised pork belly, caramelised plums • Chocolate & violet fondant, warm wild cherry
WINE GUIDE ♀ Castera Jurançon Sec Gzos Manseng £23 • ♀ Domaine de Granajolo Nieluccio £18.50 • 27 bottles over £20, 7 bottles under £20 • 10 by the glass (£3.50-£5.90)
PRICE GUIDE Fixed L £17.50 • Fixed D £29.50 • coffee £2 • min/water £2.95 • Service added but optional 12.5%

PLACE: Set among the cobbled pedestrian lanes and boutiques off Carnaby Street, the small, two-roomed La Trouvaille proves to be quite the Soho find, as the name suggests. Mustard-yellow walls, floorboards, retro mirrors and wooden furniture - including pews, window banquettes and white-clothed tables topped with brown paper - create a relaxed, rustic, authentic Gallic bistro mood.

FOOD: Unconventional French cooking - thoughtful and with easygoing invention, well-sourced ingredients and clean-cut flavours - fits the bill. Expect Herdwick mutton fillet with lavender sauce, garlic and grilled courgettes, and marinated pears with black truffle honey and tobacco ice cream.

OUR TIP: Enthusiastic staff add to the Gallic ambience
Chef: Marion David **Owners:** T Bouteloup **Times:** 12-3/6-11, Closed Xmas, Sun **Notes:** Vegetarian available **Seats:** 35, Pr/dining room 16 **Smoking:** No pipes, No cigars, Air con **Children:** Portions
Directions: Nearest station: Oxford Circus Off Carnaby St by Liberty she **Parking:** NCP (off Broadwick St) **web:** www.latrouvaille.co.uk

Umu see page 333

Vasco & Piero's Pavilion Restaurant
Italian
Friendly neighbourhood Italian with panache
☎ 020 7437 8774 15 Poland St W1F 8QE Plan 3-B2

MENU GUIDE Hand-made asparagus tortelloni • Grilled rare tuna, ginger dressing • Compote of plums & yogurt
WINE GUIDE ♀ Borgo Conventi Pinot Grigio £27.50 • ♀ Rufino Vino Nobile di Montepulciano £29.50 • 34 bottles over £20, 6 bottles under £20 • 5 by the glass (£3.60-£7.50)
PRICE GUIDE Fixed L £14.50 • Fixed D £26-£29.50 • starter £5-£9 • main £9-£17 • dessert £6.50 • coffee £2.50 • min/water £3.40 • Service added but optional

PLACE: Warm Italian hospitality makes you feel like a treasured member of the family, and the lively chatter from close-packed tables forces you to leave any cares outside. Unassumingly sited on a street corner, it's not too easy to spot, but head for the red front door.

FOOD: Many of the superb quality ingredients come fresh from Italy, and the kitchen's simple handling of them keeps flavours vivid and clear. Pasta dishes are an obvious strength, and well-loved classics like peaches with zabaglione and Amaretto are perfectly rendered.

OUR TIP: Go with a bunch of friends
Chef: Vasco Matteucci **Owners:** Tony Lopez, Paul Matteucci & Vasco Matteucci **Times:** 12-3/6-11, Closed BHs, Sun, closed L Sat

continu...

Umu

England

apanese (Kyoto Area)   **NEW**
**iophisticated Japanese restaurant offering high-
[u]ality Kyoto cuisine**
☎ 020 7499 8881   14-16 Bruton Place W1J 6LX   Plan
'-H2

MENU GUIDE Langoustine yuba roll • Grilled pigeon, Japanese
mushrooms • Individual cherry & green tea tart

PRICE GUIDE Food prices not confirmed for 2006. Please
[t]elephone for details

[P]LACE: The discreet frontage of Umu, tucked away just off
[B]erkeley Square, is almost clublike. A touch button slides open
[th]e wooden front door on to welcoming staff, a prelude to the
[s]ophisticated, modern interior, with its high-quality wood and
[m]irrors, banquettes and chef's central sushi table. Service is
[h]elpful, particularly when guiding the uninitiated through the
[m]enu.

[F]OOD: Impressive, high quality, contemporary Japanese cuisine
delivered via fixed-price lunch option and an extensive carte.

Expect vibrant, balanced flavours and imaginative presentation
from a wide range of dishes that include some less common
ingredients, like foie gras, venison, and pigeon. The extensive
carte is divided into 8 main categories: Tsukidashi (appetisers),
Suimono (soups), Tsukuri (Sashimi), Agemono (fried dishes),
Yakimono (grilled), Takiwase (simmered), Gohan (rice), Kashi
(desserts). There's also a separate selection of sushi, either
traditional or contemporary, and 6 tasting menus, ranging from
7-12 courses, with or without matched wines/sake. Dishes might
include poached oyster with ponzu sauce, sweet shrimp in sake
vinaigrette, eel kabayaki, usuzukiri (Sashimi course), sudachi
(lime) sorbet and sake jelly with guava sauce.
OUR TIP: Entrance is very low key, so be careful not to miss it
Chef: Ichiro Kubota **Owners:** Mark Groups **Times:** 12-2.30/6-11, Closed
Sun **e-mail:** eric@umurestaurant.com **web:** www.umurestaurant.com

---

[L]ONDON W1 *continued*

[N]otes: Vegetarian available, Dress Restrictions, No shorts **Seats:** 50,
['dining room 36 **Smoking:** No pipes, Air con **Children:** Min 5 yrs,
[po]rtions **Directions:** Nearest station: Oxford Circus From Oxford Circus
['tur]n right towards Tottenham Court Road, continue for 5min and turn right
[in]to Poland St. On corner of Great Marlborough Street & Noel Street.
[Pa]rking: NCP car park opposite **e-mail:** vascosfood@hotmail.com
[w]eb: www.vascosfood.com

🍴 Veeraswamy Restaurant

[I]ndian
[M]odern Indian with refined traditional Indian cooking
☎ 020 7734 1401   Mezzanine Floor, Victory House,
[15] Regent St W1B 4RS   Plan 3-B1

MENU GUIDE Prawn balchao with red chillies, vinegar &
[ga]rlic • Lamb xacutti, cooked with 20 spices & coconut • Bitter
[ch]ocolate kulfi

continued

WINE GUIDE ♀ Colchagua Valley Carmenère Reserve £17.25
46 bottles over £20, 9 bottles under £20 • 10 by the glass (£4.20-
£6.95)

PRICE GUIDE Fixed L fr £13.50 • Fixed D fr £15.50 • starter
£5.25-£9 • main £10.50-£21.50 • dessert £3.75-£5.75 • coffee
£2.50 • min/water £3.70 • Service added 12.5%
PLACE: You'll find London's oldest Indian restaurant just off
Regent Street. Stairs lead up to a tastefully decorated first-floor
dining room that blends minimalist chic with the Asian love of
vibrant colours, with imaginative use of glass, chrome and gold
leaf.
FOOD: Sensibly, the menu is not over long, successfully
combining spicy specialities from South India with classic dishes
from the north, and pleases all palates.
OUR TIP: Renowned Indian that lives up to its reputation
Chef: Gopal Kochak **Owners:** R Mathrani, C Panjabi & N Panjabi
Times: 12-2.30/5.30-11.30, Closed D Xmas **Notes:** 3 course Sun L £16,
Vegetarian available **Seats:** 130, Pr/dining room 36 **Smoking:** N/Sm
area, No pipes, No cigars, Air con **Directions:** Nearest station: Piccadilly
Entrance near junct of Swallow St and Regent St, in Victory House.
web: www.realindianfood.com

The AA Wine Awards recognise the finest
wine lists in England, Scotland and Wales. For
full details, see pages 14-15

England

⚜ *Villandry*

Modern British

Impressive restaurant, store and bar

☎ 020 7631 3131   170 Great Portland St W1W 5QB
Plan 3-A4

MENU GUIDE Prosciutto, baby leeks, truffle honey • Sea bass
fillet, white bean purée • Chocolate cake, crème Chantilly

PRICE GUIDE Food prices not confirmed for 2006. Please
telephone for details

PLACE: The restaurant is situated within a food store in this chic,
understated venue. Concrete floors, white walls and crisp linens
act as a backdrop to the buzz, and large glass windows provide
street-side views.

FOOD: Rustic, modern European dishes make the most of
produce also available in the shop. The brasserie-style menus,
changing twice daily for lunch and dinner, take heed of the
seasons, from roast goose breast in midwinter to a distinctly
summery grilled lobster with aioli.

OUR TIP: High quality ingredients and wines sold in the store
Times: 12-3/6-10, Closed 23 Dec-2 Jan, closed D Sun
Directions: Nearest station: Great Portland Street Restaurant entrance at
91 Bolsover St **e-mail:** contactus@villandry.com
web: www.villandry.com

⚜ *Westbury Hotel*

Modern British

*Inspirational cooking in exclusive Bond Street
hotel*

☎ 020 7629 7755   Bond St W1S 2YF   Plan 3-A2
MENU GUIDE Goats' cheese & basil parfait • Lamb canon
stuffed with lobster • Fruit terrine & Champagne jelly
PRICE GUIDE Food prices not confirmed for 2006. Please
telephone for details

PLACE: A stylish upgrade has added sophistication to this
luxurious hotel, which is a real refuge from the high-life hubbub
of Bond Street. Knowledgeable staff demonstrate impeccable
professionalism and friendliness.

FOOD: Cooking is accurate and well executed, while
combinations of flavours are subtle and successful. Succulent
Cornish scallops on ratatouille could be followed by a tender
fillet and shin of beef on a creamy parsnip purée.

OUR TIP: Follow the shopping spree with eminently civilised
afternoon tea
Times: 12-2.30/6-10.30, Closed L Sat, Sun **Rooms:** 247 (247 en suite)
★★★★ **Directions:** Nearest station: Oxford Circus, Piccadilly Circus
Telephone for directions **e-mail:** enquiries@westburymayfair.com
web: www.westburymayfair.com

⚜ The Wolseley

European

Sophisticated brasserie fare to suit all tastes

☎ 020 7499 6996   160 Piccadilly W1J 9EB   Plan 5-A6
MENU GUIDE Matjes herrings on pumpernickel • Pork belly,
black pudding, roast quince • Poire William in red wine
WINE GUIDE 37 bottles over £20, 8 bottles under £20 • 27 by
the glass (£3.75-£10.75)
PRICE GUIDE Starter £5.25-£18 • main £9.50-£22.50 • dessert
£3.75-£7 • coffee £2.75 • min/water £3.50 • Service optional

PLACE: Seating 170 when busy and catering to a well-heeled mix
of media types and Bond Street shoppers, this classy brasserie
has an infectious buzz despite the grandeur of its listed
architecture and domed ceilings.

FOOD: An extensive menu, served from 7am to midnight
Monday to Friday, covers everything from full meals to light
snacks, via afternoon tea and a patisserie selection. Expect
modern British fare with a strong middle European influence.

OUR TIP: Impressive breakfast menu for early birds
Chef: Chris Galvin, Ed Wilson **Owners:** Chris Corbin & Jeremy King
Times: 7am-mdnt, Closed 11pm Sun, 24(eve) & 25 Dec, 31 Dec (eve),
1 Jan, BHs, open 9am Sat & Sun **Notes:** Vegetarian available **Seats:** 170
Smoking: N/Sm area, No pipes, Air con **Children:** Portions
Directions: Nearest station: Green Park 500 mtrs from Underground
station **web:** www.thewolseley.com

⚜⚜ Yauatcha

Chinese   NEW

All day dim sum and chic tea house

☎ 020 7494 8888   15 Broadwick St W1F 0DL
Plan 3-B2
MENU GUIDE Pan-fried turnip cake • Prawn & date dumpling
WINE GUIDE ♀ Sauvignon Chenin Morgenhof
£19.50 • ♀ Grenache Merlot Cessane £16.50 • 29 bottles over
£20, 7 bottles under £20 • 6 by the glass (£3.20-£4.80)
PRICE GUIDE Food prices not confirmed for 2006. Please
telephone for details

PLACE: Owned by Alan Yau of Hakkasan, it took two years to
transform this basement restaurant in the heart of Soho, and the
results are stunning. A long fish tank divides the room in two,
and twinkling lights from the dark ceiling and tiny wall alcoves
shine down on cool grey furniture. The semi-open kitchen runs
the length of one wall. There is also a unique contemporary tea
room offering over 50 teas and exquisite French pâtisserie.

FOOD: The menu is restricted to an amazing dim sum range,
with a handful of stir fry dishes and noodles. The quality is
superb, and the variety of unusual fillings includes spinach cube
with prawn and waterchestnut.

OUR TIP: Book ahead to avoid disappointment
Chef: Soon Wah Cheong **Owners:** Alan Yau **Times:** 12-11, Closed
25 Dec **Notes:** Vegetarian available **Seats:** 109 **Smoking:** N/Sm in
restaurant, Air con **Directions:** Nearest station: Tottenham Ct Rd,
Piccadilly Circ, Oxford Circ On the corner of Broadwick and Berwick St
Parking: Poland Street - 100 yds **e-mail:** reservations@yauatcha.com

---

NEW
denotes a restaurant which is new
to the guide this year.

England

YMing
Chinese
Authentic Chinese in Soho
☎ 020 7734 2721   35-36 Greek St W1D 5DL
Plan 3-C2

MENU GUIDE Prawns in chilli & spiced salt • Double braised pork • Lychees & Chinese tea

WINE GUIDE ♀ Chene Marchand Sancerre Sauvignon Blanc £22 • ♀ Marques de Casa Concha Cabernet Sauvignon £19 29 bottles over £20, 13 bottles under £20 • 7 by the glass (£3.50-£6.50)

PRICE GUIDE Fixed L £10-£15 • Fixed D £15-£20 • starter £3-£10 • main £6.50-£15 • dessert £4-£5.50 • min/water £3.50 • Service added 10%

PLACE: Just north of Chinatown, this popular eaterie is a haven from the bustling Soho streets. Shades of jade and duck egg blue create a tranquil feel, while tables are spaciously set and well appointed with crisp white linen.

FOOD: Authentic Chinese cooking with an emphasis on regional dishes from the north. The extensive carte is complemented by a range of daily specials, such as duck with black mushroom and lily flower, or lamb with fresh lemon zest.

OUR TIP: Handy for a pre-theatre meal

Chef: Aaron Wong **Owners:** Christine Yau **Times:** noon-11.45, Closed 25-26 Dec, 1 Jan, Sun (ex Chinese New Year) **Notes:** Vegetarian available, clean and tidy dress **Seats:** 60, Pr/dining room 25 **Smoking:** N/Sm area, Air con **Parking:** China town carpark **e-mail:** cyming2000@blueyonder.co.uk **web:** www.yming.com

Yumi Restaurant
Japanese
Accessible Japanese eaterie
☎ 020 7935 8320   110 George St W1H 5RL
Plan 2-G3

PLACE: Kimono-clad waitresses and bow-tied waiters guide you through the maze of Japanese etiquette and cuisine in the small minimalist dining room and authentic private rooms of this restaurant, which could have been plucked straight from Tokyo.

FOOD: The exciting Japanese array of sushi, sashimi, tempura and teriyaki underpin the chef's recommendations and fixed-price meals, using produce of the highest quality, impeccably presented.

Times: 5.30-10.30 **Directions:** Telephone for further details

Carluccios Caffè Fenwick, New Bond St W1A 3BS ☎ 020 7629 0699 Quality Italian chain.

Carluccios Caffè 8 Market Place, Oxford Circus W1N 7AG ☎ 020 7636 2228

Carluccios Caffè St Christopher's Place W1U 1AY ☎ 020 7935 5927

Chor Bizarre 16 Albermarle St, Mayfair W1S 4HW 020 7629 9802 & 7692 8542 The London branch of New Delhi's most innovative and popular restaurant.

Marsala Zones 9 Marshall St W1F 7ER 020 7287 9966 Modern Indian with a balanced approach.

New World Chinese Restaurant 1 Gerrard Place W1D 5PA ☎ 020 7434 2508 In the heart of London's Chinatown, dim sum is a favourite here.

Patara 15 Greek St W1D 4DP ☎ 020 7437 1071 The fourth London branch of this popular modern Thai concept chain.

Sardo 45 Grafton Way W1P 5LA ☎ 020 7387 2521 Authentic and satisfying Sardinian specials in a relaxed setting.

Signor Zilli 40 & 41 Dean St W1D 4PR ☎ 020 7734 3924 Fashionable Italian at the heart of medialand. Expect celebrities and good fish.

Strada 15-16 New Burlington St W1S 3BJ ☎ 020 7287 5967 Superior pizza from quality ingredients cooked in wood-fired ovens.

Strada 9-10 Market Place W1W 8AQ ☎ 020 7580 4644

Wagamama 10a Lexington St W1R 3HS ☎ 020 7292 0990 Informal noodle bars with no booking.

Wagamama 101a Wigmore St W1H 9AB ☎ 020 7409 0111

Yo! Sushi 52 Poland St ☎ 020 7287 0443 Sushi, sashimi, noodles and more.

Yo! Sushi Selfridges Food Hall, 400 Oxford St W1A 1AB ☎ 020 7318 3944

Zilli Fish 36-40 Brewer St W1F 9TA ☎ 020 7734 8649 Fish with an Italian accent from the ebullient Aldo Zilli.

LONDON W2

Assaggi
Italian
Imaginative and authentic Italian
☎ 020 7792 5501   39 Chepstow Place W2 4TS
Plan 2-A2

MENU GUIDE Deep-fried courgette flowers • Roasted guinea fowl, black truffle • Lemon & ricotta mousse

WINE GUIDE ♀ Anselm Capitel Croce Garganega £29.50 • ♀ Umani Ronchi Cumaro Montepucciano £35 25 bottles over £20, 2 bottles under £20 • 6 by the glass (£3.95-£5.50)

PRICE GUIDE Starter £7.95-£12.95 • main £16.95-£21.95 • dessert £6.25 • coffee £1.95 • min/water £2.50 Service optional

PLACE: The easy-going staff and relaxed ambience make it a genuine pleasure to eat here. Three beautiful full length windows allow plenty of daylight in, though the pale apricot walls and a striking floral display brighten the evenings too.

FOOD: The Italian menu is translated with pleasure on request, revealing accomplished national and regional specialities that focus on a simplicity grounded in first rate ingredients. More technically skilled dishes also rate highly.

OUR TIP: Very popular, so book well ahead

Chef: Nino Sassu **Owners:** Nino Sassu, Pietro Fraccari **Times:** 12.30-2.30/7.30-11, Closed 2 wks Xmas, BHs, Sun **Notes:** Vegetarian available **Seats:** 35 **Smoking:** No pipes, No cigars, Air con **Children:** Portions **Directions:** Nearest station: Notting Hill Gate Telephone for directions **e-mail:** nino@assaggi.demon.co.uk **web:** www.assaggi.com

England

LONDON W2 continued

🌀 Island Restaurant & Bar
Modern British   🐟NEW

Stylish bar-restaurant with modern British food prepared in plain view

☎ 020 7551 6070 Royal Lancaster Hotel, Lancaster Ter W2 2TY Plan 2-D2

MENU GUIDE Cornish crab with artichoke, tomato & ginger • Lamb with sweetbreads & broad beans • Goats' cheese ice cream

PRICE GUIDE Food prices not confirmed for 2006. Please telephone for details

PLACE: Part of the Royal Lancaster Hotel but with its own entrance and identity, this contemporary restaurant offers an informal setting for relaxed, all-day dining and views over Kensington Gardens. The stylish decor has a natural feel, with earthy colours, leather seats and plenty of organic materials used.
FOOD: Competent, modern cooking is simple in style with good technical skills and use of quality ingredients. Unfussy dishes are well balanced with good flavours. Fish is a speciality.
OUR TIP: Walk off lunch in the gardens
Times: 12-3/6-10.45 **e-mail:** eat@islandrestaurant.co.uk
web: www.islandrestaurant.co.uk

🌀 Nipa Thai Restaurant
Thai

Authentic Thai within top London hotel

☎ 020 7551 6039 The Royal Lancaster Hotel, Lancaster Ter W2 2TY Plan 2-D2

MENU GUIDE Deep-fried minced prawns on toast • Roasted duck in red curry • Mixed fresh fruits

PRICE GUIDE Food prices not confirmed for 2006. Please telephone for details

PLACE: At the heart of the large Royal Lancaster Hotel, Nipa Thai has been its showpiece restaurant for over ten years. Small and intimate, the distinct feeling of authenticity is built on the decor of reds, golds and browns against which carved wooden figurines and artefacts are displayed. Even the cutlery is genuine, and the mainly male serving team are wonderfully charming and professional.
FOOD: The kitchen team too are experienced Thai chefs, whose practised methodologies continue to produce high quality dishes, including some regional specialities. One to three chilli symbols are used to indicate levels of spiciness.
OUR TIP: For parties of more than five people eating the set menu, one person goes free
Times: 12-2/6.30-10.30, Closed Xmas, New Year, BHs, Sun, closed L Sat
Rooms: 416 (416 en suite) ★★★★ **Directions:** Nearest station: Lancaster Gate Opposite Hyde Park on Bayswater Rd. On 1st floor of hotel
Parking: 30 **e-mail:** nipa@royallancaster.com
web: www.royallancaster.com

AA's Chefs' Chef is the annual poll of all the chefs included in The Restaurant Guide. Around 1800 of the country's top chefs are asked to vote to recognise the achievements of one of their peers.
This year's winner is featured on page 19.

🌀 Royal China
Chinese

Popular traditional Chinese

☎ 020 7221 2535 13 Queensway W2 4QJ Plan 2-B

MENU GUIDE Prawn dumplings • Pork & orniki mushroom noodles

PRICE GUIDE Food prices not confirmed for 2006. Please telephone for details

PLACE: Hugely popular with the Chinese community in particular, this traditional-style restaurant is resplendent with lacquered black and gold, combined with mirrored pillars and etched glass screens.
FOOD: The menu demonstrates a well-executed and subtly flavoured range of classic Chinese dishes. Several set menus off good deals for two or more diners.
OUR TIP: Go for Sunday dim sum
Times: 12-11, Closed 25-26 Dec **e-mail:** info@royalchinagroup.co.uk
web: www.royalchinagroup.co.uk

🍴 **Levantine** 26 London St, Paddington W2 1HH
☎ 020 7262 1111 Authentic Middle Eastern/Lebanese restaura in the heart of Paddington.

🍴 **Yo! Sushi** Unit 218, Whiteleys Shopping Centre W2 6LY
☎ 020 7727 9392 Sushi, sashimi, noodles and more.

🍴 **Yo! Sushi** Unit R07, The Lawn, Paddington Station
W2 1HB ☎ 020 7706 9550 Sushi, sashimi, noodles and more.

LONDON W4

🌀 The Devonshire House
British, Mediterranean   🐟

Simple gastro-pub cuisine

☎ 020 8987 2626 126 Devonshire Rd, Chiswick W4 2JJ Plan 1-D3

MENU GUIDE Pickled herrings, roast beetroot & shallot salad • Braised rabbit, Pommery mustard cream, sage buttere noodles • Bakewell tart

WINE GUIDE ♀ McLaren Vale Stump Jump Sauvignon Blanc £17 • ♀ Miranda Firefly Night Harvest Shiraz £14.50 • 29 bottle over £20, 18 bottles under £20 • 13 by the glass (£3.75-£8)

PRICE GUIDE Fixed L £10.45-£14.45 • starter £3.95-£8.95 • ma £8.95-£15.50 • dessert £4.95 • coffee £1.95 • min/water £2.50 • Group min 7 service 12.5%

PLACE: This smart gastro-pub is a real find and has a restaurar feel thanks to polished wooden tables, leather banquettes and subtle lighting.
FOOD: The Devonshire's hard-working chef-proprietor hails fro Marco Pierre White's stable and is happy to discuss dishes whe you order. The menu changes daily and features uncomplicatec modern European fare made from quality ingredients.
OUR TIP: Busy, so arrive early or book ahead
Chef: Peter Reffell **Owners:** Nicolas Gross & Peter Reffell **Times:** 12-2.30/7-10.30, Closed 25-26 Dec & 1 Jan, Mon **Notes:** Vegetarian availa
Seats: 65 **Smoking:** No pipes, No cigars, Air con **Children:** Menu, Portions **Directions:** Nearest station: Turnham Green 150yds from Chiswick High Rd, 100yds from the Hogarth rdbt on A4. **Parking:** Free street parking **e-mail:** info@thedevonshirehouse.co.uk
web: www.thedevonshirehouse.co.uk

For information on Service Charge, see p21.

England

🍴⊛ Fish hoek

South African Seafood 🐟

Upbeat South African fish restaurant

☎ 020 8742 0766 8 Elliott Rd, Chiswick W4 1PE
Plan 1-D5

MENU GUIDE Chargrilled Atlantic squid, mandarin & chilli dressing • Jumbo Mozambique prawns • Hazyview Malva pudding

PRICE GUIDE Fixed L fr £12 • Fixed D fr £14 • starter £5.50-£14 • main £10-£25 • dessert £5-£7.50 • coffee £2.50 • min/water £3 • Group min 6 service 12.5%

PLACE: Many South Africans living over here make a beeline for this unassuming restaurant to sample seafood jetted in from back home. Close set tables, large family photographs of big-game fishing and a buzzy atmosphere set the style. The friendly team are always happy to explain some unfamiliar names on the menus.

FOOD: The chef, newly arrived from Cape Town, treats the seafood with great respect resulting in clean, well-balanced flavours, as in the grilled Cape Stumpnose with butternut mash. Usefully most dishes can be ordered as starters or mains. Finish in true SA style with desserts such as koeksisters or chocolate mielie meal pudding.

OUR TIP: The amazingly good value set lunch and all South African wine list

Chef: Pete Gottgens **Owners:** Pete Gottgens **Times:** 12-2.30/6-10.30, Closed Xmas, New Year (10 Days), BH Tue, Mon **Notes:** Vegetarian available **Seats:** 50 **Smoking:** N/Sm area, No pipes, No cigars, Air con **Directions:** Nearest station: Turnham Green Telephone for directions **Parking:** Street parking **e-mail:** info@fishhoek.co.uk

🍴⊛ La Trompette

French 🍾

French-inspired cuisine in chic, popular neighbourhood restaurant

☎ 020 8747 1836 5-7 Devonshire Rd, Chiswick W4 2EU Plan 1-C3

MENU GUIDE Deep-fried plaice goujons, tartare sauce, lemon & parsley • White onion & chanterelle risotto, salsify & parmesan • Sticky toffee pudding, pecan praline ice cream

WINE GUIDE ♀ Albariño Pazo de Señorans £28.50 • ♀ Chianti Roccao di Montegrossi Sangiovese £28 • 450 bottles over £20, 55 bottles under £20 • 14 by the glass (£4.50-£11.50)

PRICE GUIDE Fixed L £21.50 • Fixed D £32.50 • coffee £3 • min/water £3 • Service added but optional 12.5%

PLACE: Potted box trees and an awning cordon off the tinted-glass sliding-door frontage to this self-assured, classy, Nigel Platts-Martin and Bruce Poole owned brasserie-style operation rooted in classic French cooking, and set on a quiet side road in fashionable Chiswick. There's alfresco dining in the summer, while the sophisticated, relaxing interior comes decked out in light oak flooring, chocolate leather banquettes and smartly dressed tables. French staff are notable for their friendliness and attentive, knowledgeable service, while oenophiles will be wowed by the wine list, and all will appreciate the bustling atmosphere and noticeable lack of pretension.

FOOD: With the departure of Olivier Couillard in May 2005 to the Dorchester's Grill Room after four highly successful years leading up the kitchens, the mantle of head chef falls to James Bennington (ex sous at sister operation, Chez Bruce, SW17). The food continues the take on French country cooking, delivered via simple brasserie-style dishes notable for their fresh quality ingredients and well-judged, balance flavours. So expect the likes

continued

of soupe paysanne with confit pork belly, ham hock, white beans and pistou, and perhaps a Valrhona chocolate and praline tartlet with chocolate ice cream.

OUR TIP: Don't arrive early on busy nights, as there is no bar or waiting area

Chef: James Bennington **Owners:** Nigel Platts-Martin, Bruce Poole **Times:** 12-2.30/6.30-10.30, Closed 3 days at Xmas **Notes:** Sun L £25, Vegetarian available **Seats:** 72 **Smoking:** N/Sm in restaurant, Air con **Children:** Portions **Directions:** Nearest station: Turnham Green From station follow Turnham Green Tce to jnct with Chiswick High Rd. Cross road & bear right. Devonshire Rd 2nd left **Parking:** On street **e-mail:** latrompette@btconnect.com **web:** www.latrompette.co.uk

⊛ Le Vacherin

French **NEW**

Chic Parisian bistro serving rustic French cuisine

☎ 020 8742 2121 76-77 South Pde W4 5LF
Plan 1-C3

MENU GUIDE Jerusalem artichoke soup, foie gras • Organic belly pork, Puy lentils • Prune & Armagnac tart

WINE GUIDE ♀ Sauvignon Elegale £13.65 • ♀ Bourdeaux de Ville £18 • 14 bottles over £20, 10 bottles under £20 • 5 by the glass (£3.95-£6.25)

PRICE GUIDE Fixed L £11.95-£14.95 • Fixed D £25-£30 • starter £4.95-£8.50 • main £9.95-£18 • dessert £4.95-£6.95 • coffee £2.50 • min/water £3.20 • Service added but optional 12.5%

PLACE: Evoking the atmosphere of a Parisian bistro, this chic restaurant in the heart of Chiswick has wooden floors, scenes of Paris on cream walls, and elegantly laid tables. French music and waitresses complete the picture.

FOOD: Classic French cooking, with simple, rustic food at lunch and more inventive, substantial and complex dishes at dinner. Good clear flavours.

OUR TIP: Parking can be a problem

Chef: Malcolm John **Owners:** Malcolm & Donna John **Times:** 12-3/6-11, Mon **Notes:** Vegetarian available, Smart Dress **Seats:** 72, Pr/dining room 30 **Smoking:** N/Sm area, No pipes **Children:** Portions **Directions:** Nearest station: Chiswick Park Nearest tube: Chiswick Park. Turn left and restaurant 400 mtrs on left **e-mail:** malcolm.john4@btinternet.com **web:** www.levacherin.co.uk

🍽 **Gravy** 142 Chiswick High Rd W4 1PU ☎ 020 8998 6816 Cosy family owned restaurant and bar where emphasis is on friendly atmosphere.

NEW
denotes a restaurant which is new
to the guide this year.

The Best Use of Seafood sponsored by Seafish In conjunction with Seafish, the Sea Fish Industry Authority, we have sought out restaurants that make the most of seafood on their menus. In addition to the four country award winners (see page 9), look out for the seafish symbol throughout the book; this denotes restaurants serving a good range of fish and shellfish dishes, where the accent is firmly on freshness.

England

LONDON W5

Momo

Japanese

Urban shop front hides friendly Japanese restaurant

☎ 020 8997 0206 14 Queens Pde, Ealing W5 3HU Plan 1-C4

MENU GUIDE Miso soup & grilled bean curd • Pickle plum sushi, fish tempura & rice • Plum ice

WINE GUIDE Muscadet de Sevre et Maine Surlie £17 • Cabernet Sauvignon Vin de Pays d'Oc £10.50 • 4 bottles over £20, 4 bottles under £20 • 2 by the glass (£2.60)

PRICE GUIDE Fixed L £8-£16.50 • Fixed D £18-£25 • starter £3.90-£14.50 • main £8.80-£23 • dessert £2.30-£4.50 • coffee £2.20 • min/water £3 • Service added 12%

PLACE: Nostalgic ex-pats craving a taste of home make up the bulk of diners at this simple but popular restaurant. You don't have to be Japanese to enjoy the food though, and there's plenty of advice for beginners.
FOOD: All the usual sushi, sashimi and tempura dishes can be found along with other traditional Japanese choices, and there's a very good value lunch menu. Fresh flavours predominate.
OUR TIP: Book, or eat at the small counter
Chef: Shigeru Kondo **Owners:** Mr Kondo **Times:** 12-3/6-11, Closed 1 wk Xmas, 1 wk Aug, Sun **Notes:** Vegetarian available **Seats:** 30 **Smoking:** Air con **Children:** Menu **Directions:** Nearest station: North Ealing 0.2m from North Ealing station **Parking:** On street

Carluccio's Caffè 5-6 The Green, Ealing W5 5DA ☎ 020 8566 4458 Quality Italian chain.

Charlotte's Place 16 St Matthews Rd, Ealing Common W5 3JT ☎ 020 8567 7541 Modern and traditional European food is the theme of this restaurant, facing Ealing Common.

Three Rosettes Outstanding restaurants that demand recognition well beyond their local area. Timing, seasoning and the judgement of flavour combinations will be consistently excellent, supported by other elements such as intelligent service and a well-chosen wine list. Around 10% of restaurants with Rosettes have been awarded three.

LONDON W6

Anglesea Arms

Modern British

Gastro-pub focussing on good, simple food

☎ 020 8749 1291 35 Wingate Rd W6 0UR Plan 1-D3

MENU GUIDE Tomato, spinach & feta tart • Roast rabbit confit, creamed potato & Savoy cabbage • St Emillion chocolate mousse

WINE GUIDE Petit Bourgeois Sauvignion Blanc £14.50 • Bodegas Urbina Rioja Crianza £16.75 • 12 bottles over £20, 30 bottles under £20 • 15 by the glass (£2.50-£4)

PRICE GUIDE Food prices not confirmed for 2006. Please telephone for details

PLACE: This fashionably shabby gastro-pub is very popular with trendy locals and students. A log fire, wooden floors, Victorian decor and an open-plan, sometimes boisterous, kitchen add to the laid-back charm.
FOOD: Good, hearty and robust cooking hits the mark every time and ensures that there is always plenty of hustle and bustle in this place. Daily changing blackboard menu with seasonal produce clearly evident.
OUR TIP: Get there early - bookings are not taken!
Times: 12.30-2.45/7-10, Closed 24-31 Dec **Directions:** Nearest station: Goldhawk Road, Ravenscourt Park. Off Goldhawk Road.
e-mail: angleseaarms@hotmail.com

The Brackenbury

Modern, European

Competent cooking in friendly neighbourhood environment

☎ 020 8748 0107 129-131 Brackenbury Rd W6 0BQ Plan 1-D3

MENU GUIDE Roast pigeon breast, braised red cabbage, chocolate oil • Loin of veal, grain mustard sabayon • Yorkshire champagne rhubarb fool

WINE GUIDE Sangoma Chenin Blanc £16 • Flagstone Blend (Merlot/Cabernet Sauvignon) £16 • 34 bottles over £20, 18 bottles under £20 • 8 by the glass (£3.20-£4.50)

PRICE GUIDE Fixed L £12.50 • starter £4-£7.50 • main £9.50-£16.50 • dessert £4-£6.50 • coffee £1.80 • min/water £2.90 • Service added but optional 12.5%

PLACE: A pair of shops, joined at the back by a bar and small seating area, is the setting for this easy-going, light and airy neighbourhood restaurant. Earthy natural colours, dark polished tables, modern wooden chairs and unadorned walls all add up to a relaxed, cool and cosy feel.
FOOD: Mediterranean inspired dishes focus on quality ingredients and a simple, unfussy approach. Cooking is accurate, presentation is appealing and promised flavours shine through.
OUR TIP: Make sure you book for Sunday lunch
Chef: Noel Capp **Owners:** Lisa Inglis **Times:** 12.30-2.45 (Last Orders 3.30 Sun)/7-10.45, Closed 24-26 Dec, 1 Jan, Easter, closed L Sat, closed D Sun **Notes:** Roast fillet of beef served every Sun, Vegetarian available **Seats:** 60 **Smoking:** N/Sm in restaurant **Children:** Portions **Directions:** Nearest station: Goldhawk Road, Hammersmith Telephone for directions **Parking:** On street
e-mail: lisa@thebrackenbury.fsnet.co.uk

Chez Kristof
NEW

French

French food in lively neighbourhood restaurant

☎ 020 8741 1177 111 Hammersmith Grove W6 0NQ
Plan 1-D4

MENU GUIDE Moules marinieres • Coq au vin • Pain perdu & apple

PRICE GUIDE Food prices not confirmed for 2006. Please telephone for details

PLACE: Occupying a corner site in Shepherd's Bush, this is very much a bustling neighbourhood restaurant where diners rub shoulders at the closely spaced tables. The restaurant owns an impressive deli next door.
FOOD: Unpretentious, straightforward French provincial cooking forms the basis of the seasonally changing menus, where there's as much wow factor in the breads and dips as the main dishes.
OUR TIP: Visit the delicatessen next door
Times: 12-3/6.30-11.15 **e-mail:** info@chezkristof.co.uk
web: www.chezkristof.co.uk

One Rosette Excellent local restaurants serving food prepared with care, understanding and skill, using good quality ingredients. These restaurants stand out in their local area. Of the total number of establishments with Rosettes around 50% have one Rosette.

The Gate

International Vegetarian

Cosmopolitan vegetarian eaterie in Hammersmith

☎ 020 8748 6932 51 Queen Caroline St W6 9QL
Plan 1-D3

MENU GUIDE Beetroot blini, dill & horseradish sour cream • Red Thai curry • Chocolate torte, Armagnac-soaked prunes, crème fraîche

PRICE GUIDE Starter £4-£6 • main £8-£13 • dessert £4-£6 • coffee £1.50 • min/water £2.50 • Service added but optional 12.50% • Group min 6 service 12.5%

PLACE: This celebrated vegetarian haunt in busy Hammersmith occupies a former artist's studio above a church, and is reached via a peaceful courtyard. It's an airy space, with big windows and a high ceiling, simply furnished with unclothed tables and colourful vases.
FOOD: Innovative vegetarian cooking with an emphasis on flavour. A globe-trotting menu promises dishes with an international feel, and indicates which meals are gluten-free or suitable for vegans.
OUR TIP: Dine alfresco in the courtyard in summer
Chef: Adrian Daniel, Joe Tyrrell **Owners:** Adrian Daniel, Michael Daniel
Times: 12-3/6-11, Closed 23 Dec-3 Jan, Easter Mon, BHs, Sun, closed L Sat
Notes: Vegetarian available **Seats:** 60 **Smoking:** N/Sm in restaurant, Air con **Children:** Portions **Directions:** Nearest station: Hammersmith Telephone for directions **Parking:** On street
e-mail: info@gateveg.co.uk **web:** www.gateveg.co.uk

 The River Café *see below*

The River Café

Italian

Thames-side trendsetter

☎ 020 7386 4200 Thames Wharf, Rainville Rd W6 9HA Plan 1-D3

MENU GUIDE Chargrilled squid, fresh red chilli & rocket • Pan-fried monkfish, potatoes, trevise, black olives, capers, sage • Lemon tart

WINE GUIDE ♀ Pieropan Calvarino Soave £27.50 • ♀ Fontodi Chianti Sangiovese £30.50 • 180 bottles over £20, 11 bottles under £20 • 14 by the glass (£3-£11)

PRICE GUIDE Fixed D £50-£65 • starter £11-£18 • main £22-£30 • dessert £7 • coffee £1.50 • min/water £3 • Service added but optional 12.5%

PLACE: People still come in their droves to Ruth Rogers' and Rose Gray's famous Hammersmith Italian. The spacious, modern, minimalist white room, with high-arched ceiling has an urban vibe (the work of Rogers' famous architect husband, David) and successfully mixes a bustling, informal, cosmopolitan atmosphere with a fine dining experience. There's plenty of steel and glass;

full length windows run along one side (opening up to the terrace in summer) and a long, shiny stainless steel kitchen/bar on the other. In between, tables are closely packed, there's the theatre of the open kitchen with its wood-burning oven, a lively cocktail bar and, amongst the buzz, the endearing charm of regulars being greeted by name with their drinks remembered.
FOOD: Authentic, unfussy, regional Italian cooking with traditional influences and modern twists, executed with panache and a lightness of touch, is the style. It's not cheap, but with the emphasis on using only the very best raw materials, simply treated and skilfully prepared without excess, it's quite the epitome of good taste. Be prepared to be wowed by fresh, vibrant combinations on the appealing, daily-changing repertoire, and anticipate making plans to return almost before you leave.
OUR TIP: Booking essential, and ask for directions
Chef: R Gray, R Rogers, Theo Randall **Owners:** Rose Gray, Ruth Rogers
Times: 12.30-3/7-11, Closed 24 Dec-1 Jan, Easter, BHs, closed D Sun
Notes: Vegetarian available **Seats:** 108 **Smoking:** N/Sm in restaurant, Air con **Children:** Portions **Directions:** Nearest station: Hammersmith 10 min walk. (Restaurant in converted warehouse). Entrance on S side of Rainville Rd at junct with Bowfell Rd **Parking:** 29
e-mail: info@rivercafe.co.uk **web:** www.rivercafe.co.uk

England

LONDON W6 continued

⊕⊕ *Sagar*
Vegetarian, Indian   NEW
South Indian vegetarian restaurant
☎ 020 8741 8563 157 King St, Hammersmith W6 9JT
Plan 1-D3
MENU GUIDE Bhajia • Masala dosa • Srikand
PRICE GUIDE Food prices not confirmed for 2006. Please telephone for details

PLACE: Located among shops in a busy Hammersmith street, this unpretentious restaurant concentrates on the cooking of the Udipi region of south west India. Service is informal and helpful.
FOOD: The large menu of vegetarian dishes ranges from uthappams (lentil pizzas) and puris to curries, dosas and thalis. Dishes are carefully created with fresh, distinct flavours and character. Served with sambar and fresh coconut chutney, the nine different varieties of dosa are a menu highlight.
OUR TIP: Order the dosa
Times: 12-2.45/5.30-10.45

⊕ Snows-on-the-Green Restaurant
Mediterranean
Very friendly and popular restaurant with Mediterranean cuisine
☎ 020 7603 2142 166 Shepherd's Bush Rd, Brook Green, Hammersmith W6 7PB Plan 1-D3
MENU GUIDE Foie gras, fried egg, balsamic • Confit of pork, fricassee of salsify & field mushrooms • Espresso crème brûlée
WINE GUIDE ♀ Il Cantico Pinot Grigio £15.50 • ♀ Trapiche Merlot/Malbec £13 • 16 bottles over £20, 26 bottles under £20 • 12 by the glass (£3.65-£8.75)
PRICE GUIDE Fixed L £13.50 • Fixed D £17.50 • starter £5-£8.75 • main £13-£16 • dessert £5-£6 • coffee £2 • min/water £1.35 • Service optional • Group min 6 service 12.5%

PLACE: Situated on the busy road between Shepherd's Bush and Hammersmith, this friendly restaurant is popular with media types and local foodies. Staff are very happy to help and service is informal.
FOOD: Mediterranean with an Italian bias, the food is honest, seasonal and unpretentious. Classic dishes like osso buco are well executed, as is the home-made baked Venetian cheesecake. Wine club nights on Monday evenings when wine is half price.
OUR TIP: Good-value set lunch
Chef: Sebastian Snow **Owners:** Sebastian Snow **Times:** 12-3/6-11, Closed 24-29 Dec, BHs, Sun, closed L Sat **Notes:** Vegetarian available
Seats: 80, Pr/dining room 30 **Smoking:** N/Sm area, No pipes, No cigars, Air con **Children:** Menu, Portions **Directions:** Nearest station: Hammersmith Broadway 300yds from station **Parking:** On street
e-mail: sebastian@snowsonthegreenfreeserve.co.uk
web: www.snowsonthegreen.co.uk

⊕ *Los Molinos* 127 Shepherds Bush Rd W6 7LP
☎ 020 7603 2229 Tapas and raciones in authentic, bustling surroundings.

🚚 denotes restaurants that place particular emphasis on making the most of local ingredients.

LONDON W8

⊕ The Ark
Italian
Decent Italian food in relaxed atmosphere
☎ 020 7229 4024 122 Palace Gardens Ter W8 4RT
Plan 4-A6
MENU GUIDE Mixed seafood broth • Grilled langoustines & lemon • Chocolate soufflé
WINE GUIDE ♀ Panizzi Vernaccia £25 • ♀ Brancaia Sangiovese/Cabernet Sauvignon/Merlot £29 • 33 bottles over £20, 13 bottles under £20 • 13 by the glass (£3.50-£7)
PRICE GUIDE Starter £6-£8 • main £14-£18.50 • dessert £6 • coffee £3 • min/water £3.50 • Service added but optional 12.5%

PLACE: This fun Italian is divided into separate restaurant and bar areas, with mirrors at either end interspersed with black and white photos. Soft lighting and candles add to the retro brasserie mood.
FOOD: The menu looks familiar with its antipasti, primi piatti, secondi piatti and dolce, but it's much better than the norm. A modern vision lifts the likes of lamb rump with rosemary well out of the ordinary.
OUR TIP: Essential to book for the small terrace
Chef: Steve Moran **Owners:** Louise Mayo **Times:** 12-3/6.30-12, Closed Sun, BHs, closed L Mon **Notes:** Light L menu Tue-Sat, Vegetarian available **Seats:** 50 **Smoking:** No pipes, Air con **Children:** Portions **Parking:** On street **e-mail:** natwalls@aol.com
web: www.thearkrestaurant.co.uk

⊕ Babylon
European, International
Imaginative food, roof garden restaurant with fabulous views
☎ 020 7368 3993 The Roof Gardens, 99 Kensington High St W8 5SA Plan 4-B4

MENU GUIDE Salt cod, lemon & spring onion fritters • Roasted sea bass, caponata & herb lasagne • Strawberry tiramisù
WINE GUIDE ♀ Jordan Sauvignon Chardonnay £24 • ♀ Jordan Cabernet Merlot £29 • 42 bottles over £20, 8 bottles under £20 • 9 by the glass (£5.50-£7)
PRICE GUIDE Fixed L £14 • Fixed D £26 • starter £6.50-£14.50 • main £14.50-£24.50 • dessert £5.75-£8 • coffee £2.50 • min/water £3.50 • Service added 12.5%

PLACE: Entering via Derry Street, diners are transported by a lift to the stylish, softly-lit restaurant with its intimate booths, impressive fish tanks and a popular rooftop garden that is a must-visit for alfresco summer evenings. A private dining room has its own sound system and terrace.

continue

FOOD: The modern British and European cuisine looks further afield for inspiration on an eclectic menu driven by quality produce, but with plenty of choice.
OUR TIP: Eat outside whenever the weather allows
Chef: Oliver Smith **Owners:** Sir Richard Branson **Times:** 12-3/7-11, Closed Xmas & New Year, other dates may vary, closed L Sat
Notes: Tasting menu 9 courses £55, with wine £85, Vegetarian available, Dress Restrictions, Smart casual **Seats:** 120, Pr/dining room 14
Smoking: N/Sm area, No pipes, No cigars, Air con **Children:** Menu, Portions **Parking:** 15 **e-mail:** babylon@roofgardens.virgin.co.uk
web: www.virgin.com/roofgardens

Belvedere

British, French

Jewel in Holland Park, with parking and stunning interior
☎ 020 7602 1238 Abbotsbury Rd, Holland House, Holland Park W8 6LU Plan 1-D3

MENU GUIDE Foie gras parfait & chicken livers • Veal cutlet, morel s • Terrine of dark chocolate, digestives, raspberries & sorbet
WINE GUIDE ♀ Jean Marc Brochard Chablis £25 • ♀ Vasse Felix abernet Merlot £28 • 60 bottles over £20, 2 bottles under 20 • 10 by the glass (£4-£9)
PRICE GUIDE Fixed L £14.95 • Fixed D £17.95 • starter £6.50-£10.50 ain £8.50-£35 • dessert £6.50 • coffee £3 • min/water £3.50 ervice added but optional 12.5% • Group min 13 service 15%
PLACE: One of London's most romantic restaurants, the vedere occupies a beautiful old orangery actually inside land Park. It was once the summer ballroom to the Jacobean nsion, Holland House, and has a vaulted ceiling, parquet ring, high windows and giant carriage lamps. In addition to main dining area, there's an intimate mezzanine and terrace.
OD: Very simple classic modern British and French brasserie king offered from a menu du jour priced for two or three rses and a carte with more of the same.
R TIP: Book a table on the terrace when the weather's good
f: Billy Reid **Owners:** Jimmy Lahoud **Times:** 12-2.30/6-10.30,

continued

Closed 26 Dec, 1 Jan, closed D Sun **Notes:** Sun L 3 courses £21, Vegetarian available **Seats:** 90 **Smoking:** No pipes, Air con
Directions: On the Kensington High Street side of Holland Park. **Parking:** 50 **e-mail:** sales@whitestarline.org.uk
web: www.whitestarline.org.uk

Clarke's

British, Mediterranean

Simple classical cooking in stylish Notting Hill Gate
☎ 020 7221 9225 • 124 Kensington Church St W8 4BH Plan 4-A5

MENU GUIDE Pear, parmesan, bitter leaves & olive salad • Marinated Welsh lamb loin, roasted & glazed • Lemon pot, candied peel, biscotti
WINE GUIDE ♀ J M Roger Sancerre Sauvignon Blanc £24 • ♀ Pavellot Savigny les Beaune Pinot Noir £35 • 105 bottles over £20, 8 bottles under £20 • 7 by the glass (£4-£7.50)
PRICE GUIDE Food prices not confirmed for 2006. Please telephone for details
PLACE: Softly lit restaurant, elegantly presented with contemporary art and fresh flowers. Tables, clothed in white linen, are closely positioned on two floors with French café-style chairs. Next door is Sally Clarke's shop, selling its celebrated bread.
FOOD: The concept is tried and tested, with stunning ingredients as the key feature of the simply prepared, seasonally inspired dishes, with lots of salads and fresh vegetables. The daily set dinner menu is quite pricey, but you can opt for two, three or four courses. Lunch offers more choice and brunch is served Saturdays.
OUR TIP: Clarke's caters for private parties
Chef: Sally Clarke, Liz Payne **Owners:** Sally Clarke **Times:** 12.30-2/7-10, Closed 8 days Xmas & New Year, Sun, closed D Mon **Notes:** Vegetarian available **Seats:** 90 **Smoking:** N/Sm in restaurant, Air con
Directions: Nearest station: Notting Hill Gate Telephone for directions **Parking:** On street **e-mail:** restaurant@sallyclarke.com
web: www.sallyclarke.com

Kensington Place

British, European

Vibrant retro-style brasserie specialising in fish
☎ 020 7727 3184 • 201-5 Kensington Church St W8 7LX Plan 4-A6

MENU GUIDE Griddled scallops, pea purée, mint vinaigrette • Bass with citrus fruits & olive oil • Hot chocolate pudding, custard
WINE GUIDE ♀ Daniel Dampt Chablis Chardonnay £26.50 ♀ Domaine Charvin Côtes du Rhône £23.50 • 120 bottles over £20, 16 bottles under £20 • 15 by the glass (£5-£8.75)
PRICE GUIDE Fixed L £18.50-£21.50 • Fixed D £24.50-£39.50 starter £6-£12.50 • main £14-£25 • dessert £6-£12 • coffee £2 • min/water £3 • Service added but optional 12.5%
PLACE: Prominently located property at the Notting Hill end of Kensington Church Street, with a long plate glass fascia giving passers by an eyeful of the 80s-style interior - all vibrant colours, closely packed tables and huge mural. Still buzzing after 20 years, locals, business people, politicians and the odd celebrity flock here at lunch and dinner, giving the young pretenders a run for their money.
FOOD: Well executed brasserie food using top quality ingredients; all very seasonal with fish as a speciality. The restaurant has its own high quality fish shop next door.
OUR TIP: Buy a copy of the chef's cook book
Chef: Rowley Leigh **Owners:** Place Restaurants Ltd. **Times:** 12-3.30/6.30-11.45, Closed 24-26 Dec, 1 Jan **Notes:** Vegetarian available **Seats:** 140, Pr/dining room 45 **Smoking:** Air con **Children:** Menu, Portions **Directions:** Nearest station: Notting Hill Gate Telephone for directions **Parking:** on street **e-mail:** kpparty@egami.co.uk
web: www.egami.co.uk

England

LONDON W8 *continued*

Launceston Place Restaurant

British

Modern British food in relaxed, upmarket, neighbourhood restaurant

☎ 020 7937 6912 1a Launceston Place W8 5RL
Plan 4-C4

MENU GUIDE Twice-baked goats' cheese soufflé, red wine poached pears • Roasted cod, pea purée, mint vinaigrette • Two brûlées, shortbread biscuits

WINE GUIDE ♀ Sancerre Sauvignon Blanc £28 • ♀ Château Vachon St Emilion £32 • 61 bottles over £20, 6 bottles under £20 • 7 by the glass (£4.50-£7.95)

PRICE GUIDE Fixed L £15.50 • starter £4-£11.50 • main £16.50-£19.50 • dessert £6.50-£7 • coffee £2.75 • min/water £3.25 • Service added but optional 12.5%

PLACE: Cosily wrapped round a corner site in a charming, leafy, well-to-do part of Kensington, Launceston Place is a haven of calm with a genteel English air. The cottagey interior of gilt mirrors, colourful prints, lamps, banquettes and chairs, and crisp white linen, is shared among a series of small townhouse rooms, where service is predictably friendly and courteous. Try for a window table up front.

FOOD: The kitchen adopts a modern British approach - with a nod to the Mediterranean - via a repertoire of simple, light and accomplished contemporary dishes that aptly suits clientele and ambience.

OUR TIP: Good value fixed-price lunch

Chef: Philip Reed **Owners:** Christopher Bodker **Times:** 12.30-2.30/7-11.30, Closed Xmas, New Year, Easter, closed L Sat **Notes:** Sun L 3 courses £22.50, Vegetarian available **Seats:** 85, Pr/dining room 14 **Smoking:** No pipes, No cigars, Air con **Directions:** Nearest station: Gloucester Road Just south of Kensington Palace.

e-mail: lpr@egami.co.uk **web:** www.egami.co.uk

Milestone Hotel & Apartments Townhouse

British

Intimate restaurant in elegant townhouse hotel

☎ 020 7917 1000 1 Kensington Court W8 5DL
Plan 4-B4

MENU GUIDE Potted lobster & crayfish, caviar butter • Chicken pot pie, baby onions, mushrooms & bacon • Chocolate fondant, mint crisp ice cream

PRICE GUIDE Food prices not confirmed for 2006. Please telephone for details

PLACE: In the heart of Kensington - opposite Kensington Palace, this elegant townhouse hotel is ideally located for weary shoppers. With an air of luxury and sophistication throughout, the restaurant has leaded Victorian windows, dark wood furniture, and shining crystal and silverware.

FOOD: Classically based dishes are perfect for the surroundings, straightforward cooking with unfussy presentation. Duck cottage pie has great mash, with a perfect contrast between the crunchy topping and smoothness beneath.

OUR TIP: Stay over and order the Midnight Feast Hamper!

Times: 12-3/5.30-11 **Rooms:** 57 (57 en suite) ★★★★★
e-mail: bookms@rchmel.com **web:** www.milestonehotel.com

Royal Garden Hotel, Tenth Floor Restaurant *see page 343*

Timo

Italian

Traditional Italian in fashionable area

☎ 020 7603 3888 343 Kensington High St W8 6NW
Plan 1-D3

MENU GUIDE Pappardelle, lamb sweetbreads & thyme • Salmo fillet, balsamic dressing • Zabaglione, mixed berries

PRICE GUIDE Food prices not confirmed for 2006. Please telephone for details

PLACE: Modern Italian decor sets the scene, with tan suede chairs and crisply dressed tables, while huge prints add a spot of colour. The restaurant is situated in one of the calmer reaches of the ever-trendy Kensington High Street.

FOOD: Classical Italian style and presentation. An all-Italian wine list has been sourced from interesting producers.

OUR TIP: Parking is difficult

Times: 12-2.30/7-11, Closed Xmas, New Yr, BHs **Directions:** Nearest station: Kensington High Street 5 mins walk towards Hammersmith, after Odeon Cinema, on left of st **Parking:** 3

e-mail: timorestaurant@tiscali.co.uk

Utsav

Indian   **NEW**

Stylish Indian dining

☎ 020 7368 0022 17 Kensington High St W8
Plan 4-B4

MENU GUIDE Lamb tawa kebab • Goan prawn balchao • Gajja ka halva

PRICE GUIDE Food prices not confirmed for 2006. Please telephone for details

PLACE: A welcome escape from the hustle and bustle of Kensington High Street, this contemporary Indian restaurant is decorated with blue glass tiles and modern artwork.

FOOD: Traditional dishes from every corner of India, prepared with skill and flair using quality ingredients. Flavours are clear and sometimes very intense, so remember to ask which dishes are particularly spicy.

OUR TIP: The lunch menu and Sunday brunch are great value

Times: 11.30-11.30 **e-mail:** mail@ustav-restaurant.co.uk
web: www.ustav-reastaurant.co.uk

Zaika

Indian

Lively restaurant serving carefully prepared, modern Indian cuisine

☎ 020 7795 6533 1 Kensington High St W8 5NP
Plan 4-B4

MENU GUIDE Tandori chicken marinated in coriander, mint & basil • Swordfish & scallop poached in coconut & chilli masala • Coconut ice cream

WINE GUIDE ♀ Dr Unger Grüner Veltliner £35 • ♀ Vergelegen Merlot £34.50 • 565 bottles over £20, 17 bottles under £20 15 by the glass (£4.75-£8.50)

PRICE GUIDE Fixed L fr £15 • starter £6.25-£12.50 • main £12.50-£18.25 • dessert £6-£6.50 • coffee £4 • min/water £3 • Service added but optional 12.5%

continued on page 3

ONDON W8

England

Royal Garden Hotel, Tenth Floor Restaurant

nternational

'anoramic views, modern cuisine and sophisticated ambience

☎ 020 7361 1910 2-24 Kensington High St W8 4PT Plan 4-B5

-mail: tenthrestaurant@royalgardenhotel.co.uk

veb: www.royalgardenhotel.co.uk

LACE: One needs a head for heights at this elevated Kensington dining room, set on the top floor of the landmark oyal Garden Hotel next door to Kensington Palace, and offering jaw-dropping views over the capital's skyline (a wide-ngle photo, converted into a brochure, helps identify the sights). Modern, elegant, sophisticated and appropriately amed, The Tenth Floor Restaurant has huge windows to exploit the fabulous views and allow light to flood in. omfortable seating, smartly appointed tables, professional, discreet but friendly service, and a comfortable bar area implete the heady package.

)OD: Modern concepts and a classical repertoire merge with exciting flavours and combinations and stylish, visually impelling presentation. The approach is via a dinner carte offering fixed prices for groups of dishes, while lunch sees value jour menu come into play alongside an abridged carte. So expect clear flavours and portions that satisfy; erhaps grilled suprême of halibut with Cornish crab risotto and cappuccino, or roast rack of English lamb with plenta and tomato tian, aubergine beignet and a thyme jus.

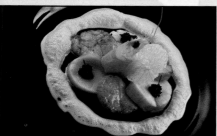

MENU GUIDE Seared scallops, veal sweetbread, Pithiviers caramelised chicory • Venison loin, Savoy cabbage, sweet potato dauphinoise, juniper sauce • Orange tartlet, honeycomb ice cream

WINE GUIDE ♀ La Croix Sauvignon Blanc £17.50 • ♀ Baron Phillipe de Rothschild Merlot £17.50 • 143 bottles over £20, 7 bottles under £20 12 by the glass (£4.50-£9.75)

PRICE GUIDE Fixed L £17.25 • starter £6.50-£12.75 • main £15-£32 • dessert £5.75 • coffee £3.75 • min/water £3.75 • Service optional

OUR TIP: Dinner and dance at one of the Manhattan nights; and try to book a window table

Chef: Norman Farquharson **Owners:** Goodwood Group **Times:** 12-2.30/5.30-11, Closed 2 wks Aug, 2 wks Jan, Sun, closed L Sat **Notes:** Vegetarian available, Civ Wed 100 **Seats:** 110 **Smoking:** N/Sm area, Air con **Children:** Portions **Rooms:** 396 (396 en suite) ★★★★★ **Directions:** Nearest station: Kensington High Street Next to Kensington Palace, Royal Albert Hall **Parking:** 200

LONDON W8 *continued*

PLACE: Zaika turns on its own distinctive flavour and style on Kensington High Street. Originally a church and then a bank, the attractive, airy interior of this listed building is pleasantly understated, its original high-ceilinged, panelled interior brightened by vibrant-coloured seating - a mix of high-backed chairs and banquettes - and range of classic Indian artefacts.
FOOD: The modern Indian repertoire delivers accomplished, well-executed and presented dishes from sound ingredients. Choose from fixed-price lunch, carte or two tasting menus.
OUR TIP: Try the tasting menu with accompanying wines
Chef: Sanjay Dwivedi **Owners:** Claudio Pulze, Raj Sharma (Cuisine Collection) **Times:** 12-2.45/6-9.45, Closed BHs, Xmas, New Year, closed L Sat **Notes:** 4 course tasting lunch £19, 6 course tasting dinner £38, 9 course gourmand £58, Vegetarian available, Dress Restrictions, Smart casual preferred **Seats:** 84 **Smoking:** No pipes, Air con
Children: Portions **Directions:** Nearest station: Kensington High Street Opposite Kensington Palace **e-mail:** info@zaika-restaurant.co.uk
web: www.zaika-restaurant.co.uk

Wagamama 26a High St Kensington W8 4PW
☎ 020 7376 1717 Informal noodle bars with no booking.

LONDON W11
E&O
Asian
Fashionable oriental haunt
☎ 020 7229 5454 14 Blenheim Crescent W11 1NN
Plan 1-D4
MENU GUIDE Duck, watermelon, cashew salad • Hot & sour braised beef, kai choy • Chocolate pudding
WINE GUIDE ♀ Vergelegen Sauvignon Blanc £20 • ♟ Boland Merlot £20 • 66 bottles over £20, 9 bottles under £20 • 10 by the glass (£3.25-£5.50)
PRICE GUIDE Starter £3-£6.50 • main £9-£21.50 • dessert £5-£6.50 • coffee £1.80 • min/water £3 • Service added but optional 12.5%

PLACE: This trendy bar-restaurant not far from Notting Hill and Portobello Road mixes oriental style with the laid-back comfort of leather booths and armchairs. Tables are simply set with a bamboo pot for cutlery and chopsticks.
FOOD: Top-notch contemporary Asian cuisine that draws inspiration from around the Pacific Rim. An extensive menu covers all the usual bases and suits grazing or sharing with friends.
OUR TIP: Book ahead to avoid disappointment
Chef: Simon Treadway **Owners:** Will Ricker **Times:** 12-3/6-11, Closed 25 & 26 Dec, 1 Jan & Aug BH **Notes:** Smart Dress **Seats:** 86, Pr/dining room 18 **Smoking:** No pipes, No cigars, Air con **Directions:** Nearest station: Notting Hill Gate At Notting Hill Gate tube station turn right, at mini rdbt turn into Kensington Park Rd, restaurant 10min down hill
Parking: Street parking available **e-mail:** info@eando.nu
web: www.eando.nu

> **Two Rosettes** The best local restaurants, which aim for and achieve higher standards, better consistency and where a greater precision is apparent in the cooking. There will be obvious attention to the selection of quality ingredients. About 40% of restaurants in the guide have two Rosettes.

Edera
Italian
Chic Italian offering great value
☎ 020 7221 6090 148 Holland Park Av W11 4UE
Plan 1-D4
MENU GUIDE Mussel soup, mixed peppers • Grilled tuna, cannellini beans, red onions • Tiramisù
WINE GUIDE 8 by the glass (£3.50-£8.50)
PRICE GUIDE Starter £6-£10 • main £11-£18 • dessert £5-£6 • coffee £2.50 • min/water £2.50

PLACE: A classic Italian eaterie with a friendly, relaxed ambience and that is modishly kitted out with light wooden floors, deep red pillars and sandstone walls. It's popular, so book ahead and leave time to find a parking space on nearby roads.
FOOD: Edera prides itself on drawing inspiration from every region of Italy and delivers a tempting menu of creative and accomplished dishes at a reasonable price. Good attention to seasonality.
OUR TIP: Limited choice for vegetarians
Chef: Gianni Andolfi **Owners:** A-Z Ltd **Times:** 12-2.30/6.30-11, Closed 25-26 & 31 Dec, closed L Sat **Notes:** Vegetarian available, Dress Restrictions, Smart casual appreciated **Seats:** 60, Pr/dining room 14 **Smoking:** Air con **Children:** Portions **Parking:** Street parking

The Ledbury
Rosettes not confirmed at time of going to press
French   **NEW**
☎ 020 7792 9090 127 Ledbury Road W11 2AQ
Plan 1-D4
This exciting new restaurant has just opened as we went to press. Owners are Nigel Platts-Martin (The Square, Chez Bruce, La Trompette and The Glasshouse) and Philip Howard, chef director at The Square. The chef is Brett Anderson, formerly sous chef at The Square, and the restaurant manager and sommelier have also moved across from that very well run restaurant. Watch our web site for an update later in the summer - www.theaa.com and click the link to Pubs & Restaurants.
Chef: Brett Anderson **Owners:** Nigel Platts-Martin & Philip Howard **Times:** 12-2/6.30-11, 12-2.30/6.30-10 Sun

Lonsdale
European
Chic eaterie with a cool clientele
☎ 020 7727 4080 48 Lonsdale Rd W11 2DE Plan 1-D4
MENU GUIDE Wild mushroom risotto • Steamed fillet of wild sea bass, choi sum, green chilli, black beans • Bitter chocolate Nemesis
WINE GUIDE ♀ Alexia Sauvignon Blanc £29 • ♟ Palena Merlot £16.95 • 21 bottles over £20, 14 bottles under £20 • 12 by the glass (£3.75-£7)
PRICE GUIDE Starter £6.25-£12.95 • dessert £5.25-£6.50 • coffee £2 • min/water £3.50 • Service added 12.5%

PLACE: Relaxed restaurant where all the formalities have been taken out of the fine dining experience, except good food and excellent service. The interior design is bold, with bar stools lining a long, brightly lit cocktail bar in the classic style. Superbly trained staff man the front desk by the entry door, and all of them know their stuff.
FOOD: The menu is inspired by the finest ingredients and culinary heritages from across Europe. Portions are starter size to encourage sharing and the enjoyment of many different flavours.

continued

England

OUR TIP: DJ playing jazz funk music
Chef: Adam Penny **Owners:** Adam & Charles Breeden **Times:** 6-12
Closed 25-26 Dec, 1 Jan, closed L Mon-Fri **Seats:** 100 **Smoking:** Air con
Children: Min 5 yrs **Directions:** Nearest station: Notting Hill One street
parallel N Westbourne Grove between Portobello Road and Ledbury Road.
e-mail: reception@thelonsdale.co.uk **web:** www.thelonsdale.co.uk

Notting Hill Brasserie
Modern French   **NEW**
*Innovative service and great food in a famous
setting*
☎ 020 7229 4481 92 Kensington Park Rd W11
Plan 4-D4
MENU GUIDE Scallops, herb gnocchi, shallots • Ragout of John
Dory, mussels & leeks • Apple tarte Tatin
WINE GUIDE 68 bottles over £20, 4 bottles under £20 • 16 by
the glass (£4.75-£10)
PRICE GUIDE Fixed L £14.50 • starter £5.50-£13.75 • main
£18.50-£22.50 • dessert £6 • coffee £2.50 • min/water
£3.50 • Service added but optional 12.5%
PLACE: Unassuming from the outside and easily missed (look for
the side alleyway entrance), this is no ordinary brasserie.
Converted from three Edwardian town houses, the three intimate
rooms ooze quality and style, from the swish, minimalist decor
and stunning floral arrangements to the unusual African artefacts
in display. Friendly service from confident staff.
FOOD: It is clear from the menus and the simple approach to
careful cooking of quality, seasonal ingredients that there's real
passion and talent in the kitchen. Awareness of aromas, textures
and flavours and not just visual presentation is impressive.
OUR TIP: Try out the Sunday jazz lunches
Chef: Mark Jankel **Owners:** Carlo Spetale **Times:** 12-4/7-1
Notes: Vegetarian available **Seats:** 110, Pr/dining room 44
Smoking: N/Sm area, No pipes, No cigars, Air con **Children:** Portions
Directions: Nearest station: Notting Hill Gate 3 mins walk from Notting
Hill station **Parking:** On street
e-mail: enquiries@nottinghillbrasserie.com

Zilli 210 Kensington Park Rd W11 1NR ☎ 020 7792 1066
Notting Hill branch of Aldo Zilli's. Fish is a speciality.

LONDON W14
Cibo
Italian
Authentic Italian cooking to linger over
☎ 020 7371 2085 3 Russell Gardens W14 8EZ
Plan 1-D3

MENU GUIDE Marinated raw swordfish & tuna • Stewed
pheasant & chestnuts • Chocolate platter   *continued*

WINE GUIDE ♀ Ca Rugate Garganenga £27.50 • ♀ S Osvaldo
Refosco £27.50 • 41 bottles over £20, 5 bottles under £20 • 4 by
the glass (£3.25-£5.95)
PRICE GUIDE Fixed L £15.50 • starter £3.95-£11.50 • main
£12.50-£25 • dessert £3.95-£7.50 • coffee £2.75 • min/water
£2 • Service added but optional 12.5%
PLACE: Rushing through a meal is not the best way to experience
the Cibo atmosphere. The place has a buzz, in part engendered
by the laid-back and charming service that still manages to be
professional, and fostered by the plain white, art-covered
surroundings.
FOOD: Another reason for not being in a hurry is the sheer
length of the menu: home-made pastas are a highlight, and the
rustic cooking style promotes plenty of fish and seafood, along
with perhaps braised veal shin and saffron risotto.
OUR TIP: Don't resist the chocolate ice cream
Chef: Piero Borrelli **Owners:** Gino Taddei **Times:** 12.15-2.30/7-11,
Closed Xmas, Easter BHs, closed L Sat, closed D Sun **Notes:** Vegetarian
available **Seats:** 50, Pr/dining room 16 **Smoking:** No pipes, Air con
Children: Portions **Directions:** Nearest station: Olympia/Shepherds
Bush Russell Gardens is a residential area off Holland Road, Kensington
(Olympia) Shepherd's Bush **e-mail:** ciborestaurant@aol.com
web: www.ciborestaurant.co.uk

Cotto
British
Chic, friendly neighbourhood restaurant
☎ 020 7602 9333 44 Blythe Rd W14 0HA Plan 1-D3

MENU GUIDE Braised Welsh lamb, aubergine cannelloni • Pan-
fried halibut, braised baby gem lettuce • Plum tarte Tatin,
chestnut ice cream
WINE GUIDE ♀ Touraine Premier Cuvée Sauvignon £17.25
♀ De Bortoli Willowglen Cabernet Sauvignon £16 • 27 bottles
over £20, 10 bottles under £20 • 8 by the glass (£3.50-£5.75)
PRICE GUIDE Fixed L £14.50 • Fixed D fr £20.50 • coffee
£2 • min/water £2.80 • Service added but optional 12.5%
PLACE: This smart yet friendly corner restaurant, in the shadow of
Earls Court, is where locals relax and enjoy good food at reasonable
prices. Decor is in shades of brown and tan, with simple, modern,
uncluttered tables and straight-backed leather chairs.
FOOD: Cotto uses independent producers (pure Hereford beef,
for example) and sticks closely to seasonal produce in short but
creative modern British menus with continental influences. The
flavoursome ingredients shine through in dishes such as pan-
fried duck breast with roasted butternut squash and beetroot.
OUR TIP: Good value for money
Chef: James Kirby **Owners:** Mr James Kirby, Mrs Jane Kirby, Mr Warren
Barton **Times:** 12-2.30/7-10.30, Closed Xmas, BHs, closed L Sat, closed D
Sun **Notes:** Tasting menu on request, Vegetarian available **Seats:** 70,
Pr/dining room 35 **Smoking:** No pipes, No cigars, Air con
Children: Portions **Directions:** Nearest station: Olympia Kensington
Directly behind Olympia Exhibition Centre **Parking:** On street also NCP
e-mail: bookings@cottorestaurant.co.uk

England

LONDON WC1
Cigala
Spanish
Appealing Spanish with separate tapas bar
☎ 020 7405 1717 54 Lambs Conduit St WC1N 3LW
Plan 3-D4

MENU GUIDE Pan-fried cuttlefish with romesco sauce • Judion bean, pigeon & wild mushroom stew • Caramelised oranges with brandy

WINE GUIDE ♀ Vina Genoli Ijalba Vivra £16.50 • ♥ Vina Izadi Tempranillo £20.50 • 180 bottles over £20, 30 bottles under £20 • 25 by the glass (£3.50-£8)

PRICE GUIDE Fixed L £15 • starter £4.50-£8 • main £10-£20 • dessert £3.50-£5 • coffee £2.50 • min/water £2.50 • Service added but optional 12.5%

PLACE: Known locally as 'the tapas bar', Cigala is much more than that: a sparse, uncluttered space with cosy tables, bare walls and plain wooden floor, laced with a friendly, efficient buzz.
FOOD: The short Spanish menu with English translations brings robust, vibrant cooking to genteel Bloomsbury. The strong chilli and garlic flavours inject interest into familiar ingredients, leaving a thrilling aftertaste.
OUR TIP: Eat tapas in the restaurant at weekends
Chef: Jake Hodges **Owners:** Jake Hodges **Times:** 12, Closed Xmas, Easter **Notes:** Special tapas menu available, Vegetarian available
Seats: 66 **Smoking:** Air con **Children:** Menu, Portions
Directions: Nearest station: Holborn Right from station into Southampton Row, right into Theobalds Rd. left at LA Gym. 2 min walk .
Parking: NCP, restricted parking outside hotel
e-mail: cigala@cigala.co.uk **web:** www.cigala.co.uk

Jurys Great Russell Street
British, European
Contemporary dining in luxury setting
☎ 020 7347 1000 16-22 Great Russell St WC1B 3NN
Plan 3-C3

MENU GUIDE Crab tian, caramelised apple • Calves' liver, potato boulangère, haricots vert, tomato confit • Lemon tart, raspberry coulis

WINE GUIDE ♀ Hardy's Riddle Chardonnay Semilion • ♥ Wynns Short Mile Bay Shiraz £17.50 • 19 bottles over £20, 31 bottles under £20 • 4 by the glass (£3.95)

PRICE GUIDE Fixed L £18.95-£29 • Fixed D £29-£65 • starter £6-£10 • main £12-£17 • dessert £9-£9 • coffee £3.25 • min/water £5.50 • Service included

PLACE: Designed by the celebrated architect Sir Edwin Lutyens in the 1920s, and restored a decade ago by the Jurys chain, this magnificent listed building houses a smart and spacious restaurant in its basement, along with a clubby bar for pre-dinner drinks.
FOOD: There's no shortage of choice here - the extensive menu aims to please and ranges from complex modern dishes to simpler fare such as steaks. Portions are generous, so bring an appetite.
OUR TIP: Handily located for Covent Garden and the West End
Chef: Paul O'Brien **Owners:** Jurys Doyle **Times:** 6-10, Closed L Mon-Sun **Notes:** Vegetarian available, Smart casual **Seats:** 120, Pr/dining room 26 **Smoking:** N/Sm in restaurant, Air con **Children:** Portions
Rooms: 170 (170 en suite) ★★★★ **Directions:** Nearest station: Tottenham Court Road Short walk from Tottenham Court Rd and Tube Station **Parking:** NCP opposite the Hotel
e-mail: great_russell@jurysdoyle.com **web:** www.jurysdoyle.com

Matsuri High Holborn
Japanese
Traditional Japanese cuisine in contemporary setting
☎ 020 7430 1970 Mid City Place, 71 High Holborn
WC1V 6EA Plan 3-E3

MENU GUIDE Salmon tataki • Chicken teriyaki • Green tea tiramisù

WINE GUIDE ♀ Venezie Pinot Grigio £18 • ♥ Bourgogne Rouge Pinot Noir £23 • 23 bottles over £20, 4 bottles under £20 • 1 by the glass (£3.75)

PRICE GUIDE Fixed L £8.50-£22 • Fixed D £20 • starter £3.50-£12 • main £15-£35 • dessert £3-£6 • coffee £2.80 • min/water £4.75 • Service added but optional 12.5%

PLACE: This futuristic Japanese restaurant offers three dining areas to sample various styles of Japanese cuisine - the sushi counter, the teppan-yaki room where everyone sits around one table with a chef in the centre, and a small private dining room.
FOOD: Not everything is raw! There is abundant choice with cooked options available. Lots of fresh fish make the dishes memorable and set menus provide an overall flavour of Japanese cuisine.
OUR TIP: The teppan-yaki tables provide great entertainment
Chef: H Sudoh, T Aso, S Mabalot, T Kurokawa **Owners:** Matsuri Restaurant Group **Times:** 12-2.30/6-10, Closed 25-26 Dec, 1 Jan, BHs, Sun **Notes:** Vegetarian available **Seats:** 120, Pr/dining room 10
Smoking: Air con **Directions:** Nearest station: Holborn On the corner of Red Lion St Opposite the Renaissance Chancery Court Hotel
Parking: On Street (pay & display) **e-mail:** eat@matsuri-restaurant.com
web: www.matsuri-restaurant.com

The Montague on the Gardens
British, International
Listed Georgian hotel offering eclectic menu
☎ 020 7637 1001 15 Montague St, Bloomsbury
WC1B 5BJ Plan 3-C4

MENU GUIDE Seared scallops, risotto, pineapple cream • Pot-roasted monkfish, pancetta, cassoulet • Chocolate brûlée, banana fritters

WINE GUIDE ♀ Bouchard Finlayson Walker Bay Sauvignon Blanc £24 • ♥ Bouchard Finlayson Galpin Peak Pinot Noir £31.50 • 43 bottles over £20, 10 bottles under £20 • 15 by the glass (£4.50-£10.95)

PRICE GUIDE Fixed L £12 • Fixed D £19.50 • starter £6.50-£9.95 • main £13.95-£26.50 • dessert £5.95-£6.95 • coffee £3.50 • min/water £4.50 • Service added but optional 12.5%

PLACE: Hotel right next door to the British Museum overlooking a secluded garden square with a pretty terrace for sitting outside

continued

The Montague on the Gardens

Divided between the Blue Door Bistro and the fine dining Chef's Table, the restaurant comprises two mahogany panelled rooms with contemporary wrought iron wall lamps.

FOOD: A diverse selection of well put together dishes, suited to all markets and tastes, from quite extensive menus. Hints of Mediterranean cuisine appear on this modern International menu.

OUR TIP: Tailor-made cocktails from an exclusive mixologist **Chef:** Neil Ramsey **Owners:** Red Carnation Hotels **Times:** 12.30-2.30/5.30-10.30 **Notes:** Sun roast lunch 3 courses £16.50, Vegetarian available, Civ Wed 90 **Seats:** 45, Pr/dining room 160 **Smoking:** N/Sm in restaurant, Air con **Children:** Menu, Portions **Rooms:** 104 (104 en suite) ★★★★ **Directions:** Nearest station: Russell Square 10 minutes from Covent Garden, adjacent to the British Museum **Parking:** Bloomsbury Square **e-mail:** bookmt@rchmail.com **web:** www.montaguehotel.com

Pearl at Renaissance London Chancery Court
Modern French
Stunning banking hall conversion, sumptuously furnished
☎ 020 7829 7000 252 High Holborn WC1V 7EN
Plan 3-D3

MENU GUIDE Sliced monkfish, herb risotto, clam gratin • Saddle of rabbit, veal sweetbread stuffing • Pineapple ravioli, coconut mousse

WINE GUIDE ♀ Nautilus Sauvignon Blanc £35 • ♛ Finca Valpiedra Rioja Reserva Tempranillo £49 • 390 bottles over £20, 18 bottles under £20 • 42 by the glass (£4.50-£39)

PRICE GUIDE Fixed L £23.50 • Fixed D £26.50 • Service added but optional 12.5%

PLACE: Now refurbished and renamed, the restaurant is housed in the old Pearl Assurance Building. The high ceilings, marble walls and columns are softened by subdued lighting and cascading pearl-like chandeliers. Interesting under-table lighting, casting a circle of light through the cloth, is totally atmospheric, and the food is beautifully presented.

FOOD: Seasonal modern French menus with a clear approach and skilful cooking of quality produce in dishes such as fillet of sea bream, stir-fried vegetables, seafood tortellini and langoustine consommé. A six-course tasting menu is also offered. Excellent wine list.

OUR TIP: Huge walnut-clad wine tower storing wines at various temperatures
Chef: Jun Tanaka **Owners:** Hotel Property Investors **Times:** 12-2.30/6-D, Closed Dec, 10 Jan, BHs (except Xmas), 2 wks Aug, Sun, closed L Sat **Notes:** 5 course tasting menu avail., Vegetarian available **Seats:** 70, Pr/dining room 12 **Smoking:** N/Sm area, No cigars, Air con

continued

Rooms: 356 (356 en suite) ★★★★★ Directions: Nearest station: Holborn 200 mtrs from Holborn tube station Parking: NCP e-mail: info@pearl-restaurant.com web: www.pearl-restaurant.com

⊕ Radisson Edwardian Kenilworth Hotel
British, International
Chic West End setting for flexible dining
☎ 020 7637 3477 Great Russell St WC1B 3LB
Plan 3-C3

MENU GUIDE Mulligatawny soup • Guinea fowl & wild mushrooms • Pear tart, vanilla cream

WINE GUIDE ♀ Fetzer Chardonnay £16.25 • ♛ Fetzer Cabernet Sauvignon £16.25 • 29 bottles over £20, 18 bottles under £20 7 by the glass (£4-£6)

PRICE GUIDE Fixed L £19.50 • Fixed D £25 • starter £6.50-£7.50 • main £13-£16 • dessert £6 • coffee £3.50 • min/water £4 • Service added but optional 12.5%

PLACE: This chic Bloomsbury hotel is ideally situated for London's theatreland. The open-plan bar and restaurant feature an impressive glass wall which puts the hardworking kitchen on show. **FOOD:** There's a flexible, hotel approach here. Anything from a simple sandwich up to four courses are available throughout the day. In the Creation Restaurant, dishes are modern British with some international touches. Good use of high quality ingredients and accurate cooking.

OUR TIP: A great venue for pre-theatre dining
Chef: Darren Woodhams **Owners:** Radisson Edwardian Hotels **Times:** 12.30-2.30/5.30-10, Sun **Notes:** Vegetarian available **Seats:** 70 **Smoking:** N/Sm area, Air con **Rooms:** 186 (187 en suite) ★★★★ **Parking:** NCP **e-mail:** resmarl@radisson.com **web:** www.radissonedwardian.com

⊕ Wagamama 14a Irving St WC1H 7AF
☎ 020 7930 7587 Informal noodle bars with no booking.

⊕ Wagamama 4a Streatham St WC1A 1JB
☎ 020 7323 9223 Informal noodle bars with no booking.

⊕ Yo! Sushi Myhotel, 11-13 Bayley St WC1B 3HD
☎ 020 7636 0076 Sushi, sashimi, noodles and more.

LONDON WC2
⊕ Adam Street Restaurant
British, International
Exclusive but easygoing basement club
☎ 020 7379 8000 9 Adam St, The Strand WC2N 6AA
Plan 3-D1

MENU GUIDE Pan-fried monkfish with chorizo • Roast rump of English lamb • Sticky toffee pudding

WINE GUIDE ♀ Picpoul Sauvignon Blanc £14.50 • ♛ Cano Shiraz £14.50 • 20 bottles over £20, 20 bottles under £20 • 20 by the glass (£3.50-£9.50)

PRICE GUIDE Fixed L £14.95 • Fixed D £17.95 • starter £4.50-£9.50 • main £9.99-£19.95 • dessert £5.50-£6.50 • coffee £2.50 • min/water £3.50 • Service added but optional 12.5%

PLACE: The menus outside give it away, but the front door is anonymous and the restaurant is tucked away in subterranean vaults beyond the clubby bar. Leather chairs and maroon banquettes (with scatter cushions) encourage you to linger.

continued

LONDON WC2 *continued*

FOOD: An enterprising carte is paired with the club's daily signature 'school dinner' dish - if it's Thursday it must be shepherd's pie etc. The no-choice Club Menu offers the best value, and service is top notch.
OUR TIP: Dinner is members only
Chef: Chris Keil **Owners:** James Minter/Tamara Minter **Times:** 12-2.15/6-11.15, Closed 25 Dec, BHs, Sun, closed L Sat, closed D members only **Notes:** Vegetarian available **Seats:** 60, Pr/dining room 60 **Smoking:** Air con **Directions:** Nearest station: Charing Cross 2 minute walk down the Strand from Charing Cross
e-mail: reception@adamstreet.co.uk **web:** www.adamstreet.co.uk

⑧ The Admiralty Restaurant
European
Nautical-themed restaurant in Thames-side location
☎ 020 7845 4646 Somerset House, The Strand WC2R 1LA Plan 3-D2

MENU GUIDE Roasted scallop, caramelised salsify • Roast saddle of rabbit, Puy lentils, tarragon mousse • Warm dark chocolate fondant

WINE GUIDE ♀ Bernard Legland Chablis 1er Cru Chardonnay £41 • ♥ Château Barrail du Blanc Cabernet Sauvignon £48 100 bottles over £20 • 14 by the glass (£4-£14.50)

PRICE GUIDE Starter £7-£11.90 • main £17.50-£23 • dessert £7 coffee £3.50 • min/water £3.75 • Service added but optional 12.5%

PLACE: Set within the Somerset House complex, this restaurant retains a distinctly nautical feel from its previous life as the Naval Headquarters. Deep greens and yellows, galleon-shaped chandeliers and the river next door make the perfect venue for business or leisure dining.
FOOD: Refined and careful presentation do justice to the skills evident in the modern European cooking. Service is professional, friendly and unobtrusive.
OUR TIP: Ideal for a trip along the Embankment
Chef: Daniel Groom **Owners:** Restaurant Associates **Times:** 12-2.15/6-10.15, Closed 24-27 Dec, closed D Sun **Notes:** Tasting menu £49.95, Vegetarian available, Smart Dress **Seats:** 55, Pr/dining room 60 **Smoking:** N/Sm area **Children:** Portions **Directions:** Nearest station: Temple, Covent Garden Telephone for directions
e-mail: maria@somerset-house.org.uk
web: www.somerset-house.org.uk

⑧⑧ Albannach
Modern Scottish   **NEW**
A taste of Scotland on Trafalgar Square
☎ 020 7930 0066 66 Trafalgar Square WC2N 5DS Plan 5-C6

MENU GUIDE Cullen skink • Venison, creamed potatoes, baby onions, game jus • Rum pannacotta, caramelised rhubarb, sabayon gratin

WINE GUIDE ♀ House white £14 • ♥ House red £15 • 40 bottles over £20, 11 bottles under £20 • 8 by the glass (£4.70-£8)

PRICE GUIDE Fixed D £30-£37.50 • starter £5.50-£9 • main £9-£17.50 • dessert £5.50 • coffee £1.50 • min/water £3 • Service added but optional 12.5%

PLACE: Art nouveau meets Highland hunting lodge in the decor of this Scottish restaurant on Trafalgar Square. Take a drink in the vaulted cocktail lounge or ground floor bar before heading upstairs to the chic dining room with its dark oak flooring and pink and cream leather chairs.

FOOD: Contemporary interpretations of traditional Scottish cuisine. Albannach makes use of the best suppliers north of the border, and delivers a tempting range of dishes such as rib-eye beef with parsnip purée, crispy potatoes and Hermitage sauce, with cranachan and soft winter berries to follow. Extensive selection of malts.
OUR TIP: Ground-floor bar has light snacks
Chef: John-Paul McLachlan **Owners:** Dan Sullam, Niall Barnes
Times: 12-4/5-10, Closed 25-26 Dec, 1 Jan **Notes:** Vegetarian available **Seats:** 70, Pr/dining room **Smoking:** N/Sm in restaurant, Air con **Children:** Min 8 yrs, Portions **Directions:** Nearest station: Charing Cross SW side of Trafalgar Square, opposite National Gallery **Parking:** NCP
e-mail: niall@albannach.co.uk **web:** www.albannach.co.uk

⑧ Asia de Cuba
Asian, Cuban
Slick Asian/Cuban fusion concept
☎ 020 7300 5588 St Martin's Hotel, 45 St Martin's Ln WC2N 4HX Plan 3-C1

MENU GUIDE Oxtail spring rolls • Palomillo of lamb • Mini Mexican doughnuts

WINE GUIDE ♀ Catena Agrelo Chardonnay £40 • ♥ Staks Leap Merlot £69 • 122 bottles over £20 • 19 by the glass (£5-£14)

PRICE GUIDE Fixed L fr £22 • starter £10-£23 • main £14.50-£45 • dessert £8.50-£14 • coffee £3.50 • min/water £4.50 • Service added but optional 15%

PLACE: A glass-fronted hotel, the coolest of minimalist lobbies and a restaurant cleverly designed by Phillipe Starck grabs the attention. Add loud Latin music, a buzzy atmosphere and a split-level dining room with bare light bulbs and pillars stacked with books, prints and plants, and you have the Asia de Cuba experience.
FOOD: The fusion of bold and colourful Latin-American-meets-Asian food comes designed for sharing, and it's well worth taking advice from the knowledgeable, upbeat staff.
OUR TIP: A must to go with friends and share in the dishes and vibrant atmosphere
Chef: Owen Stewart **Owners:** China Grill Restaurant-Jefferey Chawdorow
Times: 12-2.30/5.30-12 **Notes:** Pre theatre menu £22, Vegetarian available **Seats:** 180, Pr/dining room 100 **Smoking:** Air con **Children:** Menu, Portions **Parking:** 80
e-mail: restaurant.resuk@morganshotelgroup.com
web: www.asiadecuba-restaurant.com

⑧ Bank Aldwych Restaurant & Bar
Modern European
Metropolitan dining in Theatreland
☎ 020 7379 9797 1 Kingsway WC2B 6XF Plan 3-D2

MENU GUIDE Chicken & shrimp Nam rolls • Grilled lobster, herb & garlic butter, chips • Prune & custard tart

WINE GUIDE 66 bottles over £20, 21 bottles under £20 • 27 by the glass (£3.60-£6.70)

PRICE GUIDE Fixed L £13.50 • Fixed D £16 • starter £6.50-£12.50 • main £12.50-£24 • dessert £5-£7.50 • coffee £2.25 • min/water £3

PLACE: Located in the heart of Theatreland and just five minutes from Covent Garden, this is a bustling brasserie. Open all day, customers are served breakfast, lunch and dinner in impressive modern surroundings.
FOOD: Modern brasserie cooking where classics like omelette Arnold Bennett jostle for customers' attention with more adventurous items like roast pigeon breast with vanilla and chive

continued

continued

...otto. Sharply dressed, friendly waiting staff deliver dishes ...epared from quality, fresh ingredients.
...UR TIP: Trendy, buzzy, good-value lunch venue
...ef: Damien Pondevie Owners: Bank Restaurant Group plc
...mes: 12-2.45/5.30-11, Closed 25-26 Dec, 1-2 Jan, BHs, closed D Sun
...tes: Brunch menu - Sat/Sun, Vegetarian available, Dress Restrictions,
...art casual Seats: 230, Pr/dining room 30 Smoking: Air con
...ildren: Menu, Portions Directions: Nearest station: Holborn, Charing
...oss, Temple 2 mins from The Strand Parking: NCP Drury Lane
...mail: aldres@bankrestaurants.com
...eb: www.bankrestaurants.com

Christophers

...ontemporary American

...opular institution in Theatreland

☎ 020 7240 4222 18 Wellington St, Covent Garden
...C2E 7DD Plan 3-D2

MENU GUIDE Salmon carpaccio, ginger soy dressing • Maine ...obster, sweetcorn blini • Pecan tart, maple syrup ice cream

WINE GUIDE ♀ Columbia Crest Chardonnay £14 • ♀ Villa Mt ...den Zinfandel £18 • 122 bottles over £20, 27 bottles under ...20 • 12 by the glass (£3.50-£5)

PRICE GUIDE Fixed L £12.75 • Fixed D £16.75 • starter £5.50-...11 • main £12.50-£25 • dessert £5.50-£6.50 • coffee £2.25 ...nin/water £3.25 • Service added but optional 12.5%

PLACE: Good location in a Grade II listed Victorian building ...nich was once London's only casino. Comfortable furniture and ...rightly service keep the regulars coming back for more both ...fore the theatre and after.

FOOD: No mention of hamburgers here. This contemporary ...merican menu keeps dishes simple and effective using top ...uality ingredients. There's the occasional international influence ...ch as Asian-style slow-cooked pork belly.

OUR TIP: Try the prime aged Scottish beef from the Buccleuch ...tates

...ef: Francis Agyepong Owners: Christopher Gilmour Times: 12-3/
...1.30, Closed 24 Dec-2 Jan, 25-26 Dec, 1 Jan, closed D Sun
...tes: Vegetarian available Seats: 110, Pr/dining room 40
...noking: No pipes, No cigars, Air con Children: Menu, Portions
...rections: Nearest station: Embankment/Covent Garden Just by Strand,
...erlooking Waterloo Bridge
...mail: coventgarden@christophersgrill.com
...eb: www.christophersgrill.com

Imperial China

...antonese

...ontemporary Cantonese dining in ...hina Town

☎ 020 7734 3388 White Bear Yard, 25a Lisle St ...C2H 7BA Plan 3-B2

PLACE: A courtyard setting for this stylish restaurant. ...ontemporary Chinese decor with wood panelling, two levels for ...ning plus private rooms for karaoke and functions, and smartly ...iformed friendly and efficient staff.

FOOD: Extensive dim sum list and large carte featuring the usual ...spects as well as some more intriguing dishes. They also offer ...i interesting vegetarian set meal.

OUR TIP: Great setting for a private function
...mes: 12, Closed Xmas e-mail: mail@imperial-china.co.uk
...eb: www.imperial-china.co.uk

⊛⊛ *Incognico*

French, Mediterranean

Stylish brasserie in the heart of theatreland

☎ 020 7836 8866 117 Shaftesbury Av, Cambridge
Circus WC2H 8AD Plan 3-C2

MENU GUIDE Roasted scallops, garlic butter • Duck breast,
honey & peppercorns • Lemon tart, raspberry coulis

PRICE GUIDE Food prices not confirmed for 2006. Please
telephone for details

PLACE: Designed by David Collins, this restaurant has the
atmosphere and look of a classical French brasserie. It is situated
at the top end of Shaftesbury Avenue, close to the hustle and
bustle of theatreland. The restful interior is dark and moody, with
strip wooden floors, oak panelling, leather banquettes, and soft
uplighting. There is a champagne room for drinks parties. Service
is discreet but efficient.

FOOD: Cooking is deep-rooted in French classics with an
underlying simple approach. The focus is on letting the quality of
the luxury ingredients and organic produce speak for themselves.

OUR TIP: Great value pre-theatre menu
Times: 12-3/5.30-11 **Directions:** Nearest station: Leicester Sq Situated
behind Cambridge Circus

⊛ **The Ivy**

British, European

London theatreland legend

☎ 020 7836 4751 1 West St, Covent Garden
WC2H 9NQ Plan 3-C2

MENU GUIDE Partridge on toast • Grilled calves' liver • Baked
rice pudding

WINE GUIDE 84 bottles over £20, 11 bottles under £20 • 14 by
the glass (£4.50-£9.75)

PRICE GUIDE Fixed D £23.50 • starter £6-£15.75 • main £9.75-
£30 • dessert £6.25-£8.50 • coffee £2.75 • min/water
£3.50 • Service optional

PLACE: Legendary dining destination frequented by London's
brightest stars, and those hoping some of the glamour will rub
off onto them. It's high volume and hectic, though staff cope
pretty efficiently.

FOOD: A long brasserie menu lists no-nonsense favourites like
shepherd's pie and fishcakes, and several classics (tournedos
Rossini, eggs Benedict etc) with the odd innovation thrown in to
keep the gastronomes happy.

OUR TIP: Booking is very essential!
Chef: Alan Bird, Mark Hix **Owners:** Signature Restaurants PLC
Times: 12-3/5.30-12, Closed 25-26 Dec,1 Jan, Aug BH, closed L 27 Dec,
closed D 24 Dec **Notes:** Vegetarian available **Seats:** 100, Pr/dining room
60 **Smoking:** Air con **Children:** Portions **Directions:** Nearest station:
Leicester Square Telephone for directions **Parking:** NCP, on street

---

What makes a Restaurant of the Year?
In selecting a Restaurant of the Year, we
look for somewhere that is exceptional in its
chosen area of the market. Whilst the
Rosette awards are based on the quality of
the food alone, Restaurant of the Year takes
into account all aspects of the operation.
For full details see pages 6-7.

England

LONDON WC2 *continued*

⑯ J. Sheekey

Fish, Seafood

Veteran seafood restaurant in theatreland

☎ 020 7240 2565 St Martin's Court WC2N 4AL
Plan 3-C2

MENU GUIDE Scallops, crispy bacon, sauce diable • Pan-fried skate wing, brown butter, capers • Baked rice pudding, raspberry jam

WINE GUIDE ♀ Chablis Colombier Chardonnay £30 • ♀ Sancerre Rouge Millet Pinot Noir £31.25 • 60 bottles over £20, 6 bottles under £20 • 11 by the glass (£4.50-£9.25)

PRICE GUIDE Fixed L £18 • Fixed D £18.50 • starter £5.75-£32.50 • main £10.75-£29.75 • dessert £5.50-£8.50 • coffee £2.75 • min/water £3.75 • Service optional

PLACE: Established in 1893, this West End institution is still packing them in over a century later. Hiding behind smoked glass windows in a winding alley behind Charing Cross Road, it's a bustling, businesslike venue with dark panelled walls hung with black and white celebrity photographs.

FOOD: Ingredients of impeccable quality and freshness are at the root of Sheekey's success; expect assured and skilful cooking whether you choose a traditional dish such as jellied eels, or something more sophisticated - Cornish fish stew perhaps, or sea bass with rock shrimp mash.

OUR TIP: Vegetarian and vegan menu available on request

Chef: Martin Dickenson **Owners:** Caprice Holdings **Times:** 12-3/5.30-12, Closed 25-26 Dec, 1 Jan, BHs, closed L Sat-Sun **Seats:** 105 **Smoking:** No pipes, No cigars, Air con **Children:** Portions **Directions:** Nearest station: Leicester Square Telephone for directions **Parking:** On street

e-mail: reservations@j-sheekey.co.uk

⑯ Kingsway Hall

International

Chic, contemporary hotel dining

☎ 020 7309 0909 Great Queen St, Covent Garden
WC2B 5BZ Plan 3-D3

MENU GUIDE Stilton, walnut, & pear salad • Lemon & thyme roast chicken, Mediterranean vegetables • Classic lemon tart, raspberry sorbet

PRICE GUIDE Food prices not confirmed for 2006. Please telephone for details

PLACE: The classical façade of this stylish hotel gives way inside to the strikingly modern Harlequin Restaurant, which boasts such features as an undulating ceiling and marble floors.

FOOD: In keeping with surrounds, the extensive international menu offers contemporary takes on the classics. Salad Niçoise is

continued

Kingsway Ha

served with grilled tuna and soft boiled quail eggs, while fillet of bream is punchily paired with roast potato and chorizo.

OUR TIP: Well located for Theatreland and the Royal Opera Hous

Times: 12-2.30/5.30-10, Closed BHs, closed L Sat-Sun **Rooms:** 170 (170 en suite) ★★★★ **Directions:** Nearest station: Holborn From Holborn tube down Kingsway and R into Gt Queens St Restaurant on L

e-mail: harlequin@kingswayhall.co.uk **web:** www.kingswayhall.co.uk

⑯⑯ Maggiore's

Modern French

Romantic French restaurant in Covent Garden

☎ 020 7379 9696 33 King St, Covent Garden
WC2E 8JD Plan 3-C2

MENU GUIDE Dorset crab risotto • Corn-fed chicken, dill gnocchi, wild mushrooms • Warm chocolate fondant, banana ice cream

WINE GUIDE ♀ William Feure Chablis Montmain 1999 Chardonnay £38 • ♀ Roger Sabon Châteauneuf du Pape Olives 1999 Grenache £39 • 2400 bottles over £20 • 20 by the glass (£4-£8)

PRICE GUIDE Fixed L £14.50 • Fixed D £19.50 • starter £4.90-£12.50 • main £14.90-£17.50 • dessert £5.50-£6.50 • coffee £3.50 • min/water £2.95 • Service added but optional 12.5%

PLACE: Decorated in the style of a French country auberge, this sophisticated theatreland restaurant is an intimate concoction of smoked mirrors, blossoms and candlelight beneath a conservatory dome.

FOOD: Classy modern French cuisine with a touch of imagination: belly pork with a roast Cox apple perhaps, or venison with a celeriac and Arabica coffee purée. The wine list is worth a mention too; it's well-balanced, extensive and a definite contender for awards.

OUR TIP: Great value pre- and post theatre menus

Chef: Alan Christie **Owners:** Tyfoon Restaurants Ltd **Times:** noon-2.30/5-11, Closed 24-26 Dec & 1 Jan **Notes:** Fixed D 3 courses incl. a glass of Champagne, Vegetarian available **Seats:** 70, Pr/dining room 30 **Smoking:** N/Sm area, No pipes, Air con **Children:** Portions **Directions:** Nearest station: Covent Garden 1 min walk from The Piazza and Royal Opera House **Parking:** NCP, on street

e-mail: enquiries@maggiores.uk.com **web:** www.maggiores.uk.com

⑯ Mela

Indian

Good value innovative Indian food in the West En

☎ 020 7836 8635 152-156 Shaftesbury Av
WC2H 8HL Plan 3-C2

MENU GUIDE Murg lukmi samosa (Savoury chicken) • Gosht pasanda shirazi (Mild lamb korma) • Rasmalai milky pudding

continue

England

WINE GUIDE ♀ Chardonnay £15.95 • ♥ Merlot £17.50
' bottles over £20, 17 bottles under £20 • 8 by the glass
£3-£4.95)

PRICE GUIDE Fixed L £10.95 • Fixed D £13-£18 • starter £3.50-
[4].95 • main £5.50-£18.95 • dessert £3.25-£3.75 • coffee
1.75 • min/water £3.25 • Service added but optional 12.5%
[P]LACE: Shaftesbury Avenue has seen many restaurants open
[an]d close, but Mela's high performance at reasonable prices is a
[w]inning formula. The brightly coloured interior has an open-plan
[ki]tchen where a battalion of chefs can be seen at work.
[FO]OD: The standard of cooking is first-rate, the authenticity of
[th]e ingredients is unquestionable, and the mix of familiar dishes
[wi]th innovative new recipes will always be more than a match for
[th]e most experienced palate. Good vegetarian selection.
[O]UR TIP: Perfect setting for a pre- or post-theatre supper
[Ch]ef: Kuldeep Singh, Uday Seth **Owners:** Kuldeep Singh **Times:** 12-
[3].30-11.30, Closed Xmas, closed L Boxing Day **Notes:** Vegetarian
[av]ailable **Seats:** 105, Pr/dining room 35 **Smoking:** N/Sm area, Air con
[e-m]ail: info@melarestaurant.co.uk **web:** www.melarestaurant.co.uk

 **Mon Plaisir**
[F]rench
[St]ill sparkling, London's first French restaurant
[☎] 020 7836 7243 21 Monmouth St WC2H 9DD
[Pl]an 3-C2
MENU GUIDE Tuna & fig carpaccio • Saddle of rabbit, black olive
[s]auce • Banana tart
PRICE GUIDE Starter £5.95-£11.95 • main £14.50-£21.50
[d]essert £5.75 • coffee £1.95 • Service added but optional 12.5%
[P]LACE: The oldest French restaurant in London, and it is still
[pa]cking them in and turning them away in almost equal
[n]umbers. Inside is a warren of rooms beyond the main
[re]staurant, each with its own individual atmosphere. The white
[a]proned staff glide between the old travel posters, French
[m]emorabilia and smart tables.
[FO]OD: Expect classic starters involving terrines with foie gras,
[an]d fricassée of petit gris (little snails) to be followed by a
[ti]meless rendition of coq au vin, or the contemporary pan-fried
[du]ck breast with lime and ginger. Fish is there too, perhaps cod
[wi]th chorizo, baby squid and white beans.
[O]UR TIP: Good value pre-theatre menu
[Ch]ef: Frank Raymond **Owners:** Alain Lhermitte **Times:** 12-2.15/5.45-
[.]15, Closed Xmas, New Year, BHs, Sun, closed L Sat **Notes:** Vegetarian
[av]ailable **Seats:** 100, Pr/dining room 28 **Smoking:** No pipes, No cigars,
[Air] con **Children:** Portions **Directions:** Nearest station: Covent Garden,
[Le]icester Square Off Seven Dials **e-mail:** eatafrog@mail.com
[w]eb: www.monplaisir.co.uk

 **Neal Street Restaurant**
[It]alian
[Po]pular restaurant exemplifying the simple
[so]phistication of Italian cooking
[☎] 020 7836 8368 26 Neal St WC2H 9QW Plan 3-D2
MENU GUIDE Salad with marinated mushrooms &
[p]ancetta • Rabbit legs baked with black olives, potato cake
[F]ig tart, vanilla ice cream
WINE GUIDE ♀ Jermann Pinot Grigio £36 • ♥ Molino di Grace
[S]angiovese £31 • 10 by the glass (£4.75-£8.50)
PRICE GUIDE Fixed L £21 • Fixed D £25-£35 • starter £6.50-
[£]8 • main £15.50-£28 • dessert £6.50 • coffee
[£]2.50 • min/water £3.50 • Service added but optional 12.5%
[P]LACE: Antonio Carluccio's restaurant is located in a former

banana-ripening warehouse, providing a restful respite from the
carnival atmosphere of Covent Garden. The stylish interior sets
modern art and a collection of carved walking sticks against
whitewashed walls.
FOOD: An enticing range of dishes from every region and village
of Italy, with fresh, vibrant flavours and top quality ingredients.
Choose from the short fixed-price menu or classic Italian carte,
both in Italian with English explanations. There's plenty of
seasonal fare with mushrooms - the chef's favourite ingredient -
featuring strongly.
OUR TIP: For a good value meal, go for lunch
Chef: Andrea Cavaliere **Owners:** Antonio Carluccio, Priscilla Carluccio
Times: 12-2.30/6-11, Closed 25 Dec-2 Jan, Easter Monday, BHs, Sun
Notes: Vegetarian available, Smart casual preferred **Seats:** 65, Pr/dining
room 24 **Smoking:** N/Sm area, No pipes, No cigars, Air con
Children: Portions **Directions:** Nearest station: Covent Garden Short
walk from tube station **Parking:** Shelton Street
e-mail: dominiquec@nealstreet.co.uk **web:** www.carluccios.com

 **One Aldwych - Axis**
Modern European
Modish hotel eaterie with wide-ranging brasserie
menu
☎ 020 7300 0300 1 Aldwych WC2B 4RH Plan 3-D2

MENU GUIDE Duck noodle salad • Hay-baked leg of lamb,
colcannon, rosemary jus • Chocolate fondant, raspberry sorbet
WINE GUIDE ♀ Craggy Range Sauvignon Blanc
£34 • ♥ Murrieta Rioja £32 • 250 bottles over £20, 12 bottles
under £20 • 10 by the glass (£4.95-£12.50)
PRICE GUIDE Fixed L £16.75 • Fixed D £19.75 • starter £4.95-
£10.95 • main £12.95-£27.50 • dessert £5.50-£6.95 • coffee
£3.75 • min/water £3.95 • Service added but optional 12.5%
PLACE: Chic modern hotel just a short walk from Covent Garden
and Shaftesbury Avenue. Axis is a split-level basement brasserie
with a buzzy ambience and minimalist cream decor that's softly
lit, and lent an air of understated luxury by acres of marble.
FOOD: Close your eyes and really taste your food - this is
cooking that deserves appreciation, with an emphasis on bold
and intense flavours. Dishes come from around the world and
are surprisingly authentic; your choice might include venison with
braised onion, apple and red cabbage, or Canadian halibut with
pappardelle, pumpkin and smoked mozzarella sauce.
OUR TIP: Good value fixed price lunch
Chef: Mark Gregory **Owners:** Gordon Campbell-Gray **Times:** 12-
2.45/5.45-10.45, Closed Xmas, New Year, Sun, closed L Sat
Notes: Vegetarian available, Civ Wed 60 **Seats:** 120, Pr/dining room 40
Smoking: No cigars, Air con **Children:** Menu, Portions **Directions:**
Nearest station: Covent Garden At point where Aldwych meets the Strand
opposite Waterloo Bridge. On corner of Aldwych & Wellington St, opposite
Lyceum Theatre **Parking:** NCP - Wellington St
e-mail: axis@onealdwych.com **web:** www.onealdwych.com

continued

England

LONDON WC2 *continued*

⊛⊛ One Aldwych - Indigo

Modern European

Honest modern cuisine in fashionable hotel

☎ 020 7300 0400 1 Aldwych WC2B 4RH
Plan 3-D2

MENU GUIDE Confit of chicken & duck terrine, fruit chutney • Salmon, herb crust, roast tomatoes, creamed fennel, leeks • Plum Tatin

WINE GUIDE ♀ Terrazze Della Luna Pinot Grigio £22.50 • ♀ Burgundy Faiveley Pinot Noir £26.50 • 36 bottles over £20, 3 bottles under £20 • 14 by the glass (£4.75-£8.95)

PRICE GUIDE Fixed D £19.75 • starter £5.50-£10.25 • main £11.95-£20.75 • dessert £5.50-£6.75 • coffee £3.75 • min/water £3.95 • Service added but optional 12.5%

PLACE: One of several eating options within this oh-so-fashionable hotel, Indigo occupies a balcony terrace above the lobby and has the feel of a classical dining room, with crisp napery, high quality tableware and comfortable seats. It's a relaxed setting and a prime spot for people-watching.
FOOD: Indigo values flavour over elaborate technique and delivers simple contemporary dishes that consistently impress. The approachable menu is designed to suit all tastes and features an option to create a pasta dish of your choice.
OUR TIP: Great pre-theatre venue
Owners: One Aldwych Ltd **Times:** 12-3/6-11.15 **Notes:** Vegetarian available, Civ Wed 60 **Seats:** 62 **Smoking:** No pipes, No cigars, Air con
Children: Menu, Portions **Rooms:** 105 (105 en suite) ★★★★★
Directions: Nearest station: Covent Garden, Charing Cross Located where The Aldwych meets The Strand opposite Waterloo Bridge
Parking: Valet parking **e-mail:** indigo@onealdwych.com
web: www.onealdwych.com

⊛ Orso Restaurant

Italian

Italian food in a buzzing basement

☎ 020 7240 5269 27 Wellington St WC2E 7DB
Plan 3-D2

MENU GUIDE Braised octopus, red onions, black olives • Venison, green peppercorns, mashed potatoes Carrot cake, vanilla sauce

WINE GUIDE ♀ Brogalvini Trebbiano £14 • ♀ Brogalvini Sangiovese £14 • 41 bottles over £20, 10 bottles under £20 8 by the glass (£6.50-£10.50)

PRICE GUIDE Fixed D £18 • starter £5.50-£9.50 • main £14-£16.50 • dessert £5.50-£6 • min/water £3.50 • Service optional • Group min 8 service 12.5%

PLACE: Buzzing with energy and conversation, this Covent Garden Italian is a cavernous underground space with fanciful frescoes, herringbone floors, pastel tablecloths and friendly staff.
FOOD: The menu and its inspiration is Tuscan to the roots, and the choice - listed separately in Italian and English - creams off favourite choices from the region, be they oxtail braised in Chianti, veal and parmesan meatballs, or slow-roast crispy pork with sage potatoes.
OUR TIP: Ideal for a pre-opera supper
Chef: Martin Wilson **Owners:** Orso Restaurants Ltd **Times:** noon-mdn
Closed 24 & 25 Dec **Notes:** Fixed D is 'pre-Theatre', Vegetarian available
Seats: 100 **Smoking:** N/Sm area, No pipes, No cigars, Air con
Directions: Nearest station: Covent Garden Telephone for directions
e-mail: info@orsorestaurant.co.uk
web: www.orsorestaurant.co.uk

⊛ The Portrait Restaurant

British, European

Stylish dining with rooftop views

☎ 020 7312 2490 National Portrait Gallery, St Martins Place WC2H 0HE Plan 3-C1

MENU GUIDE Black pudding, poached egg • Rare bavette of beef, wild mushrooms & stilton butter • Baked plum tart, clotted cream

WINE GUIDE ♀ Michel Laroche Chardonnay £15 • ♀ Michel Laroche Merlot £15 • 23 bottles over £20, 10 bottles under £20 • 15 by the glass (£3.85-£6.75)

PRICE GUIDE Fixed L £19.50 • Fixed D £24.50 • starter £4.95-£9.95 • main £9.95-£18.95 • dessert £5-£5.95 • coffee £2 • min/water £3 • Service added but optional 12.5%

PLACE: Take the grand escalator past famous paintings to the top floor, where you'll find yourself nearly eye-to-eye with Nelson amidst black pillars, pale wooden floor and a sloping glass roof.
FOOD: The menu is as stylish as the setting, with a compelling display of modern British verve and imagination in the likes of crispy belly of pork with sea scallop and sweet and sour sauce.
OUR TIP: Ask for a window seat
Chef: Brendan Fyldes **Owners:** Searcys **Times:** 11.45-2.45/5.30-8.30, Closed 24-26 Dec, 1 Jan, Good Fri, closed D Sat-Wed **Notes:** Vegetarian available **Seats:** 100 **Smoking:** N/Sm in restaurant, Air con
Children: Portions **Directions:** Nearest station: Leicester Square, Trafalgar Square Telephone for directions **Parking:** NCP - Orange St
e-mail: portrait.restaurant@searceys.co.uk **web:** www.searcys.co.uk

⊛⊛⊛ Savoy Grill *see page 353*

continued

England

Savoy Grill

French, British

Flawless cooking at re-styled legendary restaurant

☎ 020 7592 1600 The Savoy, Strand WC2R 0EU

Plan 3-D1

MENU GUIDE Scallops, pea purée, tomato confit, mint-infused velouté • Lamb rump, confit shoulder, aubergine purée, black olive jus • Basil crème brûlée, strawberry sorbet

WINE GUIDE ♀ Henri Bourgeois Domaine Lavigne Sancerre £41 • ♀ Château Potensac Medoc £50 • 345 bottles over £20, 2 bottles under £20 • 8 by the glass (£5-£12.50)

PRICE GUIDE Fixed L £30-£55 • Fixed D £55 • coffee £5 • min/water £4 • Service optional • Group min 16 service 12.5%

PLACE: There's a feeling of great anticipation as you arrive at this much-loved institution, and never more so since Marcus Wareing has ushered decor and menu into the present day. The modernisation echoes a fine balance between tradition and contemporary tastes, with a lighter, more up-to-date feel, but without losing the original art-deco character. The banquettes have been retained, re-upholstered in sleek tobacco, nougat and black stripe, while crisp white linen and the shimmering gold leaf-effect ceiling combine to create an understated richness. Atmosphere and service is surprisingly unstuffy.

FOOD: Marcus Wareing has confidently stamped his authority on the Grill, the modern approach underpinned by a classical French theme. Food is classy, intelligent and measured, with quality and skill, balance and variety jumping off the pages of the menu, even before it's delivered. Stunning ingredients (including luxury items) are complemented by exemplary skills, clear flavours and fine balance. Think, ravioli of king prawns and chervil with a salad of truffle and ceps and shellfish and Armagnac emulsion to start, perhaps a lightly roasted fillet of John Dory with marinated field mushrooms and globe artichokes, and a crème fraîche and thyme sauce to follow. Impressive wine list.

OUR TIP: Try the seven-course tasting menu

Chef: Marcus Wareing **Owners:** Marcus Wareing at the Savoy Grill Ltd **Times:** 12-3/5.45-11 **Notes:** Early supper £30, Vegetarian available, Smart, jacket preferred **Seats:** 70, Pr/dining room 60 **Smoking:** N/Sm in restaurant, Air con **Children:** Menu, Portions **Rooms:** 263 (263 en suite) ★★★★★ **Parking:** on street

e-mail: savoygrill@marcuswareing.com **web:** www.marcuswareing.com

Swissotel London, The Howard

Rosettes not confirmed at time of going to press

French, Cambodia

Fusion eaterie in a smart hotel

☎ 020 7836 3555 Temple Place WC2R 2PR

Plan 3-E2

MENU GUIDE Duo of foie gras • Rack of lamb on aubergine caviar • Cream of coconut pannacotta

WINE GUIDE ♀ Villa Maria Sauvignon Blanc £31 • ♀ Crozes-Hermitage Shiraz £28 • 126 bottles over £20, 1 bottles under £20 • 15 by the glass (£6-£14)

PRICE GUIDE Fixed L £25-£33 • Fixed D £28-£38 • starter £12-£18 • main £19-£25 • dessert £6-£8 • coffee £4 • min/water £3.85 • Service added 12.5%

PLACE: The spacious Jaan Restaurant is decorated in luxurious handmade silks, with antique Asian artwork and has a peaceful, contemporary feel.

FOOD: An unusual fusion of modern French cooking with the delicate flavours of South East Asian cuisine. Seven-course tasting menu available.

OUR TIP: Great for alfresco dining

Chef: Paul Peters **Owners:** Samosir Ltd **Times:** 12-2.30/5.45-10.30, Closed L Sat-Sun **Notes:** Vegetarian available, Dress Restrictions, smart, casual, Civ Wed 100 **Seats:** 56 **Children:** Menu, Portions **Rooms:** 189 (189 en suite) ★★★★★ **Directions:** Nearest station: Temple Telephone for directions **Parking:** 30

e-mail: ask-us.london@swissotel.com

web: www.london.swissotel.com

LONDON WC2

Thyme

Modern

Sophisticated contemporary meets some of the most exciting food in London

☎ 020 7170 9200 The Hospital, 24 Endell St WC2H 9HQ Plan 3-C2

e-mail: adamb@thymeandspace.com

web: www.thymeandspace.com

PLACE: Set in the new multi-media centre, The Hospital (the vision of owner Paul Allen and Dave Stewart of The Eurythmics fame) is set on Endell Street slap bang in the middle of Covent Garden. Thyme is a classy affair, with Adam Byatt and Adam Oates transferring their critically acclaimed neighbourhood restaurant uptown to its new first floor fine-dining stage from Clapham. The interior is a sophisticated contemporary space design by Claire Nelson, the L-shaped room delivering an air of luxury with its sleek lavender and beige decor and well-spaced tables set with bespoke crockery. Service is nothing short of first class, highly professional whilst reassuringly friendly.

FOOD: Thyme's refined cooking foundation remains true to the classical but has bags of innovation and creativity. Supreme in its consistency and technical skill, the wonderful depth and accuracy of flavours and emphasis on seasonality and high quality ingredients, includes plenty of luxury items (foie gras, lobster, oysters, truffles, caviar, etc). The approach is via an enticing fixed-price repertoire that includes a brace of set lunch offerings, a pair of five-course tasting menus (accompanied by recommended wines) and an appealing four-course carte that all get the pulse racing. So expect a tasting option to deliver the likes of: cauliflower soup with winter truffles; lobster farfallini with tarragon mayonnaise; an assiette of foie gras served with raisin purée; seared hand-dived scallops with citrus-braised endive; and for the finale, Amadei chocolate emulsion with mandarin crisp, marsala ice cream and hazelnut. And be prepared to be wowed by ancillaries too, like an interesting range of canapés, fresh breads, amuse bouche and pre-desserts, that also keep up the pace and hit a high note.

MENU GUIDE Smoked eel terrine, apple gazpacho, smoked bacon • Pot-roast lamb saddle, confit lamb belly, chervil root purée, meat juices • Lemon meringue tart, crème fraîche sorbet, limoncello jelly

WINE GUIDE ♀ Francis Boudin Chablis £34 • ♀ Nittnaus Pinot Noir £29 • 270 bottles over £20, 6 bottles under £20 • 20 by the glass (£3.75-£15)

PRICE GUIDE Fixed L £20 • Fixed ALC D £40-£45 coffee £3.50 • min/water £4 • Service added 12.5%

OUR TIP: Fixed-price lunch menu offers great value at this level

Chef: Adam Byatt **Owners:** Adam Byatt & Adam Oates **Times:** 12.30-2.30/6-10.30, Closed 25-26 Dec, 1 Jan, Easter Mon & Sun, 25-26 Dec, Sun **Notes:** ALC 3 courses £40, 4 Courses £45, Tasting Menu £35-90, Vegetarian available **Seats:** 76, Pr/dining room 12 **Smoking:** N/Sm in restaurant, Air con **Children:** Min 16 yrs

LONDON WC2 *continued*

Belgo 50 Earlham St WC2H 9HP ☎ 020 7813 2233
Belgian style, extending to strong beer, good seafood (mussels of course) and staff in habits.

Café du Jardin 28 Wellington St WC2E 7BD
☎ 020 7836 8769 Mediterranean style dishes at this bustling split-level restaurant.

Loch Fyne Restaurant, Covent Garden
2-4 Catherine St WC2B 5JS ☎ 020 7240 4999 Quality seafood chain.

Strada 6 Great Queen St WC2B 5DH ☎ 020 7405 6293
Superior pizza from quality ingredients cooked in wood-fired ovens.

Wagamama 1 Tavistock St, Covent Garden WC2E 7PG
☎ 020 7836 3330 Informal noodle bars with no booking.

Zilli Fish Too 145 Drury Ln WC2B 5TA
☎ 020 7240 0011 Fish with an Italian accent from the ebullient Aldo Zilli.

LONDON, GREATER

BECKENHAM

 Mello

Modern European   **NEW**

Fashionable dining near suburban high street
☎ 020 8663 0994 2 Southend Rd BR3 1SD

MENU GUIDE Sautéed foie gras, duck ballotine • Roast skate wing, spinach purée • Hazelnut parfait, poached pear

WINE GUIDE ♀ Trebiona £12.50 • ♀ Montepulliano £12.50 • 36 bottles over £20, 12 bottles under £20 • 4 by the glass (£3.50)

PRICE GUIDE Fixed L £17 • Fixed D £21.50 • starter £4.50 • main £12.50 • dessert £4.50 • coffee £1.80 • min/water £3 • Service added but optional 10%

PLACE: A modern restaurant located in a Victorian listed building, the air-conditioned dining room has leather chairs and good quality settings. Decoration is simple and effective with neutral surfaces and modern art on the walls. Service is formal but friendly.
FOOD: Menus provide a good choice of modern European dishes with some of the more exotic items carrying a supplement. Good skills, clear flavours and adventurous combinations are apparent.
OUR TIP: Great value gourmet evenings
Chef: Christopher Bower **Owners:** V Narin, A Demirtas **Times:** 12-2.30/6-10 **Notes:** Vegetarian available **Seats:** 90, Pr/dining room 36 **Smoking:** No pipes, Air con **Children:** Portions **Directions:** 0.5m from Beckenham town centre, directly opposite Beckenham train station **Parking:** 26 **e-mail:** info@mello.uk.com
web: www.mello.uk.com

BROMLEY *See LONDON SECTION plan 1-G1*

  Chapter One *see page 356*

CROYDON MAP 06 TQ36

 Coulsdon Manor

British, French

Imaginative cooking in stunning rural setting
☎ 020 8668 0414 Coulsdon Court Rd, Coulsdon CR5 2LL

MENU GUIDE Prawn tortellini, scallops, lemongrass velouté • Pork belly, apple purée, braised white cabbage • Chocolate & ginger parfait

WINE GUIDE ♀ Linea Corte Vigna Pinot Grigio £16.50 • ♀ Hardys Shiraz Cabernet £16.25 • 61 bottles over £20, 31 bottles under £20 • 8 by the glass (£4.10-£5.90)

PRICE GUIDE Fixed L £15.50 • Fixed D £32.50 • starter £7-£13 • main £18-£23 • dessert £6.95 • min/water £3.50 • Service optional

PLACE: Only 15 miles from central London and Gatwick, this Victorian manor sits in rural splendour amid 140 acres of landscaped parkland. A brasserie menu is available on the terrace throughout the day, while more formal fare is served in a sunlit dining room overlooking the 18-hole golf course.
FOOD: Modern British dishes with French influences and good presentation: rump of lamb with creamed broad beans perhaps or monkfish in Parma ham with wild mushrooms and gratin potatoes. Extras include canapés, as well as an amuse bouche and sorbet course.
OUR TIP: Regular jazz brunches and disco dinner dances
Chef: Martin Nisbett **Owners:** Marston Hotels **Times:** 12.30-2.30/7-9.30, Closed L Sat **Notes:** Coffee incl, monthly Sun Jazz Brunch, Vegetarian available, Dress Restrictions, No jeans, shorts, sportswear, Civ Wed 60 **Seats:** 120, Pr/dining room 40 **Smoking:** N/Sm in restaurant **Children:** Menu, Portions **Rooms:** 35 (35 en suite) ★★★★
Directions: M23/M25 junct 7 N bound towards Croydon. Take right signposted Old Coulsdon B2030. Continue for 1.5m and turn left into Coulsdon Court Rd. **Parking:** 180
e-mail: coulsdonmanor@marstonhotels.com
web: www.marstonhotels.com

Selsdon Park Hotel & Golf Course

International

Jacobean mansion with imposing views
☎ 020 8657 8811 Addington Rd, Sanderstead CR2 8YA

MENU GUIDE Double baked cheese soufflé • Honey & rosemary glazed lamb, white onion Tatin • Vanilla pannacotta

PRICE GUIDE Food prices not confirmed for 2006. Please telephone for details

PLACE: While the 200 acres of parkland surrounding this Jacobean mansion offer the utmost in peace and seclusion, central London is only 20 minutes away. The Cedar Restaurant, named for a magnificent specimen planted by Elizabeth I, enjoys stunning views of the terraces and gardens.
FOOD: Attractive presentation of globally influenced dishes, with intriguing desserts including saffron ice cream and lemon balm brûlée.
OUR TIP: 18-hole golf course
Times: 12-2/7-9.45 **Rooms:** 204 (204 en suite) ★★★★
Directions: 3 miles SE of Croydon off A2022
e-mail: sales@pricipal-hotels.com

BROMLEY *See* LONDON SECTION plan 1-G1

Chapter One

European
Sophisticated cooking in suburban Bromley
☎ 01689 854848 Farnborough Common, Locksbottom BR6 8NF

e-mail: info@chaptersrestaurants.com
web: www.chaptersrestaurants.co.uk

PLACE: From the outside it might look somewhat like the neighbourhood steakhouse, handily located on the A21, but any preconceptions about this unprepossessing mock-Tudor building are completely unwarranted, as inside is a totally different story. The front door opens to chic refinement; from suave and welcoming waiting staff - who successfully mix friendliness with real service - to the spacious, elegant and stylish metropolitan-style dining room, with its wooden floors, dark blue upholstered chairs and pale walls that combine with splashes of mulberry and truffle tones. Modern stained-glass windows play their part too, while a separate, buzzy brasserie with a more casual vibe, attracts savvy foodies enjoying culinary thrills at even lower prices.

FOOD: Expect grand cru cooking and evolved classics from the talented Andrew McLeish. His modern-focused style, based around classical techniques and dishes, displays innovation, consummate technical skill and wonderfully distinct flavours and balanced combinations. The approach via monthly changing, fixed-price menus, indulges anticipation and reads like central London luxury with suburban prices. Take a winning three-course format - ravioli of lobster with cauliflower purée and a lobster cognac sauce; braised melt-in-the-mouth oxtail stuffed with pancetta and served with celeriac purée, baby beetroot, roasted silverskin onions and a foie gras mousse; and finally chocolate marquise with black cherries and cherry cappuccino. Ancillaries, like breads and petits fours, keep up the pace in equally confident and accomplished style, while the wine list not unexpectedly favours France, though Europe and the New World find their place too. Lunchtime menu offers superb value. Chapter Two, in Blackheath SE3 (see entry), is a sister restaurant.

MENU GUIDE Risotto of winter truffles • Slow-roast pork belly, Savoy cabbage, potato fondant, foie gras, caramelised apple purée • chocolate fondant

WINE GUIDE ♀ Baron Phillipe de Rothschild Sauvignon Blanc £18.50 • ♥ Baron Phillipe de Rothschild Merlot £18.50 • 103 bottles over £20, 34 bottles under £20 • 12 by the glass (£3.75-£5.50)

PRICE GUIDE Fixed L £16.50 • starter £5.95 • main £15.50 • dessert £5.50 • coffee £2.50 • min/water £3 • Service added but optional 12.5%

OUR TIP: Prices allow you to enjoy the carte

Chef: Andrew McLeish **Owners:** Selective Restaurants Group **Times:** 12-2.30/6.30-10.30, Closed 1-4 Jan **Notes:** Sun L 3 courses £16.95, Vegetarian available, Dress Restrictions, No shorts, jeans or trainers **Seats:** 120, Pr/dining room 55 **Smoking:** N/Sm in restaurant, Air con **Children:** Portions **Directions:** Situated on A21, 3m from Bromley. From M25 junct 4 onto A21 for 5m. **Parking:** 90

NFIELD MAP 06 TQ39

🏨 Royal Chace Hotel
International

ophisticated hotel brasserie

☎ 020 8884 8181 The Ridgeway EN2 8AR

MENU GUIDE Smoked haddock fishcakes, coriander & mint I • Beef fillet, red wine & shallot sauce • Spotted dick, caramel auce

WINE GUIDE ♀ Hardys Captains Chardonnay 4.95 • ♀ Delicato Zinfandel £18 • 7 bottles over £20, 5 bottles under £20

PRICE GUIDE Starter £4.20-£7.75 • main £9.45-£14.75 • dessert 4.50 • coffee £1.75 • min/water £2.95 • Service added but ptional 10%

PLACE: Smart brasserie restaurant on the first floor of a modern d popular hotel set in a peaceful north London location. oduced lighting, warm colours, wood panelling and clothed les create a sophisticated ambience. Staff are smart and ndly.

FOOD: Cooking is International in style with modern twists and extensive menu changes seasonally. Portions are generous. **OUR TIP:** Booking advisable as the brasserie is popular **Chef:** Chris Jenkins **Owners:** R Nicholas **Times:** 7-10, Closed Xmas, ed L Mon-Sat, closed D Sun **Notes:** Vegetarian available, Dress trictions, No jeans or trainers, Civ Wed 220 **Seats:** 120, Pr/dining m 50 **Smoking:** N/Sm in restaurant, Air con **Children:** Menu, tions **Rooms:** 92 (92 en suite) ★★★ **Parking:** 220 **ail:** reservations@royalchacehotel.co.uk **web:** www.royal-chace.com

ADLEY WOOD MAP 06 TQ29

🏨🏨 West Lodge Park Hotel, The edar Restaurant
itish

unty house setting for polished professionalism
☎ 020 8216 3900 Cockfosters Rd EN4 0PY

MENU GUIDE Thai spiced crab cakes, coconut broth • Venison n, parsnip mash, liquorice jus • Prune & Armagnac soufflé, uce anglaise

WINE GUIDE ♀ Santa Serena Sauvignon Blanc Chardonnay 5.10 • ♀ Santa Serena Cabernet Sauvignon/Merlot £15.10 • 49 ttles over £20, 24 bottles under £20 • 8 by the glass (£5-£6.05)

PRICE GUIDE Starter £5.95-£10.50 • main £17.50-£24.50 ssert £5.95 • coffee £2.95 • min/water £3.70 • Service optional

PLACE: Grand house visited by Elizabeth I and James I in its e, West Lodge Park is now a popular business hotel. It stands 5 acres of mature parkland and lakes, just 12 miles from tral London and a mile from the M25, with the elegant Cedar taurant overlooking the garden.
continued

FOOD: The modern British menu incorporates both modern and traditional styles to meet the needs of its clientele. Technically accomplished and well presented dishes deliver a good balance of flavours, textures and seasoning, and the quality of the ingredients is evident.
OUR TIP: Live events, regular concerts and gourmet dinners **Chef:** Wayne Turner **Owners:** Beales Ltd **Times:** 12.30-2/7.00-10.00, Closed L Sat **Notes:** Vegetarian available, Dress Restrictions, Smart casual, Jacket & tie recommended, Civ Wed 40 **Seats:** 70, Pr/dining room 54 **Smoking:** N/Sm in restaurant, Air con **Children:** Portions **Rooms:** 59 (59 en suite) ★★★★ **Directions:** On the A111, 1m S of M25 junct 24 **Parking:** 75 **e-mail:** westlodgepark@bealeshotels.co.uk **web:** www.bealeshotel.co.uk

---

HAMPTON *See* LONDON SECTION plan 1-B2
🏵🏵🏵 *Monsieur Max* *see page 358*

HARROW WEALD *See* LONDON SECTION plan 1-B6
🏵🏵 Grim's Dyke Hotel
British, French

Competent cooking in a traditional country house

☎ 020 8385 3100 Old Redding HA3 6SH
MENU GUIDE Steamed halibut in banana leaf • Beer braised pheasant • Quince tarte Tatin, pear ice cream
WINE GUIDE ♀ Kirkton Vale Semillon Chardonnay £18 • ♀ Kirkton Vale Cabernet Shiraz £18 • 72 bottles over £20, 14 bottles under £20 • 8 by the glass (£3.50-£5.50)
PRICE GUIDE Fixed L £15 • Fixed D £25-£29 • starter £6.25-£9.25 • main £15-£24.50 • dessert £6.25 • coffee £2.75 • min/water £3 • Service optional

PLACE: WS Gilbert of Gilbert & Sullivan fame lived here for 20 years, and there's plenty of memorabilia to show the link. It still feels like a country house despite the closeness of London, Wembley and Watford, and the traditional restaurant is a peaceful haven where attentive service prevails.
FOOD: The new kitchen garden has had a positive influence on the menus, where Asian and French concepts add interest to the modern British theme. The quality of the ingredients, seasonal whenever possible and matched with strong technical skills, leads to some outstanding examples.
OUR TIP: Special themed events are held
Chef: Daren Mason **Owners:** Gilberts Restaurant **Times:** 12.30-2/7-9.30, Closed L Sat **Notes:** Vegetarian available, Dress Restrictions, No jeans or trainers (Fri-Sat), Civ Wed 100 **Seats:** 45, Pr/dining room 40 **Smoking:** N/Sm in restaurant **Children:** Menu, Portions **Rooms:** 44 (45 en suite) ★★★ **Directions:** 3m from M1 between Harrow and Watford **Parking:** 100 **e-mail:** enquiries@grimsdyke.com **web:** www.grimsdyke.com

---

A Restaurant with Rooms is usually a local (or national) destination for eating out which also offers accommodation. Most have 12 bedrooms or less, and public areas may be limited to the restaurant itself. Bedrooms reflect at least the level of quality associated with a two star hotel. A red symbol indicates a restaurant with rooms that is amongst the AA's Top Hotels in Britain and Ireland.

England

HAMPTON *See* LONDON SECTION plan 1-B2

Monsieur Max

French
Gallic charm
☎ 020 8979 5546 133 High St, Hampton Hill
TW12 1NJ
MENU GUIDE Pumpkin velouté with boudin noir • Confit of duck leg, fried butternut squash • Chocolate Moelleux
PRICE GUIDE Fixed L £20-£25 • Service added but optional 12.5%
PLACE: Never mind the unassuming suburban location, tucked away in a parade of shops. Once inside, you could be forgiven for thinking you are in a Lyonnaise brasserie, as this quirky Gallic restaurant is Hampton Hill's very own little piece of France. Bare wooden floors, magnolia-coloured walls, attractive floral arrangements, art deco mirrors and paintings, eclectic furnishings, and crisp linen-clothed tables topped with sparkling glassware set the authentic tone and make it a characterful place in which to dine. Decor befits the substantial French bourgeois cuisine, while slick and attentive French staff add to the friendly, hospitable ambience.

FOOD: Classic French provincial cooking delivered by an ambitious and skilful kitchen who have successfully taken the quality ingredients and combinations to a higher, more elaborate and refined level. Expect deep robust flavours, rich textures, excellent saucing and strong presentation relying on colour and layout rather than over embellishment. The wine list is extensive and, naturally, focuses on France.
OUR TIP: Be prepared for an enthusiastic welcome
Chef: David Philpott **Times:** 12-2.30/7-10, Closed L Sat, Xmas
Smoking: No pipes, no cigars **Directions:** Telephone for directions
e-mail: monsmax@aol.com **web:** www.monsieurmax.co.uk

KEW *See* LONDON SECTION plan 1-C3

The Glasshouse

Modern British
Local favourite with a light touch
☎ 020 8940 6777 14 Station Rd TW9 3PZ
MENU GUIDE Foie gras & chicken liver parfait • Pork, apple tarte fine, crispy ham • Raspberry ripple baked Alaska
WINE GUIDE ♀ Syrah Grenache £15 • ♀ Sauvignon Semilion £15 • 360 bottles over £20, 17 bottles under £20 • 14 by the glass (£4-£10)
PRICE GUIDE Fixed L £12.50-£25 • Fixed D £32.50 • coffee £3 • min/water £2.95 • Service added but optional 12.5%
PLACE: Sister to Chez Bruce (see entry) this buzzy little eaterie in Kew Village consistently impresses, drawing a loyal local crowd of devotees with its genial atmosphere and chic, airy decor. Tables are well spaced, with an eclectic mix of furniture, antiques, cushions and drapes all helping to create a luxurious ambience. Relaxed and friendly, but with high standards of service.
FOOD: One for the wine buffs this - The Glasshouse has a notable list with an impressive spread of countries, suppliers and vintages, many available by the glass. And the food's great too:

unfussy modern British cooking distinguished by a light touch and fresh flavours. Cheese is from Neal's Yard and La Fromagerie. Book to avoid disappointment.
OUR TIP: Good value seven-course tasting menu
Chef: Anthony Boyd **Owners:** Larkbrace Ltd **Times:** 12-2.30/7-10.30, Closed Xmas, New Year **Notes:** Tasting menu £45, Vegetarian available **Seats:** 60 **Smoking:** N/Sm in restaurant, Air con **Children:** Portions **Directions:** Telephone for directions **Parking:** On street; metered

HEATHROW AIRPORT See LONDON SECTION plan 1-A3

⊚⊚ The Radisson Edwardian Heathrow

British

British fare in luxurious surroundings

☎ 020 8759 6311 Bath Rd UB3 5AW

MENU GUIDE Rock oysters, red wine shallot vinegar • Grilled corn-fed chicken breast, pearl barley risotto • Baked chocolate tart

WINE GUIDE 13 bottles over £20, 19 bottles under £20 • 8 by the glass (£4-£5.25)

PRICE GUIDE Starter £6-£12 • main £13-£24 • dessert £6 Service added but optional 12.5%

PLACE: Lavish modern airport hotel with a renowned collection of newly commissioned artwork, oriental artefacts and designer furniture. The panelling of Henleys restaurant recalls a formal but comfortable country house setting.

FOOD: The best of native ingredients, carefully sourced, provide the basis for the British carte. Expect crowd pleasers like prime rib of Scottish beef with chunky chips and sauce béarnaise alongside the likes of pan-seared turbot with asparagus and warm vinaigrette.

OUR TIP: Informal meals are served in the brasserie
Chef: Steve White **Owners:** Radisson Edwardian **Times:** 12-2.30/7-10, closed 25 Dec, New Year & BHs, Sat-Sun **Notes:** Vegetarian available, Smart Dress, Civ Wed 350 **Seats:** 60, Pr/dining room 30
Smoking: N/Sm area, Air con **Children:** Portions **Rooms:** 459 (459 en suite) **Directions:** On A4, close to Heathrow Airport and M4
Parking: 600 **web:** www.radissonedwardian.com

⊚ Simply Nico

French

French flair in airport hotel

☎ 0870 400 9140 Crowne Plaza London - Heathrow, Stockley Rd UB7 9NA

PLACE: Tucked away at the rear of this busy airport hotel (Crowne Plaza, Heathrow) is this elegant, sophisticated French brasserie. Staff are efficient and knowledgeable.
FOOD: Authentic French brasserie fare with intense flavours. The food is inspired by world class chef Nico Ladenis, renowned for taking familiar French dishes and reworking them to include modern ingredients and flavours.
OUR TIP: Good selection of wines by the glass
Times: 12-2.30/6-11, Closed Sat, closed L Sun **Rooms:** 458 (458 en suite) ★★★★ **Directions:** From M25 junct 15 take M4. At junct 4 take A408. Straight on at traffic lights. Hotel on slip road on L
web: www.london-heathrow.crowneplaza.com

KEW See LONDON SECTION plan 1-C3

⊚⊚⊚ The Glasshouse *see opposite*

KINGSTON UPON THAMES
See LONDON SECTION plan 1-C1

⊚⊚ *Ayudhya Thai Restaurant*
Thai

Authentic Thai in the heart of suburbia

☎ 020 8546 5878 0208 5495984 14 Kingston Hill KT2 7NH

MENU GUIDE Chicken satay • Steamed mussels, lemongrass, basil • Banana in coconut milk

PRICE GUIDE Food prices not confirmed for 2006. Please telephone for details

PLACE: Not far from Kingston centre, this established neighbourhood Thai is part of a parade of small shops. Step inside and you'll be greeted by friendly staff in authentic costume and the aroma of incense; oriental paintings and woodcarvings hang on the dark panelled walls.
FOOD: Quality produce and an authentic approach have won the Ayudhya a strong local following. Its lengthy menu features handy notes to guide the novice, and a takeaway service is available.
OUR TIP: Leave time to find a parking place
Times: 12-2.30/6.30-11, Closed Xmas, BHs, closed L Mon
Directions: 0.5m from Kingston town centre on A308, and 2.5m from Robin Hood rdbt at junction of A3

The AA Wine Awards recognise the finest wine lists in England, Scotland and Wales. For full details, see pages 14-15

continued

KINGSTON UPON THAMES *continued*
See LONDON SECTION plan 1-C1

Frère Jacques
French
Simple French fare in relaxed riverside bistro
☎ 020 8546 1332 10-12 Riverside Walk, Bishops Hall KT1 1QN

MENU GUIDE Snails, garlic & parsley butter • Lamb shank with mash & green lentils • Hot chocolate fondant

WINE GUIDE 9 bottles over £20, 14 bottles under £20 • 14 by the glass (£3-£7)

PRICE GUIDE Fixed L £8-£12 • Fixed D £15-£23 • starter £3.90-£8 • main £9-£20 • dessert £4-£6 • coffee £1.50 • min/water £3 • Service added but optional 12.5%

PLACE: Overlooking Kingston Bridge, the terrace of this Thames-side bistro is an ideal place to dally away an afternoon. Inside is relaxed and rustic with authentically Gallic staff, service and music.
FOOD: Expect classical French cuisine conjured from quality ingredients, and a selection that stretches from snacks to full meals. The emphasis is on simplicity rather than more elaborate, innovative fare: king prawns in garlic butter perhaps, or chicken supreme with Roquefort sauce.
OUR TIP: Good range of fixed-price menus
Chef: Yves Tatard **Owners:** John Scott **Times:** 12, Closed 25-26 Dec, 1 Jan, closed D 24 Dec **Notes:** Coffee free when booked online, Vegetarian available **Seats:** 130 **Smoking:** N/Sm in restaurant, Air con **Children:** Menu **Directions:** 50 mtrs S of Kingston side of Kingston Bridge, by the river **Parking:** Euro car park - Thames St
e-mail: john@frerejacques.co.uk **web:** www.frerejacques.co.uk

Carluccio's Caffè Charter Quay KT1 1HT
☎ 020 8549 5898 Quality Italian chain.

Wagamama 16-18 High St KT1 1EY ☎ 020 8546 1117
Informal noodle bar with no booking.

PINNER MAP 06 TQ18 *See* LONDON SECTION PLAN 1-B5
Friends Restaurant
British, European
Neighbourhood favourite given a stylish make-over
☎ 020 8866 0286 11 High St HA5 5PJ

MENU GUIDE Foie gras terrine, gold leaf gelée • Lobster, saffron & pistachio risotto, Chablis cream sauce • Champagne & berry terrine

WINE GUIDE ♀ Alamos Chardonnay £18.95 • ♥ Alamos Cabernet Sauvignon £18.95 • 40 bottles over £20, 6 bottles under £20 • 7 by the glass (£4-£5.25)

PRICE GUIDE Fixed L £16.50 • Fixed D £17.95 • starter £5.95-£12.95 • main £15.50-£30 • dessert £6.75-£7.50 • coffee £3.75 • min/water £3.50 • Service added but optional 10%

PLACE: Recently refurbished in black and white, this friendly neighbourhood restaurant, with two dining rooms, is decorated in smart modern style with high back leather chairs, crisp white linen and bold flower displays. Outside is a different affair: a black and white Tudor frontage that's awash with greenery in the summer.
FOOD: Classical cuisine with a few contemporary twists: venison with poached pear and Valrhona jus perhaps, or chicken with sweet potato mash and coconut cream sauce. New champagne bar upstairs.
OUR TIP: The deli next door is also run by the restaurant team
Chef: Terry Farr **Owners:** Mr Farr **Times:** 12-3/6.30-10.30, Closed 25 Dec, BHs, closed D Sun closed Mon during summer **Notes:** Fixed menu only avail. Mon-Fri, Vegetarian available **Seats:** 40, Pr/dining room 30 **Smoking:** N/Sm in restaurant, Air con **Children:** Portions
Directions: In centre of Pinner. 2 mins' walk from underground station **Parking:** nearby car parks x3
e-mail: info@friendsrestaurant.co.uk
web: www.friendsrestaurant.co.uk

...ICHMOND (UPON THAMES) MAP 06 TQ17
...e LONDON SECTION PLAN 1-C3

Bingham Hotel
...rench, European **NEW**

...odern cuisine in riverside setting

☎ 020 8940 0902 61-63 Petersham Rd TW10 6UT

MENU GUIDE Crab charlotte, aubergine caviar • Pheasant in ...ancetta, Puy lentils, butternut squash purée • Date & orange ...eam pudding

WINE GUIDE ♀ Franz Haaz Pinot Grigio £27 • ♥ Omrahi Shiraz ...9 • 31 bottles over £20, 12 bottles under £20 • 10 by the glass ...4-£16)

PRICE GUIDE Starter £5-£9 • main £12-£22 • dessert £6-£7.50 ...ffee £2.50 • min/water £3.50 • Service added but optional 12.5%

PLACE: Just a short walk from Richmond Bridge, this chic hotel ...terie overlooks the Thames, and is decorated in bold modern ...le with white-washed walls, splashes of red, and black leather ...ts. Candles create a romantic feel at night, and there's a ...easant balcony for alfresco dining in summer.

FOOD: Contemporary cooking with its roots in classical cuisine. A ...ll-balanced menu offers a good mix of simple and more ...mplex dishes.

OUR TIP: A delightful alfresco venue

Chef: Pierre Denoyer **Owners:** Ruth & Samantha Trinder **Times:** 12.30-...-10, Closed 26 Dec-early Jan, closed L Mon-Sat, closed D Sun **...tes:** Vegetarian available, Smart Dress, Civ Wed 50 **Seats:** 40, ...dining room 30 **Smoking:** N/Sm in restaurant **Children:** Menu, ...tions **Rooms:** 23 (23 en suite) ★★★ **Parking:** 6 **...mail:** reservations@binghamhotel.co.uk **...b:** www.binghamhotel.co.uk

La Buvette
...ench **NEW**

...assy French bistro

☎ 020 8940 6264 6 Church Walk TW9 1SN

MENU GUIDE Crab salad, herb vinaigrette • Roast beef, ...tichoke, brandy sauce • Chocolate tart

WINE GUIDE ♀ Cheverny £16.50 • ♥ Moulin a Vent £19.50 • 17 ...ottles over £20, 7 bottles under £20 • 7 by the glass (£3.25-£7.50)

PRICE GUIDE Fixed L £11 • starter £5-£8.25 • main £11-£14.75 ...essert £4.75-£5.25 • coffee £2 • min/water £3.25 • Service optional

PLACE: This intimate French bistro is prettily set beside a church ...a pedestrianised alley just off Richmond High Street. A sunny ...low decor strikes a Mediterranean note, and is teamed simply ...th wooden chairs and neatly clothed tables.

FOOD: No fuss bistro cooking based on classical French recipes. ...oose from the carte, or take advantage of the good value ...ed-price menu available at lunchtime.

OUR TIP: Courtyard for alfresco dining in summer

Chef: Buck Carter & Toby Williams **Owners:** Lawrence Hartley & Bruce ...ckett **Times:** 12-3/6-11, Closed 25-26 Dec, 1 Jan, Good Fri **...tes:** Vegetarian available **Seats:** 50 **Smoking:** N/Sm in restaurant **...ldren:** Menu, Portions **e-mail:** info@brulabistrot.com **...b:** www.la-buvette.com

Ma Cuisine Le Petit Bistrot
...ench **NEW**

...endly bistro in Kew Village

☎ 020 8332 1923 The Old Post Office, 9 Station ...proach, Kew TW9 3QB

MENU GUIDE Soupe de poisson • Fillet steak tartare with pont ...euf potatoes • Tarte au citron

continued

WINE GUIDE ♀ Santa Helena Sauvignon Blanc 2003 £14.50 • ♥ Santa Helena Merlot 2002 £14.50 • 13 bottles over £20, 8 bottles under £20 • 10 by the glass (£3-£5)

PRICE GUIDE Fixed L £13.95-£18.50 • starter £3.95-£5.95 • main £9.50-£14 • dessert £3.95 • coffee £1.80 • min/water £2.50

PLACE: This local bistro is situated in The Old Post Office in Kew Village. With high, arched ceilings, gingham red and white tablecloths, and walls adorned with Toulouse-Lautrec posters, the ambience is friendly, informal and relaxed.

FOOD: The traditional French bistro style menu offers generous portions and good value for money in dishes such as cassoulet of confit duck, Toulouse sausage and beans or a rustic coq au vin.

OUR TIP: Excellent value lunch menu

Chef: Tim Francis **Owners:** John McClements/Dominique Sejourne **Times:** 9 am-11 pm, D served fr 6 **Notes:** Vegetarian available **Seats:** 45 **Smoking:** No pipes, No cigars **Children:** Menu, Portions **Directions:** From Kew Garden Station follow signs to Royal Botanical Gardens. At fork in road keep to the right. Restaurant is 50 mtrs on right **Parking:** on street

ⓐⓐ Restaurant at The Petersham
British

Breathtaking views with cooking to match

☎ 020 8940 7471 The Petersham, Nightingale Ln TW10 6UZ

MENU GUIDE Brown shrimp cocktail • Beef en croûte, gratin dauphinoise, green peppercorn velouté • Pineapple tarte Tatin, coconut sorbet

WINE GUIDE ♀ Domaine Gonon Macon Villages Chardonnay £17.50 • ♥ Château de Beaucastel Grand Prebois Grenache and Syrah £17.50 • 98 bottles over £20, 12 bottles under £20 • 6 by the glass (£4.50-£5.50)

PRICE GUIDE Fixed L £16.50 • starter £5.50-£11.50 • main £12-£26 • dessert £5.50 • coffee £2.50 • min/water £3 • Service added but optional 10%

PLACE: Perched on Richmond Hill, this elegant Victorian pile boasts one of the most celebrated views in London: a curving stretch of the Thames winding through water meadows and woodland.

FOOD: The Petersham's dishes show accomplished skills and a serious commitment to the use of high quality produce. Expect a modern British menu with a mix of classical cuisine and more innovative fare: sea bass with a seaweed crust perhaps, or lamb cutlets with smoked aubergine caviar.

OUR TIP: Take time out to enjoy that famous view

Chef: Alex Bentley **Owners:** The Petersham Hotel Ltd **Times:** 12.15-2.15/7.15-9.45, Closed Xmas, New Year, 25-26 Dec, 1 Jan, closed D 24 Dec, Sun non-residents **Notes:** Sun L £26, Vegetarian available, Dress Restrictions, Smart casual, Civ Wed 40 **Seats:** 70, Pr/dining room 28 **Smoking:** No pipes, No cigars, Air con **Children:** Menu, Portions **Rooms:** 61 (61 en suite) ★★★★ **Parking:** 60 **e-mail:** enq@petershamhotel.co.uk **web:** www.petershamhotel.co.uk

England

RICHMOND (UPON THAMES) *continued*
MAP 06 TQ17 *See* LONDON SECTION PLAN 1-C3

🍽 Richmond Gate Hotel
British
Elegant restaurant in a prestigious hotel
☎ 020 8940 0061 Richmond Hill TW10 6RP

MENU GUIDE Seafood risotto • Beef olives, horseradish mash • Roast coconut & basil parfait

PRICE GUIDE Fixed L £17.95 • Fixed D £28.50-£31 • coffee £3.10 • min/water £3 • Service optional

PLACE: An elegant restaurant, part of the Georgian hotel that sits opposite the park gate at the top of the hill. High vaulted ceilings and ornate features match the traditional decor.
FOOD: Choose from the short 'plain and simple' menu or a more inventive set of classical dishes on the dinner menu, both at set prices according to number of courses taken. Presentation is a strength.
OUR TIP: Walk on Richmond Hill
Chef: Christopher Basten **Owners:** Folio Hotels **Times:** 12.30-2/7-9.30, Closed L Sat, BHs **Notes:** Vegetarian available, Civ Wed 70 **Seats:** 30, Pr/dining room 70 **Smoking:** N/Sm in restaurant, Air con
Children: Menu, Portions **Rooms:** 68 (68 en suite) ★★★★
Directions: At top of Richmond Hill, opposite Star and Garter, just opposite Richmond Park **Parking:** 50
e-mail: richmondgate@corus.co.uk
web: www.corushotels.com/richmondgate

🍴 **Chez Lindsay** 11 Hill Rise TW10 6UQ
☎ 020 8948 7473 Popular neighbourhood restaurant known for its crêpes.

🍕 **Strada** 26 Hill St TW1 1TW ☎ 020 8940 3141 Superior pizza from quality ingredients cooked in wood-fired ovens.

RUISLIP
🍽🍽 Hawtrey's Restaurant at the Barn Hotel
French
Ambitious hotel cuisine
☎ 01895 636057 & 679999 The Barn Hotel, West End Rd HA4 6JB

MENU GUIDE Roast scallops, artichoke risotto • Venison, braised beetroot, roast parsnips, bitter chocolate sauce • Strawberry parfait

WINE GUIDE 🍷 Monte Verde Chardonnay £18.95 • 🍷 Murua Rioja £34.10 • 72 bottles over £20, 63 bottles under £20 • 9 by the glass (£3.50-£4.90)

continued

Hawtrey's Restaurant at the Barn Hotel

PRICE GUIDE Fixed L £16.50 • Fixed D £29-£39.50 • coffee £2.50 • min/water £3.50 • Service added but optional 10%

PLACE: Unassumingly located behind Ruislip station, this comfortable modern hotel is the unexpected setting for some seriously good food. The dining room is a sedate and civilised concoction of mahogany panelling, fine oil paintings, and high quality tableware.
FOOD: Expect ambitious cooking designed to impress, with luxury ingredients used to the fore. Modern French dishes predominate, with mains along the lines of lamb with caramelised onions, buttered spinach and rosemary jus, or pan-fried duck with creamed haricots and glazed asparagus.
OUR TIP: Six-course tasting menu available
Chef: Colin Buchan **Owners:** Pantheon Hotels & Leisure **Times:** 12-2.30/7-10.30, Closed L Saturday **Notes:** Vegetarian available, Smart casual, Civ Wed 24 **Seats:** 44, Pr/dining room 20 **Smoking:** N/Sm in restaurant, Air con **Children:** Menu, Portions **Rooms:** 59 (59 en suite)
★★★ **Directions:** From M40/A40 - exit at Polish War Memorial juncts and follow A4180 towards Ruislip. After 2m turn right at mini roundabout into hotel entrance **Parking:** 50 **e-mail:** info@thebarnhotel.co.uk
web: www.thebarnhotel.co.uk

SURBITON *See* LONDON SECTION plan 1-C1
🍽 The French Table
French, Mediterranean
Modern cuisine in warm and friendly local restaurant
☎ 0208 3992 365 85 Maple Rd KT6 4AW

MENU GUIDE Deep fried skate • Pan fried beef skirt, new potato with raclette, serano ham • Ginger bread & butter pudding, roasted pear

WINE GUIDE 🍷 Ken Forrester Chenin Blanc £16.50 • 🍷 Sainte Marthe Syrah £17.50 • 45 bottles over £20, 20 bottles under £20 • 7 by the glass (£3.50-£4.50)

PRICE GUIDE Fixed L £12.50-£15.50 • starter £5.20-£9.80 • main £10.50-£15.50 • dessert £4.95 • coffee £1.95 • min/water £2.95 • Service added but optional 12.5%

PLACE: A well established modern French restaurant dedicated to offering serious 'haute-inspired' cuisine. Interior decor is bold with black-tiled floor, red banquettes and apple green walls. Beech furniture and well placed mirrors give a feeling of space. Service is warm and friendly and the ambience relaxed and calming.
FOOD: French/ Mediterranean dishes with monthly change of à la carte and weekly change of lunch menu. Seasonal ingredients delivered daily.
OUR TIP: Booking ahead essential
Chef: Eric Guignard **Owners:** Eric & Sarah Guignard **Times:** 12-2.30/7-10.30, Closed 25-26 Dec, 10 days Jan, last 2 wks Aug, Mon, closed L Tue Sat, closed D Sun **Notes:** Vegetarian available, Dress Restrictions, Smart casual **Seats:** 48 **Smoking:** N/Sm area, No pipes, No cigars, Air con **Children:** Portions **Directions:** 5 minute walk from Surbiton Station, 1 mile from Kingston **Parking:** On street
web: www.thefrenchtable.co.uk

TWICKENHAM See LONDON SECTION plan 1-C2

Brula

French

Reassuringly French neighbourhood bistro

☎ 020 8892 0602 43 Crown Rd TW1 3EJ

MENU GUIDE Foie gras ballotine, grape chutney • Sautéed king scallops, creamed endive • Chocolate marquise

WINE GUIDE ♀ Jean-Jacques Milles Sancerre Sauvignon £20 • ♀ Andre Collange Fleurie Gamay £22.50 • 12 bottles over £20, 12 bottles under £20 • 6 by the glass (£3.25-£7)

PRICE GUIDE Fixed L £10 • starter £4.50-£7.75 • main £10-£13.75 • dessert £4.50-£5 • coffee £1.50 • min/water £3 • Service optional

PLACE: There's more than a hint of the French bistro at Brula, despite its location in a shopping parade. Wooden tables, ceiling fans, mirrors and paper-covered linen tablecloths contribute to the Francophile mood. Friendly, relaxed staff.
FOOD: French country cooking meets modern European ideas on the short menus: Burgundy snails and ballotine of foie gras sit alongside smoked mozzarella, spinach and mushroom lasagne or confit Barbary duck leg with beetroot boulangère.
OUR TIP: Buy a lunchtime parking voucher from the shops opposite
Chef: Bruce Duckett and Jamie Russel **Owners:** Lawrence Hartley, Bruce Duckett **Times:** 12.30-2.30/7-10.30, Closed Xmas, BHs **Notes:** Vegetarian available **Seats:** 40, Pr/dining room 10 **Smoking:** No pipes, No cigars **Directions:** Join A305, go straight at traffic lights over the A3004, turn left onto Baronsfield Rd. Restaurant is at the end of the t-junct, immediately on the right **Parking:** On street & parking meters
e-mail: info@brulabirtrot.com **web:** www.brulabistrot.com

Ma Cuisine Le Petit Bistrot

Modern French

Bustling Parisian-style bistro in the heart of Twickenham

☎ 020 8607 9849 6 Whitton Rd TW1 1BJ

MENU GUIDE Frogs' legs Kiev, garlic mayonnaise • Cassoulet with confit duck, Toulouse sausage & beans • Crêpes Suzette

WINE GUIDE ♀ Santa Helena Sauvignon £14.50 • ♀ Santa Helena Merlot £14.50 • 13 bottles over £20, 8 bottles under £20 10 by the glass £3-£5

PRICE GUIDE Fixed L £10.95-£12.95 • starter £3.95-£5.95 • main £9.50-£14 • dessert £3.95-£4.20 • coffee £1.90 • min/water £2.50 Service added but optional 10%

PLACE: French bistro-style eaterie set in a row of shops two doors down from the chef/proprietor's main restaurant, McClements. Authentic decor takes in red gingham, wooden floors, Toulouse-Lautrec posters and a tiny bar serving French spirits.
FOOD: Rustic, classical French cuisine using good quality produce at an appealing price. The menu is hard to choose from, with its great choice of simply presented and enjoyable food.
OUR TIP: Ideal for a quick bite or a full meal
Chef: John McClements **Owners:** John McClements **Times:** 12-2.30/6.30-11, Sun **Notes:** 3 course Sun L £18.50 Vegetarian available
Seats: 70 **Smoking:** No pipes, No cigars **e-mail:** johnmac21@aol.com
web: www.mcclementsrestaurant.com

McClements Restaurant
see below

Loch Fyne Restaurant & Oyster Bar
175 Hampton Rd TW2 5NG ☎ 020 8255 6222 Quality seafood chain.

TWICKENHAM See LONDON SECTION plan 1-C2

McClements Restaurant

French

Assured cooking in a discreet shopping parade

☎ 020 8744 9610 2 Whitton Rd TW1 1BJ

MENU GUIDE Lobster ravioli, black pudding & apple • Veal sweetbread, chestnut purée • Rhubarb, lemon posset, Swiss meringue

WINE GUIDE 500 bottles over £20, 8 bottles under £20 • 18 by the glass (£4-£10)

PRICE GUIDE Fixed L fr £25 • Fixed D fr £48 • coffee £3 • min/water £5 • Service added but optional 10%

PLACE: Set unassumingly in a modest parade of shops near the station and the High Street, this staging post for fine food continues to wow the punters. Despite the location there is nothing withdrawn about McClements: the smart modern decor embraces polished wood and stylish table settings, and the service by the small friendly team is as professional as the kitchen.
FOOD: The ambitious approach to cooking depends on highly-developed technical skills matched with top notch ingredients that do much more than just nod at the seasons. This dreamchild of John McClements does all this and more, and under his direction the team handles the food in a simple but assured manner, yielding harmonious combinations and flavours that hit the top notes again and again. Choose between the luxury tasting menu and carte, with a short set menu offering genuine good value at lunchtime. Dishes along the lines of salad of cod brandade mousse followed by loin of venison in thyme crumb with beetroot fondant could make a showing.
OUR TIP: Perfect for a post-Rugby match celebration
Chef: John McClements **Owners:** John McClements **Times:** 12-2.30/7-11, Closed Sun-Mon **Notes:** Tasting menu £60 **Seats:** 40, Pr/dining room 30 **Smoking:** N/Sm in restaurant, Air con **Children:** Min 9
Directions: Close to Twickenham Station **Parking:** 8
e-mail: johnmac21@aol.com **web:** www.mcclementsrestaurant.com

England

MERSEYSIDE

BIRKENHEAD MAP 15 SJ38

 **Fraiche** *see below*

LIVERPOOL MAP 15 SJ39

🌸 Radisson SAS Hotel Liverpool
Italian, Mediterranean **NEW**
Contemporary Italian cooking in stylish new
hotel
☎ 0151 966 1500 107 Old Hall St L3 9BD
MENU GUIDE Carpaccio of beef, parmesan soufflé • Roast
pheasant, Chianti risotto • Lemon pannacotta
WINE GUIDE ⚲ Masi £14.95 • ⚲ Masi £14.95 • 14 bottles over
£20, 20 bottles under £20 • 8 by the glass (£3.50-£4.50)
PRICE GUIDE Fixed L £11.50 • starter £4.95-£8 • main £10.50-
£19.50 • dessert £4.95 • coffee £2 • min/water £3.50 • Service
optional • Group min 10 service 10%
PLACE: Formerly an eye hospital, this brand new hotel with the
sleek contemporary Filini Restaurant overlooking the River
Mersey, with the twinkling lights of the Wirral providing a
backdrop at night. Windows along the length of one wall
maximise the view.
FOOD: The modern Italian menu with influences from Sardinia
veers towards a Northern Italian theme with Piedmontese,

continued

Lombardian and Florentine dishes. Authentic ingredients include
fregola grossa, stinco, and filetto di cinghiale.
OUR TIP: Excellent value lunch menu
Chef: Chris Marshall **Owners:** Radisson SAS **Times:** 12-2.30/6-10.30,
Sun **Notes:** Vegetarian available, Civ Wed 100 **Seats:** 90, Pr/dining room
120 **Smoking:** N/Sm in restaurant, Air con **Children:** Menu, Portions
Rooms: 194 (194 en suite) ★★★★ **Parking:** 200 mtrs
e-mail: info.liverpool@radissonsas.com **web:** www.radissonsas.com

🌸 *Simply Heathcotes*
Modern British
Modern eaterie with extensive brasserie-style
menu
☎ 0151 236 3536 Beetham Plaza, 25 The Strand
L2 0XL

continued

BIRKENHEAD MAP 15 SJ38

🌸🌸🌸

Fraiche

Modern French
Fine dining in Merseyside **NEW**
☎ 0151 652 2914 11 Rose Mount CH43 5SG
MENU GUIDE Foie gras torchon, quince jelly, poached
pear • Fillet of cod, slow-cooked pork belly, lemon
dressing • Sweet & sour pineapple, poppy seed parfait, red
pepper croquant
WINE GUIDE ⚲ Dreambay Sauvignon £19.50 • ⚲ Bottle Tree
Shiraz £15.50 • 80 bottles over £20, 20 bottles under £20 • 5 by
the glass (£4-£4.50)
PRICE GUIDE Fixed D £30 • coffee £2.95 • min/water
£3 • Service optional
PLACE: This intimate little eaterie is well worth seeking out.
Designed by the chef, it's a relaxed, contemporary venue with a
subtle decor of natural shades inspired by views of the shore
from Marc Wilkinson's home. Efficient and knowlegeable staff.
FOOD: With one of the country's best chefs at the helm, Fraiche
promises great things and deserves the support of local foodies.
Expect a concise menu of forward-thinking cuisine designed to

excite the palate, through a full spectrum of flavours, textures and
temperatures and served up at a reasonable price. If you want to
really do the place justice, try the tasting menu, a heady ten
course mix of new and signature dishes. For starters, you could
expect seared scallops with muscarado glazed chicory and
mushroom espuma, before moving on to slow-cooked Loire quail
with pomelo compote and boudin noir. Desserts delight with the
likes of chilled chocolate coulant, passionfruit sorbet and cocoa
and walnut crisp, or try the pressing of roasted apple, tonka bean
and rosemary ice cream. Amazing peripherals such as black
cherry froth and lemongrass pannacotta. Fine quality ingredients
are sourced locally wherever possible. This is one to watch.
OUR TIP: Open for dinner only
Chef: Marc Wilkinson **Owners:** Marc Wilkinson **Times:** 12-1.45/7-9.30,
Closed Mon, closed D Sun **Notes:** Tasting signature menu £45, Gourmet
menu £35, Vegetarian available **Seats:** 20, Pr/dining room 20
Smoking: N/Sm in restaurant **Children:** Min 8 yrs, Portions
Directions: M53 junct 3 towards Preston. Follow for 2m then take left
towards Oxton, Fraiche on right. **Parking:** On street
e-mail: fraicherestaurant@yahoo.com

England

MENU GUIDE Mussels with crab, saffron & fennel • Slow roast pork belly, spiced honey gravy • Eve's pudding

PRICE GUIDE Food prices not confirmed for 2006. Please telephone for details

PLACE: Tucked down a side street in Manchester's newly developed old registry offices, this stunning modern eaterie has floor-to-ceiling windows and is decked out in granite, cherry wood, and Philippe Starck bucket chairs.

FOOD: The extensive brasserie-style menu offers something for everyone, from a pasta or a bowl of soup to the more contemporary and Paul Heathcote's signature dishes. Cooking is careful and attentive with high skill levels and good use of Lancashire produce.

OUR TIP: Good value set lunches

Times: 12-2.30/6-10, Closed 25-26 Dec, 1Jan **Directions:** Opposite pier head **e-mail:** liverpool@simplyheathcotes.co.uk **web:** www.heathcotes.co.uk

60 Hope Street Restaurant

British

Smart and fashionable dining

☎ 0151 707 6060 60 Hope St L1 9BZ

MENU GUIDE Goats' cheese lasagne • Grilled beef fillet, braised ox cheek • Bread & butter pudding

WINE GUIDE ♀ Sauvignon Touraine £13.95 • ♀ Brushwood Shiraz/Cabernet Sauvignon £13.50 • 60 bottles over £20, 32 bottles under £20 • 8 by the glass (£4.50-£8.50)

PRICE GUIDE Fixed L £12.95-£15.95 • starter £5.50-£12.95 main £14.95-£29.95 • dessert £5.95-£8.95 • coffee £1.95 min/water £3.50 • Service optional • Group min 8 service 10%

PLACE: An unpretentiously stylish restaurant behind a Georgian facade that manages to be relaxed and chic at the same time. A river ground floor café and upstairs private dining room are equally appealing.

FOOD: The food follows a straightforward course between grilled fillet of sea bass with celeriac cream, and roast breast of Goosnargh duck, with the odd quirky dish - deep-fried jam sandwich with Carnation milk ice cream - thrown in.

OUR TIP: Handy for the Anglican and Roman Catholic cathedrals **Chef:** Paul McEvoy **Owners:** Colin & Gary Manning **Times:** 12-2.30/6-30, Closed BHs, Sun, closed L Sat **Notes:** Vegetarian available, Smart dress **Seats:** 90, Pr/dining room 30 **Smoking:** N/Sm area, No pipes, No cigars, Air con **Children:** Portions **Directions:** From M62 follow city centre signs, then brown tourist signs for cathedral. Hope St near cathedral **Parking:** On street **e-mail:** info@60hopestreet.com **web:** www.60hopestreet.com

Prices quoted in the guide are for guidance only and are subject to change without notice.

Ziba

British

Upmarket eaterie to savour

☎ 0151 236 6676 Hargreaves Building L3 9AG

MENU GUIDE Peppered duck breast, rocket & raspberry salad • Monkfish, daal, confit tomatoes • Peanut butter brûlée, melted bananas

WINE GUIDE ♀ Monte Real Reserva Rioja £23 • ♀ J Durup Pere et Fils Chablis £24.20 • 40 bottles over £20, 40 bottles under £20 • 6 by the glass (£3.50-£4)

PRICE GUIDE Fixed L £15 • starter £4.95-£10 • main £14.95-£24 • dessert £5-£8 • coffee £1.70 • min/water £3.75 • Service optional

PLACE: Minimalist chic and Gothic exuberance combine to dazzling effect in the decor of this classy restaurant, which draws an eclectic crowd of suits, shoppers and theatre-goers alike.

FOOD: A short and sweet lunch menu gives way to a wider evening selection of thoughtful modern fare, featuring dishes such as salmon with tomato, chickpea and chorizo stew, or beef with horseradish mash. Light bite menu served in the bar.

OUR TIP: Award-winning wine list to suit all tastes and budgets

Chef: Neil Dempsey **Owners:** Martin & Helen Ainscough **Times:** 12-2.30/7-10.30, Closed 25 Dec & BHs, Sun, closed L Sat **Notes:** Vegetarian available, Civ Wed 100 **Seats:** 80, Pr/dining room 100 **Smoking:** N/Sm in restaurant, Air con **Children:** Portions **Directions:** Situated in city centre Liver buildings **Parking:** Opposite restaurant entrance **e-mail:** info@racquetclub.org.uk **web:** www.racquetclub.org.uk

SOUTHPORT MAP 15 SD31

Warehouse Brasserie

International

Chic destination with global flavours

☎ 01704 544662 30 West St PR8 1QN

MENU GUIDE Teriyaki rare beef fillet, oriental salad, wasabi • Trio of Bowland lamb • Melting chocolate & orange pudding

WINE GUIDE ♀ Plaisirs D'Printemps Sauvignon Blanc £12.50 • ♀ Plaisirs D'Automine Merlot £12.50 • 18 bottles over £20, 17 bottles under £20 • 4 by the glass (£3-£3.25)

PRICE GUIDE Fixed L £10.95-£12.95 • Fixed D £14.95-£16.95 • starter £3.50-£8.95 • main £7.95-£16.95 • dessert £3.95-£10.95 • Service added but optional • Group min 8 service 10%

PLACE: This contemporary restaurant has a definite buzz and is popular with the smart young set, stylish business executives and ladies who lunch. They all love the theatre of the kitchen and friendly atmosphere.

continued

SOUTHPORT continued MAP 15 SD31

FOOD: With good technical skills, the chef succeeds impressively in the way he uses quality ingredients. The food is not rooted in one country or indeed one continent. There are some fun combinations too, allowing oriental dishes sit comfortably alongside good old-fashioned Whitby cod.
OUR TIP: Save room for the great desserts
Chef: Marc Verité **Owners:** Paul Adams **Times:** 12-2.15/5.30-10.45, Closed 25-26 Dec, 1 Jan, Sun **Notes:** Vegetarian available **Seats:** 110, Pr/dining room 18 **Smoking:** No pipes, No cigars, Air con **Children:** Portions **Directions:** Telephone for directions **Parking:** NCP-Promenade **e-mail:** info@warehousebrasserie.co.uk
web: www.warehousebrasserie.co.uk

THORNTON HOUGH MAP 15 SJ38

ⓖ Thornton Hall Hotel
International
Elegant dining in stately surroundings
☎ 0151 336 3938 Neston Rd CH63 1JF
MENU GUIDE Spicy lentil, coriander & coconut soup • Welsh black beef fillet, oyster mushroom glaze • Warm chocolate cup, sablé biscuits
WINE GUIDE ♀ Sauvignon £14.25 • ♟ Merlot £14.25 21 bottles over £20, 31 bottles under £20 • 8 by the glass (£3.30-£4.80)
PRICE GUIDE Fixed L £9.95 • Fixed D £28 • starter £5.95-£7.50 • main £16.50-£21.50 • dessert £5.95-£6.95 • coffee £2.75 • min/water £3.95 • Service included
PLACE: The hotel's Italian Restaurant is so named following the specification by the original owner, a shipping magnate, for classic Italian decor in his mid-1800s home. The ceiling is particularly notable, in tooled leather with mother of pearl inset. The resulting ambience is elegant and comfortable, with formal but friendly service.
FOOD: International cuisine based in Europe but including fashionable flavours from afar. Regularly changing menus use seasonal ingredients and introduce occasional speciality dishes.
OUR TIP: Much favoured wedding venue
Chef: Brian Herron **Owners:** The Thompson Family **Times:** 12-2.30/7.00-9.30, Closed 1 Jan, closed L Sat **Notes:** Sun D £33 incl wine, Vegetarian available, Dress Restrictions, Smart casual, No T-shirts or jeans, Civ Wed 400 **Seats:** 45, Pr/dining room 24 **Smoking:** N/Sm in restaurant **Children:** Portions **Rooms:** 63 (63 en suite) ★★★★
Directions: M53 junct 4 onto B5151 & B5136 and follow brown tourist signs (approx 2.5 miles) to Thornton House Hotel **Parking:** 250
e-mail: reservations@thorntonhallhotel.com
web: www.thorntonhallhotel.com

Give us your views! All the rosetted restaurants in this guide have been visited by one of the AA's team of professional inspectors, but we want to hear from you! Use the report forms in the back of the guide or email us at lifestyleguides@theaa.com with your comments on any establishments featured or on the restaurants that you feel are worthy of an entry. We would also be pleased to receive your views on the guide itself and suggestions for information you would like to see included.

NORFOLK

BLAKENEY MAP 13 TG04
ⓖ The Blakeney Hotel
Traditional British NEW
Quayside hotel dining with superb views
☎ 01263 740797 The Blakeney Hotel, The Quay NR25 7NE
MENU GUIDE Salmon & lobster ravioli • Baked monkfish tail with leek fondue • Raspberry and white chocolate trifle
WINE GUIDE ♀ Lelesc Plaimont Vin Pays du Gers Blanc 2003 £11 • ♟ Les Cent Vignes Rouge Vin Pays l'Aude 2003 £11.25 • 25 bottles over £20, 25 bottles under £20 • 7 by the glass (£3.70-£4.8
PRICE GUIDE Fixed D £22.50 • starter £4.75-£8.25 • main £11.95-£22 • dessert £4.75 • coffee £2.50 • min/water £2.50 • Service optional
PLACE: Situated on the quayside, with views across the salt marshes to Blakeney Point, this privately-owned hotel boasts an elegant dining room with professional, smartly uniformed staff.
FOOD: A good use of locally sourced ingredients, particularly fi and meat, is evident in traditional British dishes such as pan-frie fillet of pork with creamed potato, redcurrant and sage sauce, although there are occasional French flourishes.
OUR TIP: Good for local fish
Chef: Danny Bozic **Owners:** Michael Stannard **Times:** 12-2/6.30-8.45 **Notes:** Vegetarian available, Smart Dress **Seats:** 100, Pr/dining room 10 **Smoking:** N/Sm in restaurant **Children:** Portions **Directions:** From th A148 between Fakenham and Holt at Letheringsett, take the B1150 to ho **Parking:** 60 **e-mail:** reception@blakeney-hotel.co.uk
web: www.blakeney-hotel.co.uk

 Morston Hall *see page 367*

BRANCASTER STAITHE MAP 13 TF74
ⓖ The White Horse
British, International
Modern dining in unusual marshland setting
☎ 01485 210262 PE31 8BY
MENU GUIDE Brancaster Staithe mussels in white wine • Pan-fried fillet of beef, wild mushroom fricassée • Lemon tart with sweet pickled raspberries
WINE GUIDE ♀ Santa Rita Sauvignon Blanc £14.40 • 16 bottle over £20, 40 bottles under £20 • 12 by the glass (£2.80-£4.10)
PRICE GUIDE Starter £4.25-£6.50 • main £9.25-£17 • dessert £4.50 • coffee £2 • min/water £1.50
PLACE: Quirky little hotel on the north Norfolk coast, with a ba and large conservatory restaurant with stunning views of the tie marshes. It can be busy but the atmosphere is relaxed and friendly, as unhurried and professional service staff ensure customers are well looked after.
FOOD: A daily changing menu majors on the freshest locally landed seafood, but meat dishes too are prepared with a mix o individual style and current culinary trends whilst preserving th best of traditional values.
OUR TIP: Book a long way ahead for a window seat
Chef: Nicholas Parker **Owners:** Cliff Nye **Times:** 12-2.30/7-9.30 **Notes:** Vegetarian available **Seats:** 98 **Smoking:** N/Sm in restaurant **Children:** Menu, Portions **Rooms:** 15 (15 en suite) ★★
Directions: On A149 coast road, between Hunstanton & Wells-next-the Sea **Parking:** 85 **e-mail:** reception@whitehorsebrancaster.co.uk
web: www.whitehorsebrancaster.co.uk

LAKENEY MAP 13 TG04

Morston Hall

British, French

Inspired set-menu cooking in small country house

01263 741041 Morston, Holt NR25 7AA

MENU GUIDE Sea bream fillet, pepper fondue, asparagus • Guinea fowl breast, parmentier potatoes, sautéed mousse, rich jus • Banana soufflé, butterscotch ice cream

WINE GUIDE ♀ Michel Giraud Sauvignon Blanc £18 Domaine Haut Chatain Blend Cabernet Sauvignon £22 • 100 bottles over £20, 10 bottles under £20 • 12 by the glass (£4-£8)

PRICE GUIDE Fixed L £28 • Fixed D £42 • Service optional

PLACE: Hidden away on the north Norfolk coast, this small, flint-and-brick Jacobean country house hotel is quite a mecca for food lovers. Not just well known for chef-patron Galton Blackiston, Morston's appeal also lies in its cookery courses, demonstrations and wine tastings.

FOOD: Galton Blackiston conjures up culinary magic on a nightly basis, the approach via no-choice, daily changing, four-course dinner served at a single sitting at the set time of 7.30pm. The kitchen pays intelligent respect to first-class, fresh local seasonal produce, skilfully allowing the main ingredient to shine. Expect simplicity, innovation and an emphasis on clean flavours.

OUR TIP: Take advantage of the cookery courses

Chef: Galton Blackiston **Owners:** T & G Blackiston **Times:** 12.30/7.30, Closed 2 wks Jan, L Mon-Sat **Notes:** Coffee incl., Vegetarian available **Seats:** 35, Pr/dining room 20 **Smoking:** N/Sm in restaurant **Rooms:** 7 (7 en suite) ★★ **Directions:** On A149 coast road **Parking:** 40 **e-mail:** reception@morstonhall.com **web:** www.morstonhall.com

BRUNDALL MAP 13 TG30

The Lavender House

British

Country dining in beautifully restored thatched setting

01603 712215 39 The Street NR13 5AA

MENU GUIDE Slow cooked pork belly • Local lamb rack, Provençale vegetables • Orange liqueur trio

WINE GUIDE ♀ Vignes de Vanel Sauvignon Blanc £14.50 • ♀ Vignes de Vanel Cabernet Sauvignon £14.50 • 8 bottles over £20, 32 bottles under £20 • 6 by the glass (£3.50-£5.50)

PRICE GUIDE Fixed L £18.50 • Fixed D £32.50 • coffee £2.50 • min/water £2.50 • Service optional

PLACE: This thatched 16th-century listed building has been sympathetically restored to provide an excellent dining venue. There's a comfortable bar with lots of deep sofas. The newly extended restaurant has well-spaced clothed tables with good quality settings. Efficient, friendly service.

FOOD: Modern British cooking using best quality, local and seasonal produce. Taster dishes appear between courses ranging from parsnip crisps in the bar to a tiny cup of cauliflower cream at your table. Starters might include soused mackerel fillets, main courses Holkham pheasant cooked with prunes and Cognac. Good cheese selection.

OUR TIP: Just 10 minutes from the centre of Norwich

Chef: Richard Hughes, Richard Knights **Owners:** Richard & Sue Hughes **Times:** 12-2/6.30-12, Closed 24 Dec-30 Dec, Sun & Mon, closed L all week **Notes:** Fixed D 6 courses £32.50, Vegetarian available **Seats:** 50,

The Lavender House

Pr/dining room 36 **Smoking:** N/Sm in restaurant **Children:** Portions **Directions:** Norwich city centre **Parking:** 16 **web:** www.thelavenderhouse.co.uk

continued

BURNHAM MARKET MAP 13 TF84

🐟 Fishes
Modern British
A fish lovers' paradise
☎ 01328 738588 Market Place PE31 8HE

MENU GUIDE Spicy crab, cucumber spaghetti • Bourride of hake, brill & langoustine • Warm rhubarb tart & clotted cream

WINE GUIDE ♀ Château de Maligny Jean Durup £23.50 • ♀ Cantina Valpaneta Falasco Corvina £15.50 41 bottles over £20, 18 bottles under £20 • 10 by the glass (£4-£8.50)

PRICE GUIDE Fixed L £14.50-£17.50 • Fixed D £33.50 • starter £6.50-£9.50 • main £10.50-£19.50 • dessert £4.75-£6 • coffee £2 • min/water £3.50 • Service optional • Group min 6 service 10%

PLACE: A double-fronted shop next to the Hoste Arms in Burnham Market's bustling centre. Scrubbed tables and pale walls and woodwork give a workmanlike appearance to the place.
FOOD: The catch landed along Norfolk's coast fills the daily menus, with Brancaster oysters and lobster, and a whole range of fish at its very freshest. The popular three-course set lunches and dinner carte show interesting modern flavours.
OUR TIP: Probably safest to book ahead
Chef: Matthew Owsley-Brown **Owners:** Matthew & Caroline Owsley-Brown **Times:** 12-2/6.45-10, Closed Xmas for 10 days, 3 wks Jan, Mon, closed D Sun **Notes:** Vegetarian available **Seats:** 42, Pr/dining room 12 **Smoking:** N/Sm in restaurant **Children:** Min pre-8yrs, Portions **Directions:** From Fakenham take B1065. 8m to Burnham Market, restaurant on the green **Parking:** On street **e-mail:** ob1@sizzel.net **web:** www.fishesrestaurant.co.uk

🐟🐟 Hoste Arms Hotel
European, Pacific-Rim
Stylish but informal inn with a vibrant menu
☎ 01328 738777 The Green PE31 8HD

continued

MENU GUIDE Sweet saffron pickled red mullet • Honey & chilli glazed ham hock • Bakewell tart

WINE GUIDE ♀ Casa La Joya Sauvignon Blanc £14.75 ♀ Reserve Vignobles Syrah-Mouvedre £11.50 • 213 bottles over £20, 33 bottles under £20 • 21 by the glass (£2.85-£12.15)

PRICE GUIDE Fixed L £14-£25 • Fixed D £22-£32 • starter £4.25-£11.50 • main £9.25-£17.50 • dessert £5.50-£7.95 • coffee £1.30

PLACE: Nelson was a Saturday morning regular here when it was first an inn, and this lovely Georgian property continues to attract sailors visiting the North Norfolk coast, and discerning others. The brasserie-style restaurant buzzes with life.
FOOD: An eclectic cooking style draws its inspiration from the Pacific Rim, Europe and, specifically, modern British innovations. The menu lists starters doubling as light meals, fish galore than to the good relationship with local fishermen, risottos and pasta and perhaps succulent best end of lamb with roasted pumpkin. Notable wine list.
OUR TIP: The Zulu wing offers exotic bedrooms
Chef: Rory Whelan **Owners:** Mr P D Whittome **Times:** 12-2/7-9, Closed L 31 Dec **Notes:** Free refills on coffee, Vegetarian available, Smart Casual **Seats:** 140, Pr/dining room 24 **Smoking:** N/Sm area, No pipes, No cigars, Air con **Children:** Menu **Rooms:** 36 (36 en suite) ★★ **Directions:** 2m from A149 between Burnham & Wells **Parking:** 45 **e-mail:** reception@hostearms.co.uk **web:** www.hostearms.co.uk

GREAT YARMOUTH MAP 13 TG50

🐟 Imperial Hotel
British, European
Traditional hotel dining
☎ 01493 842000 North Dr NR30 1EQ

MENU GUIDE Herring salad • Chargrilled chicken, polenta, green beans, pesto • Orange crème brûlée

WINE GUIDE ♀ Louis Jadot Couvent de Jacobin Chardonnay £16.95 • ♀ Louis Jadot Couvent de Jacobin Pinot Noir £16.95 • bottles over £20, 30 bottles under £20 • 8 by the glass (£2.50-£5)

PRICE GUIDE Starter £4-£8 • main £9-£22 • dessert £5-£7.50 • coffee £1.50 • min/water £3.50 • Service optional

PLACE: A friendly, family-run end of the Great Yarmouth seafront. Dinner is served in the comfortable surroundings of the Rambouillet restaurant.
FOOD: A menu of favourites and comfort food that suits the traditional seaside setting. Your meal might kick off with prawn cocktail, followed by beef Stroganoff or sausage and mash, and crêpes Suzette flambéed at the table.
OUR TIP: An easy walk into town
Chef: Stephen Duffield **Owners:** Mr N.L. & Mrs A. Mobbs **Times:** 12-2/7-10, Closed L Mon-Sat **Notes:** Sun lunch 3 courses £14.95, Vegetarian available, Dress Restrictions, Smart-casual, No shorts or trainers, Civ Wed **Seats:** 60, Pr/dining room 140 **Smoking:** N/Sm area, Air con **Children:** Portions **Rooms:** 39 (39 en suite) ★★★ **Directions:** North end of Great Yarmouth seafront **Parking:** 45 **e-mail:** reception@imperialhotel.co.uk **web:** www.imperialhotel.co.uk

England

RIMSTON MAP 12 TF72

◐◉ Congham Hall

Modern British

Imaginative, seasonal cooking in Georgian setting

☎ 01485 600250 Lynn Rd PE32 1AH

MENU GUIDE Congham gravadlax with herb salad • Partridge
ballotine, ceps & truffle sauce • Poached pear, honey & almond
cream

WINE GUIDE ♀ 2003 Cairnbrae Sauvignon Blanc £21 • ♥ Roger
Holland Burgundy San Taney 1er Cru £33.50 • 80 bottles over
£20, 12 bottles under £20 • 12 by the glass (£3.75-£4.25)

PRICE GUIDE Fixed L £14.50 • Fixed D £42 • coffee
£4 • min/water £4 • Service optional

PLACE: This elegant Georgian manor has 30 acres of mature,
landscaped parkland. Beautiful day rooms are comfortable and
relaxing. The Orangery Restaurant provides an intimate setting
for dining with rich Georgian decor and panoramic garden views.
This is everything an English country house should be.

FOOD: Imaginative cooking based on high quality local and
seasonal produce. The kitchen garden provides fresh scents and
flavours throughout the year to complement dishes of foie gras,
British beef or local game. Good vegetarian choices and
excellent cheeses.

OUR TIP: Request a tour of the impressive herb garden
Chef: Jamie Murch **Owners:** Von Essen Hotels **Times:** 12-1.45/7-9.15
Notes: Sun L £21.95, Vegetarian available, Dress Restrictions, No jeans,
shorts or trainers, Civ Wed 100 **Seats:** 50, Pr/dining room 18
Smoking: N/Sm in restaurant **Children:** Min 7yrs D, Portions
Rooms: 14 (14 en suite) ★★★ **Directions:** 6m NE of King's Lynn on
A148, turn right towards Grimston. Hotel 2.5m on left (do not go to
Congham) **Parking:** 50 **e-mail:** info@conghamhallhotel.co.uk
web: www.conghamhallhotel.co.uk

HEACHAM MAP 12 TF63

◉ Rushmore's

British **NEW**

British restaurant in Norfolk's lavender village

☎ 01485 579393 14 High St PE31 7ER

MENU GUIDE Black pudding & sweet apple fritters • Baked
Cromer crab & Shetland salmon • Lemon meringue tart

WINE GUIDE ♀ Chablis Pascal Bouchard • ♥ Pinotage
Backeburg £14.95 • 8 bottles over £20, 19 bottles under £20
• 4 by the glass (£2.65-£3.95)

PRICE GUIDE Fixed L £11.95-£13.75 • starter £5.30-£6.25 • main
£8.70-£18.75 • dessert £4.95 • coffee £1.80 • min/water
£1.95 • Service optional

PLACE: Peruse the menu over an aperitif in the entrance
conservatory, before moving into the smart restaurant which was
once a draper's shop. Pastel shades and neatly clothed tables are
as soothing as the surrounding countryside.

FOOD: Seafood from the nearby coast and game in season from
the neighbouring Sandringham Estate are staples of the menus.
Traditional dishes like lamb's liver and bacon are given an
interesting modern makeover.

OUR TIP: Visit the local lavender farm
Chef: Colin Rushmore **Owners:** P Barrett, D Askew **Times:** 12.00-
2.00/6.30-9.30, Closed Mon, closed L, Tues, Sat, closed D, Sun
Notes: Vegetarian available, Smart Dress **Seats:** 42, Pr/dining room 6
Smoking: N/Sm in restaurant **Children:** Min 5 yrs, Portions
Directions: A149 towards Hunstanton. At Heacham, turn left at Lavender
farm. Follow into village, take 1st left into High St **Parking:** 25
e-mail: norfolkchef@ukonline.co.uk **web:** www.heacham.fsnet.co.uk

HOLKHAM MAP 13 TF84

◉◉ The Victoria at Holkham

British, French

Stylish Norfolk hideaway to suit most tastes

☎ 01328 711008 Park Rd NR23 1RG

MENU GUIDE Thornham mussel, saffron & chive
risotto • Venison, fondant potato, baby carrots • Granny Smith
tarte Tatin, apple sorbet

WINE GUIDE ♀ Gaudio Pinot Grigio £14 • ♥ Jean Balmont
Merlot £12.50 • 52 bottles over £20, 23 bottles under £20
10 by the glass (£3.20-£4.50)

PRICE GUIDE Starter £5-£11 • main £10-£18 • dessert £6 • coffee
£1.75 • min/water £3.50 • Service optional • Group min 6 service
12.5%

PLACE: This Grade II listed property turned chic restaurant with
rooms is part of the Holkham Estate and only ten minutes' walk
from the sandy beaches of the north Norfolk coast. The
brasserie and its airy conservatory extension have a colonial feel
with ornately carved artefacts and furniture imported from
Rajasthan.

FOOD: Simple British cooking featuring plenty of seasonal
produce provided by the estate and nearby harbours. There is
something to suit everyone on the extensive carte, which ranges
from a ploughman's lunch to more complex dishes such as sea
bass with a lemon and thyme risotto.

OUR TIP: A drink on the terrace before dinner
Chef: Neil Dowson **Owners:** Viscount & Viscountess Coke **Times:** 12-
2.30/7-9.30 **Notes:** Vegetarian available, Civ Wed 50 **Seats:** 80,
Pr/dining room 20 **Smoking:** N/Sm in restaurant **Children:** Menu,
Portions **Rooms:** 10 (10 en suite) ★★ **Directions:** 3m W of Wells-next-
the-Sea on A149. 12m N of Fakenham **Parking:** 50
e-mail: victoria@holkham.co.uk
web: www.victoriaatholkham.co.uk

England

HOLT MAP 13 TG03

⚙ Yetman's

Modern British

Friendly village haunt, excellent local produce

☎ 01263 713320 37 Norwich Rd NR25 6SA

MENU GUIDE Crab cakes, capsicum mayonnaise • Sea bass, asparagus spears • Gooseberry & elderflower brûlée

PRICE GUIDE Food prices not confirmed for 2006. Please telephone for details

PLACE: Formed from two adjoining cottages, and boasting a pretty rear garden, this smartly painted restaurant has an airy, easy appeal. Flowers on the tables and friendly staff are just some of the details that have made this such a popular venue for locals and tourists alike.

FOOD: A brief menu treats local produce with simplicity. Chargrilling is the house speciality, and you can expect plenty of fresh, skilfully selected fish, meat and poultry.

OUR TIP: The wine list features the owners' favourites

Times: 12.30-2.30/7-10, Closed 25-26 Dec, 3wks in Nov, Mon-Tue, closed D Sun **Directions:** On A418 (Norwich road), on outskirts of Holt **web:** www.yetmans.net

HORNING MAP 13 TG31

⚙ Taps

British

Popular village restaurant in the Norfolk Broads

☎ 01692 630219 25 Lower St NR12 8AA

MENU GUIDE Baked figs with dolcelatte • Pan-fried calves' livers, plum sauce, gratin Dauphinoise • Iced bread & butter parfait

PRICE GUIDE Food prices not confirmed for 2006. Please telephone for details

PLACE: Although something of a dining destination, Taps has maintained the relaxed feel of a neighbourhood eaterie. It's set in a pretty village on the Norfolk Broads, and a smart refurbishment has only added to the appeal.

FOOD: Sourcing good local produce clearly comes high on the agenda. Dishes are in the modern British vein, drawing influences from an eclectic range of culinary traditions.

OUR TIP: Lunch for value-for-money, dinner for the adventurous

Times: 12-2/7-9.30, Closed Mon, closed L Wed, Fri, Sat, closed D Sun **Directions:** From Norwich follow signs to The Broads on A1151. Through Wroxham and turn right to Horning & Ludham. After 3m turn right into Horning, Lower Street 500yds on left **e-mail:** terry.westall@tiscali.co.uk **web:** www.tapsrestaurant.com

HUNSTANTON MAP 12 TF64

⚙ The Lodge Hotel & Amethyst Restaurant

British   **NEW**

Smart and traditional hotel restaurant

☎ 01485 532896 Old Hunstanton Rd PE36 6HX

MENU GUIDE Twice baked Stilton soufflé • Braised lamb shank, lemon thyme sauce • Chocolate & lavender bavarois

WINE GUIDE ♀ Orvieto Classico £14.25 • ♀ Santa Septima Cabernet Sauvignon £14.25 • 2 bottles over £20, 40 bottles under £20 • 9 by the glass (£2.95-£4.40)

PRICE GUIDE Fixed L £10.95 • Fixed D £24 • starter £4.50-£8.25 • main £14.95-£17.95 • dessert £4.95 • coffee £1.35 • min/water £3.20 • Service optional

continued

PLACE: Amethyst both by name and colour scheme, this hotel restaurant was once part of the dower house to Hunstanton Ha■ Service is professional and relaxed, and the well-spaced tables promote a calm atmosphere.

FOOD: The use of fresh local produce - notably fish and seafoo■ from the nearby coast - is an appealing aspect of the balanced dinner menu (carvery lunch on Sundays only). Well-made sauc■ complement unfussy dishes like honey roast quail.

OUR TIP: Hunstanton golf course within walking distance

Chef: Mr K Jackman **Owners:** Mrs & Mr Best **Times:** 12-2.30/6-9.30 **Notes:** Vegetarian available, Dress Restrictions, No jeans or T shirts **Seats:** 80 **Smoking:** N/Sm in restaurant **Children:** Menu, Portions **Rooms:** 22 (22 en suite) ★★ **Directions:** Take A149 from King's Lynn to Hunstanton - hotel on right **Parking:** 60 **e-mail:** reception@the-lodge-hotel.co.uk **web:** www.thelodge-hotel.co■

NORTH WALSHAM MAP 13 TG23

⚙⚙ Beechwood Hotel

British, Mediterranean

Enthusiastic commitment to great food in elegan■ surroundings

☎ 01692 403231 Cromer Rd NR28 0HD

MENU GUIDE Grilled sole on bed of wilted little gem, shrimp butter • Breast of corn-fed chicken on champ with rich jus • Prune & caleys chocolate tart

WINE GUIDE ♀ Wither Hills Sauvignon Blanc £25.90 • ♀ Langmeil Shiraz £26.50 • 55 bottles over £20, 26 bottles under £20 • 5 by the glass (£4)

PRICE GUIDE Fixed L £18 • Fixed D £34 • min/water £3 • Serv■ optional

PLACE: This gracious ivy-clad house used to be frequented by Agatha Christie and fans can scan her letters to the family displayed in the hallway. Inside you'll find a lounge bar reminiscent of a gentlemen's club with leather chairs, and a smartly appointed restaurant, with discreet and skilled service.

FOOD: A dedicated kitchen team, which has been together for ■

continu■

...eral years, are committed to local produce and enjoy ...perimenting resulting in some original combinations. Watch ...t for dishes featuring Morston mussels, Sheringham lobster ...d local samphire. The menu changes seasonally.
...R TIP: Booking advisable
...ef: Steven Norgate **Owners:** Don Birch & Lindsay Spalding
...nes: 12-1.45/7-9, Closed L Mon-Sat **Notes:** Coffee incl, Vegetarian
...ilable, Smart Dress **Seats:** 60, Pr/dining room 22 **Smoking:** N/Sm in
...taurant **Children:** Portions **Rooms:** 15 (15 en suite) ★★
...ections: From Norwich on B1150, 13m to N Walsham. Turn left at
...ts and next right. Hotel 150 mtrs on left **Parking:** 25
...nail: enquiries@beechwood-hotel.co.uk
...b: www.beechwood-hotel.co.uk

...ORWICH MAP 13 TG20

...⊛ Adlard's Restaurant

...ench, European

...novative cuisine in renowned restaurant
☎ 01603 633522 79 Upper St Giles St NR2 1AB
...ENU GUIDE Terrine of foie gras with consommé en gelée
...oney roast breast of guinea fowl with herb dumpling • Coffee
...ille-feuille with dark chocolate and cardamom sorbet
...INE GUIDE ♀ House £15.50 • ♥ House £15.50 • 250 bottles
...ver £20, 20 bottles under £20 • 4 by the glass (£4.25)
...ICE GUIDE Fixed L £17 • starter £6-£12 • main £17.50-£25.50
...essert £8-£9 • coffee £2.75 • min/water £3.25 • Service optional
...ACE: One of Norwich's most enduring restaurants, Adlard's
...s stood the test of time with its competent cooking. Inside
...re are stripped wooden floors, white draped tables, elegant
...ssware and crockery and impressive oil paintings. The
...bience is cheerful, with plenty of natural daylight and cream
...ge walls providing a light, airy feel.
...OD: French cooking with European influences is given a British
...ch. The approach to food is serious with care taken over
...urcing and utilising quality ingredients. Some new concepts
...d innovative ideas are also tried. Excellent wine list.
...R TIP: Lunch menu is very good value
...ef: Roger Hickman **Owners:** David Adlard **Times:** 12.30-1.45/7.30-
...30, Closed 1 wk after Xmas, Sun, closed L Mon, closed D Mon (evening
...y for big parties) **Notes:** Vegetarian available **Seats:** 40
...oking: No pipes, No cigars, Air con **Children:** Portions
...ections: City centre, 200yds behind the City Hall **Parking:** On street
...nail: info@adlards.co.uk **web:** www.adlards.co.uk

...⊛ Ah-So Japanese Restaurant

...panese

...panese culinary adventures in Norwich
☎ 01603 618901 16 Prince of Wales Rd NR1 1LB
...ENU GUIDE Tempura prawns, lemon dip • Yakitori chicken,
...weet soy & sake sauce, fried rice • Cooked ice cream
...INE GUIDE ♀ Basa £13.95 • ♥ Casa Riva Merlot £12.95
...bottles over £20, 12 bottles under £20 • 4 by the glass (£3.95)
...ICE GUIDE Fixed D £15-£32 • Service optional
...ACE: A popular choice for local businesses, this Japanese
...panyaki restaurant has a smart contemporary decor and
...asantly laid-back approach.
...OD: Dishes are rustled up table-side at stainless steel griddles,
...d if you ask your chef nicely he might throw in a culinary trick
...two. Tuck in with a cold beer or sake.
...R TIP: Egg juggling is a speciality!
...ners: John Rose **Times:** 12-2.30/6-12, Closed L Mon-Sat
...tes: Vegetarian available **Seats:** 50, Pr/dining room 24
...oking: N/Sm area, No pipes, Air con **Children:** Menu,
...tions **web:** www.ah-so.co.uk

⊛ Annesley House Hotel
British, Mediterranean

Conservatory dining in charming surroundings
☎ 01603 624553 6 Newmarket Rd NR2 2LA
MENU GUIDE Crayfish tail salad • Braised partridge, celeriac &
blue cheese risotto
WINE GUIDE ♀ Forgemill Franschoek Chenin Blanc
£12.25 • ♥ Casa Rivas Mairo Valley Merlot £13.25 • 3 bottles
over £20, 22 bottles under £20 • 7 by the glass (£3.95-£4.95)
PRICE GUIDE Fixed L £19.50 • Fixed D £22.50 • starter £4.50-
£7 • main £10-£19 • dessert £4.75 • coffee £2.45 • min/water
£4.50 • Service optional
PLACE: Close to the city centre, this Georgian property provides
the perfect retreat amid three acres of landscaped grounds. The
Conservatory restaurant is surrounded by a water garden, with a
pretty waterfall and resident Koi carp.
FOOD: The menu offers a wide choice of dishes, set price or
carte, including a daily roast, baked ham with chunky chips,
steaks and a vegetarian option.
OUR TIP: Good selection of continental coffees
Chef: Simon Woodward **Owners:** Mr & Mrs D Reynolds **Times:** 12-2/
6-10, Closed Xmas & New Year **Notes:** Vegetarian available **Seats:** 40,
Pr/dining room 18 **Smoking:** N/Sm in restaurant **Children:** Portions
Rooms: 26 (26 en suite) ★★★ **Directions:** On A11, close to city centre
Parking: 25 **e-mail:** annesleyhouse@bestwestern.co.uk
web: www.bw-annesleyhouse.co.uk

⊛ Arlington Grill & Brasserie
International **NEW**

Brasserie food in Norwich's Golden Triangle
☎ 01603 617841 The George Hotel, 10 Arlington Ln,
Newmarket Rd NR2 2DA

MENU GUIDE Pork & chicken liver terrine, pear chutney
Ribeye steak, hand-cut chips, mushroom & tomato • Tiramisù
WINE GUIDE ♀ L'Emage Sauvignon Blanc £12.95 • ♥ Moondara
Shiraz £13.95 • 4 bottles over £20, 23 bottles under £20 • 5 by
the glass (£2.65-£2.85)
PRICE GUIDE Fixed L £7.95 • Fixed D £19.95-£20.95 • starter
£4.50-£5.50 • main £9.95-£16.75 • dessert £4.25-£4.50 • coffee
£2.25 • min/water £3.75 • Service optional
PLACE: This comfortable, family-run hotel is a great base for
exploring ancient Norwich. The Arlington Grill & Brasserie has
leather banquette seating and lots of mirrors. Uniformed staff
with long white aprons provide efficient service.
FOOD: Fresh, local ingredients are the basis the modern
brasserie-style menu including some grill items. There are old
friends here such as French onion soup as well as some
newcomers like smoked chicken and Cos salad.

continued

England

NORWICH continued MAP 13 TG20

OUR TIP: Conveniently close to the city centre
Chef: Paul Branford **Owners:** David Easter/Kingsley Place Hotels Ltd
Times: 12-2/6-10 **Notes:** Sun L 2 courses £10.50, 3 courses £12.99,
Vegetarian available **Seats:** 44, Pr/dining room 60 **Smoking:** N/Sm in
restaurant, Air con **Children:** Menu, Portions **Rooms:** 43 (43 en suite)
★★★ **Directions:** 1/2 miles from Norwich City Centre, 2 miles from
Norwich City station, 30 miles from A14 **Parking:** 40
e-mail: reservations@georgehotel.co.uk
web: www.georgehotel.co.uk

Beeches Hotel & Victorian Gardens

British, Pacific Rim
City centre retreat with idyllic gardens
☎ 01603 621167 2-6 Earlham Rd NR2 3DB
MENU GUIDE Spiced roast duck leg, plum sauce • Roast lamb
saddle, balsamic dressing • Croissant & chocolate bread & butter
pudding
WINE GUIDE ♀ Fox Grove Chardonnay £14.25 • ♀ Santa
Carolina Merlot £16.50 • 4 bottles over £20, 16 bottles under
£20 • 3 by the glass (£1.90-£3.60)
PRICE GUIDE Fixed L £12.50-£19.95 • starter £5.90-£7.50 • main
£13.90-£21.90 • Service optional

PLACE: Attractive hotel a short walk from the city centre, set in a
celebrated Victorian garden. The split-level bistro-style restaurant
has clothed tables and linen napkins, and service provided by
smartly dressed staff is relaxed but professional.
FOOD: Daily changing menus in the Cardinals Restaurant offer a
range of simply cooked modern British dishes with Asian influences
using quality local produce. There's also a decent wine list with a
good choice of affordable wines and selection of small bottles.
OUR TIP: Book in advance if lunch is required
Chef: Boyke **Owners:** Mrs M Burlingham **Times:** 12-2.30/6.30-9.30
Notes: Vegetarian available, Smart Dress **Seats:** 32 **Smoking:** N/Sm in
restaurant **Children:** Min 12 yrs, Portions **Seats:** 38 (38 en suite)
★★★ **Directions:** W of City on B1108, behind St Johns R C Cathedral
Parking: 50 **e-mail:** beeches@mjbhotels.com
web: www.mjbhotels.com

Brummells Seafood Restaurant

International, Seafood
Historic setting for fresh seafood
☎ 01603 625555 7 Magdalen St NR3 1LE

MENU GUIDE Monkfish fritters, roast tomato relish • Strawberr
grouper fillet, crab & oyster sauce • Warm pear, orange &
brandy syrup
WINE GUIDE ♀ Whitehaven Sauvignon £23 • ♀ Château
Lalande Pomerol Merlot £39 • 58 bottles over £20, 33 bottles
under £20 • 3 by the glass (£3.50-£4)
PRICE GUIDE Starter £5-£14 • main £16-£35 • dessert
£5.50 • coffee £3.25 • min/water £4 • Service optional • Group
min 7 service 10%

PLACE: Quaint medieval restaurant looking out onto the street,
with exposed timber beams and stonework. Rustic in style and
relaxed in atmosphere, it's the sort of place where you would fe
comfortable in smart casual clothes or black tie, though service
properly formal.
FOOD: Well-timed seafood dishes are offered from a highly
diverse menu. Cooking styles from around the world are
represented, all using the best of fresh ingredients. Some of the
combinations are quite striking, including sea bass with a
piccalilli-type accompaniment, and a dessert of warm apple, wil
mushroom and Calvados pie.
OUR TIP: Romantic candlelit setting
Chef: A Brummell, J O'Sullivan **Owners:** Mr A Brummell **Times:** 12/6
Notes: Vegetarian available, Smart Dress **Seats:** 30 **Smoking:** N/Sm
area, Air con **Children:** Portions **Directions:** In city centre, 2 mins' wa
from Norwich Cathedral, 40yds from Colegate
e-mail: brummell@brummells.co.uk
web: www.brummells.co.uk

By Appointment

British, European
Dinner in Aladdin's cave
☎ 01603 630730 27-29 St George's St NR3 1AB
MENU GUIDE Marinated Scottish salmon with avocado ice
cream • Fillet of beef wrapped in bacon, roquefort
cheese • Elderflower sorbet
PRICE GUIDE Food prices not confirmed for 2006. Please
telephone for details

PLACE: This glass-fronted restaurant hides behind its façade of
three 15th-century merchants' houses with their labyrinth of
theatrical corridors crammed with antique furniture, Victorian
silver cutlery and fine china. Each of the four dining rooms
resembles a theatre set.
FOOD: Classically English dishes, with continental influences, ar
simple almost rustic and full of flavour. Everything from the
bread to the ice creams are made in-house.
OUR TIP: Regular themed evenings
Times: 7.30-9.30, Closed 25 Dec, Sun-Mon, closed L all Week
Directions: City centre. Entrance rear of Merchants House

Four Rosettes Amongst the very bes
restaurants in the British Isles, where the
cooking demands national recognition. These
restaurants will exhibit intense ambition, a
passion for excellence, superb technical skill
and remarkable consistency. They wi
combine appreciation of culinary tradition
with a passionate desire for furthe
exploration and improvement. Around twenty
restaurants have four Rosettes.

continued

De Vere Dunston Hall

Modern British

Elegant dining in relaxed setting

☎ 01508 470444 Ipswich Rd NR14 8PQ

MENU GUIDE Salad of pigeon with black pudding & quail's egg • Roast partridge, caramelised apples • Bitter chocolate tart

PRICE GUIDE Food prices not confirmed for 2006. Please telephone for details

PLACE: Located in an imposing Grade II listed building set midst 170 acres of landscaped grounds, this sophisticated dining room boasts attentive, friendly service.

FOOD: The Fontaine restaurant offers modern British menus. Expect dishes like seared king prawns, chorizo mash, chive sauce and baby spinach salad or pan-fried monkfish wrapped in pancetta with pesto mash, flageolet beans and claret sauce.

OUR TIP: Ask to see the list of seasonal wines by the glass

Times: 7/10, Closed Xmas, Sun, closed L Mon-Sun **Rooms:** 130 (130 en suite) ★★★★ **e-mail:** dhreception@devere-hotels.com **web:** www.devereonline.co.uk/dunstonhall

Marriott Sprowston Manor Hotel

British, French

Stylish dining in elegant hotel

☎ 01603 410871 Sprowston Park, Wroxham Rd NR7 8RP

MENU GUIDE Scallops & smoked bacon with pea soup • Chicken supreme • Brandy & raisin crème brulée

WINE GUIDE ♀ Cork Vigna Pinot Grigio £16.25 • ♀ Penfolds Cabernet £31.60 • 60 bottles over £20, 20 bottles under £20 • 20 by the glass (£3.75-£8.75)

PRICE GUIDE Fixed L £13.50 • Fixed D £31.50 • starter £5.50 main £19.50 • dessert £5.80 • coffee £2.20 • min/water £3.20 service optional

PLACE: This large, imposing property is a short drive from the city centre and surrounded by landscaped grounds with golf and leisure facilities. You can dine in either the elegant Manor restaurant or the more informal Café Zest.

FOOD: The menus are largely British influenced and the food is simpler than it was, particularly in dishes such as chargrilled salmon served with sautéed potatoes, rocket and lemon butter sauce.

OUR TIP: Spend a relaxing weekend here

Chef: Paul Danabie **Owners:** Marriott, Whitbread **Times:** 12-2/6.30-9.45, Closed L Sat **Notes:** Vegetarian available, Dress Restrictions, Smart casual, no shorts, Civ Wed 120 **Seats:** 130, Pr/dining room 150 **Smoking:** N/Sm in restaurant, Air con **Children:** Menu, Portions **Rooms:** 94 (94 en suite) ★★★★ **Directions:** From A47 take Postwick exit onto Norwich outer ring road, then take A1151. Hotel approx 3m and signed **Parking:** 100 **e-mail:** alberto.rizzo@marriotthotels.co.uk **web:** www.marriotthotels.com/nwigs

Five Rosettes The finest restaurants in the British Isles, where the cooking stands comparison with the best in the world. These restaurants will have highly individual voices, exhibit breathtaking culinary skills and set the standards to which others aspire. Around six restaurants have five Rosettes.

Old Rectory

British, International

Candlelit restaurant in Georgian rectory

☎ 01603 700772 750772 103 Yarmouth Rd, Thorpe St Andrew NR7 0HF

MENU GUIDE Pigeon & pheasant terrine, cranberry & sloe gin relish • Black bream fillet, scallop risotto • Prune & Armagnac crème brûlée

WINE GUIDE 5 bottles over £20, 9 bottles under £20 • 5 by the glass (£2.75-£3.95)

PRICE GUIDE Fixed D £21-£23 • coffee £1.75 • min/water £2.95 • Service included

PLACE: This Grade II listed building is peacefully located by the River Yare, just a few minutes' drive from the city centre. The panelled dining room overlooks pretty landscaped gardens and the tables are laid with fine linen. In winter, there's a welcoming log fire in the drawing room.

FOOD: The fixed-price daily international menu offers a balanced choice of simple yet interesting dishes based around local ingredients.

OUR TIP: Stay over in one of the delightful bedrooms

Chef: James Perry **Owners:** Chris & Sally Entwistle **Times:** 7-10, Closed Xmas & New Year, Sun-Mon, closed L all week **Notes:** Vegetarian available, Smart Dress **Seats:** 16, Pr/dining room 16 **Smoking:** N/Sm in restaurant **Children:** Portions **Rooms:** 8 (8 en suite) ★★ **Directions:** From A47 take A1042 to Thorpe, then A1242. Hotel right after 1st traffic lights. **Parking:** 16 **e-mail:** enquiries@oldrectorynorwich.com **web:** www.oldrectorynorwich.com

1 Up

British, European **NEW**

Contemporary restaurant offering modern fine dining

☎ 01603 627687 The Mad Moose Arms & 1Up, 2, Warwick St NR2 3LD

MENU GUIDE Chicken liver parfait, spiced pear chutney • Wild sea bass, saffron potatoes • Hot chocolate fondant

WINE GUIDE ♀ La Reverence Sauvignon Blanc £11.95 • ♀ Firefly Shiraz £13.95 • 15 bottles over £20, 24 bottles under £20 • 6 by the glass (£2.60-£4.95)

PRICE GUIDE Fixed D £19.95-£24.95 • starter £5.50-£8.50 • main £9.95-£16.50 • dessert £4.50-£5.50 • coffee £1.50 • min/water £3 • Service optional

PLACE: Paradoxically uplifting and soothing at the same time, the soft yellows, deep blues and natural woods of this restaurant help to create an intimate space. This is the fine dining end of the trendy downstairs gastro-pub, and the professional staff do a superb job at very busy times.

FOOD: Classical cuisine is given an interesting modern tweak, aided and abetted by a competent team committed to using only quality ingredients. Tried and tested dishes are often reinvented, like slow-cooked pork belly with marmalade, sticky onions and Puy lentils.

OUR TIP: Good value menu du jour

Chef: Eden Derrick **Owners:** Mr Henry Watt **Times:** 12-3/7-9.30, Closed 25-26 Dec, 1 Jan, closed L Mon-Sat, closed D Sun **Notes:** Vegetarian available **Seats:** 48 **Smoking:** N/Sm in restaurant **Children:** Portions **Directions:** Telephone for directions **Parking:** On street **e-mail:** madmoose@animalinns.co.uk

England

St Benedicts Restaurant

Modern British

Confident cuisine from lively local brasserie

☎ 01603 765377   9 St Benedicts St NR2 4PE

MENU GUIDE Cheese soufflé • Wild boar with juniper, thyme & winter vegetables • Steamed date & walnut pudding, Horlicks ice cream

WINE GUIDE ♀ Whitehaven Sauvignon Blanc £17.50 ♀ Piqueras Almansa £14.95 • 54 bottles under £20 • 6 by the glass (£3.50-£4.40)

PRICE GUIDE Food prices not confirmed for 2006. Please telephone for details

PLACE: Just a short walk from Norwich city centre, this popular local brasserie hides a vibrant interior behind its classy Edwardian frontage. Sunny yellows give a contemporary feel, alongside blue leather seating and the odd church pew.
FOOD: Expect confident modern British cooking with the odd French twist and some inspired combinations. Desserts are a highlight: the choice might include hazelnut roulade or a chocolate and raspberry brownie with raspberry smoothie.
OUR TIP: Look out for the daily specials
Chef: Nigel Raffles **Owners:** Nigel & Joyne Raffles **Times:** 12-2/7-10, Closed 25-31 Dec, Sun-Mon **Notes:** Vegetarian available **Seats:** 42, Pr/dining room 24 **Smoking:** N/Sm in restaurant **Children:** Portions
Directions: Just off inner ring road. Turn right by Toys-R-Us, second right onto St Benedicts St. Restaurant is on left by pedestrian crossing
Parking: On street, West Wick Pay & Display
e-mail: stbens@ukonline.co.uk

Shiki

Japanese   **NEW**

City centre sushi and high-quality Japanese cuisine

☎ 01603 619262   5 Tombland NR3 1HE

MENU GUIDE Miso soup with wakame • Tonkatsu chicken, mouli and soy sauce

PRICE GUIDE Food prices not confirmed for 2006. Please telephone for details

PLACE: Dark rosewood tables, pale walls and stripped floors add up to a sharply minimalist interior that suits the contemporary Japanese feel.
FOOD: High quality dishes with good, clear flavours are the order of the day here. A takeaway sushi bar gives plenty of freshly made options, while the main menu might include such treats as a delicate and crisp prawn and green bean tempura or grilled teriyaki chicken with garlic, apple and ginger.
OUR TIP: Try the tapas-style taster menu
Times: 12-2/5.30-10 **e-mail:** bookings@shikirestaurant.co.uk
web: www.shiki.co.uk

Three Rosettes Outstanding restaurants that demand recognition well beyond their local area. Timing, seasoning and the judgement of flavour combinations will be consistently excellent, supported by other elements such as intelligent service and a well-chosen wine list. Around 10% of restaurants with Rosettes have been awarded three.

Stower Grange

British, French

Relaxed dining in 17th-century rectory in wooded grounds

☎ 01603 860210   School Rd, Drayton NR8 6EF

MENU GUIDE Tartlet of marrow, red onions with pesto • Seared fillets of red mullet with couscous & saffron sauce • Crème brûlée with fresh strawberries

WINE GUIDE ♀ Dubard Sauvignon Blanc £11.75 • ♀ Peter Lehmann Shiraz £15.75 • 31 bottles over £20, 24 bottles under £20 • 4 by the glass (£3-£4)

PRICE GUIDE Starter £5-£7.95 • main £12.50-£17.95 • dessert £5.50 • coffee £2.50 • min/water £2.50 • Service optional

PLACE: This attractive ivy-clad hotel is situated in a residential area just outside the city centre. The restaurant is small and intimate with crisp white table linen and crockery - the atmosphere is relaxed.
FOOD: Traditional British dishes are given a French accent on a succinct menu which has wide appeal. Almost everything is made on the premises and robust flavours feature alongside more simple and subtle dishes.
OUR TIP: Pleasant rooms to extend a stay
Chef: Mark Smith, Gary Taylor **Owners:** Richard & Jane Fannon
Times: 12-2.30/7-9.30, Closed 26-30 Dec, closed D Sun **Notes:** Sun L 3 courses £19, Vegetarian available, Smart dress preferred, Civ Wed 120
Seats: 40, Pr/dining room 20 **Smoking:** N/Sm in restaurant
Children: Portions **Rooms:** 11 (11 en suite) ★★
Directions: Telephone for directions **Parking:** 40
e-mail: enquiries@stowergrange.co.uk
web: www.stowergrange.co.uk

Tatlers

British

Relaxed and stylish brasserie dining

☎ 01603 766670   21 Tombland NR3 1RF

MENU GUIDE Cromer crab ravioli, avocado salsa • Roast lamb, chou-croute, rosemary jus • Warm blonde brownie

WINE GUIDE ♀ Les Trois Bastides Sauvignon Blanc £16.45 ♀ I Vigneti del Sole Sangiovese £15.75 • 17 bottles over £20, 20 bottles under £20 • 10 by the glass (£3.50-£6.55)

PRICE GUIDE Fixed L £14 • starter £5.50-£8.50 • main £11.50-£16.50 • dessert £6 • coffee £2.45 • min/water £2.45 • Service optional • Group min 10 service 10%

PLACE: This busy, brasserie-style restaurant is situated in a converted Victorian townhouse containing a number of separate individually decorated dining rooms. All feature scrubbed tables, wooden floors and lots of period features, and have a friendly, down-to-earth feel. The bar is particularly striking.
FOOD: Modern British dishes populate this menu although there are classical French undertones to some offerings. The menu changes daily and makes good use of local produce such as Brancaster oysters and Brampton wild boar; even the bread flour comes from a nearby mill.
OUR TIP: Paintings by contemporary local artists in the bar
Chef: Christopher Johnson **Owners:** Annelli Clarke **Times:** 12-2/6.30-10, Closed 25-26 Dec, Sun **Notes:** Vegetarian available **Seats:** 75, Pr/dining room 30 **Smoking:** N/Sm area, No pipes, No cigars
Children: Portions **Directions:** In city centre in Tombland. Next to Erpingham gate by Norwich Cathedral **Parking:** Law courts, Elm Hill, Colegate **e-mail:** info@tatlers.com **web:** www.tatlers.com

Loch Fyne Restaurant 30-32 St Giles St NR2 1LL
☎ 01603 723450   Quality seafood chain.

RINGSTEAD MAP 12 TF74

The Gin Trap Inn
British **NEW**
Relaxed dining in 17th-century Inn
☎ 01485 525264 6 High St PE36 5JU

MENU GUIDE Thornham rock oysters, lemon, shallot vinegar • Roast pheasant, crushed potatoes, grapes, walnuts • Pear strudel, pear syrup

WINE GUIDE ♀ Bellefontaine Sauvignon £12.95 • 9 bottles over £20, 23 bottles under £20 • 5 by the glass (£3.50-£4.50)

PRICE GUIDE Starter £4.25-£8.25 • main £8.95-£16.25 • dessert £4.50-£6.50 • coffee £1.20 • min/water £3.50 • Service optional

PLACE: Located in a peaceful village on the outskirts of Hunstanton, this delightful 17th-century coaching inn is very much a gastro-pub, with food offered throughout. The bar is quite rustic with plain wooden tables, a huge fireplace with a wood burning stove, exposed brickwork and beams adorned with traps. The small candelit restaurant has neatly clothed tables with crisp napkins.
FOOD: The carte offers a balanced choice of fish, meat and vegetarian dishes, prepared from quality local produce. There's also a good bar snack menu and an interesting selection for children, all using fresh produce.
OUR TIP: Relax by log fires in winter, or enjoy the delightful walled garden in summer
Chef: Andy Bruce **Owners:** Don & Margaret Greer **Times:** 12-2/6-9 **Notes:** Vegetarian available **Seats:** 20 **Smoking:** N/Sm in restaurant **Children:** Menu, Portions **Rooms:** 3 (3 en suite) ♦♦♦ **Parking:** 50 **e-mail:** info@gintrap.co.uk **web:** gintrapinn.co.uk

SHERINGHAM MAP 13 TG14

Dales Country House Hotel
Classical Modern
Country house dining in National Trust parkland
☎ 01263 824555 NR26 8TJ

MENU GUIDE Asparagus & gruyère soufflé • Pan-fried plaice with crayfish tails • Chocolate torte

PRICE GUIDE Food prices not confirmed for 2006. Please telephone for details

PLACE: Grade II listed Victorian country house hotel set in extensive, landscaped grounds on the edge of Sheringham Park.
FOOD: Contemporary English cuisine is conjured from ingredients sourced from quality local suppliers, including game from local estates and fish from the North Norfolk coast. Layered chicken terrine may be followed by braised venison haunch steak with red wine sauce, red cabbage and horseradish mash.
OUR TIP: Visit in June to see 65 species of rhododendrons
Times: 12-2/7-9.30, Closed 2-16 Jan **Rooms:** 17 (17 en suite) ★★★★ **Directions:** On B1157, 1m S of Sheringham. From A148 Cromer to Holt road, take turn at entrance to Sheringham Park. Restaurant 0.5m on left **e-mail:** dales@mackenziehotels.com **web:** www.mackenziehotels.com

One Rosette Excellent local restaurants serving food prepared with care, understanding and skill, using good quality ingredients. These restaurants stand out in their local area. Of the total number of establishments with Rosettes around 50% have one Rosette.

SHIPDHAM MAP 13 TF90

Bay Tree Brasserie at Pound Green Hotel
British, International
Brasserie serving down to earth food
☎ 01362 820940 Pound Green Ln IP25 7LS

MENU GUIDE Pan-fried wild mushrooms • Seared calves' liver, red onion confit • Champagne poached whole pear

WINE GUIDE ♀ Frasers Bay Chenin Blanc £11.50 • ♀ Oakwood Shiraz Cabernet £11.75 • 1 bottles over £20, 14 bottles under £20 • 5 by the glass (£2.30-£4.75)

PRICE GUIDE Starter £3-£4.75 • main £5.95-£11 • dessert £3-£4 coffee £1.75 • Service optional

PLACE: A peacefully located brasserie with a warm gold and terracotta colour scheme. Friendly staff help the chef/patron and his wife to keep the loyal local supporters happy.
FOOD: The seasonally changing menu with daily specials promotes an uncomplicated mixture of International and traditional British flavours. From braised minted lamb shank to sea bass baked on sea salt, the choice is reliably good.
OUR TIP: No problem parking
Chef: David Ostle **Owners:** David & Sarah Ostle **Times:** 12-2/7-9, Closed First 2 wks Jan **Notes:** Sun cavery lunch, Vegetarian available **Seats:** 45 **Smoking:** N/Sm in restaurant, Air con **Children:** Menu, Portions **Rooms:** 11 (7 en suite) ♦♦♦ **Directions:** A47 to Dereham. A1075 5m to Shipdham. Take left at brown hotel sign into Pound Green Lane **Parking:** 20 **web:** www.poundgreenhotel.co.uk

SNETTISHAM MAP 12 TF63

Rose & Crown
Mediterranean, Pacific Rim
Child-friendly Norfolk gastro-pub retreat
☎ 01485 541382 Old Church Rd PE31 7LX

MENU GUIDE King scallops, peanut butter & banana samosas • Pan-fried grey mullet, horseradish beurre blanc • Chocolate brownies

WINE GUIDE ♀ Louis Alexandre Sauvignon Blanc £11.50 • ♀ La Reverence Merlot £12.50 • 7 bottles over £20, 28 bottles under £20 • 14 by the glass (£3.25-£5.95)

PRICE GUIDE Fixed L £12.50 • starter £5.50-£7 • main £8.75-£14 • dessert £4.50-£4.75 • coffee £1.25 • min/water £3 • Service optional • Group min 10 service 10%

PLACE: A stylish, relaxed pub with rooms that - in part - date back to the 14th century. There are lots of stone floors, low beams and roaring fires. Meals can be taken in the dining room or the bars. Informal, friendly service.
FOOD: This gastro-pub has an eclectic menu with well-prepared traditional British dishes as well as items from the Mediterranean, the Far East and the Pacific.
OUR TIP: A walk along the nearby Peddars Way
Chef: Philip Milner **Owners:** Anthony & Jeanette Goodrich **Times:** 12-2/6.30-9, 25 Dec **Notes:** Vegetarian available **Seats:** 60, Pr/dining room 30 **Smoking:** N/Sm in restaurant **Children:** Menu, Portions **Rooms:** 11 (11 en suite) ★★ **Directions:** From King's Lynn take A149 N towards Hunstanton. After approx 10m, into Snettisham to village centre, then into Old Church Rd towards church. Hotel is 100yds on left **Parking:** 70 **e-mail:** info@roseandcrownsnettisham.com **web:** www.roseandcrownsnettisham.co.uk

England

STOKE HOLY CROSS MAP 13 TG20
The Wildebeest Arms
British, Mediterranean

Not to be missed East Anglian safari

☎ 01508 492497   82-86 Norwich Rd, NR14 8QJ

MENU GUIDE Seared scallops, apple boudin, lardon, guacamole • Roast turbot, saffron risotto, shrimp fricassee • Hot chocolate fondant

WINE GUIDE ♀ De Stefano Pinot Grigio £11.95 • ♀ Firefly Shiraz £11.95 • 40 bottles over £20, 80 bottles under £20 • 12 by the glass (£2.95-£4.05)

PRICE GUIDE Fixed L £11.95 • Fixed D £18.50 • starter £4.50-£8.95 • main £9.95-£19.95 • dessert £4.95-£5.95 • coffee £1.40 • min/water £2.95 • Service optional

PLACE: Relaxed gastro-pub, where you can sit at rustic wooden tables (like slices of log), and watch the busy kitchen produce your food. The decor is African inspired with yellow ochre walls and African motifs, memorabilia and artefacts.
FOOD: Well-executed modern cooking with European influences. The emphasis is on quality locally sourced produce - notably fresh fish - complemented by richly flavoured sauces. Excellent wine list.
OUR TIP: Good value lunch (advisable to book)
Chef: Daniel Smith **Owners:** Henry Watt **Times:** 12-3.30/6-11.30, Closed 25-26 Dec **Notes:** Vegetarian available **Seats:** 60 **Smoking:** N/Sm area, No pipes, Air con **Children:** Portions **Directions:** From A47, take A140 turn off towards Ipswich. Turn first left signposted byway to Dunston. Continue to end of the road and turn left at the t-junct, restaurant on right **Parking:** 40
e-mail: mail@animalinns.co.uk **web:** www.animalinns.co.uk

THORNHAM MAP 12 TF74
Lifeboat Inn
British, Mediterranean

Traditional inn on the North Norfolk coast

☎ 01485 512236   Ship Ln PE36 6LT

MENU GUIDE Crispy duck parcel on rhubarb compote • Pheasant casseroled in Guinness, horseradish mash • Ginger & rum syllabub

WINE GUIDE ♀ Gaudio Veneto Pinot Grigio £12.75 • ♀ Rioja Carrizal £16.50 • 22 bottles over £20, 31 bottles under £20 12 by the glass (£2.60-£4.75)

PRICE GUIDE Fixed D £27 • coffee £1.55 • min/water £2.75 • Service optional

PLACE: This 16th-century smugglers' inn turned gastro-pub does a brisk trade, particularly in the summer. Open fires, beams and hanging lanterns create a cosy ambience, and there are beautiful views across the marshes to Thornham Harbour.
FOOD: A daily-changing menu with a notable commitment to locally sourced meat and fish. Dishes cater to most tastes, and might include lemongrass and ginger scented sea bass, or roast pork with a walnut and apricot stuffing.
OUR TIP: Good bar menu also available
Chef: Paul Atkins, Michael Sherman **Owners:** Charles & Angie Coker **Times:** 7-9.30, Closed L all week **Notes:** Vegetarian available **Seats:** 70, Pr/dining room 18 **Smoking:** N/Sm in restaurant **Children:** Portions **Rooms:** 13 (13 en suite) ★★ **Directions:** Take A149 from Kings Lynn to Hunstanton follow coast road to Thornham, take 1st left **Parking:** 100
e-mail: reception@lifeboatinn.co.uk **web:** www.lifeboatinn.co.uk

THORPE MARKET MAP 13 TG23
Elderton Lodge Hotel
British

Romantic retreat serving the best of Norfolk produce

☎ 01263 833547   Gunton Park NR11 8TZ

MENU GUIDE Norfolk mussels • Venison, pease pudding, blueberry & red wine sauce • Apple & caramel tarte Tatin, rum raisin ice cream

WINE GUIDE ♀ Villa Rosa Sauvignon Blanc £14.95 • ♀ Villa Rosa Merlot £14.95 • 16 bottles over £20, 21 bottles under £20 • 5 by the glass (£3.50-£3.75)

PRICE GUIDE Fixed D £24.50 • starter £4.95-£7.50 • main £11.2 £18.95 • dessert £4.95 • coffee £2.50 • min/water £3 • Service optional

PLACE: This former shooting lodge was a one time retreat of Lillie Langtry, and rumour has it she entertained Edward VII he Aperitifs are served in the cosy bar, before a candlelit dinner in the newly refurbished restaurant.
FOOD: Honest cooking that makes the most of quality local ingredients including fish, lobster and crab, as well as game fro nearby estates. A wide-ranging menu showcases this wonderful variety of produce.
OUR TIP: Good base for the north Norfolk coast
Chef: Nick Shingles **Owners:** Rachel Lusher & Patrick Roofe **Times:** 12-2/7-9 **Notes:** Vegetarian available, Civ Wed 55 **Seats:** 50, Pr/dining room 25 **Smoking:** N/Sm in restaurant **Children:** Portions **Rooms:** (11 en suite) ★★ **Directions:** On A149 (Cromer/North Walsham road 1m S of village **Parking:** 100 **e-mail:** enquiries@eldertonlodge.co.uk **web:** www.eldertonlodge.co.uk

TITCHWELL MAP 13 TF74
Titchwell Manor Hotel
British, International

Conservatory dining in great location to build up an appetite

☎ 01485 210221   PE31 8BB

MENU GUIDE Brancaster oysters • Roast loin of lamb • Pineapple tarte Tatin

WINE GUIDE ♀ Pinot Grigio £14.50 • ♀ Peter Lehman Merlot/Cabernet £14.95 • 22 bottles over £20, 23 bottles unde £20 • 6 by the glass (£3.15-£5)

PRICE GUIDE Fixed L £10-£15 • starter £4.50-£7.50 • main £9.! £19.50 • dessert £4.95-£5.95 • coffee £2 • min/water £3.50 • Service optional

PLACE: A lovely Victorian house in an idyllic location on the beautiful north Norfolk coast. The restaurant's conservatory

contin

Titchwell Manor Hotel

setting and modern colours create a light and airy atmosphere; food is also served in the less formal bar. Beaches, an RSPB reserve and golf courses are nearby.

FOOD: The family-run kitchen is not afraid to push the boundaries, and the locals are not deterred; beef, for example, may be served with a foie gras and bitter chocolate parfait. For the less adventurous, the menus make full use of local seafood, and good quality preparation and excellent presentation produce very enjoyable dishes.

OUR TIP: Book ahead especially in summer

Chef: Eric Snaith **Owners:** Titchwell Manor Hotel **Times:** 12-2.30/6-11 **Notes:** Sun lunch 3 courses £15, Special gourmet evenings £25, Vegetarian available, Dress Restrictions, Smart casual **Smoking:** N/Sm in restaurant, Air con **Children:** Min 7yrs at D, Menu, Portions **Rooms:** 15 (15 en suite) ★★ **Directions:** On the A149 coast road between Brancaster and Thornham **Parking:** 25 **e-mail:** margaret@titchwellmanor.com **web:** www.titchwellmanor.com

WELLS-NEXT-THE-SEA MAP 13 TF94

⊛ The Crown Restaurant

Pacific Rim

Contemporary cuisine in chic coastal hotel

☎ 01328 710209 The Buttlands NR23 1EX

MENU GUIDE Lamb shank & sweetbread terrine, brioche • Venison, roast plum, ginger & soy jus • Sticky toffee pudding, toffee sauce

PRICE GUIDE Fixed D £29.95 • min/water £2.95 • Service optional

PLACE: Overlooking a quiet green in the pretty coastal town of Wells-Next-The-Sea, this 16th-century coaching inn has been converted into a modish little hotel. The bar is a cosy mix of old and new, with ancient beams and comfy chocolate brown chairs, while the more formal restaurant is decorated with the work of local artists.

FOOD: A concise menu of refreshingly simple modern British cooking enlivened by Pacific Rim flavours. Lighter bar meals also available.

OUR TIP: Dine alfresco on the sun deck in summer

Chef: Chris Coubrough **Owners:** Chris Coubrough **Times:** 7-9, Closed L all week **Notes:** Coffee incl. Price also incl. Canapés and amuse bouche, Vegetarian available **Seats:** 30, Pr/dining room 22 **Smoking:** N/Sm in restaurant **Children:** Portions **Directions:** 9m from Fakenham. At the top Buttlands Green

e-mail: reception@thecrownhotelwells.co.uk **web:** www.thecrownhotelwells.co.uk

WYMONDHAM MAP 13 TG10

⊛ Number Twenty Four Restaurant

British, International

Sound cooking in a 17th-century townhouse

☎ 01953 607750 24 Middleton St NR18 0AD

MENU GUIDE Cromer crab cake, rocket, aioli • Sauté breast of pheasant, ginger pancetta cabbage • Glazed lemon tart, amaretto ice cream

WINE GUIDE ♀ Pinot Grigio £14.25 • ♀ Peter Lehman Shiraz £14.25 • 6 bottles over £20, 20 bottles under £20 • 5 by the glass (£3.50)

PRICE GUIDE Fixed L £13.95 • Fixed D £22.50 • coffee £1.75 • min/water £2.95

PLACE: Friendly, family-run restaurant located in a listed row of terraced cottages in an attractive market town. The dining room has well spaced tables and has been redecorated in warm and relaxing tones.

FOOD: The manageable menu offers modern British cuisine with international influences, reflecting quality daily market choices. Cooking is simple and the dishes have clear flavours.

OUR TIP: Good value three-course lunch menu

Chef: Jonathan Griffin **Owners:** Jonathan Griffin **Times:** 12-2/7-9, Closed 26 Dec, 1 Jan, Mon, closed L Tue, closed D Sun **Notes:** Sun L 2 courses £12.95, 3 courses £14.95, Vegetarian available, Smart casual **Seats:** 60, Pr/dining room 20 **Smoking:** N/Sm in restaurant **Children:** Portions **Directions:** Town centre opposite war memorial **Parking:** On street opposite. In town centre car park **web:** www.number24.co.uk

⊛ Casablanca 2 Middleton St NR18 0AD

☎ 01953 607071 High street restaurant serving great value Moroccan food.

continued

NORTHAMPTONSHIRE

CASTLE ASHBY MAP 11 SP85

Falcon Hotel

Modern British

Good food in peaceful location

☎ 01604 696200   NN7 1LF

MENU GUIDE Smoked haddock tart, poached egg • Pork fillet with forcemeat & sweet redcurrant sauce • Crème brûlée

PRICE GUIDE Food prices not confirmed for 2006. Please telephone for details

PLACE: Set in the heart of this quiet village, the Falcon comprises a large stone-built house and two neighbouring cottages. The pretty dining room overlooks the garden.

FOOD: Well-presented dishes made with quality ingredients. Local pork is excellent, and seasonal specialities like the spring asparagus and rhubarb from the garden are a feature on the menu.

OUR TIP: Look out for seasonal extras

Times: 12-2/7-9.30, Closed D 24 Dec **Rooms:** 16 (16 en suite) ★★
e-mail: falcon.castleashby@oldenglishinns.co.uk
web: www.falcon-castleashby.com

DAVENTRY MAP 11 SP56

Fawsley Hall Hotel

see page 379

FOTHERINGHAY MAP 12 TL09

The Falcon Inn

Mediterranean

Friendly local in historic village setting

☎ 01832 226254   PE8 5HZ

MENU GUIDE Spicy chicken salad, basil, pine nuts & noodles • Moroccan spiced pork cutlet, couscous, harissa, aïoli • Panettone bread & butter pudding

WINE GUIDE ♀ Hellfire Bay Chardonnay £15.95 • ♀ Magpie Estate Grenache-Shiraz £14.75 • 80 bottles over £20, 40 bottles under £20 • 16 by the glass (£3.25-£7.50)

PRICE GUIDE Fixed L £12.50 • starter £4.95-£7.95 • main £9.95-£18.95 • dessert £4.95-£6.95 • coffee £1.95 • min/water £2.75 • Service optional • Group min 10 service 10%

PLACE: Set in the mellow-stone village where Mary Queen of Scots ended her days, The Falcon has bags of character and is very much the villagers' local as well as one of the county's most renowned pub-restaurants.

FOOD: Crowd-pleasing modern menus offer a fashionable nod to the Mediterranean and beyond in unpretentious, hearty dishes delivered with panache in the sunny conservatory extension, dining room or bar. Notable wine list.

OUR TIP: Book if you want a seat in the conservatory; light meals are also served in the garden in summer

Chef: Ray Smikle   **Owners:** John Hoskins & Ray Smikle   **Times:** 12-2.15/7-9.30   **Notes:** Vegetarian available   **Seats:** 45, Pr/dining room 25   **Smoking:** N/Sm in restaurant   **Children:** Menu, Portions   **Directions:** Off A605 follow signpost Fotheringhay   **Parking:** 40   **web:** www.huntsbridge.com

HELLIDON MAP 11 SP55

Hellidon Lakes

Contemporary

Golfer's paradise

☎ 01327 262550   NN11 6GG

PLACE: Over 200 acres of beautiful countryside, which include 27 holes of golf and 12 lakes, form the stunning backdrop to this hotel. Extensive range of facilities includes swimming pool and gym.

FOOD: The menu lists uncomplicated dishes, without too much fuss and frill, that allow flavours to shine through.

OUR TIP: Window tables have great views

Times: 7-9.45   **Rooms:** 110 (110 en suite) ★★★★
e-mail: stay@hellidon.demon.co.uk   **web:** www.hellidon.demon.co.uk

Give us your views! All the rosetted restaurants in this guide have been visited by one of the AA's team of professional inspectors, but we want to hear from you! Use the report forms in the back of the guide or email us at lifestyleguides@theaa.com with your comments on any establishments featured or on the restaurants that you feel are worthy of an entry. We would also be pleased to receive your views on the guide itself and suggestions for information you would like to see included.

England

DAVENTRY MAP 11 SP56

Fawsley Hall Hotel

British, Mediterranean

Stunning country house with contemporary features in classical setting

☎ 01327 892000 Fawsley NN11 3BA

e-mail: reservations@fawsleyhall.com **web:** www.fawsleyhall.com

PLACE: Grand and majestic, this beautiful 15th-century country house enjoys 'Capability' Brown landscaping and a great hall complete with comfortable sofas and log fire for aperitifs. And, while the interior is in keeping with the country-house style, it has a contemporary edge with no chintz to be seen. The bar (and cigar room) has large windows overlooking an enclosed courtyard, while the Knightley Restaurant (once the Tudor kitchen, laundry and brew house) is split into two rooms with elegantly laid, well-spaced tables. Service is professional and attentive, yet approachable and well led.

FOOD: Classically inclined but with modern focus and adopting an intelligently simple approach that allows top notch ingredients to shine. Presentation follows the theme in confident, clean, clear-flavoured dishes on an ambitious and appealing array of menus that includes lunch (with one price per course), carte, no-choice fixed-priced tasting and set-price options, plus vegetarian and children's offerings. So expect the likes of an assiette of rabbit with langoustine, or perhaps roast breasts of Bresse squab pigeon with smoked bacon polenta, stuffed cabbage and a beetroot jus.

MENU GUIDE Seared scallops, white chocolate & caviar sauce, baby fennel • Pan-fried brill fillet, winter vegetables, mussel broth • Dandelion & burdock soufflé, lemon sorbet

WINE GUIDE ♀ Stoneburn Sauvignon Blanc £23.25 ♀ Château Lezongars Premier Cru de Bordeaux £23.75 110 bottles over £20, 18 bottles under £20 • 10 by the glass (£4.50-£5.75)

PRICE GUIDE Fixed L £20.70-£24.95 • Fixed D £35-£49.50 • starter £7-£12.50 • main £18-£25.50 • dessert £8-£9 • coffee £1.75 • min/water £3 • Service added but optional 12.5%

OUR TIP: Enjoy the full experience and stay overnight

Chef: Philip Dixon **Owners:** Fawsley Hall Hotel Ltd **Times:** 12-2.30/7-9.30 **Notes:** Vegetarian available, Smart Dress, Civ Wed 140 **Seats:** 85, Pr/dining room 140 **Smoking:** N/Sm in restaurant **Children:** Menu, Portions **Rooms:** 43 (43 en suite) ★★★★ **Directions:** From M40 junct 11 take A361, follow for 12m. Turn right towards Fawsley Hall **Parking:** 100

England

HORTON MAP 11 SP85

The New French Partridge

British, French

Fine dining in contemporary country house restaurant

☎ 01604 870033   NN7 2AP

MENU GUIDE Lobster bisque • Partridge, vanilla mash, carrots, pomegranate & port wine jus • Hot chocolate & raspberry dessert cake

WINE GUIDE ♀ Vocoret Chablis £22 • ♀ La Grav Figeac St Emilion Grand Cru £45 • 40 bottles over £20, 12 bottles under £20 • 5 by the glass (£4-£5)

PRICE GUIDE Fixed L £16-£20 • Fixed D £41.50-£46.50 • coffee £3.50 • min/water £3.95 • Service optional

PLACE: The square hallway of this appealing Georgian manor house gives way to a series of cosy lounges and dining rooms, including a restaurant decorated in vibrant style with contemporary purple drapes, striking blue glassware and a stripped wooden floor.
FOOD: A well-balanced range of modern French and English dishes, centred around complex combinations of quality ingredients. Your choice of mains might include a dish of Suffolk pork served with Calvados and apple jus, and sweet potato purée, or a simpler option such as brill with brown shrimp butter.
OUR TIP: Stay over in one of ten individually designed bedrooms.
Chef: I Oakenfull, S Addison, J Ingram **Owners:** Miss T K Banerjee & Ian Oakenfull **Times:** 12-2.30/7-10, Closed L Sat, closed D Sun **Notes:** Sun L 3 courses £25-27, coffee incl in Fixed D, Vegetarian available, Dress Restrictions, Civ Wed 70 **Seats:** 60, Pr/dining room 12 **Smoking:** N/Sm in restaurant **Children:** Portions **Directions:** On B526, 6m S of Northampton **Parking:** 35 **e-mail:** info@newfrenchpartridge.co.uk
web: www.newfrenchpartridge.co.uk

KETTERING MAP 11 SP87

Kettering Park Hotel

Traditional British

Contemporary hotel dining

☎ 01536 416666 Kettering Parkway NN15 6XT

MENU GUIDE Oak smoked duck, spiced pear chutney • Sea bass fillet, pea risotto cake, lobster cream sauce • Banana crèm

PRICE GUIDE Food prices not confirmed for 2006. Please telephone for details

PLACE: The facilities at this modern hotel are excellent, and include a gym, sauna and indoor pool. The Langberry's Restaurant is well turned out, with friendly, courteous staff.
FOOD: The British menu is full of interest. Begin with warm goats' cheese filo tart, before tucking into a well-selected grilled fillet of brill with olive and basil mash.
OUR TIP: A pianist accompanies Saturday night dining
Times: 12.30-2.30/7-9.30, Closed Xmas & New Year (ex residents), closed L Sat, Sun **Rooms:** 119 (119 en suite) ★★★★ **Directions:** Off A14 J9
e-mail: kpark.reservations@shirehotels.co.uk
web: www.shirehotels.co.uk

LOWICK MAP 11 SP98

The Snooty Fox

British   **NEV**

Gastro-pub dining in former stately home

☎ 01832 733434   NN14 3BH

PLACE: Once home to the Countess of Peterborough, this sandstone inn dates in part to the 15th century. The beams and flagstones give a sense of the age, and you can chose to dine in the friendly bar or the more formal restaurant.
FOOD: An experienced team have created a simple, crowd-pleasing menu offering classic gastro-pub fare, where steak and chips takes its place amongst more elaborate, but equally well-handled options.
OUR TIP: Popular with families. Some lunchtime opening hours may vary, so ring ahead
Times: 12-2/6-9.30, Sun 12-2/7-9.30

What makes a Restaurant of the Year?
In selecting a Restaurant of the Year, we look for somewhere that is exceptional in its chosen area of the market. Whilst the Rosette awards are based on the quality of the food alone, Restaurant of the Year takes into account all aspects of the operation. For full details see pages 6-7.

MARSTON TRUSSELL MAP 11 SP68

The Sun Inn
Modern British

Traditional inn with modern cooking and attentive service

☎ 01858 465531 Main St LE16 9TY

MENU GUIDE Confit of duck, foie gras terrine • Roast pheasant • Warm chocolate tart , pears in Sauternes

WINE GUIDE ♀ Balbi Vineyard Chardonnay £17.50 • ♀ Tinto Navajas - Rioja £15.50 • 11 bottles over £20, 12 bottles under £20 • 13 by the glass (£5-£7.50)

PRICE GUIDE Fixed L £17 • Fixed D £24 • starter £5-£10 • main £16.50-£19.50 • dessert £5.50-£6.50 • coffee £2.50 • min/water £3.50 • Service optional

PLACE: A rural inn decorated with model horses and country artefacts. There are three small and intimate dining rooms, with the two levels of the largest being the most popular.

FOOD: A seasonal carte, a fixed-price menu and a bar snacks menu offer the breadth of choice to satisfy any appetite. Careful preparation and fresh ingredients feature in the mainly British dishes.

OUR TIP: Traditional Sunday lunch available
Chef: Paul Elliott **Owners:** Paul Elliott **Times:** 12-1.45/7-9.30, Closed 26 Dec-5 Jan, BH's, closed L Sun **Notes:** Traditional Sun L, Vegetarian available **Seats:** 42, Pr/dining room 70 **Smoking:** N/Sm area **Children:** Menu, Portions **Rooms:** 20 (20 en suite) ★★
Directions: Off A4304, between the villages of Lubenham & Theddingworth **Parking:** 35 **e-mail:** manager@suninn.com
web: www.suninn.com

ROADE MAP 11 SP75

Roade House Restaurant
British

Popular village restaurant

☎ 01604 863372 16 High St NN7 2NW

MENU GUIDE Leek soup, smoked haddock & gruyère • Roast pheasant breast, leg meat sausage, red wine sauce • Strawberry & raspberry trifle

WINE GUIDE ♀ Sancerre • ♀ Fleurie £19 • 30 bottles over £20, 20 bottles under £20

PRICE GUIDE Fixed L £23-£26 • Fixed D £35-£40 • coffee £2.50 • min/water £3 • Service optional

LACE: Rurally-sited restaurant in a former village pub, now extended and attractively restored. Heavy old beams give the spacious room a stamp of authentic character.

FOOD: Offering French cuisine, the simple lunch menu makes way for a more elaborate choice in the evening, when the likes of tagliatelle with a hare, bacon and red wine sauce might be followed by grilled halibut fillet with mushroom, chilli and garlic cream.

OUR TIP: Fish dishes are a speciality
Chef: Chris Kewley **Owners:** Mr & Mrs C M Kewley **Times:** 12-2.00/7-9.30, Closed 1 wk Xmas, Sun, closed L Mon & Sat **Notes:** Vegetarian available, Dress Restrictions, No shorts for men **Seats:** 50
Smoking: N/Sm in restaurant, Air con **Children:** Portions
Directions: M1 junct 15 (A508 Milton Keynes) to Roade, left at mini rdbt, 200yds on left **Parking:** 20 **e-mail:** info@roadehousehotel.co.uk
web: www.roadehousehotel.co.uk

TOWCESTER MAP 11 SP64

Vine House Restaurant
British

High quality restaurant with rooms

☎ 01327 811267 100 High St, Paulerspury NN12 7NA

MENU GUIDE Sea scallops, cauliflower cream • Venison, fondant potatoes, port & mushroom sauce • Strawberry jam ice cream, shortbread

WINE GUIDE ♀ Louis Latour St Veran £20.50 • ♀ Fleurie £21.25 50 bottles over £20, 23 bottles under £20 • 4 by the glass (£3)

PRICE GUIDE Fixed L £26.95 • Fixed D £29.95 • coffee £2.50 • min/water £3.50 • Service added but optional 12.5%

PLACE: Run by a committed husband and wife team, this restaurant with rooms in the pretty Northamptonshire countryside isn't far from the Silverstone race track. It's a converted 17th-century farmhouse, and with its leafy gardens and village setting is just the place for an indulgent foodie getaway.
FOOD: A short menu changes daily and features quality seasonal produce, including meat sourced from rare breeds for its flavour. Dishes are a fusion of modern and traditional English as in the starter of local free range chicken with parma ham terrine and apricot and hazelnut chutney.
OUR TIP: Handy for Silverstone, but book months in advance for race meetings
Chef: Marcus Springett **Owners:** Mr M & Mrs J Springett **Times:** 12.30-1.45/7.00-9.30, Closed 2 wks from 24 Dec, Sun, closed L Sat-Mon
Seats: 26, Pr/dining room 10 **Smoking:** N/Sm in restaurant
Directions: 2m S of Towcester, just off A5 **Parking:** 20
e-mail: info@vinehousehotel.com **web:** www.vinehousehotel.com

WHITTLEBURY MAP 11 SP64

Whittlebury Hall Hotel & Spa
British, European

Fine dining in a modern hotel

☎ 01327 857857 NN12 8QH

MENU GUIDE Poached goose liver & truffles • Venison rosette, beetroot mash, chocolate sauce • Raspberry soufflé

WINE GUIDE ♀ Hardys Riddle £16 • ♀ Hardys Riddle £16 60 bottles over £20, 40 bottles under £20 • 16 by the glass (£3.50-£8.50)

PRICE GUIDE Fixed L fr £15.50 • Fixed D fr £29.95 • starter £6-£12 • main £18-£24 • dessert £6-£12 • coffee £2.95 • min/water £2.50 • Service optional

PLACE: A Georgian-style modern hotel with a small fine dining restaurant hidden in its midst. The restaurant is named after Formula One race commentator Murray Walker in a tribute to the nearby Silverstone Racecourse, and some of his more famous quotes are framed on the walls.
FOOD: The French classics are given an inventive modern interpretation on the wide-ranging menu, with local produce contributing to their success. Some unexpected combinations add to the interest, like watercress pannacotta, and rocket and turnip purée.
OUR TIP: May need to book at weekends
Chef: Wayne Asson **Owners:** Macepark (Whittlebury) Ltd **Times:** 7-10, Closed 24-26, 31 Dec, 1-7 Jan, Sun, Mon, closed L all wk
Notes: Vegetarian available, Dress Restrictions, Smart casual, no jeans, trainers or shorts, Civ Wed 200 **Seats:** 48, Pr/dining room 400
Smoking: N/Sm in restaurant **Children:** Min 12, Menu, Portions
Rooms: 210 (210 en suite) ★★★★ **Directions:** A43/A413 to Whittlebury, through village, hotel at far end on right **Parking:** 300
e-mail: sales@whittleburyhall.co.uk **web:** www.whittleburyhall.co.uk

NORTHUMBERLAND

CORNHILL-ON-TWEED MAP 21 NT83

◎◎ Tillmouth Park Hotel
Contemporary British
Modern cuisine in Victorian elegance
☎ 01890 882255 TD12 4UU

MENU GUIDE Smoked salmon, lemon, caper & gherkin • Rib-eye steak, fondant potato, spinach, mushroom jus • Winter berry brûlée

WINE GUIDE ♀ Pouilly Fumé £24.50 • ♀ Château Beaumont 1997 £24.50 • 52 bottles over £20, 44 bottles under £20 • 9 by the glass (£3.50-£4.50)

PRICE GUIDE Fixed L £13.50 • Fixed D £32.50 • min/water £4 • Service optional

PLACE: Set in secluded woodland by the River Till, this imposing Victorian manor is elegantly furnished and still rings to the sound of service bells. Savour a malt in the bar, and then move through to the wood-panelled library dining room where crisp white linen, sparkling tableware and attentive staff await.

FOOD: Tillmouth gives classical dishes a contemporary slant, teaming pheasant with rösti potato and sultana jus, or pork with cabbage, bacon, and a beetroot and mustard sauce. The three course fixed-price menu changes daily.

OUR TIP: The more informal hotel bistro serves lunches and early evening meals

Chef: Gerard Boylan, Tony McKay **Times:** 12-2/7-8.45, Closed 24 Dec, 26-28 Dec, closed L Mon-Sat **Notes:** coffee incl., Vegetarian available, Smart Dress, Civ Wed 60 **Seats:** 40, Pr/dining room 20 **Smoking:** N/Sm in restaurant **Children:** Portions **Rooms:** 14 (14 en suite) ★★★
Directions: A698, 3m E from Cornhill-on-Tweed **Parking:** 50
e-mail: reception@tillmouthpark.force9.co.uk
web: www.tillmouthpark.com

HEXHAM MAP 21 NY96

◎ De Vere Slaley Hall
British, French
Golfer's paradise with high class dining
☎ 01434 673350 Slaley NE47 0BX
MENU GUIDE Beetroot & orange marinated salmon • Daube of English beef in Newcastle Brown ale • Dark chocolate tart

WINE GUIDE ♀ Oakwood Estate Semillion/Chardonnay £14.75 • ♀ Oakwood Estate Shiraz/Cabernet Sauvignon £14.75 • 28 bottles over £20, 22 bottles under £20 • 10 by the glass (£3.50-£8)

De Vere Slaley Hall

PRICE GUIDE Fixed D £26.95 • starter £5.50-£8 • main £10-£27 dessert £6.95 • coffee £3.50 • min/water £3.50 • Service included

PLACE: Amidst a sprawling thousand acres of forest and moorland, the hotel restaurant has been designed and decorated to reflect the environment of the location, featuring sandblasted oak, slate mirrors and twisted willows for example. The service is attentive but relaxed.

FOOD: Albert Roux is food consultant to the restaurant resulting in a classical French approach to modern British cooking. Dishes are simply constructed using quality produce. The main menu is essentially brasserie in style and seasonal.

OUR TIP: Renowned golfing venue

Chef: Paul Montgomery **Owners:** De Vere Group PLC **Times:** 1-3/7-9.30, Closed L Mon-Sat **Notes:** Sun L 3 courses £17.50, Vegetarian available, Smart Dress, Civ Wed 250 **Seats:** 200, Pr/dining room 250 **Smoking:** N/Sm in restaurant, Air con **Children:** Menu, Portions **Rooms:** 139 (139 en suite) ★★★★ **Directions:** A1 from S to A68. Follow signs for Slaley Hall. From N A69 to Carbridge then take A68 S and follow signs to Slaley Hall **Parking:** 500
e-mail: slaley.hall@devere-hotels.com
web: www.devereonline.co.uk/slaleyhall

LONGHORSLEY MAP 21 NZ19

◎◎ Linden Hall Hotel
Modern British
Imposing mansion with elegant restaurant
☎ 01670 500000 NE65 8XF
MENU GUIDE Layered salmon & sole with warm king prawns, rocket salad • Pan-fried medallion of beef with tian of new potatoes & roasted shallots • Earl Grey iced parfait

PRICE GUIDE Food prices not confirmed for 2006. Please telephone for details

PLACE: An impressive Georgian mansion set in parkland in the beautiful Northumberland countryside. The restaurant overlooks the hotel's golf course.

FOOD: Dining is formal in the Dobson restaurant, where dinner might start with rabbit and bacon terrine with spiced apricot chutney, or escabeche of mackerel, roasted beetroot and pearl potatoes, and continue with braised lamb shank with confit of bacon, Savoy cabbage and stewed onions.

OUR TIP: Lunch is good value

Times: 12-2.30/7-9.30 **Rooms:** 50 (50 en suite) ★★★
Directions: Located between Longhorsley and Longframlington off A697
e-mail: stay@lindenhall.co.uk **web:** www.lindenhall.co.uk

 denotes restaurants that place particular emphasis on making the most of local ingredients.

continued

MATFEN MAP 21 NZ07

✿✿ Matfen Hall

British, French

Satisfying dining in elegant surroundings

☎ 01661 886500 NE20 0RH

MENU GUIDE Baked cheddar & spinach soufflé • Lamb Wellington, rosemary & red wine jus • Crème brûlée

WINE GUIDE ♀ Georges du Boeuf Sauvignon Blanc £14.95 • ♀ Rapel Valley Santa Rita Merlot £16.50 • 39 bottles over £20, 29 bottles under £20 • 6 by the glass (£3.25-£3.95)

PRICE GUIDE Fixed D £29.95 • starter £6.45-£8.25 • main £14.95-£20.95 • dessert £5.50-£6.25 • coffee £2.50 • Service optional

PLACE: Situated amidst classic parkland, this imposing Regency mansion overlooks a private golf course. Inside, the panelled library and the Print Room restaurant ooze atmosphere, especially by candlelight. During the daytime, there are stunning views. The service is formal but helpful.
FOOD: The menus offer modern British dishes - with the occasional French twist - using fresh, prime Northumbrian ingredients including organic lamb from the estate farm. Amongst the confit local rabbit leg with braised lentils and braised pork belly with Lyonnaise potato, there are good vegetarian options like shallot and artichoke tarte Tatin.
OUR TIP: Maybe take a round on the PGA championship golf course
Chef: Phil Hall **Owners:** Sir Hugh & Lady Blackett **Times:** 12.15-2.30/7-10, Closed L Mon-Sat **Notes:** Sun L 3 courses £16.95, Vegetarian available, Dress Restrictions, Smart casual, Civ Wed 160 **Seats:** 90, Pr/dining room 120 **Smoking:** N/Sm in restaurant **Children:** Portions
Rooms: 53 (53 en suite) ★★★★ **Directions:** A69 signed Hexham, leave at Heddon on the Wall. Then B6318, through Rudchester & Harlow Hill. Follow signs on right for Matfen **e-mail:** info@matfenhall.com
web: www.matfenhall.com

PONTELAND MAP 21 NZ17

✿ Café 21

British, European

Busy modern bistro near the airport

☎ 01661 820357 35 The Broadway, Darras Hall, Ponteland NE20 9PW

MENU GUIDE Marinated chicken salad • Aromatic steamed cod, oriental vegetables & noodles • Treacle tart, mascarpone sorbet

WINE GUIDE ♀ Georges Duboeuf Cuvée 21 Chardonnay £12 • ♀ Georges Duboeuf Cuvée 21 Pinot Noir £12 • 9 bottles over £20, 24 bottles under £20 • 6 by the glass (£3-£5.50)

PRICE GUIDE Fixed L £12 • starter £4.50-£6.50 • main £9.50-£16.50 • dessert £3.50-£5.50 • coffee £1.80 • min/water £3.50 • Service optional • Group min 10 service 10%

continued

Café 21

PLACE: Neighbourhood bistro in a small shopping precinct, popular with locals in this residential area of Ponteland. The simple interior includes quarry tiled floors, clothed tables and Victorian-style wooden chairs. The atmosphere is lively, and attentive service is provided by a young aproned team.
FOOD: British and European bistro-style food, plus a good-value two or three-course early evening menu from 5.30 until 7pm.
OUR TIP: Try the farmhouse cheeses
Chef: Ian Lowrey **Owners:** Terence Laybourne **Times:** 12-2/5.30-10, Closed BHs, Sun, closed L Mon-Fri **Notes:** Vegetarian available, Smart casual **Seats:** 68 **Smoking:** N/Sm area, No pipes, No cigars
Children: Portions **Directions:** From A696, follow signs for Darras Hall. Left at mini rdbt, restaurant in 200yds **Parking:** On street

NOTTINGHAMSHIRE

BARNBY MOOR MAP 16 SK68

✿ Restaurant 1650 at Ye Olde Bell

British, European

Accomplished cuisine in quality 300-year-old hotel

☎ 01777 705121 DN22 8QS

MENU GUIDE Pressed terrine of confit duck • Roast marinated pork fillet • Lemon sponge pudding, lavender ice cream

WINE GUIDE ♀ Admiralty House Sauvignon Blanc £13.95 • ♀ Torrean de Paredas Merlot £14.95 • 5 bottles over £20, 38 bottles under £20 • 12 by the glass (£3.25-£4.50)

PRICE GUIDE Fixed L £12.50 • Fixed D £19 • starter £3.95-£7.95 • main £10.25-£17.50 • dessert £3.95-£5.50 • coffee £1.95 • min/water £4 • Service optional

PLACE: An intimate set of three rooms with oak-panelled walls, spaciously separated tables and crisp white linen. This old London to York posting house sits in landscaped gardens.

continued

England

BARNBY MOOR continued MAP 16 SK68

FOOD: The small repertoire of dishes shows good use of seasonal produce, all the better for being simply but carefully handled. The set lunch is a bargain, and the monthly dinner choice is well balanced between fish and meat, plus a vegetarian dish.

OUR TIP: Take coffee in the welcoming lounge area
Chef: Keith Firth **Owners:** British Trust Hotels, Crerar Division
Times: 12.30-3/6.30-12, Closed 25-26 Dec, 1 Jan, Sun **Notes:** Vegetarian available, Civ Wed 250 **Seats:** 40, Pr/dining room 200 **Smoking:** N/Sm in restaurant **Children:** Portions **Rooms:** 51 (51 en suite) ★★★
Directions: From A1 take A620 (Retford junction). Turn left at T-junct and continue on A620 until taking a left signposted for Barnby Moor. Hotel is located on left at junction with A638 **Parking:** 200
e-mail: yeoldebell@crerarhotels.com

LANGAR MAP 11 SK73

Langar Hall
British
Step back in time for grand country house dining
☎ 01949 860559   NG13 9HG

MENU GUIDE Pheasant & rabbit terrine, red onion marmalade • Pan-fried sea bass, seared scallop, spinach, curry sauce • Tarte Tatin

WINE GUIDE ♀ Isabel Estate Sauvignon Blanc £29.75 • ♥ St Emilion J P Moueix Merlot Cabernet £23.50 • 72 bottles over £20, 35 bottles under £20 • 6 by the glass (£3-£4.50)

PRICE GUIDE Fixed L £13.50-£17.50 • starter £4.50-£17.50 • main £13.50-£20 • dessert £7.50 • coffee £2.50 • min/water £2.50 • Service added but optional 10%

PLACE: Country house in the Vale of Bevoir set in delightful grounds complete with medieval fishponds and a croquet lawn. Delightful public rooms with antiques and fine furnishings include several cosy lounges, a library and an elegant dining room.
FOOD: A meal at Langar Hall is always a special occasion and should not be hurried. The short daily carte is based on select British produce including game from the adjoining Belvoir Estate. Technical skills are evident and the whole team is confident and assured, which is clear in the attention to detail.
OUR TIP: Extensive wine list, plus ports, cigars and brandies
Chef: Toby Garratt, Gary Booth **Owners:** Imogen Skirving **Times:** 12-2/7-10 **Notes:** Vegetarian available, Civ Wed 40 **Seats:** 30, Pr/dining room 20 **Smoking:** N/Sm in restaurant **Children:** Portions **Rooms:** 12 (12 en suite) ★★★ **Directions:** Off A46 & A52 in village centre (behind church) **Parking:** 40 **e-mail:** imogen@langarhall.co.uk
web: www.langarhall.com

NOTTINGHAM MAP 11 SK53

Hart's Hotel
British
Sophisticated eaterie with imaginative modern menu
☎ 0115 988 1900 Standard Hill, Park Row NG1 6FN

MENU GUIDE Rabbit terrine, hazelnut dressing • Chicken, black truffle & foie gras risotto • White chocolate parfait, cassis sorbet

WINE GUIDE ♀ Kim Crawford Sauvignon Blanc £25 • ♥ Vina Urbina Tempranillo £22 • 30 bottles over £20, 30 bottles under £20 • 4 by the glass (£3.50-£5.50)

PRICE GUIDE Fixed L £11.95-£14 • Fixed D £26.50-£35 • starter £5-£14 • main £11.50-£20 • dessert £6.50-£12.50 • coffee £1.50 • min/water £2.95 • Service added but optional 12%

PLACE: Located in a quiet cul-de-sac not far from Nottingham city centre, this smart modern hotel occupies the former A&E department of the general hospital. Its restaurant is an airy contemporary venue, hung with vibrant works of abstract art that chime with colourful chairs and floral displays.
FOOD: Modern British with a European slant. Expect imaginative combinations of quality ingredients: calves' liver with crispy bacon and a shallot and sage sauce for example, or beef with rösti potato and béarnaise. Vegetarian menu available. Notable wine list.
OUR TIP: Book ahead
Chef: Alan Gleeson **Owners:** Tim Hart **Times:** 12-2/7-10.30, Closed 26 Dec & 1 Jan, closed L 31 Dec, closed D 25 Dec **Notes:** Vegetarian available, Civ Wed 110 **Seats:** 80, Pr/dining room 104 **Smoking:** N/Sm in restaurant **Children:** Portions **Rooms:** 32 (32 en suite) ★★★★
Directions: M1 junct 24 and follow A453 to city centre. Follow signs to the Castle. Once on the Maid Marion Way turn left at the Gala Casino and continue to top of the hill and turn left through black gates **Parking:** 17
e-mail: ask@hartsnottingham.co.uk
web: www.hartsnottingham.co.uk

Merchants Restaurant & Bar

ritish, French

fturbished restaurant serving brasserie food

0115 958 9898 29-31 High Pavement NG1 1HE

ENU GUIDE Somerset brie beignets with stilton • Sea bass & ngoustine duo • Hot Grand Marnier soufflé

INE GUIDE ♀ Jacky Morteau Touraine Sauvignon Loire Valley 003 £14 • ♀ Maipo Valley Chile Casa Rivas Merlot 2002 5 • 46 bottles over £20, 21 bottles under £20 • 14 by the glass 3.50-£11)

ICE GUIDE Fixed L £11.95 • starter £4.95-£11.50 • main 2.50-£18.50 • dessert £5.90-£6.50 • coffee £2.10 • min/water .10 • Service added but optional 10%

ACE: Seek out the trendy Lace Market area of the city and 'll be rewarded with this smartly refurbished restaurant upying a former merchant's house.

OD: The brasserie style of cooking appeals equally to harried siness lunchers and more relaxed evening diners - with its ckie midday menu and lengthier carte and fixed menu. vençale fish soup shows a typically rich depth of flavour.

R TIP: The sommelier offers good advice

ef: Patrick Tweedie **Owners:** Lace Market Hotel Ltd **Times:** 12-/7-10.30, Closed L Sun, Mon **Notes:** Vegetarian available **Seats:** 64, ining room 18 **Smoking:** No pipes, Air con **Children:** Min 18 ms: 42 (42 en suite) ★★★★ **Directions:** Follow town centre signs Galleries of Justice, entrance is opposite **Parking:** On street. NCP cent **e-mail:** dine@merchantsnottingham.co.uk b: www.merchantsnottingham.co.uk

estaurant Sat Bains with Rooms

settes not confirmed at time of going to press

odern European

linary adventures by the river

0115 986 6566 Old Lenton Ln NG7 2SA

ENU GUIDE Chicken liver parfait • Venison, candied carrots, e gras bon bon, chocolate sauce • Chocolate cake

INE GUIDE ♀ Genwurtztraminer (Seppi Landemann) 5 • ♀ Grant Burge Old Vine Shiraz £30 • 100 bottles over £20, bottles under £20 • 8 by the glass (£3.85-£9)

ICE GUIDE Fixed L £20 • Fixed D £50 • starter £10-£30 • main 5-£40 • dessert £6-£10 • coffee £3 • min/water £4 • Service tional

ACE: Occupying a sympathetically converted Victorian nhouse, this delightful restaurant sits along a quiet lane on banks of the Trent. Sat Bains has now taken over not just the aurant but the accommodation side also, named Restaurant Bains with Rooms. Sat has a reputation for creativity and ovation, and this new secure platform will allow him to shine e again.

continued

OUR TIP: Quality wine list with many available by the glass

Chef: Sat Bains **Owners:** Sat Bains **Times:** 7-9.30, Closed Bank Holidays, Sun, Mon, 2 wks Jan, 2 wks Aug, closed L all wk **Notes:** Set L D £50, Vegetarian available, Dress Restrictions, No jean, T-shirts **Seats:** 40, Pr/dining room 14 **Smoking:** N/Sm in restaurant **Children:** Min 8 years, Portions **Rooms:** 9 (9 en suite) **Directions:** From M1 Junct 24 take A453 for approx 8 m. Through Clifton, road divides into three - take middle lane signed 'Lenton Lane Industrial Estate', then 1st left and left again **Parking:** 22 **e-mail:** info@restaurantsatbains.net **web:** www.restaurantsatbains.net

Sonny's

British, French

Stylish city centre restaurant

0115 947 3041 3 Carlton St, Hockley NG1 1NL

MENU GUIDE Caramelised pears, walnuts & roquefort • Monkfish & scallop brochette • Lemon tart, confit lemon zest, raspberry sorbet

WINE GUIDE ♀ Casa Azul Sauvignon Blanc £17 • ♀ Apaltagua Carmenere £16.50 • 12 by the glass (£2.95-£7.50)

PRICE GUIDE Fixed L £11.50 • Fixed D £16.50 • starter £4.95-£8.50 • main £12-£21 • dessert £5.25-£6.95 • coffee £2.50 • min/water £3 • Service added but optional 10%

PLACE: Black and white framed photographs and pictures against stark white walls bring a tasteful contemporary edge to this former printworks. The businesslike atmosphere is enhanced by tan leather chairs with stainless steel frames.

FOOD: Good kitchen skills and a disciplined approach to classical themes account for many highlights among this modern food. A short set menu supplements both lunchtime and evening cartes, with winning starters like confit chicken and pearl onion terrine with truffled bean salad followed by a main course of braised oxtail with celeriac purée.

OUR TIP: Try a tisane instead of coffee

Chef: Matt Vincent **Owners:** Ms R Mascarenhas **Times:** 12-2.30/7-10.30, Closed BHs **Notes:** Vegetarian available **Seats:** 80 **Smoking:** N/Sm area, Air con **Children:** Menu, Portions **Directions:** City centre **e-mail:** nottingham@sonnys.co.uk **web:** www.sonnys.co.uk

World Service

Modern British, International   **NEW**

Eastern chic in a Georgian property

0115 847 5587 Newdiegate House, Castle Gate NG1 6AF

MENU GUIDE Chilled provençale mackerel, crispy chorizo • Pan-fried halibut, smoked bacon • Warm greengage & almond tart

WINE GUIDE ♀ Laroche Chablis St Martin Chardonnay £20.50 • ♀ Deakin Estate Wingara Wine Shiraz £17.95 48 bottles over £20, 22 bottles under £20 • 21 by the glass (£3.20-£7.50)

PRICE GUIDE Fixed L £11.50 • starter £5-£12 • main £12.50-£19.50 • dessert £5-£7.50 • coffee £1.75 • min/water £2.95 • Service added but optional 10%

PLACE: Hidden away opposite the Museum of Costume and Textiles, this buzzy restaurant is entered through an oriental garden. The Indonesian theme continues inside with lots of artefacts, and tables are companionably close.

FOOD: Simplicity is the key here, and flavours are accurately balanced. The seasonally-dictated menus show a modern approach with global touches: sag aloo with tempura cauliflower, and slow-roasted belly pork show the extremes.

OUR TIP: Have a fancy cocktail on the patio

continued

England

NOTTINGHAM continued MAP 11 SK53

Chef: Preston Walker **Owners:** Daniel Lindsay, Phillip Morgan, Ashley Walter, Chris Elson **Times:** 12-2.15/7-10, Closed Jan 1-7
Notes: Vegetarian available, Smart Dress **Seats:** 80, Pr/dining room 34
Smoking: N/Sm in restaurant **Children:** Menu, Portions
Directions: 200m from Nottingham town centre **Parking:** Car park nearby **e-mail:** enquiries@worldservicerestaurant.com
web: www.worldservicerestaurant.com

🐟 Loch Fyne Restaurant & Oyster Bar
17 King St NG1 2AY ☎ 01159 886840 Quality seafood chain.

🍜 Wagamama The Cornerhouse, Burton St NG1 4DB
☎ 0115 924 1797 Informal noodle bars with no booking.

OLLERTON MAP 16 SK66

☕ Ollerton Watermill Tea Shop NG22 9AA
☎ 01623 824094 Winner of The Tea Guild's Top Tea Place 2005.

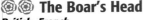

OXFORDSHIRE

ARDINGTON MAP 05 SU48
🐟🐟 The Boar's Head 🐟NEW
British, French
Accomplished cooking in a traditional setting
☎ 01235 833254 Church St OX12 8QA
MENU GUIDE Tempura of Cornish scallops • Grilled cod, red wine vinaigrette • Hot pistachio soufflé
WINE GUIDE ♀ Chablis la Colombe Paul Boutinot Chardonnay £18.50 • ♀ Côtes de Castillon Cabernet Sauvignon £17.50
36 bottles over £20, 38 bottles under £20 • 10 by the glass (£2.70-£5.65)
PRICE GUIDE Fixed L £16 • starter £5.95-£9.50 • main £13.95-£19.50 • dessert £5.95-£7.95 • coffee £2.50 • min/water £2.50 • Service optional
PLACE: A lively local crowd drinks comfortably in this lovely old village pub, where a restaurant with rooms is attracting wider attention. The flagstoned floors and exposed beams create an atmosphere to which the warm wall colours and plain pine tables bring a contemporary feel.
FOOD: Accomplished cooking noted for its clever twists and unusual flavour combinations is detailed on a printed sheet and a blackboard above the bar. Terrine of foie gras with pressed pigs' trotters, and breast of Gressingham duck with seasonal elder, beetroots and apple Tatin show typical complexity.
OUR TIP: Interesting Sunday lunches
Chef: Bruce Buchan **Owners:** Boar's Head (Ardington) Ltd **Times:** 12-2/7-10, Closed 4 days between Xmas & New Year, closed L Mon, closed D Sun-Mon **Notes:** Sun L 3 courses £20, Vegetarian available **Seats:** 40, Pr/dining room 24 **Smoking:** N/Sm in restaurant **Children:** Portions
Rooms: 3 (3 en suite) ♦♦♦♦ **Directions:** 2 m E of Wantage on A417
Parking: 10 **e-mail:** info@boarsheadardington.co.uk
web: www.boarsheadardington.co.uk

denotes a restaurant with a particularly good wine list.

BECKLEY MAP 05 SP51
🐟 The Abingdon Arms
British, International
Country inn with wide-ranging menu
☎ 01865 351311 High St, Beckley OX3 9UU
MENU GUIDE Tiger prawns, garlic butter • Lamb, mash, red wine gravy, green beans • White chocolate profiteroles
WINE GUIDE ♀ Sauvignon Blanc £12.95 • ♀ Merlot £12.95
3 bottles over £20, 12 bottles under £20 • 15 by the glass (£2.70-£3.95)
PRICE GUIDE Starter £3.95-£6.50 • main £8.95-£11.95 • dessert £2.95-£3.95 • coffee £1.75 • min/water £3.50 • Service optional
PLACE: This delightful village inn draws a friendly mix of locals and tourists, and has a relaxed country atmosphere. Book ahead to reserve a table in the non-smoking dining area, or eat in the bar.
FOOD: Quality home cooking. A lengthy menu runs to more than ten mains plus specials, and caters to all tastes, promising simple treats such as sizzling fajitas, or liver and bacon, as well as more adventurous International fare.
OUR TIP: Evelyn Waugh used to write here
Chef: Andrew Lacy **Owners:** Michelle Wass **Times:** 12-3/6-11, Closed 25 Dec, closed D Sun **Notes:** Vegetarian available **Seats:** 40
Smoking: N/Sm in restaurant **Children:** Portions **Directions:** From Headington rdbt, head towards crematorium. Turn left at end of road then take the first right, situated on left of the High St **Parking:** 20
e-mail: chequers89@hotmail.com

BICESTER MAP 11 SP52
🐟 Bignell Park Hotel
British, French
Creative cooking in country setting
☎ 01869 326550 Chesterton OX26 1UE

MENU GUIDE Ham hock terrine, red onion marmalade • Seared tuna, wilted spinach, pepper & shallot dressing • White peach brûlée, honeycomb ice
WINE GUIDE 25 bottles over £20, 25 bottles under £20 • 4 by the glass (£3.50)
PRICE GUIDE Fixed L £16.95 • Fixed D £19.95 • coffee £2 • min/water £3 • Service optional
PLACE: Combining charm and character with modern facilities, this small hotel dates from the 16th century and enjoys a peaceful country location near Bicester shopping village. Housed in a converted barn, the galleried restaurant has fine artwork, beams and a lovely open fire.
FOOD: The fixed-price dinner menu offers variety, imagination and value for money, with an enjoyable mix of modern dishes and traditional favourites.

continued

UR TIP: Definitely worth staying in for dinner
ef: Chris Coates Owners: Caparo Hotels Times: 12-2/7-9.30
otes: Vegetarian available, Smart Dress, Civ Wed 60 Seats: 60,
'dining room 18 Smoking: N/Sm in restaurant Children: Menu,
rtions Rooms: 23 (23 en suite) ★★★ Directions: M40 junct 9,
low A41 towards Bicester, turn off at Chesterton and hotel is signposted
turning Parking: 50 e-mail: enq@bignellparkhotel.co.uk
eb: www.bignellparkhotel.co.uk

RITWELL SALOME MAP 05 SU69

The Goose

ritish, European

ccomplished cuisine in a traditional pub setting

☎ 01491 612304 OX49 5LG

MENU GUIDE Ballotine of foie gras, marinated
herries • Seafood ragout, young vegetables, vermouth
auce • Hot passionfruit soufflé

WINE GUIDE ♀ Buitenverwachting Sauvignon Blanc
22.50 • ♀ Griffin Vineyards Shiraz £16.50 • 53 bottles over £20,
2 bottles under £20 • 17 by the glass (£3.25-£7.50)

PRICE GUIDE Fixed L £15 • Fixed D £18 • starter £6-£12 • main
14-£18 • dessert £6.50-£7.50 • coffee £2 • min/water
3 • Service optional • Group min 10 service 12.5%

ACE: Brick and flint pub on the main road of a lovely
fordshire village, attracting a good mix of business and leisure
stomers. The brightly decorated interior has a contemporary
el, with wooden floors and furniture set against original beams
d fireplaces. Friendly, well-informed and smartly dressed staff
ovide table service with a ready smile.
OD: The simple approach and understated style of the
odern British cooking belies the skill and hard work that goes
o it. Dishes are imaginative and some fly high, using premium
ality ingredients from leading local suppliers.
JR TIP: Patio garden with climbing roses and hanging baskets
ef: Michael North Owners: Goose Restaurant Ltd Times: 12-3/6.30-
Cosed D Sun Notes: Fixed menu not avail. Fri D, all day Sat, Sun L,
getarian available Seats: 40, Pr/dining room 25 Smoking: N/Sm area,
con Children: Menu, Portions Directions: M40 junct 6 take B4009
Watlington and on towards Benson. Pub on right, 1.5m Parking: 35
nail: thegooseatbritwellsalome@fsmail.net

URFORD MAP 05 SP21

The Bay Tree Hotel

ritish, European

cient inn with a modern menu

☎ 01993 822791 12-14 Sheep St OX18 4LW

MENU GUIDE Scallops, chorizo, parmesan tapenade, orange
il • Beef, haggis crust, parsnip confit, whisky jus • Chocolate &
um torte

WINE GUIDE ♀ Montes Estate Sauvignon Blanc
14.75 • ♀ Montes Estate Cabernet Sauvignon £14.75
bottles over £20, 25 bottles under £20 • 8 by the glass
3.65-£8.60)

PRICE GUIDE Fixed L £16.95 • Fixed D £27.95 • starter
6.95-£8.95 • main £16.50-£23.50 • dessert £6.10-£6.95 • coffee
3.25 • min/water £3.95 • Service optional

ACE: Dating back to the 16th century, this wisteria-clad inn sits
he heart of the pretty Cotswold market town of Burford. Take
rink in the bar, and then move through to the elegant
taurant, which overlooks the hotel's attractive walled garden.
OD: A mouthwatering modern European menu. Start with
eriac, butterbean and saffron soup perhaps, and then tuck into

lamb with black pudding and bubble and squeak, or seared brill
with sweet potato.
OUR TIP: Take a stroll in the garden before dinner
Chef: Brian Andrews Owners: Cotswold Inns & Hotels Times: 12-2/7-
9.30 Notes: Vegetarian available, Dress Restrictions, No jeans, Civ Wed
60 Seats: 70, Pr/dining room 24 Smoking: N/Sm in restaurant
Children: Portions Rooms: 21 (21 en suite) ★★★ Directions: From
Oxford, A40, take right at Burford rdbt. Continue half way down the hill
and turn left into Sheep St. Bay Tree 200yds on right Parking: 55
e-mail: bookings@cotswold-inns-hotels.co.uk
web: www.cotswold-inns-hotels.co.uk

Jonathan's at the Angel

Classical

Brasserie fare in Cotswolds restaurant with rooms

☎ 01993 822714 14 Witney St OX18 4SN

MENU GUIDE Scallops, chorizo, salad leaves • Venison, damson
compote, Parisian potatoes • Iced black cherry parfait

WINE GUIDE ♀ Pinot Grigio £14.75 • ♀ Rioja £15.75 • 20 bottles
over £20, 14 bottles under £20 • 9 by the glass (£3.50-£4.95)

PRICE GUIDE Food prices not confirmed for 2006. Please
telephone for details

PLACE: Decorated in simple modern style, this pretty coaching
inn dates back to the 16th century and is set in the heart of the
unspoilt Cotswolds village of Burford. Eat alfresco in the walled
garden in summer.
FOOD: A well-balanced brasserie style menu of modern fare,
ranging from tried and tested combinations to innovative pairings,
such as a tomato and paw-paw salad with a flavoursome
asparagus and red pepper tart. Vegetarian menu available.
OUR TIP: Stay over in one of the inn's three attractive bedrooms
Chef: Jonathan Lewis Owners: Jonathan & Josephine Lewis Times: 12-
2/7-9.30, Closed 18 Jan-11 Feb, Mon, closed D Sun Notes: Vegetarian
available Seats: 34, Pr/dining room 18 Smoking: N/Sm in restaurant
Children: Min 9 yrs, Portions Rooms: 3 (3 en suite) ♦♦♦♦♦
Directions: From A40, turn off at Burford rdbt, down hill 1st right into
Swan Lane, 1st left to Pytts Lane, left at end into Witney St Parking: On
street e-mail: jo@theangel-uk.com web: www.theangel-uk.com

The Lamb Inn

British

Cotswold coaching inn with contemporary appeal

☎ 01993 823155 Sheep St OX18 4LR

MENU GUIDE Cured pavé salmon, vanilla mayonnaise • Pan-
fried trout, caviar & saffron sauce • Chocolate torte, camomile
ice cream

WINE GUIDE 50 bottles over £20, 20 bottles under £20 • 6 by
the glass (£3.50-£9)

PRICE GUIDE Fixed L £27.50 • Fixed D £32.50 • coffee
£2.50 • min/water £3.60 • Service added but optional 10%

continued

continued

BURFORD *continued* MAP 05 SP21

PLACE: The 15th-century Cotswold inn has a spacious restaurant with mullioned windows overlooking a walled cottage garden and courtyard. The cheerful interior combines original features with modern fabrics, enhanced by flowers, candles and light jazz.
FOOD: Fixed-price and market menus offering a modern take on traditional dishes, making full use of seasonal local produce. You can eat in any of the public areas, with the new Fireside Menu available for a casual or lighter meal. The courtyard is perfect for alfresco dining in the warmer months.
OUR TIP: Close to the centre of Burford
Chef: Sean Ducie **Owners:** Mr & Mrs Bruno Cappuccini **Times:** 12-2.30/7-9.30 **Notes:** Vegetarian available **Seats:** 55 **Smoking:** N/Sm in restaurant **Children:** Menu, Portions **Rooms:** 15 (15 en suite) ★★★
Directions: 1st left as you descend on the High Street **Parking:** On street **e-mail:** info@lambinn-burford.co.uk
web: www.lambinn-burford.co.uk

The Navy Oak
British, Mediterranean NEW
Country pub with relaxed fine dining
☎ 01993 878496 Lower End OX29 9QQ
PLACE: This Cotswold stone building, full of character, houses a busy country inn. With exposed stonework and bare tables, a small fire place and an open plan kitchen, this is a simple, cosy place.
FOOD: The cooking is modern British, uncluttered and unfussy in style. The dinner menu is more complex than that offered at lunch. Quenelles of salmon and smoked salmon rillette are light and full of flavour, and might be followed by a hearty portion of accurately cooked pork loin on crushed minted potatoes. Finish with deliciously light lemon sponge.
OUR TIP: Look out for the Gourmet and other special event evenings
Times: 12.30-2.30/7-9.30 Closed 1-18 Jan, Mon, D Sun
e-mail: thenavyoak@aol.com **web:** www.thenavyoak.co.uk

CHARLBURY MAP 11 SP31

The Bell Hotel
British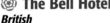
Modern cooking in historic Cotswold stone inn
☎ 01608 810278 Church St OX7 3PP
MENU GUIDE Oysters, champagne sabayon • Rosemary roasted loin of lamb, baked peppers • Chocolate marquise
WINE GUIDE ♀ Marcus Sauvignon Blanc £10.95 • ♀ Wild Pig Merlot £10.95 • 3 bottles over £20, 19 bottles under £20 • 7 by the glass (£2.75-£3.75)
PRICE GUIDE Fixed L £15.25-£19.25 • Fixed D £19.20-£23.20 • starter £5.95-£6.95 • main £13.95-£16.95 • dessert £4.50-£6.95 • coffee £1.20 • min/water £1.95 • Service optional • Group min 8 service 10%
PLACE: Dating from the 16th century, this Cotswold-stone hostelry once housed the local Customs & Excise. Popular with locals, the cosy oak-beamed and flagstoned bar is ideal for lighter meals.
FOOD: The intimate restaurant has a short carte of modern dishes, where local produce is treated with style. The bar menu offers a comprehensive range of real favourites.
OUR TIP: Great choice of real ales and vintage wines
Chef: Pete Southey **Owners:** Martin Lyall **Times:** 12-2.30/7-9.30
Notes: Vegetarian available, Dress Restrictions, ETB **Seats:** 30, Pr/dining room 20 **Smoking:** N/Sm in restaurant **Children:** Portions **Rooms:** 11

(11 en suite) ★★ **Directions:** Situated 3m off A44 between Oxford and Chipping Norton 5m NW of Woodstock. From London via M40 follow signs for Blenheim Palace, then A44 N. Hotel is in centre of town
Parking: 40 **e-mail:** reservationsatthebell@msn.com
web: www.bellhotel-charlbury.co.uk

CHINNOR MAP 05 SP70

Sir Charles Napier
Modern British
Character inn with sculptures, great views and good food
☎ 01494 483011 Sprigg's Alley OX39 4BX

MENU GUIDE Deep-fried langoustine tails with chilli jam • Leg saddle of rabbit, red chard, girolles • Strawberry soup, basil ice cream
WINE GUIDE ♀ Gravitas Sauvignon Blanc £24.50 • ♀ Lacoste Borie 1993 Cabernet Sauvignon £29.50 • 200 bottles over £20, 36 bottles under £20 • 15 by the glass (£3.50-£7)
PRICE GUIDE Fixed L £14.50 • starter £6.75-£12.50 • main £15.50-£19.50 • dessert £6.75 • coffee £2 • min/water £3.50 • Service added but optional 12.5%
PLACE: Packed with character and atmosphere, this quirky old inn sports beams and flagstones along with unmatched old chairs and tables. Sculptures are exhibited indoors and out, and the blazing log fires in winter and wisteria- and vine-shaded terrace in summer make this place a must at any time.
FOOD: Stylish handwritten menus list the daily choices, with a change of chef taking the food in a modern British direction. Mediterranean flavours bring interest to the likes of seafood risotto with chorizo, with the more simple dishes tending to work best.
OUR TIP: Go on a warm day and eat outside
Chef: Richard Berkent **Owners:** Julie Griffiths **Times:** 12-3/6.30-10.30, Closed 25-27 Dec, Mon, closed D Sun **Notes:** 2 roasts on Sun, Vegetarian available **Seats:** 75, Pr/dining room 45 **Smoking:** N/Sm area, No pipes No cigars, Air con **Children:** Min 6yrs D, Menu, Portions
Directions: M40 junct 6 to Chinnor. Turn right at rdbt, up hill for 2m to Sprigg's Alley **Parking:** 60 **web:** www.sircharlesnapier.co.uk

CHOLSEY MAP 05 SU58

The Sweet Olive
French NEW
Country pub with honest French cooking
☎ 01235 851272 Baker St OX11 9DD
PLACE: Located in the Chequers Inn, a country restaurant with bags of understated rustic charm. The wine-themed decor invokes a Parisian bistro atmosphere. Service, by an all French staff, is attentive and relaxed.
FOOD: Good honest cooking underpinned by quality ingredients

continued

continued

England

here's a strong French bias but expect the occasional English touch, such as treacle sponge with custard and ice cream. Good vegetarian options.
OUR TIP: Ideal for lazy summer lunches in the beer garden
Times: Telephone for details

CHURCH ENSTONE MAP 11 SP32

The Crown Inn
British, Italian

former coaching inn serving carefully-prepared cuisine

☎ 01608 677262 Mill Ln OX7 4NN

MENU GUIDE Spinach & feta cheese tart • Breast of duck, Calvados & apple sauce • Sharp lemon tart

WINE GUIDE 3 bottles over £20, 18 bottles under £20 • 7 by the glass (£2.75-£3.50)

PRICE GUIDE Fixed L £9-£14.50 • Fixed D £14.50-£17.50 • starter £3.50-£7.95 • main £8.50-£15.95 • dessert £4.25 • coffee £1.40 • min/water £3 • Service optional

PLACE: Enter this Cotswold inn through the bar with its blazing log fires, beams and rough stone walls, into the two restaurant areas, one with rich red walls and intimate lighting, and the other plant-filled conservatory.
FOOD: A clear commitment to good food is the hallmark here, and the choice is spread between the daily-changing menus and blackboard list of specials, each yielding well-presented substantial portions.
OUR TIP: Garden & patio in fine weather
Chef: Tony Warburton **Owners:** Mr & Mrs Warburton **Times:** 12-2/7-9, closed 24 Dec, 26 Dec, Mon, closed L Mon, closed D Sun, Mon
Notes: Vegetarian available **Seats:** 42, Pr/dining room 18
Smoking: N/Sm in restaurant **Children:** Menu, Portions
Directions: Telephone for directions **Parking:** 8
web: www.crowninnenstone.co.uk

DEDDINGTON MAP 11 SP43

Deddington Arms
Modern British

reliable fare in fine former coaching inn

☎ 0800 3287031 Horsefair OX15 0SH

MENU GUIDE Goats' cheese wrapped in courgette, chilli jam • Loin of venison, dauphinoise potatoes • Iced Irish parfait, coffee poached pear

WINE GUIDE ♀ Côtes de St Mont Plaimont Gascogne £11.50 • ♀ Concha y Toro Merlot £14.50 • 11 bottles over £20, 7 bottles under £20 • 8 by the glass (£2.60-£3)

PRICE GUIDE Fixed L £8.50 • starter £5.25-£7.25 • main £12.50-£16.95 • dessert £4.95-£5.95 • coffee £1.60 • min/water £2.70 • Service optional   *continued*

PLACE: A Cotswold stone building off the market square, the Deddington Arms' interior reflects the character of its age, with impressive stone walls and light wood panelling setting a sophisticated tone.
FOOD: Continental ideas combined well with an inventive British approach. In addition to the carte, classic specials are put on every week, such as steak Diane, duck à l'orange and lemon meringue pie.
OUR TIP: Popular, friendly and informal venue
Chef: Nick Porter **Owners:** Oxfordshire Hotels ltd. **Times:** 12-2/6.30-9.45 **Notes:** Sun L 3 courses £16.95, Vegetarian available **Seats:** 60, Pr/dining room 30 **Smoking:** N/Sm in restaurant, Air con
Children: Menu, Portions **Rooms:** 27 (27 en suite) ★★★
Directions: Telephone for directions **Parking:** 36
e-mail: deddarms@oxfordshire-hotels.co.uk
web: www.oxfordshire-hotels.co.uk

DORCHESTER (ON THAMES) MAP 05 SU59

George Hotel
British, French

Traditional coaching inn in historic village

☎ 01865 340404 25 High St OX10 7HH

MENU GUIDE Oven-baked Camembert • Spicy seafood casserole • Dark chocolate fondant with rum & raisin ice cream

WINE GUIDE ♀ La Fleurie Sancerre £18 • ♀ Wolfblass Shiraz £18 • 30 bottles over £20, 100 bottles under £20 • 10 by the glass (£1.90-£5)

PRICE GUIDE Fixed L £10-£13 • Fixed D £15-£40 • starter £4-£8 • main £8-£20 • dessert £4-£8 • coffee £2 • min/water £4

PLACE: Located next to Dorchester Abbey, this 15th-century inn has bags of character and charm, plus cosy bedrooms and comfortable dining areas with friendly service.
FOOD: British and French flavours dominate the menu, with classical dishes receiving an added twist in starters such as confit of duck and foie gras terrine served with wild mushroom purée and plum brioche.
OUR TIP: Cosy bedrooms
Chef: Ross Colledge **Owners:** Neville & Griffin Ltd **Times:** 12-2.15/7-9.30/10, Closed Xmas, New Year **Notes:** Vegetarian available **Seats:** 35, Pr/dining room 30 **Smoking:** N/Sm in restaurant **Rooms:** 17 (17 en suite) ★★★ **Directions:** In town centre, 8m south of Oxford
Parking: 70 **e-mail:** thegeorgehotel@fsmail.net
web: www.thegeorgedorchester.co.uk

White Hart Hotel
British, French

Historic coaching inn with vibrant dining

☎ 01865 340074 High St OX10 7HN

continued

England

DORCHESTER (ON THAMES) *continued*
MAP 05 SU59

MENU GUIDE Leek & ham hock terrine, sauce gribiche • Salmon confit, Pernod cream • Coffee brûlée tart

WINE GUIDE ♀ Willandra Chardonnay £17.45 • ♀ Concha y Torro Merlot £15.95 • 10 bottles over £20, 15 bottles under £20 • 6 by the glass (£2.70-£4.20)

PRICE GUIDE Fixed L £10 • starter £4.50-£7.50 • main £8.75-£16.95 • dessert £3.45-£5.95 • coffee £1.75 • min/water £1.20 • Service optional

PLACE: This 17th-century coaching inn is situated in the heart of a picturesque Oxfordshire village. The attractive, original exterior has wooden gates, beams and brickwork, while inside there are flagstone floors, stone fireplaces with roaring stoves, four-poster beds and an attractive high-beamed dining room. Genuinely attentive service.

FOOD: Dishes are modern British in style with pronounced international touches such as scallops with seared vanilla polenta and sweet chilli. The menus here make extensive use of local produce and there are well thought out and executed combinations such as the poached & grilled sea bass with lime scented cabbage, pea velouté and saffron potatoes.

OUR TIP: Look out for the special event evenings

Chef: Stuart Turvey **Owners:** Oxfordshire Hotels Ltd **Times:** 12-2.30/6.30-9.30 **Notes:** Vegetarian available, Dress Restrictions, Smart casual preferred **Seats:** 40, Pr/dining room 16 **Smoking:** N/Sm in restaurant **Children:** Portions **Rooms:** 26 (26 en suite) ★★★ **Directions:** Village centre. Just off A415/ A4074. 3 Miles from Wallingford, 6m from Abingdon **Parking:** 25

e-mail: whitehart@oxfordshire-hotels.co.uk

web: www.oxfordshire-hotels.co.uk

FARINGDON MAP 05 SU29

🏵 The Lamb at Buckland
British, International

Archetypal 18th-century Cotswold village dining pub

☎ 01367 870484 Buckland SN7 8QN

MENU GUIDE Three cheese & red onion tart • Kelmscott pork medallions, mustard sauce • Apricot & almond frangipane

WINE GUIDE ♀ Miguel Torres Sauvignon Blanc £14.95 • ♀ Cornellana Merlot £14.95 • 7 bottles over £20, 16 bottles under £20 • 9 by the glass (£3.95-£5.60)

PRICE GUIDE Fixed L £10-£18.95 • Fixed D £18.50 • starter £4.50-£9.95 • main £9.95-£23.95 • dessert £3.95-£6.50 • coffee £2.65 • min/water £3 • Service optional

PLACE: Worth seeking out (it can be tricky to find in the dark) this dining pub has a wonderful Cotswold setting. Its village exterior reveals a relaxed informal interior with gentle jazz adding to the informal ambience. Service in the beamed dining room is attentive and friendly. The menus are displayed on blackboards.

FOOD: With local produce used wherever possible, there's a loyal local following for menus of traditional British and French dishes with modern influences.

OUR TIP: Popular weekend destination so booking advisable

Chef: Paul Barnard **Owners:** The Lamb at Buckland Ltd **Times:** 12-3/7-11, Closed 24-6 Dec-6 Jan, closed D Sun **Notes:** Vegetarian available **Seats:** 65, Pr/dining room 18 **Smoking:** N/Sm in restaurant **Children:** Menu, Portions **Directions:** Midway between Oxford and Swindon on A420. 4m E of Faringdon **Parking:** 40

GORING MAP 05 SU68

🏵🏵 The Leatherne Bottel
British, Pacific Rim

Discreetly located riverside restaurant

☎ 01491 872667 RG8 0HS

MENU GUIDE Chicken liver & foie gras parfait • Seared cod with fricassee of mussels, clams, chorizo • Lemon & passionfruit tart

PRICE GUIDE Food prices not confirmed for 2006. Please telephone for details

PLACE: Tucked away on the edge of Goring, a single track road takes you right down to the Thames river front. The restaurant's large garden, terrace and decked area offers plenty of space for fine weather dining and the interior is bright and colourful with oil paintings and bronzes.

FOOD: The modern British cuisine here is simply presented and rustic in style and there is much use of herbs grown in the restaurant's own garden

OUR TIP: Great for alfresco dining

Times: 12.30-2/7-9, Closed 27-31 Dec, closed D Sun **Directions:** M4 Junct 12 or M40 Junct 6, signposted from B4009 towards Wallingford

e-mail: leathernebottel@aol.com

web: www.leathernebottel.co.uk

GREAT MILTON MAP 05 SP60

🏵🏵🏵🏵🏵 Le Manoir Aux Quat' Saisons *see page 391*

The AA Wine Awards recognise the finest wine lists in England, Scotland and Wales. For full details, see pages 14-15

The Best Use of Seafood sponsored by Seafish In conjunction with Seafish, the Sea Fish Industry Authority, we have sought out restaurants that make the most of seafood on their menus. In addition to the four country award winners (see page 9), look out for the seafish symbol throughout the book; this denotes restaurants serving a good range of fish and shellfish dishes, where the accent is firmly on freshness.

REAT MILTON MAP 05 SP60

Le Manoir Aux Quat' Saisons

ontemporary French
dream of a place
☎ 01844 278881   OX44 7PD
-**mail:** lemanoir@blanc.co.uk
eb: www.manoir.com

ACE: Come spring, summer, autumn or winter, Raymond Blanc's mellow stone, 15th-century manor house set in acres of beautiful grounds, offers the ultimate dining experience. On warm sunny days you can take aperitifs on the maculate lawn in the shade of a majestic cedar tree. No visit here, whatever the season, would be complete without troll round the gardens dotted with bronze statues and, beyond the wall, the tranquil Japanese garden and tea use and the impressive two-acre organic potager, so fundamental to the Blanc food philosophy. Inside, newcomers ght be surprised by the clean, classic-contemporary lines and understated elegance (none of the predictable untry-house chintz), but then Le Manoir is the epitome of luxury and good taste. Lounges coddle with sophistication d modernity, while the dining room is in three parts, the elegant main conservatory continues the contemporary me, while the two smaller rooms follow a more country-house style; the Grand Salle (passed through en route to conservatory) is strikingly attired in bold yellow and blue. Service is welcoming, relaxed and intelligent from a artly turned-out team that provides unrivalled attention to detail (car park valets with umbrellas even deal with the garies of the English climate).

OD: The menu is an extravagant provision of nature's finest ingredients (inspired by the kitchen garden that oplies ultra-fresh produce), cooked with breathtaking il and presented with flair and dexterity, the style ted in French classics but with contemporary focus. e approach is vibrant, colourful and exciting, the carte oviding the ultimate agony of choice with each dish ering tantalising combinations, backed by a fixed-price ich jour and gourmand offerings, plus vegetarian nus and a lovely, if unexpected, touch - a children's nu. But then they think of everything here. Luxury ns, clear precise flavours and perfect balance abound, ile a wonderful selection of oven-fresh breads, pressive canapés and dazzling petits fours keep up the w-factor pace through to the end. Superb wine list.

MENU GUIDE Pan-fried Scottish langoustines, Perigord truffle, Jerusalem artichoke • Milk-fed Devonshire lamb, baby leeks, caramelised sweatbreads, garlic purée • Platter of caramel

WINE GUIDE ♀ Pouilly Fumé Guyot Sauvignon Blanc £38 • ♀ Chorey Les Beaune Malliard Pinot Noir £38 • All bottles over £20 • 15 by the glass (£6-£24)

PRICE GUIDE Fixed L £45 • starter £28-£38 • main £38-£40 • dessert £18-£19 • coffee £4.25 • min/water £3.95 • Service optional

OUR TIP: Make sure you tour the vegetable gardens

Chef: Raymond Blanc & Gary Jones **Owners:** Mr R Blanc
Times: 12.15-2.30/7.15-9.45 **Notes:** Tasting menu, 7 courses £95, Vegetarian available, Dress Restrictions, No jeans, trainers or shorts, Civ Wed 50 **Seats:** 100, Pr/dining room 50
Smoking: N/Sm in restaurant, Air con **Children:** Menu, Portions
Rooms: 32 (32 en suite) ★★★★ **Directions:** M40 junct 7 follow A329 towards Wallingford. After 1m turn left, signposted Great Milton Manor **Parking:** 70

England

HENLEY-ON-THAMES MAP 05 SU78
The Cherry Tree Inn
British, French NEW
Contemporary rural dining
☎ 01491 680430 Stoke Rd RG9 5QA

MENU GUIDE Mushroom & leek tartlet, truffle dressing • Grilled calves' liver, bacon, roasted figs • Chocolate tart, damson ice cream

WINE GUIDE ♀ La Borgata Pinot Grigio £15.50 • ♀ McGuigan Shiraz £14.95 • 12 bottles over £20, 28 bottles under £20 • 13 by the glass (£2.95-£6.50)

PRICE GUIDE Starter £4.95-£6.95 • main £8.95-£14.95 • dessert £4.10-£6.50 • coffee £1.40 • min/water £2.95 • Service optional

PLACE: Originally three flint cottages dating back to the 1700s, this renovated inn retains bags of original features. The flagstones, beamed ceilings and fireplaces find a comfortable place alongside contemporary colours and furnishings that add a modern twist to the relaxed, informal atmosphere.

FOOD: The crowd-pleasing modern food is prepared with care and skill, delivering quality ingredients with uncomplicated presentation and an eye on value for money.

OUR TIP: Look out for the daily-changing blackboard menu

Chef: Richard Coates **Owners:** Paul Gilchrist & Richard Coates
Times: 12-3/7-10 **Notes:** Sun roast beef/lamb £12.50, Vegetarian available **Seats:** 76 **Smoking:** N/Sm in restaurant **Children:** Menu, Portions **Rooms:** 4 (4 en suite) ♦♦♦♦ **Directions:** On the A4155 from Henley-on-Thames exit B481 to Sonning Common. Follow signs for Stock Row, turn right for pub **Parking:** 25
e-mail: info@thecherrytreeinn.com
web: www.thecherrytreeinn.com

NEW
denotes a restaurant which is new
to the guide this year.

Red Lion Hotel
Modern British
Serious food beside the Thames
☎ 01491 572161 Hart St RG9 2AR
MENU GUIDE Boudin of salmon • Rump of veal, morel sauce • Warm lemon cake
PRICE GUIDE Food prices not confirmed for 2006. Please telephone for details
PLACE: A majestic old hotel sitting at the edge of the Thames, where the rustic restaurant creates a warm atmosphere under 15th-century beams. Creamy yellow walls and cosy table arrangements add to the effect.
FOOD: The unfussy handling of decent produce, local where appropriate, achieves success with the likes of mallard with beetroot dauphinoise, celeriac purée and blackcurrant jus.
OUR TIP: Sample afternoon tea with home-made jams
Times: 12-2.30/7-9.45 **Rooms:** 26 (26 en suite) ★★★
Directions: Adjacent to Henley bridge
e-mail: reservations@redlionhenley.co.uk **web:** www.redlionhenley.co

The White Hart Hotel
British, Mediterranean
Enjoyable dining in historic inn
☎ 01491 641245 High St, Nettlebed RG9 5DD
MENU GUIDE Venison carpaccio, rocket, Parmesan • Lobster cannelloni, pave of salmon, baby leeks • Blackberry soufflé
WINE GUIDE ♀ Domaine la Meuliere Chablis £24.95 • ♀ Ang 'The Bull' Cabernet Sauvignon £22.95 • 48 bottles over £20, 19 bottles under £20 • 6 by the glass (£3.75-£4.50)
PRICE GUIDE Fixed D £35 • coffee £2 • min/water £3.50 • Service optional
PLACE: This historic village coaching inn has a relaxed, moder bistro serving traditional brasserie food and a more formal restaurant offering fine dining.
FOOD: The bistro goes along the popular gastro-pub route wit well-priced pub staples - seared rib-eye of local beef with grille mushrooms and béarnaise sauce being a good example. The weekly-changing menu in the restaurant shows more ambition with dishes like seared foie gras with endive tart Tatin and ora jus taking on a more French flavour.
OUR TIP: Good children's menu available
Owners: Robyn & Tim Jones **Times:** 12-2.30/6-10, Closed Mon-Thu, closed L all week **Notes:** Tasting menu 5 courses £55, Vegetarian available **Seats:** 55, Pr/dining room 18 **Smoking:** N/Sm in restaurant **Children:** Menu, Portions **Rooms:** 12 (12 en suite)
Directions: From Henley take A4130 towards Wallingford. Approx 5m
Parking: 50 **e-mail:** info@whitehartnettlebed.com
web: www.whitehartnettlebed.com

Loch Fyne Restaurant & Oyster Bar
20 Market Place RG9 2AH ☎ 01491 845780 Quality seafood cha

KINGHAM MAP 10 SP22
Mill House Hotel
British, French
Attractive, Cotswold stone mill house in lovely rural setting
☎ 01608 658188 OX7 6UH
MENU GUIDE Seared scallops, butternut squash & sweet pota lobster vinaigrette • Pork trio, Toulouse sausage cassoulet, bu beans & bacon • Assiette of desserts

contin

Mill House Hotel

WINE GUIDE ♀ Linea Corte Vigna Pinot Grigio £16.50 • ♥ Hardy's Riddle Shiraz/Cabernet Sauvignon 56 bottles over £20, 27 bottles under £20 • 12 by the glass (£4.10-£5.15)

PRICE GUIDE Fixed L £17.50 • starter £6 • main £15 • dessert £6 • coffee £2.75 • min/water £3.75 • Service optional

PLACE: Modern hotel built around two attractive courtyards in a rural location close to the A40, with lovely country views from the back of the building. Although it is relatively new, the wood-panelled restaurant has the traditional feel of a club, with skylights giving it a light, airy atmosphere.

FOOD: A daily fixed-price menu with a monthly choice of intriguing speciality dishes available at a supplementary price.

OUR TIP: Separate monthly vegetarian menu

Chef: Robert Hubbard **Owners:** Marston Hotels **Times:** 12-2/7.30-9.30, Closed L Sat **Notes:** Vegetarian available, Civ Wed 400 **Seats:** 130, Pr/dining room 50 **Smoking:** N/Sm in restaurant, Air con **Children:** Menu, Portions **Rooms:** 130 (130 en suite) ★★★★ **Directions:** From S: M40 junct 7. Top of slip road turn right, immediate left (50yds). From N: M40 junct 8a. Top of slip road turn 1st left after golf club. Take 1st right, hotel 1m on left **Parking:** 400 **e-mail:** oxfordbelfry@marstonhotels.com **web:** www.marstonhotels.com

OXFORD MAP 05 SP50

⊚ Cotswold Lodge Hotel
British

Elegant, traditional dining near city centre
☎ 01865 512121 66a Banbury Rd OX2 6JP
MENU GUIDE Celeriac & stilton soup • Chicken supreme, roasted leeks & pommery mustard sauce • Pear & almond tart
WINE GUIDE 40 bottles over £20, 8 bottles under £20 • 4 by the glass (£3-£6)
PRICE GUIDE Fixed L £10-£15 • Fixed D £20-£30 • starter £4-£9.25 • main £9.50-£18 • dessert £3.50-£4.50 • coffee £3.25 • min/water £3 • Service included

PLACE: This city-centre, family-run Victorian hotel has well-presented public areas and a comfortable lounge. The dining room has murals of college scenes and rather luxurious high-backed chairs.

FOOD: Modern British dishes predominate here. Cooking is skilful and accurate with mains such as fillet of beef with morel sauce or poached parcel of salmon wrapped in seaweed on roasted pimento coulis. Delightful puddings too, like the brandy snap basket filled with fruit.

OUR TIP: Convenient for a shopping excursion in Oxford

Chef: Garin Chapman **Owners:** Mrs O Peros **Times:** 12-2.30/6.30-10 **Notes:** Vegetarian available, Dress Restrictions, No jeans or collarless shirts **Seats:** 48, Pr/dining room 100 **Smoking:** N/Sm in restaurant **Children:** Menu, Portions **Rooms:** 49 (49 en suite) ★★★★ **Directions:** Take A4165 (Banbury Road) off A40 ring road, hotel 1.5m on left **Parking:** 30 **e-mail:** aa@cotswoldlodgehotel.co.uk **web:** www.cotswoldlodgehotel.co.uk

WINE GUIDE ♀ Los Vilos Chardonnay £14.50 • ♥ Los Vilos Cabernet Sauvignon £14.50 • 51 bottles over £20, 33 bottles under £20 • 7 by the glass (£4.50-£5.50)

PRICE GUIDE Fixed L £16.50 • Fixed D £28 • starter £4-£8.50 • main £8-£17.50 • dessert £4.50-£5.50 • coffee £3 • min/water £3 • Service optional

PLACE: A stone-built former mill house, sympathetically converted into a comfortable, family-owned hotel and set in ten acres of lawned gardens with its own crystal-clear trout stream. The interior is rustic in style, the lounge and bar featuring agricultural artefacts from the Victorian era, flagged floors and open fireplaces. The restaurant also has a traditional feel, with elegantly laid tables and friendly and attentive service.

FOOD: The kitchen's modern British approach is delivered via appealing fixed-price carte, nine-course tasting option and separate vegetarian menu. Imaginative, intricate dishes utilise fine quality produce and generous portions.

OUR TIP: Good offering for vegetarians or non-meat eaters

Chef: Paul Haywood **Owners:** John Parslow **Times:** 12-2/6.30-10 **Notes:** Dégustation menu £40, Vegetarian available, Smart-casual, Civ Wed 80 **Seats:** 70, Pr/dining room 50 **Smoking:** N/Sm in restaurant **Children:** Menu, Portions **Rooms:** 23 (23 en suite) ★★★ **Directions:** Just off B4450, between Chipping Norton and Stow on the Wold. On S outskirts of village **Parking:** 60 **e-mail:** stay@millhousehotel.co.uk **web:** www.millhousehotel.co.uk

MILTON COMMON MAP 05 SP60

⊚ The Oxford Belfry
British, French

Ambitious food in modern hotel setting
☎ 01844 279381 OX9 2JW
MENU GUIDE Confit duck salad, plum jam • Braised lamb shank, honey mustard mash, redcurrant jus • Sticky toffee pudding, fudge sauce

⊚ Gee's Restaurant
British

Modern cooking in Victorian conservatory
☎ 01865 553540 61 Banbury Rd OX2 6PE
MENU GUIDE White crab & saffron risotto • Confit of lamb shank, mash, caramelised onions • Treacle sponge, vanilla sauce
WINE GUIDE ♀ Geo Kinross Chenin Blanc £12.95 • ♥ Gees House Vincent Lagrave Bordeaux Claret £17.75 • 14 bottles over £20, 6 bottles under £20 • 10 by the glass (£3.80-£5.95)

continued

continued

OXFORD continued MAP 05 SP50

Gee's Restaurant

PRICE GUIDE Fixed L £13.50 • Fixed D £24.95 • starter £5-£12.95 • main £10-£20 • dessert £5-£8.95 • coffee £1.95 • min/water £2.95 • Service optional • Group min 5 service 10%

PLACE: Airy Victorian conservatory in north Oxford that's bright and sunny by day, and romantic at night. Busy, so book ahead.
FOOD: Gee's tries to keep things simple and seasonal, and delivers a well-balanced modern British menu to suit most tastes. Fish-lovers should note a 6-course seafood tasting menu is available on Wednesday and Thursday evenings.
OUR TIP: Live jazz every Sunday
Chef: Michael Wright **Owners:** Jeremy Mogford **Times:** 12-2.30/6-10.30, Closed 25-26 Dec **Notes:** Seafood tasting menu Wed and Thurs eve 6 courses £45, Vegetarian available **Seats:** 85 **Smoking:** N/Sm in restaurant, Air con **Children:** Portions **Directions:** M40 junct 8. From northern ring road, follow signs to city centre through Summertown. Gee's opp Parktown on Banbury Rd **Parking:** Street parking, car park opposite **e-mail:** info@gees-restaurant.co.uk **web:** www.gees-restaurant.co.uk

The Lemon Tree

Modern Mediterranean   **NEW**

Stylish restaurant/bar offering eclectic food
☎ 01865 311936 268 Woodstock Rd OX2 7NW
MENU GUIDE Steamed mussels with saffron, garlic & chilli • Braised lamb shank, butternut squash & sage risotto • Hot chocolate pudding
WINE GUIDE ♀ Finca Lucia Unoaked Chardonnay £13.95 • ♀ Rioja Crianza Castillo d Clavijo £17.95 • 20 bottles over £20, 20 bottles under £20 • 11 by the glass (£3.25-4.95)
PRICE GUIDE Fixed L £10.95 • starter £4.95-£11.50 • main £9.95-£19.50 • dessert £5.50-£6.95 • coffee £1.75 • min/water £2.75 • Group min 5 service 12.5%

PLACE: This trendy restaurant has a relaxed wine bar/bistro feel, with a large lounge filled with wicker chairs and benches. Huge mirrors, tall palms, an orangery-style ceiling and arched windows with stained glass gives the restaurant a warm Mediterranean feel.
FOOD: Stunning flavours come through the simple modern Mediterranean cooking in dishes such as seared squid, chorizo and rocket salad with romesco sauce. Service is friendly, relaxed but professional.
OUR TIP: The sun terrace is a must in summer
Chef: John Pugsley **Owners:** Clinton Pugh **Times:** Closed 24-31 Dec, closed L Mon-Thurs **Notes:** Vegetarian available, Civ Wed 90 **Seats:** 90 **Smoking:** N/Sm in restaurant **Children:** Portions **Directions:** 1.5m from city centre heading N **Parking:** 19
e-mail: info@thelemontreeoxford.co.uk
web: www.thelemontreeoxford.co.uk

Le Petit Blanc

French, Mediterranean
Confident brasserie dining in fashionable suburb
☎ 01865 510999 71-72 Walton St OX2 6AG

MENU GUIDE Beetroot risotto • Confit of corn-fed guinea fowl, wild mushrooms & Madeira jus • Iced chestnut & meringue vacherin
WINE GUIDE ♀ Colombard Vin du Pays Gasgogne Sauvignon £12.95 • ♀ Bovey Merlot Vin du Pays Cabernet Merlot £12.95 • 15 bottles over £20, 15 bottles under £20 • 12 by the glass (£3.25-£8.15)
PRICE GUIDE Fixed L £12 • Fixed D £14.50 • starter £4.50-£7.50 • main £9.50-£17.95 • dessert £5.50-£7.75 • coffee £1.75 • min/water £3 • Group min 6 service 10%

PLACE: Located in the fashionable Jericho area of Oxford, this modern French-style brasserie is bright and airy with large windows looking onto the street. Children are positively welcome and have their own menu. Buzzy atmosphere with black-clothed staff always on the move.
FOOD: Dishes remain firmly grounded in French culinary excellence whilst incorporating British ingredients, as in deep fried goats' cheese with onion marmalade starter. The wine list is also mainly French with token items from New Zealand and Germany.
OUR TIP: Allow time for parking
Chef: Thierry Errante **Owners:** Raymond Blanc & Loch Fyne Group **Times:** 11am-11pm, Closed 25 Dec **Notes:** Vegetarian available **Seats:** 134, Pr/dining room 14 **Smoking:** N/Sm in restaurant, Air con **Children:** Menu, Portions **Directions:** From city centre. N along St Giles left into Little Clarendon St and right at end of Walton St **Parking:** Gloucester Green **e-mail:** oxford@lepetitblanc **web:** www.lepetitblanc.co.uk

Quod Restaurant & Bar

British, Mediterranean
City centre hotel serving popular brasserie fare
☎ 01865 202505 Old Bank Hotel, 92-94 High St OX1 4BN

continue

MENU GUIDE Chicken terrine, tarragon, toast • Morecombe Bay sole, tartare sauce, chips • Lemon tart

WINE GUIDE ♀ Chenin Blanc £10.65 • ♦ Shiraz/Merlot £10.65 • 17 bottles over £20, 19 bottles under £20 • 12 by the glass (£2.95-£4.15)

PRICE GUIDE Fixed L £8.75 • starter £3.95-£6.95 • main £7.95-£17.50 • dessert £3.95-£4.75 • coffee £1.85 • min/water £3 • Service optional • Group min 5 service 10%

PLACE: Housed in a former bank turned chic hotel, this all-day bar/brasserie has a slick modern interior with stone floors, wooden tables and an eclectic collection of modern art and photographs.
FOOD: A modern brasserie menu with Italian leanings featuring a range of steaks, plus spaghetti dishes and old favourites such as barbecue spare ribs and wild mushroom risotto.
OUR TIP: Close to city centre and colleges
Chef: Chris Kennedy **Owners:** Mr J Mogford, Mr G Strivens **Times:** noon-11, Closed 25-26 Dec **Notes:** Vegetarian available **Seats:** 150, Pr/dining room 24 **Smoking:** N/Sm area, No pipes, No cigars, Air con **Children:** Menu, Portions **Rooms:** 42 (42 en suite) ★★★★ **Directions:** Approach city centre via Headington. Over Magdalen Bridge into High St. Hotel 75yds on left **Parking:** 40 **e-mail:** quod@oldbank-hotel.co.uk **web:** www.quod.co.uk

The Randolph
Modern British   **NEW**
Traditional city centre hotel serving modern food
☎ 0870 400 8200 Beaumont St OX1 2LN
MENU GUIDE Seared scallops, parsley purée • Honey roast duck breast • Glazed lemon tart, raspberry coulis
PRICE GUIDE Food prices not confirmed for 2006. Please telephone for details

PLACE: Watch the world go by from behind the picture windows at this superbly located neo-Gothic hotel. A favourite with locals and tourists alike, the restaurant is richly furnished and very comfortable.
FOOD: Modern renditions of classical favourites are among the freshly-prepared dishes served here. The presentation is part of the enjoyment, but there is no doubting the skill involved in the likes of ham hock and black pudding terrine with celeriac remoulade.
OUR TIP: Great central location for touring
Times: 12-2.30/5.30-10 **Rooms:** 150 (150 en suite) ★★★★
e-mail: randolph@macdonald-hotels.co.uk
web: www.macdonaldhotels.co.uk

Wellingtonia Restaurant
British, European
Adventurous cooking in country-house hotel
☎ 01865 820416 Fallowfields Country House Hotel, Faringdon Rd, Kingston Bagpuize OX13 5BH
MENU GUIDE Local game terrine • Woodland mushroom ravioli • Calvados parfait, crushed Amaretto biscuit
WINE GUIDE ♀ Montmains Chablis Chardonnay £33.75 • ♦ Châteauneuf du Pape £29.99 • 97 bottles over £20, 10 bottles under £20 • 2 by the glass (£3.50)
PRICE GUIDE Fixed L £10-£21.25 • starter £6.50-£12.25 • main £18.75-£23.50 • dessert £7.50-£9.25 • coffee £3.75 • min/water £3.50 • Service added but optional 10%

PLACE: Situated in a small and intimate country house whose extensive herb and vegetable gardens supply the kitchen. The conservatory restaurant retains its 18th-century elegance while still managing to feel homely.

continued

FOOD: An impressive range of menus ensures a wide choice of modern British dishes from the gourmet to the casual, with plenty to interest all tastes.
OUR TIP: Enjoy a pre-lunch garden walk
Chef: Charles Leenders **Owners:** Mr & Mrs A Lloyd **Times:** 12-2.30/6-9.30, Closed 25-26 Dec **Notes:** Gourmet menu 8 courses £57.50, Sun L 2 courses £16, Vegetarian available, Civ Wed 120 **Seats:** 50, Pr/dining room 14 **Smoking:** N/Sm in restaurant **Children:** Portions **Rooms:** 10 (10 en suite) ★★★ **Directions:** From A34 at Abingdon take A415 (Witney). At mini rdbt in Kingston Bagpuize turn left. Fallowfields 1m on left **Parking:** 80 **e-mail:** stay@fallowfields.com **web:** www.fallowfields.com

⑪ **Edamame** 15 Holywell St OX1 3SA ☎ 01865 246 916 Japanese canteen-style dining.

⑪ **Loch Fyne Restaurant** 55 Walton St OX2 6AE ☎ 01865 292510 Quality seafood chain.

STADHAMPTON MAP 05 SU69
◉◉ **The Crazy Bear**
British
Excellent dining in character restaurant with rooms
☎ 01865 890714 Bear Ln OX44 7UR

MENU GUIDE Wild mushroom pie, tarragon cream • Seared calves' liver, white bean purée, Alsace bacon • Lemon posset, rumtoff raspberries

WINE GUIDE ♀ Framingham Sauvignon Blanc £24 • ♦ Madfish Cabernet Merlot Bin 157 £23 • 107 bottles over £20, 22 bottles under £20 • 16 by the glass (£3.75-£6.25)

PRICE GUIDE Fixed L £12.50-£13.50 • Fixed D £15-£16 • starter £6.50-£9.50 • main £14.50-£19.50 • dessert £6.50-£7.50 • coffee £2.50 • min/water £3.50 • Service added but optional 12.5%

PLACE: A dramatically restored 16th-century inn, this popular and attractive restaurant combines modern chic with old-world character. Mirrors, subdued lighting and mauve leather seating set the scene for some enjoyable eating. The addition of stunningly styled bedrooms some years ago makes this an very attractive option for staying over after dining.
FOOD: Modern British dishes predominate here but Asian and European influences are never far away with dishes such as cumin-scented lamb rump or Lapsang Souchong infused pork belly. Good vegetarian options. Service is relaxed and friendly. (See also entry for Thai Thai on p. 396).
OUR TIP: Long summer lunches on the terrace
Chef: Martin Gallon **Owners:** Jason Hunt **Times:** 12-3/6-10 **Notes:** Vegetarian available, Dress Restrictions, Smart casual, no jeans/trainers, Civ Wed 100 **Seats:** 40 **Smoking:** N/Sm area, No pipes, Air con **Children:** Menu, Portions **Rooms:** 12 (12 en suite) 🏠 **Directions:** From London leave M40 at junct 7 turn left onto A329, continue for 4m, left after petrol station & left again into Bear Lane **Parking:** 50 **e-mail:** enquiries@crazybear-oxford.co.uk **web:** www.crazybeargroup.co.uk

STADHAMPTON *continued* MAP 05 SU69

⚛⚛ Thai Thai
Thai
Quirky setting for authentic Thai cuisine
☎ 01865 890714 Crazy Bear Hotel, Bear Ln OX44 7UR

MENU GUIDE Sesame prawn toast, sweet chilli dip • Yellow chicken curry, roast peanuts, crispy shallots • Lemon posset
WINE GUIDE ♀ Framingham Bin 37 Sauvignon Blanc £24 • ♀ Madfish Bin 157 Cabernet Merlot £23 • 107 bottles over £20, 22 bottles under £20 • 16 by the glass (£3.75-£6.25)
PRICE GUIDE Fixed L £20 • Fixed D £26.50-£36.50 • starter £3.50-£8 • main £7.50-£18.50 • dessert £6.50-£7.50 • coffee £2.50 • min/water £3.50 • Service added but optional 12.5%

PLACE: This top notch Thai eaterie occupies the basement of the Crazy Bear, a 16th-century inn redecorated in quirky contemporary style. A red double-decker bus in the garden serves as a reception area, while the restaurant itself is a vibrant haunt with a jazz soundtrack, dark red walls and mirrored ceiling.
FOOD: High quality, truly authentic Thai cooking - and plenty of it. An extensive carte runs to more than twenty main dishes, and is supplemented by a number of good value set menus.
OUR TIP: Get directions before you set out
Chef: Anusak Thepdamrongchaikagul **Owners:** Jason Hunt **Times:** 12-3/6-10, Closed L Sun **Notes:** Vegetarian available, Dress Restrictions, Smart casual, no jeans/trainers, Civ Wed 100 **Seats:** 25 **Smoking:** N/Sm in restaurant **Children:** Menu, Portions **Directions:** From London leave M40 at junct 7 turn left onto A329, continue for 4 miles, left after petrol station and 2nd left again into Bear Lane **Parking:** 70
e-mail: enquiries@crazybear-oxford.co.uk
web: www.crazybeargroup.co.uk

SWERFORD MAP 11 SP33

⚛ The Mason's Arms
Modern British   ⚛NEW
Great pub food, popular with local diners
☎ 01608 683212 Banbury Rd OX7 4AP
MENU GUIDE Skate & potato terrine, pea vinaigrette, salsa verde Braised lamb shank, pearl barley risotto • Orange crème brûlée
WINE GUIDE ♀ Marc Xero Chardonnay £11.95 • ♀ Cape Promise Shiraz £10.95 • 6 bottles over £20, 24 bottles under £20 • 6 by the glass (£2.90-£4.50)
PRICE GUIDE Fixed L £8.95 • starter £3.95-£7.50 • main £8.50-£14.95 dessert £4.50 • coffee £1.90 • min/water £2.80 • Service included

PLACE: Stone-built roadside pub with lovely views over surrounding countryside. Inside, the traditional pub ambience gives way to a modern open-plan interior, with stripped floorboards, pine tables and panelled walls.

continued

FOOD: Competent modern cuisine to complement the style of the operation, offered from a light lunchtime menu, an evening carte and a specials list. The chef is one of the licensees and has trained with both Marco Pierre White and Gordon Ramsay.
OUR TIP: Look out for the fresh daily seafood
Chef: Bill Leadbeater **Owners:** B & C Leadbeater, Tom Aldous **Times:** 12-3/7-11, Closed 25-26 Dec, closed L 1 Jan, closed D 24 Dec **Notes:** Vegetarian available **Seats:** 75, Pr/dining room 25 **Children:** Menu, Portions **e-mail:** Themasonschef@hotmail.com

THAME MAP 05 SP70

⚛ Spread Eagle Hotel
British, French
Smart hotel dining in appealing market town
☎ 01844 213661 Cornmarket OX9 2BW

MENU GUIDE Egg Florentine • Gressingham duck, apple & Calvados sauce, gratin dauphinoise • Dark chocolate mousse, crème anglaise
WINE GUIDE ♀ Chardonnay £14.95 • ♀ Merlot £12.95 • 6 by the glass (£4-£6.25)
PRICE GUIDE Fixed D £20.95 • starter £4.30-£8.95 • main £11.95-£26.95 • dessert £4.50-£5 • coffee £2.50 • min/water £2.80 • Service included

PLACE: Former coaching inn on the main street of a pretty market town. Food is served in the informal Fothergills brasserie which takes its name from the diarist and raconteur who owned the hotel in the 1920s.
FOOD: Cooked with accuracy and care, Fothergills' dishes are modern British with French influences in style and might include châteaubriand or trout with a lemon butter sauce. The lengthy menu features a light bite selection.
OUR TIP: Look out for special promotions such as French week and Asian week
Chef: Yohan Chapelle **Owners:** Mrs S Barrington **Times:** 12.30-2.30/5.30-10 **Notes:** Vegetarian available, Civ Wed 200 **Seats:** 65, Pr/dining room 20 **Smoking:** No pipes, No cigars, Air con **Children:** Menu, Portions **Rooms:** 33 (33 en suite) ★★★ **Directions:** M40 - junct 6 from S, junct 8 from N. Town centre on A418 (Oxford to Aylesbury road) **Parking:** 80
e-mail: enquiries@spreadeaglethame.co.uk
web: www.spreadeaglethame.co.uk

⚛ The Swan at Tetsworth
Modern British
Imposing old coaching inn
☎ 01844 281182 High St, Tetsworth OX9 7AB
MENU GUIDE Duck terrine, red onion pickle • Pork & leek sausage, bubble & squeak • Bread & butter pudding

continued

The Swan at Tetsworth

PRICE GUIDE Food prices not confirmed for 2006. Please [t]elephone for details

[PL]ACE: It retains the timeless atmosphere of an Elizabethan [co]aching inn, though The Swan is now a well-known restaurant [at]tached to an award-winning antiques centre. Converted sewing [m]achine tables and plenty of antique paintings show the [pr]oprietor's other interests.

[F]OOD: The seasonal menu delivers substantial portions of fresh, [ta]sty food, with robust flavours given full expression. Roast [pa]rtridge, guinea fowl breast, and braised lamb shank are among [th]e hearty options.

[O]UR TIP: Save time for some antique hunting next door
[Ti]mes: 11.30-2.30/6-10.30, Closed 25-26 Dec, closed D Sun
[Di]rections: From London - 3m from M40 J6. From Birmingham - 5m
[fro]m M40 J8   e-mail: Restaurant@theswan.co.uk
[we]b: www.theswan.co.uk/restaurant.htm

WALLINGFORD MAP 05 SU68
Lakeside Restaurant
[Br]itish, French

[En]joyable dining in elegant Victorian setting
☎ 01491 836687 Springs Hotel, Wallingford Rd,
[N]orth Stoke OX10 6BE
MENU GUIDE Duck & pork rillettes, brandy & sultana [c]hutney • Beef medallions, mushroom duxelle • Beignets soufflé
WINE GUIDE ♀ Backsberg Chenin Blanc £15.50 • ♀ Avant [G]arde Merlot £15.50 • 37 bottles over £20, 15 bottles under [£]20 • 8 by the glass (£3.75)
PRICE GUIDE Fixed L £11.50 • Fixed D £32.50-£40 • coffee [£]2.50 • min/water £3.50 • Service optional • Group min 10 [s]ervice 10%

[PL]ACE: With its own golf course and springs, this Victorian [m]ansion has a wonderful, peaceful atmosphere. The dining room [ha]s a light and airy feel as well as some wonderful views over the [sp]ring-fed lake. Understated decor with a pleasingly muted [c]olour scheme.

[FO]OD: Dishes are modern British in style with French influences. [Sim]ple combinations allow local, seasonal ingredients to assert [th]emselves in dishes like poached chicken with basil.

[O]UR TIP: Hone your appetite with a round of golf or a lakeside [w]alk

[Ch]ef: Ian Cawkwell Owners: Lakeside Restaurant Times: 12-2/7-9.45 [No]tes: Vegetarian available, Smart Dress, No denim, trainers, t-shirts, Civ [Wed] 90 Seats: 80, Pr/dining room 30 Smoking: N/Sm in restaurant [Ch]ildren: Portions Rooms: 31 (31 en suite) ★★★ Directions: Edge [of] village of North Stoke Parking: 150
[e-]mail: info@thespringshotel.com web: www.thespringshotel.com

---

WESTON-ON-THE-GREEN MAP 11 SP51
🌸🌸 Weston Manor Hotel
British, European
Modern cuisine in baronial surroundings
☎ 01869 350621   OX25 3QL

MENU GUIDE Duck foie gras with pistachio nuts • Braised lamb shank on a herb mash • Crème brûlée with brandy snap
WINE GUIDE ♀ Marnier-Lapostonne Chateau Sancerre £27.20 • ♀ Chateau Segueronge Medoc £19.50 • 32 bottles over £20, 18 bottles under £20 • 6 by the glass (£4.25-£5.50)
PRICE GUIDE Fixed L £22.50 • Fixed D £39.50 • min/water £3 • Service optional

PLACE: During World War II, Weston Manor served as an officers' mess for American airmen, who must have been mighty impressed by this historic medieval manor; it was converted to a hotel shortly afterwards. Enjoy a stroll in the beautiful grounds before taking your seat in the baronial dining hall with gallery, high vaulted ceiling and oak-panelled walls.

FOOD: A small, regularly changing fixed menu ensures seasonality and freshness of ingredients, and helps the kitchen guard against being overstretched by the venue's success as an off-site business venue. Neat dishes of individual flavours in the modern English and European style.

OUR TIP: Popular conference and wedding venue

Chef: Michael Keenlyside Owners: Mr & Mrs Osborn Times: 12-2/7-9.30, Closed L Sat - Sun Notes: Coffee incl, Vegetarian available, Dress Restrictions, Smart Casual; no jeans, Civ Wed 90 Seats: 60, Pr/dining room 32 Smoking: N/Sm in restaurant Children: Portions Rooms: 35 (35 en suite) ★★★ Directions: 2 mins from M40 junct 9, via A34 (Oxford) on Weston-on-Green; hotel in village centre Parking: 50
e-mail: reception@westonmanor.co.uk web: www.westonmanor.co.uk

---

WOODCOTE MAP 05 SU68
🌸 Ricci's on the Green
French, European
French bistro in a pretty English village
☎ 01491 680775 Goring Rd RG8 0SD
MENU GUIDE Honey roasted parsnip & carrot soup • Gornish cod with saffron butter • Crème brûlée, rum & raisin ice cream
WINE GUIDE ♀ Chardonnay £29.50 • ♀ Merlot £45.50 5 bottles over £20, 8 bottles under £20 • 2 by the glass (£3.50-£4.95)
PRICE GUIDE Fixed L £20-£45 • Fixed D £25.50 • starter £5.25-£13 • main £12.95-£21.50 • dessert £5.50

PLACE: Cricket may be playing on the village green, but within this is Francophile heaven, stripped tables, exposed beams and cheerful Provençale colours conspire to convince that you've wandered into Aïx, while a log fire ensures cosiness in winter.

continued

WOODCOTE *continued* MAP 05 SU68

FOOD: This is traditional bistro style, where simple cooking draws attention to excellence of produce. Hearty, country-style dishes might include chicken livers with buttered fettuccini or duck breast in honey and orange sauce.
OUR TIP: Book a terrace table for summer afternoons enjoying the cricket
Chef: Stuart Sheperd **Owners:** Michael Ricci **Times:** 12-2.30/7-21.30, Closed Mid Feb, 2 wks Aug, 1 wk Nov, Mon & Tue **Notes:** Vegetarian available **Seats:** 60 **Children:** Portions **Parking:** 30
e-mail: michelricci@waitrose.com **web:** www.chezricci.co.uk

WOODSTOCK MAP 11 SP41

 **The Bear Hotel**

British, European
Modern European cooking in historic inn
☎ 0870 4008202 Park St OX20 1SZ

MENU GUIDE Carpaccio of tuna, teriyaki vinaigrette • Blade of beef, pommes purée, red wine jus • Banana crème brûlée, raspberry sorbet
WINE GUIDE ♀ Ca Lunghetta Pinot Grigio £17.50 • ♀ Marques de Caceres Rioja £20.95 • 43 bottles over £20, 37 bottles under £20 • 12 by the glass (£4.25-£7)
PRICE GUIDE Fixed L £15.95 • Fixed D £24.95 • starter £5.95-£9.95 • main £15-£23.95 • dessert £5.95-£6.95 • coffee £3.75 • min/water £4.55 • Service optional

PLACE: Dating back to the 13th century, this ancient inn draws a crowd of all ages and is always busy. An ivy-clad façade gives way to a cosy old world interior of open fires, sloping ceilings and flagstone floors. Easy parking at the rear.
FOOD: Simple dishes are distinguished by the freshest ingredients and accomplished cooking skills, paying particular attention to the season's best produce. A modern European menu features mains along the lines of pheasant with a Madeira sauce, or pan-fried tuna with a white bean and potato ragout.
OUR TIP: Visit Blenheim Palace nearby
Chef: Imad Abdul-Razzak **Owners:** Macdonald Hotels plc **Times:** 12.30-2/7-9.30 **Notes:** Vegetarian available **Seats:** 80, Pr/dining room 30 **Smoking:** N/Sm in restaurant **Children:** Menu, Portions **Rooms:** 52 (52 en suite) ★★★ **Directions:** Town centre, facing the market square **Parking:** 45 **e-mail:** bear@macdonald-hotels.co.uk
web: www.bearhotelwoodstock.co.uk

The AA Wine Awards recognise the finest wine lists in England, Scotland and Wales. For full details, see pages 14-15

Feathers Hotel

Rosettes not confirmed at time of going to press
British, French
Bistro fare in charming Georgian hotel
☎ 01993 812291 Market St OX20 1SX

PLACE: The restaurant in this handsome Georgian building in the centre of Woodstock is an elegant room with timber panelling and large casement windows.
FOOD: New chef Simon Garbutt, ex Castle at Taunton, has joined the Feathers as head chef overseeing both the dining room and busy bistro. Food in both focuses on quality, sourced ingredients. Simplicity rules the bistro menu whilst the dining room menu takes two or three ingredients and allows them centre stage.
Chef: Simon Garbutt **Owners:** Empire Ventures Ltd **Times:** 12.30-2.30/7-9.30 **Notes:** Vegetarian available, Dress Restrictions, Smart casual. No jeans/trainers **Seats:** 42, Pr/dining room 30 **Smoking:** N/Sm in restaurant **Children:** Menu, Portions **Rooms:** 20 (20 en suite) ★★★ **Directions:** 8m from Oxford on A44. Follow signs Eversham & Blenheim Palace. In Woodstock take 2nd left into the town. Hotel 20 mtrs on left **Parking:** On street **e-mail:** enquiries@feathers.co.uk
web: www.feathers.co.uk

⊚ Kings Head Inn

Mediterranean
Cosy old listed building in conservation village
☎ 01993 811340 Chapel Hill, Wootton OX20 1DX
MENU GUIDE Toasted goats' cheese, roast tomatoes • Braised leg & roasted Gressingham duck breast, sherry gravy • Three home-made ice creams
WINE GUIDE ♀ Torres Sauvignon Blanc £13.95 • ♀ Penfolds Shiraz Cabernet £13.95 • 21 bottles over £20, 23 bottles under £20 • 7 by the glass (£2.95-£4.25)
PRICE GUIDE Starter £3.95-£5.95 • main £9.50-£17.25 • dessert £4.95-£5.50 • coffee £2 • min/water £3.50

PLACE: Stone-built old world inn, set in one of Oxfordshire's prettiest villages. Inside you'll find a welcoming atmosphere, with log fires and eating areas separated by sofas. Those who prefer a less formal atmosphere are welcome to eat in the bar.
FOOD: The imaginative menu reflects modern, Mediterranean and Pacific Rim influences and many of the dishes are completely gluten-free. High quality ingredients are locally sourced.
OUR TIP: Accommodation provided in traditional-style bedrooms
Chef: Tony Fay **Owners:** Mr & Mrs T Fay **Times:** 12-2.30/7-9, Closed Xmas, closed D Sun/Mon **Notes:** Vegetarian available **Seats:** 30 **Smoking:** N/Sm in restaurant **Children:** Min 12 yrs **Rooms:** 3 (3 en suite) ♦♦♦ **Directions:** On A44 2m N of Woodstock turn right to Wootton. The inn is located near church on Chapel Hill **Parking:** 7 **e-mail:** t.fay@kings-head.co.uk **web:** www.kings-head.co.uk

England

RUTLAND

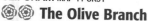

CLIPSHAM MAP 11 SK91

The Olive Branch

British, European

Great modern cooking in unpretentious gastro-pub

☎ 01780 410355 Main St LE15 7SH

MENU GUIDE Foie gras & pink peppercorn terrine • Honey-roast confit duck leg, bean cassoulet, red cabbage • Sticky toffee pudding

WINE GUIDE ♀ Domaine de Laballe 2002 Sauvignon Blanc £12 • ♀ La Croix 2003 £12.95 • 24 bottles over £20, 28 bottles under £20 • 10 by the glass (£2.25-£3.75)

PRICE GUIDE Fixed L £12.50 • starter £3.95-£8.95 • main £5.25-£18.95 • dessert £4.50-£12.95 • coffee £1.75 • min/water £3 • Service optional • Group min 12 service 10%

PLACE: This gem of a gastro-pub is always bustling thanks to a growing reputation for great food. Originally three farm labourers' cottages, it's a homely, traditional venue with wooden floors, open fires, and mismatched tables and chairs.
FOOD: They take their food seriously here - ingredients are sourced with care from around the local area, and quality breads, cheeses and other basics are sold in the pub shop. Expect accomplished modern British cooking notable for its flair and simplicity: Lincolnshire sausages with mustard mash perhaps, or pheasant with a wild rice and bacon risotto.
OUR TIP: Book ahead especially at weekends
Chef: Sean Hope **Owners:** Sean Hope, Marcus Welford, Ben Jones
Times: 12-2/7-9.30, Closed 26 Dec, 1 Jan, closed L 31 Dec, closed D 25 Dec **Notes:** Sun L 3 courses £16.50, Vegetarian available, Pr/dining room 20 **Smoking:** N/Sm area **Children:** Portions
Directions: 2m from A1 at Stretton junct, 5m N of Stamford **Parking:** 15
e-mail: info@theolivebranchpub.com
web: www.theolivebranchpub.com

OAKHAM MAP 11 SK80

Barnsdale Hall Hotel

French, International

Up-to-the-minute cooking in modern hotel

☎ 01572 757901 Barnsdale LE15 8AB

MENU GUIDE Button mushroom & Colton Basset stilton tartlet • Pan-fried chicken on crushed new potatoes • Apple pie with custard

PRICE GUIDE Food prices not confirmed for 2006. Please telephone for details

PLACE: This attractive Edwardian-style hotel is set in impressive grounds and its Osprey restaurant has stunning views over Rutland Water and the rural countryside beyond.
FOOD: The imaginative menu is very much modern hotel style, with quality ingredients and something to please everyone. Dishes might include fresh green-lipped mussels in a rich garlic, herb and white wine sauce, or grilled Scottish salmon served on oriental vegetables.
OUR TIP: Extensive leisure and beauty facilities available
Times: 12-2.30/7.30-9.30, Closed D (Sun 7-9) **Rooms:** 65 (65 en suite) ★★ **e-mail:** tim@barnsdalehotel.co.uk
web: www.barnsdalehotel.co.uk

Barnsdale Lodge Hotel

British, European

17th-century former farmhouse with Edwardian-style dining rooms

☎ 01572 724678 The Avenue, Rutland Water, North Shore LE15 8AH

MENU GUIDE Eggs Benedict • Oven baked Rutland trout basted with lemon & fish velouté • Traditional rice pudding, home-made damson jam

WINE GUIDE ♀ Pinot Grigio £13.50 • ♀ Firefly Shiraz £13.50 47 bottles over £20, 41 bottles under £20 • 7 by the glass

PRICE GUIDE Starter £3.95-£5.95 • main £10.95-£17.95 • dessert £4.50-£4.95 • coffee £1.95 • min/water £2.95 • Service added but optional 10%

PLACE: Well regarded hotel overlooking Rutland Water with six cosy dining rooms giving customers a choice between casual or more formal surroundings. The hotel is beautifully furnished with Edwardian and other antique pieces, clocks, pretty Wedgwood china, and original paintings.
FOOD: The bistro-style menu makes much use of local produce. Dinner is more serious but lunch is very popular, taken mainly in the conservatory.
OUR TIP: Sit out in the attractive courtyard garden
Chef: Richard Carruthers **Owners:** The Hon Thomas Noel **Times:** 12.15-2.15/7-9.30 **Notes:** Set Sun L £18.95, Vegetarian available, Civ Wed 100 **Seats:** 120, Pr/dining room 50 **Smoking:** N/Sm area, No pipes, No cigars **Children:** Menu, Portions **Rooms:** 46 (46 en suite) ★★★
Directions: Turn off A1 at Stamford onto A606 to Oakham. Hotel 5m on right. (2 miles E of Oakham) **Parking:** 250
e-mail: enquiries@barnsdalelodge.co.uk
web: www.barnsdalelodge.co.uk

Hambleton Hall Hotel

see page 400

Four Rosettes Amongst the very best restaurants in the British Isles, where the cooking demands national recognition. These restaurants will exhibit intense ambition, a passion for excellence, superb technical skills and remarkable consistency. They will combine appreciation of culinary traditions with a passionate desire for further exploration and improvement. Around twenty restaurants have four Rosettes.

OAKHAM MAP 11 SK80

Hambleton Hall Hotel

British *Romantic retreat serving the best of English country-house cuisine*

☎ 01572 756991 Hambleton LE15 8TH

e-mail: hotel@hambletonhall.com

web: www.hambletonhall.com

PLACE: The epitome of the English country house hotel, celebrating its 25th anniversary in 2005, this delightful Victorian house is spectacularly (not an over-used superlative in this instance) located in sweeping landscaped grounds overlooking Rutland Water. The sophisticated, traditional comforts are just as you would expect, and include a cosy bar and spacious drawing room with real winter fires and deep sofas; the perfect setting for pre-dinner drinks, cocktails and imaginative canapés. The dining room is small, intimate and comfortable, with warm traditional colours, crisp white linen, fresh flowers, heavy brocade drapes and oil paintings, accompanied by views over garden and lake. Service is suitably professional, attentive and friendly, the wine list extensive and appropriate to the occasion.

FOOD: Aaron Patterson's style is modern, underpinned by a classical theme, and perfectly fits the country-house bill. His inspired cooking showcases the finest quality ingredients and a commitment to seasonality. Bountiful local game (hare, rabbit, venison, pheasant, grouse, etc), fresh fish and seafood, together with a smattering of luxury items and the freshest vegetables, herbs and salads from Hambleton's own kitchen garden, all find their place on the table. Consummate technical skills, distinct flavours and balance all shine on the sophisticated repertoire of appealing fixed-price menus (including a vegetarian option) and carte. Expect the likes of simply roasted woodcock served with a mille-feuille of pan-fried foie gras, or roast suckling pig delivered with fondant potato and a prune and Armagnac sauce, or perhaps a tronçon of turbot, partnered with ravioli filled with scallop mousse and baby leeks to induce an agony of choice.

MENU GUIDE Veal sweetbreads, egg yolk ravioli • Sea bass fillet, tempura fried langoustine, tomato & caper couscous • Caramelised apple tart

WINE GUIDE 350 bottles over £20, 20 bottles under £20 • 8 by the glass (£4-£8)

PRICE GUIDE Fixed L £18.50 • Fixed D £35-£60 starter £16-£24 • main £20-£39.50 dessert £9-£18 • coffee £5 • min/water £3 Service included

OUR TIP: Spectacular setting for a weekend break

Chef: Aaron Patterson **Owners:** Mr T Hart **Times:** 12-1.30/7-9.30 **Notes:** Tasting menu £60, Sun L 3 courses £36, Dress Restrictions, Smart dress preferred, Civ Wed 64 **Seats:** 60, Pr/dining room 24 **Smoking:** N/Sm in restaurant **Children:** Portions **Rooms:** 17 (17 en suite) ★★★ **Directions:** 8m W of the A1 Stamford junct (A606) **Parking:** 36

England

PPINGHAM MAP 11 SP89

⑨◎ Lake Isle Restaurant & Town House Hotel

British, French

elegant town house hotel and restaurant

☎ 01572 822951 16 High St East LE15 9PZ

MENU GUIDE Salmon, prawn & lobster tart • Steak, stilton, wild mushroom sauce • Chocolate fondant tart, white chocolate ice cream

WINE GUIDE ♀ Koura Bay Sauvignon £18.50 • ♀ Andrew Hurley Shiraz Cabernet £15 • 100 bottles over £20, 45 bottles under £20 • 6 by the glass (£3.50-£10)

PRICE GUIDE Fixed D £23.50 • starter £3.95-£7.50 • main £11.50-£19 • dessert £4.50-£6 • coffee £1.95 • min/water £3.50 • Service optional

PLACE: The entrance to this elegant town house in the pretty market town of Uppingham is via a flower-filled courtyard just off the main street. Once inside, take a drink in the intimate bar, before moving through to the restaurant, an elegant blend of contemporary minimalism and William Morris inspired fabrics and antiques.

FOOD: A lengthy menu offers a tempting range of imaginative contemporary dishes, such as bacon wrapped chicken, stuffed with Somerset brie, or honey-glazed duck with roast kumquats and brandy. Extensive wine list.

OUR TIP: Cottage suites available

Chef: Stuart Mead **Owners:** Richard Burton, Janine Burton **Times:** 12-2/7-9.30, Closed L Mon, closed D Sun **Notes:** Sun L 2 course £13.50, course £16.50, Vegetarian available **Seats:** 40, Pr/dining room 16 **Smoking:** N/Sm in restaurant, Air con **Children:** Portions **Rooms:** 12 (12 en suite) ★★ **Directions:** Located on main High St **Parking:** 7 **e-mail:** info@lakeislehotel.com **web:** www.lakeislehotel.com

SHROPSHIRE

CHURCH STRETTON MAP 15 SO49

◎ Stretton Hall Hotel

British

contemporary cooking in Georgian hotel

☎ 01694 723224 All Stretton SY6 6HG

MENU GUIDE Wild mushroom risotto • Poached local duckling, Kirsch cherry compote • Citrus fruit jelly

WINE GUIDE 15 bottles over £20, 31 bottles under £20 • 7 by the glass (£2.70-£3.25)

PRICE GUIDE Starter £5.50-£7.95 • main £10.95-£18 • dessert £4-£5.50 • coffee £1.50 • min/water £2 • Service optional

PLACE: Spacious gardens surround this 18th-century country house, which has maintained many of the charms of the Georgian era. Light pours into the Lemon Tree restaurant through the stone mullioned windows, and subtle details include simply arranged flowers on the tables and warmly attentive staff at hand.

FOOD: Simple, generously proportioned dishes make the most of local produce, including saddle of local rabbit served with chicken mousse and black pudding. Good vegetarian options.

OUR TIP: Look out for the fresh fish dish of the day

Chef: Marc Cintas **Owners:** Mr C Baker **Times:** 12.30-2/7-9 **Notes:** Vegetarian available, Civ Wed 72 **Seats:** 40, Pr/dining room 14 **Smoking:** N/Sm in restaurant **Children:** Portions **Rooms:** 12 (12 en suite) ★★★ **Directions:** Off A49 Ludlow to Shrewsbury Road, in village of All Stretton **Parking:** 40 **e-mail:** enquiries@strettonhall.co.uk **web:** www.strettonhall.co.uk

◎ The Studio

Modern British

Imaginative food surrounded by interesting art and ceramics

☎ 01694 722672 59 High St SY6 6BY

MENU GUIDE Pheasant terrine, beetroot relish • Sea bass, tomato Tatin, herb vinaigrette • White chocolate pannacotta, balsamic strawberries

WINE GUIDE ♀ Privilege de Drouet Sauvignon Blanc £11.50 • ♀ Francicso de Aguirée Merlot £12.95 • 11 bottles over £20, 29 bottles under £20 • 7 by the glass (£3.50)

PRICE GUIDE Starter £4-£7 • main £14-£16.50 • dessert £4.50 • coffee £1.75 • min/water £2.50 • Service optional

PLACE: Former artist's studio in the historic centre, set amid antique shops, craft places and pubs. It's a hands-on restaurant with a husband and wife team delivering quality food and friendly service, while the simple decor provides the perfect backdrop for a great collection of art.

FOOD: The modern British menu is a manageable size for a chef-patron, and seasonality is evident. The emphasis is on local produce plus two good seafood main courses.

OUR TIP: Patio garden for warm evenings and Sunday lunch

Chef: Tony Martland **Owners:** Tony & Sheila Martland **Times:** 12-3/7-9, Closed Xmas, 3 wks Jan, Mon, closed L Mon-Sat, closed D Sun **Notes:** Sun L 3 courses £16.50, Vegetarian available **Seats:** 30 **Smoking:** N/Sm in restaurant **Children:** Portions **Directions:** Off A49 to town, left at T-junct onto High Street, 300 yds on left **Parking:** Street parking available

CLEOBURY MORTIMER MAP 10 SO67

◎ The Crown Inn

British

Classic country pub with a good range

☎ 01299 270372 Hopton Wafers DY14 0NB

MENU GUIDE Chicken liver parfait, pear chutney • Tournedos of Hereford beef, stilton mash, five spice sauce • Tiramisù

WINE GUIDE 10 by the glass (£3-£4)

PRICE GUIDE Food prices not confirmed for 2006. Please telephone for details

PLACE: The classic country pub, set in extensive gardens with a pretty duck pond, and featuring hearty log fires and a wealth of exposed timbers. Dine in Poacher's Restaurant with its traditional decor, or less formally in the bar.

continued

continued

England

CLEOBURY MORTIMER *continued* MAP 10 SO67

FOOD: Fine ales and honest cooking are the draw here; the lengthy menu offers a mix of straightforward dishes (fish and chips) and more imaginative fare such as chicken filled with banana on a korma and coriander cream.

OUR TIP: Check out the blackboard menu too

Chef: Kevin Clark **Owners:** Howard Hill-Lines **Times:** 12-2.30/6.30-9.30, Closed 25 Dec, Mon-Wed, closed D Sun **Seats:** 36, Pr/dining room 36 **Smoking:** N/Sm in restaurant **Rooms:** 7 (7 en suite) ◆◆◆◆ **Directions:** Located on A4117 between Cleobury Mortimer (3m) and Ludlow (8m) **Parking:** 40 **web:** www.crownathopton.co.uk

CLUNGUNFORD MAP 09 SO37

 Bird on the Rock Tearoom Abcott SY7 0PX
☎ 01588 660631 Winner of The Tea Guild Award of Excellence 2005.

LLANFAIR WATERDINE MAP 09 SO27

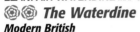 The Waterdine
Modern British
Great food in a beautiful setting
☎ 01547 528214 LD7 1TU

PLACE: Set in wonderful Shropshire countryside, the Waterdine is a former drovers' inn, dating back over 400 years and full of charm and character. Friendly, efficient hospitality from the owners puts you at your ease immediately.

FOOD: Here you'll find an experienced chef making great use of quality produce, including plenty from the local area and fruit and vegetables from the inn's own garden. Menu is seasonal and changes regularly.

OUR TIP: Stay over and sample the home-made sloe gin

Times: 12-1.45/7-9, Closed D Sun, Mon, 1 wk spring, 1 wk autumn **Rooms:** 3 (3 en suite) ◆◆◆◆◆

LUDLOW MAP 10 SO57

The Clive Restaurant with Rooms
Modern British
Converted farmhouse with contemporary design
☎ 01584 856565 Bromfield SY8 2JR

MENU GUIDE Pan-fried pigeon breast, red wine reduction • Roast venison, bacon wrapped, juniper & thyme jus • Bread & butter pudding
WINE GUIDE ♀ Altana di Vico Pinot Grigio £12.75 • ♀ San Elias Cabernet Sauvignon £11.85 • 30 bottles over £20, 45 bottles under £20 • 8 by the glass (£2.95-£4.45)

continued

PRICE GUIDE Fixed L £12.50-£21.50 • Fixed D £16.45-£25 • starter £4.95-£7.50 • main £12.95-£15.95 • dessert £4.25-£5.75 • coffee £1.85 • min/water £2.80 • Service optional

PLACE: Originally a farmhouse, located two miles north of Ludlow, the main building has been developed to retain the original Clive bar, restaurant and Cookhouse café bar. The restaurant has contemporary decor, stylish seating and tables s with elegant white linen and classy glassware and cutlery.

FOOD: The food is modern British with some Mediterranean influences, utilising as much fresh locally sourced produce as possible, such as local meats, smoked products vegetables and fish. Vegetarian dishes, such as wild mushroom cassoulet with provençale vegetables, are available every day.

OUR TIP: Bedrooms and boardroom facilities in converted period outbuildings

Chef: Peter Gartell **Owners:** Paul & Barbara Brooks **Times:** 12-3/7-9. Closed 25-26 Dec **Notes:** Sun L 3 courses £16.75, Smart Dress **Seats:** 35 **Smoking:** N/Sm in restaurant **Children:** Portions **Rooms:** 15 (15 en suite) ◆◆◆◆ **Directions:** 2m N of Ludlow on A4 **Parking:** 80 **e-mail:** info@theclive.co.uk **web:** www.theclive.co.uk

Dinham Hall Hotel
British, Italian
Comfortable hotel in the historic centre of Ludlow
☎ 01584 876464 By the Castle SY8 1EJ

MENU GUIDE Parsley velouté, poached egg • Cannon of lamb red wine jus • Caramelised lemon tart
WINE GUIDE ♀ Cotes de Duvas Sauvignon £17.50 • ♀ Concha Toro Merlot £17.50 • 43 bottles under £20 • 8 by the glass (£4.50)
PRICE GUIDE ALC £35 • Coffee £3.50 • min/water £3.50 Service optional

PLACE: Built in 1792, this building was once part of Ludlow Grammar School. All rooms are well equipped and, as an extra touch, have a decanter of sherry. The well presented dining roo has oak flooring and well-spaced tables with garden views.

FOOD: Cooking is traditional in style but with some European influences such as the lamb loin with Mediterranean vegetables and the black bream with tomato and chorizo. Good regional cheeses.

OUR TIP: Great location opposite Ludlow Castle

Chef: Peter James McGregor **Owners:** Mr J Mifsud **Times:** 12.30-1.45/7-8.45, Closed L Mon, closed D 25 Dec **Notes:** Vegetarian availab Smart Dress, Civ Wed 140 **Seats:** 34, Pr/dining room 140 **Smoking:** N/Sm in restaurant **Children:** Min 8 yrs, Menu, Portions **Rooms:** 13 (13 en suite) ★★★ **Directions:** Town centre, off Market Place **e-mail:** info@dinhamhall.co.uk **web:** www.dinhamhall.co.uk

The Feathers Hotel
British, International
Modern menu at a world-renowned 17th-century inn
☎ 01584 875261 The Bull Ring SY8 1AA

MENU GUIDE Shellfish ravioli, crushed peas, lemon sauce • Lamb, provençale vegetables, chive potatoes, confit garlic • Crème caramel
WINE GUIDE 10 bottles under £20
PRICE GUIDE Fixed L £15 • Fixed D £25 • coffee £1.50 • min/water £3.50 • Group min 12 service 10%

PLACE: Tagged by the New York Times as 'the most handsome inn in the world', this comfortable hostelry in the ancient mark town of Ludlow has a remarkable timber-framed exterior and

continue

The Feathers Hotel

...nber of beautiful Jacobean features inside.
...OD: The concise menu is a modern treat despite the sedate
...roundings. Kick off with a pork, pistachio and fennel terrine,
...d then tuck into pan-fried pork with dried cured bacon and
...amed cabbage, or wild mushroom risotto.
...R TIP: Lighter menu available in the bar
...ef: Stuart Leggett **Owners:** Ceney Developments **Times:** 12-
...)/6.30-9.30, Closed L Mon-Sat **Notes:** Vegetarian available, Dress
...trictions, Smart casual, Civ Wed 80 **Seats:** 60, Pr/dining room 30
...oking: N/Sm in restaurant **Children:** Menu, Portions **Rooms:** 40
...en suite) ★★★ **Directions:** Town centre hotel in th middle of
...low. Approximately 40 minutes from Hereford **Parking:** 36
...ail: feathers.ludlow@btconnect.com
...b: www.feathersatludlow.co.uk

Hibiscus *see page 404*

Mr Underhills *see page 405*

The Old Town House
odern British   **NEW**
aginative modern British food in relaxing
ssical setting
...01584 878777 11 Corve St SY8 1DA
ENU GUIDE Confit duck leg, orange & sesame
...lad • Monkfish, Chinese vegetables, shiitaki broth
ango parfait
INE GUIDE ♀ Aresti Sauvignon Blanc £13 • ♀ Aresti Merlot
3 • 8 bottles over £20, 10 bottles under £20 • 6 by the glass
5.50)
ICE GUIDE Starter £4.50-£7.50 • main £12-£18 • dessert
.50 • coffee £2 • min/water £2.50 • Service included
ACE: Elegant restaurant (Retro) located on the ground floor of
...stefully renovated former town house in the heart of Britain's
...nary hotspot. High-backed chairs, polished tables and a rich
...gundy decor set the comfortable scene, and there's a walled
...den for summer dining.
...OD: A modern British-style of cooking focuses on the quality
...he main ingredients rather than complicated and over
...bellished dishes. Simple, skilful cooking allows flavours to
...he through.
...R TIP: Superb bedrooms - stay the night
...f: Gareth Morgan & David Wilson-Lloyd **Owners:** David Wilson-Lloyd
...es: 12-2.30/6.30-9.30, Closed Mon, closed L Tues, closed D Sun
...ts: 34 **Smoking:** N/Sm in restaurant **Children:** Min 10 yrs, Portions
...ms: 4 (4 en suite) ♦♦♦♦ **Parking:** On street
...ail: d@velloyd.com **web:** www.theoldtownhouse.com

⊚⊚⊚ Overton Grange Country House *see page 405*

⊚⊚ The Roebuck Inn Restaurant
Modern British
Welcoming atmosphere in 15th-century inn
☎ 01584 711230 Brimfield SY8 4NE
PLACE: The old world bars are what you'd expect at this 15th-
century inn, but the dining room is a far more modern setting,
with log fires in winter, fresh flowers and linen tablecloths.
FOOD: The extensive menus make consistently brilliant use of
the freshest local produce, and everything is made on the
premises from bread to petits fours. There is a wide choice of
both traditional and more innovative dishes, with additional
blackboard specials and fish. You might begin with well
presented pan-seared scallops on truffled leek and bacon risotto,
with a light paprika butter sauce, and then follow that with moist
roast fillet of monkfish served on a crab and fennel fondue.
OUR TIP: Look out for the local cheeses
Times: 11.30-2.30/6.30-9.30, Closed 25-26 Dec **Rooms:** 3 (3 en suite)
♦♦♦♦ **e-mail:** peter@theroebuckinn.fsnet.co.uk
web: www.theroebuckinn.com

De Grey's 5-6 Broad St SY8 1NG
☎ 01584 872764 Winner of The Tea Guild Award of Excellence
2005.

MARKET DRAYTON MAP 15 SJ63

⊚ Goldstone Hall
British
Modern cooking amidst period charm
☎ 01630 661202 Goldstone TF9 2NA
MENU GUIDE Pan-fried crevettes, lemongrass, chilli
mayonnaise • Seared duck breast, rhubarb & vodka
sauce • Chocolate nemesis
WINE GUIDE ♀ Producteurs Plaimont Colombard
£12.90 • ♀ Almansa Bodegas Piqueras Tempranillo £14.75
25 bottles over £20, 57 bottles under £20 • 9 by the glass
(£3.50-£7)
PRICE GUIDE Fixed L £13.50-£23.50 • Fixed D £18-£29 • coffee
£2.40 • min/water £3.35
PLACE: A charming period property set in lovely gardens,
offering luxurious accommodation and several delightful sitting
rooms. This old manor house promises a truly rural experience.
FOOD: A well-deserved reputation for good food brings visitors
from afar, with the use of local produce and home-grown
vegetables and herbs making a strong impact on the fixed-price
dinner menu and lighter supper choice. The likes of ravioli of
crab with sun-dried tomato cream sauce, and rack of lamb with
garlic and herbs make a simple, accurate statement.
OUR TIP: Good value weekday supper menu
Chef: Carl Fitzgerald-Bloomer **Owners:** Mr J Cushing & Mrs H Ward
Times: 12-2.30/7.30-11 **Notes:** Vegetarian available, Dress Restrictions,
Smart casual, Civ Wed 100 **Seats:** 40, Pr/dining room 20
Smoking: N/Sm in restaurant **Children:** Portions **Rooms:** 11 (11 en
suite) ★★★ **Directions:** From A529, 4m S of Market Drayton, follow
signs for Goldstone Hall Gardens **Parking:** 40
e-mail: enquiries@goldstonehall.com
web: www.goldstonehall.com

LUDLOW MAP 10 SO57

Hibiscus

French *Exciting and memorable modern cooking in charming atmosphere*

☎ 01584 872325 17 Corve St SY8 1DA

PLACE: Ground-breaking chef-patron Claude Bosi may have been in Ludlow for some time (he previously worked at the town's Overton Grange, see entry) but his French roots still shine through as clear as ever. An apprenticeship served in some of France's top kitchens has brilliantly born fruit in this small, unassuming but now well-established and renowned restaurant. Ancient oak panelling and exposed brick combine with a warm, friendly welcome at the one-time 17th-century coaching inn. For a gastronomic big hitter, though, it doesn't actually shout its whereabouts, so be sure to look out for a low-key blue sign on the town's Corve Street (there's parking here too). The handful of much-in-demand, formally dressed tables and unintimidating, relaxed atmosphere is the province of Claire Bosi who delivers an ample helping of charm to the front-of-house operation.

FOOD: Bosi's cooking is innovative and exciting, and just about unique. The adventurous cooking is based firmly around his classic Lyonnaise training, but sees him couple classic French with some daring, imaginative and intriguing combinations, and the successful marriage of the sweet and savoury and the delicate and robust. Based on sound principles, it all works brilliantly; take a starter, fine beetroot and orange tart with iced feta cheese and Scottish girolle mushrooms, for instance, or dessert of classic crème brûlée of sweet garden peas, marjoram ice cream and sweetened oats. Skill, deftness of touch and passion are evident throughout, teamed with ingredients of the highest quality. Precise seasoning and balance merge with delicate flavours and refined saucing to hit the spot, and a lightness of touch even makes the nine-course tasting Menu Surprise undaunting.

MENU GUIDE Foie gras ice cream, brioche emulsion, balsamic caramel • Pigeon, chestnut royale, pumpkin & orange, beetroot confit, gaufrette potato • Tarte au chocolat

WINE GUIDE ♀ Jackson Estate Chardonnay £26 • ♀ Langmeil Shiraz (Old Vines) £32 • 400 bottles over £20, 20 bottles under £20 • 6 by the glass (£3.50-£5.25)

PRICE GUIDE Fixed L £19.50 • Fixed D £42.50 • coffee £3 • min/water £2.75 • Service optional

OUR TIP: Great value lunch, but book ahead

Chef: Claude Bosi **Owners:** Claude Bosi & Claire Bosi
Times: 12.30-1.30/7-10, Closed 2 wks Jan, 1 wk Aug, Sun & Mon, closed L Tue **Notes:** Tasting menu 7 courses £47.50, 10 courses £65 **Seats:** 36 **Smoking:** N/Sm in restaurant
Children: Portions **Directions:** Town centre, bottom of hill below Feathers Hotel **Parking:** 6

JDLOW MAP 10 SO57

Mr Underhills

odern British

npretentious dining on the river bank

☎ 01584 874431 Dinham Weir SY8 1EH

MENU GUIDE Almond velouté with crispy chorizo • Perigord
uck breast with warm winter spices, broad bean risotto
emon tart, orange & mascarpone ice cream

WINE GUIDE ♀ Brolettino Lugana Ca'deifrata £24
• Collection J Mourat Fiefs Vendeens £18 • 120 bottles over £20,
) bottles under £20 • 11 by the glass (£2.45-£7.50)

PRICE GUIDE Fixed D £40-£45 • min/water £2.50 • Service
otional

ACE: Set in a lovely position on the banks of the wooded River
ne, overlooking the weir in the shadow of the brooding castle
mparts. There's a small but pretty courtyard garden to the
toric building, once part of the castle corn mill, and interesting
e details reinforce the association, particularly among the
ious prints inside. There's a small reception room for aperitifs,
ile large picture windows offer diners views over patio and river

from the Bradley's recently refurbished restaurant with rooms.
Service, with Judy as host, is relaxed and friendly but precise.
FOOD: Dinner is a fixed-price affair of six courses plus coffee and
petits fours, and no choice before dessert. When booking, chef-
patron Chris enquires about any dietary requirements or dislikes,
then on the day you are advised on what the main dishes will be.
The cooking keeps things intelligently simple, the emphasis
concentrates on getting the best out of fresh, top-quality
ingredients and clean, clear flavours, but there are one or two
little twists along the way, take a pre-dessert white chocolate ice
cream delivered with chilli soup. Notable wine list.
OUR TIP: Worth booking early; the riverside garden is more
special then ever
Chef: Christopher Bradley **Owners:** Christopher & Judy Bradley
Times: 7.30-8.30, Closed 1 wk Jan, 1 wk July, Tue, closed L all wk, closed
D Tue (some Mon) **Notes:** Fixed D 8-9 courses, Vegetarian by request
only, Smart Dress **Seats:** 24 **Smoking:** N/Sm in restaurant
Children: Portions **Directions:** From Castle Square: with castle in front,
turn immediately left, proceed round castle, turn right before bridge,
restaurant on left **Parking:** 7 **web:** www.mr-underhills.co.uk

JDLOW MAP 10 SO57

Overton Grange Country House

ench, European

ussy cooking and stylish accommodation

☎ 01584 873500 Old Hereford Rd SY8 4AD

MENU GUIDE Foie gras terrine, brioche toast • Noisette of local
mb, wild mushroom parcel, liquorice sauce • Pear tart
ourdaloue, cinnamon ice cream

WINE GUIDE ♀ Paul Cluver Estate Elgin Sauvignon Blanc
9 • ♥ Puglia Virtuoso Primitivo Igt Casa Girelli £37
0 bottles over £20, 20 bottles under £20 • 8 by the glass
4.50-£6.50)

PRICE GUIDE Fixed L £37.50-£55.50 • Fixed D £39.50-£55.50
arter £10.50-£17.50 • main £13.95-£25 • dessert £10.50-
7.50 • coffee £3.50 • min/water £3.50 • Service added 10%

ACE: A mile or so out of town, this handsome Edwardian
ntry house hotel has a friendly charm, and stands in mature
unds with lovely views across the peaceful Shropshire
untryside. Take a pre-meal stroll on the lawn in the summer
shine, or relax by a blazing log fire in a cosy lounge over
ritifs during colder months. The oak-panelled dining room is

equally inviting, and comes decked out with comfortable,
contemporary-style furnishings, well-spaced tables and lovely
food-themed prints lining its walls.
FOOD: Chef Olivier Bossut's refined cooking elegantly blends
modern and classical French in a repertoire of crisply scripted,
fixed-price menus, including a carte and tasting dégustation
option. Intelligent use of quality fresh produce (locally derived
where possible) define sensibly balanced, stylish dishes such as a
feuilleté of langoustine with buttered baby spinach and a
langoustine coulis to open, or perhaps squab pigeon Rossini, with
creamed Savoy cabbage and a truffle périgourdine sauce.
OUR TIP: Well-chosen wines include a good selection of half
bottles
Chef: Olivier Bossut **Owners:** Indigo Hotels Ltd **Times:** 12-2.30/7-10
Notes: Tasting menu £55.50, Vegetarian available, Smart Dress, Civ
Wed 100 **Seats:** 40, Pr/dining room 32 **Smoking:** N/Sm in restaurant
Children: Min 6 yrs **Rooms:** 14 (14 en suite) ★★★ **Directions:** M5
junct 5. On B4361 opposite petrol station, approx 1.5m from Ludlow
towards Leominster **Parking:** 50 **e-mail:** info@overtongrangehotel.com
web: www.overtongrangehotel.com

England

MARKET DRAYTON *continued* MAP 15 SJ63

Rosehill Manor

British, French

Traditional fare in former manor house

☎ 01630 638532 637000 Rosehill, Ternhill TF9 2JF

MENU GUIDE Smoked salmon & prawns with dill sauce • Roast rack of lamb, rosemary & garlic • Selection of home-made desserts

WINE GUIDE ♀ Australian Chardonnay £13 • ♀ Australian Shiraz £13 • 10 bottles over £20, 15 bottles under £20 • 4 by the glass (£2.75)

PRICE GUIDE Starter £4.50 • main £16 • dessert £4.50 • coffee £1.15 • min/water £3.50 • Service optional

PLACE: Privately-owned hotel, parts of which date from the 16th century, set in mature gardens. It has a beamed bar with a log-burning stove and a large conservatory available for functions. The homely yet upmarket restaurant is equally suitable for an intimate dinner or a larger gathering.

FOOD: The fixed-price menu offers British cooking with French overtones and changes every couple of months, though your favourite dish can probably be cooked to order.

OUR TIP: Great venue for Sunday lunch

Chef: Jane Eardley **Owners:** Mr & Mrs P Eardley **Times:** 12-2/7-9.30, Closed L Mon-Sat, closed D Sun **Notes:** Tasting menu £15.75, Vegetarian available, Smart Casual, Civ Wed 100 **Seats:** 70, Pr/dining room 30 **Smoking:** N/Sm in restaurant **Children:** Menu, Portions **Rooms:** 9 (9 en suite) ★★ **Directions:** On A41 4m from Market Drayton **Parking:** 60 **web:** www.rosehillmanorhotel.co.uk

MUCH WENLOCK MAP 10 SO69

Raven Hotel

British, Mediterranean

Classic cuisine in unique historic setting

☎ 01952 727251 30 Barrow St TF13 6EN

MENU GUIDE Calves' liver, cider & mustard dressing • Slow-cooked lamb shank, redcurrant & rosemary jus • Cherry frangipane

WINE GUIDE ♀ Concha Y Toro Chardonnay £12 • ♀ Gallaire et Fils Merlot/Cabernet Sauvignon £12 • 26 bottles over £20, 54 bottles under £20 • 14 by the glass (£2.20)

PRICE GUIDE Fixed L £15-£19.50 • Fixed D £20-£25 • coffee £2.50 • min/water £3.20 • Service optional

PLACE: With an 18th-century coaching inn at its heart, the Raven rambles through several ancient almshouses, as well as a medieval great hall. It's a cosy warren of oak beams and open fires, with a tasteful restaurant that overlooks an inner courtyard filled with flowers.

continued

FOOD: A straightforward menu of classic British dishes with a nod to the Mediterranean. Mains might include bouillabaisse, or supreme of chicken with Shropshire blue cheese, smoked bacon and creamed leeks.

OUR TIP: Bar menu also available

Chef: Kirk Heywood, Steve Biggs **Owners:** Kirk Heywood, Sheila Hartshorn **Times:** 12-2.30/6.45-9.30, Closed 25 Dec **Notes:** Vegetarian available, Smart Dress **Seats:** 40, Pr/dining room 14 **Smoking:** N/Sm in restaurant **Rooms:** 15 (15 en suite) ★★★ **Directions:** 10m SW from Telford on A4169, 12m SE from Shrewsbury. In town centre **Parking:** 30 **e-mail:** enquiry@ravenhotel.com **web:** www.ravenhotel.com

NORTON MAP 10 SJ70

Hundred House Hotel

British, European

Family-run hotel with its own quirky charm

☎ 01952 730353 Bridgnorth Rd TF11 9EE

MENU GUIDE Seared scallops, pea purée, pancetta • Roast rack of Shropshire lamb, lentils, rosemary jus • Raspberry ice cream terrine

WINE GUIDE ♀ Failia Cielo Pinot Grigio £13.95 • ♀ Yvon Mau Cabernet Merlot £13.95 • 6 bottles over £20, 11 bottles under £20 • 12 by the glass (£2.65-£3.50)

PRICE GUIDE Starter £4.95-£7.95 • main £12.95-£23.95 • dess £4.95-£5.95 • coffee £1.85 • min/water £3.75 • Service optional • Group min 7 service 10%

PLACE: Fabulous former coaching inn, rich in historical detail, with aromatic herbs and flowers suspended overhead and no fewer than five log fires to ensure a warm welcome. There are exquisite gardens and a 14th-century thatched barn in the car park - the original meeting and courthouse for the local 'hundreds', where tithes were collected and justice meted out (close to the stocks and dipping pond).

FOOD: Bar brasserie and carte menus offer modern British and European dishes based on classic French training, using good fresh local ingredients.

continu

UR TIP: Romantic rooms with antique beds and indoor swings
hef: Stuart Phillips **Owners:** Mr H Phillips, Mrs S Phillips, Mr D Phillips,
r SG Phillips **Times:** 12-2.15/6-9.45 **Notes:** Fixed L Sun only 2 courses
6.95, 3 courses £19.95, Vegetarian available **Seats:** 60, Pr/dining room
■ **Smoking:** N/Sm area, No pipes, No cigars **Children:** Menu, Portions
ooms: 10 (10 en suite) ★★ **Directions:** Midway between Telford &
idgnorth on A442. In centre of Norton village **Parking:** 30
mail: reservation@hundredhouse.co.uk
eb: www.hundredhouse.co.uk

SWESTRY MAP 15 SJ22

⑩⓪ Pen-y-Dyffryn Country Iotel

ritish, International

p notch cooking in hillside haven

☎ 01691 653700 Rhydycroesau SY10 7JD

MENU GUIDE Venison terrine, redcurrant jelly • Welsh beef,
arlic mash, buttered spinach, balsamic jus • Passionfruit crème
rûlée

WINE GUIDE ♀ Trivento Viognier £13.25 • ♀ Brown Brothers
hiraz/Cabernet Sauvignon £19.75 • 36 bottles over £20,
3 bottles under £20 • 47 by the glass (£3.85-£5.90)

RICE GUIDE Fixed D £32-£33.50 • coffee £2.75 • min/water
4.25 • Service optional

ACE: This Victorian rectory turned comfortable country-house
tel is set on a Shropshire hillside in acres of pretty grounds. Its
ling room is decorated in traditional style, and there are two
mfortable lounges for pre-dinner drinks.

OD: Local produce is the mainstay of Pen-y-Dyffryn's concise
enu, which features a tempting range of modern and traditional
shes, such as steamed turbot with a salmon dumpling, and
hisky and tarragon sauce. There's no shortage of skill, so sit
ck and enjoy.

UR TIP: Take a stroll around the grounds
ef: Tim Wesley **Owners:** Tranquility Hotels Limited **Times:** 6.45-11,
sed 20 Dec-21 Jan, closed L all week **Notes:** Vegetarian available
ats: 25 **Smoking:** N/Sm in restaurant **Children:** Min 3 yrs, Menu,
rtions **Rooms:** 12 (12 en suite) ★★★ **Directions:** 3m W of
westry on B4580 **Parking:** 18 **e-mail:** stay@peny.co.uk
eb: www.peny.co.uk

HREWSBURY MAP 15 SJ41

⑩ Albright Hussey Hotel

ritish, French

odern cooking in medieval surroundings

☎ 01939 290571 & 290523 Ellesmere Rd
4 3AF

Albright Hussey Hotel

MENU GUIDE Carpaccio of tuna, herb salad, tomato salsa • Beef
fillet, raisin & Armagnac jus • Hot chocolate fondant, caramel ice
cream

WINE GUIDE ♀ Henri Germain Mersault £45 • ♀ E Loron et Fils
Fleurie £21.95 • 52 bottles over £20, 39 bottles under £20 • 4 by
the glass (£2.80)

PRICE GUIDE Fixed L £12.50-£25.10 • starter £5.25-£8.45 • main
£12.50-£20.95 • dessert £5.95 • coffee £1.50 • min/water
£3.30 • Service optional

PLACE: Fabulous medieval manor house with its own moat and
landscaped garden. There's an intimate atmosphere in the
panelled dining room, where pastel pink linen and fresh flowers
are set against original beams and large fireplaces.
FOOD: The lively choice of dishes aims to please everyone, and
the food is thoroughly enjoyable, with good use made of fresh
local ingredients.
OUR TIP: Delightfully romantic setting
Chef: John Winter **Owners:** Franco, Vera & Paul Subbiani **Times:** 12-
2.15/7-10 **Notes:** Vegetarian available, Dress Restrictions, No jeans,
trainers or T-shirts, Civ Wed 200 **Seats:** 80, Pr/dining room 40
Smoking: N/Sm in restaurant, Air con **Children:** Portions **Rooms:** 26
(26 en suite) ★★★ **Directions:** On A528, 2m from centre of
Shrewsbury **Parking:** 80 **e-mail:** info@albrighthussey.co.uk
web: www.albrighthussey.co.uk

⑩⑩ Mytton & Mermaid Hotel

British

Modern cuisine in historic riverside inn

☎ 01743 761220 Atcham SY5 6QG

MENU GUIDE Wild mushroom & bacon potato cake, poached
egg, hollandaise • Sea bass, black olive mash, roast pepper
sauce • Warm fig tart

WINE GUIDE ♀ Logan Rock Semillon/Chardonnay
£10.95 • ♀ Kamsberg Pinotage Shiraz £10.95 • 19 bottles over
£20, 30 bottles under £20 • 10 by the glass (£2.85-£5.50)

PRICE GUIDE Fixed D £27.50-£30 • starter £5.95-£6.95 • main
£13.95-£19.95 • dessert £5.95-£6.95 • coffee £2 • min/water
£3.50 • Service optional

PLACE: There's a relaxed gastro-pub feel to this ivy-clad coaching
inn, set in rural surroundings on the banks of the Severn. Lighter
meals are served in the convivial bar, while unclothed tables,
candles and fresh flowers comprise the restaurant's unfussy,
contemporary decor.
FOOD: Modern British cooking featuring some sound flavour
combinations. The kitchen sources top notch Shropshire
ingredients, with suppliers listed on the menu. Vegetarian menu
available.
OUR TIP: Take a stroll to the nearby stately home of Attingham
Park

continued   *continued*

England

SHREWSBURY *continued* MAP 15 SJ41

Chef: Adrian Badland **Owners:** Mr & Mrs Ditella **Times:** 11.30-2.30/6.30-10, Closed 25 Dec, closed D 26 Dec **Notes:** Sun lunch £15.95/£16.95, Sun D £18.95/£19.95, Vegetarian available, Civ Wed 75 **Seats:** 100, Pr/dining room 15 **Smoking:** N/Sm in restaurant **Children:** Portions **Rooms:** 18 (18 en suite) ★★★ **Directions:** Just outside Shrewsbury on the B4380 (old A5). Opposite Attingham Park **Parking:** 80 **e-mail:** admin@myttonandmermaid.co.uk **web:** www.myttonandmermaid.co.uk

Rowton Castle Hotel

Modern British

Fine dining in 17th-century house with lovely gardens

☎ 01743 884044 Halfway House SY5 9EP

MENU GUIDE Carrot & coriander soup • Baked cod, smoked bacon, spring onion & tomato risotto • Rice pudding crème brûlée

PRICE GUIDE Food prices not confirmed for 2006. Please telephone for details

PLACE: Castellated country-house hotel dating from the 17th century and set in 17 acres of tranquil grounds west of Shrewsbury. Steeped in history and swathed in oak panelling, the baronial-style restaurant features a magnificent fireplace and is softened by candlelit intimacy.
FOOD: The seasonal set-price menu offers a choice of options and variety. The kitchen takes a modern approach and uses fresh local produce whenever possible.

continued

OUR TIP: Fabulous setting with formal gardens
Times: 12-2/7-9.30 **Rooms:** 19 (19 en suite) ★★★ **Directions:** From Birmingham take M6 west. Follow M54 & A5 to Shrewsbury. Continue on A5 and exit at 6th rdbt. Take A458 to Welshpool. Rowton Castle 4m on right **e-mail:** post@rowtoncastle.com
web: www.rowtoncastle.com

TELFORD MAP 10 SJ60

Hadley Park House

Mediterranean, International   NEW

Relaxed conservatory dining in former gentleman's residence

☎ 01952 677269 Hadley Park TF1 6QJ

MENU GUIDE Confit of Gressingham duck leg, toasted sesame seed & orange salad • Chicken & spinach roulade, potato rösti, wilted greens, supreme sauce • Warm lemon & almond pudding, lemon syrup, vanilla ice cream

WINE GUIDE ♀ Logan Rock Chardonnnay £12.25 • ♀ Logan Rock Cabernet Shiraz £12.25 • 10 bottles over £20 • 8 by the glass (£4.25-£4.50)

PRICE GUIDE Starter £4-£7.50 • main £11.50-£18 • dessert £5 coffee £1.75 • min/water £3.75

PLACE: Privately-owned Georgian manor house (built by Thomas Telford's chief engineer) with an airy conservatory dining room and two acres of landscaped gardens.
FOOD: Modern British cooking with a hint of the Mediterranean. The seasonal menu changes according to availability of the finest ingredients.

continued

WORFIELD MAP 10 S079

Old Vicarage Hotel and Restaurant

European

Quality cooking in old vicarage

☎ 01746 716497   WV15 5JZ

MENU GUIDE Ham hock & foie gras terrine • Roast lamb, minted balsamic gravy • Pineapple tarte Tatin

WINE GUIDE ♀ Rousanne Vin de Pays Sauvignon £17.80 ♀ Les Mercedes Merlot £17.80 • 72 bottles over £20, 10 bottles under £20 • 9 by the glass (£4.55-£5.55)

PRICE GUIDE Fixed L £17.50 • starter £3.50-£9.95 • main £12.50-£27.95 • dessert £6.25 • coffee £3 • Service included

PLACE: Set in two acres of grounds, this converted parsonage reflects the peace and quiet of its village setting. The interior features polished wood floors and tables, fresh flowers, a relaxing lounge, and the bright, new Orangery restaurant.
FOOD: The sophisticated food has its foundation firmly based on what the region (and the kitchen garden) can produce - only the best seasonal ingredients are sourced here. The kitchen is confident and accomplished and delivers a sound range of modern dishes. Fish features well and presentation is first-class. The 100-bin wine list covers the globe and is a well planned and described list.

OUR TIP: Indulge yourself in the atmosphere and the fine food
Chef: Martyn Pearn **Owners:** Mr & Mrs D Blakstad **Times:** 12-2/7-9, Closed L Sat, (lunch by reservation only) **Notes:** Vegetarian available, Smart casual **Seats:** 42, Pr/dining room 30 **Rooms:** 14 (14 en suite) ★★★ **Directions:** A454 (Bridgnorth Road), or A442 towards Kidderminster **Parking:** 30
e-mail: admin@the-old-vicarage.demon.co.uk
web: www.oldvicarageworfield.com

OUR TIP: Local produce gives a real taste of Shropshire
Chef: Daniel Silcock **Owners:** Mark & Geraldine Lewis **Times:** 12-2/7-9.30, Closed 29 Aug, 2-5 Jan, closed L Sat, closed D Sun **Notes:** Dress Restrictions, Smart casual, Civ Wed 80 **Seats:** 80, Pr/dining room 12 **Smoking:** N/Sm in restaurant, Air con **Children:** Menu, Portions **Rooms:** 10 (10 en suite) ★★★ **Parking:** 24
e-mail: info@hadleypark.co.uk **web:** www.hadleypark.co.uk

◎◎ Valley Hotel
International
Hotel restaurant with interesting menus and rare ceramics

☎ 01952 432247 TF8 7DW

MENU GUIDE Salt cod pâté, parmesan crust, confit tomatoes • Pheasant breast, mushroom duxelle, red wine jus • Vanilla pod crème brûlée

WINE GUIDE ♀ House £8.95 • ♂ House £8.95 • 10 bottles over £20, 30 bottles under £20 • 4 by the glass (£2.60-£2.95)

PRICE GUIDE Fixed L £12-£15 • Fixed D £19-£29.45 • starter £4.50-£6.50 • main £10.50-£17.95 • dessert £4-£5 • coffee £1.70 • min/water £1.20 • Service optional

PLACE: The hotel is located by the River Severn, surrounded by beautiful parkland, close to the famous Iron Bridge. Chez Maws restaurant is a bright modern space with simple furnishings and wooden floors. The Maws family, who once owned this 18th-century house, were tile manufacturers and fine examples of their work are still visible today.
FOOD: The same carte menu is offered at lunch and dinner, listing a good choice of imaginative dishes. French and international influences crop up here and there, and good use is made of seasonal local produce.
OUR TIP: Take a stroll along the banks of the Severn before dinner
Chef: Barry Workman **Owners:** Philip & Leslie Casson **Times:** 12-2/7-9.30, Closed 26 Dec-2 Jan, closed L Sat **Notes:** Vegetarian available, Civ Wed 120 **Seats:** 50, Pr/dining room 120 **Smoking:** N/Sm in restaurant **Children:** Menu, Portions **Rooms:** 35 (35 en suite) ★★★
Directions: From M6 on to M54, take junct 6 and follow A5223 to Ironbridge for 4m. At mini island turn right, hotel 80 yds on left
Parking: 100 **e-mail:** info@thevalleyhotel.co.uk
web: www.thevalleyhotel.co.uk

WORFIELD MAP 10 SO79
◎◎◎ Old Vicarage Hotel and Restaurant *see page 408*

Three Rosettes Outstanding restaurants that demand recognition well beyond their local area. Timing, seasoning and the judgement of flavour combinations will be consistently excellent, supported by other elements such as intelligent service and a well-chosen wine list. Around 10% of restaurants with Rosettes have been awarded three.

England

SOMERSET

BATH MAP 04 ST76 *See* ALSO COLERNE, WILTS
◎◎ Bath Spa Hotel, Vellore Restaurant
International, British
Classy cuisine in timeless and elegant hotel
☎ 0870 400 8222 Sydney Rd BA2 6JF

MENU GUIDE Salmon blinis • Beef, fondant potatoes, herb purée • Coconut parfait pineapple sorbet

WINE GUIDE ♀ Torreon de Paredes Sauvignon Blanc £22.50 • ♂ Marques de Caceras Rioja Crianza £29.75 all bottles over £20 • 6 by the glass (£7.20-£9.95)

PRICE GUIDE Fixed L £13.95 • Fixed D £37.50 • starter £10-£13 • main £22-£30 • dessert £7-£10 • coffee £4.95 • min/water £4 • Service optional

PLACE: Just a short walk from Bath's city centre, this Georgian mansion has a timeless elegance that's hard to resist. Dinner is served in the airy splendour of the former ballroom.
FOOD: A well-balanced range of modern European dishes, conjured with care from quality ingredients. The carte is supplemented by a fixed-price menu, and features the likes of roast quail with ceps and caramelised chicory, or cod with a garden herb crust and nut brown butter.
OUR TIP: Take a cocktail in the Colonnade Bar before dinner
Chef: Andrew Hamer **Owners:** Macdonald Hotels **Times:** 12-2/7-9.45, Closed L Mon-Sat **Notes:** Vegetarian available, Dress Restrictions, No jeans preferred, Civ Wed 120 **Seats:** 80, Pr/dining room 120 **Smoking:** N/Sm in restaurant **Children:** Menu, Portions **Rooms:** 104 (104 en suite) ★★★★★ **Directions:** M4 junct 18, onto A46 follow signs to Bath. Continue for 8m, at rdbt turn right onto A4 and follow city centre signs for 1m. At lights turn left towards A36. At mini rdbt turn right then left into Sydney Place. Hotel 200yds on right **Parking:** 160 **e-mail:** sales@bathspahotel.com **web:** www.bathspahotel.com

BATH MAP 04 ST76

The Bath Priory Hotel and Restaurant

Rosettes not confirmed at time of going to press

French
Intimate country-house restaurant noted for accomplished cooking

☎ 01225 331922 Weston Rd BA1 2XT

e-mail: mail@thebathpriory.co.uk

web: www.thebathpriory.co.uk

PLACE: You'll find all the trappings of a country house here - four acres of beautifully landscaped gardens, tranquillity and exceptional comforts - though it's only a few minutes from the city. An exceptional approach to service is at its best in the intimate picture-lined restaurant, where customers are treated like valued friends. The atmosphere at Bath Priory is like a private residence with a collection of oil paintings adorning the walls, plush sofas and roaring fires. **FOOD:** A strong team under the direction of Chris Horridge, ex sous chef at Le Manoir uses its considerable technical skills to impressive advantage, taking prime ingredients and converting them into mouthwatering creations. Flavours in the French inspired dishes are fresh and prominent, and often sourced from the hotel's own garden. The wine list is also of interest; the selection is global but the emphasis is on French and Italian choices.

MENU GUIDE Salad of quail, nasturtiums, pickled mushrooms, beetroot syrup • Loin of pork, tortellini of braised belly, apple & butterbean cassoulet, crackling pencil • Aniseed parfait, candied fennel, pear sauce

WINE GUIDE ♀ Les Templiers Sauvignon Blanc £16.50 • ♀ Les Templiers Cabernet Sauvignon £16.50 • 180 bottles over £20, 10 bottles under £20 6 by the glass (£4.50-£5.50)

PRICE GUIDE Fixed L £20 • Fixed D £49.50 • coffee £4 • min/water £3 • Service optional

OUR TIP: Excellent wine advice from the restaurant manager

Chef: Chris Horridge **Owners:** Mr A Brownsword **Times:** 12-1.45/7-9.45 **Notes:** Vegetarian available, Dress Restrictions, No jeans or t-shirts, Civ Wed 64 **Seats:** 60, Pr/dining room 64 **Smoking:** N/Sm in restaurant **Children:** Menu, Portions **Rooms:** 28 (28 en suite) ★★★★ **Directions:** At top of Park Lane, on W side of Victoria Park, turn left into Weston Rd. 300yds on left **Parking:** 60

England

BATH *continued* MAP 04 ST76

Combe Grove Manor Hotel & Country Club

International

Georgian country house hotel dining

☎ 01225 834644 Brassknocker Hill, Monkton Combe A2 7HS

MENU GUIDE Asparagus soup with chive fromage frais • Pan-ried fillet of sea bass with linguini • Champagne jelly with strawberries

PRICE GUIDE Food prices not confirmed for 2006. Please telephone for details

PLACE: Set in over 80 acres of gardens, this mansion commands unning views over Limpley Stoke Valley. The restaurant consists a series of small vaulted rooms, and there is also a well-rnished terrace. The hotel offers superb indoor and outdoor sure facilities.

OOD: Well handled local ingredients produce a confident odern British cooking style.

UR TIP: Kids' concept menus available

mes: 12-2/7-9.30, Closed Mon-Thu, closed L Fri-Sat, closed D Sun
ooms: 40 (40 en suite) ★★★★ **Directions:** Telephone for directions
mail: julianebbutt@combegrovemanor.com
eb: www.combegrovemanor.com

The Eastern Eye

ndian

uthentic Indian in exceptional Georgian setting

☎ 01225 422323 466401 8A Quiet St BA1 2JS

THE EASTERN EYE

RESTAURANT

MENU GUIDE Chicken Chandan • Lamb Mon Passand • Coconut e cream

WINE GUIDE ♀ Vin de Pays Chardonnay £11.95 • ♀ Vin de Pays abernet Syrah £11.95 • 6 bottles over £20, 21 bottles under 20 • 2 by the glass (£2.50)

continued

PRICE GUIDE Fixed D £18-£25 • starter £2.50-£5.90 • main £5.50-£11.90 • dessert £2.50-£4.50 • min/water £3.20

PLACE: Even amidst Bath's architectural splendours, the ornately Georgian interior of this Indian restaurant stands out. Spectacular features include a glass domed ceiling. Drapes and dressings in soft colours create warmth, and quiet Indian music sets the tone.

FOOD: This family-run curry house offers unusual and authentic Bengali and North Indian dishes, all skilfully prepared.

OUR TIP: Book - and allow time to park

Chef: Harun Rashid, Nagendal Kandal **Times:** 12.30-2.15/6-11.30, Closed 25 Dec **Notes:** Vegetarian available **Seats:** 130, Pr/dining room 54
Smoking: N/Sm area, No pipes, Air con **Children:** Portions
Directions: Town centre **e-mail:** info@easterneye.co.uk
web: www.easterneye.co.uk

The Lansdown Grove

Modern British

Enjoyable dining in one of Bath's oldest hotels

☎ 01225 483888 Lansdown Rd BA1 5EH

MENU GUIDE Caruso of plum tomato & mozzarella with pesto dressing • Lemon sole fillet stuffed with spinach, chive mash, saffron sauce • Lemon tart, strawberry compote

PRICE GUIDE Food prices not confirmed for 2006. Please telephone for details

PLACE: In an elevated position overlooking the Georgian city centre to the wooded hills beyond, this Grade II listed building has a relaxed and friendly atmosphere, high ceilings and delightful period details.

FOOD: The elegant Conservatory restaurant offers innovative, interesting cuisine, making good use of quality produce in well constructed dishes.

OUR TIP: Good value fixed-price menu

Times: 12-2.30/7-9.30, Closed L Sat **Rooms:** 60 (60 en suite) ★★★
Directions: From city outskirts. Pass the Hare & Hound pub on the left, continue down hill and turn right at T-junct and 200 yds on left
e-mail: resevations.bath@swallowhotels.com
web: www.swallow.bath@swallow

The Olive Tree at the Queensberry Hotel

British

A sophisticated retreat near the centre of town

☎ 01225 447928 Russel St BA1 2QF

MENU GUIDE Pan-fried ham hock terrine • Baked cod with bouillabaisse sauce • Irish cream bread & butter pudding

WINE GUIDE ♀ Blue Ridge Sauvignon Blanc £26.50 • ♀ Pavelot Pinot Noir £37 • 182 bottles over £20, 31 bottles under £20 12 by the glass (£3.75-£7.95)

PRICE GUIDE Fixed L £13.50 • starter £6.25-£8.95 • main £13.50-£21.95 • dessert £6.50 • coffee £2.95 • min/water £2.95 • Service optional • Group min 10 service 10%

PLACE: This restaurant in the middle of Bath has understated decor with modern artwork creating a calm oasis to escape into. Bare tables during the day are clothed for evening service to add that extra bit of luxury. A local favourite, staff remember names and provide formal yet friendly table service.

FOOD: A lengthy modern British menu includes a daily fixed-price choice of adventurous, creative dishes with a Mediterranean influence and strong flavour combinations. Try the Provençale fish soup followed by the rump of Scottish beef with braised lentils and morrel jus maybe.

continued

BATH continued MAP 04 ST76

OUR TIP: Good choice of dessert wines
Chef: Marc Salmon **Owners:** Mr & Mrs Beere **Times:** 12-2/7-10, Closed L Mon **Notes:** Vegetarian available **Seats:** 60, Pr/dining room 30 **Smoking:** N/Sm in restaurant, Air con **Children:** Portions **Rooms:** 29 (29 en suite) ★★★ **Directions:** City centre. 100yds N of Assembly Rooms in Lower Lansdown **Parking:** Residents' valet parking; Street pay/display **e-mail:** reservations@thequeensberry.co.uk **web:** www.thequeensberry.co.uk

Popjoys Restaurant

British, European

Accomplished dining in elegant Regency venue

☎ 01225 460494 Beau Nash House, Sawclose BA1 1EU

MENU GUIDE Trio of smoked fish, iced Smirnoff • Aberdeen Angus beef fillet • Chocolate & orange truffle cake

WINE GUIDE 80 bottles over £20, 15 bottles under £20 • 12 by the glass (£3.40-£5)

PRICE GUIDE Fixed L £14 • Fixed D £24 • starter £7-£12 • main £15-£23 • dessert £7.50-£10.50 • coffee £2.20 • min/water £4 • Service optional • Group min 10 service 10%

PLACE: The former home of Beau Nash's mistress, Juliana Popjoy, the dining room in this Grade I listed Regency house is grand and historic - lemon coloured walls, red carpets and several portraits set the scene.
FOOD: Fresh and hearty food is traditional British with the occasional Swiss (thanks to Swiss proprietor) touch, like a selection of excellent Swiss cheeses. Use of quality local produce is in evidence.

continued

OUR TIP: Next to the theatre so ideal for pre- or post-theatre dinners
Chef: John Headley **Owners:** Tomi Gretner **Times:** 12-2/5.30-11, Closed Sun **Notes:** Smart casual **Seats:** 32, Pr/dining room 40 **Smoking:** N/Sm in restaurant **Children:** Min 6yrs **Directions:** City centre adjacent to Theatre Rotal (Bath) **e-mail:** popjoys@btinternet.com **web:** www.popjoys.co.uk

 **Royal Crescent Hotel - Pimpernels** *see below*

Give us your views! All the rosetted restaurants in this guide have been visited by one of the AA's team of professional inspectors, but we want to hear from you! Use the report forms in the back of the guide or email us at lifestyleguides@theaa.com with your comments on any establishments featured or on the restaurants that you feel are worthy of an entry. We would also be pleased to receive your views on the guide itself and suggestions for information you would like to see included.

BATH MAP 04 ST76

Royal Crescent Hotel - Pimpernels

British, Mediterranean

Contemporary fine dining in Georgian splendour

☎ 01225 823333 16 Royal Crescent BA1 2LS

MENU GUIDE Salad of rabbit with Asian flavours • Dorade Royale & red mullet • Lavender crème caramel

WINE GUIDE ♀ Vincent Pinard Sancerre Cuvée Flores £42 • ♀ Gilles Robin Crozes Hermitage Cuvée Papillon 2002 Syrah £33 • 160 bottles over £20 • 14 by the glass (£5-£9)

PRICE GUIDE Fixed L £18 • Fixed D £49 • coffee £4.50 • min/water £3.75 • Service included

PLACE: This smart hotel is located on Bath's famous Royal Crescent and is recognisable by its liveried doormen and tree tubs on which the hotel's name is discreetly written. Inside is a fanfare of Georgian splendour, with impressive paintings and artefacts. Pimpernel's restaurant matches the elegance of its surroundings and opens onto secluded gardens. Skilled, helpful staff add to the air of luxury.
FOOD: Accomplished and interesting, this contemporary British menu combines influences from the Mediterranean and the Far East. Scallops might come with butternut squash purée and chilli infused oil, while a beautifully tender duo of braised lamb could

be accompanied by aubergine caviar and provençale vegetables in all of which textures and flavours are skilfully combined.
OUR TIP: Sumptuous picnics can be provided for guests
Chef: Steven Blake **Owners:** Von Essen Hotels **Times:** 12.30-2.30/7-10.30 **Notes:** Sun L is a set menu, Vegetarian available, Dress Restriction Civ Wed 60 **Seats:** 65, Pr/dining room 36 **Children:** Menu **Rooms:** (45 en suite) ★★★★★ **Parking:** 17 **e-mail:** info@royalcrescent.co **web:** www.royalcrescent.co.uk

⊚ Sakura Restaurant

Japanese

Bath's only Japanese restaurant

☎ 01225 422100 The Windsor Hotel, 69 Great Pulteney St BA2 4DL

MENU GUIDE Wafu salad & yakitori • Sukiyaki (Wafer thin slices of beef with vegetables & noodles) • Blackcurrant sorbet

WINE GUIDE ♀ Coldndge Estate Chardonnay £11.50 • ♥ Coldndge Estate Shiraz £11.50 • 5 bottles over £20, 14 bottles under £20 • 2 by the glass (£11.50-£27.50)

PRICE GUIDE Fixed D £25-£28 • coffee £2.50 • min/water £3.50

PLACE: Japanese restaurant located at the Windsor Hotel, a Grade I listed town house a short walk from the city centre. All the elements are authentic, including the music, the sake, the garden and basic wooden seats.
FOOD: There are three set menu options: Shabu Shabu and Sukiyaki, which both centre around a main serving of beef, and Seafood Nabe. In each case the main course is cooked at the table.
OUR TIP: An excellent way to discover Japanese cuisine
Chef: Sachiko Bush **Owners:** Cary & Sachiko Bush **Times:** 6-9.30 (Last Orders 11), Closed Xmas, Sun-Mon, closed L all week **Notes:** Vegetarian by request only **Seats:** 24 **Smoking:** N/Sm in restaurant **Children:** Min 12 yrs **Rooms:** 14 (14 en suite) ★★★★ **Directions:** From E & N take M4 junct 18 towards Bath. From S & W approach Bath on A36
Parking: 8 **e-mail:** sales@bathwindsorhotel.com
web: www.bathwindsorhotel.com

⊚ *Woods Restaurant*

British, French

Popular brasserie in the heart of classic Bath

☎ 01225 314812 9-13 Alfred St BA1 2QX

MENU GUIDE Basil marinated sardines • Slow roast loin of pork, caramelised shallots & port • Caramel poached pear, cinnamon palmiers

PRICE GUIDE Food prices not confirmed for 2006. Please telephone for details

PLACE: A traditional Bath townhouse exterior conceals this bustling restaurant. There's a nice balance between formality and ease, with candlelight and a mixture of bare wood and dressed tables striking a harmonious note.
FOOD: Drawing ideas from around Europe, these imaginative and flavourful dishes use quality ingredients. Good presentation and successful combinations in dishes like seared scallops with horseradish cream and beetroot jam.
OUR TIP: Advance booking is suggested, especially in summer
Times: 12-2/5.45-10, Closed 26 Dec, 1 Jan, closed D Sun
Directions: Telephone for directions **web:** www.woods.co.uk

⑪ **Fire House Rotisserie** 2 John St BA1 2JL
☎ 01225 482070 Grills, gourmet pizzas and vegetarian dishes in a relaxed setting.

⑪ **Fishworks** Green St BA1 2JY ☎ 01225 448707 Exciting fish dishes from this café above a fishmonger's.

⑪ **Loch Fyne Restaurant** 24 Milsom St BA1 1DG
☎ 01225 750120 Quality seafood chain.

☕ **Searcey's at the Pump Rooms** Stall St BA1 1LZ
☎ 01225 444477 Winner of The Tea Guild Award of Excellence 2005.

⑪ **Tilleys Bistro** North Pde, Passage BA1 1NX
☎ 01225 484200 Tremendous variety, including an extensive vegetarian choice.

BRIDGWATER MAP 04 ST23

⊚ **Walnut Tree Hotel**

British

Good seasonal food in former coaching inn

☎ 01278 662255 North Petherton TA6 6QA

MENU GUIDE Duck spring rolls with apricot chutney • Six-hour Somerset belly pork • Warm coconut & treacle tart

WINE GUIDE ♀ Colmanari Di Santi Pinot Grigio £11.50 • ♥ One Tree Hill Cabernet/Shiraz £10.95 • 9 bottles over £20, 32 bottles under £20 • 10 by the glass (£2.75-£5.75)

PRICE GUIDE Starter £4.75-£6.50 • main £8.95-£19.50 • dessert £5.50-£6.50 • coffee £2 • min/water £3.50 • Service optional

PLACE: Less than two miles from the M5, this former 16th-century coaching inn is now a smart, stylish hotel with a modern bistro and comfortable, more formal Lemon Tree restaurant.
FOOD: An impressive use of local produce - including a list of suppliers on the menu - means that the menus are seasonal and packed with West Country ingredients. Modern British dishes include ham hock and duck foie gras terrine with home-made piccalilli or fillet of organic Exmoor lamb Wellington with spring onion croquettes, pea purée and baby roast vegetables.
OUR TIP: Large selection of West Country cheeses
Owners: Richard & Hilary Goulden **Times:** 12-2/7-9.30
Notes: Vegetarian available, Smart Dress **Seats:** 80, Pr/dining room 100 **Smoking:** N/Sm in restaurant, Air con **Children:** Menu, Portions
Rooms: 33 (33 en suite) ★★★ **Directions:** M5 junct 24 on A38
Parking: 70 **e-mail:** info@walnuttreehotel.com
web: www.walnuttreehotel.com

BRUTON MAP 04 ST63

⊚ **Truffles**

British, European

Modern food in a cosy period setting

☎ 01749 812255 95 High St BA10 0AR

MENU GUIDE Pumpkin & parmesan risotto • Pan-roasted crown of partridge • William pear tarte Tatin

WINE GUIDE ♀ Brown Brothers Everton Pinot Grigio/Chardonnay £13.75 • ♥ Brown Brothers Everton Cabernet/Shiraz/Malbec £13.75 • 26 bottles under £20 • 3 by the glass (£3.45-£3.95)

PRICE GUIDE Fixed L £10-£20 • Fixed D £26.95 • coffee £1.50 • min/water £3 • Service optional

PLACE: Creeper-clad and full of atmosphere, this town centre property is spread over two floors for dining. Colour-washed walls, high-backed chairs and fresh table settings create a relaxed, intimate mood.
FOOD: Tried and tested recipes give way to more imaginative creations, with the innovative monthly menus coming up with plenty of interest: braised oxtail wrapped in Parma ham is likely to be followed by green tea, jasmine and lime parfait.
OUR TIP: On street parking can be limited
Chef: Mark Chambers **Owners:** Mr & Mrs Chambers **Times:** 12-2/7-9.30, Closed Mon, closed L Tue-Wed, closed D Sun **Notes:** Sun L 3 courses £15.95, Vegetarian available, Dress Restrictions, Smart casual preferred **Seats:** 30, Pr/dining room 12 **Smoking:** N/Sm in restaurant, Air con **Children:** Min 6 yrs, Portions **Directions:** Town centre, at start of one-way system, on left **Parking:** On street opposite
e-mail: enquiries@trufflebruton.co.uk
web: www.trufflesbruton.co.uk

CHARD MAP 04 ST30

Bellplot House Hotel

International   **NEW**

Friendly Georgian hotel serving quality, locally sourced food

☎ 01460 62600 High St TA20 1QB

MENU GUIDE Crab cakes, ginger sauce • Roast saddle of lamb stuffed with field mushrooms, redcurrant jus • Triple chocolate marquise

WINE GUIDE ♀ Sierra Grande Sauvignon Blanc £12.50 • ♥ Château Laurents Syrah Merlot £12.50 • 3 bottles over £20, 14 bottles under £20 • 3 by the glass (£3.50)

PRICE GUIDE Starter £4-£6 • main £12-£15 • dessert £4-£6 • coffee £2.25 • min/water £2 • Service optional

PLACE: Once a Georgian home, this hotel has a comfortable restaurant, decorated in a harmonious style with apple green walls, and fine glassware giving a sense of days gone by.

FOOD: The International menu serves up the classics, although expect some modern variants, including a parsnip and apple cappuccino. Traditional dishes are well executed, with an emphasis on local produce.

OUR TIP: Try the catch of the day from Lyme Bay

Chef: Thomas Jones **Owners:** Dennis Betty, Thomas Jones **Times:** 7-9, Closed Sun, closed L Everyday **Notes:** Vegetarian available, Smart Dress **Seats:** 30 **Smoking:** N/Sm in restaurant **Children:** Menu, Portions **Directions:** M5 junct 25,/A358 signposted Yeovil. At rdbt take 4th exit A358 from Taunton, follow signs to Chard town centre. 500 mtrs from Guildhall **Parking:** 12 **e-mail:** info@bellplothouse.co.uk **web:** www.bellplothouse.co.uk

DULVERTON MAP 03 SS92

Ashwick House Hotel

British

Edwardian elegance and courteous hospitality

☎ 01398 323868 TA22 9QD

MENU GUIDE Light local blue cheese mousse • Noisettes of local lamb, port jus • Old English bread & butter pudding

WINE GUIDE ♀ Hanmer Junction Sauvignon Blanc £13 • ♥ Penfolds Shoraz £14 • 20 bottles over £20, 30 bottles under £20

PRICE GUIDE Fixed L £14.95 • Fixed D £24 • coffee £2.75 • min/water £2 • Service optional

PLACE: Six acres of delightful grounds surround this Edwardian country house, including water gardens and lily ponds. Dinner is served in a small, sunny dining room with French windows opening onto a pretty terrace. Look out for original William Morris wallpaper.

FOOD: Accomplished but unfussy cooking in the English country house style. The fixed-price four-course dinner menu offers alternative choices at the starter and dessert stage only.

OUR TIP: Treat yourself to the splendid afternoon tea

Chef: Richard Sherwood **Owners:** Richard Sherwood **Times:** 12.30-2/7.15-8.45, Closed L Mon-Sat **Notes:** No Credit Cards, Vegetarian by request only, Dress Restrictions, No shorts **Seats:** 30, Pr/dining room 10 **Smoking:** N/Sm in restaurant **Children:** Min 8 yrs, Portions **Rooms:** 6 (6 en suite) ★★ **Directions:** From M5 junct 27 follow signs to Dulverton, then take B3223 Lynton road and turn left after 2nd cattle grid **Parking:** 20 **e-mail:** ashwickhouse@talk21.com **web:** www.ashwickhouse.co.uk

Tarr Farm Inn

British Mediterranean

Homely hotel with culinary potential

☎ 01643 851507 Tarr Steps, Exmoor National Park TA22 9PY

MENU GUIDE Mussels, coriander, lime leaf • Beef, roast tomatoes, parmesan crisps, red onion & tomato salsa • White chocolate cheesecake

WINE GUIDE ♀ Chardonnay £14.40 • ♥ Cabernet Syrah £9.90 • 36 bottles over £20, 40 bottles under £20 • 6 by the glass (£3-£3.50)

PRICE GUIDE Fixed L £12-£15 • starter £4-£7.50 • main £12-£17 • dessert £4.50-£5.50 • coffee £1.85 • min/water 90p • Service optional

PLACE: Renowned for its cream teas, this 16th-century farmhouse is popular with the many walkers attracted by the Exmoor National Park. Oak beams and open fires keep things cosy, while furnishings are contemporary in style.

FOOD: Things get interesting once the day-trippers have left - expect a tempting dinner menu of carefully crafted modern English and Mediterranean dishes, created from local produce where possible. Breakfast also impresses.

OUR TIP: Bedrooms are also available

Chef: Steve Cox/Kate Lewis **Owners:** Richard Benn & Judy Careless **Times:** 11-3/6.30-12 **Notes:** Vegetarian available **Seats:** 45, Pr/dining room 20 **Smoking:** N/Sm area **Children:** Min 14 eve, Portions **Rooms:** 9 (9 en suite) ♦♦♦♦♦ **Directions:** Leave M5 junct 27, signed Tiverton. Follow signs to Dulverton, from Dulverton take B3223 signed Tarr Stepps for approx 6.5 miles **Parking:** 40 **e-mail:** enquiries@tarrfarm.co.uk **web:** www.tarrfarm.co.uk

Woods Bar & Dining Room

British   **NEW**

Accomplished cooking in relaxed setting

☎ 01398 324007 4 Banks Square TA22 9BU

MENU GUIDE Chicken liver parfait, apple & date chutney Seared swordfish, sweet chilli • Vanilla bean pannacotta

PRICE GUIDE Food prices not confirmed for 2006. Please telephone for details

PLACE: This unpretentious eaterie is run by the owners of a former AA Pub of the Year and seems to be another winning formula. Popular with Exmoor's country crowd, it's a friendly venue, done out in rough-hewn oak and decorated with bric-a-brac.

FOOD: Accomplished cooking that promises good things for the future. Dishes are straightforward in style, and range from ham, egg and chips, to pheasant with mustard mash and port sauce.

OUR TIP: The same menu is available in restaurant and bar

Times: Telephone for details

DUNSTER MAP 03 SS94

The Luttrell Arms Hotel

Traditional British

Atmospheric restaurant in small hotel

☎ 01643 821555 High St TA24 6SG

MENU GUIDE Honey confit of duck, soy & honey dressing • Loin of lamb, herb & wild mushroom mousse • Chocolate layer cake, coffee parfait, pear tart

PRICE GUIDE Food prices not confirmed for 2006. Please telephone for details

continue

England

LACE: In a great high street position, looking up towards the
astle, this medieval guest house, which once entertained the
bbots of Cleeve, has been renovated and decorated in
ontemporary style. The restaurant is split-level - an intimate,
andlelit space.
OOD: Great use of local produce including Exmoor lamb.
teresting selection of dishes on the two menus. Desserts can be
uite complex, sometimes featuring several mini dishes.
UR TIP: Good selection of lighter lunches
imes: 12-3/7-10 Rooms: 28 (28 en suite) ★★★ Directions: A39 to
inehead, Turn S towards Tiverton on the A396. Hotel is in centre of
unster Village e-mail: info@luttrellarms.fsnet.co.uk
eb: www.bhere.co.uk

XFORD MAP 03 SS83

ⓓ⓪ Crown Hotel

ritish, French

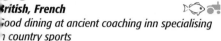

ood dining at ancient coaching inn specialising
1 country sports
☎ 01643 831554 Park St TA24 7PP

MENU GUIDE Scallops St Jacques • Exmoor beef fillet, foie gras
Lemon tart

WINE GUIDE ♀ Tindall Sauvignon Blanc £20.95 • ♀ Penfolds
Shiraz/Cabernet £17.95 • 18 bottles over £20, 18 bottles under
£20 • 6 by the glass (£4.50)

PRICE GUIDE Fixed L £16.50-£18 • Fixed D £32.50-£35 • coffee
£2.50 • min/water £3.50 • Service optional

LACE: This ancient establishment is believed by many to be the
Idest coaching inn on Exmoor. It's located in the heart of this
icturesque village and still offers weary travellers comfortable
ccommodation and good food. The candlelit dining room has a
onvivial atmosphere with its paprika and white walls, green
arpet and walls hung with old engravings.
OOD: Canapés and home-baked bread are followed by
aditional dishes based on excellent local produce. Good well-

balanced flavour combinations in dishes like turbot, truffle mash
and lobster sauce, and sea bass with a basil dressing.
OUR TIP: Book for the excellent afternoon tea
Chef: Scott Williams **Owners:** Hugo Jeune **Times:** 12-2/7-9
Notes: Vegetarian available, Dress Restrictions, Smart casual, no jeans,
T-shirts, swimwear **Seats:** 30, Pr/dining room 14 **Smoking:** N/Sm in
restaurant **Children:** Min 7 yrs, Portions **Rooms:** 17 (17 en suite)
★★★ **Directions:** From Taunton take A38 to A358. Turn left at B3224 &
follow signs to Exford **Parking:** 30
e-mail: info@crownhotelexmoor.co.uk
web: www.crownhotelexmoor.co.uk

HINTON CHARTERHOUSE MAP 04 ST75

ⓓⓓ Homewood Park

British, French

*Imaginative cuisine in romantic Georgian
house*

☎ 01225 723731 BA2 7TB

MENU GUIDE Seared scallops, mango salsa • Poached sea bass,
nori noodles, fennel jam, coconut & saffron sauce • Pineapple
tarte Tatin

WINE GUIDE ♀ Jean Max Roger Sancerre Sauvignon Blanc
£27 • ♀ R Lopez de Heredia Rioja Crianza Tempranillo
£27 • 199 bottles over £20, 15 bottles under £20 • 10 by the
glass (£3.50)

PRICE GUIDE Fixed L £16 • Fixed D £39.50 • coffee
£4 • min/water £2.75 • Service optional

PLACE: Georgian country house with comfortable public rooms
warmed by open fires. The restaurant occupies three airy rooms,
all with lovely views over the award winning gardens and
Limpley Stoke Valley. Huge vases of lilies, floral pictures and soft,
summery colour schemes complete the effect.
FOOD: Knowledgeable and accommodating staff are happy to
guide guests through the menus. These offer modern British
dishes with French influences and some imaginative innovations
such as farced lamb cutlets with oregano on chorizo cassoulet,
aubergine caviar and garlic jus.
OUR TIP: Bath is just a short drive away
Chef: Jean de la Rouzière **Owners:** Von Essen Hotels **Times:** 12-2.30/
7-11 **Notes:** Tasting menu £49, Sun L 3 courses £22.50 (incl. coffee),
Vegetarian available, Dress Restrictions, No Jeans, Civ Wed 50 **Seats:** 60,
Pr/dining room 40 **Smoking:** N/Sm in restaurant **Children:** Portions
Rooms: 19 (19 en suite) ★★★ **Directions:** 6m SE of Bath off A36,
turnleft at second sign for Freshford **Parking:** 50
e-mail: info@homewoodpark.co.uk
web: www.homewoodpark.co.uk

continued

England

HOLFORD MAP 04 ST14

⊕ Combe House Hotel
Modern European   **NEW**
Flavourful cuisine in stylish country hotel
☎ 01278 741382 TA5 1RZ

MENU GUIDE Scallops, crab & saffron cake • Guinea fowl stuffed with black pudding & apple, wine jus • Crème brûlée, strawberry coulis

WINE GUIDE 9 bottles over £20, 18 bottles under £20

PRICE GUIDE Fixed L £12.95 • starter £4.50-£7.95 • main £14.50-£17.95 • dessert £4.95 • min/water £3 • Service optional

PLACE: Peacefully located in a wooded valley in the Quantock Hills, this stylish country house hotel sits in pretty grounds near a stream. Its smart, modern restaurant is furnished with handmade Cornish oak and walnut furniture.
FOOD: Flavours pack a punch here; fresh local ingredients are handled skilfully and seasoned with care. Meat and game come direct from nearby farms and shoots, while vegetables and soft fruit are grown in the organic kitchen garden.
OUR TIP: Facilities include a pool, sauna, tennis court and croquet lawn
Chef: Laurence Prott & Pascal Prunier **Owners:** Andrew Ryan
Times: 12-2.30/7-9 **Notes:** Coffee incl, Vegetarian available, Smart Dress **Seats:** 40, Pr/dining room 8 **Smoking:** N/Sm in restaurant
Children: Portions **e-mail:** info@combehouse.co.uk
web: www.combehouse.co.uk

HUNSTRETE MAP 04 ST66

⊛⊛ Hunstrete House Hotel
British, French
Contemporary country house cooking with promise
☎ 01761 490490 BS39 4NS

MENU GUIDE Foie gras, pear & celeriac tart • Salmon, sautéed scallop, saffron potatoes, lemon & chive dressing • Dark chocolate fondant

WINE GUIDE ♀ Las Casas del Toqui Chardonnay £17.50 • ♀ Norte Chico Merlot £17.50 • 131 bottles over £20, 24 bottles under £20 • 6 by the glass (£4.50-£5.50)

PRICE GUIDE Fixed L £15.95 • Fixed D £47.75 • coffee £3.75 • min/water £2.50 • Service added but optional 5%

PLACE: The quintessential country house, this Georgian manor is just a short drive from Bath and set in acres of orchards, deer park and pasture land. The pretty restaurant is Regency in style, with elegant chandeliers and windows opening out onto a courtyard where you can dine alfresco in the summer.
FOOD: Lots of promise here, thanks to an ambitious new chef with large helpings of talent. The creative menu features local produce wherever possible, with fruit and herbs from the manor's walled garden. *continued*

OUR TIP: Make time to take a stroll around the grounds
Chef: Daniel Moon **Owners:** Culloden Associates **Times:** 12-2/7-9.30
Notes: Tasting menu £55, Sun L 3 courses £25, Vegetarian available, Dress Restrictions, No jeans, smart casual, Civ Wed 60 **Seats:** 35, Pr/dining room 50 **Smoking:** N/Sm in restaurant **Children:** Menu, Portions
Rooms: 25 (25 en suite) ★★★ **Directions:** On A368 - 8 miles from Bath **Parking:** 50 **e-mail:** reception@hunstretehouse.co.uk
web: www.hunstretehouse.co.uk

PORLOCK MAP 03 SS84

⊛⊛⊛ Andrews on the Weir
see page 41

⊕ The Oaks Hotel
British, French
Straightforward cooking on Exmoor
☎ 01643 862265 TA24 8ES

MENU GUIDE Avocado, tomato & walnut salad • Salmon & haddock fish cakes, lemon hollandaise • Crème caramel, raspberries

WINE GUIDE 15 bottles over £20, 70 bottles under £20 • 4 by the glass (£3-£4)

PRICE GUIDE Fixed D £30 • min/water £2 • Service included

PLACE: Elegant Edwardian house run by a friendly husband and wife team. Large picture windows in the restaurant look out across the village rooftops to Porlock Weir and the Bristol Channel beyond.
FOOD: Dishes are simple in style and feature the best of fresh local produce; you might start with cream of broccoli and lemon soup, and then tuck into an Exmoor venison and wild mushroom pie, or Devon beef béarnaise. The menu changes daily.
OUR TIP: A good base for Exmoor
Chef: Anne Riley **Owners:** Tim & Anne Riley **Times:** 7-8, Closed Nov-Mar **Notes:** Coffee incl., Vegetarian by request only **Seats:** 22
Smoking: N/Sm in restaurant **Children:** Min 8 yrs, Portions **Rooms:** 8 (8 en suite) ★★ **Directions:** At bottom of Dunstersteepe Road, on left on entering Porlock from Minehead **Parking:** 12
e-mail: info@oakshotel.co.uk **web:** www.oakshotel.co.uk

SHEPTON MALLET MAP 04 ST64

⊛⊛⊛ Charlton House Hotel
see page 41

SHIPHAM MAP 04 ST45

⊛⊛ Daneswood House Hotel
British
Modern cuisine in country house hotel
☎ 01934 843145 Cuck Hill BS25 1RD

MENU GUIDE Scallops, roast belly pork, Jerusalem artichoke purée • Beef, sweet potato mash, whisky & mustard sauce • Apple tarte Tatin

WINE GUIDE ♀ Bergsig Chenin Blanc £12.95 • ♀ Navajas Crianza Garnacha £16.95 • 3 by the glass (£3-£3.50)

PRICE GUIDE Fixed L £17.95 • starter £5.95-£11.95 • main £14.95-£21.95 • dessert £6.95-£7.95 • coffee £2.50 • min/water £2 • Service included • Group min 10 service 10%

PLACE: Prettily set in the Somerset countryside, this Edwardian house offers distant views of the Bristol Channel and Wales. Its restaurant is a charming affair with starched linen and friendly staff.

continued on page 41

England

Andrews on the Weir

European, British *Great local produce in superb location*

☎ 01643 863300 Porlock Weir TA24 8PB

e-mail: information@andrewsontheweir.co.uk

web: www.andrewsontheweir.co.uk

PLACE: A charming Georgian building overlooking Porlock Bay, Andrews is decorated in classic country-house style and is the perfect restaurant with rooms. What was the front bar is now a dining room, so you can watch the boats in the harbour as you eat. Assured service is well informed, very friendly and perfectly in tune with the kitchen brigade. **FOOD:** This is modern European cooking with classical roots. Local ingredients wherever possible (some suppliers are listed on the menu) and an emphasis on quality are the ideal underpinning for the high standards on show. Andrew Dixon would rather close the restaurant for the night than not be running things himself, and his almost obsessive attention to detail is clearly demonstrated by his cooking, with exact timing and spot on execution evident in all aspects of the food here. The true flavours of the ingredients are sympathetically nurtured and well chosen combinations and accomplished cookery result in memorable dishes. The boned stuffed and braised Devon Ruby oxtail with creamed parsnips, roasted butternut squash and braising juices is as near to a signature dish as Dixon gets - the meat moist, tender and rich, the braising juices deep flavoured and luxuriant. Vegetarians get their own menu at dinner, and the mini lemon tart offered as a petit four should not be missed.

MENU GUIDE Open saffron ravioli of poached oysters & scallops with oyster & Avruga butter sauce • Steamed Exmoor lamb suet pudding, root vegetables, creamed potatoes, roasted sweetbreads & rosemary • Warm creamed rice pudding with caramelised rhubarb & cardamom syrup

WINE GUIDE ♀ Sauvignon Blanc £23 • ♀ Bodegas Muga Tinto Reserva £26.60 • 30 bottles over £20, 20 bottles under £20 • 7 by the glass (£3.60-£6.05)

PRICE GUIDE Fixed L £12.50 • starter £8 • main £20 • dessert £7 • coffee £3.50 • min/water £2.50 • Service optional • Group min 7 service 10%

OUR TIP: Book well in advance to secure a window seat and a sea view

Chef: Andrew Dixon **Owners:** A Dixon, Rodney Sens **Times:** 12-3/6.30-10, Closed Jan, Mon, Tue **Notes:** Vegetarian menu £29.50, Tasting menu £55, Sun L £20.50, Vegetarian available **Seats:** 40 **Smoking:** N/Sm in restaurant **Children:** Min 12 yrs, Portions **Rooms:** 5 (5 en suite) 🛏 **Directions:** From M5 junct 25 follow A358 towards Williton, then A39 through Porlock & onto Porlock Weir. Hotel in 1.5m **Parking:** 5

England

SHEPTON MALLET MAP 04 ST64

Charlton House Hotel

British, International *Innovative cuisine in designer luxury*
☎ 01749 342008 Charlton Rd BA4 4PR
e-mail: enquiries@chaltonhouse.com
web: www.charltonhouse.com

PLACE: Owned by the founder of the celebrated design label Mulberry, this achingly chic country house hotel is decorated with imagination and theatrical panache, not to mention many of the company's signature fabrics. A dramatic red and gilt opera box frames the entrance to the restaurant, while an eclectic mix of antiques, curios, family photos and racing memorabilia decorate the entrance hall. A new spa offers a romantic retreat for those in need of pampering, while the restaurant has been extended so that most tables sit within a light and airy conservatory overlooking the manicured lawns.

FOOD: Cooking of the highest quality from an accomplished chef, Simon Crannage, who just gets better and better. Featuring the finest local produce, especially from Roger Saul's nearby organic farm, dishes impress with their simplicity and innovation, and might include venison with candied red cabbage, and dark chocolate, or salmon with sweet potato fondants. A seven-course menu gourmand is available if you want to do the place justice, in addition to carte and concise but imaginative vegetarian selection. Visit on a Friday or weekend for the full effect, as lighter lunches are served Monday to Thursday. Afternoon tea is also a tradition here and can be enjoyed on the terraces in fine weather.

MENU GUIDE Scallops, confit pork belly, truffle & parsley salad • Duo of lamb, capers, mint, winter vegetables • Passionfruit soufflé

WINE GUIDE ♀ Trevor Mast Four Sisters Sauvignon Blanc/Semillion £22 • ♀ Terrabianca Campaccio £35 • 80 bottles over £20, 10 bottles under £20 10 by the glass (£4-£10)

PRICE GUIDE Fixed L £16 • Fixed D £49.50 • coffee £4.50 • min/water £3 • Service optional • Group min 8 service 10%

OUR TIP: Snacks available throughout the day at the new spa café, Montes

Chef: Simon Crannage **Owners:** Roger Saul **Times:** 12.30-2.30/7.30-10.15 **Notes:** Tasting menu 5 courses £60, Sun L 3 courses £24.50, Vegetarian available, Civ Wed 120 **Seats:** 84, Pr/dining room 70 **Smoking:** N/Sm in restaurant, Air con **Children:** Menu, Portions **Rooms:** 25 (26 en suite) ★★★ **Directions:** On A361. Hotel is located 1m before Shepton Mallet **Parking:** 70

SHIPHAM continued MAP 04 ST45

FOOD: A modern British menu blends proven combinations with more innovative dishes. You might tuck into slow-roast duck with noodles and stir-fry vegetables, or smoked haddock with a cider and stilton glaze.
OUR TIP: Take a pre-dinner stroll around the gardens
Chef: Ross Duncan, Elise Hodges **Owners:** D. Hodges & E. Hodges **Times:** 12-2/7-9.30, Closed 26 Dec-4 Jan, closed L Sat **Notes:** Tasting menu £29.95, Vegetarian available, Smart Dress **Seats:** 50, Pr/dining room 30 **Smoking:** N/Sm in restaurant **Children:** Portions **Rooms:** 17 (17 en suite) ★★★ **Directions:** 1m from A38 between Bristol & Bridgwater **Parking:** 20 **e-mail:** info@daneswoodhotel.co.uk
web: www.daneswoodhotel.co.uk

STON EASTON MAP 04 ST65

⊕⊕ Ston Easton Park
British, Mediterranean
Fine dining in Palladian splendour near Bath
☎ 01761 241631 BA3 4DF

MENU GUIDE Symphony of foie gras • Roasted saddle of local venison • Assiette of Ston Easton desserts
WINE GUIDE ♀ Vinha Sauvignon Blanc £17.50 • ♀ Collin Bourisset Fleurie Gamay £26 • 113 bottles over £20, 16 bottles under £20 • 7 by the glass (£3.75-£6)
PRICE GUIDE Fixed L £17.50 • Fixed D £39.50 • starter £11 • main £27 • dessert £6.50 • coffee £2.75 • min/water £3 • Service included
PLACE: A fine Palladian mansion built in 1739, set in parklands with landscaped gardens and a stream. Delightful, inviting public rooms are full of comfortable furnishings, antiques and oil paintings. The Cedar Tree restaurant, with Georgian-style decor, is a wonderful setting for fine dining. Less formal, candle-lit meals can be served in the old kitchen.
FOOD: Imaginative and well executed modern British dishes use fresh local ingredients, some from the kitchen garden and the best of local producers. Vegetarian menu provided.
OUR TIP: The lunch menu provides superb value
Chef: Michael Parke **Owners:** Von Essen Hotels **Times:** 12-2/7-9.30 **Notes:** Tasting menu £34.50, Vegetarian available, Dress Restrictions, Smart Casual, Civ Wed 100 **Seats:** 40, Pr/dining room 80 **Smoking:** N/Sm in restaurant **Children:** Min 7 yrs, Menu, Portions **Rooms:** 23 (23 en suite) ★★★★ **Directions:** Follow A39 from Bath for approx. 8m. Turn onto A37 (Shepton Mallet), Ston Easton is next village **Parking:** 100 **e-mail:** info@stoneaston.co.uk
web: www.stoneaston.co.uk

TAUNTON MAP 04 ST22

⊕ Brazz
British
Unpretentious brasserie fare
☎ 01823 252000 Castle Bow TA1 1NF

MENU GUIDE Chicken liver parfait • Cumberland sausage, champ, onion gravy • Sticky toffee pudding, Chantilly cream
WINE GUIDE ♀ Guerrieri Rizzardi Pinot Grigio • ♀ Copperidge Red Zinfandel £18.95 • 12 bottles over £20, 30 bottles under £20 • 15 by the glass (£3.10-£8.50)
PRICE GUIDE Starter £3-£6 • main £8.50-£17.50 • dessert £4.50-£6.50 • coffee £1.50 • min/water £1.50 • Service added but optional 10%
PLACE: This lively Taunton brasserie, which is also a café and bar, draws a mix of diners. It's decorated in bright, contemporary style and has a comfy bar for coffee and lighter snacks.

continued

FOOD: A sister restaurant to successful eateries in Exeter and Cardiff, Brazz has been associated with a number of famous chefs over the years, and delivers a lengthy range of dishes distinguished by first class ingredients and accomplished cooking skills. Children and grazers welcome.
OUR TIP: 45 minute express menu available at lunchtime
Chef: Richard Guest **Owners:** Mr K Chapman **Times:** 12-11 **Notes:** Vegetarian available **Seats:** 100 **Smoking:** N/Sm in restaurant, Air con **Children:** Portions **Directions:** From M5 junct 25, follow signs for Town Centre/Castle Hotel **Parking:** 35 **e-mail:** taunton@brazz.co.uk
web: www.brazz.co.uk

⊕⊕⊕ Castle Hotel *see page 420*

⊕ Corner House Hotel
Modern **NEW**
Modern bistro with fresh vibrant flavours
☎ 01823 284683 Park St TA1 4DQ

MENU GUIDE Coriander & Thai mussels • Teriyaki salmon, duo of noodles • Glazed lemon tart
WINE GUIDE ♀ Pinot Grigio £9.50 • ♀ Hardy's Shiraz Cabernet £10.95 • 15 bottles over £20, 20 bottles under £20 • 6 by the glass (£2.75-£7)
PRICE GUIDE Food prices not confirmed for 2006. Please telephone for details
PLACE: A stylishly revitalised hotel that has occupied its prominent position in the heart of this old market town since Victorian times. The modern bistro atmosphere is relaxed and friendly.
FOOD: Simply prepared fresh ingredients are given a Mediterranean flavour on the large informal menu. Go for a simple sausage and Parmesan mash, try bacon wrapped pork fillet, or pick something from the chargrill like mixed grill or fillet steak.
OUR TIP: Stay over in the newly-refurbished bedrooms
Chef: David Gaughan **Owners:** Hatton Hotels **Times:** 12-2.30/6.30-9.45 **Notes:** Vegetarian available **Seats:** 100, Pr/dining room 55 **Smoking:** N/Sm area, No pipes, No cigars **Children:** Menu, Portions **Rooms:** 28 (28 en suite) ★★★ **Directions:** Telephone for details **Parking:** 40 **e-mail:** res@corner-house.co.uk
web: www.corner-house.co.uk

⊕⊕ Farthings Hotel & Restaurant
Modern British
Classic cooking of local produce in formal surroundings
☎ 01823 480664 Hatch Beauchamp TA3 6SG

continued

England

TAUNTON MAP 04 ST22

Castle Hotel

British

Refined and historical setting for fine dining

☎ 01823 272671   Castle Green TA1 1NF

MENU GUIDE Scrambled duck egg with smoked eel • Rump of Cornish lamb • Coffee & hazelnut bonfire

WINE GUIDE ⚲ Jean Marc Brochard Petits Chablis Chard £27 • ⚲ Domaine de la Madonne Fleurie Gamay £29 • 201 bottles over £20, 36 bottles under £20 • 14 by the glass (£4.50-£7.50)

PRICE GUIDE Fixed L £20-£38 • Fixed D £25-£45 • coffee £3.50 • min/water £3.50 • Service added but optional 12.5%

PLACE: This wisteria-covered hotel was built as a fortress by the Normans. Spacious public areas have tapestry hangings, thick curtains and heavy soft furnishings. The elegant restaurant is a little more contemporary in style.

FOOD: The chef's passion for sourcing good local produce is shown in dishes like excellent organic pork chops with clear flavour that are complemented by rich, well-timed pan-fried foie gras, and accompanied by a potato fruit terrine to cut through

the potential over-richness of the dish.

OUR TIP: The set menu with wine included is great value

Chef: Richard Guest **Owners:** Mr C H Chapman **Times:** 12.30-2/7-9.30, Closed D Sun **Notes:** Vegetarian available, Smart Dress **Seats:** 60, Pr/dining room 12 **Children:** Portions **Rooms:** 44 (44 en suite) ★★★ **Directions:** M5 junct 25, follow signs for town centre/castle **Parking:** 35 **e-mail:** reception@the-castle-hotel.com **web:** www.the-castle-hotel.com

TAUNTON *continued* MAP 04 ST22

MENU GUIDE Hot & cold seafood platter • Two style Quantock duck (roast breast, leg braised in Dubonnet) • Crème brûlée, fruit sorbet

WINE GUIDE ⚲ Mâcon Blanc Chardonnay £18.95 • ⚲ Hervé Varenne Pinot Noir £14.95 • 17 bottles over £20, 30 bottles under £20 • 10 by the glass (£3.95-£4.95)

PRICE GUIDE Fixed L £17.99 • Fixed D £31.95 • coffee £2.95 • min/water £3.50 • Service optional

PLACE: A comfortable lounge with a log-burning fire lies between the bar and restaurant of this traditional family-run hotel. The restaurant comprises two rooms with damask cloths and quality appointments. Service is formal.

FOOD: The classic style menu, priced for two and three courses, majors on quality local ingredients, including Quantock duck, free-range chicken and locally reared lamb and beef.

OUR TIP: Enjoy coffee and petits fours in the comfortable lounge

Chef: Stephen Murphy & Martin McMullan **Owners:** Stephen & Hilary Murphy **Times:** 12-2/7-9, Closed L Mon-Sat, closed D Sun (residents only) **Notes:** Vegetarian available, Dress Restrictions, Smart casual, Civ Wed 50 **Seats:** 30, Pr/dining room 10 **Smoking:** N/Sm in restaurant **Children:** Min 10yrs, Portions **Rooms:** 10 (10 en suite) ★★ **Directions:** From M5 take A358 towards Ilminster, 3m to sign for Hatch Beauchamp & brown tourist sign for Farthings. In village 300yds after pub on right **Parking:** 20 **e-mail:** farthing1@aol.com **web:** www.farthingshotel.com

⚜⚜ Mount Somerset Hotel

British, French

Grand old Regency house with lovely country views and elegant dining

☎ 01823 442500   Henlade TA3 5NB

MENU GUIDE Assiette of game • Pan-fried wild sea bass, fennel purée, basil butter cream • Lemon flavours (sorbet, mousse, crème brûlée)

WINE GUIDE ⚲ Domaine Grauzan Sauvignon Blanc £14.50 • ⚲ Meridian Cabernet Sauvignon £14.50 • 33 bottles over £20, 23 bottles under £20 • 4 by the glass (£3.75)

PRICE GUIDE Fixed L £13.50 • Fixed D £27.50 • starter £8 • main £22 • dessert £6 • coffee £2.95 • min/water £2.75

PLACE: Traditional country house hotel overlooking Taunton vale and the Quantock Hills. Attractive features include exquisite tableware, log fires, the sunny Somerset Room, and the

continue

conservatory and terrace leading down to the croquet lawn. The baby grand is in use most weekends over afternoon tea, and there's a helipad in the grounds so you can arrive in style.
FOOD: The daily fixed-price French and English menu combines classic favourites and imaginative new dishes using the best of ingredients: Quantock chicken, Exmoor lamb, Somerset cheeses and Brixham lobster and crab, plus speciality home-baked breads.
OUR TIP: Helicopter pleasure flights are available
Chef: Stefan Warwick **Owners:** The Von Essen Group **Times:** 12-2/7-9.30 **Notes:** Vegetarian available, Dress Restrictions, Smart casual; no jeans or trainers, Civ Wed 60 **Seats:** 40, Pr/dining room 20 **Smoking:** N/Sm in restaurant **Children:** Portions **Rooms:** 11 (11 en suite) ★★★ **Directions:** From M5 junct 25 take A358 (Chard); turn right in Henlade (Stoke St Mary), then turn left at T-junct. Hotel 400yds on right **Parking:** 50 **e-mail:** info@mountsomersethotel.co.uk **web:** www.mountsomersethotel.co.uk

The Willow Tree Restaurant
British, French
Imaginative regional cooking in intimate restaurant
☎ 01823 352835 3 Tower Ln TA1 4AR

MENU GUIDE Sautéed pork belly, home-made rabbit sausage • Fillet of bream, pumpkin gnocchi • Stem ginger crème brûlée
WINE GUIDE ♀ Grebet Pouilly Fumé Rabichattes Sauvignon Blanc £24.95 • ♀ Thomson Old Pumphouse Estate Shiraz £18.95 • 25 bottles over £20, 23 bottles under £20 • 4 by the glass (£3.50-£3.75)
PRICE GUIDE Starter £4.95-£9.95 • main £12.95-£18.95 • dessert £4.50-£6.95 • coffee £1.95 • min/water £2.50 • Service optional
PLACE: Tucked away in a period building handy for the town centre, this cosy little restaurant gains bags of atmosphere from its exposed beams and inglenook fireplace. There's a charming waterside terrace.

FOOD: A range of cooking skills is harnessed to bring the best out of star ingredients, most of them good representatives of the local region. Roast best end of Exmoor lamb is carefully enhanced by several subtly flavoured partners.
OUR TIP: Ideal for a romantic dinner
Chef: Darren Sherlock **Owners:** Darren Sherlock & Rita Rambellas **Times:** 6.30-10, Closed Jan, Aug, Sun-Mon, closed L all week **Notes:** Vegetarian available **Seats:** 25, Pr/dining room 16 **Smoking:** N/Sm in restaurant **Children:** Min 10 yrs **Directions:** 200 yds from Taunton bus station **Parking:** 20 yds 300 spaces

TRISCOMBE MAP 04 ST13
The Blue Ball Inn
British, European   **NEW**
Impressive cooking in pretty thatched pub
☎ 01984 618242 TA4 3HE
MENU GUIDE Scallops, black pudding & chorizo dressing • Pork, parsnip & parsley mash, shallot fondue • Lemon tart, raspberry sorbet
WINE GUIDE ♀ Wither Mills Sauvignon Blanc £17.95 • ♀ Paul Jaboulet Gigondas £18.95 • 20 bottles over £20, 70 bottles under £20 • 10 by the glass (£2.70-£3.50)
PRICE GUIDE Starter £4.50-£7.95 • main £12.95-£16.95 • dessert £4.75 • coffee £1.25 • Service included
PLACE: A former AA Pub of the Year, this delightful thatched country inn draws a friendly mix of diners and drinkers. Its traditional interior features an open timbered ceiling.
FOOD: Accomplished contemporary cooking that makes the most of fresh, high quality ingredients, and isn't too hard on the wallet. All dishes are cooked to order. One to watch.
OUR TIP: Superb terraced garden with views over the Vale of Taunton
Chef: Peter Alcroft **Owners:** Sharon Murdoch & Peter Alcroft **Times:** 12-2/7-9, Closed 25 Dec, Mon (Jan-Apr), closed D Sun (Jan-Apr) **Notes:** Vegetarian available **Seats:** 48 **Smoking:** N/Sm in restaurant **Children:** Menu, Portions **Directions:** 10m from Taunton, 16m from Minehead on A358. M5 junct 25 **Parking:** 20 **web:** www.blueballinn.co.uk

WELLINGTON MAP 03 ST12
Bindon Country House Hotel & Restaurant
British
Accomplished cuisine in Baroque country retreat
☎ 01823 400070 Langford Budville TA21 0RU
MENU GUIDE Sauteéd Brixham scallops • Tournedos Rossini Blackberry & Bramley apple crumble with vanilla custard
WINE GUIDE ♀ Blue Ridge Sauvignon Blanc £24 • ♀ Bertrand Bergi Fitou £24 • 110 bottles over £20, 19 bottles under £20 6 by the glass (£4-£6.50)
PRICE GUIDE Fixed L fr £12.95 • coffee £2.50 • min/water £2.95 • Service optional
PLACE: Set in idyllic and tranquil grounds, with spectacular views down to the Blackdown Hills, this Grade II listed property is the perfect backdrop for the gracious and elegant Wellesley Restaurant. Service in the restaurant is formal, yet friendly, and very efficient.
FOOD: Accomplished British classical cooking dazzles the palate with imaginative combination of flavours. Dishes might include rolled Gressingham duck and foie gras terrine with apricot chutney, followed by roast native brill with braised wild rice,

continued

continued

WELLINGTON *continued* MAP 03 ST12

leeks and tarragon reduction, and baked mango cream with raspberry sorbet to finish.

OUR TIP: The terrace is great for summer dining
Chef: Mike Davis **Owners:** Lynn & Mark Jaffa **Times:** 12.30-2.30/7.30-9.30 **Notes:** Vegetarian available, Civ Wed 50 **Seats:** 50, Pr/dining room 29 **Smoking:** N/Sm in restaurant **Children:** Min 7 yrs, Menu, Portions **Rooms:** 12 (12 en suite) ★★★ **Directions:** From Wellington B3187 to Langville Budville, through village & right towards Wiveliscombe, right at junct, past Bindon Farm, right after 450 yds **Parking:** 30
e-mail: stay@bindon.com **web:** www.bindon.com

WELLS MAP 04 ST54

Swan Hotel

British **NEW**

Generous, imaginative dishes in traditional setting

☎ 01749 836300 Sadler St BA5 2RX

MENU GUIDE Smoked tuna • Marinated duck breast, duck sausage, butternut squash • Hot banana muffin, toffee ice cream

WINE GUIDE ⚲ Berri Estate Chardonnay £13.95 • ⚱ Berri Estate Merlot £13.95 • 25 bottles over £20, 17 bottles under £20 • 6 by the glass (£3.25-£5.25)

PRICE GUIDE Fixed L £14-£17.50 • Fixed D £25.50 • starter £6.50-£9.75 • main £18-£22 • dessert £6-£7 • coffee £2.50 • min/water £2.60 • Service optional

PLACE: Enjoy wonderful views of Wells Cathedral from this former 15th-century coaching inn. The oak-panelled interior is pleasingly traditional, from the interesting antiques to the smartly clothed tables.

FOOD: An imaginative mix of modern and traditional menu with international influences makes good use of local produce such as Somerset beef and West Country cheeses. Presentation may be modern, but there are some old fashioned country style portions.
OUR TIP: Enjoy alfresco dining on the terrace in summer
Chef: Paul Mingo-West **Owners:** Christopher Chapman **Times:** 12.30-2/7-9.45 **Notes:** Smart Dress, Civ Wed 70 **Seats:** 60, Pr/dining room 100 **Smoking:** N/Sm in restaurant **Children:** Menu, Portions
Directions: A39, A371, opp Cathedral **Parking:** 30
e-mail: swan@bhere.co.uk **web:** www.bhere.co.uk

WILLITON MAP 03 ST04

⚙⚙ *White House Hotel*

British, Mediterranean

Friendly family-run hotel

☎ 01984 632306 632777 Long St TA4 4QW

PLACE: A relaxed atmosphere is the hallmark of this charming little Georgian hotel run by husband and wife team, Richard and Kay Smith. The restaurant has a warm and unpretentious feel, decorated in autumnal shades with exposed stone walls and wooden tables.

FOOD: Handwritten menus offer a concise but tempting range of dishes, notable for their use of fresh local produce. Typical mains might include pan-fried guinea fowl supreme with caramelised apples, or lamb with a roasted garlic and crème fraîche sauce.
OUR TIP: Interesting and good value wine list
Chef: Dick & Kay Smith **Owners:** Dick & Kay Smith **Times:** 7.30-9, Closed early Nov-mid May **Notes:** Seats: 26 **Smoking:** N/Sm in restaurant **Children:** Portions **Rooms:** 10 (9 en suite) ★★
Directions: On A39 in centre of village **Parking:** 14

WINCANTON MAP 04 ST72

⚙⚙ *Holbrook House Hotel*

Modern British

A lovely place to eat serious food

☎ 01963 824466 Holbrook BA9 8BS

MENU GUIDE Crisp salt cod beignets, watercress velouté • Beef fillet, Marsala jus • Dark chocolate & pear tartlet, chilli vodka sorbet

PRICE GUIDE Food prices not confirmed for 2006. Please telephone for details

PLACE: Wooded grounds and beautifully manicured gardens provide the peaceful and secluded setting for this handsome country house hotel. Retreat here for the excellent leisure facilities or for high levels of quality, comfort and the friendly atmosphere to be found within the lovely interior. There are gracious lounges with open fires and deep sofas, and an attractive, quite formal restaurant.

FOOD: An enthusiastic kitchen takes a serious approach to cooking innovative modern dishes. Impressive looking dishes are presented with a huge amount of care and attention to detail.
OUR TIP: Lovely gardens!
Times: 12.30-2/7-9, Closed L Sat, closed D Sun **Rooms:** 21 (21 en suite) ★★★ **Directions:** From A303 at Wincanton, turn left on A371 towards Castle Cary & Shepton Mallet **e-mail:** reception@holbrookhouse.co.uk **web:** www.holbrookhouse.co.uk

WINSFORD MAP 03 SS93

⚙ Karslake House

British

Country house hospitality with home cooking

☎ 01643 851242 Halse Ln TA24 7JE

MENU GUIDE Tart of Exmoor blue cheese & caramelised onion • Fillet of Brixham cod, sweet potato mash • Warm chocolate mousse

continue

England

WINE GUIDE ♀ Mâcon Uchizy Chardonnay £15.25 • ♀ Los Vascos Cabernet Sauvignon £16.50 • 10 bottles over £20, 21 bottles under £20 • 2 by the glass (£4.40-£4.80)

PRICE GUIDE Fixed D £29.50 • coffee £2.50 • min/water £1.95 • Service optional

PLACE: This listed building, originally a 15th-century malt house, has had a sympathetic conversion and decoration with preserved oak beams and an informal country house feel. Tables are beautifully set, complete with white linen and fresh flowers from the garden. Non-residents by reservation.

FOOD: The carte of three starters and three main courses is changed daily, with fresh vegetables and specials being added according to season.

OUR TIP: Special touches for special occasions

Chef: Juliette Mountford **Owners:** Mr & Mrs F.N.G. Mountford **Times:** 7.30-8.30, Closed Nov-Apr, closed D Sun-Thu (ex residents) **Notes:** Vegetarian by request only **Seats:** 18 **Smoking:** N/Sm in restaurant **Children:** Min 12yrs **Rooms:** 6 (5 en suite) ♦♦♦♦ **Directions:** A396 to Winsford. Then left up the hill **Parking:** 12 **e-mail:** enquiries@karslakehouse.co.uk **web:** www.karslakehouse.co.uk

WITHYPOOL MAP 03 SS83

🍺 Royal Oak Inn
British, International

Renowned Exmoor sporting inn with stylish dining room

☎ 01643 831506 TA24 7QP

MENU GUIDE Smoked salmon, creamed horseradish • Confit lamb shoulder, rosemary jus • Spiced apple crumble, crème anglaise

WINE GUIDE ♀ Chardonnay £11.95 • ♀ Shiraz/Cabernet Sauvignon £11.95 • 13 bottles over £20, 24 bottles under £20 • 20 by the glass (£2.85-£6)

PRICE GUIDE Fixed L £8.95-£12.95 • starter £3.75-£6 • main £7.95-£16 • dessert £3-£5 • coffee £1.25 • min/water £2.50 • Service optional

PLACE: A stylish, friendly and thoroughly laid-back country inn, well beloved of hunting and shooting parties, that has provided moorland travellers with food, drink and shelter for 300 years. There's a choice of bars, complete with beams and crackling log fires, and the strikingly decorated Acorn Restaurant is the venue for accomplished modern cuisine.

FOOD: The interesting, well-balanced carte offers a mix of traditional British and French cooking with a modern twist underpinned by fresh local produce.

OUR TIP: An ideal base for outdoor pursuits

continued

Chef: Steve Cox/Lorna Fisher **Owners:** Coast & Country Inns **Times:** 12-2/6.30-9.30 **Notes:** Vegetarian available **Seats:** 32, Pr/dining room 32 **Smoking:** N/Sm in restaurant **Children:** Portions **Rooms:** 8 (7 en suite) ★★ **Directions:** A361 via S Molton, N Molton to Withypool. M5 junct 25, take A358 then B3224 to Withypool **Parking:** 20 **e-mail:** roy.bookings@ccinns.com **web:** www.ccinns.com

YEOVIL MAP 04 ST51

⚙ Helyar Arms
British

Charming inn offering menus featuring local produce

☎ 01935 862332 Moor Ln, East Coker BA22 9JR

MENU GUIDE Soused herring fillets • Coq au vin • Hot Valrhona chocolate fondant

WINE GUIDE ♀ Masi Blend £11.50 • ♀ De Bortoli Cabernet Sauvignon/Shiraz £11.50 • 14 bottles over £20, 18 bottles under £20 • 30 by the glass (£2.95-£13.50)

PRICE GUIDE Starter £4-£7 • main £8-£18 • dessert £4-£7 coffee £2 • min/water £1.50 • Service optional

PLACE: A 15th-century inn set in a south Somerset village of chocolate box thatched roofs and mellow stone. The Apple Loft restaurant meets all the criteria for the enjoyment of good food in picturesque surroundings.

FOOD: The menu combines classic pub favourites, modern European cooking and a hint of the exotic. Local suppliers are proudly named and praised, including cheese, meat, fish, wine and breads, indicative of a kitchen producing real food, carefully thought through from preparation to plate.

OUR TIP: Children's menu included

Chef: Mathieu Eke **Owners:** Ian McKerracher **Times:** 12-2.30/6.30-9.30, Closed 25 Dec, closed D Sun (Jan-Easter) **Notes:** Vegetarian available **Seats:** 55, Pr/dining room 40 **Smoking:** N/Sm area **Children:** Menu, Portions **Rooms:** 6 (6 en suite) ♦♦♦♦ **Directions:** 3m from Yeovil. Take A37 or A30. Follow signs for East Coker. Helyar Arms is 50 mtrs from church **Parking:** 30 **e-mail:** info@helyar-arms.com **web:** www.helyar-arms.com

⚛⚛⚛ Little Barwick House Ltd
see page 424

 denotes restaurants that place particular emphasis on making the most of local ingredients.

NEW
denotes a restaurant which is new to the guide this year.

 denotes a restaurant with a particularly good wine list.

England

Little Barwick House Ltd

British, French

Exquisite cooking and bedrooms to match

☎ 01935 423902 Barwick Village BA22 9TD

MENU GUIDE Twice-baked cheese soufflé • Pink sea bream, ratatouille, langoustine sauté • Calvados pannacotta, dark chocolate ice cream

WINE GUIDE ⚲ Blue Ridge Sauvignon £18.75 • ♀ Excelsior Shiraz £17.95 • 128 bottles over £20, 28 bottles under £20 6 by the glass (£4.50-£7)

PRICE GUIDE Fixed L £16.95 • Fixed D £32.95 • starter £6.95-£14.50 • main £18.50-£24 • dessert £5.50-£7.50 • coffee £2.95 • min/water £3.25 • Service optional

PLACE: On the edge of a peaceful hamlet just a few miles from Yeovil, this listed Georgian dower house is run as a restaurant with rooms by an accomplished young husband and wife team. It blends the unstuffy friendliness of a private home with all the facilities of a modern hotel and has a strong following both among celebrating locals, and weekending Londoners looking for

a romantic retreat in the Somerset countryside. Take an aperitif in the comfortable lounge, and then move through to the elegant dining room, recently refurbished in restrained style and decorated with fresh flowers and watercolours.
FOOD: Enjoyable and accomplished cooking teamed with a tempting and impressive wine list designed to suit all budgets. Modern British dishes are the order of the day, featuring tried and tested combinations such as rump of lamb with asparagus and rosemary jus, or beef with wild mushrooms and a red wine sauce.
OUR TIP: Explore one of the many nearby walking paths
Chef: Timothy Ford **Owners:** Emma & Timothy Ford **Times:** 12-2/7-9.30, Closed New Year, 2wks Jan, Mon, closed L Tues, closed D Sun
Notes: Vegetarian available **Seats:** 40 **Smoking:** N/Sm in restaurant, Air con **Children:** Min 5 yrs, Portions **Rooms:** 6 (6 en suite) ★
Directions: Turn off A371 Yeovil to Dorchester opp Red House rdbt, 0.25m on left **Parking:** 25 **e-mail:** reservations@barwick7.fsnet.co.uk
web: www.littlebarwickhouse.co.uk

---

⑧⑧ Yeovil Court Hotel Limited

British, European

Contemporary dining in relaxed atmosphere

☎ 01935 863746 West Coker Rd BA20 2HE

MENU GUIDE Open wood pigeon pie with baby onions, celeriac & spinach • Grilled wing of skate, mussel butter sauce • Hot raised apple pie

WINE GUIDE ⚲ Montes Sauvignon Blanc £13.75 • ♀ Old Station Zinfandel £11.50 • 18 bottles over £20, 45 bottles under £20 8 by the glass (£2-£4.50)

PRICE GUIDE Fixed L £11.95 • starter £3.75-£6.50 • main £10.95-£18 • dessert £4.25-£5.50 • coffee £2.50 • min/water £2.50 • Service optional

PLACE: Unstuffy, friendly and efficient dining is the order of the day in this smart but unpretentious hotel on the edge of town, popular with both business guests and non-resident diners. The dining room is contemporary, comfortable and attractively decorated.
FOOD: A newly appointed and innovative chef produces an exciting menu with some well chosen combinations. There are a number of traditional dishes that are successfully given a contemporary twist. Local, seasonal produce is well represented
OUR TIP: Great cheese board
Chef: Lincoln Jones **Owners:** Brian & Carol Devonport **Times:** 12-1.45/7-9.30, Closed 24 Dec, 26-28 Dec, 1-2 Jan, closed L Sat
Notes: Vegetarian available **Seats:** 50, Pr/dining room 70
Smoking: N/Sm in restaurant **Children:** Portions **Rooms:** 30 (30 en suite) ★★★ **Directions:** On A30, 2.5m W of town centre **Parking:** 6
e-mail: unwind@yeovilhotel.com **web:** www.yeovilhotel.com

Two Rosettes The best local restaurants which aim for and achieve higher standards, better consistency and where a greater precision is apparent in the cooking. There will be obvious attention to the selection of quality ingredients. About 40% of restaurants in the guide have two Rosettes.

continued

STAFFORDSHIRE

URTON UPON TRENT MAP 10 SK22

⑨ Meynell and Deer Park estaurant

ternational

ood country pub atmosphere - worth a detour

☎ 01283 575202 Hoar Cross DE13 8RB

ENU GUIDE Roast pigeon breast, niçoise salad • Herb crusted alibut fillet, spinach & shallot linguine • Passionfruit delice

INE GUIDE ⚲ Ladera Verde Sauvignon Blanc 12.50 • 🍷 Ladera Verde Merlot £12.50 • 4 bottles over £20, 3 bottles under £20 • 4 by the glass (£2.95-£4.50)

RICE GUIDE Fixed L £12-£17 • Fixed D £15-£22.95 • starter 5.50-£8 • main £11.50-£18.95 • dessert £4.95-£5.75 • coffee 1.75 • min/water £3 • Service optional

ACE: Good looking brick-built country inn in a very rural ting. It has a typical pub interior with exposed beams in veral rooms, oak floors, open fires, polished tables and lots of dded benches.

OD: The good-value food is an obvious attraction here. The ekly changing International menu runs through the bar and taurant. Dishes, slightly rustic in style, are based on produce m local suppliers.

IR TIP: Real ales served at the bar

ef: Tony Holland **Owners:** Mike and Jane Chappell **Times:** 12-0/7-9.30, closed D Sun **Notes:** Theme nights £17.50, Vegetarian ilable, Dress Restrictions, Smart casual **Seats:** 30, Pr/dining room 44 **oking:** N/Sm in restaurant **Children:** Portions **Directions:** 7m W of ton on Trent, 2 minute drive off the A515 main road between Lichfield the A50 **Parking:** 50 **e-mail:** themeynell@btopenworld.com

HEADLE MAP 10 SK04

⑨ Thornbury Hall Rasoi

itish, Indian

vard-winning Pakistani restaurant in historic untry house

☎ 01538 750831 Lockwood Rd ST10 2DH **ENU GUIDE** Vegetable samosa • Karhai rogan josh • Pistachio lfi

INE GUIDE ⚲ Carmen Reserve Chardonnay £12.50 🍷 Marques de Crianza - Rioja £15.35 • 4 bottles over £20, 5 bottles under £20 • 3 by the glass (£2-£2.20)

PRICE GUIDE Fixed L £9-£12 • Fixed D £10-£13 • starter £2-£4 main £5.90-£12.99 • dessert £2-£3 • coffee £1.50 • min/water £2 • Service optional

PLACE: There's a lively buzz at this unusual set-up, an authentic Pakistani restaurant in a Georgian hall with Tudor origins. Rich red and gold wallpaper warms the long room, and staff are cool in black and white.

FOOD: Choose from over 60 dishes on the menu, where a mixture of the familiar and the less well known is carefully cooked and well presented, along with poppadoms, hot towels and a refreshing orange.

OUR TIP: Set in beautiful countryside

Chef: Nir D Vassaramo **Owners:** Mr & Mrs Siddique **Times:** 12-2/6-10 **Notes:** Vegetarian available, Smart Dress, Civ Wed 40 **Seats:** 60, Pr/dining room 60 **Smoking:** N/Sm in restaurant **Children:** Menu, Portions **Directions:** 7m from Stoke-on-Trent **Parking:** 80 **e-mail:** info@thornburyhall.com **web:** www.thornburyhall.com

LEEK MAP 16 SJ95

⑧ Number 64

British

Refined cooking in charming Georgian townhouse

☎ 01538 381900 64 St Edwards St ST13 5DL

MENU GUIDE Smoked bacon & thyme risotto • Pork fillet, chasseur sauce • Apricot & almond tart

WINE GUIDE ⚲ Domaine du Gouyat Sauvignon Blanc £11.95 • 🍷 Cruz Del Castillo Rioja £11.45 • 8 bottles over £20, 24 bottles under £20 • 10 by the glass (£2.35-£2.95)

PRICE GUIDE Fixed L fr £15 • Fixed D £20-£30 • starter £4.75-£8.50 • main £10-£22.50 • dessert £4.50-£6 • coffee £2.50 min/water £1.50 • Service optional

PLACE: The well-proportioned room with full-length windows and polished wooden floor makes for a relaxed restaurant, while this Georgian townhouse also boasts a cellar wine bar and upstairs coffee lounge.

FOOD: A sophisticated choice includes a signature menu with a glass of wine for each course, and an imaginative carte detailing beautifully-presented regional and seasonal cuisine like carpaccio of venison with red onion marmalade, and noisettes of salt marsh lamb.

OUR TIP: Impossible to park outside - nearby car park

Chef: Paul Owens **Owners:** Nigel Cope **Times:** 12-2.30/7-9, Closed D Sun **Notes:** Vegetarian available, Smart casual, Civ Wed 50 **Seats:** 35, Pr/dining room 14 **Smoking:** N/Sm in restaurant, Air con **Children:** Portions **Rooms:** 3 (3 en suite) 🏨 **Directions:** In town centre near junct of A520 and A53, at bottom of hill **Parking:** Parking available 50 mtrs away **e-mail:** enquiries@number64.com **web:** www.number64.com

continued

LEEK *continued* MAP 16 SJ95

Three Horseshoes Inn
International

Pretty inn serving exciting international cuisine

☎ 01538 300296 Buxton Rd, Blackshaw Moor ST13 8TW

MENU GUIDE Crab cakes, noodle salad • Stir fry of beef fillet on fragrant Thai rice • Iced nougatine, toffee sauce

PRICE GUIDE Food prices not confirmed for 2006. Please telephone for details

PLACE: This family-owned farmhouse inn stands in its own large garden complete with play area. The restaurant has superb views and is decorated in brasserie style with stripped wood floors and bare tables. In the evenings the atmosphere is enhanced by candlelight and romantic music.

FOOD: Expect fresh ingredients and flavours from around the world. The chef demonstrates a good grasp of far eastern cooking techniques. Traditional food is available in the adjoining carvery.

OUR TIP: There is a dinner dance most Saturdays

Times: 12-2/6.30-9, Closed 26 Dec-30 Dec, closed L Mon-Sat **Rooms:** 6 (6 en suite) ★★ **Directions:** M6 J15 or 16 onto A500. Exit A53 towards Leek. Turn left onto A50 (Burslem) **e-mail:** mark@threeshoesinn.co.uk **web:** www.threeshoesinn.co.uk

Greystones 17th Century Stockwell St ST13 6DH
☎ 01538 398522 Winner of The Tea Guild Award of Excellence 2005.

LICHFIELD MAP 10 SK10

Bratz
Modern European

Modern cuisine with lovely views

☎ 01543 253788 Minster House, Pool Walk WS13 6QT

MENU GUIDE Warm crab tartlet, herb salad • Grilled calves' liver, Puy lentils & crispy ham • Raspberry crème brûlée

PRICE GUIDE Food prices not confirmed for 2006. Please telephone for details

PLACE: Sweeping views over Minster Pool and the cathedral give a sense of space to the crooked staircases and low ceilings of this Georgian minster house. Upstairs has a light, airy feel with contemporary decor, and service is notably friendly.

FOOD: The international-influenced menu offers an elegant blend of the traditional and modern with a European edge. Appealing dishes include ham hock terrine with gruyère, or roast smoked haddock with coriander and mussel velouté.

OUR TIP: Book a table by the window

Times: 12-2/7-10, Closed Mon, closed L Tue-Sat, closed D Sun, Mon **Directions:** City centre. Please phone for further directions. **web:** www.bratzrestaurant.co.uk

The Four Seasons Restaurant
European

Impressive mansion and proficient cooking

☎ 01543 481494 Swinfen Hall Hotel, Swinfen WS14 9RE

MENU GUIDE Pan-fried John Dory • Loin of Cornish lamb • Banana tarte Tatin

WINE GUIDE ♀ Fournier Verdigny Vielles Vignes Sancerre Sauvignon Blanc £26 • ♀ Bodegas Artesanas Campo Viejo Gran Reserva £32 • 73 bottles over £20, 3 bottles under £20 • 7 by the glass (£5.95)

PRICE GUIDE Fixed L £14.95 • Fixed D £39.50 • coffee £3.50 • Service optional

PLACE: Swinfen Hall is an imposing mansion with spacious, elegant rooms that overlook the equally striking gardens. A superb restoration has resulted in sumptuous decorations including ornate frescoes and plasterwork. The tasteful split-level restaurant is a calm and elegant oasis.

FOOD: The cooking is as accomplished as the surroundings warrant, with the fixed-price menu demonstrating advanced skill. A strong initial impression from the beautifully-presented food is borne out by an interesting use of flavours, with a starter of roasted foie gras ravioli and sautéed sweetbreads suggesting the delights to follow.

OUR TIP: Ideal for a romantic evening

Chef: Neil Peers **Owners:** Helen & Vic Wiser **Times:** 12.30-2.30/7-9.30, Closed L Sat, closed D Sun **Notes:** Sun L £23.50-£29.50, Vegetarian available, Dress Restrictions, No trainers or jeans, Civ Wed 120 **Seats:** 50 Pr/dining room 20 **Children:** Portions **Rooms:** 19 (19 en suite) ★★★★ **Directions:** 2m S of Lichfield on A38 between Weeford rdbt and Swinfen rdbt. Follow A38 to Lichfield, hotel is 0.5m on right **Parking:** 80 **e-mail:** info@swinfenhallhotel.co.uk **web:** www.swinfenhallhotel.co.uk

Chandlers Corn Exchange Buildings, Conduit St WS13 6JU
☎ 01543 416688 Large brasserie with modern British menu.

RUGELEY MAP 10 SK01

The Plum Pudding Brasserie
Mediterannean

Canal-side dining in this cheerful brasserie

☎ 01543 490330 Rugeley Rd, Armitage WS15 4AZ

MENU GUIDE Scallops, fondant potatoes, lemon dressing • Staffordshire beef, shallot & shitake jus • Sticky toffee pudding, pecan ice

WINE GUIDE ♀ Lizard Point Chardonnay £11.95 • ♥ Logan Rock Shiraz £9.95 • 7 bottles over £20, 29 bottles under £20 by the glass (£2.60-£4.75)

PRICE GUIDE Fixed L £12 • Fixed D £15 • starter £3.95-£6.25 • main £8.95-£16.55 • dessert £4.75 • coffee £1.50 • min/water £1.90 • Service optional

PLACE: Converted pub on the Trent and Merseyside Canal, with bright red walls, colourful prints, and part pine panelling in the bar and lounge area. A lot of boaters stop by for a meal and enjoy the friendly and relaxed atmosphere.
FOOD: The brasserie menu lists a good choice of bistro/gastro-style dishes including some with Mediterranean influences. The lunch menu offers doorstep sandwiches, salads and larger plates.
OUR TIP: Take a stroll along the canal before or after dining
Chef: Richard Light **Owners:** Mr & Mrs J Takhar **Times:** 12-3.30/6-11.30, Closed 1 Jan **Notes:** Vegetarian available, Smart Dress **Seats:** 70 Smoking: N/Sm in restaurant **Children:** Portions **Rooms:** 4 (4 en suite) ♦♦♦♦ **Directions:** M6 junct 11 follow signs for Cannock to Rugeley. Situated on A513 through Rugeley to Lichfield **Parking:** 50
e-mail: enquiries@theplumpudding.co.uk
web: www.theplumpudding.co.uk

STAFFORD MAP 10 SJ92

Moat House
British, Mediterranean

Conservatory dining in canal-side hotel

☎ 01785 712217 Lower Penkridge Rd, Acton Trussell ST17 0RJ

MENU GUIDE Foie gras terrine, port, figs, brioche • Rosette of beef, Madeira truffle sauce • Chocolate fondant, white chocolate sorbet

WINE GUIDE ♀ Marlborough Silverlake Sauvignon Blanc £15.95 • ♥ Pelican Cove Shiraz £15.95 • 49 bottles over £20, 5 bottles under £20 •

PRICE GUIDE Fixed L £10 • starter £5.95-£8.50 • main £18-£21 • dessert £6-£7 • coffee £2.95 • min/water £4.50

PLACE: Busy hotel occupying a 15th-century Grade II listed property - a moated former manor house - with a striking canal-side setting. The main building is full of oak panelling and

Moat House

exposed beams, while the conservatory restaurant is light and airy with great views of the Staffordshire and Worcestershire Canal.
FOOD: Quality produce is sourced locally where possible and the classically based menu benefits from a sense of flair and adventure. Mediterranean influences are also evident. A separate vegetarian menu is available.
OUR TIP: For a lighter meal, there's a good bar menu
Chef: Matthew Davies **Owners:** The Lewis Partnership **Times:** 12-2/7-9.30, Closed 25 Dec, 1-2 Jan **Notes:** Tasting menu 7 courses £39.50, Sun D 5 courses £37.50, Vegetarian available, No jeans, Civ Wed 120 Seats: 120, Pr/dining room 150 **Smoking:** N/Sm in restaurant, Air con **Children:** Menu, Portions **Rooms:** 32 (32 en suite) ★★★★ **Directions:** M6 junct 13 towards Stafford, 1st right to Acton Trussell, hotel by church **Parking:** 200 **e-mail:** info@moathouse.co.uk
web: www.moathouse.co.uk

The Swan Hotel
British   **NEW**

Innovative cooking in smartly renovated hotel

☎ 01785 258142 46 Greengate St ST16 2JA

MENU GUIDE Smoked salmon, creamed guacamole • Pan-fried mackerel, baby spinach • Rich chocolate truffle

WINE GUIDE ♀ Logan Rock Chardonnay £9.95 • ♥ Logan Rock Shiraz £9.95 • 8 bottles over £20, 29 bottles under £20 • 15 by the glass (£3.45-£4.75)

PRICE GUIDE Fixed L £5-£10 • starter £3.75-£6.50 • main £8.50-£31 • dessert £3.95-£4.75 • Service optional

PLACE: This timber-framed old coaching inn was virtually derelict before being rescued and transformed into a premier dining venue. The split-level brasserie is smart, contemporary and welcoming.
FOOD: An innovative cooking style that relies as much as possible on quality Staffordshire produce has proved a winner here. Good clear flavours in dishes like seared sea bass fillets with cherry tomato sauce show the depth of skill and accuracy.
OUR TIP: Check out the daily specials
Chef: Mark Williams **Owners:** Chris Lewis **Times:** 12-2.30/5.30-10, Closed 25-26 Dec **Notes:** Vegetarian available **Seats:** 80 **Smoking:** N/Sm in restaurant, Air con **Children:** Menu, Portions **Rooms:** 27 (27 en suite) ★★★ **Directions:** M6 junct 13//14 then to town. Follow signs to rail station, turn right after station at mini rdbt. 1st left into Water St. Hotel on left. (Access via Mill St) **Parking:** 30 **e-mail:** info@theswanstafford.co.uk
web: www.theswanstafford.co.uk

continued

England

STOKE-ON-TRENT MAP 10 SJ84

The Elms, Passion of India

Indian

Indian restaurant offering healthy options

☎ 01782 266360 Snowhill, Shelton ST1 4LY

MENU GUIDE Murg malai tikka • Chicken tawa • Gajja ka halva

WINE GUIDE 8 bottles over £20, 15 bottles under £20 • 2 by the glass (£3.25)

PRICE GUIDE Fixed D £20-£30 • starter £4.50-£14.99 • main £8.25-£13.95 • dessert £3.95-£4.25 • coffee £1.80 • min/water £3.65 • Service optional

PLACE: Once home to famous pottery manufacturer John Ridgway, and a pub in Victorian times. Now tastefully converted to an upmarket Indian restaurant, its status is reflected in gold cornices, crisp linen and rich wall coverings. Lots of smiles and enthusiastic exchanges between kitchen and table.
FOOD: Authentic Ayurvedic dishes are the hallmark, with plenty of advice for novices. This holistic approach leads to health-promoting balanced combinations. Everything is freshly made, with spices ground to order.
OUR TIP: You can try something unusual with confidence
Chef: Sanjeev Kumar, Harish Kumar **Owners:** Pritpal Singh Nagi
Times: 6-11.30, Closed 25 Dec, Sun, closed L Mon-Sat, closed D Sun
Notes: Vegetarian available, Smart Dress **Seats:** 120, Pr/dining room 30
Smoking: N/Sm in restaurant **Children:** Portions
Directions: Telephone for directions **Parking:** 80

Haydon House Hotel

British, European

Modern cooking in a Victorian ambience

☎ 01782 711311 Haydon St, Basford ST4 6JD

MENU GUIDE Butterflied king prawns • Fillet of pork Marsala • Sticky toffee pudding

WINE GUIDE 3 by the glass (£2.40-£3.40)

PRICE GUIDE Fixed D £17.50 • starter £4.20-£7.95 • coffee £1.95 • min/water £3.50 • Service included

PLACE: Heavy drapes, chinzy table settings and evening candlelight characterise the Victorian Town House restaurant in this family-run hotel. Formally-dressed staff preside.
FOOD: The British cooking is popular locally, with a simple format and generous portions proving popular. Choose between a reasonably priced set menu and a lengthier carte, the latter including flambéed dishes prepared at your table. All dishes are prepared to order.
OUR TIP: Wine list helpfully listed by type
Chef: Michael Spink **Owners:** Mr J F Machin **Times:** 12-1.30/7-9.30, Closed L Sat & Sun **Notes:** Vegetarian available, Civ Wed 80 **Seats:** 45, Pr/dining room 20 **Smoking:** N/Sm in restaurant **Children:** Menu, Portions **Rooms:** 23 (23 en suite) ★★★ **Directions:** From M6 junct 15 to Stoke-on-Trent, then A53 signed Hanley/Newcastle. At rdbt take 1st exit, up hill, 2nd on left at top. (St before traffic lights) **Parking:** 50
e-mail: enquiries@haydon-house-hotel.co.uk
web: www.haydon-house-hotel.co.uk

UTTOXETER MAP 10 SK03

 Restaurant Gilmore at Strine's Farm

British

Converted farmhouse and confident cooking

☎ 01889 507100 Beamhurst ST14 5DZ

continued

MENU GUIDE Ham hock & goats' cheese terrine • Poached blade of beef • Bread & butter pudding, sauce Anglaise

WINE GUIDE ♀ Sunshine Bay Sauvignon Blanc £22.50 • ♀ Navajas Rioja Tinto £14.50 • 35 bottles over £20, 20 bottles under £20 • 4 by the glass (£3.75)

PRICE GUIDE Fixed L £15 • Fixed D £30 • coffee £3 • min/water £3.75 • Service optional • Group min 8 service 10%

PLACE: Individual dining rooms with their own personalities - an inglenook fireplace in one, a huge Welsh dresser in another - characterise this converted farmhouse filled with elegant antiques.
FOOD: A confident menu highlights true home cooking from the breads to the ice creams, and terrific ingredients are sensitively handled throughout the short lunch and longer dinner choices. Lemon and olive risotto with pan-fried sole typically exceeds expectations.
OUR TIP: Book for weekends, lunch & dinner
Chef: Paul Gilmore **Owners:** Paul & Dee Gilmore **Times:** 12.30-2/7.30-9, Closed 2 wks Aug, 1 wk Easter, 1 wk Jan, Mon, closed L Sat & Tue, closed D Sun **Notes:** Sun L 3 courses incl coffee £21, Vegetarian available, Dress Restrictions, Smart casual **Seats:** 24 **Smoking:** N/Sm in restaurant **Children:** Portions **Directions:** 1.5m N of Uttoxeter on A522 to Cheadle. Set 400yds back from the road along a fenced farm track **Parking:** 12
e-mail: paul@restaurantgilmore.com **web:** www.restaurantgilmore.com

SUFFOLK

ALDEBURGH MAP 13 TM45

152 Aldeburgh

Modern European

Well-tuned cooking in popular resort

☎ 01728 454594 152 High St IP15 5AX

celebrating great food

MENU GUIDE Skate & leek terrine • Pot roasted quail, red cabbage, parsnip purée • Classic peach Melba

WINE GUIDE ♀ Casa Rivas Chardonnay £11.75 • ♀ Casa Rivas Cabernet Sauvignon £11.75 • 12 bottles over £20, 31 bottles under £20 • 8 by the glass (£2.75-£6.65)

PRICE GUIDE Fixed L £13 • Fixed D £16 • starter £4.95-£9.50 • main £10.50-£18 • dessert £4-£5 • coffee £1.80 • min/water £2.50 • Service included

PLACE: A light space reflecting the huge Suffolk sky brings minimalism to this busy resort's High Street, close to the beach. Lots of fresh flowers add their own beauty, and stand out against pale walls and stripped wooden floors.
FOOD: Top quality fish landed locally mingles with game in season, meats like braised lamb shank or venison sausage, and vegetarian dishes that all receive the same relaxed treatment. Clear flavours abound.

continued

England

UR TIP: Several good value eating options available
hef: Garry Cook **Owners:** Garry Cook / Andrew Lister **Times:** 12-3/
10 **Notes:** Petits fours only at dinner, Vegetarian available **Seats:** 56
moking: N/Sm in restaurant **Children:** Portions **Parking:** On-street
arking on High St & Kings St **e-mail:** info@152aldeburgh.co.uk
eb: www.152aldeburgh.co.uk

The Brudenell

ritish, International
elaxed brasserie dining with lovely
each views

☎ 01728 452071 The Parade IP15 5BU
MENU GUIDE Crab, dill mustard mayonnaise • Seafood
asserole, parsley & crab dumplings • Fresh strawberries
WINE GUIDE ♀ La Grange Grenache Chardonnay £12.90 • ♀ La
Grange Grenache Merlot £12.90 • 19 bottles over £20, 20 bottles
under £20 • 19 by the glass (£3.40-£6.50)
PRICE GUIDE Fixed D £22.50 • starter £3.75-£5.50 • main £7.50-
17.95 • dessert £4.95-£5.95 • coffee £2 • min/water
3.50 • Service optional
LACE: Overlooking the beach of this delightful Suffolk town, this
arming hotel enjoys wonderful views when the weather is
ood. The long, open plan bar/restaurant is light and
ontemporary in style with pastel shades and stripped wooden
bles with modern settings.
OOD: Modern British dishes predominate here with the
casional Mediterranean influence showing in seared scallops
th crispy pancetta, rocket and parmesan or toasted goats'
eese on croutons with roasted red pepper and pine nuts.
ere's very good use of the high quality seafood which is landed
ily here by local fishermen.
UR TIP: One step and you're on the beach
hef: Mark Clements **Owners:** Thorpeness & Aldeburgh Hotels Ltd
mes: 12-2.30/6-10 **Notes:** Vegetarian available, Smart casual **Seats:** 80
moking: N/Sm in restaurant **Children:** Menu, Portions **Rooms:** 42
2 en suite) ★★★ **Parking:** 15 **e-mail:** info@brudenellhotel.co.uk
eb: www.brudenellhotel.co.uk

Regatta Restaurant

ritish
reat seafood in seaside restaurant

☎ 01728 452011 171 High St IP15 5AN
MENU GUIDE Mediterranean fish soup • Whole sea bass with
hilli, coriander & lime • Crème brulée
PRICE GUIDE Food prices not confirmed for 2006. Please
elephone for details
LACE: Bistro-style restaurant with nautical murals paying tribute
Aldeburgh's maritime tradition. Casually dressed staff help to
eate a relaxed atmosphere.
OOD: This predominantly seafood and fresh fish menu strikes a
od balance between the classics and more adventurous cooking.
home-made gravadlax doesn't grab you for starters, try the
ared scallops on a carrot purée with smoked bacon and salad.
JR TIP: Good for families
mes: 12-2/6-10, Restricted opening in winter, Mon,Tue,Sun evening
ov-Mar), closed D Sun **Directions:** Middle of High Street, town centre
mail: regatta.restaurant@aldeburgh.sagegost.co.uk
eb: www.regattaaldeburgh.com

Wentworth Hotel

International
Elegant seaside hotel with busy restaurant
☎ 01728 452312 Wentworth Rd IP15 5BD

MENU GUIDE Duck liver pâté, poached plums • Fillet of black
bream, pancetta, olives & parsley dressing • Lemon syllabub,
red fruits
PRICE GUIDE Food prices not confirmed for 2006. Please
telephone for details
PLACE: This traditional-style hotel, run by the same family since
1920, is located at the quiet end of Aldeburgh looking out over
the beach. The restaurant, with burgundy drapes and wallpaper,
is intimate by candlelight and has views of the promenade and
fish sheds.
FOOD: Locally caught seafood is a feature of the menu and you
can see it being landed right opposite. Cooking is straightforward
and almost everything is made on the premises, including breads
and ice creams. The decent wine list includes some affordable
bottles, particularly the French house white.
OUR TIP: Not far from Snape Maltings
Times: 12-2/7-9, Closed 28 Dec-10 Jan **Rooms:** 35 (35 en suite) ★★★
Children: Menu, Portions **Rooms:** 42
Directions: From A12 take A1094 to Aldeburgh. In Aldeburgh straight on
at mini-rdbt, turn left at x-roads into Wentworth Rd. Hotel on right
e-mail: stay@wentworth-aldeburgh.co.uk
web: www.wentworth-aldeburgh.com

White Lion Hotel

British **NEW**
Popular seaside hotel with choice
of dining

☎ 01728 452720 Market Cross Place IP15 5BJ
MENU GUIDE Gravad lax, dill, fennel & rocket • Monkfish
medallions, mussels, champagne fricassee • Glazed lemon tart,
raspberry sorbet
WINE GUIDE ♀ Touraine Sauvignon Blanc £13.75 • ♀ Cande
Tree Shiraz/Cabernet Sauvignon £13.75 • 23 bottles over £20,
31 bottles under £20 • 18 by the glass (£3.50-£6.75)
PRICE GUIDE Fixed L £12.95 • Fixed D £13.50-£22.50 • starter
£4.25-£7.25 • main £8.95-£14.50 • dessert £4.25-
£5.95 • min/water £3.25 • Service optional
PLACE: Aldburgh's oldest hotel dates back to 1563 and is
situated at the quiet end of town overlooking the sea. Public
areas include two lounges and an oak-panelled restaurant, plus a
modern brasserie.
FOOD: There's a strong focus on fresh, locally caught fish and
other locally sourced items, such as Suffolk strawberries and
asparagus. The menu in the brasserie is more or less the same
but also offers fish and chips.

continued

ALDEBURGH continued MAP 13 TM45

OUR TIP: Pre-concert meals or late suppers during the festival and proms
Chef: Eleanor Richmond **Owners:** Thorpness and Aldeburgh Hotels Ltd.
Times: 12-2.30/6.30-9.30 **Notes:** Vegetarian available, Civ Wed 90
Seats: 60, Pr/dining room 50 **Smoking:** N/Sm in restaurant
Children: Menu, Portions **Rooms:** 38 (38 en suite) ★★★ **Parking:** 15
e-mail: whitelionaldeburgh@btinternet.com
web: www.whitelion.co.uk

BECCLES MAP 13 TM48

🕮 Swan House
British, International
Informal venue for good food with music and art
☎ 01502 713474 By The Tower NR34 9HE
MENU GUIDE Sautéed wild mushrooms • Pan-fried loin of venison • Pecan & honey tart
WINE GUIDE 9 bottles over £20, 42 bottles under £20 • 8 by the glass (£3-£6.50)
PRICE GUIDE Fixed L £14.90-£14.90 • Fixed D £20.50-£20.50 • starter £4.20-£6.50 • main £11.50-£19.50 • dessert £4.90-£5.50 • coffee £1.70 • min/water £2.50 • Service optional • Group min 8 service 10%

PLACE: Once a small coaching inn, this wine bar-style restaurant has scrubbed tables, wooden floors and log fires burning throughout the winter. Live musicians and modern art exhibitions feature, plus special events such as vegetarian and pudding nights.
FOOD: The menu gives helpful tips on wines to accompany chosen courses, and local suppliers are identified. Simple treatments of good quality produce are efficiently served in a relaxed atmosphere.
OUR TIP: Can get very busy at weekends
Chef: Jonathan Casewell **Owners:** M R Blunk, Ms L Dumphie
Times: 12-2.45/6.45-10.00, Closed 26 Dec, 1 Jan, 1 Jan, closed L 25 Dec, closed D 26 Dec **Notes:** Fixed L Sun only, Fixed D Tue/Thur, reserve 1 day in advance, Vegetarian available **Seats:** 40 **Smoking:** N/Sm in restaurant **Children:** Min 14yrs **Directions:** Next to church tower in Market Place **Parking:** On street & nearby car parks
e-mail: info@swan-house.com **web:** www.swan-house.com

BROME

🕮 The Snailmakers at Brome Grange
European
Good choice on a journey
☎ 01379 870456 IP23 8AP

MENU GUIDE Sautéed mussels & shallots, champagne • Rack of lamb, apricot & honey jus • Apple strudel

continued

WINE GUIDE ♀ Champs du Moulin Colombard/Chardonnay £12.95 • ♥ Champs du Moulin Syrah/Grenache £12.95 • 30 bottles over £20, 45 bottles under £20 • 8 by the glass (£3-£4)
PRICE GUIDE Fixed L £15-£25 • Fixed D £24.95-£34.95 • starter £4.95-£10 • main £14.95-£29.95 • dessert £5.95-£6.95 • coffee £1.50 • min/water £3.50

PLACE: The oddly entitled but smartly refurbished Snailmakers - named after a bronze statue by David Good - has the atmosphere of an old inn, with its rich burnt-red walls, oak panelling and tapestry-style fabrics to chairs.
FOOD: The carte offers abundant choice and good use of seasonal produce, specialising in locally-caught fish. Well-executed dishes might take in a whole lobster or baked fillet of halibut with sweet chilli sauce.
OUR TIP: Changing menu offers lots of choices
Chef: Alan Lunn, John Shead **Owners:** Paul A Meredew **Times:** 12-2.30/6.30-9.30 **Notes:** Sun L 2 courses £14.95, 3 courses £18.95, Vegetarian available, Smart Dress **Seats:** 34, Pr/dining room
Smoking: N/Sm in restaurant **Children:** Portions **Rooms:** 19 (19 en suite) ★★★ **Directions:** A12 take A140 towards Norwich, approx 20m on left **Parking:** 60 **e-mail:** bromegrange@fastnet.co.uk
web: www.bromegrange.co.uk

BUNGAY MAP 13 TM38

🕮 Earsham Street Café
British, Mediterranean
Simple modern fare in unpretentious café
☎ 01986 893103 11-13 Earsham St NR35 1AE

MENU GUIDE Sticky pork belly, mango, spring onion, cherry tomato salad • Halibut, pea & parmesan risotto • Plum & almond tart
WINE GUIDE ♀ Vanel Nobles Vignes Sauvignon Blanc £13.95 • ♥ Ernst Gouws Hoopenburg Merlot £14.50 • 36 bottle over £20, 18 bottles under £20 • 15 by the glass (£2.75-£8)
PRICE GUIDE Starter £3.50-£8 • main £6.25-£14 • dessert £2.20 £5.50 • coffee £1.20 • min/water £2.50 • Service optional

PLACE: Popular with locals and tourists alike, this buzzy little ca and restaurant has ambience a-plenty and a queue out the door Booking essential.
FOOD: Down-to-earth rustic cooking, in variable portion sizes to suit both café and restaurant guests. Dishes make sympathetic use of good quality ingredients and might include calves' liver with truffle mash, or a lobster and crayfish fricassée with fettuccine. Dinner parties and picnics catered for.
OUR TIP: The café also runs the deli next door
Chef: Stephen David, Christopher Rice **Owners:** Rebecca Mackenzie, Stephen David **Times:** 9.30-5/7-9, Closed Xmas, New Year, Sun, closed ex last Fri & Sat of month 7-9 **Notes:** Vegetarian available **Seats:** 55, Pr/dining room 16 **Smoking:** N/Sm in restaurant **Children:** Menu, Portions **Directions:** In the centre of Bungay **Parking:** Parking opposi
e-mail: www.earshamstcafe@aol.com

BURY ST EDMUNDS MAP 13 TL86

⊕⊕ Angel Hotel
British, European

Imposing hotel dining in perfect location on Angel Hill

☎ 01284 714000 Angel Hill IP33 1LT

MENU GUIDE Confit terrine of poultry livers • Aberdeen Angus beef, grain mustard crust, red wine sauce • Maple & pecan crème brûlée

WINE GUIDE ⌾ Sauvignon de Touraine £14.30 • ⚑ Livor Rioja £14.80 • 27 bottles over £20, 22 bottles under £20 • 21 by the glass (£3.20-£7.15)

PRICE GUIDE Fixed D £24.85-£40 • coffee £2.15 • min/water £3 • Service optional

PLACE: Impressive building situated a few minutes walk from the town centre in one of Britain's prettiest squares, with views across the cathedral. There have been some notable guests over the past 400 years, including Charles Dickens, reputed to have written part of the *Pickwick Papers* here. The restaurant is elegantly presented with neatly laid tables and classy tableware.
FOOD: Simple dishes made from quality ingredients. Examples are superb scallops, pan-seared and served with rocket, crispy lardons and a good Caesar salad; or a wonderfully rich hot chocolate fondant.
OUR TIP: Great range of fresh coffees
Chef: Simon Barker **Owners:** Robert Gough **Times:** 7-9.30, Closed L Mon-Sat **Notes:** Vegetarian available, Smart casual, Civ Wed 85 **Seats:** 50, Pr/dining room 85 **Smoking:** N/Sm in restaurant **Children:** Portions **Rooms:** 64 (64 en suite) ★★★ **Directions:** Town centre, right from Northgate St traffic lights **Parking:** 30
e-mail: sales@theangel.co.uk
web: www.theangel.co.uk

⊕ Clarice House
Modern European   NEW

Upmarket health & beauty spa with tempting food

☎ 01284 705550 Horringer Court, Horringer Rd P29 5PH

MENU GUIDE Smoked salmon & lobster terrine • Nage of seafood with star anise • Maple & walnut tart

WINE GUIDE ⌾ Dolmen De Fees Sauvignon Blanc 2003 £12 • ⚑ Dolmen De Fees Merlot 2002 £12 • 6 bottles over £20, 22 bottles under £20 • 4 by the glass (£2-£3)

PRICE GUIDE Fixed L £14.95 • Fixed D £21.95 • main £4.50-£13.95 • dessert £3.95 • coffee £1.50 • min/water £3 • Service optional

PLACE: A residential health spa in a superb country house set in peaceful grounds. The oak-panelled restaurant is spacious and relaxing, with intimate table settings.
FOOD: Healthy diets are seriously catered for, but it's not all carrot juice and steamed rice, and there's a decent wine list. Expect sliced duck breast marinated in orange with salad leaves, and pork tenderloin baked in pastry with spinach and puréed longroise potatoes.
OUR TIP: Fantastic range of health and beauty treatments
Chef: Steve Winser **Owners:** King Family **Times:** 11-3/6-11, Closed Xmas, Boxing Day, New Year's Day **Notes:** Vegetarian available, Smart dress, for dinner **Seats:** 40 **Smoking:** N/Sm in restaurant **Rooms:** 13 (13 en suite) ♦♦♦♦ **Directions:** On A143 towards Horringer and Haverhill, hotel 1m from town centre on right **Parking:** 82
e-mail: enquiry@clarice-bury.fsnet.co.uk **web:** www.clarice.co.uk

⊕ The Leaping Hare Restaurant & Country Store
British

Bistro in ancient barn with distinctive seasonal food and home-grown wines

☎ 01359 250287 Stanton IP31 2DW

MENU GUIDE Seared scallops, citrus oil • Cannon of Suffolk lamb • Glazed lemon tart

WINE GUIDE ⌾ Wyken Bacchus £16.50 • ⚑ Wyken Triomphe D'Alsace £16.50 • 13 bottles over £20, 12 bottles under £20 6 by the glass (£3.50-£4.95)

PRICE GUIDE Starter £4.75-£8.95 • main £11.95-£16.95 • dessert £4.50-£4.95 • coffee £1.75 • min/water £2.95 • Service optional • Group min 6 service 10%

PLACE: A magnificent 400-year-old barn is home to this relaxed bistro style restaurant. There are wood-burning stoves to keep things cosy, and wonderful beams, while lofty ceilings and large windows give the conversion an airy feel.
FOOD: Accomplished cooking using organic local ingredients: the weekly farmers' market supplies organic eggs, local cheeses and seasonal vegetables, and all meat is reared in Suffolk or Norfolk. Award-winning wine comes from the Wyken Estate vineyard next door.
OUR TIP: Take a wander around the Wyken Hall gardens
Chef: Nicholas Claxton-Webb **Owners:** Kenneth & Carla Carlisle **Times:** 12-2.30/7-9, Closed 2 wks Xmas, closed D Sun-Thu **Notes:** Vegetarian available **Seats:** 55 **Smoking:** N/Sm in restaurant **Children:** Portions **Directions:** 8m NE of Bury St Edmunds, 1m off A143. Follow brown signs at Ixworth to Wyken vineyards **Parking:** 50
e-mail: info@wykenvineyards.co.uk
web: www.wykenvineyards.co.uk

⊕ Maison Bleue
French, Mediterranean

Popular seafood bistro

☎ 01284 760623 30-31 Churchgate St IP33 1RG

MENU GUIDE Thai haddock & coriander fishcake • Poached salmon, fennel, parsley sauce • Warm apple & cinnamon tart, caramel sauce

WINE GUIDE ⌾ A Pabiot Pouilly Fumé £24.10 • ⚑ R Passot Morgan £18.65 • 36 bottles over £20, 53 bottles under £20 6 by the glass (£2.10-£2.50)

PRICE GUIDE Fixed L £10.95-£13.95 • Fixed D £23.95 • starter £4.95-£9.15 • main £8.95-£18.95 • dessert £4.95 • coffee £1.80 • min/water £2.50 • Service optional

PLACE: Centrally located in historic Bury St Edmunds, this friendly French bistro has plenty of atmosphere thanks to its well-deserved popularity with locals. It's a chic affair, with a seated bar and colourful marine murals.
FOOD: Seafood is the raison d'être, although the odd meat dish ensures carnivores can dine happy too. Expect accomplished cooking with a rustic feel: seared tuna with olive oil mash perhaps, or steak meunière.
OUR TIP: Book a day ahead for the extensive seafood plateau
Chef: Pascal Canevet **Owners:** Regis Crepy **Times:** 12-2.30/7-9.30, Closed Jan, 1 wk in summer, Sun-Mon **Notes:** Group service charge only applies to Dec, Vegetarian available **Seats:** 65, Pr/dining room 35 **Smoking:** N/Sm in restaurant **Children:** Portions **Directions:** Town centre. Churchgate Street is opposite cathedral **Parking:** On street
e-mail: info@maisonbleue.co.uk
web: www.maisonbleue.co.uk

England

BURY ST EDMUNDS *continued* MAP 13 TL86
The Priory Hotel
British, European
Accomplished manor house hotel dining
☎ 01284 766181 Tollgate IP32 6EH

MENU GUIDE Venison sausage, parsnip & ginger purée, cranberry jus • Lamb shank, grain mustard mash, rosemary jus • Pecan & whiskey tart, crème Anglaise

WINE GUIDE ♀ Kleine Sauvignon Blanc £16.50 • ♀ Hardys Riddle Shiraz Cabernet £15 • 49 bottles over £20, 55 bottles under £20 • 6 by the glass (£3.75-£4.50)

PRICE GUIDE Fixed L £17-£26 • Fixed D £31-£45 • min/water £2.95 • Service added but optional 10%

PLACE: Built on the site of an historic friary founded in 1263, this listed 18th-century manor sits in pretty grounds on the edge of Bury town centre. The hotel has a comfortable lounge for pre-dinner drinks, and a smartly presented restaurant decorated with modern art.
FOOD: A skilful kitchen delivers on the promise of a wide-ranging menu, which features traditional British combinations as well as more modern European fare. Dishes might include chicken with leeks and rösti potato, or seared sea bass with lime and ginger couscous and balsamic dressing.
OUR TIP: Take a stroll in the landscaped gardens
Chef: Jon Ellis **Owners:** Priory Hotel Ltd. **Times:** 12.30-2/7-10, Closed L Sat **Notes:** Coffee incl, Vegetarian available **Seats:** 74, Pr/dining room 26 **Smoking:** N/Sm in restaurant **Children:** Portions **Rooms:** 39 (39 en suite) ★★★ **Directions:** From Bury St. Edmunds follow signs for Mildenhall A1011. 1m out of town centre **Parking:** 60
e-mail: reservations@prioryhotel.co.uk **web:** www.prioryhotel.co.uk

Ravenwood Hall Hotel
British, Continental
Fine dining in Tudor mansion
☎ 01359 270345 Rougham IP30 9JA

MENU GUIDE Goats' cheese & pear strudel • Seared tuna, warm citrus salsa • Chocolate torte

WINE GUIDE 48 bottles over £20, 29 bottles under £20 • 10 by the glass (£3.60-£5.80)

PRICE GUIDE Fixed L £25.75 • Fixed D £25.75-£34.95 • coffee £2.50 • min/water £2.90 • Service optional

PLACE: An elegant restaurant with a formal yet welcoming ambience, set in a charming 15th-century hotel. The carved timber beams and massive inglenook fireplace date from Tudor times when the dining room was the living hall.
FOOD: The kitchen makes good use of quality, local produce, especially seasonal game, and you'll also find fish and vegetarian choice on the menus, as well as an excellent cheese board.

Preserved fruit and vegetables, and smoked meat and fish, are prepared on the premises.
OUR TIP: Walk in the landscaped grounds
Chef: David White **Owners:** Craig Jarvis **Times:** 12-2/7.30-9.30
Notes: ALC price includes 3 courses, Vegetarian available, Smart Dress, C Wed 200 **Seats:** 50 **Smoking:** N/Sm in restaurant **Children:** Menu, Portions **Rooms:** 14 (14 en suite) ★★★ **Directions:** 3m from Bury St Edmunds, just off A14 **Parking:** 150
e-mail: enquiries@ravenwoodhall.co.uk **web:** www.ravenwoodhall.co.uk

CAVENDISH MAP 13 TL84
The George
International
Informal dining in village green surroundings
☎ 01787 280248 The Green CO10 8BA
PLACE: A delightful and charming inn situated in the heart of Cavendish village between Long Melford and Clare. The George retains a wealth of its original features - exposed brickwork and beams jostle with dark wooden tables, seagrass carpeting and eggshell and light sage hues.
FOOD: The eclectic menu makes good use of fresh local produce. Flavours are bold and international.
OUR TIP: Walled gardens for summer dining
Times: 12-3/6-10, Mon (Jan-Apr), closed D Sun (Jan-Apr) **Rooms:** 5 (5 en suite) ♦♦♦♦ **Directions:** 6 miles from Sudbury, 3 miles from Long Melford **e-mail:** reservations@georgecavendish.co.uk
web: www.georgecavendish.co.uk

DEBENHAM MAP 13 TM16
The Angel Inn
Modern French, British   **NEW**
Flavourful cooking in rustic restaurant with rooms
☎ 01728 860954 5 High St IP14 6QL
MENU GUIDE Smoked haddock & crab chowder • Chicken, wild mushroom risotto, Madeira sauce • Chocolate & walnut brownie, mascarpone cream

PLACE: This village inn turned restaurant with rooms has kept its country roots, serving food at rustic wooden tables in a dining room hung with pictures of rural scenes. Lighter snacks are available in the bar.
FOOD: Modern French and British cuisine with a touch of Asian spice. The carte changes seasonally and is complemented by daily blackboard specials.
OUR TIP: Real ale served in the bar
Times: Telephone for details **Rooms:** 3 (3 en suite) 🏠
e-mail: dgiven@btconnect.com **web:** www.angelinn.org

The Best Use of Seafood sponsored by **Seafish** In conjunction with Seafish, the Sea Fish Industry Authority, we have sought out restaurants that make the most of seafood on their menus. In addition to the four country award winners (see page 9), look out for the seafish symbol throughout the book; this denotes restaurants serving a good range of fish and shellfish dishes, where the accent is firmly on freshness.

continued

FRESSINGFIELD MAP 13 TM27

Fox & Goose Inn
British, French

Excellent cooking in quintessential English village

☎ 01379 586247   IP21 5PB

MENU GUIDE Duck leg confit, salsify purée • Halibut, Parma ham, spinach risotto, vanilla & rosemary sauce • Grande Marnier crème brûlée

WINE GUIDE ♀ Daniel Bessiere Sauvignon Blanc £12.95 • ♀ Richmond Ridge Shiraz/Merlot £12.95 • 21 bottles over £20, 31 bottles under £20 • 6 by the glass (£2.95-£3.50)

PRICE GUIDE Fixed L £11.50 • starter £4.50-£7.95 • main £10.95-£17.50 • dessert £4.50-£4.95 • coffee £1.95 • min/water £2.50 • Service optional

PLACE: Village inn dating from 1509, peacefully located by the church. Inside you'll find open fires, exposed timbers and walls hung with modern art. There is a handsome bar and two glamorous dining areas with lovely fabrics and well-laid tables. Light jazz plays in the background and the atmosphere is pretty relaxed.

FOOD: Expect a few classical touches in an otherwise modern take on British and French ideas, with good use made of local produce, notably game. Dishes are quite complex but the various elements blend well together.

OUR TIP: Very good wine list both by the bottle and the glass **Chef:** P Yaxley, M Wyatt **Owners:** Paul Yaxley **Times:** 12-2/7-9, Mon **Notes:** Tasting menu 7 courses £35, Sun L £12.95-£15.95, Vegetarian available **Seats:** 48, Pr/dining room 25 **Smoking:** N/Sm in restaurant **Children:** Min 9 yrs, Portions **Directions:** A140 & B1118 (Stradbroke) left after 6m - in village centre by church **e-mail:** foxandgoose@uk2.net **web:** www.foxandgoose.net

HINTLESHAM MAP 13 TM04

Hintlesham Hall *see below*

HORRINGER MAP 13 TL86

The Ickworth Hotel
International

Quality cooking in stately home

☎ 01284 735350   IP29 5QE

MENU GUIDE Viennese beef bouillon • Seared salmon on miso onion • Cinnamon rice pudding

PRICE GUIDE Food prices not confirmed for 2006. Please telephone for details

PLACE: A classic country house dining room in this National Trust property, part of which is now a luxury hotel. High ceilings and huge swathes of taffeta curtains add a surprisingly modern feel to the imposing room, while candles and flowers add a traditional touch.

FOOD: In these light surroundings the cooking is intense and complicated. A Bavarian influence leads to the likes of white truffle, thyme and potato soup, and ox ragout with herb dumplings. Tiramisù, by comparison, is light years away, as are Austrian wild boar and Chinese Oysters.

OUR TIP: Sample the health and leisure facilities **Times:** 12-2/7-9.30 **Rooms:** 38 (38 en suite) ★★★★ **Directions:** From A14 take 1st exit for Bury St Edmunds (Junct 42). Follow signs for Westley & Ickworth Estate **e-mail:** ickworth@luxuryfamilyhotels.com **web:** www.ickworthhotel.com

---

HINTLESHAM MAP 13 TM04

Hintlesham Hall

British, French

Fine dining in outstanding country house

☎ 01473 652334   IP8 3NS

MENU GUIDE Ham hock & beetroot gâteau • Grilled fillet of turbot • Poire William parfait

PRICE GUIDE Fixed L £27.50 • Fixed D £30 • starter £10-£17.50 • main £22-£27.50 • dessert £8-£13

PLACE: A magnificent Grade I listed country house, dating from the 16th century, Hintlesham Hall is surrounded by 175 acres of open countryside. The main restaurant, the Salon, has recently been redecorated in pale creams, and is an amazingly grand room, the high domed ceiling decorated with gold leaf, ornate cornices and a huge branched chandelier. Service is formal, and the dress code is enforced.

FOOD: Quality of ingredients for true flavours, sound execution, good depths of flavour. Traditional ingredients and dishes appear on the menu to match the surroundings, but there are some interesting combinations of flavours and some modern influences that bring the style up to date. This really is classic country house cooking, consistent, effective and pleasing. For example, to begin, a warm venison, celeriac and roasted courgette salad with goats' cheese ravioli with tenderloin of pork, wild mushroom and truffle risotto to follow. Canapés, bread and petits fours are all home made.

OUR TIP: Lunch is exceptional value **Chef:** Alan Ford **Owners:** Ms Dee Ludlow **Times:** 12-1.30/7-9.30, Closed L Sat **Notes:** Set price L&D mid week only, strict dress restrictions **Seats:** 80, Pr/dining room 80 **Smoking:** N/Sm in restaurant **Rooms:** 33 (33 en suite) ★★★★ **Directions:** 5m W of Ipswich on A1071 **e-mail:** reservations@hintleshamhall.com **web:** www.hintleshamhall.com

England

IPSWICH MAP 13 TM14

Il Punto
French
Solid brasserie cooking in full sail!

☎ 01473 289748 Neptune Quay IP4 1AX

MENU GUIDE Roasted goats' cheese tart • Grilled fillet of sea bass with horseradish mash • Iced apricot & pistachio nougat

PRICE GUIDE Fixed L £11.95 • Fixed D £23.95 • starter £4.95-£6.95 • main £11.95-£17.50 • dessert £4.95 • coffee £1.80 • min/water £2.50 • Service optional

PLACE: Located on a ship moored at Neptune Quay, a short walk from the town centre, the dining room is split between the two decks. Polished wood, blue and white fabrics add a suitably nautical feel.

FOOD: Solid French brasserie-style dishes form the basis of the menus on this floating venue. Dishes are nicely presented, well-executed and complemented with good sauces in main courses such as pan-fried fillet of turbot and scallops meunière.

OUR TIP: Perfect for sunny alfresco lunches

Chef: Frederic Lebrun **Owners:** Mr R Crepy **Times:** 12-2.30/7-9.30, Closed Jan, Sun-Mon, closed L Sat **Notes:** Vegetarian available **Seats:** 80 **Smoking:** N/Sm in restaurant **Children:** Portions

Directions: Telephone for directions

e-mail: info@ilpunto.co.uk **web:** www.ilpunto.co.uk

Salthouse Harbour Hotel
British, Mediterranean
Great contemporary brasserie dining amidst breathtaking views

☎ 01473 226789 No 1 Neptune Quay IP4 1AS

MENU GUIDE Ham hock terrine, quince jelly • Cuban-spiced lamb rump, sweet potato mash • Sticky toffee pudding, fudge sauce

WINE GUIDE ♀ J Bouchon Sauvignon Blanc £12.95 ♀ J Bouchon Merlot £12.95 • 12 bottles over £20, 17 bottles under £20 • 27 by the glass (£3.20-£8.30)

PRICE GUIDE Fixed L £8.50-£11.50 • starter £3.95-£6.95 • main £8.25-£14.25 • dessert £3.95-£4.95 • coffee £2.35 • min/water £3.10 • Service optional

PLACE: Occupying a unique setting within an early 19th-century warehouse, this renovated hotel overlooks the new trendy area of Neptune Marina. Mixing original features and contemporary style, it offers spacious and luxurious accommodation and stunning views. Bustling ground floor brasserie with smart banquette seating, huge windows, up-to-the-minute decor and award-winning food.

FOOD: Draws local diners for well-executed contemporary brasserie dishes that are simply and confidently produced using quality fresh ingredients. There are two dozen wines and champagne by the glass to choose from.

OUR TIP: Check out the daily specials on the blackboard

Chef: Tim Keeble **Owners:** Robert Gough **Times:** 12-2.30/6-10 **Notes:** Civ Wed 80 **Seats:** 60 **Smoking:** N/Sm in restaurant **Children:** Menu, Portions **Rooms:** 43 (43 en suite) ★★★★ **Directions:** A14 junct 53, A1156 to town centre and harbour, off Key St **Parking:** 30 **e-mail:** staying@salthouseharbour.co.uk **web:** salthouseharbour.co.uk

IXWORTH MAP 13 TL97

Theobalds Restaurant
British
Long established and popular village restaurant

☎ 01359 231707 68 High St IP31 2HJ

MENU GUIDE Twice baked cheese soufflé • Beef tournedos, horseradish crust, caramelised apples/sultanas, Beaujolais sauce • Crème brûlée

WINE GUIDE ♀ Moa Ridge Marlborough Sauvignon Blanc £15.75 • ♀ Coudert Clos de Roilette Fleurie £22.70 • 42 bottles over £20, 19 bottles under £20 • 5 by the glass (£2.95-£3.95)

PRICE GUIDE Fixed L £20 • Fixed D £25 • starter £6.25-£8.75 • main £14.50-£18.50 • dessert £6.50 • coffee £2.25 • min/water £2.50 • Service optional

PLACE: Smart upmarket restaurant, housed in a 16th-century property, in the main street of a small village. The oak-beamed restaurant is simply decorated with pink floral curtains and lots of paintings by local artists. The husband and wife team work well together and have a loyal following.

FOOD: Very accomplished and precise with good flavours and use of quality, well sourced produce. The menu changes with the seasons and tends towards modern British restaurant classics.

OUR TIP: Enjoy a drink on the patio in summer

Chef: Simon Theobald **Owners:** Simon & Geraldine Theobald **Times:** 12.15-1.30/7-9, Closed 10 days in Summer, Mon, closed L Tues, Thurs, Sat, closed D Sun **Notes:** Fixed D Tue-Thur, Vegetarian available **Seats:** 42, Pr/dining room 16 **Smoking:** N/Sm in restaurant **Children:** Min 8yrs D, Portions **Directions:** 7m from Bury St Edmunds on A143 Bury/Diss Road **Parking:** On street **web:** www.theobaldsrestaurant.co.uk

LAVENHAM MAP 13 TL94

Angel Hotel
British
Popular inn with quality food and plenty of character

☎ 01787 247388 Market Place CO10 9QZ

MENU GUIDE Duck, orange & chestnut terrine, Cumberland sauce • Calves' liver & bacon, red onion marmalade • Lemon meringue roulade

WINE GUIDE ♀ Concha y Toro Chardonnay £10.95 • ♀ Concha y Toro Merlot £10.95 • 8 bottles over £20, 38 bottles under £20 • 7 by the glass (£3)

PRICE GUIDE Starter £3.95-£6.75 • main £8.95-£16.95 • dessert £4.25 • coffee £1.50 • min/water £3 • Service optional

PLACE: Fifteenth-century inn at the heart of this lovely little medieval town, popular with both locals and the numerous tourists throughout the year. Eat in relaxed style in the bar or dining areas at sturdy wooden tables, but do book in advance.

FOOD: Quality ingredients, carefully prepared and cooked in a simple style with an emphasis on flavours. There's lots of comfort food, such as steak and ale pudding, and steamed syrup sponge.

OUR TIP: Local real ales in the bar

Chef: Michael Pursell **Owners:** Mr R Whitworth & Mr J Barry **Times:** 12.15/6.45-9.15, Closed 25-26 Dec **Notes:** Vegetarian available, Dress Restrictions, Smart casual **Seats:** 100, Pr/dining room 15 **Smoking:** N/Sm in restaurant **Children:** Portions **Rooms:** 8 (8 en suite) ★★ **Directions:** From Bury St Edmunds towards Sudbury on A134, then A1141 to Lavenham. In town centre, nr Tourist Information **Parking:** 50 **e-mail:** angellav@aol.com **web:** www.theangelhotel-lavenham.co.uk

Great House Restaurant

French, European

Gallic charm in Tudor setting

☎ 01787 247431 Market Place CO10 9QZ

MENU GUIDE Gravadlax & onions quiche • Poached halibut fillet, orange & butter sauce • Tarte au citron

WINE GUIDE ♀ Côtes de St Mont Sauvignon £13.50 • ♥ Bergerac Merlot £13.50 • 50 bottles over £20, 80 bottles under £20 • 10 by the glass (£2.50-£5.50)

PRICE GUIDE Fixed L £15.95 • Fixed D £24.95 • starter £6-£9.50 • main £11-£19.50 • dessert £4.75-£6.50 • coffee £1.95 • min/water £2.50 • Service optional

PLACE: A little pocket of France in a medieval English village is what you'll find here. The beamed Tudor restaurant might have the uneven walls and huge fireplace typical of the Elizabethan period, but it is French through and through.
FOOD: Plenty of luxury ingredients appear on the menu but, indulgent or plain, all are well sourced. An accomplished kitchen favours an elaborate style, with terrine of duck foie gras, and veal fillet with a lime butter sauce scoring well, and a superb cheese board perhaps tempting connoisseurs away from the dessert menu.
OUR TIP: Book early, and stay over if you can
Chef: Regis Crépy **Owners:** Mr & Mrs Crépy **Times:** 12-2.30/7-9.30, Closed Jan, Mon, closed D Sun **Notes:** Sun lunch £24.95, Vegetarian available **Seats:** 40, Pr/dining room 12 **Smoking:** N/Sm in restaurant **Children:** Portions **Rooms:** 5 (5 en suite) ♦♦♦♦ **Directions:** In Market Place (turn onto Market Lane from High Street) **Parking:** Market Place **e-mail:** info@greathouse.co.uk **web:** www.greathouse.co.uk

The Swan

British, French **NEW**

Fine dining in an atmospheric old hotel

☎ 01787 247477 High St CO10 9QA

MENU GUIDE Crayfish risotto, saffron butter sauce • Rump of lamb, wild mushrooms • Warm apple crumble

WINE GUIDE ♀ Casa Rivas Sauvignon Blanc £15.25 • ♥ Casa Rivas Merlot £15.25 • 100 bottles over £20, 30 bottles under £20 • 9 by the glass (£3.50-£6.50)

PRICE GUIDE Fixed L £19.95-£24.95 • Fixed D £28.50 • starter £5.50-£12 • main £16.50-£30 • dessert £5.50-£9.50 • coffee £2.75 • min/water £3 • Service optional

PLACE: The 14th-century Swan retains much of its original charm, not least in the restaurant where the dark beams and log fire are at their most atmospheric. There is a lighter eating option in the informal brasserie, and a charming bar where aperitifs can be enjoyed.
FOOD: Fine dining is promised from a team with sound technical skills and access to Suffolk's freshest produce. The modern British style of cooking with French influences is displayed on the seasonal and house menus.
OUR TIP: Stay over in one of the tasteful bedrooms
Owners: Thorpeness & Aldeburgh Hotels Ltd **Times:** 12-2.30/7-9.30, Closed L Sat **Notes:** Vegetarian available, Dress Restrictions, No jeans or trainers, Civ Wed 80 **Seats:** 80, Pr/dining room 30 **Smoking:** N/Sm in restaurant **Children:** Min 10 yrs, Portions **Rooms:** 51 (51 en suite) ★★★★ **Directions:** From Bury St Edmunds take A134 for 6m. Lavenham is 6m along B1071 **Parking:** 50
e-mail: info@theswanatlavenham.co.uk
web: www.theswanatlavenham.co.uk

LONG MELFORD MAP 13 TL84

The Black Lion Hotel

British, Mediterranean

Ivy clad hotel on the green

☎ 01787 312356 Church Walk, The Green CO10 9DN

MENU GUIDE Crab spring rolls, lemongrass & pimento salad • Baked salmon, curry dressing • Apple & plum strudel

WINE GUIDE 48 bottles over £20, 29 bottles under £20 • 10 by the glass (£3.60-£5.80)

PRICE GUIDE Fixed L £18.95 • Fixed D £23.75 • min/water £2.80 • Service optional

PLACE: Overlooking the green, this charming and stylish hotel mixes period charm with contemporary furnishings. High-back leather chairs and white linen set the mood in the restaurant, while the cosy bar offers a more informal option.
FOOD: A range of fixed-price menus, which include home-made chutneys and breads, deliver competent dishes with some modern ideas.
OUR TIP: Take afternoon tea in the Victorian walled garden
Chef: Annette Beasant **Owners:** Craig Jarvis **Times:** 12-2/7-9.30 **Notes:** ALC 2 courses £27.95, 3 courses £31.95, Vegetarian available, Smart Dress **Seats:** 50, Pr/dining room 20 **Smoking:** N/Sm in restaurant **Children:** Menu, Portions **Rooms:** 10 (10 en suite) ★★★ **Directions:** From Bury St Edmunds take A134 to Sudbury. Turn right onto B1064 to Long Melford. right onto A1092 to Cavendish. Black Lion on the green **Parking:** 10 **e-mail:** enquiries@blacklionhotel.net **web:** www.blacklionhotel.net

Scutchers Restaurant

Modern British

Friendly bistro serving imaginative fare

☎ 01787 310200 Westgate St CO10 9DP

MENU GUIDE Lobster omelette, thermidor sauce • Grilled halibut, prawn & curry risotto, coriander oil • Crème brûlée, cherry compôte

PRICE GUIDE Food prices not confirmed for 2006. Please telephone for details

PLACE: Bright bistro, with yellow and blue decor and light pine furniture, situated on the edge of the attractive village of Long Melford. The atmosphere is relaxed and informal, and the well turned out staff provide particularly friendly service.
FOOD: The cooking style is modern British with an emphasis on fish, and the carte offers a comprehensive choice of dishes. There are some unusual ideas, as in a nicely timed, rich foie gras on a corned beef rösti with Puy lentil gravy providing a rustic contrast.
OUR TIP: Special event catering available
Times: 12-2/7-9.30, Closed 25 Dec, 1-11 Jan, last wk Aug, Sun-Mon **Directions:** About 1m from Long Melford towards Clare **web:** www.scutchers.com

---

AA's Chefs' Chef is the annual poll of all the chefs included in The Restaurant Guide. Around 1800 of the country's top chefs are asked to vote to recognise the achievements of one of their peers.
This year's winner is featured on page 19.

England

England

LOWESTOFT MAP 13 TM59
 The Crooked Barn
European, Thai
Charming old farmhouse with inventive kitchen
☎ 01502 501353 Ivy House Country Hotel, Ivy Ln, Beccles Rd, Oulton Broad NR33 8HY

MENU GUIDE Borshchock, parsley croûtons • Roast Norfolk duck breast, celeriac purée • Soft baked meringue, home-made lemon curd, raspberries
WINE GUIDE 4 by the glass (£2.75-£2.95)
PRICE GUIDE Fixed L £12.95-£13.95 • Fixed D £25 • starter £3.95-£9.95 • main £13.95-£21.95 • dessert £3.95-£8.95 • coffee £2.75 • min/water £3.75 • Service optional
PLACE: An ancient farmhouse and its outbuildings were the basis for this modern, well-equipped hotel and its charming restaurant. The old barn has been sympathetically converted into a spacious dining room with large windows overlooking the gardens. Creaking floors, restored brickwork and crooked beams all add to the character of the place.
FOOD: High quality, locally sourced, seasonal produce is turned into an eclectic mix of skilfully cooked and well-presented dishes. Simple combinations allow the quality of ingredients to shine through in dishes like the asparagus and wild mushroom chowder.
OUR TIP: A walk along the nearby Oulton Broad footpath
Chef: Richard Pye **Owners:** Caroline Coe **Times:** 12-1.45/7-9.30, Closed 20 Dec- 5 Jan **Notes:** Vegetarian available **Seats:** 45, Pr/dining room 16 **Smoking:** N/Sm in restaurant **Children:** Portions **Rooms:** 19 (19 en suite) ★★★ **Directions:** A146 into Ivy Lane **Parking:** 7
e-mail: aa@ivyhousefarm.co.uk **web:** www.ivyhousecountryhotel.co.uk

Flying Fifteens 19a the Esplanade NR33 0QG
☎ 01502 581188 Winner of The Tea Guild Award of Excellence 2005.

MILDENHALL MAP 12 TL77
Riverside Hotel
British, French
Attractive riverside hotel with enjoyable dining
☎ 01638 717274 Mill St IP28 7DP
MENU GUIDE Oak smoked chicken & pine nuts • Wild mushroom risotto • Steamed lemon sponge, lemon sauce
WINE GUIDE ♀ Pinot Grigio £12.50 • ♀ Kells Edge Blenox £14.50 • 8 bottles over £20, 29 bottles under £20 • 27 by the glass (£2-£4)
PRICE GUIDE Fixed L £19.50 • Fixed D £22.50 • coffee £2 • min/water £3 • Service optional
PLACE: Built around 1720, this imposing red-brick Georgian hotel was recently renovated to a high standard and includes a choice of venue for food. The Terrace Bar provides informal dining and, weather permitting, alfresco dining. The bright conservatory-style Terrace Restaurant offers more formal meals.
FOOD: Classical dishes using good quality, fresh produce could include pan-fried monkfish, cassoulet and chorizo.
OUR TIP: A pre-dinner garden stroll along the River Lark
Chef: Terry Ungless **Owners:** Mr B Keane **Times:** 12-2/6.30-9.30
Notes: Sun lunch £16, 3 courses, Vegetarian available, Civ Wed 150
Seats: 100, Pr/dining room 50 **Smoking:** N/Sm area **Children:** Menu, Portions **Rooms:** 23 (23 en suite) ★★★ **Directions:** From M11 junct take A11 for Norwich. At Fiveways Rdbt take A1101 into town. Left at mini rdbt, hotel last on left before bridge **Parking:** 70
e-mail: bookings@riverside-hotel.net **web:** www.riverside-hotel.net

NAYLAND MAP 13 TL93
The White Hart Inn
British, European
First-rate gastro-pub cuisine
☎ 01206 263382 High St CO6 4JF
MENU GUIDE Game en croûte, cranberry chutney • Pan-fried pork, tagliatelle, foie gras sauce • Vanilla & lychee crème brûlée
WINE GUIDE ♀ Domaine les Arnaud Sauvignon Blanc £11 • ♀ Meridian Estate Cabernet Sauvignon £11 • 50% bottles over £20, 50% bottles under £20 • 10 by the glass (£2.95-£3.95)
PRICE GUIDE Fixed L £10.95 • Fixed D £21.50 • starter £3.80-£8.40 • main £10.40-£17.60 • dessert £4.40-£5.80 • coffee £1.80 • min/water £2.80 • Service optional • Group min 6 service 10%
PLACE: Surrounded by quaint timber-framed houses, this ancient inn is set in a pretty Suffolk village in the heart of Constable country. Old-fashioned charm comes courtesy of the bar's heavy wooden beams, tiled floors and feature fireplaces, while the dining room is a more elegant affair.
FOOD: A French twist on the White Hart's accomplished cooking betrays Michel Roux's ownership, but the kitchen draws inspiration from around the globe, delivering dishes distinguished by an attention to seasonality and the use of high quality local ingredients. Lunchtimes see a lighter selection but no drop in standards.
OUR TIP: Menu rapide available for speedy lunches
Chef: Carl Shillingford **Owners:** Mr M Roux **Times:** 12-2.30/6.30-9.30, Closed 26 Dec-9 Jan **Notes:** Vegetarian available, Dress Restrictions, Smart casual, Civ Wed 70 **Seats:** 55, Pr/dining room 36 **Smoking:** N/Sm in restaurant **Children:** Portions **Rooms:** 6 (6 en suite) ♦♦♦♦ **Directions:** 6m N of Colchester on A134 towards Sudbury **Parking:** 22
e-mail: nayhart@aol.com **web:** www.whitehart-nayland.co.uk

NEWMARKET MAP 12 TL66

Bedford Lodge Hotel
British, International

Hunting lodge with elegant restaurant

☎ 01638 663175 Bury Rd CB8 7BX

MENU GUIDE Rabbit terrine, grain mustard • Beef fillet, foie gras, hazelnut jus • Chocolate tart, ivory chocolate ice cream

WINE GUIDE ♀ Whitehaven Winery Sauvignon Blanc £22.95 • ♀ Marques de Caceres Rioja Crianza £20 • 40 bottles over £20, 18 bottles under £20 • 7 by the glass (£3.85-£5)

PRICE GUIDE Starter £4.95-£10.95 • main £8.95-£21.95 • dessert £3.95-£5.95 • coffee £2.25 • min/water £3.50 • Service optional

PLACE: An imposing 18th-century Georgian hunting lodge set in three acres of secluded landscaped grounds. Extended and refurbished, it has contemporary bedrooms and first-rate leisure facilities. Service is professional from uniformed staff.
FOOD: Race days see the hotel's elegant Orangery restaurant packed with punters, the attraction being the imaginative, inspired menu of classic British dishes with International influences.
OUR TIP: Great place to stay for Newmarket Races
Chef: Richard Duckworth **Owners:** Barnham Broom Golf Club **Times:** 12-2.30/7-9.30, Closed L Sat **Notes:** Sun lunch - 2 course £17.95, 3 course £19.95, Vegetarian available, Dress Restrictions, No shorts, sandals, vests, Civ Wed 80 **Seats:** 47, Pr/dining room 150 **Smoking:** N/Sm in restaurant, Air con **Children:** Menu, Portions **Rooms:** 55 (55 en suite) ★★★★ **Directions:** From town centre follow A1303 towards Bury St Edmunds for 0.5m **Parking:** 100 **e-mail:** info@bedfordlodgehotel.co.uk **web:** www.bedfordlodgehotel.co.uk

Star Inn The Street, Lidgate CB8 9PP ☎ 01638 500275
Catalan-influenced cooking from Mediterranean fish soup to tortillas.

ORFORD MAP 13 TM45

The Crown & Castle
International

Fun and fine dining on the Suffolk coast

☎ 01394 450205 IP12 2LJ

MENU GUIDE Duck liver & orange parfait, courgette pickles • Guinea fowl, Puy lentils, gingery pak choi • Hot bitter chocolate mousse

WINE GUIDE ♀ Stormy Cape Chenin £12.50 • ♀ Wilsons Quay £12.50 • 19 bottles under £20 • 18 by the glass (£3.25)

PRICE GUIDE Fixed L £16.50-£19.50 • Fixed D fr £32.50 • starter £6.50-£8.95 • main £11.50-£16.50 • dessert £5.50 • coffee £1.75 min/water £2.75 • Service optional • Group min 8 service 10%

PLACE: Set in Orford's old market square, next to a picture-book Norman keep, this red-brick Victorian inn is a foodie haven and great base for the Suffolk heritage coast with its nature reserves and unspoilt beaches. Decor is contemporary throughout, the restaurant a spacious room with stripped floors, simply set tables and a friendly ambience.
FOOD: Proprietor Ruth Watson is a renowned cookery writer, and the Crown's food reflects a genuine commitment to the use of high quality local produce. Skills are high and creativity in no short supply – this is one to watch.
OUR TIP: Alfresco dining in the garden in summer
Chef: Ruth Watson, Max Dougal **Owners:** David & Ruth Watson **Times:** 12.15-2.15/7-9.30, Closed 19-22 Dec, 3-4 Jan **Notes:** Vegetarian available **Seats:** 60, Pr/dining room 10 **Smoking:** N/Sm in restaurant

Children: Min 8 yrs D, Menu, Portions **Rooms:** 18 (18 en suite) ★★ **Directions:** 9m E of Woodbridge, off A12 **Parking:** 20 **e-mail:** info@crownandcastle.co.uk **web:** www.crownandcastle.co.uk

The Butley-Orford Oysterage
Market Hill IP12 2LH ☎ 01394 450277 Salmon, eels, cod roe, mackerel and kippers smoked on the premises.

SAXMUNDHAM MAP 13 TM36

Harrisons Restaurant
British, European

Relaxed, enjoyable dining in 17th-century surroundings

☎ 01728 604444 Main Rd, Kelsale IP17 2RF

MENU GUIDE Gloucester Old Spot terrine & pickles • Roast venison, figs & chestnuts • Buttermilk pudding, rhubarb

WINE GUIDE ♀ Bollini Pinot Grigio £16.50 • ♀ Norte Chico Cabernet Sauvignon £12.95 • 6 bottles over £20, 24 bottles under £20 • 2 by the glass (£2.95)

PRICE GUIDE Fixed L £13.95 • starter £4.95-£6.95 • main £11.95-£15.95 • dessert £4.95 • coffee £1.75 • min/water £2.95 • Service optional • Group min 8 service 10%

PLACE: This ancient, timber-framed thatched cottage has a well-presented beamed dining room with old brick floors and open fireplaces. White crockery and crisp napkins complement mahogany furniture. Professional staff add to the whole attractive offering which has a keen local following.
FOOD: Modern dishes characterised by simple and effective combinations of flavour and texture. Lunch might comprise a mushroom and parmesan tart or local lamb with bubble and squeak, while dinner could feature grilled duck hearts with tartare sauce to start with Heritage coast sea bass with leeks in white sauce main course.
OUR TIP: Wonderful home-made bread & pickles
Chef: Peter Harrison **Owners:** Peter Harrison **Times:** 12-2.30/from 7, Closed 2 wks Xmas, Mon **Notes:** Vegetarian available **Seats:** 55, Pr/dining room 25 **Smoking:** N/Sm in restaurant **Children:** Portions **Directions:** On A12, 0.5m N of Saxmundham near Kelsale junct **Parking:** 20 **e-mail:** mel@harrisonsrestaurant.com

SOUTHWOLD MAP 13 TM57

The Crown
Traditional European

Enjoyable dining in historic seaside inn

☎ 01502 722275 90 High St IP18 6DP

MENU GUIDE Crab cakes, orange vinaigrette • Wild sea trout, crushed peas & tsatziki • Apple tarte Tatin

PRICE GUIDE Fixed L £18.50 • Fixed D £29 • coffee £1.50 • min/water £2.85 • Service optional

PLACE: This delightful old town centre posting inn combines a pub, wine bar, intimate restaurant and elegant first-floor lounge with superb accommodation. Food is available in the bar and the dining room, and there's a snug at the back serving real ales. The wine list is impressive plus a list of wines by the glass.
FOOD: Good, accurate cooking here with simple combinations prepared and presented in an accomplished manner. The daily-changing, fixed-price menu specialises in local fish and suggests wines to accompany each course. High quality ingredients used throughout.
OUR TIP: Lots of parking space

continued

continued

England

SOUTHWOLD continued MAP 13 TM57

Chef: Sue Miles **Owners:** Adnams Brewery/Adnams Hotels **Times:** 12-2/7-9.30 **Notes:** Vegetarian available **Seats:** 30 **Smoking:** N/Sm in restaurant **Children:** Min 5 yrs, Portions **Rooms:** 13 (12 en suite) ★★ **Directions:** Take A1095 from A12; hotel at the top of High Street **Parking:** 15 **e-mail:** crown.reception@adnams.co.uk **web:** www.adnams.co.uk

 ## The Randolph
British, European
Stylish gastro-pub meets upmarket restaurant
☎ 01502 723603 41 Wangford Rd, Reydon IP18 6PZ

MENU GUIDE Spicy fish kebabs • Baked fillet of sea bass on smoked salmon linguine • Chocolate brownie, white chocolate ice cream

WINE GUIDE ⚲ Canoe Tree Semillion/Chardonnay £10.50 • ⚑ Canoe Tree Cabernet Sauvignon £10.50 • 2 bottles over £20, 15 bottles under £20 • 5 by the glass (£2.70-£3.20)

PRICE GUIDE Starter £3.50-£6.10 • main £7.95-£12.95 • dessert £4.95-£5.95 • coffee £1.75 • min/water £3 • Service optional

PLACE: Ideally located in the small village of Reydon on the outskirts of Southwold, this popular converted pub is often busy so expect a lively buzz.
FOOD: Simple modern British food with European influences is well executed and packed with big flavours, ranging from Thai fishcakes with chilli and ginger to steamed game pudding with mustard mash.
OUR TIP: Good value set-price lunches
Chef: Martin Page **Owners:** David Smith **Times:** 12-2/6.30-9, Closed D 25 Dec **Notes:** Sun lunch menu and specials available, Vegetarian available **Seats:** 65 **Smoking:** N/Sm in restaurant **Children:** Menu, Portions **Rooms:** 12 (4 en suite) **Directions:** 1m from Southwold **Parking:** 40 **e-mail:** reception@randolph.co.uk **web:** www.therandolph.co.uk

 ## Swan Hotel
British, French
Accomplished cooking in seaside inn
☎ 01502 722186 Market Place IP18 6EG

MENU GUIDE Scallops, pink fir apple salad • Beef, mustard mash, wild mushrooms, roast onions • Chocolate fondant, pistachio ice cream

WINE GUIDE ⚲ Cave Talmard Chardonnay £14.50 • ⚑ La Capalla Volpaia Sangiovese £14.50 • 53 bottles over £20, 64 bottles under £20 • 9 by the glass (£2.35-£6.50)

PRICE GUIDE Fixed L £20-£25 • Fixed D £30-£35 • starter £4-£6 • main £9-£15 • dessert £4-£6 • coffee £2 • min/water £3

PLACE: Set in the bustling market square of the pretty seaside town of Southwold, this former coaching inn has been welcoming guests for over 300 years. These days it's decorated in cosy contemporary style, and has a comfortable bar and lounge for pre-dinner drinks or afternoon tea. Book ahead in summer.
FOOD: The lunch menu changes daily and offers a concise choice, with a wider range available at dinner. Expect accomplished modern English and French cooking: sea bass with purple broccoli and salsa verde perhaps, or beetroot and rocket risotto. Strong wine list.
OUR TIP: The Admiral's room comes complete with telescope to survey the sea
Chef: Ian Howell **Owners:** Adnams PLC **Times:** 12-2/7-9.30 **Notes:** Fixed-menu prices vary on special dates (Xmas, New Yr), Vegetarian available, Dress Restrictions, Smart casual - no jeans, Civ Wed 40 **Seats:** 65, Pr/dining room 36 **Smoking:** N/Sm in restaurant
continued

Children: Min 5 yrs, Menu, Portions **Rooms:** 42 (42 en suite) ★★★ **Directions:** Turn right off A12 signposted Southwold/Reydon, and continue for 4m into Southwold. Follow main street into Market Place, hotel on left **Parking:** 36 **e-mail:** swan.hotel@adnams.co.uk **web:** www.adnamshotels.co.uk

STOKE-BY-NAYLAND MAP 13 TL93
 ## The Angel Inn
British, French
Imaginative dining in charming coaching inn
☎ 01206 263245 Polstead St CO6 4SA

MENU GUIDE Grilled goats' cheese, mushroom, red onion jam • Beef, cumin rösti, tomato salsa, onion rings • Orange cheesecake

WINE GUIDE ⚲ Vina Arinita Chardonnay £12.25 • ⚑ Eagle Hawk Shiraz £11.25 • 4 bottles over £20, 26 bottles under £20 • 10 by the glass (£2.65-£5.50)

PRICE GUIDE Starter £3.25-£6.95 • main £7.75-£16.95 • dessert £4.25 • coffee £1.50 • min/water £2.35 • Service optional

PLACE: Well known locally for its food, this 16th-century coaching inn offers guests a choice of dining casually in the bar, or more formally in a cosy restaurant. Character comes courtesy of hearty fires, exposed brickwork, and a wealth of ancient beams.
FOOD: The blackboard menu changes daily and features a good range of dishes especially fish and including some traditional crowd-pleasers. Fresh local produce is used whenever possible. It's complemented by a decent wine list and selection of beers.
OUR TIP: The restaurant contains the Angel's original water well
Chef: Neil Bishop **Owners:** Horizon Inns **Times:** 12-2/6.30-9.30, Closed 25-26 Dec, 1 Jan **Notes:** Vegetarian available **Seats:** 28 **Smoking:** N/Sm in restaurant **Children:** Portions **Rooms:** 6 (6 en suite) ◆◆◆ **Directions:** From A12, take Colchester right turn, then A135, 5m to Nayland from A125, take B1068 **Parking:** 20 **e-mail:** theangel@tiscali.co.uk **web:** www.horizoninns.co.uk

WESTLETON MAP 13 TM46
 ## The Westleton Crown
British, European
Historic inn with inventive menu
☎ 01728 648777 Main St IP17 3AD

MENU GUIDE Roast quail, wild mushroom mousse • Whole grilled bream, sprouting broccoli, fennel chips • Apple & cardamom tarte Tatin

WINE GUIDE 50% bottles over £20, 50% bottles under £20 10 by the glass (£2.50-£6.50)

continued

PRICE GUIDE Starter £5.25-£6 • main £13.50-£17.50 • dessert £4.95-£5.95 • coffee £2.45 • min/water £3.50 • Service optional

PLACE: This handsome red-brick coaching inn, believed to be one of England's oldest, is located in a village setting just a few minutes from the A12 and within easy reach of the Suffolk Heritage Coast. You can eat in the rustic chic restaurant, the lounge or the busy bar. In summer, there's a conservatory restaurant, floodlit at night, overlooking the pretty terraced gardens.
FOOD: An interesting choice of dishes offered from a daily carte. Ingredients are seasonal and locally sourced where possible, fish is a speciality and bread is home made.
OUR TIP: A selection of local ales is served in the bar **Chef:** Richard Bargewell **Owners:** Agellus Hotels Ltd **Times:** 12-2.30/7-9.30 **Notes:** Vegetarian available **Seats:** 80, Pr/dining room 20 **Smoking:** N/Sm in restaurant **Children:** Portions **Directions:** Turn off A12 (N bound) just past Yoxford northbound. Follow tourist signs for 2m **Parking:** 30 **e-mail:** reception@westletoncrown.com **web:** www.westletoncrown.com

WOODBRIDGE MAP 13 TM24

Captain's Table

British, European

Busy town-centre bistro

☎ 01394 383145 3 Quay St IP12 1BX

MENU GUIDE Spiced Egyptian lentil soup • Local fillet of cod with tartare butter sauce • Iced hazelnut nougat & raspberry coulis

WINE GUIDE ♀ Jean des Vignes Colombard £9.95 • ♀ Tin Hat Victoria Shiraz/Cabernet Sauvignon £14.25 • 8 bottles over £20, 32 bottles under £20 • 5 by the glass (£2.20-£2.80)

PRICE GUIDE Starter £3-£6.50 • main £6.50-£15.50 • dessert £4.25 • coffee £1.25 • min/water £2.50 • Service included

PLACE: Originally three 16th-century cottages just off the main street, this popular bistro has a relaxed but efficient air with bright decor and wooden floors and beams. Outside is a wonderful 100-year-old magnolia tree and a rose just 20 years its junior climbs over the front door.
FOOD: The well-balanced menu offers a mixture of classic dishes such as game pie to more exotic hot pot of prawns with thermidor sauce. The food is full of flavour and well presented.
OUR TIP: Alfresco dining available in the summer
Chef: Pascal Pommier **Owners:** Mr P & Mrs J M Pommier **Times:** 12-2/6.30-9.30, Closed 2 wks Jan, Mon (ex BHs), Tues, closed D Sun (ex BHs) **Seats:** 50, Pr/dining room 34 **Smoking:** N/Sm in restaurant **Children:** Menu, Portions **Directions:** From A12, (Garden centre on left). Quay St is opposite rail station & theatre, restaurant 100 yds on left **Parking:** 4 **web:** www.captainstable.co.uk

Seckford Hall Hotel

British, International

Magnificent Elizabethan experience

☎ 01394 385678 IP13 6NU

MENU GUIDE Home cured foie gras • Thai-style lobster • Tarte Tatin au poire

WINE GUIDE ♀ Domaine de Clementele Chardonnay £19.95 • ♀ Crista Rolfe Syrah Grenache £19.95 • 39 bottles over £20, 46 bottles under £20 • 10 by the glass (£3-£6)

PRICE GUIDE Fixed L £16.50-£22 • Fixed D £28.50-£38.50 min/water £3.25 • Service included

PLACE: From the commanding Tudor façade with tall chimneys and huge carved oak door to the lovely landscaped gardens surrounding Seckford Hall will awe you with its majestic splendour.
FOOD: With informal yet attentive service, the kitchen delivers fresh, clean flavours produced from the highest quality

ingredients largely sourced locally. Lobster and Suffolk pork are a speciality, with good vegetarian options.
OUR TIP: Enjoy the leisure facilities in the Tudor tithe barn **Chef:** Mark Archer **Owners:** Mr & Mrs Bunn **Times:** 12.30-1.45/7.30-9.30, Closed 25 Dec, closed L Mon **Notes:** Vegetarian available, Dress Restrictions, No jeans or trainers, Civ Wed 125 **Seats:** 70, Pr/dining room 100 **Smoking:** N/Sm in restaurant, Air con **Children:** Menu, Portions **Rooms:** 32 (32 en suite) ★★★ **Directions:** Hotel signposted on A12 (Woodbridge by-pass). Do not follow signs for town centre **Parking:** 100 **e-mail:** reception@seckford.co.uk **web:** www.seckford.co.uk

YAXLEY MAP 13 TM17

The Bull Auberge

British, French

Simple good food in charming country inn

☎ 01379 783604 Ipswich Rd IP23 8BZ

MENU GUIDE Crayfish & Bloody Mary terrine • Pigeon stuffed with foie gras with Puy lentils • Rhubarb & ginger crumble

WINE GUIDE ♀ Louis Latour Macon Lugny £17.50 • ♀ Paul Ja Boulle Côtes du Rhône £19.50 • 32 bottles over £20, 34 bottles under £20 • 8 by the glass (£2.70-£5.30)

PRICE GUIDE Fixed L £10.95 • Fixed D £18.95 • starter £3.15-£7.35 • main £7.50-£18.95 • dessert £4.95 • coffee £2.40 • min/water £3.50

PLACE: With its exposed brickwork and beams, this charming, family-owned 15th-century inn with rooms provides a warm atmosphere and the elegant restaurant is comfortable and cosy.
FOOD: Although starters of garden pea and ham soup, and mains of Norfolk fillet of beef served with wild mushroom and Madeira sauce demonstrate a British style with French influences, international influences crop up in Moroccan salmon fillet and Goan tiger prawn curry. The Tuesday to Friday fixed-price menu offers good value for money.
OUR TIP: Good selection of wines by the glass **Chef:** John Stenhouse **Owners:** John & Dee Stenhouse **Times:** 12-2/7-9.30, Closed Xmas, Sun & Mon, closed L Sat **Notes:** Vegetarian by request only, Smart Dress **Seats:** 30 **Smoking:** N/Sm in restaurant, Air con **Children:** Portions **Rooms:** 4 (4 en suite) ♦♦♦♦ **Directions:** 5m S of Diss on A140 **Parking:** 25 **e-mail:** deestenhose@fsmail.net **web:** www.the-auberge.co.uk

YOXFORD MAP 05 TM36

Satis House Hotel

Malaysian

Adventurous and authentic Malaysian food

☎ 01728 668418 IP17 3EX

MENU GUIDE Laksa (Curried noodle soup) • Rendang (Spicy coconut beef) • Pulut hitam (Black rice pudding)

continued

continued

England

YOXFORD *continued* MAP 05 TM36

WINE GUIDE ♀ Hawkes Bay Sauvignon Blanc £17.95 • ♥ Bimbaugon Shiraz £19.95 • 8 bottles over £20, 24 bottles under £20 • 3 by the glass (£3.75-£4.95)

PRICE GUIDE Fixed D fr £29 • starter £4.95-£9 • main £10.50-£16.75 • dessert £4.75-£5.75 • coffee £1.75 • min/water £2.75 • Service optional

PLACE: The restaurant's oriental decor and ornamentation provide a striking contrast with the rest of this hotel. It is an 18th-century Grade II listed property set in three acres of parkland and was once frequented by Charles Dickens. The name Satis House is actually mentioned in *Great Expectations*.

FOOD: An intriguing menu specialising in Malaysian cuisine with some Chinese and Indian ideas thrown in. The kitchen uses the freshest of ingredients to create authentic dishes with a combination of spices and herbs. A banquet menu is available at weekends.

OUR TIP: Try the range of Malaysian nibbles to start

Chef: Ms D Ferrance, Mrs C Blackmore **Owners:** Mrs Y C Blackmore **Times:** 7-9.30, Closed 25-26 Dec, Sun, closed L (by arrangement only) **Notes:** Vegetarian available **Seats:** 30, Pr/dining room 16 **Smoking:** N/Sm in restaurant **Children:** Min 5 yrs, Portions **Rooms:** 8 (8 en suite) ★★ **Directions:** Between Ipswich and Lowestoft on A12, N of village **Parking:** 30 **e-mail:** yblackmore@aol.com

SURREY

ABINGER HAMMER MAP 06 TQ04

⊛⊛ Drakes on the Pond

British

Classy village restaurant

☎ 01306 731174 Dorking Rd RH5 6SA

MENU GUIDE Terrine of chicken foie gras & artichoke, pepper caramel • Rabbit, beetroot & potato dauphinoise, chestnut purée • Rhubarb crumble, crème fraîche sorbet

WINE GUIDE ♀ Touraine Sauvignon Blanc £18 • ♥ Mountadam Shiraz £19.50 • 80 bottles over £20, 12 bottles under £20 • 10 by the glass (£4.50-£5.50)

PRICE GUIDE Fixed L £18.50 • starter £8.50-£16 • main £21-£25 • dessert £7-£9 • coffee £3.50 • min/water £3.50 • Service optional • Group min 8 service 10%

PLACE: Located in a friendly Surrey village, this classy restaurant has a light, uncluttered interior and serves its guests at well-spaced tables dressed with crisp linen and polished glassware. Service is formal but friendly with the proprietor always on hand.

FOOD: Expect quality ingredients teamed in classic combinations: Scotch beef with parsnip fondant and horseradish jus perhaps, or duck breast with a white bean and bacon cassoulet. Lunch is a concise affair with three choices at each stage, while dinner sees a wider range of more complex dishes.

OUR TIP: Buzzy atmosphere on Fridays and Saturdays

Chef: Jonathan Clarke **Owners:** John Morris & Tracey Honeysett **Times:** 12-2/7-10, Closed 2 wks Aug-Sep, Xmas, New Year, BHs, Sun, Mon, closed L Sat **Notes:** Vegetarian available, Smart Dress **Seats:** 32 **Smoking:** N/Sm in restaurant, Air con **Children:** Min 10 yrs **Directions:** On the A25 between Dorking and Guildford **Parking:** 20 **e-mail:** info@drakesonthepond.com

BAGSHOT MAP 06 SU96

⊛⊛⊛ Pennyhill Park Hotel & The Spa *see page 441*

CAMBERLEY MAP 06 SU86

⊛ *Frimley Hall Hotel & Spa*

Traditional, Modern

All change at a country house hotel

☎ 0870 400 8224 Lime Av GU15 2BG

MENU GUIDE Caesar salad • Pan-roast chicken in pancetta, thyme reduction • Vanilla crème brûlée, tuile biscuits

PRICE GUIDE Food prices not confirmed for 2006. Please telephone for details

PLACE: Set in the heart of rural Surrey, this ivy-clad Victorian manor is currently undergoing a four and a half million pound refurbishment that will see its contemporary restaurant completely transformed.

FOOD: Menus are in line for a makeover too, and include a tempting carte, plus a daily changing fixed-price selection.

OUR TIP: Check with hotel for refurbishment schedule

Times: 12-2/7-9.30, Closed L Sat **Rooms:** 86 (86 en suite) ★★★ **Directions:** From M3 junct 3 follow signs for Bagshot. Turn left onto A30 signed Camberley/Basingstoke. At rdbt branch left onto A325, then right into Conifer Dr & Lime Ave to Hotel **e-mail:** gm.frimleyhall@macdonald-hotels.co.uk **web:** www.macdonaldhotels.co.uk

CHARLWOOD MAP 06 TQ24

⊛⊛ Langshott Manor

see entry under Horle

⊛ Restaurant 1881

French, European **NEW**

Fine dining in a country house

☎ 01293 862166 Stanhill Court Hotel, Stanhill Rd, RH6 0EP

MENU GUIDE Scallops, cauliflower & cumin purée • Pork, apple mash, wild mushrooms, Calvados gravy • Vanilla pannacotta, figs & berries

WINE GUIDE ♀ Chenin Blanc £15.95 • ♥ Côtes du Roussillon £15.95 • 160 bottles over £20, 27 bottles under £20 • 14 by the glass (£3.50-£3.70)

PRICE GUIDE Fixed L £13.95-£18.95 • Fixed D £21.95-£25.95 • starter £4.95-£9.75 • main £13.25-£22.99 • dessert £5.95-£7.95 • coffee £3.95 • min/water £3.95 • Service added but optional 10%

PLACE: A country-house hotel in classical style complete with library, wood-panelled dining room and views over the Downs. Take a stroll outside if there's time - the 35-acre grounds include an amphitheatre and Victorian walled garden.

FOOD: An ambitious kitchen utilises quality ingredients that shine through in French and European dishes such as steak with a chorizo and basil mash, or duck with creamed Savoy cabbage.

OUR TIP: Very handy for Gatwick Airport, just 10 minutes away

Chef: Roger John Gadsden **Owners:** Antony Colas **Times:** 12-3/7-11 **Notes:** Vegetarian available, no jeans or T-shirts, Civ Wed 140 **Seats:** 120 Pr/dining room 260 **Smoking:** N/Sm in restaurant, Air con **Children:** Portions **Rooms:** 15 (15 en suite) ★★★ **Parking:** 150 **e-mail:** enquiries@stanhillcourthotel.co.uk **web:** www.stanhillcourthotel.co.uk

Prices quoted in the guide are for guidance only and are subject to change without notice.

BAGSHOT MAP 06 SU96

Pennyhill Park Hotel & The Spa

British, French

Innovative cuisine in luxurious country-house hotel

☎ 01276 471774 London Rd GU19 5EU

e-mail: enquiries@pennyhillpark.co.uk

web: www.exclusivehotels.co.uk

PLACE: There's a nostalgic grandeur to the exterior of this romantic Victorian manor with its picture-perfect ivy-clad façade and stunning gardens, that's also a feature of its fine dining restaurant, the Latymer Room. It's a classical venue, oak-panelled with leaded windows, and decorated with heavy tapestries and artistic flower displays. Build up an appetite by making the most of the hotel's facilities, which include a jogging trail, golf course and rugby pitch, or take a dip in the pool at one of the finest spas in Britain and enjoy the softly piped underwater music.

FOOD: The setting may be historic, but the food's certainly not; expect innovative and elaborate modern cuisine distinguished by high quality ingredients and clear flavours with mains such as loin of pork en cocotte, braised belly, glazed aromatic cheek, with jelly of apple and Calvados. An extensive wine list offers a comprehensive selection from around the globe, with many bottles available by the glass.

MENU GUIDE Langoustine, pork belly, asparagus • Duck breast, chestnut tortellini, figs, raisins, verjus • Banana parfait in crisp chocolate

WINE GUIDE ♀ Mango Bay Semillion Chardonnay £19 • ♀ Mango Bay Shiraz £19 • 212 bottles over £20 • 23 by the glass (£6-£33)

PRICE GUIDE Fixed L £10-£20 • Fixed D £50 • starter £15 • main £30 • dessert £15 • coffee £4.50 • min/water £3.95 • Service optional

OUR TIP: Try the organic café at the spa for a healthy treat

Chef: Duncan Ray **Owners:** Exclusive Hotels **Times:** 12-2.30/7-10, Closed BHs, Sun-Mon, closed L Sat **Notes:** Vegetarian available, Civ Wed 160 **Seats:** 36, Pr/dining room 160 **Smoking:** N/Sm in restaurant, Air con **Children:** Min 12 yrs, Portions **Rooms:** 123 (123 en suite) ★★★★ **Directions:** On A30 between Bagshot & Camberley **Parking:** 500

DORKING MAP 06 TQ14

The Burford Bridge

British, French

Enjoyable dining in historic hotel setting

☎ 0870 400 8283 Burford Bridge, Box Hill RH5 6BX

MENU GUIDE Poached oysters & fennel mousse • Turbot, smoked cheddar glaze • Chocolate & banana fondant

WINE GUIDE ♀ Ca' Lunghetta Pinot Grigio £17.50 • ♀ Marques de Caceres Rioja £20.95 • 52 bottles over £20, 28 bottles under £20 • 12 by the glass (£4.25-£7)

PRICE GUIDE Fixed L £13.95 • Fixed D £26.50 • starter £8.95-£10.95 • main £20.50-£28.50 • dessert £6.50-£6.95 • coffee £3.75 • min/water £4.55 • Service added but optional 12.5%

PLACE: This is a hotel with a history as it is rumoured to be the final meeting place of Lord Nelson and Lady Hamilton before the Battle of Trafalgar, and it is said that the surrounding landscape has inspired poets. The restaurant offers formal elegance overlooking the stunning gardens.
FOOD: The menus continue to be modern British in style with strong European, particularly French, influences, as in mosaic of foie gras, baby apple soufflé, cranberry brioche and cinnamon sauce.
OUR TIP: Visit the RHS gardens at Wisley
Chef: John Forestier **Owners:** Macdonald Hotels **Times:** 12-2.30/7-9.30, Closed D 25-26 Dec **Notes:** Vegetarian available, Dress Restrictions, No Jeans, Civ Wed 200 **Seats:** 60, Pr/dining room 18 **Smoking:** N/Sm in restaurant **Children:** Menu, Portions **Rooms:** 57 (57 en suite) ★★★★
Directions: M25 junct 9. Towards Dorking, the hotel is on the A24 at the Burford Bridge roundabout **Parking:** 140
e-mail: burfordbridge@macdonald-hotels.co.uk
web: www.macdonaldhotels.co.uk

☕ Haskett's Tea & Coffee Shop

86 South St RH4 2EW ☎ 01306 885833 Winner of The Tea Guild Award of Excellence 2005.

EGHAM MAP 06 TQ07

Great Fosters

Modern, International

Regal Elizabethan setting for top-notch cuisine

☎ 01784 433822 Stroude Rd TW20 9UR

MENU GUIDE Foie gras terrine, apple brioche, peach jelly • Rabbit, prunes, celeriac fondant, herb gnocchi • Poached raspberry meringue

WINE GUIDE ♀ Jose Pariente Rueda Superior Verdejo £24 • ♀ Bodegas Los Llanos Pata Negra Gran Reserva Tempranillo £26 • 290 bottles over £20, 8 bottles under £20 15 by the glass (£4-£6.50)

PRICE GUIDE Fixed L £19.50 • Fixed D £34.50 • starter £9-£12 • main £22-£25 • dessert £8-£9 • coffee £3.75 • min/water £3.95 • Service added but optional 10%

PLACE: A truly exceptional dinner destination, this majestic Elizabethan manor has served as a sumptuous retreat for everyone from Henry VIII to Charlie Chaplin. Dark woods, deep sofas and magnificent tapestries blend with exquisite period features inside, while a wander in the grounds reveals a knot garden and Saxon moat.
FOOD: A well-balanced menu of accomplished modern cooking from an ambitious kitchen. Ingredients are first-rate and thoughtfully combined in dishes such as beef with a horseradish fritter, steak and kidney ravioli, and watercress cream. Notable wine list.

continued

OUR TIP: Afternoon tea in the cocktail bar or drawing room
Chef: Jerry Davies **Owners:** Great Fosters (1931) Ltd **Times:** 12.30-2/7-9.30, Closed L Sat **Notes:** Vegetarian available, Civ Wed 170 **Seats:** 60, Pr/dining room 20 **Smoking:** N/Sm in restaurant **Children:** Portions
Directions: 1m from town centre **Parking:** 200
e-mail: enquiries@greatfosters.co.uk **web:** www.greatfosters.co.uk

EPSOM MAP 06 TQ26

Chalk Lane Hotel

British, French

Country hotel dining close to Epsom Racecourse

☎ 01372 721179 Chalk Ln, Woodcote End KT18 7BB

MENU GUIDE Seared scallops, cauliflower pannacotta • Duo of lamb (navarin & roast chump), ratatouille • Prune & vanilla tartlet

WINE GUIDE ♀ Jean de Vigne Sauvignon Blanc/Colombard £14.50 • ♀ Casa Rivas Merlot £19.50 • 52 bottles over £20, 23 bottles under £20 • 11 by the glass

PRICE GUIDE Fixed L £10-£16.50 • starter £5-£12 • main £14-£24 • dessert £4.50-£7.50 • coffee £2.25 • min/water £3.50 • Service added but optional 12.5%

PLACE: An intimate hotel restaurant only a ten-minute walk from the racecourse. It is a Grade II listed property located in a conservation area of the town. The restaurant has contemporary decor, with clothed tables and upholstered chairs.
FOOD: An imaginative range of modern dishes is skilfully produced from good quality ingredients, with producers and suppliers credited in the menu. A choice of simply cooked grillades is offered in addition to the carte, such as poached salmon or seared rib-eye.
OUR TIP: A separate vegetarian menu is available
Chef: Greg Lewis **Owners:** Steven McGregor **Times:** 12.30-2.30/7-10, Closed L Sat **Notes:** Vegetarian available, Dress Restrictions, Smart casual **Seats:** 40, Pr/dining room 20 **Smoking:** N/Sm in restaurant **Children:** Portions **Directions:** M25 junct 9 then A24 towards Ashtead & Epsom. Just in Epsom turn right at BP garage, then left into Avenue Road & follow hotel signs **Parking:** 60
e-mail: smcgregor@chalklanehotel.com **web:** www.chalklanehotel.com

FARNHAM MAP 05 SU84

⊛⊛ Bishop's Table Hotel

British, French

Robust flavours amidst Georgian surroundings

☎ 01252 710222   27 West St GU9 7DR

MENU GUIDE Assiette of foie gras, griottine cherries • Roast monkfish, oxtail ravioli, pancetta • Sticky toffee soufflé, apricot sorbet

WINE GUIDE ♀ Charente Sauvignon £11.40 • ♀ Domaine Virginie Vin de Pays de l'Herault Grenache/Syrah £11.40 • 88 bottles over £20, 22 bottles under £20 • 6 by the glass (£3.50-£4.25)

PRICE GUIDE Fixed L £15-£17.50 • starter £6.95-£9.80 • main £16.50-£18.20 • dessert £6.75-£6.95 • coffee £3.50 • min/water £3.60 • Service optional

PLACE: Georgian townhouse, which has in its time been a school for the clergy and residence of the Bishop of Winchester. Small and intimate, the restaurant is elegantly furnished and decorated in pastel shades for a calm and relaxing atmosphere. Tables are laid with white china on white linen, and effective modern lighting enhances the period effect.
FOOD: Modern British with hints of classical French, making good use of fresh, seasonal produce. Some of the dishes are complex, but all are full of flavour and delivered with style.
OUR TIP: There's a resident ghost called William
Chef: James Cooper **Owners:** Mr K Verjee **Times:** 12.30-1.45/7-9.45, Closed 26 Dec-5 Jan, closed L Mon **Notes:** Sun L £15, Vegetarian available, No jeans or T shirts **Seats:** 55, Pr/dining room 36
Smoking: N/Sm in restaurant **Children:** Portions **Rooms:** 17 (17 en suite) ★★★ **Directions:** A331 to town centre, next to public library
Parking: Street parking, pay & display (300 yds)
e-mail: welcome@bishopstable.com **web:** www.bishopstable.com

GODALMING MAP 06 SU94

⊛ La Luna

Modern Italian

Stylish two-tone Italian restaurant

☎ 01483 414155   10 Wharf St GU7 1NN

MENU GUIDE Roasted suckling pig, vin santo sauce, chickpea pancake • Wild boar rolls, ragu gnocchi • Chocolate & pear torte

WINE GUIDE ♀ Roberto Anselmi Capital Croce Garganega £30 • ♀ Forador Teroldego £28 • 130 bottles over £20, 11 bottles under £20 • 8 by the glass (£5)

PRICE GUIDE Fixed L £11.95 • starter £5.95-£9.50 • main £12.95-£16.95 • dessert £4.75-£5.95 • coffee £2 • min/water £3.75

PLACE: Sophisticated venue in the centre of Godalming, bright by day and romantic by night with its black and white decor and smooth jazz. Professional service is provided by friendly, formally attired Italian staff.

La Luna

FOOD: Rustic Italian food offered from a comprehensive selection in traditional style: anti pasta, primi, secondi and dessert. A shortened lunch menu is also available at a very good price.
OUR TIP: Superb list of Italian wines including many unusual bottles
Chef: Giovanni Puglisi, **Owners:** Daniele Drago & Orazio Primavera **Times:** 12-2/7-10, Closed early Jan, 2 wks in Aug, Sun-Mon **Notes:** Tasting menu 5 courses £50-60 (incl. wine), Vegetarian available **Seats:** 58, Pr/dining room 24 **Smoking:** N/Sm in restaurant, Air con **Children:** Portions **Directions:** In centre of Godalming, junction of Wharf St & Flambard Way **Parking:** Public car park behind restaurant **e-mail:** laluna@tiscali.co.uk **web:** www.lalunarestaurant.co.uk

GUILDFORD MAP 06 SU94

⊛ Café de Paris

French

Really popular French brasserie & restaurant

☎ 01483 534896   35 Castle St GU1 3UQ

MENU GUIDE French onion soup • Roast halibut fillet, almond & basil crust • Delice au chocolat tiède

WINE GUIDE ♀ Le Lesc Plaimont Ugni Blanc/Colombard £11.95 • ♀ Les Clairieres Jean d'Alibert Merlot £11.95 • 40 bottles over £20, 22 bottles under £20 • 13 by the glass (£2.95-£7)

PRICE GUIDE Fixed L £12.50 • starter £3.95-£11.50 main £8.50-£24 • dessert £3.95-£6.50 • coffee £2 min/water £2.95 • Service added but optional 10%

PLACE: In a restaurant-filled street in the oldest part of Guildford, this one really stands out from the crowd. The setting is authentically French, from the posters and wine racks to the tiled floor and circular white-clad tables.
FOOD: All the classics are there, from Châteaubriand (for two) to foie gras-stuffed pigeon breasts, carré d'agneau and magret de canard. The restaurant is pricier than the brasserie, but offers more choice.
OUR TIP: Great venue for homesick Francophiles

continued

continued

GUILDFORD continued MAP 06 SU94

Chef: Eric Devaux **Owners:** Frank & Maya Kraus/Cafe De Paris Ltd
Times: 12-2.30/6.00-10.30, Closed Xmas Wk, BHs, closed D Sun
Notes: Vegetarian available, Smart casual **Seats:** 80, Pr/dining room 50
Smoking: N/Sm area, No pipes, Air con **Children:** Portions
Directions: Guildford town centre, corner of Castle and Chapel Streets
Parking: NCP **web:** www.cafedeparisguildford.co.uk

HASLEMERE MAP 06 SU93

Lythe Hill Hotel

French

Sumptuous hotel dining in Surrey countryside

☎ 01428 651251 Petworth Rd GU27 3BQ

MENU GUIDE Tuna carpaccio, foie gras • Confit duck leg, Madeira jus • Roast baby pineapple, orange sorbet

WINE GUIDE ♀ Miguel Torres Curico Valley Sauvignon Blanc £18 • ♀ Domaine Corne-Loup Côtes du Rhône Shiraz £24 • 6 by the glass (£5.50-£6.50)

PRICE GUIDE Fixed L £10.95 • starter £7-£12 • main £17-£29 • dessert £8 • coffee £3 • min/water £4.75 • Service optional

PLACE: There's a choice of ancient and modern dining venues at this privately owned hotel and spa surrounded by its own 30 acres of parkland. The 15th-century Auberge de France offers fine dining in wood-panelled splendour whilst diners in the Italian Garden can enjoy lighter dishes in a more contemporary setting.
FOOD: Classic French dishes are given a fusion twist here with crispy pork belly arriving with a Vietnamese salad and baked piquillo peppers being served with couscous and mozzarella. Good quality ingredients attractively presented.
OUR TIP: Experience the hotel spa
Chef: Neil Wackrill **Owners:** Auberge De France **Times:** 12.30-2.15/7.15-9.15, Closed L Sat **Notes:** Sun L £25.50, Vegetarian available, Civ Wed 130 **Seats:** 60, Pr/dining room 35 **Smoking:** N/Sm in restaurant **Children:** Menu, Portions **Rooms:** 41 (41 en suite) ★★★★
Directions: 1 mile E of Haslemere on B2131 **Parking:** 150
e-mail: lythe@lythehill.co.uk **web:** www.lythehill.co.uk

HORLEY

Langshott Manor

British, European

Stylish Tudor house hotel amidst award-winning gardens

☎ 01293 786680 Langshott Ln RH6 9LN

MENU GUIDE Trio of Scottish salmon • Braised & roasted lamb • Assiette of Swiss chocolate

WINE GUIDE ♀ La Croisade Sauvignon Blanc £18.95 • ♀ Marques de Riscal Reserve Tempranillo £34.50 • 95 bottles over £20, 6 bottles under £20 • 4 by the glass (£5-£6.50)

continued

Langshott Manor

PRICE GUIDE Fixed L £17.50 • Fixed D £38 • starter £7.50-£11 • main £18-£25 • dessert £7-£7.50 • coffee £4 • min/water £3.50 • Service added 12.5% • Group service 12.5%

PLACE: Charming timber-framed Tudor house hotel set in three acres of beautifully landscaped gardens. The stylishly decorated public areas boast plushly furnished lounges with polished-oak panelling, exposed beams and log fires. The Mulberry restaurant has an intimate atmosphere and overlooks a picturesque pond.
FOOD: A classical menu with modern twists - the use of local and high quality produce is the key to the successful cooking here. Preparation is precise and allows flavours of ingredients to shine through. Herbs and vegetables are often grown in the adjoining garden. Friendly and efficient service.
OUR TIP: Convenient for Gatwick Airport
Chef: Stephen Toward **Owners:** Peter & Deborah Hinchcliffe **Times:** 12.30/7-9.30 **Notes:** Vegetarian available, Dress Restrictions, No Jeans, jacket and tie, Civ Wed 60 **Seats:** 55, Pr/dining room 22
Smoking: N/Sm in restaurant **Children:** Min 12 yrs, Portions
Rooms: 22 (22 en suite) ★★★ **Directions:** From A23, Horley, take Ladbroke Rd turning off Chequers Hotel rdbt, 0.75m on right **Parking:** 2
e-mail: admin@langshottmanor.com **web:** www.langshottmanor.com

OCKLEY MAP 06 TQ14

Bryce's Seafood Restaurant

British, Seafood

Busy fish restaurant in quiet village

☎ 01306 627430 The Old School House RH5 5TH

MENU GUIDE Tian of Portland crab, cucumber & mint crème fraîche • Sea bream, smoked garlic risotto • Orange & stem ginger pudding, spiced crème anglaise

WINE GUIDE ♀ Honore de Berticot Sauvignon Blanc £12.50 • ♀ Ochoa Garnacha/Tempranillo £12.50 • 19 bottles over £20, 25 bottles under £20 • 15 by the glass (£3.20-£4.25)

PRICE GUIDE Fixed L £22 • Fixed D £27.50 • coffee £1.50 min/water £3.50 • Service optional • Group min 8 service 10%

PLACE: A former boys' boarding school, dating from 1825, with

continue

the building split between a traditional pub and a restaurant. Full of charm and character, with exposed beams and brickwork, and a warming log fire in the bar.
FOOD: Fresh fish and seafood is the mainstay of the printed menu and ever-changing blackboards. Meat-eaters are not forgotten and there's a separate vegetarian menu.
OUR TIP: Look out for special event evenings
Chef: B Bryce and Richard Attkins **Owners:** Mr B Bryce **Times:** 12-2.30/7-9.30, Closed 25 Dec, 1 Jan, closed D Sun in Nov, Jan & Feb **Notes:** Vegetarian available **Seats:** 50 **Smoking:** N/Sm in restaurant **Children:** Portions **Directions:** From M25 junct 9 take A24, then A29. 8m S of Dorking on A29 **Parking:** 35 **e-mail:** bryces.fish@virgin.net **web:** www.bryces.co.uk

---

PEASLAKE MAP 06 TQ04

 **Hurtwood Inn Hotel**
Modern British
Inviting country dining room offering modern cooking
☎ 01306 730851 Walking Bottom GU5 9RR
MENU GUIDE Stilton & red onion parcels, balsamic & tomato chutney • Lamb rump, garlic pomme purée, rosemary jus • Rhubarb pannacotta
WINE GUIDE ♀ Sauvignon Blanc £12.95 • ♥ Merlot £12.95 33 bottles over £20, 18 bottles under £20 • 8 by the glass (£2.75-£3.95)
PRICE GUIDE Starter £5-£5.95 • main £14.95-£18.95 • dessert £4.95-£5.95 • coffee £2 • min/water £2.95 • Service optional
PLACE: Recently refurbished, this intimate restaurant has a cosy traditional feel and its elegantly skirted tables are attended by friendly staff.
FOOD: A concise menu of classy cuisine that's also available in the hotel's more informal bistro. Dishes are modern British in style, and might include supreme of guinea fowl in pancetta with sweet potato mash.
OUR TIP: Try the bar for snacks
Chef: Gerry Dee **Owners:** Mrs S Best **Times:** 12-2/7-9.30, Closed 26-30 Dec, 1 Jan, closed L Mon-Sat, closed D Sun **Notes:** Sun L 2 courses £13.95, 3 courses £15.95, Vegetarian available, Smart Dress, No trainers or shorts **Seats:** 30, Pr/dining room 25 **Smoking:** N/Sm in restaurant **Children:** Portions **Rooms:** 21 (21 en suite) ★★★ **Directions:** Leave A25 in Gomshall, follow signs to Peaslake, turn opposite Jet Garage, follow hotel signs **Parking:** 22 **e-mail:** sales@hurtwoodinnhotel.com **web:** www.hurtwoodinnhotel.com

---

REDHILL MAP 06 TQ25

 **Nutfield Priory**
British, European
Victorian mansion with commanding country views
☎ 01737 824400 Nutfield RH1 4EL
MENU GUIDE Seared scallops, duck confit • Poached lamb, chervil mousse, tomato sauce • Vanilla pannacotta, strawberry mille-feuille
WINE GUIDE ♀ La Serre Sauvignon Blanc £18 • ♥ La Serre Merlot £18 • 76 bottles over £20, 11 bottles under £20 • 8 by the glass (£4.50-£11)
PRICE GUIDE Fixed L £18.50-£22.50 • Fixed D £35-£40 • starter £6-£13.50 • main £15-£25 • dessert £6.50-£9 • coffee £3.50 • min/water £4 • Service optional
PLACE: Built in the 1870s, this imposing property is styled after Westminster Palace. Architectural features include stone and wood carvings, lofty ceilings, leaded stained glass windows and impressive chandeliers. The priory is set in 40 acres of grounds, high up on Nutfield Ridge, with great views.

continued

FOOD: Cooking is fairly classical in the main with some European twists, and strong use is made of quality ingredients. The two-course lunch is good value with just slightly less choice than at dinner.
OUR TIP: Only 8 miles from Gatwick Airport
Chef: Neil Davidson **Owners:** Handpicked Hotels **Times:** 12-2/7-9.30, Closed L Sat **Notes:** Dress Restrictions, No jeans, Civ Wed 80 **Seats:** 60, Pr/dining room 100 **Smoking:** N/Sm in restaurant **Children:** Portions **Rooms:** 60 (60 en suite) ★★★★ **Directions:** On A25, 1m E of Redhill **Parking:** 130 **e-mail:** nutfieldpriory@handpicked.co.uk **web:** www.handpicked.co.uk/nutfieldpriory

---

REIGATE MAP 06 TQ25

 The Dining Room
Modern British
Understated modern restaurant dining
☎ 01737 226650 59a High St RH2 9AE
MENU GUIDE Scallops, Thai crab cake, hot & sweet syrup • Roast duck, chorizo risotto • Dark chocolate & cashew tart, cashew praline ice cream
WINE GUIDE ♀ Pouilly Fumé £26 • ♥ Mansion House Pinot Noir £26 most bottles over £20, 2 bottles under £20 • 4 by the glass (£4.50)
PRICE GUIDE Fixed L £16 • Fixed D £39.95 • starter £9 • main £19.50 • dessert £7.95 • coffee £3.50 • min/water £3.50 • Service added but optional 12.5%
PLACE: Classy contemporary eaterie, with a stylish, uncomplicated decor and a 'dining club' atmosphere, located above the shops at one end of the High Street. Foodie paintings and modern landscapes blend well with exposed beams and quality linen and glassware. Service is attentive and friendly.
FOOD: Exotic influences from the Mediterranean and Asia lift the flavours of the more traditional dishes on the seasonally changing and predominantly modern British menu. Cooking is simple and enjoyable.
OUR TIP: Champagne bar upstairs
Chef: Tony Tobin **Owners:** Tony Tobin **Times:** 12-2/7-10, Closed Xmas & BH's, closed L Sat, closed D Sun **Notes:** Vegetarian available **Seats:** 75, Pr/dining room 28 **Smoking:** N/Sm in restaurant, Air con **Children:** Portions **Directions:** 1st floor restaurant on Reigate High Street **Parking:** On street, car park

---

RIPLEY MAP 06 TQ05

 Drake's *see page 446*

SHERE MAP 06 TQ04

Kinghams
British
Innovative cuisine in intimate setting
☎ 01483 202168 Gomshall Ln GU5 9HE

continued

England

RIPLEY MAP 06 TQ05

Drake's

French, European
Skilled cooking in village restaurant
☎ 01483 224777 The Clock House, High St GU23 6AQ
MENU GUIDE Scallops, duck & sesame salad • Venison, wild mushrooms, peppercorn sauce • Banana parfait, caramel sauce
WINE GUIDE ♀ Henri Bourgeios Sauvignon Blanc £34.50
♣ Domaine des Grands Fers Christian Bernard Pinot Noir £25
72 bottles over £20, 24 bottles under £20 • 8 by the glass (£4-£6)
PRICE GUIDE Fixed L £18 • Fixed D £33.50-£39.50 • coffee £3.50 • min/water £3.50 • Service optional

PLACE: Occupying a Georgian house on the village high street, Drake's is a friendly place to dine. A lemon and green colour scheme is complemented by interesting artwork and smartly appointed tables, with a pretty garden for summer drinks.
FOOD: Expect modern European cooking of great skill and flair from Steve Drake, created from quality local ingredients where possible. Classical favourites are delivered with eclectic modern twists, and presented with elegant simplicity. You might start with a foie gras and chicken terrine served with peppered pineapple,

followed by lamb saddle with a parsley and mint crumb.
OUR TIP: Leave space for the amazing petits fours
Chef: Steve Drake **Owners:** Steve & Serina Drake **Times:** 12-1.30/7-9.30, Closed 2 wks Xmas, 2 wks Aug, Sun, Mon, L Sat **Notes:** Vegetarian available, Smart casual **Seats:** 34, Pr/dining room 10 **Directions:** A3 Ripley turn off after M25 junct **Parking:** 4
web: www.drakesrestaurant.co.uk

SHERE *continued* MAP 06 TQ04
MENU GUIDE Fresh crab & orange steamed in a won ton wrapper • Medley of lamb • Light chilled citrus soufflé
WINE GUIDE ♀ Hawkes Bridge Sauvignon £22.50 • ♣ Avila Cabernet Sauvignon £26.50 • 24 bottles over £20, 22 bottles under £20 • 4 by the glass (£3-£3.50)
PRICE GUIDE Fixed L £14.95 • Fixed D £21.70 • starter £5.95-£8.95 • main £10.95-£22.95 • dessert £5.75-£5.95 • coffee £2.50 • min/water £3 • Service optional • Group min 8 service 10%

PLACE: A 1640s building constructed when Shere's wool trade was prospering, though previous owners reputedly included sheep thieves, one of whom was hung from the gibbet outside town. Today the low ceilings and beams, crisp white linen and friendly serving staff ensure a relaxed and intimate dining experience; a heated gazebo in the garden is a summer option.
FOOD: Imaginative and creative cooking uses high quality ingredients from local companies and farms; fresh fish is delivered daily. Attention to detail and artistic presentation are the icing on the cake.
OUR TIP: Desserts are amazing
Chef: Paul Baker **Owners:** Paul Baker **Times:** 12.15-2.30/7-9.30, Closed 25 Dec-4 Jan, Mon, closed D Sun **Notes:** Vegetarian available **Seats:** 48, Pr/dining room 24 **Smoking:** N/Sm in restaurant **Children:** Portions **Directions:** On A25 between Guildford and Dorking. 12 mins from M25 junct 10 **Parking:** 16 **e-mail:** paul@kinghams-restaurant.co.uk **web:** www.kinghams-restaurant.co.uk

STOKE D'ABERNON MAP 06 TQ15
Woodlands Park Hotel
Modern European
Grand country house cooking
☎ 01372 843933 Woodlands Ln KT11 3QB
MENU GUIDE Salmon & langoustine ballottine • Cajun-spiced mackerel fillet • Spiced apple & pear tartlet
WINE GUIDE ♀ La Serre Sauvignon Blanc £17.50 • ♣ La Serre Merlot £17.50 • 85 bottles over £20, 8 bottles under £20 • 10 by the glass (£5.50-£13)
PRICE GUIDE Fixed D £39 • min/water £3.50 • Service optional

PLACE: Edward VII and Lillie Langtry were seduced by its grandeur and beauty, and Oscar Wilde's stays here are the stuff of legend. The restaurant's splendours still draw breaths of admiration from modern visitors.
FOOD: A light touch brings out the uncomplicated flavours of crab samosas on mango carpaccio with coriander and chives, while a top quality seared foie gras sits comfortably with a dish of squab pigeon. Quality ingredients are consistently handled with assurance.
OUR TIP: Try the Quotes Bar & Brasserie
Chef: Ian Howard **Owners:** Hand Picked Hotels **Times:** 12-2.30/7-10, Closed Mon, closed L Mon-Sat, closed D Sun **Notes:** Coffee incl., Vegetarian available, Dress Restrictions, No jeans or trainers, Civ Wed 200 **Seats:** 35, Pr/dining room 130 **Smoking:** N/Sm in restaurant **Children:** Menu, Portions **Rooms:** 57 (57 en suite) ★★★★ **Directions:** From M25 junct 10, A3 towards London. Through Cobham centre and Stoke D'Abernon, left at garden centre into Woodlands Lane. Hotel 0.5m on left **Parking:** 150
e-mail: woodlandspark@handpicked.co.uk **web:** www.handpicked.co.u

TADWORTH MAP 06 TQ25

🖤🏵 *Gemini*

International

Modern, unfussy food in a stylish setting

☎ 01737 812179 28 Station Approach KT20 5AH

MENU GUIDE Spring onion & goats' cheese tartlet • Roast monkfish, mussel risotto • Caramelised banana charlotte, ice cream

PRICE GUIDE Food prices not confirmed for 2006. Please telephone for details

PLACE: Hidden in a row of shops, Gemini's unassuming exterior masks a stylish, elegant interior. The restaurant is split into two halves: a small, comfy bar and seating area, and the main restaurant. The decor is warm and relaxing, with mellow sunshine yellows and oranges, carpeted floors and tables clothed in white and cream.

FOOD: You're as likely to find onion bhajis or waffles as roast British lamb on this eclectic, modern menu. The cooking is technically very good, and allows all the flavours to come through.

OUR TIP: Plenty of parking within walking distance

Times: 12-2/7-9.30, Closed 2 wks Xmas, Mon, closed L Sat, closed D Sun **Directions:** A217/B290, on left before Tadworth station **e-mail:** comments@gemini-reataurant.com **web:** www.gemini-restaurant.com

SUSSEX, EAST

BATTLE MAP 07 TQ71

🖤🏵 Powder Mills Hotel

European, British

Elegant Georgian mansion adjoining the 1066 battlefield

☎ 01424 775511 Powdermill Ln TN33 0SP

MENU GUIDE Foie gras & leek terrine, Chardonnay/truffle gelée • Lamb loin in bacon, bubble & squeak, redcurrant jus • Pineapple parfait

WINE GUIDE ♀ Georges Duboeuf £12.50 • ♀ Georges Duboeuf £12.50 • 4 by the glass (£2.80-£3)

PRICE GUIDE Fixed L £18.50 • Fixed D £30 • coffee £1.75 • min/water £2.75 • Service added but optional 10% • Group service 10%

PLACE: Handsome country house set amid 200 acres of landscaped grounds with lakes and woodlands. A gunpowder works produced explosives here during the Napoleonic wars, and the house was built in 1796 after the previous one blew up. Public rooms include a lounge bar, music room, drawing room, library and conservatory, in addition to the marble-floored orangery restaurant, where wicker chairs and elegant tables are surrounded by Greek statues.

FOOD: The menu is modern English with European influences, using fresh local produce whenever possible. Cooking is accomplished and dishes are well presented. Lighter meals can be taken in the Library and Conservatory.

OUR TIP: There's a steam boat on the lake for weddings

Chef: James Penn **Owners:** Mr & Mrs D Cowpland **Times:** 12-2/7-9 **Notes:** Fixed ALC £35, Vegetarian available, Dress Restrictions, No jeans, shorts or T-shirts, Civ Wed 100 **Seats:** 90, Pr/dining room 16 **Smoking:** N/Sm in restaurant **Children:** Not at D, Menu, Portions **Rooms:** 40 (40 en suite) ★★★ **Directions:** A21/A2100 past Battle Abbey. Turn into Powder Mill Lane, first right **Parking:** 100 **e-mail:** powdc@aol.com **web:** www.powdermillshotel.com

BRIGHTON MAP 06 TQ30

🏵 Alias Hotel Seattle

Mediterranean 🐟🍴

Contemporary dining by Brighton Marina

☎ 01273 679 799 The Strand, Brighton Marina BN2 5WA

MENU GUIDE Steamed mussels in ouzo, smoked velouté • Red mullet, angel hair pasta, orange sauce • Bitter chocolate fondant, tuaca ice

WINE GUIDE ♀ Veramonte Sauvignon Blanc £14.50 • ♀ Don Jacobo Tempranillo £16.95 • 39 bottles over £20, 38 bottles under £20 • 12 by the glass (£3.60-£4.80)

PRICE GUIDE Starter £4.25-£9.55 • main £7.95-£25 • dessert £4.75 • coffee £1.10 • min/water £3 • Service optional

PLACE: Floor to ceiling glass-fronted restaurant with stunning views of Brighton Marina. Inside, expect antique French chandeliers and pre-war German mannequins dressed in trendy gear. There's a bar area with retro leather chairs and a slick, separate cocktail bar called Black & White.

FOOD: Modern Mediterranean meets updated British classics on the Café Paradiso menu specialising in fresh fish and gourmet pizzas from the wood-fired oven. There's plenty to interest vegetarians, too.

OUR TIP: Check out the Seattle supper club

Chef: Fabien Figuet **Owners:** Alias Hotels Plc **Times:** 12-3/6-10.30 **Notes:** Vegetarian available, Civ Wed 8 **Seats:** 96, Pr/dining room 100 **Smoking:** N/Sm area **Children:** Portions **Rooms:** 71 (71 en suite) ★★★★ **Directions:** Follow signs to the seafront, turn left along seafront. Follow signs to Brighton Marina **Parking:** Mulit Storey 100m (free) **e-mail:** info@aliasseattle.com **web:** www.aliashotels.com

For information on Service Charge, see p21.

England

BRIGHTON MAP 06 TQ30

Due South

British ↷◇NEW

Ethically sound food by the sea

☎ 01273 821218 139 Kings Rd Arches BN1 2FN

MENU GUIDE Due South fish soup • Sirloin, garlic button onion confit, mushrooms, red wine jus • Elderflower & vanilla pannacotta

WINE GUIDE ♀ Curious Grape Flint Dry £13.95 • ♥ Clos de Torribas Crianza Pinord £14.95 • 21 bottles over £20, 15 bottles under £20 • 10 by the glass (£3.50-£4.70)

PRICE GUIDE Food prices not confirmed for 2006. Please telephone for details

PLACE: A modern glass-fronted restaurant located within an arch on Brighton's promenade. Located at beach level, it has excellent sea views and alfresco dining in the summer. A popular restaurant with a buzzing, yet relaxed atmosphere, its distinct character is enhanced by busy young staff who are passionate about its ethos.

FOOD: The simple, uncomplicated menu is underpinned by a commitment to environmentally sustainable, fresh, locally sourced, seasonal produce. Seafood is a speciality.

OUR TIP: Great for sea views

Chef: Richard Hodgeson **Owners:** Robert Shenton **Times:** 12-4/6-9.30, Closed 2 wks Xmas & New Yr, closed D Sun **Notes:** Vegetarian available **Seats:** 55, Pr/dining room 14 **Smoking:** N/Sm in restaurant **Children:** Min 14 D, Portions **Parking:** NCP Churchill Sq **e-mail:** eat@duesouth.co.uk **web:** www.duesouth.co.uk

The Gingerman Restaurant

British, French 🍴

Popular, relaxed and unpretentious restaurant

☎ 01273 326688 21A Norfolk Square BN1 2PD

MENU GUIDE Scallops, aubergine tortellini • Slow-roasted lamb, mustard potato, rosemary jus • Spiced apple soufflé, Calvados cream

WINE GUIDE ♀ Domaine Daulny Sancerre le Clos de Chaudenay Sauvignon Blanc £25 • ♥ Château Treytins St Emilion Treytins Cabernet/Merlot £23 • 23 bottles over £20, 15 bottles under £20 • 2 by the glass (£3.50)

PRICE GUIDE Fixed L £12.95 • Fixed D £29 • coffee £2 • min/water £3 • Group min 6 service 10%

PLACE: A long, narrow but cosy room in warm shades of cream, with stripped floorboards and simple artwork, draws a savvy local crowd to this bustling, relaxed and friendly little restaurant just off one of the Regency squares. Many customers here are greeted on first name terms.

FOOD: Owner and executive chef Ben McKellar creates a fashionable, modern-focused menu that is underpinned by a French classical theme. Quality produce, locally sourced whenever possible, and excellent flavour combinations, without over-complication, illustrate the kitchen's skill, via value fixed-price menus.

OUR TIP: Quality lunch at a bargain price, but be sure to book early for dinner

Chef: Ben McKellar/David Keates **Owners:** Ben & Pamela McKellar **Times:** 12.30-2/7-10, Closed 2 wks winter, Sun-Mon **Notes:** Vegetarian available **Seats:** 32 **Smoking:** No pipes, No cigars, Air con **Children:** Portions **Directions:** Telephone for directions **e-mail:** info@gingermanrestaurants.com **web:** www.gingermanrestaurants.com

Hotel du Vin Brighton

French, European

Stylish brasserie dining in metropolitan hotel setting

☎ 01273 718588 Ship St BN1 1AD

MENU GUIDE Chicken liver & foie gras parfait • Châteaubriand & Béarnaise sauced • Tarte Tatin

WINE GUIDE 700 bottles over £20, 50 bottles under £20 • 16 by the glass (£3.50-£15)

PRICE GUIDE Starter £6.75-£8.75 • main £14.95-£16.95 dessert £6.50 • coffee £2.75 • min/water £3.50 • Service optional

PLACE: Situated in a tastefully converted, mock-Tudor building, this stylish hotel is in a quiet side street close to the sea front. Decor has a strong wine theme. There are comfortable bedrooms, a split-level bar and a relaxed brasserie style restaurant.

FOOD: Cooking is modern European in style with a pronounced French accent. Nice to see dishes like seared duck's heart with provençale sauce and robust coq au vin with mash. Helpful service. Excellent wine list.

OUR TIP: Location makes parking difficult so plan ahead

Chef: Rob Carr **Owners:** Marylebone Warwick Balfour **Times:** 12-2/7-10, closed L Dec 31 lunch only **Notes:** Set price lunch Sun only £23.50, (private dining £33.50), Vegetarian available **Seats:** 85, Pr/dining room 5 **Smoking:** N/Sm in restaurant **Children:** Menu, Portions **Rooms:** 37 (37 en suite) ★★★★ **Directions:** A23 to seafront, at rdbt take right, then 3rd right **Parking:** 10 **e-mail:** info@brighton.hotelduvin.com **web:** www.hotelduvin.com

One Paston Place

European

Imaginative cooking in plush surroundings

☎ 01273 606933 1 Paston Place BN2 1HA

continue

MENU GUIDE Tuna carpaccio, rocket & lemon mousseline • Pancetta, apple compote, broccoli • Sadler tiramisù

WINE GUIDE ♀ Sancerre Clos Des Bouffants Sauvignon Blanc £26 • ♀ Auxey-Duresses Les Clous Pinot Noir £29 • 7 bottles over £20, 12 bottles under £20 • 5 by the glass (£4.50)

PRICE GUIDE Fixed L £16.50-£32.50 • Fixed D £39 • coffee £3.50 • min/water £3.50 • Service optional

PLACE: The baroque and classical interior here has well-spaced tables, crisp table linen, beautiful fresh flowers and oil lamps which, combined with the large chandeliers, give a wonderful theatrical light to this dining room. Claret and gold drapes and antique mirrors add an opulent touch. Hidden down a road between the Palace Pier and the Marina, it is easy to miss but a delight to find. Exemplary service.

FOOD: Contemporary European cooking using carefully sourced ingredients, such as Fir Honey Dew from Northern Italy, hand-dived scallops and local Sussex lamb. With signature dishes like seared scallops with white truffle fondant, port sauce and Alba white truffle shavings, dining here is a sensory experience. Notable wine list.

OUR TIP: Parking is difficult. Call a cab

Chef: Francesco Furriello **Owners:** Gusto Ltd **Times:** 12-2/19-10, Closed Sun-Mon **Notes:** Vegetarian available **Seats:** 40 **Smoking:** N/Sm in restaurant, Air con **Children:** Min 7 yrs, Portions **Directions:** Between Palace Pier & Marina **Parking:** Street parking available
e-mail: info@onepastonplace.co.uk
web: www.onepastonplace.co.uk

Sevendials

European

An epicurean oasis in busy Sevendials
☎ 01273 885555 1-3 Buckingham Place
BN1 3TD

MENU GUIDE Sautéed sweetbreads, pancetta, peas & broad beans • Pork belly, apple & orange compote • Strawberry & vanilla cream tart

WINE GUIDE ♀ Le Charme Sauvignon £12.50 • ♀ Pure Merlot £13 • 53 bottles over £20, 15 bottles under £20 • 6 by the glass (£2.75-£3.75)

PRICE GUIDE Fixed L £10-£21.50 • Fixed D £26.50 • starter £5 • main £10 • dessert £5 • coffee £1.70 • min/water £3 • Service added but optional 12%

PLACE: A masterly conversion of a bank has resulted in this lofty eaterie in one of Brighton's most popular areas. The elegant space rises up from dark wooden floors, and there's a smart terrace for summer dining.

FOOD: Intense flavours and vivid colours bring an unmistakeable taste of Europe to the English seaside. Excellent fish dishes include céviche of monkfish delicately balanced with the sharper red onions, chilli and avocado, and cherry crème brûlée is simply sublime.

OUR TIP: Short walk to the seafront
Chef: Sam Metcalfe **Owners:** Sam Metcalfe **Times:** 12-2.30/7-10.30, Closed Xmas & New Year, Mon **Notes:** Vegetarian available, Civ Wed 55 **Seats:** 55, Pr/dining room 20 **Smoking:** N/Sm area, No pipes, No cigars **Children:** Menu, Portions **Directions:** From Brighton station turn right 5m up hill, restaurant situated at Seven Dials rdbt **Parking:** Two mins from restaurant **e-mail:** sam@sevendialsrestaurant.co.uk
web: www.sevendialsrestaurant.co.uk

Terre à Terre
Modern Vegetarian
The ultimate vegetarian dining in stylish venue
☎ 01273 729051 71 East St BN1 1HQ

MENU GUIDE Truffled Jerusalem risotto • Fondue soufflé • Quince & fairy quills

PRICE GUIDE Food prices not confirmed for 2006. Please telephone for details

PLACE: Deceptively large, funkily colourful restaurant with only a few tables on show at the front. Staff are so natural and knowledgeable that the uninitiated will feel confident ordering the many unfamiliar choices. Forget any faddish hippie associations - this is the Mecca of modern vegetarian dining.
FOOD: Lengthy dish descriptions involving multiple ingredients and some quirky produce are balanced by clear guidelines given about dishes (vegan, gluten free, organic etc). Rizola are fried rice patties crammed with palm hearts and Masai Mara stuffing, and röstibrown is pan-fried potato and onion with optional toppings.
OUR TIP: Take home some divine piccalilli
Chef: Glen Lester **Owners:** Ms A Powley & Mr P Taylor **Times:** 12-3/6-10.30, Closed 24-26 Dec, 1 Jan, Mon, closed L Tue & Wed **Notes:** Vegetarian available **Seats:** 110 **Smoking:** N/Sm in restaurant, Air con **Children:** Menu, Portions **Directions:** Town centre near casino, close to Palace Pier & The Lanes **Parking:** NCP, on street
e-mail: mail@terreaterre.co.uk
web: www.terreaterre.co.uk

Loch Fyne Restaurant 95-99 Western Rd BN1 2LB
☎ 01273 716160 Quality seafood chain.

Regency Restaurant 131 Kings Rd BN1 2HH
☎ 01273 325014 Classic seafood restaurant dating back to the 1930s.

England

EASTBOURNE MAP 06 TV69

⚙️⚙️ Grand Hotel (Mirabelle)

British, European

Accomplished cooking in seafront Victorian surroundings

☎ 01323 412345 King Edward's Pde BN21 4EQ

MENU GUIDE Pike soufflé, smoked salmon • Roast French black-legged chicken, truffle jus • Banana & cardamom Tatin

WINE GUIDE 210 bottles over £20, 190 bottles under £20 • 11 by the glass (£3.70-£5.70)

PRICE GUIDE Fixed L £16.50 • Fixed D £35-£42 • min/water £3 • Service added but optional 10%

PLACE: This famous Victorian hotel situated on King Edwards Parade overlooks the beach and has been sympathetically restored to its former glory. The dining room with separate street entrance is light and airy. The jacket and tie dress code is less rigorously enforced than in the past and the atmosphere is relaxed with attentive and thoughtful service throughout.

FOOD: Modern interpretations of classic dishes populate a fixed price, an à la carte and a tasting menu. Good recommendations for wines to accompany each course are available for a supplement. Notable wine list.

OUR TIP: Take afternoon tea in the impressive Grand Hall

Chef: Keith Mitchell, Gerald Roser **Owners:** Elite Hotels **Times:** 12.30-2/7-10, Closed 1-14 Jan, Sun-Mon **Notes:** Tasting menu £55, incl. wine £84, coffee incl., Vegetarian available, Dress Restrictions, Jacket or tie for D, Civ Wed 200 **Seats:** 50 **Smoking:** N/Sm in restaurant, Air con **Children:** Min 12 yrs **Rooms:** 152 (152 en suite) ★★★★★
Directions: Western end of the seafront **Parking:** 50
e-mail: reservations@grandeastbourne.com
web: www.grandeastbourne.com

FOREST ROW MAP 06 TQ43

⚙️⚙️ Ashdown Park Hotel

British, European

Innovative cuisine in magnificent country-house hotel

☎ 01342 824988 Wych Cross RH18 5JR

MENU GUIDE Pan-fried foie gras, roasted squab, Sauternes jus • Saddle of venison, cracked pepper sauce • Lemon pannacotta, crushed meringues & blueberries

WINE GUIDE ⚲ Colombard Soave Classico Garganega £20 ⚲ Gerard Bertrand 6 eme Sens Syrah/Grenache £18 357 bottles over £20, 21 bottles under £20 • 16 by the glass (£4.50-£8)

PRICE GUIDE Fixed L £16 • Fixed D £35 • coffee £3.25 min/water £3 • Service added 10%

PLACE: The impressive Victorian country mansion, set in many acres of woods and parkland deep in the Ashdown Forest, was a convent and a training centre before becoming a fine hotel. Enjoy cocktails on the terrace, or in one of the smart drawing rooms, before dining in the formal but relaxed Anderida Restaurant, which boasts wonderful views over lake and parkland.

FOOD: Quality English ingredients are used to create modern British dishes with European influences, with some innovative interpretations. Emphasis is on accuracy of technique and flavour Knowledgeable service and excellent wine list.

OUR TIP: Wonderful afternoon tea

Chef: John McManus **Owners:** Elite Hotels **Times:** 12-2/7-10
Notes: Set speciality menu £46, Sun L £25, Vegetarian available, Jacket and Tie for gentlemen after 7pm, Civ Wed 150 **Seats:** 120, Pr/dining room 160 **Smoking:** N/Sm in restaurant **Children:** Menu, Portions
Rooms: 106 (106 en suite) ★★★★ **Directions:** A22 towards Eastbourne, pass through Forest Row, continue on A22 for 2m. At Wych Cross turn left, hotel 0.75m on right **Parking:** 120
e-mail: reservations@ashdownpark.com
web: www.ashdownpark.com

England

HASTINGS & ST LEONARDS MAP 07 TQ80

🍽 The Chatsworth Hotel
Indian NEW

Exciting Indian dining by the seaside

☎ 01424 457300 Carlisle Pde TN13 1JG

MENU GUIDE Mumbai Koliwada • Pan flash bazaar • Gajar ka Halwa

WINE GUIDE ♀ Pinot Grigio £17 • ♀ Short Mile Bay Shiraz £18 • 10 bottles over £20, 19 bottles under £20 • 6 by the glass (£4.30)

PRICE GUIDE Starter £4.25-£12 • main £11.45-£18.50 • dessert £3.25-£3.75 • coffee £1.75 • min/water £3.50 • Service optional

PLACE: An unusual but successful combination of a traditional seaside hotel with an Indian restaurant. The dining room has a contemporary feel with bright tomato red walls, Jali fretwork and Indian prints. There's a small, mirrored bar and tables have comfortable banquette seating.

FOOD: A selection of carefully prepared North Western style and tandoori dishes mixed with regional specialities from Mumbai, Hyderabad and Kashmir beautifully presented on square plates.

OUR TIP: Take a stroll along the pier before tiffin

Chef: Ramesh Angre **Owners:** Trimiri Group **Times:** 12-2.30/6-11, closed L Mon-Sat **Notes:** Vegetarian available, Smart Dress **Seats:** 52 **Smoking:** N/Sm area, No pipes, No cigars, Air con **Children:** Portions **Directions:** On Hastings seafront, near railway station **Parking:** 8 **e-mail:** info@chatsworthhotel.com **web:** www.jailbarandrestaurant.co.uk

---

HERSTMONCEUX MAP 06 TQ61

🍽 Sundial Restaurant
French

Pretty cottage setting for classic French cuisine

☎ 01323 832217 BN27 4LA

MENU GUIDE Foie gras terrine • Red mullet fillet, king tiger prawns, confit veg & risotto • Mille-feuille, tutti frutti yogurt mousse

WINE GUIDE ♀ Steenberg Sauvignon Blanc £22.75 • ♀ Auxey Duresses 1er Cru Bourgogne £32.50 • 110 bottles over £20, 22 bottles under £20 • 4 by the glass (£3.75-£4.95)

PRICE GUIDE Fixed L £17.50-£19.50 • Fixed D £27.50 • starter £8.50-£19.75 • main £18.75-£19.75 • dessert £5.50-£10.75 • coffee £2.50 • min/water £3.25 • Service added but optional 10%

PLACE: Cosy red brick cottage with black oak beams and whitewashed walls in the pretty village of Herstmonceux. The proprietor invests in the finest china, silver and glassware to heighten guests' experience and this quality is reflected in the prices.

FOOD: An extensive choice of classic French dishes is offered from the carte and two fixed-price menus, using only the best of ingredients.

OUR TIP: Try the chocolate taster plate

Chef: Vincent Rongier **Owners:** Mr & Mrs V & Mary Rongier **Times:** 12-2/7-10, Mon, Closed D Sun **Notes:** Tasting menu 8 courses £45, vegetarian available, Dress Restrictions, Smart casual preferred **Seats:** 50, Pr/dining room 22 **Smoking:** N/Sm in restaurant **Children:** Portions **Directions:** In village centre, on A271, between Bexhill & Hailsham **Parking:** 16 **e-mail:** sundialrestaurant@hotmail.com **web:** www.sundialrestaurant.co.uk

---

JEVINGTON MAP 06 TQ50

🍽 Hungry Monk Restaurant
British, French

Charming 15th-century cottage restaurant

☎ 01323 482178 BN26 5QF

MENU GUIDE Local scallops with crisp bacon • Roast rack of English lamb with Moroccan spices • Pear & ginger tarte Tatin

WINE GUIDE ♀ Honore de Berticot Sauvignon Côtes de Duras £15 • ♀ Château les Hauts de Perey Bordeaux Superior £16.80 • 75 bottles over £20, 41 bottles under £20 • 6 by the glass (£3.43-£7.76)

PRICE GUIDE Fixed L £28.95 • Fixed D £29.95 • coffee £2.90 • min/water £3 • Group min 8 service 12.5%

PLACE: Village restaurant with a good local reputation since at least 1972, when the ubiquitous banoffi pie was invented here. The Tardis-like interior has three antique-furnished lounges and a dining room full of character, with intimate spaces, beams and open fireplaces.

FOOD: Simple dishes with French influences offer plenty of comfort food and steaming plates of vegetables - the sort of thing you might expect at a dinner party with friends in the country.

OUR TIP: Four first-floor dining rooms available for parties

Chef: Gary Fisher, Matt Canbem **Owners:** Mr & Mrs N Mackenzie **Times:** 12-2/6.45-9.45, Closed 24-26 Dec, BHs, closed L Mon-Sat **Notes:** Vegetarian available, Smart Dress **Seats:** 38, Pr/dining room 16 **Smoking:** N/Sm in restaurant, Air con **Children:** Min 4 yrs, Portions **Directions:** A22, turn towards Wammock at Polegate x-rds. Continue for 2.5m, restaurant on right **Parking:** 14 **web:** www.hungrymonk.co.uk

England

LEWES MAP 06 TQ41

⚙ Circa
International
Trendy fusion food in historic market town
☎ 01273 471777   145 High St BN7 1XT

MENU GUIDE Paper smoked scallops, flying egg dim sum • Beef fillet, chickpea fluff, macadamia pesto • Cassia kulfi, blood lassia

WINE GUIDE ♀ Pouilly Vinzello Fleurie • ♥ Nebbiolo £23.50 20 bottles over £20, 30 bottles under £20 • 8 by the glass (£4.50-£7.50)

PRICE GUIDE Fixed L £14-£15 • starter £4.50-£9 • main £10.50-£17.50 • dessert £6-£7 • coffee £2.50 • min/water £2.80 • Service added but optional 10%

PLACE: Circa stands out for its distinctive contemporary design, more Brighton than Lewes. The interior is divided into two areas, similarly decorated in art deco-style with a curvy cream ceiling, linen blinds, coffee coloured faux suede banquettes and wooden floors.
FOOD: Exuberant cooking offered from an eclectic clipboard menu with some intriguing ingredients, vibrant salsas and vivacious desserts. Eat first with your eyes – the presentation is superb.
OUR TIP: Great cocktails, dessert wines and single malts
Chef: Marc Bolger **Owners:** Ann Renton Biles **Times:** 12-2.30/6-10, Closed Mon & Sun **Notes:** Vegetarian available **Seats:** 85
Smoking: N/Sm area, No pipes, Air con **Children:** Menu, Portions
Directions: At top of High St, just past the Castle Gate **Parking:** On street **e-mail:** eat@circacirca.com
web: www.circacirca.com

⚙⚙ The Shelleys
Modern British
Elegant market town hotel dining
☎ 01273 472361   High St BN7 1XS

The Shelley

PLACE: This elegant 16th-century hotel, set high on the hill in the historic market town of Lewes, was once owned by the Earl of Dorset and also by the poet Shelley. The airy, spacious dining room is romantically candlelit, and overlooks the pretty enclosed gardens
FOOD: Sourcing of high-quality Sussex produce is a knack of this kitchen, which aims to use organic where possible. The modern British menu takes influences from across Europe in dishes such as tempura of oysters with cauliflower and almond soup, or seared fillet of local bream with caramelised chicory.
OUR TIP: Ideal for the opera at Glyndebourne
Times: 12-2.15/7-9.15 **Rooms:** 19 (19 en suite) ★★★
e-mail: info@shelleys-hotel-lewes.com
web: www.shelleys-hotel.com

NEWICK MAP 06 TQ42

⚙⚙ Newick Park Hotel & Country Estate
European
Accomplished cooking in elegant country house room
☎ 01825 723633   BN8 4SB

continued

continue

MENU GUIDE Scallop & lobster tortelloni, shellfish bisque • Beef, galette salardaise, garlic sauce • Roast pineapple, coconut ice cream

WINE GUIDE ♀ Montes Sauvignon Blanc £14.10 • ♥ Montes Reserve Merlot £15.20 • 80 bottles over £20, 20 bottles under £20 • 4 by the glass (£3.50)

PRICE GUIDE Fixed L £14.50 • starter £7.50-£12 • main £17.50-£27 • dessert £7-£9.50 • coffee £3.50 • min/water £3 • Service optional

PLACE: Take a stroll around this imposing Georgian mansion if there's time; it's set in 250 acres of glorious Sussex parkland and boasts its own walled kitchen garden and trout lake. Inside, the elegant restaurant is an ideal venue for special occasions, decorated in summery yellows with striking floral displays and art.
FOOD: Newick's kitchen impresses consistently and looks set for greater things. The modern European menu is crafted from well-sourced local produce, including game and vegetables from the estate, while dishes are presented simply to keep attention focused on flavour.
OUR TIP: Great for a romantic weekend break
Chef: Chris Moore **Owners:** Mr and Mrs Childs **Times:** 12-2/7-9, Closed New Year **Notes:** Vegetarian available, Dress Restrictions, Smart casual, Civ Wed 120 **Seats:** 60, Pr/dining room 54 **Smoking:** N/Sm in restaurant **Children:** Min 1yr, Portions **Rooms:** 16 (16 en suite) ★★★ **Directions:** From village turn S on A272, continue along lane for 1m, past pubs and garage to t-junct. Turn left and continue to entrance on right **Parking:** 100 **e-mail:** Bookings@newickpark.co.uk **web:** www.newickpark.co.uk

RYE MAP 07 TQ92

🐟 The Fish Café

Modern British 🐟NEW

Relaxed fish and seafood restaurant
☎ 01797 222226 17 Tower St TN31 7AT
MENU GUIDE Smoked haddock cakes, kipper sauce, creamed leek • Lemon sole, mussel & Indian spice sauce • Pear Tatin, blueberry ice cream

WINE GUIDE ♀ La Huerta Sauvignon Blanc £12.50 • ♥ La Huerta Merlot £12.50 • 21 bottles over £20, 33 bottles under £20 • 6 by the glass (£3.50)

PRICE GUIDE Starter £4-£10 • main £9-£23 • dessert £4-£5.50 • coffee £2.25 • min/water £2.75 • Service optional

PLACE: Former antiques warehouse, sympathetically converted to a smart modern fish restaurant. Downstairs is a laid-back café or lunch or snacks, while the first floor is a more formal dining room decorated in neutral shades of beige and brown with high back leather chairs.
FOOD: An accomplished kitchen keeps things simple, combining good quality fresh fish with one or two other ingredients designed to enhance the flavour. Meat dishes also available.
OUR TIP: The third floor can be hired for private functions
Chef: Paul Webbe **Owners:** Paul & Rebecca Webbe **Times:** 6-9.30, closed 25-26 Dec, closed D Sun-Mon **Notes:** Vegetarian available, Smart Dress **Seats:** 52, Pr/dining room 70 **Smoking:** N/Sm in restaurant, Air Con **Children:** Menu, Portions **Parking:** Cinque Port Street **e-mail:** info@thefishcafe.com **web:** www.thefishcafe.com

🐟 Mermaid Inn

British, French

Accurate cooking in romantic Tudor inn
☎ 01797 223065 223788 Mermaid St TN31 7EY
MENU GUIDE Lobster bisque with brandy cream • Roast grouse, game chips & red wine jus • Banoffee pie

continued

Mermaid Inn

WINE GUIDE ♀ L'Emage Sauvignon Blanc £16.75 • ♥ Eaglehawk Merlot £16.75 • 30 bottles over £20, 24 bottles under £20 • 8 by the glass (£3.85)

PRICE GUIDE Fixed L £18.50 • Fixed D £37.50 • starter £6.50-£10 • main £19.50-£36 • dessert £6 • coffee £3.50 • min/water £5.50 • Service added but optional 10%

PLACE: This Tudor inn on a cobbled side street was rebuilt in 1420 and has an interesting history and great atmosphere. All areas have retained original character with huge fireplaces, dark beams and, reportedly, several haunted bedrooms. The tables are draped with quality white linen and antique silver.
FOOD: A marriage of British and French styles on the menu, using good quality ingredients. Accurate cooking with great combinations that work well.
OUR TIP: Antique lovers will relish the decor and furniture
Chef: Roger Kellie **Owners:** Mrs J Blincow & Mr R I Pinwill **Times:** 12-2.30/7-9.30 **Notes:** Vegetarian available, Dress Restrictions, No jeans or T-shirts **Seats:** 64, Pr/dining room 12 **Smoking:** N/Sm in restaurant **Children:** Menu, Portions **Rooms:** 31 (31 en suite) ★★★ **Directions:** Rye is situated on A259 between Ashford and Hastings **Parking:** 26 **e-mail:** mermaidinnrye@btclick.com **web:** www.mermaidinn.com

🍴 Landgate Bistro 5-6 Landgate TN31 7LH
☎ 01797 222829 Bustling bistro with varied menu.

TICEHURST MAP 06 TQ63

🐟 Dale Hill Hotel & Golf Club

British, International

Formal dining in modern golfing hotel
☎ 01580 200112 TN5 7DQ

MENU GUIDE Asparagus & spring onion rolls, plum sauce • Barbary duck, caramelised oranges, rosemary jus • Coconut parfait, Malibu syrup

WINE GUIDE ♀ Les Calades Colombard/Ugni Blanc £12.50 • ♥ Les Calades Merlot/Grenache £12.50 • 20 bottles under £20 • 8 by the glass (£2.75-£8)

continued

England

TICEHURST continued MAP 06 TQ63

PRICE GUIDE Fixed D £25-£27 • starter £4-£6 • main £13-£30 • dessert fr £6 • min/water £3.50 • Service optional

PLACE: This smart modern golfing hotel offers lighter snacks at the conservatory brasserie, or more formal dining in the main restaurant, which overlooks the 18th green.
FOOD: The kitchen delivers a tempting range of modern British dishes with international influences. Tee off with split pea soup with crème fraîche and smoked salmon, and then try sea bass with broad beans and herb tagliatelle, or chicken supreme in pancetta.
OUR TIP: Build up an appetite with a round of golf
Chef: Mark Carter **Owners:** Wealden View Restaurant **Times:** 6.30-9, Closed L Mon-Sun **Notes:** Sun L £17.50, Dress Restrictions, Smart casual, Civ Wed 150 **Seats:** 70, Pr/dining room 24 **Smoking:** N/Sm in restaurant, Air con **Children:** Menu, Portions **Rooms:** 35 (35 en suite) ★★★★ **Directions:** At junction of A21 & B2087 follow signs for Ticehurst & Flimwell; Dale Hill is 1m on left **Parking:** 220 **e-mail:** info@dalehill.co.uk **web:** www.dalehill.co.uk

UCKFIELD MAP 06 TQ42

Buxted Park

British, European
Masterful cooking in classical surroundings
☎ 01825 733333 Buxted TN22 4AY
MENU GUIDE Roulade of foie gras & confit duck leg with toasted brioche • Cannon of Welsh lamb, osso bucco • Warm banana pancake with butterscotch sauce
WINE GUIDE ♀ Graham Beck Sauvignon Blanc £24 • ♀ Alta Palena Pinot Noir £28 • 89 bottles over £20, 6 bottles under £20 • 12 by the glass (£4.50-£8.50)
PRICE GUIDE Fixed L £17.50 • Fixed D £36.50 • starter £9.50 • main £18 • dessert £9 • coffee £3.95 • min/water £3.95 • Service optional

PLACE: Dating back to the 17th century, this charming Georgian Grade II listed property sits amidst a stunning estate comprising 300 acres of parklands and formal gardens. It has a glorious past as a prime ministerial home and a playground of Hollywood stars and directors. The Victorian Orangery Restaurant and the adjoining Crystal Bar are well presented with orange trees and glass-topped wrought iron tables, overlooking formal gardens.
FOOD: The kitchen delivers accomplished modern British and European cuisine using top quality ingredients, locally sourced whenever possible. Expect mains such as confit fillet of sea bass, lime mash, caviar velouté and seaweed oil.
OUR TIP: Pre-dinner drinks in The Crystal Bar
Chef: Pramod Pillai **Owners:** Hand Picked Hotels **Times:** 12-2.30/7-9.30, Closed L Sat **Notes:** Vegetarian available, Smart casual, Civ Wed 130 **Seats:** 40, Pr/dining room 120 **Smoking:** N/Sm in restaurant, Air con **Children:** Menu, Portions **Rooms:** 44 (44 en suite) ★★★★
Directions: Turn off A22 Uckfield by-pass (London-Eastbourne road), then take A272 to Buxted. Cross traffic lights, entrance to hotel 1m on right **Parking:** 100 **e-mail:** buxtedpark@handpicked.co.uk **web:** www.handpicked.co.uk/buxtedpark

Horsted Place

Modern British
Imposing setting for high quality cuisine
☎ 01825 750581 Little Horsted TN22 5TS
MENU GUIDE Seared swordfish, Caesar salad • Venison on noodles, cep mushrooms • Summer pudding, thick cream, blackberry sauce

WINE GUIDE ♀ Muscadet £17.50 • ♀ Vaucluse Syrah £17.50 94 bottles over £20, 12 bottles under £20 • 9 by the glass (£4)
PRICE GUIDE Fixed L £14.95 • starter £6.95-£10.95 • main £17-£21 • dessert £6.20-£7.95 • coffee £2.80 • min/water £3.50 • Service optional

PLACE: With an interior largely designed by Augustus Pugin, this country-house hotel abounds in gothic features, and is one of the finest examples of revivalist architecture in the country. There are extensive grounds to explore plus the adjacent East Sussex golf club and nearby Glyndebourne Opera House.
FOOD: A concise menu allows attention to detail and showcases the kitchen's panache in presentation and all-round skill. Modern British in style, it includes some intriguing uses of high quality ingredients, in dishes such as beef on a banana shallot cobbler.
OUR TIP: Comprehensive wine list with some good half bottles
Chef: Allan Garth **Owners:** Perinon Ltd **Times:** 12-2/7-9.30, Closed L Sat **Notes:** Sun lunch £25, Vegetarian available, Dress Restrictions, No jeans, Civ Wed 100 **Seats:** 40, Pr/dining room 100 **Smoking:** N/Sm in restaurant **Children:** Min 7 yrs, Portions **Rooms:** 20 (20 en suite) ★★★ **Directions:** 2M S on A26 towards Lewes **Parking:** 50 **e-mail:** hotel@horstedplace.co.uk **web:** www.horstedplace.co.uk

WADHURST MAP 06 TQ63

The Best Beech Inn   NEW

French, European
Enjoyable dining in an ancient country inn
☎ 01892 782046 Mayfield Ln TN5 6JH
MENU GUIDE Tomato tarte Tatin, rocket salad • Rib eye, onion jam • Lemon tart, lemon & lime sorbet
WINE GUIDE ♀ Pinot Grigio £11.95 • ♀ Chilean Merlot £12.95 6 by the glass
PRICE GUIDE Fixed D £16.95 • starter £5.95-£8.95 • main £10.25-£17.95 • dessert £5.95-£6.95 • coffee £2.50 • min/water £2.50 • Service included • Group min 6 service 10%

PLACE: This 17th-century pub with food is the social hub of the village. Even after extensive refurbishment its essential character and charm were retained providing a bar, two comfortable dining rooms and several bedrooms.
FOOD: Three chefs labour in the kitchen to produce modern dishes with French and European influences. A tapas menu is also available in the bar. Friendly staff serve well cooked food, simply presented and properly seasoned.
OUR TIP: Visit Bodiam Castle and Chartwell
Chef: Stephan Santin **Owners:** Roger Felstead **Times:** 12-2/7-9, Closed 25-26 Dec, closed D Sun **Notes:** Vegetarian available, Dress Restrictions, Smart casual **Seats:** 64, Pr/dining room 34 **Smoking:** N/Sm in restaurant **Children:** Min 10 yrs, Portions **Directions:** From Wadhurst take B2100 to Mark Cross, continue for 1m **Parking:** 35 **e-mail:** roger_felstead@hotmail.com **web:** www.bestbeech.net

WESTFIELD MAP 07 TQ81

The Wild Mushroom Restaurant

British
Accomplished cooking in converted farmhouse setting
☎ 01424 751137 Woodgate House, Westfield Ln TN35 4SB
MENU GUIDE Tiger prawn tempura • Breast & confit of duckling, Szechuan pepper sauce • Baked apple, Calvados ice cream
WINE GUIDE ♀ Trivento Viognier £12.75 • ♀ Trivento Shiraz/Malbec £12.75 • 28 bottles over £20, 20 bottles under £20 • 6 by the glass (£2.50-£5)

continued

continued

PRICE GUIDE Fixed L £13.95-£15.95 • Fixed D £29 • starter £5-£8 • main £10.50-£18 • dessert £4.50-£7 • coffee £2.50 • min/water £2.75 • Service optional

PLACE: Converted farmhouse that's stayed true to its country roots with a cosy rustic decor of bare wood, Welsh dressers and white linen. Mint green chairs and yellow walls hung with local watercolours complete the picture.

FOOD: Sound cooking skills and an attention to quality ingredients ensure a menu of first-rate fare. Temptations on the lengthy evening carte might include pheasant in pancetta, or beef with wild mushroom sauce.

OUR TIP: Good value Sunday lunch (book ahead)

Chef: Paul Webbe/Matthew Drinkwater **Owners:** Mr & Mrs P Webbe **Times:** 12-2.30/7-10, Closed 25 Dec, 2 wks at New Year, Mon, closed L Sat, closed D Sun **Notes:** Vegetarian available **Seats:** 40 **Smoking:** N/Sm in restaurant **Children:** Portions **Directions:** From A21 towards Hastings, turn left onto A28 to Westfield. Restaurant 1.5m on left **Parking:** 20 **e-mail:** info@wildmushroom.co.uk **web:** www.wildmushroom.co.uk

WILMINGTON MAP 06 TQ50

Crossways Hotel

British

Local favourite offering confident cooking

☎ 01323 482455 BN26 5SG

MENU GUIDE Seafood pancake • Guinea fowl with Puy lentils • Trio of desserts

WINE GUIDE ♀ Saget Sancerre £21.75 • ♥ Rosemount Cabernet Sauvignon £15.95 • 17 bottles over £20, 27 bottles under £20 • by the glass (£3.40)

PRICE GUIDE Fixed D £34.95 • min/water £3.25 • Service optional

PLACE: This small, Georgian country house with its well established, traditional restaurant sits in well-kept gardens at the heart of the Cuckmere Valley. Enjoying a meal here feels just like attending a private dinner party, with close-set tables and relaxed service by the convivial owners creating a friendly, intimate atmosphere.

FOOD: The monthly-changing, set-price menu makes sound use of prime local produce, with starters and desserts (which have concise menu descriptions, like mushroom cornucopia or gingered peaches) explained in detail at the table.

OUR TIP: English wines available by the glass

Chef: David Stott **Owners:** David Stott, Clive James **Times:** 7.30-8.30, closed 24 Dec-24 Jan, closed Sun-Mon, closed L all week **Notes:** Coffee incl., Vegetarian by request only **Seats:** 24 **Smoking:** N/Sm in restaurant **Children:** Min 12 yrs **Rooms:** 7 (7 en suite) **Directions:** On A27, 2m E of Polegate **Parking:** 20 **e-mail:** stay@crosswayshotel.co.uk **web:** www.crosswayshotel.co.uk

WINCHELSEA

The Tea Tree Winner of The Tea Guild Award of Excellence 2005.

SUSSEX, WEST

AMBERLEY MAP 06 TQ01

Amberley Castle

British, French

Fine dining in fairy tale castle

☎ 01798 831992 BN18 9LT

MENU GUIDE Mille-feuille of marinated foie gras • Mignon of lamb & minted lamb pudding • Hot pistachio soufflé

continued

WINE GUIDE ♀ Bellevue Touraine Sauvignon Blanc £21.50 • ♥ Peter Lehmann Shiraz £28.50 • 400 bottles over £20, 5 bottles under £20 • 3 by the glass (£4.50)

PRICE GUIDE Fixed L £20-£43 • Fixed D £50 • coffee £3.10 • min/water £4 • Service optional • Group min 30

PLACE: A half-ruined medieval castle in fabulous grounds, now home to a luxury family-run hotel. From the impressive gatehouse and portcullis to antique rooms with vaulted ceilings and massive fireplaces, this historic place is superb.

FOOD: The atmospheric Queen's Room plays host to accomplished cooking where the freshest of South Downs ingredients contribute to the overall enjoyment. The cooking is intricate and elaborate. Breast of wood pigeon with thyme crust, foie gras sausage, globe artichoke purée, caramelised shallot cream and pâté negra is a typically delicious starter.

OUR TIP: Try the golf putting course

Chef: James Peyton **Owners:** Joy & Martin Cummings **Times:** 12.30-2/7-9.30 **Notes:** Sun lunch £30, dinner includes coffee, Vegetarian available, Dress Restrictions, Jacket or Tie, Civ Wed 48 **Seats:** 39, Pr/dining room 48 **Smoking:** N/Sm in restaurant **Children:** Min 12 yrs, Portions **Rooms:** 19 (19 en suite) ★★★ **Directions:** Off B2139 between Amberley and Houghton **Parking:** 48 **e-mail:** info@amberleycastle.co.uk **web:** www.amberleycastle.co.uk

BOSHAM MAP 05 SU80

Millstream Hotel

British, European

Quality fare in an idyllic village location

☎ 01243 573234 Bosham Ln PO18 8HL

MENU GUIDE Spiced crab mousse, herb oil • Guinea fowl breast stuffed with sun-blushed tomatoes • Profiteroles

WINE GUIDE ♀ Montes Sauvignon Blanc £15.50 • ♥ Cedar Creek Shiraz/Cabernet Sauvignon £15.50 • 54 bottles over £20, 32 bottles under £20 • 11 by the glass (£3.50-£6.50)

PRICE GUIDE Fixed L £15.50 • Fixed D £27 • coffee £2.25 • min/water £3 • Service optional

PLACE: An 18th-century flint-built property by the millstream in picturesque Bosham, a well-known sailing village on the shores of Chichester Harbour. Patio doors from the restaurant open onto the pretty garden.

FOOD: Accurately cooked and well presented dishes from the traditional British and European repertoire, using the best quality produce. Desserts are a particular strength.

OUR TIP: Eat in the garden during fine weather

Chef: Bev Boakes **Owners:** The Wild Family **Times:** 12.30-2/6.45-9.15 **Notes:** Vegetarian available, Dress Restrictions, No jeans in the evenings, smart casual, Civ Wed 92 **Seats:** 60, Pr/dining room 92 **Smoking:** N/Sm in restaurant, Air con **Children:** Portions **Rooms:** 35 (35 en suite) ★★★ **Directions:** Take A259 exit from Chichester rdbt and in village follow signs for quay **Parking:** 40 **e-mail:** info@millstream-hotel.co.uk **web:** www.millstream-hotel.co.uk

BRACKLESHAM MAP 05 SZ89

Cliffords Cottage Restaurant

French

French dining in intimate country cottage

☎ 01243 670250 Bracklesham Ln PO20 8JA

MENU GUIDE Fruits de Mer with saffron • Rack of lamb, herb crust, orange & redcurrant sauce • Honey & ginger parfait

WINE GUIDE ♀ House White • ♀ House Merlot • 1 bottle over £20, 29 bottles under £20 •

PRICE GUIDE Fixed L £13.95 • Fixed D £21 • starter £3.75-£6.95 • main £11.95-£18.95 • dessert £3.95-£4.50 • coffee £1.65 • min/water £2.75 • Service optional • Group min 10 service 10%

PLACE: This 16th-century thatched roof cottage is located just outside this popular summer resort. There's a loyal local following which gives the place an appealing, lively buzz.
FOOD: The menu comprises classics with a pronounced French accent and cooking is competent and consistent. There's a good choice of well-executed dishes using local meat and fish although vegetarians should maybe ring ahead to check what's on offer.
OUR TIP: Competitively priced wine list
Chef: Tony Shanahan **Owners:** Mr & Mrs Shanahan **Times:** 12.30-2/7-9.15, Closed 1-14 Nov, 1-7 Feb, Mon-Tue, closed L Wed-Sat, closed D Sun **Notes:** Vegetarian available, Dress Restrictions, Smart casual preferred **Seats:** 28 **Smoking:** N/Sm in restaurant, Air con **Children:** Min 5 yrs, Portions **Directions:** From A27 follow signs for The Witterings. A286 to Birdham, B2198 to Bracklesham **Parking:** 16

BURPHAM MAP 06 TQ00

George & Dragon

British, French

Traditional inn with loyal local following

☎ 01903 883131 BN18 9RR

MENU GUIDE Home-smoked turkey fillet salad • Slow roasted shoulder of lamb • Pear & ginger crème brûlée

WINE GUIDE 9 bottles over £20, 19 bottles under £20 • 6 by the glass (£3.50-£4.50)

PRICE GUIDE Starter £4.95-£6.95 • main £8.95-£12.95 • dessert £5.25 • coffee £1.75 • Group service 10%

PLACE: A charming old inn tucked away in a pretty village, the George & Dragon is a local favourite and bustles with a friendly crowd of all ages.
FOOD: Arrive in the evening if you want to experience the George at its best, as only a bar menu is available at lunchtime. Standards are consistently high, with good quality ingredients handled with confident simplicity.
OUR TIP: Booking is essential, it's a very popular place
Chef: Cavill Perrin, Andy Field, Eric Cassar **Owners:** Alastaire & Angela Thackeray **Times:** 12-2/7-9, Closed 25 Dec **Notes:** Vegetarian available, Dress Restrictions, Smart casual preferred **Seats:** 45 **Smoking:** N/Sm in restaurant **Children:** Portions **Directions:** 2.5m along no-through road signed Burpham off A27, 1m E of Arundel **Parking:** 40

CHICHESTER MAP 05 SU80

Comme Ça

French

A little Normandy in Chichester

☎ 01243 788724 536307 67 Broyle Rd PO19 6BD

MENU GUIDE Sautéed duck liver & shallots • Seared medallions of monkfish with shrimp & port coulis • Strawberry cheesecake

PRICE GUIDE Food prices not confirmed for 2006. Please telephone for details

PLACE: Whether for a Sunday lunch en famille or a lingering romantic supper, this family-owned restaurant offers the finest French cuisine. The decor in the two dining rooms is colourful with old Victorian and Edwardian prints and objets d'art.
FOOD: The best traditions of French cuisine with some hints of other exotic flavours feature in the extensive menu. The daily 'specials' reflect seasonal changes with good vegetarian choices.
OUR TIP: A very thorough wine list concentrating on France
Chef: Michael Navet, Mark Howard **Owners:** Mr & Mrs Navet **Times:** 12-2/6-10.30, Closed Xmas week & New Year week, BHs, Mon, closed L Tue, closed D Sun **Notes:** Vegetarian available, Dress Restrictions, Smart casual preferred **Seats:** 100, Pr/dining room 14 **Smoking:** N/Sm in restaurant **Children:** Menu, Portions **Directions:** On A286 near Festival Theatre **Parking:** 46
e-mail: comme.ca@commeca.co.uk **web:** www.commeca.co.uk

Croucher's Country Hotel & Restaurant

British, French

Family-run hotel dining in former farmhouse

☎ 01243 784995 Birdham Rd PO20 7EH

MENU GUIDE Roasted sea scallops • Baked halibut fillet, herb crust, crab spring roll • Mango crème brûlée

WINE GUIDE ♀ Sancerre Sauvignon Blanc £21.50 • ♀ Brampton Old Vine Merlot Shiraz Blend £15.95 • 18 bottles over £20, 20 bottles under £20 • 4 by the glass (£3-£4.50)

PRICE GUIDE Fixed L £12.50 • Fixed D £17.50 • starter £4.95-£8.25 • main £13.50-£17.95 • dessert £5.25 • coffee £2.50 • min/water £2.80 • Service optional

PLACE: This friendly, appealing hotel is situated in the open countryside near Chichester. The main hotel is a sympathetically converted farmhouse with more rooms in the adjoining barn and coach house. The newly built restaurant features an open timber roof and oak beams.
FOOD: Seafood dishes dominate the menu although there are good choices for meat-eaters. Modern British in style with Mediterranean touches.
OUR TIP: Take a stroll round nearby Chichester Harbour
Chef: Gavin Wilson, Nick Markey, Alistair Craig **Owners:** Mr D P Wilson **Times:** 12.30-2.30/7-9.30, 26 Dec, 1 Jan **Notes:** Vegetarian available, Dress Restrictions, No shorts **Seats:** 80, Pr/dining room 20 **Smoking:** N/Sm in restaurant **Children:** Menu, Portions **Rooms:** 18 (18 en suite) ★★★ **Directions:** From A27, S of Chichester, take A286 to The Witterings. Hotel 2m on left **Parking:** 35
e-mail: crouchers_bottom@btconnect.com
web: www.crouchersbottom.com

Hallidays

International

Smart thatched cottage village restaurant

☎ 01243 575331 Funtington PO18 9LF

MENU GUIDE Crab cakes with shaved fennel • Well-hung Aberdeen Angus sirloin steak, wild mushrooms • Hot chocolate fondant, mascarpone cream

WINE GUIDE ♀ Millberg Cellars Chenin Blanc £11.75 • ♀ Campero Merlot £12.50 • 57 bottles over £20, 31 bottles under £20 • 4 by the glass (£2.95-£3.25)

PRICE GUIDE Fixed L £14.50 • Fixed D £29 • starter £5-£7.50 • main £13.75-£18 • dessert £5.50-£7 • coffee £2.75 • min/water £2.50 • Service optional

continued

continued

England

ACE: At the foot of the South Downs a few miles west of ...ichester, Hallidays was originally three 16th-century thatched ...ttages. Now knocked together, they form an intimate two-...omed restaurant with a bar area between and oak beams ...lenty.
OD: The menu changes in tune with the seasons, using local ...d organic produce when possible. Game in winter with ...propriate sauces, and unpretentious fish dishes are two ...llmarks.
UR TIP: Once found, easy off-lane parking
...ef: Andrew Stephenson **Owners:** Mr A Stephenson & Mr P Creech
...mes: 12-1.45/7-9.45, Closed 2 wks Mar, 1 wk Sep, Mon-Tue, closed L
...t, closed D Sun **Notes:** 3 course Sun lunch £19.00, Vegetarian available,
...ess Restrictions, No shorts **Seats:** 26 **Smoking:** N/Sm area
...ildren: Portions **Directions:** Telephone for directions **Parking:** 12

Royal Oak Inn
ritish, Mediterranean
njoyable dining in village inn
01243 527434 Pook Ln PO18 0AX

ENU GUIDE Crab cakes, mango salsa • Calves' liver & bacon, ...namp, red wine, lentils • Crème brûlée
INE GUIDE ♀ Mansion House Sauvignon Blanc
...8.50 • ♥ Marques de Caceres Rioja £18 • 10 bottles over £20, ...2 bottles under £20 • 12 by the glass (£3.10-£6)
RICE GUIDE Fixed D £21 • starter £5-£9 • main £9.50-
...7 • dessert £4-£5.50 • coffee £1.90 • min/water £2.70
...ervice optional
ACE: Old character inn with beams, flagstone floors, smart ...cor and a ghost. It's a popular haunt with both locals and ...lkers, so book ahead.
OD: A good range of enjoyable traditional dishes with ...ropean touches, using fresh local produce whenever possible. ...rt with crispy whitebait perhaps, with a lemon and caper ...yonnaise, and then try chicken with a smoked bacon mash, or ...nb cutlets with a mint and red wine jus.
IR TIP: Eat alfresco in the garden in summer
...ef: Malcolm Goble **Owners:** Nick & Lisa Sutherland **Times:** 12-
...15-9.30 **Notes:** Sun lunch £11, Vegetarian available **Seats:** 47
...oking: N/Sm area, No pipes, No cigars, Air con **Children:** Menu,
...tions **Rooms:** 6 (6 en suite) ♦♦♦♦ **Directions:** From Chichester
...e A286 towards Midhurst, 2m to mini rdbt take right, signposted East
...ant. Royal Oak on the left **Parking:** 23
...nail: nickroyaloak@aol.com
...b: www.sussexlive.co.uk/royaloakinn

Shepherd's Tearooms 35 Little London PO19 1PL
...01243 774761 Winner of The Tea Guild Award of Excellence
...05.

CHILGROVE MAP 05 SU81
The White Horse
British, Mediterranean
Confident cooking in 18th-century inn
☎ 01243 525219 PO18 9HX

MENU GUIDE Seafood stuffed sweet red peppers • Slow-roasted Gressingham duck • Chocolate Diablo
WINE GUIDE ♀ Chilean Chardonnay £15.50 • ♥ Chilean Cabernet Sauvignon £15.50 • 400 bottles over £20, 30 bottles under £20 • 10 by the glass (£3-£7.50)
PRICE GUIDE Fixed L £24.50 • Fixed D £24.50 • starter £7.50-£11.95 • main £14.95-£17.95 • dessert £5.50-£8.95 • Service added 10%
PLACE: Dating back to 1765, this quintessential English country inn retains all the charms of yesteryear. And while its cosy bar is a great place to mentally kick off your shoes, the dining room offers a more formal experience with friendly service. Totally non-smoking establishment.
FOOD: Expect confident cooking with interesting Mediterranean and Spanish twists. The ambitious kitchen offers an exciting menu that might have fillet steak grill alongside baked crab thermidor. Excellent wine list.
OUR TIP: Over 600 wines available
Chef: Juanna Otero **Owners:** C Burton **Times:** 12-2/7-10, Closed Mon, closed D Sun **Notes:** Fixed L 2 courses, Fixed D 3 courses Tue-Fri (Nov-Mar) **Seats:** 80, Pr/dining room 14 **Smoking:** N/Sm in restaurant, Air con **Children:** Portions **Rooms:** 8 (8 en suite) ♦♦♦♦
Directions: 7m N of Chichester off B2141. 3m W of A286 **Parking:** 60
e-mail: info@whitehorsechilgrove.co.uk
web: www.whitehorsechilgrove.co.uk

CLIMPING MAP 06 SU90
Bailiffscourt Hotel & Health Spa
British, French
Impressive dining in stylish coastal hotel
☎ 01903 723511 BN17 5RW
MENU GUIDE Sautéed foie gras, oakleaf & orange salad • Honey-glazed duck, plum sauce • Caramelised lemon tart, gin & tonic sorbet
WINE GUIDE ♀ Millman Campero Sauvignon Blanc £17 • ♥ Millman Campero Merlot £17 • 175 bottles over £20, 10 bottles under £20 • 7 by the glass (£4.50-£10)
PRICE GUIDE Fixed L £11-£24.50 • Fixed D £43.50-£60 • coffee £3.95 • min/water £3.25 • Service optional

continued

England

CLIMPING continued MAP 06 SU90

PLACE: Set in 32 acres of parkland and constructed almost entirely of recycled 13th-century building materials, the faux-medieval manor, built by Lord Moyne in 1927, creates a genuinely mellow atmosphere with lots of old timbers, heavy iron-studded doors and old stone fireplaces. The spacious dining room has wooden ceilings, mullioned windows and a magnificent medieval fireplace. Professional service is overseen with Gallic efficiency.

FOOD: Cooking is refined, modern and classy. Dishes are simply presented, the concentration here is all on the flavours of the high quality ingredients rather than appearance.

OUR TIP: Private beach is just 200 yards away
Chef: Russell Williams **Owners:** Pontus & Miranda Carminger
Times: 12-1.30/7-9.30 **Notes:** Vegetarian available, Dress Restrictions, Smart casual, Civ Wed 60 **Seats:** 70, Pr/dining room 70 **Smoking:** N/Sm in restaurant **Children:** Menu, Portions **Rooms:** 39 (39 en suite) ★★★
Directions: From A27 (Arundel), take A284 towards Littlehampton. Continue to the A259, Bailiffscourt is signposted towards Climping Beach
Parking: 60 **e-mail:** bailiffscourt@hshotels.co.uk
web: www.hshotels.co.uk

COPTHORNE MAP 06 TQ33

⊛ Copthorne Hotel London Gatwick
European, International
Elegant restaurant with food to match
☎ 01342 348800 Copthorne Way RH10 3PG
MENU GUIDE Seared foie gras & duck terrine • Pan-fried scallops, roast fennel, orange & cardamom beurre blanc • Passionfruit tart
WINE GUIDE ♀ Nobilo Sauvignon Blanc £19.90 • ♀ Veramonte Merlot £21 • 69 bottles over £20, 22 bottles under £20 • 6 by the glass (£4.20-£8.95)
PRICE GUIDE Fixed L £19.50-£24.50 • Fixed D £30-£35 • starter £6.95-£10.50 • main £16.75-£35 • dessert £7.50-£9.50 • coffee £2.50 • min/water £4.45 • Service included

PLACE: Built around a 16th-century farmhouse, the hotel is located in 100 acres of wooded and landscaped gardens, complete with jogging tracks, a putting green and petanque pit. Diners are spoilt for choice, with an elegant fine dining room, the main restaurant and an inn on site.
FOOD: The formal menu focuses on European cooking with International influences. The quality of the produce is high with Loch Fyne seafood featuring strongly.
OUR TIP: Formal dress code applies at dinner
Chef: Andrew Davidson **Owners:** Millennium and Copthorne Hotels
Times: 12.30-2/7-10, Closed BHs, Sun, Closed L Sat **Notes:** Vegetarian available, Smart Dress, Civ Wed 120 **Seats:** 54, Pr/dining room 10
Smoking: N/Sm in restaurant **Children:** Portions **Rooms:** 227 (227 en suite) ★★★★ **Directions:** M23 junct 10 follow A264 signed East Grinstead, take 3rd exit off 1st rdbt **Parking:** 350
e-mail: sales@mill-cop.com **web:** www.millennium-hotels.com

⊛⊛ The Old House Restaurant
British, French
Honest cooking in historic cottage
☎ 01342 712222 Effingham Rd RH10 3JB
MENU GUIDE Chicken liver parfait, fig & date chutney • Duck, plum & port wine sauce, sautéed sweet potatoes • Apple tarte Tatin

The Old House Restaurant

WINE GUIDE 89 bottles over £20, 38 bottles under £20 • 14 by the glass (£3.95-£7.95)
PRICE GUIDE Fixed L £17-£40 • Fixed D £34-£41 • starter £4.50-£8.50 • main £12.50-£31 • dessert £6 • coffee £3 • min/water £3.50 • Service optional • Group service 10%

PLACE: Dating back to the 16th century, this black and white timbered cottage blends ancient beams and hearty fires with country house comfort. Sink into a sofa in the bar for an aperitif and then take your seat in the romantic candlelit dining room. Book ahead.
FOOD: Expect old favourites with a few modern twists from a kitchen that knows its stuff. Mains range from the hearty (lamb chump with minted mousse and rosemary jus) to simpler fare, such as grilled Dover sole with lemon and crushed sea salt.
OUR TIP: Handy for Gatwick Airport
Chef: Alan Pierce **Owners:** Mr & Mrs C Dormon **Times:** 12.15-2/6.30-9.30, Closed Xmas, New Year, 1 wk spring, BHs, Mon, closed L Sat, closed D Sun **Notes:** Vegetarian available, Dress Restrictions, No jeans or trainers **Seats:** 80, Pr/dining room 35 **Smoking:** N/Sm in restaurant, Air con **Children:** Min 10 yrs **Directions:** From M23 junct 10 follow A264 to East Grinstead, take 1st left at 2nd rdbt, left at crossroads, restaurant 0.75m on left **Parking:** 45
e-mail: info@oldhouserestaurant.co.uk
web: www.oldhouserestaurant.co.uk

CUCKFIELD MAP 06 TQ32

⊛⊛⊛ Ockenden Manor see page 459

EAST GRINSTEAD MAP 06 TQ33

⊛⊛⊛ Gravetye Manor Hotel
see page 4

GOODWOOD MAP 06 SU80

⊛⊛ Marriott Goodwood Park Hotel / Richmond Room
British, European
Adventurous cuisine near Goodwood
☎ 0870 400 7225 PO18 0QB
MENU GUIDE Spiced salmon & crab ballantine, Japanese dressing • Beef tournedos, rösti potato, wild mushroom ragout • Banana tarte Tatin, caramel ice cream
WINE GUIDE ♀ Chablis £21 • ♀ Reinares £17 • 10 bottles over £20, 10 bottles under £20 • 10 by the glass (£3-£5)
PRICE GUIDE Fixed L £16.95 • Fixed D £25 • starter £6.95-£13.95 • main £18.95-£22.50 • dessert £7.50 • coffee £1.95 • min/water £3.25 • Service optional

continued

continued on page 4

UCKFIELD MAP 06 TQ32

Ockenden Manor

Modern French

serious cooking in elegant surroundings

☎ 01444 416111 Ockenden Ln RH17 5LD

MENU GUIDE Crab ravioli, crab velouté • Red mullet, roasted Provençale vegetables • Lemon tart, blackcurrant sorbet

WINE GUIDE ♀ Chablis £25.50 • ♥ Fleurie £29 • 188 bottles over £20, 38 bottles under £20 • 12 by the glass (£3.95)

PRICE GUIDE Fixed L £13.95–£15.95 • Fixed alc £46 • Service optional • Group min 10 service 5%

PLACE: This charming Elizabethan manor-house hotel nestles down a narrow lane behind the pretty village of Cuckfield, with views over the South Downs from its delightful gardens. Beautiful in rich reds and yellows, the formal dining room has striking historic features; carved-stone fireplace, dark-oak panelling, Victorian hand-painted ceiling and stained-glass windows.
FOOD: Though the manor may offer an endearing step back in time, the serious approach to cooking is anything but. The cuisine speaks with a modern Gallic accent, using top-notch, seasonal produce in well-balanced, clean flavoured and accurately delivered dishes that show an intelligently simple approach.

Fixed-price menus, including lunch, vegetarian offering, carte and tasting options, deliver the appealing repertoire.
OUR TIP: Enjoy the Tasting Menu
Chef: Steve Crane **Owners:** Goodman & Carminger Family **Times:** 12-2/7-9 **Notes:** Civ Wed 74 **Seats:** 40, Pr/dining room 75 **Rooms:** 22 (22 en suite) ★★★ **Directions:** Village centre **Parking:** 45
e-mail: reservations@ockenden-manor.com
web: www.hshotels.co.uk

EAST GRINSTEAD MAP 06 TQ33

Gravetye Manor Hotel

British

seriously beautiful hotel, gardens and food

☎ 01342 810567 RH19 4LJ

MENU GUIDE Red mullet, saffron vermicelli, caviar • Venison, parsnip purée, blackcurrant jus • Prune & Armagnac soufflé

WINE GUIDE ♀ Louis Latour Macon Lugny £17 • ♥ J Faiveley Pinot Noir £24 • 300 bottles over £20, 7 bottles under £20 • 8 by the glass (£5.50-£7.50)

PRICE GUIDE Fixed L £21-£21 • Fixed D £35-£37 • starter £12 • main £30 • dessert £10 • coffee £4 • Service included

PLACE: Rich dark wood, open fires, opulent fabrics and antiques abound and make for a refined first impression at this handsome Elizabethan mansion set in 30 acres. The oak-panelled restaurant complete with a carved white ceiling.
FOOD: Mark Raffan's style is modern but underpinned by a classical theme, his sophisticated, intelligently simple touch allowing first-rate local produce (some from Gravetye's estate) to shine. Clear flavours, superb execution, timings and high-skill levels are a hallmark of the excellent cooking, with well-

constructed menus echoing the seasons. Impressive wine list.
OUR TIP: Make time to walk in the gardens
Chef: Mark Raffan **Owners:** A Russell & M Raffan **Times:** 12.30-1.45/7-9.30, Closed 25 Dec eve (ex residents) **Notes:** Sun L £35, Vegetarian available, Civ Wed 45 **Seats:** 50, Pr/dining room 20 **Rooms:** 18 (18 en suite) ★★★ **Directions:** Telephone for directions **Parking:** 45
e-mail: info@gravetyemanor.co.uk
web: www.gravetyemanor.co.uk

England

GOODWOOD continued MAP 06 SU80

PLACE: Handily located for Goodwood's equestrian and motor sports centres, this smart hotel and country club has extensive facilities including a golf course and spa. Subdued lighting and comfy seats make its cocktail bar a relaxing place for a pre-dinner drink, while food is served in the chic rustic setting of a former barn.
FOOD: Classic cuisine with a touch of things modern and the odd adventurous twist. Dishes are elaborate and might include veal with a truffle risotto and béarnaise sauce, or Scottish lobster with lemon butter sauce, and a coriander and mango salad.
OUR TIP: Explore the 12,000 acre Goodwood estate
Chef: Darran Kimber **Owners:** Whitbread Plc **Times:** 12.30-2/7-10
Notes: Sun carvery L £14.95, Vegetarian available, Dress Restrictions, Smart casual, no jeans or T-shirts, Civ Wed 150 **Seats:** 90, Pr/dining room 100 **Smoking:** N/Sm in restaurant **Children:** Menu, Portions
Rooms: 94 (94 en suite) ★★★★ **Directions:** Just off A285, 3m NE of Chichester. Follow signs for Goodwood, once in estate follow signs for hotel **Parking:** 350 **web:** www.marriotthotels.com/mpegs

HAYWARDS HEATH MAP 06 TQ32
⑧ Jeremy's at Borde Hill
British, Mediterranean
Attractive restaurant with a creative kitchen
☎ 01444 441102 Balcombe Rd RH16 1XP

MENU GUIDE Seared squid, mussel risotto • Braised belly pork, smoked bacon, black pudding • White chocolate & vanilla pannacotta
WINE GUIDE ⚑ Antonio San Vina Sofraga Verdejo/Sauvignon £13 • ⚑ Inurrieta Navarra Garnacha/Carignan £14 • 60 bottles over £20, 12 bottles under £20 • 7 by the glass (£3-£4)
PRICE GUIDE Fixed L £16.50 • Fixed D £20.50 • starter £7-£9 • main £13.50-£19.50 • dessert £5 • coffee £2.20 • min/water £2.80 • Service optional • Group min 8 service 10%
PLACE: Gastro-pub cum country house, located in a converted stable block with an award-winning walled garden. Friendly service and a relaxed atmosphere ensure a strong local following. The terrace lends itself to lighter meals, accompanied by a glass of chilled wine, in the summer sun.
FOOD: Creative cooking with influences from France, Spain and Italy. Local suppliers provide organic vegetables, free-range eggs and meat.
OUR TIP: On the doorstep of Borde Hill Gardens
Chef: Jeremy Ashpool, Vera Ashpool, Rupert Gleadow **Owners:** Jeremy & Vera Ashpool **Times:** 12-2.30/7-9.30, Closed 1st wk Jan, Mon, closed D Sun **Notes:** Tasting menu avail. 6 courses, Vegetarian available, Civ Wed 55 **Seats:** 55 **Smoking:** N/Sm in restaurant **Children:** Portions
Directions: 1.5m N of Haywards Heath. From M23 junct 10a take A23 through Balcombe **Parking:** 20
e-mail: reservations@jeremysrestaurant.com
web: www.homeofgoodfood.co.uk

HORSHAM MAP 06 TQ13
⑧ Les Deux Garçons
French, Mediterranean
French dining in the heart of town
☎ 01403 271125 Piries Place RH12 1DF

MENU GUIDE Beef confit ravioli, celeriac velouté, foie gras Seared monkfish fillet, courgette linguine • Warm chocolate fonda
WINE GUIDE ⚑ Berticot Sauvignon Blanc £12.90 • ⚑ Pennauti Merlot £12.90 • 22 bottles over £20, 15 bottles under £20 • 9 b the glass (£3.50-£4.50)
PRICE GUIDE Fixed L £9.90 • Fixed D £11.90 • starter £5.90-£9.90 • main £12-£25 • dessert £5.90 • coffee £1.95 • min/wate £2.50 • Service optional • Group min 9 service 10%
PLACE: Small restaurant on the first floor of a courtyard property, with a crisp blue and white colour scheme and mirror creating an illusion of space. It appeals to a wide range of customers who appreciate its relaxed atmosphere.
FOOD: Modern approach to classic French dishes. Choose from the carte, six-course dégustation or brasserie menu, the latter offering lighter options. Children are welcome and have their own menu.
OUR TIP: Catering service for any party or event
Chef: Norbet Kettnor **Owners:** Bob Emmott **Times:** 12-3/7-11, Closed Xmas wk, Sun, Mon **Notes:** Dégustation menu 6 courses £39, Vegetaria available **Seats:** 60, Pr/dining room 20 **Smoking:** N/Sm in restaurant, Air con **Children:** Menu, Portions **Directions:** Follow town centre sig then sign for Piries Place & car park, situated bottom of car park at entrance to Piries Place **Parking:** Parking adjacent to restaurant
e-mail: info@lesdeuxgarcons.com **web:** www.lesdeuxgarcons.com

LICKFOLD MAP 06 SU92
⑧ The Lickfold Inn
Mediterranean, International
Busy family character inn
☎ 01798 861285 Lickfold GU28 9EY
MENU GUIDE Warm chorizo salad • Guinea fowl breast, bread sauce • White chocolate & orange brûlée
WINE GUIDE ⚑ Montes Sauvignon Blanc £14.50 • ⚑ Domaine Come Loupe Grenache/Syrah Lirae (Rhône) £18.50 • 20 bottle over £20, 15 bottles under £20 • 10 by the glass (£3.25-£4.50)
PRICE GUIDE Starter £4.95-£10.95 • main £8.95-£21.95 • dessert £3.50-£7.25 • coffee £1.50 • min/water £4.50 • Service optional
PLACE: This 15th-century, Grade II listed pub has many architectural features including herringbone brickwork, hanging tile frontage, leaded lights and huge grounds. Outside, there ar paved courtyards and ample parking for its loyal following. Insi it's all inglenooks, flagstones, beams and a busy, noisy, lively atmosphere.

continu

...OD: High quality, seasonal ingredients locally sourced are the ...asis of some enjoyable modern dishes, such as fillet of venison ...h herb sautéed potatoes, celeriac purée and braised red ...bbage.

...UR TIP: A visit to nearby Petworth
...ef: Simon Goodman Owners: James Hickey & Andrea Walkinshaw
...mes: 12-2.30/7-9.30, Closed 25-26 Dec, Mon, closed D Sun
...tes: Sun L menu avail., Vegetarian available, Dress Restrictions, No
...tball shirts Seats: 40, Pr/dining room 40 Children: Portions
...rections: Signposted from A272, 6m E of Midhurst. From A285 6m S of
...slemere, follow signs for Lurgashall Winery and continue on to Lickfold
...age Parking: 40 e-mail: thelickfoldinn@aol.com

...OWER BEEDING MAP 06 TQ22

...◎◎◎ The Camellia Restaurant at ...outh Lodge Hotel *see page 462*

...ANNINGS HEATH MAP 06 TQ22

...◎ Mannings Heath Golf Club

...ternational

...assical cooking in welcoming golf club

☎ 01403 210228 Hammerpond Rd RH13 6PG

MENU GUIDE Lamb faggots, mash, port jus • Halibut, buttered
...pinach, red wine jus • Almond & cherry sponge pudding,
...maretto custard

WINE GUIDE ♀ Les Vigeaux Sauvignon Blanc £15.50 • ♀ Andes
...eak Merlot £18.50 • 18 bottles over £20, 18 bottles under
...20 • 2 by the glass (£3.50)

PRICE GUIDE Fixed L £13.50-£21.50 • Fixed D £16.99-£30
...offee £1.25 • min/water £4 • Service optional

...ACE: Overlooking the green, the Goldings restaurant of this
...ember's only golf course is open to all and has a friendly
...bhouse charm. Take a pre-dinner drink in the bar or on the
...rrace in warmer weather, and then move through to the wood
...nelled dining room with its traditional decor.

...OD: A classical menu, with international influences, to match
...e setting. Expect dishes such as a Barbary duck and girolle
...shroom pie with a shallot Tatin, and confit cabbage.

...UR TIP: A bar menu offers a lighter selection of dishes
...ef: Robby Pierce Owners: Exclusive Hotels Times: 12.30-2.30/7-9,
...osed D Sun-Wed (Winter only) Notes: Vegetarian available, Dress
...strictions, No jeans, trainers. Collared shirt required, Civ Wed 100
...ats: 43, Pr/dining room 12 Smoking: N/Sm in restaurant
...ildren: Menu, Portions Directions: From Horsham A281, for 2m.
...proaching Mannings Heath, left at the Dun Horse. Follow road to T-
...ct, left then follow road past village green. At T-junct, right then right
...in Parking: 120 e-mail: enquiries@manningsheath.com
...b: www.manningsheath.com

...IDHURST MAP 06 SU82

...◎ The Angel Hotel

...itish, European

...ntemporary menu in classically influenced ...vironment

☎ 01730 812421 North St GU29 9DN

MENU GUIDE Blue cheese cheesecake • Top-roasted fillet of
...ill • Yogurt pannacotta

WINE GUIDE ♀ La Huerta Chardonnay £13.95 • ♀ Moondara
...iraz £14.50 • 27 bottles over £20, 17 bottles under £20 • 10 by
...e glass (£2.85-£5.25)

continued

PRICE GUIDE Fixed L £10 • starter £4.25-£7.95 • main £13.25-
£17.95 • dessert £5.95 • coffee £2.50 • min/water £2.75 • Service
optional • Group min 8 service 10%

PLACE: This old building dates to 1539, and has served as a
coaching inn and courthouse. Its town centre site is fronted by a
bar and brasserie, with more formal dining at the rear - Gabriel's
restaurant is decorated in soft golds, and vibrant blues with
plenty of natural daylight.

FOOD: Modern British cooking with European influences,
attractively presented. The frequently changing carte aims to use
seasonal produce.

OUR TIP: Explore the town after dinner
Chef: Alan Randall Owners: John Cooper, Ian Webb Times: 12-2.30/7-
9.30 Notes: Sun L 2 courses £14.95, 3 courses £19.95, Vegetarian
available, Dress Restrictions, No Seats: 40, Pr/dining room 20
Smoking: N/Sm in restaurant Children: Menu, Portions Rooms: 28
(28 en suite) ★★★ Directions: Town centre, junct of A286 and A272
Parking: 75 e-mail: info@theangelmidhurst.co.uk
web: www.theangelmidhurst.co.uk

◎◎ Spread Eagle Hotel and Health Spa

British, European

Character inn steeped in history offering modern cuisine

☎ 01730 816911 South St GU29 9NH

MENU GUIDE Roasted cep soup with croûtons • Grilled south
coast cod • Warm pear & frangipane tart

WINE GUIDE ♀ Château Laulerie Bergerac £15.95 • ♀ Château
Laulerie Bergerac £17.50 • 88 bottles over £20, 29 bottles under
£20 • 9 by the glass (£4-£5)

PRICE GUIDE Fixed D £35-£36 • starter £7.50-£7.75 • main £20-
£20.50 • dessert £7.50-£7.75 • coffee £2.50 • min/water
£3.95 • Service optional

PLACE: Standing in its own picturesque grounds, people have
sought sustenance here since the early 15th century. The building
is rich in antiquity, with the restaurant decorated with copper
artefacts and Christmas puddings hanging from the overhead
beams.

FOOD: Expensive ingredients abound in the modern British
cooking with European influences, and a six-course tasting menu
will tempt the bon viveur. The cheeseboard offers the best of
England and France.

OUR TIP: Enjoy the tasting menu
Chef: Lee Williams Owners: The Goodman Family Times: 12.30-2/7-
9.30 Notes: Tasting menu £49, Sun L 3 courses £19.95, Vegetarian
available, Dress Restrictions, Smart casual, Civ Wed 80 Seats: 50,
Pr/dining room 12 Smoking: N/Sm in restaurant Children: Menu,
Portions Rooms: 39 (39 en suite) ★★★ Directions: Town centre
Parking: 70 e-mail: reservations@spreadeagle-midhurst.com
web: www.hshotels.co.uk/spread/spreadeagle-main.htm

ROWHOOK MAP 06 TQ13

◎ Neals Restaurant at The Chequers Inn

British, Mediterranean

Lively rural pub with separate restaurant

☎ 01403 790480 RH12 3PY

MENU GUIDE Scottish smoked salmon on saffron
blini • Seared calves' liver on bubble & squeak • William pear
& apple crumble

continued on page 463

England

The Camellia Restaurant at South Lodge Hotel

British, French
Country-house cuisine overlooking the South Downs
☎ 01403 891711 Brighton Rd RH13 6PS
e-mail: enquiries@southlodgehotel.co.uk
web: www.exclusivehotels.co.uk

PLACE: Named after the 100-year-old camellia which still grows against the terrace wall, this impeccable Victorian country-house hotel is a haven of gracious living and stands in 90 acres of mature gardens and grounds. With its wo panelling, rich oil paintings, heavy fabrics and sense of space, it was built to impress and it certainly does. Take aperitifs in the clubroom intimacy of the lounge, before enjoying the crisp white napery, candlelight, wooden panelli and floors of the dining room, with its views over the South Downs. Service is formal but appropriately friendly.
FOOD: Lewis Hamblet's refreshingly unpretentious menus are modern-focused and based on classical roots. Cookin is intelligently simple and to the point, with the emphasis on making the best use of quality local ingredients. With clear, well-defined flavours and technical skill to the fore, enjoy the likes of a trio of South Down lamb served with basil creamed potato and honeycomb jus, or perhaps fillets of John Dory, paired with sautéed potatoes, wilted spinach, celeriac crisps and a light watercress cream.

MENU GUIDE Rabbit loin, chanterelles, sun-dried tomato tart • Angus fillet, braised shin, foie gras, truffled cream potatoes, horseradish froth • Pear Tatin, roquefort ice cream, walnuts

WINE GUIDE 200 bottles over £20 • 14 by the glass

PRICE GUIDE Fixed L £14 • Fixed D £46 • coffee £2.50 • min/water £3.95 • Service optional

OUR TIP: Take afternoon tea in the elegant lounge

Chef: Lewis Hamblet **Owners:** Exclusive Hotels & Golf Clubs
Times: 12-2/7-10 **Notes:** Vegetarian available, Dress Restrictions, Smart casual - no sportswear, Civ Wed 160 **Seats:** 40, Pr/dining room 10 **Smoking:** N/Sm in restaurant **Children:** Menu
Rooms: 45 (45 en suite) ★★★★ **Directions:** On A23, left onto B2110, take a right turn through Handcross to A281 junct
Parking: 190

England

ROWHOOK *continued* MAP 06 TQ13

WINE GUIDE ♀ Sauvigilio Pinot Grigio £14.50 • ♥ Stonefish Shiraz £12.50 • 22 bottles over £20, 29 bottles under £20 8 by the glass (£3.20-£3.40)

PRICE GUIDE Fixed L £16.50-£18.50 • Fixed D £27-£30 • starter £5.50-£8.50 • main £10.50-£18.50 • dessert £4.50-£6.50 • coffee £2 • min/water £3 • Service optional • Group min 8 service 10%

PLACE: A 15th-century cottage pub with stone-flagged floors, oak beams, open fires and traditional rustic decor. The restaurant has simple table linen and contemporary art on the walls. A loyal following of regulars makes for a buzzy atmosphere.

FOOD: Modern British food with Mediterranean influences prepared by the chef/proprietor. A bar menu offers an excellent range of options at all price points, while the restaurant menu focuses on fewer but more complex dishes.

OUR TIP: The garden is lovely in fine weather

Chef: Tim Neal **Owners:** Mr & Mrs Neal **Times:** 12-3.30/7-12.30, Closed Mon, closed D Sun **Notes:** Vegetarian available **Seats:** 40 **Smoking:** N/Sm in restaurant **Children:** Portions **Directions:** From Horsham take A281 towards Guildford. At rdbt take A29 signposted for London. After 200 mtrs turn left, follow signs for Rowhook **Parking:** 40 **e-mail:** thechequers1!@aol.com **web:** www.nealsrestaurants.biz

STORRINGTON MAP 06 TQ01

◉ Old Forge

Modern International

Interesting experience for wine lovers

☎ 01903 743402 6 Church St RH20 4LA

MENU GUIDE Seared foie gras with thyme brioche • Tuna steak, chargrilled aubergines • Iced praline & limoncello parfait

WINE GUIDE ♀ Grant Burge Colombard Chardonnay 20 bottles over £20, 30 bottles under £20 • 10 by the glass (£3.25-£5)

PRICE GUIDE Fixed L £13-£24.50 • Fixed D £32 • min/water £2.50 • Service included

PLACE: Lovely old building with remnants of its blacksmith's past intact. There are two dining rooms, one open and small, the other full of nooks and crannies. The amazingly well-stocked wine cellar is open next door for a browse.

FOOD: A short but well-balanced fixed-price modern international menu suggests pan-seared scallops and confit of rabbit saddle, and the indecisive can opt for a taste of all the listed desserts.

OUR TIP: Superb wine list with many rarities

Chef: Cathy Roberts, Will Murgatroyd **Owners:** Mr & Mrs N C Roberts **Times:** 12.15-1.45/7.15-9.30, Closed Xmas-New Year, 2 wk spring, 2 wk autumn, Mon-Wed, closed L Sat, closed D Sun **Notes:** Vegetarian available, Smart casual **Seats:** 34, Pr/dining room 12 **Smoking:** N/Sm area, No pipes **Children:** Portions **Directions:** On a side street in the village centre **Parking:** On street **e-mail:** contact@oldforge.co.uk **web:** www.fine-dining.co.uk

◉◉ Sawyards

French   **NEW**

Sharp cooking in the heart of the Sussex countryside

☎ 01903 742331 Manleys Hill RH20 4BT

MENU GUIDE White onion risotto, truffle cappuccino • Roast cannon of Cornish lamb, niçoise • Caramelised apple tart, caramel & vanilla ice cream

PRICE GUIDE Food prices not confirmed for 2006. Please telephone for details

continued

PLACE: On the outskirts of town, this restaurant has a long-standing tradition for fine food, but recently taken over, it's now called Sawyards (formerly Fleur de Sel). Interiors mix tradition (original beams and inglenook) with contemporary pastel colours and the occasional splash of art. A small bar area appeals for aperitifs, while there's a courtyard garden for fine weather drinks. At the time of going to press, a refurbishment was taking place.

FOOD: Chef Richard Davies shows pedigree (ex Restaurant Gordon Ramsay, London SW3 and Vineyard at Stockcross, Newbury) via modern-focused menus underpinned by a classical French theme. His cooking is skilful, sharp and thoughtful, with quality local produce playing a key role. Presentation is clean and unfussy allowing main ingredients centre stage and not clouding flavours. Dish compilation and beautifully prepared food leaps from the appealing, sensible length fixed-price carte (no supplements) and great value fixed-price market menu.

OUR TIP: The market menu is exceptionally good value

Chef: Richard Davies **Times:** Telephone for details **Directions:** On A283, off A24, just E of Storrington

TURNERS HILL MAP 06 TQ33

◉◉ Alexander House Hotel

British, French

Fine dining in stylish country-house setting

☎ 01342 714914 East St RH10 4QD

MENU GUIDE Warm herbed crusted goats' cheese • Medallions of monkfish • Apple & stem ginger pudding

WINE GUIDE ♀ Chablis £30 • ♥ Rioja Reserva £35 • 154 bottles over £20, 4 bottles under £20 • 5 by the glass (£5)

PRICE GUIDE Fixed L £17.50 • Fixed D £39.50 • coffee £4 • min/water £3.50 • Service added but optional 12.5%

PLACE: Surrounded by 170 acres of beautiful parkland, this stunning house with its distinctive chimneys dates in part from the 17th century. The classically elegant interior is rich in original features, fine fabrics and luxurious furniture. The dining room is decorated in warm hues with high quality linen, china and glassware.

continued

England

TURNERS HILL *continued* MAP 06 TQ33

FOOD: Touches of French influence throughout the British menu give the kitchen plenty of scope to offer classically proven combinations. Excellent English ingredients are well married with fine flavours from beyond our shores such as black truffle and olive oils, basil, herbs, Sauternes and Armagnac.

OUR TIP: Indulge someone special with an overnight stay
Chef: Brett Cambourne Paynter **Owners:** Alexander Hotels Ltd
Times: 12-2/7-9.30, Closed L Sat **Notes:** ALC 3 courses £49.50 Sun L 3 courses £26, Vegetarian available, Dress Restrictions, No jeans or trainers, Civ Wed 60 **Seats:** 60, Pr/dining room 24 **Smoking:** N/Sm in restaurant
Children: Min 7 yrs, Portions **Rooms:** 18 (18 en suite) ★★★
Directions: On B2110 between Turners Hill & East Grinstead; 6m from M23 junct 10 **Parking:** 50 **e-mail:** info@alexanderhouse.co.uk
web: www.alexanderhouse.co.uk

WORTHING MAP 06 TQ10

Ardington Hotel
International

Seaside hotel with contemporary cuisine
☎ 01903 230451 Steyne Gardens BN11 3DZ

MENU GUIDE Chicken liver & foie gras parfait • Pork, apple & stilton stuffing, beer sauce • Belgian chocolate truffle torte

WINE GUIDE ♀ Dalwood Chardonnay • ♀ Nal d'Obieu Merlot £12.50 • 2 bottles over £20, 6 bottles under £20 • 6 by the glass (£2.50)

PRICE GUIDE Fixed L £16 • Fixed D £25 • starter £4.95-£7.85 • main £9.85-£17.15 • dessert £4.75 • coffee £2.10 • min/water £3 • Service added

PLACE: Friendly hotel set in a pretty gardened square near the seafront. Dinner is served in the colourful and airy Indigo restaurant, which is decorated in contemporary style with bold artwork and hand-made high-back chairs.
FOOD: Simple modern British dishes with International influences and a touch of flair. You might begin with fresh local mussels in white wine and garlic, and then move on to sweet potato curry, or smoked cod with saffron mash and pesto cream.
OUR TIP: Take a walk along the front before dinner
Chef: John Gettings **Owners:** Mr & Mrs B Margaroli **Times:** 12-2/7-8.45, Closed 22 Dec-7 Jan, closed L Mon-Sat **Notes:** Vegetarian available
Seats: 70, Pr/dining room 50 **Smoking:** N/Sm in restaurant
Children: Menu, Portions **Rooms:** 45 (45 en suite) ★★★
Directions: Telephone for directions **web:** www.ardingtonhotel.co.uk

TYNE & WEAR

GATESHEAD MAP 21 NZ26

Eslington Villa Hotel
British, French

Victorian setting for modern cuisine
☎ 0191 487 6017 & 420 0666 8 Station Rd, Low Fell NE9 6DR

MENU GUIDE Chicken liver parfait • Roast pork, Parma ham, black pudding, parsley mash • Sticky toffee pudding

WINE GUIDE ♀ Stoney Vale Semillion/Chardonnay £13.90 • ♀ BMW Shiraz £20.60 • 13 bottles over £20, 18 bottles under £20 • 6 by the glass (£3.35-£3.50)

PRICE GUIDE Fixed L £12.50 • Fixed D £18.50 • starter £4.50-£8.50 • main £12.50-£18 • dessert £4-£6.50 • coffee £2 min/water £3.25 • Service optional

PLACE: The Eslington blends period and contemporary style, its Victorian features tastefully complemented by low-key modern shades and furnishings. Food is served in an airy modern conservatory, or amid the more classical surroundings of the 19th-century dining room.
FOOD: Modern British dishes with French influences distinguishe by care and attention. You might start with a paysanne salad of crisp pancetta, mushrooms and sauté potatoes, and move on to sole with a chive butter sauce, or chargrilled chicken with blue cheese polenta and roasted peppers.
OUR TIP: Great value fixed-price lunch
Chef: Andy Moore **Owners:** Mr & Mrs N Tulip **Times:** 12-2/7-9.45, Closed 25-26 Dec, 1 Jan, BHs, closed L Sat, closed D Sun **Notes:** Sun lunch £16, Vegetarian available, Smart casual **Seats:** 80, Pr/dining room 30 **Smoking:** N/Sm in restaurant **Children:** Portions **Rooms:** 17 (17 e suite) ★★★ **Directions:** From A1 (M) turn off to Team Valley Trading Estate, up Eastern Avenue. Turn left at PDS car showroom. Hotel is 100 yd on left **Parking:** 21 **e-mail:** eslingtonvilla@freeuk.com

NEWCASTLE UPON TYNE MAP 21 NZ26

Blackfriars
International, Pacific Rim

Informal dining in historic setting
☎ 0191 261 5945 Friars St NE1 4XN

MENU GUIDE Pearl barley risotto, smoked chicken and apple • Spiced duck, char sui crab, sweet kumquat chutney • Coconut tart, honeyed yoghurt

WINE GUIDE ♀ Jim Barry Riesling £17 • ♀ J & F Lurton Pinot Noir £16.50 • 4 bottles over £20, 17 bottles under £20 • 6 by the glass (£3.25-£4)

PRICE GUIDE Fixed L £9.90 • Fixed D £12.90 • starter £3.95-£6.95 • main £8.95-£22.50 • dessert £3.95-£5 • coffee £1.70 min/water £2.80 • Service optional • Group min 6 service 10%

PLACE: Built in 1239 as a refectory for the adjacent priory, you could say that this informal café bar/restaurant is one of the oldest purpose-built restaurants in the country. Expect plenty of exposed stone, wooden floors, terracotta walls, thick church candles, and relaxed and friendly service.
FOOD: Use of fresh ingredients, interesting flavours and simple, contemporary presentation will impress. Menus are modern with clever international twists.
OUR TIP: Dine in the peaceful courtyard on fine days
Chef: Andy Drape **Owners:** Andy & Sam Hook **Times:** 12-2.30/6-12, Closed BHs except Good Fri, Mon, closed D Sun **Notes:** Vegetarian available **Seats:** 65, Pr/dining room 20 **Smoking:** N/Sm in restaurant, Air con **Children:** Portions **Directions:** Take the only small cobbled road off Stowel St (China Town). Blackfriars 100yds on left **Parking:** Car park next to restaurant
e-mail: info@blackfriarscafebar.co.uk
web: www.blackfriarscafebar.co.uk

🍽 Café 21 Newcastle

British, French

Good quayside dining in fashionable metropolitan setting

☎ 0191 222 0755 Quayside NE1 3UG

MENU GUIDE Roast beetroot salad, goats' cheese • Salt cod, provençale vegetables • Date & Jamaica rum soufflé

WINE GUIDE ♀ Delibori Delle Venezie Pinot Bianco £14.90 ♥ Monte Real Reserva Rioja Tempranillo £23.50 • 32 bottles over £20, 24 bottles under £20 • 8 by the glass (£3.40-£4.60)

PRICE GUIDE Fixed L £13.50 • starter £5-£10.50 • main £11.50-£21.50 • dessert £4.50-£6.50 • coffee £2 • min/water £3

PLACE: This bustling, busy bistro in Newcastle's trendy Quayside area enjoys quite a local following. Expect smart settings, lots of artwork and racks of wine bottles.

FOOD: With well presented accurate cooking, the menu of modern British dishes is punctuated by French bistro classics. Boeuf Bourguignon can follow cheddar soufflé with spinach. French bread is served as soon as you're seated by helpful staff. Blackboard specials change daily.

OUR TIP: Still a place to see and be seen in Newcastle **Chef:** Christopher Dobson **Owners:** Mr and Mrs T Laybourne **Times:** 12-2.30/6-10.30, Closed Xmas, BHs, Sun **Notes:** Vegetarian available **Seats:** 60 **Smoking:** N/Sm area, No pipes, Air con **Children:** Portions **Directions:** Telephone for directions **Parking:** On street, NCP **e-mail:** ns@cafetwentyone.co.uk

🍽🍽 The Fishermans Lodge

British, French

A fashionable out-of-town setting for fine dining

☎ 0191 281 3281 Jesmond Dene, Jesmond NE7 7BQ

MENU GUIDE King prawn tempura, Asian salad • Grilled halibut supreme, lemon & herb butter • Apple crumble soufflé

WINE GUIDE ♀ Mezza Corona Pinot Grigio £19.95 • ♥ Bulanda Tempranillo £23.95 • 145 bottles over £20, 14 bottles under £20 • 21 by the glass (£4.50-£18.50)

PRICE GUIDE Fixed L £17.50-£22.50 • Fixed D £50 • coffee £3.95 • min/water £3.75 • Service optional

PLACE: The sophisticated setting attracts all sorts from business people to old friends and romantic couples, all confident that this sister restaurant to Seaham Hall will deliver the same quality product. It's located outside Newcastle in a secluded little valley where the traditional shooting lodge-type exterior conceals a tastefully decorated and elegant set of rooms. Service is pitched at just the right level.

FOOD: With consistent accuracy, the forward-looking menu introduces some interesting combinations and exciting variations whilst continuing to acknowledge a strongly classical background. Fish, not surprisingly, plays a starring role, with pan-fried fillet of cod, monkfish braised in red wine, and wild sea bass with crab beignets among the inspired choices. You'll find some tastefully presented meat and game dishes too: perhaps grilled Northumbrian beef fillet with wild mushroom gratin, or supreme of roast pheasant, each with its own carefully chosen accompaniments.

OUR TIP: The set lunch menu is ideal for slender budgets **Chef:** Paul Amer **Owners:** Tom and Jocelyn Maxfield **Times:** 12-2/7-10.30, Closed BHs, Sun, closed L 31 Dec, closed D Sun **Notes:** Vegetarian available, Smart casual, Civ Wed 60 **Seats:** 60, Pr/dining room 40 **Smoking:** N/Sm in restaurant **Children:** Portions **Directions:** 2.5m from city centre, off A1058 (Tynemouth road). Turn into Jesmond Rd then 2nd right on Jesmond Dene Rd. Follow signposts **Parking:** 40 **e-mail:** enquiries@fishermanslodge.co.uk **web:** www.fishermanslodge.co.uk

🍽 *Malmaison Hotel*

French

Good brasserie dining in trendy location

☎ 0191 245 5000 Quayside NE1 3DX

MENU GUIDE Chicken liver & foie gras parfait • Cheviot lamb shank • Treacle tart, cinnamon ice cream

PRICE GUIDE Food prices not confirmed for 2006. Please telephone for details

PLACE: Stripped wooden floorboards remind you of this building's warehouse past; the deep purple decor, beautiful staff and slick table service prove that it is now a chic modern hotel. The dining room is contemporary in style with chestnut leather sofas, tub chairs and round banquettes.

FOOD: The menu is packed with traditional, brasserie classics like steak frites, salade niçoise and warm duck salad with caramelised kumquats. The cheese selection is also impressive.

OUR TIP: Booking is required as there is a loyal local following **Times:** 12-2.30/6-11 **Rooms:** 116 (116 en suite) ★★★ **Directions:** Telephone for directions **e-mail:** newcastle@malmaison.com **web:** www.malmaison.com

🍽🍽 Newcastle Marriott Hotel, Gosforth Park

British, French

Modern hotel with an extensive range

☎ 0191 236 4111 High Gosforth Park, Gosforth NE3 5HN

MENU GUIDE Ham hock terrine, apricot chutney • Pork belly, braised fennel, black pudding ravioli • Cointreau & white chocolate truffle

continued *continued*

England

NEWCASTLE UPON TYNE continued MAP 21 NZ26

WINE GUIDE ♀ Australia Semillion £19.55 • ♀ Chile Merlot £16.25 • 34 bottles over £20, 27 bottles under £20 • 19 by the glass (£5.10-£7.85)

PRICE GUIDE Fixed L £16.95 • Fixed D £26 • starter £4.95-£8.45 • main £15.50-£19.75 • dessert £4.95 • coffee £3.50 • min/water £3.95 • Service optional

PLACE: Overlooking Gosforth Park, this popular hotel restaurant is smartly decked out in muted browns and reds with luxurious cream drapes. The Marriott has extensive conference and leisure facilities and is handily located for both the racecourse and airport.
FOOD: Catering to all tastes, the menu features a lengthy selection of dishes that range from straightforward fare (a grill or roast of the day) to more complex modern combinations, such as a cannon of beef with leek and potato rösti and a morel jus.
OUR TIP: Less formal dining available in Chats Bar
Chef: Simon Devine **Owners:** Whitbread Hotel Co **Times:** 12.30-2/7-10, Closed 25, 31 Dec, closed L Sat (Mon-Fri for conferences only)
Notes: Vegetarian available, Civ Wed 200 **Seats:** 120, Pr/dining room 30
Smoking: N/Sm area, No pipes, No cigars, Air con **Children:** Menu, Portions **Rooms:** 178 (178 en suite) ★★★★ **Directions:** From A1 take A1056 (Killingworth/Wideopen) 3rd exit to hotel ahead **Parking:** 300
e-mail: frontdesk.gosforthpark@whitbread.com
web: www.marriotthotels.com/ncglf

◎◎ *Treacle Moon*
International
Fashionable little restaurant near the quay
☎ 0191 232 5537 5-7 The Side NE1 3JE
MENU GUIDE Hot charred tiger prawns • Poached whiting, crab & chive crust • Tonka bean rice pudding
PRICE GUIDE Food prices not confirmed for 2006. Please telephone for details

PLACE: Modern images of the city and its connecting bridges grace the walls of this stylish little eaterie near the quayside. Romantically candlelit at night, it boasts chic table settings with fresh roses and tall glassware. Staff are attentive and friendly.
FOOD: The short menu has made a big impact on local diners, with flavours drawn from classical, modern and International inspirations and brought together with great panache. The no-nonsense cooking is supported by an effectively simple presentation, ably demonstrated by braised shoulder of pork with prunes and chestnuts, and a well-judged cider jus.
OUR TIP: Enjoy a quayside walk
Times: 7-10.30, Closed Xmas, 2 wks Aug, BHs, Sun, closed L all week
Directions: On the quayside **e-mail:** john@treaclemoonrestaurant.co.uk
web: www.treaclemoonrestaurant.com

◎ **Vermont Hotel**
British, European
Stylish hotel restaurant in prime location with great views
☎ 0191 233 1010 Castle Garth NE1 1RQ
MENU GUIDE Roast pepper & potato terrine, thyme crème fraîche • Crispy duck, chive mash, red wine jus • Chocolate & hazelnut sponge, caramel ice cream
WINE GUIDE ♀ L'Emage White £14.50 • ♀ L'Emage Red £14.50 • 50 bottles over £20, 40 bottles under £20 • 8 by the glass (£3.50-£5.20)
PRICE GUIDE Fixed L £14 • Fixed D £22 • coffee £2.80 • min/water £3.50

PLACE: Plumb in the city centre next to the castle and close to the bustling quayside, the Vermont occupies a grand old building formerly the County Hall. With views over the Tyne and Millennium Bridges, and decorated in an elegant, modern style, the Bridge Restaurant is the hotel's fine dining option.
FOOD: Fixed-price menus have been simplified and read well, the style being modern British and French with European influences.
OUR TIP: Sample Newcastle's vibrant nightlife
Chef: Kristian Branch **Owners:** Lincoln Group **Times:** 12-2.30/6-11
Notes: Vegetarian available, Dress Restrictions, Very smart; no casual dress, no jeans, Civ Wed 150 **Seats:** 80, Pr/dining room 80
Smoking: N/Sm in restaurant **Children:** Portions **Rooms:** 101 (101 en suite) ★★★★ **Directions:** City centre, by high level bridge and castle keep **Parking:** 80 **e-mail:** info@vermont-hotel.co.uk
web: www.vermont-hotel.co.uk

◎ **Barn Again Bistro** 21a Leazes Park Rd NE1 4PF
☎ 0191 230 3338 Fun, safari-tinged surroundings with a global menu to match.

TYNEMOUTH MAP 21 NZ36
◎ **Sidney's Restaurant**
Modern British
Friendly neighbourhood bistro
☎ 0191 257 8500 & 0191 213 0284 3-5 Percy Park Rd NE30 4LZ

MENU GUIDE Asian fishcakes, sweet chilli dipping sauce • Lamb hotpot, mash & pickled cabbage • Crème brûlée
WINE GUIDE ♀ De Gras Sauvignon Blanc £13.50 • ♀ Thorne Hill Shiraz £14 • 4 bottles over £20, 17 bottles under £20 • 6 by the glass (£3.25-£4)
PRICE GUIDE Fixed L £9.95 • Fixed D £12.95 • starter £3.95-£7 • main £9.95-£19.50 • dessert £4-£5 • coffee £1.70 • min/water £2.80 • Service optional • Group min 6 service 10%

PLACE: An unobtrusive façade, forming part of a town-centre shopping street, surprisingly conceals this bang-up-to-date, bright contemporary bistro. Art-conscious - from its lower studio that doubles as a gallery to the burnt orange and purples and polished floorboards - Sidney's hits all the right cosmopolitan notes.
FOOD: The modern, bistro-style dishes are accurate, clean-cut and play to the gallery, delivering the likes of seared salmon with Puy lentils and chorizo stew.
OUR TIP: Ale lovers should check out the bottled beer selection
Chef: Christopher Slaughter **Owners:** Andy & Sam Hook **Times:** 12-2.30/6-12, Closed BHs ex Good Friday, Sun **Notes:** Vegetarian available
Seats: 50, Pr/dining room 20 **Smoking:** N/Sm in restaurant, Air con
Children: Menu, Portions **Directions:** From Newcastle take A1058 to Tynemouth. Restaurant on corner of Percy Park Rd & Front St
Parking: On street **e-mail:** bookings@sidneys.co.uk
web: www.sidneys.co.uk

continued

WARWICKSHIRE

ABBOT'S SALFORD MAP 10 SP05

Salford Hall Hotel

British, European

Historic hotel with traditional atmosphere

☎ 01386 871300 WR11 5UT

MENU GUIDE Home-smoked duck breast • Pan-fried fillet of lamb • Sticky date pudding

WINE GUIDE ♀ Brampton Sauvignon Blanc £16.25
♥ Rowlands Brook Shiraz Cabernet £13.50 • 120 bottles over £20, 25 bottles under £20 • 14 by the glass (£3.95-£6.75)

PRICE GUIDE Fixed D £25-£30 • coffee £2.50 • min/water £3.50 • Service optional

PLACE: Brimming with history and fine period features, this delightful 15th-century manor house boasts a newer restaurant that is itself full of atmosphere. Oak panelling, polished brass chandeliers and muted reds make a comforting traditional statement.
FOOD: An heraldic shield fronting the menu signals some fine old recipes, brought up to date with plenty of modern ideas: braised blade of beef, and pavé of Old Spot pork with wholegrain mash, are sure winners.
OUR TIP: Ideal for a weekend break
Chef: Paul Napper **Owners:** Charter Hotels Ltd **Times:** 12.30-2/7-10, closed Xmas, closed L Sat **Notes:** Coffee incl, Vegetarian available, Dress restrictions, No jeans or trainers, Civ Wed 60 **Seats:** 50, Pr/dining room
● **Smoking:** N/Sm in restaurant **Children:** Min 2 yrs, Portions **Rooms:** 33 (33 en suite) ★★★ **Directions:** Off A46 between Stratford upon Avon & Evesham. Take road signposted Salford Priors, Abbots Salford 1.5 miles on left **Parking:** 60
e-mail: reception@salfordhall.co.uk **web:** www.salfordhall.co.uk

ALCESTER MAP 10 SP05

Kings Court Hotel

British, European

Modern cooking in old world setting

☎ 01789 763111 Kings Coughton B49 5QQ

MENU GUIDE Tomato & mozzarella tower, basil & pine nut oil • Beef fillet glazed with stilton, bordelaise sauce • Bittersweet lemon tart

WINE GUIDE ♀ Moondara Chardonnay £10.75 • ♥ Moondara Shiraz £10.75 • 2 bottles over £20, 18 bottles under £20 • 12 by the glass (£2.50-£4.65)

PRICE GUIDE Fixed L £9.20 • starter £4.25-£5.95 • main £9.75-£13.95 • dessert £3.95-£4.95 • coffee £1.35 • min/water £2.50 • Service optional

PLACE: The hotel, originally a Tudor farmhouse, is set in open countryside on a main road near Stratford-upon-Avon. The spacious courtyard restaurant has a great atmosphere, and you can also eat well in the bar from a different menu.
FOOD: The restaurant offers a good range of dishes using well-researched local produce, with fresh fish as a feature. Blackboard specials are written up in the bar.
OUR TIP: The gunpowder plot was hatched in the village
Chef: David Price **Owners:** Thomas Aldous **Times:** 12-2/7-10, Closed Xmas **Notes:** Sun L 2 courses £8.95, 3 courses £11.50, Vegetarian available, Smart Dress, Civ Wed 100 **Seats:** 70, Pr/dining room 100
Smoking: N/Sm in restaurant **Children:** Menu, Portions **Rooms:** 41 (41 en suite) ★★★ **Directions:** 1m N of Alcester on the A435, 8m outside of Stratford-upon-Avon **Parking:** 100
e-mail: info@kingscourthotel.co.uk **web:** www.kingscourthotel.co.uk

ALDERMINSTER MAP 10 SP24

❀❀ Ettington Park Hotel

British, French   ✎🐟

Dine in Gothic splendour

☎ 01789 450123 CV37 8BU

MENU GUIDE Roasted saddle of rabbit • Pan-fried monkfish tail, lime herb butter sauce • Lemon pudding

WINE GUIDE ♀ Spy Valley Sauvignon Blanc £26 • ♥ Huia Pinot Noir £35 • 111 bottles over £20, 6 bottles under £20 • 12 by the glass (£5.50-£7.50)

PRICE GUIDE Fixed L £19.50-£27.50 • Fixed D £41.50-£57.45 coffee £3.95 • min/water £3.95 • Service optional

PLACE: A house 'built for pleasure' is just the place for a spot of self-indulgence, and the magnificent Oak Room Restaurant epitomises the glamour and hedonism of this Gothic hotel. The original architectural features add dignity, while the friendly staff bring a lighter touch.
FOOD: The cooking is ambitious, and the carte and menu gourmand are its ideal showcases. Chef's specialities like assiette of tuna with chilled gazpacho are created from top-class ingredients, and there are delicate sauces to match most dishes, as in breast of Perigord duck with a pickled girolle sauce.
OUR TIP: Enjoy a walk around the delightful grounds
Chef: Ben Davies **Owners:** Handpicked Hotels **Times:** 12-2/7-9.30, Closed L Mon-Fri **Notes:** Gourmet tasting menu £55, Vegetarian available, Smart Dress, Smart casual, Civ Wed 96 **Seats:** 50, Pr/dining room 80 **Smoking:** N/Sm in restaurant **Children:** Menu, Portions **Rooms:** 48 (48 en suite) ★★★★ **Directions:** M40 junct 15/A46 towards Stratford-upon-Avon, then A439 into town centre onto A3400 5m to Shipston. Hotel 1/2m on left **Parking:** 80
web: www.handpicked.co.uk

ATHERSTONE MAP 10 SP39

❀ Chapel House Hotel

British, French   **NEW**

Elegant hotel offering accomplished cuisine

☎ 01827 718949 Friar's Gate CV9 1EY

MENU GUIDE St James' baked scallops • Pork fillet, cider brandy sauce & glazed apple balls • Almond paste soufflé, raspberry coulis

WINE GUIDE ♀ Echeverria unwooded Chardonnay £15.45 • ♥ Michel Torino Cabernet Sauvignon £14.35
49 bottles over £20, 44 bottles under £20 • 8 by the glass (£2.50-£3.95)

PRICE GUIDE Starter £4.50-£9 • main £18-£22 • dessert £4.95-£8.95 • coffee £2.45 • min/water £2.40 • Service optional

PLACE: This 18th-century former dower house for Atherstone Hall, where Florence Nightingale often stayed, now provides the setting for this elegant, unfussy dining room, where candlelight and classical music set a relaxing note.
FOOD: In keeping with surroundings, this sophisticated menu, drawing on classic French dishes, makes good use of local produce, including some succulently well-timed lamb.
OUR TIP: Relax in the pretty walled garden
Chef: Richard Henry Napper **Owners:** Richard & Siobhan Napper
Times: 7-9, Closed 24 Dec-3 Jan, Sun, closed L all wk **Notes:** Vegetarian available, Dress Restrictions, Smart casual **Seats:** 24, Pr/dining room 12
Smoking: N/Sm in restaurant **Children:** Portions **Rooms:** 12 (12 en suite) ★★ **Directions:** Off Market Sq in Atherstone, behind High St
Parking: On street **e-mail:** info@chapelhousehotel.co.uk
web: www.chapelhousehotel.co.uk

England

England

FARNBOROUGH MAP 11 SP44

The Inn at Farnborough

Modern British

Smart village inn offering accomplished cuisine

☎ 01295 690615 Main St OX17 1DZ

MENU GUIDE Sautéed scallops, orange & ginger • Roast pavé of Lighthorne lamb, thyme & port jus • Sticky toffee pudding, butterscotch sauce

WINE GUIDE ♀ Colli Orientali Pinot Grigio £14.95 • ♀ Marques di Caceres Rioja Tempranillo £17.95 • 21 bottles over £20, 40 bottles under £20 • 12 by the glass (£2.75-£7)

PRICE GUIDE Fixed L £10.95 • Fixed D £12.95 • starter £4.95-£9.95 • main £8.95-£22.95 • dessert £4.95 • coffee £2.25 • min/water £2.95 • Service optional

PLACE: Once the village butcher's shop, this Grade II listed building dates from around 1700 and incorporates a village pub and restaurant set in beautiful landscaped gardens. The restaurant is stylish and relaxed with both contemporary and traditional features, including exposed stonework and mullioned windows. Service is friendly and knowledgeable.

FOOD: The cooking is mainly modern British with Mediterranean and Asian influences and an emphasis on locally sourced produce.

OUR TIP: Close to the National Trust property Farnborough Hall

Chef: Anthony Robinson **Owners:** Oyster Inns Ltd **Times:** 12-3/6-10, Closed 25 Dec, Christmas Day Vegetarian available **Seats:** 80, Pr/dining room 16 **Smoking:** N/Sm in restaurant **Children:** Portions **Directions:** M40 junct 11 - (Banbury). 3rd rdbt turn right onto A423 to Southam. After 4m turn left down road signposted Farnborough. After 1m turn right into the village - the Inn at Farnborough is on the right hand side **Parking:** 40 **e-mail:** enquiries@innatfarnborough.co.uk **web:** www.innatfarnborough.co.uk

HENLEY-IN-ARDEN MAP 10 SP16

Edmunds

British, European

Accomplished cooking in local village eaterie

☎ 01564 795666 64 High St B95 5BX

MENU GUIDE Girolles risotto, truffle oil • Scotch beef, roast salsify, crispy pancetta, Madeira jus • Brioche & butter pudding

WINE GUIDE ♀ Brocard Chablis £20.25 • ♀ Stimpson Estate Merlot £14 • 30 bottles over £20, 26 bottles under £20 • 7 by the glass (£3.25-£4)

PRICE GUIDE Fixed L £10-£24.50 • Fixed D £26.95 • coffee £2.50 min/water £3 • Service optional • Group min 6 service 10%

PLACE: Step past the black and white frontage of this pretty 16th-century cottage, and you'll find an understated contemporary interior, where terracotta tones and leafy green plants form a warm backdrop to tables dressed in quality linen and glassware. Popular, so book ahead.

FOOD: Accomplished modern British cooking from a kitchen that likes to conjure the odd culinary adventure (pan-fried trotter and scallop) alongside more familiar fare. Fish dishes are a particular strength, though there's tough competition from mains such as slow-roasted Gressingham duck and red cabbage.

OUR TIP: Great value menu du jour, lunchtimes Tuesday to Friday

Chef: Andy Waters **Owners:** Andy & Beverly Waters **Times:** 12-1.45/7-9.45, Closed 1 wk May, Aug, Sep, Nov, Dec, Sun-Mon, closed L Sat **Notes:** Vegetarian available **Seats:** 44 **Smoking:** N/Sm in restaurant **Children:** Menu, Portions **Directions:** M40, junct 15. Located on the A3400 Henley in Arden High St **Parking:** On street

KENILWORTH MAP 10 SP27

⊚⊚ Simply Simpsons

French

Newly refurbished town-centre bistro with modern cooking

☎ 01926 864567 101-103 Warwick Rd CV8 1HL

MENU GUIDE Simpsons fishcakes, tartare sauce • Duck breast, prune & Armagnac sauce • Vanilla pannacotta, berry compote

WINE GUIDE ♀ Oyster Bay Sauvignon Blanc £19 • ♀ Conde de Valdemar Rioja Reserva £25 • 50 bottles over £20, 28 bottles under £20 • 6 by the glass (£3.25-£3.50)

PRICE GUIDE Starter £4.75-£5.50 • main £9.50-£15.50 • dessert £4.95 • coffee £1.95 • min/water £3 • Service added but optional 10%

PLACE: Andreas Antona's glass-fronted, double shop conversion in Kenilworth's high street is now an informal, bistro-style operation. Refurbished in modern style, high-backed chairs and linen cloths have given way to polished wooden tables, flagged floors, with long mirrors and poster-style pictures on the walls.

FOOD: Fine dining may now be at Simpsons in Edgbaston, but diners looking for simple, modern cooking in a bustling atmosphere will not be disappointed. Good use of fresh local produce and first-class presentation.

OUR TIP: Enjoy the bustle and the friendly staff

Chef: Iain Miller **Owners:** Andreas & Alison Antona **Times:** 12.30-2/7-10, Closed Last 2 wks of Aug, BHs, Sun, Mon **Notes:** Vegetarian available **Seats:** 70, Pr/dining room 40 **Smoking:** N/Sm in restaurant, Air con **Children:** Portions **Directions:** In main street in Kenilworth centre **Parking:** 15 **e-mail:** info@simplysimpsons.com **web:** www.simplysimpsons.com

LEAMINGTON SPA (ROYAL) MAP 10 SP36

⊚⊚⊚ Mallory Court Hotel

see page 46

Solo

European

Chic little eaterie

☎ 01926 422422 23 Dormer Place CV32 5AA

MENU GUIDE Salad of black pudding & smoked bacon • Braised shoulder of lamb, white beans • Lemon tart, raspberry coulis

WINE GUIDE ♀ Plenio Verdichio £28 • ♀ Noceto Sangiovese £28 • 65 bottles over £20, 7 bottles under £20 • 10 by the glass (£4-£7.50)

PRICE GUIDE Fixed L £15 • Fixed D £30 • coffee £2 • min/water £3.25 • Service optional • Group min 6 service 10%

PLACE: This little gem of a restaurant has only eight tables, each comfortably furnished with high-backed padded chairs, and set with quality crockery and glassware. Take a seat and watch the chefs rustle up your meal in the open kitchen.

FOOD: The quality of ingredients is all important at Solo, as a list of local suppliers on the daily-changing menu attests. There's no unnecessary embellishment, just an honest emphasis on seasonality and freshness that results in simple dishes such as Brixham plaice with a lemon and herb dressing, or Cotswold pheasant with chestnuts and prunes.

OUR TIP: Vegetarians should ring ahead

Chef: Ian Buckle **Owners:** The Wallace Family **Times:** 12-2/7-9.30, Closed Xmas, BHs, Sun, Mon **Notes:** Vegetarian by request only, Business casual preferred **Seats:** 24 **Smoking:** N/Sm in restaurant, Air con **Children:** Min 12 yrs **Directions:** Telephone for directions **Parking:** Lots of street parking **e-mail:** solorestaurant@hotmail.com **web:** www.solorestaurant.co.uk

LEAMINGTON SPA (ROYAL) MAP 10 SP36

Mallory Court Hotel

British, European

Exquisitely prepared dishes in sumptuous country-house hotel

☎ 01926 330214 Harbury Ln, Bishop's Tachbrook CV33 9QB

e-mail: reception@mallory.co.uk

web: www.mallory.co.uk

PLACE: An elegant Lutyens-style manor house of grand proportions, set in 10 acres of landscaped gardens, offers an impeccable country hideaway. Despite oozing quality and style – a choice of richly furnished, sumptuous and deeply comfortable lounges for aperitifs – there's a delightful, mellow, homely atmosphere. Leaded-light and mullioned windows, oak-panelling and crisp white linen provide the backdrop for elegant dining, while enthusiastic, dedicated and professional staff contrive to make the occasion a memorable experience.

FOOD: The modern cooking, underpinned by a classical theme, is appealing and smacks of confidence and class. Dishes are creatively presented, pay due respect to the finest ingredients and are prepared with the utmost attention to detail. Clear flavours, skilful combinations, balance and texture, simplicity and a lightness of touch all hit the mark. There's nothing too over-pretentious about the cooking either, which admirably complements the endearing philosophy behind the whole hotel.

MENU GUIDE Croustade of mushrooms, wood pigeon & pan-fried foie gras • Brill fillet, dressed crab, saffron sauce • Lemon tartlet, honey ice cream, autumnal fruits

WINE GUIDE ♀ Dog Point Sauvignon £38 • ♀ Dona Paula Malbec £27.50 • 153 bottles over £20, 4 bottles under £20 • 10 by the glass (£5.50-£6.50)

PRICE GUIDE Fixed L £19 • Fixed D £39.50 • starter £7.50-£12.50 • main £22-£28 • dessert £10.50-£12.50 • coffee £3.75 • min/water £3.50 • Service optional

OUR TIP: Make time to take a stroll in the gardens

Chef: Simon Haigh **Owners:** Sir Peter Rigby **Times:** 12-2/7-9.30
Notes: Vegetarian available, Dress Restrictions, No jeans or sportswear, Civ Wed 160 **Seats:** 50, Pr/dining room 27
Smoking: N/Sm in restaurant **Children:** Min 9 yrs, Portions
Rooms: 29 (29 en suite) ★★★ **Directions:** M40 junct 13 N-bound. Turn left, and left again towards Bishops Tachbrook. Continue for 0.5m and turn right up Harbury Lane. M40 junct 14 S-bound. Follow A452 for Leamington. At 2nd rdbt take left into Harbury Lane **Parking:** 50

England

STRATFORD-UPON-AVON MAP 10 SP25

⊕⊕ Billesley Manor Hotel

British, European

Modern food in a baronial setting

☎ 01789 279955 Billesley, Alcester B49 6NF

MENU GUIDE Scallops St Jacques, risotto nero, ginger velouté • English lamb three ways, sweet potatoes & artichokes • Banana tarte Tatin

WINE GUIDE ♀ Delle Venezie Pinot Grigio £17 • ♥ Delle Venezie Merlot £17 • 47 bottles over £20, 18 bottles under £20 • 7 by the glass (£3.95-£5.45)

PRICE GUIDE Fixed L £24.95 • Fixed D £27.95 • starter £7.25-£10.95 • main £18.95-£23.50 • dessert £6.50-£7.50 • coffee £3.25 • min/water £3.25 • Service added but optional 5%

PLACE: The Stuart Restaurant is a splendid oak-panelled dining room with a huge stone fireplace, chandeliers, tapestry and silver pheasants. The room also has fine views over the garden and fountain - do take time to see the yew topiary if you can. William Shakespeare is among the manor's former guests, and is reputed to have written part of *As You Like It* here.

FOOD: A modern approach is taken to food, with dishes based on few key ingredients carefully handled. Produce is fresh and locally sourced.

OUR TIP: Speciality and liqueur coffees served

Chef: Christopher Short **Owners:** Haydn Fentum/Furlong Hotels **Times:** 12.30-2/7-9.30 **Notes:** Vegetarian available, Dress Restrictions, No denims, trainers or T-shirts, Civ Wed 73 **Seats:** 42, Pr/dining room 40 **Smoking:** N/Sm in restaurant **Children:** Menu, Portions **Rooms:** 71 (71 en suite) ★★★★ **Directions:** M40 junct 15, then take A46 S towards Stratford/Worcester. Follow the A46 E over three rdbts. Continue for 2m then take a right for Billesley **Parking:** 100

e-mail: enquiries@billesleymanor.co.uk **web:** www.billesleymanor.co.uk

⊕ Fox and Goose

British, European

Busy country inn offering imaginative food

☎ 01608 682293 Armscote CV37 8DD

MENU GUIDE Sardines, lime & coriander dressing • Slow-roast lamb shank, mash, rosemary & redcurrant jus • Sticky toffee pudding

WINE GUIDE ♀ Willowglen Chardonnay £12.50 • ♥ Willowglen Shiraz Cabernet £12.50 • 5 bottles over £20, 17 bottles under £20 • 6 by the glass (£2.90-£3.15)

PRICE GUIDE Starter £3.75-£6 • main £9.95-£15 • dessert £4.75-£5.50 • coffee £1.60 • min/water £3 • Service optional

PLACE: This ivy-clad inn sits in the heart of an unspoilt country village not far from Stratford-upon-Avon. Converted from cottages and a blacksmith's forge, its rustic interior comprises a cosy bar, a pretty candlelit dining room with deep red walls and rustic tables and chairs, and four eccentric bedrooms styled to a Cluedo theme.

FOOD: Imaginative British cooking with European influences that consistently impresses. Expect hearty portions and a good smattering of local produce, with game in season. Daily-changing menu.

OUR TIP: Look out for special evenings during the year

Chef: Dean Hawker **Owners:** Paul Stevens **Times:** 12-2.30/7-9.30, Closed 25 Dec, 1 Jan **Notes:** Sun D 1 course £10.50, Vegetarian available **Seats:** 45, Pr/dining room 20 **Smoking:** N/Sm area **Children:** Portions **Rooms:** 4 (4 en suite) ◆◆◆◆ **Directions:** From Stratford-upon-Avon take A3400 S for 7m. After Newbold-on-Stour turn R towards Armscote (signed). 1m to village **Parking:** 20 **e-mail:** email@foxandgoose.co.uk **web:** www.foxandgoose.co.uk

⊕ Menzies Welcombe Hotel and Golf Course

British   NEW

A class above standard hotel fare

☎ 01789 295252 Warwick Rd CV37 0NR

MENU GUIDE Saffron & crab risotto • Spiced pork tenderloin, mustard sauce • Mille-feuille of chocolate, summer berries

PRICE GUIDE Fixed L £14.50 • Fixed D £45 • Service optional

PLACE: A Jacobean manor house, set in landscaped parkland, with an impressive wood-panelled lounge and clubby bar. Its Trevelyan Restaurant, overlooking formal gardens, continues the theme, a grand ballroom-style space in sage green with Venetian-style glass sidelights.

FOOD: An appropriately classical theme runs through the modern, fixed-price menus. So expect the likes of medallions of beef fillet, served with sauté girolles, baby carrots and onions, pancetta, thyme-crushed potatoes and a red wine jus.

OUR TIP: Try one of the more complex dishes

Chef: Wayne Thomson **Owners:** Menzies Hotels **Times:** 12-2/6-10 **Notes:** Coffee incl, Sun L available, Tasting Menu 7 courses £55, Civ Wed 160 **Seats:** 70, Pr/dining room 160 **Smoking:** N/Sm in restaurant **Children:** Menu, Portions **Rooms:** 73 (73 en suite) ★★★★ **Directions:** 1m from Stratford-upon-Avon **Parking:** 90 **e-mail:** welcombe@menzies-hotels.co.uk **web:** www.bookmenzies.co.uk

⊕⊕ The Shakespeare

International   NEW

Imaginative cooking in historical setting

☎ 0870 4008182 Chapel St CV37 6ER

PLACE: Dating back to the 17th century this picture-perfect building in the heart of Stratford is reputed to be the oldest in town. It retains plenty of old-world charm, with exposed wooden beams inside and out and a flagstone floor. The restaurant has bags of character, plus modern comforts such as well-spaced tables and polished, efficient service.

FOOD: Imaginative, modern cooking with attention to detail, timing and accuracy. Expect well thought out combinations such as fillet of black bream with seared scallops, Vale of Evesham asparagus tomato dress of wild salmon with truffle cream.

OUR TIP: An ideal base for exploring Stratford-upon-Avon

Chef: Chris McPherson **Owners:** Macdonald Hotels **Times:** Telephone for details **Notes:** Vegetarian available **Seats:** 80 **Directions:** Telephone for details **Rooms:** 74 (74 en suite) ★★★★ **web:** www.macdonaldhotels.co.uk

⊕ Stratford Manor

Traditional British   NEW

Assured cooking in modern hotel

☎ 01789 731173 Warwick Rd CV37 0PY

MENU GUIDE Quail ravioli, cep reduction • Venison, fondant potatoes, spring greens, liquorice jus • Chocolate crème brûlée

WINE GUIDE ♀ Hardys Riddle Chardonnay £16.25 • ♥ Hardys Riddle Shiraz Cabernet £16.25 • 62 bottles over £20, 27 bottles under £20 • 12 by the glass (£4.10-£6.85)

PRICE GUIDE Fixed L fr £13.95 • Fixed D fr £32.50 • min/water £2.95 • Service optional

PLACE: Purpose-built 4 star hotel set in attractive countryside just outside Stratford-upon-Avon. Well-spaced tables ensure privacy in the restaurant, which caters to a mixed audience of business and leisure guests. Facilities include a spa, treatment centre and tennis court.

continued

FOOD: Simple cooking that interests without unnecessary fuss or fanfare. A changing daily menu supplements the carte, in addition to a tasting selection.
OUR TIP: A good base for Shakespeare country
Chef: Darren Proud **Owners:** Marston Hotels **Times:** 12-2.30/6-9.30, Closed L Sat **Notes:** Vegetarian available, Smart Dress, Civ Wed 200 **Seats:** 140, Pr/dining room 250 **Smoking:** N/Sm in restaurant, Air con **Children:** Menu, Portions **Parking:** 200
e-mail: stratfordmanor@marstonhotels.com
web: www.marstonshotels.com

Stratford Victoria
British, European
Classic dishes in a traditional hotel setting
☎ 01789 271000 Arden St CV37 6QQ
MENU GUIDE Chicken & red pepper roulade • Pork, apple mille-feuille, spinach, forest mushroom sauce • Raspberry pannacotta
WINE GUIDE ♀ Hardys Riddle Chardonnay Semillion £16.25 • ♦ Hardys Riddle Shiraz/Cabernet Sauvignon £16.25 • 23 bottles over £20, 23 bottles under £20 • 12 by the glass (£4.10-£5.90)
PRICE GUIDE Fixed L £15.50 • Fixed D £27 • starter £4.50-£7.50 • main £12.95-£19.95 • dessert £4.50 • coffee £3.75 • min/water £3.75 • Service included
PLACE: Within walking distance of the centre of Stratford, this modern hotel is built in red-brick Victorian style, and has a traditional decor featuring leather chesterfield sofas, exposed beams, and an old-fashioned red telephone box.
FOOD: Classic cuisine to suit the setting. You might start with cream of mushroom and tarragon soup, and then try lamb with a whole grain mustard and sherry sauce, or a seafood medley with spring onion and prawn risotto.
OUR TIP: Worth taking time out in the gym and spa
Chef: Mark Grigg **Owners:** Marston Hotels **Times:** 12.30-2/6-9.45 **Notes:** Vegetarian available, Smart Dress, Civ Wed 160 **Seats:** 90, Pr/dining room 90 **Smoking:** N/Sm in restaurant, Air con **Children:** Menu, Portions **Rooms:** 100 (100 en suite) ★★★★
Directions: From town centre, follow A3400 to Birmingham. Turn left at traffic lights towards Arden Street, hotel 150yds on right **Parking:** 102
e-mail: stratfordvictoria@marstonhotels.com
web: www.marstonshotels.com

Lambs of Sheep Street 12 Sheep Streeet
CV37 6EF ☎ 01789 292554 Modern British fare handy for the theatre.

The Opposition 13 Sheep St CV37 6EF
☎ 01789 269980 Related (literally) to Lambs above and similar in style.

WARWICK MAP 10 SP26

Ardencote Manor Hotel
British, International
Rustic wooden lodge in hotel grounds
☎ 01926 843111 Lye Green Rd CV35 8LS
MENU GUIDE Wild mushroom & artichoke ravioli, lemon cream • Roast rabbit saddle, Madeira & truffle jus • Orange & thyme brûlée
WINE GUIDE ♀ Ladera Verde Sauvignon Blanc £14.50 • ♦ Marques de Caceres Rioja £16.50 • 26 bottles over £20, 37 bottles under £20 • 7 by the glass (£2.50-£5.25)
PRICE GUIDE Starter £6-£8 • main £15.50-£25 • dessert £5-£8.50 • coffee £1.20 • min/water £2.60 • Service included

Ardencote Manor Hotel

PLACE: The Lodge Restaurant is built log cabin-style by the lake in the grounds of the Ardencote Manor Hotel. The Lodge is on two levels featuring plenty of wood inside and out, including the rustic tables, and there's a central bar with sofa seating. The overall effect is warm and inviting, comfortable and unpretentious. The smart country-club hotel has extensive facilities including a spa, golf course and indoor pool.
FOOD: An appealing menu of British classics alongside more elaborate French and international dishes – all with excellent presentation. Good fresh fish and vegetarian choices.
OUR TIP: Try the new La Plancha menu in the evening
Chef: Lee Childs **Owners:** TSB Developments Ltd **Times:** 12-3/6-11 **Notes:** Vegetarian available, Civ Wed 150 **Seats:** 60, Pr/dining room 28 **Smoking:** N/Sm in restaurant **Children:** Menu, Portions **Rooms:** 75 (75 en suite) ★★★★ **Directions:** 4m from Warwick. Off A4189 (Warwick/Henley-in-Arden Rd). In Claverdon follow signs for Shrewley and brown tourist signs for Ardencote Manor. Approx 1.5m **Parking:** 250
e-mail: hotel@ardencote.com **web:** www.ardencote.com

WISHAW MAP 10 SP19

The De Vere Belfry
European
Contemporary cuisine at celebrated golf hotel
☎ 01675 470301 B76 9PR
MENU GUIDE Wild boar, quince • Sea bass, artichoke fricassee, salt cod fritter, wasabi sauce • Vanilla crème brûlée, sorbet
WINE GUIDE ♀ Laroche Petit Chablis £30.10 • ♦ Firefly Shiraz £22.40 • most bottles over £20, 1 bottle under £20 • 4 by the glass (£4.95-£8.65)
PRICE GUIDE Fixed D fr £34.95 • starter £9.95-£15.95 • main £18.95-£27.95 • dessert £7.50 • coffee £2.95 • min/water £3.55
PLACE: Golfers will need no introduction to the Belfry - it's a former Ryder Cup venue and boasts no fewer than three challenging courses, as well as a range of other leisure facilities. The sophisticated restaurant is a haven amid the bustle.

continued

continued

England

WISHAW continued MAP 10 SP19

FOOD: Straightforward modern cooking, with dishes along the lines of beef Wellington with pomme fondant and a port wine jus, or sautéed halibut with Vermouth sauce.
OUR TIP: Good value fixed-price lunch menu
Chef: Mark Barker & Ian Boden **Owners:** De Vere Hotel Group
Times: 12.30-2/7.30-10, Closed L Mon-Sat **Notes:** Sun lunch £19.95, Tasting menu 7 courses £54.95, Vegetarian available, Dress Restrictions, No jeans or T-shirts. Jacket & tie preferred, Civ Wed 70 **Seats:** 70
Smoking: N/Sm in restaurant, Air con **Children:** Min 14 yrs
Rooms: 324 (324 en suite) ★★★★ **Directions:** At junct of A446 & A4091, 1m NW of M42 junct 9 **Parking:** 915
e-mail: enquiries@thebelfry.com
web: www.devereonline.co.uk/thebelfry

WEST MIDLANDS

BALSALL COMMON MAP 10 SP27

🏵 Haigs Hotel

British, French

Modern cooking in popular family-run hotel
☎ 01676 533004 Kenilworth Rd CV7 7EL
MENU GUIDE Oak smoked salmon, citrus dressing • Beef, braised red cabbage, parsnips, potato rösti • Chocolate orange pot
PRICE GUIDE Fixed D £26.95 • starter £5.50-£7.50 • main £5.75-£17.95 • dessert £4.75-£7.50 • coffee £1.75 • min/water £2.50 • Service optional
PLACE: This popular modern hotel has a cosy bar for a pre-dinner drink, and a recently refurbished restaurant that overlooks pleasant gardens. Service is friendly but formal, and tables are well appointed with quality glassware and cutlery.
FOOD: Simple modern cooking, with dishes along the lines of pork belly with mash and Savoy cabbage. Expect quality ingredients all round, with fish particularly well sourced.
OUR TIP: Five miles from the M6 and well positioned for the Birmingham NEC
Chef: Sean Cullen **Owners:** Bill & Diane Sumner **Times:** 12.30-2.30/7.30-9.30, Closed New Year, closed L Mon-Sat, closed D Sun
Notes: Sun L 2 courses £13.95, 3 courses £17.95, Vegetarian available, Smart Dress **Seats:** 60, Pr/dining room 28 **Smoking:** N/Sm in restaurant
Children: Portions **Rooms:** 23 (23 en suite) ★★★ **Directions:** On A452, 6m SE of NEC/airport, on left before village centre **Parking:** 25
e-mail: info@haigsemail.co.uk **web:** www.haigshotel.co.uk

🏵🏵 Nailcote Hall

British, French

Fine dining in small 17th-century stately home
☎ 024 7646 6174 Nailcote Ln, Berkswell CV7 7DE

Nailcote Hall

MENU GUIDE Salmon gravadlax with crisp salad • Lamb chump with potato pancake • Iced raspberry & white chocolate parfait, fruit coulis
WINE GUIDE ♀ Chardonnay £15.50 • ♟ Merlot £15.50
80 bottles over £20, 22 bottles under £20 • 8 by the glass
PRICE GUIDE Fixed L £19.75 • Fixed D £31.50 • starter £8.95-£11.50 • main £19.95-£28 • dessert £6.65-£7.95 • coffee £2.50 • min/water £3 • Service optional
PLACE: Set in 15 acres of wonderful Warwickshire countryside with its own nine-hole golf course, this is one of England's most beautiful small stately homes. The Oak Room restaurant, with its grand fireplace, is softly candlelit in the evenings, and some tables overlook the garden. There's a pianist on Saturday nights.
FOOD: A menu du jour and a carte offer food that is modern and international, or you can choose a simple grill. Sunday lunch is the classic roast followed by English puddings.
OUR TIP: Perfect retreat for a romantic weekend
Chef: Neil Oates **Owners:** Mr R W Cressman **Times:** 12-2/7-10, Closed L Sat, closed D Sun **Notes:** Wed D 3 courses £25, Vegetarian available, Dress Restrictions, No jeans or trainers, Civ Wed 120 **Seats:** 45, Pr/dining room 140 **Smoking:** N/Sm in restaurant **Children:** Menu, Portions
Rooms: 40 (40 en suite) ★★★★ **Directions:** On B4101 towards Tile Hill/Coventry, 10 mins from NEC/Birmingham Airport **Parking:** 100
e-mail: info@nailcotehall.co.uk **web:** www.nailcotehall.co.uk

BARSTON MAP 10 SP27

🏵 The Malt Shovel

British, International

Country pub and restaurant offering modern cooking, especially fish
☎ 01675 443223 Barston Ln B92 0JP

MENU GUIDE Scallops, courgette & tarragon mousse • Rib-eye steak, wild mushroom jus • Bread-and-butter pudding
WINE GUIDE ♀ Vistamar Sauvignon Blanc • ♟ Stony Cape Cabernet Sauvignon £12.95 • 10 bottles over £20, 17 bottles under £20 • 6 by the glass (£2.20-£4.50)

continued

continued

PRICE GUIDE Fixed L fr £24 • Fixed D £25 • starter £3.95-£7.95 main £9.95-£16.95 • dessert £4.95-£6.95 • coffee £1.50 min/water £2.50 • Service optional • Group min 6 service 10%
PLACE: Stylish dining in a converted malt barn, or go casual in the easy-going bar at this bustling country pub and restaurant. Modern soft furnishings, interesting art and artefacts and a minimalist feel set the informal scene for enjoying carefully sourced and cooked food.
FOOD: Modern British cooking with emphasis on core ingredients without over embellishments. The menu includes reliable favourites alongside more creative dishes. Good vegetarian options.
OUR TIP: Excellent daily fish selection
Chef: Max Murphy **Owners:** Caroline Furby & Chris Benbrook **Times:** 12-2.30/6.30-9.30, Closed 25 Dec, closed D Sun **Notes:** Vegetarian available, Smart Dress **Seats:** 40 **Smoking:** N/Sm in restaurant, Air con **Children:** Min 10 yrs, Portions **Directions:** M42 junct 5, take turn towards Knowle. 1st left on Jacobean Lane, right turn at T-junct (Hampton Lane). Sharp left into Barston Lane. Restaurant 0.5m **Parking:** 30

BIRMINGHAM MAP 10 SP08
Bank Restaurant & Bar
Modern European
Successful lively brasserie with great views
☎ 0121 633 4466 4 Brindley Place B1 2JB
MENU GUIDE Prosciutto, dolcelatte & pear salad • Pork belly, red cabbage, potato & sage gâteau • Vanilla pannacotta, mulled wine plums
WINE GUIDE 62 bottles over £20, 22 bottles under £20 • 12 by the glass (£2.90-£6.75)
PRICE GUIDE Fixed L £12.50 • Fixed D £15 • starter £4.30-£10.50 • main £11-£21 • dessert £4.50-£5.45 • coffee £2 min/water £2.50 • Service added but optional 12.5%
PLACE: Allied to the London restaurants of the same name, this vibrant brasserie has an enviable city centre location overlooking Birmingham canal. Its spacious interior features a comfortable lounge and smart dining areas with leather seating, crisp linen and quality tableware.
FOOD: An extensive modern British selection with some crowd-pleasers thrown in; your choice might range from Bank fish and chips to a classier dish such as roast lobster with a saffron broth. Children's menu available.
OUR TIP: Open for breakfast from 7.30 am
Chef: David Colcombe, Stephen Woods **Owners:** Bank Restaurant Group Plc **Times:** 12-2.45/5.30-10.30, Closed 1-2 Jan, 1 May, BHs **Notes:** Brunch menu - Sat/Sun, Vegetarian available, Smart casual **Seats:** 250, Pr/dining room 100 **Smoking:** N/Sm area, No pipes, Air con **Children:** Menu, Portions **Directions:** Located off Broad St (A456) **Parking:** 100 yds away (Sheepcoat St) **e-mail:** birmingham@bankrestaurants.com **web:** www.bankrestaurants.com

Birmingham Marriott
European, International
Elegant brasserie restaurant in traditional hotel
☎ 0121 452 1144 12 Hagley Rd, Five Ways B16 8SJ
MENU GUIDE Roquefort soufflé, pear & walnut salad • Chicken supreme, tarragon mash, café au lait sauce • Syllabub, ginger biscuits
WINE GUIDE 20 bottles over £20, 12 bottles under £20 • 10 by the glass (£4.50-£9)

PRICE GUIDE Starter £5-£8 • main £12-£22 • dessert £5-£7 min/water £3.75 • Service optional
PLACE: Part of an elegant Edwardian hotel on the outskirts of the city centre, this contemporary brasserie, West 12, is a popular destination for leisure and commercial wining and dining.
FOOD: The Marriott aims to suit most tastes, offering a wide-ranging menu that stretches from international dishes such as Thai pasta with crab in coconut sauce, to British favourites like Cumberland sausage with herby mash, or calves' liver with pancetta and onion jam.
OUR TIP: Good value lunch menu
Chef: Toby Buet **Owners:** Marriott Group **Times:** 12-2.30/6-10, Closed L Sat **Notes:** Sun lunch £15.50, Vegetarian available, Civ Wed 80 **Seats:** 60, Pr/dining room 60 **Smoking:** N/Sm area, Air con **Children:** Menu, Portions **Rooms:** 104 (104 en suite) ★★★★ **Directions:** City end of A456, at the Five Ways roundabout **Parking:** 60 **e-mail:** birmingham.marriott@whitbread.com **web:** www.marriott.com/marriot/bhxbh

Chung Ying Garden
Chinese
Extensive choice of Cantonese dishes
☎ 0121 666 6622 & 622 1668 17 Thorp St B5 4AT

MENU GUIDE Steamed scallops with garlic & spring onion • Deep-fried chicken stuffed with banana
WINE GUIDE ♀ Peter Lehmann Chardonnay £15.50 ♥ El Coto Rioja £16 • 8 bottles over £20, 24 bottles under £20 2 by the glass (£2.80)
PRICE GUIDE Fixed L £14-£30 • starter £2.20-£15 • main £7-£36 • dessert £1.50-£5 • coffee £1.40 • min/water £3.50 • Service optional
PLACE: Downstairs it's high ceilings, Andy Warhol-style prints – modern European in style with a touch of Chinese influence. Upstairs is more traditional, and includes a dance floor and disco facilities for karaoke. Very popular with the local Chinese community.

continued

continued

England

BIRMINGHAM continued MAP 10 SP08

FOOD: An immense menu (the same at lunch and dinner) with around 400 dishes, including 59 dim sum. Traditional Cantonese food with some unusual dishes, like deep-fried stuffed duck with crabmeat sauce.

OUR TIP: Big menu needs time to digest
Chef: Mr Siu Chung Wong **Owners:** Mr S C Wong **Times:** Noon-mdnt, Closed Xmas Day **Notes:** Vegetarian available, Smart casual preferred **Seats:** 380, Pr/dining room 200 **Smoking:** Air con **Directions:** City centre, just off Hurst St, nr Hippodrome Theatre & shopping centre, just off A38 **Parking:** 50 **e-mail:** chungyinggarden@aol.com
web: www.chungying.co.uk

Goldsmiths
British, International
Classy city-centre hotel
☎ 0121 200 2727 Copthorne Hotel Birmingham, Paradise Circus B3 3HJ

MENU GUIDE Game & port terrine • Best end of lamb, herb & mushroom risotto • Pear tarte Tatin
WINE GUIDE ⚲ Grenache Merlot £14.95 • ⚑ Colombard Sauvignon £14.95 • 35 bottles over £20, 22 bottles under £20 • 14 by the glass (£3.50-£7)
PRICE GUIDE Fixed D £35 • starter £5-£9 • main £11-£20 dessert £4-£8 • coffee £2.90 • min/water £3.95

PLACE: A well located hotel in the city centre with extensive lounges and bars, and a very smart restaurant furnished and decorated along traditional lines. Staff are pleasantly attentive.
FOOD: The choice of dining venues is a bonus for guests, with the contemporary Goldies brasserie and more formal Goldsmiths Restaurant bringing an interesting variety. The classical menu shows flair with, perhaps, wild mushroom and goats' cheese Charlotte, and baked turbot fillet with lemon rösti.
OUR TIP: Take advantage of the excellent parking
Chef: John Stephens **Owners:** Millennium Hotels and Resorts
Times: 12-2.30/6-10.30, Closed 25 Dec, closed L Sat **Notes:** Vegetarian available, Civ Wed 200 **Seats:** 85, Pr/dining room 30 **Smoking:** N/Sm in restaurant, Air con **Children:** Menu, Portions **Rooms:** 212 (212 en suite) ★★★★ **Directions:** In city centre, telephone for further directions **Parking:** 80 **e-mail:** reservations.birmingham@mill-cop.com
web: www.stay-with-us.com

AA's Chefs' Chef is the annual poll of all the chefs included in The Restaurant Guide. Around 1800 of the country's top chefs are asked to vote to recognise the achievements of one of their peers.
This year's winner is featured on page 19.

Hotel Du Vin
British, Mediterranean
Imaginative bistro with great wine list
☎ 0121 200 0600 25 Church St B3 2NR
MENU GUIDE Mushroom & chorizo tagliatelle, caper butter • Pan-fried lemon sole meunière, new potatoes • White chocolate & raspberry mousse
PRICE GUIDE Starter fr £6.95 • main fr £14.95 • dessert fr £6.75 • coffee £2.50 • min/water £3 • Service optional

PLACE: This chic boutique hotel and bistro, created from a former Victorian eye hospital, cuts a stylish stance. As with the groups' other hotels, the hallmark wine theme reigns over the decor, the relaxed bistro decked out with wood floors, polished tables and comfortable chairs. A superb wine list and professional wine service proves a key strength.
FOOD: Cooking is modern-styled bistro, the simple, light approach delivering trademark classics alongside more contemporary parings.
OUR TIP: Relax in one of the two bars pre or post dining
Chef: Nick Turner **Owners:** Hotel Du Vin Ltd **Times:** 12-2/6-10
Notes: Sun L £24.50, Vegetarian available, Civ Wed 60 **Seats:** 85, Pr/dining room 120 **Smoking:** N/Sm in restaurant **Children:** Menu, Portions **Rooms:** 66 (66 en suite) ★★★★ **Directions:** Telephone for directions **Parking:** 20 **e-mail:** info@birmingham.hotelduvin.com
web: www.hotelduvin.com

Jessica's
Modern British
Discreet suburban dining meets bold, accomplished cooking
☎ 0121 455 0999 1 Montague Rd, Edgbaston B16 9HN
MENU GUIDE Scallops, crab & chilli beignets, cucumber, red pepper • Brill, red lentils, Indian cauliflower, coconut milk • Lemon tart, chocolate sorbet
WINE GUIDE ⚲ Touraine Sauvignon Blanc £19.95 • ⚑ Côte de Rhône Shiraz £15.95 • 75 bottles over £20, 26 bottles under £20 • 9 by the glass (£4.75-£5.75)
PRICE GUIDE Fixed L £15 • Service added but optional 12.5% • Group min 6 service 12.5%

PLACE: The modish, airy, conservatory-styled restaurant at Jessica's is slickly designed in minimalist style to ensure the focus is strictly on the food. Top quality parades everywhere, from crisp napery to cutlery and refined, professional service. It's situated in a leafy suburb just off the Hagley Road, with discreet entrance and small bar area.
FOOD: Jessica's takes food seriously, its innovative modern menus delivering superb combinations that promote an agony of choice. Refined dishes of bold, finely balanced, clear flavours exceed expectations, while five- or seven-course tasting options and a vegetarian menu bolster the exciting repertoire. One to watch.
OUR TIP: World class bread rolls
Chef: Glynn Purnell **Owners:** Mr K & Mrs D Stevenson, Glynn Purnell
Times: 12.30-2.30/7.00-10.30, Closed 1 wk Xmas, 1 wk Etr, last 2 wks Jul, Sun, closed L Sat & Mon **Notes:** Tasting menu 5 courses £36.50, 7 courses £42.50, Vegetarian available **Seats:** 36 **Smoking:** N/Sm in restaurant, Air con **Children:** No Children **Parking:** On street
web: www.jessicasrestaurant.co.uk

England

⚜ Malmaison Birmingham

French

French brasserie food in stylish surroundings

☎ 0121 246 5000 1 Wharfside St, The Mailbox
B1 1RD

MENU GUIDE Pressed ham & lentil terrine • Polenta crusted sea bass • Lemon posset

PRICE GUIDE Fixed L £9.95-£18.50 • Fixed D £20.95-£31.95 • starter £4.50-£8.50 • main £9.95-£24.95 • dessert £4.95 • min/water £2.75 • Service added but optional 10%

PLACE: This first floor hotel brasserie is set in a stylish development of fashionable shops and restaurants.
FOOD: Simple modern cooking with the odd interesting twist appears on the trendy French brasserie menu, including a grill section and daily specials. The quality produce yields up clear flavours in dishes like fillet of brill en crôute with buttered spinach and warm tartare sauce.
OUR TIP: Stone's throw from Harvey Nichols
Chef: Nigel Grantham **Owners:** Malmaison Ltd **Times:** 12-2.30/6-10.30
Notes: Vegetarian available, Smart Dress **Seats:** 155, Pr/dining room
Children: Portions **Rooms:** 189 (189 en suite) ★★★ **Directions:** M6 Junct 6, follow the A38 towards Birmingham, hotel is located within The Mailbox **Parking:** Mailbox carpark
e-mail: birmingham@malmaison.com **web:** www.malmaison.com

⚜⚜⚜ Paris Restaurant Patrick McDonald *see below*

⚜⚜⚜ Simpsons *see page 476*

2006

The
Bed & Breakfast
Guide

Britain's best-selling B&B guide featuring over 4,000 great places to stay.

www.theAA.com

AA

BIRMINGHAM MAP 10 SP08

Paris Restaurant Patrick McDonald

French

Sophisticated, luxury city-centre dining

☎ 0121 632 1488 109-111 Wharfside St, Mailbox B1 1RF

MENU GUIDE Lobster ravioli, braised celery • Sea bass tranche, aubergine caviar, baby fennel • Assiette of pineapple

WINE GUIDE ⚲ South Africa Sauvignon Blanc £26
🍷 D'Arenberg Shiraz/Viognier £37 • 6 by the glass (£4.50-£7)

PRICE GUIDE Fixed L £16.50 • starter £9.50-£15.50 • main £19.50-£26.50 • dessert £7.50-£9.50 • coffee £5 • min/water £3.75 • Service added but optional 12.5%

PLACE: Set on the top floor of the city's Mailbox shopping complex, sophistication and chic mark out the Paris Restaurant from its less-so neighbouring eateries. Step through the huge black smoked doors into a shining glass-backed bar with large champagne ice bucket, and you're in a different world, that of chef-patron Patrick McDonald and wife Claire, who designed this elegant dining experience. Modernistic and richly furnished, with high ceilings, spacious tables, candlelight and striking contemporary oils by Roberto Bernardi on chocolate walls, all echo style, panache and an understated sense of luxury. Charming, informed and unfussy service.
FOOD: As its name might suggest, there's a clear French influence – modern and classic – in Patrick McDonald's fantastically assured cooking, with quality and finesse stamped all over it. His approach is precise, measured and exacting, so that flavours flourish and race across the palate with gusto. Think roasted squab pigeon with Swiss chard, duck foie gras and pigeon jus, or tournedos Rossini, and toasted pistachio soufflé with chocolate sauce. A seven-course tasting gourmand wraps up the account of a rising star.
OUR TIP: Good-value lunch; you need to book for weekends
Chef: Patrick McDonald & Richard Turner **Owners:** Patrick McDonald
Times: Noon-2.30/7-10, Closed 1wk Xmas, 1wk Etr & 2 wks Aug, Sun & Mon **Notes:** Tasting menu 7 courses £55, Vegetarian available **Seats:** 40, Pr/dining room 12 **Smoking:** N/Sm in restaurant, Air con **Parking:** 250
e-mail: paris.restaurant@virgin.net **web:** www.restaurant-paris.co.uk

BIRMINGHAM MAP 10 SP08

Simpsons

French   **NEW**
One to watch
☎ 0121 454 3434   20 Highfield Rd B15 3DU
MENU GUIDE Ham hock & chicken terrine • Venison, chestnut gnocchi, creamed leeks, grand veneur sauce • Peanut butter parfait

WINE GUIDE ♀ Domaine Hamilin Chablis Chardonnay £24 • ♀ Terrazas Reserve Malbec £26.50 • 275 bottles over £20, 50 bottles under £20 • 19 by the glass (£3.85-£11)

PRICE GUIDE Fixed L £20 • Fixed D £30 • starter £8.50-£11.50 • main £19.50-£21.50 • dessert £7.50-£8.50 • coffee £3.25 • min/water £3.50 • Service added but optional 10%

PLACE: Just outside the city centre, this listed Georgian house is the restrained setting for a gastronomic extravaganza. The Orangery restaurant plays host to an eclectic mix of diners and is an airy, contemporary venue with stripped oak floors, smartly appointed tables, and pretty views over the leafy garden.

FOOD: Highly skilful and accomplished cuisine, conjured from the finest luxury ingredients. Simpsons takes a neo-classical approach to cooking, offering eye-catching modern interpretations of tried and tested combinations: sea bream with potato scales and Sevruga caviar sauce for example, or squab pigeon with foie gras and juniper berry sauce. It's all washed down with wine from an extensive list, featuring a tempting choice of both old and New World producers, and an interesting range of champagnes. Set menus complement the carte, with lunch offering particularly good value at two courses for £20, or three for £25.
OUR TIP: Treat yourself to a night in one of four luxury bedrooms
Chef: Andreas Antona, Luke Tipping **Owners:** Andreas & Alison Antona **Times:** 12.30-2/7-10 **Notes:** Sun L £27.50, Vegetarian available **Seats:** 70, Pr/dining room 18 **Smoking:** N/Sm in restaurant, Air con **Children:** Menu, Portions **Parking:** 15
e-mail: info@simpsonsrestaurant.co.uk
web: www.simpsonsrestaurant.co.uk

BIRMINGHAM *continued* MAP 10 SP08

⊛ Thai Edge Restaurant
Thai
True Thai cooking in a modern setting
☎ 0121 643 3993   Brindley Place B12HS
MENU GUIDE Stuffed chicken wings • Prawns in Panang curry

WINE GUIDE ♀ Mâcon Villages Chardonnay £16 • ♀ Rioja Crianza £15.75 • 10 bottles over £20, 20 bottles under £20

PRICE GUIDE Fixed L £9.90 • Fixed D £19.80-£29.80 • starter £5-£8.50 • main £7-£28 • dessert £4.50 • coffee £1.50 • min/water £3 • Service added but optional 10%

PLACE: The city's rejuvenated canal area is the setting for this popular Thai restaurant, where smart contemporary designs work in harmony with traditional Oriental influences to create a restful balance.
FOOD: Promising an exciting dining experience, the lengthy menu lists dishes from all four regions of Thai cooking, with explicit translations to guide you through the choices. Ask for advice from experienced staff.
OUR TIP: The fixed-price menus are a good introduction to Thai food
Chef: Mit Jeensanthia **Owners:** Harish Nathwani **Times:** 12-2.30/5.30-11, Closed 25-26 Dec, 1 Jan **Notes:** Vegetarian available **Seats:** 100 **Smoking:** N/Sm area, Air con **Directions:** Brindley Place is just off Broad St (approx 0.5m from B'ham New Street station) **Parking:** Brindley Place
e-mail: manager777@btconnect.com **web:** www.thaiedge.co.uk

⊛⊛ La Toque d'Or
French
Modern authentic French cuisine in the jewellers' quarter
☎ 0121 233 3655   27 Warstone Ln, Hockley B18 6JQ
MENU GUIDE Dodine of Périgord duck foie gras • Médaillons of monkfish tail, wilted spinach • Tarte Tatin, vanilla ice cream

WINE GUIDE ♀ Louis Latour Chardonnay £12.90 • ♀ Bellefontaine Merlot £12.90 • 30 bottles over £20, 14 bottles under £20 • 5 by the glass (£3.20-£4.60)

PRICE GUIDE Fixed L £16.50 • Fixed D £24.50 • coffee £3.75 • min/water £3.50 • Service included

PLACE: Walk down the narrow alley and enjoy the sense of theatre as you enter the early 20th-century ambience of quarry floors, exposed brick walls, stained glass windows, and lofty wooden ceilings of this old precious metal rolling mill. Francophiles gravitate here just to soak up the whole experience: Parisian banquettes and mirrors, knowledgeable staff, and classic French cuisine with modern overtones.
FOOD: Didier Philipot is an anglophile who is proud to print his menus in English. But he hasn't forgotten his roots, and uses first-rate ingredients to deliver precisely what's described; a blackboard lists seasonal additions.
OUR TIP: Good-value two-course lunch
Chef: Didier Philipot **Owners:** SSPG Consulting Ltd **Times:** 12.30-1.30/7-9.30, Closed 1 wk Xmas, 1 wk Etr, 2 wks Aug, Sun-Mon, closed L Sat **Notes:** Vegetarian available **Seats:** 36 **Smoking:** No pipes, No cigars, Air con **Children:** Portions **Directions:** 1m N of city centre, 400 mtrs from clock tower (in Jewellery Quarter). Telephone for further directions **Parking:** NCP - Vyse Street **e-mail:** didier@latoquedor.co.uk
web: www.latoquedor.co.uk

⊚ **Imran's Balti** 264-266 Ladypool Rd, Sparkbrook
B12 8JU ☎ 0121 449 1370 Longstanding balti.

⊚ **Maharaja** 23-25 Hurst St B5 4AS ☎ 0121 622 2641
Indian serving superior versions of familiar dishes.

▮ **San Carlo** 4 Temple St B2 5BN ☎ 0121 633 0251
Traditional Italian with pizzas, pasta and good fish.

COVENTRY MAP 10 SP37

⊚ Brooklands Grange Hotel
British, European
Quality cooking in traditional hotel
☎ 024 7660 1601 Holyhead Rd CV5 8HX

MENU GUIDE Crab ravioli, red pepper coulis • Beef medallions,
potato rösti • Rhubarb cheesecake

WINE GUIDE ⚲ Chilean Chardonnay £11.50 • ⚱ Chilean Merlot
£11.50 • 12 bottles over £20, 28 bottles under £20 • 6 by the
glass (£3.25-£3.85)

PRICE GUIDE Fixed L £8.90-£14.90 • Fixed D £16.95-£25.95
starter £3.95-£6.95 • main £10.95-£18.95 • dessert £4.95 • coffee
£1.65 • min/water £3.95

PLACE: This 16th-century former farmhouse is now a well-run
modern and comfortable hotel. The restaurant is traditional in
style with a relaxed atmosphere. Over the years many celebrities
have stayed here, including The Beatles.
FOOD: The menu offers both traditional, modern and
international style dishes made from the best local produce.
Fresh daily fish dishes. Skilful saucing and excellent presentation.
OUR TIP: Book a room with a four-poster bed
Chef: Jonathan Beard **Owners:** Brooklands Grange Ltd **Times:** 12-2/
7-10, Closed BHs, closed L Sat **Notes:** Vegetarian available **Seats:** 80,
Pr/dining room 16 **Smoking:** N/Sm in restaurant **Children:** Menu,
Portions **Rooms:** 31 (31 en suite) ★★★ **Directions:** From M42 junct 6
take A45 towards Coventry. Then A4114 (Pickford Way) and 3rd exit at rdbt
(continue on A4114). Hotel on left **Parking:** 52
e-mail: info@brooklands-grange.co.uk
web: www.brooklands-grange.co.uk

DORRIDGE MAP 10 SP17

⊚⊚ Forest Hotel
European
Reliable cooking in a modern, boutique hotel
☎ 01564 772120 25 Station Approach B93 8JA

MENU GUIDE Moules marinière, home-made bread • Rump of
lamb, basil couscous, ratatouille • Hot chocolate fondant,
malted-milk ice cream

WINE GUIDE ⚲ Riddle Chardonnay/Semillion £11.75 • ⚱ Riddle
Shiraz/Cabernet Sauvignon £11.75 • 15 bottles over £20,
25 bottles under £20 • 9 by the glass (£2.95-£4)

PRICE GUIDE Food prices not confirmed for 2006. Please
telephone for details

PLACE: The light and airy downstairs restaurant and bar at this
sophisticated, boutique-style hotel set in a Birmingham suburb,
sons a contemporary vogue and stylish designer decor.
FOOD: The broadly European style is delivered via an extensive
range of menu and dish options that play to the gallery,
delivering intelligently conceived, precise and skilful cooking.
Simplicity is a keynote, backed by quality produce, competitive
pricing and informal, professional service.
OUR TIP: Try the excellent-value, fixed-price menu
Chef: Dean Grubb **Owners:** Gary & Tracy Perkins **Times:** 12-2.30/6.30-
continued

10, Closed 25 Dec **Notes:** Sun L 2 courses £14.50, 3 courses £17.50,
Vegetarian available, Civ Wed 100 **Seats:** 70, Pr/dining room 150
Smoking: N/Sm in restaurant, Air con **Children:** Menu, Portions
Rooms: 12 (12 en suite) ⋔ **Directions:** From M42 junct 5, go
through Knowle village, right to Dorridge village, turn left before bridge
Parking: 40 **e-mail:** info@forest-hotel.com
web: www.forest-hotel.co.uk

HOCKLEY HEATH MAP 10 SP17

Nuthurst Grange Country House Hotel
Rosettes not confirmed at the time of going to press
British, French
Fine dining in imposing country house
☎ 01564 783972 Nuthurst Grange Ln B94 5NL

MENU GUIDE Smoked chicken risotto • Medallions of pork with
carrot & coriander purée • Malibu pannacotta

WINE GUIDE ⚲ Logan Rock Semillon Chardonnay
£19.75 • ⚱ Logan Rock Shiraz/Cabernet Sauvignon £19.75 •
12 bottles under £20 • 6 by the glass (£3.95)

PRICE GUIDE Fixed L £15.95-£19.95 • Fixed D £29.50-£50
starter £6.95-£7.95 • main £14.95-£17.50 • dessert £6.50-£7.50
coffee £2.95 • min/water £4.95 • Service optional

PLACE: A long sweeping drive sets the scene for grand dining in
this imposing country house. Set in well-tended grounds,
Nuthurst Grange boasts stunning country views, and an elegant
and sunny dining room.
FOOD: This hotel has recently changed hands, with changes in
the kitchen also. Stuart Nicholson remains in charge and has
been joined by Oliver Ritchings as head chef.
Chef: Stuart Nicholson & Oliver Ritchings **Owners:** Mr & Mrs Pike
Times: 12-2/7-9.30, Closed 25-26 Dec, L Sat **Notes:** Tasting menu
£59.50, Sun L £24.95, Vegetarian available, Dress Restrictions, Civ Wed 90
Seats: 80, Pr/dining room 95 **Smoking:** N/Sm in restaurant
Rooms: 15 (15 en suite) ★★★ **Directions:** Off A3400, 0.5 mile S of
Hockley Heath, turn at sign into Nuthurst Grange Lane **Parking:** 80
e-mail: info@nuthurst-grange.com
web: www.nuthurst-grange.com

MERIDEN MAP 10 SP28

🏵 Manor Hotel

British, French

Modern dining in Georgian manor

☎ 01676 522735 Main Rd CV7 7NH

MENU GUIDE Scallops, black pudding, pea purée • Canon of lamb, shepherd's pie, fine ratatouille • Banana pannacotta

WINE GUIDE ♀ Honore de Benticot Sauvignon Blanc £14.50 • ♀ Honore de Benticot Merlot £14.50 • 19 bottles over £20, 28 bottles under £20 • 6 by the glass (£2.40-£3.50)

PRICE GUIDE Fixed L £23-£24 • Fixed D £25-£26 • starter £6.50-£10.50 • main £12.95-£22.95 • dessert £4.95-£5.25 • coffee £2.95 • min/water £3.50 • Service included

PLACE: A refurbished Georgian manor in a village setting not far from the medieval cross marking the centre of England. The bright and airy Regency Restaurant is conveniently close to the M6, M42, and NEC.

FOOD: The full range of British dishes with French influences in a choice of menus - carte, two- or three-course fixed-price lunches, Sunday lunch and children's choices.

OUR TIP: Courtyard for summer drinks or coffee

Chef: Peter Griffiths **Owners:** Mr R Richards **Times:** 12-2/7-9.45, Closed 27-30 Dec, closed L Sat **Notes:** Vegetarian available, Civ Wed 120 **Seats:** 150, Pr/dining room 220 **Smoking:** N/Sm in restaurant, Air con **Children:** Menu, Portions **Rooms:** 110 (110 en suite) ★★★ **Directions:** M42 junct 6 take A45 towards Coventry then A452, signed Leamington. At rdbt join B4102, signed Meriden, hotel 0.5m on left **Parking:** 180 **e-mail:** reservations@manorhotelmeriden.co.uk **web:** www.manorhotelmeriden.co.uk

SOLIHULL MAP 10 SP17

🏵 *The Town House Restaurant & Bar*

Modern European   **NEW**

All-day restaurant and bar in a central location

☎ 0121 704 1567 727 Warwick Rd B91 3DA

PLACE: Trendy modern café bar with a lemon wash exterior, opposite the main shopping centre. The spacious open-plan interior is furnished with an abundance of leather and steel, and provides the perfect atmosphere for light meals, a glass of wine or serious dining.

FOOD: All carte options, with smaller portions of certain dishes at lunch and dinner and sandwiches 12 noon until 6pm. Very good fish and vegetarian selection.

OUR TIP: Oysters and champagne that won't break the bank **Times:** Telephone for details

---

What makes a Restaurant of the Year?
In selecting a Restaurant of the Year, we look for somewhere that is exceptional in its chosen area of the market. Whilst the Rosette awards are based on the quality of the food alone, Restaurant of the Year takes into account all aspects of the operation. For full details see pages 6-7.

WALSALL MAP 10 SP09

🏵🏵 The Fairlawns at Aldridge

International

Elegant hotel dining offering high standards

☎ 01922 455122 178 Little Aston Rd, Aldridge WS9 0NU

MENU GUIDE Risotto of leeks & warm goats' cheese • Stuffed saddle of wild rabbit, creamed Savoy • Trio of chocolate desserts

WINE GUIDE ♀ Tapestry Vineyards Sauvignon Blanc £16.50 • ♀ Tapestry Vineyards Cabernet Sauvignon £16.50 22 bottles over £20, 45 bottles under £20 • 6 by the glass (£3.20-£6.50)

PRICE GUIDE Fixed L £14.95-£22.50 • Fixed D £18.95-£30 coffee £1.95 • min/water £2.50 • Service optional

PLACE: Contemporary elegance best describes the dining room of this popular rural hotel, with rich woods, cream decor and well-dressed tables traditionally set with crisp linen and sparkling place settings. Excellent standards of service are practised by friendly staff.

FOOD: The Fairlawns team prepare International dishes with traditional values, for menus that remain consistent throughout the seasons. The fixed-price menu offers two or three courses for lunch, three courses for dinner, and the kitchen will do its best to satisfy requests for personal favourites.

OUR TIP: 'Early bird' offers and seasonal specialities

Chef: Mark Bradley **Owners:** John Pette **Times:** 12-2/7-10, Closed 1 Jan, Good Fri, Easter Mon, May Day, Whit Mon, closed L Sat, closed D 25 & 26 Dec **Notes:** Sun lunch/dinner 3 courses £17.50, Vegetarian available, Dress Restrictions, No jeans, trainers, sports clothing, Civ Wed 100 **Seats:** 80, Pr/dining room 100 **Smoking:** N/Sm in restaurant, Air con **Children:** Menu, Portions **Rooms:** 50 (50 en suite) ★★★ **Directions:** Outskirts of Aldridge, 400 yds from junction of A452 (Chester Rd) & A454 (Little Aston Road) **Parking:** 120 **e-mail:** welcome@fairlawns.co.uk **web:** www.fairlawns.co.uk

WIGHT, ISLE OF

BEMBRIDGE MAP 05 SZ68

🌀 *Windmill Inn Hotel*

Modern British   **NEW**

Friendly island hotel featuring quality local produce

☎ 01983 875806 1 Steyne Rd PO35 5UH

PLACE: The hotel is located on the island's most easterly point close to Bembridge Harbour. The fine dining option is the Windmill Restaurant, with a separate menu offered in the bar and gallery, where paintings by local artists are displayed.

FOOD: Both menus draw on fine local produce with seafood as a speciality. Bembridge crab, island lamb and rare breed beef feature, and home-made bread is made daily from Calbourne Mill flour.

OUR TIP: Island ales are served in the bar

Times: 12.15-2.30/6.30-9.30 **Rooms:** 14 (14 en suite) ★★★
e-mail: info@thewindmillhotel.co.uk
web: www.eatatthewindmill.co.uk

FRESHWATER MAP 05 SZ38

🌀 **Farringford**

International, British

Increasingly popular dining venue in country hotel

☎ 01983 752500 Bedbury Ln PO40 9TQ

MENU GUIDE Avocado & mango timbale • Roasted supreme of cod • Iced passionfruit & lemongrass parfait

WINE GUIDE ♀ Concha y Toro Sauvignon Blanc £17 • ♀ Louis Latour Bourgogne Rouge Pinot Noir £21 • 26 bottles over £20, 29 bottles under £20 • 5 by the glass (£2.90-£4.50)

PRICE GUIDE Fixed L £16 • Fixed D £27 • coffee £1.50 min/water £3

PLACE: Farringford was the home of Lord Tennyson for over 40 years, and it is easy to see why he fell in love with it. Among other attractions, the views from the conservatory-style restaurant are magnificent.

FOOD: A short, punchy menu achieves a well-balanced choice, with flavours left clean and simple. A progressive approach yields cinnamon-marinated lamb rump, and stir-fried shitake mushrooms with grilled Aberdeen Angus beef.

OUR TIP: Interesting historic house

Chef: Brian Kerr **Owners:** Lisa Hollyhead **Times:** 12-2/6.30-9, Closed L Mon-Sat **Notes:** Fixed L Sun only, Vegetarian available, Dress Restrictions, No sports clothes or denim, Civ Wed 150 **Seats:** 100, Pr/dining room 20 **Smoking:** No pipes **Children:** Menu, Portions **Rooms:** 18 (18 en suite) ★★★ **Directions:** Follow signs for Yarmouth, over bridge for 1m, take left at Pixie Hill. Continue for 2m. At rdbt take left into Afton Rd. Turn left at the bay. Turn into Bedbury Ln. Farringford is 0.5m from bay **Parking:** 50
e-mail: enquiries@farringford.co.uk
web: www.farringford.co.uk

England

How do I find my perfect place?

New editions on sale now!

Available from all good bookshops,
on www.theAA.com or call 01256 491524

England

SEAVIEW MAP 05 SZ69

 Priory Bay Hotel

Modern French

Coastal country-house hotel dining

☎ 01983 613146 Priory Dr PO34 5BU

MENU GUIDE Tomato soup with asparagus ravioli • Pan-fried monkfish tail, saffron potatoes, lemongrass sauce • Rhubarb soufflé

WINE GUIDE ♀ Carmen Central Valley Chardonnay £12.50 • ♀ Carmen Central Valley Merlot £12.50 • 20 bottles over £20, 15 bottles under £20 • 7 by the glass (£3.50-£7.90)

PRICE GUIDE Fixed L £15.50 • Fixed D £27.50 • coffee £2.30 • min/water £3.50 • Service optional

PLACE: Relaxed and candlelit, the elegant dining room in this historic house makes for an ideal romantic dinner setting. There are views over the grounds and across the Solent.

FOOD: Modern French in style, with a good use of local produce, the seasonally changing menu demonstrates good technical skills and a flair for adventurous flavours and textures, especially in a main course of local sea bass fillet on a bed of tagliatelle and anchovy sun-dried tomato butter.

OUR TIP: Book a window table for great views

Chef: Chris Turner **Owners:** Mr R Palmer & Mr J Palmer **Times:** 12.30-2.15/7-9.30 **Notes:** Vegetarian available, Dress Restrictions, Smart/smart casual recommended, Civ Wed 100 **Seats:** 70, Pr/dining room 50 **Smoking:** N/Sm in restaurant **Children:** Menu, Portions **Rooms:** 31 (31 en suite) ★★★ **Directions:** On B3330 to Nettlestone, 0.5 miles from St Helens **Parking:** 50 **e-mail:** enquiries@priorybay.co.uk **web:** www.priorybay.co.uk

VENTNOR MAP 05 SZ57

 The Pond Café

Modern British, French

Contemporary village dining

☎ 01983 855666 Bonchurch Village Rd, Bonchurch PO38 1RG

MENU GUIDE Crisp fried confit pork belly, seared scallops • Sea bass, lobster butter sauce, new potatoes • Assiette of chocolate, merlot cherry ice cream

PRICE GUIDE Fixed L £17.50 • Fixed D £25 • coffee £2.40 min/water £2.80 • Service included

PLACE: Situated in the scenic and historic village of Bonchurch, this classically designed restaurant with a simple, modern interior is set in a Victorian house that overlooks the village pond. There is a small terrace for alfresco dining. Service is relaxed, professional and friendly.

FOOD: Good quality and fresh local produce, especially fish, is used where possible on the regularly changing menu. Cooking style reflects modern British with French and Pacific-rim influences. Cookery classes and gourmet evenings are available.

OUR TIP: Tempting cocktail menu and excellent range of coffees

Times: 12-5/5-10 **e-mail:** pondcafe@aol.com

web: www.thepondcafe.com

The Royal Hotel

British, French

Modern cuisine in formal seaside hotel

☎ 01983 852186 Belgrave Rd PO38 1JJ

MENU GUIDE Poached salmon & pancetta salad • Scotch beef, mushroom gâteau, dauphinoise potatoes, port jus • White chocolate pannacotta

WINE GUIDE ♀ Vinedos Terranoble Valle Andino Sauvignon Blanc £13.50 • ♀ La Diva Donatien Bahaug Merlot/Cab. Sauvignon £12.60 • 16 bottles over £20, 35 bottles under £20 5 by the glass (£3.40-£4)

PRICE GUIDE Fixed L £18-£20 • Fixed D £32.50-£38 • min/water £3 • Service optional

PLACE: Stately hotel dining room decked out in Victorian style with crystal chandeliers, oil paintings and rich fabrics. The Appuldurcombe dining room has pretty views of The Royal's carefully tended gardens.

FOOD: Modern British dishes with French influences that depend on quality produce for distinction. Choose from simpler seafood options (Dover sole meunière, or sea bass with a white wine and parsley sauce) or heartier fare such as roast pork with a potato and apple gratin, caramelised apples, and a rosemary jus.

OUR TIP: Daily fresh fish is brought straight to the hotel by local fishermen

Chef: Alan Staley **Owners:** William Bailey **Times:** 12-1.45/7-9, Closed 2 wks Jan, closed L Mon-Sat in Apr-Oct **Notes:** Vegetarian available, Dress Restrictions, No jeans, Civ Wed 150 **Seats:** 100, Pr/dining room 40 **Smoking:** N/Sm in restaurant **Children:** Min 5 yrs, Portions **Rooms:** 55 (55 en suite) ★★★★ **Directions:** On A3055 coastal road, into Ventnor. Follow the one way system, turn left at lights into Church St. At top of hill bear left into Belgrave Rd, hotel on right **Parking:** 50 **e-mail:** enquiries@royalhoteliow.co.uk **web:** www.royalhoteliow.co.uk

 Rex Piano Bar Kingsview, Church St PO38 1SG

☎ 01983 853355 Classic French cuisine using local produce, in stylish art deco surroundings.

YARMOUTH MAP 05 SZ38

 George Hotel *see page 481*

continued

...ARMOUTH MAP 05 SZ38

George Hotel

...uropean

...omantic and dramatic dining by the Solent

☎ 01983 760331 Quay St PO41 0PE

MENU GUIDE Seared scallop with toasted rice broth • Pan-fried ...ngus rib eye, cottage pie, red wine jus • Chocolate fondant

WINE GUIDE 60 bottles over £20, 20 bottles under £20 • 13 by ...e glass (£3.95)

PRICE GUIDE Fixed D £45 • Service included

...ACE: Set by the water's edge in this bustling yachting village the ...orge is a haven of rich character and gracious living, with cosy ...r and inviting lounge. The fine-dining, chic and intimate George ...staurant is an evenings-only affair – and its decor adds a touch of ...mance to the occasion. (The sunny Brasserie, awash with bright ...lours, is the more informal eating option.)

...OD: The cuisine suits the occasion and bold George Restaurant ...cor, the emphasis on high technique and dramatic, svelte ...esentation rather than simplicity, with an admirable mix of textures ...d temperatures and subtle, meticulous cooking. The fixed-price ...nner menu changes on a rolling basis but has seasonal intent.

OUR TIP: Enjoy pre-dinner drinks in the garden
Chef: Kevin Mangeolles **Owners:** Mr J Willcock, Mr J Illsley **Times:** 7-9.30, Closed L all wk, D Sun-Mon (Brasserie open daily)
Notes: Vegetarian available, Civ Wed 100 **Seats:** 40, Pr/dining room 25
Smoking: No pipes, No cigars, Air con **Children:** Min 10 yrs **Rooms:** 17 (17 en suite) ★★★ **Directions:** Adjacent to fort **Parking:** Pay & Display **e-mail:** res@thegeorge.co.uk **web:** www.thegeorge.co.uk

WILTSHIRE

...RADFORD-ON-AVON MAP 04 ST86

⑩ The Georgian Lodge Restaurant

...ternational

...iendly restaurant by the river offering ...ternational cuisine

☎ 01225 862268 25 Bridge St BA15 1BY

MENU GUIDE Smoked salmon blinis, crème fraîche, ...aviar • Rack of lamb, black pudding, apple mash • Sticky toffee ...udding

WINE GUIDE ⚲ Sauvignon £14.75 • ⚲ Merlot £14.75 ...5 bottles over £20, 22 bottles under £20 • 8 by the glass ...£2.95-£6)

PRICE GUIDE Food prices not confirmed for 2006. Please telephone for details.

PLACE: This relaxed restaurant with rooms occupies a Georgian building, originally a bakers and confectioners. The building stands in the centre of town, near the river. Its restful interior offers dining on two floors.
FOOD: The International menu displays a wealth of influences, notably Mediterranean, but traditional British meals such as roast pork tenderloin are also featured.
OUR TIP: The express lunch is good value
Chef: Alex Stock **Owners:** Brain Howe & Alex Stock **Times:** 12-2.30/6.30-10 **Notes:** Vegetarian available **Seats:** 60, Pr/dining room 24
Smoking: N/Sm in restaurant **Children:** Portions **Directions:** In town centre, just off town bridge **Parking:** Across rd
e-mail: georgianlodge.hotel@btinternet.com

⑩⑩ The Tollgate Inn

British, Mediterranean

Country inn and restaurant full of character

☎ 01225 782326 Ham Green BA14 6PX

MENU GUIDE Confit duck leg, mulled wine sauce • Roast pork tenderloin, brie & Meaux mustard sauce • Chocolate terrine, fruit coulis

WINE GUIDE ⚲ Wither Hills Sauvignon Blanc £17.50 • ⚲ Heartland Stickleback Merlot £13.50 • 5 bottles over £20, 25 bottles under £20 • 7 by the glass (£2.95-£4.50)

PRICE GUIDE Fixed L £9.95 • starter £4.50-£6.50 • main £10.50-£16.95 • dessert £3.50-£4.75 • coffee £2.50 • min/water £2.50 • Service optional • Group min 6 service 10%

continued

continued

England

BRADFORD-ON-AVON continued MAP 04 ST86

The Tollgate Inn

PLACE: A colourful history involving a weavers' shed, Baptist chapel and slaughter house lies behind this successful operation, more a restaurant with rooms than plain restaurant, or gastro-pub. The downstairs Buttery has a cosy farmhouse feel, while upstairs is more formal, with oak tables and a large open fire.
FOOD: Home-made breads and ice creams, traceable meat and game, fresh fish and seasonal vegetables are behind the Tollgate's surge in popularity. Tastes of the Mediterranean bring a light touch to the menus, including a short set lunch and interesting light choices in the bar.
OUR TIP: Seasonal game is very popular
Chef: Alexander Venables **Owners:** Alexander Venables, Alison Ward-Baptiste **Times:** 11.30-2.30/5.30-11, Closed Dec 25-26, Mon, closed D Sun **Notes:** Sun roast £9.95, Vegetarian available **Seats:** 60, Pr/dining room 38 **Smoking:** N/Sm in restaurant, Air con **Children:** Min 12 yrs **Rooms:** 4 (4 en suite) ♦♦♦♦ **Directions:** M4 junct 18, take A46 and follow signs for Bradford-on-Avon, take A363 then turn left onto B3105, in Holt turn left onto B3107 towards Melksham. The Tollgate Inn is 100yds on right **Parking:** 40 **e-mail:** alison@tollgateholt.co.uk **web:** www.tollgateholt.co.uk

Widbrook Grange
British
Confident cooking in relaxed country house
☎ 01225 864750 Trowbridge Rd, Widbrook BA15 1UH

MENU GUIDE Pigeon breast, potato rösti, juniper berry sauce • Brill fillet, mussels, oyster & prawn broth • Pineapple & rum parfait, Malibu sauce

WINE GUIDE ♀ Fairvalley Sauvignon Blanc £14.50 • ♀ Norte Chico Merlot £14.50 • 9 bottles over £20, 19 bottles under £20 • 4 by the glass (£3)

PRICE GUIDE Fixed D £26-£32.50 • starter £5.50-£7.50 • main £15-£18.50 • dessert £5.50 • coffee £2.50 • min/water £3.50 • Service included

continued

PLACE: A family-owned, tastefully renovated, 18th-century Georgian country house, Widbrook's has a relaxed style and plenty of personal attention. The Medlar Restaurant is elegantly furnished, with tables traditionally dressed in starched white linen, backed by a choice of two sitting rooms for aperitifs.
FOOD: Modern British dishes use quality fresh, local produce, intelligently simply prepared to let the main ingredient do the talking. The carte comes with a wine recommendation for each course selection.
OUR TIP: Stay the night in Widbrook's comfortable bedrooms
Chef: Michael Collom **Owners:** Peter & Jane Wragg **Times:** 7-11, Close 24-31 Dec, Sun, closed L Mon-Sat **Notes:** Diners club, Scottish Banquet for Burns Night, Vegetarian available, Dress Restrictions, No jeans or tracksuits, Civ Wed 48 **Seats:** 45 **Smoking:** N/Sm in restaurant **Children:** Portions **Rooms:** 20 (19 en suite) ♦♦♦♦ **Directions:** 1 S of Bradford-Upon-Avon on A363 **Parking:** 50
e-mail: stay@widbrookgrange.com **web:** www.widbrookgrange.com

ⓐⓐ Woolley Grange
British
Family-friendly manor house offering home-grow food
☎ 01225 864705 Woolley Green BA15 1TX

MENU GUIDE Steak & kidney pudding, oysters, Parma ham • Braised brill, white bean, chorizo & winter veg casserole • Banana soufflé

WINE GUIDE 70 bottles over £20, 7 bottles under £20 • 4 by th glass (£4)

PRICE GUIDE Fixed L £15.50 • Fixed D £25-£35 • starter £4.50-£8.50 • main £8-£12.50 • dessert £5 • coffee £2.50 • min/water £3.50 • Service optional

PLACE: A 16th-century Cotswold manor house with delightful surrounding gardens. Take a drink on the patio in summer, and then move in to the pleasant restaurant with its well-spaced tables, white linen and candles.
FOOD: The emphasis is on home-grown organic produce from the hotel's walled garden. The menu changes regularly accordir to which freshly harvested items are at their best. Excellent fresh Cornish fish also features, and there are some very effective flavour combinations. Various eating options are also provided for children, along with special activities.
OUR TIP: The hotel has its own nanny
Chef: Phillip Rimmer **Owners:** Nigel Chapman & Luxury Family Hotels **Times:** 12-2/7-9.30 **Notes:** Vegetarian available **Seats:** 40, Pr/dining room 22 **Smoking:** N/Sm in restaurant **Children:** Menu, Portions **Rooms:** 26 (26 en suite) ★★★ **Directions:** Telephone for directions **Parking:** 25 **e-mail:** info@woolleygrange.com **web:** www.woolleygrange.com

☕ The Bridge Tea Rooms 24a Bridge St BA15 1BY
☎ 01225 865537 Winner of The Tea Guild Award of Excellence 2005.

Two Rosettes The best local restaurants which aim for and achieve higher standards better consistency and where a greate precision is apparent in the cooking. There wil be obvious attention to the selection of quality ingredients. About 40% of restaurants in the guide have two Rosettes.

CASTLE COMBE MAP 04 ST87

⊕◎ The Bybrook Restaurant at Manor House

British, European

Atmospheric country retreat with modern cuisine

☎ 01249 782206 SN14 7HR

continued

MENU GUIDE Smoked salmon, traditionally garnished • Cannon of lamb, crushed new potatoes, crown of asparagus, five-herb jus • Four presentations of apple

WINE GUIDE ♀ Brocard Chablis Chardonnay £34 • ♀ Vinnaioli Venezia Giula Pinot Nero £45 • 205 bottles over £20 • 10 by the glass (£5-£10)

PRICE GUIDE Fixed L £14.95-£25 • coffee £4.95 • min/water £3.95 • Service optional

PLACE: The epitome of the country-house retreat, this striking, mellow-stone 14th-century manor house nestles in 365 acres of parkland beside its quintessentially English, picture-postcard village. The rolling manicured grounds are not to be missed, where waterfalls, meandering streams and romantic Italian garden – lovely at any time of the year – are joined by a golf course. Indoors, it's all exposed stonework, mullioned windows and the traditional comforts of cosy lounges and roaring fires. There's more than a hint of romance about the classic, candlelit setting of the dining room; a long hall with exposed beams, wood panelling and stained glass, with service a pleasing blend of professionalism and friendliness.

FOOD: The modern repertoire with classic roots admirably treads a sensible line between conservatism and unfettered experimentation, with a clear focus on the use of top quality local seasonal produce. So expect a threesome – lobster bisque (with poached langoustines), roast fillet of Wiltshire beef, chorizo spiced cabbage and horseradish foam, and glazed lemon tart with orange Pavlova – from the crisply scripted menus that belie their more elaborate presentation on the plate. The repertoire of fixed-price menus is backed by two set gourmet options, refreshingly, one a vegetarian offering.

OUR TIP: Great choice for a weekend break

Chef: David Campbell **Owners:** Exclusive Hotels **Times:** 12-2/7-10.30 **Notes:** Vegetarian available, Smart Dress, Civ Wed 100 **Seats:** 90, Pr/dining room 90 **Smoking:** N/Sm in restaurant **Children:** Menu, Portions **Rooms:** 48 (48 en suite) ★★★★ **Directions:** M4 junct 17, follow signs for Castle Combe **Parking:** 100
e-mail: enquiries@manor-housecc.co.uk
web: www.exclusivehotels.co.uk

AA 2006
The **Bed & Breakfast** Guide

Britain's best-selling B&B guide featuring over 4,000 great places to stay.

AA

www.theAA.com

AA 2006
The **Pub** Guide

Over 2,200 pubs hand-picked for their great food and authentic character.

AA

www.theAA.com

AA 2006
The **Hotel** Guide

Britain's best-selling hotel guide for all your leisure needs.

AA

www.theAA.com

AA 2006
The **Golf Course** Guide

Britain's best-selling Golf Course Guide featuring over 2,500 courses.

AA

www.theAA.com

Wine Award Winner for England and Overall Winner

The Harrow Inn at Little Bedwyn

(see page 485)

CASTLE COMBE *continued* MAP 04 ST87

⚜ Castle Inn

British, European

NEW

Picturesque inn with stylish dining

☎ 01249 783030   SN14 7HN

MENU GUIDE Pineapple piri piri • Sole meunière • Summer pudding

WINE GUIDE ♀ Montana Marlborough Sauvignon Blanc £16.95 • ♀ Chilean Merlot £14.50 • 18 bottles over £20, 14 bottles under £20 • 5 by the glass (£2.95-£5)

PRICE GUIDE Starter £3.95-£6.95 • main £10.95-£18.50 • dessert £4.50 • coffee £1.85 • min/water £3.70 • Service optional

PLACE: A quaint and pretty inn in this picture-postcard village, dating from the 12th century but tastefully modernised and atmospheric. The understated elegance of the restaurant is appealing and reassuringly intimate.

FOOD: In this quintessentially English setting, the food is traditional and popular, with a whole section of the menu devoted to fresh fish from Brixham, and favourites like calves' liver and bacon, or slow-roasted shoulder of lamb on the meat and grill list.

OUR TIP: Take a stroll through this picturesque village
Chef: Michael Rees **Owners:** Vanessa Rees **Times:** 12-2.30/7-10.00, Closed 25 Dec (ex residents), closed D 26 Dec **Notes:** Sun lunch, 1 course £8.95, Vegetarian available, Smart casual **Seats:** 28, Pr/dining room 20 **Smoking:** N/Sm area, No pipes, No cigars **Children:** Menu, Portions **Rooms:** 11 (11 en suite) ★★ **Directions:** M4 junct 17. Head S on A350 towards Bath, then right onto A420. Take right for Yatton Keynall and continue to Castle Combe **Parking:** On street
e-mail: enquiries@castle-inn.info
web: www.castle-inn.info

COLERNE MAP 04 ST87

⚜⚜⚜ **Lucknam Park** *see page 486*

LITTLE BEDWYN MAP 05 SU26

⚜⚜⚜ **The Harrow Inn at Little Bedwyn** *see below*

continued

LITTLE BEDWYN MAP 05 SU26

The Harrow Inn at Little Bedwyn

British

Wine Award Winner for England and Overall Winner

☎ 01672 870871   SN8 3JP

MENU GUIDE Foie gras, scallop & black pudding • Turbot, pea mash, wild mushrooms • Lemon tart

WINE GUIDE ♀ Tin Shed Riesling £21 • ♀ Mitolo Jester Shiraz £21 • 800 bottles over £20, 58 bottles under £20 • 24 by the glass (£4-£12)

PRICE GUIDE Fixed L £20-£25 • starter £8-£12 • main £18-£24 • dessert fr £7.50 • coffee £2.50 • min/water £2.50 • Service optional

PLACE: This unassuming Victorian pub has been converted into a restaurant with outdoor patio. The dining room is split into two sections. Decor is bright and contemporary and features well-spaced tables with high-back leather chairs, white tablecloths, colourful crockery and good quality glassware and cutlery. There's a small garden to the rear. Service is friendly and relaxed.

FOOD: This is modern British cooking with a strong commitment to local, seasonal ingredients with a special emphasis on fresh fish. If it isn't local, then it is always of the highest quality such as razor clams from Scotland, seafood from Cornwall, meat from North Wales, Scotland and Northumberland. The British cheese selection is exemplary. After home-made bread drizzled with olive oil, expect dishes with clear strong flavours using minimal amounts of cream and butter. Dishes like the caramelised squid and confit Gloucester Old Spot combine both flavour and freshness. Exceptional wine list.

OUR TIP: A loyal local following makes booking essential
Chef: Roger Jones **Owners:** Roger & Sue Jones **Times:** 12-3/7-11, Closed 3 wks Jan & Aug, Mon-Tue, closed D Sun **Notes:** Dress Restrictions, Smart casual **Seats:** 38 **Smoking:** N/Sm in restaurant **Children:** Menu, Portions **Directions:** Between Marlborough & Hungerford, well signed **Parking:** On street
e-mail: bookings@harrowinn.co.uk **web:** www.harrowinn.co.uk

England

COLERNE MAP 04 ST87

Lucknam Park

British *Faultless country-house cuisine*
☎ 01225 742777   SN14 8AZ
e-mail: reservations@lucknampark.co.uk
web: www.lucknampark.co.uk

PLACE: The mile-long drive of beech and elm trees gives a hint of the treats in store at this wonderful Palladian mansion. Aperitifs are taken in the luxurious splendour of the 17th-century drawing room of this classical country house, which has as many deep sofas, chandeliers, ornate cornicing, theatrical flower arrangements and oil paintings as you could wish for. On a quiet day, the atmosphere is serene and relaxed, perhaps punctuated by the dreamy ticking of a mantelpiece clock or the discreet whispers of unstuffy, genuinely friendly, professional staff. The dining room, in the mansion's former bow-fronted ballroom, is equally awe inspiring, replete with crystal chandeliers, gold silk curtains and views over the estate. It's a dimly-lit, gastronomic haven, laid with double-clothed tables, starched napery and enough gleaming silver to dazzle.

FOOD: The fixed-price menus (including a separate vegetarian repertoire) match expectation with a wish-list of appealing dishes that reflect the seasons. Chef Hywel Jones has obvious pedigree (ex Mandarin Oriental Hyde Park – Foliage, Lola's and the ill-fated Pharmacy – all in London), his style is modern-focused, underpinned by classical root the nigh-faultless cooking dripping with luxury ingredients, self-assurance, imagination and balance, with peripherals like canapés, amuse bouche and petits fours equally impressive.

MENU GUIDE Diver scallops, fricassee of snails & ceps, turnip purée, creamed parsley • Sea bass, crushed peas, linguini of crayfish • Organic lemon three ways

WINE GUIDE ♀ Marquis de Maupas Menatou Salon 2003 Sauvignon Blanc £30 • ♀ Fairview Primo Pinotage 2001 Pinot Noir Cinsaut £38 • 350 bottles over £20, 2 bottles under £20 • 6 by the glass (£4.50-£10)

PRICE GUIDE Fixed L £30 • Fixed D £55 • coffee £4.50 • min/water £3.50 • Service included

OUR TIP: Stay overnight and enjoy the wonderful atmosphere at this superb country house and its grounds

Chef: Hywel Jones **Owners:** Lucknam Park Hotels Ltd
Times: 12.30-2.30/7-10, Closed L Mon-Sat **Notes:** Vegetarian available, Dress Restrictions, Jacket & tie, Civ Wed 64 **Seats:** 80, Pr/dining room 30 **Smoking:** N/Sm in restaurant **Children:** Min 8 yrs, Menu, Portions **Rooms:** 41 (41 en suite) ★★★★
Directions: From M4 junct 17 take A350 to Chippenham, then A420 towards Bristol for 3m. At Ford turn towards Colerne. After 4m turn right into Doncombe Ln. Then 100yds **Parking:** 80

MALMESBURY MAP 04 ST98

Mayfield House Hotel

British, European

Cotswolds hotel to suit most tastes

☎ 01666 577409 Crudwell SN16 9EW

MENU GUIDE Exmoor blue soufflé, celery & apple chutney • Venison with black olives, garlic & thyme • Eton mess, rose petal sauce

WINE GUIDE ♀ Hardys Semillion/Chardonnay £11.25 • ♀ Hardys Shiraz/Cabernet Sauvignon £11.25 32 bottles over £20, 3 bottles under £20 • 5 by the glass

PRICE GUIDE Starter £3.95-£4.95 • main £9.95-£12.50 • dessert £4.25 • coffee £2.50 • min/water £3.25 • Service optional

PLACE: Comfortable country-house hotel on the edge of the Cotswolds offering pretty garden views from its restaurant.
FOOD: A lengthy menu of modern British dishes with European touches, offering old favourites (shepherd's pie) to more adventurous fare. You might kick off with York ham with a peppered pineapple sorbet, before tucking into chicken supreme with caramelised onion jus.
OUR TIP: Bar food lunches only during the week
Chef: Alastair Forster **Owners:** Mr M Strelling, Mr C Marston **Times:** 12-6.30-8.45, Closed L Mon-Sat **Notes:** Vegetarian available **Seats:** 50, Pr/dining room 35 **Smoking:** N/Sm in restaurant **Rooms:** 24 (24 en suite) ★★ **Directions:** 3m N of Malmesbury on A429, halfway through village **Parking:** 40 **e-mail:** reception@mayfieldhousehotel.co.uk
web: www.mayfieldhousehotel.co.uk

Old Bell Hotel

British

Refined cooking in an ancient hostelry

☎ 01666 822344 Abbey Row SN16 0BW

MENU GUIDE Poached scallops & Dublin Bay prawns • Roast outlet & crisp belly pork • Bread & butter pudding

WINE GUIDE ♀ Thierry Hamelin Petit Chablis Chardonnay £19.85 • ♀ Santa Rita Merlot £16.40 • 75 bottles over £20, 20 bottles under £20 • 8 by the glass (£3.50-£5.25)

PRICE GUIDE Fixed L £12.50 • starter £6-£8.50 • main £14-£21.50 • dessert £6.50-£7.50 • coffee £2.50 • min/water £3.50 • Service optional

PLACE: There's a wealth of period charm in this former hostelry to the medieval abbey, though the restaurant hints at a more recent past with its large oil paintings and subdued evening lighting. Wisteria-clad with stone mullioned windows, flagged floors and crackling fires in winter make the Old Bell perennially inviting.
FOOD: There's a sophisticated, even exciting, element to the cooking which emanates from careful sourcing of produce, a

continued

dash of inspiration, and a good eye for presentation. There is a nine-course tasting menu with a good mix of fish and meat, rounded off by delicious home-made petits fours served with coffee.
OUR TIP: Enjoy a Light Bite or well-priced lunch
Chef: Tom Rains **Times:** 12-2.30/7-9.30 **Notes:** Tasting menu £45, Vegetarian available, Dress Restrictions, Smart dress preferred; No jeans, Civ Wed 80 **Seats:** 60, Pr/dining room 24 **Smoking:** N/Sm in restaurant **Children:** Menu, Portions **Rooms:** 31 (31 en suite) ★★★
Directions: In town centre, next to Abbey. 5 m from M4 junct 17
Parking: 31 **e-mail:** info@oldbellhotel.com
web: www.oldbellhotel.com

The Old Rectory

British, French

Modern cooking in delightful period setting

☎ 01666 577194 SN16 9EP

MENU GUIDE Seared scallops, mango & chilli salsa Roast guinea fowl breast, dauphinoise potato, lentils, pancetta • Glazed lemon tart

WINE GUIDE ♀ Domaine Bergon Les Petits Grains Blend Vermentino/S.Blanc £12.95 • ♀ Charles Vienot Burgundy Blend £12.95 • 70 bottles over £20, 30 bottles under £20 • 5 by the glass (£3.95-£6.60)

PRICE GUIDE Starter £4.50-£8.75 • main £11.75-£16.95 • dessert £6 • coffee £2.95 • min/water £3 • Service optional

PLACE: The original Cotswold stone-built rectory dates from the 16th century but has additional Victorian wings. Three acres of walled gardens provide a delightful setting beside the village church, and the hotel is elegant and intimate with period furnishings and sympathetic decor. Dine in the impressive wood-panelled restaurant, or in the airy conservatory overlooking the Victorian garden and ornamental pond.
FOOD: The three-course dinner menu showcases modern British dishes with French overtones, using Welsh lamb, Cornish fish and local venison featuring strongly. Organic produce is used wherever possible.
OUR TIP: The perfect setting for weddings, with a civil licence
Chef: Peter Fairclough **Owners:** Derek & Karen Woods **Times:** 12-2/7-9.30 **Notes:** Vegetarian available, Civ Wed 45 **Seats:** 55, Pr/dining room 30 **Smoking:** N/Sm in restaurant **Children:** Min 6 yrs, Menu, Portions
Rooms: 12 (12 en suite) ★★★ **Directions:** Follow A429 to Cirencester. The Old Rectory is in village centre, next to village church **Parking:** 70
e-mail: office@oldrectorycrudwell.co.uk
web: www.oldrectorycrudwell.co.uk

Whatley Manor *see page 488*

The Best Use of Seafood sponsored by Seafish In conjunction with Seafish, the Sea Fish Industry Authority, we have sought out restaurants that make the most of seafood on their menus. In addition to the four country award winners (see page 9), look out for the seafish symbol throughout the book; this denotes restaurants serving a good range of fish and shellfish dishes, where the accent is firmly on freshness.

MALMESBURY MAP 04 ST98

Whatley Manor

French 🍴

French cuisine in new-style country-house hotel

☎ 01666 822888 Easton Grey SN16 0RB

MENU GUIDE Langoustine tails, smoked ham hock ravioli, braised celery, pork cider jus • Venison loin, cauliflower purée, brandy & peppercorn jus • Chocolate trio

WINE GUIDE ♀ Domaine Nichelot Chardonnay £72 • ♟ Wallace Barossa Valley Cabernet Shiraz £45 • 228 bottles over £20, 6 bottles under £20 • 10 by the glass (£4-£12.50)

PRICE GUIDE ALC (3 course) £60 • coffee £2.95 • min/water £2.50 • Service added but optional 10%

PLACE: This stunning country house delivers the highest levels of luxury. The Swiss-style Le Mazot restaurant is brasserie-style and the Dining Room is the fine-dining option.

FOOD: The cooking is classical French with a contemporary touch. Top-class produce, with luxury items in abundance yet the kitchen also finds a place for more traditional and humble ingredients like snails or pig's trotter. Light, beautifully presented dishes suit the venue perfectly, with peripherals such as canapés,

amuse bouche, pre-dessert, breads and petits fours all impressive. Notable wine list.

OUR TIP: Unwind in the stunning spa

Chef: Martin Burge **Owners:** C Landolt **Times:** 7-10, Closed Mon-Tues, L Mon-Sat **Notes:** Tasting menu £75, Vegetarian **Seats:** 40, Pr/dining 20 **Children:** Min 12, Portions **Rooms:** 23 en suite ★★★★ **Parking:** 100 **e-mail:** reservations@whatleymanor.com **web:** www.whatleymanor.com

MARTEN MAP 05 SU26

 The Windmill

British ⚗️**NEW**

Classic country restaurant on the way up

☎ 01264 731372 Salisbury Rd SN8 3SH

MENU GUIDE Crab tortellini, rocket salad • Beef, oxtail & mushroom ragout, confit potatoes, thyme sauce • Valrhona chocolate fondant, orange syrup

WINE GUIDE ♀ Plaimont Colombard £13.95 • ♟ Papillon Vin de Pays Merlot/Cabernet £14.50 • 450 bottles over £20, 40 bottles under £20 • 18 by the glass (£3.80-£6.50)

PRICE GUIDE Fixed L fr £15.95 • starter £6.50-£9.95 • main £15.50-£19.90 • dessert fr £7.50 • coffee £2.50 • min/water £2.95 • Service optional

PLACE: Recently refurbished, this sophisticated restaurant in the rolling Wiltshire countryside blends period Edwardian charm with contemporary chic. Split into three rooms and candlelit by night, its pale red walls are hung with local art, while large wooden tables are set with fine white china and antique wine decanters.

FOOD: A commitment to the use of first-rate local produce is at the heart of The Windmill's success, along with a simple cooking style that highlights rather than masks its quality. The modern British menu with European influences changes regularly to reflect the seasons and is complemented by an extensive wine list.

OUR TIP: Dine alfresco on the terrace and enjoy the view of nearby Wilton Windmill.

Chef: Gary Fisher **Owners:** Chris Ellis **Times:** 11.45-2/6.45-9, Closed 25-26 Dec, 1 Jan, Mon, closed D Sun **Notes:** Vegetarian available **Seats:** 44, Pr/dining room 14 **Smoking:** N/Sm in restaurant **Children:** Portions **Directions:** Please ring for directions **Parking:** 30

PURTON MAP 05 SU08

 The Pear Tree at Purton

British

Tempting modern British cooking in the Wiltshire countryside

☎ 01793 772100 Church End SN5 4ED

MENU GUIDE Salmon & spring onion terrine • Guinea fowl, foie gras mousseline, Sauternes sauce • Burnt Catalan cream, peanut shortbreads

WINE GUIDE ♀ Domaine de Tariquet Ugni Blanc/Colombard £12.50 • ♟ Domaine Grande Courtade Merlot £12.50 57 bottles over £20, 25 bottles under £20 • 12 by the glass (£3.75-£5.50)

PRICE GUIDE Fixed L £19.50 • Fixed D £34.50 • min/water £2.50 • Service optional

PLACE: Dating back to the 15th century, this former vicarage is made of mellow Cotswold stone and sits amid rolling Wiltshire countryside not far from Swindon. Its restaurant is housed in an airy conservatory overlooking pretty gardens with a pond and water feature.

FOOD: Thoughtful combinations distinguish a lengthy menu of modern British fare: you might start with cream of fennel soup, mussels and curry oil perhaps, before moving on to pork tenderloin with apricots, bacon and a brandy sauce, or a simple dish such as seared tuna with tapenade and roast peppers.

OUR TIP: Visit Ringsbury Camp, an ancient hill fort nearby

Chef: Alan Postill **Owners:** Francis and Anne Young **Times:** 12-2/7-9.1, Closed 26-30 Dec, closed L Sat **Notes:** Coffee incl., Vegetarian available, Dress Restrictions, No jeans or shorts, Smart casual, Civ Wed 50 **Seats:** 50, Pr/dining room 50 **Smoking:** N/Sm in restaurant

continue

Children: Portions **Rooms:** 17 (17 en suite) ★★★ **Directions:** From M4 junct 16, follow signs to Purton. Turn right at Spa shop, hotel 0.25m on right **Parking:** 70 **e-mail:** stay@peartreepurton.co.uk **web:** www.peartreepurton.co.uk

REDLYNCH MAP 05 SU22

🌸 Langley Wood Restaurant

British

Country dining room with well-balanced menu

☎ 01794 390348   SP5 2PB

MENU GUIDE Griddled goats' cheese, chilli tomato jam • Pan-fried fillet steak, stilton & walnut crust • Chocolate Amaretto truffle torte

WINE GUIDE ♀ Sauvignon Blanc £11.50 • ♀ Villa Magna Sangiovese £9.75 • 17 bottles over £20, 49 bottles under £20 6 by the glass (£2.50-£3)

PRICE GUIDE Fixed L £17.75 • starter £4-£6.95 • main £9.75-£15 • dessert £4 • coffee £2 • min/water £2.50 • Service optional

PLACE: Once belonging to Horatio Nelson's estate, this enlarged 17th-century country house stands in five acres of wooded grounds within the New Forest National Park. The husband and wife team run a reassuringly traditional dining room dominated by a huge fireplace, and three bedrooms contribute to the relaxed private house atmosphere.

FOOD: A short, pleasing carte well balanced between meats, fish, game in season and a vegetarian choice. Classically English dishes do not eschew fine use of continental herbs and ingredients.

OUR TIP: Leave room for dessert

Chef: Sylvia Rosen **Owners:** David and Sylvia Rosen **Times:** 12.30-2.30/7-10.30, Closed Xmas-New Year, Mon & Tue, closed L Wed-Fri, closed D Sun **Notes:** Unlimited coffee, Vegetarian available, Dress Restrictions, Smart casual **Seats:** 30 **Smoking:** N/Sm in restaurant **Directions:** Between A338 Salisbury to Ringwood road and A36 Salisbury to Southampton road **Parking:** 30 **e-mail:** therestaurant@langleywood.freeserve.co.uk

ROWDE MAP 04 ST96

🌸 George & Dragon

British, European

Simple modern cooking in charming gastro-pub

☎ 01380 723053   High St SN10 2PN

MENU GUIDE Smoked haddock & salmon tartlet • Rack of lamb, braised cabbage, red wine jus • Apple & blueberry crumble, clotted cream

WINE GUIDE ♀ Bornos Verdejo £14 • ♀ Casablanca Merlot £14 • 16 bottles over £20, 17 bottles under £20 • 8 by the glass (£2.90-£4.65)

George & Dragon

PRICE GUIDE Fixed L fr £11 • coffee £2 • min/water £3.50 • Service optional

PLACE: This charming old inn mixes original features with a relaxed gastro-pub atmosphere, and draws an eclectic blend of regulars. Beams and wood panelling abound in the restaurant and bar, where an open log fire keeps things homely.

FOOD: Fresh ingredients are handled in a simple, modern style, with seafood a speciality – fresh from Cornwall, and featuring on its very own menu. Mains might include a cassoulet of Wiltshire sausages, or smoked haddock risotto with rocket.

OUR TIP: Pub cat Rupert has been known to scrounge

Chef: Christopher Day **Owners:** Mr & Mrs Hale & Mr C Day **Times:** 12-3/6-11, Closed L Mon, closed D Sun **Notes:** Set 3 course Sun L £15.50, Vegetarian available **Seats:** 35 **Smoking:** N/Sm in restaurant **Children:** Portions **Directions:** 1.5m out of Devizes towards Chippenham on A342 **Parking:** 12 **e-mail:** thegandd@tiscali.co.uk

SWINDON MAP 05 SU18

🌸 The Ridge Restaurant

British, European

Modernised country-house hotel with up-to-date facilities

☎ 01793 721701   Blunsdon House Hotel, Blunsdon SN26 7AS

MENU GUIDE Foie gras ballotine, pear chutney • Sweet & sour pork fillet, bok choi • Pannacotta, pineapple sorbet

WINE GUIDE ♀ Libertad Pinot Blanc £13.50 • ♀ Libertad Merlot £13.50 • 15 bottles over £20, 14 bottles under £20 • 6 by the glass (£3.20-£4.60)

PRICE GUIDE Food prices not confirmed for 2006. Please telephone for details

PLACE: Set in 30 acres of lovely grounds, this hotel has a choice of dining. Christophers is the carvery/buffet option, whilst The Ridge is more formal complete with a carte menu, walnut panelling and lots of natural light.

FOOD: Modern British dishes are occasionally given a European twist. Expect starters of lobster & chive risotto and main courses of roast pheasant with smoky bacon & celeriac purée.

OUR TIP: Handy helipad for those in a hurry

Chef: Glen Bent **Owners:** Mr & Mrs P Clifford and Family **Times:** 12.15-2/7-10, Closed L Mon-Sat, closed D Sun **Notes:** Vegetarian available, Civ Wed 100 **Seats:** 65, Pr/dining room 10 **Smoking:** N/Sm in restaurant, Air con **Children:** Menu, Portions **Rooms:** 118 (118 en suite) ★★★★ **Directions:** M4 junct 15, 200 yds off A419. Northern edge of Swindon at Blunsdon **Parking:** 200 **e-mail:** info@blunsdonhouse.co.uk **web:** www.blunsdonhouse.co.uk

continued

TROWBRIDGE MAP 04 ST85

The Linnet

Modern British, International

Pleasant country inn

☎ 01380 870354 Great Hinton BA14 6BU

MENU GUIDE Lemon sole terrine • Confit duck leg, stuffed with sage and pine nuts, mustard mash • Lime & gingernut cheesecake

PRICE GUIDE Food prices not confirmed for 2006. Please telephone for details

PLACE: You will find a relaxing and welcoming atmosphere in this country inn – although it might not be necessarily the easiest place to find.

FOOD: The modern British cooking uses good quality ingredients, often with an international twist. Great menu choice ranging from light lunches and separate lunch special to full dinner menu.

OUR TIP: Best to book ahead; weekends can be very busy

Times: 12-2/6.30-9.30, Closed 25, 26 Dec, 1 Jan, Mon **Directions:** Off A342, 4m W of Devizes, 3m E of Trowbridge

WARMINSTER MAP 04 ST84

Bishopstrow House Hotel

British, Mediterranean

Charming Georgian country house setting for fine contemporary cuisine

☎ 01985 212312   BA12 9HH

MENU GUIDE Ravioli of smoked haddock, creamed leeks Pan-fried Longleat pheasant, onion & garlic tarte Tatin • Melting chocolate fondant

WINE GUIDE ♀ Vinha d'or Chardonnay £17 • ♀ Vinha d'or Merlot £17 • 95 bottles over £20, 15 bottles under £20 • 6 by the glass (£4-£5)

PRICE GUIDE Fixed L £12 • Fixed D £38 • starter £4-£12 • main £9-£18 • dessert £4-£7.50 • coffee £2.75 • min/water £3.75 • Service added but optional 15%

PLACE: This fine Georgian country house is situated in 27 acres of rolling parklands. Public areas are traditional in style warmed by cosy open fires in winter and crammed with antiques. A spa, tennis court and several country walks ensure there is something for everyone.

FOOD: The Mulberry Restaurant serves quality contemporary cuisine executed skilfully with well-timed combinations. Organic local produce is used wherever possible, with herbs and vegetables coming from their own gardens. There is a separate vegetarian and children's menu.

OUR TIP: Themed evenings throughout the year

Chef: Frank Bailey **Owners:** Von Essen Hotels **Times:** 12.15-2/7.30-9.30 **Notes:** Vegetarian available, Civ Wed 70 **Seats:** 65, Pr/dining room 28 **Smoking:** N/Sm in restaurant **Children:** Menu, Portions **Rooms:** 32 (32 en suite) ★★★★ **Directions:** From Warminster take B3414 (Salisbury). Hotel is signposted. **Parking:** 100 **e-mail:** info@bishopstrow.co.uk **web:** www.bishopstrow.co.uk

Prices quoted in the guide are for guidance only and are subject to change without notice.

WHITLEY MAP 04 ST86

The Pear Tree Inn

British, Italian

Convivial rustic setting for a culinary treat

☎ 01225 709131 Top Ln SN12 8QX

MENU GUIDE Crisp pork belly, black pudding, apple sauce • Beef, polenta with gorgonzola, bacon, red wine sauce • Sticky date pudding

WINE GUIDE ♀ Con Class Cuevas de Castilla Sauvignon Blanc £15.50 • ♀ Chacmas Bark Shiraz £13.75 • 28 bottles over £20, 22 bottles under £20 • 10 by the glass (£3.15-£5.35)

PRICE GUIDE Fixed L £13.50 • starter £4.75-£6.95 • main £11.25-£18 • dessert £4.75-£5.50 • coffee £2.50 • min/water £2.95 • Service optional

PLACE: This one-time pig farm turned cosy hotel draws diners from a wide area with its tasty food and convivial atmosphere. Pretty grounds surround the mellow stone building, while inside is divided into a comfy bar, intimate dining area and bright garden room – all furnished with old farming implements and simple wooden tables.

FOOD: The Pear Tree is proud of its commitment to seasonal ingredients, and champions local farmers who are passionate about their produce in turn. Cooking is honest and the lengthy menu good value, with lighter snacks available at lunchtime.

OUR TIP: Treat yourself to a weekend break

Chef: Steven Terry **Owners:** Martin & Debbie Still **Times:** 12-2.30/6.30-9.30, Closed 25-26 Dec, 1 Jan **Notes:** Vegetarian available **Seats:** 60, Pr/dining room 40 **Smoking:** N/Sm in restaurant **Children:** Menu, Portions **Rooms:** 8 (8 en suite) 🏠 **Directions:** Telephone for directions **Parking:** 60 **e-mail:** enquiries@peartreeinn.co.uk **web:** www.peartreeinn.co.uk

WORCESTERSHIRE

ABBERLEY MAP 10 SO76

The Elms Hotel & Restaurant

British

Queen Anne architecture with relaxed ambience and fine dining

☎ 01299 896666 Stockton Rd WR6 6AT

MENU GUIDE Confit pork, seared scallops, shallots & bacon • Saddle of venison, confit spiced fig & claret • Banana crème brûlée, malt ice cream

WINE GUIDE ♀ Santa Rita Chardonnay £18 • ♀ Croix Belle Merlot £16.50 • 200 bottles over £20, 18-20 bottles under £20 • 10 by the glass (£4.25-£4.75)

continued

The Elms Hotel & Restaurant

PRICE GUIDE Fixed L £12.50 • Fixed D £32.50 • starter £9.50 main £19.50 • dessert £8.50 • coffee £2.25 • min/water £4 • Service optional

PLACE: Built in 1710 by a pupil of Sir Christopher Wren, this imposing mansion is set in rolling parkland in the Teme Valley. Dotted with antiques and filled with period features, day rooms have a gracious, country-house feel, and the grand restaurant overlooks the gardens.

FOOD: Well-balanced menus feature classic dishes with some modern twists. Local ingredients are well used; many sourced from the hotel's large kitchen garden. Service is relaxed and welcoming.

OUR TIP: Well-kept cheese selection

Chef: Daren Bale **Owners:** Von Essen Hotels **Times:** 12-2.30/7-9.30 **Notes:** Sun L 3 courses £21.95, Vegetarian available, Dress Restrictions, Smart casual, no jeans, no T-shirts, Civ Wed 30 **Seats:** 50, Pr/dining room 50 **Smoking:** N/Sm in restaurant **Children:** Menu, Portions **Rooms:** 21 (21 en suite) ★★★ **Directions:** Located on A443 near Abberley **Parking:** 40 **e-mail:** info@theelmshotel.co.uk **web:** www.theelmshotel.co.uk

BROADWAY MAP 10 SP03

Dormy House Hotel

British, French

Elegant country location with sophisticated food

☎ 01386 852711 Willersey Hill WR12 7LF

MENU GUIDE Brioche-crusted Somerset brie • Baked fillet of brill, prawn & crab risotto • Chocolate fondant pudding

WINE GUIDE ♀ Alain Bretin Chablis Chardonnay £19.50 • ♀ Almansa Marius Reserve £15 • 70 bottles over £20, 10 bottles under £20 • 10 by the glass (£2.95-£4.50)

PRICE GUIDE Fixed L £21 • Fixed D £34 • starter £7.50-£11.50 • main £15-£23 • dessert £5.95-£6.95 • coffee £2.50 • min/water £2.65 • Service optional

PLACE: A converted Cotswold-stone farmhouse with a fine reputation for hospitality. The elegant dining room is housed in a conservatory extension overlooking well-tended lawns, and service, like the dress code, manages to be formal and relaxed at the same time.

FOOD: Traditional English flavours like garden sage, local asparagus and strawberries make a vibrant but controlled impact on the seasonal menus. Sophisticated ingredients are handled with a refreshing simplicity, with some classic results like Dijon roasted loin of lamb and Madeira jus, and medallions of beef fillet with pan-fried foie gras.

OUR TIP: A few minutes' walk from the beautiful Nidd Gorge

Chef: Alan Cutler **Owners:** Mrs I Philip-Sorensen **Times:** 12-2/7-7.30, Closed 24-27 Dec, closed L Mon-Sat **Notes:** Sun L £21, Vegetarian available, Civ Wed 100 **Seats:** 80, Pr/dining room 170 **Smoking:** N/Sm

in restaurant, Air con **Children:** Menu, Portions **Rooms:** 48 (48 en suite) ★★★ **Directions:** From A44 take turn signed 'Saintbury', after 0.5m turn left **Parking:** 80 **e-mail:** reservations@dormyhouse.co.uk **web:** www.dormyhouse.co.uk

The Lygon Arms *see page 492*

Russell's

Modern British   **NEW**

A chic setting for contemporary cuisine

☎ 01386 853555 20 High St WR12 7DT

MENU GUIDE Boudin of lamb sweetbreads, onion purée Pork, sautéed foie gras, caramelised apples • Banana parfait, chocolate ravioli

PRICE GUIDE Food prices not confirmed for 2006. Please telephone for details

PLACE: On the high street of a picturesque village, this chic restaurant with rooms blends period features such as Cotswold stone walls and wooden beams with a muted modern decor of wood flooring, dark colours and contemporary art.

FOOD: Contemporary British cuisine conjured from good quality produce. Lunch sees a concise fixed price menu in operation, plus a snack selection, while dinner brings more complex fare and a longer carte.

OUR TIP: Good value early bird dinner

Times: 12-2.30/6-9.30 **Rooms:** 4 (4 en suite) **e-mail:** info@russellsofbroadway.com **web:** www.russellsofbroadway.com

BROMSGROVE MAP 10 SO97

Grafton Manor Restaurant

British, Indian

Indian-influenced modern British cuisine in elegant period setting

☎ 01527 579007 Grafton Ln B61 7HA

MENU GUIDE Wild mushroom risotto • Lamb infused with coconut milk, dhal, Basmati rice • White chocolate & saffron pannacotta

WINE GUIDE ♀ J & F Lurton Sauvignon Blanc £13.35 • ♀ Stonefish Shiraz £14.10 • 39 bottles over £20, 29 bottles under £20 • 3 by the glass (£3.65)

PRICE GUIDE Fixed L £18.50-£20 • Fixed D £27.85 • coffee £2.60 • min/water £3.25 • Service optional

PLACE: Large manicured grounds, complete with lake, provide the perfect backdrop to this impressive 16th-century manor house. Attractive features include moulded ceilings, log fires, a sumptuous drawing room and smartly furnished dining room.

FOOD: Modern British with the option of authentic Indian cuisine. The chef has travelled extensively in India and carefully sources his ingredients to achieve the correct flavours. Vegetarians are very welcome and have a separate menu.

OUR TIP: Fully subscribed annual Indian festival

Chef: Simon Morris **Owners:** The Morris Family **Times:** 12.30-1.30/7-9.30, Closed BHs, closed L Sat, closed D Sun **Notes:** Vegetarian available, Civ Wed 120 **Seats:** 60, Pr/dining room 60 **Smoking:** N/Sm in restaurant **Children:** Portions **Directions:** Off B4091, 1.5m SW of Bromsgrove **Parking:** 60 **e-mail:** stephen@graftonmanorhotel.co.uk **web:** www.graftonmanorhotel.co.uk

continued

England

BROADWAY MAP 10 SP03

The Lygon Arms

International, Latvian
Bold and inventive cuisine in delightful location
☎ 01386 852255 High St WR12 7DU

MENU GUIDE Borsch terrine, sour cream, shredded beef & onion pirags • Seared scallops, scallop butter sauce • Peach Melba

WINE GUIDE ♀ Alain Bretin Chablis £27.50 • ♀ Concha y Toro Merlot £21.50 • 148 bottles over £20, 2 bottles under £20 • 12 by the glass (£6-£9)

PRICE GUIDE Fixed L £26.50 • Fixed D £39.50 • starter £8.50-£16 • main £19.50-£26.50 • dessert £6-£8.50 • coffee £3.50 • min/water £3.25 • Service optional

PLACE: The Great Hall – as impressive as the name suggests with oak floor, barrel-vaulted ceiling, minstrels' gallery, huge stone fireplace, suits of armour and stags' heads – is the baronial-style main dining room at this landmark, 16th-century former inn at the heart of the beautiful Cotswold village of Broadway. Oak panels, beams, flagstone floors, snugs and inglenooks – reflecting the history of one of Britain's best recognised hotels (you'll be walking in the footsteps of Oliver Cromwell and Charles I too) – find their place alongside modern comforts, including a health spa. At the time of going to press room star rating was not confirmed due to ongoing refurbishment.

FOOD: The distinctive cooking of Martin Blunos proves a highlight of any visit. His creative menus (which include a nine-course tasting option), are well conceived, innovative and ambitious, inspired by the cooking of his native Latvia and fused with French classics. Elaborate, technically challenging and accomplished dishes reflect fresh, quality ingredients and the expertise of the kitchen, and include typical Blunos theatrical signature dishes. Breads are of the best. Excellent wine list.

OUR TIP: Afternoon teas are also a treat

Chef: Martin Blunos **Owners:** Furlong Hotels Ltd **Times:** 12-2.30/7-9.30 **Notes:** Vegetarian available, Dress Restrictions, Smart casual, No jeans, T-shirts, trainers, Civ Wed 80 **Seats:** 90, Pr/dining room 80 **Smoking:** N/Sm in restaurant, Air con **Children:** Min 12 yrs, Menu, Portions **Directions:** A40 to Burford, A424 through Stow-on-the-Wold, then A44 **Parking:** 100 **e-mail:** info@thelygonarms.co.uk **web:** www.thelygonarms.co.uk

---

BROMSGROVE MAP 10 SO97

Hanover International Hotel & Club
Contemporary
Mediterranean-themed hotel just off the M5
☎ 01527 576600 Kidderminster Rd B61 9AB

MENU GUIDE Chicken liver parfait • Pan-fried sea bass & prawns, herb velouté • Lemon & lime crème brûlée

PRICE GUIDE Food prices not confirmed for 2006. Please telephone for details

PLACE: There's an airy, Mediterranean feel to this striking hotel. Whitewashed walls reflect light and a courtyard garden soaks up the sun. The Parador restaurant continues the theme with Spanish-style terracotta tiles and big rugs.

FOOD: Articulate cooking matches flavours intelligently. There's an appealing blend of traditional and modern cuisine, and dishes are compiled simply and effectively.

OUR TIP: Leisure facilities include steam room and pool

Times: 12.30-2/7-9, Closed Xmas, closed L Sat **Rooms:** 114 (114 en suite) ★★★★ **Directions:** On A448 Kidderminster road 1m W of Bromsgrove centre

e-mail: banqueting.bromsgrove@hanover-international.com **web:** www.hanover-international.com

---

CHADDESLEY CORBETT MAP 10 SO87

Brockencote Hall
French
Elegant French dining in fine country house
☎ 01562 777876 DY10 4PY

MENU GUIDE Roast scallops, cauliflower purée • Veal, honey-roast lamb sweetbreads, girolles, port reduction • Coconut soufflé

WINE GUIDE ♀ Montes Sauvignon Blanc £15.50 • ♀ Bodegas Murua Rioja Tempranillo £28 • 80 bottles over £20, 20 bottles under £20 • 5 by the glass (£3.50-£7)

PRICE GUIDE Fixed L £13-£20 • Fixed D £26.30-£44.50 • starter £6.30-£13.50 • main £14.50-£22.50 • dessert £5.50-£8.50 • coffee £3.20 • min/water £3 • Service included

PLACE: Set in elegantly landscaped gardens, this peaceful country house has the feel of a provincial French château. The dining room is an airy ensemble of pastel colours, chandeliers and flowered fabrics, with pretty views over the grounds.

continued   *continue*

Brockencote Hall

FOOD: A concise lunch menu gives way to a longer carte and fixed-price selection at dinner. Expect accomplished modern French cuisine with a touch of imagination: lemon sole with coriander and Noilly Prat cream perhaps, or Normandy rabbit with a Madeira and mustard jus. Vegetarian menu on request.
OUR TIP: Six-course tasting menu also available
Chef: Jerome Barbancon **Owners:** Mr & Mrs Petitjean **Times:** 12-1.30/7-9.30, Closed L Sat **Notes:** Tasting menu £48, £70 (incl. wine), Vegetarian available, Civ Wed 40 **Seats:** 60, Pr/dining room 30 **Smoking:** N/Sm in restaurant **Children:** Menu, Portions **Rooms:** 17 (17 en suite) ★★★
Directions: On A448 just outside village, between Kidderminster & Bromsgrove **Parking:** 45 **e-mail:** info@brockencotehall.com
web: www.brockencotehall.com

EVESHAM MAP 10 SP04

The Evesham Hotel
International, Eclectic
Strong following for imaginative food with personality
☎ 01386 765566 Coopers Ln, Off Waterside WR11 1DA
MENU GUIDE Marinated pork, chilli apple sauce • Poached & gratinated sea bass, pine nut & basil crust • Dried fruit, cider & walnut tart
WINE GUIDE ♀ Château Ste Michelle Pinot Blanc £18.30 • ♀ Diekrans Tinta Barocca £15.50 • 100 bottles over £20, 100 bottles under £20 • 6 by the glass (£2.60)
PRICE GUIDE Starter £3.20-£8.50 • main £11.35-£18.45 • dessert £4.75 • coffee £1.80 • min/water £2.30 • Service included
PLACE: Run by the Jenkinson family for 30 years, with their own brand of jokey good humour, this former farmhouse dates from 1540 but was remodelled as a Georgian mansion. The Cedar Restaurant overlooks extensive grounds set around a spectacular cedar tree.

FOOD: Imaginative menu descriptions for a great variety of dishes, featuring some rare and local items (Harper's pheasant, Oakfield pork fillet, golden wild boar cutlets); vegetarians are also well served.
OUR TIP: Good choice lunchtime buffet popular with regulars
Chef: Sue James **Owners:** John Jenkinson **Times:** 12.30-2/7-10, Closed 25-26 Dec **Notes:** Vegetarian available **Seats:** 55, Pr/dining room 12 **Smoking:** N/Sm in restaurant **Children:** Menu, Portions **Rooms:** 40 (40 en suite) ★★★ **Directions:** Coopers Lane is off road along River Avon **Parking:** 45 **e-mail:** reception@eveshamhotel.com
web: www.eveshamhotel.com

Riverside Hotel
International
Good honest cooking in secluded setting by the River Avon
☎ 01386 446200 The Parks, Offenham Rd WR11 8JP

MENU GUIDE Goujons of plaice, tartare sauce • Gressingham duck breast, sweet potato chilli • Passionfruit mousse
WINE GUIDE ♀ Corte Giara Pinot Grigio £14.95 • ♀ Mas Montel Cuvée Psalmodi £14.95
PRICE GUIDE Fixed L £25.95-£35.95 • Fixed D £28.95 • starter £4.95-£6.95 • main £6.95-£13.95 • dessert £4.95-£5.95 • coffee £2 • min/water £2.50
PLACE: Standing in three acres of gardens sloping down to the River Avon, this rural, family-run hotel is a genuine hideaway, and even has a couple of cruisers for hire for pre-dinner cocktails. On warm summer evenings, the terrace is a popular alfresco dining destination and staff are well-drilled and customer-focused.
FOOD: Cooking remains one of the hotel's strong points and the International menu is constantly changing, sometimes during the service. With its blackboard menu, lunch is less formal, but dinner offers an equally wide-ranging selection of well-executed dishes.
OUR TIP: Perfect for sunny alfresco lunches
Chef: Julie Groves, Racheal Taylor **Owners:** Deborah Sinclair **Times:** 12.30-2/7.30-9, Closed 25 Dec, 1st 2 wks Jan, closed L Mon, closed D Sun **Notes:** Vegetarian by request only **Seats:** 48 **Smoking:** N/Sm in restaurant **Children:** Portions **Rooms:** 10 (7 en suite) ★★
Directions: From A46 Evesham follow signs for Offenham, then take a right onto B4510. Hotel 0.5m on left down private drive **Parking:** 20
e-mail: info@river-side-hotel.co.uk
web: www.river-side-hotel.co.uk

 denotes a restaurant with a particularly good wine list.

continued

EVESHAM MAP 10 SP04

◎◎ Wood Norton Hall

British, French

Fine dining in grand country-house hotel

☎ 01386 425780 Wood Norton WR11 4YB

MENU GUIDE Asparagus & lemongrass soup • Pork, cider potato, apple tarte Tatin • Lemon tart, orange sorbet

WINE GUIDE ⚲ Les Pierriers Sancerre £24.25 • ⚲ Château Sicard St Emilion £32 • 50 bottles over £20, 3 bottles under £20 • 5 by the glass (£3.95-£9.95)

PRICE GUIDE Fixed L £21.50 • Fixed D £37.50 • coffee £2.95 • Service included

PLACE: Imposing Victorian manor set in 170 acres of Worcestershire countryside. Extensive facilities mean there's no excuse for not arriving in the oak-panelled dining room with an appetite, unless you're waylaid by the photos on the walls recording the use of the house in an episode of Dr Who.
FOOD: Expect classic combinations of high quality seasonal ingredients in the Le Duc restaurant. Each course offers half a dozen choices, with typical mains along the lines of salmon with wild mushrooms and spinach, or duck with boulangère potatoes, parsnip purée and port jus.
OUR TIP: Take a stroll in the grounds before dinner
Chef: Mark Streeter **Times:** 12-2/7-9.30, Closed L Sat **Notes:** Vegetarian available, Dress Restrictions, No jeans or trainers, Civ Wed 70 **Seats:** 70, Pr/dining room 40 **Smoking:** N/Sm in restaurant **Children:** Portions **Rooms:** 45 (45 en suite) ★★★★ **Directions:** Take A4538 then A44 to Wood Norton Hall. Approximately 3.5 miles from Evesham Town Centre **Parking:** 150 **e-mail:** info@wnhall.co.uk **web:** www.wnhall.co.uk

KIDDERMINSTER MAP 10 S087

◎ The Granary Hotel & Restaurant

British, International

Comfortable dining in modern hotel restaurant

☎ 01562 777535 Heath Ln, Shenstone DY10 4BS

MENU GUIDE Thai crab cakes • Beef fillet & wild mushroom sauce • Vanilla pannacotta, wild strawberry compote

WINE GUIDE ⚲ Dalwood Semillon Chardonnay £12.75 • ⚲ Paarl Heights Cinsault/Shiraz £11.75 • 7 bottles over £20, 34 bottles under £20 • 8 by the glass (£2.60-£4.50)

PRICE GUIDE Fixed L £8.50 • Fixed D £12-£14 • starter £4.50-£7.50 • main £9.95-£19.95 • dessert £4.50-£5.50 • coffee £1.75 • min/water £3.25 • Service optional

PLACE: This attractive, modern hotel restaurant with its stylish open-plan layout and Lloyd Loom furniture was once a haulage yard. Staff contribute to a relaxed and friendly atmosphere.

continued

FOOD: Modern British dishes populate the menu with the occasional Asian or Continental accent. Good use of British ingredients like black pudding and game. The emphasis is on fresh ingredients simply prepared and presented.
OUR TIP: Great value weekday carvery lunch
Chef: Tom Court **Owners:** Richard Fletcher **Times:** 12-2.30/7-11, Closed L Mon/Sat, closed D Sun **Notes:** Vegetarian available, Civ Wed 200 **Seats:** 60, Pr/dining room 40 **Smoking:** N/Sm in restaurant, Air con **Children:** Portions **Rooms:** 18 (18 en suite) ★★★ **Directions:** Situated on A450 between Worcester and Stourbridge. 2m outside Kidderminster **Parking:** 95 **e-mail:** info@granary-hotel.co.uk **web:** www.granary-hotel.co.uk

MALVERN MAP 10 S074

◎◎ Cottage in the Wood

British

Country retreat with stunning views

☎ 01684 575859 Holywell Rd, Malvern Wells WR14 4LG

MENU GUIDE Wild duck consommé, sautéed scallop • Pork loin, boudin noir, Calvados sauce • Chocolate fondant, poached cherries

WINE GUIDE ⚲ Torres Sauvignon Blanc £15.95 • ⚲ Thompsons Merlot £17.50 • 405 bottles over £20, 87 bottles under £20 • 8 by the glass (£3.95-£4.50)

PRICE GUIDE Fixed L £15.95 • starter £7.50-£11 • main £17-£22 • dessert £8.50 • coffee £3.25 • min/water £3

PLACE: Hidden away among woodland in the Malvern hills, this friendly family-run hotel overlooks a wide green expanse of the Severn plain and prides itself on having the most beautiful view in England. Diners get the best of it, thanks to the elegant restaurant's floor to ceiling windows.
FOOD: Lots of ambition and creativity here with a modern British menu that has a strong emphasis on seasonality and best quality local produce. There is an excellent wine list - over 600 bins, plus a separate list of half bottles all presented with enthusiasm and a refreshing lack of pretension.

continued

OUR TIP: A beautiful setting for a pre-dinner stroll
Chef: Dominic Pattin **Owners:** The Pattin Family **Times:** 12.30-2/7-9.30
Notes: Vegetarian available, Dress Restrictions, Smart casual preferred. No jeans, trainers **Seats:** 70, Pr/dining room 20 **Smoking:** N/Sm in restaurant, Air con **Children:** Portions **Rooms:** 31 (31 en suite) ★★★
Directions: 3m S of Great Malvern off A449. From Great Malvern, take 3rd turning on right after Railway pub **Parking:** 40
e-mail: proprietor@cottageinthewood.co.uk
web: www.cottageinthewood.co.uk

Foley Arms Hotel
British

Handsome Georgian hotel with traditional values
☎ 01684 573397 14 Worcester Rd WR14 4QS

MENU GUIDE Red snapper & king prawn brochette • Lamb noisettes, minted green pea mash, sherry & redcurrant jus • Ginger & lime soufflé

PRICE GUIDE Food prices not confirmed for 2006. Please telephone for details

PLACE: The Foley Arms is possibly the oldest hotel in Malvern and has spectacular views over the Severn Valley. Public areas include a popular bar and the Elgar Restaurant, with a warm and comfortable atmosphere throughout.
FOOD: Wherever possible, fresh local produce is used to create the dishes offered from the fixed-price menu. A vegetarian option is included, such as baked red pepper filled with spiced risotto on a pesto dressing.
OUR TIP: Themed short breaks are a feature
Times: 12-2/7-9.15, Closed L Sat **Rooms:** 28 (28 en suite) ★★★
Directions: M5 junct 8 from south (junct 7 from north). Follow signs for Upton/Malvern, approx 8m from motorway on A449, in centre of town
e-mail: reservations@foleyarmshotel.com
web: www.foleyarmshotel.co.uk

Seasons Restaurant at Colwall Park Hotel
British

Modern country-house hotel dining
☎ 01684 540000 Walwyn Rd, Colwall WR13 6QG
MENU GUIDE Crab & chive risotto, avocado crème fraîche • Pork, cabbage, bacon, apple fondant, sage juices Hot raspberry soufflé

WINE GUIDE ♀ Sauvignon Blanc £12.99 • ♀ Claret £12.99 • 60 bottles over £20, 40 bottles under £20 • 7 by the glass (£3.15-£4.50)

PRICE GUIDE Fixed D £17.95 • starter £5.75-£7.95 • main £15.95-£19.95 • dessert £5.95-£7.95 • coffee £1.95 • min/water £2.95 • Service included

PLACE: This elegant country-house hotel was built in the early 20th century to meet the needs of the local race track. Dinner is served in the civilised surroundings of the oak-panelled Seasons restaurant, with its high vaulted ceiling and grand piano.
FOOD: Plenty of choice here, with the carte complemented by a range of fixed-price menus and a five-course tasting option. Expect modern British dishes created from quality seasonal ingredients: pan-seared scallops to start perhaps, then organic lamb with braised lentils and bacon, and a rosemary jus.
OUR TIP: Bar menu also available
Chef: James Garth **Owners:** Mr & Mrs I Nesbitt **Times:** 12.30-2.30/7.30-9, Closed L all week ex by arrangement **Notes:** Vegetarian available **Seats:** 40, Pr/dining room 100 **Smoking:** N/Sm in restaurant
Children: Menu, Portions **Rooms:** 22 (22 en suite) ★★★
Directions: On B4218, off A449 from Malvern to Ledbury **Parking:** 40
e-mail: hotel@colwall.com **web:** www.colwall.com

OMBERSLEY MAP 10 SO86

The Venture In Restaurant
Modern British, French

Confident cooking in cottage setting
☎ 01905 620552 Main Rd WR9 0EW

MENU GUIDE Roquefort soufflé, red wine poached pear • Pheasant, game & cranberry faggot, pickled red cabbage • Sticky toffee pudding

WINE GUIDE 44 bottles over £20, 25 bottles under £20 • 5 by the glass (£3.50-£4.50)

PRICE GUIDE Fixed L £16.95 • Fixed D £31.50-£34 • min/water £3 • Service optional

PLACE: Behind an ancient black and white timbered exterior, this pretty restaurant has a cottage feel with its comfortable sofas and warm yellow and terracotta colour scheme. It dates back to 1430 and comes complete with heavy beams, an inglenook fire, and the rumour of a ghost.
FOOD: Simple cooking executed with confidence and care. The modern British menu with French influences has plenty to tempt with mains along the lines of navarin of lamb, or calves' liver with bacon and mash, and there's also a gourmet fish menu offering dishes such as steamed fillet of silver dorade with a crab and coriander risotto.
OUR TIP: Good value lunch menu
Chef: Toby Fletcher **Owners:** Toby Fletcher **Times:** 12-2/7-9.30, Closed 25 Dec-1 Jan, 2wks summer & 2wks winter, Mon, closed D Sun
Notes: Vegetarian available, Smart casual **Seats:** 32, Pr/dining room 32
Smoking: N/Sm in restaurant, Air con **Children:** Min 12 yrs D
Directions: From Worcester N towards Kidderminster - A449 (approx 5m). Turn left at Ombersley turning - 0.75m on right **Parking:** 15

continued

England

STOURPORT-ON-SEVERN MAP 10 SO87
Menzies Stourport Manor
International
Modern manor with spacious brasserie
☎ 01299 289955 Hartlebury Rd DY13 9JA
MENU GUIDE Spinach & mushroom ravioli • Lamb rump on parsley mash • Banoffee pie
WINE GUIDE ♀ Penfolds Chardonnay £18.65 • ♀ Merlot £18.95 • 8 bottles over £20, 12 bottles under £20 • 6 by the glass (£2.75-£4.50)
PRICE GUIDE Fixed L £9.95 • Fixed D £24.50 • starter £4.50-£7.95 • main £12.95-£19.95 • dessert £4.50-£5.95 • coffee £2.50 • min/water £3.15 • Service included

PLACE: Set in pretty grounds, this country house has been extended to offer all the trappings of a modern hotel including a range of lounges, a leisure club and conference facilities.
FOOD: The split-level brasserie offers a wide-ranging menu to suit most tastes, featuring both hearty, comfort fare (pheasant with a black pudding and red wine casserole) and lighter fish and pasta dishes. Vegetarian menu available on request.
OUR TIP: Former family home of prime minister Stanley Baldwin
Chef: Stuart Cockayne **Owners:** Menzies Hotels Plc **Times:** 12-2.15/7-9.15 **Notes:** Vegetarian available, Smart Dress, Civ Wed 100 **Seats:** 100, Pr/dining room 20 **Smoking:** N/Sm in restaurant **Children:** Menu, Portions **Rooms:** 68 (68 en suite) ★★★★ **Directions:** M5 junct 6 and follow A449 towards Kidderminster. Take the B4193 sign posted Stourport Hotel, on right **Parking:** 250 **e-mail:** stourport@menzies-hotels.co.uk **web:** www.bookmenzies.com

TENBURY WELLS MAP 10 SO56
Cadmore Lodge
British, French
Secluded hotel with extensive grounds
☎ 01584 810044 Berrington Green, St Michaels WR15 8TQ
MENU GUIDE Smoked salmon platter, caper & lemon dressing • Beef stroganoff, scented rice • White chocolate truffle cake
WINE GUIDE ♀ Concha y Toro Chardonnay £11.50 • ♀ Georges Duboeuf £10.50 • 5 bottles over £20, 20 bottles under £20 • 2 by the glass (£2-£2.70)
PRICE GUIDE Fixed L £9-£11.50 • coffee £1.10 • min/water £1.10

PLACE: This hotel and country club's secluded lakeside setting – within a private estate deep in the Worcestershire countryside – proves quite the draw card. Interiors are colourful and cosy, and the country-style restaurant offers lake and valley views.
FOOD: Descriptions may be concise on the daily-changing menus, but they deliver simply cooked, traditional dishes of quality; utilising fresh local produce and careful presentation.
OUR TIP: Try the plums and fresh fruit from their own garden
Chef: Mark Griffiths, Wayne Rimmer **Owners:** Mr & Mrs J Weston **Times:** 12-2/7-9.15, Closed 25 Dec, closed L Mon **Notes:** Vegetarian available, Smart Dress, Civ Wed 100 **Seats:** 50, Pr/dining room 50 **Smoking:** N/Sm in restaurant, Air con **Children:** Menu, Portions **Rooms:** 15 (14 en suite) ★★ **Directions:** A4112 from Tenbury Wells to Leominster. 2m from Tenbury Wells, turn right opposite St Michaels Church **Parking:** 100 **e-mail:** info@cadmorelodge.co.uk **web:** www.cadmorelodge.co.uk

The Peacock Inn
International
Relaxed dining in ancient roadside inn
☎ 01584 810506 Worcester Rd, Boraston WR15 8LL
MENU GUIDE Deep-fried goats' cheese, apricot chutney • Sea bass, scallops, beurre blanc • Crème brûlée
PRICE GUIDE Food prices not confirmed for 2006. Please telephone for details

PLACE: Wood-panelling, beams and low ceilings ensure this ancient pub isn't short on character; it dates back to the 14th century and has acquired its own ghost over the years in the spectral form of a previous landlady.
FOOD: Popular with the locals, the sound cooking skills bring a modern touch to traditional British and French dishes with international influences.
OUR TIP: Popular so arrive early for a table
Chef: Eric Celton, James Vidler **Owners:** Mr J Vidler **Times:** 12-2.15/6.30-9.15 **Notes:** Vegetarian available **Seats:** 40 **Smoking:** N/Sm area **Children:** Menu, Portions **Rooms:** 4 (4 en suite) 🏠 **Directions:** On A456, 1m from Tenbury Wells towards Worcester **Parking:** 30 **e-mail:** jamesvidler@btconnect.com **web:** www.thepeacockinn.com

UPTON UPON SEVERN MAP 10 SO84
White Lion Hotel
British, Mediterranean
Lively modern menu at historic inn
☎ 01684 592551 21 High St WR8 0HJ
MENU GUIDE Monkfish & scallops skewered with rosemary, tomato & onion relish • Duck confit, plum & peppercorn compote • Iced raspberry & passionfruit parfait, vanilla cream & mini meringues
WINE GUIDE ♀ Chardonnay £13.75 • ♀ Merlot £13.75 6 bottles over £20, 33 bottles under £20 • 3 by the glass
PRICE GUIDE Fixed L £12.50 • starter £4-£7.50 • main £13.50-£17 • dessert £5 • coffee £1.40 • min/water £2.50 • Service optional

PLACE: Immortalised in Henry Fielding's 18th-century novel, *Tom Jones*, the White Lion dates back to 1510 and has been welcoming guests for nearly 500 years. The intimate candlelit restaurant is decorated in deep red and gold with traditional table settings. Staff are relaxed, attentive and friendly.
FOOD: Modern British cooking with some Mediterranean/European influences – Welsh rarebit comes with crispy pancetta and a fried quail's egg.
OUR TIP: Strong Civil War associations
Chef: Jon Lear, Richard Thompson **Owners:** Mr & Mrs Lear **Times:** 12-2/7-9.15, Closed 1 Jan **Notes:** Set price L Sun only, Vegetarian available **Seats:** 45 **Smoking:** N/Sm in restaurant **Children:** Portions **Rooms:** 13 (11 en suite) ★★★ **Directions:** From A422 take A38 towards Tewkesbury. After 8m take B4104 for 1m, after bridge turn left to hotel **Parking:** 16 **e-mail:** info@whitelionhotel.biz **web:** www.whitelionhotel.biz

 denotes restaurants that place particular emphasis on making the most of local ingredients.

WORCESTER MAP 10 SO85

Brown's Restaurant
Classical

Popular waterside restaurant

☎ 01905 26263 The Old Cornmill, South Quay WR1 2JJ

MENU GUIDE Carpaccio of tuna, tapenade, lemon & basil oil • Pan-fried saddle of venison, braised red cabbage • Baked rice pudding with roasted rhubarb

WINE GUIDE ♀ Laroche Chardonnay £22 • ♀ Louis Latour Fleurie • 80 bottles over £20, 30 bottles under £20 • 6 by the glass (£4.95-£6.95)

PRICE GUIDE Fixed D £33.50 • starter £4.95-£8.25 • main £9.50-£16.95 • dessert £5.50 • coffee £2.50 • min/water £3.50 • Service included

PLACE: Set in a former Victorian corn mill, with large picture windows overlooking the river Severn, this restaurant has a modern, fresh, airy decor with plenty of natural light.

FOOD: The classically based menu offers modern British dishes with classical French influences using quality ingredients. Expect mains such as breast of Gressingham duck, leg meat dumplings and red wine sauce.

OUR TIP: Opposite the Worcestershire county cricket ground
Chef: Gary Phipps **Owners:** Mr R Everton **Times:** 12.30-1.45/7.30-9.45, Closed 1wk Xmas, Mon, closed L Sat, closed D Sun **Notes:** Vegetarian available, Dress Restrictions, Smart casual preferred **Seats:** 110
Smoking: N/Sm in restaurant **Children:** Portions **Directions:** From M5 junct 7 to city centre. At lights turn into Copenhagen St, car park adjacent to restaurant **Parking:** Large car park adjacent to the restaurant

Glass House Restaurant
British, International

Nothing old school about these dinners

☎ 01905 611120 Church St WR1 2RH

MENU GUIDE Air-dried Shropshire ham, creamed goats' cheese • Braised lamb neck fillet, bubble & squeak • Glass House puddings in miniature

WINE GUIDE ♀ Les Bories Sauvignon Blanc £13.75 • ♀ Rocheburg Cinsault Pinotage £14.50 • 6 bottles over £20, 18 bottles under £20 • 8 by the glass (£3.50-£4.75)

PRICE GUIDE Fixed L £10 • starter £4.50-£6.95 • main £14.50-£18.50 • dessert £4.75-£10.95 • coffee £1.75 • min/water £2.60 • Service optional • Group min 8 service 10%

PLACE: Former school house that once belonged to Worcester's foremost grammar, with records dating back to around 1598; its town centre location, polished floors and stained-glass windows make it an atmospheric location. A cosy brick vaulted cellar bar is ideal for an aperitif, and a flagged courtyard offers alfresco dining in summer.

FOOD: Contemporary British cooking treats quality ingredients with care, producing consistently good results. Fresh fish has its own menu, delivered daily from Fowey in Cornwall.

OUR TIP: The 'quick' lunch menu delivers the same quality
Chef: Calum MacCrimmon **Owners:** Brandon Weston, Calum MacCrimmon **Times:** 12-2/6.30-10, Closed Xmas, 2 wks Jan, Sun
Notes: Vegetarian available **Seats:** 42 **Smoking:** N/Sm in restaurant, Air con **Children:** Portions **Directions:** Off north end of High St, next to St withuns church **Parking:** St. Martins Multi Storey
e-mail: Brandon.Weston@talk21.com
web: www.theglasshouse.co.uk

YORKSHIRE, EAST RIDING OF

BEVERLEY MAP 17 TA03

The Manor House
British

City style in a country-house setting

☎ 01482 881645 Northlands, Walkington HU17 8RT

MENU GUIDE Tempura of tiger prawns, aubergine caviar Venison medallions, celeriac purée • Trio of crème brûlée

WINE GUIDE ♀ Pouilly Fumé Château de Tracy £32.50 • ♀ Château La Tour St Bonnet £28.50 • 31 bottles over £20, 27 bottles under £20 • 4 by the glass (£3.50-£6)

PRICE GUIDE Fixed L £10.95-£12.95 • Fixed D £18.95 • coffee £2.50 • min/water £3 • Service optional

PLACE: Two very different dining rooms – the elegant Blue Room with its silk walls and crystal chandeliers, and the conservatory overlooking the terrace and gardens – but the same fine dining experience. This Victorian country manor house makes an impressive destination.

FOOD: Inspired cooking from a talented team that stands out from the crowd. Prime ingredients may be behind this restaurant's success, but the technical skill that converts them into superb creations (check out the roast cod with brioche herb crust, brown shrimp and Nero risotto) lift it into another league. One to watch.

OUR TIP: Be sure to book so you don't miss out
Chef: Neil Armstrong **Owners:** Ann Pickering **Times:** 11.30-2.30/7-9.15, Closed L Sat, closed D Sun **Notes:** Set price (A L C) £34.00, Sun lunch 3 courses £18.95, Vegetarian available, Smart Dress, Civ Wed 70 **Seats:** 60, Pr/dining room 30 **Smoking:** N/Sm in restaurant **Children:** Min 12 yrs, Portions **Rooms:** 7 (7 en suite) ★★ **Directions:** 4m SW off B1230 **Parking:** 30 **e-mail:** info@walkingtonmanorhouse.co.uk **web:** www.walkingtonmanorhouse.co.uk

Tickton Grange Hotel
British

Country-house hotel with exciting food

☎ 01964 543666 Tickton HU17 9SH

MENU GUIDE Langoustine tarragon & lemongrass salad • Beef medallions, foie gras ravioli • Rhubarb assiette

WINE GUIDE ♀ Caprice VDP Sauvignon Blanc £13.50 • ♀ Caprice VDP Merlot £13.50 • 29 bottles over £20, 34 bottles under £20 • 8 by the glass (£3.25-£4.75)

PRICE GUIDE Fixed L £15-£17 • Fixed D £35-£40 • starter £5-£10 • main £15-£20 • dessert £5-£10 • coffee £2.50 • min/water £3.50 • Service optional

PLACE: This charming Georgian country-house hotel has four acres of private grounds and attractive gardens. There is a comfortable library lounge for pre-dinner drinks and a newly refurbished elegant restaurant with marble fireplace overlooking the gardens. Helpful, welcoming service.

FOOD: Modern British in style proudly showcasing local and seasonal produce such as starters of Whitby crab or local wood pigeon and main courses of Hutton Cranswick lamb or Hornsea guinea fowl. Combinations are imaginative and skilfully executed. The four-course fixed-price dinner includes a glass of Taittinger champagne to start.

OUR TIP: Convenient for Humberside airport

continued

BEVERLEY continued MAP 17 TA03

Chef: David Nowell **Owners:** Mr & Mrs Whymant **Times:** 12-2/7-9.30
Notes: Fixed D 4 courses, Vegetarian available, Smart Dress, Civ Wed 150
Seats: 45, Pr/dining room 20 **Smoking:** N/Sm in restaurant
Children: Menu, Portions **Rooms:** 17 (17 en suite) ★★★
Directions: From Beverley take A1035 towards Bridlington. After 3m hotel
on left, just past Tickton **Parking:** 75 **e-mail:** info@ticktongrange.co.uk
web: www.ticktongrange.co.uk

WILLERBY MAP 17 TA03

⑧⑧ Willerby Manor Hotel

British, Mediterranean

Fine dining in modern, comfortable surroundings

☎ 01482 652616 Well Ln HU10 6ER

MENU GUIDE Beef carpaccio • Confit pork belly • Passionfruit
brûlée

WINE GUIDE ♀ Portal del Alto Sauvignon Blanc
£12.75 • ♥ Santa Martha Cabernet Sauvignon £12.60 • 8 bottles
over £20, 23 bottles under £20 • 4 by the glass (£3.70-£4.70)

PRICE GUIDE Fixed D £20.50 • starter £4.40-£5.60 • main
£11.75-£14 • dessert £4.10-£4.50 • coffee £1.80 • min/water
£3.20 • Service optional

PLACE: A smart country-house hotel with plenty of original
features intact, set in extensive grounds including a renowned
rose garden. A choice of eating styles includes the bar and
brasserie, though the really fine dining is the preserve of the
discreet, stylish Icon Restaurant.
FOOD: Excitingly combined ingredients – think potato, onion and
feta cheese soup, or duck breast and grape chutney – yield
delicate flavours that don't disguise their natural origins in this
modern European menu. The skilful cooking extends to tempting
desserts like dark chocolate torte with clotted cream.
OUR TIP: Don't miss the home-smoked chicken
Chef: David Roberts, Ben Olley **Owners:** Alexandra Townend
Times: 12.30/7-9.30, Closed 1st wk Jan, last 2 wks Aug, BHs, Sun, closed L
Mon-Sat, closed D Sun **Notes:** Vegetarian available, Civ Wed 300
Seats: 40, Pr/dining room 40 **Smoking:** N/Sm in restaurant, Air con
Children: Portions **Rooms:** 51 (51 en suite) ★★★
Directions: M62/A63, follow signs for Humber Bridge, then signs for
Beverley until Willerby Shopping Park. Hotel signed from rdbt next to
McDonald's **Parking:** 200 **e-mail:** willerbymanor@bestwestern.co.uk
web: www.willerbymanor.co.uk

YORKSHIRE, NORTH

ALDWARK MAP 19 SE46

⑧⑧ Aldwark Manor

British, European

*Contemporary cooking in 19th-century manor
house*

☎ 01347 838146 YO61 1UF

MENU GUIDE Risotto of smoked haddock, saffron &
parmesan • Roast breast of chicken with celeriac
fondant • Grand Marnier parfait

WINE GUIDE ♀ Hardys Chardonnay £16.25 • ♥ Hardys Shiraz
£16.25 • 64 bottles over £20, 30 bottles under £20 • 12 by the
glass (£4.10-£7.85)

PRICE GUIDE Fixed L £18.95 • Fixed D £32.50 • min/water
£3.95 • Service optional

PLACE: This rambling 19th-century manor is set in peaceful
scenic grounds with an 18-hole golf course, and the River Ure
meandering through it. The modern contemporary restaurant,
done up with stylish modern paintings, has a bright and airy
feel. The service is professional and attentive without being
obtrusive.
FOOD: The enthusiastic kitchen uses quality local produce to
good effect producing well-conceived and unusual dishes with
clean flavours. The cooking is simple, with good saucing and
accurate timing.
OUR TIP: Stay the weekend and sample the excellent spa and
golf course
Chef: David Spencer **Owners:** Marston Hotels **Times:** 12-2.30/7-9.30
Notes: Vegetarian available, Dress Restrictions, No trainers, Civ Wed 140
Seats: 90, Pr/dining room 150 **Smoking:** N/Sm in restaurant, Air con
Children: Menu, Portions **Rooms:** 60 (60 en suite) ★★★★
Directions: From A1, A59 towards Green Hammerton, then B6265
towards Little Ouseburn, follow signs Aldwark Bridge/Manor. A19 through
Linton on Ouse to Aldwark **Parking:** 200
e-mail: reception@aldwarkmanor.co.uk
web: www.aldwarkmanor.co.uk

ARNCLIFFE MAP 18 SD97

⑧⑧ Amerdale House Hotel

European

*Enjoyable dining in the beautiful
Yorkshire Dales*

☎ 01756 770250 BD23 5QE

MENU GUIDE Grilled black pudding, herb mustard
sauce • Roast leg of lamb, garlic & rosemary • Yorkshire
curd tart, liquorice ice cream

WINE GUIDE ♀ Jordan Chardonnay £13.50 • ♥ Logan Merlot
£13.95 • 46 bottles over £20, 54 bottles under £20 • 2 by the
glass (£2.95)

PRICE GUIDE Fixed D fr £34.50 • min/water £2.50 • Service
included

PLACE: Charming Victorian country-house hotel set in the steep-
sided valley of the River Skirfare, in what must be one of the
most delightful villages in the Yorkshire Dales. The dining room is
elegantly furnished with Regency-style tables and scroll-back
chairs. Service is relaxed and friendly.
FOOD: The emphasis is on local ingredients – superb local lamb
and old breed pork from Colin Robinson in Grassington, and
Dales cheeses. The menu is concise and restrained, avoiding
fussiness or over saucing to allow the true flavours of the
produce to come through.
OUR TIP: Impressive wine list with pudding wines by the glass
Chef: Nigel Crapper **Owners:** Paula & Nigel Crapper **Times:** 7.30-8.30,
Closed mid Nov-mid Mar, closed L all week **Seats:** 24 **Smoking:** N/Sm
in restaurant **Children:** Min 8 yrs **Rooms:** 11 (11 en suite) ★★
Directions: On the outskirts of village **Parking:** 20
e-mail: amerdalehouse@littondale.com
web: www.amerdalehouse.co.uk

One Rosette Excellent local restaurants
serving food prepared with care,
understanding and skill, using good quality
ingredients. These restaurants stand out in
their local area. Of the total number of
establishments with Rosettes around 50%
have one Rosette.

continued

ASENBY MAP 19 SE37

◎◎ Crab and Lobster Restaurant

French, British 🐟

Character restaurant serving mainly seafood

☎ 01845 577286 Dishforth Rd YO7 3QL

MENU GUIDE Baked queenie scallops with gruyère & garlic • Sea bass fillet with crab & pancetta • Lemon pannacotta with poached strawberries

WINE GUIDE ♀ Georges Duboeuf £15 • ♀ Georges Duboeuf Cabernet Sauvignon £15 • 18 bottles over £20, 12 bottles under £20 • 13 by the glass (£2.70-£3.20)

PRICE GUIDE Fixed L fr £11 • Fixed D fr £29.50 • starter £6-£8.75 • main £10.50-£17.50 • dessert £6-£7.95 • coffee £2.25 • min/water £1.50 • Service optional

PLACE: Reputedly one of the only two thatched pubs in North Yorkshire, the Crab and Lobster is a slightly unconventional restaurant set in seven acres of grounds. The walls are decorated with an eccentric mix of music, racing and food memorabilia. **FOOD:** As the name suggests seafood dominates, although the meat dishes are equally well executed. A clever menu marries traditional and more unusual, but well-conceived dishes with flair, ensuring there is something for everyone. **OUR TIP:** Check out the Marilyn Monroe themed men's room! **Chef:** Steve Dean **Owners:** Vimac Leisure **Times:** 12-2.30/7-9.30 **Notes:** Vegetarian available, Civ Wed 24 **Seats:** 55, Pr/dining room 24 **Smoking:** N/Sm in restaurant **Children:** Portions **Directions:** From A19/A168 take A167, drive through Topcliffe follow signs for A1. On left, 8m from Northallerton **Parking:** 80 **e-mail:** enquiries@crabandlobster.co.uk **web:** www.crabandlobster.com

AUSTWICK MAP 18 SD76

◎ The Austwick Traddock

Classic, Modern British **NEW**

Inviting country-house with classic cooking

☎ 015242 51224 LA2 8BY

MENU GUIDE Moules marinère • Rack of lamb hot pot • Belgian dark chocolate ganache

PLACE: A friendly, elegant restaurant in a family-run, country-house hotel with plenty of charm and character. The sympathetic decor retains plenty of original Georgian features. A large wine rack dominates one wall of the restaurant, whose tables are candlelit in the evenings. **FOOD:** Classic and modern British cooking with an emphasis on organic and locally sourced ingredients. Don't miss the selection of local cheeses. **OUR TIP:** A perfect base for walking or touring **Times:** Telephone for details **e-mail:** info@austwicktraddock.co.uk **web:** www.austwicktraddock.co.uk

BILBROUGH MAP 16 SE54

◎◎ The Three Hares Country Inn

British, French 🐟

Country pub with good restaurant food

☎ 01937 832128 Main St YO23 3PH

MENU GUIDE Whitby fish cake, parsley sauce • Nidderdale lamb hotpot, pickled red cabbage • Rhubarb soup, liquorice mousse

WINE GUIDE ♀ J Moreau Petit Chablis • ♀ Houghton Shiraz • 10 bottles over £20, 16 bottles under £20

PRICE GUIDE Starter £4.75-£9.95 • main £9.50-£16.95 • dessert £4.95-£6.50 • coffee £2.95 • Service optional

PLACE: The only pub in the village, stone-built and atmospheric, with beams, stone floors and modern rural decor. Four rooms are divided into bar and restaurant areas, the latter more intimate, with stylish tableware and contemporary pictures. Service is relaxed and attentive. **FOOD:** The same menu runs through all areas: a carte supplemented by daily specials. Food is modern British with influences from France, Spain and Italy, following the seasons of the year with quality supplies. A choice of dishes from the grill includes rib-eye Yorkshire beef and speciality sausages. **OUR TIP:** Sunday brunch 11am until 4pm **Chef:** Nick Robinson **Owners:** Charles Oliver **Times:** 12-2/7-9, Closed 2 wks at start of year, Mon (ex BHs), closed D Sun **Notes:** Vegetarian available **Seats:** 34, Pr/dining room 16 **Smoking:** N/Sm in restaurant **Children:** Portions **Directions:** From York take A64 towards Leeds and follow signs for Bilbrough on right **Parking:** 35 **e-mail:** info@thethreehares.co.uk **web:** www.thethreehares.co.uk

England

BOLTON ABBEY MAP 19 SE05

⚜⚜⚜ Devonshire Arms Country House Hotel *see below*

BOROUGHBRIDGE MAP 19 SE36

⚜⚜ The Dining Room

British, European

Formal dining in relaxed surroundings

☎ 01423 326426 20 St James Square YO51 9AR

MENU GUIDE Lightly spiced king prawns • Wild mushroom ravioli, Parmesan cream • Malted crème brûlée, bitter chocolate sorbet

WINE GUIDE ♀ Chardonnay £14.95 • ♀ Rioja £18.95 • 40 bottles over £20, 40 bottles under £20 • 8 by the glass (£3.95)

PRICE GUIDE Fixed L £15-£20 • Fixed D £26.95 • starter £5-£6 • main £15 • dessert £5-£6 • coffee £2.50 • min/water £3 Service included

PLACE: Upstairs a comfortable lounge and bar is in contrast to the bright and modern dining room, with its muted creams offset by colourful paintings.

FOOD: There is nothing restrained about the cooking, where tried and trusted menu choices are spiced up with interesting accompaniments: an onion marmalade with chargrilled fillet of beef, and lightly curried leeks with fillet of halibut, perhaps, and a Bacardi lime breezer sorbet served with a glazed lemon tart.

OUR TIP: Enjoy your coffee by the fire

Chef: Christopher Astley **Owners:** Mr & Mrs C Astley **Times:** 12-2/7-9.30, Closed 25 Dec, 10 days Apr, 10 days Sept, Mon, closed L Tue-Sat, closed D Sun **Notes:** Vegetarian available, Smart Dress **Seats:** 32

continued

The Dining Room

Smoking: N/Sm in restaurant **Children:** Min 3 yrs, Portions
Directions: A1(M), Boroughbridge junct, sign to town. Opposite fountain in the town square **Parking:** On street/Private on request
e-mail: thediningrooms@wanadoo.co.uk

BOLTON ABBEY MAP 19 SE05

Devonshire Arms Country House Hotel

British, French

Beautiful country-house hotel fine dining

☎ 01756 710441 BD23 6AJ

MENU GUIDE Boudin of corn-fed chicken, girolles, beetroot Venison loin, choucroute, caramelised apples, ravioli of black pudding • Crème brûlée, almond sablé, apple sorbet

WINE GUIDE ♀ Malborough Gravitas Sauvignon Blanc ♀ Vina Leyda Rafael Urrejola Pinot Noir • 1950 bottles over £20, 100 bottles under £20 • 13 by the glass (£3.90-£11.75)

PRICE GUIDE Food prices not confirmed for 2006. Please telephone for details

PLACE: With stunning views of the Wharfedale countryside, this beautiful country-estate hotel, owned by the Duke and Duchess of Devonshire, dates back to the 17th century and has the feel of a private country mansion. Devonshire family oils adorn lounges (with open winter fires and comfy sofas) and the fine dining Burlington Restaurant where antiques and immaculately dressed tables cut a formal edge. And, while the main dining room is classic country house, the adjoining conservatory comes with

views over the Italian garden, wicker chairs and stone floor. Staff are professional, friendly and have natural flair. (The Devonshire Brasserie provides a lighter, informal option.)

FOOD: Michael Wignall's elegant dishes of modern French influence display accomplished technical skills and intricate but clear-flavoured style. Excellent fresh produce is either carefully sourced from suppliers, or comes direct from the estate and kitchen garden. Expect a cannon of lamb with wilted spinach, braised onions and ceps, and a classic hot chocolate fondant with milk ice cream on the dinner carte, which is backed by the nine-course tasting Menu Prestige. A knowledgeable sommelier is at hand to navigate the vast global wine list.

OUR TIP: A walk along the River Wharfe to Bolton Abbey helps work up an appetite

Chef: Michael Wignall **Owners:** Duke & Duchess of Devonshire **Times:** 12.30-2.30/7-10, Closed Mon, closed L Tue-Sat **Notes:** Coffee inc Tasting menu, Sun L available, Vegetarian available, No jeans, no trainers, Civ Wed 90 **Seats:** 70, Pr/dining room 90 **Smoking:** N/Sm in restaurant **Children:** Menu **Rooms:** 41 (41 en suite) ★★★ **Directions:** On B6160 to Bolton Abbey, 250 yds N of junct with A59 rdbt junction **Parking:** 100 **e-mail:** reservations@thedevonshirearms.co.uk **web:** www.devonshirehotels.co.uk

BUCKDEN MAP 18 SD97

The Buck Inn Hotel

Classic

Delightful old-fashioned English inn with hospitality and food to match

☎ 01756 760228   BD23 5JA

MENU GUIDE Chicken & ham terrine • Confit of Dales lamb hock on creamed mash, redcurrant & rosemary sauce • Apple & honey tart Tatin

PRICE GUIDE Food prices not confirmed for 2006. Please telephone for details

PLACE: Very friendly and helpful staff makes a visit to this traditional Georgian inn a pleasure. The beamed Courtyard restaurant has bags of character.

FOOD: The chef demonstrates impressive skills creating delicious, perfectly timed dishes, using quality local produce; plenty of game, lamb and cheese in evidence. Presentation is a strong point too – so not only is the food fresh, vibrant and full of flavour, it looks good as well.

OUR TIP: Many dishes also feature on blackboard menu in bar
Times: 6.30-9, Closed L all week   **Rooms:** 14 (14 en suite) ★★
Directions: In centre of village   **e-mail:** thebuckinn@buckden.yorks.net
web: www.thebuckinn.com

BURNSALL MAP 19 SE06

Red Lion Hotel

British

Picturesque inn serving hearty favourites

☎ 01756 720204   By the Bridge BD23 6BU

MENU GUIDE Smoked haddock florentine • Beef & kidney pie in Theakstons ale gravy • Apple & blackberry crumble, custard

WINE GUIDE ♀ Bourgogne Blanc £13.50 • ♟ Mouchac/ Bordeaux £14.25 • 18 bottles over £20, 66 bottles under £20 ♦1 by the glass (£2.95-£6.50)

PRICE GUIDE Fixed L £18.95 • Fixed D £29.95 • starter £4.25-£8.50 • main £9.50-£18.95 • dessert £5-£6.95 • coffee £2 • min/water £2.95 • Service optional

PLACE: This ancient hostelry sits beside the picturesque River Wharfe in the tiny Dales village of Burnsall. Dine in the cosy surroundings of the oak-panelled bar, or more formally in the restaurant overlooking the green and maypole.

FOOD: A tempting modern British menu that makes the most of local lamb and beef, with game coming fresh from nearby estates. You might tuck into pot-roast pork with baked apple, or calves' liver with bubble and squeak.

OUR TIP: Very popular so book at weekends
Chef: James Rowley   **Owners:** Andrew & Elizabeth Grayshon   **Times:** 12-2.30/6-9.30   **Notes:** Vegetarian available, Smart casual, Civ Wed 100
Seats: 50, Pr/dining room 90   **Smoking:** N/Sm in restaurant
Children: Menu, Portions   **Rooms:** 11 (11 en suite) ★★
Directions: 10m from Skipton on B6160   **Parking:** 70
e-mail: redlion@daelnet.co.uk   **web:** www.redlion.co.uk

CRATHORNE MAP 19 NZ40

Crathorne Hall Hotel

British, European

Edwardian country house with impressive cuisine

☎ 01642 700398   TS15 0AR

MENU GUIDE Seared salmon on Caesar salad • Pan-fried Barbary duck, honeyed figs, braised cabbage • White chocolate truffle tart

WINE GUIDE ♀ Michel la Roche Chardonnay £21 • ♟ Deakin Estate Cabernet Sauvignon £20 • 60 bottles over £20, 20 bottles under £20 • 12 by the glass (£3.25-£5.75)

PRICE GUIDE Food prices not confirmed for 2006. Please telephone for details

PLACE: Former stately home set in its own private grounds with lovely views of the Leven valley and Cleveland hills. Ornate ceilings, imposing oil paintings and elegant antiques create an air of grandeur, but there is also a warmly welcoming feel. The Leven Restaurant is half panelled in mahogany and, at its focal point is a carved stone fireplace.

FOOD: Technically impressive food with modern presentation and very good quality ingredients, many sourced locally. The European menu offers a range of interesting dishes, but the simplest are the clear winners.

OUR TIP: Take a walk in the extensive grounds
Chef: Gary Edfon   **Owners:** Hand Picked Hotels   **Times:** 12.30-2.30/7-10
Notes: Vegetarian available, Civ Wed 120   **Seats:** 45, Pr/dining room 26
Smoking: N/Sm in restaurant   **Children:** Min 2 yrs D, Menu, Portions
Rooms: 37 (37 en suite) ★★★★   **Directions:** Off A19, 2m E of Yarm.
Access to A19 via A66 or A1, Thirsk   **Parking:** 80
e-mail: crathornehall@handpicked.co.uk
web: www.crathornehall.com

ESCRICK MAP 16 SE64

The Parsonage Country House Hotel

British, French

Country-house hotel serving classy cuisine

☎ 01904 728111   York Rd YO19 6LF

MENU GUIDE King scallops, creamed leeks • Salmon, mustard mash, wild mushroom fricassee • Belgian chocolate soufflé

PRICE GUIDE Fixed D fr £25 • starter £5-£9.50 • main fr £14.95 • dessert £5-£9.50 • coffee £2.50 • min/water £3.10

continued

continued

ESCRICK continued MAP 16 SE64

PLACE: Just a few miles outside York, this Victorian parsonage has been sympathetically restored and mixes period charm with all the facilities of a modern hotel.

FOOD: A tempting blend of adventurous modern dishes and old favourites, using locally sourced ingredients. Tuck into a lamb hotpot perhaps, with a redcurrant and port jus, or a more complex creation such as rarebit crusted halibut, with a ratatouille lasagne and parmesan vinaigrette.

OUR TIP: Enjoy afternoon tea

Chef: Neal Birtwell **Owners:** P Smith **Times:** 12-2/7-9, Closed L Sat **Notes:** Vegetarian available, Dress Restrictions, No jeans, Civ Wed 100 **Seats:** 50, Pr/dining room 20 **Smoking:** N/Sm in restaurant **Children:** Portions **Rooms:** 46 (46 en suite) ★★★ **Directions:** S from York on A19, Parsonage on right, 4m out of town in Escrick village **Parking:** 80 **e-mail:** sales@parsonagehotel.co.uk **web:** www.parsonagehotel.co.uk

GUISBOROUGH MAP 19 NZ61

⬡ Pinchinthorpe Hall

Modern British

Modern cooking using home-grown produce

☎ 01287 630200 Pinchinthorpe TS14 8HG

MENU GUIDE Seared king scallops & fried pancetta salad Pot-roast Helmsley partridge with chestnuts, prunes & Madeira sauce • Chocolate espresso pudding

WINE GUIDE ♀ Sacchetto Pinot Grigio £15.30 • ♥ Premium Vina Tarapaca Maipo Valley Merlot £15 • 25 bottles over £20, 35 bottles under £20 • 2 by the glass (£2.95)

PRICE GUIDE Fixed L £7.95 • Fixed D £15.95 • starter £4.75-£7.25 • main £12.95-£21.95 • dessert £3.95-£5.95 • coffee £1.85 • min/water £2.65 • Service optional

PLACE: Elegant 17th-century moated manor house whose Brewhouse Bistro serves award-winning cuisine with flair and creativity. Situated in North Yorkshire moors but within easy reach of industrial Teesside.

FOOD: Game and fish feature highly as local to the area. Many ingredients on the menu come from the Georgian kitchen garden. Cooking shows a twist of imagination, combining nostalgic dishes with modern trends.

OUR TIP: On-site organic micro-brewery with tours

Chef: Kevin Mulraney **Owners:** George Tinsley, John Warnock & Alison Foster **Times:** 12-5.30/5.30-10 **Notes:** Vegetarian available, Smart casual, Civ Wed 80 **Seats:** 45, Pr/dining room 40 **Smoking:** N/Sm in restaurant **Children:** Portions **Rooms:** 6 (6 en suite) 🏠 **Directions:** 10 miles S of Middlesborough **Parking:** 150 **e-mail:** nyb@pinchinthorpe.freeserve.co.uk **web:** www.pinchinthorpehall.co.uk

HAROME MAP 19 SE68

⬡⬡ *The Star Inn*

Modern British

Picture-postcard 14th-century thatched inn

☎ 01439 770397 YO62 5JE

MENU GUIDE Risotto of partridge, braised chestnuts, black trumpet mushrooms, hazelnut pesto • Wild turbot with Yorkshire Blue rarebit, salad of seared celery • Baked apple tarte Tatin, cheese ice cream

PRICE GUIDE Food prices not confirmed for 2006. Please telephone for details

PLACE: While this cosy family-run inn is clearly a quality operation, the accent is definitely on enjoyment. With ancient

continued

beams, leaning walls and a Mousey Thompson bar and bar furniture, the atmosphere is welcoming. There's a quirky attic-style coffee loft, an enchanting private dining room and a restaurant decorated with wine paraphernalia, and wine labels stuck all over the ceiling.

FOOD: Excellent quality fresh ingredients are simply prepared. Flavours burst on to the palate from a chef who combines prime ingredients with natural ease. Fish, mussels and Loch Fyne oysters feature strongly, as does local game.

OUR TIP: Excellent deli across the road

Times: 11.30-3/6.30-11, Closed 25 Dec, 2 wks spring, 1wk summer, BHs, Mon, closed D Sun **Directions:** From Helmsley take A170 towards Kirkbymoorside, after 0.5m turn right towards Harome. After 1.5m Inn is 1st building on right **web:** www.thestaratharome.co.uk

HARROGATE MAP 19 SE35

⬡⬡ The Boar's Head Hotel

British

Charmingly British setting and food

☎ 01423 771888 Ripley Castle Estate HG3 3AY

MENU GUIDE Sweet vine tomatoes stuffed with fromage frais and poached quails' eggs • Tournedos of pork fillet, fondant roots, scrumpy & thyme jus • Iced honey & Drambuie nougat

WINE GUIDE ♀ Concha y Toro Chardonnay £12.95 • ♥ Concha y Toro Merlot £12.95 • 100 bottles over £20, 30 bottles under £20 • 10 by the glass (£2.95-£6)

PRICE GUIDE Fixed L £15 • coffee £2.50 • min/water £3 • Service optional

PLACE: The Boar's Head is located in the private village belonging to Ripley castle, and was opened in 1990 by the castle's current occupiers Sir Thomas and Lady Ingilby, who also donated some of their paintings and furniture, giving this former coaching inn an aristocratic elegance.

FOOD: Inspired by modern, regional British food, the menu is imbued with inspiration both in presentation and flavour. You could expect perhaps Yorkshire beef fillet, oxtail mash, baby vegetables and Balmoral sauce.

OUR TIP: Specially prepared vegetarian selection

Chef: Marc Guilbert **Owners:** Sir Thomas Ingilby & Lady Ingilby **Times:** 12-2/7-9 **Notes:** Vegetarian available, Civ Wed 80 **Seats:** 40, Pr/dining room 40 **Smoking:** N/Sm in restaurant **Children:** Menu, Portions **Rooms:** 25 (25 en suite) ★★★ **Directions:** On A61 (Harrogate/Ripley road). In village centre **Parking:** 45 **e-mail:** reservations@boarsheadripley.co.uk **web:** www.boarsheadripley.co.uk

The AA Wine Awards recognise the finest wine lists in England, Scotland and Wales. For full details, see pages 14-15

The Clocktower at Rudding Park

International, British

Civilised hotel with excellent dining

☎ 01423 871350 Rudding Park Hotel, Rudding Park, Follifoot HG3 1JH

MENU GUIDE French onion soup • Venison, sloe gin sauce & dauphinoise potato • Chocolate baked Alaska

WINE GUIDE ♀ Sauvignon de Touraine Sauvignon Blanc £14.50 • ♀ Echeverria Chile Merlot £16 • 24 bottles over £20, 24 bottles under £20 • 12 by the glass (£3.75-£5.95)

PRICE GUIDE Starter £4.75-£8.95 • main £12-£19.50 • dessert £6.50 • coffee £3 • min/water £4.25 • Service included

PLACE: This modern hotel is set in the midst of this 200-year-old landscaped park. The modern dining room has bare wood tables with good quality settings and glassware. Large canvasses depicting vegetables fill the walls. Service is professional and attentive but still friendly. There's also a spacious and comfortable bar and lounge.

FOOD: Modern British dishes based on fresh, local and seasonal produce. Skilful preparation ensures satisfying and flavoursome dishes like roast pigeon breast with mushroom risotto or roast Nidderdale lamb shank.

OUR TIP: Take a round of golf on the renowned course

Chef: Stephanie Moon **Owners:** Simon Mackaness **Times:** 12-3/7-9.30 **Notes:** Vegetarian available, Dress Restrictions, Smart casual preferred, Civ wed 180 **Seats:** 160, Pr/dining room 250 **Smoking:** N/Sm in restaurant, air con **Children:** Menu, Portions **Rooms:** 50 (50 en suite) ★★★★ **Directions:** A61 at rdbt with A658 follow signs 'Rudding Park' **Parking:** 250 **e-mail:** sales@ruddingpark.com **Web:** www.ruddingpark.com

The Courtyard

Modern British

Attractive mews dining venue

☎ 01423 530708 1 Montpellier Mews HG1 2TQ

MENU GUIDE Goats' cheese & avocado torte • Confit duck leg, Asian risotto cake • Passionfruit pannacotta

PRICE GUIDE Food prices not confirmed for 2006. Please telephone for details

PLACE: This modern courtyard restaurant is tucked away in a cobbled mews in this popular Yorkshire resort. The interior is brightly coloured and well furnished; an ideal setting for summer dining.

FOOD: The menus comprise interesting dishes with some surprising combinations of texture and flavour. Expect local

The Courtyard

delicacies like Nidderdale beef, roast tomato and horseradish champ, beetroot relish and borderlaise sauce.

OUR TIP: Dine alfresco in the cobbled courtyard

Times: 12-2.30/6.30-9.30, Closed 25-26 Dec, 1 Jan, Sun

Directions: Telephone for directions

Dusty Miller

British, French

Inspired cooking in traditional alehouse

☎ 01423 780837 780065 Low-Laithe, Summerbridge HG3 4BU

MENU GUIDE Sautéed chicken livers, chutney brioche • Roast halibut, roasted Mediterranean vegetables • Rhubarb tartlet

WINE GUIDE ♀ Sauvignon Blanc £12.90 • 40 bottles over £20, 20 bottles under £20 • 6 by the glass (£3.50)

PRICE GUIDE Fixed D £24.90 • starter £4.90-£12.90 • main £22 • dessert £4.90 • coffee £2 • Service optional

PLACE: Covered in ivy, this old ex-alehouse was built for 19th-century railway workers. The lounge area has a clubby feel to it emphasised by the open fires in winter and deep armchairs and sofas. The dining room has an informal atmosphere despite its crisp white table linen and efficient service, and there are good views down the valley.

FOOD: This is a highly skilled kitchen where best quality, local, seasonal produce such as Whitby crab are used creatively in a display of interesting and innovative combinations. Flavours are clear and timing exact.

OUR TIP: Canapés alone make the visit worthwhile

Chef: Brian Dennison **Owners:** Brian & Elizabeth Dennison **Times:** 7-11, Closed 1 wk Jul, 24-26 Dec, 1 Jan, Sun, Mon, closed L all week **Notes:** Fixed D coffee and water incl., Vegetarian available **Seats:** 28, Pr/dining room 18 **Smoking:** N/Sm in restaurant **Children:** Min 9 yrs, Portions **Directions:** On B6165, 10m from Harrogate **Parking:** 7

The Best Use of Seafood sponsored by Seafish In conjunction with Seafish, the Sea Fish Industry Authority, we have sought out restaurants that make the most of seafood on their menus. In addition to the four country award winners (see page 9), look out for the seafish symbol throughout the book; this denotes restaurants serving a good range of fish and shellfish dishes, where the accent is firmly on freshness.

continued

England

HARROGATE continued MAP 19 SE35

🏨 Harrogate Brasserie Hotel
British, French, Mediterranean
Relaxed venue, informal dining experience
☎ 01423 505041 28-30 Cheltenham Pde HG1 1DB

MENU GUIDE Chicken liver pâté, red onion marmalade • Baked joint of lamb • Brandy snap basket

PRICE GUIDE Food prices not confirmed for 2006. Please telephone for details

PLACE: A collector's dream, this lively brasserie is filled with artefacts, and richly decorated in bright colours. With its distinctly continental style and live jazz three times a week, it remains a popular destination.

FOOD: Traditional dishes with a hint of the Mediterranean sit alongside more adventurous choices on the carte, fixed dinner menu and blackboard specials. Everything is cooked to order by a well-trained team.

OUR TIP: Good for a night out with friends
Times: 12-2/6-10, Closed 26 Dec, 1 Jan, BHs, closed L all week (ex residents) **Rooms:** 17 (17 en suite) 🏠 **Directions:** In town centre, 500 mtrs from railway station, behind theatre, 150 mtrs from Conference Centre **e-mail:** info@brasserie.co.uk **web:** www.brasserie.co.uk

🏨 Hotel du Vin & Bistro
British, Mediterranean
Dynamic hotel with cracking food
☎ 01423 856800 Prospect Place HG1 1LB

MENU GUIDE Seared pigeon breast, Puy lentils • Roasted cod, saffron braised leeks • Apricot soufflé, rum & raisin ice cream

PRICE GUIDE Fixed L £12.50 • starter £6.95 • main £14.95 • dessert £6.75 • coffee £2.50 • min/water £3 • Service optional • Group service 10%

PLACE: A well-appointed townhouse overlooking the Stray – the town's green heart – is this boutique-hotel chain's northernmost outpost. The stylish, French-inspired bistro is decked out with wooden floors, wine-themed prints, black leather banquettes and smart table settings. A galaxy of wines and predominantly French staff fit the bill.

FOOD: The menu is a crisply scripted, appealing repertoire of uncomplicated, well-constructed combinations served with modern simplicity and flair. There's also a list of Simple Classics.

OUR TIP: The hot place in town; and the value two-course lunch includes a glass of wine
Chef: Gareth Longhurst **Owners:** Hotel du Vin Ltd **Times:** 12-1.45/6.30-9.45 **Notes:** Sun L £24.50, Vegetarian available, Civ Wed 75 **Seats:** 86, Pr/dining room 60 **Smoking:** No pipes, No cigars **Children:** Menu, Portions **Rooms:** 43 (43 en suite) ★★★★ **Directions:** From A1 follow signs for Harrogate & town centre. Take 3rd exit on Prince of Wales rdbt (marked town centre). Hotel is 400yds on right **Parking:** 33
e-mail: info@hotelduvin.com **web:** www.hotelduvin.com

🏨 Quantro
International
Fashionable restaurant and good value food
☎ 01423 503034 3 Royal Pde HG1 2SZ

MENU GUIDE Duck spring roll, plum compôte, Hoi sin sauce • Fillet steak, julienne chips, peppercorn sauce • Cointreau & milk chocolate bread & butter pudding

WINE GUIDE 12 bottles over £20, 35 bottles under £20 • 12 by the glass (£3.15-£6)

PRICE GUIDE Fixed L £9.95 • starter £3.90-£6.90 • main £10.20-£16.90 • dessert £3.90-£4.50 • coffee £1.60 • min/water £2.20 Service added but optional 10%

PLACE: An informal restaurant with lots of natural wood, and large windows overlooking the street. The chic aubergine and lime colour scheme goes down well with a trendy clientele.

FOOD: The food strikes a modern chord, whether with the light lunch menu – particularly popular – or carte offerings like monkfish and hot chilli squid with black ink tagliatelli and currie veloute, which are soundly cooked from quality components.

OUR TIP: Centrally located in town
Chef: Neil Ballinger **Owners:** T & K Burdekin **Times:** 12-2/6-10, Closed 25-26 Dec, 1 Jan, Sun, closed D Sun (ex trade shows) **Notes:** Vegetarian available, Smart Dress, Smart casual preferred **Seats:** 40 **Smoking:** N/Sm in restaurant, Air con **Children:** Min 8 **Directions:** Telephone for directions **Parking:** On street **e-mail:** info@quantro.co.uk **web:** www.quantro.co.uk

☕ Bettys Café Tea Rooms 1 Parliament Square
HG1 2QU ☎ 01423 502746 Winner of The Tea Guild Award of Excellence 2005.

HELMSLEY MAP 19 SE68

🏨 Feversham Arms Hotel
British, French
Friendly, stylish conservatory restaurant
☎ 01439 770766 1 High St YO62 5AG

MENU GUIDE Whitby crab salad • Goosnargh duck breast, caramelised chicory • Traditional rice pudding

WINE GUIDE 136 bottles over £20, 47 bottles under £20 • 10 by the glass (£3.75-£7.15)

PRICE GUIDE Fixed L £17.95 • Fixed D £32 • starter £9.50-£11.50 • main £16.50-£23 • dessert £8.50 • coffee £2.95 min/water £2.60 • Service optional

PLACE: A sumptuously decorated hotel, with an eclectic mix of comfortable modern furniture and artworks jostling with the older features. The dining room is in the stylish conservatory, where a friendly and relaxed atmosphere pervades.

FOOD: Uncomplicated dishes have a modern Anglo/French influence. Ingredients from the surrounding area feature strongly, particularly lamb, game and seafood fresh from Whitby.

OUR TIP: The cheeseboard is worth a visit
Chef: Charlie Lakin **Owners:** Simon Rhatigan **Times:** 12-2/7-9.30 **Notes:** ALC D only, Sun L £18.50, Vegetarian available, Dress Restrictions, Smart casual, No jeans, No T-shirts, Civ Wed 120 **Seats:** 50, Pr/dining room 25 **Smoking:** N/Sm in restaurant **Children:** Portions **Rooms:** 17 (17 en suite) ★★★ **Directions:** From A1(M) take A168 to Thirsk then A170 for 14 miles to Helmsley **Parking:** 50
e-mail: info@fevershamarmshotel.com
web: www.fevershamarmshotel.com

HETTON MAP 18 SD95

🌸🌸 The Angel Inn

British

One of the original gastro-pubs

☎ 01756 730263 BD23 6LT

MENU GUIDE Black pudding topped with foie gras • Goosnargh duck breast, red cabbage, prunes, thyme jus • Vanilla pannacotta

WINE GUIDE ♀ Domaine Picard Sauvignon Blanc £13.05 ♥ Michael Picard Merlot £13.05 • 200 bottles over £20, 50 bottles under £20 • 25 by the glass (£2.25-£4.96)

PRICE GUIDE Fixed D fr £15.95 • starter £5.25-£6.95 • main £10.95-£16.95 • dessert £4.50-£6.50 • coffee £2.75 • min/water £1.75 • Service optional

PLACE: A cosy, welcoming gastro-pub with original beams, exposed stonework, roaring log fires and its stylish restaurant. A very popular, bustling place that attracts families, farmers and foodies.

FOOD: The British cuisine served here has a strong Yorkshire influence, with plenty of local produce used and listed on the blackboard and carte menus. There is an international twist to some dishes, with Asian-style crisp belly of pork accompanied by the Northern English staple of black pudding. Seafood and fish is also a major strength.

OUR TIP: Visit the well-stocked 'Wine Cave' so you can take a bottle or two home

Chef: Bruce Elsworth **Owners:** Denis & Juliet Watkins **Times:** 12-3/6-10.30, Closed 25 Dec, 1 Jan & 1wk in Jan, closed L Mon-Sat, closed D Sun **Notes:** Vegetarian available, Dress Restrictions, Smart casual, Civ Wed 40 **Seats:** 56, Pr/dining room 40 **Children:** Portions **Rooms:** 5 (5 en suite) **Parking:** 50 **e-mail:** info@angelhetton.co.uk **web:** www.angelhetton.co.uk

HOVINGHAM MAP 19 SE67

🌸 Worsley Arms Hotel

British

Country-house dining in spa hotel

☎ 01653 628234 High St YO62 4LA

MENU GUIDE Duck liver parfait, port & orange sauce • Medallions of beef fillet, horseradish mash, Madeira sauce • Sticky toffee pudding

WINE GUIDE ♀ Olivier Merlin Mâcon Village Vielles Viones £19 • ♥ Rioja Vega Tinto Crianza £19.75 • 23 bottles over £20 6 by the glass (£3.50-£7.95)

PRICE GUIDE Fixed D £25-£30 • starter £4.50-£7.95 • main £13.95-£18.95 • dessert £4.50-£5.50 • coffee £2.50 • min/water £3.50 • Service optional

PLACE: An impressive stone-built hotel in the centre of the village overlooking the green. It has a country house-style interior with comfortable lounges, open fires and a traditional candlelit restaurant with quality table appointments.

FOOD: Sound cooking based on good quality local produce is at the heart of the kitchen's output.

OUR TIP: Food available in the Cricketers bar at lunchtime **Chef:** Jonathon Murray **Owners:** Mr & Mrs A Finn **Times:** 12-2/7-9.45, Closed L Mon-Sat **Notes:** Vegetarian available, Civ Wed 90 **Seats:** 70, Pr/dining room 40 **Smoking:** N/Sm in restaurant **Children:** Portions **Rooms:** 20 (20 en suite) ★★★ **Directions:** 20 mins N of York on the B1257, between Malton and Helmsley **Parking:** 30 **e-mail:** worsleyarms@aol.com **web:** www.worsleyarms.com

KIRKHAM MAP 19 SE76

🌸 Stone Trough Inn

British

Good quality gastro-pub dining

☎ 01653 618713 Kirkham Abbey, Whitwell on the Hill YO60 7JS

continued

KIRKHAM continued MAP 19 SE76

MENU GUIDE Venison, quince & pear vinaigrette • Calves' liver, black pudding, caramelised apple, damson jus • Banoffee cheesecake

PRICE GUIDE Starter £3.95-£7.50 • main £10.95-£16.50 • dessert £4.25 • coffee £1.95 • min/water £2.95 • Service optional

PLACE: Recently revamped by one of the BBC's *Home Front* programme team, this cosy country inn prides itself in offering a warm Yorkshire welcome to its guests. It's very popular, particularly at weekends.
FOOD: Quality gastro-pub fare created from good quality local produce. The modern British menu features tempting dishes such as beef with a horseradish rösti, or tenderloin of pork stuffed with brandied apricots.
OUR TIP: All meals served in the bar
Chef: Adam Richardson **Owners:** Adam & Sarah Richardson **Times:** 12-2.15/6.45-9.30, Closed 25 Dec, 3-7 Jan, Mon, closed L Tue-Sat, closed D Sun **Notes:** Sun L 3 courses £17.50, Vegetarian available **Seats:** 55
Smoking: N/Sm in restaurant **Children:** Menu, Portions
Directions: 1.5m off the A64, between York & Malton **Parking:** 100
e-mail: info@stonetroughinn.co.uk
web: www.stonetroughinn.co.uk

KNARESBOROUGH MAP 19 SE35

General Tarleton Inn
Regional British

Choice of dining rooms and quality cooking
☎ 01423 340284 Boroughbridge Rd, Ferrensby HG5 0PZ

MENU GUIDE Ham hock & foie gras terrine • Roast suckling pig loin • Dark chocolate timbale

WINE GUIDE ♀ Grauzan Sauvignon Blanc £12.95 • ♀ Echeverria Merlot £13.95 • 60 bottles over £20, 30 bottles under £20 • 10 by the glass (£2.20-£5)

PRICE GUIDE Fixed D £29.50 • min/water £3 • Service optional

PLACE: Handy for the A1 yet firmly located in the countryside is this 18th-century coaching inn that has also served as a granary. Inside it is brightly decorated and airy, with a modern conservatory, a formal dining room and a rustic bar/brasserie all serving meals in comfortable surroundings.
FOOD: An uncomplicated approach to cooking ensures that flavours are left intact, with the quality ingredients allowed to speak for themselves. A wide range of interesting dishes can be chosen from the carte, fixed-price menu (dining room only) and blackboard listings.
OUR TIP: Eating in the brasserie is the cosiest option
Chef: John Topham, Robert Ramsden **Owners:** John & Claire Topham
Times: 12-1.45/6-9.15, Closed L Mon-Sat, Closed D Sun **Notes:** Sun Fixed L menu £18.95, coffee incl. in price, Vegetarian available **Seats:** 64,

Pr/dining room 36 **Smoking:** N/Sm in restaurant **Children:** Menu, Portions **Rooms:** 14 (14 en suite) ★★★ **Directions:** From A1 junct 48 take A6055 towards Knaresborough. Continue for 4 mins, Inn is situated on right in the village of Ferrensby **Parking:** 40
e-mail: gti@generaltarleton.co.uk **web:** www.generaltarleton.co.uk

Restaurant 48
British, International

Simple cooking in relaxed hotel setting
☎ 01423 863302 Dower House Hotel, Bond End HG5 9AL

MENU GUIDE Game terrine, piccalilli • Pheasant, fondant potato, cranberry & chestnut relish • Wild blackberry & crème fraîche brûlée

WINE GUIDE ♀ Sandford Eagles Point Semillon Chardonnay £12.95 • ♀ Sandford Eagles Point Cabernet Merlot £12.95 20 bottles over £20, 46 bottles under £20 • 9 by the glass (£2.95-£4.95)

PRICE GUIDE Starter £3.95-£7.95 • main £9.95-£17.95 • dessert £5.50 • coffee £2.50 • min/water £3 • Service optional

PLACE: Now refurbished, the restaurant of this ivy-clad hotel has a relaxed and comfortable atmosphere and overlooks pretty gardens. There's a cosy bar or non-smoking lounge for aperitifs.
FOOD: Traditional dishes with a contemporary twist: pork encrusted with pistachios perhaps, or venison with a redcurrant glaze and blueberry drop scone. Lighter bar menu also available.
OUR TIP: A few minutes' walk from the beautiful Nidd Gorge
Chef: Michael Wright **Owners:** Mr M J Davies **Times:** 12-2/7-9.30
Notes: Vegetarian available, Dress Restrictions, No shorts, T-shirts. Smart casual preferred, Civ Wed 70 **Seats:** 100, Pr/dining room 20
Smoking: N/Sm in restaurant **Children:** Menu, Portions **Rooms:** 31 (31 en suite) ★★★ **Directions:** 2m W of Harrogate on A59. At Harrogate end of Knaresborough High Street **Parking:** 100
e-mail: enquiries@bwdowerhouse.co.uk
web: www.bwdowerhouse.co.uk

MALTON MAP 19 SE77

Burythorpe House Hotel
British

Elegant country-house hotel
☎ 01653 658200 Burythorpe YO17 9LB

MENU GUIDE Stilton-stuffed bread mushrooms • Roast duckling with orange & Grand Marnier sauce • Lemon tart

WINE GUIDE 5 by the glass (£2.95-£3.95)

PRICE GUIDE Fixed D £21 • coffee £2.20 • min/water £2.60 • Service optional

PLACE: Set in peaceful, wooded grounds, this family-run hotel dates back to 1750 and boasts a Regency façade and an oak-panelled dining room. Food can also be taken in the conservatory.
FOOD: The unpretentious, traditional selection of dishes on the menu might include smoked salmon and asparagus terrine with toast and pink mayonnaise as a starter, followed by a home-made steak and kidney suet pudding with rich gravy.
OUR TIP: Enjoy the peaceful location
Chef: Mr & Mrs T Austin **Owners:** Mr & Mrs T Austin **Times:** 12-2/7-9.30 **Notes:** Coffee price - cafetiere for 2, Vegetarian available **Seats:** 60, Pr/dining room 20 **Smoking:** N/Sm in restaurant, Air con **Children:** Min 7 yrs, Menu, Portions **Rooms:** 16 (16 en suite) ★★★ **Directions:** Edge of Burythorpe village, 4 miles S of Malton **Parking:** 30
e-mail: reception@burythorpehousehotel.com
web: www.burythorpehousehotel.com

continued

MARTON MAP 19 SE78

The Appletree Country Inn
British **⇥NEW**

Delicious quirky food in cosy gastro-pub

☎ 01751 731457   YO62 6RD

MENU GUIDE Grilled fig & cob nut salad • Suckling pig, pork & apricot casserole • Marbled chocolate pyramid

WINE GUIDE ♀ Oyster Bay Sauvignon Blanc £15 • ♀ Hardys Captain's Table Shiraz Cabernet Sauvignon £11 • 32 bottles over £20, 62 bottles under £20 • 13 by the glass (£3-£5.50)

PRICE GUIDE Starter £3.90-£6.50 • main £9-£15 • dessert £3.50-£5.50 • Service optional

PLACE: A lovely little dining pub in a former farm, full of character and set in a tiny village. The dining room was once a piggery, but a tasteful restoration, plus candles and open fires in winter, have produced a great ambience. There is also a relaxing coffee lounge filled with huge squashy sofas.

FOOD: A passion for cooking and an inventive mind bring an air of excitement to the menus, with lots of home-grown produce leading to interesting combinations.

OUR TIP: Visit the foodie shop counter

Chef: TJ Drew **Owners:** TJ & Melanie Drew **Times:** 12-2/6.30-9.30, closed Xmas, 2 wks January, Mon-Tue **Notes:** Mineral water incl., vegetarian available **Seats:** 24, Pr/dining room 8 **Smoking:** N/Sm in restaurant **Children:** Portions **Directions:** 2m from Kirkbymoorside on A170 towards Pickering, turn right to Marton **Parking:** 30

e-mail: appletreeinn@supanet.com

web: www.appletreeinn.co.uk

MASHAM MAP 19 SE28

◉◉◉ **Swinton Park** *see below*

NORTHALLERTON MAP 19 SE39

The Three Tuns
Modern European

Wholesome cooking in rustic restaurant with rooms

☎ 01609 883301   9 South End, Osmotherley DL6 3BN

MENU GUIDE Pigeon breast, peppered blueberry compote • Dover sole, tartare salsa • Rhubarb pudding, nutmeg ice cream

continued

MASHAM MAP 19 SE28

Swinton Park

British, European

Elegant and atmospheric luxury castle hotel

☎ 01765 680900   HG4 4JH

MENU GUIDE Crab tian, sautéed scallops • Venison, faggot, parsnip purée, artichoke, bay leaf jus • Lemon tart, raspberry sorbet

WINE GUIDE ♀ Mudhouse Sauvignon Blanc £17 • ♀ Los Vascos Cabernet Sauvignon £15.50 • 131 bottles over £20, 50 bottles under £20 • 13 by the glass (£3.65-£5.50)

PRICE GUIDE Fixed L £14 • Fixed D £35-£49 • coffee £3 min/water £3.95 • Service optional

PLACE: A 17th-century castle set in a 200-acre estate, complete with turrets, gatehouse and sweeping drive, is the romantic setting for a sophisticated, formal, yet relaxing dining experience. Crisp white linen, subtle candlelight and garden views befit the professional service.

FOOD: Superb ingredients, much coming from the Swinton estate; particularly game, herbs and vegetables. Balanced flavours, seasonality and immaculate presentation illustrate the kitchen's technical skill. The approach is modern British, delivered via appealing fixed-price menus, though dotted with a few supplements. Excellent wine list.

OUR TIP: Try the upgraded spa and new treatment rooms

Chef: Andrew Burton **Owners:** Mr & Mrs Cunliffe-Lister **Times:** 12.30-2/7-9.30 **Notes:** Vegetarian available, Smart Dress, Civ Wed 100 **Seats:** 60, Pr/dining room 20 **Rooms:** 30 (30 en suite) ★★★★ **Directions:** On B6267, follow brown signs for hotel **Parking:** 80 **e-mail:** enquiries@swintonpark.com **web:** www.swintonpark.com

England

NORTHALLERTON continued MAP 19 SE39

The Three Tuns

PRICE GUIDE Food prices not confirmed for 2006. Please telephone for details

PLACE: Pretty Osmotherley lies on the flanks of the Cleveland Hills and this popular restaurant with rooms stands among 17th-century stone cottages on the main street. The modern, elegantly designed dining room has a rustic feel with stone floors, lots of bare wood, log fire and intimate evening candlelight.
FOOD: The imaginative menu is an assured blend of modern British and European influences. Good, wholesome cooking with some interesting twists to classic dishes.
OUR TIP: Lighter options also available at lunchtimes
Times: 12-2.30/5.30-9.30 **Directions:** Telephone for directions
web: www.the3tuns.net

Bettys Café Tea Rooms 188 High St DL7 8LF
☎ 01609 775154 Winner of The Tea Guild Award of Excellence 2005.

PICKERING MAP 19 SE78

⊛ Fox & Hounds Country Inn
British
Imaginative cuisine in traditional country pub
☎ 01751 431577 Main St, Sinnington YO62 6SQ

MENU GUIDE Black pudding & ham ballantine fritters, dressed mixed leaves & skordalia • Steamed monkfish fillet, shrimp & sweet potato rösti, gravadlax & schnapps dressing • Glazed apple Bakewell, Calvados caramel & clotted cream
WINE GUIDE ♀ Echeverria Sauvignon Blanc £11.75
♀ Echeverria Cabernet Sauvignon £11.75 • 2 bottles over £20, 24 bottles under £20 • 6 by the glass (£3)
PRICE GUIDE Fixed L £11.90 • starter £3.95-£7.25 • main £9.25-£15.75 • dessert £4.65-£5.95 • coffee £1.95 • min/water £2.50 • Service optional

PLACE: A former coaching inn dating from the 18th century set in a charming village with riverside and woodland walks within easy reach. Efficient, friendly service.
FOOD: Modern British cooking with some interesting flavour combinations showing flair and imagination, such as slow-roast Goosnargh duck with honey & lavender scented sauce, celeriac remoulade. There are more traditional dishes like steak pie and lamb cutlets too, plus fresh fish from Whitby.
OUR TIP: Good range of bar meals
Chef: Mark Wilson **Owners:** Mr & Mrs A Stephens **Times:** 12-2/6.30-9, Closed 25 Dec **Notes:** Set L Sun only, Vegetarian available, Dress Restrictions, Smart casual; No shorts **Seats:** 40, Pr/dining room 12
Smoking: N/Sm in restaurant **Children:** Menu **Rooms:** 10 (10 en suite)
★★ **Directions:** In centre of Sinnington, 300 yds off A170 between Pickering & Helmsley **Parking:** 35 **e-mail:** foxhoundsinn@easynet.co.uk
web: www.thefoxandhoundsinn.co.uk

⊛ White Swan
Modern British
Family-run gastro-pub that caters for all
☎ 01751 472288 Market Place YO18 7AA

MENU GUIDE Spiced mussel soup, garlic crisp breads • Calves' liver, blue cheese mash, wilted spinach • Lemon tart, lime syrup
WINE GUIDE ♀ Villa Sandi Pinot Grigio Sauvignon Blanc £16.50 • ♀ St Emillion Merlot £17.95 • 102 bottles over £20, 46 bottles under £20 • 18 by the glass (£2.45-£3.75)
PRICE GUIDE Fixed L £10.95-£15.95 • Fixed D £15.95-£35 • starter £3.95-£8.95 • main £9.95-£19.95 • dessert £4.95-£5.25 • coffee £2.50 • min/water £2.50 • Service optional
PLACE: This 16th-century coaching inn doesn't overplay its old-world charm, favouring a cosy modern decor of comfortable sofas and roaring fires to complement its beams and flagstone floors.
FOOD: There's a lot to choose from on a menu that caters both to fashion-conscious foodies and those in search of plainer fare. The use of local produce is a strength in dishes such as Whitby fish, leek and cider pie, or game terrine. Excellent wine list.
OUR TIP: Comprehensive wine list and selection of malts
Chef: Darren Clemmit **Owners:** The Buchanan Family **Times:** 12-2/7-9
Notes: Vegetarian available **Seats:** 60, Pr/dining room 14
Smoking: N/Sm in restaurant **Children:** Menu, Portions **Rooms:** 12 (12 en suite) ★★ **Directions:** Between the church and steam railway station **Parking:** 35 **e-mail:** welcome@white-swan.co.uk
web: www.white-swan.co.uk

RAMSGILL MAP 19 SE17

⊛⊛⊛ Yorke Arms see page 509

continued

RAMSGILL MAP 19 SE17

Yorke Arms

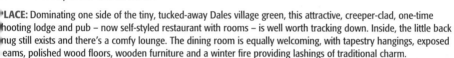

European *Poised, sophisticated and dedicated to quality*
☎ 01423 755243   HG3 5RL

e-mail: enquiries@yorke-arms.co.uk
web: www.yorke-arms.co.uk

PLACE: Dominating one side of the tiny, tucked-away Dales village green, this attractive, creeper-clad, one-time shooting lodge and pub – now self-styled restaurant with rooms – is well worth tracking down. Inside, the little back snug still exists and there's a comfy lounge. The dining room is equally welcoming, with tapestry hangings, exposed beams, polished wood floors, wooden furniture and a winter fire providing lashings of traditional charm.

FOOD: Clean-cut flavours, balance and high-quality ingredients are key components of Frances Atkins' sophisticated and appealing repertoire, backed by refreshingly simple presentation. Menus are modern–focused but supported by classical roots; the approach via fixed-price lunch, carte, daily specials and a tasting option that come sprinkled with luxury items. Expect venison fillet with foie gras ravioli, wild mushrooms and leeks, or perhaps sea bass and scallops, served with a shrimp tagliatelle, roast artichoke and pak choi. Notable wine list.

MENU GUIDE Lobster ravioli, fennel & tomato confit • Roast veal fillet, fricassee of veal sweetbreads • Assiette of chocolate

WINE GUIDE ♀ Domaine Ramonet Chassagne Muntrachet Boudriottes £66 • ♀ Merriman Rustenburg-John X Stellenbosch £35 • 180 bottles over £20, 7 bottles under £20 • 16 by the glass (£3-£6.50)

PRICE GUIDE Fixed L £17.50-£26 • starter £5.95-£11.50 • main £17.50-£24 • dessert £6.95-£10.50 • coffee £3.50 • min/water £3.50 • Service optional

OUR TIP: Lunch is great value, but book ahead

Chef: Frances Atkins, Roger Olive **Owners:** Mr & Mrs G Atkins **Times:** 12-2/7-9, Closed D Sun (ex residents) **Notes:** Tasting menu £70, Vegetarian available, Dress Restrictions, No jeans or trainers **Seats:** 60, Pr/dining room 20 **Smoking:** N/Sm in restaurant **Children:** Min 12 yrs **Rooms:** 14 (14 en suite) **Directions:** From Pateley Bridge, turn right onto Low Wath road and continue for 5m, turn right into Ramsgill, Yorke Arms is beside village green **Parking:** 20

England

England

RICHMOND MAP 19 NZ10
🏵 *Frenchgate Hotel*
British   **NEW**

Inspiring food in atmospheric restaurant full of charm

☎ 01748 822087   59-61 Frenchgate DL10 7AE

MENU GUIDE Home-made fettuccine, crispy bacon, mushrooms
Rump of lamb, shallot purée, French beans • Mixed spice pannacotta

PRICE GUIDE Food prices not confirmed for 2006. Please
telephone for details

PLACE: Converted in the 1950s from a Georgian gentlemen's
residence this hotel sits on a cobbled street in a historic part of
the town. Colourful artwork by local artists adorns the walls, and
oak floors and feature fireplaces combine with antique chairs to
create a cosy, relaxing atmosphere.
FOOD: A simple, short menu with quality ingredients demonstrates
good technical skills and results in clean flavours. Ex Gidleigh Park
chef Michael Benjamin will expand the menu in due course.
OUR TIP: The artwork is available for purchase
Times: 12.30-2.30/7-9.30 **Notes:** Closed L Mon-Sat
e-mail: info@frenchgatehotel.com **web:** www.frenchgatehotel.com

SCARBOROUGH MAP 17 TA08
🏵 *Beiderbecke's Hotel*
Modern International

International cuisine and all that jazz

☎ 01723 365766   1-3 The Crescent YO11 2PW

MENU GUIDE Slow-cooked belly pork, black pudding • Char-grilled
tuna, Creole spices, mango salsa • Light lemon sponge pudding

PRICE GUIDE Food prices not confirmed for 2006. Please
telephone for details

PLACE: Located in a Georgian terrace, this jazz-themed restaurant
offers regular live music, showcasing the best of local talent.
FOOD: International cuisine with a modern twist is served in
Marmalade's Restaurant using local, high-quality ingredients. Try
the grilled Mediterranean crevettes with garlic, lemon and chilli
butter, before tucking into grilled sea bass fillet, soft parsley crust
with a white wine and crab chive sauce.
OUR TIP: Watch out for the special events
Times: 12-2.30/6-9.30 **Rooms:** 27 (27 en suite) ★★★ **Directions:** In
town centre, 200 mtrs from rail station **e-mail:** info@beiderbeckes.com
web: www.beiderbeckes.com

STADDLE BRIDGE MAP 19 SE49
🏵 McCoys (Tontine Inn)
British

Lively bistro with contrasting eating areas

☎ 01609 882671   DL6 3JB

MENU GUIDE Wild mushroom & spinach tart • Sea bass with
pak choi & noodles • Apple pie & custard

WINE GUIDE ♀ Dom de Montmarin Sauvignon Blanc
£28.50 • ♥ Perrin Côtes de Rhône £14.95 • 72 bottles over £20,
3 bottles under £20 • 4 by the glass (£5-£7)

PRICE GUIDE Fixed L fr £12.95 • starter £3.95-£8.35 • main
£16.95-£18.95 • dessert fr £5.75 • coffee £2.25 • min/water
£4.50 • Service optional

PLACE: A delightfully rambling collection of buildings housing a
lively bistro, where the period characteristics of low ceilings and
quarry tiled floors provide an atmospheric backdrop for the
crisply-laid tables.

continued

FOOD: Short set menus are offered along with the cartes, bringing
a range of appetising, well-judged bistro dishes to lunch and
dinner guests. Black pudding with apple purée, and chicken with
chorizo and chickpea cassoulet suggest international influences.
OUR TIP: Good selection of desserts
Chef: Stuart Hawkins **Owners:** Mr E & Mr T McCoy **Times:** 12-2/6.45-9,
Closed 25-26 Dec, 1 Jan **Notes:** Vegetarian available **Seats:** 54,
Pr/dining room 30 **Smoking:** No pipes, Air con **Children:** Portions
Directions: At the junction of A19 & A172, Stokesley Road
web: www.mccoysatthetontine.co.uk

SUTTON-ON-THE-FOREST MAP 19 SE56
🏵 Rose & Crown
Modern British   **NEW**

Converted village pub focusing on good food

☎ 01347 811333   Main St YO61 1DP

MENU GUIDE Salmon ballotine • Posh fish & chips • Sticky
toffee pudding

WINE GUIDE ♀ Wither Hill Sauvignon Blanc
£15.50 • ♥ Salisbury Shiraz £14.95 • 4 bottles over £20,
20 bottles under £20 • 9 by the glass (£2.50-£4.95)

PRICE GUIDE Fixed L £9.95-£12.95 • Fixed D £12.95-
£14.95 • starter £3.50-£6.95 • main £8.95-£16.95 • dessert fr
£4.50 • coffee £1.95 • min/water £1.95 • Service optional

PLACE: A former roadside pub in a village setting midway
between York and Helmsley. There's a simple beamed interior
with open fires, wooden floors and unclothed wooden tables; a
brasserie-style restaurant area incorporating contemporary
design features, and a snug bar for drinking or eating lunch.
FOOD: Local lamb, fish and game feature in an inventive menu,
delivering traditional food with an imaginative twist. Some dishes
are inspired by famous chefs.
OUR TIP: Canopied terrace with outside seating
Chef: Adam Jackson, Russel Johnson **Owners:** Martin Burgess
Times: 12-3/5.30-9.30, Closed 1st wk Jan, Mon, closed D Sun
Notes: Vegetarian available **Seats:** 44 **Smoking:** N/Sm in restaurant
Children: Portions **Directions:** 8m N of York towards Helmsley on
B1363 **Parking:** 12 **e-mail:** enquiries@rose-crown.freeserve.co.uk

TADCASTER MAP 16 SE44
🏵🏵 Hazlewood Castle
Modern French

Refurbished restaurant in a converted castle

☎ 01937 535354   Paradise Ln, Hazlewood LS24 9NJ

MENU GUIDE Mosaic of corn-fed chicken, shitaki & foie
gras • Venison saddle, celeriac, red cabbage, sauce
opera • Burnt orange soufflé

continued

WINE GUIDE ♀ Côtes du Luberon 2002 £19.50 • ♀ Côtes du Ventoux 2003 £19.50 • 67 bottles over £20, 8 bottles under £20 • 10 by the glass (£3–£6.50)

PRICE GUIDE Fixed L £15.95 • Fixed D £19.95 • starter £8–£13 main £17–£22 • dessert £7–£10 • coffee £2.95 • min/water £3.50

PLACE: The hotel is an imaginative conversion of a 950-year-old astle; a fascinating building, which has been a monastery and etreat in its time and stands in 77 acres of parkland. The staurant has been revamped, and now looks very stylish and corporates a bar. Alternatively, there is a pizza and pasta bistro erving light meals all day.

FOOD: An interesting carte of modern French cooking is offered ong with wine recommendations for each dish, available by the ass. Mains might include oven roasted fillet of turbot with clam age, salsify pomme vapeur with persillade and potato croquant.

UR TIP: Check out the extensive wine list

hef: Paul Rowntree **Owners:** Hazlewood Castle Ltd **Times:** 12-2/6-30 **Notes:** Vegetarian available, Civ Wed 120 **Seats:** 80, Pr/dining oom 120 **Smoking:** N/Sm in restaurant **Children:** Min 12 yrs D, Menu, ortions **Rooms:** 21 (21 en suite) ★★★ **Directions:** Signed from A64, of Tadcaster, 0.5 mile from A1/M1 **Parking:** 120

mail: info@hazlewood-castle.co.uk **web:** www.hazlewood-castle.co.uk

WEST TANFIELD MAP 19 SE27

The Bruce Arms

Modern British

Popular pub-bistro in a village setting

☎ 01677 470325 Main St HG4 5JJ

MENU GUIDE Duck liver mousse, pickled pineapple • Roast cod, mustard grain mash, watercress sauce • Crème caramel, soft fruits

WINE GUIDE ♀ Santa Rita Sauvignon Blanc £13.95 • ♀ Georges Duboeuf Cuvée Rouge £11.95 • 17 bottles over £20, 41 bottles under £20 • 11 by the glass (£3.25–£5)

PRICE GUIDE Starter £4.50–£6.50 • main £13.50–£17.95 • dessert £4.50 • coffee £1.95 • min/water £3 • Service optional • Group min 10 service 10%

PLACE: There's a strong following for this early 18th-century inn cated in the heart of a North Yorkshire village. It is stone built ith high ceilings and open fires, and you can stay over in one of ree smart bedrooms.

FOOD: A modern British menu featuring Masham beef and Dales mb along with an interesting selection of half a dozen English eeses, such as Wigmore, Mrs Kirkham's and Stinking Bishop.

UR TIP: Lunch on Saturday and Sunday only

hef: Geoff Smith **Owners:** Geoff Smith **Times:** 12-2.30/6.30-9.30, osed 2 wks Feb, Mon, closed L Tue-Sat, closed D Sun

otes: Vegetarian by request only **Seats:** 30, Pr/dining room 20 **moking:** N/Sm area, No pipes **Children:** Portions **Rooms:** 3 (3 en ite) ◆◆◆ **Directions:** Telephone for directions **Parking:** 15 **mail:** geoffsmith@bruceams.com **web:** www.bruceams.com

WHITBY MAP 19 NZ81

Dunsley Hall

European, International

maginative cooking in a classic country-house setting

☎ 01947 893437 Dunsley YO21 3TL

MENU GUIDE Asparagus mousse, roast shallot purée • Monkfish llet & chorizo • Liquorice sponge, apple sorbet, chocolate & lime custard

WINE GUIDE ♀ Beelgara Chardonnay £12.95 • ♀ Opel Ridge Shiraz/Cabernet Sauvignon £12.95 • 19 bottles over £20, 33 bottles under £20 • 12 by the glass (£3.30–£3.50)

continued

Dunsley Hall

PRICE GUIDE Fixed L £6.95 • Fixed D £27.95 • coffee £1.50 • min/water £3.50 • Service optional

PLACE: An imposing Victorian mansion where a shipping magnate once reared a family of thirteen children. Beautiful oak panelling and stained-glass windows have been faithfully preserved for today's visitors to the elegant dining room.

FOOD: The cooking soars above the ordinary, and the menus reveal plenty of imagination and novelty. Tiny glass tasses contain artistic accompaniments to dishes, like cider jelly with a ham hock ballontine, and flavours are reliably strong.

OUR TIP: Try a dessert wine with the interesting puddings

Chef: Mike Boyle Cook **Owners:** Mr & Mrs W Ward **Times:** 12-2/7.30-9.30, Closed L Mon-Sat **Notes:** Fixed ALC £37.50, Tasting menu avail., Vegetarian available, Dress Restrictions, No shorts, Civ Wed 60 **Seats:** 85, Pr/dining room 30 **Smoking:** N/Sm in restaurant **Children:** Min 5 yrs, Menu, Portions **Rooms:** 18 (18 en suite) ★★★ **Directions:** 3.5m from Whitby off A171 Teeside road **Parking:** 18

e-mail: reception@dunsleyhall.com

web: www.dunsleyhall.com

Estbek House

European 🐟 ⬦ **NEW**

An upstairs-downstairs seafood restaurant

☎ 01947 893424 East Row, Sandsend YO21 3SU

MENU GUIDE Skate in parsleyed jelly • Halibut, Sauvignon Blanc cream sauce • Lemon cheesecake

WINE GUIDE ♀ Santa Rita Sauvignon Blanc £13.95 • ♀ Santa Rita Cabernet Sauvignon £13.95 • 17 bottles over £20, 26 bottles under £20 • 5 by the glass (£3.85–£5.85)

PRICE GUIDE Starter £4.50–£6.95 • main £12.74–£22.95 • dessert £4.75 • coffee £1.75 • Service optional

PLACE: A small unspoilt village down the coast from Whitby shelters this stylish Georgian hotel. Downstairs is a lively bistro, while upstairs the period candlelit setting is ideal for a relaxed romantic evening.

FOOD: Fish is the king here, and the simple cooking means it arrives on the table in peak condition. From seared crayfish and samphire salad to local cod with a lemon cream sauce, it's carefully paired with herbs and vegetables from the garden.

OUR TIP: Try the superbly cooked fish

Chef: Tim Lawrence **Owners:** D Cross, T Lawrence **Times:** 6-9 **Notes:** Menu changes daily dependent upon ingredients, Vegetarian available **Seats:** 40, Pr/dining room 28 **Smoking:** N/Sm in restaurant **Children:** Menu, Portions **Rooms:** 5 (4 en suite) 🛏 **Directions:** From Whitby follow A174 towards Sandsend, Estbek just before bridge **Parking:** 6 **e-mail:** reservations@estbekhouse.co.uk **web:** www.estbekhouse.co.uk

England

WHITBY continued MAP 19 NZ81

⊚ The White Horse & Griffin

British, International

Bistro fare in coaching inn

☎ 01947 825026 604857 Church St YO22 4BH

MENU GUIDE Bouillabaisse (starter or main) • Châteaubriand, Madeira sauce, vegetable gratin • Vanilla crème brûlée, winter berries

PRICE GUIDE Fixed L £10 • starter £4.70-£7.95 • main £4.95-£17.95 • dessert £4.95-£6.95 • coffee £1.90 • min/water £2.95 • Service added 10%

PLACE: As quaint as the cobbled street in which it lies, this restaurant with rooms is steeped in history. Original wood and flagstone floors and panelling remain, and there are three dining areas: a rustic room off the street, a 'warmer' bistro-style room at the back, and an old-world room upstairs.

FOOD: Bistro cooking with hearty portions. Fish is a speciality, fresh from the boat and simply handled.

OUR TIP: Breakfast 8.30-10.30 and Fastrack menu 12-7pm

Chef: S Perkins, K Healy, B Davies **Owners:** June & Stewart Perkins **Times:** 12-3/5-9, Closed D 25 Dec **Notes:** Specials and fasttrack menu available, Vegetarian available **Seats:** 75, Pr/dining room 36 **Smoking:** N/Sm area **Children:** Portions **Rooms:** 10 (10 en suite) ♦♦♦ **Parking:** 50 yds **e-mail:** info@whitehorseandgriffin.co.uk **web:** www.whitehorseandgriffin.co.uk

☕ **E Botham and Sons** 35/39 Skinner St YO21 3AH
☎ 01947 602823 Winner of The Tea Guild Award of Excellence 2005.

🍴 **Magpie Café** 14 Pier Rd YO21 3PU ☎ 01947 602058 Overlooking Whitby harbour, this is an ideal location to enjoy local fish, seafood and Magpie Café's specialities.

YARM MAP 19 NZ41

⊚⊛ Judges Country House Hotel

British, French

Gracious mansion in extensive grounds

☎ 01642 789000 Kirklevington TS15 9LW

MENU GUIDE White bean & garlic soup, truffle oil • Sea bass, pesto mash, spinach & oyster beignets, mussel, olive oil & caviar butter sauce • Lemon tart, soufflé milanaise, red berry sauce

WINE GUIDE ♀ Domaine de Martindales Chardonnay £18 • ♀ Hubert de Bouvey Merlot £18 • 340 bottles over £20, 13 bottles under £20 • 8 by the glass (£3.50-£4.95)

PRICE GUIDE Fixed L £12.95 • Fixed D £32.50 • coffee £4 • min/water £4.50 • Service optional

Judges Country House Hotel

PLACE: This Victorian mansion with its 42 acres of landscaped gardens and woodland walks offers a haven of peace and tranquility. Once the lodging of circuit judges on location in the North East – hence the name – it still proves an ideal country retreat for calm deliberation. The lounge has plump cushioned armchairs and a roaring winter fire, while there are two elegant dining rooms; a traditional oak-panelled room and a lighter, more airy conservatory extension with views over the lovely gardens. Genuinely friendly and attentive, professional staff enhance the experience.

FOOD: Unfussy, simply presented modern British dishes – underpinned by a classical theme – uses the finest, local seasonal produce and intelligently lets the main ingredient shine. Expect accomplished cooking, clean flavours and assured balance, the approach via a fixed-price repertoire of dinner carte, lunch menu plus an abridged lunch carte. So consider the case of a brace of trios; veal (roasted loin, sautéed sweetbreads and shin with foie gras), served with parmentier potatoes and asparagus in a rich Madeira sauce, and a trio of chocolate finish, before pronouncing your judgement.

OUR TIP: Enjoy a pre- or post-meal stroll in the gardens

Chef: Neal Bullock **Owners:** Mr M Downs **Times:** 12-2/7-10 **Notes:** Tasting menu £45, Vegetarian available, Dress Restrictions, Jacket & tie preferred, No jeans, Smart dress, Civ Wed 300 **Seats:** 60, Pr/dining room 40 **Smoking:** N/Sm in restaurant **Children:** Menu, Portions **Rooms:** 21 (21 en suite) ★★★ **Directions:** 1.5m from junct W A19, take A67 towards Kirklevington, hotel 1.5m on left **Parking:** 110 **e-mail:** enquiries@judgeshotel.co.uk **web:** www.judgeshotel.co.uk

YORK MAP 16 SE65

⊚ Blue Bicycle

European

Crowd-pleasing cooking in bustling York institution

☎ 01904 677688 34 Fossgate YO1 9TA

MENU GUIDE Thai fishcakes • Chicken, garlic mushrooms, sautéed potatoes, black pudding • Raspberry crème brûlée tartlet, berry coulis

continued

continued

Blue Bicycle

Dean Court Hotel

WINE GUIDE ♀ Trentino Pinot Grigio £17 • ♀ Concha y Toro Merlot £14 • 43 bottles over £20, 33 bottles under £20 • 18 by the glass (£3.50-£5.50)

PRICE GUIDE Starter £5.75-£9.50 • main £14.50-£19.50 • dessert £6-£7.50 • coffee £2.60 • min/water £3.50 • Service added but optional 10%

PLACE: One of York's best-loved restaurants, this buzzy city centre eaterie is popular with locals and tourists alike, and has a bright decor, full of character.

FOOD: A creative chef brings touches of imagination to popular dishes, delivering a wide-ranging modern European menu with an emphasis on fish and game in season. Local ingredients get top billing.

OUR TIP: Popular, so book ahead

Chef: Kenny Noble **Owners:** Lawrence Anthony Stephenson **Times:** 12-2.30/6-9.30, Closed 25-26 Dec, 1 Jan, closed L 24, 31 Dec **Notes:** Vegetarian available **Seats:** 83 **Smoking:** N/Sm in restaurant **Children:** Portions **Directions:** Located in centre of York, just off Parliament St **Parking:** On street & NCP **e-mail:** info@thebluebicycle.com **web:** www.thebluebicycle.com

⊚⊚ Dean Court Hotel

British, French

Contemporary hotel restaurant with a menu designed to please

☎ 01904 625082 Duncombe Place YO1 7EF

MENU GUIDE Ballotine of rabbit, elderflower dressing • Slow-cooked lamb, saffron & orange dressing • Trio of rhubarb desserts

WINE GUIDE ♀ Hawkes Bay Mills Reef Sauvignon Blanc £20.50 • ♀ Central Wines Merlot £15.95 • 64 bottles over £20, 26 bottles under £20 • 12 by the glass (£3.50-£10)

PRICE GUIDE Fixed L £13-£14 • starter £5.75-£7.50 • main £13.75-£19.50 • dessert £5.75-£7.50 • coffee £3.50 min/water £3

PLACE: Standing in the shadow of the Minster, this luxurious hotel is an ideal base from which to explore the historic city of York. The restaurant is a relaxed contemporary setting, boasting impressive views of its ecclesiastical neighbour.

FOOD: Showcasing the best of Yorkshire produce, Dean Court offers a wide-ranging menu of dishes that stretches from familiar fare such as steak and kidney pudding to more modern options - venison with a rosemary glaze perhaps, or roast monkfish, scallops and mussels in a coconut, lime and chilli broth.

OUR TIP: Light snacks served all day in Terry's conservatory café

Chef: Andrew Bingham **Owners:** Mr B A Cleminson and D Brooks **Times:** 12.30-2/7-9.30, Closed L 31 Dec, closed D 25 Dec **Notes:** Lunch coffee incl., Vegetarian available, Civ Wed 54 **Seats:** 60, Pr/dining room 40 **Smoking:** N/Sm in restaurant, Air con **Children:** Menu, Portions **Rooms:** 39 (39 en suite) ★★★ **Directions:** City centre, directly opposite York Minster **Parking:** 30 **e-mail:** sales@deancourt-york.co.uk **web:** www.deancourt-york.co.uk

⊚⊚ The Grange Hotel

British, European

Listed townhouse with three dining options

☎ 01904 644744 1 Clifton YO30 6AA

MENU GUIDE Roast squab, tarragon cream • Rabbit saddle, gnocchi, morels, asparagus • Chocolate & peanut parfait, berries, amaretto sabayon

WINE GUIDE ♀ Jacques Veritier £12.50 • ♀ VDP Cuvée Paul Bocuse £12.50 • 34 bottles over £20, 32 bottles under £20 • 7 by the glass (£3.50-£4)

PRICE GUIDE Fixed L £12.95-£16.95 • Fixed D £28-£35 • starter £5.50-£9.50 • main £18-£22 • dessert £5.50-£8.95 • coffee £2 • min/water £3 • Service optional

continued

continued

YORK continued MAP 16 SE65

PLACE: An elegant Regency town house just a few minutes' walk from the city centre, The Grange offers a choice of restaurants. For fine dining in lavish surroundings it has to be The Ivy. Alternatively there's the seafood bar (dinner only), where striking murals reflect York's racing history, or the Brasserie in the brick-vaulted cellars.

FOOD: The Ivy's ambitious menu is carried off with great panache. It offers classics, favourites and modern introductions, underpinned by good culinary sense and no small measure of skill.

OUR TIP: The Brasserie is ideal for pre-theatre suppers
Chef: Philip Upton **Owners:** Jeremy & Vivien Cassel **Times:** 12-2/7-10, Closed L Mon-Sat, closed D Sun **Notes:** Vegetarian available, Dress Restrictions, Smart casual preferred, Civ Wed 60 **Seats:** 35, Pr/dining room 60 **Smoking:** N/Sm in restaurant **Children:** Portions **Rooms:** 30 (30 en suite) ★★★ **Directions:** A19 York/Thirsk road, approx 400 yds from city centre **Parking:** 30 **e-mail:** info@grangehotel.co.uk **web:** www.grangehotel.co.uk

Melton's

British

Eclectic dining in long-established and friendly family-run restaurant
☎ 01904 634341 7 Scarcroft Rd YO23 1ND

MENU GUIDE Poached egg, polenta, deep-fried artichoke shavings, truffle oil • Ox tongue, sauce charcuterie • Hot chocolate indulgence

WINE GUIDE ♀ Les Yeuses Sauvignon Blanc £13.50 • ♀ Les Yeuses Syrah £13.50 • 30 bottles over £20, 50 bottles under £20 • 7 by the glass (£3)

PRICE GUIDE Fixed L £16.50 • Fixed D £25 • starter £4.50-£7.90 main £12.90-£18.90 • dessert £4.90-£6.60 • Service optional

PLACE: The restaurant has a suburban shop-front opening into a bright, modern dining room with lively murals of people dining. Comfortable furnishings and quality table settings combine with

continued

---

relaxed yet professional service to ensure that the mood of diners matches those in the murals.
FOOD: Here is a kitchen that reliably turns out attractively presented modern British cooking, with well-balanced flavours and generous portions. An eclectic choice of dishes is offered, including interesting vegetarian options (aubergine, mozzarella and roast pepper Charlotte), and a decent wine list.
OUR TIP: Good value early bird menu
Chef: Michael Hjort, Annie Prescott **Owners:** Michael & Lucy Hjort **Times:** 12-2/5.30-10, Closed 3 wks Xmas, 1wk Aug, Sun, closed L Mon **Notes:** Coffee/min water included, Vegetarian available **Seats:** 30, Pr/dining room 16 **Smoking:** N/Sm in restaurant, Air con **Children:** Portions **Directions:** South from centre across Skeldergate Bridge, restaurant opposite Bishopthorpe Road car park **Parking:** Car park opposite **e-mail:** greatfood@meltonsrestaurant.co.uk **web:** www.meltonsrestaurant.co.uk

Middlethorpe Hall Hotel, Restaurant & Spa see page 515

Sous le Mont

British

Stylish hotel restaurant, accessible to racecourse
☎ 01904 619444 Mount Royale, The Mount YO24 1GU

MENU GUIDE Tian of crab, Parmesan crisp • Sea bass fillets, rosemary mash, asparagus & Hollandaise • Home-made chocolate ice cream

WINE GUIDE ♀ Tierra Arena Sauvignon Blanc £12.95 ♀ Castillo d'Clavijo Rioja Tempranillo £14.95 • 68 bottles over £20, 48 bottles under £20 • 10 by the glass (£2.40-£3.70)

PRICE GUIDE Fixed L £9.95 • Fixed D £19.95 • starter £3.50-£7.95 • main £9.95-£19.95 • dessert £4.50-£5.95 • coffee £1.25 • min/water £2.50 • Service included

PLACE: Two William IV properties house this welcoming hotel and smart restaurant, close to the city centre. Burgundy and gold are the predominant colours, used throughout the restaurant and conservatory, the latter boasting serene garden views.
FOOD: Traditional British food with modern twists produces clear cut flavours and successful combinations. There's plenty of choice among straightforward dishes like crispy duck salad, and roast rump of lamb, with plenty of fish always available.
OUR TIP: Extensive, well-priced wine list
Chef: Richard Howes **Owners:** R Chamberlain, M Chamberlain, M Osborne, K Hooper **Times:** 12-2.30/6-9.30, Closed 1-6 Jan, Sun **Notes:** Vegetarian available **Seats:** 80, Pr/dining room 18 **Smoking:** N/Sm area, Air con **Children:** Portions **Rooms:** 24 (24 en suite) ★★★ **Directions:** W on B1036, towards racecourse **Parking:** 25 **web:** www.mountroyale.co.uk

---

What makes a Restaurant of the Year?
In selecting a Restaurant of the Year, we look for somewhere that is exceptional in its chosen area of the market. Whilst the Rosette awards are based on the quality of the food alone, Restaurant of the Year takes into account all aspects of the operation. For full details see pages 6-7.

ORK MAP 16 SE65

Middlethorpe Hall Hotel, Restaurant & Spa

odern British *Inventive cooking in traditional country house*
☎ 01904 641241 Bishopthorpe Rd, Middlethorpe YO23 2GB
-mail: info@middlethorpe.com
web: www.middlethorpe.com

PLACE: This imposing, mellow red-brick William III country house, gloriously located on the fringes of the city in acres of gardens and parkland, exudes style. Built in 1699, it was once the home of the famous diarist, Lady Mary ortley Montagu. Public rooms, in keeping with the hotel's traditional theme, are full of antiques and fine paintings nd include a stately drawing room (where afternoon tea is an event) and the smart, formality of the oak-panelled, andlelit dining room, which overlooks the gardens.

FOOD: Surprisingly, there are plenty of modern combinations from the kitchen of such a traditional hotel, with avoury ice creams and foams all finding a place on the repertoire, with its imaginative spin on modern British cuisine. ead chef Lee Heptinstall is a Yorkshireman and takes pride in sourcing the best local and regional produce (Moors' mb, wild Yorkshire venison, fresh fish and seafood from the East Coast), with herbs and fruits coming from iddlethorpe's own gardens in season. Technically adept dishes are delivered with skill and flair on fixed-price menus at also offer a special vegetarian selection, while table service is formal, efficient and friendly.

MENU GUIDE John Dory, tomato risotto, haricot vert • Belly pork, pommes mousseline, black pudding • Chocolate fondant, milk ice cream, griottine cherries

WINE GUIDE 164 bottles over £20, 15 bottles under £20 • 7 by the glass (£3.75-£7.95)

PRICE GUIDE Fixed L £17 • Fixed D £39 • coffee £3.50 • min/water £3.50 • Service included

OUR TIP: Take time to enjoy the garden before dinner

Chef: Lee Heptinstall **Owners:** Historic House Hotels
Times: 12.30-2.15/7-9.45, Closed (L residents only 25 Dec & 31 Dec) **Notes:** Sun L £23.50, Vegetarian available, Dress Restrictions, Jacket required; no jeans/shorts/trainers, Civ Wed 56
Seats: 60, Pr/dining room 56 **Smoking:** N/Sm in restaurant
Children: Min 8 yrs **Rooms:** 29 (29 en suite) ★★★
Directions: 1.5m S of York, beside York racecourse **Parking:** 70

England

YORK *continued* MAP 16 SE65

◎◎ York Pavilion Hotel
British, Mediterranean

Brasserie-style food in elegant Georgian surroundings

☎ 01904 622099   45 Main St, Fulford YO10 4PJ

MENU GUIDE Duck confit, celeriac purée • Roast cod, girolles & pea ragout • Vanilla mousse, citrus salad

WINE GUIDE ♀ Le Charme Sauvignon Blanc £14 • ♀ Le Charme Merlot £14 • 6 bottles over £20, 12 bottles under £20 • 7 by the glass (£3.40-£4.90)

PRICE GUIDE Fixed L £14.95-£18.95 • Fixed D £25-£30 • starter £4.95-£7.95 • main £12.95-£19.95 • dessert £4.95-£6.25 • coffee £2.20 • min/water £4 • Service optional

PLACE: An impressive Grade II listed Georgian house hotel just on the outskirts of York. The wood-floored Langtons Brasserie is light and airy thanks to high ceilings and large windows overlooking the gardens.
FOOD: The regularly changing menu includes both traditional and modern dishes, mostly British but with the occasional Mediterranean or Asian influence as in the seared king scallops with a minted pea velouté followed by a dish of honey roast Harome duck with red onion tart Tatin.
OUR TIP: Don't miss the good choice on the blackboard menu
Chef: David Spencer **Owners:** Irene & Andrew Cossins **Times:** 12-2/6.30-9.30 **Notes:** Vegetarian available, Civ Wed 90 **Seats:** 60, Pr/dining room 150 **Smoking:** N/Sm in restaurant **Children:** Menu, Portions **Rooms:** 57 (57 en suite) ★★★ **Directions:** S from York city centre on A19 (Selby), hotel 2m on left. On A1 from N or S take A64 to York, then take Selby/York City Centre A19 junct **Parking:** 50
e-mail: reservations@yorkpavilionhotel.com
web: www.yorkpavilionhotel.com

♨ Bettys Café Tea Rooms 6-8 St Helen's Square
YO1 2QP ☎ 01904 659142 Winner of The Tea Guild Award of Excellence 2005.

♨ Little Bettys 46 Stonegate YO1 8AS
☎ 01904 622865 Winner of The Tea Guild Award of Excellence 2005.

> **One Rosette** Excellent local restaurants serving food prepared with care, understanding and skill, using good quality ingredients. These restaurants stand out in their local area. Of the total number of establishments with Rosettes around 50% have one Rosette.

YORKSHIRE, SOUTH

CHAPELTOWN MAP 16 SK39

◎ Greenhead House
British, French

Exciting cooking in sophisticated surroundings

☎ 0114 246 9004   84 Burncross Rd S35 1SF

MENU GUIDE Rabbit terrine with Calvados & cinnamon toast • Roast breast of mallard with balsamic & honey Apple tart

WINE GUIDE ♀ Trinity Hill Hawkes Bay Sauvignon £16.95 • ♀ Brown Brothers Shiraz £19.50 • 24 bottles over £20, 17 bottles under £20 • 5 by the glass (£4.25-£4.50)

PRICE GUIDE Starter £5.25-£5.50 • main £10-£10.50 • dessert £5.25-£5.50 • min/water £2.50 • Service included

PLACE: Set in a 17th-century stone villa which still retains many of its original features, the cottage-style restaurant has an informal, relaxed atmosphere.
FOOD: Cooking is inspired, the head chef being keen on original recipes and an expert on traditional cooking; and an Italian second chef brings in his own distinctive influence to the food.
OUR TIP: Small restaurant, so booking is essential
Chef: Neil Allen **Owners:** Mr & Mrs N Allen **Times:** 12-1/7-9, Closed Xmas-New Year, 2wks Etr, 2wks end Aug, Sun-Tue, closed L Wed, Thu & Sat **Notes:** ALC L only, Fixed D 5 courses £36-40, Vegetarian available **Seats:** 32 **Smoking:** N/Sm in restaurant **Children:** Min 7 yrs, Portions **Directions:** 1m from M1 junct 35 **Parking:** 10

ROSSINGTON MAP 16 SK69

◎ Mount Pleasant Hotel
British, International

Creative cooking in country-house hotel

☎ 01302 868696 & 868219 Great North Rd DN11 0HW

MENU GUIDE Mussels, ginger, lemongrass, chilli, coconut milk • Guinea fowl spring roll, paw-paw salad, cashew, coriander • Individual treacle tart

WINE GUIDE ♀ Chardonnay £17.50 • ♀ Shiraz/Rioja Tempranillo £13.95 • 16 bottles over £20, 19 bottles under £20 • 7 by the glass (£4.50-£5.85)

PRICE GUIDE Fixed L £15.45-£27.90 • Fixed D £21.40-£34.70 • starter £4.95-£6.95 • main £10.50-£20.95 • dessert £5.95-£6.50 • coffee £2.10 • min/water £3.50

PLACE: The Garden Restaurant is decorated in traditional style, with exposed brickwork, wide tapestries and stylish high-back chairs. It's a spacious room with tables set apart for privacy.
FOOD: Creative dishes in the simple modern style with international influences, created from seasonal local produce. Try a traditional shepherd's pie with an Asian twist, or braised beef bourguignon with baby beetroot and hand-made brioche dumplings.
OUR TIP: A grill selection features less complex dishes
Chef: Dave Booker **Owners:** Richard McIlroy **Times:** 12-2/6.45-9.30, Closed 25 Dec **Notes:** Vegetarian available, Smart casual preferred, Civ Wed 150 **Seats:** 72, Pr/dining room 200 **Smoking:** N/Sm in restaurant, Air con **Children:** Menu, Portions **Rooms:** 45 (45 en suite) ★★★★ **Directions:** Located on A638 between Bawtry and Doncaster **Parking:** 100 **e-mail:** reception@mountpleasant.co.uk
web: www.bw-mountpleasant.co.uk

England

SHEFFIELD MAP 16 SK38

Rafters Restaurant

British, European

Popular neighbourhood restaurant

☎ 0114 230 4819 220 Oakbrook Rd, Nethergreen
S11 7ED

MENU GUIDE Chargrilled boneless quail with Mauritian spices • Pan-fried Gressingham duck breast on a risotto of Jerusalem artichoke, peas & sage • Hot chocolate fondant

WINE GUIDE ♀ Sancerre Loire Valley Sauvignon Blanc £19.95 • ♀ Rioja Reserva Tempranillo £21.50 • 40% bottles over £20, 60% bottles under £20 • 4 by the glass (£2.60-£3.20)

PRICE GUIDE Fixed D £27.50 • coffee £2.80 • min/water £2.80 • Group min 8 service 10%

PLACE: In a leafy suburb of Sheffield, this busy restaurant is situated above a row of bustling shops and is very popular with locals, many of whom are regulars. Original rafters and beams, exposed brick walls, quality appointments and overhanging contemporary lighting contribute to the refined, relaxed atmosphere.

FOOD: The well-travelled chef makes good use of fresh, seasonal ingredients. European influences result in some unusual touches like courgette flower filled with sweet potatoes. Presentation is a strong point; the food not only tastes great, it looks appealing as well. The home-made bread is excellent.

OUR TIP: Bring your own wine on Wednesday (corkage charge applies)

Chef: Marcus Lane, M Sabin **Owners:** Marcus Lane, Michael Sabin **Times:** 7-10, Closed 25-26 Dec, 1wk Jan, 2 wks Aug, Sun, Tue, closed L all week **Notes:** Vegetarian available, Smart casual **Seats:** 38 **Smoking:** N/Sm in restaurant, Air con **Children:** Min 5 yrs, Portions **Directions:** 5 mins from Ecceshall road, Hunters Bar rdbt **Parking:** 15 **web:** www.raftersrestaurant.co.uk

 Richard Smith at Thyme

see page 518

Staindrop Lodge Hotel

British, European

Art deco brasserie in smart hotel

☎ 0114 284 3111 Ln End, Chapeltown S35 3UH

MENU GUIDE Saffron & parmesan risotto, poached egg • Grilled plaice, lemon butter • Vanilla crème brûlée

WINE GUIDE 6 bottles over £20, 33 bottles under £20 • 7 by the glass (£2-£4.45)

PRICE GUIDE Starter £3.50-£5.50 • main £4.25-£15.95 • dessert £4.75 • coffee £1.15 • min/water £2 • Service optional

PLACE: Fully refurbished and extended, this bar, brasserie and hotel occupy a 200-year-old building that offers smart, modern public areas and accommodation. The split-level restaurant sports lots of glass, solid floors and an art deco theme. Service is relaxed and friendly.

FOOD: The modern British and European menu sits well with the stylish surroundings. All-day menus are also available in the bar.

OUR TIP: First come, first served at weekends

Chef: Andrew Roebuck **Owners:** David Slade, John Wigfield **Times:** 12-9.30 **Notes:** Sunday roast £7.95, Vegetarian available, Smart Dress, Civ Wed 80 **Seats:** 100 **Smoking:** N/Sm in restaurant, Air con **Children:** Menu, Portions **Rooms:** 31 (31 en suite) ★★★ **Directions:** Take A629 towards Huddersfield, go straight at first rdbt, at mini rdbt take right fork. Restaurant is 0.5 miles on the right **Parking:** 60 **e-mail:** info@staindroplodge.co.uk **web:** www.staindroplodge.co.uk

A Restaurant with Rooms is usually a local (or national) destination for eating out which also offers accommodation. Most have 12 bedrooms or less, and public areas may be limited to the restaurant itself. Bedrooms reflect at least the level of quality associated with a two star hotel. A red symbol indicates a restaurant with rooms that is amongst the AA's Top Hotels in Britain and Ireland.

Give us your views! All the rosetted restaurants in this guide have been visited by one of the AA's team of professional inspectors, but we want to hear from you! Use the report forms in the back of the guide or email us at lifestyleguides@theaa.com with your comments on any establishments featured or on the restaurants that you feel are worthy of an entry. We would also be pleased to receive your views on the guide itself and suggestions for information you would like to see included.

England

SHEFFIELD MAP 16 SK38

Richard Smith at Thyme

British, International
Modern bistro with star quality

☎ 0114 266 6096 32-34 Sandygate Rd S10 5RY
web: www.thymeforfood.co.uk

PLACE: A modern-look, corner-sited building in the city suburbs, Richard Smith (at Thyme) draws the crowds with his imaginative cooking. Light wood, etched glass, modern spotlighting, plain walls with vibrant modern art and cartoons create a cool, chic contemporary edge to proceedings in this busy, light and airy bistro-style outfit. The wooden floors, high-back chairs and plain tables (decked out with sparkling glassware and cutlery) further reinforce the minimalist, design-led styling, with partly open-to-view kitchens bearing witness to the serious intent of the cooking. A separate bar up front completes the upbeat package.

FOOD: Richard Smith's imaginative cooking goes from strength to strength at this long-established restaurant. His modern British, crowd-pleasing repertoire encompasses the classical and contemporary; take speciality châteaubriand of beef fillet or Marseille bouillabaisse, or traditional British classics like Yorkshire fish and chips to more adventurous and complex tasting of lamb (including braised shoulder, chargrilled cutlet, mini shepherd's pie, sautéed lambs' liver and roast lamb gravy). Informal, highly flexible menus see things crank up a gear with more serious culinary intent in the evenings, but presentation and combinations of flavours are quite outstanding, based around carefully sourced, high-quality fresh produce and high-level skill at either service.

MENU GUIDE Local venison & foie gras terrine • Pot-roast belly pork, chorizo, saffron mash, Portuguese white bean stew, olive oil • Key lime cheesecake, brie ice cream

WINE GUIDE ♀ Waipara Hills Sauvignon Blanc £24 • ♀ Rioja £16 • 40 bottles over £20, 40 bottles under £20 • 12 by the glass (£3-£6)

PRICE GUIDE Fixed L £12 • Fixed D £22-£24 • starter £4-£12 • main £12-£20 • dessert £5-£10 • coffee £3 • min/water £3 • Service optional • Group min 12 service 10%

OUR TIP: Save room for excellent desserts; bargain lunches

Chef: S Wild, Joe Horvath **Owners:** Richard & Victoria Smith
Times: 12-2/6-10, Closed 26 Dec, 1 Jan **Notes:** Sun lunch 3 courses £22, Vegetarian available **Seats:** 70, Pr/dining room 24 **Smoking:** N/Sm in restaurant, Air con **Children:** Portions
Directions: From Sheffield centre take A57; at Crosspool turn right onto Sandygate Road. 100yds on right

YORKSHIRE, WEST

LIFTON MAP 16 SE12

The Black Horse Inn

ritish, Mediterranean

joyable dining with wonderful coastal views

01484 713862   HD6 4HJ

MENU GUIDE Salmon & coriander fishcakes • Beer battered
od, mint pea purée • Tangy lemon tart

WINE GUIDE Babich Sauvignon Blanc £14.75 • La Heurta
erlot £12.95 • 57 bottles over £20, 45 bottles under £20
by the glass (£2.95-£6.95)

PRICE GUIDE Starter £4-£9.50 • main £9-£18 • dessert £3-
• coffee £1.85 • min/water £2.25 • Service optional

ACE: The atmosphere in this 17th-century inn is traditional and
axed. Starched white linen and full settings seem strangely at
ds with the building's history as a Luddite meeting place. In
60s and 70s, the inn was a favourite stopover for Roy
bison, Danny La Rue, Shirley Bassey and many other
ertainers who were performing at the Batley Variety Club.
OD: Gastro-pub menus bring together classic, traditional and
dern British dishes with occasional Mediterranean influence.
ly specials on blackboard.
R TIP: Good choice of wines by the glass
ef: Kevin Grady **Owners:** Andrew & Jane Russell **Times:** 12-9.30,
sed 1 Jan, closed D 25-26 Dec **Notes:** Vegetarian available, Smart
ss, Civ Wed 60 **Seats:** 80, Pr/dining room 50 **Smoking:** N/Sm in
aurant **Children:** Portions **Parking:** 60
nail: mail@blackhorseclifton.co.uk **web:** www.blackhorseclifton.co.uk

EWSBURY MAP 16 SE22

Healds Hall Hotel

ritish, Mediterranean

untry-house dining

01924 409112   Leeds Rd, Liversedge WF15 6JA

MENU GUIDE Pan-fried king scallops, caramelised
lsify • Gressingham duck, black pepper crust • Vanilla rice
dding & blackberry jam

WINE GUIDE Jean Didier Chardonnay Cuvée Menhir
2.75 • Santa Helena Cabernet Sauvignon £13.75 • 14 bottles
er £20, 34 bottles under £20 • 8 by the glass (£3.30)

PRICE GUIDE Fixed L £7.50 • starter £3.25-£6 • main £11-
7.50 • dessert £4.25-£4.50 • coffee £1.70 • min/water
.70 • Service optional

ACE: Built in 1764, this West Yorkshire country house was once
ne to Rev Hammond Robertson, memorable to literary types

continued

---

as the inspiration for Rev Matthew Helston in Charlotte Brontë's
Shirley. Dining choices are between the brightly decorated
brasserie and the more formal Harringtons restaurant.
FOOD: Influences come from the Mediterranean, interpreted via
a selection of fresh British produce.
OUR TIP: Good range of Yorkshire cheeses
Chef: Phillip McVeagh, David Winter **Owners:** Mr T Harrington
Times: 12-2/6-10, Closed 1 Jan, BHs, closed L Sat, closed D Sun (ex
residents) **Notes:** Sun L £13.50, Vegetarian available, Smart casual, Civ
Wed 130 **Seats:** 46, Pr/dining room 30 **Smoking:** N/Sm in restaurant,
Air con **Children:** Portions **Rooms:** 24 (24 en suite) ★★★
Directions: M1 junct 40, A638, From Dewsbury take the A652 (signed
Bradford). Turn left at A62 and then 50 yds on right **Parking:** 90
e-mail: enquire@healdshall.co.uk **web:** www.healdshall.co.uk

HALIFAX MAP 19 SE02

Holdsworth House Hotel

British, European

Magnificent Jacobean manor-house dining

01422 240024   Holdsworth HX2 9TG

MENU GUIDE Guinea fowl, foie gras & Parma ham terrine
Whole lemon sole with parsley butter • Rhubarb & ginger crumble

WINE GUIDE Beringer Fumé Blanc £19.10 • Whistling Duck
Shiraz/Cabernet £16.50 • 60 bottles over £20, 30 bottles under
£20 • 11 by the glass (£2.95-£4.50)

PRICE GUIDE Fixed L fr £12.95 • starter £4.95-£8.50 • main
£11-£20 • dessert £5.50-£10.50 • coffee £2.95 • min/water
£2.95 • Service optional

PLACE: Owned by the same family for the past 40 years, the
restaurant is in the oldest part of this historic 17th-century manor
house and comprises three rooms, the Stone Room, the oak-
panelled Panel Room and the Mullion Room with its mullioned
windows overlooking the well-kept gardens.
FOOD: There is a real focus on quality British produce and the
menu names where certain produce originates - sea bass from
Anglesey, Gressingham duck, Reg Johnson's corn-fed chicken,
Galloway steak from the Lake District.

continued

HALIFAX continued MAP 19 SE02

OUR TIP: Delightful wedding venue
Chef: Garry Saunders **Owners:** Gail Moss, Kim Wynn **Times:** 12-2/ 7-9.30, Closed Xmas, Sun, closed L Sat **Notes:** Vegetarian available, Dress Restrictions, Smart casual, no shorts, Civ Wed 120 **Seats:** 45, Pr/dining room 120 **Smoking:** N/Sm in restaurant **Children:** Portions **Rooms:** 40 (40 en suite) ★★★ **Directions:** From Halifax take A629 (Keighley), 2 miles turn right at garage to Holmfield, hotel 1.5 miles on right **Parking:** 60 **e-mail:** info@holdsworthhouse.co.uk **web:** www.holdsworthhouse.co.uk

⑳⑳ Shibden Mill

British
Candlelit restaurant with a menu to draw the crowds

☎ 01422 365840 Shibden Mill Inn, Shibden Mill Fold, Shibden HX3 7UL

MENU GUIDE Gravadlax, sour cream, blinis • Venison, red cabbage, apples, roast chestnut sauce • Stem ginger sponge pudding

PRICE GUIDE Starter £4.25-£5.75 • main £10.95-£16.95 • dessert £4.50 • coffee £1.30 • Service optional

PLACE: Always busy, this traditional inn serves food in a candlelit loft conversion beneath a beamed ceiling hung with chandeliers. Tables are smartly dressed with crisp linen, and waited on by attentive and professional staff. The same menu is also available in the bar or garden in summer.
FOOD: A lengthy menu to suit most tastes, ranging from old favourites such as cottage pie, or ham hock, egg and chips to classier dishes brought to life by intriguing twists: sea bream with spinach rösti perhaps, or rabbit with smoked bacon, prunes and pine nuts.
OUR TIP: Great real ales served in the bar
Chef: Steve Evans **Owners:** Mr S D Heaton **Times:** 12-2/6-9.30, Closed 25 Dec (Eve), closed D 26 Dec, 31 Dec **Notes:** Vegetarian available, Civ Wed 70 **Seats:** 50, Pr/dining room 10 **Children:** Menu, Portions **Rooms:** 12 (12 en suite) ◆◆◆ **Directions:** Telephone for directions **Parking:** 100 **e-mail:** enquiries@shibdenmillinn.com **web:** www.shibdenmillinn.com

HAWORTH MAP 19 SE03

⑳ Weavers Restaurant with Rooms

British
Atmospheric weavers' barn close to the Brontë parsonage

☎ 01535 643822 15 West Ln BD22 8DU

continued

MENU GUIDE Smoked haddock soup, bacon & potato • Rare breed pork tenderloin, sausage stuffing, pancetta, cider sauce • Rhubarb brûlée

WINE GUIDE ⚲ Georges Duboeuf Sauvignon Blanc £14.95 • ⚲ Mataro Kingston Estate Shiraz £13.50 • 8 bottles over £20, 47 bottles under £20 • 10 by the glass (£3-£4)

PRICE GUIDE Fixed L £13.50 • Fixed D £16.50 • starter £4.95-£6.95 • main £9.95-£16.95 • dessert £4.95-£5.95 • coffee £1.75 min/water £2.75 • Service optional • Group min 6 service 10%

PLACE: Formerly part of a hand loom weaving complex, the building has lots of cottage features. The busy interior with its rich colours, church candles, mood lighting and mismatched furniture makes for an atmospheric place to eat - relaxed and full of character. Jazz and blues play discreetly in the background.
FOOD: British cooking, in modern and traditional styles, with a northern English bias. There's plenty of choice, including some old favourites.
OUR TIP: Bedrooms with period charm available
Chef: Colin, Tim & Jane Rushworth **Owners:** Colin & Jane Rushworth (& Family) **Times:** 11.30-2.30/6.30-9.30, Closed 1 wk Xmas, Mon, closed L Tue & Sat, closed D Sun **Notes:** Vegetarian available, Smart Dress, Clean & Tidy **Seats:** 65, Pr/dining room 14 **Smoking:** N/Sm in restaurant, Air con **Children:** Portions **Rooms:** 3 (3 en suite) 🏠 **Directions:** From A629 take B6142 towards Haworth, by Brontë Museum car park **Parking:** Brontë Museum car park (free 6pm-8am) **e-mail:** weaversinhaworth@aol.com **web:** www.weaverssmallhotel.co.uk

HUDDERSFIELD MAP 16 SE11

⑳⑳ The Weavers Shed Restaurant with Rooms

Modern British
Modern cooking with home-grown ingredients

☎ 01484 654284 Knowl Rd, Golcar HD7 4AN

MENU GUIDE Croustade tart of caramelised wild mushrooms • Chargrilled fillet of locally-bred Limousin beef • Soup-soufflé of bitter chocolate

WINE GUIDE 51 bottles over £20, 30 bottles under £20 • 6 by the glass (£3.50)

PRICE GUIDE Fixed L £11.50 • starter £6.95-£12.95 • main £14.95-£25.95 • dessert £6.25-£9.50 • coffee £2 • min/water £2.50 • Service optional

PLACE: Housed in an 18th-century converted cloth-finishing mill that retains many original features, the recently redecorated and contemporary furnished restaurant (its stone walls hung with framed menus from the world's famous restaurants) is driven by an amazing kitchen garden, supplying fruit, herbs, vegetables and free-range eggs from its ducks, chickens and quail.
FOOD: Freshness and seasonality of ingredients is of the highest quality, fed by home-grown, wild picked and locally-reared produce, the modern British cooking displaying flair and imagination, with clear flavours that shine through. Excellent wine list.
OUR TIP: Lovely, spacious and well-equipped rooms
Chef: S Jackson, I McGunnigle, C Sill **Owners:** Stephen & Tracy Jackson **Times:** 12-2/7-9, Closed 25 Dec-7 Jan, Sun, Mon, closed L Sat **Notes:** Vegetarian available **Seats:** 36, Pr/dining room 16 **Smoking:** N/Sm in restaurant **Rooms:** 5 (5 en suite) ◆◆◆◆ **Directions:** 3m W of Huddersfield off A62. (Please telephone for further directions) **Parking:** 30 **e-mail:** info@weaversshed.co.uk **web:** www.weaversshed.co.uk

LKLEY MAP 19 SE14

🌸🌸🌸 **Box Tree** *see below*

🌸🌸 **Rombalds Hotel & Restaurant**

uropean

egant Georgian town house with robust
ining

☎ 01943 603201   11 West View, Wells Rd
529 9JG

MENU GUIDE Confit duck & roast fig salad • Poached pheasant,
rain mustard mash • Apple & toffee tart

continued

WINE GUIDE ♀ Louis Chatel Sauvignon Blanc £10.75 • ♀ Louis
Chatel Cabernet Sauvignon/Merlot £10.75 • 43 bottles over £20,
56 bottles under £20 • 6 by the glass

PRICE GUIDE Fixed L £8.95 • Fixed D £14.95 • starter £3.95-
£5.95 • main £11.95-£24.95 • dessert £5.25 • coffee
£2.65 • min/water £2.75 • Service optional

PLACE: Set between the town centre and Ilkley Moor, this
elegant Georgian property enjoys a peaceful terrace setting.
Delightful day rooms include a choice of comfortable lounges
and an attractive restaurant with relaxed ambience.
FOOD: Modern European dishes are prepared with skill and
flair by enthusiastic young kitchen staff. Expect dishes like
scallop skewers on sweet-pickled vegetable salad or rosemary &
apricot stuffed pork fillet wrapped in Parma ham on an apple
rösti.
OUR TIP: A walk on the moors to build up your appetite
Chef: Michael Trowbridge **Owners:** Colin & Jo Clarkson **Times:** 12-
2.30/6.30-9, Closed 28 Dec-2 Jan **Notes:** Sun L 2 courses £11.95, 3
courses £13.95, Vegetarian available, Smart casual, Civ Wed 70 **Seats:** 34,
Pr/dining room 70 **Smoking:** N/Sm in restaurant **Children:** Menu,
Portions **Rooms:** 18 (18 en suite) ★★★ **Directions:** From Leeds take
A65 to Ilkley. At 3rd main lights turn left & follow signs for Ilkley Moor. At
junct take Wells Rd, by bank. Hotel 600 yds on left **Parking:** 22
e-mail: reception@rombalds.demon.co.uk
web: www.rombalds.co.uk

☕ **Bettys Café Tea Rooms** 32-34 The Grove
YO1 2QP ☎ 01943 608029 Winner of The Tea Guild Award of
Excellence 2005.

KLEY MAP 19 SE14

Box Tree

ritish, French

uperb cooking in legendary restaurant

☎ 01943 608484 35-37 Church St LS29 9DR
MENU GUIDE Niçoise of roasted langoustines • Pot-roast squab
igeon, grilled polenta, roasted ceps, red wine fumet • Crème
rûlée, jus Granny Smith
WINE GUIDE ♀ Chablis Durup Chardonnay £29.90
♀ Domaine Chaintreuil Fleurie Gamay £29.90 • 400 bottles over
£20, 12 bottles under £20 • 6 by the glass (£4-£5.50)
PRICE GUIDE Fixed L £18 • Fixed D £28 • starter £10.50-£15
ain £23-£36 • dessert £7.50 • coffee £4 • min/water £3.50

PLACE: Chef-patron Simon Gueller has made a welcome return
the stove at the legendary Box Tree and looks determined to
tore it to its former glory. The cottage-style town-centre
taurant features an interesting collection of art and antiques
t define the style and luxury for which the Box Tree is famed,
d open fires feature in colder months. It's welcoming and
mate, backed by professional, highly attentive yet friendly
vice.

FOOD: Simon Gueller continues the style that made his name at
Rascasse and Guellers in Leeds; modern French classical cuisine
with a serious commitment to sourcing the best, freshest local
ingredients. The approach, via prix-fixe lunch and enticing carte,
comes dotted with luxury items and brimming with clear flavours
and assured combinations. A fillet of turbot with a velouté of
oysters and chervil, or tournedos Rossini, and a prune and
Armagnac soufflé with sauce anglaise ensure the Box Tree is a
culinary delight.
OUR TIP: Excellent value lunch and extensive wine list
Chef: Mr S Gueller **Owners:** Mrs R Gueller **Times:** 12-2/7-9.30, Closed
Xmas-New Year, 1-15 Jan, Mon, closed L Tue-Thur, closed D Sun
Notes: Dress Restrictions, Smart casual **Seats:** 50, Pr/dining room 16
Smoking: N/Sm in restaurant, Air con **Children:** Min 10 yrs (Sun)
Directions: On A65 from Leeds through Ilkley, main lights approx
200 yds on left **Parking:** NCP **e-mail:** info@theboxtree.co.uk
web: www.theboxtree.co.uk

KEIGHLEY MAP 19 SE04

The Harlequin Restaurant
British
Popular neighbourhood bistro
☎ 01535 633277 139 Keighley Rd, Cowling BD22 0AH

MENU GUIDE Warm salad of king scallops & fillet steak Duckling, savoury apple crumble, rhubarb sauce • Trio of chocolate desserts
WINE GUIDE ♀ Beelgara Chardonnay £11.50 • ♀ Beelgara Shiraz £11.50 • 150 bottles over £20, 100 bottles under £20 10 by the glass (£2-£6)
PRICE GUIDE Starter £3.50-£7 • main £9.50-£19 • dessert £4.50-£6.25 • coffee £2.75 • min/water £2.50

continued

PLACE: This cosy high-street bistro has ambience a-plenty and is so popular that you'll need to book a table a month or so in advance. Closed Mondays and Tuesdays.
FOOD: The Harlequin's secret is its varied and extensive menu, a cunning blend of culinary nostalgia and modern British cuisine. Puddings particularly impress, and there's a good range of dessert wines by way of accompaniment.
OUR TIP: The restaurant menu is available in the bar
Owners: Mr & Mrs S Robinson **Times:** 12-3/6.30-11, Closed 4 days at Xmas, Mon-Tue, closed L Wed-Sun, closed D Wed-Sun **Notes:** Sun menu 3 courses (incl. coffee) £14.95, Vegetarian available **Seats:** 42
Smoking: N/Sm in restaurant **Children:** Min 6 yrs D, Portions
Directions: On A6068 in Cowling village, between Crosshills and Colne. (6m from M65) **Parking:** 10
e-mail: simon@harlequin.fsbusiness.co.uk

LEEDS MAP 19 SE23

 ### Anthony's Restaurant
see below

 ### Brasserie Forty Four
Mediterranean, British
Vibrant brasserie on the waterfront
☎ 0113 234 3232 44 The Calls LS2 7EW
MENU GUIDE Mulligatawny soup • Duck, roast beetroot, shallots, sour cream • Amaretto cheesecake, glazed fruits, bitter chocolate

continue

LEEDS MAP 19 SE23

Anthony's Restaurant

European **NEW**
A rising star
☎ 0113 245 5922 19 Boar Ln LS1 5DA
MENU GUIDE Cep velouté, salt cod, kikos • Suckling pig, quinoa, rhubarb • Pineapple & black olive Tatin, cardamom ice cream
WINE GUIDE ♀ Tasman Bay Sauvignon Blanc £22.95 • ♀ Brentino Maculan Merlot/Cabernet £27.95 • 68 bottles over £20, 8 bottles under £20 • 4 by the glass (£4.95-£6.95)
PRICE GUIDE Fixed L £18.95 • starter £6.95-£12.50 • main £21.95-£25 • dessert £6.45-£12.95 • coffee £2.95 • min/water £2.85 • Service optional
PLACE: Two floors comprise this innovative Leeds' eaterie: a curved dining room downstairs decorated in clean, minimalist style, and above, a chic bar for pre- and post-dinner drinks. Relaxed and friendly service encourages a leisurely meal, as does a 2 am licence.

FOOD: Bold modern cuisine from a chef, Anthony Flinn, with an impressive pedigree (he has trained with John Campbell and worked at the famous El Bulli in Spain). This is food designed to wow – superbly presented, always exciting, and achingly modish with dishes along the lines of roast duck with malt loaf cannelloni, or confit monkfish with baby octopus and pumpkin ravioli. Amazing pre-starters, amuses bouches (red mullet, langoustine 'horchata'), pre-desserts (banana sorbet on white chocolate cookie) and petits fours. Not to be missed.
OUR TIP: Be adventurous when choosing your meal
Chef: Anthony Flinn **Owners:** Anthony Flinn **Times:** 12-2.30/7-9.30, Closed 1 wk early Sep, BH Mon & Tue, Sun, Mon **Notes:** Vegetarian available, Dress Restrictions, Smart dress **Seats:** 36 **Smoking:** N/Sm in restaurant, Air con **Children:** Portions **Directions:** Close to railway station and Corn Exchange **Parking:** NCP
e-mail: reservations@anthonysrestaurant.co.uk
web: www.anthonysrestaurant.co.uk

WINE GUIDE ♀ Concha y Toro Chardonnay £14.95 • ♂ Concha y Toro Merlot £14.95 • 32 bottles over £20, 36 bottles under £20 • 3 by the glass (£3.65)

PRICE GUIDE Fixed L £12.50 • Fixed D £16 • starter £4.25-£12 main £10.95-£15.50 • dessert £5 • coffee £1.90 • min/water £1.95 • Service added but optional 10%

PLACE: This breezy brasserie is a fun and relaxed setting, designed to suit all ages and occasions. Set in an old grain store on the waterfront, it's decorated in vibrant shades of terracotta and yellow, and has large windows overlooking the Leeds-Liverpool canal.

FOOD: Something to suit everyone here; expect straightforward dishes with a fashionable edge and cosmopolitan flavour. A lengthy selection of mains ranges from crowd-pleasers such as steak or chicken Kiev, to more modish combinations: Scottish salmon with a leek and tarragon risotto perhaps.

OUR TIP: Great value lunchtime and early diner menus

Chef: Jeff Baker **Owners:** Michael Gill **Times:** 12-2/6-10.30, Closed BHs, Sun, closed L Sat **Notes:** Vegetarian available **Seats:** 110, Pr/dining room 50 **Smoking:** No pipes, No cigars, Air con **Children:** Portions **Directions:** From Crown Point Bridge, left past Church, left into High Court Lane. On river **Parking:** On street, NCP

e-mail: info@brasserie44.com **web:** www.brasserie44.com

🏵 De Vere Oulton Hall

British

Impressive hotel with reliably good food

☎ 0113 282 1000 Rothwell Ln, Oulton LS26 8HN

MENU GUIDE Tartare of trout • Roast partridge, blackberry sauce • Spiced Bakewell tart

WINE GUIDE ♀ Sancerre £20.50 • ♂ Rioja £21.95 • 30 bottles over £20, 20 bottles under £20 • 20 by the glass (£5.50-£6.25)

PRICE GUIDE Fixed L £14 • starter £4.50-£7.95 • main £13-£22 • dessert £5-£7.50 • coffee £3.95 • min/water £3.50

PLACE: Clever lighting and the strategic siting of solid pillars creates some privacy in this huge dining room. The dark reds, clarets and creams perfectly complement the elegant Victorian property.

FOOD: The menu has distinctly classical leanings in spite of its modern French avowal, enhanced by clever pastry work and great ingredients. A game menu in season is popular, as is the separate vegetarian list.

OUR TIP: Excellent breads, amuses bouches and petits fours

Chef: Steve Collinson **Owners:** De Vere Hotels **Times:** 12.30-2.30/7-9.45 **Notes:** Vegetarian available, Dress Restrictions, No jeans **Seats:** 200, Pr/dining room 60 **Smoking:** N/Sm in restaurant, Air con **Children:** Menu, Portions **Rooms:** 152 (152 en suite) ★★★★★ **Directions:** Telephone for directions **Parking:** 150

e-mail: oulton.hall@devere-hotels.com **web:** www.devereonline.co.uk/oultonhall

🏵🏵 Haley's Hotel & Restaurant

British, French

Cooking with flair in stylish hotel in leafy suburb

☎ 0113 278 4446 Shire Oak Rd, Headingley LS6 2DE

MENU GUIDE Lobster risotto, parmesan foam • Venison, fig tart, celeriac rösti, port jus • Passionfruit sorbet, posset & soufflé

WINE GUIDE ♀ Le Charme Sauvignon Blanc £16.95 • ♂ El Picador Merlot £16.95 • 90 bottles over £20, 15 bottles under £20 • 8 by the glass (£4-£10)

PRICE GUIDE Fixed L £18.95 • Fixed D £35 • coffee £2.50 • min/water £4.50 • Service optional

Haley's Hotel & Restaurant

PLACE: This townhouse hotel has a real country feel, tucked away down a tree-lined cul-de-sac, yet it's only a couple of miles from the city centre and has the Headingley cricket ground on the doorstep. The smart, richly furnished, traditionally styled dining room comes complete with professional service, swagged-and-tailed curtains, white linen and walls hung with contemporary art.

FOOD: The appealing modern menu is sensibly concise and dotted with French influence and luxury ingredients. The kitchen style is minimalist and modern, clean cut and unfussy, with slick cooking and presentation to the fore.

OUR TIP: Popular as an event venue

Chef: Jon Vennell **Owners:** John Appleyard **Times:** 12-2.30/7-10, Closed 26-30 Dec, closed L Mon-Sat, closed D Sun **Notes:** Vegetarian available, Dress Restrictions, No jeans, Civ Wed 100 **Seats:** 60, Pr/dining room 24 **Smoking:** N/Sm in restaurant, Air con **Children:** Portions **Rooms:** 28 (28 en suite) ★★★★ **Directions:** 2m N of city centre off A660, between HSBC & Starbucks **Parking:** 29

e-mail: info@haleys.co.uk **web:** www.haleys.co.uk

🏵 Malmaison Hotel

Modern French

Funky French brasserie food in stylish hotel

☎ 0113 398 1000 Sovereign Quay LS1 1DQ

MENU GUIDE Greek salad with pan-fried halloumi • Roasted guinea fowl on polenta cake with baby vegetables • Banana iced parfait with caramelised bananas

PRICE GUIDE Food prices not confirmed for 2006. Please telephone for details

PLACE: A stylish, fashionable venue with a contemporary ground floor oak-panelled restaurant, where tables are closely set and staff are welcoming and knowledgeable.

FOOD: Brasserie food with a twist - like the hotel, it's contemporary, with simple, clear flavours and quality ingredients. Expect dishes like loin of rabbit stuffed with tomato, shallots and thyme, served with mushrooms à la grecque and confit potato.

continued

continued

England

OUR TIP: Ask for the local specials
Times: 12-2.30/6-11 **Rooms:** 100 (100 en suite) ★★★
Directions: City centre. 5 mins walk from Leeds railway station. On junct
16 of Loop Road, Sovereign St & Swingate
e-mail: leeds@malmaison.com **web:** www.malmaison.com

⚜⚜ Pool Court at 42

French

Stylish dining in waterfront location

☎ 0113 244 4242 44 The Calls LS2 7EW

MENU GUIDE Sea scallops, carrot purée • Roast turbot, leek
risotto, oxtail jus • Valrhona chocolate soufflé

WINE GUIDE ♀ Babich Sauvignon Blanc £19.50 • ♟ Trentham
Shiraz £19.95 • 121 bottles over £20, 13 bottles under £20 • 3 by
the glass (£4.50)

PRICE GUIDE Fixed L £25-£39.50 • Fixed D £30-£47.50 • coffee
£2.45 • min/water £2.95 • Service added 10%

PLACE: This restaurant has a cool, waterfront location in an old
grain store building. The modern but intimate interior has a fine
dining restaurant - with a balcony for smokers - and a buzzy
bistro next door. Friendly, efficient and knowledgeable staff.
FOOD: Menus are classic French in style lightened by modern
techniques with imaginative combinations like the Jerusalem
artichoke confit, chestnuts and little onions, wild mushrooms and
potato espuma or whipped brie mille-feuille with Perigord truffle
and apple coleslaw.
OUR TIP: Try the excellent breads and sound puddings
Chef: Jeff Baker **Owners:** Michael Gill **Times:** 12-2/7-10, Closed BHs,
Sun, closed L Sat **Notes:** Tasting menu 8 courses £59 incl. coffee,
Vegetarian available **Seats:** 38 **Smoking:** N/Sm in restaurant, Air con
Children: Min 3 yrs, Portions **Directions:** From Crown Point, left past
church, left into High Court Lane **Parking:** On street, NCP
e-mail: info@poolcourt.com **web:** www.poolcourt.com

⚜ Quantro

International

Imaginative cooking in stylish surroundings

☎ 0113 288 8063 62 St Lane LS8 2DQ

MENU GUIDE Ravioli of Dublin Bay prawns • Calves' liver with
pancetta • Dark chocolate soufflé, milk chocolate parfait

WINE GUIDE ♀ Santa Rita Sauvignon Blanc £15.30 • ♟ Martinez
Bujanda Tempranillo £13.95 • 12 bottles over £20, 35 bottles
under £20 • 12 by the glass (£3.15-£6)

PRICE GUIDE Fixed L £9.95-£14.10 • Fixed D £12.95-
£18.30 • starter £4.20-£5.50 • main £10.20-£16.90 • dessert
£3.90-£4.50 • coffee £1.60 • min/water £2.20 • Service added
but optional 10%

PLACE: Chunky banquettes with dark wood tables and floors
characterise the bright interior of this contemporarily minimalist
eaterie, where a lime green and aubergine colour scheme adds
to the sophisticated ambience.
FOOD: International cooking with hints of modern and traditional
British, all mixed in confidently cosmopolitan dishes and served
in a slick but unobtrusive way.
OUR TIP: Low-cost lunches and Saturday evening post-theatre deals
Chef: Andrew Brooks **Owners:** Tim and Kath Burdekin **Times:** 12-2/6-
10, Closed 25-26 Dec, 1 Jan, Sun **Notes:** Vegetarian available, Dress
Restrictions, Smart casual preferred **Seats:** 60 **Smoking:** N/Sm in
restaurant, Air con **Children:** Min 8 yrs **Directions:** Near Roundhay
rdbt, Leeds **Parking:** On Street **e-mail:** info@quantro.co.uk
web: www.quantro.co.uk

⚜⚜ Simply Heathcotes Leeds

British

Canal-side brasserie

☎ 0113 244 6611 Canal Wharf, Water Ln LS11 5PS

MENU GUIDE Steamed mussels, crab, saffron, fennel • Slow-
roast pork, spiced honey gravy • Bread & butter pudding

WINE GUIDE ♀ Vision Chardonnay £16 • ♟ Vision Merlot
Cabernet £16 • 60 bottles over £20, 13 bottles under £20 • 10 by
the glass (£3.85-£5.25)

PRICE GUIDE Fixed L £14 • Fixed D £16 • starter £2.75-£8 • main
£9.95-£19.50 • dessert £5.50 • coffee £1.80 • min/water
£3.25 • Service optional • Group min 8 service 10%

PLACE: Trendy brasserie housed in a former warehouse
overlooking the Leeds-Liverpool canal. Its old stone walls and
beams are complemented by a low-key modern decor.
FOOD: The menu is a mix of old and new like the setting, and
features a lengthy range of classic English dishes updated with
contemporary panache. Black pudding is a typical starter, served
with a sauté of chestnuts, bacon & onion, while mains might
include braised beef with horseradish mash.
OUR TIP: Lunch is good value
Chef: Simon Peacock **Owners:** Paul Heathcote **Times:** 12-2.30/6-10,
Closed 25-26 Dec, 1-2 Jan, BH Mons **Notes:** Sun D 2 courses £14.50,
3 courses £17, Vegetarian available **Seats:** 110 **Smoking:** N/Sm in
restaurant, Air con **Children:** Menu, Portions **Directions:** 0.5m from
M621 junct 3; follow signs to city centre, turn left into Water Lane, then
right on Canal Wharf. On Canal Basin **Parking:** 20
e-mail: leeds@heathcotes.co.uk **web:** www.heathcotes.co.uk

⚜ Thorpe Park Hotel & Spa

Italian

Contemporary food in spacious modern setting

☎ 0113 264 1000 Century Way, Thorpe Park LS15 8Z

MENU GUIDE Whitby crab cakes, aioli, celeriac remoulade
Lamb shank, minted peas, mash, burgundy wine sauce • Hot
blackberry sponge

WINE GUIDE ♀ Domaine Sarry Sancerre £22.95 • ♟ Domaine
Rion Pinot Noir £21.95 • 42 bottles over £20, 17 bottles under
£20 • 13 by the glass (£4.95-£9.75)

PRICE GUIDE Fixed L £14.50 • starter £5.50-£12.50 • main
£12.50-£21.50 • dessert £5.95-£6.95 • coffee £3.95 • min/water
£3.65 • Service optional

PLACE: Just off the M1 near Leeds, this modern hotel is a have
of contemporary comfort with a state-of-the-art spa. A range of
food options includes a spacious open-plan restaurant modishly
done out in light woods and leather.
FOOD: Expect a tempting range of contemporary European
dishes, with a bias towards Italy. Your choice might include lem

continu

sole with caper butter and fries, or heartier fare such as calves' liver with bacon, mash and onion gravy.
OUR TIP: Lighter meals available beneath a stunning glass atrium in the courtyard
Chef: Darren Winder **Owners:** Shire Hotels **Times:** 12-2/6.45-9.30, Closed L Sat & Sun **Notes:** Vegetarian available, Civ Wed 90 **Seats:** 120, Pr/dining room 50 **Smoking:** N/Sm in restaurant, Air con
Children: Menu, Portions **Rooms:** 123 (123 en suite) ★★★★
Parking: 200 **e-mail:** thorpepark@shirehotels.co.uk
web: www.shirehotels.co.uk

Bibis Minerva House, 16 Greek St LS1 5RU
☎ 0113 243 0905 Bustling contemporary Italian.

MARSDEN MAP 16 SE01

Hey Green Country House Hotel

British **NEW**

Modern brasserie in elegant surroundings
☎ 01484 844235 Waters Rd HD7 6NG
MENU GUIDE Wild mushroom risotto with Parmesan • Salmon with crushed potatoes & chive butter sauce • Lemon tart with raspberry sorbet
PRICE GUIDE Food prices not confirmed for 2006. Please telephone for details

PLACE: This delightful Victorian country house style property sits in extensive landscaped gardens. The restaurant has a contemporary turquoise and terracotta decor, giving it an airy Mediterranean feel.
FOOD: The cooking is highly accomplished – dishes are uncomplicated and well judged using good ingredients and producing great flavours. Even the bread is good. Definitely one to watch.
OUR TIP: Fantastic wedding venue
Chef: Nigel Skinkiss **Owners:** S. Hunter, M. Dolman **Times:** 7-9
Rooms: 12 (12 en suite) ★★ **e-mail:** info@heygreen.com
web: www.heygreen.com

OTLEY MAP 19 SE24

Chevin Country Park Hotel

British, European

Ambitious cuisine in country retreat
Scandinavian style
☎ 01943 467818 Yorkgate LS21 3NU
MENU GUIDE Chargrilled asparagus, truffled hollandaise • Sea bass, basil mash, pesto • Lime cheesecake, Horlicks ice cream
WINE GUIDE 50 bottles over £20, 39 bottles under £20 • 12 by the glass (£2.85-£4.95)

continued

PRICE GUIDE Fixed L £16.95 • Fixed D £21.95 • starter £5.95-£7.95 • main £13.95-£21.50 • dessert £5.95-£13.50 • coffee £2.95 • min/water £2.95 • Service included
PLACE: At the heart of Chevin's fifty-acre country park stands this huge Scandinavian-style log-built hotel. Rooms are split between the main building and chalet-style accommodation. Window tables in the split-level restaurant overlook the wildlife-rich lake and woodland.
FOOD: Two- and three-course fixed-price menus and an ambitious carte list a good range of modern British dishes.
OUR TIP: Well-equipped leisure centre
Chef: Simon Forsey **Owners:** Chevin Lodge Limited **Times:** 12-2/6.30-9.15, Closed L Mon, Sat **Notes:** Vegetarian available, Dress Restrictions, Smart casual minimum, Civ Wed 120 **Seats:** 70, Pr/dining room 30
Smoking: N/Sm in restaurant **Children:** Menu, Portions **Rooms:** 49 (49 en suite) ★★★ **Directions:** Take A658 towards Harrogate. Left at 1st turning towards Carlton turn 2nd left towards Yorkgate **Parking:** 100
e-mail: reception@chevinhotel.com
web: www.chevinhotel.com

PONTEFRACT MAP 16 SE42

Wentbridge House Hotel

British, French

Classical cuisine in elegant country house
☎ 01977 620 444 WF8 3JJ

MENU GUIDE Goats' cheese bruschetta • Crisp confit of duck leg • Pecan nut tart, amaretto ice cream
WINE GUIDE Jean Marc Brocard Chablis Manants £25.50 • Louis Latour Fleurie 'Les Garans' £26.50 • 100 bottles over £20, 50 bottles under £20 • 10 by the glass (£3.50-£4.50)
PRICE GUIDE Fixed L £12.50 • Fixed D £28 • starter £6-£15 • main £16-£30 • dessert £5.50-£7 • coffee £2.95 • min/water £2.95 • Service optional

PLACE: An oasis off the A1, this country house dates back to the early 18th century and sits in beautifully landscaped gardens. Choose between the modern brasserie and more formal dining room.
FOOD: The quality of cooking, combining British and French influences, is consistently high in both dining areas, though the more casual brasserie menu offers several dishes as starter or main course, such as chargrilled tuna with niçoise salad, and pan-fried calves' liver.
OUR TIP: Enjoy a pre-meal stroll in the grounds
Chef: Steve Turner **Owners:** Mr G Page **Times:** 12.15-2.30/7.15-9.30, Closed 25 Dec eve, closed D Sun **Notes:** Vegetarian available, Smart Dress, Civ Wed 130 **Seats:** 60, Pr/dining room 24 **Smoking:** No pipes
Children: Portions **Rooms:** 18 (18 en suite) ★★★ **Directions:** 0.5m off A1, 4m S of M62/A1 junct **Parking:** 100
e-mail: info@wentbridgehouse.co.uk
web: www.wentbridgehouse.co.uk

SHIPLEY MAP 19 SE13

⊚⊚ Beeties Gallery Restaurant
Modern British

Parisian café dining in West Yorkshire

☎ 01274 595988 581718 7 Victoria Rd, Saltaire Village BD18 3LA

MENU GUIDE Seared scallops, sauce vierge, roast tomatoes, rocket • Smoked haddock, poached egg, mustard sauce • Banana tarte Tatin

WINE GUIDE ♀ Veilies Vignes Sauvignon Blanc £14.50 • ♀ Veilies Vignes Merlot £14.50 • 10 bottles over £20, 15 bottles under £20 • 12 by the glass (£2.95-£5.50)

PRICE GUIDE Fixed L £9.95-£13.95 • Fixed D £15.95-£25 • starter £4.50-£6.95 • main £9.95-£16.95 • dessert £4.50-£5.95 • coffee £1.95 • min/water £3.20 • Service optional • Group min 10 service 10%

PLACE: Converted Victorian mill in the World Heritage Site of Saltaire model industrial village. There is a tapas bar and bistro serving light meals and drinks on the ground floor, while the fine dining restaurant is located upstairs. The restaurant interior is decorated in the style of a French café; service is friendly and the atmosphere is happy and relaxed.
FOOD: Well-presented dishes are offered from fixed-price menus. The emphasis is on seasonal local produce, including good quality fresh fish daily.
OUR TIP: Wide choice of hot beverages and liqueurs
Chef: Wayne Brimicombe **Owners:** Jayne Dixon-Hill, Wayne Brimicombe **Times:** 12-2/6-10, Closed 2 days between Xmas & New Year **Notes:** Vegetarian available, Dress Restrictions, Smart casual preferred **Seats:** 50 **Smoking:** N/Sm in restaurant **Children:** Portions **Rooms:** 5 (5 en suite) 🐕 **Directions:** 50 yds from Saltaire Railway Station **Parking:** On street, nearby car park **e-mail:** info@beeties.co.uk **web:** www.beeties.co.uk

⊚ Marriott Hollins Hall Hotel & Country Club
British

Stylish and formal dining in beautiful countryside

☎ 01274 530053 Hollins Hill BD17 7QW

MENU GUIDE Coarse pork terrine, home-made piccalilli • Herb-rolled lamb loin, broad bean cassoulet • Mulled poached pear, brandy snap

WINE GUIDE ♀ Penfolds Sauvignon £17.60 • ♀ Galope Merlot £16.25 • 46 bottles over £20, 30 bottles under £20 • 20 by the glass (£5.10-£7.85)

PRICE GUIDE Fixed L £11.95-£25 • Fixed D £25 • starter £4.75-£8.95 • main £13-£20.50 • dessert £5.25-£5.95 • coffee £2.25 • min/water £3.75 • Service optional

PLACE: This Victorian mansion built in the Elizabethan style sits in 200 acres of grounds. Formal table service and smart casual dress code set the tone for a traditional dining venue, topped off with soft piano music in the background and views over the gardens.
FOOD: Dishes are prepared in the modern style, with roots in classical French cuisine and flavours from Asia adding to the cosmopolitan feel of the menu.
OUR TIP: Desserts are worth saving room for
Chef: Sean Kelly **Owners:** Marriott International **Times:** 12.30-2.00/6.30-9.30, Closed L Sat, Closed D BHs **Notes:** Sun L from £11.95, Vegetarian available, Civ Wed 120 **Seats:** 120, Pr/dining room 30 **Smoking:** N/Sm in restaurant, Air con **Children:** Menu, Portions
continued

Rooms: 122 (122 en suite) ★★★★ **Directions:** From A650 follow signs to Salt Mill. At lights in Shipley take A6038. Hotel 3m on left **Parking:** 250 **e-mail:** reservations.hollinshall@marriotthotels.co.uk **web:** www.marriotthotels.com/lbags

TODMORDEN MAP 18 SD92

⊚ The Old Hall
Modern British

Elizabethan manor serving seasonal sensations

☎ 01706 815998 OL14 7AD

MENU GUIDE Filo parcel of black pudding, pear, chives, pine nuts • Roast pork fillet with pancetta • Yorkshire parkin with ginger sauce

WINE GUIDE ♀ Riunite Pinot Grigio/Chardonnay £11.95 • ♀ Wilsons Quay Cabernet Sauvignon/Sangiovese £11.95 • 67 bottles over £20, 62 bottles under £20 • 10 by the glass (£2.30-£4.75)

PRICE GUIDE Fixed L £10 • starter £4.50-£7.50 • main £12.50-£15.50 • dessert £4.95 • coffee £1.50 • min/water £3.25 • Service optional • Group min 10 service 10%

PLACE: Records of the Old Hall start in 1294, and some of the original timbers and wattle and daub still exist. It was extended in 1603. The reception has a magnificently carved mantelpiece and wood panelling.
FOOD: The motto on the enscribed mantelpiece says it all: 'Native soil is sweet'. This is the inspiration for the kitchen, where fresh and locally sourced ingredients are prepared with skill and presented in an attractive modern British style.
OUR TIP: Customer comfort and satisfaction are paramount
Chef: Chris Roberts **Owners:** Nick & Madeleine Hoyle **Times:** 12-2/7-9.30, Closed Xmas, 1 Jan, 1st wk Jan, Mon, closed L Tue, Wed, Sat, closed D Sun **Notes:** Sun L 3 courses £16, Vegetarian available, Civ Wed 50 **Seats:** 70, Pr/dining room 24 **Smoking:** N/Sm area, No pipes **Children:** Portions **Directions:** Near town centre & rail station. Between Hall St & Rise Lane, off A6033 (Rochdale road) **Parking:** 5

WAKEFIELD MAP 16 SE32

⊚ Brasserie Ninety Nine
British, European

Brasserie in unusual business environment

☎ 01924 377699 Trinity Business Park WF2 8EF

MENU GUIDE Wild mushroom & sherry soup • Pan-roasted salmon with spinach • Baileys crème brûlée

WINE GUIDE ♀ De Gras Sauvignon Blanc Reserva £16.50 • ♀ De Gras Merlot Reserva £16.50 • 18 bottles over £20, 24 bottles under £20 • 6 by the glass (£3-£4.25)

PRICE GUIDE Fixed L £8.99 • starter £3.50-£8.95 • main £12.95-£17.95 • dessert £4.95 • coffee £1.95 • min/water £3.50 • Service optional • Group min 10 service 10%
continued

England

PLACE: An all-day brasserie located in the unusual setting of a high-tech business park. The restaurant has a bar area and the dining room is unashamedly modern with portholes instead of windows, lots of steel, glass and coral pink paintwork. Service is cheerful and well informed.

FOOD: Modern European in style, the menu uses best quality ingredients sourced from around the UK. Dishes are at their best when simply constructed as in roasted rack of lamb with garlic and herb crust.

OUR TIP: Value for money wine list

Chef: Alan Gazeley **Owners:** Mr N Parkin **Times:** 12-5.30/5.30-9.30, Closed 25 Dec, 1 Jan, BHs, Sun **Notes:** Vegetarian available, Dress Restrictions **Seats:** 120, Pr/dining room 40 **Smoking:** N/Sm in restaurant, Air con **Children:** Menu, Portions **Parking:** 40

Waterton Park Hotel

British, International   **NEW**

Simple fare in unique island setting

☎ 01924 257911 Walton Hall, The Balk, Walton WF2 6PW

MENU GUIDE Game terrine, pear & apple chutney • Monkfish, lime couscous, lemongrass oil • Dark chocolate & prune terrine

WINE GUIDE ♀ Moondarra Chardonnay £11.95 • ♀ Momre Brook Shiraz £24.95

PRICE GUIDE Fixed L £15 • Fixed D £24.95 • starter £5.25-£6.95 • main £14.95-£17.25 • dessert £4.25 • coffee £1.80 • min/water £2.75 • Service optional

PLACE: Idyllically set on an island in the midst of a lake and wildfowl park, this friendly hotel is a popular choice for wedding functions, and boasts two bars and a leisure centre as well as its waterside restaurant.

FOOD: Waterton's cooking has been quietly improving for some time, and is characterised by simple combinations of locally sourced ingredients. The menu changes daily.

OUR TIP: Definitely save room for dessert

Chef: David Wrend **Owners:** The Kaye Family **Times:** 12-2/7-9.30 **Notes:** Vegetarian available, Smart casual, Civ Wed 150 **Seats:** 50, Pr/dining room 35 **Smoking:** N/Sm in restaurant **Children:** Portions **Rooms:** 61 (61 en suite) ★★★ **Directions:** From Wakefield follow A61 to Walton and follow brown signs. M1 junct 39, A638 (Crofton) **Parking:** 130 **e-mail:** watertonpark@bestwestern.co.uk **web:** watertonparkhotel.co.uk

WETHERBY MAP 16 SE44

⊛⊛ Wood Hall Hotel

British, European   ⌀

Grand dining in luxurious and romantic Georgian weekend country retreat

☎ 01937 587271 Trip Ln, Linton LS22 4JA

continued

MENU GUIDE Spiced foie gras, gingerbread crumb • Buccleuch beef, oxtail faggot • Lemon & lime tart, bay leaf ice cream

WINE GUIDE ♀ Michel Laroche Chardonnay £22 • ♀ Graham Beck Shiraz/Cabernet Sauvignon £24 • 98 bottles over £20, 2 bottles under £20 • 12 by the glass (£4.50-£11)

PRICE GUIDE Fixed L £18.50-£25 • Fixed D £32.50-£46 • starter £6-£9 • main £22-£24 • dessert £6-£7.95 • coffee £3.50 min/water £3.75 • Service optional

PLACE: This 18th-century country-house hotel in 100 acres of beautiful parkland provides a strikingly opulent setting for The Georgian Restaurant. The dining room is richly furnished with fine oils on the walls and impressive views over the rolling Yorkshire countryside.

FOOD: The French menu offers dishes characterised by bold and adventurous flavour combinations, and minimalist descriptions. Loin of Perthshire venison with a gin and juniper jus might follow a velouté of Jerusalem artichokes scented with white truffle. Timing and sauces are both well handled and there's good use of seasonal produce, notably baby vegetables.

OUR TIP: Great selection of farmhouse cheeses

Chef: Ian Samson **Owners:** Hand Picked Hotels **Times:** 1-3/6.30-9.30, Closed L Mon-Sat **Notes:** Coffee incl., Vegetarian available, Dress Restrictions, No jeans, No trainers, Civ Wed 120 **Seats:** 35, Pr/dining room 100 **Smoking:** N/Sm in restaurant **Children:** Menu, Portions **Rooms:** 44 (44 en suite) ★★★★ **Directions:** From Wetherby take A661(Harrogate road) N for 0.5m. Left to Sicklinghall/Linton. Cross bridge, left to Linton/Woodhall. Right opp Windmill Inn, 1.25m to hotel, (follow brown signs) **Parking:** 100 **web:** www.handpicked.co.uk

CHANNEL ISLANDS

GUERNSEY

CASTEL MAP 24

⊛ La Grande Mare Hotel, Golf and Country Club

International   🐟

Well-located hotel with ocean views

☎ 01481 256576 The Coast Rd, Vazon Bay GY5 7LL

MENU GUIDE French onion soup • Poached sole roulade • Lemon citrus tart, Chantilly cream

WINE GUIDE ♀ Fire Finch Sauvignon Blanc £15.95 • ♀ McGuigans Black Label Merlot £15.95 • 33 bottles over £20, 49 bottles under £20 • 12 by the glass (£2.85-£6.65)

PRICE GUIDE Fixed L £12.95 • Fixed D £19.95 • starter £5.95-£8.50 • main £12.95-£17.95 • dessert £5.95-£6.50 • coffee £1.50 • min/water £2.75 • Service optional

PLACE: A setting that includes a beautiful sandy bay, an 18-hole golf course, private grounds with a lake, and the backdrop of wooded hills is a hard one to beat. In the midst of all this, the hotel restaurant is serene and welcoming.

FOOD: Flambées at the table are a fine way to round off a meal that favours freshly caught fish, locally grown vegetables, and a worthy wine list.

OUR TIP: Relax in the private health suite

Chef: Bill Kay **Owners:** The Vermeulen Family **Times:** 12-2/6.30-9.30 **Notes:** Vegetarian available **Seats:** 70, Pr/dining room 40 **Smoking:** N/Sm in restaurant **Children:** Menu, Portions **Directions:** From airport turn right and continue for 5 min and then turn right onto coast road and continue for a further 5 min **Parking:** 200 **e-mail:** hotellagrandemare@cwgsy.net **web:** www.lgm.guernsey.net

CASTEL *continued* MAP 24

 Hotel Hougue du Pommier

French, European

Intimate dining in converted farmhouse

☎ 01481 256531 Hougue du Pommier Rd GY5 7FQ

MENU GUIDE Assiette of Guernsey fish & shellfish, warm saffron brioche • Roast saddle of Welsh lamb, black pudding & rosemary fondant • Iced tiramisù torte

WINE GUIDE ♀ Muscadet Surlie £12.95 • ♥ Rioja £18.50 • 1 bottle over £20, Most bottles under £20 • 4 by the glass (£3.80)

PRICE GUIDE Fixed D £19.75 • starter £4.75-£6.95 • main £9.95-£17.50 • dessert £5.50-£7.50 • coffee £2.50 • min/water £3.50

PLACE: This 18th-century converted farmhouse retains much of its charm and character. A relaxing atmosphere permeates the spacious 90-seating restaurant that comprises a number of interconnecting rooms - all with individual names like cider room, tack room and so on.

FOOD: The menu combines the richness of classical French cuisine with a European twist. Good use of fresh and local ingredients is in evidence throughout.

OUR TIP: Try the freshest seafood dishes

Chef: Andrew Till **Owners:** Hougue Du Pommier Holdings Ltd **Times:** 12-2.30/6.30-9.30, Closed L Mon-Sat **Notes:** Fixed L 3 courses Sun only, Vegetarian available, No jeans or T-shirts **Seats:** 90 **Smoking:** N/Sm in restaurant **Children:** Menu, Portions **Rooms:** 43 (43 en suite) ★★★ **Directions:** 2m W of St Peter Port towards Cobo. Turn at Rue de Friquet **Parking:** 60 **e-mail:** hotel@houguedupommier.guernsey.net **web:** www.hotelhouguedupommier.com

COBO MAP 24

Cobo Bay Hotel

British, European

Accomplished modern cooking in classy seaside hotel

☎ 01481 257102 GY5 7HB

MENU GUIDE Tiger prawn tails in tempura, sweet & sour sauce • Chicken in pancetta, mushroom & tarragon cream sauce • Crème brûlée

WINE GUIDE 20 bottles over £20, 32 bottles under £20 • 3 by the glass (£2.25-£5.25)

PRICE GUIDE Fixed L £14.95 • Fixed D £19.95-£23.50 • starter £3.50-£6.50 • main £9.95-£13.50 • dessert £3.95-£4.95 • coffee £1.50 • min/water £2.95 • Service optional

PLACE: It's worth timing your visit to this elegant candlelit restaurant to catch the sunset if you can - the coastal views are stunning and enjoyed by almost every table. The hotel overlooks Cobo Bay which, with its soft white sands and shallow water, is the perfect spot for a pre-dinner stroll.

FOOD: A varied modern European menu showcases the kitchen's skill, and makes the most of fresh local fish. Carnivores aren't forgotten either, with mains ranging from pork with apple and mustard mash to parsley-crusted salmon with lemon and sage beurre blanc.

OUR TIP: Book ahead for a window table

Chef: John Chapman **Owners:** Mr D Nussbaumer **Times:** 12-2/7-9.30, Closed 1st wk Jan-end Feb, closed L Mon-Sat **Notes:** Lunch only available on Sun, Vegetarian available, Smart casual **Seats:** 120 **Smoking:** N/Sm in restaurant, Air con **Children:** Menu, Portions **Rooms:** 36 (36 en suite) ★★★ **Directions:** From St Peter Port follow signs for Castel/Cobo/West Coast. At coast road turn right, Hotel 100m on right **Parking:** 100 **e-mail:** info@cobobayhotel.com **web:** www.cobobayhotel.com

PERELLE MAP 24

Atlantique Hotel

European

Seafood and sea views on Guernsey's lovely west coast

☎ 01481 264056 Perelle Bay GY7 9NA

MENU GUIDE Pan-fried scallops, crab risotto, pancetta, pea velouté • Whole lobster thermidor • Tangy lemon tart, strawberry ice cream

WINE GUIDE ♀ Bouchard Alne and Fils £10 • ♥ Bouchard Alne and Fils £10 • 15 bottles over £20, 33 bottles under £20 • 3 by the glass

PRICE GUIDE Fixed L £10-£13.50 • Fixed D £17 • starter £3.95-£7.95 • main £8.95-£23 • dessert £3.95-£7.95 • min/water £3 • Service optional

PLACE: This 70s style building has fabulous views over Perelle Bay. The decor is simple and service relaxed, to the accompaniment of restrained background music. Diners can also avail themselves of a separate cocktail bar and sitting room.

FOOD: Reliable cooking delivers everything promised in the menu. Local seafood stars - including Guernsey crab and lobster - alongside chef's daily hors d'oeuvre, and classics like châteaubriand for two with béarnaise sauce, a selection of traditional grills and crêpes Suzette. Vegetarians are also offered a choice, maybe pancakes, mushroom medley or tagliatelle.

OUR TIP: Great place to watch the sun set over the bay

Chef: Derek Hill **Owners:** Carey Olsen Trustees/L'Atlantique 2003 Ltd **Times:** 12-2/6.30-9.30, Closed 1 Jan-end Mar, closed L Mon-Sat **Notes:** Vegetarian available, Smart casual **Seats:** 80, Pr/dining room 40 **Smoking:** N/Sm in restaurant, Air con **Children:** Portions **Rooms:** 23 (21 en suite) ★★★ **Directions:** Off west coast road overlooking Perelle Bay **Parking:** 30 **e-mail:** enquiries@perellebay.com **web:** www.perellebay.com

ST MARTIN MAP 24

La Barbarie Hotel

British, French

Local favourite with colourful past

☎ 01481 235217 Saints Rd, Saints Bay GY4 6ES

MENU GUIDE Foie gras & chicken liver parfait, apple chutney • Sea bass, bacon, Niçoise potatoes, pesto cream • Lemon tart, confit zest

WINE GUIDE ♀ Mill Reef Sauvignon Blanc £15.95 • ♥ McGuigans Merlot £12.95 • 10 bottles over £20, 22 bottles under £20 • 8 by the glass (£2.10-£2.95)

PRICE GUIDE Fixed L £9.95 • Fixed D £17.95-£28 • starter £3.50 • main £11.95 • dessert £4.45 • coffee £1.20 • min/water £2.60 • Service optional

PLACE: Popular hotel that takes its name from the Barbary Coast pirates who kidnapped its owner in the 17th century. Lunch is served in the bar, and dinner in the brightly coloured restaurant.

FOOD: La Barbarie takes a pride in food and offers a good range, with mains such as chicken fricassee or rack of lamb supplemented by steak options, and a daily selection of fresh fish.

OUR TIP: Pop in during Guernsey's October 'Tenner Fest' and eat for £10

Chef: David Hayden **Owners:** LaBarbarie Ltd **Times:** 12-1.45/6.15-9.30, Closed 3 Nov-28 Feb **Notes:** Vegetarian available, Smart casual **Seats:** 75 **Smoking:** N/Sm in restaurant **Children:** Menu **Rooms:** 22 (22 en suite) ★★★ **Directions:** At traffic lights in St Martin take road to Saints Bay - hotel on right at end of Saints Road **Parking:** 60 **e-mail:** reservations@labarbariehotel.com **web:** www.labarbariehotel.com

🏵 Hotel Jerbourg

British, European

Elaborate modern cuisine in cliff-top hotel

☎ 01481 238826 Jerbourg Point GY4 6BJ

MENU GUIDE Tempura tiger prawns, yellow chilli & coriander dip • Scotch beef, foie gras & peppercorn terrine • Iced white peach parfait

WINE GUIDE ♀ Oyster Bay Sauvignon Blanc £16 • ♀ McGuigan Bin 2000 Shiraz £16 • 15 bottles over £20, 25 bottles under £20 • 3 by the glass (£2.75)

PRICE GUIDE Fixed L £10-£18 • Fixed D £20 • starter £5 • main £15 • dessert £5 • coffee £1.75 • min/water £3 • Service optional

PLACE: Cliff-top hotel with an airy conservatory dining room that offers stunning sea views towards the other Channel Islands. An elegant lounge is available for pre-dinner drinks.

FOOD: An extensive modern British carte with European influences is complemented by a selection of daily specials, especially seafood. Dishes are elaborate in style and might include cannon of lamb with a burgundy and marjoram jus, or a scallop and monkfish galette with Lyonnaise potatoes and salsa verde.

OUR TIP: A 'dine and dip' option includes pool access and a bar meal

Chef: Tim Cribben **Owners:** Arthenella Guernsey Ltd **Times:** 12-2/7-9, Closed Nov-Mar **Notes:** Vegetarian available, Smart Dress **Seats:** 80, Pr/dining room 20 **Smoking:** N/Sm in restaurant, Air con
Children: Menu, Portions **Rooms:** 32 (32 en suite) ★★★
Directions: From St Peter Port follow signs for St Martins, at traffic lights by Manor stores turn left. Hotel at end of road on right **Parking:** 30
e-mail: stay@hoteljerbourg.com
web: www.hoteljerbourg.com

ST PETER PORT MAP 24

🏵 The Absolute End

Italian, International

Cottage restaurant by the sea, specialising in fish

☎ 01481 723822 Longstore GY1 2BG

MENU GUIDE Scallops in white wine, cream, onion & mushroom sauce • Turbot, hollandaise sauce, sauté potatoes • Almond & chocolate torte, pistachio ice cream

WINE GUIDE ♀ Rongopai NZ Sauvignon Blanc £16 • ♀ Navajas Rioja £17.90

PRICE GUIDE Fixed L £15 • Fixed D £20 • starter fr £3.95 • main £10-£18.50 • dessert £3.95-£6 • coffee £1.50 • min/water £2.50

PLACE: Ranging over two floors of a traditional fisherman's cottage, this well-established little eaterie is just metres from the sea and has a smart terrace for alfresco dining.

FOOD: Fresh produce simply cooked is what makes this place so popular; fish is a speciality, straight from the boat and handled with care. There's plenty to tempt on the lengthy menu including regular Italian specials.

OUR TIP: Great value fixed-price lunch menu

Chef: Antonio Folmi **Owners:** Antonio Folmi **Times:** 12-2/7-10, Closed Jan, Sun **Notes:** Vegetarian available, Civ Wed 50 **Seats:** 55, Pr/dining room 22 **Smoking:** N/Sm in restaurant, Air con **Children:** Portions
Directions: Less than 1 mile from town centre, going N on seafront road to St Sampson **Parking:** On street
e-mail: theabsoluteend@cwgsy.net

🏵 Da Nello

Italian, Mediterranean

Atmospheric and popular Italian restaurant

☎ 01481 721552 46 La Pollet GY1 1WF

MENU GUIDE Brandadi of smoked haddock • Chargrilled venison sausage • Sloe gin tiramisù

WINE GUIDE ♀ Vernaccia Terruzzi and Puthod £16.75 • ♀ Rocca delle Macié Chianti Sangiovese £17.50 20 bottles over £20, 36 bottles under £20 • 2 by the glass (£2.75-£4.50)

PRICE GUIDE Fixed L £11.95-£12.95 • Fixed D £21.50 • starter £3.50-£9.50 • main £8.50-£19.50 • dessert £4.50-£4.95 • coffee £1.60 • min/water £2.75 • Service optional

PLACE: The smartly painted frontage with dishes inscribed on the windows leads into a much extended space, where marble and terracotta floors and a covered piazza are unashamedly Mediterranean. A good local following keeps the place buzzing.

FOOD: Plenty of pasta and fresh local fish bring their own nostalgic taste of Italy to the Guernsey capital, with poached brill fillet on a saffron sauce, chosen from the blackboard, delivering lovely clean flavours.

OUR TIP: Try the chef's recommendations

Chef: Tim Vidamour **Owners:** Nello Ciotti **Times:** 12-2/6.30-10, Closed 24 Dec-23 Jan **Notes:** Vegetarian available **Seats:** 90, Pr/dining room 20
Smoking: N/Sm area, No pipes, No cigars, Air con **Children:** Portions
Directions: In town centre, 100 yds from North beach car park
Parking: 900

> **One Rosette** Excellent local restaurants serving food prepared with care, understanding and skill, using good quality ingredients. These restaurants stand out in their local area. Of the total number of establishments with Rosettes around 50% have one Rosette.

England

ST PETER PORT *continued* MAP 24

La Frégate

British, French

Guernsey hotel specialising in seafood

☎ 01481 724624 Les Cotils GY1 1UT

MENU GUIDE Lobster bisque • Peppered duck, honey roasted vegetables, foie gras sauce • Crêpes Suzette

PRICE GUIDE Food prices not confirmed for 2006. Please telephone for details

PLACE: It's worth phoning ahead for directions to this friendly hotel as it can be hard to find, but it's well worth the trouble, as crowded tables attest.

FOOD: Expect an extensive selection of accomplished British and French cuisine, and lots (and lots) of fresh Guernsey fish. Meat lovers aren't forgotten, so if brill with a champ mash and hollandaise isn't your choice, you might tuck into calves' liver with pancetta, or roast rack of lamb.

OUR TIP: Try the menu gourmand for more adventurous fare

Chef: Neil Maginnis **Owners:** GSH Ltd **Times:** 12-2.30/6.30-9.45
Notes: Vegetarian available **Seats:** 70, Pr/dining room 30
Smoking: N/Sm in restaurant, Air con **Rooms:** 13 (13 en suite) ★★★
Directions: Town centre, above St Julian's Avenue **Parking:** 25
e-mail: enquiries@lafregatehotel.com **web:** www.lafregatehotel.com

Le Nautique Restaurant

French, International

Popular seafront restaurant with great fish

☎ 01481 721714 Quay Steps GY1 2LE

MENU GUIDE Crab gratin thermidor • Seared scallops, cauliflower risotto, Guernsey love apples • Amaretto parfait, roast bananas

WINE GUIDE ♀ M Laroche Chablis 1'er Cru Chardonnay £28 • ♀ Ogier Châteauneuf-du-Pape £25 • 40 bottles over £20, 28 bottles under £20 • 6 by the glass (£2.80-£4)

PRICE GUIDE Fixed L £12.50 • starter £4.50-£9.50 • main £10.50-£22.50 • dessert £5.50-£8.50 • coffee £1.60 • min/water £2.50

PLACE: Located in a former warehouse and sailmaker's yard, this restaurant occupies two floors with stunning views over the harbour and across to the smaller islands. The upstairs room, the former sail loft, is used for private parties.

FOOD: A fairly extensive French and International menu is offered, but most people come for the excellent selection of fresh local fish dishes, changing daily according to the catch.

OUR TIP: There's a good range of vegetarian dishes

Chef: Gunter Botzenhardt **Owners:** Gunter Botzenhardt **Times:** 12-2/6.30-10, Closed Sun, closed L Sat **Notes:** Vegetarian available
Seats: 56, Pr/dining room 30 **Smoking:** N/Sm area, No pipes, Air con
Children: Portions **Directions:** Seafront opposite harbour and Victoria Marina **Parking:** On street

Old Government House Hotel

Modern British

Fine dining with island views

☎ 01481 724921 Ann's Place GY1 4AZ

MENU GUIDE Lobster risotto, poached egg, red pepper essence • Roast lamb cannon, niçoise garnish, dauphinoise potatoes • Crème brûlée

PRICE GUIDE Food prices not confirmed for 2006. Please telephone for details

PLACE: Formerly the Governor's residence, affectionately known as OGH, this is one of the island's leading hotels. The Regency Room restaurant is elegantly furnished and has splendid views over the neighbouring islands. It's a professional operation, with an attentive welcome by friendly staff.

FOOD: Menus are based on fresh local and continental ingredients and seafood figures strongly. A good choice is offered for vegetarians.

OUR TIP: Brasserie-style food in the Centenary Restaurant
Times: 12-2/7.30-9.30, Closed 2-7 Jan **Rooms:** 68 (68 en suite)
★★★★ **Directions:** Telephone for directions
e-mail: ogh@guernsey.net **web:** www.theoghhotel.com

St Pierre Park Hotel

International

A taste of French elegance

☎ 01481 728282 Rohais GY1 1FD

MENU GUIDE Brandied lobster & crab bisque • Lamb cutlet provençale, tian of roast vegetables, garlic potato • Summer pudding, fresh berries

WINE GUIDE ♀ Boslundal Sauvignon Blanc • ♀ Meuigwan Shiraz 30 bottles over £20, 50 bottles under £20 • 8 by the glass (£3-£4)

PRICE GUIDE Fixed D £23.50 • starter £5.50-£8.50 • main £10.50-£16 • coffee £2.20 • min/water £2.75

PLACE: Elegance, glamour and luxury converge at this purpose-built hotel. Set in 45 acres of mature, peaceful parkland on the

continued

utskirts of St Peter Port, this attractive establishment has its own olf course. Expect chandeliers, large mirrors, gentle beiges and reams, Regency-style chairs and French waiting staff in the ormal Victor Hugo restaurant.

OOD: The stylish setting matches the kitchen's approach, elivering smartly presented, sometimes ambitious, dishes with ocal seafood taking a lead role.

UR TIP: Good for business meetings and a game of golf
hef: Julian Prosser **Owners:** C I Traders **Times:** 7-9.30, Closed 26 Dec, Jan, Sun, closed L Mon-Sat **Notes:** Vegetarian available, Dress estrictions, Smart casual, No trainers/jeans/sandals **Seats:** 70, Pr/dining oom 24 **Smoking:** N/Sm in restaurant, Air con **Children:** Menu, ortions **Rooms:** 131 (131 en suite) ★★★★ **Directions:** Located 1.5m om St Peter Port on road to Cobo Bay **Parking:** 150
-**mail:** info@stpierreparkhotel.com
eb: www.stpierreparkhotel.com

Saltwater

Modern British

NEW

Chic harbourside restaurant
☎ 01481 720823 Albert Pier GY1 1AD

MENU GUIDE Lobster Benedict • Slow-roasted shoulder of lamb • Rich chocolate tart
PRICE GUIDE Food prices not confirmed for 2006. Please telephone for details

PLACE: A bit unassuming on the outside, this restaurant is nevertheless well located overlooking the marina and fish quay. The newly revamped interior is smart, tasteful and very welcoming.

OOD: The modern British cooking draws on French influences, and the menu is relaxed and versatile. Pick a simple seafood dish, construct your own seafood platter, or choose from set items like Catalan fish stew, or mushroom Stroganoff. Presentation is pretty impeccable.

UR TIP: Game dishes are a feature in season
imes: 12-2/6-10, Closed Sun, closed L Sat **e-mail:** info@saltwater.gg
eb: www.saltwater.gg

HERM

HERM MAP 24

White House Hotel

Mediterranean, International

Country-house dining in peaceful island retreat
☎ 01481 722159 GY1 3HR

MENU GUIDE Shredded, potted duck, hoi sin sauce • Local whiting, Welsh rarebit • Kiwi Pavlova

continued

WINE GUIDE ♀ Château du Grand Moueys Sauvignon Blanc/Semillion £10.75 • ♥ M J Maynard Château Thilede Grillon Cabernet/Merlot £10.75 • 70 bottles over £20, 97 bottles under £20 • 4 by the glass (£2.50-£4.50)
PRICE GUIDE Fixed D £24.50 • min/water £3 Service optional

PLACE: This former residence of a Prussian princeling has a unique island setting and panoramic sea and island views. A wonderful country-house hotel destination with excellent hospitality and well-tended gardens that surround the main house and comfortable cottages.

FOOD: Classical dishes with an occasional modern accent such as the tomato and brie tian or raspberry delice with cranberry compôte.

OUR TIP: Certainly the place to 'get away from it all'
Chef: Neil Southgate **Owners:** Wood of Herm Island **Times:** 12.30-2/ 7-9.30, Closed Oct-Apr **Notes:** Fixed L 4 courses £24.50, Coffee included, Vegetarian available, Dress Restrictions, Jacket & tie at D **Seats:** 100 **Smoking:** N/Sm in restaurant **Children:** Portions **Rooms:** 40 (40 en suite) ★★★ **Directions:** By regular 20 min boat trip from St Peter Port, Guernsey **e-mail:** hotel@herm-island.com
web: www.herm-island.com

JERSEY

GOREY MAP 24

Jersey Pottery, The Garden Restaurant

French, International

Strong and confident cooking in a vine-decked conservatory
☎ 01534 850850 Gorey Village JE3 9EP

MENU GUIDE Tempura king prawns • Crispy oriental duck salad • Soft maple cheesecake
WINE GUIDE ♀ Mulderbosch Sauvignon Blanc £19.95 • ♥ Chateldon Cabernet Sauvignon £19.50 • 29 bottles over £20 • 18 by the glass (£3.25-£9.50)
PRICE GUIDE Fixed L £15.50 • starter £4.75-£7.55 • main £9.50-£31.50 • dessert £5.95 • coffee £1.95 • min/water £2.95 • Service included

PLACE: A great place to try out the wares before buying, this is the classier of the two Jersey Pottery eating options. The bright and lively conservatory also welcomes children, who can paint pottery while you relax over a digestif.

FOOD: Seafood and fish are strongly represented in an accomplished menu that demonstrates a good range of skills and styles. Sushi and sashimi are favourites, along with impressive steaks and simple lamb cutlets.

OUR TIP: Check out the Sunday lunches
Chef: Tony Dorris **Owners:** The Jones Family **Times:** 12-2.30, Closed Xmas, Jan, Mid Feb, Mon, closed D all week **Notes:** Vegetarian available, Civ Wed 180 **Seats:** 180, Pr/dining room 180 **Smoking:** N/Sm in restaurant **Children:** Menu, Portions **Directions:** On main road to Gorey Castle. Turn left before Gorey Village. Follow signs **Parking:** 300
e-mail: enquiries@jerseypottery.com
web: www.jerseypottery.com

GOREY *continued* MAP 24

⊛⊛ Suma's
British, Mediterranean
Sea views, skilful cuisine and excellent service
☎ 01534 853291 Gorey Hill JE3 6ET

MENU GUIDE Pan-fried scallops, baby leeks, Serrano ham, sweet potato purée • Steamed brill, shellfish chowder, saffron potatoes • Apple dessert trio

WINE GUIDE 39 bottles over £20, 25 bottles under £20 • 8 by the glass (£3-£5.25)

PRICE GUIDE Fixed L £12.50 • Fixed D £25 • starter £6.75-£12.75 • main £12.75-£20 • dessert £5.75-£9 • coffee £2.25 • min/water £3.25 • Service included

PLACE: A stunning setting with views over Gorey's pretty fishing harbour and Mont Orgueil Castle from inside, or under a parasol on the terrace, proves an ace drawcard. The chic, modern, minimalist feel fits the bill, and is as bright and fresh as the food-and wine-themed artwork that adorns the walls. The mood is relaxed and friendly, service charming and efficient.
FOOD: The kitchen takes a modern approach with a dash of fashionable European flair, along light, intelligently simple lines. Clear flavoured, appealing, balanced dishes showcase fresh, seasonal produce, with superb fish from local boats.
OUR TIP: Try the Big Breakfast on Saturdays
Chef: Danial Ward **Owners:** Ms S Dufty & Mr M Lewis **Times:** 12-2.30/6.30-9.30, Closed 20 Dec-20 Jan **Notes:** Fixed D not avail. Fri-Sat, Sun L 3 courses £20, Vegetarian available **Seats:** 40 **Smoking:** Air con **Children:** Menu, Portions **Directions:** Take A3 E, continue for 4m from St Helier to Gorey. Before castle tale sharp left. Restaurant 100 yds before harbour on left **Parking:** On street

⊛ The Village Bistro
British, Mediterranean
Friendly restaurant in village surroundings
☎ 01534 853429 Gorey Village JE3 9EP
MENU GUIDE Sautéed squid, chorizo, tomato, red onion • Rack of lamb, cabbage, pancetta, potato dauphinoise • Prune & Armagnac tart

WINE GUIDE ♀ Roger Neveu Sancerre £17.50 • ♀ Lennards Crossino Shiraz/Malbec £14.50 • 10 bottles over £20, 20 bottles under £20 • 4 by the glass (£2.75-£3)

PRICE GUIDE Starter £4.95-£8.50 • main £12.50-£16.50 • dessert £3.75-£4.95 • coffee £1.65 • min/water £2.30 • Service optional • Group min 8 service 10%

PLACE: Once part of the village church, this friendly family-run bistro is still at the heart of the community, drawing a crowd of locals and tourists alike. Dine alfresco on the terrace in summer.
FOOD: There's plenty to choose from with an extensive carte supplemented by a good value fixed-price selection and daily *continued*

specials. Expect hearty portions of modern British and Mediterranean fare, conjured from quality ingredients and delivered in a rustic style.
OUR TIP: Seafood is a strength
Chef: Sarah Copp **Owners:** Sean & Sarah Copp **Times:** 12-2.30/7-10.30, Closed Mon **Notes:** Fixed L 4 courses £13.50, Vegetarian available **Seats:** 40 **Smoking:** N/Sm in restaurant **Children:** Portions **Directions:** Take A3 E from St Helier to Gorey. Restaurant in village centre **Parking:** On street and public car park
e-mail: thevillagebistro@yahoo.co.uk **web:** www.village-bistro.com

ROZEL MAP 24

⊛⊛ Château La Chaire
British, Mediterranean
Robust dining in comfortable surroundings
☎ 01534 863354 Rozel Bay JE3 6AJ

MENU GUIDE Boudin blanc, apple Calvados sauce & shitake • Sea bass, provençal vegetables & polenta • Crème brûlée

WINE GUIDE 43 bottles over £20, 18 bottles under £20 • 15 by the glass (£2.75-£8.95)

PRICE GUIDE Fixed L £11.95 • Fixed D £27.50 • starter £6.25-£8.95 • main £15.95-£22.95 • dessert £6.95 • coffee £2.75 • min/water £2.80 • Service added but optional 10%

PLACE: Built as a gentleman's residence in 1843, this hotel enjoys a peaceful setting within its own secluded wooded valley. The spacious and beautifully maintained terraced gardens that surround the house are an added bonus in summer. The restaurant is an attractive mixture of wood-panelled interior and new, light and airy conservatory. Service is excellent.
FOOD: Dishes here are British in style with strong French influences. Tradtional, well-prepared favourites such as prawn cocktail or roast lamb rump jostle Mediterranean chargrilled provençal vegetables and red mullet with saffron risotto for diners' attention.
OUR TIP: Visit the picturesque harbour at Rozel
Chef: Simon Walker **Owners:** The Hiscox Family **Times:** 12-3/7-10

continue

England

Notes: Sun lunch £17.50, Vegetarian available, Dress Restrictions, No jeans. Jackets required evening, Civ Wed 30 **Seats:** 60, Pr/dining room 28 **Smoking:** N/Sm in restaurant **Children:** Portions **Rooms:** 14 (14 en suite) ★★★ **Directions:** From St Helier NE towards Five Oaks, Maufant, then St Martin's Church & Rozel; 1st left in village, hotel 100 mtrs **Parking:** 30 **e-mail:** res@chateau-la-chaire.co.uk **web:** www.chateau-la-chaire.co.uk

ST AUBIN MAP 24

⑨⑩ Somerville Hotel
Mediterranean, International
Harbour-side hotel with something for everyone
☎ 01534 741226 Mont du Boulevard JE3 8AD
MENU GUIDE Chancre crab salad • Scotch beef, potato rösti, foie gras, Madeira • Raspberry & lime crème brûlée
WINE GUIDE ♀ Chardonnay £12.50 • ♀ Côtes du Rhône £12.50 • 18 bottles over £20, 26 bottles under £20 • 5 by the glass (£2.95-£3.45)
PRICE GUIDE Fixed L £10.95-£16.50 • Fixed D £19.50 • starter £3.95-£7.50 • main £10.95-£16.50 • dessert £3.95-£4.95 • coffee £1.40 • min/water £2.95 • Service optional
PLACE: With a picture-postcard setting high on the hillside overlooking St Aubin's Bay, the Somerville offers views all the way to St Helier. Both the lounge and restaurant make the most of the panorama, and pull an appreciative crowd of locals, suits and tourists alike.
FOOD: Plenty of fresh fish of course, but a wide-ranging international and French menu caters for carnivores too, so if salmon and hollandaise doesn't appeal, you might plump for roast saddle of venison. Desserts aren't in short supply either - expect some pleasurable dithering between the likes of dark chocolate tart, or banana parfait.
OUR TIP: Book a window table
Chef: Wayne Pegler **Owners:** Mr W Dolan **Times:** 12.30-2/7-9 **Notes:** Vegetarian available, Dress Restrictions, Smart casual at D **Seats:** 120 **Smoking:** N/Sm in restaurant, Air con **Children:** Portions **Rooms:** 59 (59 en suite) ★★★ **Directions:** From village follow harbour, then take Mont du Boulevard **Parking:** 30 **e-mail:** somerville@dolanhotels.com **web:** www.dolanhotels.com

ST BRELADE MAP 24

⑨⑩⑩ Ocean Restaurant at The Atlantic Hotel see page 534

⑨ Hotel La Place
British, French
Enjoyable dining in 17th-century farmhouse with comfortable rooms
☎ 01534 744261 Route Du Coin, La Haule JE3 8BT

continued

Hotel La Place

MENU GUIDE Tomato tart • New season lamb, crushed peas • Fried banana, basil brûlée, caramel syrup
WINE GUIDE ♀ Chablis £25 • ♀ Bordeaux £19.50 • 40 bottles over £20, 19 bottles under £20 • 6 by the glass (£3.50-£4.50)
PRICE GUIDE Fixed L £10-£20 • Fixed D £22-£25 • starter £4.50-£9 • main £10-£19 • dessert £5-£7 • coffee £1.75 • min/water £3 Service added 10%
PLACE: This friendly hotel is a renovated and considerably extended traditional Jersey farmhouse near the harbour but still in the countryside. Its oak-beamed dining room overlooks a pleasant courtyard. The stylish cocktail bar is a popular rendezvous for pre-dinner drinks, and the comfortable bedrooms have private patios and direct access to the pool.
FOOD: Interesting modern menus based on local produce, include plenty of fish. Expect classic dishes such as Dover sole filleted at table and served with Jersey potatoes.
OUR TIP: Quiet base for some island exploration
Chef: Steven Walker **Owners:** Mylncroft Trading Ltd **Times:** 12-6/7-9 **Notes:** Sun lunch £15, Vegetarian available, Smart Dress, No shorts or T-shirts, Civ Wed 100 **Seats:** 80, Pr/dining room 50 **Smoking:** N/Sm in restaurant **Children:** Menu, Portions **Rooms:** 42 (42 en suite) ★★★★ **Directions:** Telephone for directions **Parking:** 100 **e-mail:** hotlaplace@aol.com **web:** www.hotellaplacejersey.com

⑩⑩ Hotel L'Horizon, The Grill
British
Accomplished cooking in atmospheric coastal retreat
☎ 01534 743101 Route de la Baie JE3 8EF
MENU GUIDE Tian of crab & avocado • Fillet of beef, with osso buco, & truffled celeriac purée • Tarte brûlée
WINE GUIDE ♀ Michael Laroche Chardonnay £19 ♀ Michael Laroche Merlot £19 • 80 bottles over £20, 40 bottles under £20
PRICE GUIDE Fixed L £15.50-£25 • Fixed D £37 • coffee £2.50 • min/water £3.50 • Service included
PLACE: The smart Grill Room makes the most of the stunning coastal setting, with a whole wall of glass doing justice to the views. Comfortable banquette seating separated by wood and glass partitions make it perfect for lingering.
FOOD: Fish and seafood dominate the menu - hardly surprising with St Brelades Bay just beyond the window. Radical choices like Japanese pancakes 'Dorayaki' with chocolate cream, sweet chestnut jelly and jasmine tea sorbet appear on the carte with classics like roast pigeon breast, pan-fried fillet of turbot, and grilled beef fillet.
OUR TIP: Ask for a window seat

continued on page 535

England

ST BRELADE MAP 24

Ocean Restaurant at Atlantic Hotel

Modern British
Sophisticated dining with Atlantic views

☎ 01534 744101   Le Mont de la Pulente JE3 8HE
e-mail: info@theatlantichotel.com
web: www.theatlantichotel.com

PLACE: The fantastic views across St Ouen's Bay and the peaceful setting amid sub-tropical gardens add to the decided air of luxury at this elegant hotel. The modern design of the recently refurbished restaurant is influenced by the hotel's coastal setting. Highly assured, polished service is friendly and attentive.

FOOD: Modern cuisine, striking in its simplicity, from a chef with a real track record. When it comes to local produce you can't get much closer than fish landed less than half a mile from where you eat it, and a similar attitude extends to meat, vegetables and other ingredients where possible. Expect dishes such as fillet of Jersey sea bass with crushed Jersey royals, confit tomato and salsify with pea sauce, or honey and five spice duck with girottine cherry jus. Desserts and petits fours are particularly attractive and demonstrate the skills at work in the kitchen.

MENU GUIDE Flash seared scallops, Vichy carrot purée, caviar • Poached & seared canon of guinea fowl, sautéed wild mushrooms • Hot passionfruit soufflé

WINE GUIDE ♀ Malborough Chardonnay £17.50 ♀ Clancy's Shiraz/Merlot £17.50 • 162 bottles over £20, 22 bottles under £20 • 11 by the glass (£4.50-£8.75)

PRICE GUIDE Fixed L fr £15 • Fixed D fr £35 • coffee £2.50 • min/water £3 • Service optional

OUR TIP: Summer dining by the pool

Chef: Mark Jordan **Owners:** Patrick Burke **Times:** 12.30-2.30/7.30-9.30, Closed 20 Jan-2 Feb **Notes:** Sun L £21, Tasting menu £55 5 course, Vegetarian available, Smart Dress, Civ Wed 60 **Seats:** 65, Pr/dining room 20 **Smoking:** N/Sm in restaurant **Children:** Menu, Portions **Rooms:** 50 (50 en suite) ★★★★ **Directions:** From St Brelade take the road to Petit Port, turn into Rue de Sergente and right again, signed to hotel **Parking:** 60

T BRELADE *continued* MAP 24

hef: Peter Fleming **Owners:** Hand Picked Hotels **Times:** 7-10, Closed
un-Mon, closed L All wk **Notes:** Sun brunch £22, 6-course celebration
enu £60 incl champagne, Vegetarian available, Smart casual, Civ Wed
0 **Seats:** 46, Pr/dining room 250 **Smoking:** N/Sm in restaurant, Air
n **Children:** Min 10 yrs, Menu, Portions **Rooms:** 106 (106 en suite)
★★★ **Directions:** 2m from Jersey Airport, 5m from St Helier
arking: 150 **e-mail:** lhorizon@handpicked.co.uk
eb: www.handpicked.co.uk/lhorizon

T CLEMENT MAP 24

Green Island Restaurant

Mediterranean

The most southerly restaurant in the British Isles

01534 857787 Green Island JE2 6LS

MENU GUIDE Salt cod & crab croquettes • Lamb, parmesan
polenta cake, roast vine tomatoes, basil fondue • Citrus tart,
raspberry sorbet

WINE GUIDE ♀ J Moreau & Fils Sauvignon Blanc • ♀ Andes
Peaks Rapel Valley Cabernet Sauvignon • 15 bottles over £20,
5 bottles under £20 • 3 by the glass (£3.25-£5)

PRICE GUIDE Fixed L £12.95 • starter £5.50-£8.95 • main £11.95-
£15.50 • dessert £4-£5 • coffee £1.60 • min/water £2.75 • Service
optional • Group min 8 service 10%

PLACE: Buzzy little beach hut-type restaurant on the sands that
draws a crowd, particularly in summer. It's a laid-back local haunt
with brightly painted walls, coconut matting on the floor, and
stunning views across to Green Island. Book ahead.

continued

FOOD: Fresh and flavourful ingredients handled with simplicity
by a confident kitchen. Expect a modern European and
Mediterranean menu with dishes such as chicken in Parma ham
with spring cabbage and bacon, or turbot with a grain mustard
dauphinoise.
OUR TIP: A must during any trip to Jersey
Chef: Lee Rogers **Owners:** Alan M Winch **Times:** 12-2.30/7-9.30,
Closed 10 days Oct, Xmas week, 3 wks Jan, Mon, closed D Sun
Notes: Vegetarian by request only **Seats:** 40 **Children:** Portions
Directions: Telephone for directions **Parking:** Public car park adjacent
e-mail: greenislandrestaurant@jerseymail.co.uk
web: www.greenislandrestaurant.com

ST HELIER MAP 24

Bohemia *see below*

Pomme D'Or Hotel

British, French

French cuisine in upmarket hotel

☎ 01534 880110 Liberation Square JE1 3UF

MENU GUIDE Confit of duck leg & foie gras terrine • Rack of
lamb, provençal galette, leek & tarragon cream • Chocolate
fondant

WINE GUIDE ♀ Chantelle des Vins House Wine £11 • ♀ Paul
Bouchard House Wine £11 • 30 bottles over £20, 43 bottles
under £20 • 13 by the glass (£2.75-£4.10)

PRICE GUIDE Fixed D £25-£27.50 • min/water £2.40 • Service
optional

continued

T HELIER MAP 24

Bohemia

French, International

Classical cooking in contemporary Jersey restaurant

☎ 01534 880588 The Club Hotel & Spa, Green St
2 4UH

MENU GUIDE Crab velouté, scallop ravioli • Pork belly, apple
pavé, foie gras, langoustine brochette • Lemon soufflé

WINE GUIDE ♀ Selaks Sauvignon Blanc £20 • ♀ Fleurie Gamay
21 • 91 bottles over £20, 18 bottles under £20 • 15 by the glass
(£3.50-£6.75)

PRICE GUIDE Fixed L £16.50 • Fixed D £33-£38 • coffee
2.20 • min/water £2.50 • Service added but optional 10%

PLACE: A smart modern hotel near the centre of St Helier with a
contemporary eaterie, decorated in shades of earthy brown and
natural materials such as polished granite, leather and wood.
FOOD: Refined and creative cooking with its roots in French
classical cuisine with International influences. Expect traditional
combinations such as Scotch beef with roast foie gras and
pommes Anna, as well as more intriguing blends of taste and
texture: like pigeon with pumpkin gnocchi and Savoy cabbage.

Fresh Jersey seafood is a particular draw: scallops wrapped in
pancetta with an artichoke salad, or sea bass served simply with
a sauce vièrge. **OUR TIP:** Enjoy the tasting menu
Chef: Shaun Rankin **Owners:** Lawrence Huggler **Times:** 12-2.30/6.30-
10.30, Closed Sun, L Sat **Notes:** Smart casual **Seats:** 40, Pr/dining room
6 **Smoking:** N/Sm in restaurant **Directions:** Centre of St Helier
Parking: 20 **e-mail:** bohemia@huggler.com
web: www.bohemiajersey.com

ST HELIER continued MAP 24

PLACE: Overlooking Liberation Square and the marina, this historic hotel is an upmarket dinner destination. The most formal of its several different eateries is the 'Petite Pomme' restaurant, an attractive dining room with views across St Helier harbour.
FOOD: A wide-ranging French menu offers plenty of choice, with fish a speciality. Dishes are complex and deftly done: beef with oyster mushrooms and a Madeira jus perhaps, or grilled brill with a roast lobster bisque.
OUR TIP: There's also has a carvery restaurant and coffee shop
Chef: James Waters **Owners:** Seymour Hotels **Times:** 7-10, Closed 26-30 Dec, Sun, closed L all week **Notes:** Vegetarian available **Seats:** 50, Pr/dining room 50 **Smoking:** N/Sm in restaurant, Air con
Children: Menu, Portions **Rooms:** 143 (143 en suite) ★★★★
Directions: 5 m from Airport, 0.5 m from ferry terminal
Parking: 100 yds from Hotel **e-mail:** enquiries@pommedorhotel.com
web: www.pommedorhotel.com

ST SAVIOUR MAP 24

 Longueville Manor *see below*

TRINITY MAP 24

 **Water's Edge Hotel**
British, French
Wonderfully atmospheric with amazing views
☎ 01534 862777 Bouley Bay JE3 5AS

continued

MENU GUIDE Scallop, pancetta & pine nut salad • Seafood panache, coriander, prawn noodles, oyster sauce • Prune & chocolate crème brûlée
WINE GUIDE ♀ McGuigan Brothers Chardonnay £14.95 • ♀ McGuigan Brothers Shiraz £13.95 • 21 bottles over £20, 51 bottles under £20 • 10 by the glass (£2.40-£5.50)
PRICE GUIDE Fixed L £10 • Fixed D £19.50-£22.50 • starter £5-£12 • main £10-£25 • dessert £5-£9 • coffee £1.50 • min/water £2.50 • Service included

PLACE: Stunning location at the bottom of Bouley Hill with view over the bay to the coastline of Normandy. Formal service is provided to well-spaced tables in the traditionally-styled restaurant.
FOOD: The fixed-price, four-course menu is based on local produce, notably seafood, reflecting British and French influence from roast beef to potage garbure. There are four options for starter, main and dessert, plus soup or sorbet between. Local produce sourced whenever possible.
OUR TIP: Good value for money
Chef: George Callum **Owners:** M Wavell/Water's Edge Hotel Ltd
Times: 12.30-2/7-9.15, Closed Oct-Apr **Notes:** Vegetarian available, Dres Restrictions, Smart casual, No trainers, Civ Wed 100 **Seats:** 100, Pr/dinin; room 40 **Smoking:** N/Sm in restaurant **Children:** Min 7 yrs, Menu, Portions **Rooms:** 51 (51 en suite) ★★★ **Directions:** 10-15 mins from St Hellier, A9 N to the A8 to the B31, follow signs to Bouley Bay
Parking: 20 **e-mail:** mail@watersedgehotelhotel.co.je
web: www.watersedgehotel.co.je

ST SAVIOUR MAP 24

Longueville Manor

Contemporary British
Historic manor with contemporary cooking
☎ 01534 725501 JE2 7WF
MENU GUIDE Grilled scallops, potted baby leeks, Parma ham • Sea bass, chicken confit, langoustines, shellfish sauce • Passionfruit soufflé, raspberry sorbet
PRICE GUIDE Fixed L £12.50 • starter £12.50-£17.50 • main £28-£30 • dessert £8.75-£16.75 • Service included

PLACE: There's a romantic film-set air about arriving at this manor house, which dates from the 13th century, set in 17 acres of grounds that include a lake with black swans. It has two dining rooms: the Jacobean dark-panelled Oak Room and the more modern Garden Room rich in fabrics and antiques.
FOOD: Quality local produce, particularly fish and seafood, features on the modern, classically-inspired repertoire. Andrew Baird's approach is via an appealing array of fixed-price menus, which include the Taste of Jersey and Menu Prestige tasting options. Cooking is confident and sophisticated, flavour combinations are contemporary and skilfully managed to

showcase the main ingredients.
OUR TIP: Fixed-price lunch is great value
Chef: Andrew Baird **Owners:** Malcolm Lewis **Times:** 12.30-2/7-10
Notes: Gourmet Menu, Vegetarian available, Jacket minimum, Civ Wed 4
Seats: 65, Pr/dining room 22 **Smoking:** N/Sm area **Children:** Menu, Portions **Rooms:** 30 (30 en suite) ★★★★ **Directions:** A3 to Gorey, hotel 0.75m on left **Parking:** 45 **e-mail:** info@longuevillemanor.com
web: www.longuevillemanor.com

SARK

SARK MAP 24

⊚⊚ La Sablonnerie
British, International
Enchanting old farmhouse hotel in unique location
☎ 01481 832061   GY9 0SD

MENU GUIDE Terrine of monkfish & salmon • Sark lobster with lime butter • Coffee & cardamom mousse

WINE GUIDE ♀ Château du Nozet Pouilly Fumé £20.80 • ♀ Louis Latour Côte de Beaune Village £16.80 • 9 bottles over £20, 41 bottles under £20 • 6 by the glass (£2-£3)

PRICE GUIDE Fixed L £16.80-£22.30 • Fixed D £23.60-£30.10 • starter £5.80-£7.80 • main £11-£14.50 • dessert £5.80-£6.80 • coffee £1 • min/water £1.25

PLACE: Modernity is replaced by horse and carriage or good old Hank's pony once you land on this traffic-free island, and the trip to the delightful former farmhouse through idyllic countryside is one to be savoured. The charming rustic restaurant and old-fashioned hospitality are entirely captivating.

FOOD: Simple fresh fish and shellfish, and produce from the island and the hotel's own farm and gardens, bring a unique flavour to the menu. French inspiration informs the contemporary menu, and style and presentation are very much to the fore.

OUR TIP: You can hire a bike near the harbour

Chef: Martin Cross **Owners:** Elizabeth Perrée **Times:** 12-2.30/7-9.30, closed mid Oct-Etr **Notes:** Tasting menu available, charged according to request, Vegetarian available **Seats:** 39 **Smoking:** N/Sm area, No pipes, No cigars **Children:** Menu, Portions **Directions:** On southern part of island. Horse & carriage is transport to hotel.

ISLE OF MAN

DOUGLAS MAP 24 SC37

⊛ Sefton Hotel
Modern European
Modern cooking in Victorian hotel by the sea
☎ 01624 645500   Harris Promenade IM1 2RW

MENU GUIDE Blueberry melon fruit salad • Cep-dusted lamb medallions • Toffee & orange pudding

PRICE GUIDE Food prices not confirmed for 2006. Please telephone for details

PLACE: An informal restaurant in this elegant hotel, where a local artist's work is highlighted - literally - on the pale yellow walls. Quarry tiled floors sustain the minimalist look.

FOOD: The Gallery Restaurant menu may be short but it is well conceived and carefully cooked, with the unmissable fish of the day appearing alongside other Manx specialities in an impressive line-up of quality produce.

OUR TIP: Try the Manx queenies (scallops)
Times: 12.30-2/7.30-10 **Rooms:** 100 (100 en suite) ★★★★
e-mail: info@seftonhotel.co.im **web:** www.seftonhotel.co.im

AA 2006
The **Pub** Guide

Over 2,200 pubs hand-picked for their great food and authentic character.

www.theAA.com   **AA**

AA 2006
The **Golf Course** Guide

Britain's best-selling Golf Course Guide featuring over 2,500 courses.

www.theAA.com   **AA**

Scotland

Restaurant of the Year for Scotland

étain,
Glasgow

(see p580)

ABERDEEN CITY

ABERDEEN MAP 23 NJ90

Ardoe House

European

Sophisticated food in baronial-style mansion

☎ 01224 867355 Blairs, South Deeside Rd AB12 5YP

MENU GUIDE Pressed ham hough & foie gras terrine • Roast loin of Highland venison with sloe gin & cranberry compote • Ardoe apple tart, layered with raspberries & frangipane

PRICE GUIDE Food prices not confirmed for 2006. Please telephone for details

PLACE: A baronial-style mansion set in 30 acres of beautiful countryside on the banks of the Dee, enjoying great views. Blairs restaurant is full of character and retains the original ornate ceilings and stained glass.

FOOD: A good range of European-influenced British dishes, well constructed and accurately cooked, using fresh, local produce and the finest international ingredients. Expect mains like seared sea bass with crispy pancetta, creamed Savoy cabbage and saffron pommes cocotte.

OUR TIP: Wide range of malt whiskies and Cuban cigars **Times:** 12-2/6.30-9.45, Closed L Sat **Rooms:** 117 (117 en suite) ★★★★ **Directions:** 3m from Aberdeen on B9077, on left **e-mail:** ardoe@macdonald-hotels.co.uk

Copthorne Hotel Aberdeen

British, Scottish

Good hotel dining in quiet and convenient location

☎ 01224 630404 122 Huntly St AB10 1SU

MENU GUIDE Warm scallop & tiger prawn tart • Braised lamb rump, baby vegetables, herb mash • Chocolate assiette, pistachio ice cream

WINE GUIDE ♀ Hardys Chardonnay/Semillion £16.90 • ♀ Hardys Shiraz/Cabernet Sauvignon £17.90 • 5 bottles over £20, 37 bottles under £20 • 14 by the glass (£3.50-£6.15)

PRICE GUIDE Starter £4-£6 • main £13-£22 • dessert £4-£7 • coffee £2.50 • min/water £4.95 • Service optional

PLACE: This conveniently located hotel houses the smart Poachers restaurant and enjoys views of the Balmoral Estate. There's the relaxing Mac's Bar for pre-dinner drinks and well-maintained bedrooms and public areas – a far cry from its origins as a furniture factory!

FOOD: The Poacher's Restaurant, which offers traditional Scottish favourites and some modern dishes, has a loyal local following and attracts destination diners. There's extensive use of local and Scottish ingredients ranging from Loch Fyne mussels, salmon and oysters through to home-made haggis and local beef.

OUR TIP: A useful base in a convenient location **Chef:** Dave Barron **Owners:** Copthorne **Times:** 12-2/7-10, Closed 25-26 Dec, closed L Sat-Sun **Notes:** Vegetarian available, Civ Wed 100 **Seats:** 80, Pr/dining room 12 **Smoking:** N/Sm area, No pipes, Air con **Children:** Menu, Portions **Rooms:** 89 (89 en suite) ★★★★ **Directions:** City centre. 200 yds off Union St, at top of Huntly Street **Parking:** 16 **e-mail:** reservations.aberdeen@mill-cop.com **web:** www.millenniumhotels.com

Maryculter House Hotel

Scottish, French

Cosy dining in historic mansion house

☎ 01224 732124 AB12 5GB

MENU GUIDE Smoked salmon, potato scone, dill cream • Sliced beef fillet, shallot compote, bordelaise sauce • Sticky rice, poached figs

WINE GUIDE 19 bottles over £20, 23 bottles under £20 • 1 by the glass (£2.65)

PRICE GUIDE Starter £2.95-£5.50 • main £7.50-£18 • dessert £3.95-£5.50 • coffee £2.25 • min/water £4.25 • Service optional

PLACE: Home to the Knights Templar dating back to 1225, Maryculter House has a fascinating history. These days it's a busy country house hotel standing in its own grounds on the banks of the River Dee. Dinner is served by candlelight in the stone-walled Priory restaurant.

FOOD: Expect a modern menu - French with a twist of Scottish - produced from fresh local produce, especially beef and salmon.

OUR TIP: Popular venue for weddings and conferences **Chef:** Sebastian Schroeder **Owners:** James Gilbert **Times:** 7-9.30, Closed Sun, closed L all week **Notes:** Vegetarian available, Dress Restrictions, No jeans or T-shirts, Civ Wed 150 **Seats:** 40, Pr/dining room 30 **Smoking:** N/Sm in restaurant **Children:** Min 4 yrs, Menu, Portions **Rooms:** 23 (23 en suite) ★★★ **Directions:** Off A90 to S of Aberdeen and onto B9077. Hotel is located 8m on right. 0.5m beyond lower Deeside Caravan Park **Parking:** 150 **e-mail:** info@maryculterhousehotel.com **web:** www.maryculterhousehotel.com

Norwood Hall

British, European

Modern food in historic setting

☎ 01224 868951 Garthdee Rd, Cults AB15 9FX

MENU GUIDE Confit of duck & pear terrine • Shellfish linguini with lobster, langoustine, mussels & cockles • Lemon tart with citrus sorbet

WINE GUIDE ♀ Chardonnay £18.50 • ♀ Torreon de Paredes Ca'Lunghetta Botter Merlot £17.50 • 38 bottles over £20, 27 bottles under £20 • 9 by the glass (£3.55-£7.35)

PRICE GUIDE Fixed L £13.75-£30 • Fixed D £18.50-£36.93 • starter £3.25-£7.50 • main £10.50-£22.50 • dessert £4.75-£6.95 • coffee £2.75 • min/water £5

PLACE: Richly furnished, imposing Victorian mansion with oak-panelled restaurant fronted by friendly, helpful staff. Well-spaced, candlelit tables.

FOOD: The Tapestry Restaurant offers a selection of traditional dishes and steaks from the grill, but more adventurous cooking shows in roasted sea bass with saffron linguine and coriander infusion, as well as desserts such as banana and marshmallow bavarois.

Scotland

continued

continued

Scotland

ABERDEEN *continued* MAP 23 NJ90

OUR TIP: Good selection of seafood
Chef: Mike McGarrie **Owners:** Monument Leisure **Times:** 12-2.30/7-9.45 **Notes:** Vegetarian available, Smart casual, Civ Wed 180 **Seats:** 28, Pr/dining room 180 **Smoking:** N/Sm in restaurant **Children:** Menu, Portions **Rooms:** 37 (37 en suite) ★★★★ **Directions:** From S, off A90 at 1st rdbt cross bridge and turn left at rdbt into Garthdee Road, continue 1.5m **Parking:** 100 **e-mail:** info@norwood-hall.co.uk
web: www.norwood-hall.co.uk

The Silver Darling
French, Seafood
Romantic restaurant with stunning harbour views
☎ 01224 576229 Pocra Quay, North Pier AB11 5DQ
MENU GUIDE Squid & tiger prawns à la plancha • Wild sea bass, spinach chartreuse, sauce vierge • Espresso bavarois, crunchy ganache
WINE GUIDE ♀ Sancerre £24.50 • ♀ Châteauneuf du Pape £29.50 • 26 bottles over £20, 9 bottles under £20 • 3 by the glass (£3.95-£4.50)
PRICE GUIDE Starter £8.50-£10.50 • main £18.50-£22.50 dessert £6.50 • coffee £2.40 • min/water £2.95 • Service optional
PLACE: A walkway of cobbled stone leads to this former customs house at the harbour entrance. The restaurant is a first floor conservatory extension with large windows, accessed by a spiral staircase. Food is delivered from the ground floor kitchen by dumb waiter.
FOOD: Specialising in freshly caught, locally landed seafood along with other excellent local produce, correctly cooked and beautifully served. The sophisticated evening menu is strongly French influenced.
OUR TIP: Look out for dolphins in the bay - binoculars available
Chef: Didier Dejean **Owners:** Didier Dejean & Karen Murray **Times:** 12-2/6.30-9.30, Closed Xmas-New Year, Sun, closed L Sat **Notes:** Smart Dress **Seats:** 50 **Smoking:** N/Sm in restaurant **Children:** Portions
Directions: Situated at Aberdeen Harbour entrance beside Harbour Pilots Round Tower in Footdec **Parking:** on quayside

ABERDEENSHIRE

BALLATER MAP 23 NO39

Balgonie House Hotel
British, French
Thoughtful cooking with a rural outlook
☎ 013397 55482 Braemar Place AB35 5NQ
MENU GUIDE Grilled halibut, parmesan salad, basil oil • Breast & braised leg of pheasant, parsnip tarte Tatin • Passionfruit mousse
WINE GUIDE ♀ William Fevre Chardonnay £22 • ♀ Crozes-Hermitage Cave de Tain L'Hermitage £19.50 • 35 bottles over £20, 20 bottles under £20 • 4 by the glass (£4.50-£4.95)
PRICE GUIDE Fixed L £19.50-£22.50 • Fixed D £35-£40 min/water £2.75
PLACE: Secluded country house set back from the road in Ballater, at the heart of beautiful Royal Deeside. The hotel is popular with country sports enthusiasts and local business folk. Delightful hosts ensure informal but attentive service in the contemporary-styled dining room.
FOOD: Carefully planned menus offer three choices at each stage (four courses at lunch and five at dinner). The well balanced and

accurately timed dishes make full use of the area's fine produce, such as salmon from the River Dee, Aberdeen Angus beef, East Coast seafood and local game.
OUR TIP: Just five minutes' walk from the village
Chef: John Finnie **Owners:** Mr J & Mrs P Finnie **Times:** 12.30-2/7-9, Closed 5 Jan-10 Feb, closed L all ex by arrangement **Notes:** Vegetarian b request only, Smart Dress **Seats:** 30 **Smoking:** N/Sm in restaurant **Children:** Portions **Rooms:** 9 (9 en suite) ★★ **Directions:** On outskirts of Ballater, signposted off A93 (Ballater-Perth) **Parking:** 10
e-mail: balgoniech@aol.com **web:** www.balgonie-hotel.co.uk

Darroch Learg Hotel

see page 54

Glen Lui Invercauld Rd AB35 5RP ☎ 013397 55402
Delightful country-house dining set in lovely grounds.

BANCHORY MAP 23 NO69
Raemoir House Hotel
British
Best local produce in fine country house
☎ 01330 824884 Raemoir AB31 4ED

MENU GUIDE Seared smoked salmon, lobster ravioli, bisque • Fillet of Aberdeen Angus, wild mushroom sauce • Lemon tart, raspberry sauce
WINE GUIDE ♀ Raemoir Sauvignon Blanc £16.50 • ♀ Raemoir Merlot £17.50 • 78 bottles over £20, 32 bottles under £20 • 12 b the glass (£3.50-£4.50)
PRICE GUIDE Fixed L £10.75-£17.50 • Fixed D £31.50 • coffee £2 • min/water £2.50 • Service optional
PLACE: It is hard to imagine a more romantic setting for dinner than the oval ballroom at Raemoir House, with its Victorian velve wall coverings, huge log fires, masses of fresh flowers and candlelight. The house itself is impressive enough, with its opulent public rooms and beautiful setting amid 3,500 acres of parkland and forest in Royal Deeside.
FOOD: The daily changing modern British menu is priced for thre or four courses and offers a good choice of dishes. Cooking is accurate and the quality of the locally sourced produce is evident.
OUR TIP: Warm hospitality is a highlight
Chef: Grant Walker **Owners:** Mr & Mrs R Bishop-Milnes **Times:** 12-2/7-9 **Notes:** Vegetarian available, Civ Wed 40 **Seats:** 40, Pr/dining room 3 **Smoking:** N/Sm in restaurant **Children:** Portions **Rooms:** 20 (20 en suite) ★★★ **Directions:** (A93 to Banchory then A980, hotel at x-rds after 2.5 m.) **Parking:** 50 **e-mail:** relax@raemoir.com
web: www.raemoir.com

continued

Darroch Learg Hotel

Modern Scottish

flawless cooking in stunning setting

☎ 013397 55443 Braemar Rd AB35 5UX

MENU GUIDE Langoustine tortellini • Beef, parsnip purée, crispy shallots, oxtail & mushroom sauce • Lemon tart

PRICE GUIDE Fixed D £37.50

PLACE: Perched high above the village of Ballater, this renowned hotel offers a panorama of the spectacular country of Royal Deeside. Inside, the restaurant is decorated in bright modern style with well-appointed tables, and extends into a conservatory that overlooks the well-kept gardens.

FOOD: Ingredients such as foie gras and truffle oil reveal the classical roots of Darroch Learg's inspiring cuisine, but the style is generally modern, an honest and unpretentious approach that showcases the finest local produce, from Highland game and beef to West Coast scallops and salmon. Add flawless technique and a touch of imagination and the result is cooking to savour - and there's a seven-course tasting menu to help you do just that, at only £5 more than the three-course fixed price option. It's all complemented by an extensive wine list.

OUR TIP: Sandwiches and afternoon tea served on the terrace **Chef:** David Mutter **Owners:** The Franks Family **Times:** 12.30-2/7-9, Closed Xmas, last 3wks Jan, L Mon-Sat **Notes:** Sun L 3 courses, Smart casual **Seats:** 48 **Smoking:** N/Sm in restaurant **Rooms:** 17 (17 en suite) ★★★ **Directions:** On A93 at the W end of village **e-mail:** info@darrochlearg.co.uk **web:** www.darrochlearg.co.uk

Scotland

🍴 Tor-na-Coille Hotel

British, European

Elegant dining in charming Victorian country hotel

☎ 01330 822242 AB31 4AB

MENU GUIDE Marinated salmon & cucumber salad, beetroot tortellini • Aged fillet of Aberdeen Angus beef • Soft chocolate pudding with plum purée

WINE GUIDE 30 bottles over £20, 27 bottles under £20 • 5 by the glass (£2.75-£3.25)

PRICE GUIDE Fixed L £13.75 • Fixed D £27.50 • coffee £1.90 • min/water £3.60 • Service optional

PLACE: Built as a private house in 1873, Tor-na-Coille was converted into a hotel at the turn of the century. Original Victorian features have been preserved, and refurbishments

Tor-na-Coille Hotel

sympathetically carried out, have created an elegant, homely and warm dining room.

FOOD: Modern British and European dishes feature local game and salmon in consistent menus, with plenty of choice at each course.

OUR TIP: Good base for touring Deeside and Balmoral **Chef:** Paul Fyvie **Owners:** Roxanne Sloan-Maris **Times:** 12-2/6.30-9, Closed 24-28 Dec, closed L Mon-Sat **Notes:** Vegetarian available, Civ Wed 90 **Seats:** 65, Pr/dining room 100 **Smoking:** N/Sm in restaurant **Children:** Menu, Portions **Rooms:** 22 (22 en suite) ★★★ **Directions:** From Aberdeen take A93 (18 miles) **Parking:** 500 **e-mail:** tornacoille@btinternet.com **web:** www.tornacoille.com

🍴 **Milton Restaurant** On A493 Royal Deeside Rd, E of Banchory AB31 5YR ☎ 01330 844566 Modish roadside restaurant with craft shop.

continued

Scotland

STONEHAVEN MAP 23 N088

Tolbooth

British, European

AA Seafood Restaurant of the Year for Scotland

☎ 01569 762287 Old Pier Rd AB3 2JU

MENU GUIDE Tolbooth crab soup • Grilled lobster with garlic & lemon butter • Warm pear & honey polenta cake, saffron syrup, vanilla marscapone sorbet

WINE GUIDE ♀ Pinot Grigio £14.50 • ♀ Fleurie £19.50 13 bottles over £20, 26 bottles under £20 • 2 by the glass (£2.95)

PRICE GUIDE Fixed L £12 • starter £3.50-£6.75 • main £9.75-£17.95 • dessert £5.25-£5.95 • coffee £1.75 • min/water £2.50 • Service optional

PLACE: Sitting on the harbour wall at Stonehaven, this former 18th-century prison and excise house successfully blends the rustic charm of its traditional whitewashed stone walls with a contemporary interior and modern tableware.

FOOD: Locally sourced fish and seafood is a major selling point here with some of the fish still landed outside. You will find the day's catch marked up on the blackboard. Chef patron Robert Cleaver cooks the freshest of ingredients with great flair and integrity. Meat eaters are not forgotten though, with several options available.

OUR TIP: Great harbour views

Chef: Robert Cleaver, John Pattillo **Owners:** Robert Cleaver **Times:** 12-2/6-9.30, Closed 3 wks after Xmas, Sun & Mon **Notes:** Vegetarian available **Seats:** 46 **Smoking:** N/Sm in restaurant **Children:** Portions **Directions:** 15 miles S of Aberdeen on A90 **Parking:** Public car park, 100 spaces web: www.tolboothrestaurant.co.uk

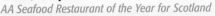

ANGUS

BRIDGEND OF LINTRATHEN MAP 23 N025

Lochside Lodge & Roundhouse Restaurant

British, International

Accomplished cooking beside Loch of Lintrathen

☎ 01575 560340 DD8 5JJ

MENU GUIDE Dunsyre Blue cheese brûlée • Grilled wild sea bass fillet • Glazed lemon & orange tart

WINE GUIDE ♀ Georges Duboeuf £13.95 • ♀ Georges Duboeuf £13.95 • 14 bottles over £20, 22 bottles under £20 • 4 by the glass (£2.50-£3.95)

PRICE GUIDE Fixed L £12-£14.50 • Fixed D £29.50-£31 • coffee £1.20 • min/water £2.75 • Service optional • Group min 20 service 10%

PLACE: Horses once walked in circles operating the threshing machinery in the unusual circular restaurant. The former farmhouse shows little sign of its original functions, though it remains cosy with a spacious bar containing church pews, and sunny dining room.

FOOD: Working single-handedly in the kitchen may be a challenge for chef/proprietor Graham Riley, but the results are accomplished and full of delight. Quality ingredients underpin dishes like oven roasted duck breast with confit leg and apple crumble crust. Gail Riley is a charming hostess.

OUR TIP: Arrive early for a walk around the loch

Chef: Graham Riley **Owners:** Graham & Gail Riley **Times:** 12-1.30/6.30-8.30, Closed 1-25 Jan, 25-26 Dec, Mon, closed D Sun **Notes:** Vegetarian available, Dress Restrictions, Smart casual, no jeans **Seats:** 35, Pr/dining room 40 **Smoking:** N/Sm in restaurant **Children:** Portions **Rooms:** 4 (4 en suite) **Directions:** From Kirriemuir, take B951 towards Glenisla for 7m, turn left towards Lintrathen and follow to village, restaurant on left **Parking:** 40 e-mail: enquiries@lochsidelodge.com web: www.lochsidelodge.com

CARNOUSTIE MAP 21 N053

11 Park Avenue

British, French

Friendly restaurant with loyal local following

☎ 01241 853336 11 Park Av DD7 7JA

MENU GUIDE Crispy duck confit, chilli & lime sauce • Seared sea bass fillet, scallop & butter sauce • Caramel poached pear, caramel ice

WINE GUIDE ♀ Sauvignon Blanc £14.95 • ♀ Merlot £14.95 39 bottles over £20, 20 bottles under £20 • 2 by the glass (£3.75-£4.25)

PRICE GUIDE Fixed L £15-£17.50 • starter £4.25-£9.75 • main £14.50-£19.95 • dessert £6.25-£6.95 • coffee £2.25 • min/water £2.95 • Service included

PLACE: The restaurant, in a side street of the seaside town, has in its time been a wartime hospital, a school meals centre and a masonic hall. The golfing collectibles on display inside are a clue to a local passion.

FOOD: Accurately cooked and simple food with finely judged flavour combinations and no nonsense. The home-made tablet that comes with the coffee is a must.

OUR TIP: Perfect place for post-putting relaxation

Chef: Stephen Collinson, Scott Kidd **Owners:** Stephen Collinson **Times:** 12-2/7-10, Closed 25 Dec, 1st wk Jan, Mon, Sun, closed L Tue -Thu & Sat **Notes:** Vegetarian available, Smart casual **Seats:** 50 **Smoking:** N/Sm in restaurant **Children:** Min 10 yrs, Portions **Directions:** From Dundee take A92 N (Arbroath). After 10-12m turn right to Carnoustie; at x-rds left, then right at mini-rdbt. Restaurant on left **Parking:** 50 e-mail: parkavenue@o2.co.uk web: www.11parkavenue.co.uk

GLAMIS MAP 21 N034

Castleton House Hotel

see page 54

continued

GLAMIS MAP 21 N034

Castleton House Hotel

British, French
Victorian country house with culinary flair
☎ 01307 840340 Castleton of Eassie DD8 1SJ
MENU GUIDE Tortellini of Usan lobster • Carved fillet of Scotch beef, dauphinoise potatoes • Baked pear Tatin, lemon sorbet
WINE GUIDE ♀ Santa Ema Sauvignon Blanc £14 • ♀ El Coto Rioja £17.50 • 50 bottles over £20, 30 bottles under £20 • 3 by the glass (£2.75-£3)
PRICE GUIDE Fixed L £30 • Fixed D £35 • starter £4.50-£7.25 main £9.50-£15.95 • dessert £4.95-£5.25 • Service optional
PLACE: Set in its own grounds with a moat, this impressive Victorian house offers a warm greeting from the owners. Clearly their hospitality and enthusiasm is infectious as the entire team go out of their way to make your evening one to remember.
FOOD: Flawlessly timed dishes are built around excellent regional ingredients kept simple to allow the flavours to shine through - the Castleton belongs to the 'less is more' school of thought. The British menu with French influences might include marbled Glen Isla venison terrine with truffled celeriac, pan-fried home-reared Tamworth pork fillet with caramelised apples and

muscovite sauce, and iced vanilla parfait with rhubarb compôte.
OUR TIP: Not far from Glamis Castle
Chef: Andrew Wilkie **Owners:** D & V Webster **Times:** 12-2/6.30-9, Closed New Year **Notes:** a la carte Sun L, Smart casual **Seats:** 50, Pr/dining room 35 **Smoking:** N/Sm in restaurant **Rooms:** 6 (6 en suite)
★★★ **Directions:** On A94, 3m W of Glamis **Parking:** 50
e-mail: hotel@castletonglamis.co.uk
web: www.castletonglamis.co.uk

Scotland

NVERKEILOR MAP 23 N064

Gordon's
Modern Scottish   NEW
Fine dining in Scottish village setting
☎ 01241 830364 Main St DD11 5RN
MENU GUIDE Arbroath smokie & salmon terrine • Seared halibut, mussel fricassee • Valrhona chocolate soufflé
PRICE GUIDE Food prices not confirmed for 2006. Please telephone for details
PLACE: This friendly, family-run restaurant with rooms in a pleasant village location has bags of character. Mother and daughter look after the front-of-house. The dining room has beams, a carpeted wooden floor and a huge log fire in the middle of an exposed stone wall.
FOOD: The father and son team in the kitchen take locally sourced, seasonal ingredients into dishes of imagination and flair. The cauliflower and artichoke velouté with miniature herb scones is just one example.
OUR TIP: Don't miss the excellent breakfast
Chef: Gordon Watson **Owners:** Gordon & Maria Watson **Times:** 12-.45/7-9 **e-mail:** gordonsrest@aol.com
web: www.gordonsrestaurant.co.uk

MONTROSE MAP 23 N075

Best Western Links Hotel
French, Scottish   NEW
Exciting menu in trendy bistro
☎ 01674 671000 Mid Links DD10 8RL
MENU GUIDE Scottish smoked salmon roulade, aubergine caviar • Roast monkfish, mussel cream • Whisky & orange bread & butter pudding
PRICE GUIDE Food prices not confirmed for 2006. Please telephone for details
PLACE: There's an air of a Paris bistro to this trendy restaurant located in a stylishly refurbished Edwardian hotel. A semi-opaque screen means you can watch kitchen proceedings unfold, while friendly front-of-house staff provide service with a flourish.
FOOD: Extensive, daring menus are matched by an accomplished cooking style that keeps flavours intact. Complex combinations are well orchestrated, and presentation is sleekly minimalist.
OUR TIP: Popular jazz venue
Chef: Franc Riveult **Owners:** Casper Mintemen **Times:** 12-2.30/6-9
Rooms: 25 (25 en suite) ★★★ **e-mail:** reception@linkshotel.com
web: www.linkshotel.co.uk

NEW
denotes a restaurant which is new
to the guide this year.

denotes restaurants that place
particular emphasis on making the
most of local ingredients.

Scotland

ARGYLL & BUTE

ARDUAINE MAP 20 NM71
◎◎ Loch Melfort Hotel
French, European
Romantic dining in West Coast hideaway
☎ 01852 200233   PA34 4XG

MENU GUIDE Trout & red onion tartlet • Barbary duck, braised red cabbage, caramelised orange sauce • Strawberry mousse, melon frappe

WINE GUIDE ♀ Santa Ema Sauvignon Blanc £12.95 • ♀ Santa Ema Cabernet Sauvignon £12.95 • 26 bottles over £20, 42 bottles under £20 • 4 by the glass (£2.70-£2.95)

PRICE GUIDE Fixed D £25 • min/water £2.90 • Service optional

PLACE: Backed by the wooded slopes of the Argyll mountain range, this family-run hotel enjoys one of the finest locations on the West Coast. The airy candlelit restaurant makes the most of the views, with large windows offering a panorama across the Sound to Jura.
FOOD: A daily-changing menu highlights fish - the catch comes straight from loch to kitchen and is as fresh as it gets. Expect thoughtful and accomplished cooking, with mains such as parsley-crusted cod and champ, or guinea fowl with redcurrant jus.
OUR TIP: Visit the beautiful Arduaine Gardens next door
Chef: Colin Macdonald **Owners:** Kyle & Nigel Schofield **Times:** 7.30-9, Closed 3 Jan-10 Feb, closed L all week **Notes:** Coffee incl. Sun buffet served Sun Evenings in season, Vegetarian available, Smart Dress
Seats: 75 **Smoking:** N/Sm in restaurant **Children:** Menu, Portions
Rooms: 27 (27 en suite) ★★★ **Directions:** From Oban, 20 m S on A816; from Lochgilphead, 19 m N on A816 **Parking:** 65
e-mail: reception@lochmelfort.co.uk **web:** www.lochmelfort.co.uk

BOWMORE MAP 20 NR35
◎◎ The Harbour Inn
Scottish, International
Island retreat with wonderful views and great food
☎ 01496 810330   The Square PA43 7JR
MENU GUIDE Local crab fish cakes • Baked Gruinart oysters • Hazelnut & date steamed pudding

PRICE GUIDE Starter £3.95-£9.50 • main fr £14.75 • dessert fr £5.25 • coffee £2.50 • min/water £3.65 • Service optional

PLACE: An old whitewashed building in the centre of town, with views over the harbour to the loch beyond, the hotel provides

The Harbour Inn

an unexpectedly sophisticated environment. There's a cosy locals' bar, a conservatory lounge with fabulous views over Loch Idaal and the peaks of Jura, and a contemporary-style restaurant.
FOOD: Modern Scottish dishes use local game, lamb and beef, as well as some of the best seafood to be found in the British Isles. Menus are according to the seasons, and presentation is accomplished.
OUR TIP: Many dishes are paired with whiskies from the island's distilleries
Chef: Carol Scott, Kevin Hanlon **Owners:** Carol Scott, Neil Scott
Times: 12-2.30/6-9.30 **Notes:** Vegetarian available, Smart casual
Seats: 44 **Smoking:** N/Sm in restaurant **Children:** Min 10 yrs, Portions
Rooms: 7 (7 en suite) ♦♦♦♦♦ **Directions:** Bowmore is situated approx 8m from both ports of Port Ellen & Port Askaig
e-mail: info@harbour-inn.com **web:** www.harbour-inn.com

CLACHAN MAP 20 NR75
◎ Balinakill Country House Hotel
Scottish, French   **NEW**
Victorian setting for contemporary cuisine
☎ 01880 740206   PA29 6XL
MENU GUIDE Pan-fried Islay scallops with bacon and lemon butter • Fillet of Kintyre sika venison, claret reduction • Warm organic chocolate tart

WINE GUIDE ♀ Marlborough Francesca Bay Sauvignon Blanc £18.50 • ♀ Campillo Tempranillo Rioja Crianza £19.50 • 7 bottles over £20, 24 bottles under £20 • 2 by the glass (£2.50)

PRICE GUIDE Fixed D £26.95 • coffee £1.80 • min/water £2.50 • Service optional

PLACE: A family-run hotel set in 7 acres of grounds on the Kintyre peninsula. Its Victorian heritage is evident in the wonderful wood panelling, plasterwork and antiques, with a traditional, elegant dining room.
FOOD: Fresh Scottish produce, largely free range or organic, features heavily on the daily changing contemporary menu. Classical French techniques are showcased in the style of cooking.
OUR TIP: Chocolate lovers will find desserts to die for
Chef: Angus MacDiarmid **Owners:** Angus & Susan MacDiarmid
Times: 7-9 **Notes:** Vegetarian available **Seats:** 24 **Smoking:** N/Sm in restaurant **Children:** Portions **Directions:** 10m S of Tarbert Loch Fyne. The entrance is located on the left off A83 travelling S towards Campbeltown **Parking:** 20 **e-mail:** info@balinakill.com
web: www.balinakill.com

continued

Scotland

CLACHAN-SEIL MAP 20 NM71

 Willowburn Hotel

British, French

Welcoming hotel in tranquil setting

☎ 01852 300276 PA34 4TJ

MENU GUIDE Vegetable & almond terrine, sweet pepper sauce • Breast of duck on red cabbage, port & pear compote • Chocolate & mango Charlotte

WINE GUIDE 45 bottles over £20, 46 bottles under £20 • 4 by the glass (£3.25-£3.50)

PRICE GUIDE Fixed D £35-£37 • min/water £2.50

PLACE: This welcoming little gem of a hotel enjoys a peaceful setting with grounds running down to the water's edge of Clachan Sound. Watch the wildlife from the dining room window.
FOOD: The service is friendly and unobtrusive - since you'll want to linger over the modern British menu with French influences. Food is prepared by a kitchen committed to using the freshest and best quality local produce. On the dinner menu, expect dishes such as crab wrapped in marinated salmon and local lobster served on a dill and mascarpone cheesecake.
OUR TIP: The breakfasts and canapés are excellent
Chef: Chris Wolfe **Owners:** Chris & Chris Wolfe **Times:** 7-8.30, Closed Dec-Feb **Notes:** Set price D, 5 courses, Coffee incl, Vegetarian available, Dress Restrictions, Tidy & comfortable **Seats:** 20 **Smoking:** N/Sm in restaurant **Children:** Min 8 yrs **Rooms:** 7 (7 en suite) ★★
Directions: 11m S of Oban via A816 and B844 (Easdale) over Atlantic bridge **Parking:** 20 **e-mail:** willowburn.hotel@virgin.net
web: www.willowburn.co.uk

DERVAIG MAP 22 NM45

Druimard Country House Hotel

Scottish

Friendly small hotel restaurant featuring local fare

☎ 01688 400345 PA75 6QW

MENU GUIDE Caramelised onion tarte Tatin • Gressingham duck breast, lemon & asparagus risotto • Iced cranachan, raspberry compôte

WINE GUIDE Madfish Bay Chardonnay £21.75 • Saint-Hilaire Coteaux D'aix en Provence £12.95 • 14 bottles over £20, 18 bottles under £20 • 2 by the glass (£2.75)

PRICE GUIDE Fixed D £31.50 • coffee £2 • min/water £2.75 Service optional

PLACE: Personally-run small hotel in an elevated position overlooking the Glen and River Bellert on the outskirts of the village. The restaurant is the focal point of the house; a cosy room with rich dark red decor and a home-from-home atmosphere.
FOOD: The cooking has a modern slant on locally sourced meat, game and seafood, using items from the island wherever possible. Dishes are offered from a short, daily fixed-price menu.
OUR TIP: Located in one of the prettiest villages on Mull
Chef: Louise Palmer **Owners:** Louise Palmer **Times:** 7-8 Closed L all wk
Notes: Vegetarian available **Seats:** 26 **Smoking:** N/Sm in restaurant
Children: Min 10 yrs, Menu, Portions **Rooms:** 7 (7 en suite)
Directions: 8m from Tobermory on Tobermory to Dervaig road. Turn left at x-rds before bridge and left before Glen Houses **Parking:** 10
e-mail: druimard.hotel@virgin.net **web:** www.druimard.co.uk

ERISKA MAP 20 NM94

Isle of Eriska

Modern Scottish

Culinary retreat in stunning island setting

☎ 01631 720371 PA37 1SD

MENU GUIDE Crab risotto, scallops, vanilla froth • Duck, black pudding, apple & potato gâteau, roast fig • Prune d'Agen crème brûlée

WINE GUIDE Latour Ardeche Chardonnay £10.50 • 40 bottles over £20, 60 bottles under £20 • 4 by the glass (£3.50-£5)

PRICE GUIDE Fixed D £38.50 • min/water £3 • Service optional

PLACE: Set on a private island off the west coast of Scotland, this late-Victorian manor is a secluded haven for foodies. Now in its second generation of family ownership, the hotel has developed a strong local following over the years and draws a friendly mix of old and young alike. Food is served in a large dining room with a classical decor, and an airy conservatory extension that overlooks the gardens.

FOOD: Modern Scottish cuisine at its best. The six-course menu changes daily and features a concise range of dishes that showcase the kitchen's technical accomplishment and respect for local seasonal produce. It's all washed down with an extensive - and great-value - wine list, presided over by a sommelier of considerable knowledge. Vegetarians catered for by request.
OUR TIP: Stroll on the beach or enjoy a round of golf on the hotel's mini course
Chef: Robert MacPherson **Owners:** Mr Buchanan-Smith **Times:** 8-9, Closed Jan **Notes:** Coffee incl, Fixed D 4 courses, Vegetarian available, Dress Restrictions, Jacket & Tie, Civ Wed 110 **Seats:** 40, Pr/dining room 20 **Smoking:** N/Sm in restaurant, Air con **Children:** Menu, Portions
Rooms: 17 (17 en suite) ★★★★ **Directions:** A82 from Glasgow to Tyndrum. A85 towards Oban; at Connel bridge take A828 to Benderloch village for 4m **Parking:** 50 **e-mail:** office@eriska-hotel.co.uk
web: www.eriska-hotel.co.uk

Scotland

ERISKA MAP 20 NM94
 Isle of Eriska *see page 545*

KILCHRENAN MAP 20 NN02
The Ardanaiseig Hotel
French, British
Breathtaking food with breathtaking scenery
☎ 01866 833333 by Loch Awe PA35 1HE

MENU GUIDE Stornoway black pudding, foie gras & apple • Halibut, lobster, shellfish essence • Chocolate tart

WINE GUIDE ⌾ Ca'dei Frati Lugana £21 • ⌾ Apaltagua Carmenere £23 • 86 bottles over £20, 10 bottles under £20 16 by the glass (£4.50-£10.50)

PRICE GUIDE Fixed D £42-£45 • coffee £2.50 • min/water £3.50 • Service optional

PLACE: Idyllic and tranquil, this 19th-century country house by William Burn sits in its own gardens on the shores of Loch Awe. Inside, rooms are expansive and feature log fires. There's a wealth of antique furniture in the bedrooms, drawing room and library bar. The elegant dining room and relaxed and friendly service set the scene for some fine dining.
FOOD: French in style using fresh, seasonal Scottish and French ingredients. Imaginative dishes are carefully prepared and attractively and effectively presented. Garnishing and saucing are exact and contribute to the success of dishes like best end of lamb, provençale vegetables, spinach, garlic, black olive and caper jus. Excellent wine list.
OUR TIP: Book a table window to enjoy the wonderful views
Chef: Gary Goldie **Owners:** Bennie Gray **Times:** 12.00-2/7-9, Closed 3 Jan- 10 Feb **Notes:** Vegetarian available, Dress Restrictions, Smart casual, no jeans or trainers, Civ Wed 50 **Seats:** 36 **Smoking:** N/Sm in restaurant **Children:** Min 9 yrs, Portions **Rooms:** 16 (16 en suite)
★★★ **Directions:** Take A85 to Oban. At Taynuilt turn left onto B845 towards Kilchrenan. In Kilchrenan turn left by pub. Hotel in 3m
Parking: 16 **e-mail:** info@ardanaiseig.com
web: www.ardanaiseig.com

 ## Taychreggan Hotel
British
One of Scotland's most romantic dining locations
☎ 01866 833211 833366   PA35 1HQ

MENU GUIDE Whole roasted quail • Scottish lamb saddle, sweet potato fondant & ratatouille • Cranachan Tower

PRICE GUIDE Food prices not confirmed for 2006. Please telephone for details

PLACE: A tastefully renovated former ferry and cattle drovers' inn by the loch's edge. The dining room here is simply furnished so as not to detract from the majestic mountain and loch views through the huge arched windows.
FOOD: The modern British dishes make full use of abundant local, seasonal ingredients. The precise modern, minimalist presentation contrasts nicely with the traditional combinations. There's a light touch to dishes like the gazpacho served in a demitasse and the pork fillet with green beans and sauce poivrade.
OUR TIP: A lavish choice of outdoor pursuits
Chef: Paul Higgins **Owners:** North American Country Inns
Times: 12.30-2/7.30-8.45 **Notes:** Fixed D, 5 courses £37.50, Vegetarian available, Civ Wed 70 **Seats:** 45, Pr/dining room 18 **Smoking:** N/Sm in restaurant **Children:** Min 14 yrs **Rooms:** 19 (19 en suite) ★★★
Directions: W from Glasgow on A82 to Crainlarich. W on A85 to Taynuilt. On B845 to Kilchrenan & Taychreggan **Parking:** 40
e-mail: taychreggan@btinternet.com **web:** www.taychregganhotel.co.uk

LOCHGILPHEAD MAP 20 NR88
Cairnbaan
British, European
Canal-side cuisine
☎ 01546 603668 Crinan Canal, Cairnbaan PA31 8SJ

MENU GUIDE Smoked venison, rowan jelly, redcurrants • Ardfern lobster, garlic butter • Dark chocolate marquise

continue

Scotland

WINE GUIDE ♀ Cape Bay Chardonnay £11.90 • ♀ Cape Bay Pinotage £11.90 • 20 bottles over £20, 30 bottles under £20 6 by the glass (£2.90-£3.50)

PRICE GUIDE Fixed L £9-£20 • starter £3.45-£8 • main £8-£18 dessert £5.50 • coffee £1.60 • min/water £3 • Service optional

PLACE: The restaurant of this friendly hotel is decorated in contemporary Scottish style with acres of tartan and stripped wooden floors. Wide windows show off an idyllic canal-side setting.
FOOD: Sensational ingredients handled with respect and confident simplicity. A wide-ranging menu offers a choice of over ten main dishes, but seafood is the draw; tuck into Jura scallops with grilled figs and a raspberry vinaigrette, or jumbo langoustines with citrus mayonnaise and salad.
OUR TIP: The hotel's bar/bistro is also popular
Chef: David Galt, Vicki Ure **Owners:** Darren & Christine Dobson
Times: 12-2.30/6-9.30 **Notes:** Civ Wed 120 **Seats:** 40, Pr/dining room 30 **Smoking:** N/Sm in restaurant **Children:** Menu, Portions **Rooms:** 12 (12 en suite) ★★★ **Directions:** Cairnbaan is 2m N of Lochgilphead on A83, Hotel first on left **Parking:** 30 **e-mail:** info@cairnbaan.com
web: www.cairnbaan.com

LUSS MAP 20 NS39
🌸🌸 Colquhoun's
International
Informal dining in lochside setting
☎ 01436 860201 The Lodge on Loch Lomond, Hotel & Restaurant G83 8PA

MENU GUIDE Scallop & prawn brochette • Pan-fried loin of wild venison • Warm chocolate tart

WINE GUIDE ♀ 1 Wine Ltd Pinot Grigio £13.95
♀ Stellenbosch Farmers Winery Pinotage £15.50 • 18 bottles over £20, 27 bottles under £20 • 5 by the glass (£3.35-£4.75)

PRICE GUIDE Fixed D £24.95 • coffee £1.55 • min/water £3.25 • Service optional

PLACE: Divided into three distinct styles according to the dates of

development, this much-extended hotel set at the water's edge is renowned for its views. You can savour these in the older lodge-style restaurant, where timber cladding and open-plan architecture are at ease with the rural setting.
FOOD: A short carte allows the kitchen to focus on freshness, with quality ingredients being used to interesting effect. Follow an inventive starter like haggis fritter, champ potatoes and turnip fondant with, perhaps, marinated loin of Perthshire lamb strikingly paired with tomato and rosemary risotto.
OUR TIP: Stay over, and try out the new leisure suite
Chef: David Friel **Owners:** Niall Colquhoun **Times:** 12-5/6-9.45
Notes: Vegetarian available, Civ Wed 100 **Seats:** 100, Pr/dining room 40
Smoking: N/Sm in restaurant **Children:** Menu, Portions **Rooms:** 46 (46 en suite) ★★★ **Directions:** 30m N of Glasgow on A82
Parking: 70 **e-mail:** res@loch-lomondhotel.co.uk
web: www.loch-lomond.co.uk

OBAN MAP 20 NM82
🌸 Eeusk
British
Fresh fish served right on the pier
☎ 01631 565666 North Pier PA34 5QD

MENU GUIDE Loch Etive mussels • Wild halibut, creamed leeks, sautéed potatoes • Clootie dumpling

WINE GUIDE ♀ Shiraz £12.75 • 8 bottles over £20, 23 bottles under £20 • 4 by the glass (£2.85)

PRICE GUIDE Starter £3.95-£8.95 • main £9.95-£17.95 • dessert £3.95-£4.50 • coffee £1.40 • min/water £3.50 • Service optional

PLACE: A privately-owned building on one of Oban's piers, where diners are treated to views over the bay and passers-by strolling or fishing from the pier. The chic interior is split into levels with tiled floors and light wood furniture.
FOOD: The freshness of the fish is the great strength here, simply prepared and attractively presented. The shellfish suppliers haven't changed in years, and all but two of the wet fish are landed in the harbour.
OUR TIP: People-watch and bay-watch from a window table
Chef: Marianne Macdonald **Owners:** The Macleod Family **Times:** 12-2.30/6-9.30, Closed 25-26 Dec, 1 Jan **Notes:** Vegetarian available
Seats: 100, Pr/dining room 24 **Smoking:** N/Sm in restaurant
Children: Min 6 yrs D, Portions **Directions:** 85 miles from Glasgow, North-West A85 **Parking:** Public car park at rear
e-mail: eeusk.fishcafe@virgin.net

🌸 Manor House Hotel
British
Quality produce and classical elegance by the sea
☎ 01631 562087 Gallanach Rd PA34 4LS

continued

continued

Scotland

OBAN continued MAP 20 NM82

MENU GUIDE Warm beef, red onion & stilton salad • Rack of lamb with herb crust • Brioche bread & butter pudding, apples & apricots

WINE GUIDE ♀ Grenache Blanc 2004 £12.95 • ♥ Grenache Noir 2004 £12.95 • 10 bottles over £20, 22 bottles under £20 4 by the glass

PRICE GUIDE Fixed L £18.95 • Fixed D £29.50 • coffee £1.95 min/water £3.50 • Service optional

PLACE: A classically elegant Georgian hotel overlooking the harbour. The dining room has a real country house feel, with heavy drapes complementing dark green walls and tartan.
FOOD: High quality local produce is transformed into a fixed-price evening menu with a modern slant. Bar menu only at lunchtime, with lower prices but the same standards.
OUR TIP: Try the iced gingerbread and Cointreau parfait
Chef: Patrick Freytag **Owners:** Mr PL Crane **Times:** 12-2/6.45-9, Closed 25 Dec **Notes:** Vegetarian available, Dress Restrictions, No jeans
Seats: 30 **Smoking:** N/Sm in restaurant **Children:** Min 12 yrs, Portions
Rooms: 11 (11 en suite) ★★★ **Directions:** 300 mtrs past Oban ferry terminal **Parking:** 20 **e-mail:** manorhouseoban@aol.com
web: www.manorhouseoban.com

PORT APPIN MAP 20 NM94

 Airds Hotel *see below*

STRACHUR MAP 20 NN00

 Creggans Inn
British, French
Skilful cooking in stunning loch-side setting
☎ 01369 860279 PA27 8BX

MENU GUIDE Scallops in filo, mussel & saffron cream sauce • Chicken, black pudding, apple rösti, foie gras sauce • Warm hazelnut torte

WINE GUIDE ♀ J&F Lurton Sauvignon Blanc £12.50 • ♥ Domaine de Courberoc Merlot £14 • 35 bottles over £20, 35 bottles under £20 • 6 by the glass (£3.20-£3.50)

PRICE GUIDE Fixed D £28-£35 • min/water £3 • Service optional

PLACE: Set on the shores of Loch Fyne, this friendly hotel offers breathtaking views of wide Scottish skies and far away hills across the water. Come at sunset to see it at its best, from one of the smart restaurant's crisply clothed, well-spaced tables.
FOOD: An ambitious kitchen delivers a well-balanced daily changing menu, and makes the most of what the loch and local area has to offer.
OUR TIP: Lunch and dinner also served in the bar
Chef: A Watson, Calum Williamson **Owners:** Mr T A Robertson, Mr T A Robertson Jnr & Mrs O Robertson **Times:** 7-9, Closed 25-26 Dec, closed L all week **Notes:** Coffee included, Vegetarian available **Seats:** 35
Smoking: N/Sm in restaurant **Children:** Min 8 yrs, Menu, Portions
Rooms: 14 (14 en suite) ★★★ **Directions:** From Glasgow A82, along Loch Lomond, then W on A83, onto A815 to Strachur. Or by ferry from Gourock to Dunoon onto A815 **Parking:** 25
e-mail: info@creggans-inn.co.uk **web:** www.creggans-inn.co.uk

---

PORT APPIN MAP 20 NM94

Airds Hotel

British, European
Lochside gastronomic retreat
☎ 01631 730236 PA38 4DF

MENU GUIDE Pigeon, foie gras, pancetta • Turbot, scallops, spinach, Vermouth velouté • Prune & Armagnac soufflé

WINE GUIDE ♀ Lowe Chardonnay £24 • ♥ Montes Cabernet Sauvignon £18.50 • 108 bottles over £20, 11 bottles under £20 10 by the glass (£4.75-£6.50)

PRICE GUIDE Fixed L £17.95 • Fixed D £47.50 • Service optional

PLACE: Country-house comfort meets sophisticated modern chic in the decor of this luxury hotel on the shores of Loch Linnhe. The elegant restaurant has wide windows making it the perfect place to watch the sun set over loch and mountain.
FOOD: Expect modern British cuisine with a Scottish twist. Airds handles world-class local ingredients with a clean cooking style that lets the flavours of key elements flourish. A starter of sautéed scallops is served with slow-cooked fennel and a delicate pesto. Mains demonstrate the emphasis on simplicity.

OUR TIP: Ask helpful staff about a personalised walk
Chef: J Paul Burns **Owners:** Mr & Mrs S McKivragan **Times:** 12-2/7.30-8.30, Closed 5-26 Jan **Notes:** Coffee incl, Gourmet nights £70 incl wine, Vegetarian by request, Civ Wed 40 **Seats:** 36 **Smoking:** N/Sm in restaurant **Rooms:** 12 (12 en suite) ★★★ **Directions:** A828, follow signs for Port Appin. Continue for 2.5m, hotel on left. **Parking:** 20
e-mail: airds@airds-hotel.com **web:** www.airds-hotel.com

TARBERT LOCH FYNE MAP 20 NR86

Stonefield Castle Hotel

British ★NEW

Enjoyable dining accompanied by superb views across Loch Fyne

☎ 01880 820836 PA29 6YJ

MENU GUIDE Grilled Loch Fyne herring • Pan-fried medallions of beef fillet, wild mushroom risotto • Strawberry Romanoff

WINE GUIDE ♀ One Tree Hill Columbard Chardonnay £12.50 • ♀ One Tree Hill Shiraz £12.50 • 19 bottles over £20, 36 bottles under £20 • 5 by the glass (£3.25)

PRICE GUIDE Fixed D £25-£30 • coffee £3 • min/water £3.50 • Service optional

PLACE: Built in 1837 in Scottish baronial style, Stonefield Castle has gardens renowned for their rhododendron collection, and a wonderful setting on the shores of Loch Fyne. The restaurant is rich in baronial elegance, but the atmosphere is light and spacious. There are exceptional picture-window views over the woodland gardens and across the loch.

FOOD: Well sourced mainly local produce, especially seafood, lamb and venison, with beef coming from the Buccleuch estates. The excellence of the ingredients shines through in well presented dishes.

OUR TIP: Visit in late spring to see the gardens at their best
Chef: Angus MacFarlane **Owners:** Stonefield Castle Group **Times:** 12-2/7-9 **Notes:** Vegetarian available, Dress Restrictions, Smart casual, Civ Wed 120 **Seats:** 120, Pr/dining room 10 **Smoking:** N/Sm in restaurant **Children:** Menu, Portions **Rooms:** 33 (32 en suite) ★★★
Directions: 2m N of Tarbert Village **Parking:** 33
e-mail: enquiries@stonefieldcastle.co.uk
web: www.stonefieldcastle.co.uk

TIGHNABRUAICH MAP 20 NR97

The Royal at Tighnabruaich

Modern Scottish

Innovative cuisine in loch-side setting

☎ 01700 811239 Shore Rd PA21 2BE

MENU GUIDE Peat-smoked haddock chowder • Scallops, monkfish in bacon, celeriac mash, Bloody Mary reduction • Clootie dumpling

WINE GUIDE ♀ Del Veneto Pinot £15.95 • ♀ Coldridge Estate Shiraz £13.95 • 51 bottles over £20, 15 bottles under £20 • 4 by the glass (£3.95-£4.50)

PRICE GUIDE Starter £3.95-£10.95 • main £16.95-£27.95 • dessert £3.95-£4.50 • coffee £1.50 • min/water £3.95 • Service optional

PLACE: This smart modern hotel run by a family team sits just a few steps from the shore, and offers stunning views over the Kyle of Bute from its candlelit conservatory dining room.

FOOD: Local produce is at the heart of The Royal's menu, which name-checks suppliers in friendly fashion, and features modern Scottish dishes such as beef with black ratte potatoes, chanterelle mushrooms and a white wine reduction.

OUR TIP: The hotel has its own masseuse
Chef: Roger McKie, Claire McKie, Louise McKie **Owners:** Mr & Mrs R McKie **Times:** 12-3/7-8.45, Closed Xmas period, Mon-Tue, closed L all week (groups by prior arrangement) **Notes:** Set price D £35 (5 courses), Seafood menu, Vegetarian available **Seats:** 35, Pr/dining room 20 **Smoking:** N/Sm in restaurant **Children:** Portions **Rooms:** 11 (11 en suite) ★★ **Directions:** From Strachur, on A886, turn right onto A8003 to Tighnabruaich. Hotel on right at bottom of hill. Dunoon ferry terminal take left onto B8000 to Tighnabruaich **Parking:** 20
e-mail: info@royalhotel.org.uk **web:** www.royalhotel.org.uk

---

TOBERMORY MAP 22 NM55

⊚⊚ Highland Cottage

Modern Scottish

A real home-from-home to enjoy highland hospitality

☎ 01688 302030 Breadalbane St PA75 6PD

MENU GUIDE Smoked haddock risotto • Ardnamurchan venison, juniper berry sauce • Spiced pear, ginger ice cream

WINE GUIDE ♀ Katherine Hills Colombard Chardonnay £16.95 • ♀ Torreon de Paredes Merlot £18.75 • 21 bottles over £20, 22 bottles under £20 • 10 by the glass (£4.50-£6.50)

PRICE GUIDE Fixed D £35 • Service included

PLACE: Small, family-run Hebridean hotel set above the West Coast town of Tobermory in a conservation area. The country-style restaurant has a welcoming fire and the atmosphere is relaxed and informal.

FOOD: The plain and simple approach to cooking adopted here perfectly showcases the high quality, seasonal ingredients. Carefully prepared and well-balanced dishes use local crab, smoked haddock, monkfish, beef and venison.

OUR TIP: The Isle of Mull provides an endless list of sights and activities so make a weekend of it
Chef: Josephine Currie **Owners:** David & Josephine Currie **Times:** 7-9, Closed mid Oct-mid Nov, Xmas, part Jan-Mar, closed L all week
Notes: Vegetarian available, Dress Restrictions, Smart casual **Seats:** 24 **Smoking:** N/Sm in restaurant **Children:** Min 10 yrs, Portions **Rooms:** 6 (6 en suite) ★★ **Directions:** Opposite fire station. Main Street up Back Brae, turn at top by White House. Follow road to right, left at next junction **Parking:** On street **e-mail:** davidandjo@highlandcottage.co.uk
web: www.highlandcottage.co.uk

⊚ Tobermory Hotel

Modern Scottish, Mediterranean

Delightful seafront hotel retreat on Isle of Mull

☎ 01688 302091 53 Main St PA75 6NT

MENU GUIDE Inverlussa moules marinières • Sgriob-ruadh apricot & rosemary stuffed pork loin • Chef's strawberry cheesecake

WINE GUIDE ♀ Château Billot Sauvignon/Semillon £11.95 • ♀ Torreon de Paredes Merlot £12.90 • 11 bottles over £20, 34 bottles under £20 • 5 by the glass (£2.75)

PRICE GUIDE Fixed D £25.50 • coffee £1.95 • min/water £3.50 • Service optional

PLACE: This friendly hotel with its pretty pink frontage sits amidst an appealing row of brightly coloured former fishing cottages on the seafront. There's a comfortable lounge where drinks are

continued

Scotland

Scotland

TOBERMORY continued MAP 22 NM55

served before dining in the cosy Water's Edge restaurant.
Friendly, helpful service.
FOOD: Freshly caught fish figure prominently on the modern
Scottish menu with Mediterranean influences although local pork
and lamb also get a look in.
OUR TIP: Excellent value light lunches in the summer
Chef: Helen Swinbanks **Owners:** Mr & Mrs I Stevens **Times:** 7-9,
Closed Xmas, closed L all week **Notes:** Vegetarian available **Seats:** 30
Smoking: N/Sm in restaurant **Children:** Menu, Portions **Rooms:** 16 (15
en suite) ★★ **Directions:** Telephone for directions **Parking:** On street
e-mail: tobhotel@tinyworld.co.uk **web:** www.thetobmoryhotel.com

AYRSHIRE, EAST

SORN MAP 20 NS52

⊚⊚ The Sorn Inn
British
Fine dining in the heart of Ayrshire
☎ 01290 551305 35 Main St KA5 6HU
MENU GUIDE West coast crab, ginger foam • Guinea fowl, black
pudding potatoes • Autumn berry baked Alaska
WINE GUIDE ♀ Pinot Grigio £11.50 • ♀ Paul Skalli Merlot
£11.50 • 15 bottles over £20, 29 bottles under £20 • 8 by the
glass (£3-£3.50)
PRICE GUIDE Fixed L £11.95 • Fixed D £23.50 • coffee
£1.75 • min/water £3 • Service optional
PLACE: This well-run restaurant with rooms, once an 18th-
century coaching inn, is situated in the middle of deepest
Ayrshire with good local shooting and fishing. There's a cosy
lounge area, bar, fine dining restaurant and a chophouse bistro.
A little bit out of the way so it might be a good idea to stay over
in one of the individually decorated comfortable bedrooms.
FOOD: Dishes are cooked with finesse and flair and are mainly
modern British in style with good use of local and Scottish game,
seafood and locally grown vegetables.
OUR TIP: Fishing permits available on River Ayr
Chef: Craig Grant **Owners:** The Grant Partnership **Times:** 12-2.30/6.30-
9.30, Closed Mon, closed L Sat, closed D Sun **Notes:** Sun L 2 courses
£12.95, 3 courses £15.95, Vegetarian available, Smart Dress **Seats:** 42
Smoking: N/Sm in restaurant **Children:** Menu, Portions **Rooms:** 4 (4
en suite) 🐕 **Directions:** From A77, take the A76 to Mauchline join
B743, 4m to Sorn **Parking:** 9 **e-mail:** craig@thesorninn.com
web: www.thesorninn.com

AYRSHIRE, NORTH

BRODICK MAP 20 NS03

⊚⊚ Auchrannie Country House Hotel
Modern Scottish
Fine dining on Arran
☎ 01770 302234 KA27 8BZ
MENU GUIDE Highland game terrine, tomato chutney • Beef,
garlic mash, wild mushrooms, anise jus • Raspberry & Drambuie
brûlée

WINE GUIDE ♀ Eagle Hawk Chardonnay £13 • ♀ Eagle Hawk
Cabernet Shiraz £13 • 27 bottles over £20, 31 bottles under
£20 • 6 by the glass (£3.75-£7.95)
PRICE GUIDE Fixed D £25.95 • coffee £1.20 • min/water
£3 • Service included
PLACE: This imposing Victorian manor has been converted into a
popular resort hotel, and offers a choice of formal dining in the
Garden restaurant, or lighter meals in a more relaxed brasserie.
Its landscaped gardens feature an impressive spa complete with
games hall, beauty parlour and pool.
FOOD: The Garden Restaurant delivers an accomplished range of
modern Scottish dishes. Expect mains like truffle-crusted loin of
venison served on a slow cooked potato and pink peppercorn
jus. Pre-dinner drinks and coffees are served in a comfortable
adjacent lounge.
OUR TIP: Indulge yourself with a trip to the spa
Chef: Craig Beedie **Owners:** Mr I Johnston **Times:** 6.30-9.30
Notes: Vegetarian available, Smart Dress, Civ Wed 100 **Seats:** 52,
Pr/dining room 22 **Smoking:** N/Sm in restaurant **Children:** Menu,
Portions **Rooms:** 28 (28 en suite) ★★★ **Directions:** From Brodick Pier
turn right onto main road. Continue for 0.5m turn left at signs for
Auchrannie **Parking:** 25 **e-mail:** info@auchrannie.co.uk
web: www.auchrannie.co.uk

⊚⊚ Kilmichael Hotel
Mediterranean, International
Country-house hotel offering competent cooking
☎ 01770 302219 Glen Cloy KA27 8BY
MENU GUIDE Carrot, parsnip & peanut soup • Breast of
Gressingham duck, Savoy cabbage with ginger & Arran
mustard • Arran berry mousse
WINE GUIDE 19 bottles over £20, 31 bottles under £20 • 2 by
the glass (£2.15-£6.45)
PRICE GUIDE Fixed D £38 • min/water £2.45
Service included
PLACE: Listed property believed to be the oldest house on the
island, set in attractive gardens with mature trees. The
proprietors aim for a private house feel with interesting
collectibles from around the world. Drinks are served in the
lounges rather than a bar and there is a domestic feel to the
Georgian-style dining room, but with individual tables.
FOOD: Modern British fare with strong Italian and International
influences is well represented on the daily four-course dinner
menu. Dishes are creative using the best of local produce with
good flavour combinations. Everything is home-made including
bread and ice cream.
OUR TIP: Lots of useful info on the island can be found in each
room
Chef: Antony Butterworth **Owners:** G Botterill & A Butterworth
Times: 7-8.30, Closed Nov-Mar, Tue **Notes:** Coffee incl., Vegetarian
available, Smart Dress **Seats:** 18 **Smoking:** N/Sm in restaurant
Children: Min 12 yrs **Rooms:** 7 (7 en suite) ★★ **Directions:** Turn
right on leaving ferry terminal, through Brodick & left at golf club. Follow
brown sign. Continue past church & onto private drive. **Parking:** 12
e-mail: enquiries@kilmichael.com
web: www.kilmichael.com

The AA Wine Awards recognise the finest
wine lists in England, Scotland and Wales. For
full details, see pages 14-15

continued

DALRY MAP 20 NS24

Braidwoods
Modern Scottish

Cooking with creative flair in rustic setting
☎ 01294 833544 Drumastle Mill Cottage
KA24 4LN

MENU GUIDE Pressed mosaic of duck confit & foie gras • Roast best end of Ayrshire lamb, parcel of slow-cooked lamb, rosemary essence • Truffle terrine of dark, milk & white chocolate

PRICE GUIDE Food prices not confirmed for 2006. Please telephone for details

PLACE: A redecoration has given this charming rustic cluster of old millers' cottages a touch of the Provençal and a more modern look. The result is cosy and inviting, with fresh flowers and local artists' work to brighten the two dining rooms.
FOOD: Keith Braidwood's menus display a healthy respect for quality ingredients (mostly sourced locally), belief in freshness (starting with the stocks and sauces), and terrific attention to detail - as displayed in his home-made pastas, breads and chocolates. The straightforward menu delivers exactly what it promises, without undue garnishes or saucing. Service, hosted by Nicola Braidwood, is relaxed and attentive.
OUR TIP: Perfect for an intimate meal
Times: 12-2.15/7-9.30, Closed 25-26 Dec, 1st 3 wks Jan, 2 wks Sep, Mon, closed L Tue. (Sun May-Sep), closed D Sun **Directions:** 1 mile from Dalry on the Saltcoats Road **e-mail:** keithbraidwood@btconnect.com **web:** www.braidwoods.co.uk

AYRSHIRE, SOUTH

AYR MAP 20 NS32

 Enterkine House
British, French

Fine dining in stylish country house
☎ 01292 520580 Annbank KA6 5AL
MENU GUIDE Home-smoked venison, red onion marmalade • Lamb noisette, veal bordelaise jus • Apple tart Tatin, crème anglaise
WINE GUIDE ♀ Nelsons Creek Sauvignon Blanc £19.25 • ♀ Domaine de Saissac Cabernet Sauvignon £18 59 bottles over £20, 10 bottles under £20 • 10 by the glass (£4.95-£11)
PRICE GUIDE Fixed L £12.50-£15 • Fixed D £25-£32 • coffee £2.25 • min/water £4 • Service added but optional 10% • Group min 6 service 10%
PLACE: Built in the 1930s, this beautifully appointed country house hotel, a private home until 2000, stands in an idyllic setting with lovely countryside views. Period features have been retained and hospitality is very much in the country-house tradition, especially in the elegant dining room.
FOOD: Well-balanced fixed-price menus utilise local fish and game and other Scottish produce. Expect interesting flavour combinations and a modern approach to cooking some classic dishes.
OUR TIP: Enjoy views of the Ayr valley from the sun room
Chef: Paul Moffat **Owners:** Mr Browne **Times:** 12-2/7-9
Notes: Vegetarian available, Dress Restrictions, Jacket for men, Civ Wed 00 **Seats:** 40, Pr/dining room 12 **Smoking:** N/Sm in restaurant

continued

Children: Menu, Portions **Rooms:** 6 (6 en suite) ★★★
Directions: Telephone for directions. 5m E of Ayr on B743 **Parking:** 20
e-mail: mail@enterkine.com **web:** www.enterkine.com

 Fairfield House Hotel
Classic

Modern cooking in seaside hotel
☎ 01292 267461 12 Fairfield Rd KA7 2AR
PLACE: This friendly hotel draws a convivial mix of business and local diners, offering a choice of two eating options: a more formal dining area, and a lounge area with comfortable leather sofas and low tables for more casual dining. Quietly set just off the Esplanade, the hotel boasts stunning sea views to the Isle of Arran and at the time of going to press is undergoing full refurbishment.
FOOD: The more formal dining area offers classic fare; its dishes based around simple combinations with little extra embellishment.
OUR TIP: Great sunsets over Arran
Chef: Bruce Morrison **Owners:** George Martin **Times:** 12-2/7-9
Rooms: 44 (44 en suite) ★★★★
e-mail: reservations@fairfieldhotel.co.uk
web: www.fairfieldhotel.co.uk

 Fouters
Modern Scottish

Basement restaurant and ambitious cooking
☎ 01292 261391 2A Academy St KA7 1HS
MENU GUIDE Salmon & spinach terrine • Breast of Gressingham duck • Caramelised orange tart
WINE GUIDE ♀ Domaine le Verger Chablis Chardonnay £23.45 • ♀ J P Moueix Fronsac Merlot £20.75 • 17 bottles over £20, 14 bottles under £20 • 2 by the glass (£2.75-£3.75)
PRICE GUIDE Starter £3.50-£8 • main £9-£20 • dessert £4.75-£6.50 • coffee £3 • min/water £3.95 • Service optional
PLACE: A friendly family-run restaurant tucked away in the basement of an old bank, located off the main street. The vaulted ceiling and flagstoned floors are full of atmosphere and appeal.
FOOD: Chef/owner Brian Murphy gets the best out of his quality ingredients with some skilful, unfussy cooking. An outstanding confit of duck leg presented simply with sautéed potatoes and green beans might share the menu with loin of Perthshire venison, and supreme of Ayrshire chicken, all at the peak of freshness.
OUR TIP: Try the daily fish dish
Chef: Brian Murphy, James Macintosh **Owners:** Mr & Mrs Murphy, Henrietta Fleming **Times:** 12-2.30/5-10, Closed 4-11 Jan, Sun-Mon
Notes: Vegetarian available **Seats:** 38, Pr/dining room 24
Smoking: N/Sm in restaurant, Air con **Children:** Min 5/10 yrs
Directions: Town centre, opposite Town Hall, down Cobblestone Lane
Parking: On street **e-mail:** qualityfood@fouters.co.uk
web: www.fouters.co.uk

Prices quoted in the guide are for guidance only and are subject to change without notice.

Scotland

BALLANTRAE MAP 20 NX08

Glenapp Castle

British

Stunning castle, stunning cuisine, stunning views

☎ 01465 831212   KA26 0NZ

MENU GUIDE Tempura of courgette flower with ratatouille • Breast of duck with pan-fried foie gras & Madeira jus • Pavé of white & dark chocolate with griottine cherries

WINE GUIDE ♀ Domaine Denis Race Chablis ler Cru £32.80 • ♀ Château Lamothe Cissac Haut Médoc £25 150 bottles over £20 • 6 by the glass (£6.50)

PRICE GUIDE Fixed D £55 • min/water £3 • Service included

PLACE: This magnificent late-Victorian castle, set in extensive grounds overlooking the Isle of Arran and Ailsa Craig, has been lovingly restored by Fay and Graham Cowan. Sumptuous lounges, richly decadent decor and fabulous antiques grace the elegant interior. Service is led from the top, with the family ever present to look after their guests. Staff are equally friendly, beautifully turned out and skilled. Book a window table to best enjoy the extensive views.

FOOD: Chef Matt Weedon (ex L'Ortolan restaurant in Berkshire) turns on the style in the kitchen. There's no choice on the daily-changing dinner menu (plus coffee and chocolates), but then you're in talented hands. The repertoire is intelligently simple yet extremely accomplished, with accuracy and quality local produce - some of it grown in the hotel grounds - keys to success. Flavours are clear, seasoning is spot on, combinations balanced. This is dynamic food. ***Winner of the AA Hotel of the Year Award for Scotland 2005-2006***

OUR TIP: Be sure to enjoy a walk round the grounds and gardens

Chef: Matt Weedon **Owners:** Graham & Fay Cowan **Times:** 1-2/7-9, Closed 30 Oct -1 Apr **Notes:** Set price D, 6 courses, Vegetarian available, Civ Wed 34 **Seats:** 34, Pr/dining room 20 **Smoking:** N/Sm in restaurant **Children:** Min 5 yrs, Menu, Portions **Rooms:** 17 (17 en suite) ★★★ **Directions:** Drive through Ballantrae, over bridge, 1st right - 1m to gates of lodge house **Parking:** 20 **e-mail:** info@glenappcastle.com **web:** www.glenappcastle.com

---

MAYBOLE MAP 20 NS20

🌸 Ladyburn

Traditional French

Traditional dining in gracious surroundings

☎ 01655 740585   KA19 7SG

MENU GUIDE Asparagus & smoked salmon soufflé • Ayrshire lamb & mint jelly • Apple & syrup sponge

WINE GUIDE ♀ Château la Coudraie Bourdeaux £16.50 • ♀ Château la Coudraie Bourdeaux £16.50 • 22 bottles over £20, 18 bottles under £20 • 3 by the glass

PRICE GUIDE Fixed L £15.50-£17.50 • Fixed D £32.50-£45 coffee £3 • min/water £2 • Service added but optional 10%

PLACE: This charming, family-run 16th-century former dower house is the perfect setting for elegant dining and candlelit dinners with formal table service. Fine china, silverware, old-fashioned crystal glasses and formal table service set the scene. **FOOD:** A carefully thought-out traditional menu offers mainly British dishes with French overtones. The seasonal dishes make good use of local produce.

OUR TIP: 24 hours notice required when booking

Chef: Mrs Jane Hepburn **Owners:** Jane Hepburn & Catriona Hepburn **Times:** 12.30-2/7.30-8.30, Closed Xmas, New Year, Mon-Thurs **Notes:** Vegetarian available, Dress Restrictions, Jacket and Tie, Civ Wed 60 **Seats:** 12 **Smoking:** N/Sm in restaurant **Children:** Min 16 yrs **Rooms:** 5 (5 en suite) ★★ **Parking:** 10 **e-mail:** jh@ladyburn.co.uk **web:** www.ladyburn.co.uk

---

PRESTWICK MAP 20 NS32

🌸 Restaurant 1933

Modern Scottish

Family-run hotel on the seafront

☎ 01292 477286 Parkstone Hotel, Esplanade KA9 1QN

MENU GUIDE Beef salad, new potatoes, chive oil • Pan-fried lamb steak, potato rösti, roast vegetables • Pavlova, fresh raspberries

WINE GUIDE ♀ Rocheberg Chenin Blanc £13.95 • ♀ Villa Rosa Merlot £13.95 • 1 bottles over £20, 17 bottles under £20 • 4 by the glass (£2.70-£3.25)

PRICE GUIDE Starter £4.95-£5.95 • main £9.95-£15.95 • dessert £4.35-£4.95 • coffee £1.95 • min/water £3.95 • Service optional

PLACE: This well-presented, family-run hotel offers spectacular views over the Firth of Clyde. Both its proximity to the golf courses of Turnberry, Royal Troon and Prestwick and its special formal dining experience make it quite the draw card. **FOOD:** Good value modern Scottish cooking from well-sourced local produce hits the spot and keeps things admirably simple, like the pan-fried fillet of Galloway beef, teamed with celeriac mash, slow-cooked baby vegetables and a red wine jus.

OUR TIP: An after-meal stroll along the beach is recommended

Chef: Mark Wares **Owners:** Stewart Clarkson **Times:** 12-2/5-9 **Notes:** Vegetarian available, Civ Wed 100 **Seats:** 32 **Smoking:** N/Sm in restaurant **Children:** Menu, Portions **Rooms:** 22 (22 en suite) ★★★ **Directions:** Telephone for directions **Parking:** 30 **e-mail:** info@parkstonehotel.co.uk **web:** www.parkstonehotel.co.uk

Scotland

Lochgreen House

French

Winning country-house hotel and highly rated restaurant

☎ 01292 313343 Monktonhill Rd, Southwood KA10 7EN

MENU GUIDE Velouté of smoked haddock • Steamed Atlantic halibut, lobster potatoes • Banana crème brûlée

WINE GUIDE 80 bottles over £20, 24 bottles under £20 • 10 by the glass

PRICE GUIDE Fixed L £19.95-£25 • Fixed D £27.50-£35 • starter £4.50-£6.95 • main £8.50-£17.95 • dessert £4.50-£5.75 • coffee £2.20 • min/water £4

PLACE: This hotel continues to excel, with new luxury accommodation being added in a couple of nearby properties. The beautiful grounds, which incorporate woodlands and immaculately tended gardens, provide a wonderful outlook from the formal Tapestry Restaurant. The panoramic windows, high ceilings and dramatic chandeliers in this grand dining room guarantee brightness at any time of day or night.

FOOD: The precise handling of the freshest of ingredients is responsible for the consistent results achieved here. Classical favourites like chicken liver with foie gras parfait, and roast loin and braised shoulder of Ayrshire lamb, will be found on the four-course dinner menu, but there are surprises too: a warm treacle scone and crème fraîche accompany gravadlax salmon, while escalope of seared salmon comes with creamed basil couscous. Rich flavours and artistic presentations are the icing on the cake.

OUR TIP: Lunch is served in the brasserie

Chef: Andrew Costley **Owners:** Bill & Cath Costley **Times:** 12-2.30/7-9.30 **Notes:** Vegetarian available, Civ Wed 130 **Seats:** 80, Pr/dining room 70 **Smoking:** N/Sm in restaurant, Air con **Rooms:** 40 (40 en suite) ★★★ **Parking:** 60 **e-mail:** lochgreen@costleyhotels.co.uk **web:** www.costleyhotels.co.uk

---

TROON MAP 20 NS33
 **Lochgreen House** *see above*

TURNBERRY MAP 20 NS20

 Malin Court

Modern British, Traditional Scottish

Modern cooking in coastal setting

☎ 01655 331457 KA26 9PB

MENU GUIDE Cream of tomato & basil soup • Duck, honey-roast vegetables, orange sauce • Mango filo parcels, caramelised pineapple

PRICE GUIDE Food prices not confirmed for 2006. Please telephone for details

PLACE: Comfortable hotel next to the famous Turnberry golf course. The Cotters restaurant has lounge areas for pre-dinner drinks, and overlooks the Firth of Clyde.

FOOD: Lots of imagination here, particularly in presentation, with traditional Scottish favourites sitting alongside more contemporary dishes, such as pan-fried duck breast with lavender and raspberry sauce. Plump for the four-course fixed price menu, or choose from a concise carte.

OUR TIP: A convivial end to a day's golfing

Times: 12.30-2/7-9 **Rooms:** 18 (18 en suite) ★★★ **e-mail:** info@malincourt.co.uk **web:** www.malincourt.co.uk

 The Westin Turnberry Resort Hotel

French, Scottish

Fine dining amidst dramatic mountain and sea views

☎ 01655 331000 KA26 9LT

MENU GUIDE Oysters, shallot & Cabernet Sauvignon vinegar • Rack of Dornoch lamb, braised Puy lentils, natural juices • Caramelised lemon tart, fresh raspberries

WINE GUIDE 180 bottles over £20 • 13 by the glass (£4.90-£7.50)

PRICE GUIDE Starter £14-£17 • main £24-£36 • dessert £7-£9.50 • coffee £4 • Service optional

PLACE: This splendid Edwardian hotel, opened in 1906, stands in 800 acres overlooking the two world-famous golf courses and endlessly fascinating views over the Firth of Clyde to Arran and the Mull of Kintyre. Spacious and comfortable public rooms provide grand settings in which to relax, and there are three elegant eating venues - the Turnberry Restaurant offering the fine dining experience.

FOOD: Cooking throughout is of a consistently high standard and modern seasonal menus, blended with classical French influences, focus on quality local ingredients, notably Scottish beef and seafood. Professional and welcoming service. Notable wine list.

OUR TIP: Dine while the sun sets over the Mull

Chef: Ralph Porciani **Owners:** Starwood Hotels & Resorts **Times:** 7-10, Closed Xmas, closed L Mon-Sun **Notes:** Fixed D 6 courses £49, Vegetarian available, Smart casual, no jeans, Civ Wed 150 **Seats:** 200, Pr/dining room 16 **Smoking:** N/Sm in restaurant **Children:** Menu, Portions **Rooms:** 221 (221 en suite) ★★★★★ **Directions:** Just off A77 S towards Stranraer, through Maybole. 2m after Kirkoswald turn right & follow signs for Turnberry. Hotel 0.5m on right **Parking:** 200 **e-mail:** turnberry@westin.com **web:** www.westin.com/turnberry

DUMFRIES & GALLOWAY

AUCHENCAIRN MAP 21 NX75

⚫⚫ Balcary Bay Hotel
British, French
Friendly family-run hotel at the water's edge
☎ 01556 640217   DG7 1QZ

MENU GUIDE Pan-seared Kircudbright scallops & sweetbreads
Roast fillet of prime local beef • Banana & rum crème brûlée
WINE GUIDE ♀ Sauvignon Blanc £17.50 • ♀ Fleurie £19.25 • 60
bottles over £20, 40 bottles under £20 • 3 by the glass (£2.20-£5.50)
PRICE GUIDE Fixed L £16 • starter £6.20-£7.75 • main £16-£19
dessert £6.20 • coffee £4.75 • min/water £2.75 • Service optional

PLACE: Built in 1622 by a company of smugglers importing
liquor from the Isle of Man, this atmospheric hotel is named after
the bay on which it stands. It is right on shore with views of the
sea and distant hills.
FOOD: Cooking is creative with a clever take on traditional dishes
- like Caesar salad with home-smoked pigeon and parmesan
custard - accurately executed and stylishly presented. Fresh
flavours are delivered from quality produce, including local fish,
seafood and beef. A vegetarian menu is available, and lunch can
be served with prior notice.
OUR TIP: Fabulous sea views from the elegant restaurant
Chef: Andrew Lipp **Owners:** Graeme A. Lamb & Family **Times:** 12-2/7-
8.30, Closed Mid Dec-Mid Feb, closed L Prior booking only Mon-Sat
Notes: Set L Sun only. Fixed D 5 courses £31, Vegetarian available, Smart
Dress **Seats:** 55 **Smoking:** N/Sm in restaurant **Children:** Menu,
Portions **Rooms:** 20 (20 en suite) ★★★ **Directions:** Situated on the
A711 between Dalbeattie & Kirkcudbright. On reaching Auhencairn follow
signs to Balcary along The Shore Rd for 2 miles **Parking:** 45
e-mail: reservations@balcary-bay-hotel.co.uk
web: www.balcary-bay-hotel.co.uk

CASTLE DOUGLAS MAP 21 NX76

⚫⚫ Plumed Horse Restaurant
Modern British
Accomplished handling of premier produce in this
intimate restaurant
☎ 01556 670333 Main St, Crossmichael DG7 3AU
PLACE: Though it's well off the beaten track in the tiny village of
Crossmichael, it is worth making a detour or a longer trek to find
this place. The whitewashed barn conversion opens onto a fresh
yellow and white interior, simply furnished with large tables,
starched linen and classy tableware.
FOOD: Tony Borthwick creams off the best of the abundant local

continued

larder - scallops, game in season, fish, beef - and matches it with
his top notch skills and natural artistry. The result is a serious
display of creative cooking.
OUR TIP: Try the simpler upstairs brasserie
Times: 12.30-1/7-9, Closed D Sun, Mon, 25-26 Dec, 2 wks Jan, 2 wks Sep
e-mail: plumedhorse@aol.com **web:** www.plumedhorse.co.uk

⬛ **Carlo's** 211 King St DG7 1DT ☎ 01556 503977 Family-
run Italian offering familiar dishes from pizza to shellfish stew.

☕ **Designs** 179 King St DG7 1DZ ☎ 01556 504552
A popular lunch spot below the shop of the same name. Food
has an organic slant.

DUMFRIES MAP 21 NX97

☕ **Abbey Cottage Tea Rooms** 26 Main St, New
Abbey DG2 8BY ☎ 01387 850377 Winner of The Tea Guild
Award of Excellence 2005.

ESKDALEMUIR MAP 21 NY29

⚫ Hart Manor
British
Traditional cooking straight from the Aga in
civilised surroundings
☎ 013873 73217 DG13 0QQ
MENU GUIDE Roast pepper & tomato soup • Roast loin of pork
with crackling, roast apples, cream & haggis sauce • Chocolate
velvet
WINE GUIDE ♀ Chablis £23.50 • ♀ Château Leon £13.95 • 10
bottles over £20, 10 bottles under £20 • 3 by the glass (£3.50)
PRICE GUIDE Fixed D £28 • min/water £3

PLACE: The hotel is run solely by the hospitable Leadbeaters,
with John front of house and Kathleen cooking. It's a former
shooting lodge, surrounded by lovely countryside, hills and
forests. The dining room features some fine antiques and a
collection of patterned jugs.
FOOD: Kathleen produces wholesome country food with
vegetables like you've never tasted before. The short blackboard
menu (dinner only) has plenty of irresistibly nostalgic dishes.
OUR TIP: Special place with delightful proprietors
Chef: Kathleen Leadbeater **Owners:** John & Kathleen Leadbeater
Times: 7-7.30, Closed Xmas & New Yr **Notes:** Vegetarian available
Seats: 12, Pr/dining room 10 **Smoking:** N/Sm in restaurant
Children: Min 10 yrs **Rooms:** 4 (4 en suite) ◆◆◆◆◆
Directions: From M74 junct 17 follow signs for Eskdalemuir. Approx 14m.
Through Eskdalemuir village, hotel approx 1m left on road to Langholm
Parking: 10 **e-mail:** visit@hartmanor.co.uk **web:** www.hartmanor.co.uk

GATEHOUSE OF FLEET MAP 20 NX55

⚫ Cally Palace Hotel
British
Modern cooking with dining in the grand style
☎ 01557 814341 DG7 2DL
MENU GUIDE Roast garlic bubble & squeak, poached quail's
egg • Grilled fillet of halibut, lemon & parsley crust, tomato
nage • Dark chocolate fondant
WINE GUIDE ♀ La Ronciere Sauvignon Blanc
£14.50 • ♀ McGregor Cabernet Sauvignon/Merlot £14.50
36 bottles over £20, 48 bottles under £20 • 7 by the glass
(£3.10-£3.60)

continued

Cally Palace Hotel

PRICE GUIDE Fixed D £28 • starter £2.50-£3.50 • main £7.25-£15 • dessert £3.20 • min/water £3.50 • Service optional

PLACE: A resort hotel with extensive leisure facilities, including its own golf course, grace this grand, one-time 18th-century palace set in 500 acres of forest and parkland. Opulent public rooms herald a formal dining experience in the elegant restaurant. Service is attentive and friendly.

FOOD: Contrasting with its formal surroundings, the compact, daily changing, fixed-price, four-course dinner menu surprises with its modernity.

OUR TIP: Jacket, collar and tie obligatory for dinner

Chef: Jamie Muirhead **Owners:** McMillan Hotels **Times:** 12-1.30/6.45-9, Closed 3 Jan-early Feb **Notes:** Vegetarian available, Dress Restrictions, Jacket, Collar and tie **Seats:** 110 **Smoking:** N/Sm in restaurant, Air con **Children:** Menu, Portions **Rooms:** 55 (55 en suite) ★★★★
Directions: From A74(M) take A75, at Gatehouse take B727. Hotel on left **Parking:** 70 **e-mail:** info@callypalace.co.uk **web:** www.callypalace.co.uk

KIRKBEAN MAP 21 NX95

Cavens

British, French

Elegant country-house dining

☎ 01387 880234 DG2 8AA

MENU GUIDE Parcels of smoked salmon & mackerel Breast of corn-fed chicken in cream, mushrooms & tarragon Chocolate pots

WINE GUIDE ♀ Santa Ema Sauvignon Blanc £13.95 • ♀ Santa Ema Cabernet Sauvignon £14.50 • 14 bottles over £20, 6 bottles under £20 • 6 by the glass (£4.50-£4.95)

PRICE GUIDE Fixed D £29.50 • min/water £2 • Service included

PLACE: Set in parkland gardens, Cavens offers an intimate country-house dining experience, with warm hospitality and fine table settings.

FOOD: There's no choice on the set four-course dinner menu, but the emphasis on home made more than compensates, with high quality locally-sourced produce and freshness to the fore. Nothings overworked, just accurate cooking with fresh flavours a hallmark.

OUR TIP: Non-residents should book well in advance

Chef: A Fordyce **Owners:** A Fordyce **Times:** 7-8.30, Closed Dec-1 Mar, closed L all week **Notes:** Coffee included, Vegetarian by request only, Civ Wed 100 **Seats:** 14, Pr/dining room 20 **Smoking:** N/Sm in restaurant **Children:** Min 12 yrs **Rooms:** 6 (6 en suite) ★★
Directions: Telephone for directions **Parking:** 20
e-mail: enquiries@cavens.com **web:** www.cavens.com

LOCKERBIE MAP 21 NY18

⊛ *Dryfesdale Hotel*

Modern European

Creative dining in country-house hotel

☎ 01576 202427 DG11 2SF

MENU GUIDE Duck leg confit, orange syrup • Angus beef fillet, glazed shallots, tomato compote, red wine jus • Apple flan, caramel sauce

PRICE GUIDE Food prices not confirmed for 2006. Please telephone for details

PLACE: An 18th-century former manse set in manicured gardens approached through an avenue of beech trees. The airy Kirkhill Restaurant has a grand piano in one corner and now extends into an attractive terrace. Tables are smartly appointed with crisp napery and the mood is formal, but with friendly and well-drilled staff.

FOOD: A wide choice of modern European food is offered from the restaurant carte, bar meals, afternoon tea selection and separate children's menu. Creative, good value dinners make excellent use of local produce.

OUR TIP: Helicopter landing site for stylish arrivals

Times: 12-2.30/6-9 **Rooms:** 16 (16 en suite) ★★★ **Directions:** M74 junct 17 (0.5m) to Lockerbie **e-mail:** reception@dryfesdalehotel.co.uk **web:** www.dryfesdalehotel.co.uk

MOFFAT MAP 21 NT00

⊛ The Dining Room, Bridge Guest House

Traditional, Modern   **NEW**

Friendly guest house serving enjoyable cuisine

☎ 01683 220558 Bridge House, Well Rd DG10 9JT

MENU GUIDE Smoked haddock & leek chowder, parmesan straws • Confit of duck, masala beans, mango jam • Lemon posset, raspberries

WINE GUIDE ♀ Pinot Grigio £13.95 • ♀ Marques de Grinon Temparillo £15.95 • 2 by the glass (£2.25)

PRICE GUIDE Fixed D £18.95 • min/water £2.95 • Service optional

PLACE: This friendly family-run guest house sits in attractive gardens in a quiet residential area on the edge of town. Its airy dining room is decorated in simple modern style, and lit by candles at night. Booking essential.

FOOD: A concise menu of contemporary fare with a touch of imagination. 'Posh bangers and mash' features venison sausages and sweet potato mash, while glazed lamb shank is served with a red wine jus.

OUR TIP: Dinner only

Chef: Russell Pearce **Owners:** Russell & Danyella Pearce **Times:** 7-8.30, Closed Xmas, Sun, closed L all wk **Notes:** Vegetarian by request only, Smart Dress **Seats:** 20 **Smoking:** N/Sm in restaurant **Children:** Menu, Portions **Rooms:** 7 (7 en suite) ◆◆◆◆ **Directions:** Take A109 from Moffat centre, 1st left into Burnside, follow into Well Rd, 0.5m on left **Parking:** 7 **e-mail:** info@bridgehousemoffat.co.uk **web:** www.bridgehousemoffat.co.uk

Scotland

MOFFAT *continued* MAP 21 NT00

Well View Hotel

European

Dignified Victorian hotel with delightful food

☎ 01683 220184 Ballplay Rd DG10 9JU

MENU GUIDE Melon, avocado & Parma ham salad • Roast saddle of venison, red cabbage & apple, redcurrant & red wine jus • Ecclefechan tart

WINE GUIDE ♀ Pouilly Fumé £26 • ♀ Dudet Fleurie £22 • 40 bottles over £20, 6 bottles under £20 • 5 by the glass (£3-£5)

PRICE GUIDE Fixed L £16 • Fixed D £30 • min/water £2 • Service included

PLACE: Small family-run hotel occupying a handsome property built in 1864 and named after the local sulphurous well, which led to Moffat's growth as a Victorian spa town. The hotel has a restful ambience, with traditional furnishings and original features. Dinner is the highlight of any stay.

FOOD: The comfortable dining room is the setting for meals based on the best Borders produce, carefully prepared in the classical style. The daily six-course tasting menu includes recommendations for accompanying wines. Extras are delicious: home-made breads, canapés and petits fours.

OUR TIP: Regular events include special dinners and culinary master classes

Chef: Janet & Lina Schuckardt **Owners:** John & Janet Schuckardt **Times:** 12.30/7.30, Closed L Mon-Sat **Notes:** Set price D 4 courses £30 Coffee incl, tasting menu **Seats:** 10, Pr/dining room 6 **Smoking:** N/Sm in restaurant **Children:** Min 10 yrs, Portions **Rooms:** 6 (6 en suite) **Directions:** From Moffat take A708 (Selkirk); turn left after fire station in Ballplay Road, 300 yds to hotel **Parking:** 6 **e-mail:** info@wellview.co.uk **web:** www.wellview.co.uk

NEWTON STEWART MAP 20 NX46

Kirroughtree House

British, European

Serious dining in imposing surroundings

☎ 01671 402141 Minnigaff DG8 6AN

MENU GUIDE Garden pea soup, truffle oil • Panaché of seafood • Mango bavarois

WINE GUIDE ♀ Plunkett Unwooded Chardonnay £19.50 • ♀ Aromo Cabernet Sauvignon £15.75 • 56 bottles over £20, 38 bottles under £20 • 3 by the glass (£3.50)

PRICE GUIDE Fixed L £16 • Fixed D £32.50 • starter £2.50-£5.25 • main £10.75-£15.50 • dessert £3.75-£5.25 • min/water £2 • Service optional

PLACE: Within the magnificent setting of its landscaped grounds, this imposing 17th-century mansion is as elegant and comfortable

as you would expect. The hushed dining room is suitably formal, and the staff are committed and courteous.

FOOD: Clear flavours from quality ingredients are a strength of the kitchen, and the fixed-price menus show the cream of the Scottish pantry: seared Solway scallops with a maple and chive sauce, breast of wood pigeon, and loin of Scottish lamb are sure to set the taste buds tingling.

OUR TIP: Great landscaped grounds for a pre-dinner stroll

Chef: Rolf Mueller **Owners:** Mr D McMillan **Times:** 12-1.30/7-9, Closed 3 Jan-mid Feb **Notes:** Vegetarian available, Dress Restrictions, Jacket must be worn after 6.30pm **Seats:** 45 **Smoking:** N/Sm in restaurant **Children:** Min 10 yrs **Rooms:** 17 (17 en suite) ★★★ **Directions:** From A75 turn left onto A712 (New Galloway), hotel entrance 300 yds on left **Parking:** 50 **e-mail:** info@kirroughtreehouse.co.uk **web:** www.kirroughtreehouse.co.uk

PORTPATRICK MAP 20 NW95

 Fernhill Hotel

British, European

Conservatory dining with a view

☎ 01776 810220 Heugh Rd DG9 8TD

MENU GUIDE Langoustines, truffle mayonnaise, asparagus • Duck, galette potato, celeriac mousse, Drambuie jus • Coconut crème brûlée

WINE GUIDE ♀ Sauvignon Blanc Chenin Blanc £9.75 • ♀ Grenache Merlot £9.75 • 11 bottles over £20, 45 bottles under £20 • 5 by the glass (£2.50)

PRICE GUIDE Fixed L £12.50 • Fixed D £32.50-£53.50 • coffee £1.95 • min/water £3.50 • Service included

PLACE: On clear days you can see the coast of Ireland from the lounge of this genteel hotel, while the airy conservatory dining room offers pretty views across the fishing and yachting village of Portpatrick.

FOOD: Plenty of ambition here - expect ostentatious creations from a kitchen that likes to impress. A pork belly main shows the style, served with charcroute, parsley potatoes, pancetta lardons, and a pork jus.

OUR TIP: Tee off at the nearby cliff-top golf course

Chef: Marc Wohner **Owners:** McMillan Hotels **Times:** 12-1.30/6.30-9.00, Closed mid Jan-mid Feb **Notes:** Vegetarian available, Dress Restrictions, No jeans, Civ Wed 40 **Seats:** 70, Pr/dining room 24 **Smoking:** N/Sm in restaurant **Children:** Menu, Portions **Rooms:** 36 (36 en suite) ★★★ **Directions:** A77 from Stranraer, right before war memorial. Hotel 1st left **Parking:** 45 **e-mail:** info@fernhillhotel.co.uk **web:** www.fernhillhotel.co.uk

 Knockinaam Lodge

see page 55

continued

PORTPATRICK MAP 20 NW95

Knockinaam Lodge

British, French

Relaxed dining in stunning coastal setting

☎ 01776 810471   DG9 9AD

MENU GUIDE Seared blue tuna niçoise • Roast Gressingham duck breast, thyme pomme purée, haggis beignet, confit shallot, ginger & coriander jus • Hot pistachio soufflé

WINE GUIDE ♀ Nelsons Creek Sauvignon Blanc £18 • ♀ Tantalus Shiraz/Cabernet Sauvignon £20 • 330 bottles over £20, 16 bottles under £20 • 10 by the glass (£4-£6)

PRICE GUIDE Fixed L £35 • Fixed D £45 • min/water £3.50 • Service optional

PLACE: A haven of tranquility and relaxation, this welcoming country-house hotel, set in lovely gardens and spacious lawns, is back from its own secluded pebble beach, sheltered by majestic cliffs and rolling woodland. A one-time shooting lodge dating from the 1800s, Churchill and Eisenhower are reputed to have met here just before the D-Day invasion of 1944. The deep red walls of the richly furnished Victorian dining room contrast with the sea views from window tables, while in winter, the flickering flames from the roaring fire dance across the ceiling.
FOOD: The modern-focused cooking, underpinned by a classical theme, showcases top-notch local produce as well as the slick skills of Tony Pierce. His cooking is exacting and precise, allowing the main ingredient centre stage, with key flavours never compromised, only enhanced. Presentation is succinct and unfussy, the lightness of touch compelling on the daily changing, enticing menus which offer a choice only between dessert or cheese selection. Peripherals, such as amuse bouche, pre-dessert, breads and petits fours, are equally accomplished, while service is friendly yet professional. Excellent wine list.
OUR TIP: The dinner, bed & breakfast package is irresistible
Chef: Antony Pierce **Owners:** David & Sian Ibbotson **Times:** 12.30-2.30/7-9.30 **Notes:** Tasting menu, 4 course Sun lunch £22.50, Vegetarian available, Dress Restrictions, No jeans, Civ Wed 40 **Seats:** 32
Smoking: N/Sm in restaurant **Children:** Min 12 yrs, Menu **Rooms:** 9 (9 en suite) 🏠 **Directions:** From A75, follow signs to Portpatrick, follow tourist signs to Knockinaam Lodge **Parking:** 20
e-mail: reservations@knockinaamlodge.com
web: www.knockinaamlodge.com

STRANRAER MAP 20 NX06

Corsewall Lighthouse Hotel

British

Unique lighthouse restaurant

☎ 01776 853220 Corsewall Point, Kirkcolm DG9 0QG

MENU GUIDE Velouté of roast parsnip & celeriac • Monkfish with pesto, redcurrant & port jus • Lemon & mango cheesecake

WINE GUIDE ♀ La Combe de Grinon Sauvignon Semillon £13.95 • ♀ Cabernet Sauvignon Domaine de Saissac £13.95 • 17 bottles over £20, 27 bottles under £20 • 2 by the glass (£3.25)

PRICE GUIDE Fixed L £10.60-£24.25 • starter £2.85-£5.75 • main £15.95-£19.50 • dessert £5.25 • coffee £1.85 • min/water £3 Service optional

PLACE: Perched on the rocky coastline at the end of a single-track road, this unique hotel is attached to a lighthouse and offers dramatic views. The restaurant is an intimate setting, with close-set tables and attentive service.
FOOD: A concise modern menu features safer choices (steak with café de Paris butter) as well as more complex fare (pan-roasted pork with a brandy, redcurrant and red onion marmalade). Desserts are a strength.
OUR TIP: A great place to switch off and unwind
Chef: A Downie, D. McCubbin **Owners:** Gordon, Kay, & Pamela Ward **Times:** 12-2/7-9 **Notes:** Set D £32.50-£36.25 (5 courses), Vegetarian available, Dress Restrictions, Preferably no jeans, Civ Wed 28 **Seats:** 28
Smoking: N/Sm in restaurant **Children:** Portions **Rooms:** 9 (9 en suite) ★★★ **Directions:** Take A718 from Stranraer to Kirkcolm, then follow B718 signposted Lighthouse **Parking:** 30
e-mail: info@lighthousehotel.co.uk **web:** www.lighthousehotel.co.uk

Britain's best-selling hotel guide for all your leisure needs.

The **Hotel** *Guide*   2006

www.theAA.com   **AA**

Britain's best-selling Golf Course Guide featuring over 2,500 courses.

The **Golf Course** *Guide*   2006

www.theAA.com   **AA**

Scotland

DUNBARTONSHIRE, WEST

BALLOCH MAP 20 NS38

 De Vere Cameron House

see below

CLYDEBANK MAP 20 NS47

 Beardmore

Scottish, French

Circular restaurant in modern hotel

☎ 0141 951 6000 Best Western Beardmore Hotel, Beardmore St G81 4SA

continued

MENU GUIDE Lobster & vanilla consommé, crab ravioli • Venison loin, cauliflower, beetroot & spinach • Ginger bread & butter pudding

WINE GUIDE ♀ Deakin Estate Chardonnay £17 • ♦ Deakin Estate Cabernet Sauvignon £17 • 22 bottles over £20, 26 bottles under £20 • 12 by the glass (£2.30-£7.95)

PRICE GUIDE Starter £5-£9 • main £12-£20 • dessert £5-£7 coffee £1.75 • min/water £3.75 • Service optional

PLACE: Impressive modern hotel on the banks of the River Clyde, with grounds shared with the neighbouring medical centre. The fine dining Citrus Restaurant is a circular room, contemporary in style, decorated in soft pastels to emphasise the light, airy ambience. Tables are well spaced, affording privacy to diners, and service is efficient and discreet with a professional edge.

FOOD: Dinner only is served - modern Scottish cuisine with classical French influences. The menu is seasonal, changing every two months, and offers a good choice inspired by top quality ingredients. Special themed events, exploring the various cuisine of the world, are held regularly.

OUR TIP: Popular venue for conferences and weddings

Chef: John McMahon **Owners:** Scottish Executive **Times:** 7-10, Closed Festive period, Sun, Mon, closed L all week **Notes:** Vegetarian available, Civ Wed 174 **Seats:** 60, Pr/dining room 16 **Smoking:** N/Sm in restaurant, Air con **Children:** Min 12 yrs, Menu, Portions **Rooms:** 168 (168 en suite) ★★★★ **Directions:** M8 junct 19, follow signs for Clydeside Expressway to Glasgow road, then Dumbarton road (A814), the signs for Clydebank Business Park. Hotel on left **Parking:** 400
e-mail: info@beardmore.scot.nhs.uk
web: www.bw-beardmorehotel.co.uk

BALLOCH MAP 20 NS38

De Vere Cameron House

French

Fine dining on the shores of Loch Lomond

☎ 01389 755565 G83 8QZ

MENU GUIDE Scallop tortellini, basil purée, chive, ginger, white wine foam • Turbot, glazed trotter, confit fennel, saffron potatoes, mussel & curry jus • Banana five ways

WINE GUIDE ♀ Springfield Estate Sauvignon Blanc £23 • ♦ Latour-Giraud Meursault Domaine Pinot Noir £55 159 bottles over £20 • 6 by the glass (£6.50-£9.50)

PRICE GUIDE Fixed L £23.50 • Fixed D £49.50 • coffee £2.25 • min/water £4 • Service included

PLACE: Nestling on the shores of Loch Lomond and enjoying beautiful views, this Scots baronial-style mansion dates back to the 17th century and was once the ancestral home of the Smollett family. In the past it played host to many great statesmen and women, including Winston Churchill and Queen Victoria, today though, it's a leisure-orientated hotel and entertains with a host of indoor and outdoor sporting activities and smart spa. The elegant, fine-dining Georgian Room restaurant is traditional in

style, with chandeliers, oil paintings, rich fabrics, pristine table settings and an intimate atmosphere. Service follows suit, being formal, attentive but friendly.

FOOD: The accomplished kitchen's modern style is steeped in classical French roots and makes intelligent use of fresh, high-quality produce, particularly from the abundant Scottish larder; take an assiette of Loch Fyne oysters three ways, or tranche of line-caught sea bass viennoise, with grain mustard sabayon and courgette blossom beignet. Highly creative technical skills and deft execution deliver with style, the approach a fixed-price affair, via weekly-changing dinner market menu or tasting gourmet option.

OUR TIP: An acoustic guitarist sometimes plays in the restaurant

Chef: Simon Whitley, Paul Tamburrini **Owners:** De Vere Hotels **Times:** 12-2.30/7-9.30, Closed Mon, Tue, closed L Wed-Sat **Notes:** Tasting menu 6 courses £57.50, Dress Restrictions, Jacket and Tie, Civ Wed 200 **Seats:** 42 **Smoking:** N/Sm in restaurant, Air con **Children:** Min 14 yrs **Rooms:** 96 (96 en suite) ★★★★★ **Directions:** M8 junct 30, over toll bridge and follow signs for Loch Lomond (A82). Hotel is on right **Parking:** 250
e-mail: reservations@cameronhouse.co.uk
web: www.devereonline.co.uk/cameronhouse

DUNDEE CITY

DUNDEE MAP 21 NO43

 Metro

French, Scottish   **NEW**

Cutting-edge cuisine by the harbour

☎ 01382 202404 Apex City Quay Hotel & Spa, 1 West Victoria Dock Rd DD1 3JP

MENU GUIDE Fig tart Tatin, seared foie gras • Sea bass with truffle pommes purée & lime froth • Valrhona chocolate fondant

WINE GUIDE ♀ Sauvignon Blanc £19.50 • ♀ Shiraz £19.50 • 18 bottles over £20, 2 bottles under £20 • 6 by the glass (£5-£8.50)

PRICE GUIDE Starter £7.50-£9.50 • main £15-£24 • dessert £6.50-£14 • coffee £3.25 • min/water £3 • Service optional

PLACE: Part of a modern hotel and spa overlooking the redeveloped harbour area, the ground floor dining area is split between the Metro restaurant and Metro brasserie, allowing flexibility. Service is attentive and friendly.

FOOD: French with a Scottish influence, the seasonally changing menu features some exciting and challenging contemporary creations - starters may include carpaccio of venison with cherry and black pepper sorbet and honey oil, or cauliflower pannacotta with walnut tuile. Tasting menus are divided into 'garden', 'highland' and 'ocean'.

OUR TIP: Seek out the brasserie's fine dining area
Chef: Bruce Price **Owners:** Apex Hotels **Times:** 7-9.30, Closed 25 Dec-10 Jan, Closed Sun-Mon **Notes:** Tasting menus, Ocean £35, Garden £29, Highland £36, Vegetarian available, Dress Restrictions, Smart casual, no jeans, T-shirts **Seats:** 30, Pr/dining room 12 **Smoking:** N/Sm in restaurant **Children:** No Children **Rooms:** 153 (153 en suite) ★★★★
Directions: A90 from Perth. A85 along riverside for 2m. With Discovery Quay on right, at rdbt follow signs for Aberdeen. At next rdbt turn right into city quay **Parking:** 150 **e-mail:** dundeemetro.restaurant.co.uk **web:** www.apexhotels.co.uk

CITY OF EDINBURGH

EDINBURGH MAP 21 NT27

 Atrium

British, Mediterranean

Modish theatre venue offering modern European cuisine

☎ 0131 228 8882 10 Cambridge St EH1 2ED

MENU GUIDE Seared scallops, crab & dill hollandaise • Roast pigeon, creamed cannelloni beans, cabbage & bacon • Banana parfait, coconut tuile

WINE GUIDE ♀ Stadt Krems Gruner Veltliner £19 • ♀ Simon Hackett Cabernet Sauvignon £20 • 270 bottles over £20, 16 bottles under £20 • 300 by the glass (£4-£100)

PRICE GUIDE Fixed L £13.50 • Fixed D £25 • starter £6.50-£12 • main £17-£22 • dessert £5.50 • coffee £3 • min/water £3.50 • Service optional • Group min 5 service 10%

PLACE: Strikingly bold in design, with aluminium ventilation ducts, railway sleeper tables, flickering oil lamps and canvas chairs, this stylish restaurant is located within the Traverse Theatre. Enjoy drinks in the stylish atrium bar and quality modern cooking in the glass-walled restaurant. Well informed and attentive staff.

FOOD: Confident and consistent modern brasserie-style cooking offers Mediterranean influences with sound use of local Scottish produce. Choose from the carte, or a fixed three-course dinner or lunch option.

OUR TIP: The excellent wine list deserves serious study
Chef: Neil Forbes & Andrew Jenkins **Owners:** Andrew & Lisa Radford **Times:** 12-2/6-10, Closed 25-26 Dec, 1-2 Jan, Sun (apart from Aug), closed L Sat (apart from Aug) **Notes:** Vegetarian available, Civ Wed 200 **Seats:** 80, Pr/dining room 20 **Smoking:** N/Sm in restaurant, Air con **Children:** Portions **Directions:** From Princes St, turn into Lothian Rd, 2nd left & 1st right, by the Traverse Theatre **Parking:** Castle Terrace Car Park and on street **e-mail:** eat@atriumrestaurant.co.uk **web:** www.atriumrestaurant.co.uk

Best Western Bruntsfield Hotel

British

Smart contemporary hotel restaurant

☎ 0131 229 1393 69/74 Bruntsfield Place EH10 4HH

MENU GUIDE Crayfish, avocado & asparagus salad • Venison medallions, beetroot sauce • Lemon posset

WINE GUIDE ♀ B Phillip Chardonnay • ♀ B Phillip Merlot £14.75 • 19 bottles over £20, 29 bottles under £20 • 6 by the glass (£3.50-£4.90)

PRICE GUIDE Starter £3.50-£6.25 • main £5.95-£17.50 • dessert £5.65 • coffee £2.50 • min/water £3.95 • Service optional

PLACE: Cardoon is the brasserie-style operation that serves this smart hotel close to the city centre. The conservatory extension matches the stylish public rooms, and there's a lively pub too.

FOOD: The carte has a contemporary flavour in the modern Scottish idiom, reinforced by locally sourced produce. Cullen skink tart and loin of border lamb with olive and mint crust are typical of the imaginative cuisine, and grills and light dishes are also offered.

OUR TIP: Leave room for the Scottish cheeses

continued   *continued*

Scotland

EDINBURGH continued MAP 21 NT27

Chef: Martyn Dixon **Owners:** Mrs C A Gwyn **Times:** 5.30-9.30, Closed Xmas, closed L Mon-Sun **Notes:** Vegetarian available, Civ Wed 75 **Seats:** 70, Pr/dining room 65 **Smoking:** N/Sm area, No pipes, No cigars **Children:** Menu, Portions **Rooms:** 73 (73 en suite) ★★★ **Directions:** From S enter Edinburgh on A702. Continue for 3m. Hotel overlooks Bruntsfield Links Park. 1m S of the W end of Princes Street **Parking:** 30 **e-mail:** sales@thebruntsfield.co.uk **web:** www.thebruntsfield.co.uk

⊛ Blue

British, Mediterranean

Chic modern brasserie

☎ 0131 221 1222 Cambridge St EH1 2ED

MENU GUIDE Pea, bacon & mushroom risotto • Chicken breast, garlic, thyme, chorizo, bean purée • Poached winter fruits, aniseed ice cream

WINE GUIDE ♀ Santa Ema Sauvignon Blanc £15.50 • ♀ Candidato Tempranillo £13.95 • 7 bottles over £20, 15 bottles under £20 • 11 by the glass (£3.40-£4.50)

PRICE GUIDE Fixed L £9.95 • Fixed D £13.95 • starter £3.95-£6 • main £11.95-£14 • dessert £4-£4.50 • coffee £1.80 • Service optional • Group min 8 service 10%

PLACE: In the heart of Edinburgh's theatre district, this trendy modern brasserie shares the same building as its big brother Atrium and the Traverse Theatre. The interior is minimalist, with fashionable hardwood floors, huge windows and blue chairs.

FOOD: Consistency is the key here and Blue's imaginative and flexible modern European menus continue to please, as evidenced by the need to book ahead. Dishes are hearty, full flavoured and simply presented.

OUR TIP: Daily papers and magazines for single diners **Chef:** Neil Forbes, Duncan McIntyre **Owners:** Andrew & Lisa Radford **Times:** 12-2.30/5.30-11, Closed 25-26 Dec, 1st Jan, Sun **Notes:** Vegetarian available, Civ Wed 150 **Seats:** 110 **Smoking:** N/Sm area, Air con **Children:** Menu, Portions **Directions:** From Princes Street turn into Lothian Road, 2nd left, 1st right, above the Traverse Theatre **Parking:** Cambridge Street, & NCP - Castle Terrace **e-mail:** eat@bluebarcafe.com **web:** www.bluebarcafe.com

⊛ Le Café St Honore

Scottish, French

Authentic bistro

☎ 0131 226 2211 34 NW Thistle St Lane EH2 1EA

MENU GUIDE Grilled oysters, bacon, hollandaise, tiger prawns Saddle of Venison, red cabbage, boudin noir, Dijon crust • Crème brûlée

WINE GUIDE ♀ Billecary-Salmon Champagne £39.50 • ♀ Cubzac-les-Ponts Bordeaux Blend £15.75 • 69 bottles over £20, 25 bottles under £20 • 10 by the glass (£2.95-£5.25)

continued

PRICE GUIDE Fixed D fr £19.95 • starter £3.75-£9.25 • main £8.75-£19.95 • dessert £4.95 • coffee £1.25 • min/water £2.95 • Group min 8 service 10%

PLACE: Surely cloned from a back street Parisian bistro, this hugely popular café has an authentic feel, with a well-worn decor of tightly packed tables, rattling ceiling fans and balloon-backed wooden chairs.

FOOD: Forget fad and fashion, St Honore sticks to the basics delivering a great value menu with more than a touch of yesteryear charm. Prawn cocktail and steak au poivre make their culinary comebacks and suit the unique venue.

OUR TIP: Eat early for the good value fixed-price menu **Chef:** C Colverson, H Barclay **Owners:** Chris & Gill Colverson **Times:** 12-2.15/7-10, Closed 24-26 Dec, 3 days at New Year, **Notes:** Vegetarian available, Fixed D pre-theatre wkdys 5.30-6.45, Sun 6-7.15 **Seats:** 56, Pr/dining room 18 **Smoking:** N/Sm area **Children:** Portions **Directions:** City centre, between Hanover & Frederick Street **web:** www.cafesthonore.com

⊛⊛ Channings Restaurant

French

Intimate dining in townhouse hotel

☎ 0131 315 2225 15 South Learmonth Gardens EH4 1EZ

MENU GUIDE Chilled rocket purée • Foie gras assiette, poached tamarillo • Chilled pineapple & dark rum soup

PRICE GUIDE Fixed L £16.50 • min/water £3.50 • Service optional • Group min 10 service 10%

PLACE: Situated in an attractive row of five Edwardian townhouses, this privately run hotel has inviting, comfortable lounges and a choice of dining. There's the Ochre Vita winebar with its Mediterranean offerings or the more classically inclined, wood-panelled basement dining room.

FOOD: The seven-course tasting menu is the star attraction here. Seasonal Scottish ingredients are skilfully prepared to good effect in dishes such as the roast mallard with artichokes and beetroot reduction and the warm lobster with winter vegetable hot pot.

OUR TIP: Opt for the different wine with each course **Chef:** Hubert Lamort **Owners:** Mr P Taylor **Times:** 12-2/7-10, Closed Sun-Mon **Notes:** Fixed D 7 courses £39.50, Vegetarian available **Seats:** 28, Pr/dining room 20 **Smoking:** N/Sm in restaurant **Children:** Portions **Rooms:** 46 (46 en suite) ★★★★ **Directions:** From Princes St follow signs to Forth Bridge (A90), cross Dean Bridge and take 4th right into South Learmonth Ave. Follow road to bottom of hill **Parking:** on street **e-mail:** f&bchannings@channings.co.uk **web:** www.channings.co.uk

⊛⊛ Dalhousie Castle and Aqueous Spa

Scottish, French

A unique castle dungeon setting for contemporary cooking

☎ 01875 820153 Bonnyrigg EH19 3JB

MENU GUIDE Confit of duck leg, cep cream sauce • Trout, oyster & chive beurre blanc • Chocolate fudge & whisky torte, vanilla cream

WINE GUIDE ♀ Currabridge Unwooded Chardonnay £18.90 • ♀ Currabridge Shiraz Cabernet £18.90 • 60 bottles over £20, 25 bottles under £20 • 8 by the glass (£4.50-£8.50)

PRICE GUIDE Fixed D £34 • coffee £1.80 • min/water £3.95 • Service included

continued

Dalhousie Castle and Aqueous Spa

FOOD: Classic carte cooked with imagination and expertise using fresh Scottish produce. International touches make for creative but confident dishes. Excellent wine list.
OUR TIP: Good value fixed-price lunch
Chef: David Scouller **Owners:** Mr M K Duck **Times:** 12-2.30/7-10.30, Closed 25-26 Dec, closed L Sat-Mon **Notes:** Vegetarian available **Seats:** 60, Pr/dining room 51 **Smoking:** N/Sm area **Directions:** Princes St, Hanover St, Dundas St, right at traffic lights **Parking:** On street
e-mail: bookings@ducks.co.uk **web:** www.ducks.co.uk

La Garrigue
French
Rustic surroundings match the food at this provincial French restaurant
☎ 0131 557 3032 31 Jeffrey St EH1 1DH

MENU GUIDE Pheasant terrine, chicory salad • Confit duck leg, flageolet bean casserole • Lavender crème brûlée
WINE GUIDE 12 bottles over £20, 14 bottles under £20 • 4 by the glass (£3.50-£4)
PRICE GUIDE Fixed L £6-£10.50 • Fixed D £27.50 • starter £3.50-£7 • main £9.50-£18 • dessert £4.50-£6.50 • coffee £1.80 • min/water £2.95 • Service added but optional 10%

PLACE: Taking its name from an area of the Languedoc, from where the chef-proprietor hails, the rustic and informal French restaurant showcases the region's food. Cool blue walls, wooden floor and handsome wooden furniture succeed in giving the dining room the required Mediterranean feel, and you could be forgiven for thinking yourself in France!
FOOD: This is French provincial cooking at its best. Expect hearty, no frills Gallic cooking, where intense, gutsy flavours are complemented with simple, unfussy presentation. Wines are from the Languedoc, personally sourced by the proprietor.
OUR TIP: Go for the cassoulet for a real flavour of France
Chef: Jean Michel Gauffre **Owners:** J M Gauffre **Times:** 12-3/6.30-10.30, Closed 25-26 Dec, 1-2 Jan **Notes:** Vegetarian available **Seats:** 48, Pr/dining room 11 **Smoking:** N/Sm area, No pipes **Children:** Portions **Directions:** Halfway down Royal Mile towards Holyrood Palace, turn left at lights into Jeffrey St **Parking:** On street
e-mail: lagarrigue@btconnect.com **web:** www.lagarrigue.co.uk

PLACE: About 700 years is time enough to notch up some serious history and this magnificent 13th-century castle doesn't disappoint, having played host to Oliver Cromwell, Queen Victoria and Sir Walter Scott among others. Descend to the dungeon for dinner, a unique and atmospheric setting with rough stone walls decorated by medieval weapons and the odd suit of armour.
FOOD: The daily changing menu is a blend of accomplished French cuisine and contemporary Scottish inspiration; your choice might include pork with a mustard and kaffir leaf sauce perhaps, or monkfish wrapped in pancetta. Lighter meals are served all day in the airy Orangery.
OUR TIP: The castle has its own falconry
Chef: Francois Graud Owners: Von Essen Hotels Times: 7-10, Closed L 1 week Notes: Vegetarian available, Smart Dress, Civ Wed 100 Seats: 45, Pr/dining room 100 Smoking: N/Sm in restaurant Children: Portions Rooms: 33 (33 en suite) ★★★ Directions: From A720 (Edinburgh bypass) take A7 south, turn right onto B704. Castle 0.5m on right Parking: 150 e-mail: info@dalhousiecastle.co.uk web: www.dalhousiecastle.co.uk

Duck's at Le Marche Noir
International, British
Scottish accents in historic newtown tenement
☎ 0131 558 1608 14 Eyre Place EH3 5EP
MENU GUIDE Hot smoked salmon, marinated fennel & radish • Roast duck breast, butternut squash purée • Baileys bavarois, toasted marshmallow
WINE GUIDE ♀ Whistling Duck Semillion Chardonnay £14.50 • ♀ Whistling Duck Shiraz Cabernet £14.50 • 177 bottles over £20, 38 bottles under £20 • 4 by the glass (£3.50-£5)
PRICE GUIDE Fixed L £12 • starter £4-£7.25 • main £12.50-£21.50 • dessert £3.90-£5.90 • coffee £1.95 • min/water £1.75 • Service optional
PLACE: Relaxed and rustically comfortable ambience, with ducks featuring numerously in the decor of this inviting restaurant. Friendly but formal table service goes well with the white linen and evening candlelight.

continued

One Rosette Excellent local restaurants serving food prepared with care, understanding and skill, using good quality ingredients. These restaurants stand out in their local area. Of the total number of establishments with Rosettes around 50% have one Rosette.

⊕ Hadrians, The Balmoral Hotel

British, European

Retro-style brasserie

☎ 0131 557 5000 1 Princes St EH2 2EQ

MENU GUIDE Moules marinière • Pork medallion, baby boudin • Bread & butter pudding

WINE GUIDE ♀ Mezzacorana Pinot Grigio £18 • ♀ Vinicola di Apollinio 1998 Puglia £20 • 35 bottles over £20, 15 bottles under £20 • 10 by the glass (£4.25-£5.95)

PRICE GUIDE Fixed L £11.95 • Fixed D £14.95 • starter £5.50-£8.95 • main £6.50-£14.95 • dessert £3.75-£5.95 • coffee £2.65 min/water £3 • Service optional • Group min 8 service 10%

PLACE: The Balmoral Hotel's spacious second eating option has a retro feel to it, with its lime green and dark brown decor, and attracts a real mix of customers.

FOOD: Uncomplicated brasserie food ranges from the classic eggs Benedict, and omelette Arnold Bennett to calves' liver and mash, with haggis, neeps and tatties with whisky sauce making an appropriate appearance. The cooking is simple, unfussy and well presented.

OUR TIP: Great central location for tourists and business people
Chef: Jeff Bland **Owners:** Rocco Forte Hotels **Times:** 12-2/6.30-10
Notes: Vegetarian available, Civ Wed 60 **Seats:** 100, Pr/dining room 30
Smoking: N/Sm area, No pipes, No cigars, Air con **Children:** Menu, Portions **Directions:** Hotel at E end of Princes Street, next to Waverley Station **Parking:** 40 **e-mail:** hadrians@thebalmoralhotel.com
web: www.roccofortehotels.com

⊕⊕ Haldanes

Modern Scottish

Tranquil oasis in the heart of the city

☎ 0131 556 8407 39A Albany St EH1 3QY

MENU GUIDE Warm salad of West Coast scallops • Fillet of beef topped with black pepper sabayon • Caramelised lemon tart

WINE GUIDE ♀ Cicila Beretta Pinot Grigio £25 • ♀ Valpiedra Rioja £34 • 142 bottles over £20, 24 bottles under £20 • 10 by the glass (£5-£9)

PRICE GUIDE Fixed L £17.50 • starter £5.95-£12.50 • main £16.95-£28 • dessert £4.75-£6.75 • coffee £2.50 • min/water £3.50 • Service added but optional

PLACE: Occupying the basements of three Georgian townhouses, the Haldanes has two dining areas. One overlooks a very pretty patio garden, which allows diners to enjoy the sunshine in summer, while the other is more intimate. There is also a comfortable lounge for guests to relax in before or after dinner.
FOOD: The philosophy is to keep it simple - and it works. The freshest of ingredients are used to conjure up dishes like open ravioli of scallops, chive and lemon butter and roast breast of maize-fed guinea fowl, sherry vinegar sauce.

OUR TIP: Make time to study the excellent wine list
Chef: George Kelso, Steven Falconer **Owners:** Mr and Mrs G Kelso
Times: 12-2.15/6-10.15, Closed 25 Dec, closed L Sat-Sun **Notes:** Seasonal specials offered at weekends, Vegetarian available, Smart casual preferred
Seats: 60, Pr/dining room 26 **Smoking:** N/Sm in restaurant
Children: Portions **Directions:** Telephone for directions **Parking:** on street **e-mail:** dinehaldanes@aol.com
web: www.haldanesrestaurant.com

⊕ Holyrood Hotel

Contemporary

Impressive hotel with honest, modern cooking

☎ 0131 550 4500 Holyrood Rd EH8 6AU

MENU GUIDE Pan-fried foie gras, sweet pea purée • Scottish lamb stew • Summer pudding

PRICE GUIDE Food prices not confirmed for 2006. Please telephone for details

PLACE: Located next to the Scottish Parliament building, this impressive modern hotel is just a short walk from the Queen's official Scottish residence. The attractive split-level restaurant is built on the site of a glass blowing workshop.
FOOD: Expect simple, modern cooking combining classic techniques and Scottish ingredients, with choices ranging from grilled lamb cutlets with fennel and potato gratin to summer vegetable risotto.

OUR TIP: A chance to spot politicians and journalists
Times: 12-2.30/6-10, Closed L all week (ex group bookings) **Rooms:** 157 (157 en suite) ★★★★ **Directions:** City centre near the Royal Mile
e-mail: holyrood@macdonald-hotels.co.uk
web: www.macdonaldhotels.co.uk

⊕ The Howard Hotel

NEW

Traditional Scottish

Elegant townhouse with intimate restaurant

☎ 0131 557 3500 34 Great King St EH3 6QH

MENU GUIDE Red pimento & orange soup, pesto • Roast salmon, bacon & split pea casserole, sherry vinegar dressing • Baileys pannacotta, winter berries

WINE GUIDE ♀ Charles Deloire Pouilly Fumé • ♀ Cabernet Sauvignon Reserve Vina Haras de Pirque • 24 bottles over £20, 7 bottles under £20 • 10 by the glass (£3.40-£4.20)

PRICE GUIDE Fixed L fr £28 • Fixed D fr £32.50 • Service optional

PLACE: Offering quiet luxury and comfort, the Howard is a beautifully converted terraced town house in the Georgian 'New Town' area of the city. Looking out over wide cobbled streets, the intimate restaurant has an exclusive club feel and service is efficient and traditional.
FOOD: The short, enticing modern menu is seasonally Scottish in style with local ingredients a key feature. Cooking is straightforward and presentation of dishes is simple.

OUR TIP: Elegant base close to the city centre
Chef: Martin Bell **Owners:** Peter Taylor **Times:** 12-2/7-9, Closed Xmas
Notes: Vegetarian available, Smart Dress, Civ Wed 35 **Seats:** 18, Pr/dining room 18 **Smoking:** N/Sm in restaurant **Children:** Portions
Parking: 10 **e-mail:** reserve@thehoward.com
web: www.thehoward.com

NEW
denotes a restaurant which is new to the guide this year.

Scotland

Iggs

Spanish

Convivial and welcoming taste of Spain

☎ 0131 557 8184 15 Jeffrey St EH1 1DR

MENU GUIDE Squid risotto, courgette ribbons • Marinated Shetland lamb, creamed mash, pancetta, Savoy cabbage • Chocolate fondant

WINE GUIDE ♀ Rioja Vilira £13.75 • ♀ Rioja Tempranillo £13.75 • 70 bottles over £20, 30 bottles under £20 • 4 by the glass (£3.50-£7)

PRICE GUIDE Fixed L £12.50 • Fixed D £18.50-£21.50 • starter £4.75-£8.25 • main £13.75-£25 • dessert £6-£7.50 • coffee £2.50 • min/water £3.50 • Service optional

PLACE: Just off the city's historic high street, Iggs strikes a colourful Mediterranean pose with its warm mustard walls, tall wrought-iron candlesticks and Spanish music and owners.

FOOD: The menu follows a contemporary Spanish theme, embellished with international flair - take châteaubriand of organic Highland beef with béarnaise sauce. Fine breads and olives bolster the repertoire, while fixed-price lunch and pre-theatre options back up an appealing carte.

OUR TIP: Excellent choice of Spanish wines

Chef: Andrew MacQueen **Owners:** Mr I Campos **Times:** 12-2.30/6.00-10.30, Sun **Notes:** Vegetarian available **Seats:** 80, Pr/dining room 40 **Smoking:** N/Sm area **Directions:** At the heart of Edinburgh's Old Town .5m from castle, just off the Royal Mile **Parking:** On street **e-mail:** iggsbarioja@aol.com

Malmaison Hotel & Brasserie

French

Chic hotel brasserie

☎ 0131 468 5001 & 468 5001 One Tower Place, Leith EH6 7DB

MENU GUIDE Buffalo mozzarella, plum tomato, pesto • Steak frites, béarnaise sauce • Summer berry gratin, champagne sabayon

PRICE GUIDE Food prices not confirmed for 2006. Please telephone for details

PLACE: Overlooking the port of Leith, this sophisticated hotel belongs to one of the nation's classiest hotel chains. Its ground floor brasserie offers views of the marina across a cobbled courtyard, and is a popular Edinburgh haunt.

FOOD: French brasserie fare with a Scottish flavour. Dishes range from regional specialities to straightforward grills, and are distinguished by quality ingredients and contemporary simplicity.

OUR TIP: The hotel's café/bar offers lighter meals

Times: 12-2/6-11, Closed 25 Dec (evening) **Rooms:** 101 (101 en suite) ★★★ **Directions:** From the city centre follow Leith Docklands, through sets of lights and left into Tower St **e-mail:** edinburgh@malmaison.com **web:** www.malmaison.com

---

The Best Use of Seafood sponsored by Seafish In conjunction with Seafish, the Sea Fish Industry Authority, we have sought out restaurants that make the most of seafood on their menus. In addition to the four country award winners (see page 9), look out for the seafish symbol throughout the book; this denotes restaurants serving a good range of fish and shellfish dishes, where the accent is firmly on freshness.

Marriott Dalmahoy

Scottish, British

Intimate fine dining in Georgian splendour

☎ 0131 333 1845 Kirknewton EH27 8EB

MENU GUIDE Tart of goats' cheese, red onion marmalade • Rack of lamb with mustard & herb crust • Mascarpone pannacotta

WINE GUIDE ♀ Chablis AC Chardonnay £22.50 • ♀ Faustino V Reserva Rioja Tempranillo £23.40 • 23 bottles over £20, 19 bottles under £20 • 23 by the glass (£5.10-£8.50)

PRICE GUIDE Fixed L £16.95 • Fixed D £25 • starter £6.95-£10 • main £18.50-£25 • dessert £4.95-£6.50 • coffee £2.45 • min/water £3.90 • Service optional

PLACE: The rolling Pentland Hills and well-kept parkland provide a stunning backdrop for this imposing Georgian mansion, with its two championship golf courses and impressive health and beauty club. The restaurant offers fine dining with professional and helpful staff.

FOOD: A strong Scottish theme to the cooking shows in the use of top quality seafood and game dishes, as well as the retro roast trolley. More contemporary cooking can be spotted in dishes like seared scallops with pea purée, pancetta and creamed cauliflower.

OUR TIP: Great golf and leisure facilities

Chef: Alan Matthew **Owners:** Marriot Group/Whitbread Hotels Ltd **Times:** 12.30-2/7-10, Closed L Sat & Sun **Notes:** Vegetarian available, Civ Wed 200 **Seats:** 120, Pr/dining room 16 **Smoking:** N/Sm in restaurant, Air con **Children:** Menu, Portions **Rooms:** 215 (215 en suite) ★★★★ **Directions:** On A71 city bypass. Take Calder exit & follow signs for A71. 7m and hotel clearly signed on left **Parking:** 350 **e-mail:** fandb.dalmahoy@marriothotels.co.uk **web:** www.marriothotels.com

Martins Restaurant

British, Mediterranean

Simple, honest cooking in good, owner-run, urban restaurant

☎ 0131 225 3106 70 Rose St, North Ln EH2 3DX

MENU GUIDE Asparagus & herb risotto, baby vegetables Halibut, braised squid & mussel stew • Date & walnut parfait

WINE GUIDE ♀ Domaine Goisot Sauvignon de St Bris £22 • ♀ Warwick Estate Pinotage £24 • 77 bottles over £20, 8 bottles under £20 • 6 by the glass (£2.40-£3.60)

PRICE GUIDE Fixed L fr £14 • starter £6-£10 • main £15-£22 • dessert fr £6 • coffee £2.50 • min/water £3 • Group min 6 service 10%

PLACE: Just off the beaten track, down a cobbled back street, this intimate, owner-run restaurant is in its 22nd year of offering simple, carefully prepared food to a loyal clientele. Bright green and white walls, fresh flowers, neat clothed tables and contemporary artwork sum up the appealing ambience. Service is attentive, discreet and personal.

FOOD: Sound and simple modern British cooking has been the key to its longevity and it comfortably holds it own in a city full of vibrant new restaurants.

OUR TIP: Magnificent cheese selection

Chef: Sean Lawson **Owners:** Mr & Mrs Irons **Times:** 12-2/7-10, Closed 5 wks from 24 Dec,1 wk May-Jun,1 wk Oct, Sun-Mon, closed L Sat **Notes:** Vegetarian available **Seats:** 30, Pr/dining room 30 **Smoking:** N/Sm in restaurant **Children:** Min 8 yrs **Directions:** North Lane is off Rose St between Frederick St & Castle St **Parking:** George Street/Castle Terrace Multi Storey **e-mail:** martinirons@fsdial.co.uk **web:** www.edinburghrestaurants.co.uk

EDINBURGH *continued* MAP 21 NT27

 Melville Castle Hotel
British   **NEW**
Cosy vaulted cellar bar & restaurant
☎ 0131 654 0088 Melville Gate, Gilmerton Rd
EH18 1AP
MENU GUIDE Pressed terrine of rabbit & olives • Casserole of
seasonal game • Warm sticky toffee pudding
WINE GUIDE ♀ Rizzaedi £18.95 • ♀ Santa Helena £16.95
23 bottles over £20, 16 bottles under £20 • 5 by the glass
(£3.20-£4)
PRICE GUIDE Fixed L £13 • starter £3.80-£5.50 • main £13-£16
dessert £4.50-£5 • coffee £2.50 • min/water £3.95 • Service optional

PLACE: The old castle cellars and dungeons make an
atmospheric setting for a restaurant, and at night when the
candles are lit, it is pretty impressive. Red-painted walls and the
odd handcuffs maintain the theme.
FOOD: A brasserie-style operation delivers a straightforward
handling of local produce, with natural flavours kept well to the
fore. Dishes like roast halibut, bacon and cabbage are given an
interesting modern slant.
OUR TIP: Try one of the galleried suites
Chef: Stephen Linsey **Owners:** The Hay Trust **Times:** 12-2.30/7-9.30
Notes: Fixed L Sun only, Vegetarian available, Dress Restrictions, Smart
casual, no jeans, Civ Wed 80 **Seats:** 50, Pr/dining room 70
Smoking: N/Sm in restaurant **Children:** Menu, Portions **Rooms:** 30
(30 en suite) ★★★ **Directions:** 2 min from city bypass (A720),
Sheriffhall rdbt **Parking:** 100 **e-mail:** reception@melvillecastle.com
web: www.melvillecastle.com

  Norton House Hotel *see below*

 Number One,
The Balmoral Hotel
Scottish, French
French influenced, fine dining hotel restaurant
☎ 0131 557 6727 1 Princes St EH2 2EQ
MENU GUIDE Twice-baked smoked haddock soufflé, lime
velouté • Venison, caramelised red onion & peppercorn
sauce • Banana & almond tart, vanilla ice cream
WINE GUIDE ♀ Les Setille Olivere Lafavie £24 • ♀ Santa Ema
Merlot £28.50 • 300 bottles over £20, 15 bottles under £20
8 by the glass (£5.50-£7.50)
PRICE GUIDE Fixed L £16.95 • starter £11.95-£15.95 • main
£22.50-£25.50 • dessert £7.95-£8.95 • Service included • Group
min 6 service 12.5%

PLACE: Just the place for a romantic meal, this chic eatery
occupies the basement of one of Edinburgh's top hotels. Enjoy a
pre-dinner drink in the intimate cocktail bar (which stocks over
30 types of champagne), and then take your seat in the dining
room, an opulent confection of gold velvet and maroon with
discreetly spaced tables.
FOOD: Accomplished cooking that's distinguished by imagination
and the use of high quality seasonal produce. Expect a modern
Scottish menu influenced by French cuisine: sea bass en papillote
perhaps, or local beef with curried oxtail and spinach. Notable
wine list.
OUR TIP: Enjoy the city and have a spot of lunch here

continue

EDINBURGH MAP 21 NT27

Norton House Hotel

Modern British
Small sophisticated restaurant in elegant hotel
☎ 0131 333 1275 Ingliston EH28 8LX
MENU GUIDE Smoked salmon terrine, beetroot
sorbet • Dornoch lamb, parsnip & vanilla ice cream, rosemary
jus • Valrhona chocolate fondant, lavender ice cream
WINE GUIDE ♀ Lamborti Pinot Grigio £22 • ♀ Castillo de
Clauijo Rioja £23 • 168 bottles over £20, 6 bottles under £20
PRICE GUIDE Starter £7.50-£10.95 • main £17.50-£23.95 • dessert
£6.50 • coffee £3.50 • min/water £3.50 • Service optional

PLACE: Extended Victorian mansion set amid 50 acres of
parkland, convenient for the airport and city centre. The hotel
has a relaxed, contemporary feel blending well with original
features. There is a conservatory bar lounge, an adjoining
brasserie and Ushers fine dining restaurant.
FOOD: Food is locally sourced and treated with skill and a simple
touch allowing vibrant flavours to shine through, as in lobster
ravioli with braised red cabbage and langoustine dressing. The
carte covers 6 choices at each course and typifies the current

modern British trends, while the tasting menu is full of surprises.
OUR TIP: Courtesy transport to and from the airport for guests
Chef: Graeme Shaw & Glen Bilins **Owners:** Handpicked Hotels
Times: 7-9.30, Closed 1 Jan, Sun-Mon, L all wk **Notes:** Vegetarian, Civ
Wed 140 **Seats:** 22, Pr/dining room 40 **Smoking:** Air con **Rooms:** 47
(47 en suite) ★★★★ **Directions:** Off A8, 0.5m past airport
Parking: 100 **web:** www.handpicked.co.uk/nortonhouse

Scotland

Chef: Jeff Bland **Owners:** RF Hotels **Times:** 12-2/7-10, Closed 1st 2 wks Jan, closed L Sat-Sun **Notes:** Tasting menu 6 courses £60-£90 (not avail. after 9.30pm), Vegetarian available, Dress Restrictions, Smart casual preferred, Civ Wed 60 **Seats:** 50, Pr/dining room 50 **Smoking:** N/Sm area, No pipes, No cigars, Air con **Children:** Portions **Rooms:** 188 (188 en suite) ★★★★★ **Directions:** Hotel at E end of Princes Street, next to Waverley Station **Parking:** 40
e-mail: numberone@thebalmoralhotel.com
web: www.roccofortehotels.com

Off the Wall Restaurant

British, French

Dine in style on the Royal Mile

☎ 0131 558 1497 105 High St, Royal Mile EH1 1SG

MENU GUIDE Scallops, crab fettuccini, pea & mint velouté, cauliflower fritter • Halibut & langoustines, tomato consommé • Chocolate torte

WINE GUIDE ♀ Domaine de la Villaudiere Sancerre Sauvignon Blanc £26.60 • ♥ Iona-Elgin Mr D Gunn Merlot £22.75 70 bottles over £20, 10 bottles under £20 • 8 by the glass (£3.95-£4.95)

PRICE GUIDE Fixed L £16.50 • Fixed D £35 • starter £7.95-£12.95 • main £19.95-£21.95 • dessert £6.95-£7.95 • coffee £2 • min/water £3.50 • Service optional

PLACE: The location in the heart of the city's Royal Mile is certainly a bonus, the relaxed atmosphere contrasting with the hustle and bustle on the street below. Arched leaded-glass windows, warm colours of terracotta and claret, white linen and friendly, professional service create just the right mood.
FOOD: The style is classically based but with a modern approach, utilising quality Scottish produce. Expect confident handling and a studied approach in well-presented dishes on an appealing menu, perhaps a fillet of Scottish beef with caramelised chicory, roasted shallots, sautéed potatoes and beef jus.
OUR TIP: Not easily found, take heed of directions
Chef: David Anderson **Owners:** David Anderson/Aileen Wilson
Times: 12-2, Closed 25-26 Dec, 1-2 Jan, Sun **Notes:** Tasting menu £65, Vegetarian available **Seats:** 44, Pr/dining room 20 **Smoking:** N/Sm area, No pipes, No cigars **Children:** Portions **Directions:** On Royal Mile near John Knox House - entrance via stairway next to Baillie Fyfes Close (first floor) **Parking:** NCP **e-mail:** otwedinburgh@aol.com
web: www.off-the-wall.co.uk

The Restaurant at the Bonham

Modern European

Trendy townhouse combining classical elegance with contemporary cuisine

☎ 0131 623 9319 35 Drumsheugh Gardens EH3 7RN

MENU GUIDE Scallop brochette, truffle risotto, tomato coulis • Sea bass fillet, lemon fettucine, salsa verde • Blood orange crème brûlée

WINE GUIDE ♀ Domaine de la Vallaudiere Sancerre £26 • ♥ Crozes-Hermitage Syrah £23 • 26 bottles over £20, 12 bottles under £20 • 11 by the glass (£4-£6.50)

PRICE GUIDE Fixed L £13.50 • starter £4.50-£8.50 • main £16-£21.50 • dessert £5-£7.50 • coffee £2.70 • min/water £3.50 Service added but optional 10% • Group min 6 service 10%

PLACE: A classic Edinburgh townhouse provides the setting for this contemporary hotel with a strong sense of style. The high-ceilinged dining rooms are handsome in black, burgundy, brown and taupe; and white walls are hung with bright modern abstract paintings.

continued

FOOD: Contemporary European cooking from a kitchen that is not afraid to take chances. Good use is made of local and organic ingredients in simple and effective combinations, like an imaginative crab, leek and sun blushed tomato petit pain.
OUR TIP: The chef's speciality fish pie on Fridays
Chef: Michel Bouyer **Owners:** Peter Taylor, The Town House Company
Times: 12-2.30/6.30-10 **Notes:** Sea Market Menu Fri D 5 courses £37.50, Vegetarian available **Seats:** 60, Pr/dining room 26 **Smoking:** N/Sm in restaurant **Children:** Portions **Rooms:** 48 (48 en suite) ★★★★
Directions: Located to the W end of Princes Street **Parking:** 16
e-mail: restaurant@thebonham.com
web: www.thebonham.com

Restaurant Martin Wishart *see page 567*

Rhubarb - the Restaurant at Prestonfield

Scottish, British

Fine dining in opulent setting

☎ 0131 225 1333 Prestonfield, Priestfield Rd EH16 5UT

MENU GUIDE Asparagus millefeuille, lemon hollandaise • Sea bass, oxtail, brown lentil & port stew • Rhubarb assiette

WINE GUIDE ♀ Hollick Chardonnay Reserve £27 • ♥ Haris de Pirique Cabernet Sauvignon £19 • 181 bottles over £20, 20 bottles under £20 • 15 by the glass (£4-£8)

PRICE GUIDE Fixed L £14.95 • starter £5.95-£10.95 • main £14.95-£25.95 • dessert £6.95-£7.95 • coffee £2.95 • min/water £3.50 • Service optional 10% • Group min 8 service 10%

PLACE: Hidden within the lavishly restored Prestonfield, this restaurant has become a byword for opulence. In addition to the richly appointed dining rooms individually decorated in Stuart, Italian or Garden style, there are separate bars and salons for aperitifs or coffee. Staff are friendly and focused.

continued

Scotland

EDINBURGH continued MAP 21 NT27

FOOD: Ambitious, extensive menus offer dishes to titillate the eye and the stomach. Mostly modern European but influences from elsewhere pop up randomly. High quality ingredients used throughout. Expect turbot steak in milk and cloves to follow sweet garlic cod on pea purée with a sauce vièrge.
OUR TIP: All this just ten minutes from Edinburgh's centre
Chef: Kenny Coltman **Owners:** James Thomson **Times:** 12.00-3/6-11
Notes: Theatre supper daily 6-7pm, 10-11pm, Vegetarian available, Smart Dress, Civ Wed 500 **Seats:** 90, Pr/dining room 500 **Children:** Min 12 yrs, Portions **Rooms:** 26 (26 en suite) ★★★★ **Directions:** Proceed out of city centre on Nicholson St, join Dalkeith Rd. At lights turn left into Priestfield Rd. Prestonfield is on the left **Parking:** 200
e-mail: reservations@prestonfield.com
web: www.rhubarb-restaurant.com

 ## Santini

Italian

Chic venue for modern Italian food

☎ 0131 221 7788 8 Conference Square EH3 8AN

MENU GUIDE Selection of Italian cured meats • Lobster & salmon cannelloni • Tiramisù, expresso ice cream
WINE GUIDE ♀ Pinot Grigio Haas £29.50 • ♀ Chianti Leonardo £26.50 • 47 bottles over £20, 5 bottles under £20 • 3 by the glass (£3.75-£4.75)
PRICE GUIDE Fixed L £23 • starter £5.50-£10 • main £14.50-£22 • dessert £5 • coffee £2 • min/water £3.20 • Service included
PLACE: Stylish minimalist restaurant, bistro and cocktail bar occupying the same building as the Sheraton Grand's impressive One Spa. From the central cocktail bar the bistro, to the right, has diners sitting high on padded stools and the bright and airy restaurant, to the left, offers more traditional seating. Expect five-star service with genuine smiles from the staff.
FOOD: Perfectly executed dishes full of Italian flavours. Even Scottish ingredients benefit from the kitchen's thoughtful use of herbs and oils. Two cartes - one classic, the other seasonal - both with the traditional Italian structure, plus fixed-price lunch options.
OUR TIP: Try the bistro for lunch and the restaurant for dinner
Chef: Richard Glennie **Owners:** Sheraton Hotel **Times:** 12-2.30/6.30-10.30, Closed 1 Jan, Sun, closed L Sat **Notes:** Vegetarian available, Smart Dress **Seats:** 45 **Smoking:** N/Sm in restaurant, Air con **Children:** Portions **Parking:** 121

The AA Wine Awards recognise the finest wine lists in England, Scotland and Wales. For full details, see pages 14-15

 ## The Scotsman

Contemporary Scottish

Opulent setting and fine dining

☎ 0131 556 5565 20 North Bridge EH1 1YT

MENU GUIDE Jellied tomato & tea consommé • Roast ling, parsley sauce • Chocolate truffle, banana Anglaise
WINE GUIDE ♀ Domaine Laroche Chablis St Martin Chardonnay £28.50 • ♀ Château Grand Corbin Bordeaux £42 • 66 bottles over £20, 4 bottles under £20 • 8 by the glass (£5.50-£9.50)
PRICE GUIDE Fixed D £35 • starter £8-£12 • main £17-£26 • dessert £7 • coffee £3 • min/water £4.50 • Service optional
PLACE: Once the head office of *The Scotsman* newspaper, this grand old building is as magnificent as in its journalistic heyday. From the marble reception hall you go down to the fine dining restaurant, Vermillion, where a soft and sophisticated atmosphere awaits amidst much opulence.
FOOD: Technical skills remain high here, though some flavour combinations can be a surprise. Great Scottish produce is evident throughout, the short menu might include wood pigeon, parsley porridge and caramelised ceps, and some superb desserts such as the highly successful orange pannacotta with fennel and lemongrass.
OUR TIP: The pre-starters are sure to delight
Chef: Geoff Balharrie/Chris Smart **Owners:** The Scotsman Hotel Group **Times:** 7-10, Mon & Tue, closed L all week **Notes:** Tasting menu 5 courses (Fri, Sat) £50, Vegetarian available, Smart Dress, Civ Wed 80 **Seats:** 32, Pr/dining room 80 **Smoking:** N/Sm in restaurant **Children:** Portions **Rooms:** 69 (69 en suite) ★★★★★
Directions: Town centre, next to railway station **Parking:** 17
e-mail: reservations@thescotsmanhotelgroup.co.uk
web: www.thescotsmanhotel.co.uk

 ## The Sheraton Grand Hotel & Spa

International

Scottish fine dining in metropolitan elegance

☎ 0131 221 6422 1 Festival Square EH3 9SR

MENU GUIDE Oyster & langoustine bouillon • Cabernet Sauvignon poached salmon • Passionfruit mousse
WINE GUIDE 42 bottles over £20
PRICE GUIDE Fixed L £21-£26 • Fixed D £30.50 • starter £7-£12.50 • main £14.50-£27 • dessert £6.50 • coffee £3 • min/water £3.95 • Service included
PLACE: The Grill Room is one of three dining rooms in this modern, stylish metropolitan hotel. The long, narrow dining room is traditionally decorated and furnished with wood panelling, tartan cladding and upholstery, as well as comfortable leather chairs. Scottish paintings and prints adorn the walls. Tables are crisply presented with white linen and fresh flowers. Silver service and friendly Franco-Scottish staff.
FOOD: Traditional dishes prepared using the best Scottish produce occasionally lightened by modern touches. This opulent dining experience might include monkfish with lobster risotto, veal fillet with sweetbreads or tea-smoked lamb.
OUR TIP: Best spa in Scotland
Chef: Philip Garrod **Owners:** Hotel Corporation of Edinburgh **Times:** 12-2/7-10, Closed Jan, Sun & Mon, closed L Sat **Notes:** Vegetarian available, Smart Dress, No jeans, trainers **Seats:** 40, Pr/dining room 485 **Smoking:** N/Sm in restaurant, Air con **Children:** No Children **Rooms:** 260 (260 en suite) ★★★★★ **Directions:** Off Lothian Road. Entrance to hotel behind Standard Life building **Parking:** 121
e-mail: grandedinburgh.sheraton@sheraton.com
web: www.sheraton.com/grandedinburgh

EDINBURGH MAP 21 NT27

Restaurant Martin Wishart

French

Imaginative, memorable cooking in intimate, fashionable waterfront venue

☎ 0131 553 3557 54 The Shore, Leith EH6 6RA

e-mail: info@martin-wishart.co.uk **web:** www.martin-wishart.co.uk

PLACE: This eponymous restaurant on the fashionable Leith waterfront is perhaps a surprisingly small venue in which to find one of Scotland's top chefs. The chic, intimate, minimalist-style room is decorated in shades of cream and beige enlivened by colourful, contemporary artwork. Orchids set off double-clothed tables laid with shiny cutlery and glistening glassware, while highly professional and knowledgeable service is delivered by an enthusiastic, mainly French team.

FOOD: Martin Wishart's style is modern-focused, underpinned by a classic French theme, his approach via an eye-catching repertoire of value fixed-price lunch, six-course tasting option (a difficult concept) and enticing carte, which comes admirably backed up by an appealing vegetarian menu. Ingredients are of the very best, with plenty of luxury items to the fore, with Wishart going to great lengths to source the finest produce - locally where possible, from artisan producers, but he's not afraid to travel further for the right quality either. Exquisite cooking, demonstrated by flawless execution and flair, find their place in complex, refined dishes of clean, distinct flavours and consummate balance, with ancillaries like bread and canapés keeping up the pace and proving a real strength too. So expect something like a quite superb lobster tortellini with pig's trotter, spinach and lobster cappuccino to start, a classic finish of tarte aux pommes accompanied by Calvados ice cream and, in between, roast turbot and langoustines served with Perigord truffle butter and braised leeks. Anticipate a memorable meal. Impressive wine list.

MENU GUIDE Mushroom & Madeira consommé, partridge & venison ravioli • Beef shin, veal sweetbreads, pomme purée, red wine jus • Ginger crème brûlée, rhubarb sorbet

WINE GUIDE ♀ Pernaud Vergelesse Burgundy £34 • ♀ Châteaux Lucas St Emilion Cabernet Sauvignon £26.50 • 200 bottles over £20, 4 bottles under £20 • 15 by the glass (£4.50-£8)

PRICE GUIDE Fixed L £18.50-£22 • starter £11.50-£16.50 • main £24-£27 • dessert £9.50 • coffee £4.50 • min/water £3.75 • Service optional • Group min 6 service 10%

OUR TIP: Fixed-price lunch is super value

Chef: Martin Wishart **Owners:** Martin Wishart **Times:** 12-2/7-10, Closed 25 Dec, BHs, Sun-Mon, closed L Sat **Notes:** Tasting Menu, 5 courses £50, 6 courses £60, Vegetarian available, Smart Dress **Seats:** 45, Pr/dining room 16 **Smoking:** N/Sm in restaurant **Directions:** Telephone for directions/map on website

EDINBURGH *continued* MAP 21 NT27

⊚ Stac Polly
Scottish, British

Fine Scottish cuisine in the city centre

☎ 0131 229 5405 8-10 Grindlay St EH3 9AS

MENU GUIDE Haggis parcels, plum & red wine sauce • Parsley crusted cod, spinach & mascarpone mash, asparagus • Vanilla crème brûlée

WINE GUIDE ♀ Lofthouse Sauvignon Blanc £17.95 • ♥ Palomar Cabernet Sauvignon £17.95 • 52 bottles over £20, 28 bottles under £20 • 9 by the glass (£3.75-£3.95)

PRICE GUIDE Fixed L £10-£14.95 • Fixed D £25.85-£32.45 • starter £5.95-£7.55 • main £13.95-£18.95 • dessert £5.95 • coffee £2.45 • min/water £3.55 • Service added but optional 10%

PLACE: Situated close to Edinburgh Castle and the main shopping areas, this convivial restaurant is a warren of richly furnished rooms. Tartan-clad chairs offset a mossy green carpet, while tables are double clothed and prettily set.
FOOD: A simple cooking style retains the flavour of quality ingredients. Expect a modern Scottish menu, with dishes along the lines of pheasant with an apricot and sage stuffing, or pork with an apple and cider jus.
OUR TIP: Vegetarians catered for - ask the staff
Chef: Steven Harvey **Owners:** Roger Coulthard **Times:** 12-2/6-11, Closed L Sat-Sun **Notes:** Tasting menu & Burn's Night menu £40, Vegetarian available **Seats:** 50, Pr/dining room 10 **Smoking:** N/Sm area, No pipes, No cigars **Children:** Portions **Directions:** In town centre. Situated beneath the castle, near Lyceum Theatre **Parking:** NCP - Castle Street; parking meters **web:** www.stacpolly.co.uk

⊚ Stac Polly
Scottish, British

Get a flavour of Scotland at this basement restaurant

☎ 0131 556 2231 29-33 Dublin St EH3 6NL

MENU GUIDE Cullen skink • Aberdeen Angus beef fillet, potato cake, oxtail galette, cognac/green peppercorn jus • Bread & butter pudding

WINE GUIDE ♀ Lofthouse Sauvignon Blanc £17.95 • ♥ Palomar Cabernet Sauvignon £17.95 • 52 bottles over £20, 28 bottles under £20 • 9 by the glass (£3.75-£3.95)

PRICE GUIDE Fixed L £10-£14.95 • Fixed D £25.85-£32.45 • starter £5.95-£7.55 • main £13.95-£18.95 • dessert £5.95 • coffee £2.45 • min/water £3.55 • Service added but optional 10%

PLACE: Basement restaurant in Edinburgh's New Town with a labyrinth of private rooms. Named after a Scottish mountain (like

continued

its sister restaurant in Grindlay Street), there's no mistaking the theme, with stone walls, tartan fabrics and Highland music.
FOOD: The Scottish theme is handled deftly, with some old favourites given a modern twist, as in filo parcels of haggis with plum and red wine sauce.
OUR TIP: Good value lunches are worth a try
Chef: Andre Stanislas **Owners:** Roger Coulthard **Times:** 12-2/6-11, Closed 25-26 Dec, 1 Jan, closed L Sat-Sun **Notes:** Vegetarian available **Seats:** 100, Pr/dining room 54 **Smoking:** N/Sm area **Children:** Portions **Parking:** On street - after 6.30 pm **web:** www.stacpolly.co.uk

⊚ Tower Restaurant & Terrace
British 🍸

Rooftop restaurant on the landmark Museum of Scotland

☎ 0131 225 3003 Museum of Scotland, Chambers St EH1 1JF

MENU GUIDE Confit duck, foie gras, beetroot • Fillet of cod, chorizo frittata, asparagus • Vanilla, rhubarb & blueberry brûlée

WINE GUIDE ♀ Montravel Château Pique-Segue Semillon/Sauvignon £15 • ♥ Marchesi Antinori Santa Christina Sangiovese Merlot £16.50 • 136 bottles over £20, 17 bottles under £20 • 12 by the glass (£3.50-£8)

PRICE GUIDE Fixed L £9.95 • starter £6.50-£11 • main £9.50-£22 • dessert £5.95-£7.95 • coffee £1.95 • min/water £3.75 • Service optional • Group min 8 service 10%

PLACE: The stunning fifth-floor location over the Museum of Scotland provides views across the rooftops to Edinburgh Castle and St Giles's Cathedral. The interior is chic and contemporary with light, pale wood, and in summer diners can take advantage of the spacious terrace.
FOOD: Competent cooking with some modern ingredients and fairly restrained treatment, which allows the flavours to come through. There's a grill section with great quality beef and a notable wine list.
OUR TIP: Good-value theatre suppers 5-6.30pm

continue

Scotland

Scotland

hef: Gavin Elder **Owners:** James Thomson **Times:** 12/12-11, Closed
5-26 Dec **Notes:** Theatre supper daily 5-6.30 pm, Vegetarian available
eats: 96, Pr/dining room 90 **Smoking:** N/Sm in restaurant, Air con
irections: Above the Museum of Scotland building at corner of George
  Bridge & Chambers St, on level 5 **Parking:** On street
mail: reservations@tower-restaurant.com
eb: www.tower-restaurant.com

The Vintners Rooms

rench

ormer wine auction room for fine French cuisine

☎ 0131 554 6767 The Vaults, 87 Giles St, Leith
H6 6BZ

MENU GUIDE Scallops in pancetta, cider beurre blanc • Duck
with honey & lime sauce • Hot chocolate fondant, pistachio ice
ream

WINE GUIDE ♀ Falchini Vernaccia £17 • ♀ St Antonins Cabernet
auvignon £17 • 184 bottles over £20, 10 bottles under £20

PRICE GUIDE Fixed L £14.50 • starter £5.50-£10.50 • main £15-
22 • dessert £5.50-£6.50 • coffee £2 • min/water £3 • Service
added but optional 10% • Group min 5 service 10%

LACE: Romantic venue with large helpings of atmosphere. The
andlelit restaurant is housed in a unique former auction room
r wine and still retains many period features, alongside a smart
nc bar and sumptuous Persian wall hangings.
OOD: Traditional French cooking in a modern style. Expect
stic dishes presented with serious artistry: sea bass with mussel
oth perhaps, or rack of lamb provençale with olive jus. A ham
ock starter shows the style, full of flavour and served with a leek
d carrot 'flower' set in aspic.
UR TIP: The wine bar has a great buzz
hef: P Ginistière **Owners:** Patrice Ginistière, Laure Pages **Times:** 12-
7/-10, Closed 15 days from 1st Jan, Mon, closed D Sun
otes: Vegetarian available **Seats:** 64, Pr/dining room 34
noking: N/Sm area **Children:** Portions **Directions:** At the end of
ith Walk; left into Great Junction St, right into Henderson St. Restaurant
old warehouse on right **Parking:** 4
mail: enquiries@thevintnersrooms.com
eb: www.thevintnersrooms.com

Witchery by the Castle

cottish

*ontemporary cooking in historic Gothic
etting*

☎ 0131 225 5613 Castlehill, Royal Mile EH1 2NF

MENU GUIDE Tian of buckie crab • Roast Atlantic cod, confit
atte potatoes • Iced mango parfait

continued

Witchery by the Castle

PRICE GUIDE Fixed L £9.95 • starter £5.95-£11 • main £12.95-
£24 • dessert £5.95-£7.95 • coffee £1.95 • Service
optional • Group min 8 service 10%

PLACE: Now established for nearly 25 years, the Witchery's
historic building - a merchant's house - dates back to 1595. The
restaurant takes its name from the hundreds of witches burned at
the stake on Castlehill during the reign of James VI. Heraldic
painted and gilded ceilings, tapestry-hung walls and oak-panelled
walls set the scene.
FOOD: First-class mainly Scottish ingredients served in
contemporary style, accompanied by a world-class wine list.
Expect mains like chargrilled Aberdeen Angus fillet, celeriac and
seared foie gras.
OUR TIP: Watch out for celebrities
Chef: Douglas Roberts **Owners:** James Thomson **Times:** 12-4/5-11.30,
Closed 25-26 Dec **Notes:** Theatre supper 5.30-6.30, 10-11, Vegetarian
available **Seats:** 120, Pr/dining room 70 **Smoking:** Air con
Children: Menu, Portions **Rooms:** 7 (7 en suite) **Directions:** At
the gates of Edinburgh Castle, at the top of the Royal Mile
e-mail: mail@thewitchery.com **web:** www.thewitchery.com

☕ **The Tea Room** 158 Canongate, Royal Mile EH8 8DD
☎ 07771 501679 Winner of The Tea Guild Award of Excellence
2005.

⑪ **David Bann** 56/58 St Mary St EH1 1SX
☎ 0131 556 5888 Smart vegetarian restaurant and bar, off the
Royal Mile.

⑪ **Henderson's Salad Table** 94 Hanover St
EH2 1DR ☎ 0131 225 2131 Pioneering vegetarian/ health food
restaurant with deli and farm shop.

◉ **Lancer's Brasserie** 5 Hamilton Place, Stockbridge
EH3 5BA ☎ 0131 332 3444 Bengal Lancers theme with North
Indian and Bangladeshi dishes.

◉ **Shamiana** 14 Brougham St EH3 9JH ☎ 0131 228 2265
Relatively small and extremely popular, serving Kashmiri/North
Indian dishes.

♀ **Valvona & Crolla** 19 Elm Row EH7 4AA
☎ 0131 556 6066 Legendary deli, wine merchants and caffe-bar
serving Italian delights.

♀ **Waterfront Wine Bar and Bistro** 1c Dock
Place, Leith EH6 6LU ☎ 0131 554 2530 Former steamship
waiting room, now a warren of rooms offering decent food and
friendly service.

⑪ **Zinc** Ocean Terminal, Ocean Dr, Leith EH6 7DZ
☎ 0131 553 8070 Conran grill and bar on the waterfront.

Scotland

FALKIRK

BANKNOCK MAP 21 NS77

⊛⊛ Glenskirlie House Restaurant

British

Country house that consistently impresses

☎ 01324 840201 Kilsyth Rd FK4 1UF

MENU GUIDE Chicken liver & black truffle pâté • Sea bass, potato & clam chowder • Lemon delice, white chocolate & vanilla ice cream

WINE GUIDE ⚲ Colombette Chardonnay £29.95 • ⚑ Rimbert Cabernet/Syrah £24.50 • 35 bottles over £20, 30 bottles under £20 • 6 by the glass (£2.75)

PRICE GUIDE Fixed L £15.75 • starter £6.50-£9.95 • main £18-£21 • dessert £7.25 • coffee £3.25 • min/water £2.95 • Service optional

PLACE: This welcoming country house in the heart of Scotland exudes Edwardian elegance, its softly lit restaurant tastefully decorated with luxurious fabrics, unusual knick knacks and mirrors.

FOOD: The cooking at Glenskirlie just gets better and better; expect delicious modern interpretations of classic dishes, made from high quality Scottish produce. A wide-ranging menu offers plenty of choice, from a simple steak to a more involved option such as venison with skirlie, creamed cabbage, pancetta and game gravy.

OUR TIP: A romantic wedding venue

Chef: Daryl Jordan **Owners:** John Macaloney, Colin Macaloney
Times: 12-2/6-9.30, Closed 26-27 Dec, 1-3 Jan, closed D Mon
Notes: Vegetarian available, Civ Wed 94 **Seats:** 54, Pr/dining room 150
Smoking: N/Sm in restaurant, Air con **Children:** Menu, Portions
Directions: From Glasgow take A80 towards Stirling. Continue past Cumbernauld & Auchenkilens rdbt. At junct 4 take A803 signed Kilsyth/Bonnybridge. At T-junct turn right. Hotel 1m on right **Parking:** 100
e-mail: macaloneys@glenskirliehouse.com
web: www.glenskirliehouse.com

AA's Chefs' Chef is the annual poll of all the chefs included in The Restaurant Guide. Around 1800 of the country's top chefs are asked to vote to recognise the achievements of one of their peers.
This year's winner is featured on page 19.

GRANGEMOUTH MAP 21 NS98

⊛⊛ The Grange Manor

British, French

Manor house hotel with Scottish influenced British/French food

☎ 01324 474836 Glensburgh FK3 8XJ

MENU GUIDE Haggis, neeps & tatties, whisky sauce • Rack of lamb, spicy coucous, salad, sweet chilli sauce • Baileys crème brûlée

WINE GUIDE 35 bottles over £20, 17 bottles under £20 • 6 by the glass (£3.50-£5)

PRICE GUIDE Fixed L £13.95 • Fixed D £26.85-£29.85 • starter £4-£9 • main £13.50-£21.95 • dessert £5-£8.50 • coffee £3 min/water £3.50 • Service optional

PLACE: The Grange Manor is an impressive country-house-style hotel located south of town near the M9. It benefits from the personal touch of family ownership and friendly welcoming staff Le Chardon (which translates as The Thistle) is the hotel's smart restaurant - comfortable, spacious and airy, decorated in neutral tones.

FOOD: The extensive menu provides nine or ten choices at each course, and while its base is modern British with French influences, good use is made of top quality Scottish meat, game and seafood. The cooking style is simple, effective, consistent and timed to perfection.

OUR TIP: There is also a bar/bistro in the grounds

Chef: Eric Avenier **Owners:** Mr W Wallace **Times:** 12-2/7-9.30, Closed 26 Dec, 1-2 Jan, Sun, closed L Sat **Notes:** Vegetarian available, Dress Restrictions, Smart casual, Civ Wed 160 **Seats:** 65, Pr/dining room 40
Smoking: N/Sm area, No pipes, No cigars, Air con **Children:** Portions
Rooms: 36 (36 en suite) ★★★ **Directions:** M9 (eastward) junct 6 200 mtrs on right, M9 (westward) junct 5, then A905 for 2m
Parking: 150 **e-mail:** info@grangemanor.co.uk
web: www.grangemanor.co.uk

FIFE

ANSTRUTHER MAP 21 NO50

 Cellar Restaurant *see page 573*

CUPAR MAP 21 NO31

Ostlers Close Restaurant

Modern Scottish

long-established restaurant with an eye on modern trends

☎ 01334 655574 Bonnygate KY15 4BU

MENU GUIDE Pot roast breast of wood pigeon • Roast roe venison, red wine sauce • Apricot & almond tart

WINE GUIDE 52 bottles over £20, 38 bottles under £20 • 6 by the glass (£3.65-£4.50)

PRICE GUIDE Starter £4.50-£10 • main £10.25-£19 • dessert £5.25-£6.50 • coffee £2.30 • min/water £2.50 • Service optional

PLACE: The warmth of the hospitality tallies well with the cosiness of this three-tiered restaurant. Amanda Graham's beautiful displays of garden flowers and seasonal produce lend it a relaxed rustic feel, though there's no doubting the stylishness of the setting.

FOOD: Jimmy Graham has been cooking here for over 23 years, but his enthusiasm and expertise are undiminished. His passion for wild mushrooms is matched by a near obsession with proper, often organic, food, and an appreciation of well-balanced flavours; ably represented by pan-fried mixed fish fillets with a chervil sauce.

OUR TIP: Some cracking wine bargains

Chef: James Graham **Owners:** James & Amanda Graham **Times:** 12.15-1.30/7-9.30, Closed 25-26 Dec, 1-2 Jan, 2 wks Oct, Sun-Mon, closed L Tue-Sat **Notes:** Vegetarian available **Seats:** 26 **Smoking:** N/Sm in restaurant **Children:** Min 6 yrs D, Portions **Directions:** In small lane off main street, **Parking:** On street, public car park **web:** www.ostlersclose.co.uk

---

DUNFERMLINE MAP 21 NT08

Cardoon

European, International

Contemporary cooking in relaxed conservatory restaurant

☎ 01383 736258 Best Western Keavil House Hotel, Crossford KY12 8QW

MENU GUIDE Flash-fried prawns, herb salad, chilli vinaigrette • Thai-roasted monkfish, lemongrass, coriander & mussel risotto • Tiramisù, amaretto crisps

continued

PRICE GUIDE Food prices not confirmed for 2006. Please telephone for details

PLACE: Cardoons is the smart, contemporary, conservatory restaurant at this former 16th-century manor house, now modern business and leisure hotel. Traditional design, rich colours, garden views and a bright, airy, relaxed ambience awaits diners.

FOOD: The appealing, modern style has a touch of brasserie and proves a crowd pleaser, with an array of light dishes and grills to bolster the usual three-course format. Locally sourced, quality ingredients and creative presentation hit the mark.

OUR TIP: The selection of light dishes offers plenty of menu options

Chef: Phil Yates **Owners:** Queensferry Hotels Ltd **Times:** 12-2/6.30-9.30 **Notes:** Vegetarian available, Civ Wed 100 **Seats:** 65, Pr/dining room 24 **Smoking:** N/Sm in restaurant **Children:** Menu, Portions **Rooms:** 47 (47 en suite) ★★★ **Directions:** M90 junct 3, 7m from Forth Road Bridge, take A985, turning right after bridge. From Dunfermline, 2m W on A994 **Parking:** 175 **e-mail:** sales@keavilhouse.co.uk **web:** www.keavilhouse.co.uk

---

Town House Restaurant

European, International

Mediterranean flavours in a slick setting

☎ 01383 432 382 48 Eastport KY12 7JB

MENU GUIDE Mussel & lemongrass risotto • Grilled monkfish, Thai curry cream • Passion fruit pannacotta

WINE GUIDE ♀ La Baume Sauvignon Blanc £13.95 • ♀ Elementos Shiraz £14.35 • 38 bottles over £20, 34 bottles under £20 • 6 by the glass (£3.35-£5.50)

PRICE GUIDE Fixed L £9.95-£13.95 • Fixed D £19.95-£23.45 • starter £3.75-£7.55 • main £7.95-£19.95 • dessert £5.45-£5.95 • coffee £1.50 • min/water £3.75 • Service optional

PLACE: More like a night club in the evenings with its lively atmosphere, this fashionable city-centre eaterie is stylishly split on two levels. A central area features black leather sofas against a crimson background for pre-dinner drinks.

continued

Scotland

DUNFERMLINE *continued* MAP 21 NT08

FOOD: The brasserie-style food looks as good as it tastes, with a Mediterranean influence infusing the likes of confit of duck with red onion marmalade, and hot smoked salmon and polenta cake.
OUR TIP: Good dinner deals Sunday-Thursday
Chef: Paul Mathieson Brown **Owners:** Paul & Diane Brown **Times:** 12-6/6-10, Closed 26 Dec, 1 Jan **Notes:** Vegetarian available **Seats:** 110, Pr/dining room 45 **Smoking:** N/Sm area, Air con **Children:** Menu, Portions **Directions:** From M90 follow signs for town centre. At Sinclair rdbt take exit for town centre. Restaurant is on left after Carnegie Hall Theatre **Parking:** NCP. On Street parking
e-mail: townhouserestaurant@btconnect.com
web: www.townhouserestaurant.co.uk

ELIE MAP 21 NO40

 Sangsters
Modern British
Relaxed and friendly restaurant with a great reputation
☎ 01333 331001 51 High St KY9 1BZ
MENU GUIDE Seared Isle of Mull scallops • Slow cooked shoulder noisette of lamb • Lemon & blueberry moulee
WINE GUIDE ♀ Vincent Girardin Ruilly les Croux Chardonnay £23 • ♀ Matakana Moro Merlot/Cabernet Sauvignon £20
21 bottles over £20, 23 bottles under £20 • 4 by the glass (£4)
PRICE GUIDE Fixed L £15.75 • Fixed D £30 • min/water £2.50 • Service optional
PLACE: Highly acclaimed restaurant on the main street of the small coastal town, run by husband and wife team Bruce and Jackie Sangster. The simple white interior has large well-spaced tables laid with crisp white linen, and high-backed chairs upholstered in gold suede. Funky cutlery, big plates and oversized glassware complete the contemporary look.
FOOD: The short dinner menu, with a choice of three starters, mains and desserts, is priced for two, three or four courses. Commitment is made to high quality local produce, particularly excellent Scottish beef.
OUR TIP: The set lunch is very good value
Chef: Bruce R Sangster **Owners:** Bruce & Jacqueline Sangster **Times:** 12.30-1.30/7-9.30, Closed 25-26 Dec, 1st 2 wks Jan, 2wks mid Feb/Oct, 1 wk mid Nov, Mon, closed L Tue & Sat, closed D Sun **Notes:** Coffee incl, Vegetarian by request only, Dress Restrictions, Smart casual **Seats:** 28 **Smoking:** N/Sm in restaurant **Children:** Min 12 yrs **Directions:** From St Andrews on the A917, take the B9131 to Anstruther, turn right at rdbt and follow A917 to Elie. 11m from St Andrews **Parking:** On street **e-mail:** bruce@sangsters.co.uk
web: www.sangsters.co.uk

FALKLAND MAP 21 NO20

☕ Kind Kyttock's Kitchen Cross Wynd KY15 7BE
☎ 01337 857477 Winner of The Tea Guild Award of Excellence.

GLENROTHES MAP 21 NO20

⊕ Rescobie House Hotel & Restaurant
British, European
Intimate dining with relaxed ambience
☎ 01592 749555 6 Valley Dr, Leslie KY6 3BQ

continued

Rescobie House Hotel & Restaurant

MENU GUIDE Crispy haggis & clapshot parcel, whisky cream • Roast monkfish, Parma ham, risotto, red wine glaze • Sticky toffee pudding
WINE GUIDE ♀ Yalumba Unwooded Chardonnay £21 • ♀ Masi Tupungato Passo Doble Malbec £17 • 28 bottles over £20, 17 bottles under £20 • 4 by the glass (£3.50-£4.75)
PRICE GUIDE Fixed D £24.95 • coffee £1.95 • min/water £3 • Service optional

PLACE: Small family-run hotel and restaurant set in secluded gardens on the edge of the village of Leslie. The original house is a listed building dating from the 1930s and retains much of its period character, enhanced by a combination of modern and art deco decor.
FOOD: Cooking shows flair without fussiness in a balanced choice of modern Scottish dishes with European influences.
OUR TIP: Hospitality and service is second to none
Chef: Oscar Sinjorgo **Owners:** Mr & Mrs K Wilkie **Times:** 12-2/6.30-9, Closed 1-2 Jan, closed L Mon-Sat **Notes:** Sun L 3 courses £14.95 (coffee incl), Vegetarian available, Civ Wed 24 **Seats:** 24, Pr/dining room 10 **Smoking:** N/Sm in restaurant **Children:** Portions **Rooms:** 10 (10 en suite) ★★ **Directions:** From A92 at Glenrothes, take A911 to Leslie. At end of High Street follow straight ahead. First left, hotel 2nd on left **Parking:** 12 **e-mail:** rescobiehotel@compuserve.com
web: www.rescobie-hotel.co.uk

KIRKCALDY MAP 21 NT29

⊕ Dunnikier House Hotel
British
Traditional cooking in atmospheric mansion house
☎ 01592 268393 Dunnikier Park KY1 3LP
MENU GUIDE Cullen skink • Steak, grain mustard & mushroom stovies, whisky pepper sauce • Raspberry & Drambuie crème brûlée
PRICE GUIDE Fixed L £17.50 • Fixed D £24 • starter £3-£4.95 • main £6.95-£15.50 • dessert £3-£4.95 • coffee £1.25 • min/water £1.25 • Service optional

PLACE: Set in parkland, this atmospheric Adam-style mansion has been tastefully furnished in keeping with its 18th-century origins. A wide selection of malts is available in the bar.
FOOD: The kitchen treats quality produce with care, conjuring traditional dishes with a distinctive Scottish flavour. Start your meal with spicy parsnip soup perhaps, and then move on to salmon with olive oil mash, and an apple and blackcurrant crumble with hot crème anglaise.
OUR TIP: Adjacent to Dunnikier golf course
Chef: Stuart Archibald **Owners:** Brian & Jane Maloney **Times:** 12-2/6-9 **Notes:** Vegetarian available **Seats:** 22, Pr/dining room 15 **Smoking:** N/Sm in restaurant **Children:** Menu **Rooms:** 15 (15 en suit ★★★ **Directions:** Turn off A92 at Kirkcaldy West, take 3rd exit at rdbt signed hospital/crematorium, then 1st left past school **Parking:** 100 **e-mail:** recp@dunnikier-house-hotel.co.uk
web: www.dunnikier-house-hotel.co.uk

ANSTRUTHER MAP 21 NO50

Cellar Restaurant

Seafood, European
Atmospheric, intimate, chic cellar seafood restaurant

☎ 01333 310378 24 East Green KY10 3AA

PLACE: Peter Jukes's renowned Cellar seafood restaurant – Anstruther's answer to Padstow's Rick Stein – comes awash with the fruits of the sea, tucked away in a quiet road just a net cast from the harbour. It occupies the ground-floor cellar (not subterranean) of the family home, a 400-year-old former cooperage. An archway entrance to a small cobbled courtyard leads to the restaurant's cosy bar area. Exposed stone walls, flagstone floors, roaring winter fires and candlelit tables provide the backdrop, while pieces of art and pottery decorate in eclectic style. Set across two rooms, the atmosphere's cosy, relaxed and convivial but chic service is unfussy but attentive and efficient.

FOOD: Peter Jukes's style has a French influence, his cooking displaying an intelligent simplicity that allows the very freshest, prime-quality local seafood to shine with clear, clean flavours. Think, fathoms-deep fish soup (crayfish bisque glazed with gruyère and cream), perhaps grilled fillet of North Sea halibut, served with greens, pine nuts, chopped smoked bacon and pot of hollandaise, followed by classic crème brûlée with lime. Excellent wine list.

MENU GUIDE Roast Pittenweem langoustines, herb & garlic butter • Steamed John Dory fillets, rosemary beurre blanc • Date & ginger sponge, toffee pecan sauce, cinnamon ice cream

WINE GUIDE ♀ Chablis Chardonnay £22.50 • 8 by the glass (£4.25-£5.50)

PRICE GUIDE Fixed L £16.50-£19.95 • Fixed D £32.50 coffee £1.75 • min/water £1.50 • Service optional

OUR TIP: Do call ahead, to confirm opening times

Chef: Peter Jukes **Owners:** Peter Jukes **Times:** 12.30-1.30/7-9.30, Closed Xmas, Mon, closed L Tue **Notes:** Fixed D 4 courses (incl. coffee) £35, Vegetarian by request only **Seats:** 40 **Smoking:** N/Sm in restaurant **Children:** Min 8 yrs, Portions **Directions:** Located behind Scottish Fisheries Museum **Parking:** outside

Scotland

LUNDIN LINKS MAP 21 NO40

 Old Manor Hotel

Modern European

Fine dining with stunning views over the Firth of Forth

☎ 01333 320368 Leven Rd KY8 6AJ

MENU GUIDE Crab, lemon grass, sweet chilli dressing • Loin of lamb, rosemary risotto • Iced chocolate orange parfait

WINE GUIDE ♀ Joseph Drouhin Chardonnay £24.50 • ♥ Hawkes Bay Cabernet Sauvignon/Merlot £21 32 bottles over £20, 25 bottles under £20 • 6 by the glass (£2.50-£3.50)

PRICE GUIDE Fixed L £9.50-£17 • Fixed D £21.50-£35 • starter £3.50-£8.50 • main £12.75-£19.95 • dessert £5.25 • coffee £2.75 • min/water £3.50 • Service optional • Group min 12 service 10%

PLACE: There are two dining options at this well-located hotel. The Terrace Brasserie is in the conservatory, which enjoys superb views out over the beautiful Fife coast, and the informal grill in the Coachman's Bistro next door, much favoured by locals.
FOOD: Seafood, fish and seasonal game dominate the starters, while main courses tend towards local lamb and beef (seared medallions with a grain mustard sauce, perhaps, or a pepper-studded steak), with a separate grill section. Some traditional desserts are given a modern twist, like vanilla rice pudding crème brûlée.
OUR TIP: Take a stroll in the well-tended grounds
Chef: Roberta Drummond, James McKay **Owners:** The Clark Family **Times:** 12-5/5-10.30, Closed Sun **Notes:** Sun L roast beef, Vegetarian available, Dress Restrictions, No jeans, Civ Wed 100 **Seats:** 60, Pr/dining room 22 **Smoking:** N/Sm in restaurant, Air con **Children:** Min 10 yrs **Rooms:** 24 (24 en suite) ★★★ **Directions:** On A915 Leven St Andrews road in Lundin Links **Parking:** 100
e-mail: enquiries@oldmanorhotel.co.uk **web:** www.oldmanorhotel.co.uk

MARKINCH MAP 21 NO20

 Balbirnie House

Modern British

Accomplished cuisine in a candlelit orangery

☎ 01592 610066 Balbirnie Park KY7 6NE

MENU GUIDE Beef bresaola, lime, tomatoes, parmesan, rocket • Pork loin, creamed cabbage, sage jus • Poached pear, liquorice ice cream

WINE GUIDE ♀ Colombard Chardonnay £14.50 • ♥ Cabernet Sauvignon £14.50 • 135 bottles over £20, 48 bottles under £20 10 by the glass (£3.65-£6.75)

PRICE GUIDE Fixed L fr £11.50 • Fixed D fr £32.50 • coffee £2.50 • min/water £3.75 • Service optional

PLACE: Waiting imposingly at the end of a winding drive, this listed Georgian manor has played host to a starry list of celebrities over the years. It's a secluded haven of gracious living set in acres of scenic parkland, with a pretty glass-roofed restaurant that's candlelit by night and overlooks the gardens.
FOOD: Accomplished modern British cooking. Supporting items are chosen with care to enhance main ingredients, with dishes along the lines of salmon with mushroom cream and saffron potatoes, or duck with mixed bean gnocchi and Toulouse sausage cassoulet.
OUR TIP: The hotel has a challenging golf course
Chef: Ian MacDonald **Owners:** The Russell family **Times:** 12-2.30/7-9.30 **Notes:** Coffee incl at D, Vegetarian available, Dress Restrictions, Smart casual for dinner. No trainers, Jeans, Civ Wed 150 **Seats:** 65, Pr/dining room 216 **Smoking:** N/Sm in restaurant **Children:** Menu, Portions **Rooms:** 30 (30 en suite) ★★★★ **Directions:** M90 junct 13, follow signs for Glenrothes and Bay Bridge, right onto B9130 to Markinch and Balbirnie Park **Parking:** 100 **e-mail:** info@balbirnie.co.uk **web:** www.balbirnie.co.uk

PEAT INN MAP 21 NO40

 The Peat Inn see page 575

ST ANDREWS MAP 21 NO51

Inn at Lathones

Modern European

International cooking in 16th-century inn

☎ 01334 840494 Largoward KY9 1JE

MENU GUIDE Marinated sardine fillets, chilli dressing • Baked haddock & ginger salsa • Profiteroles, ice cream & chocolate sauce

WINE GUIDE ♀ Cape Bay Chenin Blanc £12.50 • ♥ Cape Bay Pinotage £12.50 • 102 bottles over £20, 19 bottles under £20 10 by the glass (£3.50-£5.50)

continued on page 5

PEAT INN MAP 21 NO40

The Peat Inn

French
The original restaurant with rooms
☎ 01334 840206   KY15 5LH
e-mail: reception@thepeatinn.co.uk
web: www.thepeatinn.co.uk

PLACE: From the outside this 300-year-old, whitewashed coaching inn looks like just another gastro-pub, but inside it's full of surprises: wonderfully sumptuous fabrics, gleaming crystal glasses and polished silver cutlery in the smartly decorated dining room indicate a serious homage to fine dining. There are three separate dining rooms, each with its own character in the style of a French 'auberge'. If you choose to stay overnight there are luxurious, individually styled suites in an adjacent block, split-level in design and each with an Italian-marble bathroom.

FOOD: After more than three decades running this successful enterprise, the Wilsons have it down to a fine art. The kitchen's strengths - technical proficiency, consistency, innovation and plenty of talent - yield exceptionally good results, offering a classic French cooking style utilising the finest Scottish ingredients. To showcase the chef's talents there is a tasting menu which diners should seriously consider choosing; lobsters from Anstruther, West Coast scallops and mussels, and locally supplied pigeon and fillet of beef can all be found on the menus. Notable wine list.

MENU GUIDE Monkfish medallion on herb & lobster risotto • Cassoulet of lamb, pork & duck • Little pot of chocolate & rosemary

WINE GUIDE ♀ Koura Bay Sauvignon Blanc £22 ♀ Château Haut Cheon Shiraz Grenache Mournedre £22 • 320 bottles over £20, 12 bottles under £20 2 by the glass (£3.80)

PRICE GUIDE Fixed L £22 • Fixed D £32 • starter £8-£11.50 • main £16-£22.50 • dessert £5.50-£7 • coffee £3.50 • Service optional

OUR TIP: Stay in one of the super-special rooms

Chef: David Wilson, Richard Turner   **Owners:** Mr & Mrs D Wilson
Times: 12.30-1/7-9.30, Closed 25 Dec, 1 Jan, Sun-Mon
Notes: Tasting menu £48, mineral water incl at D, Vegetarian available   **Seats:** 48, Pr/dining room 36   **Smoking:** N/Sm in restaurant   **Children:** Portions   **Rooms:** 8 (8 en suite) ★★
Directions: At junction of B940/B941, 6 miles SW of St Andrews
Parking: 24

ST ANDREWS continued MAP 21 N051

Inn at Lathones

PRICE GUIDE Fixed L £12.50 • starter £3.95-£11.50 • main £12.50-£23.50 • dessert £5.95-£9.50 • coffee £3.50 • min/water £3.50 • Service optional

PLACE: With a 400-year-old past and plenty of character, this delightful country inn was sure to be a favourite with locals and visiting golfers to nearby St Andrews. The open fires and exposed beams combine with genuinely hospitable staff to make it irresistible.

FOOD: Modern ideas from Scotland and further afield bring an interesting flavour to the various menus, ranging from a market menu to the Gastronomes choice of delicacies. Hand-dived scallops with pastrami, and Thai-flavoured crab cake indicate the breadth of the global sweep.

OUR TIP: Stay over in a smart contemporary bedroom
Chef: Martin Avey **Owners:** Mr N White **Times:** 12-2.30/6-9.30, Closed 25-26 Dec, 4-18 Jan **Notes:** Tasting menu £45.00, Vegetarian available, Dress Restrictions, Smart casual **Seats:** 34, Pr/dining room 30 **Smoking:** N/Sm in restaurant **Children:** Menu, Portions **Rooms:** 13 (13 en suite) **Directions:** 5m SW of St Andrews on A915. In 0.5m before Largoward on left, just after hidden dip **Parking:** 34 **e-mail:** lathones@theinn.co.uk **web:** www.theinn.co.uk

Macdonald Rusacks Hotel

Contemporary

Stylish split-level dining with famous views

☎ 0870 4008128 Pilmour Links KY16 9JQ

MENU GUIDE Crab bisque, Cognac cream • Loin of lamb & ratatouille • Gaelic whisky cage

WINE GUIDE ♀ Pinot Grigio £16.95 • ♀ Vegaval Clasico • 20 bottles over £20, 17 bottles under £20 • 11 by the glass (£3.75-£6.65)

PRICE GUIDE Fixed L £12.95 • Fixed D £24.95 • starter £5.50-£8.50 • main £12.50-£22.50 • dessert £5.50-£7.50 • coffee £2.95 • min/water £4

PLACE: An almost unrivalled position overlooking the renowned golf course guarantees this hotel's popularity with golfers, though not exclusively so. The stylish restaurant and classical hotel accommodation continue to exert a universal appeal.

FOOD: The modern style of cooking works well with both the tourist and local trades, with some strong dishes like chicken liver and foie gras parfait with red onion and sultana chutney and toasted brioche setting a cracking pace from the starter menu. The kitchen demonstrates good skills, timing and execution.

OUR TIP: For best views of the golf course, ask for a window seat
Chef: John Kelly **Owners:** Macdonald Hotels **Times:** 12-2.30/6.30-9, Closed L Mon-Sat **Notes:** Vegetarian available, Civ Wed 60 **Seats:** 66, Pr/dining room 65 **Smoking:** N/Sm in restaurant **Children:** Menu, Portions **Rooms:** 68 (68 en suite) ★★★★ **Directions:** From M90 junct 8 take A91 to St Andrews. Hotel on left on entering the town **Parking:** 23 **e-mail:** general.rusacks@macdonald-hotels.co.uk **web:** www.macdonald-hotels.co.uk

The Road Hole Grill

see page 577

Rufflets Country House

British

Country-house dining in beautiful surroundings

☎ 01334 472594 Strathkinness Low Rd KY16 9TX

MENU GUIDE Smoked pigeon breast, rosemary jus • Collop of venison, dauphinoise potatoes, raspberry tea syrup • Bitter chocolate tart

PRICE GUIDE Fixed D £36 • coffee £1.75 • min/water £3 • Service optional • Group min 20 service 10%

PLACE: A turreted mansion built in 1924 for the wife of a Dundee jute baron, Rufflets is set in extensive gardens and is only a few minutes' drive from the town centre. The house has been carefully extended, and personal memorabilia adds visual interest. The Garden Restaurant has recently been refurbished with bold colours and vibrant artwork.

FOOD: Dinner only is served in the restaurant, from a fixed-price three-course menu. The kitchen has a modern approach to cooking and presentation, with effective use of local ingredients. Lunch is available in the brasserie-style bar. Excellent wine list.

OUR TIP: Take a walk in the beautiful gardens
Chef: Mark Pollock **Owners:** Ann Murray-Smith **Times:** 12.30-2/7-9, Closed 2-5 Jan, closed L Mon-Sat **Notes:** Vegetarian available, Dress Restrictions, No shorts, Civ Wed 35 **Seats:** 80, Pr/dining room 80 **Smoking:** N/Sm in restaurant **Children:** Menu, Portions **Rooms:** 24 (24 en suite) ★★★ **Directions:** 1.5m west of St Andrews on B939 **Parking:** 50 **e-mail:** reservations@rufflets.co.uk **web:** www.rufflets.co.uk

Russell Hotel

French, Scottish

Imaginative food in an intimate setting

☎ 01334 473447 26 The Scores KY16 9AS

continue

The Road Hole Grill

British, Scottish

Sumptuous dining in golfing heaven

☎ 01334 474371 Old Course Hotel, Golf Resort & Spa KY16 9SP

MENU GUIDE Scottish salmon assiette • Roast Scottish lobster, scallop tortellini, bouillon • Valrhona trio

WINE GUIDE ♀ Montes Alpha Cabernet Sauvignon Curico Cuvée £34 • ♀ Koura Bay Whalesback Sauvignon Blanc £33 223 bottles over £20

PRICE GUIDE Fixed D £40 • starter £9-£13.95 • main £17.50-£29.50 • dessert £8.50-£12.75 • coffee £3.50 • min/water £4

PLACE: Expect sumptuous eating in the Grill of this renowned hotel. Dine in the Sands seafood bar or traditional Grill with its open kitchen, floor-to-ceiling window and sea views.
FOOD: Traditional classics are given a modern twist and with consistency and quality being bywords here, with full use made of seasonal, local Scottish produce. To start, expect delicate langoustine soup, trompette mushrooms and caviar crème fraîche. To follow, Angus beef with oxtail and wild mushrooms.

OUR TIP: Find time for the well-equipped spa
Chef: Drew Heron **Owners:** Jonathan Stapleton **Times:** 7-10, Closed 24-28 Dec, L all week **Notes:** Vegetarian available, No jeans. Smart dress requested, Civ Wed 150 **Seats:** 60, Pr/dining room 20 **Smoking:** N/Sm in restaurant **Children:** Menu, Portions **Rooms:** 134 (134 en suite)
★★★★★ **Directions:** Close to A91. 5 mins from St Andrews
e-mail: info@oldcoursehotel.co.uk **web:** www.oldcoursehotel.co.uk

PLACE: A comfortable and intimate hotel restaurant that would not be out of place in Paris or Brussels. The convivial atmosphere and close-packed tables are much sought after.
FOOD: The pick of the east coast's produce is strongly represented on an imaginative Scottish menu with French leanings. Roast loin of Perthshire lamb, and seared fillet of Tay salmon are joined by tender slices of duck breast with a kumquat and red onion marmalade.
OUR TIP: Charming bedrooms might tempt you to stay over
Times: 11-2.30/6.30-9.30, Closed Xmas **Rooms:** 10 (10 en suite) ★★
e-mail: russellhotel@talk21.com **web:** www.russellhotelstandrews.co.uk

🚜 St Andrews Bay Golf Resort & Spa

Mediterranean

Mediterranean cooking at golfing hotel

☎ 01334 837000 KY16 8PN

MENU GUIDE Red mullet & baby leek terrine • Fillet of veal with sweetbreads • Seville marmalade tart, blood orange sorbet

WINE GUIDE ♀ Esk Valley Hawkes Bay Sauvignon Blanc £27.50 ♀ Crest View Estate Cabernet Sauvignon £22 • 76 bottles over £20, 11 bottles under £20 • 8 by the glass (£4.30-£9.40)

PRICE GUIDE Fixed D £39.50 • coffee £2.50 • min/water £3.95 • Service optional

PLACE: Set on a windswept headland overlooking the bay, this modern hotel is flanked by its two golf courses. A central atrium forms the focal point of the hotel, with the Mediterranean-inspired fine dining Esperante restaurant overlooking the atrium.
FOOD: Unfussy presentation and a lightness of touch here, where Italian and French influences dominate the cooking and high quality local ingredients can appear in open lasagne of rabbit with shitake mushrooms or seared fillet of brill with braised fennel, aubergine caviar and garlic chips.
OUR TIP: Book a balcony table for a romantic dinner
Chef: Scott Dougall **Owners:** Dr Don Panoz & Mr Henk Evers
Times: 6.30-10, Closed Mon-Tues, closed L all wk **Notes:** Tasting menu (7 course), Dress Restrictions, No denim, Civ Wed 600 **Seats:** 60, Pr/dining room 80 **Smoking:** N/Sm in restaurant, Air con **Children:** Min 14 yrs **Rooms:** 217 (217 en suite) ★★★★★ **Parking:** 250
e-mail: info@standrewsbay.com
web: www.standrewsbay.com

🚜 denotes restaurants that place particular emphasis on making the most of local ingredients.

continued

Scotland

St Andrews Golf Hotel

Scottish, French

Contemporary cuisine in golfing hotel

☎ 01334 472611 40 The Scores KY16 9AS

MENU GUIDE Confit of duck leg, parsnip purée, honey jus • Lamb, chanterelles, fondant potatoes, piquant sauce • Chocolate fondant

WINE GUIDE ♀ J & F Lurton Les Salice Sauvignon Blanc £13.50 • ♀ Angoves Butterfly Ridge Shiraz/Cabernet £13.75 61 bottles over £20, 32 bottles under £20 • 5 by the glass (£3.75-£4.25)

PRICE GUIDE Fixed L £9.50 • Fixed D £28.50 • coffee £2 min/water £3.50 • Service optional

PLACE: Friendly family-run hotel with stunning views of the coastline and famous golf course. Professional staff are on hand in the wood-panelled dining room with smartly set tables.
FOOD: Honest modern cooking that delivers on its promises. There's no shortage of skill in the kitchen, and dishes are pleasingly simple and based around fine Scottish produce. Arrive hungry as portions are hearty.
OUR TIP: Great value lunch menu
Chef: Mark Pollock **Owners:** Justin Hughes **Times:** 12.30-2/7-9.30, Closed 26-28 Dec **Notes:** Vegetarian available, Dress Restrictions, No jeans, shorts, trainers, baseball caps, Civ Wed 180 **Seats:** 60, Pr/dining room 20 **Smoking:** N/Sm in restaurant, Air con **Children:** Menu, Portions **Rooms:** 21 (21 en suite) ★★★ **Directions:** Enter town on A91, cross both mini rdbts, turn left at Golf Place and 1st right into The Scores. Hotel 200 yds on right **Parking:** 5
e-mail: reception@standrews-golf.co.uk **web:** www.standrews-golf.co.uk

Sands Bar & Restaurant

Mediterranean   **NEW**

Stylish brasserie within the Old Course Hotel

☎ 01334 474371&468228 The Old Course Hotel, KY16 9SP

MENU GUIDE Home-cured bresaola, roasted figs • Osso buco, rocket & roasted vegetables • Classic Tiramisù

WINE GUIDE 24 bottles over £20 • 18 by the glass (£4.50)

PRICE GUIDE Starter £6.25-£10.50 • main £14.50-£21.50 • dessert £5.50 • coffee £2.95 • min/water £4 • Service included

PLACE: St Andrews Old Course Hotel needs no introduction, especially to golfing enthusiasts, and this, its second restaurant, is one more feather in its illustrious cap. It provides a cool, elegant setting under a lofty ceiling.
FOOD: A crisp, upbeat menu offers a short choice that includes antipasto for two, intermezzo/salads, and some memorable desserts like cinnamon pannacotta. Several dishes marked for healthy eating are ideal for the calorie-conscious diner.
OUR TIP: Try a great latte, cappuccino or espresso
Chef: Mark Lindsey **Times:** 12.00-6.00/6.00-10.00, Closed 22-28 Dec
Notes: Vegetarian available, Smart casual, Civ Wed 200 **Seats:** 80, Pr/dining room 40 **Smoking:** N/Sm in restaurant **Children:** Menu, Portions **Directions:** M90 junct 8. Situated close to A91 and 5 mins walk from St Andrews **Parking:** 100
e-mail: reservations@oldcoursehotel.co.uk
web: www.oldcoursehotel.co.uk

The Seafood Restaurant

Seafood

Accomplished cooking in stunning glass building by the bay

☎ 01334 479475 The Scores KY16 9AS

MENU GUIDE Seared scallop & foie gras, beans & pesto • Baked halibut, shellfish risotto, Thai coconut sauce • Pineapple pain perdu

WINE GUIDE ♀ Maison Blondells Pouilly Fumé £26 • ♀ Albert Morel Fleurie £19 • 152 bottles over £20, 11 bottles under £20 • 9 by the glass (£4-£6)

PRICE GUIDE Fixed L fr £20 • Fixed D fr £40 • coffee £2.75 • min/water £3.50 • Group min 8 service 10%

PLACE: Stunning glass-walled building virtually suspended over the bay, with views of West Sands and St Andrews golf course. Sister to the Seafood Restaurant at St Monans, down the coast, where Tim Butler and Craig Millar first joined forces, the restaurant is uncompromisingly contemporary in style with an open-plan kitchen and clean interior decor.

FOOD: Craig and his team cook in full view of diners, adding much to the anticipatory excitement. There's a huge emphasis on ingredients, with classic combinations mixed up with some quite daring juxtapositions. Pan-seared fillet of sea bass with tapenade crisped skin, tomato chutney, curly kale, wild mushrooms, pine kernels and rösti potato with Sauternes sauce sounds complicated, but most of the ingredients combine to form a hot salad as a base for the perfectly cooked bass. You can expect some variety in the wine list too, as the restaurant's team of experienced wine enthusiasts descend en masse to wine tastings, and everyone has their say.
OUR TIP: Last year's AA Restaurant of the Year for Scotland
Chef: Craig Millar **Owners:** Craig Millar, Tim Butler **Times:** 12-2.30/6.30-10.00, Closed 25-26 Dec, Jan 1 **Notes:** Vegetarian by request only **Seats:** 60 **Smoking:** N/Sm area, Air con **Children:** Min 12 yrs, Portions **Parking:** 50m away **e-mail:** info@theseafoodrestaurant.com
web: www.theseafoodrestaurant.com

ST ANDREWS

 The Seafood Restaurant

see page 578

ST MONANS MAP 21 NO50

 The Seafood Restaurant

Seafood

Harbour-side seafood eatery

☎ 01333 730327 16 West End KY10 2BX

MENU GUIDE Lobster cocktail, tomato sorbet • Halibut, curried shellfish risotto, pea velouté • Lemon thyme pannacotta, strawberry sauce

WINE GUIDE ♀ Kim Krawford Sauvignon £20 • ♟ Jeff Merrill Shiraz £23 • 79 bottles over £20, 18 bottles under £20 • 6 by the glass (£4-£5)

PRICE GUIDE Fixed L fr £20 • Fixed D fr £35 • min/water £3.50

PLACE: Just 15 minutes drive from St Andrews, this light modern restaurant occupies a former fisherman's cottage in the picturesque village of St Monans. A harbour-side setting makes for stunning views, as do large windows and the dining room's circular design, which ensures most tables offer a glimpse of crashing waves. Alfresco dining in summer.

FOOD: Great ingredients and a touch of imagination result in a menu of tempting dishes, such as cod with smoked bacon mash and onion ice cream, or scallops with noodles, mussels and coriander. The restaurant holds regular wine tasting events with matched meals.

OUR TIP: Great value lunch menu

Chef: George Scott **Owners:** Roybridge Ltd **Times:** 12-2.30/6-9.30, Closed 25-26 Dec,1-2 Jan, Mon, Tues **Seats:** 44 **Smoking:** N/Sm in restaurant **Children:** Portions **Directions:** Take A959 from St Andrews o Anstruther, then head W on A917 through Pittenweem. In St Monans to harbour then right **Parking:** 10 **e-mail:** info@theseafoodrestaurant.com **web:** www.theseafoodrestaurant.com

CITY OF GLASGOW

GLASGOW MAP 20 NS56

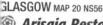 **Arisaig Restaurant & Bar**

Scottish

Unique Scottish dining in Glasgow

☎ 0141 552 4251 Merchant City, 24 Candleriggs G1 1LD

PLACE: Flickering candles, moody black and white seascapes and bright oil paintings bring Scotland's rugged west coast to the heart of Glasgow.

FOOD: The motto seems to be 'keep it simple, keep it Scottish.' Arisaig specialises in resurrecting traditional Scottish ingredients, so watch out for kale, nettles, and red seaweed on the menu, as well as a hearty spattering of haggis and quality whisky.

OUR TIP: A must for haggis lovers

Times: 12-3/5-12, Closed L Mon-Thu, 26 Dec & 1 Jan **e-mail:** info@arisagrestaurant.com

La Bonne Auberge

French, Mediterranean

Popular restaurant with a good range of menu deals

☎ 0141 352 8310 Holiday Inn Theatreland, 161 West Nile St G1 2RL

MENU GUIDE Lobster & crab bisque • Pork cutlet, emmenthal & Chinese shallot mash, apple & rosemary sauce, Stornoway black pudding • Warm pear & frangipane tart

WINE GUIDE ♀ Ca'Lungheith Pinot Grigio £13.95 • ♟ Katherine Hills Shiraz/Cabernet Sauvignon £13.95 • 11 bottles over £20, 20 bottles under £20 • 4 by the glass (£3-£4.75)

PRICE GUIDE Fixed L £7.50-£12.95 • Fixed D £17.95-£23.95 starter £4.50-£7.50 • main £8-£20 • dessert £5-£7.50 • coffee £2.25 • min/water £3.50 • Service added but optional 10%

PLACE: Handy for the shops and theatreland, La Bonne Auberge in the city's contemporary Holiday Inn is a popular French brasserie-style restaurant.

FOOD: The repertoire plays to the crowd, with a range of accomplished, honest, modern dishes. Menu variations include fixed-priced options, specialities and grills to suit every occasion, pocket and taste.

OUR TIP: Keep an eye on special promotions

Chef: Gerry Sharkey **Owners:** Chardon Leisure Ltd **Times:** 12-2.15/5-10 **Notes:** Vegetarian available **Seats:** 90, Pr/dining room 100 **Smoking:** N/Sm area, No pipes, No cigars, Air con **Children:** Menu, Portions **Rooms:** 113 (113 en suite) ★★★ **Directions:** Telephone for directions **e-mail:** info@higlasgow.com **web:** www.labonneauberge.co.uk

Brian Maule at Chardon d'Or

French, British

Smart, modern city-centre restaurant

☎ 0141 248 3801 176 West Regent St G2 4RL

MENU GUIDE Confit duck & foie gras, pear salad • Roast monkfish, horseradish-flavoured spaghetti, light jus • Apple tarte Tatin, vanilla ice cream

WINE GUIDE ♀ Le Verger Chablis Chardonnay £24.75 • ♟ Laboure Roi Pinot Noir £29.85 • 145 bottles over £20, 5 bottles under £20 • 4 by the glass (£4.25-£4.95)

PRICE GUIDE Fixed L £15.50 • starter £5.50-£9.50 • main £19-£23 • dessert £6.25-£6.50 • coffee £3.50 • min/water £3.50 • Service optional

PLACE: This stylish, cool, chef-driven, cosmopolitan restaurant, situated in a terraced property off Blythwood Square, draws an appreciative crowd.

continued

Scotland

GLASGOW *continued* MAP 20 NS56

FOOD: Unsurprising for a former Le Gavroche head chef, menus are modern-focused but underpinned by a classical French theme. With a good-value lunch, a celebration menu and a pretheatre menu backing up the appealing carte, this restaurant will have you spoilt for choice.

OUR TIP: Enjoy a power lunch

Chef: Brian Maule **Owners:** Brian Maule at Chardon d'Or **Times:** 12-2.30/6-10.30, Closed 2 wks Jan, 2 wks Summer & BHs, Sun, closed L Sat **Notes:** Pre Theatre 2 courses £15.50, 3 courses £18.50, Vegetarian available **Seats:** 90, Pr/dining room 60 **Smoking:** N/Sm in restaurant **Children:** Portions **Directions:** 10 minute walk from Glasgow central station **Parking:** Metered parking on street **e-mail:** info@brianmaule.com **web:** www.brianmaule.com

The Buttery

British, International

Vibrant flavours in Glaswegian grandee

☎ 0141 221 8188 652 Argyle St G3 8UF

MENU GUIDE Trio of Scottish shellfish • Venison, goats' cheese & tarragon spätzle, cranberry & crab apple chutney • Calvados brûlée

WINE GUIDE ♀ Barossa Valley Estates Chardonnay £27 ♀ Casa la Joya Cabernet Sauvignon £26 • 77 bottles over £20, 4 bottles under £20 • 8 by the glass (£4-£5.50)

PRICE GUIDE Fixed L £16 • Fixed D £38 • starter £5-£6 • main £12-£15 • dessert £5-£6 • coffee £2.50 • min/water £3 • Service optional

PLACE: Set in a quiet part of town behind a low-key frontage, this Glasgow veteran wears its heritage lightly - at least on the outside. The city's oldest restaurant, it dates back to 1869, and has a luxurious decor that combines original Victorian fittings with fashionable modern touches.

FOOD: First-rate modern Scottish cooking from Willie Deans and his team that your taste buds will savour. This is heady stuff - fresh and vibrant flavours brought together in nicely judged combinations. Choose from the carte or a budget fixed-price menu at lunch.

OUR TIP: Get directions before you set out

Chef: Willie Deans **Owners:** Ian Fleming **Times:** 12-2/7-10, Closed 25-26 Dec, 1-2 Jan, Sun, Mon, closed L Sat **Notes:** Vegetarian available **Seats:** 60, Pr/dining room 40 **Smoking:** N/Sm in restaurant, Air con **Children:** Portions **Directions:** From St Vincent St (city centre) first left onto Elderslie St, at rdbt, left onto Argyle St. Restaurant 600 yds on left **Parking:** 36

Cafe Ostra

Seafood

Relaxed seafood café in Glasgow's Italian centre

☎ 0141 552 4433 The Italian Centre, 15 John St G1 1HP

MENU GUIDE Fish soup with crab, ginger & herb oil • Salmon & leek quiche, green salad • Sticky toffee pudding, vanilla ice cream

WINE GUIDE ♀ Cantavida Sauvignon Blanc £12.95 • ♀ Vina Borgia Garnacha £12.95 • 13 bottles over £20, 14 bottles under £20 • 9 by the glass (£3.50-£5.50)

PRICE GUIDE Starter £4.50-£9.95 • main £7.50-£14.95 • dessert £4.50-£5.95 • coffee £1.60 • min/water £3.15 • Service optional • Group min 6 service 10%

Cafe Ostra

PLACE: Laid-back seafood restaurant that caters to a friendly mix of students, shoppers and suits. Unclothed tables and low lighting create a down-to-earth bistro atmosphere, aided by a toe-tapping jazz soundtrack.

FOOD: This is a kitchen that respects its ingredients. Seafood is handled simply, so that flavours are preserved rather than lost in complex cooking procedures. Meanwhile, the few non-fish options aim to please, and might include steak with caramelised onion mash.

OUR TIP: A great place to pop into

Chef: John Gillespie **Owners:** Alan Tomkins & Derek Marshall **Times:** 11-10, Closed 25-26 Dec, 1-2 Jan **Notes:** Vegetarian available **Seats:** 80, Pr/dining room 15 **Smoking:** N/Sm area, Air con **Children:** Portions **Directions:** Heart of Glasgow City Centre, 2 min from George Square **Parking:** NCP car park Glassford Street **e-mail:** info@cafeostra.com **web:** www.cafeostra.com

étain

British, French

AA Restaurant of the Year for Scotland

☎ 0141 225 5630 Princes Square G1 3JX

MENU GUIDE Poached Loch Fyne oysters, Champagne sabayon • Grilled beef rib, bacon, wild mushrooms • Banana soufflé, caramel ice cream

WINE GUIDE ♀ Plantagenet Omrah Sauvignon Blanc £24.50 • ♀ Château Grand-Puy-Lacoste-Borie Cabernet/Merlot £36 • 234 bottles over £20, 16 bottles under £20 • 8 by the glass (£4-£7.25)

PRICE GUIDE Fixed L £21 • Fixed D £32 • coffee £2.85 min/water £2.95 • Service added but optional 12.5%

PLACE: Accessed by lift from the street or through Zinc bar and brasserie, this emphatically contemporary restaurant is located on the top storey of a glass-fronted building. The interior is styled in wood, leather and earthy colours - typically Conran - set against shining pewter-clad pillars. ('Etain' is French for pewter - a metal rather more precious than zinc.)

FOOD: Very competent cooking with clear technical skills, high quality Scottish produce and strong flavours - modern British menu with strong French overtones. There's a daily carte with a vegetarian option and a six-course epicurean menu. Excellent wine list.

OUR TIP: Smart place to be seen at affordable prices

Chef: Geoffery Smeddle **Owners:** Conran Restaurants Ltd **Times:** 12-2.30/7-11, Closed 25 Dec & 1 Jan, closed L Sat, closed D Sun **Notes:** Tasting menu £39, Vegetarian available **Seats:** 65 **Smoking:** N/Sm in restaurant, Air con **Parking:** NCP Mitchell Street, street parking available **e-mail:** etain@conran.com **web:** www.etain-restaurant.co.uk

continued

⊛⊛ Gamba
Seafood

Modern city-centre restaurant focusing on fish
☎ 0141 572 0899 225a West George St G2 2ND

MENU GUIDE Warm salad of scallops • Snapper with garlic gravy • Blackcurrant, cassis & champagne jelly

WINE GUIDE ♀ Trinity Hill Sauvignon Blanc • ♂ Trinity Hill Pinot Noir £17.95 • 50 bottles over £20, 10 bottles under £20 8 by the glass (£4.50-£7)

PRICE GUIDE Fixed L £15.95 • starter £8-£12 • main £13-£25 dessert £5-£8 • coffee £2.25 • min/water £3.25 • Service optional • Group min 6 service 10%

PLACE: Warm colours, light woods and soft lighting combine to create an appealing atmosphere that just hints of the Mediterranean, despite the northerliness of the latitude. A small bar area enhances the spacious dining room.
FOOD: Seafood and fish, the subjects of the artwork, dominate the menu where Asian influences conspire with those of several other global regions to define the food style. It's not all fruits de mer, with fillet of Angus beef, and asparagus, blue cheese and apple risotto perhaps making an appearance.
OUR TIP: Don't miss the fish soup
Chef: Derek Marshall **Owners:** Mr A C Tomkins & Mr D Marshall
Times: 12-2.30/5-10.30, Closed 25-26 Dec, 1-2 Jan, BHs, Sun
Notes: Vegetarian available **Seats:** 66 **Smoking:** N/Sm in restaurant, Air con **Children:** Min 14 yrs **Directions:** Telephone for directions
e-mail: info@gamba.co.uk **web:** www.gamba.co.uk

⊛ Killermont Polo Club
Indian

Great value Indian eaterie with polo theme
☎ 0141 946 5412 2002 Maryhill Rd, Maryhill Park G20 0AB

MENU GUIDE Jhinga tikka • Murgh laziz • Gulab jamon

WINE GUIDE ♀ Cachile Villa Rose £13.75 • ♂ Rocheburg Pinotage, Western Cape £16.25 • 9 bottles over £20, 18 bottles under £20 • 4 by the glass (£2.75-£3.50)

PRICE GUIDE Fixed L £6.95-£8.95 • Fixed D £11.95 • starter £2.95-£6.95 • main £5.95-£15.95 • dessert £2.50-£3.50 • coffee £1.50 • min/water £3.75

PLACE: A former manse is an unusual setting for an Indian restaurant, but then Killermont is no ordinary Indian, as its distinctive polo-themed decor declares from the off.
FOOD: A traditional court cuisine, dum pukht, is the speciality, so this is your chance to eat like a Moghul emperor. Sound Indian cooking, with a great value two-for-the-price-of-one offer available at lunchtime.
OUR TIP: Be warned: the hot dishes here aren't for the faint of stomach

continued

Chef: Belbir Farwaha **Owners:** P Thapar **Times:** 12-2.30/5-11.30, Closed New Year **Notes:** Vegetarian available, Smart Dress **Seats:** 80, Pr/dining room 30 **Smoking:** N/Sm area **Children:** Menu, Portions
Directions: Telephone for directions **Parking:** 40
web: www.killermontpoloclub.co.uk

⊛⊛ Langs Hotel
Contemporary Scottish

Fine dining in a modern city-centre hotel
☎ 0141 333 1500 2 Port Dundas Place G2 3LD

MENU GUIDE Scallop & lobster risotto • Loin of Highland venison • Chocolate & crisp praline mousse

WINE GUIDE ♀ Veramonte Sauvignon Blanc £19 • ♂ Kleine Zalze Cabernet Sauvignon £18 • 28 bottles over £20, 20 bottles under £20 • 12 by the glass (£3.25-£5.95)

PRICE GUIDE Fixed D £15.50 • starter £3.75-£5.50 • main £8.75-£19 • dessert £4.25-£6 • coffee £1.65 • min/water £2.75 • Service optional

PLACE: Glasgow's vibrant theatreland is home to this chic and stylish hotel where you can relax in comfort and watch the world go by. Dine in the mezzanine-level Aurora where the friendly, attentive service is one of the many attractions.
FOOD: The importance of sourcing quality Scottish produce is detailed on the dinner menu, where Orkney scallops and lobster, Highland venison, Perthshire lamb and Shetland salmon are among the ingredients handled with a light touch that maintains the natural intensity of their flavours.
OUR TIP: Very handy for theatreland
Chef: Craig Dunn **Owners:** Prestwick Hotels Ltd **Times:** 5-10, Closed Sun, Mon, closed L all wk **Notes:** Vegetarian available, Dress Restrictions, Smart casual preferred, no trainers, Civ Wed 120 **Seats:** 50
Smoking: N/Sm in restaurant, Air con **Children:** Portions **Rooms:** 100 (100 en suite) ★★★★ **Directions:** Telephone for directions
Parking: 1200 spaces available, discounted
e-mail: cathy.owen@langshotel.co.uk **web:** www.langshotels.co.uk

⊛ The Living Room
British

Dynamic restaurant with a real buzz to it
☎ 0870 220 3028 150 St Vincent St G2 5NE

MENU GUIDE Roast leek & mushroom tart, gorgonzola & pesto • Grilled lamb cutlets, sweet onion marmalade • Hot chocolate fudge cake

WINE GUIDE ♀ Chablis Deloux £26.50 • ♂ Oomoo Shiraz £28 • 18 bottles over £20, 15 bottles under £20 • 5 by the glass (£3.75-£5)

PRICE GUIDE Starter £3.45-£5.75 • main £5.95-£15.95 • dessert £4.25-£4.75 • coffee £1.25 • min/water £3.95 • Service optional • Group min 6 service 10%

continued

GLASGOW *continued* MAP 20 NS56

PLACE: Formerly Eurasia, and then Opus, the restaurant has been transformed into a richly furnished dining room with acres of leather, dark wood partitions, mood lighting, a smooth sound track and appealingly informal service.
FOOD: Cutting edge menu to satisfy both the grazing public and the serious diner expecting the works. Pacific Rim fusion dishes sit alongside fish and chips, with home comforts, lunch club and salad options.
OUR TIP: Outstanding value for money
Chef: Raymond Corrie **Owners:** Living Ventures **Times:** 11am-mdnt, Closed 25-26 Dec, 1-2 Jan, BHs **Notes:** Sun brunch menu, Vegetarian available **Seats:** 140, Pr/dining room 11 **Smoking:** Air con **Children:** Menu, Portions **Directions:** City Centre location between Hope St & Wellington St **Parking:** On street
e-mail: glasgow@thelivingroom.co.uk
web: www.thelivingroom.co.uk

Lux
Modern Scottish
Converted station building with exemplary cooking
☎ 0141 576 7576 1051 Great Western Rd G12 0XP

MENU GUIDE Tomato & dahl lentil soup • Pan-fried duck, apple & black pudding risotto • Lemon meringue pie, dark berry compôte

WINE GUIDE 36 bottles over £20, 6 bottles under £20 • 4 by the glass (£3.95-£4.25)

PRICE GUIDE Fixed L £26 • Fixed D £35.50 • coffee £1.80 min/water £3.45 • Service optional • Group min 6 service 10%

PLACE: A stylish conversion on the first floor of a Victorian railway station, with smartly set tables given plenty of space across the polished wooden floor. A mixture of banquettes and dining chairs assures guest comfort, and service is pleasantly attentive.
FOOD: The unusual combination of ingredients featured on the short menu contribute to Lux's success, with an exactness of cooking and well-prepared sauces that make this place stand out. Some popular staples also appear, but include more unusual dishes like pork fillet with mango salsa and coriander cream cheese mash.
OUR TIP: Ask about the special early dining promotions
Chef: Stephen Johnson **Owners:** Stephen Johnson **Times:** 6, Closed 25-26 Dec, 1-2 Jan, Sun ex by arrangement, closed L all week ex by arrangement **Notes:** Vegetarian available, Smart casual **Seats:** 64, Pr/dining room 14 **Smoking:** N/Sm area, No pipes, No cigars, Air con **Children:** Min 12 yrs **Directions:** At traffic lights signed Gartnavel Hospital, on Great Western Rd. 0.25m E of Anniesland Cross **Parking:** 16
e-mail: luxstazione@bt.connect.com **web:** www.lux.5pm.co.uk

Malmaison
Traditional French, British
French brasserie food in stylish church conversion
☎ 0141 572 1001 278 West George St G2 4LL

MENU GUIDE Seared foie gras, apple compôte • Confit of duck, Sarladeise potatoes, tarragon jus • Mango pannacotta, passionfruit coulis

PRICE GUIDE Food prices not confirmed for 2006. Please telephone for details

PLACE: A stylish conversion of an old church in the historic Charing Cross area houses the latest addition to the Malmaison chain. To enter the atmospheric brasserie, located in the former crypt, you must go down a spiral staircase to reach the restaurant below.
FOOD: French brasserie style has been given a clean, contemporary reworking, with simple dishes making the most of quality produce and artful combinations.
OUR TIP: Wine advice from newly installed sommeliers
Times: 12-2.30/5.30-10.30 **Rooms:** 72 (72 en suite) ★★★
Directions: From George Square take Vincent Street to Pitt Street. Hotel on corner with West George Street **e-mail:** glasgow@malmaison.com
web: www.malmaison.com

Millennium Hotel Glasgow
British   NEW
Superb Scottish ingredients in modern stylish brasserie
☎ 0141 332 6711 George St G2 1DS

MENU GUIDE Scallops, black pudding, pommes soufflé, pancetta crisps • Lamb rump, tomato confit, jus • Banana & praline parfait

WINE GUIDE ♀ Crusan Colombard-Sauvignon £14.95 • ♀ Crusan Granache-Merlot £14.95 • 19 bottles over £20, 31 bottles under £20 • 10 by the glass (£3.50-£8.95)

PRICE GUIDE Fixed L £9-£15 • Fixed D £15-£17.95 • starter £5.25-£9 • main £11.50-£22.50 • dessert £4.60-£7.25 • coffee £2.50 • min/water £4.50 • Service optional

PLACE: A modern, minimalistic design rarely evokes an invitation of appealing warmth, yet this is effortlessly achieved within this eye-catching hotel dining room. Stripped wooden floors, multi-shades of beiges and browns, palm fronds and smartly appointed tables all blend seamlessly together.
FOOD: Menus unashamedly showcase Scotland's natural larder of seafood and game. Cooking style and presentation is simple and uncomplicated allowing the honest, first-class flavours of the superbly fresh ingredients to burst through.
OUR TIP: Take a conservatory seat and watch the world go by
Chef: Stewart Goldie **Owners:** Millennium & Copthorne Hotels
Times: 12-2.15/6-10.15, Closed 25-26 Dec, closed L Sun
Notes: Vegetarian available, Smart Dress **Seats:** 140, Pr/dining room 40 **Smoking:** N/Sm area, No pipes, No cigars, Air con **Children:** Menu, Portions **Rooms:** 117 (117 en suite) ★★★★ **Directions:** M8 junct 15, follow directions to George Square, brasserie is in Millennium Hotel
Parking: On street, NCP **e-mail:** reservations.glasgow@mill-cop.com
web: www.millenniumhotels.com

The AA Wine Awards recognise the finest wine lists in England, Scotland and Wales. For full details, see pages 14-15

Scotland

No5 Restaurant

British, European

Intimate restaurant at renowned boutique hotel

☎ 0141 339 2001 One Devonshire Gardens Hotel, Devonshire Gardens G12 0UX

MENU GUIDE Foie gras parfait, pear chutney • John Dory, scallop mousseline • Cherry assiette (tart, compôte, sorbet)

WINE GUIDE ♀ Pouilly Fumé Patrice Moreux Sauvignon Blanc • ♀ Domaine de Fontabou Gamay Fleurie • 60 bottles over £20, 2 bottles under £20 • 6 by the glass (£4.95)

PRICE GUIDE Fixed D £39-£42 • coffee £3 • min/water £3.50 • Service optional

PLACE: An elegant, intimate restaurant set in one of Glasgow's premier-league hotels, the boutique-style One Devonshire Gardens, which has been created from five Victorian townhouses. The aptly named restaurant is in the fifth, and is discreet and understated, elegantly furnished and professionally staffed.
FOOD: The modern approach - with classical grounding and European influence - extends to the cooking, which utilises the best of Scottish produce on appealing, sensibly compact, fixed-price, seasonal menus. There's a vegetarian plat du jour main course on the concise repertoire, with at least one starter catering for non-meat eaters too.
OUR TIP: It's a sin not to stay over to enjoy the luxurious bedrooms
Chef: David Clark **Owners:** Citrus Hotels **Times:** 6.30-10.15, Closed 25-26 Dec, closed L Private lunches only **Notes:** Vegetarian available, Civ Wed 48 **Seats:** Pr/dining room 50 **Smoking:** N/Sm in restaurant **Children:** Portions **Rooms:** 36 (38 en suite) ★★★★ **Directions:** M8 Junct 17, follow signs for A82 after 1.5 miles turn left into Hyndland Rd **Parking:** Parking available, residential area
e-mail: events@onedevonshiregardens.com
web: www.onedevonshiregardens.com

Papingo Restaurant

Modern Scottish

Well-established city-centre restaurant with a modern menu

☎ 0141 332 6678 104 Bath St G2 2EN

MENU GUIDE Thai-spiced salmon, chilli jam • Roast rump of lamb • Steamed chocolate pudding, apricot coulis

WINE GUIDE ♀ Côte du Rhône £18.95 • ♀ Castillo de Montblanc £14.95 • 15 bottles over £20, 20 bottles under £20 8 by the glass (£3.90-£5.90)

PRICE GUIDE Fixed L £7.95 • Fixed D £15 • starter £4.95-£6.95 • main £12.95-£20.95 • dessert £4.95 • coffee £2.25 • min/water £2.95 • Group min 6 service 10%

PLACE: A bright, uncluttered restaurant in a split-level basement, with light wood floors and wooden-topped tables. Understated artwork helps to break up the extensive space.
FOOD: The modern Scottish cooking is consistently produced, with the short lunch menu (very good value) and evening carte reflecting the seasons. Expect shitake mushroom risotto, roast breast of guinea fowl, and tournedos of pork from an autumn showing.
OUR TIP: Check out the special offers
Chef: David Clunas **Owners:** Mr A Tomkins **Times:** 12-2.30/5-10.30, Closed 25-26 Dec, 1-2 Jan, BH Mon, closed L Sun **Notes:** Vegetarian available **Seats:** 75 **Smoking:** N/Sm area, No pipes, Air con **Children:** Portions **Directions:** City centre. At junct of Bath St & Hope St **Parking:** NCP 50 yds **e-mail:** info@papingo.co.uk **web:** www.papingo.co.uk

Quigley's

Modern

One of the city's popular eating and drinking venues

☎ 0141 331 4060 158 Bath St G2 4TB

PLACE: High vaulted ceilings, wooden floors, plain mirrored walls lined with dark banquettes and cloth-clad chairs hit exactly the right note at this Victorian-era building - formerly an auction house - now a popular three-in-one restaurant, bar and nightclub.
FOOD: The brasserie-style menus (the 'Lowdown') play to the gallery with simple, balanced, modern combinations and competitive prices. Service is predictably youthful, but attentive and friendly.
OUR TIP: Ideal for pre- and post-theatre, with free parking outside after 6pm
Times: 5-10.45, Closed L all, Sun, 25 Dec, 1 Jan
e-mail: mail@quigleysglasgow.com **web:** www.quigleysglasgow.com

Rococo

French, Scottish

Chic basement eaterie, one of Glasgow's best

☎ 0141 221 5004 202 West George St G2 2NR

continued   *continued*

Scotland

GLASGOW *continued* MAP 20 NS56

MENU GUIDE Oven roasted crown of quail • Boneless saddle of Normandy rabbit • Banana three ways

WINE GUIDE ♀ John Hancock Trinity Hill Sauvignon Blanc £28 • ♀ Marques des Caceres Tempranillo £39 • 210 bottles over £20, 19 bottles under £20 • 8 by the glass (£5-£6.75)

PRICE GUIDE Fixed L £14 • Fixed D £36.50 • starter £6.75-£8.50 • main £16.50-£22.50 • dessert £6.50-£7.50 • coffee £3.50 • Service optional • Group min 6 service 10%

PLACE: Though it occupies a basement in the heart of the city, there's a hint of clear starry nights from the sparkly lights dotting the ceiling. Bold modern glass pieces and artwork add to the chic effect, and service is formal and exact.

FOOD: An additional choice of menus caters for business lunches, theatre-goers and very early diners, with a set two- or three-course dinner. Fresh produce using the finest ingredients and light portions are sometimes reminiscent of nouvelle cuisine, with a mixture of traditional and contemporary styles.

OUR TIP: Ideal for business lunches

Chef: Mark Tamburrini **Owners:** Alan & Audrey Brown **Times:** 12-3/5-10, Closed 1 Jan, Sun **Notes:** Vegetarian available **Seats:** 60, Pr/dining room 30 **Smoking:** N/Sm area, No pipes, Air con **Children:** Menu **Directions:** City centre **Parking:** On street parking or NCP **e-mail:** res@rococoglasgow.com **web:** www.rococoglasgow.com

Room

British, Contemporary   NEW

Old school cuisine in chic brasserie

☎ 0141 341 0000 1 Devonshire Gardens G12 0UX

MENU GUIDE Prawn & avocado cocktail • Posh pie & peas • Fruit crumble, ice cream

WINE GUIDE ♀ Loire Sauvignon Les Nuages Sancerre £19.50 • ♀ Spy Valley Pinot Noir £27 • 18 bottles over £20, 19 bottles under £20 • 17 by the glass (£3.25-£5.75)

PRICE GUIDE Fixed L £16.50-£20 • Fixed D £18.50-£25 • starter £5.25 • main £14.75 • dessert £5-£12 • coffee £2.30 • min/water £3 • Service added but optional 10%

PLACE: Part of the prestigious hotel complex that is One Devonshire Gardens, this upmarket brasserie strives for a laid-back neighbourhood feel and comprises a lounge bar and smart dining room.

FOOD: No-nonsense British cuisine with an element of fun. Room aims to suit most tastes and pockets, with dishes ranging from fish and chips to halibut Veronique, and duck 'pot noodle'. Lunch is straightforward, while dinner sees the introduction of more complex options.

OUR TIP: Vegetarian menu also available

Chef: Mark Greenaway **Owners:** John Pallagi, Simon Wright **Times:** 11-10 **Notes:** Vegetarian available, Civ Wed 20 **Seats:** 130, Pr/dining room 50 **Smoking:** N/Sm in restaurant **Children:** Portions **Directions:** 10 mins from city centre, situated in West End district **Parking:** 20 **e-mail:** glasgowreception@roomrestaurants.com **web:** www.roomrestaurants.com

Saint Judes

Modern British

Stylish restaurant in Victorian town house

☎ 0141 352 8800 190 Bath St G2 4HG

MENU GUIDE Parma ham & spinach crêpes, wensleydale sauce • Seafood in a saffron nage, sautéed potatoes • Vanilla soufflé, baby apples

WINE GUIDE ♀ Lafitte Chablis Chardonnay £23 • ♀ Portone Valpolicella £15 • 15 bottles over £20, 13 bottles under £20 6 by the glass (£3.50-£3.95)

PRICE GUIDE Food prices not confirmed for 2006. Telephone for details

PLACE: Slick, relaxed, unpretentious minimalism meets Victorian grandeur at this first-floor city-centre restaurant and basement bar. Polished wooden floors, banquettes - some arranged in bays - striking contemporary art and black-clad staff set a modern tone.

FOOD: The kitchen moves with the times and a degree of innovation, the populist menus ranging from cha-cha monkfish with stir-fry vegetables and egg noodles to an unusual greengage and damson Tatin with mascarpone.

OUR TIP: Good value set prices at lunchtime

Chef: Jenny Burn **Owners:** Jenny Burn, Walter Barratt **Times:** 12-2.30/5-10.30, Closed 25 Dec, 1-2 Jan, closed L Sat-Sun **Notes:** Vegetarian available, Civ Wed 33 **Seats:** 60, Pr/dining room 25 **Smoking:** No pipes, Air con **Children:** Portions **Directions:** City centre **Parking:** On street, NCP **e-mail:** reservations@saintjudes.com **web:** www.saintjudes.com

Shish Mahal

British, Indian

Heady tandoori nights in town

☎ 0141 339 8256 & 334 7899 60-68 Park Rd G4 9JF

MENU GUIDE Chicken Tikka tandoori • Shish Special bhoona

WINE GUIDE ♀ Chablis £19.95 • ♀ Shiraz £14.95 • 1 by the glass (£2.70)

PRICE GUIDE Fixed D £15.95-£19.95 • starter £1.95-£6.95 • main £5.95-£14.95 • dessert £1.70-£3.50 • coffee £1.15 • min/water £3.95 • Service optional • Group min 5 service 10%

PLACE: For over 30 years the Shish Mahal, in the trendy west end of Glasgow, has established a huge following thanks to its smart, attentive service and mind-boggling choice of dishes.

FOOD: The North Indian cuisine gets the best out of the traditional tandoor oven, and sets standards for others in Scotland. 'Ali's Old Favourites' on the menu are specially recommended.

OUR TIP: Lunch set-price menus offer especially good value

Chef: Mr I Humayun **Owners:** Ali A Aslam, Nasim Ahmed **Times:** 12-2/5-11, Closed Xmas, closed L Sun **Notes:** Fixed L 4 courses £5.50-6.75, Sun D 5-11pm, Vegetarian available **Seats:** 95, Pr/dining room 14 **Smoking:** N/Sm in restaurant, Air con **Children:** Portions **Directions:** From M8/A8 take exit towards Dumbarton, drive along Great Western Rd and turn 1st left into Park Rd, restaurant is at number 66-68 **Parking:** Side street, Underground station **e-mail:** reservations@shishmahal.co.uk **web:** www.shishmahal.co.uk

continued

Stravaigin
European, International
Lively basement restaurant, eclectic and eccentric cooking
☎ 0141 334 2665 30 Gibson St G12 8NX

MENU GUIDE Coconut, oyster mushroom, prawn soup • Veal osso buco, basil & parmesan pappardelle • Chocolate truffle & lavender beignet

WINE GUIDE ♀ Hueues de Beauvignon Picpoul £13.25 • ♀ Santa Ema Carmeners £13.25 • 26 bottles over £20, 24 bottles under £20 • 4 by the glass (£3.35-£4.65)

PRICE GUIDE Fixed D £13.95-£28.95 • starter £3.45-£10.95 • main £13.45-£22.50 • dessert £4.95-£6.25 • coffee £2.50 • min/water £2.85 • Service optional

PLACE: In a busy street close to the university, Stravaigin draws the crowds to its popular bar and bright, modern basement restaurant below with its split-level seating. It's fashionably metropolitan, lively and friendly, with attentive service and a great cocktail menu.
FOOD: The Stravaigin motto, 'think global, eat local', sums up the repertoire. Its menu is fused with exotic flavours from around the world; Pacific Rim, Asia and the Mediterranean blend with ingredients from the Scottish larder. Lots of spicing, great ingredients and fine presentation hit the mark.
OUR TIP: There's something for everyone at reasonable prices
Chef: Daniel Blencowe **Owners:** Colin Clydesdale **Times:** 12-2.30/5-11, Closed 25-26 Dec, 1 Jan, Mon, closed L Tue-Thu **Notes:** Vegetarian available **Seats:** 76 **Smoking:** N/Sm in restaurant, Air con **Children:** Portions **Directions:** Next to Glasgow University. 200 yds from Kelvinbridge underground **Parking:** On street
e-mail: bookings@stravaigin.com **web:** www.stravaigin.com

Ubiquitous Chip
Scottish
A Glaswegian legend
☎ 0141 334 5007 12 Ashton Ln G12 8SJ

MENU GUIDE Rabbit, pear & pistachio sausage • Wild boar, paprika potatoes, Calvados vinaigrette • Oatmeal ice cream, fruit compôte

WINE GUIDE ♀ Henri Bourgeois Sauvignon Blanc £26.90 • ♀ Campbells of Rutherglen Shiraz £22.75 • 263 bottles over £20, 68 bottles under £20 • 32 by the glass (£2.40-£3.95)

PRICE GUIDE Fixed L £21.80 • Fixed D £37.80 • min/water £3.15 • Service optional

PLACE: This culinary legend has treated the people of Glasgow to top-notch Scottish cuisine for more than three decades now and is still as popular as ever. It's a unique setting - a glass-covered mews complete with cobbled floor, water fountain, and enough greenery for an arboretum. An upstairs brasserie offers lighter fare, and there's a bar with a range of over 150 malts.
FOOD: Traditional Scottish cooking untouched by fad or fashion. Quality ingredients are conjured into an enjoyable range of unpretentious dishes: Aberdeen Angus with stovies and wild mushrooms maybe, or salmon with lime and vanilla mash.
OUR TIP: A serious wine list
Chef: Ronnie Clydesdale **Owners:** Ronnie Clydesdale **Times:** 12-2.30/5.30-11, Closed 25 Dec, 1 Jan **Notes:** Coffee incl, 3 course Sun lunch £17.95, Vegetarian available **Seats:** 180, Pr/dining room 45 **Smoking:** Air con **Children:** Portions **Directions:** In the West End of Glasgow, off Byres Rd. Beside Hillhead subway station **Parking:** Lilybank gardens (50m) **e-mail:** mail@ubiquitouschip.co.uk
web: www.ubiquitouschip.co.uk

Bouzy Rouge 111 West Regent St G2 2RU
☎ 0141 221 8804 Relaxed bistro with a great buzz.

Café Gandolfi 65 Albion St G1 1NY ☎ 0141 552 6813
Hugely popular cross between a traditional Glasgow tea room and a continental-style restaurant.

Mother India 28 Westminster Ter, Sauchiehall St
G3 7RU ☎ 0141 221 1663 Popular, cosy Indian.

Willow Tea Rooms 97 Buchanan St G1 3HF
☎ 0141 204 5242 Winner of The Tea Guild Award of Excellence 2005.

Give us your views! All the rosetted restaurants in this guide have been visited by one of the AA's team of professional inspectors, but we want to hear from you! Use the report forms in the back of the guide or email us at lifestyleguides@theaa.com with your comments on any establishments featured or on the restaurants that you feel are worthy of an entry. We would also be pleased to receive your views on the guide itself and suggestions for information you would like to see included.

Scotland

Scotland

HIGHLAND

ACHILTIBUIE MAP 22 NC00

The Summer Isles Hotel

European

Remote hideaway for foodies

☎ 01854 622282 IV26 2YG

MENU GUIDE Pan-seared pigeon, duxelles of mushroom, brioche • Halibut, mussels in white wine & saffron • Syrup pudding, lemon ice cream

PRICE GUIDE Food prices not confirmed for 2006. Please telephone for details.

PLACE: This peaceful gem of a hotel is remotely located in the Scottish wilds, but worth a special trip as its well-heeled regulars would attest. Simple style and quality distinguish everything from the cooking to the comfortable bedrooms, while outside some of the most beautiful and rugged landscape in Britain waits to be explored. Dine at sunset for stunning views across the bay to the Hebrides.

FOOD: A culinary haven. Expect a short and pricey menu of dishes featuring the finest home grown and locally caught produce, treated with intelligence, simplicity and respect.

OUR TIP: A local boat ferries visitors around the islands to spot seals and rare birds

Chef: Chris Firth-Bernard **Owners:** Mark & Gerry Irvine **Times:** 12.30-2/8, Closed mid Oct-Easter **Notes:** Fixed D 5 courses £47, coffee incl., Vegetarian available **Seats:** 28 **Smoking:** N/Sm in restaurant **Children:** Min 8 yrs, Portions **Directions:** 10 m N of Ullapool. Turn left off A835 onto single track road. 15m to Achiltibuie. Hotel 100 yds after post office on left **Parking:** 15 **e-mail:** summerisleshotel@aol.com **web:** www.summerisleshotel.co.uk

BALLACHULISH MAP 22 NN05

Ballachulish House

Modern Scottish

Traditional Scottish hospitality with formal flourish

☎ 01855 811266 PH49 4JX

PLACE: Surrounded by breathtaking scenery, guests at this 17th-century laird's house will feel they are truly in the heart of the Highlands. The setting is idyllic, and exciting (and rather bloodthirsty) events here in the 18th century are said to have inspired RL Stevenson to write *Kidnapped*. You will find dark wood tables and plenty of silver in the Victorian dining room.

FOOD: Modern Scottish in style, the inventive daily changing five-course menus offer a choice only on the main course. Some

continued

---

dishes are quite complex, with ambitious and successful flavour combinations as in the butternut squash soup with its foam of coriander, lemongrass and chilli.

OUR TIP: Work up an appetite walking nearby Glencoe

Times: 12-2.15/7-8 **Rooms:** 8 (8 en suite) ♦♦♦♦♦

e-mail: mclaughlins@btconnect.com

web: www.ballachulishhouse.com

BOAT OF GARTEN MAP 23 NH91

Boat Hotel – The Capercaille

Modern Scottish

Station hotel that's well-placed for steam enthusiasts

☎ 01479 831258 Deshar Rd PH24 3BH

MENU GUIDE Scallops, timbale of celeriac & leek • Caramelised halibut, fennel & tomato compôte • Vanilla Savarin, poached fruit

PRICE GUIDE Fixed D fr £32.50 • coffee £1.95 • Service optional

PLACE: In the heart of the Spey valley, this Victorian hotel is set next to the restored Strathspey steam railway. Its elegant restaurant has dark smart blue decor and open fire, and there's also a cocktail bar for lighter meals, or a quiet malt.

FOOD: Classically based cuisine with a modern Scottish twist. Plump for the three- or four-course fixed-price selection, or choose from the extensive carte; local and seasonal produce is a feature of both.

OUR TIP: Meet the opera-singing head waiter

Chef: Tony Allcott **Owners:** Ian & Shona Tatchell **Times:** 7-9.30, Closed last 2 wks in Jan, closed L all week **Notes:** Vegetarian available, Dress Restrictions, No jeans **Seats:** 40, Pr/dining room 40 **Smoking:** N/Sm in restaurant **Children:** Min 12 yrs **Rooms:** 28 (28 en suite) ★★★ **Directions:** Turn off A9 N of Aviemore onto A95. Follow signs to Boat of Garten **Parking:** 36 **e-mail:** holidays@boathotel.co.uk **web:** www.boathotel.co.uk

BREAKISH MAP 22 NG62

Rendezvous Restaurant

French, European

French skill and dedication on Scottish island

☎ 01471 822001 Old School House IV42 8PY

MENU GUIDE Venison terrine, onion marmalade • Seared diver scallops, apple & ginger velouté • Chocolate & almond tart, crème anglaise

WINE GUIDE ♀ Pouilly Fumé Sauvignon £21.50 • ♀ Alistair Maling £14.20 • 6 bottles over £20, 5 bottles under £20 • 1 by the glass (£2.90)

PRICE GUIDE Starter £4.50-£6.80 • main £11.50-£18 • dessert £4.60 • coffee £1.80 • min/water £2.80 • Service optional

continued

PLACE: The windows in this former Victorian schoolhouse were set high to deter daydreaming pupils. These days, local artwork and fishing paraphernalia have taken the place of the blackboards, providing a much more inviting interior.
FOOD: The chef's French classical background is apparent in the faultless execution of dishes that handles the abundant local game and seafood with accuracy, precision and flair. Lightly grilled sea bass demonstrates just how good fresh fish can be.
OUR TIP: Lovely views over the Minch
Chef: Denis Woodtli **Owners:** Denis Woodtli **Times:** 6.15-9, Closed 2 wks Oct, Jan, Feb, Tue, Closed L all week **Notes:** Vegetarian available
Seats: 32 **Smoking:** N/Sm in restaurant **Children:** Portions
Directions: 10 minutes N of Skye Bridge **Parking:** 15
e-mail: rosemary@woodtli.fsnet.co.uk

BRORA MAP 23 NC90

Royal Marine Hotel
Scottish, French
Edwardian hotel much loved by golfers
☎ 01408 621252 Golf Rd KW9 6QS
MENU GUIDE Cullen skink • Stuffed chicken breast, black pudding mash
WINE GUIDE ♀ Santa Ema Sauvignon £12.95 • ♀ Jacobite Ridge Shiraz £14.95 • 15 bottles over £20, 60 bottles under £20 • 12 by the glass (£3.50-£5)
PRICE GUIDE Starter £3-£7 • main £12-£20 • dessert £4-£5 • coffee £1.75 • min/water £2.95
PLACE: With views over Dornoch Firth and the Highlands, this Edwardian hotel commands an excellent position. The interior is very much in the country house tradition, luxuriously appointed and instantly relaxing.
FOOD: The menu makes the most of local produce in a range of dishes that draw inspiration from Scottish classics and country house favourites. Saddle of Sutherland venison with stewed plums gives a sense of the style.
OUR TIP: Bring your golf clubs for a round on the adjacent links
Chef: Mikael Helies **Owners:** Duncraggie Ltd **Times:** 12-2/6.30-8.45, Closed L (pre booking only) **Notes:** Vegetarian available, Smart Dress, Civ Wed 60 **Seats:** 50, Pr/dining room 12 **Smoking:** N/Sm in restaurant
Children: Menu, Portions **Rooms:** 22 (22 en suite) ★★★
Directions: Turn off A9 in village toward beach and golf course.
Parking: 40 **e-mail:** info@highlandescape.com
web: www.highlandscape.com

COLBOST MAP 22 NG24

Three Chimneys
Restaurant *see page 588*

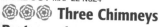

The Best Use of Seafood sponsored by Seafish In conjunction with Seafish, the Sea Fish Industry Authority, we have sought out restaurants that make the most of seafood on their menus. In addition to the four country award winners (see page 9), look out for the seafish symbol throughout the book; this denotes restaurants serving a good range of fish and shellfish dishes, where the accent is firmly on freshness.

DORNOCH MAP 23 NH78

2 Quail Restaurant & Rooms
International
Classic cooking in tiny Highland restaurant
☎ 01862 811811 Inistore House, Castle St IV25 3SN
MENU GUIDE Duck & foie gras terrine, pear & rosemary chutney Tournedo Rossini • Raspberry mousse, Drambuie sauce
WINE GUIDE ♀ Bourgogne les Setilles Le Flaive Chardonnay £16.95 • ♀ Campillo Rioja Crianza Tempranillo/Grenache £23.50 51 bottles over £20, 8 bottles under £20 • 8 by the glass (£3.50-£10)
PRICE GUIDE Fixed D £35.50 • coffee £2 • min/water £1.25 • Service optional
PLACE: With only four tables to its name, this book-lined little restaurant is a cosy, intimate place to dine. It's run by a husband and wife team and is located close to Dornoch's town centre and historic cathedral. Reservations essential.
FOOD: Creative Highland cooking with International influences. The range of dishes is concise but nicely judged - you might kick off with Skye scallops with fresh pea purée and crispy bacon, followed by venison with celeriac dauphinoise and a red wine jus. Reduced hours in winter.
OUR TIP: Book a room to make the most of your evening
Chef: Michael Carr **Owners:** Michael and Kerensa Carr **Times:** 7.30-9.30, Closed Xmas, 2 wks Feb-Mar, Sun-Mon **Notes:** Vegetarian by request only **Seats:** 14 **Smoking:** N/Sm in restaurant
Children: Portions **Rooms:** 3 (3 en suite) ♦♦♦♦♦ **Directions:** 200 yds past war memorial on left side of main street, just before Cathedral
Parking: On street **e-mail:** theaa@2quail.com **web:** www.2quail.com

DUNDONNELL MAP 22 NH08

Dundonnell Hotel
British, Scottish
Remote and breathtaking location for modern hotel
☎ 01854 633204 Little Loch Broom IV23 2QR
MENU GUIDE Roast Queen scallops, herb couscous, coral butter sauce • Pan-fried sea bass & halibut, smoked haddock mash, braised fennel • Orange Cointreau & chocolate cheesecake, whole poached pears
PRICE GUIDE Food prices not confirmed for 2006. Please telephone for details
PLACE: A beautiful and isolated location at the head of Little Loch Broom, with mountains all around, might sound like the last place you would expect to find this smart and extensively developed hotel. The hotel's interior exudes traditional charm and many of the bedrooms enjoy fine views.
FOOD: Modern British cooking that ranges from trusty favourites to unusual combinations.
OUR TIP: Local seafood is well worth trying
Times: 7-9, Closed Jan, closed L All wk **Rooms:** 32 (32 en suite) ★★★
Directions: On A832 Ullapool/Gairloch road, 14m from Braemore junction **e-mail:** enquiries@dundonnellhotel.co.uk
web: www.dundonnellhotel.com

FORT WILLIAM MAP 22 NN17

 # Inverlochy Castle Hotel

see page 589

COLBOST MAP 22 NG24

The Three Chimneys

Modern Scottish
Foodie hideaway on Skye

☎ 01470 511258   IV55 8ZT

e-mail: eatandstay@threechimneys.co.uk
web: www.threechimneys.co.uk

PLACE: Nestled between hills, this whitewashed crofter's cottage sits in glorious countryside beside a loch that teams with seals, cormorants and other wildlife. The natural theme continues inside, with wood, stone and slate used to create a decor of chic simplicity that extends through the restaurant to The House Over-By, a stylish extension with a handful of tasteful rooms.

FOOD: Expect deft and skilful cooking that plunders the wilderness for quality ingredients in this romantic cottage restaurant. Local seafood is a highlight; as fresh as can be and put to use in complex dishes such as citrus-baked halibut with seared scallops, crispy potatoes and an orange sauce. The menu changes daily and features subtle Scottish touches - Drambuie custard with hot marmalade pudding perhaps - alongside more contemporary combinations. Award-winning wine list.

MENU GUIDE Crab risotto • Lamb loin & kidney, golden pearl barley, spinach, rowan & port wine gravy • Rhubarb & ruby orange compôte

WINE GUIDE ♀ Domaine del Labelle Colombard £17.95 • ♀ Lopez Christobal Tempranillo £21.75 155 bottles over £20, 5 bottles under £20 • 7 by the glass (£4.45-£5.75)

PRICE GUIDE Fixed L £18.50 • Fixed D £48-£52 coffee £3.45 • min/water £3.25 • Service optional • Group min 8 service 10%

OUR TIP: Stay over and enjoy the wind-swept scenery

Chef: Michael Smith, Shirley Spear **Owners:** Eddie & Shirley Spear **Times:** 12.30-2/6.30-9.30, Closed 3 wks Jan, 1 wk Dec, closed L Sun **Notes:** 7 course tasting L £60, incl coffee, Vegetarian available, Dress Restrictions, Smart casual preferred **Seats:** 30 **Smoking:** N/Sm in restaurant **Children:** Min 8 yrs D, Portions **Rooms:** 6 (6 en suite) 🏠 **Directions:** 5m W of Dunvegan take B884 to Glendale

FORT WILLIAM MAP 22 NN17

Inverlochy Castle Hotel

Scottish
Luxurious Highland setting for dazzling dishes
☎ 01397 702177 Torlundy PH33 6SN

MENU GUIDE Skate wing, belly pork, capers, lemon • Turbot, parmesan crust, lentil salad • Lemon tart, blackcurrant sorbet

WINE GUIDE ♀ Cloudy Bay Sauvignon Blanc £75 • ♀ Cape Mentelle Cabernet Sauvignon/Merlot £45 • 300 bottles over £20 • 8 by the glass (£5.50-£12.50)

PRICE GUIDE Fixed L £23.50 • Fixed D £52.50 • coffee £5.50 • Service optional

PLACE: Ben Nevis provides a majestic backdrop for this gracious castle, set at the edge of a loch. Pre-dinner drinks are served in a luxurious lounge, while the lavishly furnished restaurant offers stunning mountain views, particularly at sunset.
FOOD: Classical concepts are given a modern treatment by a chef with dazzling technique; expect a concise but seductive range of interesting dishes, based around simple combinations of the finest ingredients Scotland has to offer.

OUR TIP: The notable wine list offers over 50 half bottles
Chef: Matthew Gray **Owners:** Inverlochy Ltd **Times:** 12.30-1.45/6.30-9.15, Closed 6 Jan-1 Feb **Notes:** Mineral water incl., Vegetarian available, Jacket & tie, Civ Wed 50 **Seats:** 40, Pr/dining room 20 **Smoking:** N/Sm in restaurant **Rooms:** 17 (17 en suite) ★★★★ **Directions:** 3m N of Fort William on A82, just past Golf Club **Parking:** 20
e-mail: info@inverlochy.co.uk **web:** www.inverlochycastlehotel.com

FORT WILLIAM *continued* MAP 22 NN17
Moorings Hotel
British
Contemporary cuisine in the heart of the Highlands
☎ 01397 772797 Banavie PH33 7LY

MENU GUIDE Smoked salmon & crab terrine • Roast chump of local lamb with roasted vegetables • Iced blackcurrant parfait

WINE GUIDE ♀ Los Vilos Chardonnay £12.75 • ♀ Los Vilos Cabernet Sauvignon £12.75 • 10 bottles over £20, 28 bottles under £20 • 6 by the glass (£3.10-£3.60)

PRICE GUIDE Fixed L £13-£18 • Fixed D £18-£27 • starter £4-£9 • main £10-£19 • dessert £4-£6 • coffee £1.25 • min/water £3 • Service optional

PLACE: A spacious Jacobean-styled dining room in a comfortable hotel alongside the Caledonian Canal at the famous Neptune's

Staircase. The hotel is popular as a base for Highland tourists and offers magnificent views of Ben Nevis and Aonach Mor.
FOOD: Solid, British and European contemporary dishes produced from locally-sourced ingredients, especially salmon and lamb.
OUR TIP: Enjoy the panoramic views of Ben Nevis
Chef: Paul Smith **Owners:** Mr S Leitch **Times:** 7-9.30, Closed L all wk **Notes:** Sun L £9.50, Vegetarian available, Dress Restrictions, Smart casual, Civ Wed 130 **Seats:** 60, Pr/dining room 120 **Smoking:** N/Sm in restaurant **Children:** Portions **Rooms:** 28 (28 en suite) ★★★
Directions: From A82 take A830 W for 1 mile. 1st right over Caledonian Canal on B8004 **Parking:** 50
e-mail: reservations@moorings-fortwilliam.co.uk
web: www.moorings-fortwilliam.co.uk

GLENFINNAN MAP 22 NM88
The Prince's House
British ⚞NEW
A star in the making in the rural Highlands
☎ 01397 722246 PH37 4LT

MENU GUIDE Mallaig seafood soup • Fillets of Dover sole, scallops, parsley pesto, chargrilled potatoes • Dark chocolate soufflé, praline cream

WINE GUIDE ♀ Lofthouse Sauvignon Blanc £21 • ♀ Rioja Marques de Murietto Tempranillo £22 • 20 bottles over £20, 10 bottles under £20 • 2 by the glass (£2.95-£3.24)

PRICE GUIDE Fixed D £23-£29 • coffee £1.85 • min/water £2.95 • Service included

PLACE: Horses pulling the old Mallaig to Fort William coach were once changed in what is now this delightful hotel's restaurant, and the intimate space is still unfussy, with stunning views.

continued

GLENFINNAN continued MAP 22 NM88

FOOD: The theme here is simplicity, and with fine local game and seafood at its disposal, the very seasonal cooking allows flavours their natural expression. The short menu and broader bar choice work well together.

OUR TIP: Shellfish cannot be eaten fresher

Chef: Kieron Kelly **Owners:** Kieron & Ina Kelly **Times:** 7-9, Closed Xmas, Jan-Feb, Low season - booking only, closed L all wk **Notes:** Vegetarian available **Seats:** 30 **Smoking:** N/Sm in restaurant **Children:** Portions **Rooms:** 9 (9 en suite) ★★ **Directions:** From Fort William N on A82 for 2 m. Turn left onto A830 Mallaig rd for 15 m to Hotel **Parking:** 18 **e-mail:** princeshouse@glenfinnan.co.uk **web:** www.glenfinnan.co.uk

GRANTOWN-ON-SPEY MAP 23 NJ02

Culdearn House

Scottish, British

Relaxed country-house dining

☎ 01479 872106 Woodlands Ter PH26 3JU

MENU GUIDE Garlic prawns with sweet chilli • Roast guinea fowl, lemon & pistachio stuffing • Mint ice cream, pickled strawberries

WINE GUIDE ♀ Blenheim Point Chardonnay £18.50 • ♀ Angus the Bull Cabernet Sauvignon £20 • 18 bottles over £20, 18 bottles under £20 • 4 by the glass (£3.75)

PRICE GUIDE Fixed D £30 • coffee £2 • min/water £2 • Service optional

PLACE: Set in its own gardens in a lovely Speyside village, this small country-house hotel extends its visitors excellent hospitality. The small dining room is appealingly Victorian, and lawn-side views provide a sense of space.

FOOD: Honesty is a distinct virtue here, with simple dishes made with great charm from the very best of local produce. Game and seafood are particular specialities of the seasonally changing menu.

OUR TIP: Enjoy a guided tour through the extensive malt whisky list

Chef: Feona Laing **Owners:** Mr & Mrs Marshall **Times:** 7, Closed Dec-Mar, closed L all week **Notes:** Vegetarian by request only, Dress Restrictions, No jeans, sportswear or T-shirts **Seats:** 16 **Smoking:** N/Sm in restaurant **Children:** Min 10 yrs **Rooms:** 7 (7 en suite) ★★ **Directions:** Enter Grantown from SW on A95, left at 30mph sign **Parking:** 11 **e-mail:** enquiries@culdearn.com **web:** www.culdearn.com

Muckrach Lodge Hotel

British

Flavoursome dining in well-presented Scottish hunting lodge

☎ 01479 851257 PH26 3LY

MENU GUIDE Asparagus mousse, prawn & caviar wine sauce • Seared Highland venison, root vegetable purée • Vanilla cheesecake

WINE GUIDE 80 bottles over £20, 32 bottles under £20 • 14 by the glass (£3.50-£7.50)

PRICE GUIDE Fixed D £32.50 • coffee £1.95 • min/water £2.50 • Service optional

PLACE: This privately owned Victorian former hunting lodge is set in wonderful Highland scenery with the Cairngorms looming dramatically in the distance. The location and lovely landscaped grounds ensure that the Finlarig Restaurant has excellent views should you need to look beyond the elegant decor, comforting log fire and sumptuous candlelit settings.

FOOD: Dishes are characterised by freshness, true, clear flavours and judicious combinations. This kitchen possesses good technical skills and makes the most of top-class ingredients from the locality and beyond.

OUR TIP: Local shooting, fishing & walking

Chef: Stephen Robertson **Owners:** Dawn & James Macfarlane **Times:** 12.15-2/7-8.30, Closed 4-21 Jan, Mon, Tue (Nov-Mar only) **Notes:** Vegetarian available **Seats:** 28, Pr/dining room 60 **Smoking:** N/Sm in restaurant **Children:** Menu, Portions **Rooms:** 13 (13 en suite) ★★★ **Directions:** From A95 Dulnain Bridge exit follow A938 towards Carrbridge, hotel 500m on right **Parking:** 25 **e-mail:** info@muckrach.co.uk **web:** www.muckrach.co.uk

The Pines

Scottish, British   **NEW**

Genteel woodside dining

☎ 01479 872092 Woodside Av PH26 3JR

MENU GUIDE Warm pigeon salad, lentils & bacon • Sea bass, herb risotto • Chocolate torte, brandied cherries

WINE GUIDE ♀ Christian Salmon Sancerre £18 • ♀ Delheim Cabernet Sauvignon Bejorua £20 • 4 bottles over £20, 20 bottles under £20 • 2 by the glass (£3.50)

PRICE GUIDE Fixed D £30 • min/water £4 • Service optional

PLACE: On the outskirts of town close to an impressive pine forest, this Victorian country house is comfortably decked out with lots of period pieces and paintings. Striking red dining room with charming service is the setting for some enjoyable dining.

FOOD: Traditional and skilfully prepared modern Scottish and British dishes with an emphasis on local game and other produce. What the menu lacks in choice (pre-ordered during the afternoon) it more than makes up for in quality.

OUR TIP: Watch the red squirrels playing on the lawns

Chef: Gwen Stewart **Owners:** Gwen & Michael Stewart **Times:** 7, Closed Nov-Feb **Notes:** Coffee incl., Vegetarian by request only, Smart Dress **Seats:** 20, Pr/dining room 10 **Smoking:** N/Sm in restaurant **Children:** Min 12 yrs, Portions **Rooms:** 8 (8 en suite) ★★ **Directions:** A95 N to Grantown-on-Spey, right at traffic lights on to A939 towards Tomintoul, then 1st right into Woodside Avenue **Parking:** 8 **e-mail:** info@thepinesgrantown.co.uk **web:** www.thepinesgrantown.co.uk

---

Two Rosettes The best local restaurants, which aim for and achieve higher standards, better consistency and where a greater precision is apparent in the cooking. There will be obvious attention to the selection of quality ingredients. About 40% of restaurants in the guide have two Rosettes.

continued

INVERGARRY MAP 22 NH30

Glengarry Castle

British, Scottish

Honest, flavoursome cuisine by the lochside

☎ 01809 501254 PH35 4HW

MENU GUIDE Chicken liver parfait, compôte of forest berries & oatcakes • Fillet of venison, juniper berry scented sauce • Rhubarb & pannacotta ice cream

WINE GUIDE ♀ Domaine de Bois D'Yver Chardonnay £19 • ♀ De Bertoli Shiraz £13 • 16 bottles over £20, 37 bottles under £20 • 7 by the glass (£2.80)

PRICE GUIDE Fixed D £24 • coffee £1.70 • min/water £2.80 • Service included

PLACE: A charming Victorian country house with great views, set on the shores of Loch Oich in 50 acres of grounds. Panelled reception hall, marble fireplaces, mellow oil paintings, a choice of sitting rooms and an elegant, traditional dining room are among the archetypal luxuries at this comfortable and welcoming hotel.
FOOD: The traditional approach, via fixed-price four-course menus, showcase the best Scottish produce (local game and fish) in uncomplicated, assured and flavoursome dishes.
OUR TIP: Try for a window seat
Chef: John McDonald **Owners:** Mr & Mrs MacCallum **Times:** 7-8.30, Closed mid Nov to mid Mar, closed L Mon-Sun **Notes:** Vegetarian available **Seats:** 40 **Smoking:** N/Sm in restaurant **Children:** Menu, Portions **Rooms:** 26 (26 en suite) ★★★ **Directions:** 1m S of Invergarry on A82 **Parking:** 30 **e-mail:** castle@glengarry.net **web:** www.glengarry.net

---

INVERMORISTON MAP 23 NH41

Glenmoriston Arms Hotel & Restaurant

Traditional Scottish

Scottish cooking in historic former drovers' inn

☎ 01320 351206 IV63 7YA

MENU GUIDE Haggis, neeps & tatties, whisky sauce • Roasted pork fillet • Lemon meringue

WINE GUIDE ♀ Francesca Bay £24.99 • ♀ Château le Fleur £29.99 • 39 bottles over £20, 42 bottles under £20 • 4 by the glass (£3.45-£4.85)

PRICE GUIDE Fixed D £27.50 • starter £4.55-£6.95 • main £15.95-£19.95 • dessert £5.95-£9.95 • coffee £1.75 • min/water £3.45 • Service optional

PLACE: This old drovers' inn dates back to before the Battle of Culloden, and is packed with historic associations. The formal dining room is cosy and welcoming, with exemplary Highland hospitality.
FOOD: The food enjoys a good local reputation, and a skilled kitchen team introduce plenty of innovation to the various menus: a bar carte can also be taken in the dining room, with choices including home-made pies, and a burger collection. Otherwise expect smoked venison loin, and rosemary roasted rack of lamb.
OUR TIP: Sample some of the 146 malt whiskies
Chef: Paul Lumby & Robert Jackson **Owners:** Nik & Hazel Hammond **Times:** 12-2.30/7-9, Closed Jan & Feb **Notes:** Vegetarian available, Dress restrictions, Smart casual **Seats:** 28 **Smoking:** N/Sm in restaurant **Children:** Min 5 yrs, Portions **Rooms:** 8 (8 en suite) ★★ **Directions:** At the junction of A82 & A877 **Parking:** 24 **e-mail:** reception@glenmoristonarms.co.uk **web:** www.glenmoristonarms.co.uk

---

INVERNESS MAP 23 NH64

⊛⊛ Bunchrew House Hotel

Scottish, French

Confident simplicity in imposing Highland manor

☎ 01463 234917 Bunchrew IV3 8TA

MENU GUIDE Cromarty smoked trout, prawn salsa • Saddle of venison, juniper & rosemary sauce • Caramelised raspberry tart, Armagnac syrup

WINE GUIDE ♀ Katherine Hills £16.25 • ♀ Torreon de Parades Merlot £15 • 49 bottles over £20, 25 bottles under £20 • 4 by the glass (£3.60)

PRICE GUIDE Fixed L £21 • Fixed D £34.50 • coffee £1.75 • min/water £3.85 • Service optional

PLACE: Built by the 8th Earl of Lovat in 1621 to satisfy his wife's ambitions, this grand old Highland mansion still impresses, perched on the shore by the Beauly Firth and surrounded by pretty gardens and woodland. Ancestral portraits, wood panelling and open fires keep things stately inside, and even the hotel ghost can't stay away from the restaurant with its artfully constructed cuisine. Book ahead for a window table.
FOOD: Scottish cooking with a French influence. Local produce and home-grown herbs are handled with deft simplicity, and the menu changes daily.
OUR TIP: Take time to explore the splendid surroundings
Chef: Walter Walker **Owners:** Terry & Irina Mackay **Times:** 12-1.45/7-8.45, Closed 22-28 Dec **Notes:** Vegetarian available, Civ Wed 92 **Seats:** 40, Pr/dining room 14 **Smoking:** N/Sm in restaurant **Children:** Portions **Rooms:** 14 (14 en suite) ★★★ **Directions:** 3m W of Inverness on A862 towards Beauly **Parking:** 40 **e-mail:** welcome@bunchrew-inverness.co.uk **web:** www.bunchrew-inverness.co.uk

⊛⊛ Culloden House Hotel

British, French

A timeless setting for intelligent cuisine

☎ 01463 790461 Culloden IV2 7BZ

MENU GUIDE Grilled Arran goats' cheese, grainy mustard dressing • Duck, raisin mousse, beetroot purée, Marcela jus • Atholle brose

WINE GUIDE ♀ Inverarity Chablis £32.50 • ♀ Inverarity Bordeaux £28.95 • all bottles over £20, 1 bottle under £20 7 by the glass (£3.25-£5.95)

PRICE GUIDE Fixed L £16-£24.40 • Fixed D £33 • coffee £1.95 • min/water £3.50 • Service added but optional 10%

PLACE: There's such a timeless ambience to this opulent Palladian mansion, it feels as if its glistening chandeliers have only just been hung, its ornate cornicing only just finished. The house is surrounded by gently rolling Scottish countryside, and isn't far from the battlefield of the same name.
FOOD: Unusual combinations stretch the imagination, but make sense both on the palate and the plate. Expect a modern translation of classical dishes, with familiar flavours delivered in a modish style.
OUR TIP: Descend to the dungeons to find the hotel's sauna
Chef: Michael Simpson **Owners:** Culloden House Associates Ltd **Times:** 12.30-2/7-9, Closed 2 wks Jan/Feb **Notes:** Petits Fours with D only, Vegetarian available, Dress Restrictions, Smart casual, Civ Wed 65 **Seats:** 50, Pr/dining room 17 **Smoking:** N/Sm in restaurant **Children:** Portions **Rooms:** 28 (28 en suite) ★★★★ **Directions:** From A96, take left turn at junction of 'Balloch, Culloden, Smithton'. Continue for 2m, hotel is on right **Parking:** 50 **e-mail:** info@cullodenhouse.co.uk **web:** www.cullodenhouse.co.uk

Scotland

Scotland

INVERNESS *continued* MAP 23 NH64

 Glenmoriston Town House Hotel

Modern French

Townhouse hotel with refurbished riverside restaurant

☎ 01463 223777 20 Ness Bank IV2 4SF

MENU GUIDE Scallops, asparagus, frothy fennel milk • Wild Scottish duck in two sauces • Hot Grand Marnier soufflé, exotic fruits

WINE GUIDE ♀ Sancerre £30 • ♀ Château Beausejour St Emilion £65 • 103 bottles over £20, 26 bottles under £20 • 6 by the glass (£3.50-£5.20)

PRICE GUIDE Fixed D £42 • coffee £4.50 • min/water £3.50 • Service optional • Group min 10 service 12.5%

PLACE: Listed town house beside the River Ness with a sophisticated restaurant Abstract – the fine dining option, but for lighter meals try La Terrazza. Highly professional and attentive service is provided by a mainly French team, and a new look has been created for both the restaurant and menu.

FOOD: The chef describes his cooking as French modern with influences from Japan and North Africa. High quality local produce stars and technical skills are evident at every stage, as in dishes such as line-caught sea bass, fricassee of gnocchi, chanterelles, Parma ham and hazelnut. Notable wine list.

OUR TIP: One to watch

Chef: Loic Lefebrvre **Owners:** Larsen & Ross South **Times:** 12-2/7-9.30 **Notes:** Vegetarian available, Dress Restrictions, Smart casual **Seats:** 50, Pr/dining room **Smoking:** N/Sm in restaurant **Children:** Menu, Portions **Rooms:** 30 (30 en suite) ★★★ **Directions:** 2 mins from city centre, on river opposite theatre **Parking:** 50 **e-mail:** glenmoriston@cali.co.uk **web:** www.glenmoriston.com

 Riverhouse

British

Formal dining on the riverbank

☎ 01463 222033 1 Greig St IV3 5PT

MENU GUIDE Highland game terrine • Seared shark, lemon, dill & pine pesto • Espresso crème brûlée

WINE GUIDE ♀ Monte Cass Sauvignon Blanc £22.75 • ♀ Paradyskloof Pinotage £24.55 • 29 bottles over £20, 3 bottles under £20 • 6 by the glass (£4.25-£5.95)

PRICE GUIDE Fixed L £10.50-£13.50 • Fixed D £28.95 • coffee £2 • min/water £4

PLACE: Attractively located small restaurant on the banks of the River Ness, with an intimate wood-panelled interior, and formal table settings.

FOOD: Great use is made of seafood, with lots of innovation seen in grilled mackerel fillets on a spicy sausage and potato hash, and sea bream with roasted celery, cherry tomatoes, mussels and crab. The lunch and pre-theatre menus offer particularly good value.

OUR TIP: The open kitchen is interesting to watch

Chef: Allan Little **Owners:** Allan Little **Times:** 12-2.15/5.30-10.00, Closed Mon, closed L Sun **Notes:** Vegetarian available, Smart casual **Seats:** 30 **Smoking:** N/Sm in restaurant **Children:** Min 8 yrs, Portions **Directions:** On corner of Huntly Street and Greig Street **Parking:** Parking available 200 yds **e-mail:** riverhouse@netbreeze.co.uk

Rocpool

Modern European   **NEW**

Lively cosmopolitan atmosphere offering international cuisine

☎ 01463 717274 1 Ness Walk IV3 5NE

PLACE: Richly coloured Mediterranean artwork and a tapas bar bring a touch of glamour to this part of the Scottish Highlands. Sitting improbably opposite the River Ness, the Rocpool is a bright and lively presence with a cosily lit interior. Staff are relaxed and fuss-free.

FOOD: The cooking is an innovative take on a theme that encompasses Italy (mainly Tuscany), the rest of Europe and the Pacific Rim. Locally sourced produce is lovingly handled by the four-strong team, leading to interesting combinations like chilli crusted lamb cutlets with crisp polenta.

OUR TIP: Booking almost essential

Times: Telephone for details. Closed Sun, 25 Dec

 Café 1 75 Castle St IV2 3EA ☎ 01463 226200 Modern-style city centre restaurant with a good range of contemporary dishes.

 Harry Ramsdens Inshes Retail Park IV2 3TW ☎ 01463 713345 Famous fish & chip shop.

ISLE ORNSAY MAP 22 NG71

Duisdale Country House Hotel

French, Scottish

Country-house hotel dining with stunning views

☎ 01471 833202 IV43 8QW

MENU GUIDE Lochcarron oysters, croft cream, Black Douglas cheese • Roast turbot, mussels, saffron herb sauce • Sticky toffee pudding

PRICE GUIDE Food prices not confirmed for 2006. Please telephone for details

PLACE: Delightfully situated country-house hotel set in landscaped gardens 300 yards from the beach, with views across the Sound of Sleat to distant hills. A feature of the restaurant is a collection of blue and white china plates complementing the Delft tiles, which have been in place since the house was built.

FOOD: Classically inspired menus with traditional Scottish flavours making full use of excellent local produce.

OUR TIP: Originally a hunting lodge for the Chief of Clan Macdonald

Times: 7-9 **Rooms:** 17 (17 en suite) ★★★ **Directions:** 7miles N of Armadale ferry, and 12 miles south of Skye Bridge on A851 **Parking:** 20 **e-mail:** info@duisdale.com **web:** www.duisdale.com

continued

Wine Award Winner for Scotland

The Cross, Kingussie

(see page 594)

Scotland

ISLE ORNSAY continued MAP 22 NG71

 Hotel Eilean Iarmain

Scottish

Complex modern cuisine on Skye

☎ 01471 833332 IV43 8QR

MENU GUIDE Scallops, prosciutto, olives, roast tomatoes, goats' cheese • Venison, black pudding galette, port wine sauce • Iced banana parfait

PRICE GUIDE Food prices not confirmed for 2006. Please telephone for details

PLACE: This thriving hotel is built around a 19th-century inn, and boasts beautiful views across the sea lochs to the mainland. There's a cosy country-house lounge with a roaring fire for pre-dinner drinks, or you can brave the lively bar with its traditional Gaelic charm.

continued

FOOD: An ambitious kitchen plunders the local area for high quality produce, with local shellfish and game featuring strongly. Expect showy and elaborate dishes designed to wow.
OUR TIP: Take a stroll by the pier
Times: 7.30-8.45, Closed L all week (ex bookings), (open 6-10 summer)
Rooms: 16 (16 en suite) ★★ **Directions:** Overlooking harbour - cross bridge at Kyle of Lochalsh then take A850 and A851, then to harbour front
e-mail: hotel@eileaniarmain.co.uk **web:** www.eileaniarmain.co.uk

KINGUSSIE MAP 23 NH70

The Cross *see below*

LOCHINVER MAP 22 NC02

The Albannach

Modern Scottish, French

Gastronomic haven in the Scottish wilds

☎ 01571 844407 Baddidarrach IV27 4LP

MENU GUIDE Cheese soufflé, red onion marmalade • Beef, parsley mash, root vegetable parcel • Apple tart, Calvados gelato, caramel sauce

WINE GUIDE ♀ Olivier Lefaive Rully 1er Cru Chardonnay £23 • ♀ Hubert Lamy St Aubin le Paradis Pinot Noir £25 180 bottles over £20, 80 bottles under £20 • 4 by the glass (£4-£9)

PRICE GUIDE Food prices not confirmed for 2006. Please telephone for details

continued

KINGUSSIE MAP 23 NH70

The Cross

Modern Scottish

AA Wine Award Winner for Scotland

☎ 01540 661166 Tweed Mill Brae, Ardbroilach Rd PH21 ILB

MENU GUIDE Seared mackerel, rhubarb salsa • Rump of Shetland salt-marsh lamb, baked aubergine, dauphinoise • Crème caramel, crème brûlée ice cream

WINE GUIDE ♀ Haras de Pirque Sauvignon Blanc £19.50 • ♀ La Rareza Malbec £19.50 • 110 bottles over £20, 20 bottles under £20 • 3 by the glass (£5-£6)

PRICE GUIDE Fixed D £35 • min/water £3.50 • Service included

PLACE: Set in woodland beside a tumbling burn, this inviting restaurant has whitewashed stone walls, beams, open fire, modern art and a riverside terrace. Quality, simplicity and hospitality are genuine features.

FOOD: Top-notch, fresh, seasonal ingredients (mainly Scottish and local; perhaps scallops or organic salmon from Skye, local venison, salt-marsh lamb), prepared and presented with deceptive simplicity, with balanced flavours all hitting the mark.

OUR TIP: Former water-powered tweed mill
Chef: Becca Henderson, David Young **Owners:** David & Katie Young
Times: 7-8.30, Closed Xmas & Jan (excl New Year), Sun-Mon, L all wk
Seats: 20 **Smoking:** N/Sm in restaurant **Rooms:** 8 (8 en suite)
Directions: From lights in centre of Kingussie, uphill along Ardbroilach Rd for 300 mtrs **Parking:** 12 **e-mail:** relax@thecross.co.uk
web: www.thecross.co.uk

The Albannach

LACE: Sociable little hotel based in a character Victorian manor
ouse not far from the bustling fishing village of Lochinver. Take
drink in the conservatory or wood-panelled snug, before
noving through to the dining room with its stunning views of sea
nd mountain.
OOD: Come hungry: the Albannach delivers a daily-changing
x-course menu that combines French techniques with Scottish
avours. It's a showcase for the finest local produce, making use
f fish from the loch, deer from the nearby forest, and lamb and
eef from Moray's pastures. Notable wine list.
UR TIP: Take a pre- or post-dinner drink in the conservatory
hef: Colin Craig, Lesley Crosfield **Owners:** Colin Craig, Lesley Crosfield
imes: 8, Closed mid Nov-mid Mar, Mon, closed L all week **Notes:** Fixed
5 courses £45, Vegetarian by request only, Dress Restrictions, Smart
sual **Seats:** 16 **Smoking:** N/Sm in restaurant **Children:** Min 12 yrs
ooms: 5 (5 en suite) **⚑ Directions:** From main Ullapool road into
ochinver, turn right over old stone bridge signposted for Baddidarrach.
ontinue for 0.5m take left turn after Highland Stoneware Pottery
arking: 80 **e-mail:** the.albannach@virgin.net
eb: www.thealbannach.co.uk

🏵 Inver Lodge

ritish, French

riendly hotel in wonderful location

☎ 01571 844496   IV27 4LU

MENU GUIDE Partridge, black pudding, red onion
narmalade • Lamb cutlets, mint risotto, pear & rosemary
us • Deep-fried ice cream

WINE GUIDE ♀ Calina Chardonnay £14.50 • ♀ Château
Richotey £17.95 • 3 bottles over £20, 44 bottles under £20
5 by the glass (£3.25-£3.50)

PRICE GUIDE Fixed D £38 • min/water £3 • Service included

LACE: High on a hillside above a small fishing village, this
elightful modern hotel boasts views across the bay to the
ebrides beyond.
OOD: A skilful kitchen conjures a concise menu from local
roduce, offering three choices for each course. Fresh fish is a
articular draw in dishes such as Inver Bay lobster thermidor, or
alibut with a butternut squash purée.
UR TIP: Book ahead for a window table
hef: Peter Cullen **Owners:** Anne & Edmund Vestey **Times:** 7-9, Closed
ec-Mar, closed L Mon-Sun **Notes:** Coffee incl, Vegetarian available,
ress Restrictions, No Jeans, shorts, tracksuit trousers **Seats:** 50
noking: N/Sm in restaurant **Children:** Min 10 yrs, Portions
ooms: 20 (20 en suite) ★★★ **Directions:** A835 to Lochinver, left at
llage hall, private road for 0.5m **Parking:** 30
mail: stay@inverlodge.com **web:** www.inverlodge.com

MUIR OF ORD MAP 23 NH55

🏵 Ord House Hotel

British, French   **NEW**

*Modern cosmopolitan and traditional Scottish
cooking*

☎ 01463 870492   IV6 7UH

MENU GUIDE Wood pigeon salad • Venison fillet & game
sauce • Grape brûlée

WINE GUIDE ♀ Joseph Drouhin Chablis £19.50 • ♀ Château Bel
Air Medoc Cabernet Sauvignon £18.75 • 10 bottles over £20,
29 bottles under £20 • 4 by the glass (£2.50-£4)

PRICE GUIDE Fixed D £18-£24 • starter £5-£12 • main £10-£21
dessert £6.50-£8.50 • coffee £1.95 • min/water £1.50 • Service
included

PLACE: You might lose yourself in the 60 acres of gardens and
woodland that surround this fine 17th-century country house, but
be sure to get a fix on the first floor restaurant in time for dinner.
FOOD: Expect high-quality dinner-party food, with crisp, clear
flavours a feature of the uncomplicated cooking. Roast loin of
lamb is cooked to perfection, while boiled Irish cream and frozen
raspberries is a triumph of imagination.
OUR TIP: Plenty of traditional outdoor sports
Chef: Eliza Allen **Owners:** Eliza & John Allen **Times:** 12-2/7-9, Closed
Nov-end Feb **Notes:** Vegetarian by request only **Seats:** 26
Smoking: N/Sm in restaurant **Children:** Portions **Rooms:** 11 (11 en
suite) ★★ **Directions:** A832 to Muir of Ord. Over x-rd and rail bridge,
1st left signed Ullapool & Ord Distillery. Hotel 1/2m on left **Parking:** 24
e-mail: admin@ord-house.co.uk **web:** www.ord-house.co.uk

NAIRN MAP 23 NH85

🏵🏵🏵 The Boath House see page 596

🏵 Newton Hotel

International

Historic house in beautiful grounds

☎ 01667 453144   Inverness Rd IV12 4RX

PLACE: Set in 21 acres of mature parkland and gardens, this
luxurious and comfortable hotel dating to 1650 was completely
refurbished recently. Facilities consist of a 14m swimming pool,
spa and gym.
FOOD: The cooking is International using quality Scottish
ingredients, with a focus on local game and seafood.
OUR TIP: Try the excellent health and beauty treatments
Times: 12-2/7-9 **Rooms:** 56 (56 en suite) ★★★★ **Directions:** West
of the town centre, 10 minutes walk **web:** www.swallowhotels.com

---

Four Rosettes Amongst the very best
restaurants in the British Isles, where the
cooking demands national recognition. These
restaurants will exhibit intense ambition, a
passion for excellence, superb technical skills
and remarkable consistency. They will
combine appreciation of culinary traditions
with a passionate desire for further
exploration and improvement. Around twenty
restaurants have four Rosettes.

Scotland

Scotland

NAIRN MAP 23 NH85

The Boath House

Scottish, French

Stunning food and effortless service in small country-house hotel

☎ 01667 454896 Auldearn IV12 5TE

MENU GUIDE Cep velouté, potato & chive crisp • Lamb cannon, pressed shoulder, dauphinoise, caramelised sweetbreads Chocolate & nutmeg soup, morello cherries & sorbet

WINE GUIDE ♀ Olivier Leflaive Bourgogne £16.50 • ♀ Domain Chandon Savigny les Beaunes £35.75 • 38 bottles over £20, 40 bottles under £20 • 8 by the glass (£5-£7.50)

PRICE GUIDE Food prices not confirmed for 2006. Please telephone for details

PLACE: Guest and diners are treated like friends at this lovingly restored Georgian mansion hotel set in 20 acres of lawns, mature woodland and streams. Open fires flicker in the lounge, while the elegant dining room boasts comfortable high-backed chairs and well-appointed tables, and vibrant, contemporary Highland art vies for attention with views over gardens and trout-filled lake.

FOOD: Talented chef Charles Lockley's repertoire is classically based with modern techniques and presentation, using stunning quality ingredients from the abundant Highland larder, including produce from the hotel's own walled garden. The cooking has great balance, with clean, clear flavours and silky technical skills. The approach is via memorable, fixed-price, five-course dinners that offer just one choice at mains and dessert. The imaginative culinary journey may take in roasted cannon of red deer saddle, served with a pear tart Tatin and foie gras, or perhaps fillet of West Coast halibut, with open ravioli, split yellow peas and ham knuckle.

OUR TIP: Stay in one of the six beautiful bedrooms, and wander in the gardens or enjoy a spa treatment

Chef: Charles Lockley **Owners:** Mr & Mrs D Matherson **Times:** 12.30-1.45/7-8.30, Closed Xmas, closed L Mon-Wed **Notes:** Fixed L 4 courses £32.50, Fixed D 5 courses £45, Vegetarian available, Smart casual, No shorts/T-shirts/jeans, Civ Wed 30 **Seats:** 28, Pr/dining room 8 **Smoking:** N/Sm in restaurant **Children:** Portions **Rooms:** 6 (6 en suite) ★★ **Directions:** 2 miles E of Nairn on A96 (Inverness to Aberdeen road) **Parking:** 20 **e-mail:** info@boath-house.demon.co.uk **web:** www.boath-house.com

---

NETHY BRIDGE MAP 23 NJ02

 The Restaurant at The Mountview Hotel

British

Inspired Highland cooking amidst amazing surroundings

☎ 01479 821248 Grantown Rd PH25 3EB

MENU GUIDE Scallops, Arbroath smokie, saffron cream • Rack of lamb, onion & rosemary jus • Treacle & ginger pudding, butterscotch sauce

WINE GUIDE ♀ La Diva Chardonnay £11.95 • ♀ La Diva Cabernet Sauvignon £11.95 • 1 bottle over £20, 16 bottles under £20 • 4 by the glass (£3)

PRICE GUIDE Starter £3.50-£6.50 • main £12-£17 • dessert £4.25-£6 • coffee £2 • Service optional

PLACE: Set in the Cairngorm National Park, this friendly country-house hotel is a favoured base for bird-watchers and walking groups, and offers stunning views across the mountains from its elevated position.

FOOD: The kitchen works with the freshest seasonal ingredients, picking salad leaves and herbs from the hotel garden in summer. Expect imaginative and accomplished cooking: duck with a port wine sauce perhaps, or pork with a gruyère and sage potato cake.

OUR TIP: The hotel specialises in guided holidays

Chef: Lee Beale **Owners:** Kevin & Caryl Shaw **Times:** 6-11, Closed Xmas, Mon-Tue, closed L all week, closed D Mon-Tue **Notes:** Vegetarian available **Seats:** 24 **Smoking:** N/Sm in restaurant **Children:** Menu,

Portions **Rooms:** 12 (11 en suite) ★★ **Directions:** From Aviemore follow signs for Nethy Bridge, through Boat-of-Garten. In Nethy Bridge over humpback bridge & follow hotel signs **Parking:** 20
e-mail: mviewhotel@aol.com
web: www.members.aol.com/mviewhotel

ONICH MAP 22 NN06

 Lodge on the Loch Hotel

Modern Scottish

A stunning lochside setting for ambitious cuisine

☎ 01855 821237 PH33 6RY

MENU GUIDE Pheasant salad, vanilla poached pear • Beef, dauphinoise potatoes, confit garlic, beetroot jus • Sticky toffee pudding

PRICE GUIDE Food prices not confirmed for 2006. Please telephone for details

PLACE: This idyllically set hunting lodge offers some of the finest views in the country, with towering mountains and Glen Coe in one direction and open sea in the other. Its public rooms have been recently refurbished and combine striking design with country-house comfort.

FOOD: Complex and ambitious cooking with bold flavours. Superb presentation ensures a great first impression. The concise menu changes daily with vegetarian options.

OUR TIP: Cosy lounge with real fire for drinks or coffee

Times: 7.30-8.30, Closed L all week, Mon-Fri Nov-Easter, (Open 23 Dec-5 Jan) **Rooms:** 16 (16 en suite) ★★★
e-mail: reservations@freedomglen.co.uk
web: www.freedomglen.co.uk/ll

continued

Onich Hotel
European
Superb quality cooking right on the shores of Loch Linnhe
☎ 01855 821214   PH33 6RY

MENU GUIDE Hand-dived Loch Leven scallops, creamed leeks & bacon • Trio of Aberdeen Angus beef on celeriac mash, red wine truffle jus • Highland toffee cheesecake

WINE GUIDE ♀ Los Vilos Chardonnay £12.50 • ♀ Los Vilos Cabernet Sauvignon £12.50 • 7 bottles over £20, 25 bottles under £20 • 6 by the glass (£3.20-£3.75)

PRICE GUIDE Fixed D £28 • min/water £3 • Service optional

PLACE: A traditional and elegantly decorated dining room with fabulous views over Loch Linnhe and the Morvern Hills. Serves dinner only.

FOOD: The fixed-price menu has three or four choices at each course, and includes coffee and petits fours. Lots of skill and a genuine enthusiasm for food, with starters and desserts giving special scope for the kitchen's artistic touches, for example roasted baby pineapple, coconut risotto & black pepper parfait. Dishes are classically based with European influences. Fresh seasonal produce of the best quality is sourced whenever possible.

OUR TIP: Perfect for a lochside stroll before or after dinner
Chef: Robert Ramsey **Owners:** Mr S Leitch **Times:** 7-9, Closed Xmas, Closed L all week **Notes:** Coffee incl, Vegetarian available, Smart casual **Seats:** 50, Pr/dining room 24 **Smoking:** N/Sm in restaurant **Children:** Menu, Portions **Rooms:** 25 (25 en suite) ★★★
Directions: Beside A82. Located in village of Onich, 9m S of Fort William **Parking:** 50 **e-mail:** enquiries@onich-fortwilliam.co.uk
web: www.onich-fortwilliam.co.uk

POOLEWE MAP 22 NG88

Pool House Hotel
Modern British
Fine dining in lochside restaurant with views
☎ 01445 781272   IV22 2LD
MENU GUIDE Chicken & Puy lentil soup • Fillet of venison with haggis, sweet potato • Hot caramel fruit pudding
PRICE GUIDE Food prices not confirmed for 2006. Please telephone for details
PLACE: Set on the shores of Loch Ewe, where the river meets the bay, this former military base may have an unassuming façade, but it boasts a stunning interior. The stylish North By North West dining room has unrestricted views of Loch Ewe, where otters and seals can be easily spotted.

FOOD: Predominantly local produce is handled with care and respect in a parade of modern Scottish dishes that may include scallops from the loch outside the hotel, as well as Kinlochbervie halibut and Scottish lamb.
OUR TIP: Keep an eye open for seals and otters
Times: 12-2/6.30-8.15, reservations required at all times **Rooms:** 5 (5 en suite) ★★★ **Directions:** 6M N of Gairloch on A832. Hotel by bridge on River Ewe **e-mail:** enquiries@poolhousehotel.com
web: www.poolhousehotel.com

PORTREE MAP 22 NG44

Cuillin Hills Hotel
British, French
Perfect Highland retreat with great food and views
☎ 01478 612003   IV51 9QU

MENU GUIDE Pan-fried fishcakes • Duck breast confit, white pudding • Clootie dumpling, Drambuie & cream
WINE GUIDE 20 bottles over £20, 45 bottles under £20 • 7 by the glass (£3.25)
PRICE GUIDE Fixed D £31.50 • coffee £1.50 • min/water £2.95 • Service optional
PLACE: Built in 1870, this imposing MacDonald hunting lodge with 15 acres of grounds has spectacular views over Portree Bay to the Cuillin Hills beyond. The split-level dining room allows as many tables as possible to enjoy the views from this wonderful location.
FOOD: Meat, game and fish are all locally sourced. Traditional dishes like roast pheasant and venison loin with plum chutney feature alongside the menu's more continental-style items such as grilled chicken with pancetta & polenta with balsamic reduction. Accomplished cooking.
OUR TIP: Visit the nearby Talisker Distillery
Chef: Robert Macaskill **Owners:** Wickman Hotels Ltd **Times:** 12-2/6.30-9, Closed L Mon-Sat **Notes:** Vegetarian available, Smart Dress, Civ Wed 70 **Seats:** 48, Pr/dining room 20 **Smoking:** N/Sm in restaurant **Children:** Menu, Portions **Rooms:** 28 (28 en suite) ★★★
Directions: 0.25 miles N of Portree on A855 **Parking:** 56
e-mail: info@cuillin-hotel-skye.co.uk
web: www.cuillin-hotel-skye.co.uk

What makes a Restaurant of the Year?
In selecting a Restaurant of the Year, we look for somewhere that is exceptional in its chosen area of the market. Whilst the Rosette awards are based on the quality of the food alone, Restaurant of the Year takes into account all aspects of the operation. For full details see pages 6-7.

Scotland

continued

PORTREE continued MAP 22 NG44

Rosedale Hotel

British

Scottish cuisine in friendly hotel with stunning views

☎ 01478 613131 Beaumont Crescent IV51 9DB

MENU GUIDE Cullen skink (smoked haddock soup) • Tuna steak, prawn & saffron risotto, prawn bisque • Skye strawberry crème brûlée

WINE GUIDE ♀ Sacred Hill Semillon/Chardonnay £14.95 • ♀ Sacred Hill Cabernet/Shiraz £14.95 • 6 bottles over £20, 28 bottles under £20 • 7 by the glass (£3)

PRICE GUIDE Fixed D £22-£26.50 • coffee £1.50 • min/water £3 • Service optional

PLACE: Converted from fishermen's cottages on the water's edge, this friendly family-run hotel is a labyrinth of rooms with comfortable lounges, a bar, and an attractive restaurant that overlooks Portree harbour.

FOOD: Modern Scottish dishes made from local produce where possible, with seafood a speciality. Hake is served with a coriander crust and pink peppercorn sauce, while lamb arrives with a sweet potato and black pudding crumble.

OUR TIP: Save room for dessert

Chef: Kirk Moir, Tony Parkyn **Owners:** Mr & Mrs P Rouse **Times:** 7-9, Closed 1 Nov-1 Apr, closed L all wk **Notes:** Vegetarian available **Seats:** 30 **Smoking:** N/Sm in restaurant **Children:** Menu, Portions **Rooms:** 18 (18 en suite) ★★ **Directions:** On harbour front **Parking:** On street **e-mail:** rosedalehotelsky@aol.com **web:** www.rosedalehotelskye.co.uk

SCOURIE MAP 22 NC14

Eddrachilles Hotel

British, French   **NEW**

Enjoyable dining in spectacular surroundings

☎ 01971 502080 Badcall Bay IV27 4TH

MENU GUIDE Haggis & potato stack • Lemon & basil poached chicken breast • Raspberry frangipane tart

WINE GUIDE ♀ Mâcon Villages £14.50 • ♀ Randall Bridge £12 • 40 bottles over £20, 20 bottles under £20 • 4 by the glass (£2.20-£4.50)

PRICE GUIDE Food prices not confirmed for 2006. Please telephone for details

PLACE: Stunning sea and island views make this peaceful hotel a magnificent haven. After walking on deserted beaches, watching the seals and otters, and climbing rugged hills, make a beeline for the cosy restaurant.

FOOD: The straightforward, homely cooking makes much use of local produce, leading to sighs of unqualified pleasure. Light salmon fishcakes, and halibut with lime butter sauce, are just two of the excellent reasons for dining here.

OUR TIP: Fish is a must!

Chef: Fiona Deakin **Owners:** Graham & Fiona Deakin **Times:** 6.30-8.30, Closed Nov-Feb, closed L everyday **Notes:** Vegetarian available, Dress Restrictions, No trainers or shorts **Seats:** 30 **Children:** Min 3 yrs, Menu, Portions **Rooms:** 11 (11 en suite) ★★ **Directions:** 2m S of Scourie village on A894 **e-mail:** fiona@eddrachilles.com **web:** www.eddrachilles.com

SHIELDAIG MAP 22 NG85

Tigh an Eilean Hotel

Modern Scottish

Accomplished cooking in thoroughly hospitable, seafront hotel

☎ 01520 755251 IV54 8XN

MENU GUIDE Timbale of Shieldaig crab & basil, sweet & sharp tomato dressing • Pan-cooked tenderloin of outdoor reared pork, juniper-braised Savoy cabbage, Dijon grain mustard sauce • Warm plum tart with chilled crème Anglaise

WINE GUIDE ♀ Domaine de Thelin Chardonnay £12.60 • ♀ Château Lauriol Cabernet £15.50 • 36 bottles over £20, 17 bottles under £20 • 4 by the glass (£3.15-£6)

PRICE GUIDE Fixed D fr £37.50 • min/water £3.75 • Service optional

PLACE: However long your journey to reach Shieldaig, an 18th-century fishing village perched on the shore of Loch Torridon, you'll know it was worth it as you arrive at this delightful white painted hotel. The restaurant is airy and light, with an atmosphere of relaxed chic, and fabulous views across the loch to the open sea beyond.

FOOD: The daily-changing menus are driven by the availability of fresh fish, seafood and other local produce, and this passion for the very best ingredients is evident in the constantly evolving dishes. The commitment of the owners is clear, and no wonder people travel considerable distances to eat here. A spring menu might feature risotto of Loch Torridon langoustines, langoustine broth and fresh herbs, to be followed by rack of Blackface lamb with a herb-scented crust - straightforward, accurately prepared dishes where nothing is more important than flavour.

OUR TIP: Great local cheeses

Chef: Christopher Field **Owners:** Christopher & Cathryn Field **Times:** 7-8.30, Closed end Oct-mid Mar, closed L all week **Notes:** Coffee incl, Vegetarian available, Smart casual, Civ Wed 40 **Seats:** 28, Pr/dining room 28 **Smoking:** N/Sm in restaurant **Children:** Menu, Portions **Rooms:** 11 (11 en suite) ★ **Directions:** From A896 follow signs for Shieldaig. Hotel in village centre on water's edge **e-mail:** tighaneilanhotel@shieldaig.fsnet.co.uk

SKEABOST BRIDGE MAP 22 NG44

Skeabost Country House Hotel

Scottish, French   **NEW**

Accurate cooking in countryside surroundings

☎ 01470 532202 01470 532215 IV51 9NP

MENU GUIDE Asparagus wrapped in pancetta & filo pastry • Lamb rack, mushroom risotto, rosemary mint jus • Banana loaf, butterscotch sauce

continue

PRICE GUIDE Food prices not confirmed for 2006. Please telephone for details

PLACE: The smart, wood-panelled, regal-designed dining room of this 19th-century house, set beside the picturesque shore of Loch Snizort, looks out over 12 acres of wooded gardens. Crisp white napery, comfortable chairs and attentive service complete the setting.

FOOD: The kitchen's simple treatment allows superb quality ingredients from the Highland larder to shine, with local seafood and game finding top billing.

OUR TIP: Delightful, romantic venue

Times: 12-3/7-9.30, Closed Jan, Feb, closed L all week **Rooms:** 21 (21 en suite) ★★★ **Directions:** Telephone for directions
e-mail: reception@skeabostcountryhouse.com
web: www.skeabostcountryhouse.com

STEIN MAP 22 NG25

Loch Bay Seafood Restaurant
Seafood

Homely setting for fantastic fish

☎ 01470 592235   IV55 8GA

MENU GUIDE Grilled oysters, parmesan & herbs • Monkfish with garlic & herb butter, chips • Clootie dumpling with cream

WINE GUIDE Domaine de Berthiers Pouilly Fumé Sauvignon Blanc £19.95 • Veldt Range Robertson Region Shiraz £11.50 • 11 bottles over £20, 25 bottles under £20 • 6 by the glass (£2.25-£4.25)

PRICE GUIDE Starter £2.75-£7 • main £8.50-£31 • dessert £4.25-£5 • coffee £1.30 • min/water £2.50 • Service optional

PLACE: Set a pebble's skim from the loch in a pretty fishing village, this small cottage restaurant does a brisk trade no matter what the time of year.

FOOD: Some of the world's finest seafood, delivered with a confident lack of fanfare and fuss. It's cooked simply with just a brush of olive oil and served with delicious home-made chips and island herbs.

OUR TIP: No meat or vegetarian dishes available

Chef: David Wilkinson **Owners:** David & Alison Wilkinson **Times:** 12-2.30/6-9, Closed Nov-Easter (excl. 1wk over Hogmanay), Sun, closed L Sat **Notes:** Blackboard menu continuously changing, Vegetarian by request only **Seats:** 26 **Smoking:** N/Sm in restaurant **Children:** Portions **Parking:** 6 **e-mail:** david@lochbay-seafood-restaurant.co.uk **web:** www.lochbay-seafood-restaurant.co.uk

STRONTIAN MAP 22 NM86

Kilcamb Lodge Hotel
Scottish, International

Accomplished cooking in peaceful, friendly lochside hotel

☎ 01967 402257   PH36 4HY

MENU GUIDE Roast loin of hare • Turbot fillet, smoked halibut brandade • Warm bitter chocolate tart

WINE GUIDE Chablis Chardonnay £18 • Santa Ema Merlot £19.50 • 40 bottles over £20, 40 bottles under £20 • 8 by the glass (£3.75-£7.50)

PRICE GUIDE Fixed L £12-£30 • Fixed D £38 • coffee £1.75 min/water £2.50 • Service optional • Group min 5 service 10%

PLACE: Used as a barracks during the Highland Clearances, Kilcamb Lodge has a friendlier reputation nowadays, and its comforts are considerably improved. The lochside setting makes an ideal winter and summer retreat, and the restaurant is as tasteful as the food.

Kilcamb Lodge Hotel

FOOD: Accomplished country-house cooking with the freshest of local produce at its core continues to get a good review. Imaginative dishes like pan-fried sea bream with langoustine beignets are superbly presented on the plate, and the short fixed-price menu is ideally balanced between fish, meat and a vegetarian choice.

OUR TIP: Well worth the journey, and a delightful place to stay

Chef: Neil Mellis & Bill Fowler **Owners:** Sally & David Fox **Times:** 12-2.30/7.30-8.30, Closed 3 Jan-15 Feb, closed L Mon **Notes:** Vegetarian available, Dress Restrictions, Smart casual, Civ Wed 60 **Seats:** 26 **Smoking:** N/Sm in restaurant **Children:** Min 12 yrs **Rooms:** 11 (11 en suite) ★★ **Directions:** Take the Corran ferry off A82. Follow A861 to Strontian. First left over bridge after village **Parking:** 28 **e-mail:** enquiries@kilcamblodge.co.uk **web:** www.kilcamblodge.co.uk

TAIN MAP 23 NH78

Glenmorangie Highland Home at Cadboll
British, Scottish

Dinner-party style in individual hotel

☎ 01862 871671   Cadboll, Fearn IV20 1XP

MENU GUIDE Baked halibut fillet & scallops • Seared, whisky-marinated loin of lamb • Drambuie & vanilla pannacotta

WINE GUIDE Domaine Gitton Sancerre £26.99 • Frank Phelan Bordeaux £27.50 • 25 bottles over £20, 7 bottles under £20 • 4 by the glass (£3.50-£5)

PRICE GUIDE Fixed D £42.50

PLACE: Guests meet each other over drinks prior to being seated at a large oak table for dinner, where firm friendships are often forged. Owned by a renowned Scottish malt whisky company, the dining room is richly furnished in traditional lodge style.

FOOD: Home-grown vegetables and fruit bring a fresh flavour to the set four-course menu (no choices), where old Scottish favourites like wild duck breast marinated in whisky are given a contemporary twist with beetroot and apple tartare.

OUR TIP: Take a walk in the walled gardens where the ruins of Cadboll Castle remain

Chef: David Graham, **Owners:** Glenmorangie Plc **Times:** 8, Closed 23-26 Dec, 4-18 Jan, closed L except by prior arrangement **Notes:** Monthly gourmet nights £47.50, Vegetarian by request only, Smart Dress, Civ Wed 24 **Seats:** 24, Pr/dining room 12 **Smoking:** N/Sm in restaurant **Children:** Min 14 yrs, Portions **Rooms:** 9 (9 en suite) ★★ **Directions:** N on A9 turn right onto B9175 (just before Tain) & follow signs for hotel **Parking:** 30 **e-mail:** relax@glenmorangieplc.co.uk **web:** www.glenmorangie.com

continued

TONGUE MAP 23 NC55

⊚ Ben Loyal Hotel

British, Scottish

Ambitious cooking and stunning highland views

☎ 01847 611216 Main St IV27 4XE

MENU GUIDE Wild salmon gravalax with deep-fried oysters
Brochette of local langoustines in Thai spice • Poached peach
Pavlova

WINE GUIDE ♀ Hidden Falls Chardonnay £14 • ♟ Hidden Falls
Merlot £14 • all bottles under £20 • 2 by the glass (£3.50)

PRICE GUIDE Starter £4.50-£7.15 • main £10.95-£15.50 • dessert
£4.95 • coffee £2.15 • min/water £2.35 • Service optional

PLACE: Fabulous views of the Kyle of Tongue, Castle Varrich and
both Ben Loyal and Ben Hope in the distance form the stunning
backdrop to this traditional hotel restaurant.
FOOD: The menu is extensive with emphasis on use of local
produce - hence, the stress on game and seafood. The chef offers
a menu where all the elements are superbly handled and
flavours shine through.
OUR TIP: Summer sunsets are beautiful
Chef: Elizabeth Warburton **Owners:** Mr & Mrs P Lewis **Times:** 12-
2.30/6-8, Closed end Oct-end Mar, closed L all week **Notes:** Vegetarian
available **Seats:** 50, Pr/dining room **Smoking:** N/Sm in restaurant
Children: Menu, Portions **Rooms:** 11 (11 en suite) ★★
Directions: Hotel in centre of village at junction of A836 & A838
Parking: 20 **e-mail:** benloyalhotel@btinternet.com
web: www.benloyal.co.uk

TORRIDON MAP 22 NG95

⊚⊚ Loch Torridon Country House Hotel

British, French

Country house with awe inspiring views and modern cooking

☎ 01445 791242 IV22 2EY

MENU GUIDE Scallops, ginger, lemon & dill butter, noodles &
vegetable spaghetti • Peppered lamb loin, polenta, ratatouille,
spinach, sweetbreads, caper & oregano jus

WINE GUIDE ♀ Santa Ema Sauvignon Blanc £19 • ♟ Jacobite
Ridge Shiraz £19 • 150 bottles over £20, 30 bottles under £20
8 by the glass (£5-£6)

PRICE GUIDE Fixed D £44 • coffee £4.50 • min/water
£3.75 • Service optional

PLACE: Magnificent views over untamed Highland mountains
and the waters of Loch Torridon await diners at this elegant,
Victorian era, country-house hotel. The plushly furnished
restaurant, with original Scots pine panelling, ornate ceiling and
fireplace, is formal yet relaxed, while the conservatory area takes
in that scenery. There's a serious, well-chosen wine list, while 300
malt whiskies await in the bar.
FOOD: The intricate, assured, modern-focused cooking is
underpinned by a French theme and utilises top quality, fresh,
local produce from the Highland larder and the hotel's kitchen
garden.
OUR TIP: Perfect setting for a romantic break or to escape the
pressures of life
Chef: Kevin Broome **Owners:** Daniel & Rohaise Rose-Bristow
Times: 12-2/7-8.45, Closed 2 Jan for 4 wks **Notes:** Light lunches
available, £6-£20, Vegetarian available, Dress Restrictions, No jeans or
trainers **Seats:** 38, Pr/dining room 16 **Smoking:** N/Sm in restaurant
Children: Min 12 yrs, Menu, Portions **Rooms:** 19 (19 en suite) ★★★

Directions: From Inverness take A9 N, follow signs to Ullapool (A835). At
Garve take A832 to Kinlochewe; take A896 to Torridon. Do not turn off to
Torridon Village. Hotel on right after Annat village **Parking:** 20
e-mail: enquiries@lochtorridonhotel.com
web: www.lochtorridonhotel.com

LANARKSHIRE, SOUTH

BIGGAR MAP 21 NT03

⊚⊚ Shieldhill Castle

International

Fine food and wine in historic castle setting

☎ 01899 220035 Quothquan ML12 6NA

MENU GUIDE Monkfish & scallop, turbot consommé • Wood
pigeon, Puy lentils, artichoke ravioli • Liquorice soufflé,
blackcurrant smoothie

WINE GUIDE ♀ Miguel Torres Marimar £40 • ♟ Jim Barry
Cover Drive Cabernet Sauvignon £23 • 16 bottles under £20

PRICE GUIDE Fixed L £12.95-£18.95 • Fixed D £17.95-
£23.95 • starter £7.45-£15.95 • main £12.50-£24.95 • dessert
£6.50-£7.45 • coffee £2 • min/water £4 • Service optional

PLACE: Set amid tranquil Scottish countryside, this imposing
castle wears its grandeur lightly and has a friendly house party
ambience. Dinner is served in the impressive surroundings of
Chancellor's restaurant, which offers panoramic views of the
Clyde Valley.
FOOD: Shieldhill offers a pleasing combination of imaginative
modern European cuisine and an award-winning wine list,
designed by the proprietor. The menu teams the two, providing a
choice of wine to accompany each dish and also features a
speciality selection of sauces to enjoy with local mussels. Diners
are welcome to mix and match from any of the menus, not
necessarily selecting the standard three courses.
OUR TIP: Game comes fresh from the estate
Chef: Ashley Gallant **Owners:** Mr & Mrs R Lamb **Times:** 12-1.45/7-8.45
Notes: Vegetarian available, Civ Wed 150 **Seats:** 32, Pr/dining room 30
Smoking: N/Sm in restaurant **Children:** Portions **Rooms:** 16 (16 en
suite) ★★★ **Directions:** From Biggar take B7016 to Carnwath. After
approx 2.5m turn left onto Shieldhill Road. Castle is 1m on right
Parking: 60 **e-mail:** enquiries@shieldhill.co.uk
web: www.shieldhill.co.uk

The AA Wine Awards recognise the finest
wine lists in England, Scotland and Wales. For
full details, see pages 14-15

EAST KILBRIDE MAP 20 NS65

Crutherland Hotel
British

Enjoyable dining in landscaped grounds
☎ 01355 577000 Strathaven Rd G75 0QZ
MENU GUIDE Scallops, pancetta, rocket • Rib-eye steak,
dauphinoise potatoes, peppercorn sauce • Poached white pear,
butterscotch sauce
WINE GUIDE ♀ Chablis £26.50 • ♀ Shiraz £17.95 • 80 bottles
over £20, 27 bottles under £20 • 12 by the glass (£5.75-£7)
PRICE GUIDE Fixed D £26.50-£28.50 • starter £5.50-£8.50 • main
£10.50-£22.50 • dessert £4.50-£5.75 • coffee £2.95 • min/water
£4.40 • Service optional
PLACE: This country-house hotel is popular with the conference
market thanks to its extensive leisure and banqueting facilities.
Tables are well spaced in the richly furnished dining room and
staff are attentive.
FOOD: Straightforward and enjoyable cooking. Plump for steak
with one of a range of sauces, or a more involved dish such as wild
mushroom risotto, or calves' liver with bacon, mash and sage jus.
OUR TIP: The fixed-price menu offers good value
Chef: Stephan Frost **Owners:** Macdonald Hotels **Times:** 12-2.30/7-9.30,
Closed L Sat **Notes:** Vegetarian available, Civ Wed 250 **Seats:** 64,
Pr/dining room 36 **Smoking:** N/Sm in restaurant, Air con
Children: Menu, Portions **Rooms:** 75 (75 en suite) ★★★★
Directions: From E Kilbride take A726 towards Strathaven. 1.5m, &
beyond Torrance rdbt, hotel on left **Parking:** 200
e-mail: crutherland@macdonald-hotels.co.uk
web: www.macdonaldhotels.co.uk

STRATHAVEN MAP 20 NS74

Rissons Restaurant at the Springvale Hotel
Modern Scottish

Relaxed restaurant with modern Scottish cuisine
☎ 01357 520234 18 Lethame Rd ML10 6AD
MENU GUIDE Chicken & leek terrine, pear chutney • Roast
pheasant, black pudding, cider sauce • Marmalade pudding,
honey oatmeal ice cream
WINE GUIDE ♀ Vinakoier Pinot Grigio £13.95 • ♀ Los
Camachos Merlot £15.95 • 20 bottles under £20 • 4 by the glass
(£2.50-£3.50)
PRICE GUIDE Fixed L £11.95 • Fixed D £13.95 • starter £3.50-
£6.95 • main £8.50-£16.50 • dessert £3.95-£4.75 • coffee
£1.75 • min/water £3 • Service optional
PLACE: Just off town centre, with up-to-date minimalist decor,
this smart restaurant offers a relaxed, friendly and homely
experience.
FOOD: The chef creates simply presented, seasonal dishes with a
modern twist; in winter months he introduces ideas based on
comfort foods to add that feel good factor. Expect layered haggis
gateau and roast mallard with sweet red cabbage and roasted
cod, lentils and capers on the menu.
OUR TIP: Great value Sunday menu
Chef: Scott Baxter, Sandra Law **Owners:** Scott Baxter, Anne Baxter
Times: 12.30-2.30/5.30-9.30, Closed New Year, 1 wk Jan, 1st wk July,
Mon-Tue, closed L Wed-Sat **Notes:** Vegetarian available **Seats:** 50
Smoking: N/Sm in restaurant **Children:** Portions **Rooms:** 11 (11 en
suite) ♦♦♦ **Directions:** From M74 junct 8 follow A71, through
Stonehouse and onto Strathaven **Parking:** 10
e-mail: rissons@msn.com

LOTHIAN, EAST

DIRLETON MAP 21 NT58

The Open Arms Hotel
Modern Scottish

Charming hotel making the most of local produce
☎ 01620 850241 EH39 5EG
MENU GUIDE Tempura hake, seafood risotto • Lamb loin, herb
& redcurrant stuffing • Passionfruit cheesecake, maple & walnut
ice cream
PRICE GUIDE Food prices not confirmed for 2006. Please
telephone for details
PLACE: A hotel of considerable charm and character, set by the
village green and with views over Dirleton Castle. There are two
dining options, the popular and informal Brasserie, and the
elegant, intimate Library.
FOOD: A smartly modern menu makes thorough use of Scottish
produce; Craigdan venison perhaps, or Kirkcudbright scallops.
The Angus fillet, pan-fried and wrapped in pancetta with a Gruth-
Dhu and chive mash, shows the style well.
OUR TIP: Walk the Castle grounds before supper
Times: 12-2/7-9, Closed D Sun **Rooms:** 10 (10 en suite) ★★★
Directions: From A1 (S) take A198 to North Berwick, then follow signs for
Dirleton - 2 miles W. From Edinburgh take A6137 leading to A198
e-mail: openarmshotel@clara.co.uk **web:** www.openarmshotel.com

GULLANE MAP 21 NT48

Greywalls Hotel
British

Good food in elegant surroundings
☎ 01620 842144 Muirfield EH31 2EG
MENU GUIDE Langoustine ravioli, wilted rocket, langoustine &
brandy bisque • Aberdeen Angus beef cooked two ways,
melange raisins • Hot chocolate fondant, Tahitian vanilla ice
cream
WINE GUIDE ♀ Babich Sauvignon Blanc £20 • ♀ Lunnards
Crossing Shiraz/Malbec £18.50 • 300 bottles over £20, 35 bottles
under £20 • 10 by the glass (£4-£6)
PRICE GUIDE Fixed D £45 • min/water £3.50 • Service optional
PLACE: Beautiful Lutyens country house and Gertrude Jekyll
gardens backing onto the estuary, providing elegant Edwardian
comfort. The stylish two rooms of the restaurant overlook the
famous Muirfield golf course, and traditional formalities include
the wearing of jackets and ties by gentlemen.
FOOD: Scottish sourcing of ingredients where possible (halibut
from Forth, Eyemouth lobster and East Lothian pheasant) is a key
feature of the short dinner menu, though the refined choice can
be supplemented by steaks and pastas if requested.
OUR TIP: Play a round on the world-famous course
Chef: David Williams **Owners:** Mr & Mrs G Weaver **Times:** 7.30-9.00,
Closed Nov-Mar, closed L all **Notes:** Vegetarian available, Dress
Restrictions, Jacket & tie requested **Seats:** 40, Pr/dining room 20
Smoking: N/Sm in restaurant **Children:** Portions **Rooms:** 22 (22 en
suite) ★★★ **Directions:** From Edinburgh take A1 to North Berwick slip
road, then follow A198 along coast to far end of Gullane - Greywalls in last
road on left **Parking:** 40 **e-mail:** hotel@greywalls.co.uk
web: www.greywalls.co.uk

Scotland

601

GULLANE *continued* MAP 21 NT48

◎◎ La Potinière

Modern British

Ambitious cooking in cottage-style restaurant

☎ 01620 843214 Main St EH31 2AA

MENU GUIDE Thai coconut soup, West Coast scallops • Roast venison, damson & juniper jus • Duo of chocolate mousses with raspberry & Drambuie

WINE GUIDE ♀ Hugel Fleur d'Alsace Riesling, Muscat £17.50 • ♀ Simon Hackett Old Vine Grenache £15.50 • 21 bottles over £20, 9 bottles under £20 • 4 by the glass (£3-£4)

PRICE GUIDE Fixed L £16.50 • Fixed D £36.50 • min/water £2.50 • Service optional

PLACE: A delightful cottage-style restaurant of fairytale proportions in a Scottish coastal village that remains a favourite with the locals. Smart crisp linen and quality tableware show serious intent.

FOOD: A concise modern British menu offers just two choices at each course, with accomplished dishes distinguished by succulent flavours, as in duck foie gras and Armagnac parfait with rhubarb and cinnamon compôte and cinnamon brioche. Great use is made of fresh local ingredients, especially seafood and game. The sensibly priced global wine list is hand-picked by the chefs themselves and shows their enthusiasm.

OUR TIP: Excellent tasting notes on the wine list
Chef: Mary Runciman & Keith Marley **Owners:** Mary Runciman & Keith Marley **Times:** 12.30-2/7-9, Closed Xmas, BHs, Mon-Tue, closed D Sun (Oct-Mar) **Notes:** Sun D avail. between Apr-Sept, coffee incl., Vegetarian available, Smart casual **Seats:** 28 **Smoking:** N/Sm in restaurant **Children:** Portions **Directions:** 20m SE of Edinburgh. 5m from North Berwick on A198 **Parking:** 10 **web:** www.la-potiniere.co.uk

---

HADDINGTON MAP 21 NT57

◎◎ Bonars Restaurant

Contemporary

A choice of brasserie or fine dining in idyllic riverbank setting by old watermill

☎ 01620 822100 Poldrate Mill, Tyne House EH41 4AD

MENU GUIDE Pan-fried veal liver, port wine onions, pancetta • Sea bass, chilli & sesame seed tiger prawns • Date pudding, espresso anglaise

PRICE GUIDE Food prices not confirmed for 2006. Please telephone for details

PLACE: The Bonars have expanded their restaurant operation within the refurbished buildings by an old watermill on the River Tyne. You can now dine informally in the all-day Poldrates Brasserie or enjoy the fine dining experience in Bonars itself, the latter sporting a Mediterranean feel with stone walls, spot lighting and terracotta tiles.

FOOD: Cooking is contemporary with emphasis on artistic presentation. Well judged, simplified dishes are cooked with flair and imagination resulting in harmony and accuracy of flavours.

OUR TIP: Ask about the themed food nights and cookery classes
Chef: Douglas & Annabel Bonar **Owners:** D & A Bonar **Times:** 12-2.30/6-9, Closed Mon, Tues **e-mail:** bonars@lineone.net

⑪ Waterside Bistro 1-5 Waterside EH41 4AT

☎ 01620 825674 Relatively formal eaterie located in a picturesque setting and known for generous portions.

LOTHIAN, WEST

LINLITHGOW MAP 21 NS97

◎◎ Champany Inn

British

Unrivalled steak restaurant in country lodge

☎ 01506 834532 EH49 7LU

MENU GUIDE Highland black pudding • Entrecote steak with mushroom sauce • Champany cheesecake

WINE GUIDE ♀ Champany own label house Chenin Blanc £14.50 • ♀ Champany own label house Shiraz £15.50 650 bottles over £20, 10 bottles under £20 • 5 by the glass (£3.75-£9)

PRICE GUIDE Fixed L £16.75 • starter £8.90-£13.50 • main £17.50-£32.50 • dessert £6.50 • coffee £3.75 • min/water £3.75 • Service added 10%

PLACE: With the atmosphere and ambience of a Scottish country lodge, this unusual little hotel is welcoming and hospitable. Stone walls and an old water mill add to the setting. There is a sommelier to help you select from the huge wine list.

FOOD: This is the Rolls Royce of steak houses, specialising in beef steaks from cattle sourced and prepared by the restaurant's own butchery. The juiciest cuts are heated over the charcoal grill, and served in prime condition. Other choices run to lamb double loin chops, and baked chicken with tarragon mousse, and there a few seafood options as well. Finish with a light apricot cheesecake.

OUR TIP: Round off the meal with coffee and a wee dram in the bar
Chef: C Davidson, D Gibson, K Hope **Owners:** Mr & Mrs C Davidson **Times:** 12.30-2/7-10, Closed 25-26 Dec, Sun, closed L Sat **Notes:** Vegetarian available, Dress Restrictions, No Jeans **Seats:** 50, Pr/dining room 30 **Children:** Min 8 yrs **Directions:** 2m NE of Linlithgow. From M9 (N) junct 3, at top of slip road turn right. Champany is 500 yds on right **Parking:** 50 **e-mail:** reception@champany.com **web:** www.champany.com

◎◎ Livingston's Restaurant

British French

Hidden gem serving fine Glenfarg, Perthshire and Wester Ross produce

☎ 01506 846565 52 High St EH49 7AE

MENU GUIDE Pot of smoked Arbroath haddock • Saddle of venison, crème de cassis sauce • Hot chocolate fondant, white chocolate ice cream

WINE GUIDE ♀ JGJ Basilicata Pinot Grigio £17.75 • ♀ Hellfire Bay Grenache-Shiraz £17.50 • 29 bottles over £20, 23 bottles under £20 • 4 by the glass (£3.30)

continue

PRICE GUIDE Fixed L £14.95 • Fixed D £33.95 • coffee £2 • min/water £3 • Service optional • Group min 8 service 10%
PLACE: When Linlithgow Palace was in its hey-day and Mary Queen of Scots used this building to stable the royal horses, the town acquired the status of 'Royal Burgh'. Almost hidden away off the main street, this family-run restaurant has a wonderful garden setting, where you can catch a glimpse of the loch through the trees. The hospitable ambience and candlelight complete this restaurant's irresistible allure.
FOOD: Julian Wright was highly commended at the Scottish Chef Awards in 2004. His modern Scottish cuisine with French influences continues to demonstrate inventive combinations with an excellent balance of ingredients and consistency.
OUR TIP: A place for romance
Chef: Julian Wright **Owners:** Ronald & Christine Livingston **Times:** 12-2.30/6-9.30, Closed 1 wk Jun, 1 wk Oct, 2wks Jan, Sun-Mon **Notes:** Vegetarian available, Smart Dress **Seats:** 40 **Smoking:** N/Sm in restaurant **Children:** Min 8 yrs, Portions **Directions:** Opposite post office **Parking:** NCP-Lilithgow Cross, on street

Marynka 57 High St EH49 7ED ☎ 01506 840123
Glass-fronted restaurant with modern Scottish cooking.

UPHALL MAP 21 NT07
⊛ Houstoun House
British, French
Intimate dining in turreted 17th-century hotel
☎ 01506 853831   EH52 6JS
MENU GUIDE Roast goat cheese, tomato chutney, salad • Sea bass, mushroom risotto cake, tomato salpicon • White chocolate & raspberry parfait
WINE GUIDE ♀ Katherine Hills Colombard/Chardonnay £17.50 • ♀ Domaine de Massia Cabernet Sauvignon £16.95 42 bottles over £20, 38 bottles under £20 • 12 by the glass (£4.25-£7)
PRICE GUIDE Fixed L £15.50 • Fixed D £27.50 • starter £5.25-£7.95 • main £14.50-£21.75 • dessert £5.50-£5.95 • coffee £3.95 • min/water £4.55 • Service optional
PLACE: A 17th-century tower house transformed into a four star hotel. The fine dining restaurant occupies three interconnecting rooms - the former drawing room, great hall and library - each of which provides its own intimate atmosphere. The vaulted bar with its open fire is the perfect place to relax with an after-dinner dram.
FOOD: A modern approach to traditional Scottish ingredients and dishes, with influences from further afield.
OUR TIP: Enjoy the grounds and delightful spa
Chef: Claus Nielsen **Owners:** Macdonald Hotels **Times:** 12.30-2/7-9.30, Closed L Sat **Notes:** Vegetarian available, No jean, no trainers, Civ Wed 100 **Seats:** 65, Pr/dining room 30 **Smoking:** N/Sm in restaurant **Children:** Menu, Portions **Rooms:** 71 (71 en suite) ★★★★ **Parking:** 200 **e-mail:** houstoun@macdonald-hotels.co.uk **web:** www.macdonaldhotels.co.uk/houstoun.house

Five Rosettes The finest restaurants in the British Isles, where the cooking stands comparison with the best in the world. These restaurants will have highly individual voices, exhibit breathtaking culinary skills and set the standards to which others aspire. Around six restaurants have five Rosettes.

MORAY

CRAIGELLACHIE MAP 23 NJ24
⊛⊛ Craigellachie Hotel
Scottish, International
Impressive Victorian hotel dining in the heart of Speyside
☎ 01340 881204   AB38 9SR
MENU GUIDE Craigellachie smoked salmon • Pan-fried rib of Aberdeen Angus beef • Iced mocha terrine
WINE GUIDE ♀ Torreon de Paredes Sauvignon Blanc £17.50 • ♀ Torreon de Paredes, Merlot £17.50 • 59 bottles over £20, 22 bottles under £20 • 8 by the glass (£2.50-£8.25)
PRICE GUIDE Fixed D £34.50 • coffee £2.50 • min/water £3.75 • Service optional
PLACE: Built in 1893, this impressive Victorian hotel on the River Spey is located on the Malt Whisky Trail. Log fires, hunting artefacts and traditional Scottish decor make for a relaxing, comfortable experience. The Ben Aigan Restaurant offers fine dining with formal service.
FOOD: Prime local produce appears in modern dishes. Lamb comes from Cabrach, beef is Aberdeen Angus and smoked salmon is from Craigellachie. Traditional haggis, neeps and tatties also makes an appearance, as do Highland pancakes for dessert, followed by Scottish cheeses.
OUR TIP: More than 500 malts to try
Chef: Addy Daggert **Owners:** Craigellachie Hotel Ltd **Times:** 12-2/6-10 **Notes:** Vegetarian available, Civ Wed 40 **Seats:** 30, Pr/dining room 40 **Smoking:** N/Sm in restaurant, Air con **Children:** Menu, Portions **Rooms:** 25 (25 en suite) ★★★ **Directions:** 12m S of Elgin, in the village centre **Parking:** 20 **e-mail:** info@craigellachie.com **web:** www.craigellachie.com

CULLEN MAP 23 NJ56
⊛ The Seafield Hotel
Mediterranean   ⚑NEW
Traditional country house-style hotel dining
☎ 01542 840791   Seafield St AB56 4SG
MENU GUIDE Scallops on black pudding & orange sauce • Loin of venison with red onion tart & redcurrant jus • Pink grapefruit and orange jelly
WINE GUIDE ♀ Santa Ema Sauvignon Blanc £16.25 • ♀ Santa Ema Cabernet Sauvignon £16.75 • 50 bottles over £20, 25 bottles under £20 • 8 by the glass (£3-£6.50)
PRICE GUIDE Starter £2.75-£9.50 • main £8.25-£19.50 • dessert £4.75-£6.95 • coffee £1.50 • min/water £3.50 • Service optional
PLACE: Standing in the heart of Cullen, this former coaching inn boasts a split level restaurant with tartan carpets, Mediterranean-style seating and unclothed tables. Service is relaxed and friendly.
FOOD: There is a good use of local produce here, with the simple cooking style making for unfussy dishes that allow flavours and ingredients shine. Accompaniments and garnishes are non-intrusive and in harmony with the key elements.
OUR TIP: Great for seafood
Chef: Allan Ritchie **Owners:** Alison & Herbert Cox **Times:** 12-2/6-9, Closed Closed for lunch Nov, Jan-Feb **Notes:** Civ Wed 120 **Seats:** 70, Pr/dining room 14 **Smoking:** N/Sm in restaurant **Children:** Menu, Portions **Rooms:** 19 (19 en suite) ★★★ **Directions:** In centre of Cullen, on main thoroughway **Parking:** 30
e-mail: herbert@theseafieldhotel.com **web:** www.theseafieldhotel.com

Scotland

Scotland

ELGIN MAP 23 NJ26

⊚ *Mansion House Hotel*

Modern British

Contemporary cooking in intimate, classical restaurant

☎ 01343 548811 The Haugh IV30 1AW

PLACE: Set in its own grounds by the River Lossie, this baronial mansion is decorated in traditional country house style. The intimate restaurant reflects the elegance of the building with its crisp white linen and shining glassware. There's also a separate bistro.

FOOD: Modern cooking, artistically presented with an emphasis on Scottish seafood, meat and game. Dishes show consistency and skill, and you might start with plump pan seared scallops on black pudding with saffron butter sauce and follow that with a grilled loin of lamb, braised Savoy cabbage and rosti with minted lamb jus.

OUR TIP: Have your post-dinner drinks in the cosy lounge

Times: 12-2/7-9 **Rooms:** 23 (23 en suite) ★★★
e-mail: reception@mhelgin.co.uk
web: www.mansionhousehotel.co.uk

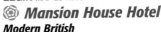
ORKNEY

ST MARGARET'S HOPE MAP 24 ND49

⊚⊚ Creel Restaurant

Modern Scottish/Seafood

Successful little seafront restaurant

☎ 01856 831311 Front Rd KW17 2SL

MENU GUIDE Slow-baked belly pork • Seared scallops, avocado & pink grapefruit salsa • Rhubarb crumble

WINE GUIDE ♀ Kim Crawford Sauvignon Blanc • 4 by the glass (£3-£3.60)

PRICE GUIDE Starter £7-£8 • main £18-£25 • dessert £6-£7 coffee £2 • min/water £1.90 • Service optional

PLACE: A charming restaurant standing as a beacon for good food on the island. The informal dining room looks out over the seafront in the pretty village of St Margaret's Hope.

FOOD: Fish features heavily on the menu, including the less well known megrim (perhaps steamed with seared hake), and wolf fish (roasted, and served with aubergine tartlet). It's not all fish though: pot roasted seaweed-fed lamb shoulder with lamb casserole has a distinctive flavour, and desserts like glazed lemon tart with marmalade ice cream shows a kitchen working well up to expectations.

OUR TIP: Book a window table for the bay views

Chef: Alan Craigie **Owners:** Alan & Joyce Craigie **Times:** 6.45-9, Closed Jan-Mar, Nov, closed L all week **Notes:** Vegetarian available **Seats:** 34, Pr/dining room 14 **Smoking:** N/Sm in restaurant **Children:** Portions
Directions: 13m S of Kirkwall on A961, on seafront in village
Parking: 12 **e-mail:** alan@thecreel.freeserve.co.uk
web: www.thecreel.co.uk

PERTH & KINROSS

ABERFELDY MAP 23 NN84

⊚ Farleyer Restaurant & Rooms

Modern French ⟨🐟⟩ ●**NEW**

Stylish dining in country-house setting

☎ 01887 820332 Farleyer House PH15 2JE

MENU GUIDE Pheasant roulade • Braised pig's trotter Passionfruit parfait

WINE GUIDE ♀ Pinot Grigio £14 • ♀ Pinotage £18 • 6 by the glass (£2.95-£3.95)

PRICE GUIDE Starter £2.90-£5.50 • main £9.95-£17.50 • dessert £3.95-£4.95 • coffee £1.50

PLACE: A bright, spacious dining room cuts a contemporary swathe through this 16th-century former dower house to nearby Menzies Castle. With its cool colours and starry lighting, it makes an undeniably stylish venue.

FOOD: The adventurous French menu reads well, with the likes of rosemary smoked pork cutlet with turnip and sage sponge and apple mash showing real imagination and skill.

OUR TIP: Choice of dining rooms except on Wednesdays

Chef: Paric Faherty **Owners:** Jake Scharrel **Times:** 12-3/6-9.30, Closed 2 wks Feb, Mon (Winter months) **Notes:** Vegetarian available **Seats:** 45, Pr/dining room 30 **Smoking:** N/Sm in restaurant **Children:** Menu
Rooms: 6 (6 en suite) 🏠 **Directions:** Please ring for directions
Parking: 15 **e-mail:** info@farleyer.com **web:** www.farleyer.com

AUCHTERARDER MAP 21 NN91

⊚⊚⊚⊚ Andrew Fairlie at Gleneagles *see page 605*

⊚ *Cairn Lodge*

Scottish

Fine country house dining

☎ 01764 662634 Orchil Rd PH3 1LX

MENU GUIDE Prawn & avocado pasta salad • Chicken pasta with pepperoni & char-grilled mixed peppers • Pear puffs with lemon curd ice cream

PRICE GUIDE Food prices not confirmed for 2006. Please telephone for details

PLACE: Close to Gleneagles and dozens of golf courses, this turreted country house is a romantic setting in extensive grounds. Fine dining takes place in the Capercaillie restaurant, and there's also an informal bar menu.

FOOD: Traditional, well executed dishes, making use of great ingredients. You'll find classic dishes like supreme of chicken cooked in French mustard, mushroom sauce, cream and brandy, and really excellent steaks, all locally sourced and hung for a minimum of 21 days.

OUR TIP: Named after Queen Victoria's nearby jubilee cairn

Times: 12-2/6-9.30 **Rooms:** 10 (10 en suite) ★★ **Directions:** From A9 take A824 (Auchterarder). Hotel at S end of town; on road to Gleneagles.
e-mail: email@cairnlodge.co.uk **web:** www.cairnlodge.co.uk

AUCHTERARDER MAP 21 NN91

Andrew Fairlie at Gleneagles

Modern French
Dramatic setting, inspired food
☎ 01764 694267   PH3 1NF

PLACE: Set between the main bar and the Strathern restaurant of the revered golfing hotel, Andrew Fairlie's is an autonomous business and a dinner/evening-only affair. A small bar leads through to the intimate, chic and high-ceilinged dining room, where dramatic blue-black walls contrast with vibrant artwork, floor-to-ceiling raw silk drapes and opulent fabrics. Tables are elegantly appointed, with dramatic downlighting picking out the crisp tableware, while service is rightly highly professional and knowledgeable from a well organised, well presented front-of-house team. The stylish and lavishly produced menu booklet and a wine list of serious pedigree further set the tone ... this is fine dining through and through! And, as it's Scotland's hardest-to-get-into restaurant, book months in advance for weekends.

FOOD: A progressive take on classic French cuisine from one of Scotland's leading chefs, is the Andrew Fairlie style, with the emphasis on flavour - uncluttered, precise, clean-cut, classy dishes. Impeccable quality, ultra-fresh local and luxury produce is superbly handled with great technical skill, and showcased on an enticing, fixed-price dinner carte and seven-course dégustation menu. So expect the likes of home-smoked lobster with a warm herb and lime butter sauce, perhaps a classic daube of beef with pommes purée or braised fillet of line-caught sea bass served with creamed parsnip and vanilla to follow, and finish on a rich vein with hot truffled Valrhona chocolate biscuit accompanied by milk ice cream. Notable wine list.

MENU GUIDE Roasted Skye scallops, parsley butter, garlic crisps • Pan-fried halibut, chorizo, confit fennel • Tarte Tatin, vanilla ice cream

WINE GUIDE ♀ Chablis 1er Cru Montmains Louis Michel Chardonnay £45 • ♀ Châteauneuf du Pape Dom Senechaux Syrah Blend £50 • 230 bottles over £20 • 12 by the glass (£7.50-£24.50)

PRICE GUIDE Fixed D £55 • starter £18 • main £27 • dessert £10 • coffee £5 • min/water £3.50 • Service optional

OUR TIP: Reservations essential

Chef: Andrew Fairlie **Owners:** Andrew Fairlie **Times:** 7-10, Closed 3 wks Jan, Sun, closed L all week, closed D Sun **Notes:** Tasting Menu £75, Vegetarian available **Seats:** 45 **Smoking:** N/Sm in restaurant, Air con **Children:** Min 12 yrs **Directions:** Take "Gleneagles" exit from A9, contiue for 1m **Parking:** 300 **e-mail:** andrew.fairlie@gleneagles.com **web:** www.gleneagles.com

AUCHTERARDER *continued* MAP 21 NN91

⊛⊛ Strathearn at Gleneagles
British, French
Grand dining in famous golfing hotel
☎ 01764 694270 PH3 1NF

MENU GUIDE Carpaccio of Aberdeen Angus beef • Pan roast turbot, oxtail ravioli • Queen of puddings

WINE GUIDE ♀ Bois d'Yuer Chablis £48 • ♀ Château de Raosset, Fleurie £35 • 16 by the glass (£8-£18.50)

PRICE GUIDE Fixed L £35-£40 • Fixed D £47-£50 • coffee £3.95 • min/water £3.95 • Service optional

PLACE: This celebrated Scottish haunt needs little introduction to golfers but others might appreciate the old-fashioned grandeur of this international hotel. From the piano bar to the open, bustling public spaces, there is a real feeling of razzmatazz here. Naturally there's a choice of places to eat but Strathearn, a beautifully grand room, has an air of timelessness about it.
FOOD: This is traditional dining with a capital T. Speciality dishes from chafing dish, or trolley, are carved or flambéed at table, perfectly executed. Menus change seasonally and the choices are excellent. Vegetarians have their own menu of equally impressive dishes. Notable wine list.
OUR TIP: Rare malt whiskies are available
Owners: Diageo **Times:** 12.30-2.30/7-10, Closed L Mon-Sat
Notes: Vegetarian available, Dress Restrictions, Smart casual, Civ Wed 250 **Seats:** 322 **Smoking:** N/Sm in restaurant **Children:** Menu, Portions **Rooms:** 270 (270 en suite) ★★★★★ **Directions:** Just off A9, well signed. Between Stirling and Perth **Parking:** 1000
e-mail: resort.sales@gleneagles.com **web:** www.gleneagles.com

BLAIRGOWRIE MAP 21 NO14

⊛⊛ Kinloch House Hotel
British
Formal country-house dining
☎ 01250 884237 PH10 6SG
MENU GUIDE Sole mousseline • Hare fillet, port wine sauce • Drambuie pannacotta with raspberries

WINE GUIDE ♀ Francesca Bay 2003 Sauvignon Blanc £21.50 • ♀ Château Grand-Puy-Lacoste Bordeaux Blend £27.50 • 224 bottles over £20, 4 bottles under £20 • 6 by the glass (£5-£7.50)

PRICE GUIDE Fixed D £39.50 • starter £4.50-£9 • main £9-£15 • dessert £4.50-£6 • min/water £3 • Service optional • Group min 12 service 10%

PLACE: Grand dining is the order of the day at this Victorian manor hotel, with flanks of staff waiting to treat guests like visiting royalty. The huge conservatory is softened by the use of candlelight, and majestic drawing rooms cosily warmed by log fires are fine settings for an after-dinner coffee.
FOOD: Scottish produce and classic French recipes bring an interesting style to the ever-changing choice. A steak menu featuring Aberdeen Angus beef is popular locally. Excellent wine list.
OUR TIP: Try one of the many malt whiskies
Chef: Bill McNicoll, Graeme Pallister **Owners:** The Allen Family
Times: 12-2/7-9, Closed 17-29 Dec **Notes:** Coffee incl, ALC lunch only, Vegetarian available, Dress Restrictions, Jacket & tie preferred, Civ Wed 55
Seats: 38, Pr/dining room 18 **Smoking:** N/Sm in restaurant
Children: Min 7 yrs, Portions **Rooms:** 18 (18 en suite) ★★★
Directions: 2.5m W of Blairgowrie on the A923 heading towards Dunkeld **Parking:** 36 **e-mail:** reception@kinlochhouse.com
web: www.kinlochhouse.com

COMRIE MAP 21 NN72

⊛ Royal Hotel
British, French
Traditional food in an elegant environment
☎ 01764 679200 Melville Square PH6 2DN

MENU GUIDE Arbroath smokey fritters • Highland venison steak, roasted vegetables • Poached pears in red wine, cinnamon ice cream

WINE GUIDE 38 bottles over £20, 57 bottles under £20 • 4 by the glass (£2.20-£4)

PRICE GUIDE Fixed D £26.50 • starter £3.75-£5.75 • main £7.50-£16.50 • dessert £4.25-£4.50 • coffee £2.75 • min/water £4 • Service optional

PLACE: The traditional antique façade gives little indication of the extensive and elegant refurbishment that has transformed this long established village centre hotel. There's a bar, library and a bright, modern dining room or conservatory brasserie.
FOOD: The menu is predominantly traditional and Scottish in style but lighter, Mediterranean dishes are being introduced as in the roast vegetable risotto. Local game and other ingredients such as Glenartney venison, seasonal partridge and haggis figure prominently.
OUR TIP: Try just of a few of the 170 whiskies on offer!
Chef: David Milsom, Michael Ludgate **Owners:** The Milsom Family
Times: 12-2/6.30-9 **Notes:** Roast sirloin carved from trolley £8.95, Vegetarian available **Seats:** 60 **Smoking:** N/Sm in restaurant
Children: Menu, Portions **Rooms:** 11 (11 en suite) ★★★
Directions: In main square, 7m from Crieff, on A85 **Parking:** 25
e-mail: reception@royalhotel.co.uk
web: www.royalhotel.co.uk

continued

CRIEFF MAP 21 NN82

The Bank Restaurant

British, French

Victorian former bank with today's quality standards

☎ 01764 656575 32 High St PH7 3BS

MENU GUIDE Mull cheddar beignets, chilli caramel • Saddle of venison with foie gras • Passionfruit tart, coconut ice cream

WINE GUIDE ♀ Torreon de Paredes Sauvignon £15.95 • ♀ San Rafael Malbec £13.50 • 25 bottles over £20, 21 bottles under £20 • 4 by the glass (£3.30)

PRICE GUIDE Starter £3.30-£5.95 • main £9.95-£15.50 • dessert £3.75-£4.25 • Service included

PLACE: Classified as A-listed (equivalent to Grade I in England), this former banking hall in the home of Scotland's oldest distillery has rich wood panelling, elaborate cornices and high ceilings which set the tone for an elegant airy dining room with a hint of formality.

FOOD: The style is modern with classic French influences, and local traceability is a prime focus. The Glenfarg beef spends three weeks maturing on the hook.

OUR TIP: The wine list is small but beautifully formed

Chef: Bill McGuigan **Owners:** Mr B & Mrs L McGuigan **Times:** 12-2.15/7-9.30, Closed 25-26 Dec, 2 wks mid Jan, Mon/Sun **Notes:** Booking essential, Vegetarian by request only **Seats:** 22 **Smoking:** N/Sm in restaurant, Air con **Children:** Portions **Directions:** Telephone for directions **Parking:** Parking available 150 yds

e-mail: mail@thebankrestaurant.co.uk

web: www.thebankrestaurant.co.uk

DUNKELD MAP 21 NO04

Kinnaird *see below*

KILLIECRANKIE MAP 23 NN96

Killiecrankie House Hotel

Scottish, European

Modern cooking in a delightful country-house hotel

☎ 01796 473220 PH16 5LG

MENU GUIDE Seared scallops, pea & smoked bacon risotto, chive & tomato oil • Corn-fed chicken supreme, chorizo & truffle mash, red onion jus • Dark chocolate tart

WINE GUIDE ♀ Meyer Fonne Alsace Pinot Blanc £18.90 • ♀ D'Arenberg Custodian Grenache £22.90 • 112 bottles over £20, 39 bottles under £20 • 8 by the glass (£3.75-£4.50)

PRICE GUIDE Fixed D £25 • starter £5 • main £15 • dessert £5 • coffee £3 • min/water £3.60 • Service optional

PLACE: Understated elegance is the byword at this long-established, whitewashed, Victorian dower house surrounded by splendid gardens, offering relaxing views from its delightfully comfortable, newly refurbished dining room. There's a bar here too, serving more informal fare.

FOOD: Expect modern dishes with Scottish overtones and the skilful matching of flavours, based around fresh local produce and the likes of vegetables and herbs from the kitchen garden. Spot-on wine recommendations for all main courses come helpfully annotated to set-price menus.

continued

DUNKELD MAP 21 NO04

Kinnaird

Scottish

Exquisite country house in remote setting serving innovative food

☎ 01796 482440 Kinnaird Estate PH8 0LB

MENU GUIDE Scallops, Arbroath smokie, smoked butter velouté • Saddle of venison, elderberry sauce • Black fig carpaccio

PRICE GUIDE Fixed L £30-£35 • Fixed D £50-£55 • Service included

PLACE: With superb views, overlooking the River Tay valley and surrounded by its own beautifully landscaped gardens and 9,000 acres of breathtaking countryside, this late 18th-century house is a haven of relaxed and civilised luxury. Kinnaird has all the facilities associated with a fine country hotel, yet retains the atmosphere of a private home - flower-filled day rooms with rare antiques, coal fires, impressive paintings and deep-cushioned sofas. The elegant dining room has glittering chandeliers, original Italianate frescoed walls and fine views across the estate from picture windows. While jacket and tie are required at dinner, the atmosphere overall is tranquil and relaxed.

FOOD: Food is creative and imaginative, with abundant local produce being a highlight of the short, carefully compiled menus, notably game from the estate, salmon from the Tay, smoked haddock and cheese from the hotel's smokehouse, and vegetables from the walled garden. Cooking is classically based but there's also an exciting and inventive strand, using fashionable flavours in unusual ways. Precise, accurate cooking allows the first-class ingredients to retain their bold, distinctive flavours. Excellent wine list.

OUR TIP: Enjoy the stunning location and scenery

Chef: Trevor Brooks **Owners:** Mrs C Ward **Times:** 12-1.45/7-9.30 **Notes:** Vegetarian available, Jacket & tie D, Civ Wed 45 **Seats:** 35, Pr/dining room 20 **Smoking:** N/Sm in restaurant **Children:** Min 12 yrs **Rooms:** 9 (9 en suite) ★★★ **Directions:** From A9 N take B898 for 4.5m. Hotel on right **e-mail:** enquiry@kinnairdestate.com

web: www.kinnairdestate.com

KILLIECRANKIE continued MAP 23 NN96

OUR TIP: Keep an eye out for the red squirrels in the garden
Chef: Mark Easton **Owners:** Mr & Mrs Waters **Times:** 7-11, Closed Jan/Feb, closed L all week **Notes:** Vegetarian available, No shorts **Seats:** 30, Pr/dining room 12 **Smoking:** N/Sm in restaurant **Children:** Min 9 yrs, Menu, Portions **Rooms:** 10 (10 en suite) ★★ **Directions:** From A9 take B8079 N of Killiecrankie, hotel is 3m on right, just past village signpost **Parking:** 20
e-mail: enquiries@killiecrankiehotel.co.uk
web: www.killiecrankiehotel.co.uk

KINCLAVEN MAP 21 NO13

⊛⊛ Ballathie House Hotel

British
Fine dining in a Victorian shooting lodge
☎ 01250 883268   PH1 4QN

MENU GUIDE Home-cured salmon & marinated oyster
Caramelised pork belly & scallops • Steamed lemon pudding
WINE GUIDE ♀ Santa Ema Sauvignon Blanc £14.50 • ♥ Montel Cabernet Sauvignon £16 • 173 bottles over £20, 42 bottles under £20 • 11 by the glass (£3.50-£5)
PRICE GUIDE Fixed D £37 • coffee £2.75 • min/water £3.50 • Service optional

PLACE: This sprawling Victorian shooting lodge built in the French style around 1850 is a riot of turrets situated in delightful grounds where tree-lined lawns lead invitingly to the River Tay. Inside, classical grandeur combines happily with modern comfort, and the bright dining room enjoys good views across the river.
FOOD: Modern Scottish cooking using the best fresh, local ingredients. Dishes are simply conceived and executed with flair. Presentation is excellent as is the wine list.
OUR TIP: Enjoy the views along the Tay
Chef: Kevin MacGillivray **Owners:** Ballathie House Hotel Ltd **Times:** 12.30-2/7-9 **Notes:** Vegetarian available, Dress Restrictions, Jacket and tie preferred, no jeans/T-shirts, Civ Wed 60 **Seats:** 70, Pr/dining room 32 **Smoking:** N/Sm in restaurant **Children:** Portions **Rooms:** 42 (42 en suite) ★★★ **Directions:** From A9 take Luncanty/Stanley exit, follow the B9099. Then follow signs for Ballathie after 0.5m **Parking:** 100
e-mail: email@ballathiehousehotel.com
web: www.ballathiehousehotel.com

PERTH MAP 21 NO12

⊛ Huntingtower Hotel

Scottish, French
Elegant Edwardian country-house dining
☎ 01738 583771   Crieff Rd PH1 3JT
MENU GUIDE Smoked salmon, onion & capers • Roast Aberdeen Angus beef, seared foie gras, truffle jus • Ginger creel, Perthshire berry cream   *continued*

WINE GUIDE ♀ Santa Ema Sauvignon Blanc £13.95 • ♥ Ken Forrester Petit Pinotage £13.95 • 24 bottles over £20, 26 bottles under £20 • 5 by the glass (£3.50-£4.95)
PRICE GUIDE Fixed D £21.95 • starter £4-£5.95 • main £14.95-£22.95 • dessert £5.95 • coffee £3.95 • min/water £4.95 • Service optional

PLACE: An imposing, tastefully upgraded and extended Edwardian mansion enjoying a rural setting on the western outskirts of the city. Traditional fine dining in the intimate, wood-panelled Oak Room restaurant furnished in neo-classical Scottish style.
FOOD: There's plenty of choice on the generous menus, from contemporary to more traditional dishes, with the adventurous carte taking in Scottish seafood and game.
OUR TIP: Ideal venue for special occasions
Chef: Sean Gallacher **Owners:** J A Brown & Colin Paton **Times:** 6-9.30, Closed L Mon-Sun **Notes:** Vegetarian available, Civ Wed 200 **Seats:** 70, Pr/dining room 30 **Smoking:** N/Sm in restaurant **Children:** Menu, Portions **Rooms:** 34 (34 en suite) ★★★ **Directions:** 10 minutes from Perth on A85 towards Crieff **Parking:** 200
e-mail: reservations@huntingtowerhotel.co.uk
web: www.huntingtowerhotel.co.uk

⊛⊛ Let's Eat

British, European
Modern bistro serving simple, quality food
☎ 01738 643377   77/79 Kinnoull St PH1 5EZ

MENU GUIDE Salad of William pear, pecorino & rocket • Fillets of Stornaway halibut, John Dory & brill • Fresh pineapple pannacotta
WINE GUIDE ♀ L'Avenir Unwooded Chardonnay £18.75 • ♥ Cave de Tain L'Hermitage Syrah £19.75 • 35 bottles over £20, 65 bottles under £20 • 7 by the glass (£3.10-£3.50)
PRICE GUIDE Starter £3.50-£7.25 • main £8.95-£18.50 • dessert £4.95-£6 • coffee £1.40 • Service optional

PLACE: Built as a theatre in the 1820s, the restaurant's unique club-like ambience is enduringly attractive for locals and visitors alike. The front-of-house team hasn't changed in nearly ten years; honest prices, warm colours and bookcases of cookbooks add to the reassuring feel. The 'sit ootery' lounge area is the hub of the business.
FOOD: Scottish produce used in a modern and energetic way. The chef/proprietor continues to impress with his lightness of touch and simple but well-constructed dishes. Look to the specials board if you fancy something more complex.
OUR TIP: Book ahead for both lunch and dinner
Chef: Tony Heath, Lewis Pringle **Owners:** Mr T Heath & Ms S Drysdale **Times:** 12-2/6.30-9.45, Closed 2 wks Jan, 2 wks Jul, Sun-Mon **Notes:** Specials board avail., Vegetarian available **Seats:** 65 **Smoking:** N/Sm in restaurant **Children:** Portions **Directions:** On corner of Kinnoull Street & Atholl Street, close to North Inch **Parking:** Multi storey car park (300 yds)
e-mail: enquiries@letseatperth.co.uk **web:** www.letseatperth.co.uk

⊛⊛ Murrayshall Country House Hotel

British, French

Modern Scottish cuisine in golfing paradise

☎ 01738 551171 New Scone PH2 7PH

MENU GUIDE Salmon & squid cannelloni, bouillabaisse • Rump of lamb, gratin dauphinoise, roast shallots • Warm berry soufflé

WINE GUIDE ♀ Rocheburg Chenin Blanc £12.95 • ♀ Montes Cabernet Sauvignon £13.50 • 60% bottles over £20, 40% bottles under £20 • 4 by the glass (£2.50-£3.30)

PRICE GUIDE Fixed L £11.50 • Fixed D £27.20-£35 • coffee £2.25 • min/water £2.95 • Service optional

PLACE: Set in 350 acres of grounds, this imposing country house is a paradise for golfers, boasting two courses, one of which is of championship standard. Recently refurbished, the elegant restaurant offers wonderful views of the Grampians and is reached via a cosy lounge with deep sofas and a roaring fire in winter.

FOOD: Murrayshall's cooking is distinguished by a refreshing simplicity and focus on quality Scottish ingredients. Expect modern dishes and some interesting combinations: roast deer with poached pear and juniper jus perhaps, or Aberdeen Angus on a ham, gruyère and potato rösti.

OUR TIP: The club house café serves light meals and snacks all day

Chef: Clive Lamb **Owners:** Old Scone Ltd **Times:** 12-2.30/7-9.45, Closed 26 Dec, closed L Sat **Notes:** Vegetarian available, Smart Dress, Civ Wed 100 **Seats:** 55, Pr/dining room 40 **Smoking:** N/Sm in restaurant, Air con **Children:** Menu, Portions **Rooms:** 41 (41 en suite) ★★★ **Directions:** From Perth A94 (Coupar Angus) turn right signed Murrayshall before New Scone **Parking:** 90 **e-mail:** lin.murrayshall@virgin.net **web:** www.murrayshall.com

⊛ Parklands Hotel

British

Enjoyable contemporary food in comfortable Victorian setting

☎ 01738 622451 St Leonards Bank PH2 8EB

MENU GUIDE Lamb terrine, home-made chutney • Turbot, vodka & smoked fish risotto • Bramley & Calvados parfait

WINE GUIDE ♀ Stella Bella Sauvignon Semillon £15.95 • ♀ Stella Bella Cabernet Merlot £15.95 • 14 bottles over £20, 58 bottles under £20 • 4 by the glass (£2.95-£5.35)

PRICE GUIDE Fixed D £27.50 • coffee £1.50 • min/water £3.95 • Service optional • Group min 8 service 8%

PLACE: Previously the residence of The Lord Provost, this Victorian hotel enjoys an impressive location with extensive views over the South Inch. Bedrooms are decorated with an eye to contemporary style. There's a choice of dining - for fine dining, head for light and stylish Acanthus Restaurant.

FOOD: Modern dishes with light saucing and adventurous combinations. Expect dishes like salmon and monkfish terrine followed by best end of lamb with herb and garlic crust.

OUR TIP: Visit the nearby River Tay

Chef: Graeme Pallister **Owners:** Scott and Penny Edwards **Times:** 7-9, Closed 26th Dec, 1st & 2nd Jan, Sun, Mon, closed L Tue-Sat **Notes:** Vegetarian available, Dress Restrictions, No shorts or jeans, Smart casual, Civ Wed 30 **Seats:** 36, Pr/dining room 22 **Smoking:** N/Sm in restaurant **Children:** Menu, Portions **Rooms:** 14 (14 en suite) ★★★ **Directions:** Adjacent to Perth station, overlooking South Inch Park **Parking:** 25 **e-mail:** info@theparklandshotel.com **web:** www.theparklandshotel.com

⊛⊛ 63 Tay Street

British, Scottish

Exciting food in chic urban Tayside surroundings

☎ 01738 441451 63 Tay St PH2 8NN

MENU GUIDE Shanghai shellfish risotto, herb oil • Perthshire venison, braised red cabbage • Banana crème brûlée

WINE GUIDE ♀ Pinot Blanc • ♀ Merlot • 40 bottles over £20, 30 bottles under £20 • 8 by the glass (£2.50-£7)

PRICE GUIDE Fixed L £14.45 • Fixed D £26.95-£29.95 • starter £5.95 • main £15.50-£18.50 • dessert £5.50 • coffee £2.25 • min/water £3 • Group min 20 service 10%

PLACE: Right next door to Perth's council offices and accessed via a flight of steps, the interior of this restaurant is stylishly modern with wooden floors, white walls and modern paintings. Blue chairs contrast nicely with white tablecloths. Enjoy good views of the River Tay as it meanders past.

FOOD: Modern style, good detailed preparation and accurate cooking characterise the dishes here. Fancy garnishes and accessories are avoided. Simple presentation allows clean, clear flavours of top quality ingredients to be appreciated such as grilled tuna with basil mash.

OUR TIP: Popular lunchtime venue so booking may be advisable

Chef: Jeremy Wares **Owners:** Shona & Jeremy Wares **Times:** 12-2/6.30-9, Closed 1st 2 wk Jan, last wk Jun, 1st wk Jul, Sun, Mon **Notes:** Gourmet wine dinners avail. over winter, Vegetarian available **Seats:** 32 **Smoking:** N/Sm in restaurant **Children:** Portions **Directions:** On the Tay River in centre of Perth **Parking:** On Street **e-mail:** www.63taystreet.co.uk

PITLOCHRY MAP 23 NN95

⊛ Donavourd House

International

Unpretentious country-house cooking

☎ 01796 472100 PH16 5JS

MENU GUIDE Minted pea & broad bean soup • Parmesan crusted chicken, buttered tagliatelle, mange-tout • Rhubarb & ginger mousse

WINE GUIDE ♀ Chardonnay £10 • ♀ Merlot £12 • 5 bottles over £20, 10 bottles under £20 • 4 by the glass (£2.50)

PRICE GUIDE Fixed D £25 • coffee £3 • min/water £2.50 • Service optional • Group min 6 service 10%

PLACE: Once home to the local laird, this country house sits among fields and woodland overlooking the town of Strathtummel.

FOOD: A concise menu offers a choice of just two dishes for each course, but you're in safe hands here - the cooking is sound and unfussy with a noteworthy emphasis on local meats, game and fresh fish. Expect simple classics with the odd twist.

OUR TIP: Vegetarians should make requests in advance

Chef: Andrea Geary **Owners:** Nicole McKechnie, John Thomson **Times:** 6.30-8.30, Closed Jan, Feb, closed L all week **Notes:** Vegetarian by request only, Smart Dress, Civ Wed 50 **Seats:** 30 **Smoking:** N/Sm in restaurant **Children:** Min 10 yrs, Portions **Rooms:** 9 (9 en suite) ★★ **Directions:** Southbound on main rd from Pitlochry, before entrance to A9 follow signs to hotel. Take Pitlochry exit off A6 northbound, turn right under railway bridge and follow signs **Parking:** 20 **e-mail:** reservations@donavourdhousehotel.co.uk **web:** www.donavourdhousehotel.co.uk

Scotland

609

PITLOCHRY *continued* MAP 23 NN95

Green Park Hotel

British, European

Hotel dining in a scenic setting

☎ 01796 473248 Clunie Bridge Rd PH16 5JY

MENU GUIDE Venison & chicken terrine, hazelnut bread • Duck confit with bean & chorizo stew • Tiramisù

WINE GUIDE ♀ Echo Point Chardonnay £11.50 • ♀ Torreon de Paredes Cabernet Sauvignon £9.95 • 3 bottles over £20, 60 bottles under £20 • 6 by the glass (£2.50)

PRICE GUIDE Fixed D £21.50 • min/water £3.20 • Service optional

PLACE: Boasting stunning views across Loch Faskally, this busy family-run hotel has beautiful landscaped gardens. Interesting works of art grace both the walls and grounds.

FOOD: A short daily-changing menu showcases quality local produce alongside ingredients fresh from the hotel gardens. Expect appealing fare rather than culinary adventuring: halibut in a cider and sesame seed batter perhaps, or warm chicken salad with figs and pecans.

OUR TIP: Booking essential

Chef: Chris Tamblin **Owners:** Green Park Ltd **Times:** 6.30-8.30, Closed L all week (ex residents) **Notes:** Complimentary sherry reception before dinner, Vegetarian available, Dress Restrictions, Reasonably smart dress **Seats:** 100 **Smoking:** N/Sm in restaurant **Children:** Menu, Portions **Rooms:** 39 (39 en suite) ★★★ **Directions:** Off A9 at Pitlochry, follow signs **Parking:** 52

e-mail: bookings@thegreenpark.co.uk
web: www.thegreenpark.co.uk

Knockendarroch House Hotel

British, European

Victorian mansion with scenic views and cuisine

☎ 01796 473473 Higher Oakfield PH16 5HT

MENU GUIDE Prawn & smoked salmon gâteau • Roast chicken breast, herb stuffing, fettucine, white wine cream • Apple & raisin crumble

WINE GUIDE ♀ Sauvignon Blanc £13.75 • ♀ Merlot £14.75 12 bottles over £20, 30 bottles under £20 • 5 by the glass (£2.75-£3.95)

PRICE GUIDE Fixed D £26 • min/water £2

PLACE: An immaculate Victorian mansion with amazing views overlooking the town and the Tummel Valley. There's no bar, but you can enjoy a drink in the delightful lounge while studying the menu.

FOOD: A daily menu of freshly prepared British dishes with European influences. There's the occasional modern flourish but traditional cooking is the real strength, using local produce whenever possible.

OUR TIP: The wine list is worth a study

Chef: Jane Ross **Owners:** Mr & Mrs A Ross **Times:** 6-8.30, Closed Nov-Feb, closed L all week **Notes:** Vegetarian available, Dress Restrictions, Smart casual preferred, no jeans, T-shirts **Seats:** 24 **Smoking:** N/Sm in restaurant **Children:** Min 10 yrs **Rooms:** 12 (12 en suite) ★★ **Directions:** On entering town from Perth, 1st right (East Moulin Road) after railway bridge, then 2nd left, last hotel on left **Parking:** 20

e-mail: info@knockendarroch.co.uk
web: www.knockendarroch.co.uk

ST FILLANS MAP 20 NN62

Four Seasons Hotel

British

Adventurous cooking in scenic setting

☎ 01764 685333 Loch Earn PH6 2NF

MENU GUIDE Seared scallops, chorizo & artichoke cream • Pork belly, boudin blanc, parsnip mash • Orange & almond cake, figs, Greek yoghurt

WINE GUIDE ♀ Forge Mill Chenin Blanc £13.95 • ♀ Casa de Piedra Cabernet Sauvignon £13.95 • 60 bottles over £20, 40 bottles under £20 • 4 by the glass (£3.65)

PRICE GUIDE Fixed D £30-£37 • coffee £1.95 • min/water £3.20 • Group

PLACE: Tucked away beneath steeply forested hills on the edge of Loch Earn, this hotel offers a range of comfortable lounges, log fires and stunning views.

FOOD: What's on the plate looks good too in the Meall Reambar restaurant - the cooking here is bold and technically advanced, and you can expect imaginative dishes conjured from fresh, flavourful produce. Mains might include venison with a liquorice sauce or John Dory with a black olive and pimento relish, while desserts are creative confections along the lines of blueberry jelly and doughnuts with a Granny Smith sorbet.

OUR TIP: Informal dining available in the Tarken Room

Chef: David Errington **Owners:** Andrew Low **Times:** 12-2.30/6-9.30, Closed Jan-Feb **Notes:** Set price D 4 courses, Vegetarian available, Civ Wed 100 **Seats:** 60, Pr/dining room 20 **Smoking:** N/Sm in restaurant **Children:** Menu, Portions **Rooms:** 18 (18 en suite) ★★★ **Directions:** From Perth take A85 W, through Crieff & Comrie. Hotel at west end of village **Parking:** 30

e-mail: info@thefourseasonshotel.co.uk
web: www.thefourseasonshotel.co.uk

SPITTAL OF GLENSHEE MAP 23 NO17

Dalmunzie House Hotel

British

Enjoyable dining in splendid isolation

☎ 01250 885224 PH10 7QG

MENU GUIDE Twice baked cheese & mushroom soufflé • Braised lamb shank, chicken & horseradish dumpling • Raspberry crème brûlée

WINE GUIDE ♀ Prieure St Com Chablis Chardonnay £26 • ♀ Saigoba Rioja Tempranillo £18 • 36 bottles over £20, 42 bottles under £20 • 2 by the glass (£3)

PRICE GUIDE Fixed D £30-£33 • coffee £2 • min/water £1.80

PLACE: For those seeking privacy, this isolated turreted mansion, set within a 6,500-acre private estate, could well be the answer. When skiers, golfers and shooting parties are not in residence,

continued

Scotland

peace and seclusion reign. The formal yet relaxed restaurant is traditional in style.

FOOD: An honest approach treats excellent local game and meat with simplicity and respect. Contemporary country-house dishes include a roast salmon fillet partnered by a creamy leek and mushroom risotto with mussel and Sauterne broth.

OUR TIP: Don't give up - the drive is over a mile long
Chef: Aaron Campbell **Owners:** Scott & Brianna Poole **Times:** 12-2.30/7.30-9, Closed 1-28 Dec **Notes:** Vegetarian available, Dress Restrictions, Jacket and Tie preferred, Civ Wed 70 **Seats:** 40, Pr/dining room 18 **Smoking:** N/Sm in restaurant **Children:** Menu, Portions **Rooms:** 19 (16 en suite) ★★ **Directions:** 15m S of Braemar on A93 at the Spittal of Glenshee **Parking:** 40
e-mail: dalmunzie@glenlochsie.freeserve.co.uk
web: www.dalmunzie.com

RENFREWSHIRE

HOWWOOD MAP 20 NS36

🏵 Bowfield Hotel & Country Club
British

Conveniently situated hotel with traditional fare

☎ 01505 705225   PA9 1DB

MENU GUIDE Bacon & black pudding boudin • Baked salmon fillet with prawn butter • Lemon bavarois

WINE GUIDE ♀ One Tree Hill Chardonnay £12.45 • ♀ One Tree Hill Shiraz £12.45 • 10 bottles over £20, 10 bottles under £20 3 by the glass (£2.65)

PRICE GUIDE Fixed D £19.50 • coffee £1.20 • min/water £2.65 • Service optional

PLACE: A former cotton mill and riding club, this modern hotel and sports club is conveniently situated close to the airport, as well as the coast and other local attractions. The relaxed restaurant has a country feel to it.
FOOD: Traditional Scottish cooking using as much local produce as possible. Service is attentive and helpful.
OUR TIP: Visit the leisure facilities or beauty salon
Chef: Ronnie McAdam **Owners:** Stonefield Castle Group **Times:** 12, Closed L all week **Notes:** Vegetarian available, Dress Restrictions, Smart casual **Seats:** 50, Pr/dining room 40 **Smoking:** N/Sm in restaurant **Children:** Menu, Portions **Rooms:** 23 (23 en suite) ★★★
Directions: From M8. Take A737 (Irvine Rd), exit at Howwood and take second right up country lane, turn right at top of hill **Parking:** 100
e-mail: enquiries@bowfield.co.uk **web:** www.bowfieldcountryclub.co.uk

RENFREWSHIRE, EAST

UPLAWMOOR MAP 10 NS45

🏵🏵 Uplawmoor Hotel
British

Warm and friendly inn serving the best of Scottish fare

☎ 01505 850565   Neilston Rd G78 4AF

MENU GUIDE Scallops, bacon & black pudding • Gaelic steak fillet, haggis crouton • Home-made bread & butter pudding

WINE GUIDE ♀ Andes Peak Chardonnay £12.95 • ♀ Lichine Red Merlot/Grenache £11.95 • 1 bottles over £20, 19 bottles under £20 • 7 by the glass (£2.90-£4)

Uplawmoor Hotel

PRICE GUIDE Fixed L £12-£15 • Fixed D £21 • starter £3.75-£8 • main £12-£19 • dessert £3.75-£4.75 • coffee £2.50 • min/water £2.50 • Service included

PLACE: Charles Rennie Mackintosh-inspired exterior touches to the 1958 extension of this mid-1700s coaching inn, which has reputedly hidden away a few smugglers in its time. The restaurant has been fashioned from an old barn, where a large beaten copper canopy over the central fireplace and Ercol chairs set the traditional tone. Genuinely warm hospitality puts customers immediately at their ease.
FOOD: Head chef has just celebrated his tenth year here, and there's no looking back. Cuisine is distinctly Scottish without gimmicks, based on superb products from Scottish pastures and waters - the beef from nearby, especially when flambéed in whisky, is exceptional.
OUR TIP: Handy for Glasgow airport
Chef: Paul Brady **Owners:** Stuart & Emma Peacock **Times:** 6-9.30, Closed 26 Dec, 1 Jan, closed L all week **Notes:** Vegetarian available **Seats:** 30 **Smoking:** N/Sm in restaurant **Children:** Min 12 yrs, Menu, Portions **Rooms:** 14 (14 en suite) ★★ **Directions:** From Glasgow follow M8 & M77 to junct 2, follow signs for Barrhead & Irvine A736. 5m past Barrhead take village road left signposted to Uplawmoor **Parking:** 38 **e-mail:** enquiries@uplawmoor.co.uk
web: www.uplawmoor.co.uk

SCOTTISH BORDERS

JEDBURGH MAP 21 NT62

🏵🏵 Jedforest Hotel
French, European

Inspiring country-house cooking

☎ 01835 840222   Camptown TD8 6PJ

MENU GUIDE Pheasant & foie gras terrine • Braised beef, chestnut mash, Bordeaux wine sauce • Apple cider Charlotte, cassis sorbet

WINE GUIDE ♀ Colombelle Sauvignon Blanc £13.50 • ♀ Cranswick Smith Shiraz/Merlot £13.50 • 29 bottles over £20, 36 bottles under £20 • 4 by the glass (£3.50-£4.50)

PRICE GUIDE Fixed L £15.95-£19.50 • Fixed D £19.95-£23.35 coffee £1.95 • min/water £2.60 • Service optional

PLACE: This former shooting lodge turned comfortable country-house hotel is set in 35 acres of landscaped gardens, within a short putt of a number of challenging golf courses. Several eating options are available, of which the most formal is Bardoulets Restaurant, a sophisticated dining room with low lighting and intimate alcoves.

continued

continued

JEDBURGH *continued* MAP 21 NT62

FOOD: The three-course menu of modern European cuisine changes daily, and bears testament to a kitchen that's not shy of innovation or short on flair. Desserts are a particular strength and - almost - too beautiful to eat.
OUR TIP: The Jedforest has its own private fly-fishing lock
Chef: Patrick Bardouiet **Owners:** Nigel & Carol Hollingworth **Times:** 12-2/6.30-9 **Notes:** 1 course £9.95-10.45/6 courses £32/Sun L 3 courses £13.95, Vegetarian available, Smart Dress **Seats:** 40, Pr/dining room 24 **Smoking:** N/Sm in restaurant **Children:** Min 12 yrs, Portions **Rooms:** 12 (12 en suite) ★★★ **Directions:** Just off A68, 3m S of Jedburgh **Parking:** 20 **e-mail:** info@jedforesthotel.com **web:** www.jedforesthotel.com

KELSO MAP 21 NT73

⊛⊛ *The Roxburghe Hotel*
Traditional Scottish
Fine dining and vintage wine in historic sporting estate
☎ 01573 450331 TD5 8JZ

MENU GUIDE Tuna tartare, soy sauce • Peppered roast duck breast • Lemon & sultana cheesecake
PRICE GUIDE Food prices not confirmed for 2006. Please telephone for details

PLACE: This impressive Jacobean mansion, owned by the Duke of Roxburghe, is set in 500 acres of mature wood and parkland. Decor is traditional country-house style punctuated by modern touches. The impressive dining room has well-spaced tables set with the best quality glassware, linen and china. Professional, friendly service makes an occasion of any meal here.
FOOD: Accomplished chef produces well-balanced dishes from ingredients mostly grown, raised or shot on the estate. Traditional game dishes are especially good such as roast pheasant with trimmings and pan-fried venison with goats' cheese mash.
OUR TIP: Great choice of malts in the library
Times: 12.30-2/7.30-9.45 **Notes:** Dress restrictions, No jeans or trainers **Rooms:** 22 (22 en suite) ★★★ **Directions:** From A68, 1m N of Jedburgh, take A698 for 5m to Heiton **e-mail:** hotel@roxburghe.net **web:** www.roxburghe.net

MELROSE MAP 21 NT53

⊛⊛ **Burt's Hotel**
British, European
Quality fare from a market town favourite
☎ 01896 822285 The Square TD6 9PL

MENU GUIDE Game terrine, red onion jam • Seared salmon, lobster ravioli, beurre blanc • Banana tarte Tatin, maple walnut ice cream
WINE GUIDE ♀ Côte de Thau Sauvignon Blanc £12.75 • ♀ Santa Rita Cabernet Sauvignon £12.75 • 40 bottles over £20, 40 bottles under £20 • 5 by the glass (£2.85-£4.50)
PRICE GUIDE Fixed L £13.50-£18.50 • Fixed D £31.50-£35 coffee £2.25 • min/water £2.50 • Service optional

PLACE: Owned and run by the same family for over thirty years, Burt's is a Melrose institution, known locally and throughout Scotland for warm hospitality and high standards. It stands in the heart of town, a white-fronted 18th-century building in the bustling market square.
FOOD: A crowd-pleasing bar selection offers plenty to tempt and is deservedly popular, but the restaurant's the real draw. The food is unfussy but skilfully done, and the daily changing menu features a hefty helping of Scottish produce and some good quality local meats.
OUR TIP: A handy base for fishing enthusiasts
Chef: David Haetzman **Owners:** The Henderson Family **Times:** 12-2/7-9, Closed 26 Dec **Notes:** Vegetarian available, Dress Restrictions, Jacket & tie preferred **Seats:** 50, Pr/dining room 25 **Smoking:** N/Sm in restaurant **Children:** Min 10 yrs, Portions **Rooms:** 20 (20 en suite) ★★★ **Directions:** Town centre in Market Square **Parking:** 40 **e-mail:** burtshotel@aol.com **web:** www.burtshotel.co.uk

The Bed & Breakfast Guide 2006

Britain's best-selling B&B guide featuring over 4,000 great places to stay.

www.theAA.com

AA

The Pub Guide 2006

Over 2,200 pubs hand-picked for their great food and authentic character.

www.theAA.com

AA

PEEBLES MAP 21 NT24

 Castle Venlaw Hotel

British, Mediterranean

Romantic castle in the Borders

☎ 01721 720384 Edinburgh Rd EH45 8QG

MENU GUIDE Black pudding brioche • Scottish salmon, roast sweet potato, lobster bisque • Shortbread & passion fruit mille-feuille

WINE GUIDE ♀ Castillo de Montblanc Chardonnay £14.95 • ♀ Castillo de Montblanc Tempranillo £14.95
50 bottles over £20, 23 bottles under £20 • 8 by the glass (£3.50-£7.50)

PRICE GUIDE Fixed D £28.50-£35 • coffee £1.75 • min/water £3 • Service optional

PLACE: A family-owned 18th-century castle-style hotel in the scenic Borders overlooking the historic town of Peebles. Interiors are in the country-house style with comfortable public rooms and a bar. The restaurant is elegant with tall windows, an ornamental fireplace and corniced ceiling. Service friendly and knowledgeable.

FOOD: Traditional British fixed-price menus are given a boost with the occasional Mediterranean influence. Technical skills demonstrated by the accomplished cooking of the kitchen team provide dishes that are well balanced and flavoured.

OUR TIP: Sir Walter Scott & John Buchan country
Chef: David Harrison **Owners:** Mr & Mrs J Sloggie **Times:** 12-2.45/7-9
Notes: Vegetarian available, Smart Dress, Civ Wed 35 **Seats:** 35,
Pr/dining room 30 **Smoking:** N/Sm in restaurant **Children:** Min 5 yrs,
Menu, Portions **Rooms:** 13 (13 en suite) ★★★ **Directions:** From
Peebles at east end of High Street, turn left at rdbt signed A703 to
Edinburgh. After 0.75m hotel is signed on right **Parking:** 25
e-mail: stay@venlaw.co.uk **web:** www.venlaw.co.uk

 Cringletie House

British, French

Romantic dining inspired by quality Scottish ingredients

☎ 01721 725750 Edinburgh Rd EH45 8PL

MENU GUIDE Scallops, curried cod croquette, pannacotta • Roast beef, braised oxtail, foie gras Pithiviers • Assiette of Granny Smith

WINE GUIDE ♀ Willowglen de Bortoli Semillon Chardonnay ♀ Joostenberg Paarl Cabernet Sauvignon £24 • 90 bottles over £20, 18 bottles under £20 • 6 by the glass (£4.50-£4.75)

PRICE GUIDE Fixed L £15 • Fixed D £32.50 • coffee £2.50 • min/water £2.75 • Service optional

PLACE: Pink sandstone baronial mansion set in its own 28 acres of gardens and woodland. Highlights are the 400-year-old walled garden and equally ancient yew hedge. The first floor dining room is Scottish country house in style, with a frescoed ceiling, an ornately carved oak fireplace, rich velvet drapes and dramatic views of the Tweed Valley and Moorfoot Hills.

FOOD: A choice of menus is offered, taking a modern slant on classical Scottish influenced cuisine, featuring home-grown produce alongside the best of Scottish meats and seafood.

OUR TIP: The perfect setting for a romantic occasion
Chef: Paul Hart **Owners:** Jacob & Johanna van Houdt **Times:** 12-2/7-9,
Closed Jan-Feb **Notes:** 8 course tasting menu, Vegetarian available, Dress
Restrictions, Smart/casual no jeans, no trainers, Civ Wed 45 **Seats:** 60,
Pr/dining room 16 **Smoking:** N/Sm in restaurant **Children:** Portions
Rooms: 14 (14 en suite) ★★★ **Directions:** 2.5m N of Peebles on A703
Parking: 30 **e-mail:** enquiries@cringletie.com
web: www.cringletie.com

ST BOSWELLS MAP 21 NT53

 Dryburgh Abbey Hotel

British, French

Baronial hospitality in the Borders

☎ 01835 822261 TD6 0RQ

MENU GUIDE Scallops, roast belly pork, soy dressing • Lamb rack, honey & sultana infusion • Lemon tart, vanilla & orange sauce

WINE GUIDE ♀ Sauvignon Blanc £14.95 • ♀ Merlot £14.95
43 bottles over £20, 70 bottles under £20 • 10 by the glass (£2.95-£4.95)

PRICE GUIDE Fixed D £30-£55 • Service included

PLACE: Enjoying a splendid setting beside the historic ruins of Dryburgh Abbey, this impressive, red sandstone baronial mansion is popular with the shooting and fishing fraternity and has fine views of the River Tweed. The elegant, first-floor restaurant is decorated in traditional, country-house style, with heavily draped curtains framing the river views.

FOOD: The fixed dinner menu changes daily and offers stylish, modern cooking with French influences.

OUR TIP: Good selection of Scottish cheeses
Chef: Rene Gate **Owners:** The Grose Family **Times:** 12-2/7-9.15, Closed
L Mon-Sat **Notes:** Vegetarian available, Dress Restrictions, No jeans or
sportswear, Civ Wed 110 **Seats:** 70, Pr/dining room 42 **Smoking:** N/Sm
in restaurant **Children:** Min 12 yrs, Menu, Portions **Rooms:** 38 (38 en
suite) ★★★ **Directions:** 4m from the A68 **Parking:** 50
e-mail: enquires@dryburgh.co.uk **web:** www.dryburgh.co.uk

SWINTON MAP 21 NT84

The Wheatsheaf at Swinton

British, Mediterranean

Notable cooking in a classic country inn

☎ 01890 860257 Main St TD11 3JJ

MENU GUIDE Chargrilled sardines & salsa • Poached halibut fillet, coriander butter sauce • Sticky ginger & pear pudding

WINE GUIDE ♀ Le Saumon Sauvignon Blanc £12.50 • ♀ Aromo Cabernet Sauvignon £12.95 • 63 bottles over £20, 48 bottles under £20 • 10 by the glass (£2.95-£4.75)

PRICE GUIDE Starter £4.70-£8.95 • main £10.65-£18.95 • dessert £4.75-£4.95 • coffee £2.60 • min/water £3.50 • Service optional • Group min 12 service 10%

PLACE: Still the focal point of the village, though most people know this traditional country inn for its food nowadays. A pine-clad conservatory restaurant and a traditional bar lounge are among the cosy eating areas, with a blazing log fire to dispel any winter chills.

FOOD: The imaginative menu is aimed at all tastes and appetites, with a host of modern and more tried-and-tested choices sure to bring the taste buds alive. A simple handling of prime ingredients is the key to this kitchen's consistent success.

OUR TIP: Stay over in one of the stylish bedrooms
Chef: John Kier **Owners:** Mr & Mrs Chris Winson **Times:** 12-2/6-9,
Closed 25-27 & 31 Dec, 1 Jan, closed D Sun (Dec, Jan) **Notes:** Vegetarian
available, Civ Wed 50 **Seats:** 45, Pr/dining room 18 **Smoking:** N/Sm in
restaurant **Children:** Menu, Portions **Rooms:** 7 (7 en suite) 🎎
Directions: From Edinburgh turn off A697 onto B6461. From East Lothian
turn off A1 onto B6461 **Parking:** 6
e-mail: reception@wheatsheaf-swinton.co.uk
web: www.wheatsheaf-swinton.co.uk

Scotland

STIRLING

BALQUHIDDER MAP 20 NN52

🌸🌸 Monachyle Mhor Hotel
Scottish, French
Modern Scottish cuisine amid loch and mountain scenery
☎ 01877 384622 FK19 8PQ

MENU GUIDE Seared scallops, Parma ham parcel, beurre blanc • Roast guinea fowl breast, pistachio & chorizo stuffing • Chocolate fondant

PRICE GUIDE Fixed D £38 • coffee £1.40 • min/water £3 Service optional

PLACE: This 18th-century former farmhouse is stunningly located at the end of a four-mile track, right in the heart of the Trossachs, next to a loch. An intimate bar and cosy lounge provide the venue for pre-dinner drinks, and the conservatory restaurant features exposed stone walls, abstract paintings and fashionable fabrics.
FOOD: The emphasis is on local and organic produce from the kitchen garden, local rivers, lochs and hills of the estate. The cooking style is complex and some unusual combinations work really well, for example seared sea bass fillet with roasted chestnuts, ginger and Brussels sprouts, speck and coriander jus.
OUR TIP: Great buzz at busy times in the bar
Chef: Tom Lewis **Owners:** Tom Lewis **Times:** 12-1.45/7-8.45, Closed 4 Jan-14 Feb **Notes:** Sun L set menu £22.50, Vegetarian available, Smart Dress **Seats:** 40, Pr/dining room 12 **Smoking:** N/Sm in restaurant
Children: Min 12 yrs, Portions **Rooms:** 11 (11 en suite) ★★
Directions: On A84 from Stirling, 11m N Callander turn right at Kingshouse Hotel. Monachyle Mhor 6m
e-mail: info@monachylemhor.com **web:** www.monachylemhor.com

CALLANDER MAP 20 NN60

🌸🌸🌸 Roman Camp Country House Hotel *see page 615*

Three Rosettes Outstanding restaurants that demand recognition well beyond their local area. Timing, seasoning and the judgement of flavour combinations will be consistently excellent, supported by other elements such as intelligent service and a well-chosen wine list. Around 10% of restaurants with Rosettes have been awarded three.

DUNBLANE MAP 21 NN70

🌸🌸 Cromlix House Hotel
Modern British
Modern cooking and refreshing hospitality in historic house
☎ 01786 822125 Kinbuck FK15 9JT

MENU GUIDE Chicken & crab ravioli, lemongrass froth • Roast turbot, langoustine & vanilla sauce • Cherry clafoutis tart, vanilla pannacotta

WINE GUIDE 250 bottles over £20, 12 bottles under £20 • 6 by the glass (£5.90-£7)

PRICE GUIDE Fixed L £18-£20 • Fixed D £39-£42 • starter £7-£12 • main £19-£28 • dessert £7-£11 • coffee £3.50 • min/water £6 • Group min 8 service 10%

PLACE: Roaring log fires ensure a soporific, relaxing atmosphere at this imposing and rather opulent Edwardian country house, set in sweeping gardens and surrounded by a 2,000-acre estate of lochs, woodland and moorland. Two elegant dining rooms of contrasting decor provide the backdrop to some innovative modern cooking. Service is friendly and informal despite the grand setting.
FOOD: The modern British menu is traditional in theme and offers a good choice of luxury, seasonal and regional produce, much of its sourced from the estate. Cooking is accurate and dishes well crafted.
OUR TIP: A perfect romantic location
Chef: Paul Devonshire **Owners:** Mr & Mrs D Assenti **Times:** 12.30-1.15/7-8.30, Closed 1-21 Jan, L by reservation Oct-Apr **Notes:** Trad Sun lunch; light lunch May-Oct, Vegetarian available, Dress Restrictions, No jeans or trainers, Civ Wed 55 **Seats:** 42, Pr/dining room 70
Smoking: N/Sm in restaurant **Children:** Min 6 yrs D, Portions
Rooms: 14 (14 en suite) ★★★ **Directions:** From A9 take B8033 (Kinbuck), through village, 2nd left after small bridge **Parking:** 50
e-mail: reservations@cromlixhouse.com **web:** www.cromlixhouse.com

KILLEARN MAP 20 NS58

🌸 Black Bull Hotel
British, International   **NEW**
Modern Scottish cooking in restored village inn
☎ 01360 550215 2 The Square G63 9NG

MENU GUIDE Tartare of salmon • Pavé of veal with sage sauce & buttered noodles • Baked saffron rice pudding

WINE GUIDE ♀ Maule Valley Sauvignon Blanc £14.95 27 bottles over £20, 18 bottles under £20 • 6 by the glass (£3.50-£5)

PRICE GUIDE Fixed L £12.95 • Fixed D £29.50 • starter £2.95-£8.90 • main £8.95-£16.95 • dessert £3.95-£4.25 • coffee £1.95 • min/water £3.95

PLACE: This former village inn has been much restored and now offers a lively bistro and an elegant, more formal conservatory dining room.
FOOD: The modern Scottish cooking is beautifully presented and although traditional dishes dominate the bistro menus, the Conservatory menu is more adventurous: roast guinea fowl and quail could be served with gin and juniper berries, pannacotta is accompanied by peppered strawberries.
OUR TIP: Try the more informal bistro
Chef: Campbell Cameron **Owners:** Daniel Stewart **Times:** 12-10
Notes: Civ Wed 80 **Seats:** 65, Pr/dining room 70 **Smoking:** N/Sm in restaurant **Children:** Menu, Portions **Rooms:** 12 (12 en suite) ★★★
Directions: N from Glasgow on A81, through Blanefield just past Glengoyne Distillery, take A875 to Killearn **Parking:** 100
e-mail: sales@blackbullhotel.com
web: www.blackbullhotel.com

CALLANDER MAP 20 NN60

Roman Camp Country House Hotel

Scotland

British
Innovative cooking in splendid riverside setting
☎ 01877 330003   FK17 8BG
e-mail: mail@roman-camp-hotel.co.uk
web: www.roman-camp-hotel.co.uk

PLACE: Once a shooting lodge, this charming country-house hotel sits in 20 acres of pretty grounds leading down to the River Teith. The house, dating from 1625, has been a hotel since 1939 and has built up a reputation as one of Scotland's most popular country-house retreats. In the restaurant, well-spaced tables are decorated with fresh flowers, while decorative tapestries hang on the walls. Real fires warm the atmospheric rooms and service is friendly yet professional.

FOOD: High-quality Scottish produce is sympathetically treated by the talented kitchen team and the French-influenced modern British cooking is innovative: Earl Grey-roasted foie gras appears with mango compôte, a medium cooked breast of squab may turn up with truffle custard, red mullet is accompanied by goats' cheese risotto and a ragout of squid. Finish with gingerbread soufflé with honey and lavender ice cream or a selection of unpasteurised farmhouse cheeses with toasted apple and celery scones.

MENU GUIDE Boudin of chicken, foie gras & truffle
Roast veal fillet & sweetbreads, braised tongue
Green tea & lemon parfait
WINE GUIDE ♀ House White £17.50 • ♀ House Red £17.50 • 6 by the glass (£3.95)
PRICE GUIDE Fixed L £16 • Fixed D £39 • starter £8.60-£17.40 • main £25.60-£29.80 • dessert £7.90-£9.80 • coffee £2.50 • min/water £3.95 • Service optional

OUR TIP: Try the four-course dinner menu

Chef: Ian McNaught **Owners:** Eric Brown **Times:** 12.30-1.30/7-8.30 **Notes:** Vegetarian available, Smart Dress, Civ Wed 100 **Seats:** 120, Pr/dining room 30 **Smoking:** N/Sm in restaurant **Children:** Portions **Rooms:** 14 (14 en suite) ★★★ **Directions:** Telephone for further details **Parking:** 70

Scotland

STIRLING MAP 21 NS79

 Stirling Highland

British, European

Sound modern cooking in spectacular surroundings

☎ 01786 272727 Spittal St FK8 1DU

MENU GUIDE Chicken & pancetta terrine • Shetland salmon on lemon risotto with parsley cream • Wild berry parfait

WINE GUIDE ♀ Mavida Chardonnay £16 • ♀ Mavida Merlot £16 • 23 bottles over £20, 15 bottles under £20 • 20 by the glass (£4-£9)

PRICE GUIDE Fixed L £10.95-£12.95 • Fixed D £24.50-£26.50 • starter £4.95-£6.95 • main £14.95-£19.95 • dessert £4.95-£5.95 • coffee £2.30 • min/water £2.95 • Service included

PLACE: With its lofty clock tower, this former Victorian school is an imposing affair located close to Stirling Castle and historic old town. Former classrooms make spacious public areas, and alongside leisure and conference facilities, there's a fully working observatory to entertain guests.

FOOD: The wood-panelled Scholars restaurant offers a safe but winning range of modern Scottish cuisine with just the occasional twist. Dishes are soundly executed and seasonal where possible.

OUR TIP: Good base to explore Stirling

Chef: Clark Gillespie **Owners:** Paramount Hotels **Times:** 12.30-2.00/7-9.50, Closed L Sat **Notes:** Vegetarian available, Civ Wed 100 **Seats:** 96, Pr/dining room 100 **Smoking:** N/Sm in restaurant **Children:** Menu, Portions **Rooms:** 96 (96 en suite) ★★★★ **Directions:** In road leading to Stirling Castle - follow Castle signs **Parking:** 106

e-mail: stirling@paramount-hotels.co.uk
web: www.paramount-hotels.co.uk

STRATHYRE MAP 20 NN51

 Creagan House

French, Scottish

Cosy hotel with baronial-style dining room

☎ 01877 384638 FK18 8ND

MENU GUIDE Veal sweetbreads, prawns, truffle sauce • Salmon, foie gras & chanterelles, sauce albert • Chocolate hazelnut mousse cake

WINE GUIDE ♀ Santa Ema Sauvignon Blanc £11.20 • ♀ Academy Pinotage £15.70 • 32 bottles over £20, 41 bottles under £20 • 8 by the glass (£2.15-£3)

PRICE GUIDE Fixed D £23.50-£27.50 • coffee £2.25 • min/water £1.75 • Service optional

PLACE: Small hotel in the heart of Rob Roy country, run by the Gunns, a capable husband and wife team. Gordon cooks while Cherry provides attentive service and caring hospitality. The building dates from the 17th century, but dinner is served in a mock baronial addition: a surprisingly grand room with a roaring fire, long wooden tables and stoneware from Skye.

FOOD: Expect classical dishes conjured from quality ingredients, carefully sourced from small local suppliers. Gordon cooks alone, putting a great deal of love and care into each dish on the concise menu.

OUR TIP: Bedrooms are delightful and very reasonable

Chef: Gordon Gunn **Owners:** Gordon & Cherry Gunn **Times:** 7.30-8.30, Closed 22 Jan-3 Mar, 5-23 Nov, closed L (ex parties), closed D Thu, (24 Nov-20 Dec Tue-Wed) **Notes:** Vegetarian by request only, Smart Dress **Seats:** 15, Pr/dining room 6 **Smoking:** N/Sm in restaurant **Children:** Min 10 yrs, Portions **Rooms:** 5 (5 en suite) ★ **Directions:** 0.25m N of village, off A84 **Parking:** 25

e-mail: eatandstay@creaganhouse.co.uk **web:** www.creaganhouse.co.uk

How do I find my perfect place?

New editions on sale now!

Available from all good bookshops,
on www.theAA.com or call 01256 491524

Wales

Restaurant of the Year for Wales

Gilby's Restaurant, Cardiff

(see p620)

ANGLESEY, ISLE OF

BEAUMARIS MAP 14 SH67

⚜ Bishopsgate House Hotel
European, Welsh
Elegant restaurant, period house, accomplished cuisine
☎ 01248 810302 54 Castle St LL58 8BB

MENU GUIDE Leek & caerphilly tart, apple chutney • Salt marsh lamb rack, redcurrant & rosemary sauce • Bara brith & butter pudding

WINE GUIDE ♀ Villa Rosa Sauvignon Blanc £12.50 • ♀ Puente del Inca Cabernet Sauvignon £12.50 • 12 bottles over £20, 26 bottles under £20 • 4 by the glass (£2.90-£3.90)

PRICE GUIDE Fixed L £9.50-£12 • Fixed D £16.50-£17.50 • starter £3.95-£6.25 • main £9.50-£16.50 • dessert £4.50-£4.95 • coffee £1.95 • min/water £4 • Service optional

PLACE: Close to the seafront, this 300-year-old, sympathetically renovated, small townhouse hotel is privately owned and personally run. Fine Chinese Chippendale staircase, wood panelling, club-style lounge, cosy bar and a tastefully furnished, intimate and subtly lit restaurant awaits diner. Friendly, well-informed service and well-spaced tables.

FOOD: The imaginative, uncomplicated cooking uses carefully sourced quality local and regional produce to advantage. Generous portions and fixed-price vegetarian menu.

OUR TIP: Superb bedrooms with antique beds
Chef: Hazel Johnson Ollier, Ian Sankey **Owners:** Hazel Johnson Ollier **Times:** 12.30-2.30/7-10, Closed L Mon-Sat **Notes:** Vegetarian available, Smart Dress, Civ Wed 55 **Seats:** 40 **Smoking:** N/Sm in restaurant **Children:** Portions **Rooms:** 9 (9 en suite) ★★ **Directions:** From Britannia Bridge follow A545 into Beaumaris town centre. Hotel is 2nd on the left in the main street **Parking:** 10
e-mail: hazel@johnson-ollier.freeserve.co.uk
web: www.bishopgatehousehotel.co.uk

⚜⚜ Ye Olde Bulls Head Inn
British, European
Historic inn with two attractive restaurants
☎ 01248 810329 Castle St LL58 8AP

MENU GUIDE Quail breast, truffled pea velouté, pancetta • Braised shoulder & roast cannon of lamb • Chocolate tart, pistachio ice cream

WINE GUIDE ♀ Macon Uchizy Chardonnay £15.50 • ♀ Painter Bridge Zinfandel £15.50 • 77 bottles over £20, 25 bottles under £20 • 4 by the glass (£3.95)

PRICE GUIDE Fixed D £33-£35 • coffee £2.75 • min/water £3.50 • Service optional

continued

Ye Olde Bulls Head Inn

PLACE: The Bull is a 500-year-old inn complete with beams, fireplaces and antique weaponry. There are two contrasting eateries, the lively brasserie and the elegant fine dining restaurant, freshly refurbished, which provides a haven of calm. The new decor is sympathetic to the building's history but is distinctively contemporary.

FOOD: There has also been a radical review of the restaurant operation. Presentation is essentially modern British but combinations and content follow a European style. The standard vegetable serving has been replaced by bespoke items for each dish.

OUR TIP: Charles Dickens and Samuel Johnson were regulars
Chef: Lee Scott **Owners:** D. Robertson, K. Rothwell **Times:** 7-9.30, Closed 25-26 Dec, 1 Jan, Sun, closed L Mon-Sat **Notes:** Chefs Grazing menu, 7 course £45, Vegetarian available, Smart Dress **Seats:** 45 **Smoking:** N/Sm in restaurant **Children:** Min 7 years **Rooms:** 13 (13 en suite) ★★ **Directions:** Town centre, main street **Parking:** 10
e-mail: info@bullsheadinn.co.uk **web:** www.bullsheadinn.co.uk

BRIDGEND

BRIDGEND MAP 09 SS97

⚜⚜ The Great House
Modern European
Something for everyone in historic setting
☎ 01656 657644 Laleston CF32 0HP

MENU GUIDE Green-lipped mussels, fresh tomato sauce & basil crumbs • Medallions of fillet Welsh Black beef, sautéed wild mushrooms & butternut squash, Drambuie beef jus, grilled baked potatoes • Selection of desserts

PRICE GUIDE Food prices not confirmed for 2006. Please telephone for details

PLACE: An imposing Grade 11 listed 16th-century hall, with original features including oak beams, inglenook fireplaces, mullioned windows and flagstone floors.

continue

FOOD: A large choice is available in Leicester's restaurant, with the carte supplemented by half a dozen blackboard specials and an extensive bistro style menu with some lighter options. Here you might find grilled fillet of Welsh beef with chips, or whole roasted sea bass with garlic and new potatoes, while choices from the carte could include carpaccio of fillet of tea-smoked Black beef with mustard crust and poached beetroot with sour cream to start, followed perhaps by confit duck leg, haricot bean casserole, Savoy cabbage and foie gras.
OUR TIP: Civil wedding ceremony licence
Times: 12-2/6.45-9.45, Closed 3 days Xmas, BHs, Mon, closed D Sun
Rooms: 16 (16 en suite) ★★★ **Directions:** M4 J35, A473 then A48 signed Porthcawl & Laleston
e-mail: enquiries@great-house-laleston.co.uk
web: www.great-house-laleston.co.uk

CARDIFF

CARDIFF MAP 09 ST17

🏵 Brazz
Modern Welsh   NEW
Modern buzzing brasserie in the Wales Millennium Centre offering something for everyone
☎ 029 2045 9000 Wales Millennium Centre, Bute Place, Cardiff Bay CF10 5AL
MENU GUIDE Chicken liver & truffle parfait • Cockle, leek & mussel pie • Rhubarb pannacotta
WINE GUIDE ♀ £11.95 • ♟ £11.95 • 16 bottles over £20, 24 bottles under £20 • 12 by the glass (£3.10-£8.50)
PRICE GUIDE Starter £4.95-£8.50 • main £6.95-£17.50 • dessert £4.50-£5 • coffee £1.60 • Service added but optional 10%
PLACE: Modern stylish brasserie located in the Millennium Centre building in the heart of the revitalised Cardiff Bay area. Dine in the larger, bustling brasserie or in the club-style dining area, both look out over the Bay. Friendly service from efficient and polite staff.
FOOD: Brazz at its best, offering tasty, unpretentious fare that includes snacks and more serious modern British dishes. Good use of Welsh produce and plenty of Mediterranean influences.
OUR TIP: The speciality 'vincisgrassi maceratese' is an irresistible pasta dish
Chef: Simon Kealy **Owners:** Brazz plc **Times:** 12-3/3-10.30, Closed 25 Dec **Seats:** 120, Pr/dining room 400 **Smoking:** N/Sm in restaurant, Air con **Children:** Portions **Directions:** Within Wales Millenium Centre in Cardiff Bay **e-mail:** cardiff@brazz.co.uk **web:** www.brazz.co.uk

🏵 Copthorne Hotel Cardiff-Caerdydd
International
Cooking with quality ingredients in a modern setting
☎ 029 2059 9100 Copthorne Way, Culverhouse Cross CF5 6DH
MENU GUIDE Foie gras & chicken terrine, truffle oil • Oriental braised belly pork, cider jus • Warm chocolate parcel, pear sorbet
WINE GUIDE ♀ Crusan Sauvignon £14.95 • ♟ Crusan Merlot £14.95 • 48 bottles over £20, 31 bottles under £20 • 14 by the glass (£3.50-£7)

continued

PRICE GUIDE Fixed L £28-£33 • Fixed D £28-£33 • starter £5.50-£9.75 • main £13.95-£18.95 • dessert £5.50-£6.25 • coffee £1.70 • min/water £3.95 • Service optional
PLACE: Raglans, the Copthorne's oak-panelled restaurant, enjoys a lakeside setting at this comfortable, popular and modern hotel. Service is traditional but the atmosphere is informal. A raft of wines are available by the glass.
FOOD: The menu offers a wide variety of imaginative International dishes at every stage, from carefully prepared starters to complex mains or simple chargrilled steaks. Cooking is traditional with contemporary influences and shows commitment to quality Welsh produce.
OUR TIP: Leave room for well-presented desserts
Chef: Manuel Monzon **Owners:** Millennium & Copthorne Hotels
Times: 12.30-2/6.30-10 **Notes:** Vegetarian available, Dress Restrictions, Smart casual, Civ Wed 120 **Seats:** 100, Pr/dining room 180
Smoking: N/Sm in restaurant, Air con **Children:** Menu, Portions
Rooms: 135 (135 en suite) ★★★★ **Directions:** M4 junct 33 take A4232 (Culverhouse Cross), 4th exit at rdbt (A48). 1st left **Parking:** 225
e-mail: sales.cardiff@mill-cop.com **web:** www.Millenniumhotels.com

🏵 Cutting Edge
British, International   🐟
Simple modern menu at bay-side restaurant
☎ 029 2047 0780 Discovery House, Scott Harbour, Cardiff Bay CF10 4PJ

MENU GUIDE Carpaccio of beef, rocket & parmesan • Pan-fried cod, seafood garnish • Sticky toffee pudding
WINE GUIDE ♀ Domaine de Montmarin Viognier £14.25 • ♟ La Toureue Merlot/Cabernet Sauvignon £13.50 • 45 bottles over £20, 33 bottles under £20 • 10 by the glass (£2.75-£5)
PRICE GUIDE Starter £4.50-£6.25 • main £8.50-£16.75 • dessert £5-£6 • coffee £1.75 • min/water £3 • Group min 10 service 10%
PLACE: Part of a group of Cardiff restaurants including Woods and the Old Post Office, this chic modern restaurant overlooks the Bay

continued

Wales

Wales

CARDIFF *continued* MAP 09 ST17

opposite the Welsh Assembly. It's a popular lunch venue for local businesses, so book ahead or aim to eat before or after the rush.
FOOD: A simple cooking style lets the quality and flavour of ingredients shine through; expect modern British dishes with a hint of the Mediterranean, such as venison and red wine sausages, or Thai fish cakes.
OUR TIP: Often closed in the evenings for private functions
Chef: Paul Thomas **Owners:** R Crane, C Nott **Times:** 12-2.30/7-9.30, Closed 25-26 Dec, 31 Dec, BHs, Sun, closed L Sat, closed D Mon-Thurs
Notes: 2 course pre-theatre menu £14.50, Vegetarian available **Seats:** 45
Smoking: N/Sm area, Air con **Children:** Menu, Portions
Directions: Opposite National Assembly of Wales and Millennium Centre
Parking: Street parking - vouchers required

da Venditto

Italian, European

Delectable Italian in stylish surroundings
☎ 029 2023 0781 7-8 Park Place CF10 3DP

MENU GUIDE Scallop & asparagus risotto • Monkfish, pancetta, spring vegetable casserole • Lemon ricotta & almond cake

WINE GUIDE ♀ Anselmi Garganenga £29.50 • ♀ Jerman Pinot Nero £27 • 70 bottles over £20, 20 bottles under £20 • 18 by the glass (£3.50-£5.50)

PRICE GUIDE Fixed L £14.50 • Fixed D £32.50 • starter £6.50-£11.50 • main £14.50-£22 • dessert £6.50 • coffee £1.90 • min/water £4 • Service added but optional 10%

PLACE: Locate Cardiff's new theatre to find this hidden gem, a chic Italian restaurant in the basement of two imposing Victorian town houses. All that indicates a restaurant is the sign and menu case at street level. The chic, modern interior, designed by a leading Italian architect, is filled with marble, stainless steel and cherry wood and is very impressive.
FOOD: Modern Italian cooking at its best. Here you can choose from a range of sophisticated dishes or tuck into simple, perfectly cooked and very memorable risotto and ravioli dishes.
OUR TIP: Pre- and post-theatre menus
Chef: Mark Turner, Roberto Barone **Owners:** Toni Venditto **Times:** 12-2.30/6-10.45, Closed Xmas, New Yr, BHs, Sun/Mon **Notes:** Gourmet nights on various dates, Vegetarian available, Smart Dress **Seats:** 55
Smoking: N/Sm in restaurant, Air con **Children:** Portions
Directions: In the city centre, opposite the new theatre **Parking:** 30
e-mail: sherry@venditogroup.co.uk
web: www.topogigio.co.uk

Gilby's Restaurant

British, European

AA Restaurant of the Year for Wales
☎ 029 2067 0800 Old Port Rd, Culverhouse Cross CF5 6DN

MENU GUIDE Pigeon, peas & bacon • Pistachio crusted cod, braised Savoy cabbage, tomato & chive beurre blanc • Assiette of chocolate

WINE GUIDE ♀ Francois de Blossac Chardonnay £14.95 • ♀ Grenache/Syrah £12.95 • 14 bottles over £20, 18 bottles under £20 • 10 by the glass (£3-£3.65)

PRICE GUIDE Fixed L £12.95-£13.95 • Fixed D £16.95 • starter £4.95-£12.95 • main £14.50-£19.95 • dessert £4.95-£5.95 • coffee £1.95 • min/water £2.95 • Service optional

PLACE: Something of a Cardiff institution, Gilby's is set in a converted tithe barn close to the fast-growing Culverhouse Cross shopping area. It's popular and bustling, with a modern open-plan kitchen, yet its decor is traditional and cosy. Carpeted floors, high ceilings and original beams characterise the split-level dining areas.
FOOD: The lengthy, populist, modern menus offer something for everyone, with fish taking centre stage, as in grilled skate wing with mussels and saffron and chorizo mash.
OUR TIP: Good value fixed-price lunch menu
Chef: Anthony Armelin, Michael Jones **Owners:** Mr A Armelin **Times:** 12-2.30/5.45-10, Closed 1 wk Jan, 2 wks Sep, BHs, Mon, closed D Sun **Notes:** Sun L £17.95, Vegetarian available **Seats:** 100
Smoking: N/Sm area **Children:** Portions **Directions:** From M4 junct 33 follow signs for Airport/Cardiff West. Take A4050 Barry/Airport road and right at 1st rdbt **Parking:** 50 **e-mail:** info@Gilbysrestaurant.co.uk
web: www.Gilbysrestaurant.co.uk

Holland House Hotel

British, European **NEW**

Mediterranean cooking in contemporary restaurant

☎ 0870 122 0020 24-26 Newport Rd CF24 0DD

MENU GUIDE Pan-fried foie gras, sweet pea purée • Tagliatelle, arrabiata sauce • Honey & citrus soufflé

WINE GUIDE ♀ Ca'langhetta Pinot Grigio £15.50 • ♥ Marques de Caceres Rioja £20.50 • 18 bottles over £20, 18 bottles under £20 • 11 by the glass (£3.75-£6.25)

PRICE GUIDE Fixed L £16.50 • Fixed D £20 • starter £4.95-£7.95 main £9.95-£19.95 • dessert £5-£6 • coffee £2.95 • min/water £3.50

PLACE: A brand new hotel with a stylish contemporary image and an exciting buzz. The restaurant has a look of understated quality that glows under the constantly changing coloured lamps.
FOOD: You can watch the chefs at work in the open-plan kitchen while tucking into a wide choice of bistro-style dishes. From a simple Caesar salad starter to roasted monkfish and four onion risotto, there is something for everyone.
OUR TIP: Live piano bar on selected evenings
Chef: David Woodford **Owners:** MacDonald Hotels **Times:** 12-2/6-10
Notes: Vegetarian available, Smart Dress, Civ Wed 700 **Seats:** 120, Pr/dining room 500 **Smoking:** N/Sm in restaurant, Air con
Children: Menu, Portions **Rooms:** 165 (165 en suite) ★★★★
Directions: Telephone for directions **Parking:** 90
e-mail: general.holland@macdonald-hotels.co.uk
web: www.macdonaldhollandhouse.co.uk

Izakaya Japanese Tavern

Japanese

Authentic Japanese-style tavern overlooking Mermaid Quay

☎ 029 2049 2939 Mermaid Quay, Cardiff Bay CF10 5BW

continued

MENU GUIDE Skewered chicken meat balls, mustard, hot dipping sauce • Steam fried dumplings (prawn or vegetable filling) • Chocolate ice cream

WINE GUIDE ♀ Trentino Pinot Grigio £16.50 • ♥ Les Templiers Cabernet Sauvignon £11.50 • 1 bottles over £20, 25 bottles under £20 • 6 by the glass (£2.90-£4.70)

PRICE GUIDE Fixed D £17-£26 • Main £1.50-£13.50 • Service optional

PLACE: For a lively and theatrical dining experience you can't beat Izakaya, built and furnished in the style of a rural Japanese tavern (or izakaya). It's fun and friendly and gets very busy at weekends.
FOOD: A selection of mini dishes (pictured on the menu) with plenty of sushi, home-made specials and some cooked options for the less adventurous, plus a choice of four set meals (one vegetarian).
OUR TIP: Go in a group and swap dishes
Chef: Y Evans, A Shiraishi **Owners:** Iestyn and Yoshiko Evans **Times:** 12-2.30/5-11, Closed 23-26, 1 Jan **Notes:** Fixed D 6 courses £17, 7 courses £22, 9 courses £26, Vegetarian available **Seats:** 85, Pr/dining room 20
Smoking: N/Sm area **Directions:** M4 junct 33, then A4232 (Techniquest exit). Restaurant on 1st floor of Mermaid Quay **Parking:** 45
e-mail: ayakazi@aol.com **web:** www.izakaya.japanese.tavern.com

Le Gallois-Y-Cymro

British, French

Exquisite, value-for-money cooking in the city centre

☎ 029 2034 1264 6-10 Romilly Crescent CF11 9NR

MENU GUIDE Wild mushroom & truffle risotto • Oven-roasted monkfish, Jerusalem artichokes, vegetable nage • Lemon tart, cassis sorbet

WINE GUIDE ♀ Christian Marou Côtes de Gascogne Colombard-Ugni Blanc £13.95 • ♥ Vignobles Bois Costieres de Nimes Grenache-Syrah £13.95 • 60 bottles over £20, 20 bottles under £20 • 4 by the glass (£3.75-£4.50)

PRICE GUIDE Fixed L £14.95 • Fixed D £35 • coffee £2.80 min/water £2.50 • Service optional • Group min 6 service 10%

PLACE: Its big blue canopy catches the eye on a residential street in the Canton area of the city. Inside the style is minimalist, a split-level dining room with plain walls of sunflower yellow and navy blue, leather and wood chairs, wooden floors and iron railings dividing the dining areas. Closely-packed, polished veneer tables ensure there's a buzzy, bustling atmosphere.
FOOD: The British and French style cooking is based around contemporary classics, with quality seasonal ingredients - flavour and innovative combination to the fore. Sophisticated menus make interesting reading with plenty of appealing options.
OUR TIP: Lunch is exceptional value
Chef: Padrig Jones **Owners:** Jones & Dupuy Family **Times:** 12-2.30/6.30-10.30, Closed Xmas, 1 wks Aug, New Year, Sun & Mon
Notes: Vegetarian available, Smart casual **Seats:** 60 **Smoking:** N/Sm area, No pipes, No cigars, Air con **Children:** Portions **Directions:** From town centre follow Cowbridge Rd East. Turn right to Wyndham Crescent, then to Romilly Crescent. Restaurant on right **Parking:** 7
e-mail: info@legallois-ycymro.com **web:** www.legallois-ycymro.com

Manor Parc Country Hotel

British, Mediterranean

Unpretentious favourites in country manor

☎ 029 2069 3723 Thornhill Rd, Thornhill CF14 9UA

MENU GUIDE Sole goujons • Sirloin steak, port & stilton sauce

WINE GUIDE ♀ Greganico £15.50 • ♥ Sangiovese £15.50 2 bottles under £20 • 4 by the glass (£3-£4.50)

PRICE GUIDE Fixed L £16.95-£22 • Fixed D £21.95-£25 • coffee £2.50 • min/water £4.50 • Service optional • Group min 6 service 10%

continued

Wales

PLACE: Overlooking leafy grounds, the Orangerie dining room is airy and spacious with a magnificent domed skylight and long windows. There is a cocktail lounge for aperitifs.
FOOD: A lengthy menu of straightforward fare, with mains along the lines of salmon with citrus butter, or orange-glazed duck. On Mondays to Thursdays, an early diners' option offers three courses for the price of two between 6 and 7.30pm.
OUR TIP: Ten minutes' drive from central Cardiff
Chef: Giovanni Morabito, Dale Holland **Owners:** Mr S Salimeni
Times: 12-2/6-9, Closed 26 Dec-1 Jan, closed D Sun **Notes:** Sun lunch £20, Vegetarian by request only, Smart Dress, Civ Wed 100 **Seats:** 70, Pr/dining room 100 **Smoking:** N/Sm in restaurant **Rooms:** 21 (21 en suite) ★★★ **Directions:** off A469 Cardiff-Caerphilly road **Parking:** 85
e-mail: reception@manorparchotel.fsnet.co.uk **web:** www.manorparc.com

New House Hotel
British, International
Enjoyable dining in attractive country retreat with wonderful views
☎ 029 2052 0280 Thornhill CF14 9UA
MENU GUIDE Duck & Armagnac pâté, Cumberland sauce • Veal medallions, mustard hollandaise • Chocolate pannacotta
WINE GUIDE ♀ Peter Lehmann Chardonnay £15.95 • ♥ L'Olivier Merlot £14.95 • 28 bottles over £20, 38 bottles under £20 • 8 by the glass (£3.25-£4.75)
PRICE GUIDE Fixed L £17.50-£26 • Fixed D £26-£34 • coffee £2.95 • min/water £3.25 • Service optional

PLACE: From the traditional dining room of this extended Georgian residence you can savour unrivalled views across the capital and, on a clear day, you can see the Somerset coastline. The hotel stands isolated high in the hills above Cardiff and there's an elegant patio area for alfresco dining.
FOOD: Simple, straightforward cooking is classical in style with a few International influences. Seasonal foods are well represented.
OUR TIP: Good geographical spread of wines
Chef: Neil Davies **Owners:** Mr J Hitchcock **Times:** 12-2/6-9.45, Closed 26 Dec, 1 Jan **Notes:** 3-course Sun lunch £16.95, Vegetarian available, Civ Wed 200 **Seats:** 35, Pr/dining room 50 **Smoking:** N/Sm in restaurant **Children:** Min 8 yrs, Portions **Rooms:** 36 (36 en suite) ★★★
Directions: Take A469 to N of city. Entrance on left shortly after crossing M4 flyover **Parking:** 95 **e-mail:** enquiries@newhousehotel.com
web: www.newhousehotel.com

The Old Post Office
British, European
Carefully prepared menu in New England-style dining room
☎ 029 2056 5400 Greenwood Ln, St Fagans CF5 6EL
MENU GUIDE Roquefort soufflé • Fillet of Welsh beef with wild mushrooms • Bailey's & chocolate cheesecake
WINE GUIDE ♀ Sauvignon Blanc £18.95 • ♥ Shiraz £18.95 • 80 bottles over £20, 13 bottles under £20 • 2 by the glass (£4.50-£5)
PRICE GUIDE Fixed L £13.95-£15.95 • Fixed D £35 • coffee £2.50 min/water £3.50 • Service optional • Group min 6 service 10%

PLACE: Situated just five miles from Cardiff, this former police station and post office offers contemporary style with a New England design. The dining room has a fresh, clean feel, with white walls and spotlights.
FOOD: Plenty of local produce is sourced, with an emphasis on Welsh lamb and beef. The modern European cooking is well executed and simply presented.

OUR TIP: Stay over in the pleasant rooms
Chef: Wesley Hammond **Owners:** Choice Produce **Times:** 12-2/7-9.30, Closed Mon & Tue, closed L Wed, closed D Sun **Notes:** Vegetarian available **Seats:** 26 **Smoking:** N/Sm in restaurant, Air con **Children:** Menu, Portions **Rooms:** 6 (6 en suite) 🏠 **Directions:** A48 E through Cardiff to St Fagans sign. Right at lights, 1.4m. In village turn right into Croft-y-Genau Rd, right into Greenwood Lane **Parking:** 30
e-mail: heidi.theoldpost@aol.com
web: www.old-post-office.com

The St David's Hotel & Spa
Modern European
Dining in stunning waterfront location
☎ 029 2045 4045 Havannah St, Cardiff Bay CF10 5SD

MENU GUIDE Carpaccio of beef • Dover sole • Coffee pannacotta with chocolate hazelnut ice cream
WINE GUIDE ♀ Fairtrade Chenin Blanc £17 • 115 bottles over £20, 15 bottles under £20 • 23 by the glass (£5-£7.50)
PRICE GUIDE Fixed L £19.50 • Fixed D fr £22.50 • starter £8-£12.50 • main £15.50-£35 • dessert £7 • coffee £3.25 • Service added but optional 10%

PLACE: Delightfully set on the edge of Cardiff Bay, Tides Bar and Grill makes the best of its sea views, with a patio for summer dining.
FOOD: The Tides Grill menu delivers contemporary modern cuisine classicaly underpinned, using the finest fresh produce sourced from local Welsh suppliers with a selection of meats and fish from the grill.
OUR TIP: Visit the stylish cocktail bar and well equipped spa
Chef: Stephen Carter **Owners:** Rocco Forte Hotels **Times:** 12.30-2.15/6.30-10.30 **Notes:** Vegetarian available, Civ Wed 160 **Seats:** 98, Pr/dining room 40 **Smoking:** N/Sm in restaurant, Air con **Children:** Menu, Portions **Rooms:** 132 (132 en suite) ★★★★★ **Directions:** From M4 junct 33 take A432, 9m to Cardiff Bay. At rdbt over Queens Tunnel take 1st left, then immediate right **Parking:** 60
e-mail: tides@thestdavidshotel.com
web: www.thestdavidshotel.com

continued

Wales

Woods Brasserie

ritish, European

opular brasserie on the edge of Cardiff Bay

☎ 029 2049 2400 Pilotage Building, Stuart St, Cardiff ay CF10 5BW

MENU GUIDE Smoked haddock & white bean soup • Roasted ork belly, piquant sauce • Prune & Armagnac clafoutis

WINE GUIDE ♀ Villa Antinori Orvieto £15.95 • ♥ Plantagenet Vines Shiraz Grenache £19.50 • 31 bottles over £20, 20 bottles under £20 • 15 by the glass (£3.75-£5.25)

PRICE GUIDE Fixed L £12.50 • Fixed D £29.95 • starter £4.95-8.95 • main £9.95-£18.45 • dessert £5.50 • coffee £1.50 • min/water 1.95 • Service optional • Group min 6 service 10%

PLACE: Right in the middle of the newly developed Cardiff Bay ea, this was the port's pilotage building that dates back to the 60s. Huge glass windows lend a lovely modern, light and acious feel, and there's plenty of outdoor seating on the patio. formal service is relaxed and welcoming.

OOD: Shoppers, businessmen and tourists mingle happily as ey choose from the modern brasserie menu, which includes ropean flavours, in addition to French favourites.

UR TIP: Break here for lunch when visiting Cardiff Bay hef: Sean Murphy **Owners:** Choice Produce **Times:** 12-2/7-10, Closed -26 Dec & 1 Jan, closed D Sun **Notes:** Sun L 2 course £14.95, 3 course 7.95, Vegetarian available **Seats:** 90, Pr/dining room 36 moking: N/Sm area, Air con **Children:** Menu, Portions **Directions:** In art of Cardiff Bay **Parking:** Multi Storey car park opposite eb: www.woods-brasserie.com

⑪ Ana Bela 5 Pontcanna St CF11 9HQ ☎ 029 2023 9393 formal and good fun, with chefs from Argentina.

⑨ Juboraj 11 Heol-y-Deri, Rhiwbina CF14 6HA ☎ 029 2062 8894 Interesting and varied Bangladeshi cooking.

⑫ La Brasserie 60 Saint Mary St CF1 1FE ☎ 029 2023 4134 Bustling venue offering quality meats and afood.

⑪ Le Monde Fish Bar & Grill 60-62 Saint Mary St 10 1FE ☎ 029 2038 7376 Seafood restaurant where food is oked in a bustling open kitchen.

CARMARTHENSHIRE

ARMARTHEN MAP 08 SN42

Falcon Hotel

ritish, Mediterranean

riendly town centre restaurant

☎ 01267 234959 & 237152 Lammas St SA31 3AP

MENU GUIDE Penclawdd cockle tartlet & laver bread • Roast ump of Towy valley lamb, redcurrant, rosemary jus • Brioche & utter pudding

WINE GUIDE ♀ Boisett Cuvée Blend £9.95 • ♥ Boisett Cuvée Blend £9.95 • 5 bottles over £20, 25 bottles under £20 • 3 by the glass (£1.85-£4.50)

PRICE GUIDE Fixed L £8.95-£11.95 • Fixed D £18.95-£22.50 starter £3.50-£6.95 • main £9.95-£17.95 • dessert £4.50-£5.95 coffee £1.25 • min/water £2.50

continued

Falcon Hotel

PLACE: Small hotel in the centre of Carmarthen, run by the Exton family for over 45 years. There are two restaurants: one a small beamed room with a log fire and the other a large contemporary room, light and airy, with air conditioning.

FOOD: The food is modern British with Mediterranean influences and some traditional Welsh dishes. Fresh Welsh produce is very much to the fore.

OUR TIP: Wedding receptions and other functions catered for Chef: Lubomir Sörm **Owners:** J R Exton **Times:** 12-2.15/6.30-9, Closed 26 Dec, closed D Sun, 25 Dec **Notes:** Sun L £13.95-£15.95, Smart Dress **Seats:** 100, Pr/dining room 25 **Smoking:** N/Sm in restaurant, Air con **Children:** Portions **Rooms:** 14 (14 en suite) ★★ **Directions:** Located in the centre of Carmathern, 200 yds from bus station **Parking:** 40 **e-mail:** reception@falconcarmarthen.co.uk **web:** www.falconcarmarthen.co.uk

LAUGHARNE MAP 08 SN31

⑧⑧ The Cors Restaurant

Modern Welsh

Culinary adventure in former vicarage

☎ 01994 427219 Newbridge Rd SA33 4SH

continued

Wales

LAUGHARNE *continued* MAP 08 SN31

MENU GUIDE Roasted figs with gorgonzola & Parma ham
Pan-fried calves' liver with caramelised red onions • Lemon tart
PRICE GUIDE Food prices not confirmed for 2006. Please telephone for details

PLACE: The rather traditional exterior of The Cors, a former vicarage just off the main street in this village made famous by Dylan Thomas, will not prepare you for the adventure inside. The entire restaurant is done up in bold colours throughout, making it very atmospheric. This is accentuated by the windows that look out on to the equally colourful garden.
FOOD: The menu makes good use of quality regional produce like Carmarthenshire organic black beef and local mussels. Carefully prepared dishes include some regulars like roasted rack of salt marsh lamb.
OUR TIP: Limited opening time so book in advance
Times: 7-9.30, Closed Sun-Wed, 25 Dec **Directions:** From Carmarthen follow A40, turn left at St Clears & 4m to Laugharne

LLANDEILO MAP 08 SN62

The Angel Salem
Modern British   **NEW**
Top Welsh cooking in friendly inn
☎ 01558 823394   Salem SA19 7LY
MENU GUIDE Smoked haddock tart, sweet potato, lime dressing • Shoulder of beef, mash, onion, bacon jus • Lemon curd brûlée
WINE GUIDE ♀ Georges Dueboeuf Grand Cuvée £10.95 • ♀ Georges Dueboeuf Grand Cuvée £10.95 • 10 bottles over £20, 32 bottles under £20 • 4 by the glass (£2.60)
PRICE GUIDE Starter £4-£7 • main £14-£19 • dessert £5-£7 coffee £2.50 • min/water £3 • Service optional

PLACE: Extensively refurbished by new proprietors, this stylish pub in the Welsh countryside is furnished with a mix of modern wood tables and more character antiques. Friendly, attentive service.
FOOD: Tempting modern British fare prepared by one of the top chefs in Wales. An experienced track record and passion for top quality produce results in a well-balanced menu of straightforward dishes, such as duckling with parsnip purée and port jus, or salmon with crayfish ravioli and fennel.
OUR TIP: Lunch options are all from the blackboard specials
Chef: Rod Peterson **Owners:** Rod Peterson & Liz Smith **Times:** 12-3/7-9, Closed 2 wks in Jan, Sun-Mon (ex BHs), closed L Tues
Notes: Vegetarian available **Seats:** 70 **Smoking:** N/Sm in restaurant
Children: Portions **Parking:** 25

CEREDIGION

ABERAERON MAP 08 SN46

Harbourmaster Hotel
Modern Welsh   **NEW**
Good, honest cooking enjoyed by the sea
☎ 01545 570755   Pen Cei SA46 0BA
MENU GUIDE Marinated Ceredigion beef • Boiled ham, chive mash, parsley sauce • Chocolate pot

WINE GUIDE ♀ Domaine la Gemière Sancerre £19
♀ Domaine du Calvaire de Roche Grès Fleurie £16 • 15 bottles over £20, 30 bottles under £20 • 19 by the glass (£2.60-£5)
PRICE GUIDE Starter £4-£7.50 • main £10.50-£17.50 • dessert £5 • coffee £2.20 • min/water £2.75 • Service optional • Group min 6 service 10%

PLACE: This former harbourmaster's house sits right beside the quay, with great views over the water. The bistro-style restaurant is in keeping with the Grade II listed building.
FOOD: Cornish shellfish and Welsh country lamb, beef, venison and goats' cheese make a strong impact on the menu, and everything here is home-made, including the excellent bread. The careful preparation results in good, honest flavours, and service hits the right level.
OUR TIP: Book a window seat for the harbour views
Chef: Sebastian Bodewes **Owners:** Glyn & Menna Hevlyn **Times:** 12-2/6.30-9, Closed 24 Dec-9 Jan, closed L Mon, closed D Sun **Notes:** Sun D £17.50 3 course, Vegetarian available **Seats:** 44 **Smoking:** N/Sm in restaurant **Children:** Portions **Rooms:** 9 (9 en suite) ♦♦♦♦
Directions: A487 coastal road, follow signs for town-centre tourist information centre **Parking:** 3 **e-mail:** info@harbour-master.com **web:** www.harbour-master.com

ABERYSTWYTH MAP 08 SN58

Belle Vue Royal Hotel
French, International
Good eating in comfortable seaside hotel
☎ 01970 617558   Marine Ter SY23 2BA

MENU GUIDE Poached eggs Florentine • Classic steak stroganoff • Bread & butter pudding
WINE GUIDE 2 bottles over £20, 25 bottles under £20 • 5 by the glass (£2.50-£5)
PRICE GUIDE Fixed L £9.95 • Fixed D £21 • starter £2.95-£7.95 • main £9.95-£18.95 • dessert £1.95-£3.95 • coffee £1.50 • min/water £2.50 • Service optional

PLACE: This large hotel has stood on Aberystwyth's famous promenade for 170 years. Meals are served in the bar or the more formal restaurant which has quite a local following.
FOOD: Menus here mix traditional, continental and modern dishes based on local produce. There's a carved roast every day with choice of vegetables and items like the beef daube or the sea bass and asparagus stack respectively. Good vegetarian choices.
OUR TIP: A bracing walk along the promenade
Chef: Andrew Turner **Owners:** Mr R Kuller & Mr G Sandhar
Times: 12.30-2/6.30-9.30 **Notes:** Vegetarian available, Civ Wed 60 **Seats:** 50, Pr/dining room 120 **Smoking:** N/Sm area, No pipes, No cigars, Air con **Children:** Menu, Portions **Rooms:** 37 (34 en suite) ★★★ **Directions:** Town centre, located on seafront **Parking:** 10 **e-mail:** reception@bellevueroyalhotelfsnet.co.uk **web:** www.bellevueroyal.co.uk

continued

Ynyshir Hall

British

Adventurous and stunning country-house cuisine

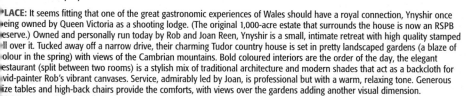

☎ 01654 781209   SY20 8TA

e-mail: ynyshir@relaischateaux.com
web: www.ynyshir-hall.co.uk

PLACE: It seems fitting that one of the great gastronomic experiences of Wales should have a royal connection, Ynyshir once being owned by Queen Victoria as a shooting lodge. (The original 1,000-acre estate that surrounds the house is now an RSPB reserve.) Owned and personally run today by Rob and Joan Reen, Ynyshir is a small, intimate retreat with high quality stamped all over it. Tucked away off a narrow drive, their charming Tudor country house is set in pretty landscaped gardens (a blaze of colour in the spring) with views of the Cambrian mountains. Bold coloured interiors are the order of the day, the elegant restaurant (split between two rooms) is a stylish mix of traditional architecture and modern shades that act as a backcloth for vivid-painter Rob's vibrant canvases. Service, admirably led by Joan, is professional but with a warm, relaxing tone. Generous size tables and high-back chairs provide the comforts, with views over the gardens adding another visual dimension.
FOOD: Impressive, refined cooking is the style, the modern repertoire rooted in classical technique. Head chef Adam Simmonds has obvious pedigree, having worked in some top kitchens (most recently at The Greenway near Cheltenham and notably at Le Manoir aux Quat' Saisons) and makes intelligent use of the high quality Welsh larder; including fish and seafood from Cardigan Bay, meats from a traditional butcher in Machynlleth, and herbs and salads from Ynyshir's walled garden. Dishes are innovative and creative, big on clean flavours, with good texture contrasts, balance and colour that surprise and delight the palate and allow the main ingredient to shine. The appealing, seasonal fixed-price menus are sensibly compact and include a six-course tasting option, while the wine list is an oenophile's dream with a powerful selection of fine first growths from Bordeaux and Burgundy.

Wales

MENU GUIDE Roast quail, beetroot, apricot & Earl Grey • Sea bass, courgette flower, lemon confit & vanilla • Plum soufflé, cardamom ice cream, plum sauce

WINE GUIDE ♀ Jean Marc Brocard Petit Chablis Chardonnay £26 • ♂ Claude Amadian Gigondas Domaine Grand Romanee Grenache £32 • 304 bottles over £20, 5 bottles under £20 • 12 by the glass (£3.50-£8.50)

PRICE GUIDE Fixed L £29.50-£34 • Fixed D £52-£58 coffee £3.50 • min/water £3.50 • Service optional

OUR TIP: Stay overnight and enjoy the whole Ynyshir Hall experience

Chef: Adam Simmonds **Owners:** Rob & Joan Reen
Times: 12.30-1.30/7-8.45, Closed Jan **Notes:** Tasting menu avail., Vegetarian available, Dress Restrictions, No jeans, beach-wear or shorts, Civ Wed 40 **Seats:** 30, Pr/dining room 16
Smoking: N/Sm in restaurant **Children:** Min 9 yrs **Rooms:** 9 (9 en suite) ★★★ **Directions:** On A487, 6m S of Machynlleth
Parking: 15

Wales

ABERYSTWYTH *continued* MAP 08 SN58

⑥⑥ Conrah Hotel
British, International
Innovative food in a classy setting
☎ 01970 617941 Ffosrhydygaled, Chancery SY23 4DF
MENU GUIDE Tuna sushi nori rolls • Pan-fried fillet of beef,
roast onion mash • Banoffee pie, caramelised pineapple & toffee
sauce
WINE GUIDE ♀ Franschoek Cellars Chenin Blanc
£12 • ♥ Franschoek Cellars Cinsault/Cabernet £13 • 52 bottles
over £20, 48 bottles under £20 • 6 by the glass (£3-£4)
PRICE GUIDE Fixed D £32 • starter £4-£8 • main £8-
£15 • dessert £4.50-£6 • coffee £3 • min/water £4 • Service
optional
PLACE: Warm hospitality is matched with the luxurious setting of
a smart country house surrounded by beautiful gardens and
woods. The mountain views in the Edwardian-style restaurant
immediately draw the eye, but the menu offers fierce
competition.
FOOD: The cooking has been revitalised, achieving consistently
high standards with its modern take on a host of international
cuisines. There's plenty of innovation, from chilled fruit soup with
mint and camomile tea water ice to roast pavé of sea trout with
Parmesan and crab risotto. The 'keep it simple' philosophy works
a treat.
OUR TIP: Stay a few days if you can
Chef: David Carney **Owners:** F J & P Heading **Times:** 12-2/7-9, Closed
1 wk Xmas, closed D Sun (low season) **Notes:** ALC lunch only, Sun L 2
courses £15, 3 courses £19, Vegetarian available, Civ Wed 60 **Seats:** 40
Smoking: N/Sm in restaurant **Children:** Min 5 yrs, Portions **Rooms:** 17
(17 en suite) ★★★ **Directions:** On A487, 3m S of Aberystwyth
Parking: 40 **e-mail:** enquiries@conrah.co.uk
web: www.conrah.co.uk

⑥ Harry's
British, French
Sound dining experience in a classic bistro
☎ 01970 612647 40-46 North Pde SY23 2NF
MENU GUIDE Salmon langoustine rilettes • Monkfish tail in
Parma ham • Chocolate truffle torte
PRICE GUIDE Starter £3.50-£5.80 • main £8.50-£16.50 • dessert
£3.50-£4.50 • coffee £1.20 • Service included
PLACE: The ever-popular Harry's restaurant continues to make a
positive contribution to Aberystwyth's food scene. Split into two
separate areas, it is cheerfully reminiscent of a rural French
bistro.
FOOD: Quality local produce cooked well is the proud boast
here. Much of it comes from the nearby sea, with the extensive
choice also extending to braised Welsh mountain lamb, pan-
seared calves' liver, and roasted half duck.
OUR TIP: Stay over in one of the rooms
Chef: Harry Hughes, Chris Williams **Owners:** Harry Hughes **Times:** 12-
2.30/6-10.00, 25 Dec **Notes:** Vegetarian available **Seats:** 120, Pr/dining
room 40 **Smoking:** N/Sm in restaurant **Children:** Portions **Rooms:** 24
(24 en suite) ★★ **Directions:** Town centre **Parking:** 14
web: www.harrysaberyswyth.com

EGLWYSFACH MAP 14 SN69

⑥⑥⑥⑥ Ynyshir Hall *see page 625*

LAMPETER MAP 08 SN54

⑥ Falcondale Mansion   **NEW**
British, European
Country house hotel and carefully-cooked food
☎ 01570 422910   SA48 7RX
MENU GUIDE Welsh cheese soufflé, beetroot salsa • Guinea
fowl & duck breast • Baked Alaska, red berry coulis
WINE GUIDE ♀ Veramonte Sauvignon Blanc £14.95
♥ Penfolds Shiraz/Cabernet £15.95 • 13 bottles over
£20, 39 bottles under £20 • 12 by the glass (£3.50-£6.50)
PRICE GUIDE Fixed D £30-£35 • starter £5-£9 • main £10-
£18 • dessert £5 • coffee £3 • min/water £3.25 • Service
optional • Group min 10 service 10%
PLACE: Italianate-style hotel overlooking the university town of
Lampeter, surrounded by lovely parkland and gardens. Blazing
fires cheer the lounges on cold days.
FOOD: A competent kitchen team produces a concise carte with
even the most subtle flavours readily discernable, as in lavender-
scented cheesecake, a delicate dessert.
OUR TIP: A brasserie offers a lighter eating option
Chef: Michael Green, Stephane Biteau **Owners:** Chris & Lisa Hutton
Times: 12-2/7-9, Closed L 1 Jan **Notes:** Sun lunch £16.95, Smart Dress,
Civ Wed 60 **Seats:** 40, Pr/dining room 28 **Smoking:** N/Sm in restaurant
Children: Portions **Rooms:** 20 (20 en suite) ★★★ **Parking:** 60
e-mail: info@falcondalehotel.com **web:** www.falcondalehotel.com

CONWY

BETWS-Y-COED MAP 14 SH75

⑥ The Royal Oak Hotel
British, Modern Welsh
Good food in Snowdonian setting
☎ 01690 710219 Holyhead Rd LL24 0AY

continue

MENU GUIDE Wild mushroom fricassee • Venison, celeriac mash, red wine & cinnamon poached pear • Chocolate & orange Charlotte

WINE GUIDE ♀ Cranswick Castle Creek Chardonnay £14.25 • ♀ Gannet Rock Totara Hill Cabernet Merlot £16.75 17 bottles over £20, 29 bottles under £20 • 6 by the glass (£3.25-£5.25)

PRICE GUIDE Fixed L £9.95-£11.95 • Fixed D £19.50-£27.50 starter £4.95-£8.25 • main £10.95-£17.50 • dessert £4.95-£5.75 • coffee £2.20 • min/water £4 • Service optional

PLACE: Set in the heart of a popular Snowdonian village, this former coaching inn boasts a range of different eating options designed to suit all occasions. Light meals are available in the two bars, while the airy restaurant delivers upmarket cuisine.

FOOD: Modern British with a commitment to the use of quality Welsh produce. Mains might include locally farmed steak served on a black pudding potato cake, or cod with a Welsh rarebit glaze.

OUR TIP: An ideal base to explore Snowdonia National Park **Chef:** Dylan Edwards **Owners:** The Royal Oaks Hotel **Times:** 12-2/6.30-9.45, Closed 25,26 Dec, Mon-Tue, closed L Wed-Sat, closed D Sun **Notes:** Vegetarian available, Dress Restrictions, No jeans, trainers, Civ Wed 75 **Seats:** 40, Pr/dining room 20 **Smoking:** N/Sm in restaurant **Children:** Portions **Rooms:** 27 (27 en suite) ★★★ **Directions:** Situated on A5 trunk road **Parking:** 100 **e-mail:** royaloakmail@btopenworld.com **web:** www.royaloakhotel.net

Tan-y-Foel Country House

see below

COLWYN BAY MAP 14 SH87

Café Niçoise

Modern European

A taste of the Mediterranean in Colwyn Bay

☎ 01492 531555   124 Abergele Rd LL29 7PS

MENU GUIDE Seared scallop salad, truffle vinaigrette • Gressingham duck breast, mandarins & ginger • Chocolate brownie, fudge sauce

WINE GUIDE ♀ Whitehaven Winery Sauvignon Blanc £17.45 • ♀ The Montes Estate Merlot £15.75 • 12 bottles over £20, 29 bottles under £20 • 6 by the glass (£2.50-£4.80)

PRICE GUIDE Fixed L £14.95 • Fixed D £18.95 • starter £4-£6 • main £11.75-£16.15 • dessert £4.50-£6.95 • coffee £2.50 • min/water £2.95 • Service optional

PLACE: Popular and well established, this small bistro-style establishment is located on the edge of the seaside town. Behind the Victorian frontage, the restaurant has a rich, warm interior and relaxed, friendly staff.

FOOD: Simple and very accurate modern European dishes using quality ingredients are offered from the carte, plus a short two or three-course menu touristique (not available Saturday evening).

OUR TIP: Good wine advice on what to drink with what **Chef:** C Jackson **Owners:** E & C Kershaw **Times:** 12-2/7-10, Closed 26-30 Dec,1 wk Jan,1 wk Jun,1 wk Nov,BHS, Sun-Tue **Notes:** Vegetarian available **Seats:** 26 **Smoking:** N/Sm area, No pipes, No cigars **Children:** Min 7 yrs D, Portions **Directions:** From A55 take old Colwyn exit, left at slip road, right at mini rdbt, right towards bay; Restaurant on left **Parking:** On street **web:** www.cafe-nicoise.co.uk

---

BETWS-Y-COED MAP 14 SH75

Tan-y-Foel Country House

Modern British

Divine cooking in chic Snowdonia hideaway

☎ 01690 710507   Capel Garmon LL26 0RE

MENU GUIDE Seared scallops, nero sauce • Lamb loin, green pea & corn filo parcel, mint cream sauce • Lemon sponge, lemon curd sauce

WINE GUIDE ♀ Cloudy Bay Sauvignon Blanc • ♀ Gaston Hochar Syrah • 81 bottles over £20, 7 bottles under £20 • 3 by the glass (£3.50-£4.25)

PRICE GUIDE Fixed D £39-£41 • coffee £4 • min/water £3 • Service optional

PLACE: The name translates as 'the house under the hillside', and Tan-y-Foel sits high in a tranquil valley above Betws-y-Coed with superb views from the part 16th-century manor house. The traditional stone façade of this old farmhouse masks a stylish, sophisticated little hotel and is a must for travellers seeking a modern, eclectic hotel. Although 16th-century features remain, the interior design and furnishings are minimalist and highly contemporary. Dinner is taken in the smartly appointed, intimate restaurant, with its beamed ceiling, elegant square tables, wood-burning stove, and conservatory extension. It is presided over by a hard-working and friendly family team.

FOOD: The kitchen is an area of particular expertise, where vibrant, modern dishes are executed with flair, skill and simplicity, using local, organic produce wherever possible. Lively interpretations are given to familiar dishes, with imaginative combinations of ingredients, but dishes remain simple and uncomplicated in presentation. Choice is limited to just two options per course on the concise, innovative menu. Some of the best cooking in Wales.

OUR TIP: Spectacular views over the Conwy valley **Chef:** Janet Pitman **Owners:** Mr & Mrs P Pitman **Times:** 7.30-8.15, Closed 1 Dec-14 Jan, closed L all week **Notes:** Vegetarian by request only, Dress Restrictions, No Jeans, trainers, tracksuits, walking boots **Seats:** 12 **Smoking:** N/Sm in restaurant **Children:** Min 7 yrs **Rooms:** 6 (6 en suite) ★★ **Directions:** A5 onto A470; 2m N towards Llanrwst, then turning for Capel Garmon. Country House on left before village **Parking:** 14 **e-mail:** enquiries@tyfhotel.co.uk **web:** www.tyfhotel.co.uk

Wales

⚜️⚜️ The Castle Hotel

British, Welsh

Contemporary cooking and friendly service at smart hotel

☎ 01492 582800 High St LL32 8DB

MENU GUIDE Smoked haddock omelette, hollandaise sauce • Turbot, boulangère potatoes • Rhubarb & walnut tart, vanilla ice cream

WINE GUIDE ♀ Alpha Zeta Pinot Grigio £12.50 • ♀ Persimmon Grenache £11.75 • 20 bottles over £20, 30 bottles under £20 13 by the glass (£3.95-£6)

PRICE GUIDE Fixed L £15.95-£17.95 • starter £5.95-£7.50 • main £15.95-£21 • dessert £5.50-£6 • coffee £1.95 • min/water £3.25 • Service added but optional 10%

PLACE: Nestling within the walls of Conwy town, the family owned and run Castle is a photogenic building dating back to the 15th century that counts Wordsworth and Stephenson among famous past guests. With a recent classy makeover, the hotel's aptly named Shakespeare's restaurant is dominated by original paintings of scenes from the Bard's plays by Victorian theatrical artist John Dawson-Watson.

FOOD: Locally sourced, quality, seasonal produce takes a leading role on the appealing modern British repertoire, which shows imagination in well executed, well-balanced, assured dishes that confirm the kitchen's technical skill. ***Winner of the AA Hotel of the Year Award for Wales 2005-2006***

OUR TIP: The popular Dawsons Bar also serves food

Chef: Graham Tinsley **Owners:** Lavin Family & Graham Tinsley **Times:** 12.30-2.30/7-9.30, Closed L Mon-Sat **Notes:** Vegetarian available, Dress Restrictions, Smart casual, no collarless T-shirts **Seats:** 50 **Smoking:** N/Sm in restaurant **Children:** Menu, Portions **Rooms:** 28 (28 en suite) ★★★ **Directions:** From A55 junct 18 towards town centre. Follow signs for town centre and continue on one-way system. Hotel halfway up High Street **Parking:** 36 **e-mail:** mail@castlewales.co.uk **web:** www.castlewales.co.uk

⚜️ The Groes Inn

British

Real ale and good cooking at an ancient inn

☎ 01492 650545 Tyn-y-Groes LL32 8TN

MENU GUIDE Poached salmon terrine, dill cream • Supreme of chicken, white wine cream, mushrooms, tarragon • Chocolate mocha pot

WINE GUIDE 5 bottles over £20, 22 bottles under £20

PRICE GUIDE Fixed L £16.50 • Fixed D £28 • starter £3.95-£7.50 • main £7.95-£16.50 • dessert £3.95-£4.95 • Service optional

PLACE: This pretty inn was the first licensed premises in Wales, and has provided a hospitable welcome to travellers for more than four centuries. It's an intimate warren of cosy nooks and crannies, that includes a tasteful restaurant and conservatory extension, which opens onto the garden.

FOOD: Hearty favourites conjured from quality local produce, such as lamb from the Conwy Valley, and Anglesey shellfish. Mains might include beef stroganoff, or braised rabbit and bacon

OUR TIP: A good base for Snowdonia and North Wales

Chef: Gary Mason **Owners:** Dawn & Justin Humphreys **Times:** 12-2.15/6.30-9.00, Closed 25 Dec **Notes:** Set price Sun L £16.50, Vegetarian available, Dress Restrictions, Smart casual **Seats:** 54, Pr/dining room 20 **Smoking:** N/Sm in restaurant **Children:** Min 12 yrs **Rooms:** 14 (14 en suite) ★★★ **Directions:** In B5106, 3m from Conwy **Parking:** 100 **web:** www.groesinn.com

⚜️⚜️⚜️ The Old Rectory see page 629

🍺 **The Mulberry** Morfa Dr, Conwy Marina LL32 8EP ☎ 01492 583350 Pub with scenic views overlooking the Conwy estuary. Food includes fresh fish and local mussels.

⚜️⚜️⚜️ Bodysgallen Hall and Spa

see page 63?

Three Rosettes Outstanding restaurants that demand recognition well beyond their local area. Timing, seasoning and the judgement of flavour combinations will be consistently excellent, supported by other elements such as intelligent service and a well-chosen wine list. Around 10% of restaurants with Rosettes have been awarded three.

CONWY MAP 14 SH77

The Old Rectory

British, French

Food to savour in elegant country-house hotel

☎ 01492 580611 Llanrwst Rd, Llansanffraid Glan
LL28 5LF

MENU GUIDE Monkfish, vanilla risotto, red wine sauce • Rack of lamb, anchovy & olive crust, boulangère potatoes • Fruit sorbet

WINE GUIDE ♀ Hugues de Beauvienac Picpuul de Pinet £15.90 • ♀ Gerard Mouton Pinot Noir £19.90 • 64 bottles over £20, 50 bottles under £20 • 4 by the glass (£3.95-£4.95)

PRICE GUIDE Fixed D £39.50 • coffee £3.95 • Service optional

PLACE: Committed proprietors have poured money and heart into this little country-house hotel resulting in a welcoming haven, with uninterrupted vistas from Conwy Castle to Snowdonia.

FOOD: Expect to have your culinary likes and dislikes quizzed on booking. Don't mind this. The Rectory is keen to please and will create ingenious meals on classical lines, using fresh local produce.

OUR TIP: Harpist plays at weekends

Chef: W Vaughan, C Jones **Owners:** M & W Vaughan **Times:** 7.30-11, Closed 15 Dec-18 Jan, Sun, L all week **Notes:** Vegetarian by request only, Dress Restrictions, No jeans, smart casual **Seats:** 14 **Smoking:** N/Sm in restaurant **Children:** Min 5 yrs, Portions **Rooms:** 6 (6 en suite) ★★ **Directions:** On A470, 0.5 mile S of junct with A55 **Parking:** 10

e-mail: info@oldrectorycountryhouse.co.uk

web: www.oldrectorycountryhouse.co.uk

Empire Hotel

British, European

Modern cooking in elegant split-level dining room

☎ 01492 860555 Church Walks LL30 2HE

MENU GUIDE Pear, bacon, walnut salad • Roast herb-crusted Welsh lamb, red wine sauce • Dark chocolate brownie, butterscotch sauce

WINE GUIDE ♀ Paarl Chenin Blanc £13.50 • ♀ Marktree Cabernet Sauvignon £13.50 • 40 bottles over £20, 58 bottles under £20 • 6 by the glass (£3.25-£4.50)

PRICE GUIDE Fixed L £14.50 • Fixed D £25-£30 • coffee £2 • min/water £3 • Service optional

PLACE: In the hands of the same family for over sixty years who, along with their dedicated staff, provide high levels of customer care. The Watkins & Co restaurant is named after a wine and spirit merchant who previously occupied this part of the building.

FOOD: The cooking is traditional British with modern and European influences. The six-course, fixed-price seasonal dinner menu may be a little too generous for smaller appetites.

OUR TIP: Expect to be well looked after

Chef: Michael Waddy, David Thompson **Owners:** Len & Elizabeth Maddocks **Times:** 12.30-2/6.45-9.30, Closed 17-30 Dec, closed L Mon-Sat **Notes:** Vegetarian available **Seats:** 110, Pr/dining room 18 **Smoking:** N/Sm in restaurant, Air con **Children:** Portions **Rooms:** 59 (59 en suite) ★★★ **Directions:** From Chester take A55 junct 19 then follow signs towards Llandudno. Follow signs to town centre, take 2nd exit at the Millennium Clock rdbt. **Parking:** 44

e-mail: reservations@empirehotel.co.uk **web:** www.empirehotel.co.uk

Imperial Hotel

Traditional

Grand Victorian hotel dining with great sea views

☎ 01492 877466 The Promenade LL30 1AP

MENU GUIDE Crab cakes, tartare sauce • Roast lamb, tapenade crust, dauphinoise potatoes, natural jus • Fig Bakewell, apricot sabayon

continued

continued

Wales

LLANDUDNO continued MAP 14 SH78

PRICE GUIDE Fixed L £15-£20 • Fixed D £25-£30

PLACE: Impressive Victorian seafront hotel in a prime location, close to the town centre. It has extensive conference, leisure and fitness facilities in addition to the elegant Chantrey's Restaurant, overlooking Llandudno Bay.

FOOD: Quality Welsh produce stars in the monthly menu. Simple crowd-pleasers (steaks) sit happily alongside more elaborate fare (roasted breast of free-range chicken stuffed with black pudding and tarragon mousse, served with creamed leeks and saffron scented crushed potatoes).

OUR TIP: Perfect location for a pre-dinner stroll

Chef: Arwel Jones **Owners:** Greenclose Ltd **Times:** 12.30-2/6.30-9 **Notes:** Vegetarian available, Civ Wed 120 **Seats:** 150, Pr/dining room 30 **Smoking:** N/Sm in restaurant **Children:** Menu, Portions **Rooms:** 100 (100 en suite) ★★★ **Directions:** On the Promenade **Parking:** 20 **e-mail:** imphotel@btinternet.com **web:** www.theimperial.co.uk

Osborne House
British, European
A luxurious setting for a meal or light bite
☎ 01492 860330 17 North Rd LL30 2LP

MENU GUIDE Crispy duck salad, Thai dressing • Pork & apple sausage, spring onion mash • Belgian chocolate sponge pudding

WINE GUIDE ♀ False Bay Chenin Blanc £15.75 • ♟ Palmeros Reserve Merlot £15.25 • 16 bottles over £20, 25 bottles under £20 • 6 by the glass (£3.25-£5.25)

PRICE GUIDE Starter £3.75-£7 • main £9-£16 • dessert £4 coffee £2 • Service optional

PLACE: Opulently restored, this Victorian townhouse is a glittering concoction of crystal chandeliers, gilt-edging and sumptuous fabric.

FOOD: The Osborne's café grill is situated in a stylish and elegant dining room and is open all day. It offers an extensive menu designed to cater for both casual and more formal diners. Tiger prawn wontons with sweet chilli pickle is a typical starter, while mains might include rack of lamb with rosemary jus, or halibut with lemon and herb butter.

OUR TIP: Range of afternoon teas available

Chef: Michael Waddy & David Thompson **Owners:** Len & Elizabeth Maddocks **Times:** 12-4/5-10, Closed 17-30 Dec **Notes:** Vegetarian available, Smart Dress **Seats:** 70, Pr/dining room 18 **Smoking:** N/Sm in restaurant **Children:** Portions **Rooms:** 6 (6 en suite) ★★★★ **Directions:** A55 at junct 19. Follow signs for Llandudno then promenade located at opposite entrance to pier **Parking:** 6 **e-mail:** sales@osbornehouse.com **web:** www.osbornehouse.co.uk

⊚⊚ St Tudno Hotel and Restaurant
Modern British
Accomplished cuisine in traditional seaside hotel
☎ 01492 874411 The Promenade LL30 2LP

MENU GUIDE Seafish soup, fennel & herbs • Glazed pork belly, leek & mustard risotto cake • Lemon tart

WINE GUIDE ♀ Rongapai Sauvignon Blanc £20 • ♟ Casa Rivas Merlot £16 • 165 bottles over £20, 42 bottles under £20 • 12 by the glass (£3.50-£6)

PRICE GUIDE Fixed L fr £14 • Fixed D £38.50 • starter £6-£9.50 • main £17.50-£22.50 • dessert £7.50-£8 • coffee £3.75 • min/water £4.20 • Service optional

PLACE: This listed, family-owned-and-run Victorian hotel on Llandudno's seafront promenade has a slightly elevated position which gives good views of the beach and the Victorian Pier. The Garden restaurant is decked out with murals of sunny Mediterranean scenes and a fountain. The friendly and helpful proprietors and staff are ubiquitous. Excellent wine list.

FOOD: The modern British dishes with international influences make good use of fresh, Welsh, seasonal produce by an enthusiastic kitchen team. Expect dishes of Thai crab cakes with pickled cucumber and scallops or rump of Welsh lamb with leek and potato dauphinoise. **OUR TIP:** A classic seafront location

Chef: Stephen Duffy **Owners:** Mr & Mrs Bland **Times:** 12.30-2.15/7-9.30 **Notes:** Vegetarian available, Dress Restrictions, Smart casual requested. No shorts/tracksuits **Seats:** 60 **Smoking:** N/Sm in restaurant, Air con **Children:** Min 6 yrs D, Menu, Portions **Rooms:** 19 (19 en suite) ★★ **Directions:** Town centre, on Promenade opposite the pier entrance(near the Great Orme) **Parking:** 9 **e-mail:** sttudnohotel@btinternet.com **web:** www.st-tudno.co.uk

continued

Wales

LLANDUDNO MAP 14 SH78

Bodysgallen Hall and Spa

British
Grand stately home offering fine country-house hospitality

☎ 01492 584466   LL30 1RS

e-mail: info@bodysgallen.com

web: www.bodysgallen.com

Wales

PLACE: Magnificent views of Snowdonia and Conwy Castle from 200 acres of parkland, await diners at the imposing, 17th-century Bodysgallen Hall, which takes country-house style gracefully in its stride. Beautiful grounds include a box-hedge parterre, walled rose garden and several follies, while the interior is equally impressive, with oak panelling, fireplaces, stone mullioned windows, soft-cushioned sofas, antiques and fine paintings. The traditional-styled restaurant continues the theme, is split between two dining rooms, and offers views over the well-kept gardens.
FOOD: The very best of local produce is skilfully brought to life in John Williams' appealing, fixed-price, modern menus. Intelligent restraint, clean, clear flavours, slick handling and sound combinations deliver in assured, well-conceived dishes. Service fits the bill, being formal but relaxed and attentive. Notable wine list.

MENU GUIDE Salmon ballotine, smoked haddock brandade • Roast lamb loin, lemon & garlic sauce, sweetbread sausage • Apple tart Tatin, clotted ice cream

WINE GUIDE ♀ Ironstone Chardonnay Semillon £22.50 • ♀ Cloudy Bay Pinot Noir £45 • 200 bottles over £20, 5 bottles under £20 • 8 by the glass (£3.50-£12)

PRICE GUIDE Fixed L £17-£20 • Fixed D £38 • coffee £3.50 • min/water £3.75 • Service included

OUR TIP: Enjoy a walk in the delightful grounds

Chef: John Williams **Owners:** Historic House Hotels Ltd **Times:** 12.30-1.45/7-9.30 **Notes:** Vegetarian available, Dress Restrictions, Gentlemen wear jacket at dinner, tie optional, Civ Wed 45 **Seats:** 60, Pr/dining room 40 **Smoking:** N/Sm in restaurant, Air con **Children:** Min 8 yrs, Portions **Rooms:** 35 (37 en suite) ★★★★ **Directions:** From A55 junct 19 follow A470 towards Llandudno. Hotel 2m on right **Parking:** 40

LLANDUDNO *continued* MAP 14 SH78

🍴 Badgers Café & Patisserie The Victoria Shopping Mall, Mostyn St LL30 2RP ☎ 01492 871649 Winner of The Tea Guild Award of Excellence 2005.

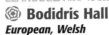

DENBIGHSHIRE

LLANDEGLA MAP 15 SJ25

🏵 Bodidris Hall

European, Welsh

Baronial dining

☎ 01978 790434 LL11 3AL

MENU GUIDE Monkfish beignets, sweet chilli dressing • Calves' liver, olive oil mash with crispy pancetta, lime sauce • Passionfruit tart

WINE GUIDE ♀ Concha y Toro Chardonnay £14.95 • ♀ Concha y Toro Cabernet Sauvignon £14.95 • 22 bottles over £20, 16 bottles under £20 • 2 by the glass (£2.99-£3.99)

PRICE GUIDE Fixed L £9.95 • Fixed D £29.95 • coffee £2.50 • min/water £4.50 • Service included

PLACE: A wealth of character and charm, Bodidris is a 15th-century manor house that is set amid ornamental gardens, woodland and lake. Oak beams and inglenook fireplaces set the scene; the dining room offering that extra medieval touch, located in the old baronial hall.

FOOD: The cooking befits the surroundings, blends the familiar alongside more modern ideas, and delivers these via fixed-price menus that offer plenty of choice.

OUR TIP: Lunch under £10 is a steal
Chef: Kevin Steel **Owners:** S & D Booth **Times:** 12-3/7-11 **Notes:** Sun L 3 courses £14.95, Fixed D 3 courses £29.95, Vegetarian available, Civ Wed 65 **Seats:** 55, Pr/dining room 22 **Smoking:** N/Sm in restaurant **Children:** Min 12 yrs, Menu, Portions **Rooms:** 9 (9 en suite) ★★★ **Directions:** Llandegla is on A525 (Wrexham-Ruthin). In village (from Wrexham direction) turn right onto A5104. Hotel signed 1m on left **Parking:** 50 **e-mail:** info@bodidrishall.com **web:** www.bodidrishall.com

LLANDRILLO MAP 15 SJ03

🏵🏵 Tyddyn Llan

British ⬧NEW

Comfortable Georgian manor with a genius for simplicity

☎ 01490 440414 LL21 0ST

MENU GUIDE Crispy crab cake, tomato salsa • Gressingham duck, potato pancake, cider, apples • Crème brûlée

WINE GUIDE ♀ Gérard Morin Sancerre Sauvignon Blanc £24 • ♀ Prince Albert Pinot Noir £28.50 • 176 bottles over £20, 43 bottles under £20 • 15 by the glass (£3.50-£5.25)

PRICE GUIDE Fixed L £19.50 • Fixed D £37.50 • coffee £3.50 min/water £3.50

PLACE: It's hard not to relax at this charming Georgian house set in pretty grounds amid beautiful countryside. You can start or end your meal in the comfort of one of several cosy lounges, and savour delicious cooking in an elegant restaurant with American-style tongue-and-groove painted walls.

FOOD: An accomplished chef strives to enhance rather than mask the flavour of top quality ingredients, delivering a tempting

---

menu of unpretentious modern British dishes. Expect confident simplicity rather than more intricate fare: Welsh Black beef au poivre, perhaps, or lamb with a shallot and thyme purée. Notable wine list.

OUR TIP: Come and stay - breakfast is as good as dinner
Chef: Bryan Webb **Owners:** Bryan & Susan Webb **Times:** Closed 3 wks Jan/Feb, closed L Mon **Notes:** Sun L 3 courses £21.50, Vegetarian available, Civ Wed 40 **Seats:** 40, Pr/dining room 40 **Smoking:** N/Sm in restaurant **Children:** Portions **Parking:** 20 **e-mail:** tyddynllan@compuserve.com **web:** www.tyddynllan.co.uk

LLANGOLLEN MAP 15 SJ24

🏵 The Wild Pheasant Hotel & Restaurant

British, European

Smart hotel dining in the beautiful Vale of Llangollen

☎ 01978 860629 Berwyn Rd LL20 8AD

MENU GUIDE Black pudding, smoked bacon, red onion chutney • Medallion of Welsh black beef, cured ham • Barabrith bread & butter pudding

WINE GUIDE ♀ Chardonnay £11.25 • ♀ Shiraz £11.25 8 bottles over £20, 39 bottles under £20 • 7 by the glass (£2.30-£4.45)

PRICE GUIDE Fixed L £9.95-£11.50 • Fixed D £19.95-£21.95 starter £4.95-£5.75 • main £8.85-£11.75 • dessert £4.25-£4.35 coffee £1.25 • min/water £2.80 • Service optional

PLACE: A 19th-century property with the charm and comfort of a country house and the addition of a striking modern wing. The Cinnamon Restaurant and Bistro Bar are renowned for good food based on local produce, and there's a lounge area with sofas by the fire.

FOOD: There's plenty of choice with a daily fixed-price modern and traditional menu in the restaurant; a carte in the bistro bar, and a separate vegetarian selection.

OUR TIP: A popular venue for weddings
Chef: Donald Craig **Owners:** P Langhorn **Times:** 6.30-9.30, Closed L Mon-Sat **Notes:** Vegetarian available, Civ Wed 80 **Seats:** 60, Pr/dining room 12 **Smoking:** N/Sm in restaurant, Air con **Children:** Menu, Portions **Rooms:** 46 (46 en suite) ★★★ **Directions:** 1.5m outside Llangollen on the A5 towards Holyhead **Parking:** 200 **e-mail:** wild.pheasant@talk21.com **web:** www.wildpheasanthotel.co.uk

RUTHIN MAP 15 SJ15

🏵 Ruthin Castle

Traditional, International

Ancient castle with imaginative modern food

☎ 01824 702664 Castle St LL15 2NU

continued

MENU GUIDE Diver-caught scallops, celeriac purée, fennel velouté • John Dory, shellfish nage, langoustine brandy sauce • Assiette of Valrhona chocolate miniatures

PRICE GUIDE Food prices not confirmed for 2006. Please telephone for details

PLACE: The main part of this impressive castle was built in the early 19th century but many ruins in the grounds date back much further. The elegantly panelled public areas include a bar, medieval banqueting hall and tea shop. The elegant dining room overlooks the garden terrace.

FOOD: Creative, modern British cooking using fresh regional produce such as Welsh Black beef (Black beef, salladaise potatoes, spring vegetables, confit Savoy cabbage and Alsacienne pancetta, Madeira jus) and Carmarthen ham.

OUR TIP: Medieval banquets are a speciality

Times: 12-2/7-9.45 **Rooms:** 58 (58 en suite) ★★★

Directions: Telephone for directions

e-mail: reservations@ruthincastle.co.uk **web:** www.ruthincastle.co.uk

FLINTSHIRE

EWLOE MAP 15 SJ36

⚙ De Vere St David's Park

International   **NEW**

International flavours in a modern hotel

☎ 01244 520800 St David's Park CH5 3YB

MENU GUIDE Carpaccio of Welsh beef fillet • Wild mushroom, boursin & courgette tartlet • Apple & cinnamon pie

WINE GUIDE ⚲ De Neuville Sauvignon Blanc £14.50 • ⚑ De Neuville Merlot £14.50 • 27 bottles over £20, 34 bottles under £20 • 24 by the glass (£3.65-£8.40)

PRICE GUIDE Fixed L £16.50 • Fixed D £21 • starter £4.95-£7.45 • main £13.45-£23.95 • dessert £4.95 • coffee £2 min/water £3.50 • Service optional • Group min 8 service 10%

PLACE: Superb leisure facilities at this purpose-built hotel include a golf course and spa, while the smart modern restaurant also stands out.

FOOD: The carte and set menu offer a choice of well-executed dishes with a marked international flavour. Presentation of the end result is taken seriously, as in an attractive lamb chump served with a fruit tangine couscous with raspberry jelly and a rosemary cream.

OUR TIP: Stay over and enjoy all the facilities, including a children's club

Chef: Stuart Duff **Owners:** De Vere Group Plc **Times:** 12.30-2/7-10, Closed L Sat **Notes:** Vegetarian available, Dress Restrictions, No trainers, T-shirts, Civ Wed 220 **Seats:** 150, Pr/dining room 45 **Smoking:** N/Sm in restaurant, Air con **Children:** Menu, Portions **Rooms:** 145 (145 en suite) ★★★★ **Directions:** 1m from Hawarden station **Parking:** 125

e-mail: reservations.stdavids@devere-hotels.com

web: www.devereonline.co.uk/stdavids

AA's Chefs' Chef is the annual poll of all the chefs included in The Restaurant Guide. Around 1800 of the country's top chefs are asked to vote to recognise the achievements of one of their peers.

This year's winner is featured on page 19.

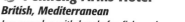

GWYNEDD

ABERDYFI MAP 14 SN69

⚙ Penhelig Arms Hotel

British, Mediterranean   🍶 🐟

Inn popular with locals for fish and classic dishes

☎ 01654 767215 LL35 0LT

MENU GUIDE Crisp fried squid with sweet chilli dip • Grilled fillet of plaice, lemon & fresh herbs • Raspberry frangipane tart

WINE GUIDE 30 by the glass (£2.75-£6)

PRICE GUIDE Fixed L £16 • Fixed D £17 • starter £2.95-£6.95 • main £7.95-£14.50 • dessert £4.25 • coffee £1.50 • min/water £2.50 • Service optional

PLACE: Situated opposite the old harbour, this delightful 18th-century hotel overlooks the Dyfi estuary. The public bar retains its original character and is much loved by the locals, who enjoy the real ale selection as well as excellent meals, many based on seafood.

FOOD: The modern British menu with Mediterranean influences has something for everyone, and it's all good. Especially popular are the fish dishes, simply cooked and served with sauces or salsa. Excellent wine list.

OUR TIP: Dine alfresco in the summer

Chef: J Griffithe, B Shaw **Owners:** Mr & Mrs R Hughes **Times:** 12-2/6-9.30, Closed 25-26 Dec **Notes:** Fixed L applies to Sunday, Vegetarian available **Seats:** 36, Pr/dining room 20 **Smoking:** N/Sm in restaurant, Air con **Children:** Portions **Rooms:** 15 (15 en suite) ★★

Directions: From Machynlleth take A439 coastal route (9 miles)

Parking: 12 **e-mail:** info@penheligarms.com

web: www.penheligarms.com

ABERSOCH MAP 14 SH32

⚙ Neigwl Hotel

British, International

Welcoming hotel with superb sea views

☎ 01758 712363 Lon Sarn Bach LL53 7DY

MENU GUIDE Hot banana in bacon • Breast of chicken, lightly spiced Creole sauce • Crème caramel

WINE GUIDE ⚲ Chardonnay £15.50 • ⚑ Cabernet Sauvignon £16.25 • 12 bottles over £20, 17 bottles under £20 • 2 by the glass (£2.50)

PRICE GUIDE Fixed D £29 • min/water £4 • Service optional

PLACE: Its setting beside the sea, and views to die for, account in part for the popularity of this traditional hotel and restaurant, where customer care from the friendly family owners is warm and genuine.

FOOD: The uncomplicated cooking provides another powerful reason for a visit; enjoyable dishes like deep-fried Brie with spicy chilli jam, and duck breast fillet with a prune and Armagnac confit are a hit with return visitors.

OUR TIP: Evening meals only

Chef: Nigel Higginbottom **Owners:** Steven & Ruth Heptonstall **Times:** 7-9, Closed Jan, closed L all week **Notes:** Coffee included, Vegetarian available, Dress Restrictions, Smart casual **Seats:** 40 **Children:** Portions **Rooms:** 9 (9 en suite) ★★ **Directions:** A499 from Pwllheli to Abersoch. On entering village turn right at bank. Hotel is 400 yds on left **Parking:** 30 **e-mail:** relax@neigwl.com **web:** www.neigwl.com

Wales

Wales

ABERSOCH continued MAP 14 SH32

@@ **Porth Tocyn Hotel**

British, International

Ambitious modern cooking in country hotel with great views

☎ 01758 713303 Bwlch Tocyn LL53 7BU

MENU GUIDE Mussel & saffron soup • Slow-roast duck, leek & apple rösti, spinach, wild mushroom cream • Chocolate truffle torte

PRICE GUIDE Fixed D £37 • min/water £2.75 • Service included

PLACE: Once a row of lead miners' cottages, this friendly hotel is a cosy warren of interconnecting lounges, furnished with country antiques and comfy chairs. Dinner is served in a pretty blue dining room decorated with watercolours, which offers stunning views through a picture window over Cardigan Bay to Snowdonia.
FOOD: Built around seasonal local produce, the menu changes daily and offers a short range of ambitious modern dishes. A beef main shows the style, the meat marinated in Conwy mustard and maple syrup, and served with sautéed potatoes and a claret jus.
OUR TIP: The restaurant will serve plainer versions of its dishes if asked
Chef: L Fletcher-Brewer, Michael Beatty **Owners:** The Fletcher-Brewer family **Times:** 12.15-2/7.30-9, Closed Mid Nov, wk before Easter, closed L Mon-Sat **Notes:** Sunday Buffet adults £21.25 children £12.50, coffee incl, Vegetarian available, Smart Dress **Seats:** 50 **Smoking:** N/Sm in restaurant **Children:** Min 7 yrs D, Portions **Rooms:** 17 (17 en suite) ★★★ **Directions:** 2m S of Abersoch, through Sarn Bach & Bwlch Tocyn. Follow brown road signs **e-mail:** porthtocyn.hotel@virgin.net **web:** www.porth-tocyn-hotel.co.uk

BALA MAP 14 SH93

@ **Palé Hall**

British, French

Formal yet relaxed dining in enchanting mansion

☎ 01678 530285 Palé Estate, Llandderfel LL23 7PS

MENU GUIDE Goats' cheese soufflé • Venison loin, tomato & onion tartlet, pomme dauphinoise, blackberry & Madeira jus • Milk chocolate & Earl Grey délice, saffron coulis

WINE GUIDE ♀ Chablis 1er Cru £27.95 • ♀ St Emilion Pierre Moueix £20.95 • 45 bottles over £20, 49 bottles under £20 4 by the glass (£3.25-£4.75)

PRICE GUIDE Fixed L £14-£19 • coffee £3 • min/water £3.50

PLACE: A magnificent entrance hall with stained-glass lantern ceiling, galleried oak staircase, library bar and choice of two elegant lounges, greet diners at this enchanting 19th-century mansion set in extensive grounds. The smart, intimate country-house restaurant is also impressive, with oak panelling, hand-carved fireplace and dresser. Service is predictably formal, but

Palé Hall

relaxed and friendly and, in the evenings, tall candles add a touch of romance to proceedings.
FOOD: The cooking is classically based, with strong British and French leanings and showcases quality local produce, including Welsh lamb and game in season.
OUR TIP: Don't miss the exquisite carving and artwork, and take a stroll in the grounds
Chef: Karl Cheetham **Owners:** Mr & Mrs Nahed **Times:** 12-1.30/7-8.30 **Notes:** Vegetarian available, Dress Restrictions, Jacket (or shirt) & tie for D, smart for L, Civ Wed 40 **Seats:** 40, Pr/dining room 24 **Smoking:** N/Sm in restaurant **Children:** **Rooms:** 17 (17 en suite) ★★★ **Directions:** Just off B4401, 4m from Llandrillo **Parking:** 40 **e-mail:** enquiries@palehall.co.uk **web:** www.palehall.co.uk

BARMOUTH MAP 14 SH61

@ **Bae Abermaw**

British   **NEW**

Modern cuisine with panoramic accompaniment

☎ 01341 280550 Panorama Hill LL42 1DQ

MENU GUIDE Steamed mussels, white wine & cream • Red bream, herb butter, saffron potatoes • Strawberry shortcake, champagne sabayon

PRICE GUIDE Food prices not confirmed for 2006. Please telephone for details

PLACE: Offering panoramic views of Barmouth Bay from its hillside position, this historic manor house has a surprisingly contemporary interior. The restaurant teams wooden floors with fresh white walls hung with modern art; its tables are elegantly laid with quality glassware and simple silver cutlery.
FOOD: A modern British menu featuring a well-balanced range of simple dishes and more adventurous fare. Local produce gets top billing in mains such as Welsh Black beef with port wine sauce.
OUR TIP: Book ahead for a window table at sunset
Times: Telephone for details **e-mail:** enquiries@baeabermaw.com **web:** www.baeabermaw.com

continued

CAERNARFON MAP 14 SH46

 Seiont Manor

Welsh, British

Country hotel with simple, locally sourced food

☎ 01286 673366 Llanrug LL55 2AQ

MENU GUIDE Smoked trout, pickled samphire • Pan-fried pork medallions, black pudding, mushrooms • White chocolate & lime cheesecake

PRICE GUIDE Food prices not confirmed for 2006. Please telephone for details

PLACE: Peaceful country hotel a short distance from Caernarfon and Mount Snowdon. The building itself is an upmarket, sensitively refurbished Welsh farmhouse with stone slabs, exposed brickwork and subtle decorative techniques creating a thoroughly calming environment. The beamed restaurant has traditional napery and well structured, friendly service.
FOOD: The food is fresh, honest and traditional with an emphasis on regional dishes and locally sourced produce.
OUR TIP: Do try the Welsh specialities
Times: 12-2/7-9.30 **Rooms:** 28 (28 en suite) ★★★ **Directions:** From Bangor follow signs for Caernarfon. Leave Caernarfon on A4086. Hotel 3m on left **e-mail:** seiontmanor@handpicked.co.uk
web: www.handpicked.co.uk/seiontmanor

CRICCIETH MAP 14 SH53

 Bron Eifion Country House Hotel

International   **NEW**

Enjoyable food in gracious country house

☎ 01766 522385 LL52 0SA

MENU GUIDE Chicken liver pâté • Braised lamb shank, red wine & thyme jus • Orange & Baileys torte

PRICE GUIDE Fixed L £13.50-£14.25 • coffee £1.95 • min/water £3.50 • Service optional

PLACE: Imposing Victorian mansion set in peaceful grounds that run down to the sea. Take a drink in the Great Hall before dinner, a stately room with a minstrels' gallery and lofty timbered roof, and then move through to the traditional elegance of the Conservatory Restaurant.
FOOD: Tempting International cuisine created from quality produce, sourced locally where possible. The carte is supplemented by a daily-changing fixed price selection.
OUR TIP: A good base for Snowdonia and the beautiful Lleyn Peninsula
Owners: Mr & Mrs Thompson **Times:** 12-1.45/7-8.30 **Notes:** Fixed choices £23.95-£39, incl coffee, Vegetarian available, No jeans **Seats:** **Smoking:** N/Sm in restaurant **Children:** Menu, Portions
Rooms: 19 (19 en suite) ★★★ **Directions:** A497 Between Porthmadog and Pwllheli **Parking:** 40 **web:** www.broneifion.co.uk

One Rosette Excellent local restaurants serving food prepared with care, understanding and skill, using good quality ingredients. These restaurants stand out in their local area. Of the total number of establishments with Rosettes around 50% have one Rosette.

DOLGELLAU MAP 14 SH71

Dolserau Hall

British

Traditional British cooking in Snowdonia

☎ 01341 422522 LL40 2AG

MENU GUIDE Pan-seared pigeon, onion & honey confit • Salmon, Chinese leaves, strawberries, balsamic dressing • Baileys crème brûlée

PRICE GUIDE Fixed D £24.95 • min/water £2.85

PLACE: Just a few miles from the foot of Cader Idris in the Snowdonia National Park, this imposing Victorian manor stands in farm meadows and offers pretty views in every direction.
FOOD: Quality ingredients are handled simply in a concise range of traditional dishes. You might begin with a Waldorf salad, and then move on to a leg of Welsh lamb with roast potatoes and parsnips.
OUR TIP: Dinner orders taken in the lounge from 7 to 8.30pm
Chef: John Charnley **Owners:** Peter & Marion Kaye **Times:** 7-9, Closed Nov-mid Feb, closed L all week **Notes:** coffee incl., Vegetarian available **Seats:** 40 **Smoking:** N/Sm in restaurant **Children:** Min 6 yrs **Rooms:** 15 (15 en suite) ★★★ **Directions:** 1.5m from Dolgellau on unclass road between A470/A494 to Bala **Parking:** 40
e-mail: aa@dhh.co.uk **web:** www.dhh.co.uk

Penmaenuchaf Hall Hotel

British, European

Enjoyable dining in Victorian manor

☎ 01341 422129 Penmaenpool LL40 1YB

MENU GUIDE Roast plum tomato velouté • Roasted monkfish, pea risotto • Lemon posset

WINE GUIDE ♀ Domaine Berland Sauvignon Blanc £14.75 • ♀ Allegrini Valpolicella Molingra Corvina Ronduella £15.75 • 60 bottles over £20, 44 bottles under £20 • 5 by the glass (£4)

PRICE GUIDE Fixed L £15.95 • Fixed D £32.50 • starter £7.40-£8.50 • main £23-£24.50 • dessert £7-£8.50 • coffee £2.50 • min/water £3.50 • Service optional

PLACE: Built in 1860, this impressive Victorian manor house stands in 20 acres of formal gardens high above the River Mawddach. Careful restoration has resulted in a warm and hospitable interior and a dining room with three-quarter polished oak panelling.
FOOD: Fresh, local seasonal produce is prepared in the modern British style although there are French and Mediterranean influences here as well. The emphasis is on clear flavours and texture. Herbs, vegetables and fruit are garden grown. Especially noteworthy is the locally sourced Welsh Black beef and the Cambrian coast seafood including sewin.
OUR TIP: Good spot for river fishing
Chef: J Pilkington, A Reeve, T Reeve **Owners:** Mark Watson, Lorraine Fielding **Times:** 12-2/7-9.30 **Notes:** Vegetarian available, Dress Restrictions, No jeans or T-shirts, Civ Wed 50 **Seats:** 36, Pr/dining room 16 **Smoking:** N/Sm in restaurant **Children:** Min 6 yrs, Portions **Rooms:** 14 (14 en suite) ★★★ **Directions:** A493 (Tywyn/Fairbourne), entrance 1.5m on left by sign for Penmaenpool **Parking:** 36
e-mail: eat@penhall.co.uk **web:** www.penhall.co.uk

The AA Wine Awards recognise the finest wine lists in England, Scotland and Wales. For full details, see pages 14-15

Wales

⬡ Castle Cottage
Welsh
Good Welsh dining in a modern setting
☎ 01766 780479 Pen Llech LL46 2YL

MENU GUIDE Rhydlewis smoked salmon • Brochette of monkfish in pesto crust • Treacle tart with berries & Drambuie cream

WINE GUIDE ♀ Sauvignon Blanc £14 • ♀ Merlot £14
27 bottles over £20, 38 bottles under £20 • 4 by the glass (£2.50-£3.50)

PRICE GUIDE Fixed D £27.50 • coffee £2 • min/water £3
Service optional

PLACE: Dating from the 16th century, this coaching inn with spacious bedrooms is just 100 metres from Harlech Castle. There's a light, modern dining room where original paintings are displayed
FOOD: Modern in style, simple in presentation with lots of local, seasonal ingredients such as seafood from Barmouth, Welsh Black beef and Welsh cheeses.
OUR TIP: Build up an appetite walking around the castle
Chef: Glyn Roberts **Owners:** Mr & Mrs G Roberts **Times:** 7-9, Closed 3 wks Jan, closed L all week **Notes:** Vegetarian available **Seats:** 45
Smoking: N/Sm in restaurant **Children:** Portions **Rooms:** 7 (7 en suite) ◆◆◆◆ **Directions:** Just off High Street (B4573) 100 yds from Harlech Castle **Parking:** 3 **e-mail:** glyn@castlecottageharlech.co.uk
web: www.castlecottageharlech.co.uk

 Cemlyn Restaurant & Tea Shop High St
LL46 2YA ☎ 01766 780425 Winner of The Tea Guild Award of Excellence 2005.

⬡ Y Bistro
Modern Welsh
Imaginative Welsh cuisine in relaxed bistro setting
☎ 01286 871278 Glandwr, 43-45 Stryd Fawr (High Street) LL55 4EU

MENU GUIDE Conwy mussels, Cariad white wine • Sliced duck and pheasant breast, Puy lentils, Cointreau sauce • Pannacotta, mulled wine cranberries

WINE GUIDE ♀ Claudeval Blend £11.50 • ♀ Vin du Pays du Torgan Carignan £11.50 • 12 bottles over £20, 50 bottles under £20 • 5 by the glass (£2.25)

PRICE GUIDE Starter £5.50-£10 • main £14-£18.50 • dessert £6 • coffee £1.90 • min/water £3 • Service optional

PLACE: Danny and Nerys Roberts have run Y Bistro for 25 years and are proud of their Welsh heritage. The terraced exterior

belies the warm and inviting interior, with its cosy lounge areas and intimate dining room.
FOOD: Consistent standards are maintained and there is always something interesting on the daily-changing menu. A good choice is offered, but not at the expense of quality, and many Welsh dishes have been created in-house.
OUR TIP: Local produce to the fore
Chef: Nerys Roberts **Owners:** Danny & Nerys Roberts **Times:** 7.30-10.15, Closed 2 wks Jan, Sun (Mon in winter), closed L Open for functions, closed D Sun (Mon in winter) **Notes:** Vegetarian available, Smart casual
Seats: 40 **Smoking:** N/Sm in restaurant **Children:** Portions
Directions: In the centre of the village at the foot of Mount Snowdon by Lake Padam **Parking:** On street **e-mail:** ybistro@fsbdial.co.uk
web: www.ybistro.co.uk

⬡ Castell Deudraeth
Modern Welsh
Modern brasserie in Italianate setting
☎ 01766 772400 LL48 6EN

MENU GUIDE Fish terrine • Grilled halibut with red onion marmalade • Crème brulée

PRICE GUIDE Starter £3.50-£5.50 • main £8.50-£20.50 • dessert £4.75 • Service optional

PLACE: Part of the refurbished castellated mansion overlooking Snowdonia, this contemporary dining room (in a former Victorian solarium) is light and airy with garden views. The hotel is part of the famous Italianate village featured in the cult 60s TV series, *The Prisoner.*
FOOD: Good local ingredients used as much as possible in accurately cooked modern Welsh dishes.
OUR TIP: Eat here and explore the Italianate village and the sea
Chef: Steven Rowlands **Owners:** Portmeirion Limited **Times:** 12.00-2/6.9.30 **Notes:** Vegetarian available, Civ Wed 40 **Seats:** 80, Pr/dining room 40 **Smoking:** N/Sm area, Air con **Children:** Menu, Portions **Rooms:** 1 (11 en suite) ★★★ **Directions:** Off A487 at Minfford. Between Porthmadog & Penryndeudraeth **Parking:** 40
e-mail: castell@portmeirion-village.com **web:** www.portmeirion.com

⬡ Hotel Portmeirion
Modern Welsh
Delightful hotel in fantasy village
☎ 01766 770000 LL48 6ET

MENU GUIDE Celeriac velouté • Loin of Welsh lamb with Mediterranean vegetables • Plum sponge pudding

PRICE GUIDE Fixed L £16 • Fixed D £37.50 • Service optional

PLACE: This elegant hotel enjoys one of the finest settings in Wales. Located beneath the wooded slopes of the charming fantasy village of Portmeirion, the dining room looks out across the estuary towards Snowdonia.
FOOD: With menus printed in Welsh (translations are available), local produce is to the fore here, although dishes like loin of Welsh lamb on a beetroot and cumin galette show the kitchen takes note of international influences.
OUR TIP: Book a window table for stunning views of Snowdonia
Chef: David Doughty, Billy Taylor **Owners:** Portmeirion Ltd **Times:** 12-2/6.30-9, Closed 4-16 Jan **Notes:** Vegetarian available, Civ Wed 100 **Seats:** 100, Pr/dining room 30 **Smoking:** N/Sm in restaurant
Children: Menu, Portions **Rooms:** 51 (51 en suite) ★★★
Directions: Off A487 at Minffordd **Parking:** 100
e-mail: hotel@portmeirion-village.com
web: www.portmeirion-village.com

continued

PWLLHELI MAP 14 SH33

 Plas Bodegroes

Modern British

Contemporary style in traditional country house

☎ 01758 612363 Nefyn Rd LL53 5TH

MENU GUIDE Smoked haddock & leek tart • Quail, stuffed & pot roast, bacon • Cinnamon biscuit, apple & rhubarb, elderflower custard

PRICE GUIDE Food prices not confirmed for 2006. Please telephone for details

PLACE: Restaurant with an elegant contemporary look set within a Georgian manor house surrounded by lovely secluded gardens. The atmosphere is relaxed, with classical music playing in the background and a mixed clientele of locals and tourists. Comfortable public room include a bar and a drawing room with an open fire.
FOOD: Cooking takes a modern approach to traditional and regional dishes and makes imaginative use of local produce, particularly seafood. The restaurant is open for dinner only and Sunday lunch.
OUR TIP: Comprehensive wine list with plenty of halves
Times: 12-2.30/7-9, Closed Dec-Feb, Mon, closed L Tue-Sat, closed D Sun
Directions: On A497, 1m W of Pwllheli
e-mail: gunna@bodegroes.co.uk **web:** www.bodegroes.co.uk

TALSARNAU MAP 14 SH63

 Hotel Maes y Neuadd

French, Welsh

Accomplished cooking in historic house with stunning views of Snowdonia

☎ 01766 780200 LL47 6YA

MENU GUIDE Smoked fish roulade, herb and lemon yoghurt Brecon venison, juniper sauce • Raspberry pannacotta, vanilla cream

WINE GUIDE ♀ Churton Sauvignon Blanc £19.95 • ♥ Joseph Fellow Gamay £25 • 100 bottles over £20, 74 bottles under £20 • 7 by the glass (£3-£5)

PRICE GUIDE Fixed L £15.75 • Fixed D £33 • starter £3.25-£7.50 • main £6.95-£7.50 • dessert £4 • coffee £2.50 • min/water £3.25 • Service optional • Group min 15 service 10%

PLACE: This comfortable and welcoming 14th-century manor enjoys a tranquil setting in an almost secret valley, overlooking the kitchen gardens and the Snowdonia National Park beyond. Updated over the years, with 16th- 18th- and 20th-century additions, the typically country-house dining room is furnished with antiques.
FOOD: Cooking is uncomplicated modern Welsh, French and classical British in style. Well-prepared dishes make good use of prime Welsh produce, notably venison and cheeses, and raw ingredients from the garden play their role in creating the four-course menu.
OUR TIP: Wine selection for each menu
Chef: Peter Jackson, John Owen Jones **Owners:** Mr & Mrs Jackson & Mr & Mrs Payne **Times:** 12-1.45/7-8.45 **Notes:** Coffee incl at dinner, Vegetarian available, Smart casual, no denim jeans or sports wear, Civ Wed 65 **Seats:** 50, Pr/dining room 14 **Smoking:** N/Sm in restaurant
Children: Menu, Portions **Rooms:** 16 (16 en suite) ★★
Directions: 3m NE of Harlech, signed off B4573 **Parking:** 60
e-mail: maes@neuadd.com **web:** www.neuadd.com

The AA Wine Awards recognise the finest wine lists in England, Scotland and Wales. For full details, see pages 14-15

MONMOUTHSHIRE

ABERGAVENNY MAP 09 S021

 Angel Hotel

Traditional British

Great choice of food in atmospheric surroundings

☎ 01873 857121 15 Cross St NP7 5EN

MENU GUIDE Pappardelle pasta, rabbit & Guinness broth • Roast monkfish, courgette, tomato salsa • Chocolate fondue, dipping biscuits

WINE GUIDE ♀ Rooiberg Sauvignon Blanc £12.50 • ♥ Andes Sur Shiraz/Bonarardo £10.50 • 26 bottles over £20, 42 bottles under £20 • 6 by the glass (£2.80-£3.30)

PRICE GUIDE Fixed L £9.25 • Fixed D £26.25 • starter £3-£5.10 • main £5.70-£17.25 • dessert £5.10 • coffee £2.10 • min/water £3 • Service optional

PLACE: Georgian coaching inn with a contemporary-style restaurant achieving a perfect balance between quality and understated elegance. Service is friendly and relaxed, enhancing the wonderful atmosphere created by candlelight, soft music and comfortable furnishings.
FOOD: Innovative British menus provide an excellent choice of real food with more than a hint of a modern American influence. There's a two-course special lunch and a main menu, which combines bar snacks with more elaborate restaurant dishes.
OUR TIP: Eat here now before it gets too popular
Chef: Mark Turton, Paul Tulip **Owners:** Mr & Mrs W J C Griffiths
Times: 12-2.30/7-10.00, Closed 25 Dec, closed D 24 & 26 Dec
Notes: Sun L £14.80, Vegetarian available, Smart Dress, Civ Wed 200
Seats: 70, Pr/dining room 120 **Smoking:** N/Sm in restaurant
Children: Portions **Rooms:** 29 (29 en suite) ★★★ **Directions:** From A4042/A465/A40 rdbt S of Abergavenny, follow signs for town centre. Continue past railway and bus station on left **Parking:** 40
e-mail: mail@angelhotelabergavenny.com
web: www.angelhotelabergavenny.com

 The Foxhunter

Modern British

Impressive gastro-pub

☎ 01873 881101 Nantyderry NP7 9DN

MENU GUIDE Black pasta with crab meat • Mixed seafood bourride, spiced rouille • St Emillion au chocolat, mint ice cream

WINE GUIDE ♀ Domaine de Grauzan Sauvignon £13.50 • ♥ Ladera Verde Merlot £13.50 • 30 bottles over £20, 20 bottles under £20 • 4 by the glass (£2.50-£3.50)

PRICE GUIDE Fixed L £18 • starter £5.95-£9.95 • main £13.95-£19.95 • dessert £4.95-£6.95 • coffee £2.75 • min/water £2.50 • Service optional • Group min 8 service 10%

PLACE: The contemporary setting belies the Victorian origins of this former stationmaster's house and pub, with restored Welsh flagstones and modern furniture making an almost minimalist statement.
FOOD: The cooking stays true to the flavours of the fresh, often organic, ingredients, with popular traditional choices like cod goujons with tartare sauce vying for attention with baby chard risotto, mascarpone and goats' cheese. Excellent wine list.
OUR TIP: Home-made bread is a real treat
Chef: Matt Tebbutt **Owners:** Lisa & Matt Tebbutt **Times:** 12-2.30/7-9.30, Closed Xmas, 1 Jan, 2 wks Feb, Sun-Mon **Notes:** Vegetarian available
Seats: 60, Pr/dining room 30 **Smoking:** N/Sm in restaurant
Children: Portions **Directions:** Just off A4042 between Usk & Abergavenny **Parking:** 25 **e-mail:** info@thefoxhunter.com
web: www.thefoxhunter.com

⚜⚜ Llansantffraed Court Hotel

Modern Welsh

High-class dining with great views

☎ 01873 840678 Llanvihangel Gobion NP7 9BA

MENU GUIDE Ballotine of foie gras, pickled girolles • Tronçon of halibut, fennel broth • Pineapple tart Tatin, rum & raisin ice cream

WINE GUIDE ♀ Mills Reef Sauvignon Blanc £18 • ♀ Los Vascos Cabernet Sauvignon £20 • 44 bottles over £20, 28 bottles under £20 • 30 by the glass (£3.25-£5.50)

PRICE GUIDE Fixed L £13 • Fixed D £29.50-£34.50 • starter £6.50-£11 • main £17-£24 • dessert £6.50-£9 • coffee £2.50 • min/water £3.75 • Service optional

PLACE: Set in a commanding position, this red brick, William and Mary period country house in 20 acres of landscaped grounds, offers enviable views of the Brecon Beacons. Relaxing, sumptuous lounges and log fires are just as expected, while the comfortable, beamed dining room - with its country furniture and pretty floral prints - is attractively decked out in crisp white linen, fresh flowers and candlelight by evening.

FOOD: Carefully sourced top quality local produce, much of it organic, is a hallmark of the kitchen's classically influenced, accomplished, simply cooked dishes presented in modern vogue.

OUR TIP: Take afternoon tea on the lawn in summer

Chef: Simon King **Owners:** Mr M Morgan **Times:** 12-2/7-8.45 **Notes:** Tasting menu £47.50, Sun L £20, Vegetarian available, Civ Wed 150 **Seats:** 50, Pr/dining room 30 **Smoking:** N/Sm in restaurant **Children:** Menu, Portions **Rooms:** 21 (21 en suite) ★★★ **Directions:** From junction of A40 & A465 at Abergavenny, take B4598 signed to Usk. Hotel 4.5m on left (with white gates). 0.5m along drive **Parking:** 250 **e-mail:** restaurant@llch.co.uk **web:** www.llch.co.uk

⚜⚜ Walnut Tree Inn

Italian, Mediterranean

A stunning Welsh setting for top-notch cuisine

☎ 01873 852797 Llandewi Skirrid NP7 8AW

MENU GUIDE English Channel oysters • Braised lamb shank, peperonata, potatoes • Grand Marnier soufflé, clementine sorbet

WINE GUIDE ♀ Banfi Le Rime Chardonnay/Pinot Grigio £13.50 • ♀ Banfi Col Di Sasso Cabernet Sauvignon £13.50 60% bottles over £20, 40% bottles under £20 • 12 by the glass (£3.50-£11)

PRICE GUIDE Starter £3.50-£14.50 • main £14.75-£21.50 • dessert £5.50-£6 • coffee £1.75 • Service optional

PLACE: Nestled in the foothills of the Black Mountains overlooking Abergavenny, this ancient inn has a relaxed and friendly ambience. Food is served in a stylish, rustic dining room, with rows of canteen-style tables and monochrome photos on the walls.

FOOD: An eclectic mix of Italian and modern European favourites that will see you dithering between, typically, lasagne or honey-roast sea bass with pumpkin and Swiss chard. Dishes are prepared with care and make the most of seasonal ingredients and good quality Welsh lamb and beef.

OUR TIP: Call ahead for a table with a view

Chef: Spencer Ralph **Owners:** Francesco Mattioli **Times:** 12-3/7-9.30, Closed Mon, closed D BHs, Sun **Notes:** Vegetarian available **Seats:** 70, Pr/dining room 26 **Smoking:** N/Sm area, No pipes **Children:** Portions **Directions:** 3m NE of Abergavenny on B4521 **Parking:** 30 **e-mail:** francesco@thewalnuttreeinn.com **web:** www.thewalnuttreeinn.co.uk

⚜⚜ Wye Knot Restaurant

British, Mediterranean

Experienced cooking in friendly cottage restaurant

☎ 01291 622929 The Back NP16 5HH

MENU GUIDE Tartare of organic salmon, smoked halibut & horseradish • Welsh Black beef, sautéed foie gras, spinach parcel of black pudding • Pineapple Tatin, coconut milk

WINE GUIDE ♀ Chenin Blanc £14.95 • ♀ Blend of Negrette £15.50 • 14 bottles over £20, 19 bottles under £20 • 8 by the glass (£3.25-£3.75)

PRICE GUIDE Fixed L £12.95 • Fixed D £23.50 • starter £3.50-£7.95 • main £12.95-£18.95 • dessert £4.95 • coffee £2.25 • min/water £3.50 • Service optional

PLACE: A pretty cottage overlooking the Wye river, where the Chartist ringleaders were held for their last night before being deported to Van Diemen's Land in 1840 (which became Tasmania in 1853). Linen-clothed tables are surrounded by an assortment of chairs and decorated with candles and fresh flowers.

continued on page 640

Wales

Wine Award Winner for Wales

The Bell at Skenfrith

(see page 640)

CHEPSTOW continued MAP 04 ST59

FOOD: Expect modern British cooking with Mediterranean twists on menus that change with the seasonal availability of quality local produce. Solid experience is on show here, reflected in reliable dishes - fillet of sea bass and scallops with mustard cream sauce, baby leeks and wild mushrooms.
OUR TIP: Alfresco eating in summer
Chef: Kevin Brookes, Emma Williams **Owners:** Kevin Brookes, Emma Williams **Times:** 12.30-2.30/7-10, Closed 26 Dec, 1 Jan, BHs, Mon-Tues, closed L Sat **Notes:** Vegetarian available **Seats:** 40 **Smoking:** N/Sm in restaurant **Children:** Menu, Portions **Directions:** From M4 take M48, then onto Chepstow, following signs for Chepstow Castle & Riverbank

LLANTRISANT MAP 09 ST39

Brookes Restaurant & Private Dining Room

British, International
Welcoming restaurant offering globally-influenced dining
☎ 01443 239600 79-81 Talbot Rd, Talbot Green CF72 8AE
MENU GUIDE Oriental salmon tempura, wok fried noodles • Chicken supreme, red pepper & wild mushroom tagliatelle • Iced mango parfait
WINE GUIDE 24 bottles over £20, 21 bottles under £20 • 3 by the glass (£3.25-£4.50)
PRICE GUIDE Starter £4.50-£8.95 • main £13.95-£18.95 • dessert £5.50 • coffee £1.95 • min/water £3.25 • Service optional
PLACE: Behind the lilac frontage lies this relaxed restaurant. The large dining room offers plenty of nooks and crannies, as well as unashamedly chic, contemporary decor, including bold paintings on striking whitewashed walls.
FOOD: The lengthy modern menu takes its influences from Europe and Asia. Excellent local produce sourced, including fresh fish from Cardiff.
OUR TIP: Relax in the first floor café bar
Chef: Craig Brookes **Owners:** Craig & Kevin Brookes **Times:** 12-2.30/7-10.30, Closed 24 Dec, 1 Jan & BHs, Mon, closed L Sat, closed D Sun **Notes:** Sun L from £8.95, Vegetarian available **Seats:** 91, Pr/dining room 26 **Smoking:** No pipes, Air con **Children:** Portions **Directions:** M4 junct 34, follow signs for Llantristant, turn left at 2nd set of lights **Parking:** On street **e-mail:** staffbrookes@btconnect.com

SKENFRITH MAP 09 SO42

The Bell at Skenfrith

British
AA Wine Award Winner for Wales
☎ 01600 750235 NP7 8UH
MENU GUIDE Chicken liver parfait, toasted brioche • Poached & grilled best end of lamb • Pineapple Tatin, pear sorbet
WINE GUIDE ♀ Plozner Pinot Grigio £16 • ♀ Montagne Noire Merlot £12 • 96 bottles over £20, 50 bottles under £20 • 13 by the glass (£3-£4.70)
PRICE GUIDE Starter £4.50-£9.50 • main £14.95-£19.50 • dessert £5.50 • coffee £2.50 • min/water £2.75 • Service optional
PLACE: This former coaching inn continues to impress on all counts. It stands beside the River Monmow in a lush green village setting. Beams, flagstone floors and big fires contribute to an understated elegance, and hospitality and service are exemplary.

FOOD: The owners are proud to display the provenance of their excellent produce, using the best of Welsh fish, lamb, pork and beef. The suppliers are listed on the back of the modern British menu. The wine list is first class.
OUR TIP: Fine British cheeses include some unpasteurised
Chef: Kurt Fleming **Owners:** Mr & Mrs W Hutchings **Times:** 12-2.30/7-9.30, Closed Mon Nov-Mar,10 days end Jan-beg Feb **Notes:** Vegetarian available **Seats:** 40, Pr/dining room 40 **Smoking:** N/Sm in restaurant **Children:** Min 8 yrs, Menu **Rooms:** 8 (8 en suite) 🐾
Directions: From A40 at rdbt in Monmouth take Hereford road. 4m left turn onto B4521 towards Abergavenny. Restaurant 3m left **Parking:** 35 **e-mail:** enquiries@skenfrith.co.uk **web:** www.skenfrith.co.uk

TINTERN PARVA MAP 04 SO50

Parva Farmhouse Hotel

European
Welcoming 17th-century farmhouse
☎ 01291 689411 & 689511 NP16 6SQ
MENU GUIDE Welsh cheese filo parcel, sour cream & chive dressing • Fresh monkfish Portugaise • Blackberry trifle
WINE GUIDE ♀ Wyndham Estate Chardonnay £12.85 • ♀ Château Terre Rouge Medoc £16.85 • 9 bottles over £20, 50 bottles under £20 • 5 by the glass (£3-£3.50)
PRICE GUIDE Fixed D £21 • coffee £2.25 • min/water £2 Service optional
PLACE: Set on a sweep of the River Wye, this friendly hotel has great views of the Wye Valley. The cosy lounge and atmospheric restaurant owe a good deal of their charm to original 17th-century features, like the amazing 14 foot beamed inglenook fireplace that dominates the dining room.
FOOD: Welsh lamb, beef and venison feature regularly, together with locally caught trout and salmon and local cheese. Vegetables and fruits are always seasonal. The European style cooking may be simple, but the emphasis on fresh local produce effectively brings out the flavours.
OUR TIP: Good value fixed-price four-course menu includes cheese
Chef: Dereck Stubbs **Owners:** Mr & Mrs D R Stubbs **Times:** 7-9, Closed L all week **Notes:** Vegetarian available, Dress Restrictions, Smart casual, no jeans **Seats:** 24 **Smoking:** N/Sm in restaurant **Children:** Min 4 yrs, Menu, Portions **Rooms:** 9 (9 en suite) ★★ **Directions:** North end of Tintern on A466 alongside the Wye, 0.75 mile from the Abbey **Parking:** 14 **e-mail:** parva_hoteltintern@hotmail.com **web:** www.hoteltintern.co.uk

USK MAP 09 SO30

The Newbridge

International, British
Rural inn with an environment redolent of Tuscany
☎ 01633 451000 Tredunnock NP15 1LY

continued

continued

Wales

MENU GUIDE Pressing of local game, foie gras, Puy lentils • Roast sea bass, vanilla beurre blanc • Parkin, spiced syrup, caramel ice

WINE GUIDE ♀ Louis Michel Chablis £25 • ♀ Château Thibault Gamay £19.50 • 49 bottles over £20, 35 bottles under £20 10 by the glass (£2.50-£6)

PRICE GUIDE Fixed L £15.50 • starter £4.50-£8 • main £12.50-£18.50 • dessert £5 • coffee £1.95 • min/water £3.10 • Service optional

PLACE: Last year's AA Restaurant of the Year for Wales is idyllically located on a bridge overlooking the River Usk. It is an open bar/bistro-style restaurant - a former inn - with a warm Tuscan influence to the decor, and candlelit tables providing rustic charm in the evenings. The atmosphere is relaxed, and the staff friendly and efficient.

FOOD: An unusual set-up for this area, combining elements of a bistro, gastro-pub and fine dining restaurant. The modern British and European cooking with international flavours include local meats, carefully selected and presented in a not over-complicated style. Fish specials feature depending on the best catch.

OUR TIP: Look out for wine tasting dinner events

Chef: Iain Sampson **Owners:** Glen Rick Court Ltd **Times:** 12-2.30/6.30-9.30, Closed 26 Dec **Notes:** Vegetarian available, Dress Restrictions, No Shorts or Flip flops, Civ Wed 60 **Seats:** 80, Pr/dining room 16 **Smoking:** N/Sm area, No pipes, Air con **Children:** Portions **Rooms:** 6 (6 en suite) 🏰 **Directions:** A449 towards Usk. Continue through Usk and take B route to Llangibby for approx 5m. From Llangibby continue for approx 0.5m until sign for Tredunnock. Turn left through Tredunnock to the back of the river **Parking:** 60

e-mail: thenewbridge@tinyonline.co.uk **web:** www.thenewbridge.co.uk

🍴 Raglan Arms

Modern British   **NEW**

Smart country pub dining

☎ 01291 690800 Llandenny NP15 1DL

MENU GUIDE Pork rillettes with apple chutney • Baked salmon with leeks & brie • Apple oatflake crumble & custard

WINE GUIDE ♀ Sauvignon Blanc £9.75 • ♀ Merlot £9.75 2 bottles over £20, 18 bottles under £20 • 4 by the glass (£2.50-£3.75)

PRICE GUIDE Starter £3.50-£7.50 • main £9.50-£18 • dessert fr £4.50 • coffee £1.75 • min/water £2 • Service optional

PLACE: Set in a beautiful village in a scenic part of Monmouthshire, this friendly, two-storey flint-built inn is a cosy, stone-floored pub with restaurant seating around the bar and in a conservatory extension.

FOOD: Unpretentious, solid home cooking with an eye on seasonality and local, organic produce wherever possible. Portions are substantial, particularly bolstering winter dishes like oxtails, beer and root vegetables.

OUR TIP: Reservations recommended

Chef: Ian Black, Stuart Bonen **Owners:** Ian and Carol Black **Times:** 12-2/7-9, Closed Mon, closed D Sun **Notes:** Vegetarian available **Seats:** 50 **Smoking:** N/Sm area, No pipes **Children:** Portions **Directions:** Llandenny is situated halfway between the market towns of Usk and Raglan **Parking:** 30

🍴 Three Salmons Hotel

International

17th-century coaching inn in scenic environment

☎ 01291 672133 Bridge St NP15 1RY

MENU GUIDE Thai-spiced crab cake, crisp salad • Poached haddock fillet, glazed with Tintern rarebit, tomato salsa • Apple tart Tatin, vanilla ice cream

continued

WINE GUIDE 20 bottles over £20, 10 bottles under £20

PRICE GUIDE Fixed L £9.95 • starter £3.95-£7.95 • main £6.95-£15.95 • dessert £4.50 • coffee £1.25 • min/water £1.30 • Service optional

PLACE: Set in the heart of Usk town, the Three Salmons is a popular place with a friendly atmosphere and well frequented by locals.

FOOD: A good range of crowd-pleasing, carefully prepared dishes that keep things simple is the kitchen's style, utilising fresh ingredients (especially the daily fish specials), with regular offerings taking in a traditional prawn cocktail to spicy stir-fried Szechuan chicken or range of steaks.

OUR TIP: Daily changing fish specials are the recommended main course

Chef: Scott Sheldon **Owners:** Tracey Lewis, Clive Hughes **Times:** 12-2/7-10, Closed D Sun **Notes:** Vegetarian available, Civ Wed 100 **Seats:** 34, Pr/dining room 22 **Smoking:** N/Sm area, No pipes, No cigars **Children:** Menu, Portions **Rooms:** 24 (24 en suite) ★★★ **Directions:** M4 junct 24, A449 N, first left A472 to Usk. Hotel in centre of village **Parking:** 40 **e-mail:** threesalmons.hotel@talk21.com

◉◉ Crown at Whitebrook

British, French

Innovative cuisine in 17th-century inn

☎ 01600 860254 NP25 4TX

MENU GUIDE Duck & foie gras terrine • Baked saddle of rabbit with Savoy cabbage • Dark chocolate & ginger parkin, parsnip ice cream

WINE GUIDE ♀ Le Petit Ferme Sauvignon Blanc £18 ♀ Kaapzicht Shiraz £22 • 6 by the glass (£3.50-£7.50)

PRICE GUIDE Fixed L £15 • Fixed D £35 • coffee £3 • min/water £3 • Service optional

PLACE: Whitewashed 17th-century drover's inn set in a delightful, wooded part of the Wye Valley. There are ten comfortable rooms to tempt diners to stay overnight after their meal.

FOOD: An ambitious kitchen isn't afraid to send out innovative dishes and interesting flavour combinations - pan-fried mackerel being married with pea and horseradish purée and beetroot jelly, butternut squash making an appearance on the dessert menu in the form of a cannellini with Muscovado toffee. Good-value lunch menu with five choices per course.

OUR TIP: Interesting wine list

Chef: James Sommerin **Owners:** Jonathan & Nicola Davies **Times:** 12-2/7-9.30, Closed 2 wks Xmas, New Year, closed D Sun **Notes:** Vegetarian available, Dress Restrictions, Smart casual preferred **Seats:** 32, Pr/dining room 12 **Smoking:** N/Sm in restaurant **Children:** Min 12 yrs **Rooms:** 10 (10 en suite) 🏰 **Directions:** W off A66 immediately S of Bigsweir Bridge (5m from Monmouth), 2m on unclassified road **Parking:** 20 **e-mail:** crown@whitebrook.demon.co.uk **web:** www.crownatwhitebrook.co.uk

NEWPORT

NEWPORT MAP 09 ST38

⊚⊚ The Chandlery

European

High quality cuisine in former ships' chandlery

☎ 01633 256622 77-78 Lower Dock St NP20 1EH

MENU GUIDE Sweet potato, rosemary & chilli soup • Grey mullet, sauté potato, spinach & chive velouté • Tonka bean tart, raspberry ice cream

WINE GUIDE ⚲ Hanmer Junction Sauvignon Blanc £17.50 • ⚲ Aresti Merlot £14.50 • 18 bottles over £20, 24 bottles under £20 • 6 by the glass (£2.90-£4.05)

PRICE GUIDE Fixed L £9.95 • starter £3.95-£8.50 • main £9.50-£16.95 • dessert £4.95-£6.95 • coffee £1.50 • min/water £2.95 • Group min 6 service 10%

PLACE: A large and impressive listed Georgian building on two levels, this renovated ships' chandlery has been painstakingly refurbished. The interior is light and airy, service attentive yet relaxed and friendly, the decor smart but unpretentious, with wooden tables and furniture from the 1930s and 40s.

FOOD: The modern European menu plays to the crowd, offering something for everyone from its repertoire of set-price lunch and light bite options to appealing carte. Expect an unfussy approach that promotes well-sourced local Welsh produce simply prepared.

OUR TIP: Excellent value business lunch is highly recommended **Chef:** Simon Newcombe, Carl Hammet **Owners:** Simon Newcombe, Jane Newcombe **Times:** 12-2/7-10, Closed 1 wk Xmas, Sun-Mon, closed L Sat **Notes:** Tasting menu available, Vegetarian available **Seats:** 80, Pr/dining room 60 **Smoking:** N/Sm area, Air con **Children:** Portions **Directions:** Situated on A48, 0.5m from the Royal Gwent Hospital at the foot of George St Bridge **Parking:** 20 **web:** www.thechandleryrestaurant.com

⊚ The Inn at the Elm Tree

European

Chic silver and white restaurant

☎ 01633 680225 St Brides, Wentlooge NP10 8SQ

MENU GUIDE Assiette of hot & cold seafood • Breast of Llanover pheasant, leg confit, chestnuts • Burnt lemon tart, blackcurrant sorbet

PRICE GUIDE Food prices not confirmed for 2006. Please telephone for details

PLACE: This stylish barn conversion sits in a peaceful setting on the coastal road between Cardiff and Newport. The restaurant

has a cool minimalist interior and there's a pleasant courtyard for summer evenings.

FOOD: The extensive European menu offers the very best of fresh, local produce, with an emphasis on lobsters and oysters from Cardigan Bay and Welsh beef and lamb.

OUR TIP: Delightfully furnished bedrooms

Times: 12-2.30/6-9.30 **Rooms:** 13 (13 en suite) ♦♦♦♦♦ **Directions:** From M4 J28 take A48 towards Castleton. At 1st rdbt turn L , continue 1.5m, right onto Morgan Way. Turn right at T-junct onto B4239. Inn 2.5m **e-mail:** inn@the-elm-tree.co.uk **web:** www.the-elm-tree.co.uk

⊚⊚ Owens at the Celtic Manor Resort

British, Welsh

Luxury resort hotel with a fine food restaurant

☎ 01633 413000 Coldra Woods NP18 1HQ

MENU GUIDE Mosaic of rabbit & foie gras • Roast loin of Brecon venison • Irish Mist & cocoa cappuccino

WINE GUIDE ⚲ Rothbury Estate Broken Back Shiraz £36.50 • ⚲ Domaine Cherrier Sancerre £27.50 • 150 bottles over £20 • 8 by the glass (£4.75-£9.50)

PRICE GUIDE Fixed D fr £45 • Service optional

PLACE: There's a host of amenities at this impressive hotel, including a range of conference facilities, three golf courses and a spa and leisure centre. Serious diners can ignore them all if they wish, and head straight for the stylish Owens Restaurant, one of several eating options here.

FOOD: A variety of contemporary twists transforms the quality Welsh ingredients into an interesting international menu. The strongest dishes are the most simply constructed.

OUR TIP: Owens is not large - don't forget to book **Chef:** Michael Bates **Owners:** Sir Terence Matthews **Times:** 7-10.30, Closed 1-12 Jan, Sun, closed L all week **Notes:** Chef's Surprise menu 10 courses £95, Vegetarian available, Dress Restrictions, No jeans, Civ Wed 100 **Seats:** 50, Pr/dining room 26 **Smoking:** N/Sm in restaurant, Air con **Children:** No Children **Rooms:** 400 (400 en suite) ★★★★★ **Directions:** From M4 junct 24 take A48 towards Newport, turn right after 300 yds **Parking:** 1000 **e-mail:** postbox@celtic-manor.com **web:** www.celtic-manor.com

🚜 denotes restaurants that place particular emphasis on making the most of local ingredients.

continued

PEMBROKESHIRE

HAVERFORDWEST MAP 08 SM91

Wolfscastle Country Hotel
International

Traditional country-house hotel with service to match

☎ 01437 741225 741688 Wolf's Castle SA62 5LZ

MENU GUIDE Warm balsamic onion tartlet • Roast Pembrokeshire duck • Chocolate truffle cake with orange & Grand Marnier sauce

WINE GUIDE ♀ Paarl Heights Chenin Blanc £11.50 • ♀ Andes Peak Caernet Sauvignon £11.50 • 19 bottles over £20, 43 bottles under £20 • 9 by the glass (£2.50-£4.80)

PRICE GUIDE Starter £3.40-£6.95 • main £6.95-£16.95 • dessert £3.50-£3.95 • coffee £1.50 • min/water £2.50 • Service optional

PLACE: Traditional country-house service is one of the delights of a stay or meal visit to this former vicarage. The high-ceilinged dining room was due to receive a complete makeover early in 2005.
FOOD: The international repertoire uses excellent ingredients, including lamb from the Preseli Hills and fish and seafood from Milford Haven. Old favourites like deep-fried brie, and melon, are joined by a more adventurous smoked haddock and apricot roulade.
OUR TIP: Experience the silver service at Sunday lunch
Chef: Steve Brown **Owners:** Mr A Stirling **Times:** 12-2/7-9, Closed 24-26 Dec **Notes:** Vegetarian available, Civ Wed 60 **Seats:** 55, Pr/dining room 32 **Smoking:** N/Sm in restaurant **Children:** Menu, Portions
Rooms: 24 (24 en suite) ★★ **Directions:** From Haverfordwest take A40 towards Fishguard. Hotel in centre of Wolf's Castle **Parking:** 50
e-mail: info@wolfscastle.com **web:** www.wolfscastle.com

PORTHGAIN MAP 08 SM83

The Shed
Seafood, European

AA Seafood Restaurant of the Year for Wales

☎ 01348 831518 SA62 5BN

MENU GUIDE Celtic mussels with bacon & tomato • Lobster thermidor • Home-made ginger & vanilla ice cream

WINE GUIDE 18 bottles over £20, 6 bottles under £20 • 6 by the glass (£3-£3.95)

PRICE GUIDE Fixed D £28.95 • coffee £1.80 • min/water 80p

PLACE: It's hard to believe that this friendly harbourside eaterie used to be a warehouse and old machine shed. White washed walls, chequered tablecloths and the relaxed atmosphere complete the rustic, beach hut feel.
FOOD: This is the place for fish and shellfish lovers - there is a wealth of local produce and the proprietors, Mr and Mrs Jones, pride themselves on their own-caught crab and lobster. Try the Porthgain plate of shellfish to share.
OUR TIP: Most of the fish caught and cooked on the day by Mr Jones
Chef: Caroline Jones **Owners:** Rob & Caroline Jones **Times:** 9-5/7-11.30, Jan-March open only weekends **Notes:** Min charge for children during Jul-Aug £15, Vegetarian by request only **Seats:** 36
Smoking: N/Sm in restaurant **Directions:** 7m from St. Davids. Off A40
Parking: On village street **e-mail:** caroline@theshedporthgain.co.uk
web: www.theshedporthgain.co.uk

ST DAVID'S MAP 08 SM72

Morgan's Restaurant
British, European

Intimate brasserie near the cathedral

☎ 01437 720508 20 Nun St SA62 6NT

MENU GUIDE Crispy fried tiger prawns in spiced batter with chilli jam • Roasted rack of Welsh lamb, pearl barley & winter vegetable broth • Chocolate & raspberry terrine

WINE GUIDE ♀ Uitkyk Chardonnay £15.50 • ♀ Nekas Tempranillo Merlot £13.85 • 4 bottles over £20, 16 bottles under £20 • 3 by the glass (£3.75)

PRICE GUIDE Fixed L £20-£25 • starter £4.50-£7.95 • main £11.95-£18.95 • dessert £4.95-£6.95 • coffee £2.50 • min/water £3.50 • Service optional

PLACE: Once the home of the village school headmistress, and now a showcase for local artistic talent, including local views and abstracts. The cosy interior is intimate and atmospheric.
FOOD: Carefully sourced local food takes pride of place on the menu, and appears on the plate without fuss or unnecessary embellishments. The blackboards shows the day's catch and chef's specials, backed up by say, fillet of Welsh Black beef on a parsnip and horseradish rösti.
OUR TIP: Look out for the themed menu special events
Chef: Richard Drakeley **Owners:** Linda Hurley, Richard Drakeley, Lynsey Draycott **Times:** 12.30-2.30/5.00-10, Closed Jan **Notes:** Themed menus for special events, Vegetarian available, Dress Restrictions, Smart casual
Seats: 36, Pr/dining room **Smoking:** N/Sm in restaurant
Children: Portions **Directions:** Haverfordwest 16m. On A487 to Fishguard, just off main square **Parking:** Car park opposite
e-mail: morgans@stdavids.co.uk **web:** www.morgans-in-stdavids.co.uk

Warpool Court Hotel
British, French

Spacious hotel restaurant with wonderful sea views

☎ 01437 720300 SA62 6BN

continued

Wales

ST DAVID'S continued MAP 08 SM72

MENU GUIDE Seared scallops, carrot & cumin purée, pancetta • Pan-fried sea bass, sesame vegetable stir-fry Apple tarte Tatin & sorbet

WINE GUIDE ♀ Jean Durup Chablis Chardonnay £26.50 • ♥ Domaine André Fleurie Gamay £27 • 71 bottles over £20, 23 bottles under £20 • 3 by the glass (£2.75)

PRICE GUIDE Fixed D £49-£55 • min/water £3.65 • Service included

PLACE: This friendly hotel was once the choir school for St David's Cathedral. The building has 3,000 unique hand-painted tiles in all the downstairs rooms and some of the older bedrooms. The restaurant provides a relaxed setting overlooking the gardens towards the sea. Furnishings are country-house style with linen tablecloths.

FOOD: The cooking style has been developed from sound technical skills and the use of fresh produce, much of it from the Welsh hills and fish markets. Fully plated service delivers the appropriate textures and flavours for each dish.

OUR TIP: Close to St David's Cathedral

Chef: John Daniels **Owners:** Peter Trier **Times:** 12-1.45/7-9.15, Closed Jan **Notes:** Vegetarian available, Civ Wed 130 **Seats:** 50, Pr/dining room 22 **Smoking:** N/Sm in restaurant **Children:** Menu, Portions **Rooms:** 25 (25 en suite) ★★★ **Directions:** From Cross Square, left by HSBC Bank into Goat St, at fork follow hotel signs **Parking:** 100 **e-mail:** warpool@enterprise.net **web:** www.warpoolcourthotel.com

TENBY MAP 08 SN10

⊛ Panorama Hotel
British, International

Seaside hotel offering plenty of choice

☎ 01834 844976 The Esplanade SA70 7DU

MENU GUIDE Salmon roulade, whisky & maple dressing • Moroccan lamb, apricots, minted couscous

WINE GUIDE ♀ Jackmans Landing Chardonnay £11.45 • ♥ Niel Joubert Pinotage £11.75 • 2 bottles over £20, 34 bottles under £20 • 4 by the glass (£1.95)

PRICE GUIDE Fixed D £23-£25 • min/water £2 • Service optional

PLACE: Part of an imposing Victorian terrace, this friendly family-run hotel has a prestigious seafront location overlooking Tenby's South Beach. Robin's restaurant makes the most of the view and is decorated in traditional style.

FOOD: A lengthy menu should suit most tastes and features local produce where possible. Start with a Thai crab cake perhaps, and then move onto pork with woodland mushrooms and cream, or salmon with a light Pernod and seafood sauce.

OUR TIP: Take a stroll into Tenby

Chef: Robin Wright **Owners:** Robin & Carol Wright **Times:** 7-9, Closed Xmas, Sun, closed L All, closed D Sun **Notes:** Vegetarian available **Seats:** 25 **Smoking:** N/Sm in restaurant **Children:** Portions **Rooms:** 7 (7 en suite) ★★ **Directions:** From A478 follow South Beach & town centre signs, sharp left at mini-rdbt, under railway and up Greenhill Road. Along South Parade to Esplanade **Parking:** On street **e-mail:** mail@tenby-hotel.co.uk **web:** www.tenby-hotel.co.uk

⊛ Penally Abbey Hotel
Traditional, Modern

Delightful country house dining

☎ 01834 843033 Penally SA70 7PY

MENU GUIDE Sautéed lamb kidneys, mushroom & bacon • Welsh lamb fillet, port & redcurrants • Dark chocolate torte, Baileys ice cream

Penally Abbey Hotel

PRICE GUIDE Food prices not confirmed for 2006. Please telephone for details

PLACE: This country house enjoys glorious sea views over Carmarthen Bay. The restaurant is romantically candlelit, while an attractively appointed drawing room and bar makes it the kind of place it's a pleasure to linger in.

FOOD: Local meat and fish are dealt with in a simple, traditional fashion. Start with Pembrokeshire crab Mornay, before a tender fillet of Welsh beef served with stilton and a rich red wine jus.

OUR TIP: There's a swimming pool and games room

Times: 12.30-2/7.30-9.30, closed L (ex by arrangement only) **Rooms:** 12 (12 en suite) ★★★ **Directions:** From Tenby take A4139 to Penally **e-mail:** penally.abbey@btinternet.com **web:** www.penally-abbey.com

POWYS

BRECON MAP 09 S002

⊛⊛ The Felin Fach Griffin
British

Quietly stylish gastro-pub with high standards

☎ 01874 620111 Felin Fach LD3 0UB

MENU GUIDE Quail skewer, braised Puy lentils, cep cappuccino • Local Welsh rib-eye steak • Sticky toffee pudding

WINE GUIDE ♀ Casa Silva Chardonnay £14.50 • ♥ De Gras Merlot £12.95 • 20 bottles over £20, 30 bottles under £20 • 6 by the glass (£2.80-£6.50)

PRICE GUIDE Fixed L £14-£18 • starter £4.80-£8.95 • main £10.50-£15.95 • dessert £5.50 • coffee £1.80 • Service optional • Group min 10 service 10%

PLACE: A great pub to seek out in the Brecon Beacons that commands stunning upland views. The warren of colourful atmospheric rooms include bedrooms that have four-posters

continued

continued

Wales

from Rajasthan and Morocco (no chintz here!). You might indeed get the feeling that you're staying at a friend's farmhouse where the food is really rather good.

FOOD: There's a commitment to using local, seasonal and organic produce including home-grown vegetables. The modern British dishes are created using simple and effective combinations, and the unhurried cooking produces flavours with a reassuring depth. Consistently high standards keep diners coming back for more.

OUR TIP: Dine alfresco with a view of the Beacons

Chef: Ricardo Van Ede **Owners:** Charles Inkin, Edmund Inkin **Times:** 12.30-2.30/7-9.30, Closed 24-26 Dec, closed L Mon (exc BH's) **Notes:** Sun L 1 course £12.50, 2 courses £16.50, 3 courses £21.50, Vegetarian available **Seats:** 45, Pr/dining room 20 **Smoking:** N/Sm in restaurant **Children:** Portions **Directions:** 3.5m N of Brecon on A470. Large terracotta building on left, in village of Felin Fach **Parking:** 60 **e-mail:** enquiries@eatdrinksleep.ltd.uk **web:** www.eatdrinksleep.ltd.uk

🎖 Peterstone Court Hotel

European   **NEW**

Bistro dining in scenic country setting

☎ 01874 665387 Llanhamlach LD3 7YB

MENU GUIDE Smoked haddock risotto, poached egg, parmesan • Sea bass, couscous, ratatouille • Rhubarb trifle, apple mousse

PRICE GUIDE Food prices not confirmed for 2006. Please telephone for details

PLACE: Peterstone is an imposing destination, but its restaurant is a relaxed affair and all the more popular as a result. The grand old house is set on the edge of the Brecon Beacons National Park overlooking the river Usk, just a few miles from Brecon itself.

FOOD: A bistro menu brings a touch of the Mediterranean to high-quality local ingredients. Expect simple and delicious dishes such as chicken on soft polenta with a mushroom truffle sauce.

OUR TIP: A good base for the National Park

Times: Telephone for details **e-mail:** info@peterstone-court.com **web:** www.peterstone-court.com

🎖 The Usk Inn

British, Mediterranean

Well-presented restaurant in a village setting

☎ 01874 676251 Station Rd, Talybont-on-Usk LD3 7JE

MENU GUIDE Mussels in white wine & garlic • Monmouthshire wild boar steak • Rhubarb crème brûlée

WINE GUIDE ♀ Orsola Pinot Grigio £12.95 • ♦ Concha y Toro Cabernet Sauvignon £14.95 • 8 by the glass (£3.25-£5.95)

PRICE GUIDE Fixed L £10 • starter £5.95-£8.95 • main £11.95-£25 • dessert £2.95-£5.95 • coffee £1.90 • min/water £3.50 • Service optional   *continued*

PLACE: A relaxed inn in a quiet village. And, though the open fire, polished wooden tables and flagstone floors remain, a refurbishment has brought a little more style. The bright, airy restaurant is bistro-styled with beige table linen contrasting with green napkins and candles.

FOOD: A blackboard list of specials supplements the bistro-style menu, with Welsh beef, venison and lamb making a positive impression.

OUR TIP: Walk, cycle or arrive by canal boat

Chef: Mike Taylor, Sean Gibbs **Owners:** Mike & Barbara Taylor **Times:** 12-3/6.30-9.30, Closed 25-27 Dec **Notes:** Sun Dinner 6.30-7.30 subject to reservation, Vegetarian available, Dress Restrictions, No slogan T-shirts, etc **Seats:** 60 **Smoking:** N/Sm in restaurant, Air con **Children:** Portions **Rooms:** 11 (11 en suite) ♦♦♦♦ **Directions:** 250 yds off A40, 6m E of Brecon **Parking:** 35 **e-mail:** dine@uskinn.co.uk **web:** www.uskinn.co.uk

🎖🎖 The White Swan

British, European   🚜

Accomplished modern cuisine in village inn

☎ 01874 665276 LD3 7BZ

MENU GUIDE Avocado, leek & goats' cheese tart • Honey-glazed lamb, elderflower & rosemary jus • Baileys & white chocolate torte

WINE GUIDE ♀ Concha y Toro Chardonnay £11.95 • ♦ Concha y Toro Cabernet Sauvignon £11.95 • 15 bottles over £20, 30 bottles under £20 • 8 by the glass (£2.95)

PRICE GUIDE Starter £3.75-£6.95 • main £10.95-£15.95 • dessert £3.95-£4.25 • coffee £1.20 • min/water £2.50

PLACE: Traditional village pub in the Brecon Beacons with a cosy decor of old beams, flagstone floors and exposed stone walls. Eat in the spacious dining room, or more informally in the bar, which also offers a lighter snack menu.

FOOD: Unpretentious gastro-pub cooking with fish a particular strength. Choose from the carte or plump for a daily blackboard special, and expect modern dishes with European flavour: venison with a port and cranberry sauce perhaps, or lamb with sweet potato mash.

OUR TIP: Spacious function room available

Chef: Lee Havard, Scott Howells, Stephen Way **Owners:** Richard Griffiths **Times:** 12-2/7-11.30, Closed 25-26 Dec, 1 Jan, Mon-Tue **Notes:** Vegetarian available **Seats:** 60, Pr/dining room 40 **Smoking:** N/Sm in restaurant **Children:** Menu, Portions **Directions:** 3m E of Brecon, off A40. Take B4558 following signs for Llanfrynach **Parking:** 40 **e-mail:** stephen.way@tiscali.co.uk **web:** www.the_white_swan.com

Wales

Wales

BUILTH WELLS

☺☺ The Drawing Room
Modern British **NEW**

Stylish restaurant with rooms starring local produce

☎ 01982 552493 Cwmbach, Newbridge-on-Wye LD2 3RT

MENU GUIDE Chicory salad, Carmarthen ham • Guinea fowl en crèpinette, byaldi • Ile flottante meringue, chocolate mousse

WINE GUIDE ♀ Cepage Colombard £12.95 • ♀ Costiere de Nimes £12.95 • 20 bottles over £20, 47 bottles under £20 6 by the glass (£3.75-£4.50)

PRICE GUIDE Fixed L £17.50 • starter £5.75-£8 • main £14.75-£18.50 • dessert £6.25 • coffee £2.75 • min/water £2.50 • Service included

PLACE: A relative newcomer, The Drawing Room attracted local diners right from the start. It's an extensively renovated Georgian country house with comfortable lounges, log fires, a private dining room and intimate restaurant, where French-themed watercolours relieve the neutral decor and candlelit tables are graced with good linen and high-backed chairs.
FOOD: Quality cuisine is cooked simply and skilfully, using the best locally sourced ingredients. The menu changes seasonally and features classical dishes with modern interpretations.
OUR TIP: Weekend cookery breaks are available
Chef: Colin and Melanie Dawson **Owners:** Colin and Melanie Dawson
Times: 12-2/7-9, Closed 2 wks Jan, 2 wks Oct, Sun-Mon **Seats:** 20, Pr/dining room 8 **Smoking:** N/Sm in restaurant **Children:** Min 12 yrs
Rooms: 3 (3 en suite) 🛏 **Directions:** From Builth Wells, take A470 towards Rhayader, 3m on left **Parking:** 14
e-mail: post@the-drawing-room.co.uk
web: www.the-drawing-room.co.uk

CRICKHOWELL MAP 09 SO21

☺ Bear Hotel
British, French 🐟

Cosy coaching inn

☎ 01873 810408 High St NP8 1BW

MENU GUIDE Crab risotto • Honey-glazed duck, Madeira jus • Lemon tart, blackberry sorbet

WINE GUIDE ♀ Wolf Blass Chardonnay £14.95 • ♀ Wolf Blass Shiraz £15.75 • 15 bottles over £20, 35 bottles under £20 • 16 by the glass (£2.10-£4.80)

PRICE GUIDE Starter £4.75-£8.25 • main £14.50-£19.50 • dessert £5-£6 • coffee £1.80 • min/water £2.80 • Service optional

PLACE: The 15th-century Bear bristles with personality and continues its tradition of hospitality as the focal point of the

Bear Hotel

market town. Evocative, busy bars have low black beams and rug-strewn flagstone floors. The main dining room is intimate and romantic with lace tablecloths and candlelight.
FOOD: Local meats such as lamb and venison are mainstays of the modern British menu, which covers a broad spectrum of dishes, from the contemporary to traditional classics.
OUR TIP: Close to the Brecons
Chef: Brian Simmonds, Justin Howe **Owners:** Mrs. J Hindmarsh, Stephen Hindmarsh **Times:** 12-2/7-9.30, Closed 25 Dec, Mon, closed D Sun
Notes: Vegetarian available **Seats:** 60, Pr/dining room 30
Children: Menu, Portions **Rooms:** 26 (26 en suite) ★★★
Directions: Town centre, off A40 (Brecon road). 6m from Abergavenny
Parking: 60 **e-mail:** bearhotel@aol.com **web:** www.bearhotel.co.uk

☺ Gliffaes Country House Hotel
British, Mediterranean

Inspired cooking in impressive mansion

☎ 01874 730371 NP8 1RH

MENU GUIDE Honey-roast figs & Parma ham • Italian fish stew (brodetta) • Pannacotta & strawberry compôte

WINE GUIDE ♀ Spy Valley Sauvignon Blanc £17.80 • ♀ Finca Carbonell Tempranillo £12.30 • 36 bottles over £20, 39 bottles under £20 • 8 by the glass (£3.30-£5.75)

PRICE GUIDE Fixed D £29.50 • coffee £2.50 • Service included

PLACE: The River Usk runs alongside this Italianate mansion in delightful grounds, while elegance prevails inside: the wood-panelled restaurant is dominated by a large carved fireplace, and lighting is attractively subdued at night.
FOOD: The cooking is a robust fusion of local and other Welsh produce and a European inspiration that can lead to success stories like sautéed lambs sweetbreads and kidneys with pea and mint on toast.
OUR TIP: Enjoy a walk in the lovely grounds
Chef: Gordon Jones **Owners:** Mr/s Brabner & Mr/s Suter **Times:** 12-2.30/7.30-9.15, Closed 2-16 Jan, closed L Mon-Sat **Notes:** Vegetarian available, Smart Dress, Civ Wed 40 **Seats:** 70, Pr/dining room 35
Smoking: N/Sm in restaurant **Children:** Menu, Portions **Rooms:** 22 (22 en suite) ★★★ **Directions:** 1m off A40. 2.5m W of Crickhowell
Parking: 30 **e-mail:** calls@gliffaeshotel.com
web: www.gliffaeshotel.com

☺ Manor Hotel
Modern European

Good quality food with a view to match

☎ 01873 810212 Brecon Rd NP8 1SE

MENU GUIDE Smoked salmon & tagliatelle • Lamb shank with herb mash • Black velvet meringue, blackcurrant sorbet

WINE GUIDE 12 bottles over £20, 38 bottles under £20

continued

continued

PRICE GUIDE Food prices not confirmed for 2006. Please telephone for details

PLACE: The Everest Restaurant enjoys panoramic views over the Brecon Beacons from its hillside setting in an imposing manor house. The evening atmosphere, inspired by candelabras and warm red walls, is also memorable.

FOOD: Keeping the cooking simple is the key to success here, with innovative ideas merging well with quality ingredients to produce something for everyone. All ducks, chickens and lamb are organically reared and free range from their farm.

OUR TIP: Prepare to be stunned by the view!

Chef: Shaun Ellis **Owners:** Mr G Bridgeman **Times:** 12-2/7-9 **Notes:** Vegetarian available, Civ Wed 250 **Seats:** 54, Pr/dining room 26 **Smoking:** N/Sm in restaurant **Children:** Portions **Rooms:** 22 (22 en suite) ★★★ **Directions:** 0.5m W of Crickhowell on A40, Brecon road **e-mail:** info@manorhotel.co.uk **web:** www.manorhotel.co.uk

Nantyffin Cider Mill Inn
British, International

Ever busy gastro-pub with plenty of character

☎ 01873 810755 Brecon Rd NP8 1SG

MENU GUIDE Scallops & rocket with chilli jam • Confit of home-reared lamb • Treacle tart with sauce anglaise

WINE GUIDE ♀ Norte Chico Chardonnay £13 • ♥ Payral Rouge Cabernet Blend £13 • 37 bottles over £20, 34 bottles under £20 • 8 by the glass (£3.25-£5.95)

PRICE GUIDE Fixed L fr £10 • Fixed D fr £12.95 • starter £3.50-£8.95 • main £7.95-£16.50 • dessert fr £4.95 • coffee £1.60 • min/water £3.50 • Service optional

PLACE: Former drovers' inn and cider mill dating from the 16th century with contemporary-style furnishings. It has a small dining room and lounge, and food is also available in the adjacent bar.

FOOD: Genuine use of local and home-reared produce, including organically reared free-range chickens, ducks, pork and lamb from the proprietor's farm. Expect traditional dishes and flavours from Asia, North Africa and the Mediterranean.

OUR TIP: Good value fixed-price Drovers Menu

Chef: Sean Gerrard **Owners:** Glyn Bridgeman & Sean Gerrard **Times:** 12-2.30/6.30-10, Closed 1 wk Jan, Mon, closed D Sun(winter) **Notes:** Vegetarian available **Seats:** 65 **Smoking:** N/Sm in restaurant **Children:** Menu, Portions **Directions:** 1m W of Crickhowell on A40 at junct with A479 **Parking:** 40 **e-mail:** info@cidermill.co.uk **web:** www.cidermill.co.uk

HAY-ON-WYE MAP 09 SO24

Old Black Lion Inn
British, International

Robust dining in an historic coaching inn

☎ 01497 820841 26 Lion St HR3 5AD

MENU GUIDE Twice-baked shropshire blue & chive soufflé • Beef Wellington, pâté & duxelle, red wine sauce • Lavender crème brûlée

WINE GUIDE ♀ Veneto Pinot Grigio £15.25 • ♥ Bodegas Naujas Rioja £15.25 • 14 bottles over £20, 19 bottles under £20 • 6 by the glass (£3)

PRICE GUIDE Starter £4.95-£7.50 • main £12.50-£17.50 • dessert £3.75-£4.25 • coffee £1.50 • min/water £2 • Service optional

PLACE: This fine old coaching inn in the middle of charming Hay-on-Wye is privately owned and personally run. The bar and dining rooms are full of old beams, charm and character. Comfortable and well-equipped bedrooms are located in an adjacent building.

FOOD: A robust and traditional style of international cooking, using locally sourced, good quality ingredients, is tempered by some modern influences. The service is both friendly and informative.

OUR TIP: Take time for a walk in the nearby Brecon Beacons

Chef: Peter Bridges **Owners:** Vanessa King **Times:** 12-2.30/6.30-9.30, Closed 25-26 Dec, 2 wks early Jan **Notes:** Sun roast L 1 course £8, 2 courses £10.50, 3 courses £12, Vegetarian available **Seats:** 60, Pr/dining room 20 **Smoking:** N/Sm in restaurant **Children:** Min 5 yrs **Rooms:** 10 (9 en suite) ★★ **Directions:** 1m off A438. From TIC car park turn right along Oxford Rd, pass Nat West Bank, next left (Lion St), hotel 20 yds on right **Parking:** 20 **e-mail:** info@oldblacklion.co.uk **web:** www.oldblacklion.co.uk

KNIGHTON MAP 09 SO27

Milebrook House
British, International

Creative cuisine in charming hotel

☎ 01547 528632 Milebrook LD7 1LT

MENU GUIDE Smoked chicken & truffle risotto • Pork belly, foie gras, scrumpy glazed popcorn, apple purée • Cherry & almond tart

WINE GUIDE ♀ Lurton Sauvignon Blanc £12.90 • ♥ Central Valley Chile Cabernet Sauvignon/Merlot £12.90 • 27 bottles over £20, 38 bottles under £20 • 5 by the glass (£2.30-£3.10)

PRICE GUIDE Fixed L £9.95-£18.50 • Fixed D £27.50 • starter £7-£11 • main £17.95-£24.50 • dessert £6.50-£9 • coffee £2.50 • min/water £2.40 • Service optional

PLACE: Friendly little country-house hotel set in the rolling Marches landscape. Explore the pretty gardens if you've time; as well as supplying all the vegetables for the kitchen, they include a croquet lawn, wildlife pond and range of exotic plants.

FOOD: Modern British cooking with international influences and a dash of wit. Expect creative combinations, such as a dish of smoked haddock with curried mussels, carrot bhaji, and a lime and coriander smoothie, as well as more familiar fare.

OUR TIP: Take a stroll along nearby Offa's Dyke

Wales

continued

continued

Wales

KNIGHTON continued MAP 09 SO27

Chef: Lee Jones **Owners:** Mr & Mrs R T Marsden **Times:** 12-2/7-9, Closed L Mon, closed D Sun/Mon (open for residents) **Notes:** Sun L 3 courses, Tasting menu 7 courses available, Vegetarian available **Seats:** 40, Pr/dining room 16 **Smoking:** N/Sm in restaurant **Children:** Min 8 yrs **Rooms:** 10 (10 en suite) ★★ **Directions:** 2m E of Knighton on A4113 (Ludlow) **Parking:** 24 **e-mail:** hotel@milebrook.kc3ltd.co.uk **web:** www.milebrookhouse.co.uk

LLANDRINDOD WELLS MAP 09 SO06

⊛ Hotel Metropole
British, European   **NEW**
Stylishly redesigned dining room with well-balanced menus
☎ 01597 823700 Temple St LD1 5DY

MENU GUIDE Smoked eel salad, wasabi crème fraîche Ballontine of guinea fowl leg • Sticky toffee pudding

WINE GUIDE ♀ House Tanners Sauvignon £11.95 • ♀ House Tanners Merlot • 20 bottles over £20, 50 bottles under £20 8 by the glass (£3.40-£4.75)

PRICE GUIDE Fixed L £12.50-£18 • Fixed D £22-£26 • coffee £1.80 • min/water £3.50 • Service included

PLACE: Elegance has been reinstated at this smartly refurbished dining room, where contemporary high-backed chairs in leather and suede are stylishly paired with ivory linen and classic white crockery.
FOOD: The food is skilfully prepared from fresh locally sourced produce, and caters for most tastes with its range and variety. Slow-roasted shoulder of local lamb shows the quality of home-grown meat, and freshly caught fish is well represented too.
OUR TIP: Relax before dinner in one of the bars
Chef: Nick Edwards **Owners:** Justin Baird-Murray **Times:** 12.30-1.45/7-9.30 **Notes:** Vegetarian available, Civ Wed 200 **Seats:** 200, Pr/dining room 250 **Smoking:** N/Sm in restaurant, Air con **Children:** Menu, Portions **Rooms:** 120 (120 en suite) ★★★ **Directions:** In centre of town off A483 **Parking:** 140
e-mail: info@metropole.co.uk
web: www.bw-metropole.co.uk

LLANFYLLIN MAP 15 SJ11

⊛ Seeds
British, Mediterranean
Quality ingredients handled with skill in Grade II listed building
☎ 01691 648604 5 Penybryn Cottage, High St SY22 5AP

MENU GUIDE Home-smoked mackerel pâté • Sauteed lambs' kidneys • Lemon posset, blackcurrant sauce

WINE GUIDE ♀ Beauroy Chablis Premier Cru £23.50 • ♀ Echeveria Merlot £18.50 • 36 bottles over £20, 91 bottles under £20 • 3 by the glass (£3.25)

PRICE GUIDE Fixed D £23 • starter £3.50-£6.95 • main £8.95-£14.50 • dessert £3.50-£4.50 • coffee £1.65 • min/water £3 • Service optional

PLACE: A timber-framed, listed building with exposed beams, slate floors and fresh flowers on the tables. Local paintings and masks from around the world adorn the cosy space.
FOOD: Choose lunch from the blackboard, or peruse the short set menu for an evening meal that shows modern British cooking

continued

in a good light. Dishes are geared towards market availability, and are likely to include roast rack of Welsh lamb.
OUR TIP: Great wine list
Chef: Mark Seager **Owners:** Felicity Seager, Mark Seager **Times:** 11-2.15/7-8.30, Closed 2 wk Oct, 25 Dec, Mon-Tue, closed L Wed in winter, closed D Sun **Notes:** Coffee included, ALC lunch only, Vegetarian available **Seats:** 22 **Smoking:** N/Sm in restaurant **Children:** Portions **Directions:** Village centre, on A490, 15 mins from Welshpool, follow signs to Llantyllin **Parking:** Free car park in town, street parking

LLANGAMMARCH WELLS MAP 09 SN94

⊛⊛ Lake Country House Hotel
British, European
Candlelit restaurant with old-fashioned charm
☎ 01591 620202 LD4 4BS

MENU GUIDE Smoked haddock tail, wen cheese, poached duck egg • Braised pork belly, black pudding, apple fondant • Malted chocolate soufflé

WINE GUIDE ♀ Château Tiregaud £21.50 • ♀ E Loront Pinot £23.50 • 150 bottles over £20, 40 bottles under £20 • 8 by the glass (£4.75-£5.50)

PRICE GUIDE Fixed D £37.50-£42.50 • coffee £3 • min/water £3.60 • Service optional

PLACE: Edwardian mansion and former health spa set in the heart of mid-Wales' countryside, with extensive grounds and a river flowing past. Well-proportioned public rooms allow for plenty of windows, wood panelling and space between tables. Service is delightfully old-fashioned, almost quirky, and dinner attracts a good mixture of residents and locals.
FOOD: The simple format of the four-course dinner menu belies the complexity and skill of the cooking. Dishes are soundly executed and good use is made of locally sourced and seasonal produce.
OUR TIP: Extensive wine list with good descriptions
Chef: Sean Cullingford **Owners:** J Mifsud **Times:** 12.30-2/7.30-9.15 **Notes:** Set price L 4 courses £23.50, Vegetarian available, Dress Restrictions, Prefer no jeans; collar at all times, Civ Wed 70 **Seats:** 40, Pr/dining room 30 **Smoking:** N/Sm in restaurant **Children:** Min 8 yrs, Menu, Portions **Rooms:** 19 (19 en suite) ★★★ **Directions:** 6m from Builth Wells on A483 from Garth, turn left for Llangammarch Wells & follow signs to hotel **Parking:** 80
e-mail: info@lakecountryhouse.co.uk
web: www.lakecountryhouse.co.uk

NEW
denotes a restaurant which is new to the guide this year.

LLANWDDYN MAP 15 SJ01

⚜ Lake Vyrnwy Hotel

British 🍷🚜

Enjoyable modern cooking in magnificent setting

☎ 01691 870692 Lake Vyrnwy SY10 0LY

Lake Vyrnwy Hotel

MENU GUIDE Seafood bouillabaisse • Duo of spring rabbit, tarragon sauce • Dark chocolate fudge cake, mint choc-chip ice cream

WINE GUIDE ♀ Château de Tiregand £18.50 • ♀ Merlot £14.95 • 88 bottles over £20, 18 bottles under £20 • 8 by the glass (£3.85-£4.70)

PRICE GUIDE Fixed L £19.50-£22.50 • Fixed D £32.50 • coffee £2.50 • min/water £2.50 • Service included

PLACE: Set in 26,000 acres of forests and moorland, this country-house hotel serves food in an airy conservatory that offers *continued*

magnificent views of the length of Lake Vyrnwy. Lighter meals are available in the bar.

FOOD: Enjoyable modern British cuisine created from local produce where possible, including lamb from the hotel's own flock, and game shot nearby. The menu offers plenty of choice, ranging from steak with horseradish butter, to duck cassoulet.

OUR TIP: Terrace for alfresco dining in summer

Chef: David Green **Owners:** The Bisiker family **Times:** 12-2.30/7-9.15 **Notes:** Vegetarian available, Dress Restrictions, Smart casual preferred, Civ Wed 125 **Seats:** 80, Pr/dining room 120 **Smoking:** N/Sm in restaurant **Children:** Portions **Rooms:** 35 (35 en suite) ★★★ **Directions:** Follow Tourist signs on A495/B4393, 200 yds past dam at Lake Vyrnwy **Parking:** 80 **e-mail:** res@lakevyrnwy.com **web:** www.lakevyrnwy.com

LLANWRTYD WELLS MAP 09 SN84

⚜⚜⚜ Carlton House Hotel *see below*

LLANWRTYD WELLS MAP 09 SN84

Carlton House Hotel

French, British 🍷🚜

Impressive cooking in restaurant with rooms

☎ 01591 610248 Dolycoed Rd LD5 4RA

MENU GUIDE Cream of leek & potato soup • Salmon fillet, lemon couscous • Chocolate fondant, raspberry sorbet

WINE GUIDE ♀ Andre Dezat Sancerre Sauvignon Blanc £19.95 ♀ Luis Canas Rioja Tempranillo £21 • 25 bottles over £20, 30 bottles under £20 • 4 by the glass (£3.50)

PRICE GUIDE Fixed L £19.95 • Fixed D £24.50 • starter £5.50-£8 main £22-£26 • dessert £5.50-£8 • Service optional

PLACE: There is a relaxed and friendly atmosphere at the Gilchrist's charming restaurant with rooms, housed in a three-storey Victorian building. The sunny and colourful dining room has Rennie Mackintosh-style high-backed chairs and tongue-and-groove wood panelling which sets the tone.

FOOD: The food takes centre-stage with Mary Ann Gilchrist running a one-woman kitchen with great panache. Though the daily-changing dinner menus are short, there's a strong emphasis on clear flavours and quality local Welsh produce. Expect the likes

of a rack of Irfon Valley lamb with potato and fennel dauphinoise.

OUR TIP: Extensive global wine list

Chef: Mary Ann Gilchrist **Owners:** Dr & Mrs Gilchrist **Times:** 12.30-2/7-9, Closed 10-30 Dec, Sun, L (reservation only), D Sun **Notes:** Coffee incl, Vegetarian by request **Seats:** 14 **Smoking:** N/Sm in restaurant **Rooms:** 6 (5 en suite) 🏨 **Directions:** In the town centre **Parking:** On street **e-mail:** info@carltonrestaurant.co.uk **web:** www.carltonrestaurant.co.uk

Wales

LLANWRTYD WELLS *continued* MAP 09 SN84

🏵 Lasswade Country House Hotel

British, Mediterranean 🍴

Enjoyable dining in very friendly hotel

☎ 01591 610515 Station Rd LD5 4RW

MENU GUIDE Pressed ham hock terrine & sage • Roast rack of local organic lamb • Poached plums in spiced wine

WINE GUIDE ♀ Cousino Macul Chardonnay £17.03 • ♀ Sunnycliff Shiraz £13.80 • 9 bottles over £20, 20 bottles under £20 • 2 by the glass (£2.93)

PRICE GUIDE Fixed D £26.50 • min/water £1 • Service optional

PLACE: An Edwardian country-house dining room with elegant features, where customers are treated more as house guests. A large lounge with wood burner and extensive book collection establishes the warm and relaxed atmosphere.

FOOD: The Welsh Black beef is raised only a quarter of a mile away, and the lamb within two miles, with vegetables grown organically - the cooking lets the flavours speak for themselves.

OUR TIP: Proprietor/chef is a cheese specialist

Chef: Roger Stevens **Owners:** Roger & Emma Stevens **Times:** 7.30-9.30, Closed 25 Dec **Notes:** Vegetarian available, Smart Dress, Civ Wed 8 **Seats:** 20, Pr/dining room 24 **Smoking:** N/Sm in restaurant **Children:** Portions **Rooms:** 8 (8 en suite) ★★ **Directions:** On A483, follow signs for station, opposite Spar shop, adjacent to Tourist info office, 400 yds on fight before station **Parking:** 6

e-mail: info@lasswadehotel.co.uk **web:** www.lasswadehotel.co.uk

LLYSWEN MAP 09 S013

🏵🏵 Llangoed Hall

British 🍷🍴

Excellent dining with views of the Black Mountains

☎ 01874 754525 LD3 0YP

MENU GUIDE Honey-roasted smoked goose, orange & pine nut salad • Brecon venison loin, leek & Puy lentil stew • Vanilla pannacotta

WINE GUIDE ♀ Beauregard Sauvignon Blanc £17.50 • ♀ Beauregard Cabernet Sauvignon £17.50 • 68 bottles over £20, 30 bottles under £20 • 6 by the glass (£5.50-£8.50)

PRICE GUIDE Fixed L £18 • Fixed D £43 • starter £7.50-£15.50 • main £12.50-£30 • dessert £7.50-£15.50 • coffee £3 • min/water £3.75 • Service optional

PLACE: Site of the 6th-century Welsh Parliament, the current house was designed by Sir Clough William-Ellis (of Portmeirion fame). Rescued by Sir Bernard & Laura Ashley in the 1970s, it was renovated to a high standard with public rooms and bedrooms furnished with period pieces. A classic country-house hotel with easy, relaxed and well-mannered service professional international staff.

FOOD: A good mix of traditional classics and modern British and Welsh dishes populate the menus. Excellent local and seasonal ingredients and careful preparation produce elaborate dishes brimming with flavour. Exceptional puddings and notable wine list.

OUR TIP: Enjoy a glass of wine on the terrace

Chef: Sean Ballington **Owners:** Sir Bernard Ashley **Times:** 12.30-2.00/7-9.30 **Notes:** Tasting menu from £75, Vegetarian available, Dress Restrictions, Jacket at dinner, no denim jeans, Civ Wed 60 **Seats:** 50, Pr/dining room 54 **Smoking:** N/Sm in restaurant **Children:** Min 8 yrs, Portions **Rooms:** 23 (23 en suite) ★★★★ **Directions:** On A470, 2m from Llyswen towards Builth Wells **Parking:** 50

e-mail: enquiries@llangoedhall.co.uk **web:** www.llangoedhall.com

MONTGOMERY MAP 15 S029

🏵 Dragon Hotel

Welsh, Mediterranean

Historic inn serving bar and restaurant food

☎ 01686 668359 & 668287 Market Square SY15 6PA

MENU GUIDE Leek & Tintern cheese terrine, raspberry toast • Braised lamb fillet, rosemary & red wine • Banana bread & butter pudding

WINE GUIDE ♀ Terre de Griffi Frascati Superiore £10.95 • ♀ Vina Aranita Merlot £11.75 • 7 bottles over £20, 42 bottles under £20 • 5 by the glass (£1.80-£1.95)

PRICE GUIDE Fixed L £20.75-£21.75 • Fixed D £20.75 • starter £3.20-£6.90 • main £13-£20 • dessert £3.75-£4.75 • coffee £1.25 • min/water £2.50 • Service optional

PLACE: A 17th-century former coaching inn at the heart of the small town of Montgomery, where the cosy beamed restaurant has a fireplace converted from a bread oven, ancient timbers and a pane of glass signed by the local hangman.

FOOD: An extensive choice is offered from either the restaurant or bar food operation. Menus take in English, Welsh and Mediterranean dishes, making good use of local produce.

OUR TIP: Located on the square near Montgomery Castle

continued

continued

Chef: Barry Thomas **Owners:** M & S Michaels **Times:** 12-2/7-9, Closed L all week ex by prior arrangement **Notes:** Sun lunch 3 courses £14.45, Vegetarian available **Seats:** 42 **Smoking:** N/Sm in restaurant **Children:** Portions **Rooms:** 20 (20 en suite) ★★ **Directions:** Behind the town hall **Parking:** 20 **e-mail:** reception@dragonhotel.com **web:** www.dragonhotel.com

NANT-DDU MAP 09 SO01

🏵 Nant Ddu Lodge Hotel
International

Bustling bistro in contemporary hotel

☎ 01685 379111 Cwm Taf, Nant Ddu CF48 2HY

MENU GUIDE Parmesan-crusted brill, tartare sauce • Slow-roasted lamb, sweet onion & mint purée • Cinnamon & apple bread-and-butter pudding

WINE GUIDE 4 bottles over £20, 22 bottles under £20 • 8 by the glass (£2.50-£3.95)

PRICE GUIDE Starter £3.50-£5.95 • main £7.95-£15.95 • dessert £3.95 • coffee £1.50 • min/water £2.95 • Service optional

PLACE: Once a shooting lodge, this Georgian riverside house is now a delightful hotel with a bustling bistro in the heart of the Brecon Beacons National Park. Decor throughout is contemporary and you'll find vibrant colours, original art work and relaxed informal service in the bistro.
FOOD: Fresh ingredients and robust cooking are the hallmarks of the modern menu. Dishes are simply prepared using the best of Welsh produce, especially fish and game.
OUR TIP: Enjoy the health spa
Chef: Richard Wimmer **Owners:** Mr & Mrs D Ronson **Times:** 12-2.30/6.30-9.30, closed D Sun **Notes:** Vegetarian available **Seats:** 80, Pr/dining room 20 **Smoking:** N/Sm in restaurant **Children:** Menu, Portions **Rooms:** 28 (28 en suite) ★★★ **Directions:** 6m N of Merthyr Tydfil, and 12m S of Brecon on A470 **Parking:** 50
e-mail: enquiries@nant-ddu-lodge.co.uk
web: www.nant-ddu-lodge.co.uk

THREE COCKS MAP 09 SO13

🏵🏵 Three Cocks Hotel
British, Welsh

Enjoyable dining in charming old country inn

☎ 01497 847215 LD3 0SL

MENU GUIDE Papillote of grey mullet with tomatoes & sauce béarnaise • Fillet of Welsh Black beef, red wine onions, glazed with goats' cheese, roasted shallots, red wine sauce • Apple soufflé with cinnamon sauce

PRICE GUIDE Food prices not confirmed for 2006. Please telephone for details

PLACE: Set in the stunning scenery of the Brecon Beacons

continued

National Park, this charming old inn dates back to the 15th century and retains plenty of original features. The elegant restaurant overlooks the garden.
FOOD: Great ingredients feature on the interesting menu. Start with a firm, smooth duck liver parfait, rich and robustly flavoured, the redcurrant reduction providing a good contrast, and then maybe try the oak smoked peppered salmon, with distinct flavours clearly present and accompanied by orange and dill scented hollandaise. For pudding, cappucino brulée is rich and creamy with a definite flavour and aroma of coffee.
OUR TIP: Convenient roadside location
Times: 12-3/7-9 **Rooms:** 7 (7 en suite) ★★ **Directions:** On A438 in the village of Three Cocks, 4 miles from Hay-on-Wye, 11 miles from Brecon **e-mail:** info@threecockshotel.com
web: www.threecockshotel.com

RHONDDA CYNON TAFF

MISKIN MAP 09 ST08

🏵 Miskin Manor Hotel
Traditional

Enjoyable dining in traditional manor house

☎ 01443 224204 Groes Faen CF72 8ND

PLACE: There are oak-panelled dining rooms in this fine country house with lovely views over 22 acres of gardens. The silver service restaurant was created in 1800 and has preserved all its charm ever since, despite two catastrophic fires in 1922 and 1952. The manor is well known from Cardiff to the valleys.
FOOD: Much pride is taken in the use of fresh and flavoursome Welsh produce, such as lamb, venison and quail.
OUR TIP: Popular wedding venue
Times: 12-2.30/7-10, Closed L Sat **Rooms:** 43 (43 en suite)
e-mail: info@miskin-manor.co.uk **web:** www.miskin-manor.co.uk

SWANSEA

LLANRHIDIAN MAP 08 SS49

🏵🏵 The Welcome to Town
Modern Welsh

Friendly bistro in country inn

☎ 01792 390015 SA3 1EH

MENU GUIDE Laverbread in an overcoat • Grilled Oxwich Bay lobster, sauce choron • Hot chocolate soufflé with pistachio ice cream

continued

Wales

LLANRHIDIAN *continued* MAP 08 SS49

WINE GUIDE ♀ Donjon de La Tour £12 • ♥ Donjon de la Tour £12 • 15 bottles over £20, 8 bottles under £20 • 6 by the glass (£2.95-£3.25)

PRICE GUIDE Fixed L £12.95 • starter £3.95-£7.95 • main £14.95-£19 • dessert £5-£6.50 • coffee £2.75 • min/water £3 • Service optional

PLACE: This 300-year-old former coaching inn, with views over the Gower peninsula, is a little off the beaten track but worth seeking out. The whitewashed interior includes a courtroom and gaol, with blackened beams, a large stone fireplace, with culinary achievements decorating the walls. Smart/casual is the dress code, but the tone is as friendly, informal and attentive as the restaurant's name suggests.

FOOD: Only the best local ingredients make it into the kitchen, for skilled preparation of modern Welsh cuisine. With dinner offering some elaborate choices, expect dishes like fillet of Gower beef with fondant potato, glazed with red wine and herb butter.

OUR TIP: Keen prices for generous dishes of quality

Chef: Ian Bennett **Owners:** Jay & Ian Bennett **Times:** 12-2/7-9.30, Closed 25-26 Dec, 1 Jan, last 2 wks Feb, 1 wk Oct, Mon, closed D Sun **Notes:** Vegetarian available, Smart casual **Seats:** 40 **Smoking:** N/Sm in restaurant, **Children:** Portions **Directions:** 8m from Swansea on the B4231. M4 junct 47 towards Gowerton. From Gowerton take B4295 **Parking:** 12 **web:** www.thewelcometotown.co.uk

MUMBLES (NEAR SWANSEA) MAP 08 SS68

⊚ Patricks with Rooms

British, European 🐟🍴 **NEW**

Lively atmosphere and a great choice of food

☎ 01792 360199 638 Mumbles Rd SA3 4EA

MENU GUIDE Seafood risotto • Pan-fried pork tenderloin • Chocolate mocha cup

WINE GUIDE ♀ House White £8.50 • ♥ House Red £8.50 5 bottles over £20, 11 bottles under £20

PRICE GUIDE Starter £2.85-£7.80 • main £11.85-£18.80 • dessert £5-£5.50 • coffee £1.50 • min/water £3 • Service optional

PLACE: Looking straight out onto Swansea beach, this colonial-style property has a separate lounge bar and popular restaurant. The buzzy atmosphere and friendly service make this place a pleasant choice.

FOOD: With a large list of regularly changing blackboard specials and a lengthy modern British menu to pore over, there is something for everyone here. Ideas are given the 'Patrick's twist', with fresh flavours from quality local and organic produce.

OUR TIP: Stay over in the delightful stylish bedrooms

Chef: P Walsh, D Fuller, B Griffiths, I Williams **Owners:** Catherine & Patrick Walsh, Sally & Dean Fuller **Times:** 12-2.50/6.30-10.20, Closed 3 wks Sept, 2nd week Jan, closed D Sun **Notes:** Vegetarian available, Smart Dress **Seats:** 75 **Smoking:** N/Sm in restaurant, Air con **Children:** Portions **Rooms:** 8 (8 en suite) 🏠 **Directions:** Exit M4 junct 42.5 m from Swansea City. From Swansea, with sea on left, over mini rdbt at White Rose pub. Restaurant 1/2 m on right **Parking:** On street, car park opposite **e-mail:** pwr@patrickswithrooms.com **web:** www.patrickswithrooms.com

---

REYNOLDSTON MAP 08 SS48

⊚⊚ Fairyhill

British, Welsh 🍴🍽️

Modern Welsh cooking in stylish country house

☎ 01792 390139 SA3 1BS

MENU GUIDE Chicken liver & foie gras parfait, Muscat jelly • Pheasant, baked apple, cider reduction • Crème caramel, kumquat compôte

WINE GUIDE ♀ Lawsons Dry Hills Sauvignon Blanc £22.50 ♥ Vega del Reya Rioja Reserva Tempranillo £21.50 • 500 bottles over £20, 50 bottles under £20 • 7 by the glass (£3.50-£5)

PRICE GUIDE Fixed L £14.95 • Fixed D £37.50 • starter £4.50-£8.95 • main £13.95-£18.50 • dessert £5.50 • coffee £3.50 • min/water £3.75 • Service optional

PLACE: Located on the beautiful Gower peninsula, this creeper-clad Georgian house has acres of pretty gardens and woodland to explore. Inside is a comfortable sanctuary of good taste, with a charming dining room that overlooks the grounds and features an abundance of fresh flowers and changing watercolours.

FOOD: Fairyhill teams an award-winning wine list with first-rate cuisine, delivering a tempting menu of modern Welsh dishes, made from home-grown and organic local produce wherever possible. Mains are straightforward in style - beef with steak and kidney pudding and parsnip chips perhaps, or poached salmon with herb velouté.

OUR TIP: Regular wine tasting evenings held

Chef: Paul Davies, Bryony Jones **Owners:** Mr Hetherington, Mr Davies **Times:** 12.30-2/7.30-9, Closed 26 Dec, 3-21 Jan **Notes:** ALC lunch only, Sun lunch £24.50, Vegetarian available **Seats:** 60, Pr/dining room 40 **Smoking:** N/Sm in restaurant **Children:** Min 8 yrs, Portions **Rooms:** 8 (8 en suite) ★★★ **Directions:** M4 junct 47, take A483 then A484 to Llanelli, Gower, Gowerton. At Gowerton follow B4295 for approx 10m **Parking:** 45 **e-mail:** postbox@fairyhill.net **web:** www.fairyhill.net

---

SWANSEA MAP 09 SS69

⊚⊚ The Grand Hotel

British, European **NEW**

Exciting cooking from an open kitchen

☎ 01792 645898 Ivey Place, High St SA1 1NE

MENU GUIDE Pan-roasted scallops & baby squid • Confit Barbary duck • Lemon parfait

WINE GUIDE 20 bottles over £20, 9 bottles under £20 • 8 by the glass (£2.75-£5.95)

PRICE GUIDE Fixed L £10.95-£22.75 • starter £3.50-£6.75 • main £6.95-£15.95 • dessert £3.50-£5.99 • coffee £1.85 • min/water £3.50

PLACE: This restaurant was an instant hit when it opened in the summer of 2004, and continues to go from strength to strength. The large, spacious dining room is stylishly lit by nightlights set in groups of pebbles, and the open kitchen kindles a sense of contained excitement.

FOOD: Superb Welsh ingredients are treated to a real assortment of influences, from Caribbean fish tea with spicy Thai fish cakes to pan-roasted beef with lasagna and cottage pie. Despite sounding odd, each element contributes seamlessly to the whole dish.

OUR TIP: Welsh beef 'cooked 3 ways' is irresistible!

Owners: The Grand Hotel Swansea Ltd **Times:** 12-3/6.30-10 **Notes:** Smart Dress **Seats:** 52 **Smoking:** N/Sm in restaurant, Air con **Children:** Menu, Portions **Rooms:** 31 (31 en suite) ★★★★ **Directions:** M4 junct 42, signed City and Train Station. Hotel opposite train station **Parking:** Next door **e-mail:** info@thegrandhotelswansea.co.uk **web:** www.thegrandhotelswansea.co.uk

---

🍷 denotes a restaurant with a particularly good wine list.

Hanson's
British, French

Harbourside fish restaurant

☎ 01792 466200 Pilot House Wharf, Trawler Rd, Swansea Marina SA1 1UN

PLACE: Bright yellow-ochre decor provides a cheerful dining setting for this enjoyable harbourside restaurant which was the AA's Seafood Restaurant of the Year 2005. On the first floor of a striking boat-shaped building, Swansea's dock renovation will soon make this a marina-side restaurant. Helpful service.
FOOD: The fresh fish comes from the trawlers docked outside and there are usually about six fish choices on the menu everyday with a few good quality Welsh lamb, beef or duck dishes too. Simple but effective modern British cooking with occasional French influences.
OUR TIP: The best fish and chips
Times: 12-1.45/6.30-10, Closed D Sun

Morgans Hotel
European

Stylish modern dining in Swansea's redeveloped Maritime Quarter

☎ 01792 484848 Somerset Place SA1 1RR
MENU GUIDE Shredded duckling, spring rolls • Welsh Black beef fillet, black pudding, stilton glaze, port jus • Bread & butter pudding
WINE GUIDE ♀ Louis Latour Burgundy £13.95 • ♀ St Hallet Shiraz Grenache £13.95 • 70 bottles over £20, 70 bottles under £20 • 11 by the glass (£3.50-£5.45)
PRICE GUIDE Fixed L £10 • Fixed D £35 • starter £5.50-£7.50 • main £13.50-£18.95 • dessert £6-£7.50 • coffee £2.25 • min/water £3.50 • Service optional
PLACE: Conversion of an old Port Authority building, with marble and slate floors, sweeping staircases and vast chocolate brown sofas. The dining rooms are on the first floor, one in the glass-domed atrium with mural-painted walls and the other more formal in the old half-panelled boardroom.
FOOD: The kitchen delivers modern British food with European influences, offering a fresh, light touch, strong on fish and good Welsh ingredients.
OUR TIP: Café-style bar on the ground floor
Chef: Chris Keenan **Owners:** Martin & Louisa Morgan **Times:** 12-3/6.30-10.15 **Notes:** ALC Sun D reduced, Vegetarian available, Civ Wed 100 **Seats:** 120, Pr/dining room 30 **Smoking:** N/Sm in restaurant, Air con **Children:** Menu, Portions **Rooms:** 20 (20 en suite) ★★★★
Directions: Telephone for directions **Parking:** Around corner NCP
e-mail: info@morganshotel.co.uk
web: www.morganshotel.co.uk

The Best Use of Seafood sponsored by Seafish In conjunction with Seafish, the Sea Fish Industry Authority, we have sought out restaurants that make the most of seafood on their menus. In addition to the four country award winners (see page 9), look out for the seafish symbol throughout the book; this denotes restaurants serving a good range of fish and shellfish dishes, where the accent is firmly on freshness.

Restaurant 698
Modern European   **NEW**

Fuss-free fine dining overlooking the bay

☎ 01792 361616 698 Mumbles Rd SA3 4EH
MENU GUIDE Wild mushroom & parmesan risotto • Sea bass en papilotte, teriyaki sauce, stir-fried vegetables • Pear tart, caramel sauce
PRICE GUIDE Food prices not confirmed for 2006. Please telephone for details
PLACE: Happening Swansea venue on the main Mumbles Road, easily missed because of its quiet exterior. Dark wood tables, leather chairs and mellow jazz music contribute to a sophisticated yet welcoming atmosphere, and the friendliness of the service is quite remarkable. The chef can be observed at work behind a glass screen at the end of the restaurant. Alternatively seats near the front overlook Swansea Bay.
FOOD: The menu changes every four weeks to reflect seasonal changes. Local fish, beef and lamb are used as well as local vegetables from the Gower.
OUR TIP: Oursin (sea urchin) 'Richard Walton' is a starter not be missed
Owners: Mr. Ramsey-William **Times:** 12-2/7-9.30
e-mail: info@698.uk.com **web:** www.698.uk.com

VALE OF GLAMORGAN

BARRY MAP 09 ST16

Egerton Grey Country House Hotel
British

Enjoyable, traditional, country-house dining

☎ 01446 711666 Porthkerry, Rhoose CF62 3BZ
MENU GUIDE Seared scallops, rocket, white truffle oil • Rack of Welsh lamb, asparagus • Assiette of desserts
WINE GUIDE ♀ Dorjou de la Tour Chardonnay £13.50 • ♀ Dorjou de la Tour Merlot/Grenache £13.50 20 bottles over £20, 20 bottles under £20 • 6 by the glass (£3.50-£4.50)
PRICE GUIDE Fixed L £10-£25 • Fixed D £20-£30 • coffee £2.50 • min/water £3.50 • Service optional
PLACE: Dine in the former billiard room of this distinguished old country-house hotel with its seven-acre garden, woods and views down to the south Welsh coast.
FOOD: Tried and tested favourites make up the traditional menu with modern British influences and an emphasis on home-grown vegetables, Welsh Black beef and local lamb and venison. A gourmet dinner menu is also available. Well-paced, formal service.
OUR TIP: Convenient for Cardiff Airport
Chef: Katie Mitchell **Owners:** Mr R Morgan-Price & Huw Thomas
Times: 12-2/6.30-9 **Notes:** Sun L 3 courses £16.95, Vegetarian available, Dress Restrictions, Smart casual, no trainers, Civ Wed 40 **Seats:** 40, Pr/dining room 18 **Smoking:** N/Sm in restaurant **Children:** Portions
Rooms: 10 (10 en suite) ★★★ **Directions:** M4 junct 33, follow signs for Airport then Porthkerry, then turn left at hotel sign by thatched cottage
Parking: 60 **e-mail:** info@egertongrey.co.uk
web: www.egertongrey.co.uk

Wales

🏵 La Cucina
Mediterranean   **NEW**
Modern bistro in golf hotel
☎ 01443 667800 The Vale Hotel, Golf and Spa
Resort, Hensol Park, CF72 8JY

PLACE: The Vale Hotel enjoys a stunning setting overlooking its own golf course. There are several eating options - La Cucina is open and spacious with tiled floors, a vaulted wooden ceiling and well spaced tables. Staff are smiling and knowledgeable.
FOOD: Menus are much simpler at lunch while in the evening the choice broadens, with lots of local fish, Mediterranean style dressings, and pizzas from the wood fired oven. The cooking is modern and simple, focusing on the ingredients and emphasising their flavours.
OUR TIP: Plenty of spa and leisure facilities
Chef: Jamie Duncan **Owners:** Vale Hotel Ltd **Times:** 12.30-4/7.30-9.30, Closed Mon-Tues **e-mail:** reservations@vale-hotel.com
web: www.vale-hotel.com

WREXHAM

🏵🏵 West Arms Hotel
British, European
Upmarket fare in cosy country inn
☎ 01691 600665 600612   LL20 7LD

MENU GUIDE Crab, prawn & trout fishcake, sweet chilli sauce • Pork tenderloin, sage mash, port & stilton sauce • Hot chocolate soufflé

WINE GUIDE ♀ Los Vilos Chardonnay £14.95 • ♀ Los Vilos Black Label Merlot £14.95 • 27 bottles over £20, 26 bottles under £20 • 10 by the glass (£2.50-£6.50)

PRICE GUIDE Fixed D £34.50 • starter £4.90-£6.95 • main £6.95-£18.95 • dessert £4.85-£5.95 • coffee £2.50 • min/water £2.75 • Service added

PLACE: Set in the beautiful Ceiriog Valley, this cosy drovers' inn dates back to the 16th century and has a hefty helping of character, boasting ancient timbers, blazing fires and a friendly local crowd.
FOOD: A fixed-price menu built around quality local produce, plus a lighter bar selection. Mains might include Welsh Black beef and champ, or fresh sea bass from the Menai Strait, wrapped in pancetta and filled with spinach soufflé.
OUR TIP: Mountain bikes available for hire
Chef: Grant Williams **Owners:** Mr & Mrs Leigh-Ford **Times:** 12-2/7-9, Closed L Mon-Sat **Notes:** Vegetarian available, Smart Dress, Civ Wed 70

Seats: 34, Pr/dining room 10 **Smoking:** N/Sm in restaurant
Children: Menu, Portions **Rooms:** 15 (15 en suite) ★★
Directions: Exit A483 (A5) at Chirk (mid-way between Oswestry and Llangollen) and follow signs for Ceiriog Valley (B4500) - 11m
Parking: 20 **e-mail:** gowestarms@aol.com
web: www.thewestarms.co.uk

🏵 Cross Lanes Hotel
British, International
Friendly hotel brasserie in beautiful grounds
☎ 01978 780555 Cross Lanes, Bangor Rd, Marchwiel
LL13 0TF

MENU GUIDE Mussels in a Thai broth • Rump of lamb, mushroom faggot, candied onions • White chocolate tart, Milky Bar ice cream

WINE GUIDE ♀ Vina Adanita Sauvignon Blanc £13.50 • ♀ Wolf Blass Cabernet Sauvignon/Merlot £15.50 • 28 bottles over £20, 35 bottles under £20 • 15 by the glass (£2.30-£6)

PRICE GUIDE Fixed L fr £13.50 • starter £4.50-£6.95 • main £8.95-£17.50 • dessert £4.25-£5.50 • coffee £1.75 • min/water £3.50 • Service optional

PLACE: This hotel brasserie has a winningly laid-back feel thanks to its friendly staff and simple decor of rustic tables, open fires and old prints of Wrexham. It's set in an elegant late Victorian house with pretty grounds.
FOOD: A modern brasserie menu that draws inspiration from around the world. Dither over the extensive range; your choice might include herb-crusted halibut with spring onion risotto, or cider braised pork with bubble and squeak.
OUR TIP: Ample car parking
Chef: Nicholas Walton **Owners:** Michael Kagan **Times:** 12-3/6.30-9.30, Closed D 25-26 Dec **Notes:** Vegetarian available, Civ Wed 140 **Seats:** 50, Pr/dining room 60 **Smoking:** N/Sm in restaurant **Children:** Menu, Portions **Rooms:** 16 (16 en suite) ★★★ **Directions:** On A525, Wrexham to Whitchurch Rd, between Marchweil and Bangor-on-Dee **Parking:** 70
e-mail: guestservices@crosslanes.co.uk **web:** www.crosslanes.co.uk

continued

Wales

NORTHERN IRELAND

CO ANTRIM

CARNLOUGH MAP 01 D6

Londonderry Arms Hotel

British

Good-value modern cooking in genteel hotel

☎ 028 2888 5255 20 Harbour Rd BT44 0EU

MENU GUIDE Chicken liver pâté, Cumberland sauce • Chicken supreme, champ, broccoli, wild mushroom cream • Baileys parfait

PRICE GUIDE Fixed L £14.50 • starter £3.45-£5.75 • main £11.95-£14.50 • dessert £4.25 • coffee £1.20 • Service optional

PLACE: Once owned by Winston Churchill, this delightful building dates back to the mid-19th century and is set in a pretty fishing village on the stunning Antrim coast. Its traditional decor has a genteel charm, and nothing is too much trouble for the friendly staff.

FOOD: Good-value modern British cuisine prepared from high quality ingredients. Portion sizes are generous, so come hungry, and expect some elaborate dishes, plus simpler options such as scampi or steak.

OUR TIP: Stunning coastal drive to reach the hotel

Chef: Manus Jamison **Owners:** Frank O'Neill **Times:** 12.30-2.45/7-8.45, Closed 25 Dec, closed L Mon-Sat **Notes:** Vegetarian by request only **Seats:** 80, Pr/dining room 14 **Smoking:** N/Sm area **Children:** Menu, Portions **Rooms:** 35 (35 en suite) ★★★ **Directions:** 14m N of Larne on coast road **e-mail:** ida@glensofantrim.com **web:** www.glensofantrim.com

CO BELFAST

BELFAST MAP 01 D5

⬡⬡ Aldens

British, Irish

Modern classics in a setting to suit

☎ 028 9065 0079 229 Upper Newtownards Rd BT4 3JF

MENU GUIDE Dublin Bay prawns, garlic butter • Rabbit, lentils, salsa verde • Sticky toffee pudding, butterscotch sauce

WINE GUIDE ♀ Salvard Sauvignon Blanc £14.45 • ♀ Madfish Shiraz £17.95 • 60 bottles over £20, 34 bottles under £20 • 10 by the glass (£3.50-£7.95)

PRICE GUIDE Fixed D £21.95 • starter £4.50-£8.50 • main £6.50-£16.95 • dessert £4-£6 • coffee £2.95 • min/water £3.50 • Service optional • Group min 6 service 10%

PLACE: This spacious restaurant on the edge of town is decked out in contemporary style, with a bright purple canopy outside to pull in the punters, and a low-key interior. Large windows and mirrors let in the light, while varnished floorboards and wooden tables keep things fashionably understated.

FOOD: A wide selection of old favourites and classic modern dishes, which stretches from steak and chunky chips to more refined fare such as lamb with creamed French beans and bacon.

OUR TIP: Great value set menu in the evenings

Chef: Cath Gradwell **Owners:** Jonathan Davis **Times:** 12-2.30/6-10, Closed 2 wks Jul, BHs, Sunday, closed L Sat, closed D (Fri, Sat 6-11) **Notes:** Tasting menu Mon-Thur £27.50, Vegetarian available **Seats:** 70 **Smoking:** N/Sm area, No pipes, No cigars, Air con **Children:** Portions **Directions:** At x-rds with Sandown Rd **Parking:** On street **e-mail:** info@aldensrestaurant.com **web:** www.aldensrestaurant.com

⬡ Beatrice Kennedy

British, European

Busy little townhouse near the university

☎ 028 9020 2290 44 University Rd BT7 1NJ

MENU GUIDE Scallop, foie gras & apple gratin • Cod, crushed potatoes, pancetta and morels • Sticky toffee pudding

WINE GUIDE 10 bottles over £20, 20 bottles under £20 • 4 by the glass (£3.25-£4.50)

PRICE GUIDE Starter £4-£8 • main £11-£15 • dessert £5 • coffee £1.30 • min/water £3 • Group min 6 service 10%

PLACE: This three-storey townhouse was once a doctor's surgery and is named after the doctor's wife. Interior decor is 1930s-style with white linen and leather, high-backed chairs and big-band jazz. There's also a private function room upstairs.

FOOD: Fresh local ingredients simply cooked with flair and imagination. Dishes hopscotch across a variety of themes and styles, and offer good value for money. Fish and game are specialities.

OUR TIP: Romantic tables for two are very popular

Chef: Jim McCarthy **Owners:** Jim McCarthy **Times:** 12.30-3/5-10.30, Closed 24-26 Dec, 1 Jan, Easter, Mon, closed L Mon-Sat, closed D Mon **Notes:** Express menu Tue-Sun 2 courses £12, Sun L 3 courses £14.95, Vegetarian available **Seats:** 75, Pr/dining room 25 **Smoking:** No pipes, No cigars **Children:** Menu, Portions **Directions:** Adjacent to Queens University **Parking:** On street **e-mail:** reservations@beatricekennedy.co.uk **web:** www.beatricekennedy.co.uk

⬡ Bourbon

British, International

Consistent cooking in atmospheric city-centre restaurant

☎ 028 9033 2121 60 Great Victoria St BT2 7BB

MENU GUIDE Baked goats' cheese, roast beetroot, vinaigrette • Roasted pork belly, apple sauce, mash • Cinnamon apple Bakewell tart

continued

continued

Ireland

WINE GUIDE ♀ Sierra Grande Sauvignon Blanc £12.95
♀ Sierra Grande Merlot £12.95 • 29 bottles over £20, 29 bottles under £20 • 8 by the glass (£3.15-£3.40)

PRICE GUIDE Starter £2.50-£7.50 • main £7.50-£18 • dessert £4.50 coffee £1.65 • min/water £3.95 • Group min 6 service 10%

PLACE: Elaborate Gothic decor crowned by a grand staircase contrasts with the simplicity of a menu that appeals to both locals and visitors alike. The place is always busy and the kitchen performs consistently, with friendly staff in support.
FOOD: Local produce is used extensively in simple dishes where the flavours of the ingredients are never lost in overly fussy preparations. The menu ranges from gourmet pizzas through to a statuesque T-bone steak.
OUR TIP: Extra busy on Fridays and Saturdays
Chef: Stephen Taylor Winter **Owners:** Brian Smyth, Lynda Coulter **Times:** 12-11pm, Closed 24-26 Dec **Notes:** Vegetarian available **Seats:** 180, Pr/dining room 100 **Smoking:** N/Sm area, Air con **Children:** Portions **Directions:** Located in city centre opposite Europa and Opera House **Parking:** On street outside
e-mail: info@bourbonrestaurant.com **web:** www.bourbonrestaurant.com

Cayenne
Modern International
Interesting food full of Eastern promise in colourful surroundings
☎ 028 9033 1532 7 Ascot House, Shaftesbury Square BT2 7DB

continued

MENU GUIDE Pea, courgette & asparagus risotto • Slow roast rabbit • Lime mousse
WINE GUIDE ♀ Domaine Bellevue Sauvignon Blanc £15.75
♀ Deakin Estate Shiraz £15.95 • 89 bottles over £20, 23 bottles under £20 • 8 by the glass (£3.50-£4)

PRICE GUIDE Fixed L £12 • Fixed D £15.50 • starter £4.50-£12.50 main £10.50-£25 • dessert £4.75-£5.50 • coffee £2 • min/water £3.55 • Service optional • Group min 6 service 10%

PLACE: Still one of the places to be seen, where the vivid colour scheme, like the name, follows a theme of Eastern spices. A spacious lounge/aperitif area is a welcome new addition.
FOOD: A strong Oriental influence, with Pacific, Indian and Mediterranean touches, gives a kick to everything, including the great choice of vegetarian and fish dishes. Good-value set lunches, and you can try dishes like chargrilled eel with smoked chicken crisps.
OUR TIP: Put on your glad rags
Chef: Danny Millar **Owners:** Paul & Jeanne Rankin **Times:** 12-2.15/6-10.15, Closed 25-26 Dec, 12 Jul, closed L Sat & Sun **Notes:** Vegetarian available **Seats:** 130, Pr/dining room 18 **Smoking:** N/Sm area, No pipes, Air con **Children:** Portions **Directions:** Top of Great Victoria St **Parking:** Dublin Rd **e-mail:** reservations@cayennerestaurant.com **web:** www.cayennerestaurant.com

 **Restaurant Michael Deane**

see below

Restaurant Michael Deane

British, French
Exemplary modern cooking in exciting setting
☎ 028 9033 1134 34/40 Howard St BT1 6PF
MENU GUIDE Scallops, black pudding, cauliflower • Rabbit saddle, sweet potato gnocchi, ceps • Pear, four ways
WINE GUIDE ♀ Gloucester Ridge Sauvignon Blanc £29
♀ Zilzie Shiraz £23 • 200 bottles over £20, 8 bottles under £20 10 by the glass (£4.25-£8.50)
PRICE GUIDE Fixed L £32.50-£37 • Fixed D £43.50-£45 • starter £10-£15 • main £25-£30 • dessert £8 • coffee £3 • min/water £3.50 • Service optional • Group min 6 service 10%

PLACE: The chef may be a celebrity but he is still pretty 'hands on' when it comes to running this exciting, theatrical restaurant. The vibrant downstairs dining room provides the buzz and fizz whilst upstairs there's a more formal restaurant with just a few large, candlelit tables with expensive settings. The kitchen provides the theatrical element with chefs preparing dishes in full

view of expectant diners. Huge serving trays also add a bit of drama to service which is efficient and friendly.
FOOD: This is modern cooking of a refined order. Each dish has depth of flavour which comes, in part, from well selected, local and seasonal produce and, in part, from not inconsiderable kitchen skills. There's a sense of consistency and confidence here in starters like roasted quail with celeriac purée, beetroot and juniper and main courses like pan-fried bream with smoked chicken and tarragon ravioli. Excellent wine list.
OUR TIP: Very popular so booking essential
Chef: Michael Deane **Owners:** Michael Deane **Times:** 7-9, Closed Xmas, New Year, Etr, 2 wk Jul, Sun-Tue, closed L Wed-Thu & Sat **Notes:** Tasting menu £52, Vegetarian available, Smart Dress **Seats:** 30 **Smoking:** N/Sm in restaurant, Air con **Children:** Portions **Directions:** Located at rear of city hall. Howard St on left opposite Spires building **Parking:** On street **e-mail:** info@michaeldeane.co.uk **web:** www.michaeldeane.co.uk

Ireland

Shu

French, International

Minimalist eaterie for fashion-conscious foodies

☎ 028 9038 1655 253 Lisburn Rd BT9 7EN

MENU GUIDE Risotto of onion, parmesan & herbs • Tempura of cod, spiced noodles, seared pak choi, chilli dip • Chocolate brownie, ice cream & chocolate sauce

WINE GUIDE ♀ Montana Sauvignon Blanc £14 • ♀ Penfold Bin 35 Shiraz Cabernet £14 • 33 bottles over £20, 21 bottles under £20 • 8 by the glass (£3.50-£3.75)

PRICE GUIDE Starter £3.75-£7 • main £9-£16 • dessert £4.75-£5 • coffee £1.55 • min/water £4.10 • Service optional • Group min 6 service 10%

PLACE: As the name might imply, this is a cool, minimalist, contemporary outfit, decked out in warm chocolate browns, reds and creams, with swathes of suede seats, leather banquettes and wooden floors that amount to a distinctive fashion statement and draws an admiring army of fans. It's advisable to book.
FOOD: The modern, eclectic menu is as fashionable and crowd-pleasing as the surroundings, with combinations that get the taste buds tingling, and spicing that's used skilfully. Neatly turned-out staff are attentive, bright and breezy, and fit the bill.
OUR TIP: The carte offers some good value dishes
Chef: Brian McCann **Owners:** Alan Reid **Times:** 12.30-2.30/6-10, Closed 24-26 Dec, 12-14 Jul, Sun **Notes:** Vegetarian available **Seats:** 76, Pr/dining room 22 **Smoking:** N/Sm area, Air con **Children:** Portions **Directions:** From city centre take Lisburn road lower end. Restaurant in 1 m **Parking:** On street **e-mail:** eat@shu-restaurant.com **web:** www.shu-restaurant.com

Metro Brasserie European 13 Lower Crescent
BT7 1NR ☎ 028 9032 3349 A modern brasserie with crisp, contemporary cooking and an easygoing atmosphere.

Ta Tu 701 Lisburn Rd BT9 7GU ☎ 028 9038 0818
Bar/restaurant of fashionable, modish design with global food to match.

CO DOWN

Clandeboye Lodge Hotel

British, European

Creative food in woodland location

☎ 028 9185 2500 10 Estate Rd, Clandeboye BT19 1UR

MENU GUIDE Chorizo risotto with feta cheese & mint • Confit of Barbary duck with sweet & sour cabbage • Apple Tatin tartelette

WINE GUIDE ♀ Copelano Semilion/Chardonnay £12.95 • ♀ Deakin Estate Merlot £13.95 • 3 bottles over £20, 27 bottles under £20 • 5 by the glass (£2.45-£3.75)

PRICE GUIDE Fixed L £11.50 • Fixed D £37.50 • starter £2.95-£5.50 • main £5.25-£15 • dessert £4.25-£5.75 • coffee £1.50 • min/water £3.95 • Service optional

PLACE: Three miles west of Bangor, this delightful hotel stands in landscaped and wooded grounds. The redesigned Lodge Restaurant offers a casual dining environment.

FOOD: European flavours and local ingredients produce fusion-inspired dishes and innovative combinations - roast fillet of brill with prawn mash and red wine jus, perhaps, or entrecôte of Irish lamb with curry spice-infused purée of parsnip.
OUR TIP: Leave room for the puds!
Chef: Martin Wilson **Owners:** Pim Dalm **Times:** 12-2.30/6.30-9.30, Closed 25-26 Dec **Notes:** Fixed D 4 courses £45 incl. bottle of wine, Vegetarian available, Dress Restrictions, Smart casual, Civ Wed 250 **Seats:** 60, Pr/dining room 300 **Smoking:** N/Sm in restaurant **Children:** Menu, Portions **Rooms:** 43 (43 en suite) ★★★
Directions: M3 follow signs for A2 (Bangor). Before Bangor turn right at junction signposted to Newtownards, Clandeboye Lodge Hotel and Blackwood Golf Course **Parking:** 250
e-mail: info@clandeboyelodge.co.uk
web: www.clandeboyelodge.com

Shanks *see page 658*

1614

Classic, Contemporary

Flavour-led cooking in old coaching inn

☎ 028 9185 3255 Old Inn, 15 Main St, Crawfordsburn BT19 1JH

MENU GUIDE Local crab salad • Beef medallions, mushroom ravioli, red wine jus • Poached pear, star anise

WINE GUIDE ♀ Chablis AC £19 • ♀ Rosemount Shiraz £15 29 bottles over £20, 59 bottles under £20 • 8 by the glass (£3.25)

PRICE GUIDE Fixed D £30 • coffee £1.25 • min/water £4.25 • Service optional

PLACE: In business since 1614, this ancient country inn has log fires, brass chandeliers and original oak panelling bedecked with local coats of arms. The 1614 Restaurant has high, wooden-clad ceilings, formally set tables and low lighting producing an intimate feel. Helpful, friendly staff ensure an enjoyable dining experience.
FOOD: Local ingredients form the basis of robust and accurately cooked classical dishes with contemporary twists like Finnebrogue venison with sweet potato purée, shitake and smoked bacon. Asia Pacific influence is discernable in dishes like salmon with rice vermicelli, bok choi, chilli, coriander and ginger.
OUR TIP: A short drive from Belfast
Chef: Alex Taylor **Owners:** Danny Rice **Times:** 12.30-2.30/7-9.30, Closed 25 Dec, closed D Sun **Notes:** Fixed Sun L £19.50, Vegetarian available, Smart Dress **Seats:** 64, Pr/dining room 25 **Smoking:** No pipes, No cigars **Children:** Menu, Portions **Rooms:** 32 (32 en suite) ★★★ **Directions:** Take A2 E from Belfast. 5-6m turn left at Ballyrobert lights, and 400 yds to Crawfordsburn, Inn is on left **Parking:** 100
e-mail: info@theoldinn.com **web:** www.theoldinn.com

Ireland

continued

Shanks

Mediterranean
Conran-design meets inspired, skilful cooking on the golf course
☎ 028 9185 3313 The Blackwood, Crawfordsburn Rd BT19 1GB
web: www.shanksrestaurant.com

PLACE: Though far from the madding crowd, set within a country estate and part of the Blackwood golf complex, Shanks is a stylish, cool, split-level affair that has earned widespread appeal thanks to its talented husband and wife team, the Millars. The Sir Terence Conran designed interior is as fresh as ever, sleek and warm, decked out with Hockney prints, polished wood flooring and a trademark open kitchen. The upper-lounge area sports comfortable sofas for aperitifs, while the terrace offers a fair-weather option and views over the surrounding countryside. Service is slick and professional but friendly.

FOOD: Robbie Millar's cooking has a modern focus but is defined by the classical French style for which he is renowned. High quality, fresh local produce is treated with respect and restraint with flavours allowed to shine. Presentation enhances rather than dominates and there's excitement coupled with accurate, spot-on cooking. His approach, via a repertoire of fixed-price seasonal menus, might take in a fillet of wild sea bass with confit of fennel, spinach, courgette, lemon aïoli and crispy potatoes, and an espresso crème brûlée with pistachio praline and crème Chantilly. Notable wine list.

MENU GUIDE Scallops, salad of roasted apricots, toasted almonds • Monkfish, champ, mushrooms, crispy cabbage, red wine sauce • Apple tarte Tatin, cinnamon ice cream

WINE GUIDE ♀ Madwood Unwooded Chardonnay £20.50 • ♀ Drouhin Fleurie Gamay £18.50 • 67 bottles over £20, 48 bottles under £20 • 6 by the glass (£3.25-£4)

PRICE GUIDE Fixed L £21-£26.50 • Fixed D £45-£54.95 • coffee £1.75 • min/water £3.50 • Group min 6 service 10%

OUR TIP: Lunch/supper menu offers exceptional value

Chef: Robbie Millar **Owners:** Mr & Mrs R Millar **Times:** 12.30-2.30/7-10, Closed 25-26 Dec and Easter Tue, 2 wks mid Jul, Sun-Mon, closed L Sat **Notes:** Tasting menus £65-£85, Vegetarian available **Seats:** 70, Pr/dining room 36 **Smoking:** N/Sm in restaurant, Air con **Children:** Portions **Directions:** Follow A2 to Bangor, right at sign for Blackwood Golf Centre

GILFORD MAP 01 D5

⑳⑳ Oriel of Gilford

Irish, French

Friendly country-style restaurant where the food is allowed to shine

☎ 028 3883 1543 2 Bridge St BT63 6HF

MENU GUIDE Fermanagh ham ravioli, chicken & thyme consommé • Irish Hereford beef fillet, oxtail stuffed cabbage, swede fondant, truffle jus • Assiette of mango & passionfruit

WINE GUIDE ♀ Fleur du Cap Chardonnay £14.95 • ♀ Château Peymouton St Emillion £26 • 80 bottles over £20, 21 bottles under £20 • 4 by the glass (£3.95)

PRICE GUIDE Fixed L £15.95 • Fixed D £19.95 • starter £4.94-£9.95 • main £15.95-£19.95 • dessert £7.95-£8.95 • coffee £1.95 • min/water £2.95 • Service optional

PLACE: This unassuming country-style restaurant is currently making waves on the Irish restaurant scene. Hard to believe given the setting, in an unassuming village south of Belfast, and its modest decor - minimal panelling and plain yellow walls adorned with local artists' paintings. Don't be fooled though, the focus is purely on the food and you can expect some powerful and accomplished dishes from a passionate and committed team.
FOOD: Daily menus describe the cooking as modern Irish with strong French influences, with Rungis Market in Paris supplying luxury ingredients on a weekly basis. Top-notch seasonal local produce includes organic vegetables.
OUR TIP: Bring your credit card for local artists' work
Chef: Barry Smyth **Owners:** Barry Smyth **Times:** 12.30-2.30/6-9.30, Closed 25-26 Dec, 1 wk Jan, 2 wks Jul, Mon-Wed, closed L Thurs
Notes: Tasting menu £50, Vegetarian available, Dress Restrictions
Seats: 45, Pr/dining room 16 **Smoking:** N/Sm area, No pipes, Air con
Children: Portions **Directions:** From Banbridge take Tandragee road and straight ahead to mini-rdbt **Parking:** On street
e-mail: info@orielrestaurant.com **web:** www.orielrestaurant.com

---

PORTAFERRY MAP 01 D5

⑳ Portaferry Hotel
Modern

Waterside hotel with a flair for seafood

☎ 028 4272 8231 10 The Strand BT22 1PE
PLACE: A well-presented, popular hotel located almost by the ferry ramp with superb views of Strangford Lough. Expect a warm welcome and good service, overseen by the proprietor.
FOOD: A modern menu with international flavours. The hotel has a wide reputation for its seafood, which is landed daily at the fishing villages of Portavogie and Ardglass, but pride is taken in all the ingredients, which tend to be locally grown and often organic.
OUR TIP: Try the langoustines - and don't be embarrassed by the bib
Times: 12.30-2.30/7-9, Closed L Mon-Sat, Xmas Eve & Xmas Day
Rooms: 14 (14 en suite) ★★★ **e-mail:** info@portaferryhotel.com
web: www.portaferryhotel.com

For information on Service Charge, see p21.

The AA Wine Awards recognise the finest wine lists in England, Scotland and Wales. For full details, see pages 14-15

PORTAVOGIE

⑳ The Quay's Pub & Restaurant
Traditional, Modern   🐟🐟 NEW

AA Seafood Restaurant of the Year for Northern Ireland

☎ 028 4277 2225 81 New Harbour, Portavogie BT22 1EB

MENU GUIDE Seafood bruschetta, lobster bisque • Smoked lythe, summer vegetables, pink peppercorn butter • Chocolate fudge cake

WINE GUIDE ♀ Torres Vina Esmerlda £11.95 • ♀ Brown Brothers Everton £10.95 • 4 bottles over £20, 23 bottles under £20 • 10 by the glass (£2.80-£3.50)

PRICE GUIDE Fixed D £13.95-£29.95 • starter £2.95-£6.75 • main £6.75-£24.95 • dessert £3.75-£4.95 • coffee £1.20 • min/water £5.40 • Service optional

PLACE: Right on the shore with the sea in front and the harbour behind, this modern building includes a lounge, public bar and spacious split-level restaurant. Bright modern art with a sea theme is set against warm ochre walls.
FOOD: Simply as good and fresh as can be, with a fish menu dictated by that day's catch and listing up to eight specialities. All tastes are catered for, with meat, vegetarian and children's dishes in good value, generous portions.
OUR TIP: Booking essential at weekends
Chef: David Cardwell & Aaron Hanna **Owners:** Francis & Diane Adair
Times: 12-2.30/5-9, Closed 25 Dec, Tue **Notes:** Vegetarian available, Smart Dress **Seats:** 96 **Smoking:** N/Sm area **Children:** Menu, Portions
Directions: Take Portaferry road out of Newtownards and head towards Greyabbey, through Kircubbin and then Portavogie **Parking:** 100
e-mail: leighgamble1969@hotmail.com
web: www.quaysrestaurant.co.uk

Ireland

LONDONDERRY

The Lime Tree

Mediterranean

Relaxed and intimate restaurant offering quality local dishes

☎ 028 7776 4300 60 Catherine St BT49 9DB

MENU GUIDE Duck rillettes, crab apple jelly • Stir-fried pork fillet, satay sauce • Sticky toffee pudding

WINE GUIDE ♀ McGregor Sauvignon £12.75 • ♀ Armoro Vina El Aromo Carmenere £12.50 • 31 bottles under £20 • 6 by the glass (£2.95)

PRICE GUIDE Starter £3.75-£7.50 • main £12.95-£17.50 • dessert £4.75-£5.50 • coffee £1.35 • min/water £2.50 • Service optional

PLACE: An intimate little restaurant, named after the lime trees planted to commemorate a former resident who went on to become Prime Minister of New Zealand.
FOOD: Seafood consistently appears on the carte in the guise of Irish smoked salmon, seafood thermidor, and a daily fish special. Otherwise expect crowd-pleasers like leek-filled chicken breast with a rosemary and bacon sauce, and fillet steak with crushed black pepper sauce.
OUR TIP: The early bird menu is a good value option
Chef: Stanley Matthews **Owners:** Mr & Mrs S Matthews **Times:** 6-9, Closed 25-26 Dec, Sun-Mon (ex Dec), closed L Mon-Sun
Notes: Vegetarian available **Seats:** 30 **Smoking:** No pipes, No cigars **Children:** Menu, Portions **Directions:** Entering Limavady from the Derry side, the restaurant is on right on small slip road **Parking:** 15
e-mail: info@limetreerest.com **web:** www.limetreerest.com

Radisson SAS Roe Park Resort

European

Slick modern hotel restaurant

☎ 028 7772 2222 BT49 9LB

MENU GUIDE Three game terrine, apple jelly • Aromatic duck, soya noodles, tempura vegetables, orange & ginger sauce • Crêpes Suzette

PRICE GUIDE Starter £3.50-£6.50 • main £10.25-£13.95 • dessert £5.50 • coffee £1.85

PLACE: The main block of the hotel is located in an impressive 18th-century country-house, with its own golf resort, set amid glorious countryside. Greens Restaurant is a clean contemporary space with relaxed, professional and friendly service.
FOOD: Cooking is simple, modern and effective, using fresh local ingredients. The carte offers a comprehensive choice of European dishes with a hint of Pacific Rim; vegetarians are well served.
OUR TIP: Informal eating in the Coach House Brasserie
Chef: Adrian McDaid **Owners:** Mr Conn, Mr McKeever, Mr Wilton **Times:** 6.30-10, Closed Sun-Thu, Jan, closed L Mon-Sat, closed D Mon
Notes: Carvery available Sun lunch, Vegetarian available, Dress Restrictions, Smart casual, Civ Wed 250 **Seats:** 160, Pr/dining room 50 **Smoking:** N/Sm in restaurant, Air con **Children:** Menu, Portions
Rooms: 118 (118 en suite) ★★★★ **Directions:** On A6 (Londonderry-Limavady road), 0.5m from Limavady. 8m from Derry airport
Parking: 250 **e-mail:** reservations@radissonroepark.com
web: www.radissonroepark.com

Beech Hill Hotel

French, Modern

Sumptuous country-house serving innovative food

☎ 028 7134 9279 32 Ardmore Rd BT47 3QP

MENU GUIDE Crab, mango & coconut salad • Turbot, scallop and leek ravioli • Forest fruit cheesecake

WINE GUIDE ♀ Central Valley Santa Rita 120 Chardonnay £12.50 • ♀ Maipo Valley Santa Rita 120 Merlot £12.50 13 bottles over £20, 44 bottles under £20 • 6 by the glass (£3.50)

PRICE GUIDE Fixed L £14.95 • Fixed D £27.95 • starter £3.95-£8.95 • main £12.95-£20.95 • dessert £5.95 • coffee £3.95 min/water £3.75 • Service optional

PLACE: This 18th-century country mansion stands in 32 acres of glorious woodlands and gardens. Day rooms are traditionally furnished, many with open fires. The dining room is in a similar style with great woodland views.
FOOD: Modern cuisine with traditional Irish and continental influences such as John Dory fillet with chorizo and sweet pepper compôte & spiced potato. Good use of fresh, local produce and particularly good breads and petits fours.
OUR TIP: Convenient for Derry's Eglington Airport
Chef: Neil Gorham **Owners:** Mr S Donnelly, Mrs P O'Kane **Times:** 12-2.30/6-9.45, Closed 24-25 Dec **Notes:** Vegetarian available, Civ Wed 80 **Seats:** 90, Pr/dining room 80 **Smoking:** N/Sm in restaurant
Children: Portions **Rooms:** 27 (27 en suite) ★★★ **Directions:** A6 Londonderry to Belfast road, turn off at Faughan Bridge. 1m further to Ardmore Chapel. Hotel entrance is opposite **Parking:** 50
e-mail: info@beech-hill.com **web:** www.beech-hill.com

Tower Hotel Derry

Mediterranean

Stylish food and setting

☎ 028 7137 1000 Off the Diamond, Butcher St BT48 6HL

MENU GUIDE Salt cod brandade & niçoise salad • Beef sirloin, roasted celeriac, sauce béarnaise • Dark chocolate mousse

WINE GUIDE ♀ Penfolds Chardonnay £13.75 • ♀ Penfolds Shiraz Cabernet £14.25 • 10 bottles over £20, 21 bottles under £20 • 12 by the glass (£3.75-£6)

PRICE GUIDE Fixed L £13.50-£18 • Fixed D £21.95-£29.95 • starter £3.95-£7 • main £12-£25 • dessert £3.95-£5.95 • coffee £2.25 • min/water £4.95 • Service added but optional

PLACE: A stylish, new city-centre hotel delivering true Irish hospitality and a lively atmosphere in its bright, contemporary bistro or more informal Lime Tree Bar.
FOOD: The bistro's crowd-pleasing modern menus hit all the right notes, perhaps delivering the likes of marinated pork belly with sweet chilli, wild mushrooms, coconut noodles and pak choi. Bright and cheery service fits the bill too.
OUR TIP: Try the fixed-price menu
Chef: Matthew Clement **Owners:** Tower Hotel Group **Times:** 12.30-2.90/6-9.45, Closed Xmas **Notes:** Vegetarian available, Civ Wed 300 **Seats:** 100, Pr/dining room 20 **Smoking:** N/Sm in restaurant, Air con **Children:** Menu, Portions **Rooms:** 93 (93 en suite) ★★★★
Directions: From Craigavan Ridge travel into city centre. Take 2nd exit at the end of bridge into Carlisle Rd and then into Ferryquay St **Parking:** 35
e-mail: reservations@thd.ie **web:** www.towerhotelderry.com

Ireland

MAGHERA MAP 01 C5

⊛⊛ Ardtara Country House
Traditional Irish
Modern dining in stately manor
☎ 028 7964 4490 8 Gorteade Rd BT46 5SA

PLACE: Housed in the former billiard room of this stately Victorian manor, Ardtara's restaurant is lit by a grand skylight and features oak panelling and an impressively restored hunting frieze. The house is graciously furnished with antiques, and has several elegant lounges for a pre-dinner drink or doze by the fire.
FOOD: An impressive solo performance from a skilful young chef on his way up. The modern Irish menu changes daily and consistently impresses, not least for its commitment to fine quality local produce.
OUR TIP: Half an hour from Royal Portrush, one of the finest golf courses in the world
Chef: Martin Nelson **Owners:** Dr Alistar Hanna **Times:** 12.30-2.30/7-9, Closed 25, 26 Dec, closed L Mon-Sat, closed D Sun, Mon (exc Residents)
Notes: Sun D £25, Vegetarian by request only **Seats:** 30, Pr/dining room 12 **Smoking:** N/Sm in restaurant **Children:** Portions **Rooms:** 8 (8 en suite) ★★ **Directions:** Take A29 to Maghera/Coleraine. Follow B75(Kilrea) to Upperlands. Continue pass sign for W Clark & Sons, then take next left into Gorteade Rd **Parking:** 50
e-mail: valerie@ardtara.fsbusiness.co.uk **web:** www.ardtara.com

MENU GUIDE Salmon roulade, beetroot salad • Beef, buttered cabbage, fondant potato, wild mushrooms • Dark chocolate cake, toffee sauce

WINE GUIDE 12 bottles over £20, 39 bottles under £20 • 4 by the glass (£3.25)

PRICE GUIDE Fixed L £12-£14 • Fixed D £30-£32 • coffee £2 min/water £3 • Service optional

continued

Ireland

How do I find my perfect place?

New editions on sale now!

Available from all good bookshops,
on www.theAA.com or call 01256 491524

REPUBLIC OF IRELAND

CO CAVAN

BALLYCONNELL MAP 01 C5

🏵 Slieve Russell Hotel Golf & Country Club

International

Elegant resort hotel restaurant

☎ 049 9526 444

MENU GUIDE Tempura prawn, sweet chilli jam • Fillet steak, potato & bacon rösti, wine & shallot jus • Chocolate & toffee pudding

WINE GUIDE ♀ Cono Sur Sauvignon Blanc €19.50 • ♀ Cono Sur Cabernet Sauvignon €19.50 • 26 bottles over €30, 40 bottles under €30

PRICE GUIDE Fixed L €20.40-€22 • Fixed D €43-€55 • Service optional

PLACE: Work up an appetite with a stroll around the extensive grounds of this busy resort hotel, or a round of golf on its championship course. The main restaurant is open for dinner only.

FOOD: A wide-ranging menu to suit most tastes, featuring simpler dishes such as black sole with a lemon and chive butter, as well as more complex options - chicken supreme with a sun-dried tomato risotto perhaps, or roast duckling with a plum tartlette.

OUR TIP: Reservations essential for non-residents

Chef: Peter Denny **Owners:** Sean Quinn **Times:** 12.30-2.15/7-9.15, Closed L Mon-Sat **Notes:** Coffee included, Vegetarian available, Dress Restrictions, No jeans, trainers, T-shirts, jogging pants **Seats:** 180, Pr/dining room 40 **Smoking:** N/Sm in restaurant **Children:** Menu, Portions **Rooms:** 157 (157 en suite) ★★★★ **Directions:** From Dublin take N3 towards Cavan. At rdbt before Cavan, follow Enniskillen sign to Belturbet. From Belturbet go towards Ballyconnell. Hotel approx 6m from Belturbet on left **Parking:** 360 **e-mail:** slieve-russell@quinn-hotels.com **web:** www.quinnhotels.com

VIRGINIA MAP 01 C4

🏵 The Park Hotel

European, International

Elegant dining in former hunting lodge

☎ 049 8546100 Virginia Park

MENU GUIDE French onion soup • Duckling with rosemary & caramelised orange sauce • Hazelnut torte, white chocolate sauce

WINE GUIDE ♀ Wolf Blass Sauvignon Blanc €19.50 • ♀ Wolf Blass Cabernet Sauvignon €19.50 • 12 bottles over €30, 10 bottles under €30 • 4 by the glass (€4.50)

PRICE GUIDE Fixed L €12-€15 • Fixed D €25-€30 • coffee €1.75 • min/water €2.30 • Service optional

PLACE: This imposing former hunting lodge prides itself on having 'served lords and ladies since the 1750s' and sits in a 100-acre estate of mature gardens and woodland.

FOOD: Snacks are available in the bar, while the elegant Marquis restaurant offers more formal fare. The menu features a mix of modern and traditional dishes, with mains stretching from the familiar (steak with brandy and peppercorn sauce) to the more elaborate (dressed rack of lamb).

OUR TIP: Build up an appetite on the hotel's nine-hole golf course

Chef: David Gadd **Owners:** Baltimore International College **Times:** 12.30-3.30/6.30-9.30, Closed 25-26 Dec, closed L Mon-Sat **Notes:** Vegetarian available **Seats:** 35, Pr/dining room 35 **Smoking:** N/Sm in restaurant **Children:** Menu, Portions **Rooms:** 26 (26 en suite) ★★ **Directions:** Follow the N3 to Virginia and when in village take first left. Hotel entrance 500 yds on left **Parking:** 40 **e-mail:** virginiapark@eircom.net **web:** www.parkhotelvirginia.com

CO CLARE

BALLYVAUGHAN MAP 01 B3

🏵🏵 Gregans Castle

Modern French, Irish

Country-house hotel dining with splendid views of the Burren

☎ 065 7077005

MENU GUIDE Duck confit filo pastry, pecans & herbs • Roast cod en crepinette, crab & smoked trout mousse • Vanilla & almond panacotta

WINE GUIDE ♀ Sauvignon Honore de Bevicot, Côtes de Duras €25 • ♀ Canvendrell Negre/Albet i Noya Penedes €24.50 • 64 bottles over €30, 39 bottles under €30 • 6 by the glass (€6.50)

PRICE GUIDE Fixed D €49.50 • min/water €5 • Service included

PLACE: Late 18th-century country-house with dramatic views over Galway Bay and the Burren. Elegant public rooms are furnished with antiques, and the full-length windows in the dining room catch the evening light across the bay as it strikes the grey limestone mountains. The setting is semi-formal and staff are renowned for their personal service.

FOOD: Imaginative modern French cooking with an emphasis on freshness. There is an interesting spread of dishes and a good supply of fish from Rossaveale and lamb from the village butcher. Organic produce is used when availability allows.

OUR TIP: Local cheeses are a speciality

Chef: Adrian O'Farrell **Owners:** Simon Haden **Times:** 7-8.30, Closed Nov-Mar, closed L all week **Notes:** Carte menu average price €51, Vegetarian available, Dress Restrictions, No shorts **Seats:** 50, Pr/dining room 30 **Smoking:** N/Sm in restaurant **Children:** Min 7 yrs, Menu, Portions **Rooms:** 22 (22 en suite) ★★★ **Directions:** On N67, 3.5m S of Ballyvaughan **Parking:** 20 **e-mail:** res@gregans.ie **web:** www.gregans.ie

continued

Temple Gate

Irish, International

Modern dining in Gothic-style building

☎ 065 6823300 The Square

MENU GUIDE Seashore chowder • Monkfish medallions, shrimp & saffron timbale, mustard/honey velouté • Mint & vanilla pannacotta mousse

WINE GUIDE ♀ Cono Sur Chardonnay €15.20 • ♥ Cono Sur Cabernet Sauvignon €15.20 • 3 bottles over €30, 17 bottles under €30 • 2 by the glass (€4.50-€5.75)

PRICE GUIDE Fixed L €15-€25 • Fixed D €25-€35 • starter €5.95-€8.50 • main €15-€23.50 • dessert €6.50-€7.75 • coffee €2.75 • Service optional • Group min 10

PLACE: Modern hotel developed from the former Convent of Mercy, retaining a 19th-century Gothic theme. JM's Bistro is warmly decorated with natural wood, elegant drapes and intimate lighting. The Great Hall, once the convent's church, provides a fabulous setting for weddings and banquets.

FOOD: Choose from an extensive carte or good-value fixed-price menu. Quality ingredients are used in straightforward Irish dishes with European influences and imaginative titles. Well-chosen dressings and sauces provide contrast.

OUR TIP: Preachers pub with regular live music

Chef: Paul Shortt **Owners:** John Madden **Times:** 12.45-2.30/7-9.45, Closed 25-27 Dec, Good Fri, closed L Request only Mon-Sat **Notes:** Vegetarian available, Civ Wed 150 **Seats:** 90, Pr/dining room 150 **Smoking:** N/Sm in restaurant **Children:** Menu, Portions **Rooms:** 70 (70 en suite) ★★★ **Directions:** Follow signs for the Tourist Office. The hotel is in same square **Parking:** 100

e-mail: info@templegatehotel.com **web:** www.templegatehotel.com

---

LISDOONVARNA

Sheedy's Country House Hotel

Modern Irish   **NEW**

Classical cooking with a contemporary edge

☎ 065 7074026

PLACE: This modern country-house hotel dates in part from the 17th century, and is set in an unrivalled location on the edge of the Burren. Intimate and full of character, it's an ideal base for touring the area, with both Doolin and the Cliffs of Moher within reach.

FOOD: Sheedy's brings a contemporary twist to classical favourites, producing honest and straightforward cuisine with an emphasis on quality ingredients. Seasonal local produce gets top billing, with much arriving fresh from the nearby Burren Smokehouse.

OUR TIP: Seafood menu available in the bar

Times: 6.45-8.30, Closed mid Oct-mid Mar **Rooms:** 11 (11 en suite) ★★★ **e-mail:** info@sheedys.com **web:** www.sheedys.com

---

NEWMARKET-ON-FERGUS MAP 01 B3

Dromoland Castle

Irish, European

Elegant dining in historic castle on 375-acre estate

☎ 061 368144

MENU GUIDE Chicken ballotine, sage, onion & chestnut stuffing • Beef sirloin, cep & ricotta risotto, Puy lentils • Brown bread soufflé

continued

WINE GUIDE ♀ Casa la Joya Chardonnay €25 • ♥ Rosemount Shiraz/Cabernet Sauvignon €26 • 500 bottles over €30, 15 bottles under €30 • 8 by the glass (€7-€8.50)

PRICE GUIDE Fixed L €40 • Fixed D €66 • starter €16-€25 • main €29-€50 • dessert €16 • coffee €2.50 • min/water €6 • Service added 15%

PLACE: A real live castle dating from the 11th century makes a great setting for a luxury hotel, with plenty of comforts as well as character. There are two restaurants, with fine dining among the silk wall hangings and crystal chandeliers of the Earl of Thomond rooms, accompanied by music from the resident harpist.

FOOD: The four-course dinner menu offers a balanced choice, including game from the estate. The Irish cooking with European influences is sound, with saucing a particular strength. A separate vegetarian menu is available. *AA Hotel of the Year for The Republic of Ireland 2005-2006.*

OUR TIP: Pay a visit to the hermit's grotto

Chef: David McCann **Owners:** Earl of Thomond **Times:** 12.30-1.30/7-10, Closed L Mon-Sat **Notes:** Vegetarian available, Dress Restrictions, Jacket **Seats:** 80, Pr/dining room 40 **Smoking:** N/Sm in restaurant **Children:** Portions **Rooms:** 100 (100 en suite) ★★★★★ **Directions:** From Ennis take N18, follow signs for Shannon/Limerick. 7m follow Quin. Newmarket-on-Fergus sign. Hotel 0.5m. From Shannon take N18 towards Ennis **Parking:** 140 **e-mail:** sales@dromoland.ie **web:** www.dromoland.ie

---

CO CORK

BALLYCOTTON MAP 01 C2

Bay View

Irish

Accomplished cuisine in comfortable country house with dramatic sea views

☎ 021 4646746

MENU GUIDE Ketafi-wrapped Bay prawns with avocado & chilli salsa • Pan-fried John Dory, asparagus & saffron gnocchi • Warm walnut pudding & autumn berry compôte

WINE GUIDE ♀ Tulbach Sauvignon Blanc €24 • ♥ Tulbach Merlot €24 • 30 bottles over €30, 30 bottles under €30 • 4 by the glass

PRICE GUIDE Fixed L €28 • coffee €2.40 • min/water €5.60 Service optional

PLACE: The panoramic expanse of the dramatic Ballycotton Bay coastline is the breathtaking view from the dining rooms of this comfortable Cork country-house hotel, perched on a cliff edge.

FOOD: The well-constructed Irish menu states that the kitchen purchases only the best produce from Cork county and the back page lists all of the suppliers. Due to its location, seafood is

continued

Ireland

BALLYCOTTON *continued* MAP 01 C2

unsurprisingly a speciality but it doesn't dominate the menu that also makes good use of local meat. The chef's creative flair shines through in combinations which are not overfussy, allowing natural flavours to dominate.

OUR TIP: Pre-dinner drinks on the terrace
Chef: Ciaran Scully **Owners:** John & Carmel O'Brian **Times:** 1-2/7-9, Closed Nov-Apr, closed L Mon-Sat **Notes:** Fixed D 5 courses €47, Vegetarian available, Dress Restrictions, Smart casual **Seats:** 65, Pr/dining room 30 **Smoking:** N/Sm in restaurant **Children:** Portions **Rooms:** 35 (35 en suite) ★★★ **Directions:** At Castlemartyr on N25 (Cork-Waterford road) turn onto R632 to Garryvoe, then follow signs for Shanagarry & Ballycotton **Parking:** 40
e-mail: res@thebayviewhotel.com **web:** www.thebayviewhotel.com

BALLYLICKEY MAP 01 B2

 Sea View House

British, International

Enjoyable country-house dining in pretty garden restaurant

☎ 027 50073 & 50462

MENU GUIDE Warm scallop mousse, Vermouth sauce • Stuffed duckling, port & orange sauce • Brown bread ice cream, butterscotch sauce

WINE GUIDE ♀ Chardonnay • ♀ Chilean Merlot • 25 bottles over €30, 20 bottles under €30 • 10 by the glass (€4.50-€5.50)

PRICE GUIDE Fixed L €22-€25 • Fixed D €40-€42 • starter €5.50-€7.50 • main €22-€28 • dessert €5.50-€7.50 • min/water €3 • Group min 10 service 10%

PLACE: The restaurant of this friendly country-house hotel meanders through several rooms including a delightful octagonal conservatory, decorated in soft green shades to chime with the colourful garden outside. Fresh flowers, sparkling glasses and unclothed wooden tables complete the picture.
FOOD: Country-house cooking with an emphasis on quality local fish. The menu changes daily depending on what's available and often features Bantry Bay's delicious mussels and scallops, as well as meatier options such as supreme of corn-fed chicken or fillet steak garni. Lighter lunch options served in the bar.
OUR TIP: Enjoy a nightcap in the comfortable lounge after dinner
Chef: Eleanor O'Donavon **Owners:** Kathleen O'Sullivan **Times:** 12.30-1.45/7-9.30, Closed Nov-Mar, closed L Mon-Sat **Notes:** Coffee incl, Vegetarian available, Dress Restrictions, Smart casual **Seats:** 50 **Smoking:** N/Sm in restaurant **Children:** Menu, Portions **Rooms:** 25 (25 en suite) ★★★ **Directions:** 3m N of Bantry towards Glengarriff, 70 yds off main road **e-mail:** info@seaviewhousehotel.com **web:** www.seaviewhousehotel.com

BALTIMORE MAP 01 B1

⊚ *Baltimore Harbour Hotel*

Classic

Charming west-coast setting offering superb cuisine

☎ 028 20361

PLACE: A modern hotel in a charming village, with wonderful views across Baltimore harbour and the islands off the coast. The sunsets can be stunning.
FOOD: The very best of west Cork produce and seafood is sourced for the accomplished cooking in the Clipper restaurant.
OUR TIP: There is a comprehensive children's menu
Times: 6.30-9.30 **Rooms:** 64 (64 en suite) ★★★
e-mail: info@bhrhotel.ie

⊚ Casey's of Baltimore

Irish, Seafood

Friendly seaside hotel specialising in fish

☎ 028 20197

MENU GUIDE Baltimore pickled herrings, lemon dressing • Black sole on the bone • Apple pie & cream

WINE GUIDE ♀ Wolf Blass Chardonnay €22 • ♀ Wolf Blass Shiraz/Cabernet Sauvignon €24 • 4 bottles over €30, 20 bottles under €30 • 1 by the glass (€3.80)

PRICE GUIDE Fixed L €25 • Fixed D €35-€50 • starter €6.50-€14 • main €14-€45 • dessert €5.50 • coffee €1.60 • min/water €4 • Service optional

PLACE: Popular family-run hotel in the seaside village of Baltimore. After dinner, take a drink in the cosy bar where traditional folk music is played at weekends.
FOOD: Fish is the speciality here and it doesn't come fresher. Casey's kitchen takes its pick from the Baltimore fleet's daily catch and delivers simple but skilful seafood dishes, as well as locally farmed steaks and a vegetarian choice.
OUR TIP: Book ahead for a window table - the bay views are breathtaking
Chef: Victoria Gilshenan **Owners:** Ann & Michael Casey **Times:** 12.30-2.30/6.30-9, Closed 21-26 Dec **Notes:** Sun lunch menu available, Vegetarian available **Seats:** 100 **Smoking:** N/Sm in restaurant, Air con **Children:** Menu, Portions **Rooms:** 14 (14 en suite) ★★★
Directions: From Cork take N71 to Skibbereen, then take R595. Hotel is at entrance to village on right **Parking:** 40
e-mail: info@caseysofbaltimore.com **web:** www.caseysbaltimore.com

CLONAKILTY

⊚⊚ Inchydoney Island Lodge & Spa

Mediterranean, European   **NEW**

Fabulous location for coastal food and views

☎ 023 33143

MENU GUIDE Crabmeat tian, marinated tomato, guacamole • Pan-fried sea bass, stir-fry, teriyaki • Frangipane tart, maple & walnut ice cream

WINE GUIDE ♀ Neil Ellis Chardonnay €32 • ♀ Concha y Toro Cabernet Sauvignon €20 • 50 bottles over €30, 25 bottles under €30 • 4 by the glass (€6.50-€12.95)

PRICE GUIDE Starter €12 • main €30 • dessert €12 • min/water €4.95 • Service added 10%

PLACE: Spectacularly positioned hotel overlooking the Celtic sea, where the deep blues and golds of the restaurant decor reflect the ocean and the sandy beaches of its surroundings. Service is relaxed and diners are encouraged to take their time over their meal to enjoy both the food and the views.
FOOD: The five-course menu offers well-balanced dishes, including vegetarian options and lighter choices for those on a spa break. The emphasis is on the finest West Cork produce, organic where possible, with plenty of fresh seafood.
OUR TIP: Get a window table at sunset
Chef: Mark Kirby **Owners:** Des O'Dowd **Times:** 12-2/7-11, Closed 25-26 Dec, closed L Mon-Sat **Notes:** Coffee incl, Tasting menu available on request, Vegetarian available, Dress Restrictions, Smart casual **Seats:** 90, Pr/dining room 250 **Smoking:** N/Sm in restaurant, Air con **Children:** Menu, Portions **Rooms:** 67 (67 en suite) ★★★★
Directions: From Cork take N71 following 'West Cork' signs. Through Innishannon, Bandon & Clonakilty, then follow signs for Inchydoney Island **Parking:** 250 **e-mail:** reservations@inchydoneyisland.com **web:** www.inchydoneyisland.com

Ireland

CORK MAP 01 B2

⓪⓪ Hayfield Manor
French, Irish

Fine food in relaxed and elegant setting

☎ 021 4845900 Perrott Av, College Rd

MENU GUIDE Ballycotton salmon plate • Tournedos of beef, woodland mushroom sabayon, confit vegetables, Bercy sauce • Warm chocolate fondant

WINE GUIDE ⌾ Chablis 1er Cru €45 • ♥ Tullbach Merlot €34.30 • 103 bottles over €30 • 14 by the glass (€6.35-€10)

PRICE GUIDE Fixed L €25 • Fixed D €58 • min/water €6.10 • Group min 8 service 10%

PLACE: A 1920s house secluded in much older walled gardens, this delightful hotel has a tranquil atmosphere despite its city centre location. Double doors open into the Manor Room restaurant, with its classic columns, Dutch chandeliers and formal silver service creating a great sense of occasion, and French windows lead out to the garden.
FOOD: Accomplished cooking drawing on fine produce from the region's rich farmland, much of it organic. An imaginative approach is taken to dishes with both Irish and French influences and some quite elaborate combinations.
OUR TIP: Afternoon tea in the drawing room
Chef: James Rendell **Owners:** Mr J Scally **Times:** 12.30-2/7-10, Closed L Sat **Notes:** Tasting menu on request, Vegetarian available, Smart Dress **Seats:** 80, Pr/dining room 32 **Smoking:** N/Sm in restaurant, Air con **Children:** Menu, Portions **Rooms:** 88 (88 en suite) ★★★★
Directions: From Cork take N22 to Killarney. On Western Rd at University gates turn left into Donovan's Rd, then right into College Rd and immediately left into Perrott Ave **Parking:** 100
e-mail: reservations@hayfieldmanor.ie **web:** www.hayfieldmanor.ie

⓪ Maryborough House Hotel
Mediterranean, European   **NEW**

Grand hotel with wide-ranging menu

☎ 021 436 5555 Maryborough Hill

MENU GUIDE Game terrine, berry coulis • Chicken supreme, fennel & paprika pork sausage, pesto cream • Brambly apple Charlotte

WINE GUIDE ⌾ Jonkheer Chardonnay €22.50 • ♥ Jonkheer Pinotage €22.50 • 39 bottles over €30, 33 bottles under €30 • 4 by the glass (€5.20)

PRICE GUIDE Fixed L €18.50 • Fixed D €45 • starter €6.95-€14.25 • main €21.95-€29.95 • dessert €7.50 • coffee €2.50 min/water €2.35 • Service included • Group min 10 service 10%

PLACE: Dating from 1715, this imposing Georgian house has been sympathetically renovated and extended to form a luxurious hotel.
FOOD: A lengthy menu of contemporary cuisine offers plenty of tempting choices, from wild boar with mustard and apple mash to halibut with a risotto of mixed shellfish and lovage. Lighter meals available in the bar. Popular for dinner, so book ahead.
OUR TIP: Champagne afternoon tea
Chef: Gerry Allen **Owners:** Dan O'Sullivan **Times:** 12.30-2.30/6.30-10, Closed 24-26 Dec **Notes:** Vegetarian available, Smart Dress, Civ Wed 100 **Seats:** 120, Pr/dining room 60 **Smoking:** N/Sm in restaurant, Air con **Children:** Min 12 yrs not D, Menu, Portions **Parking:** 300
e-mail: info@maryborough.ie **web:** www.maryborough.com

⑨ **Café Paradiso** 16 Lancaster Quay, Western Rd
☎ 021 427 7939 Lively vegetarian with seasonal cooking.

⑨ **Jacobs** 30a South Mall ☎ 021 425 1530 Skill, creativity and top-notch ingredients in an easygoing setting.

⑨ **Jacques** Phoenix St ☎ 021 427 7387 Mediterranean style decor and food, with friendly service.

GARRYVOE MAP 01 C2

⓪ Garryvoe Hotel
Irish

Seaside dining

☎ 021 4646718 Ballyrotton Bay, Castlemartyr

MENU GUIDE Prawn cocktail • Fresh Ballycotton plaice • Squidgy chocolate log

WINE GUIDE • 15 bottles over €30, 25 bottles under €30 2 by the glass (€4)

PRICE GUIDE Fixed L €20-€22 • Fixed D €35 • starter €5.20-€11 • main €17-€25 • dessert €5 • coffee €2 • min/water €2.20 • Service optional

PLACE: Big changes have been planned for the Garryvoe for 2005. A completely new feel to its Ocean restaurant combining modern and classic decor is planned.
FOOD: Irish country cooking with locally caught fish a feature. Dishes might include baked hake with a chunky tomato and basil sauce or pan-fried swordfish with a sweet chilli salsa.
OUR TIP: Watch out for the new location
Chef: Phillip Villiard **Owners:** Carmel & John O'Brian **Times:** 1-2.30/6.45-8.45, Closed 24-25 Dec, closed D 24 Dec **Notes:** Vegetarian available **Seats:** 80, Pr/dining room 40 **Smoking:** N/Sm in restaurant **Children:** Menu, Portions **Rooms:** 38 (47 en suite) ★★
Directions: From N25 at Castlemartyr (Cork-Rosslare rd) take R632 to Garryvoe **Parking:** 80 **e-mail:** res@garryvoehotel.com
web: www.garryvoehotel.com

KINSALE MAP 01 B2

⓪ Actons Hotel
European

Waterfront hotel with a wide-ranging menu

☎ 021 4772135 Pier Rd

MENU GUIDE King prawns, garlic & dill butter sauce • Steamed seafood platter • Chocolate bread & butter pudding

WINE GUIDE 26 bottles over €30, 34 bottles under €30

PRICE GUIDE Fixed L €20 • Fixed D €35-€40 • starter €7-€9.30 • main €17.50-€35 • dessert €4-€7.50 • coffee €1.75 • min/water €6.50 • Service included

PLACE: This established modern hotel overlooks Kinsale's bustling harbour, occupying several Georgian townhouses on the waterfront. Drinks and light meals are served in the bar and adjacent garden when weather permits, while more formal fare is available in the Captain's Table restaurant - a bright, contemporary nautical themed room with polished tables and crisp linen.

continued

KINSALE *continued* MAP 01 B2

FOOD: A lengthy European and modern Irish menu offers plenty of choice, including steaks as well as more elaborate dishes. Seafood is a speciality.
OUR TIP: The hotel has an impressive health and fitness club
Chef: Paul McBride **Owners:** Candela Ltd **Times:** 12.30-3/7-9.45, Closed Xmas & Jan, closed L Mon-Sat **Notes:** Vegetarian available, Smart Dress **Seats:** 80 **Smoking:** N/Sm in restaurant, Air con
Children: Menu, Portions **Rooms:** 76 (76 en suite) ★★★ **Parking:** 60
e-mail: info@actonshotelkinsale.com
web: www.actonshotelkinsale.com

⚜ Trident Hotel
Modern European
Harbourside dining
☎ 021 4772301 Worlds End
PLACE: Set in this hotel, which is currently being extended, the attractive harbourside restaurant occupies one wing of a 17th-century corn store with views across to Scilly and Summercove.
FOOD: The carte menu offers good range for each course. The best of local produce, especially seafood, is used to create dishes with a modern European edge.
OUR TIP: Particularly good range of desserts
Times: 1-2.30/7-9, Closed L Mon-Sat, 24-26 Dec **Rooms:** 58 (58 en suite) ★★★ **e-mail:** info@tridenthotel.com
web: www.tridenthotel.com

⚜ **Fishy Fishy Café** Guardwell ☎ 021 477 4453
Seafood café serving the freshest of fish.

MACROOM MAP 01 B2
⚜ Castle Hotel
European
Popular market-town hotel
☎ 026 41074 Main St
MENU GUIDE Smoked salmon, pickled cucumber • Chicken supreme filled with goats' cheese • Tiramisù
WINE GUIDE ♀ Klein River Chenin Blanc €18.25 • ♀ Copperidge Zinfandel €18.25 • 2 bottles over €30, 10 bottles under €30
PRICE GUIDE Fixed L €25-€30 • Fixed D €35-€45 • starter €5.50-€10 • main €19-€28.50 • dessert €5.50-€6.50 • coffee €2 • min/water €2 • Service included
PLACE: A friendly town-centre hotel offering a café and bar for light snacks, and a split-level, bistro-style restaurant for more upmarket fare.
FOOD: The freshest of local produce boost a traditional and modern menu with mains along the lines of local steak with garlic butter, or grilled fillet of John Dory on a bed of spinach. Efficient, friendly and attentive service.
OUR TIP: Handy car park behind the hotel
Chef: Pat Ryan **Owners:** The Buckley Family **Times:** 12-3/6-9.30, Closed 25 Dec **Notes:** Vegetarian available **Seats:** 50, Pr/dining room 150
Smoking: N/Sm in restaurant, Air con **Children:** Menu, Portions
Rooms: 60 (60 en suite) ★★★ **Directions:** On N22, midway between Cork and Killarney **Parking:** 30 **e-mail:** castlehotel@eircom.net
web: www.castlehotel.ie

MALLOW MAP 01 B2
⚜⚜⚜ Longueville House *see below*

Longueville House

French
Charming Georgian manor house
☎ 022 47156 & 47306
MENU GUIDE Prawn ravioli, leek duxelles, sorrel dressing • Roast pork loin, artichoke mousse, Szechuan pepper jus • Hot praline fondant
WINE GUIDE ♀ Staete Landt Sauvignon Blanc €42 • ♀ Domaine de Chaintreuil Fleurie €44 • 100 bottles over €30, 7 bottles under €30 • 4 by the glass €6-€6.50
PRICE GUIDE Fixed L €30-€55 • Fixed D €55 • coffee €2.80 • min/water €4.50 • Service optional • Group min 8 service 10%
PLACE: Dating from 1720, Longueville is a splendid example of a classic Georgian manor house, full of charm and set in a 500-acre estate of romantic woodlands, walled gardens and parkland. The Turner conservatory dining room has an elegant and romantic feel with white drapes, candlelight and delicate flowers, while the Presidents dining room is lined with portraits of former Irish presidents.

FOOD: Menus reflect the kitchen's understandable enthusiasm for the top quality produce that is supplied by the estate's own farm, river and garden. It is used with great skill and flair in a predominantly classical French style of cooking. Modern creations such as spiced monkfish with chorizo couscous and chervil sauce appear alongside more traditional cooking like roast beef sirloin with smoked bacon and onion cake, mushrooms and horseradish.
OUR TIP: A perfect romantic evening venue
Chef: William O'Callaghan **Owners:** The O'Callaghan Family
Times: 12.30-5/6.30-9, Closed 8 Jan-17 Mar **Notes:** Set price D 4 courses, Tasting menu 8 courses €80, Vegetarian available, Smart dress preferred **Seats:** 100, Pr/dining room 18 **Smoking:** N/Sm in restaurant
Children: Menu, Portions **Rooms:** 20 (20 en suite) ★★★
Directions: 3m W of Mallow via N72 to Killarney, right at Ballyclough junct, hotel 200 yds on left **Parking:** 35
e-mail: info@longuevillehouse.ie **web:** www.longuevillehouse.ie

YOUGHAL

🏵 Ahernes

Modern Irish 🐟➻**NEW**

Enjoyable seafood dining in historic Irish port

☎ 024 92424 163 North Main St

MENU GUIDE Prawns in garlic butter • Youghal Bay lobster • Almond & pear flan

PRICE GUIDE Food prices not confirmed for 2006. Please telephone for details

PLACE: This long established family-owned restaurant with accommodation is situated in the southern Irish Heritage port of Youghal. There are a dozen enchanting rooms and suites each decorated to a high standard. There's also a lively bar.

FOOD: With its seaport location, it's no surprise that fish is the speciality here. A dedicated kitchen team prepares traditional and modern Irish takes on local scallops, John Dory and turbot.

OUR TIP: A great base for exploring the southern Irish coast

Chef: Mr D Fitzgibbon **Owners:** The Fitzgibbon Family

Times: Telephone for details **Notes:** Smart Dress **Seats:** 60, Pr/dining room 20 **Smoking:** N/Sm in restaurant **Children:** Portions **Rooms:** 13 (13 en suite) **Parking:** 20 **e-mail:** ahernes@eircom.net

web: www.ahernes.com

CO DONEGAL

DONEGAL MAP 01 B5

🏵🏵 Harvey's Point Country Hotel

French, Mediterranean

Sound cooking in lakeside setting

☎ 074 9722208 Lough Eske

MENU GUIDE Scallop feuilleté, asparagus cream sauce • Lamb, vegetable tian, rosemary jus • Orange chantclaire, Grand Marnier syrup

WINE GUIDE ♀ Touraine Domaine Bellevue €22 ♀ Casablanca Carmenere €29 • 62 bottles over €30, 42 bottles under €30 • 8 by the glass

PRICE GUIDE Fixed L €29 • Fixed D €50 • starter €7-€15 • main €17-€30 • dessert €5-€10 • coffee €2 • min/water €3.90 Service included

PLACE: Beautifully set in a lakeside clearing, this country hotel is an elegant dinner venue. Aperitifs are served by a cosy turf fire, while the restaurant offers stunning views across Lough Eske.

FOOD: A blend of quality local Irish ingredients with French techniques; expect assured and accurate cooking, with sauces a particular strength. The wine list is similarly Gallic and features a good range of champagnes.

OUR TIP: Crowd-pleasing buffet served Sunday lunchtimes

Chef: Frank Pasquier **Owners:** Marc Gysling, Deirdre McGlone

Times: 12.30-2.30/6.30-9.30, Closed Mon-Tue (Nov-Easter), closed D Sun **Notes:** Vegetarian available **Seats:** 100, Pr/dining room 100

Smoking: N/Sm in restaurant, Air con **Children:** Min 12 yrs **Rooms:** 20 (20 en suite) ★★★ **Directions:** 6km from Donegal **Parking:** 200

e-mail: info@harveyspoint.com **web:** www.harveyspoint.com

LETTERKENNY MAP 01 C5

🏵 Castle Grove Country House

Irish

Accomplished cooking in Georgian elegance

☎ 074 9151118 Castlegrove, Ballymaleel

PLACE: Approached by a mile-long avenue, the gracious Castle Grove is a fine example of Georgian country-house architecture set in its own parkland estate, overlooking Lough Swilly.

FOOD: The Abbey Restaurant offers accomplished cooking with a choice of wide-ranging menus. Local produce is very much to the fore.

OUR TIP: Take a walk in the grounds

Times: 12/6, Closed Sun (Nov-Mar), 22-30 Dec **Rooms:** 15 (15 en suite) ★★★ **e-mail:** marytsweeney@hotmail.com

web: www.castlegrove.com

CO DUBLIN

DUBLIN MAP 01 D4

🏵🏵 The Clarence

European, Irish 🐟➻🍴

Designer hotel with distinctive ballroom restaurant

☎ 01 4070800 6-8 Wellington Quay D2

MENU GUIDE Brochette of monkfish & prawns, sweet & sour tomatoes • Navarin of lamb, creamed potatoes, root vegetables • Pear & raisin clafoutis, lemon sorbet

continued

continued

Ireland

DUBLIN continued **MAP 01 D4**

WINE GUIDE ♀ Sherwood Sauvignon Blanc €38.50 • ♀ Hollick Cabernet Sauvignon/Merlot €38.55 • 192 bottles over €30, 8 bottles under €30 • 15 by the glass (€7-€16)

PRICE GUIDE Fixed L €26 • Fixed D €55 • coffee €3.30 min/water €4.95 • Service optional • Group service 12.5%

PLACE: Situated on Dublin's 'left bank' overlooking the River Luffey, U2's Bono and The Edge have brought a cool, contemporary look to this classic 19th-century hotel. The lofty Tea Room restaurant, originally the ballroom, evokes the best of old and modern in its elegantly simple setting, flooded with natural light from huge windows. A serious but relaxed atmosphere provides a sophisticated setting and opportunities for some great people-watching.
FOOD: The appealing, daily changing, fixed-price modern menus suit the ambience and hit all the right notes, and are based on high quality Irish produce, enhanced by a fashionable European theme.
OUR TIP: Valet parking available after 10am; the famous Octagonal Bar is here also
Chef: Antony Ely **Owners:** Bono & The Edge **Times:** 12.30-2.30/6.30-10.30, Closed 25-26 Dec, closed L Sat **Notes:** Tasting menu €65, Sun L €34.50, Vegetarian available, Dress Restrictions, Smart casual **Seats:** 80, Pr/dining room 16 **Smoking:** N/Sm in restaurant **Children:** Portions **Rooms:** 50 (50 en suite) ★★★★ **Directions:** From O'Connell Bridge, proceed W along quays **Parking:** Valet Parking
e-mail: reservations@theclarence.ie **web:** www.theclarence.ie

⊛ Clarion Hotel Dublin IFSC
Modern Irish
Sophisticated corporate hotel with a straightforward approach
☎ 01 353 433 8800 I.F.S.C
MENU GUIDE Leek & goats' cheese tart • Risotto, black pudding, blue cheese, bacon lardons • Bread & butter pudding
WINE GUIDE ♀ Fox Wood Chardonnay €23 • ♀ Four Sisters Shiraz €28 • 10 bottles over €30, 15 bottles under €30 • 14 by the glass (€5-€9.50)
PRICE GUIDE Fixed L €15-€25 • Fixed D €24.50-€60 • starter €5.50-€8 • main €18-€28 • dessert €5.50-€6.50 • coffee €2.50 • min/water €3.60 • Service optional
PLACE: In the heart of Dublin's financial area, this bright and bustling hotel eaterie caters to a mix of residents and suits. It's a smart setting with minimalist glass walls, solid oak tables clothed with white linen, and a pleasantly casual feel.
FOOD: Expect straightforward Irish and European dishes distinguished by good ingredients and clear flavours: pan-seared duck with an orange and rocket salad perhaps, or fillet steak with chunky chips.
OUR TIP: Good setting for business meetings
Chef: Andrew O'Gorman **Owners:** Giacomo Ltd **Times:** 12-2.30/6-11, Closed 24-26 Dec, closed L Sat & Sun **Notes:** Pre-theatre menu 2 courses £19.95, 3 courses £24.95, Vegetarian available, Dress Restrictions, Smart casual preferred **Seats:** 94, Pr/dining room 80 **Smoking:** N/Sm in restaurant, Air con **Children:** Menu, Portions **Rooms:** 147 (147 en suite) ★★★★ **Directions:** Financial Services Centre **Parking:** 40
e-mail: sinergie@clarionhotelifsc.com **web:** www.clarionhotelifsc.com

⊛ Finnstown Country House
International
Country retreat with a warm welcome and accurate cooking
☎ 01 6010700 Newcastle Rd

continued

MENU GUIDE Stuffed green lip mussels • Loin of venison, juniper infused red wine jus • Lemon tart, strawberry ice cream
PRICE GUIDE Fixed L €19 • Fixed D €36 • starter €5-€11 • main €18-€30 • dessert €6.50
PLACE: Close to the village of Lucan, west of Dublin, this peaceful house is set in 45 acres of woodland. The dining room has original Victorian features and an open fire.
FOOD: Choose from the traditional carte or the daily changing fixed-price menu, both of which offer a good choice of seasonal dishes. Lunch is a little less formal, and there's a very popular buffet on Sundays. Cooking is straightforward and successful.
OUR TIP: Ask for a table in the front room
Chef: Steve McPhillips **Owners:** Eoin & Nora Hickey **Times:** 12.30-2.30/7.30-9.30, Closed Sun (buffet only 1-5pm) **Notes:** Civ Wed 200 **Seats:** 80 **Smoking:** N/Sm in restaurant **Rooms:** 53 (53 en suite) ★★★ **Directions:** From M1 take 1st exit onto M50 southbound. 1st exit after Toll Bridge. Take 3rd left (N4 W). Left at lights. Over next 2 rbts, hotel on right **Parking:** 150 **e-mail:** manager@finnstown-hotel.ie **web:** www.finnstown-hotel.ie

⊛⊛ The Fitzwilliam Hotel, Citron Restaurant
Mediterranean, European   **NEW**
Contemporary and stylish hotel dining with intense flavours
☎ 01 4787000 St Stephen's Green
MENU GUIDE Roast quail with brioche, white onion purée, morel sauce • Fillet of wild sea bass with fennel & herb risotto, squid ink sauce • Warm chocolate tartlet with crème anglaise, fresh raspberries
PRICE GUIDE Fixed L €25-€35 • Fixed D €45-€65 • starter €8-€14 • main €20-€30 • dessert €8-€10 • coffee €2 • min/water €6 • Service optional
PLACE: A first floor, stand-alone restaurant in the Fitzwilliam Hotel, with great views over St Stephen's Green. The atmospheric restaurant is luxuriously decorated in shades of gold and cream, with a gilded ceiling.
FOOD: Well presented dishes prepared from great Irish ingredients show real concern for seasonality. This is serious, considered cooking, and the signature dishes, such as roast suckling pig with poitin sauce, are very popular.
OUR TIP: Lunch is great value
Chef: Daniel McHews **Times:** 12-2.30/6-10.30 **Seats:** 70, Pr/dining room 60 **Smoking:** N/Sm in restaurant, Air con **Children:** Menu, Portions **Directions:** Overlooking St Stephens Green **Parking:** 80
e-mail: enq@fitzwilliam-hotel.com **web:** www.fitzwilliam-hotel.com

⊛⊛ The Herbert Park
Mediterranean, International
Modern hotel, international cooking, Irish hospitality
☎ 01 6672200 Ballsbridge
MENU GUIDE Thai chicken salad • Beef fillet, pea mash, chocolate jus • Mocha coffee parfait
WINE GUIDE ♀ Rosario Estate Chardonnay €21 • ♀ Rosario Estate Merlot €21 • 20 bottles over €30, 29 bottles under €30
PRICE GUIDE Fixed L €19.75 • Fixed D €45 • starter €7.50-€12.40 • main €19.50-€39.50 • dessert €7-€9 • coffee €4.75 • min/water €5.70 • Service optional
PLACE: A purpose-built luxury hotel in an exclusive area of Dublin. The Pavilion restaurant, with glass all round, has a spacious, airy atmosphere and enjoys wonderful views over the 48-acre Herbert Park. Service is friendly and professional.

continued

FOOD: The Head Chef hails from South Africa, which accounts for the modern cooking style, popular international dishes and Asian flavours. But there's also a typically Irish feel in the fine local produce such as seafood from Howth and Kildare lamb. **OUR TIP:** Secure underground parking **Times:** 12.30-2.30/5.30-9.30, Closed 25-26 Dec, closed D Sun-Mon & BHs **Owners:** Herbert Park Hotel Ltd **Chef:** Henry Jonkers **Notes:** Sun Jazz Buffet L £35, Vegetarian available **Seats:** 120 **Smoking:** N/Sm in restaurant, Air con **Children:** Menu, Portions **Rooms:** 153 (153 en suite) ★★★★ **Directions:** 5 mins from city centre. S over canal into Northumberland Rd to Ballsbridge. Turn right cross bridge in Ballsbridge, first right down Anglesea Rd **Parking:** 80 **e-mail:** reservations@herbertparkhotel.ie **web:** www.herbertparkhotel.ie

⊚ *Jurys Hotel & Towers*

International

Modern hotel dining with attitude

☎ 01 6605000 Pembroke Rd, Ballsbridge

PLACE: This establishment has two identities - Jurys Hotel and the more recently opened Towers Building, which offers a choice of venues for drinking and dining. Service is helpful and friendly. **FOOD:** The head chef is proving his impressive track record by serving simple meals made from quality ingredients. Lots of good, fresh, local produce on the menu of mainly modern dishes with International influences. **OUR TIP:** Extensive buffet on Sundays **Times:** 12.15-2.15/6.15-10.15 **Rooms:** 303 (303 en suite) ★★★★ **e-mail:** ballsbridge_hotel@jurysdoyle.com **web:** www.jurysdoyle.com

⊚⊚ *The Morrison Hotel*

Modern International

Luxurious city-centre hotel with great visual impact

☎ 01 8872400 Lower Ormond Quay

PLACE: Stunning contemporary hotel designed by Douglas Wallace and John Rocha, and filled with original artwork by Clea Van der Grjin. It incorporates the façade of a Georgian townhouse and stands in the centre of the city overlooking the River Liffey. Choices for dining are the light-flooded Café Bar at the front of the hotel or the fine dining Halò Restaurant, with its high ceilings, fabulous staircase and sophisticated ambience. **FOOD:** A dinner carte and short fixed-price menu deliver beautifully presented dishes created from the best of Irish produce. **OUR TIP:** Good value special dinner Sunday to Thursday **Times:** 12.30-2.30/7-9.30, Closed 25-26 Dec **Rooms:** 94 (94 en suite) ★★★★ **e-mail:** info@morrisonhotel.ie **web:** www.morrisonhotel.ie

⊚⊚⊚⊚ Restaurant Patrick Guilbaud *see page 670*

⊚ *The Shelbourne*

European, Irish **NEW**

The Grande Dame of Dublin hotels

☎ 01 6634500 27 St Stephen's Green

PLACE: Having come under the Marriott fold, and currently undergoing a renovation programme which will culminate in a complete revamp both in decor and in the kitchen, The Shelbourne still retains its position as the timelessly elegant Georgian Dublin landmark it has held since 1824. **FOOD:** Mostly locally sourced ingredients accurately and simply cooked to best effect. The menu is interesting and can spring

delightful surprises like pan-fried sea bass, orange braised fennel and pak choi. **OUR TIP:** Quite an extensive wine cellar **Times:** 12.30/7, Closed L Sat, Mon-Tue **Rooms:** 190 (190 en suite) **web:** www.shelbourne.ie

⊚ *Stillorgan Park Hotel*

French, International **NEW**

Modern hotel with contemporary menu

☎ 01 2881621 Stillorgan Rd

PLACE: A thoroughly modern hotel located on the southern outskirts of the city. Relax in the inviting bar before moving to the contemporary dining room. Service is pleasant and attentive. **FOOD:** Modern cooking, demonstrating a consistent level of skill and accuracy. From a starter of fresh plump scallops, seared and accurately caramelised, to desserts such as dark chocolate and Cointreau bavarois nicely contrasted with orange conserve, dishes are balanced and well presented. **OUR TIP:** Good value early bird deal **Times:** Telephone for details **e-mail:** sales@stillorganpark.com **web:** www.stillorganpark.com

⊚ **Chapter One** 18/19 Parnell Square ☎ 01 873 2266 Modern twists to consistently excellent classic French cooking.

⊚ **Jacob's Ladder** 4 Nassau St ☎ 01 670 3865 Punchy modern food with an emphasis on healthy eating.

⊚ **l'Ecrivain** 109a Lower Baggot St ☎ 01 661 1919 Fine French cuisine and an admirable wine list.

⊚ **Les Frères Jacques** 74 Dame St ☎ 01 679 4555 French classic cooking with an emphasis on seafood.

⊚ **Mermaid Café** 69-70 Dame St ☎ 01 670 8236 Californian style with lovely food at this bustling venue.

⊚ **O'Connell's** Bewleys Hotel, Merrion Rd ☎ 01 647 3304 Carefully sourced contemporary cooking making the most of local produce.

⊚ **One Pico** 5-6 Molesworth Place, School House Ln ☎ 01 676 0300 Sophisticated and ambitious cuisine in stylish surrounds.

⊚ **Roly's Bistro** 7 Ballsbridge Ter ☎ 01 668 2611 Buzzing bistro with robust retro cooking.

PORTMARNOCK MAP 01 D4

⊚⊚ **Portmarnock Hotel**

Modern European

Fine cuisine beside the sea

☎ 01 8460611 Strand Rd

MENU GUIDE Ravioli of king scallops • Balsamic roast leg of lamb • Raspberry delice

WINE GUIDE ♀ Groot Constantia €36.50 • ♥ Tanca Ferra €36.50 69 bottles over €30, 16 bottles under €30 • 4 by the glass (€4.95)

PRICE GUIDE Starter €13.95-€20 • main €25.90-€29.95 • dessert €9.50-€13.50 • Service included

PLACE: Formerly the home of the Jameson whiskey family, this 19th-century house overlooks the sea and the PGA Championship Golf Links. The formal Osborne Restaurant is beside the garden, and the friendly staff go out of their way for diners.

continued

continued

Ireland

Restaurant Patrick Guilbaud

French
Ireland's finest restaurant
☎ 01 6764192 Merrion Hotel, 21 Upper Merrion St 2
e-mail: restaurantpatrickguilbaud@eircom.net
web: www.restaurantpatrickguilbaud.ie

PLACE: The city's eponymous temple of gastronomy, serving a sophisticated clientele, is fittingly set in the opulent Georgian splendour of the Merrion Hotel - a gracious terrace of buildings reputedly the birthplace of the Duke of Wellington - located on the wide boulevard-like Upper Merrion Street. Though Restaurant Patrick Guilbaud has its own independent entrance and reception, it can also be accessed via the hotel lobby. The contemporary-styled dining room is a generous size; light, airy and elegant with a serious collection of modern Irish art, profusion of glass and fronds of greenery. The high-domed ceiling gives a feeling of space and there are views over the landscaped inner-courtyard - perfect for fair-weather dining. Walls and ceilings are white, immaculate napery gracing well-spaced tables follows suit, while professional yet friendly service is delivered by an impeccable brigade of waiting staff. There's a smart bar/lounge up front, while a suitably impressive, French-influenced wine list offers the perfect partnership.

FOOD: Patrick Guilbaud's style is modern-focused, underpinned by a classical French theme, utilising the best of Irish produce in season and comes dotted with a wish-list of luxury items. And, though the technique may be rooted in Gallic tradition, there's plenty of sophisticated innovation and flair. The approach is via an array of appealing menus with detailed dish descriptions that promote an agony of choice, including a daily changing fixed-price lunch, extensive carte (including a vegetarian offering) and a nine-course Sea & Land tasting option (an innovative take on traditional Irish dishes with names like oyster & brown bread, Molly Malone's cockles & mussels, cod & mushy peas, Irish whiskey, or autumn apple). Peripherals like canapés, amuse bouche, pre-dessert and petits fours are equally impressive.

MENU GUIDE Scallops, chicory marmalade, endive salad, black truffle dressing • Squab, Savoy cabbage, pan-fried foie gras, mead & almond jus • Rum baba

WINE GUIDE ♀ Henry Natter Sancerre Sauvignon Blanc €49 • ♀ Bouissiere Gigondas Grenache €56 60 bottles over €30 • 10 by the glass (€7-€12)

PRICE GUIDE Fixed L €33 • starter €24-€42 • main €45-€55 • dessert €18-€25 • coffee €8 • min/water €6 • Service optional

OUR TIP: Great value lunch menu at this level (Tue - Fri)

Chef: Guillaume Lebrun **Owners:** Patrick Guilbaud
Times: 12.30-2.15/7-10.15, Closed 25 Dec, 1st wk Jan, Sun-Mon
Notes: Tasting Menu €130, Vegetarian available, Smart Dress
Seats: 80, Pr/dining room 25 **Smoking:** N/Sm in restaurant, Air con **Children:** Portions **Rooms:** 145 (145 en suite) ★★★★★
Directions: Opposite Government Buildings **Parking:** Parking in Square

Ireland

PORTMARNOCK *continued* MAP 01 D4

FOOD: Excellent quality raw ingredients are carefully prepared and cooked accurately. Choose from the carte or the daily changing fixed-price menus, which reflect all that is best of the current season, particularly fresh seafood from the nearby fishing village of Howth.
OUR TIP: Great for seafood
Chef: Mark Doe **Owners:** Natworth Ltd **Times:** 7-10, Closed Sun-Mon, closed L all wk **Notes:** Vegetarian available, Neat casual **Seats:** 80, Pr/dining room 24 **Smoking:** N/Sm in restaurant, Air con **Children:** Portions **Rooms:** 99 (99 en suite) ★★★★
Directions: Follow N1 towards Drogheda. At junct with R601 turn to Malahide. 2m turn left at T-junct, through Malahide & 2.2m hotel on left. Off M1 take Malahide junct, then on to Portmarnock **Parking:** 200
e-mail: sales@portmarnock.com **web:** www.portmarnock.com

SKERRIES

 Redbank House & Restaurant
Progressive Irish 🐟 ⌂ ﹁**NEW**
Popular seafood restaurant in former bank premises
☎ 01 8491005 8490439 5-7 Church St
MENU GUIDE Razor fish 'Cardy Rocks' • Rock Pollock Milberton with rosemary, crabapple & horseradish sauce • Almond & berry flan
WINE GUIDE ♀ Chardonnay €20 • ♂ Quatre Saisons Shiraz €20 50 bottles over €30, 20 bottles under €30 • 6 by the glass (€5)
PRICE GUIDE Fixed D €45 • starter €8-€16.50 • main €18-€32 dessert €10 • coffee €3 • min/water €3.50 • Service included
PLACE: Restaurant housed in a converted bank - a listed building - where the old vaults are usefully employed to guard the wine collection.
FOOD: Spanking fresh seafood straight from the trawler, offered from a range of menus to suit all tastes and budgets, matched with carefully sourced local produce. Horseradish, wild samphire and nettles all make an appearance, together with black pudding from the nearby butchers and farmhouse cheeses.
OUR TIP: Leave room for something from the dessert trolley
Chef: Terry McCoy **Owners:** Terry McCoy **Times:** 12.30-4.30/6-10, Closed 24-26 Dec, closed L Mon-Fri, closed D Sun **Notes:** Fixed L 4 courses £19.75, Vegetarian available, Dress Restrictions, Smart casual **Seats:** 60, Pr/dining room 10 **Smoking:** N/Sm in restaurant **Rooms:** 12 (12 en suite) 🏠 **Directions:** From Dublin, M1 N to Lissenhall interchange, take exit to Skerries **Parking:** On street
e-mail: info@redbank.ie **web:** www.rebank.ie

CO GALWAY

CASHEL MAP 01 A4

🌸🌸 Cashel House
British, European 🐟
Refined and classic dining in garden conservatory
☎ 095 31001
MENU GUIDE Warm parcel of quail & smoked duck • Roast crown of pork, caramelised apples • Sticky toffee pudding
WINE GUIDE ♀ Château Bonnet €24 • ♂ Château la Marche €24 30 bottles over €30, 65 bottles under €30 • 4 by the glass (€5.60)
PRICE GUIDE Fixed D €47-€49 • starter €9.95-€12.95 • main €28-€29 • dessert €11 • coffee €3.30 • min/water €5.95 Service added 12.5%

PLACE: A beautiful early Victorian country-house at the head of Cashel Bay on the Atlantic coast in Galway. The friendly and dedicated family-led team ensures the highest standards of hospitality and comfort. Quietly secluded, with 50 acres of award-winning gardens, this is where General de Gaulle and his wife once spent a holiday.
FOOD: The fixed-price dinner carte reflects the superb quality of seafood from the bay, including lobster, mussels, clams, scallops and salmon. Succulent Connemara lamb is served with a wide variety of fresh vegetables straight from the hotel's own gardens.
OUR TIP: Seashore and woodland walks
Chef: Arturo Amit **Owners:** Dermot & Kay McEvilly & family **Times:** 12.30-2.30/7-8.30, Closed 6 Jan-6 Feb **Notes:** Vegetarian available, Smart casual **Seats:** 70 **Smoking:** N/Sm in restaurant **Children:** Min 5 yrs, Menu, Portions **Rooms:** 32 (32 en suite) ★★★
Directions: S of N59. 1m W of Recess **Parking:** 30
e-mail: info@cashel-house-hotel.com
web: www.cashel-house-hotel.com

🌸🌸 Zetland Country House
European 🐟
Sea views and modern European food in refined setting
☎ 095 31111 Cashel Bay
MENU GUIDE Potato ravioli • Chargrilled rump of lamb, goats' cheese & potato mousse • Warm dark chocolate fondant
WINE GUIDE ♀ Chardonnay €27 • ♂ Syrah €27 • 25 bottles over €30, 14 bottles under €30 • 4 by the glass (€5-€8)
PRICE GUIDE Fixed L €21.50-€40 • Fixed D €49.50 • coffee €2.50 • min/water €4.95 • Service added but optional 12.5%
PLACE: An elegant country-house restaurant with dramatic sea views. Built as a sporting lodge in the 19th century, it retains a refined air, with antique plates and highly polished silver decorating the dining room.
FOOD: The kitchen makes good use of seasonal produce with many of the herbs coming from the well-tended garden. Expect creative, modern cooking with a strong European influence, with clear flavours shining through.
OUR TIP: Lobster from the sea tank is a speciality
Chef: Richard Hart **Owners:** Ruaidhri Prendergast **Times:** 12-2/7-8.30, Closed D Sun (winter) **Notes:** 5-course D £49.50, Vegetarian available, Smart Dress **Seats:** 75, Pr/dining room 20 **Smoking:** N/Sm in restaurant **Children:** Portions **Rooms:** 19 (19 en suite) ★★★ **Directions:** N59 from Galway towards Clifden, turn right after Recess onto R340, after approx 4m turn left onto R341, hotel 1m on right **Parking:** 40
e-mail: zetland@iol.ie **web:** www.zetland.com

CLIFDEN MAP 01 A4

🌸 Abbeyglen Castle Hotel
French, International
Elegant setting for dinner, country-house style
☎ 095 21201 Sky Rd
MENU GUIDE Baked seafood parcels • Fillets of beef Wellington • Warm chocolate bread & butter pudding
WINE GUIDE ♀ Montana Sauvignon Blanc €24.95 • ♂ Rosemont Shiraz €25 • 40 bottles over €30, 4 bottles under €30 • 4 by the glass (€4.90-€5.50)
PRICE GUIDE Fixed D €40 • starter €6-€10.50 • main €18.50-€34 dessert €6.50 • coffee €2 • min/water €5 • Service added 12.5%
PLACE: Relaxed fine dining at this 19th-century country house, to the accompaniment of live piano music. Friendly formal service is provided in the dining room, overlooking the landscaped

continued

continued

Ireland

CLIFDEN continued MAP 01 A4

grounds. All residents dine in-house so reservations are essential for non-residents.

FOOD: Simple treatment of prime produce, much of which is sourced locally. The daily changing menu offers Connemara lamb and fish, plus a tempting selection of seafood, and sizeable salad and dessert buffets.

OUR TIP: The kitchen will prepare any fish caught by guests **Chef:** Kevin Conroy **Owners:** Mr P Hughes **Times:** 7.15-9, Closed 6 Jan-1 Feb, closed L Mon-Sun **Notes:** Vegetarian available **Seats:** 75 **Smoking:** N/Sm in restaurant **Children:** Min 12 yrs **Rooms:** 44 (44 en suite) ★★★★ **Directions:** From Galway take N59 to Clifden. Hotel 0.6m on the Sky Road **Parking:** 40 **e-mail:** info@abbeyglen.ie **web:** www.abbeyglen.ie

Ardagh Hotel

Mediterranean, European

Enjoyable dining in stunning waterside setting
☎ 095 21384 Ballyconneely Rd

MENU GUIDE Lamb sweetbreads, mushroom feuilletage • Sole, citrus & chive butter • Yoghurt ice cream, forest fruits

WINE GUIDE ♀ Thelema Sauvignon Blanc €45.50 • ♥ Le Maine Bordeaux €32 • 48 bottles over €30, 13 bottles under €30 • 2 by the glass (€5.50)

PRICE GUIDE Fixed D €49.50 • starter €6-€15 • main €10-€40 dessert €7.50 • coffee €2.50 • min/water €4.95 • Service optional

PLACE: This quiet owner/chef-run hotel situated at the head of Ardbear Bay is in the scenic heart of Connemara. Its modern exterior hides a wealth of traditional interior features such as real fires, exposed beams and comfy sofas. The restaurant with its quarry-tiled floor, yellow walls and pine furniture has a cheerful, bright, Mediterranean feel.

FOOD: Locally caught seafood and home-grown produce feature strongly on the eclectic and lengthy menus. The style of cooking is modern European with lots of Mediterranean and Asian flavours making an appearance.

OUR TIP: A good base for Connemara Pony Show in August **Chef:** C Curran, M Bauvet **Owners:** S & M Bauvet **Times:** 7.15-9.30, Closed end Nov-end Mar **Notes:** Vegetarian available, Dress Restrictions, Smart casual. No shorts or trainers **Seats:** 50 **Smoking:** N/Sm in restaurant **Children:** Menu, Portions **Rooms:** 19 (19 en suite) ★★★ **Directions:** Galway to Clifden on N59. Signposted in Clifden, 2m on Ballyconneely road **Parking:** 40 **e-mail:** ardaghhotel@eircom.net **web:** www.ardaghhotel.com

Brown's

European, Irish

Modern Irish dining in bright, modern setting
☎ 095 21206 & 21086 Alcock & Brown Hotel

MENU GUIDE Garlic mussels, pesto, toasted breadcrumbs • Turbot with Guinness, Lakeshore mustard & herb butter • Pavlova, seasonal fruits

WINE GUIDE ♀ Symposium White Vin Pays de L'Aude €15 • ♥ Santa Rita Cabernet Sauvignon €17.50 • 4 bottles over €30, 23 bottles under €30 • 5 by the glass (€5)

PRICE GUIDE Fixed D €25 • starter €4.60-€9.95 • main €14.50-€23.95 • dessert €4.95-€6.50 • coffee €1.60 • min/water €2.30 • Service optional

PLACE: This family-owned hotel is situated in the centre of Clifden - where Alcock and Brown completed the first transatlantic crossing by aircraft. There's a cosy bar and lounge warmed by an open fire in winter. The restaurant is bright and airy with cheerful yellow and terracotta decor. In the evening,

continued

there's subdued lighting and candlelight.
FOOD: Modern Irish in style, dishes here include plenty of local produce, especially the excellent local seafood.
OUR TIP: Try a bracing walk around the Connemara clifftops **Chef:** Paddy Conroy, Eddie Devane **Owners:** Deirdre Keogh **Times:** 12.30-2/6-9.30, Closed 22-26 Dec **Notes:** Vegetarian available **Seats:** 100 **Smoking:** N/Sm in restaurant, Air con **Children:** Menu, Portions **Rooms:** 19 (19 en suite) ★★★ **Directions:** From Galway city take N59 to Clifden. Follow one-way system to centre. Hotel in town square **Parking:** Street Parking **e-mail:** alcockandbrown@eircom.net **web:** www.alcockandbrown-hotel.com

GALWAY MAP 01 B3/4

Ardilaun House Hotel Conference & Leisure Centre

Traditional, French **NEW**

Well-appointed family run hotel offering consistently fine cuisine
☎ 091 521433 Taylor's Hill

PLACE: Built in 1840, and converted into a hotel in 1962, the elegant and smart Ardilaun is set in five acres of landscaped gardens on the outskirts of Galway city near the sea at Salthill.
FOOD: The spacious and gracious restaurant, which overlooks the garden, serves Irish cuisine with French influences of consistently sound standards using best quality local fish, beef and lamb.
OUR TIP: Very comfortable bedrooms and extensive leisure facilities on offer
Times: 1/7, Closed L Sat, 22-28 Dec **Rooms:** 89 (89 en suite) ★★★★ **e-mail:** ardilaun@iol.ie **web:** www.ardilaunhousehotel.ie

Galway Bay Hotel

European

Contemporary Irish cuisine at Galway Bay
☎ 091 520520 The Promenade, Salthill

MENU GUIDE Salmon terrine, lemon & dill mayonnaise • Beef, Madeira & wild mushroom sauce • Bitter chocolate tart, cappuccino ice cream

WINE GUIDE ♀ Rosemount Chardonnay €20 • ♥ Rosemount Shiraz €20 • 20 bottles over €30, 26 bottles under €30 • 10 by the glass (€4.60-€5.75)

PRICE GUIDE Fixed L €18-€27 • starter €6.50-€7.50 • main €16.50-€35 • dessert €6.50-€7 • coffee €2.50 • min/water €5 • Service included

PLACE: Overlooking celebrated Galway Bay, this smart modern hotel offers panoramic views from the Lobster Pot, its elegant restaurant. Lighter snacks are available in Café Lido.
FOOD: High quality ingredients distinguish the cooking here; expect lots of local produce, particularly fish. The lengthy menu features a well-balanced selection of contemporary dishes, including temptations such as lobster thermidor, and garlic and pepper crusted rack of lamb.
OUR TIP: The hotel has its own leisure centre and beauty salon **Chef:** Robert Bell **Owners:** John O'Sullivan **Times:** 12.30-2.30/6.30-9.15, Closed 25 Dec (residents only) **Notes:** Vegetarian available, Smart Dress **Seats:** 220 **Smoking:** N/Sm in restaurant **Children:** Menu, Portions **Rooms:** 153 (153 en suite) ★★★★ **Directions:** 2m from Galway city centre **Parking:** 350 **e-mail:** info@galwaybayhotel.net **web:** www.galwaybayhotel.net

Ireland

Park House Hotel & Park Room Restaurant

International, Irish

Impressive cooking in city-centre hotel restaurant

☎ 091 564924 Forster St, Eyre Square

MENU GUIDE Tempura prawns • Glazed breast of duckling, pink peppercorn sauce • Bread & butter pudding

WINE GUIDE ♀ Rosemount Estate Semillon/Chardonnay €18.50 • ♀ Rosemount Estate Cabernet Sauvignon/Shiraz €18.50 • 40 bottles over €30, 61 bottles under €30 • 4 by the glass (€4.85)

PRICE GUIDE Fixed L €17-€25 • Fixed D €36-€42.50 • starter €7-€10 • main €16-€30 • dessert €7-€9 • coffee €2.50 • min/water €2.50

PLACE: Popular with locals, this city-centre establishment hides a warm, classical and elegant dining room behind its historic stone frontage. Paintings of old Galway adorn the walls, and lighting levels are comfortable.

FOOD: The menu offers something for every taste, from Irish originals to French classics, and a sprinkling of international appeal as well. Specials focus on fresh arrivals, usually the day's delivery of fish.

OUR TIP: Nearby parking in the multi-storey

Chef: Robert O'Keefe, Martin Keane **Owners:** Eamon Doyle, Kitty Carr **Times:** 12.3/6-10, Closed 24-26 Dec **Notes:** Vegetarian available **Seats:** 145, Pr/dining room 45 **Smoking:** N/Sm in restaurant, Air con **Children:** Menu, Portions **Rooms:** 57 (57 en suite) ★★★★ **Directions:** In city centre, off Eyre Square **Parking:** 40 **e-mail:** parkhousehotel@eircom.net **web:** www.parkhousehotel.ie

Radisson SAS Hotel Galway

International, European

Modern hotel restaurant with views of Galway Bay

☎ 091 538300 Lough Atalia Rd

MENU GUIDE Galway Bay smoked fish roulade • Peppered lamb rack, Puy lentil ragout, balsamic sauce • Chocolate timbale, berry compote

WINE GUIDE ♀ Rosario Estate Sauvignon Blanc €22 • ♀ Rosario Estate Merlot €22 • 27 bottles over €30, 12 bottles under €30 • 9 by the glass (€6-€7.50)

PRICE GUIDE Fixed D €32 • starter €6.50-€8.50 • main €14-€26 • dessert €7-€8 • coffee €3.20 • min/water €6.80 • Service optional

PLACE: The design of the 220-seater, split-level Marinas restaurant reflects the hotel's surroundings of blue water and light from Lough Atalia. The seating is a blend of blue upholstery and dark wood, with an infusion of warmth from the central fireplace.

FOOD: The menu offers modern Irish dishes with plenty of international influences, thanks to the wide range of international chefs. Fish is a speciality and seasonality is evident.

OUR TIP: It's very busy so booking is advisable

Chef: Sean Buckley **Owners:** Marinas Restaurant **Times:** 12.30-15.00/6-10.30, Closed L Mon-Sat **Notes:** Fixed L 4 courses €28 (Sun only), Fixed D Sat only, Vegetarian available, Smart Dress **Seats:** 220, Pr/dining room 40 **Smoking:** N/Sm in restaurant, Air con **Children:** Menu, Portions **Rooms:** 217 (217 en suite) ★★★★ **Directions:** Telephone for directions **Parking:** 260 **e-mail:** sales.galway@radissonsas.com **web:** www.galway.radissonsas.com

Ballynahinch Castle

French, European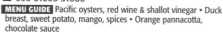

Fine dining in elegant country-house

☎ 095 31006 31086

MENU GUIDE Pacific oysters, red wine & shallot vinegar • Duck breast, sweet potato, mango, spices • Orange pannacotta, chocolate sauce

WINE GUIDE ♀ Château la Casamichef Muscadet €25.20 • ♀ Rosemount Cabernet Sauvignon €26.50 • 64 bottles over €30, 30 bottles under €30 • 5 by the glass (€5.50-€6)

PRICE GUIDE Fixed D €49 • coffee €2.35 • Service added 10%

PLACE: An air of casual elegance pervades this 16th-century castle, set in 350 acres of woodlands and lakes. Residents tend to dine in, so book ahead for a table in the popular restaurant; it's a bright, airy room with breathtaking views of the Ballynahinch river.

FOOD: Honest, unfussy cooking that allows the natural flavour of quality local ingredients to come through. Expect a lengthy and well-balanced menu of dishes rooted in classical French and European cooking.

OUR TIP: The castle has its own jail on an island in the lake

Chef: Robert Webster **Owners:** Ballynahinch Castle Hotel Inc **Times:** 6.30-9, Closed 1 wk Christmas, Feb, closed L all wk **Notes:** Set D 5 course, Vegetarian available, Dress Restrictions, Smart casual **Seats:** 90 **Smoking:** N/Sm in restaurant **Rooms:** 40 (40 en suite) ★★★★ **Directions:** Take N59 from Galway. Turn right after Recess towards Roundstone (R331) for 2m **Parking:** 55 **e-mail:** bhinch@iol.ie **web:** www.ballynahinch-castle.com

Lough Inagh Lodge

Classic French, Irish

Irish country dining with lovely mountain views

☎ 095 34706 & 34694 Inagh Valley

MENU GUIDE Seafood cake, rosemary crème fraîche • Wild lake salmon fillet • Vanilla terrine, wild berry compôte

WINE GUIDE ♀ Montanna Chardonnay Reserve €34 • ♀ Shiraz €22

PRICE GUIDE Food prices not confirmed for 2006. Please telephone for details

PLACE: This 19th-century fishing lodge on the shores of Lough Inagh is surrounded by Connemara's spectacular mountain scenery. Spacious bedrooms are smartly decorated and there's a choice of lounges and a cosy traditional bar and dining room.

FOOD: Excellent seafood and game are given simple but effective preparation with clear flavours. Home-baked breads are a treat followed by dishes like St Tola's goats' cheese in filo parcels with spinach, or local lobster or succulent fresh prawns tossed in butter with a hint of garlic.

OUR TIP: Coffee and home-made petits fours in the library, complete with log fire

Chef: Fiona Joyce **Owners:** Marie O'Connor **Times:** 7-9, Closed mid Dec-mid Mar **Notes:** Civ Wed 36 **Seats:** 30 **Smoking:** N/Sm in restaurant **Rooms:** 12 (12 en suite) ★★★ **Directions:** From Galway take N344. After 3.5m hotel on right **e-mail:** inagh@iol.ie **web:** www.loughinaghlodehotel.ie

The AA Wine Awards recognise the finest wine lists in England, Scotland and Wales. For full details, see pages 14-15

Ireland

RENVYLE MAP 01 A4
Renvyle House
Contemporary
Welcoming country hotel with literary connections
☎ 095 43511

MENU GUIDE Locally-smoked chicken & mushroom tart • Grilled brill, shrimp & spring onion risotto • Rich chocolate fondant

WINE GUIDE ♀ Tarapaca Chardonnay • ♟ Tarapaca Cabernet Sauvignon • 6 by the glass (€4.60)

PRICE GUIDE Starter €1.95-€7.95 • main €15.95-€25.95 dessert €3-€4.95 • coffee €2.55 • min/water €2.20

PLACE: Yeats honeymooned in this attractive country-house, tucked betwixt the Connemara mountains and the wild Atlantic coast, and it was also the setting for his final portrait. Dinner is a romantic affair, with soft lighting and the evocative scent of turf fires.
FOOD: An excellent sense of timing leaves well-judged flavours intact. This is vibrant, robust cooking, full of interest and demonstrating skilful sourcing of local produce.
OUR TIP: Relax by the turf fires
Chef: Tim O'Sullivan **Owners:** Tim O'Sullivan **Times:** 7-9, Closed 4 Jan-14 Feb **Notes:** Set D €45 (5 courses), Vegetarian available **Seats:** 90, Pr/dining room 150 **Smoking:** N/Sm in restaurant **Children:** Menu, Portions **Rooms:** 68 (68 en suite) ★★★ **Directions:** N59 west of Galway towards Clifden, through Oughterard & Maam Cross. At Recess turn right, Keymore turn left, Letterfrack turn right, hotel 5m **Parking:** 150 **e-mail:** info@renvyle.com **web:** www.renvyle.com

CO KERRY

CAHERDANIEL MAP 01 A2
Derrynane Hotel
Irish, European
Spectacular Atlantic backdrop for enjoyable dining
☎ 066 947 5136

PLACE: Spectacular ocean views as you relax and enjoy your meal is the highlight of visiting Derrynane Hotel, perched on a clifftop location on the Ring of Kerry. The bright, spacious dining room overlooks Derrynane Bay.
FOOD: The small dedicated kitchen brigade produce modern Irish dishes with European influences, using quality and fresh produce. A bar menu is also available and includes paninni and ciabatti alongside home-made soup, and scones.
OUR TIP: Hotel has its own herb garden
Times: 7-9, Closed Oct-mid Apr **Rooms:** 73 (73 en suite) ★★★
e-mail: info@derrynane.com **web:** www.derrynane.com

AA's Chefs' Chef is the annual poll of all the chefs included in The Restaurant Guide. Around 1800 of the country's top chefs are asked to vote to recognise the achievements of one of their peers. This year's winner is featured on page 19.

KENMARE MAP 01 B2
Sheen Falls Lodge *see opposite*

Lime Tree Sheburne St ☎ 064 41225 Pretty stone building housing a bustling, seasonally-inspired restaurant.

Packie's Henry St ☎ 064 41508 Good local ingredients treated with care and intelligence.

KILLARNEY MAP 01 B2
Aghadoe Heights Hotel
British, French
Stunning rural views and classical fine dining
☎ 064 31766

MENU GUIDE Carlingford Bay oysters, natural or Rockerfeller • Grilled Châteaubriand, sauce béarnaise • Baileys bread and butter pudding

WINE GUIDE ♀ La Ciboise Chapoutier €25.50 • ♟ La Ciboise Chapoutier €25.50 • 130 bottles over €30, 10 bottles under €30 • 10 by the glass (€6-€7.50)

PRICE GUIDE Fixed D €60 • starter €16 • main €32-€35 • dessert €13 • coffee €6 • min/water €6 • Service optional • Group min 10 service 12.5%

PLACE: Fredericks restaurant occupies a bright modern space on the third floor of the hotel, with spectacular views of Killarney's lakes and mountains. Adding to the ambiance is the resident pianist, who plays during dinner and for the famous champagne Sunday brunch. Excellent staff mingle easily with guests, exemplifying the perfect balance between professionalism and friendliness.
FOOD: The carte is supported by a short daily fixed-price menu. These draw inspiration from local produce, notably Dingle seafood served in simple, well executed dishes.
OUR TIP: Full vegetarian menu available on request
Chef: Robin Suter **Owners:** Pat & Marie Chawke **Times:** 12.30-2.00/6.30-9.30, Closed 25 Dec (residents only), Jan-March, closed L Mon-Sat **Notes:** Vegetarian available, Dress Restrictions, Jacket. No jeans and trainers **Seats:** 120, Pr/dining room 100 **Smoking:** N/Sm in restaurant, Air con **Children:** Menu, Portions **Rooms:** 75 (75 en suite) ★★★★
Directions: 2.5m from Killarney, off N22. 11m from Kerry International Airport **Parking:** 120 **e-mail:** info@aghadoeheights.com **web:** www.aghadoeheights.com

Arbutus Hotel
Traditional
Traditional Irish hospitality
☎ 064 31037 College St

PLACE: Norrie Buckley's restaurant is three interconnecting rooms with direct street access in this smart family-run hotel situated in the centre of Killarney. It seems to have a single aim – to provide traditional Irish cooking (with some international nudges) from the cream of Celtic produce.
FOOD: Traditional Irish and international cooking with excellent, fresh ingredients, mainly sourced locally.
OUR TIP: Try the amazing breakfast
Times: 12.30-2.30/6-9.30, Closed 7 Dec-15 Jan **Rooms:** 35 (35 en suite) ★★★ **e-mail:** arbutushotel@eircom.net **web:** www.arbutuskillarney.com

Sheen Falls Lodge

Modern Irish

Romantic waterfall setting for excellent cuisine

☎ 064 41600

MENU GUIDE Sautéed potato gnocchi, wild mushrooms, deep-fried quails' eggs • Fillet of hake, risotto of periwinkle, garlic & parsley • Apple & Calvados Normande, vanilla chiboust, cider apple caramel

WINE GUIDE ♀ Domaine Chizoulet Sauvignon Blanc €35 • ♀ Domaine Bouscat Cabernet/Merlot €32 • 900 bottles over €30, 10 bottles under €30 • 12 by the glass (€8.50-€18)

PRICE GUIDE Fixed D €65 • starter €16-€21 • main €30-€36 • dessert €16-€18 • coffee €5 • Service optional

PLACE: The views of the crystal cascading Sheen Falls, and occasional salmon seen leaping upstream, from the vast windows of the elegant La Cascade restaurant are magical, especially at night when floodlit. Once the summer residence of the Marquis of Landsdowne, today the former fishing lodge retains the warm, welcoming atmosphere of a country manor house.

FOOD: The emphasis here is firmly on fresh, local, organic ingredients. The chef sources fish and shellfish from Castletainbere, regional cheeses and many of the vegetables, salad and herbs are especially grown for the restaurant. Dishes are sophisticated, with clear flavours coming through, and might include loin of lamb, aubergine caviar, Mediterranean vegetables and tapenade jus.

OUR TIP: All fish is local

Chef: Aidan McGrath **Owners:** Sheen Falls Estate Ltd **Times:** 7.15-9.30, Closed 3 wks before Xmas, 2 Jan-1 Feb, closed L all week **Notes:** Vegetarian available, Smart Dress **Seats:** 120, Pr/dining room 20 **Smoking:** N/Sm in restaurant **Children:** Menu, Portions **Rooms:** 66 (66 en suite) ★★★★ **Directions:** From Kenmare take N71 to Glengarriff. Take 1st left after suspension bridge. 1m from Kenmare **Parking:** 75 **e-mail:** info@sheenfallslodge.ie **web:** www.sheenfallslodge.ie

Cahernane House Hotel

Traditional, Modern

Lakeside manor house dining

☎ 064 31895 Muckross Rd

PLACE: Once home to the Earls of Pembroke, this country mansion enjoys the most fortuitous of settings. Set by a lake, with a mountain range as dramatic background, the hotel is also at the edge of the Killarney National Park. Elegant period furniture is mixed with more modern pieces to create a relaxed, warm feel.

FOOD: Straightforward menu descriptions belie serious technical proficiency and flair. A perfectly timed roast monkfish wrapped in Parma ham, served on lemon risotto, black grape and veal jus is full of interest, demonstrating excellent combinations of flavour and texture.

OUR TIP: Killarney town is nearby

Times: 12-2.30/7-9.30, Closed L all wk ex by arrangement, Dec-Jan **Rooms:** 38 (38 en suite) ★★★★ **e-mail:** cahernane@eircom.net **web:** www.cahernane.com

One Rosette Excellent local restaurants serving food prepared with care, understanding and skill, using good quality ingredients. These restaurants stand out in their local area. Of the total number of establishments with Rosettes around 50% have one Rosette.

Killarney Park

Classical European

Sound cuisine in upmarket hotel

☎ 064 35555 Kenmare Place

MENU GUIDE Butternut squash risotto • Dover sole, lemon & caper butter • Chocolate marquise

WINE GUIDE ♀ Dampt et Fils Chablis Chardonnay €34 • ♀ Château de la Garde St Emilion €33 • 95 bottles over €30, 5 bottles under €30 • 4 by the glass (€6.75-€14)

PRICE GUIDE Fixed D €44 • starter €13.50-€14.95 • main €26-€29.50 • dessert €8.95 • coffee €3.75 • Service included

PLACE: Just on the edge of the friendly town of Killarney, this upmarket modern hotel aims to offer country-house comfort boasting deep sofas, roaring fires and a well-stocked library. A pianist plays away each evening in the elegant restaurant, where tables are well-spaced and appointed.

FOOD: Sound cooking skills and a touch of imagination make the most of local Kerry produce. A theatrical touch is added by the flambé drinks and cheese trollies.

OUR TIP: Indulge yourself at the hotel's luxurious spa

Chef: Odran Lucey **Owners:** Padraig & Janet Treacy **Times:** 7-9.30, Closed 24-26 Dec, closed L all week **Notes:** Vegetarian available, Dress Restrictions, Neat clothing required **Seats:** 90, Pr/dining room 40 **Smoking:** N/Sm in restaurant, Air con **Children:** Menu, Portions **Rooms:** 72 (72 en suite) ★★★★ **Directions:** From Cork take R22 to Killarney. Take 1st exit for town centre, then at 2nd rdbt take 2nd exit. At 3rd rdbt, take 1st exit. Hotel 2nd entrance on left **Parking:** 75 **e-mail:** info@killarneyparkhotel.ie **web:** www.killarneyparkhotel.ie

PARKNASILLA MAP 01 A2

Great Southern

Traditional

Majestic hotel dining in dramatic location

☎ 064 45122

MENU GUIDE Roast rabbit loin, Parma ham, rosemary jus • Grilled monkfish tail, braised fennel • Raspberry parfait, vanilla cream sauce

WINE GUIDE ♀ Baron de Pouilly Fumé €80 • ♥ Château Lynch Bages €110 • 23 bottles over €30, 27 bottles under €30 • 4 by the glass (€5.50-€10.50)

PRICE GUIDE Fixed D €39 • starter €9-€13 • main €26-€28 dessert €9 • coffee €3 • min/water €6 • Service included

PLACE: Parknasilla is a Victorian hotel in an extraordinary location, with stunning Atlantic, woodland and mountain views. Original architectural features include a sweeping staircase, stained glass windows and log fires. George Bernard Shaw was a frequent visitor and wrote much of *St Joan* here.

FOOD: Dinner only, offered from a daily fixed-price menu, plus a short carte of lighter fare. Excellent ingredients are simply prepared in fairly traditional dishes.

OUR TIP: The local seafood is very good

Chef: John Knightly **Times:** 7-9, Closed Sun-Wed 4 Jan-11 Feb, closed L all week **Notes:** Smart casual **Seats:** 180, Pr/dining room 24 **Smoking:** N/Sm in restaurant, Air con **Children:** Min 9 yrs, Menu, Portions **Rooms:** 83 (83 en suite) ★★★★ **Directions:** From Killarney take N71 to Kenmare. On entering town pass golf club. Hotel entrance on left at top of town **Parking:** 78 **e-mail:** res@parknasilla.gsh.ie **web:** www.gshotels.com

CO KILDARE

LEIXLIP MAP 01 D4

Leixlip House

Modern Irish

Fine dining in gracious hotel

☎ 01 6242268 Captains Hill

MENU GUIDE Beef carpaccio, red onion relish • Sea bass, crab fishcake, spinach velouté, cucumber & lime salsa • Tiramisù

WINE GUIDE ♀ Casa Viva Chardonnay €18.50 • ♥ Casa Viva Merlot €18.50 • 1 bottle over €30, 30 bottles under €30 6 by the glass

PRICE GUIDE Fixed L €25 • Fixed D €25 • starter €5.50-€8.50 main €14-€22.50 • dessert €7.50 • coffee €2.50 • min/water €4.75 • Service optional

PLACE: Gracefully decorated in keeping with its 18th-century surroundings, this bright and airy hotel restaurant offers fine dining in a friendly and relaxed ambience.

FOOD: A commitment to the use of fresh and seasonal ingredients is reflected in a menu of regularly changing dishes, such as chicken with aromatic couscous and lemon beurre blanc, or steak with confit shallot and béarnaise sauce.

OUR TIP: A short drive from Dublin

Chef: Ray Sanderson **Owners:** Frank Towey **Times:** 12.30-4/7-10, Closed 25-26 Dec, Mon, closed L Mon-Sat **Notes:** Vegetarian available **Smoking:** N/Sm in restaurant **Children:** Menu, Portions **Rooms:** 19 (19 en suite) ★★★ **e-mail:** info@leixliphouse.com **web:** www.leixliphouse.com

MAYNOOTH MAP 01 D4

⑨⑨ Moyglare Manor

French

Romantic restaurant with Georgian splendour

☎ 01 6286351 Moyglare

MENU GUIDE Smoked salmon & spring onion tart • Venison, bolletana, balsamic & red wine sauce • Walnut tart, praline chestnut ice cream

WINE GUIDE ♀ Chablis 2001- Regnard • ♥ Château Vigneaure 1999 • 6 bottles over €30, 6 bottles under €30

PRICE GUIDE Fixed L €34.95 • Fixed D €60

PLACE: Approached by a half-mile, tree-lined drive and surrounded by beautifully landscaped gardens, this stone-built 18th-century property brims with fascinating antiques and collectables. The atmospheric restaurant is decorated in period style with well-spaced tables and clever arrangements of lamps, leafy palms and screens.

FOOD: Fruit and vegetables from Moyglare's gardens are put to good use in the traditional country-house cuisine, which truly reflects the seasons. Choose from the extensive à la carte menu or more limited daily specials.

OUR TIP: Reservations are essential for non-residents

Chef: Edward Cullen **Owners:** Norah Devlin **Times:** 12.30-2.30/7-9.30, Closed 24-27 Dec, closed L Sat **Notes:** Vegetarian available, Smart Dress **Seats:** 40, Pr/dining room 22 **Smoking:** N/Sm in restaurant **Children:** Min 12 yrs **Rooms:** 17 (17 en suite) ★★★ **Directions:** 18m from Dublin city centre **Parking:** 50 **e-mail:** info@moyglaremanor.ie **web:** www.moyglaremanor.ie

NAAS MAP 01 D4

⑨ Killashee House Hotel & Villa Spa

European, Irish

Elegant dining in magnificent surroundings

☎ 045 879277

MENU GUIDE Seared scallops with flat parsley • Stuffed cannon of Irish lamb with vegetable noodles • Crêpes Suzette

WINE GUIDE ♀ Montana Chardonnay €22 • ♥ Rosemount Shiraz €24 • 70 bottles over €30, 30 bottles under €30 • 6 by the glass (€4.75-€6)

PRICE GUIDE Fixed L €32.50 • Fixed D €48.50 • starter €9.50-€14 • main €20-€34 • dessert €10.50-€12.95 • coffee €2.50 min/water €4.50 • Service included

PLACE: Set amidst acres of manicured gardens, Killashee House (once a convent) is a majestic Victorian manor house. Turner's restaurant is opulent and classically elegant, with intricate plasterwork, crystal chandeliers and gold and scarlet soft furnishings.

FOOD: The kitchen team work with top quality local produce to create daring combinations such as chicken with goats' cheese and confit banana or beef fillet with oxtail and wild mushrooms. Daily changing traditional menus with European influences, as well as the carte, reflect the changing seasons.

OUR TIP: Magnificent views of Wicklow mountains

Chef: Aziz Joudar **Owners:** Mr & Mrs Tierney **Times:** 1-2.45/7-9.45, Closed 25 Dec, closed L Sat **Notes:** Vegetarian available, Dress Restrictions, No jeans **Seats:** 220, Pr/dining room 35 **Smoking:** N/Sm in restaurant, Air con **Children:** Menu, Portions **Rooms:** 142 (146 en suite) ★★★★ **Directions:** 1m from Naas on old Kilcullen road. On left past Garda (police station) **Parking:** 600 **e-mail:** sales@killasheehouse.com **web:** www.killasheehouse.com

Ireland

STRAFFAN MAP 01 C/D4

The K Club

Irish, French
Luxurious golfing hotel with impressive French restaurant
☎ 01 6017200
e-mail: hotel@kclub.ie
web: www.kclub.ie

PLACE: Set to play host to the 2006 Ryder Cup, this truly luxurious hotel sits at the heart of a resort that includes two championship golf courses and a new spa. The golf pavilion houses two informal eateries - Legends and Monza - but it's the fine dining option that's the real draw. Dominated by a painting of the thoroughbred horse after which it's named, the Byerley Turk restaurant is a classy affair with ornate chandeliers, lavish drapes and elegantly clothed tables.

FOOD: First-rate French cuisine, with the occasional nod to things Irish. A skilful kitchen delivers modern interpretations of classical dishes, dazzling with an array of high quality ingredients and demonstrating a serious commitment to seasonality. Menus are extensive, and include a tasting selection of the chef's signature dishes; there's also an impressive - and expensive - range of wines.

Ireland

MENU GUIDE Pigeon, cep purée, pickled girolles • Sea bass, shellfish bouillabaisse, rouille flavoured mash • Rum & raisin soufflé, vanilla ice cream

PRICE GUIDE Fixed L €55 • starter €19-€29 • main €32-€48 • dessert €17.50 • coffee €6.50 • min/water €6.50 • Service included

OUR TIP: Book early for the Ryder Cup 2006

Chef: Finbarr Higgins **Owners:** Michael Smurfit **Times:** 7-9.45
Notes: Vegetarian available, Dress Restrictions, Jacket & tie
Seats: 100, Pr/dining room 16 **Smoking:** N/Sm in restaurant, Air con **Children:** Min 3 yrs, Portions **Rooms:** 79 (79 en suite)
★★★★★ **Directions:** 30 minutes from Dublin. From Dublin Airport follow M4 to Maynooth, turn for Straffan, just after village on right **Parking:** 100

Ireland

NEWBRIDGE MAP 01 C3

◎◎ Keadeen Hotel

European, French

Enjoyable dining in country hotel with racing pedigree

☎ 045 431666

MENU GUIDE Wood pigeon salad, lardons • Chicken breast, leek & asparagus cream reduction • Blackcurrant parfait

WINE GUIDE ♀ Sancerre Sauvignon Blanc €30.50 • ♀ Château du Courlat St Emilion €26.50 • 6 bottles over €30, 14 bottles under €30 • 6 by the glass (€5)

PRICE GUIDE Fixed L €21–€33 • Fixed D €35–€40 • starter €8–€13 • main €17–€28 • dessert €6.60–€9.60 • coffee €2.15 • min/water €2.60 • Service optional

PLACE: This family-owned hotel is set in eight acres of prize-winning gardens on the outskirts of Newbridge. Public areas include a spacious drawing room, a state-of-the-art leisure complex and the Derby Restaurant.

FOOD: Modern Irish cooking with French influences using the best ingredients sourced locally. There's a choice of either a fixed-price menu or a bistro carte. The latter includes pasta dishes, fish and prime Irish beef offered in various guises. The set dinner menu offers treats like wild mushroom risotto with grilled brie and Parma ham or roast rack of Wicklow lamb with Puy lentils.

OUR TIP: Good base for a visit to the famous Curragh racecourse
Chef: Michael Casey **Owners:** O'Loughlins **Times:** 12.30-2/7-10, Closed 25 Dec-4 Jan (open 31 Dec) **Notes:** Vegetarian available, Dinner Jacket & tie **Seats:** 120, Pr/dining room 32 **Smoking:** N/Sm in restaurant, Air con **Children:** Menu, Portions **Rooms:** 75 (75 en suite) ★★★★
Directions: N7 from Dublin to Newbridge. Hotel 1m from Curragh racecourse & 0.5m from Newbridge town centre. **Parking:** 100
e-mail: keadeen@iol.ie **web:** www.keadeenhotel.kildare.ie

STRAFFAN MAP 01 C/D4

◎◎ Barberstown Castle

Irish, French

Fine dining in 13th-century castle in attractive grounds

☎ 01 6288157

MENU GUIDE Crispy Kerry prawns, Puy lentils • Roast stuffed pheasant & chestnuts, rosemary potato gratin • Caramelised apple & pear tart

WINE GUIDE 70 bottles over €30, 15 bottles under €30

PRICE GUIDE Food prices not confirmed for 2006. Please telephone for details

PLACE: Little could be more romantic than dining in a castle, and this 13th-century hotel, recently extended, will not disappoint. Dinner is served in what was once the keep, and it's an atmospheric, candlelit affair. Knowledgeable staff are pleased to offer advice and post-dinner drinks can be taken in the elegantly appointed drawing room.

FOOD: The Irish country-house style has a distinctly French sophistication. Game is a real strength, and accurate cooking makes the most of the high quality ingredients.

OUR TIP: Recent addition of spacious bedrooms
Chef: Bertrand Malabat **Owners:** Kenneth Healy **Times:** 12.30-3/7-9.30, Closed 24-28 Dec, 2nd-3rd wk Jan **Notes:** Fixed price L €32.50, D €60.00, Vegetarian available **Seats:** 75, Pr/dining room 32 **Smoking:** N/Sm in restaurant **Rooms:** 58 (58 en suite) ★★★ **Directions:** Telephone for directions **e-mail:** barberstowncastle@ireland.com
web: www.barberstowncastle.com

◎◎◎ The K Club *see page 677*

CO KILKENNY

KILKENNY MAP 01 C3

◎ Kilkenny River Court

Modern Irish, European

Comfortable riverside hotel dining

☎ 056 7723388 The Bridge, John St

PLACE: This comfortable riverside hotel has a dining room that is very much in the grand scheme. Marble floors and crystal chandeliers add glamour, while huge windows command striking views over the river and Kilkenny Castle.

FOOD: A Mediterranean influence can be discerned in the simple approach which makes much of local produce. Seasonally changing menus ensure the very best of what's on offer, while combinations are subtly successful.

OUR TIP: Within walking distance of the city centre
Times: 12.30-2.30/6-9.30, Closed L Mon-Sat, 25-26 Jan **Rooms:** 90 (90 en suite) ★★★★ **e-mail:** reservations@kilrivercourt.com **web:** www.kilrivercourt.com

THOMASTOWN MAP 01 C3

◎◎ The Lady Helen Restaurant

European, Mediterranean

Fine dining in imposing 18th-century country mansion

☎ 056 7773000 Mount Juliet Conrad Hotel

MENU GUIDE Squab, Puy lentils, salsify & pear purée • Wild boar, red cabbage, truffle gallette, apple purée • Passionfruit mousse

WINE GUIDE ♀ J M Bouchard Chablis Chardonnay €36 • ♀ Domaine Pardon et Fils Fleurie/Beaujolais €36 159 bottles over €30, 26 bottles under €30 • 8 by the glass (€7–€9)

PRICE GUIDE Fixed D €52 • coffee €2.75 • min/water €5 Service optional

PLACE: Set in 1500 acres of parkland, this elegant 18th-century Palladian mansion has its own golf course, and retains many original features like Adam fireplaces. There's a choice of places to eat - Kendels for informal eating and Lady Helen for fine dining.

FOOD: The menus are a combination of European and modern Mediterranean. The formal service complements the rather grand setting. There's good use of local ingredients here especially game and seafood, and fresh vegetables and herbs come from the kitchen gardens.

OUR TIP: Equestrian centre for a pre-prandial hack
Chef: Peter Brennan **Owners:** Conrad Hotels **Times:** 7-9.45, Closed L Sun (Jan-Feb) **Notes:** Dress Restrictions, No Jeans, no T-shirts **Seats:** 60, Pr/dining room 70 **Smoking:** N/Sm in restaurant **Children:** Min 16 yrs, Menu, Portions **Rooms:** 59 (59 en suite) ★★★★ **Directions:** Just outside Thomastown heading S on N9 **Parking:** 200
e-mail: info@mountjuliet.ie **web:** www.mountjuliet.ie

Prices quoted in the guide are for guidance only and are subject to change without notice.

CO LIMERICK

ADARE MAP 01 B3

⊚⊚ Dunraven Arms
Mediterranean, International

Traditional inn with a modern approach

☎ 061 396633

MENU GUIDE Scallops, black pudding, herb mash • Roast rib of local beef from the trolley • Plum pudding, clove ice cream, brandy anglaise

PRICE GUIDE Fixed L €27-€30 • starter €8.50-€10 • main €16-€28 • dessert €6-€8 • coffee €3 • min/water €4.50 • Service added 12.5%

PLACE: The building which plays host to this well-presented and well-equipped hotel dates back to 1792. The interior is smartly decorated, comfortably furnished and warmed by open fires. Large bay windows look out to the thatched cottages of one of Ireland's prettiest villages. Service is friendly and helpful.
FOOD: The well-balanced Maigue Restaurant menu is modern Irish in style with some French and Mediterranean influences. There's extensive use of local, seasonal, fresh produce with good combinations of flavours and textures such as plum and mulled wine sorbets or crab, celery, beetroot and fennel salsa.
OUR TIP: Shed the calories in the excellent leisure centre
Chef: Sandra Earl **Owners:** Brian & Louis Murphy **Times:** 12.30-2.30/7-9.30, Closed L Mon-Sat **Notes:** Vegetarian available **Seats:** 80, Pr/dining room 30 **Smoking:** N/Sm in restaurant, Air con **Children:** Min 6 yrs, Portions **Rooms:** 75 (75 en suite) ★★★★ **Directions:** Telephone for directions **Parking:** 60 **e-mail:** reservations@dunravenhotel.com **web:** www.dunravenhotel.com

LIMERICK MAP 01 B3

⊚ McLauglins
Modern International

Contemporary hotel dining

☎ 061 335566 Castletroy Park Hotel, Dublin Rd

MENU GUIDE Pan-fried Atlantic scallops, gaufrette of seasonal leaves, walnut & mixed pepper vinaigrette • Duo of Barbary duck, orange scented polenta, cherry compote • Warm plum tart, cinnamon ice cream, saffron anglaise

WINE GUIDE ♀ Moreau Chardonnay €19 • ♀ Moreau Merlot €19 • 13 bottles over €30, 25 bottles under €30 • 3 by the glass (€5-€6)

PRICE GUIDE Fixed L €24 • Fixed D €40 • starter €5-€10 • main €15-€27 • dessert €6-€7 • coffee €2.90 • min/water €4.50 • Group min 6 service 12.5%

PLACE: Undoubtedly the only restaurant in the world named after the inventor of hydro-electric power, McLaughlins is a softly lit, spacious dining room with views across to the Clare hills.
FOOD: A lengthy modern international carte offers a range of dishes to suit most tastes. Mains might include herb crusted rack of lamb, or pan-fried fillet of John Dory with saffron potatoes. Skill is evident in the accuracy of the cooking, and presentation is stylish and modern.
OUR TIP: Great value all-inclusive weekend breaks
Chef: Tom Flavin **Owners:** Fordmount Developments **Times:** 12.30-2.30/6.00-9.30, Closed 25-31 Dec **Notes:** Vegetarian available **Seats:** 78, Pr/dining room 14 **Smoking:** N/Sm in restaurant, Air con **Children:** Menu, Portions **Rooms:** 107 (107 en suite) ★★★★ **Directions:** 5 mins from Limerick on Dublin road **Parking:** 150 **e-mail:** sales@castletroy-park.ie **web:** www.castletroy-park.ie

⊚ Radisson SAS Hotel
Mediterranean, International

Candlelit dining in modern hotel restaurant

☎ 061 326666 Ennis Rd

MENU GUIDE Tian of crabmeat & avocado, gazpacho coulis • Pan-fried monkfish, tapenade crust, fennel confit • Gratin of strawberries

WINE GUIDE ♀ Rosario Sauvignon Blanc €21 • ♀ Rosario Merlot €21 • 9 bottles over €30, 16 bottles under €30 2 by the glass (€5.25)

PRICE GUIDE Fixed L €20-€25 • Fixed D €30-€35 • starter €5-€9 • main €18-€24 • dessert €6.50 • min/water €4 • Service optional

PLACE: This is a smart new hotel located between Limerick and Shannon Airport. Candlelight and classical music create a relaxing atmosphere in the open-plan Porters restaurant, while the Irish pub provides a casual alternative.
FOOD: Mediterranean and International cooking make the best of local produce in a range of simply executed dishes, including fresh fish, lamb and game in season.
OUR TIP: Good value early bird menu
Chef: Gerard Costelloe **Owners:** St Johns Hotels Ltd **Times:** 1-2.30/6.30-10.00, Closed L Mon-Sat (ex groups), closed D Sun
Notes: Vegetarian available, Smart Dress **Seats:** 150, Pr/dining room 15 **Smoking:** N/Sm in restaurant, Air con **Children:** Menu, Portions **Rooms:** 154 (154 en suite) ★★★★ **Directions:** 3m from Limerick city centre **Parking:** 200 **e-mail:** info@radissonsas.com **web:** www.radissonsas.com

CO MAYO

BALLINA MAP 01 B4

⊚ Teach Iorrais Hotel
International

Great dining in this wild corner of County Mayo

☎ 097 86888 Geesala

MENU GUIDE Salmon & prawn Mary Rose parcels • Roast lamb rack, lemon & lime crust • Chocolate parfait

WINE GUIDE ♀ Bin 222 Chardonnay €26.95 • ♀ Fairview Shiraz €24.50 • 8 bottles over €30, 26 bottles under €30 • 3 by the glass (€4.10)

PRICE GUIDE Fixed L €10.95 • Fixed D €29.25-€41.84 • starter €4.25-€9.95 • main €18.75-€24.95 • dessert €6.25-€6.95 coffee €1.95 • Service included

Ireland

continued

BALLINA continued MAP 01 B4

PLACE: Set in the heart of the Erris peninsula, this warm, friendly hotel offers comfortable accommodation. Although this is a modern building, there's an appealing Celtic-style decor. Dine amidst the medieval-style columns and vaults of the An Néifinn restaurant. It's quieter than the lively bar.
FOOD: International style cooking using local, seasonal produce. Consistently good quality dishes cooked with flair and imagination, such as the pork saltimbocca.
OUR TIP: Visit the Céide Visitors Centre for a huge range of local activities
Chef: Darren Blincker **Owners:** Tom Gaughan **Times:** 7-10
Notes: Vegetarian available **Seats:** 70, Pr/dining room 30
Smoking: N/Sm in restaurant, Air con **Children:** Portions **Rooms:** 31
(31 en suite) ★★★ **e-mail:** teachlor@iol.ie
web: www.teachiorrais.com

FOXFORD MAP 01 B4

⊚ Healys Restaurant & Country House Hotel

Irish

19th-century shooting lodge serving traceable local fare
☎ 094 925 6443 Pontoon

MENU GUIDE Steamed mussels, white wine & Pernod sauce • Rack of lamb, mustard & herb crust, rosemary jus • Strawberry cheesecake
WINE GUIDE ⚲ Aromo Chilean €19.99 • ⚑ Belair Monsette €19.99 • 60 bottles over €30, 38 bottles under €30 • 4 by the glass (€4.45)
PRICE GUIDE Fixed D €39 • starter €3.50-€12 • main €12-€30 • dessert €6 • coffee €2 • min/water €2 • Service optional

PLACE: This grand creeper-clad former shooting lodge, delightfully converted into a hotel, is situated on the edge of Lough Cullen and is a paradise for anglers. The cosy, comfortable restaurant is decorated in typical Irish country-house style, with blues and whites and linen place settings.
FOOD: Traditional fare, served in the Louch Cullen Dining Room (and bar), offers plenty of choice, showcasing fresh local produce - traceable organic beef, pork and lamb, game, etc.
OUR TIP: Pack a rod and tackle
Chef: Ray Barrett **Owners:** John Dever **Times:** 12.30-6.30/6-10, Closed 25 Dec **Notes:** Vegetarian available, Smart Dress **Seats:** 70
Smoking: N/Sm in restaurant, Air con **Children:** Portions **Rooms:** 14 (14 en suite) ★★ **Directions:** Telephone for directions **Parking:** 150
e-mail: info@healyspontoon.com **web:** www.healyspontoon.com

WESTPORT MAP 01 B4

⊚⊚ The Atlantic Coast Hotel

Irish, European

West Coast dining with impressive views
☎ 098 29000 The Quay

MENU GUIDE Newport mussels, Asian broth • Brill fillets, spiced couscous • Grapefruit jelly, mango pannacotta
WINE GUIDE ⚲ Robertsons Winery Chardonnay €21.50 • ⚑ Gecko Ridge Blend €17.50 • 13 bottles over €30, 13 bottles under €30 • 4 by the glass (€4.70)
PRICE GUIDE Fixed D €36 • coffee €2 • min/water €3.50 • Service added but optional 12.5%

PLACE: This 19th-century wool mill has been converted into a distinctive hotel with modern facilities. Many of the rooms face the sea and have wonderful views of Clew Bay as does the Blue Wave restaurant on the fourth floor. There's a lively bar and relaxing lounge on the ground floor.
FOOD: Dishes are modern Irish in style with European references. There's good use of local ingredients especially seafood like monkfish, brill and crab with lots of strong flavours and combinations such as smoked mackerel with orange and mango dressing.
OUR TIP: Build up an appetite in the hotel's impressive leisure centre
Chef: Frank Walsh **Owners:** Masterchefs **Times:** 6.30-9.15, Closed 23-27 Dec **Notes:** Vegetarian available **Seats:** 85, Pr/dining room 140
Smoking: N/Sm in restaurant, Air con **Children:** Menu, Portions
Rooms: 85 (88 en suite) ★★★ **Directions:** From Westport take coast road towards Louisburgh for 1m. Hotel on harbour on left **Parking:** 80
e-mail: info@atlanticcoasthotel.com
web: www.atlanticcoasthotel.com

⊚ The Olde Railway Hotel

Traditional

Riverside dining with an emphasis on local produce
☎ 098 25166 & 25605 The Mall

PLACE: Situated on an avenue overlooking the river, this former coaching inn maintains a cheerful conviviality, with roaring fires and cosy lounge areas adding to the appeal. The light-drenched conservatory restaurant is a lovely spot for summer dining.
FOOD: Irish and classical roots are evident in simple food that celebrates wonderful local produce. Imaginative details include the unusual Guinness loaf.
OUR TIP: Sample the local catch
Times: 6.30-9.30 **Rooms:** 24 (24 en suite) ★★
e-mail: railway@anu.ie **web:** www.anu.ie/railwayhotel

continued

CO MONAGHAN

CARRICKMACROSS MAP 01 C4

🌸🏵 Nuremore Hotel

Irish, European

Accomplished country-house cooking

☎ 042 9961438

MENU GUIDE Assiette of rabbit, apple chutney • John Dory, pomme boulangère, buttered asparagus • Peach Melba parfait, almond cream

WINE GUIDE 🍷 Marlborough Mud House John/Jennifer Joslin Sauvignon Blanc €26 • 🍷 Marie-Claude Flavas Domaine de Granoupiac Merlot €26 • 188 bottles over €30, 1 bottle under €30 • 6 by the glass (€7.50-€10)

PRICE GUIDE Fixed L €20-€22 • Fixed D €48-€50 • coffee €3 • min/water €5 • Service included

PLACE: An embarrassment of riches awaits guests at this luxurious country-house hotel, which boasts its own 18-hole golf course, leisure centre and tennis courts, as well as some of the best food in Ireland. The restaurant is an elegant affair with well-spaced tables and views over the gardens and lake.

FOOD: One look at Nuremore's imaginative modern menu is enough to show that this is an accomplished kitchen team with talent to spare. A heady duck main shows the style, cooked with honey and spices, and served with sautéed foie gras, butternut squash purée, and a prune and Armagnac sauce.

OUR TIP: Afternoon tea in the lounge

Chef: Raymond McArdle **Owners:** Gilhooly family **Times:** 12.30-2.30/6.30-9.45, Closed L Sat **Notes:** Tasting menu €75, Sun L €35, Vegetarian available, Smart Dress **Seats:** 120, Pr/dining room 50 **Smoking:** N/Sm in restaurant, Air con **Children:** Menu, Portions **Rooms:** 72 (72 en suite) ★★★★ **Directions:** 11m from M1at Ardee turning (N33) **Parking:** 200 **e-mail:** info@nuremore.com **web:** www.nuremore.com

CO TIPPERARY

CASHEL MAP 01 C3

🌸 Cashel Palace Hotel

Irish

Traditional Irish cuisine in fine 18th-century house

☎ 062 62707

PLACE: The Rock of Cashel, floodlit at night, forms a dramatic backdrop to this elegant 18th-century former Archbishop's house, furnished with antiques, bang in the centre of town.

continued

FOOD: There's a strong bias towards fish, Aberdeen Angus beef and local lamb reflected in a menu that celebrates traditional Irish cooking with modern interpretation.

OUR TIP: Afternoon tea is served in the drawing room

Times: 12-2.30/6-9.30 **Rooms:** 23 (23 en suite) ★★★★ **e-mail:** reception@cashel-palace.ie **web:** www.cashel-palace.ie

🍽 **Chez Hans** Moor Ln ☎ 062 61177 Former Wesleyan chapel offering familiar dishes.

CO WATERFORD

LISMORE MAP 01 C2

🌸 Ballyrafter House

Modern Irish

Relaxed country-house dining

☎ 058 54002

PLACE: Popular with anglers and tourists, this is a relaxed country-house in a beautiful location.

FOOD: Expect modern Irish food with a strong bias towards fish and seafood. Fresh locally sourced produce is used whenever possible.

OUR TIP: Take a stroll around the area before dinner

Times: 1-2.30/7.30-9.30, Closed Tue (ex residents), 31 Oct-17 Mar (ex. for private parties) **Rooms:** 10 (10 en suite) ★★ **e-mail:** info@waterfordhotel.com **web:** www.waterfordhotel.com

WATERFORD MAP 01 C2

🌸🏵 Waterford Castle

Mediterranean, European

Welcoming island castle hotel dining

☎ 051 878203 The Island

MENU GUIDE Seared scallops, lentil & coriander nage • Pan-fried sea bass, soba noodles, wild mushrooms • Pistachio profiteroles

WINE GUIDE 7 bottles under €30 • 9 by the glass (€6.50)

PRICE GUIDE Fixed L €30 • Fixed D €58 • starter €10-€12 • main €30-€32 • dessert €10 • coffee €4.50 • min/water €5 • Service added but optional 10%

PLACE: Enjoying an enchanting island setting, this hotel is reached by a chain link ferry from the mainland. The Munster dining room is inviting, wood-panelled and filled with antiques and there are views across the surrounding deer park. A resident pianist often plays through dinner.

FOOD: Seasonal menus emphasise local and Irish ingredients in a good choice of modern Irish treatments. Seafood is of high quality and figures in an appealing range of international styles such as tempura of Dublin Bay prawns or brill fillet with tomato fondue, chorizo, shallots and saffron & crab risotto.

OUR TIP: Enjoy a round of golf before lunch

Chef: Michael Quinn **Owners:** Munster Dining Room **Times:** 12.30-1.45/7-8.30, Closed Xmas, early Jan, closed L Mon-Fri **Notes:** Vegetarian available, Dress Restrictions, No denim, or trainers, Jacket required for D **Seats:** 50, Pr/dining room 80 **Smoking:** N/Sm in restaurant **Children:** Menu, Portions **Rooms:** 19 (19 en suite) ★★★★ **Directions:** Telephone for directions **Parking:** 200 **e-mail:** info@waterfordcastle.com **web:** www.waterfordcastle.com

Ireland

CO WESTMEATH

ATHLONE MAP 01 C4

 Hodson Bay

European, International

Smart lakeshore hotel dining with island and country views

☎ 090 6442000 Hodson Bay

MENU GUIDE Cajun chicken salad • Fresh Ballinstelligs Bay lobster with maître d'hôtel beurre • Traditional crème brûlée, shortbread

WINE GUIDE ⚲ Rosemont Chardonnay €20 • ⚱ Rosemont Shiraz €20 • 14 bottles over €30, 26 bottles under €30

PRICE GUIDE Fixed L €18.50-€23 • starter €4-€12 • main €17-€40 • dessert €5.50-€6.50 • coffee €2 • Service optional

PLACE: Recently refurbished hotel with its own marina on the shore of Lough Ree. L'Escale restaurant is classically designed and the atmosphere is relaxed and intimate. Less formal dining is available in the buttery and conservatory.

FOOD: Evening menus are inspired by the finest produce, with fresh fish delivered each day and lobsters from the tank.

OUR TIP: Athlone Golf Course surrounds the property

Chef: Kevin Ward **Owners:** John O'Sullivan **Times:** 12.30-2.15/7-9.30 **Notes:** Fixed D 6 courses, Vegetarian available **Seats:** 180, Pr/dining room 40 **Smoking:** N/Sm in restaurant, Air con **Children:** Menu, Portions **Rooms:** 133 (133 en suite) ★★★ **Directions:** From Athlone follow signs for Roscommon. Approx 2.5m on entering Hodson Bay follow signs for the hotel on right **Parking:** 300

e-mail: info@hodsonbayhotel.com **web:** www.hodsonbayhotel.com

🕸 Wineport Lodge

Modern Classical

Wholesome cooking in lakeside setting

☎ 090 643 9010 Glasson

MENU GUIDE Rabbit & goose rillette with rocket leaves • Carved rack of lamb on celeriac cream • Chocolate mousse

WINE GUIDE ⚲ Chablis €30 • ⚱ Rioja €39 • 40 bottles over €30, 40 bottles under €30 • 10 by the glass (€7-€14)

PRICE GUIDE Fixed L fr €20 • Fixed D €55 • starter €8-€15 main €20-€35 • dessert €8-€12 • coffee €3 • min/water €5 Service optional

PLACE: It's hard to think of a more impressive location for a hotel than the shores of the inner lakes of Lough Ree on the Shannon. Customers can arrive by road or water and dine on the deck or in the attractive dining room. Spectacular views and friendly service reflects the highest standards of Irish hospitality.

FOOD: Wholesome local produce is served in generous portions. The wine list is a major attraction; regular wine dinners are hosted by visiting wine growers.

OUR TIP: Ten luxurious lakeshore bedrooms with balconies

Times: 6-10, Closed 24-26 Dec, closed L all week **Rooms:** 10 (10 en suite) 🐾 **Parking:** 100 **e-mail:** lodge@wineport.ie **web:** www.wineport.ie

CO WEXFORD

GOREY MAP 01 D3

🕸 Ashdown Park Hotel

International

Well-equipped modern hotel for enjoyable dining

☎ 055 80500 The Coach Rd

MENU GUIDE Quail, shallot stuffing • Monkfish, & calamari stirfry, red curry dressing • Nougat parfait, mint & mango salsa

WINE GUIDE ⚲ Dalwood Chardonnay €19.50 • ⚱ Dalwood Cabernet Sauvignon €19.50 • 12 bottles over €30, 12 bottles under €30 • 3 by the glass (€4-€5.50)

PRICE GUIDE Fixed L €16.95 • Fixed D €35 • starter €4.75-€10 • main €19.50-€24 • dessert €5.75-€7 • coffee €1.80 • min/water €5 • Service optional

PLACE: A modern hotel within easy reach of Wexford. There's a pub-style bar, a library bar and a full range of spa and leisure facilities. Choose to eat in the carvery or, for fine dining, in the Rowan Tree restaurant.

FOOD: The modern Irish menus with international influences feature local seasonal produce, with lots of fresh fish dishes and with some interesting and quirky twists such as a 'Bloody Mary' dressing.

OUR TIP: Take a stroll on the beautiful sands of Ballymoney Beach

Chef: Siobhain Devereux **Owners:** Pat & Tom Redmond **Times:** 12.30-3/6-9.30, Closed 24-25 Dec, closed L Mon-Sat **Notes:** Vegetarian available **Seats:** 110, Pr/dining room 90 **Smoking:** N/Sm in restaurant, Air con **Children:** Menu, Portions **Rooms:** 60 (60 en suite) ★★★★ **Directions:** On approach to Gorey Town take the N11 from Dublin. Take left signposted for Courtown. Hotel on left **Parking:** 150

e-mail: info@ashdownparkhotel.com **web:** www.ashdownparkhotel.com

🕸🕸🕸 Marlfield House see page 683

ROSSLARE MAP 01 D2

🕸🕸 Kelly's Resort

European

Smart and intimate restaurant in famous hotel

☎ 053 32114

PLACE: A truly fine hotel, owned and run by the Kelly family since 1895. Exemplary in every way, it offers extensive leisure facilities and a stylishly intimate Beaches restaurant featuring original art from the hotel's renowned collection. Casual during the day, the atmosphere is more elegant and formal in the evenings.

FOOD: The fixed-price daily changing menu may be extensive, featuring classic seafood and steaks alongside more adventurous dishes, but it champions local produce. Look for fish landed at Kilmore Quay, Wexford beef and the hotel's own lamb.

OUR TIP: Booking essential

Times: 1-2/7.30-9, Closed Dec-Feb **Rooms:** 118 (118 en suite) ★★★★ **e-mail:** kellyhot@iol.ie **web:** www.kellys.ie

Ireland

GOREY MAP 01 D3

Marlfield House

Classic
Luxurious mansion house offering assured Mediterranean classics
☎ 055 21124

MENU GUIDE Foie gras (pan-fried & terrine) • Confit of Barbary duck leg, honey-roasted butternut squash • Crème brûlée, lemon tart & chocolate pot

PRICE GUIDE Fixed L €37 • Fixed D €57

PLACE: This Regency style building has been sympathetically extended and developed into an excellent family-run hotel. An atmosphere of luxury and elegance permeates every corner of the house and is underpinned by truly professional yet friendly service. Dinner in the restaurant is a guaranteed highlight of a stay here. Each of the restaurant's three rooms has a view of the hotel's lovely gardens and the generously sized tables are laid with the best quality glass and crockery.

FOOD: The daily changing menu is full of innovative combinations and has a strong Mediterranean twist. From a

beautifully presented starter of foie gras cooked two ways to a selection of favourite desserts, the cooking is skilled, accurate and underpinned by a firm grounding in the classics. No ingredient is overworked, allowing the natural flavours to dominate. There is a clear commitment to quality ingredients, many of which come from the hotel's own kitchen garden, and is supported by an extensive wine list that includes a good selection of half bottles. A dedicated sommelier is on hand to answer any questions.
OUR TIP: Stroll through the gardens and meet the peacocks
Chef: Michael MacCurtain **Owners:** The Bowe Family **Times:** 12.30-2/7-9, Closed 15 Dec-30 Jan, closed L Mon-Sat **Notes:** Vegetarian available, Dress Restrictions **Seats:** 70, Pr/dining room 20 **Smoking:** N/Sm in restaurant, Air con **Children:** Min 8 yrs at D **Rooms:** 20 (20 en suite) ★★★ **Directions:** 1m from Gorey on R742 (Courtown road) **e-mail:** info@marlfieldhouse.ie **web:** www.marlfield.com

WEXFORD MAP 01 D3

Ferrycarrig Hotel
International
Popular modern hotel restaurant with estuary views
☎ 053 20999 Ferrycarrig Bridge

MENU GUIDE Wicklow ostrich salad • Mille-feuille of smoked haddock, café de Paris sauce • Chocolate marquis, raspberry sorbet

WINE GUIDE ⚲ Wolf Blass Chardonnay €23.50 • ⚲ Wolf Blass Cabernet Sauvignon €26.15 • 17 bottles over €30, 55 bottles under €30 • 10 by the glass (€5-€7.25)

PRICE GUIDE Fixed L €15-€24 • Fixed D €34-€40 • starter €8.50-€12 • main €17-€27 • dessert €8-€10 • coffee €1.90 • Service optional

PLACE: Built around the curve of the bay, this smart modern hotel offers stunning views of the Slaney River estuary. The Tides restaurant has well-spaced tables with elegant appointments and gets very busy making reservation essential, particularly for non-residents. Impressive leisure centre.
FOOD: With a wordy menu, the cooking impresses and features the best of seasonal local produce. Dishes are classically inspired, and range from simple combinations (cannon of lamb with rosemary jus) to more complex offerings, such as bacon-wrapped pork served with a pepper and pineapple sauce.
OUR TIP: Book for dinner when making your reservation at the hotel

Chef: Tony Carty **Owners:** Mr Griffin **Times:** 12.30-2.15/6.00-9.45 **Notes:** Mineral water is complimentary, Vegetarian available, Smart Dress, Civ Wed 250 **Seats:** 140, Pr/dining room 40 **Smoking:** N/Sm in restaurant, Air con **Rooms:** 102 (102 en suite) ★★★★ **Directions:** On N11 by Slaney Estuary, beside Ferrycarrig Castle **Parking:** 200 **e-mail:** ferrycarrig@ferrycarrighotel.com **web:** www.ferrycarrighotel.ie

denotes restaurants that place particular emphasis on making the most of local ingredients.

Give us your views! All the rosetted restaurants in this guide have been visited by one of the AA's team of professional inspectors, but we want to hear from you! Use the report forms in the back of the guide or email us at lifestyleguides@theaa.com with your comments on any establishments featured or on the restaurants that you feel are worthy of an entry. We would also be pleased to receive your views on the guide itself and suggestions for information you would like to see included.

continued

Ireland

WEXFORD *continued* MAP 01 D3

Newbay Country House & Restaurant

European, Irish 🐟NEW

Georgian country-house dining

☎ 053 42779 Newbay, Carrick

MENU GUIDE Baked scallops with leek & ginger nage • Roast breast of free-range chicken, ballontine of its leg • Pineapple baked Alaska

WINE GUIDE ♀ Concho y Toro Sauvignon Blanc €18 ♦ Concho y Toro Cabernet Sauvignon €18 • 12 bottles over €30, 13 bottles under €30 • 4 by the glass (€5)

PRICE GUIDE Starter €4.95-€10.95 • main €18.95-€28.95 dessert €6.90 • coffee €2 • min/water €4 • Service optional

PLACE: A short drive from Wexford City, this Georgian country-house hotel is set in mature, well-tended gardens. The dining room is comfortable and more formal than the relaxed bistro on the lower floor.

FOOD: High quality ingredients are treated with care, with accurate cooking and judicious seasoning, especially in seafood dishes, which are a particular strength of the kitchen.

OUR TIP: Great for seafood
Chef: Brian Heffernan **Owners:** Alec Scallan **Times:** 12-3/6-9.30
Notes: Smart Dress **Seats:** 75 **Smoking:** N/Sm in restaurant
Children: Menu, Portions **Directions:** Take Cork Rd from Wexford, left after Citroen Garage, at x-rds turn right, restaurant on right **Parking:** 70
e-mail: newbay@newbayhouse.com **web:** www.newbayhouse.com

Whitford House Hotel Health & Leisure Spa

European

Sound cooking in friendly, family-run hotel

☎ 053 43444 New Line Rd

MENU GUIDE Seafood cocktail • Honey roast duckling, egg noodle stir fry, sweet 'n' sour glaze • Apple crumble, crème anglaise

WINE GUIDE ♀ Motif Blanc €19 • ♦ Rosemount Shiraz €19 8 bottles over €30, 49 bottles under €30 • 4 by the glass (€4.25-€4.50)

PRICE GUIDE Fixed L €14.95-€17.95 • Fixed D €24.95-€31.95 • starter €4.25-€9.50 • main €15.95-€24.95 • dessert €5.95 • coffee €1.80 • min/water €2.25 • Service optional

PLACE: A long-established local favourite, this friendly hotel gets busy on weekends, so it's worth booking ahead to be sure of a table. Dinner is served in the smart and spacious surroundings of the Footprints Restaurant, often accompanied by the tinkling of ivories or a classical guitar.

FOOD: Whitford House majors in European cooking and aims to please with a menu of crowd-pleasers such as steaks, surf 'n turf, and moules marinière.

OUR TIP: Handy for Rosslare ferry port
Chef: Michael O'Connor **Owners:** The Whitty Family **Times:** 12.30-3/7-9, Closed 23 Dec-28 Dec, closed L Mon-Sat **Notes:** Vegetarian available
Seats: 100 **Smoking:** N/Sm in restaurant, Air con **Children:** Menu, Portions **Rooms:** 36 (36 en suite) ★★★ **Directions:** From Rosslare ferry port follow N25. At Duncannon Road rdbt, turn right onto R733, hotel immediately on left. 1.5m from Wexford Town **Parking:** 150
e-mail: info@whitford.ie **web:** www.whitford.ie

CO WICKLOW

BLESSINGTON MAP 01 D3

Downshire House

Irish

Country-house style cooking in friendly Georgian hotel

☎ 045 865199

PLACE: This fine Georgian house hotel, in the very attractive village of Blessington, is renowned for its relaxed atmosphere and friendly service.

FOOD: The bright, smart restaurant, with its crisp white table linen, serves Irish cuisine using locally sourced produce such as salmon, Wicklow lamb, beef and game when in season. Expect mains like roast half chicken, baked Wicklow ham and herb stuffing

OUR TIP: Don't miss the home-made chicken liver pâté
Times: 12.30-3/5.30-9.30, Closed 2 wks Xmas & New Year **Rooms:** 25 (25 en suite) ★★★ **e-mail:** info@downshirehouse.com
web: www.downshirehouse.com

MACREDDIN MAP 01 D3

The Strawberry Tree Restaurant

Modern Irish

Innovative organic and wild food cuisine

☎ 0402 36444 BrookLodge Hotel & Wells Spa

MENU GUIDE Marinated wild mackerel • Beef fillet, buttered beetroot, balsamic jus • Passionfruit mousse, poppy seed biscuits

WINE GUIDE ♀ Terra Sana J & F Lurton Charentais €25 ♦ De Martino Cabernet Malbec €25 • 60 bottles over €30, 56 bottles under €30 • 56 by the glass (€6.20)

PRICE GUIDE Food prices not confirmed for 2006. Please telephone for details

PLACE: This luxurious country-house boasts a spa and equestrian centre as well as micro-brewery, organic bakery and smoke house. The Strawberry Tree restaurant is romantic and elegant, and reservations are essential

FOOD: This award-winning restaurant is one of only a handful in Europe that serves solely organic and wild foods. Chefs are committed to the Slow Food movement and imaginative modern Irish dishes with a rustic twist make the most of wonderful produce. Vibrant flavours are preserved, as with a succulent braised widgeon served with red cabbage and blood orange, or a spankingly fresh crab gratin.

OUR TIP: 30 organic wines available by the glass
Chef: Norman Luedke, Evan Doyle **Owners:** The Doyle Family
Times: 1.30-3.30/7-9.30, Closed L Mon-Sat **Notes:** Vegetarian available, Dress Restrictions, Smart casual **Seats:** 130, Pr/dining room 50
Smoking: N/Sm in restaurant, Air con **Children:** Menu, Portions
Rooms: 40 (40 en suite) ★★★★ **Directions:** From Dublin take N11, turn off at Rathnew for Rathdrum, then through Aughrim to Macreddin (2m) **Parking:** 400 **e-mail:** brooklodge@macreddin.ie
web: www.brooklodge.com

Ireland

RATHNEW MAP 01 D3

 Hunter's Hotel

Irish

Beautiful views and 150 years of history

☎ 0404 40106

PLACE: This delightful inn is one of Ireland's oldest coaching inns and the family home of the owners for well over 150 years. Its beautiful prize-winning gardens, bordering on the River Varty, can be admired from the large restaurant windows.

FOOD: Using the best of local and seasonal produce, the dinner menu shows plenty of flair, with enjoyable dishes like fresh crab and tomato gratin or tender roast duck served on a pistachio mash.

Times: 12.45-3/7.30-9, Closed 3 days Xmas **Rooms:** 16 (16 en suite)
★★★ **e-mail:** reception@hunters.ie **web:** www.hunters.ie

WOODENBRIDGE MAP 01 D3

 Woodenbridge Hotel

European

Hotel dining in beautiful Vale of Avoca

☎ 0402 35146

PLACE: Overlooking the river and the golf course in the beautiful Vale of Avoca, you couldn't ask for a more delightful setting. The candlelit Redmond Restaurant has an air of old-world charm, and is popular with locals, tourists and golfers.

FOOD: Wexford beef, fish landed at Kilmore Quay, local vegetables and the hotel's own lamb all feature on the modern Irish fixed-price menu and the carte.

OUR TIP: Enjoy a drink by the open fire in the cosy bar

Times: 12.30-3/7-9, Closed L Mon-Sat, 25 Dec **Rooms:** 23 (23 en suite)
★★★ **e-mail:** wbhotel@iol.ie **web:** www.woodenbridgehotel.com

Ireland

How do I find my perfect place?

New editions on sale now!

Available from all good bookshops, on www.theAA.com or call 01256 491524

Late Entries

These restaurants were appointed to the scheme too late for us to include them in the main body of the guide (some of them had yet to be inspected at the time of going to press). For up-to-date reports and details of any changes affecting these and all restaurants in the guide, please see our website **www.theAA.com**

England

BERKSHIRE
HURLEY
Black Boys Inn
01628 824212 Henley Road, Hurley, SL6 5NQ
16th-century inn with contemporary feel offering modern British cuisine.

CAMBRIDGESHIRE
CAMBOURNE
⊚ The Cambridge Belfry
01954 714995 Back Street,
Cambourne, CB3 6BW
Sleek modern restaurant serves confident traditional classics in hotel overlooking lake.

DEVON
NEWTON POPPLEFORD
⊚ ⊚ Moores Restaurant & Rooms
01395 568100 6 Greenbank, High Street,
Newton Poppleford, EX10 0EB
Crisp-clothed tables in smallish restaurant serving imaginative dishes with modern interpretation.

DORSET
CORFE MULLEN
⊚ The Coventry Arms
01258 857284 Mill Street,
Corfe Mullen, BH21 3RH
Once a 15th-century watermill now serving local fish and meat cooked with modern influences.

GLOUCESTERSHIRE
GLOUCESTER
⊚ Hatton Court
01452 617412 Upton Hill, Upton St Leonards,
Gloucester, GL4 8DE
Familiar classics cooked in French style in relaxed Cotswold manor.

GREATER MANCHESTER
WIGAN
⊚ Simply Heathcotes
01257 425803 Moss Lane,
Wrightington WN6 9PB
With sleek and contempory decor, this popular restaurant offers traditional Heathcotes style of British cuisine with Mediterranean touches.

HAMPSHIRE
HIGHCLERE
⊚ The Yew Tree Inn
08452 412969 Hollington Cross, Andover
Road, Newbury, RG20 9SE
Linen-clothed tables and brasserie-style cooking in 17th-century whitewashed, low-beamed building close to Highclere Castle (Marco Pierre White is one of the directors here).

HEREFORDSHIRE
WEOBLEY
⊚ The Salutation Inn
01544 318443 Market Pitch, Weobley, HR4 8SJ
Village inn going places – busy lunchtimes and more than a hint of French to the cuisine.

KENT
AYLESFORD
Hengist Restaurant
01622 719273 7-9 High Street,
Aylesford, ME20 7AX
Chocolate suede-lined walls indicate an interior design feast to match modern French cuisine in 1560's building.

LONDON
E14
⊚ Royal China
020 7719 0888 Canary Wharf Riverside,
30 Westferry Circus, London, E14 8RR
East meets West with River Thames the backdrop to traditional Cantonese restaurant.

Metrogusto
020 7226 9400 13 Theberton Street,
London, N1 0QY
Paintings are part of the decor in this privately
owned Italian restaurant where fresh pasta is a
speciality.

Beauberry House
020 8299 9788 Gallery Road,
London, SE21 7AB
In glorious parkland with terraces, the new-look
restaurant promises regional French cooking.

Shikara
020 7581 6555 87 Sloane Avenue,
London, SW3 3DX
Northern Indian food cooked with flair and with
healthy eating in mind.

Deep
020 7736 3337 Imperial Wharf,
London, SW6 2UB
Swedish seafood creatively presented in smart
Chelsea surroundings.

Wizzy
020 7736 9171 616 Fulham Road,
London, SW6 5RP
Coolly simple decor offsets modern interpretations of classic Korean dishes from chef Whizzy
(formerly at Nobu and Hakkasan).

Yi-Ban Chelsea
020 7731 6606 No 5 The Boulevard, Imperial
Wharf, Imperial Road, London, SW6 2UB
A new addition to Imperial Wharf with moody
dark decor and upmarket modern
Chinese/Tepanyaki cuisine.

Salt Yard
020 7637 0657 54 Goodge Street,
London, W1T 4NA
Spanish and Italian tapas with flair.

Tangawizi
020 8891 3737 406 Richmond Road,
Richmond Bridge, Twickenham, TW1 2EB
Northern Indian cooking with a modern slant in
smart venue (from the stable of Vineet Bhatia)

The Neptune Inn & Restaurant
01485 532122 85 Old Hunstanton Road,
Hunstanton, PE36 6HZ
Old inn reincarnated into smart restaurant
serving quality, locally-sourced dishes.

The Cottage Restaurant & Ternhill Farm House
01630 638984 Ternhill,
Market Drayton, TF9 3PX
Georgian farmhouse now a busy rustic restaurant
where Aga slow-cooking is in tandem with
modern British style.

The Bradford Arms Hotels
01691 830582 Llanymynech,
Oswestry, SY22 6EJ
Cooking is committed to innovative modern
British food, locally produced.

Wynnstay Hotel
01691 655261 Church Street,
Oswestry, SY11 2SZ
A former coaching inn with elegantly renovated
restaurant serving traditional British dishes with a
contemporary touch.

SOMERSET
The Moody Goose At The Old Priory
01761 416784 Church Square,
Midsomer Norton, BA3 2HX
Small village-centre country hotel where classic
dishes are presented with a modern slant.

Goodfellows
01749 673866 5 Sadler Street, Wells
An amalgam of smart restaurant, café, patisserie
and fishmonger combine to create a popular
eating place serving tip-top food.

Lanes
01935 862555 West Coker, Yeovil, BA22 9AJ
Modern cooking and brasserie informality in
contemporary surroundings created within
Victorian house.

SURREY
Station Masters House
01372 466721 The Parade,
Claygate, KT10 0PB
Village surroundings to a family-run restaurant
where menu changes to sophisticated in the
evenings.

WORCESTERSHIRE
Epic Bar Brasserie
01527 871929 68 Hanbury Road, Stoke Prior,
Bromsgrove, B60 4DN
A local hub of gastronomic activity with
international menu in smart, retro-designed
restaurant of this converted inn.

Epic Bar Brasserie
01905 620000 The Half Way House,
Dunhampton, DY13 9SW
A slick ultra-modern brasserie with extensive
fashionable menus, including grazing options.

YORKSHIRE, NORTH
The Old Deanery
01765 600003 Minster Road, Ripon, HG4 1QS
Close to the Cathedral, oak-panelled dining
room, British food and sound cooking.

Scotland
CITY OF GLASGOW
Café Royale
01413 38 6606 340 Crowe Road, G11 7HT
Simplicity is the hallmark of this good-value café-
style restaurant serving fresh seafood and
traditional Scottish dishes.

HIGHLAND
Toravaig House Hotel
01471 820200 Knock Bay,
Teangue, Isle of Syke, IV44 8RE
The Iona Restaurant is a haven of peace offering
Skye's wonderful local produce – fish, game and
lamb.

PERTH & KINROSS

KINLOCH RANNOCH

🌹 Dunalastair Hotel

01882 632323 Kinloch Rannoch PH16 5PW
Great hospitality with carefully prepared dishes
served in fine wood-panelled dining room of
traditional Highland hotel.

Wales

DENBIGHSHIRE

RHYL

🌹 Barratt's at Ty'n Rhyl

01745 344138 Ty'n Rhyl,
167 Vale Road, Rhyl, LL18 2PH
16th-century stone-built house in peaceful
location offering imaginative food with fresh
fish always on menu.

POWYS

CRICKHOWELL

🌹 Ty Croeso Hotel

01873 810573 The Dardy, Llangattock,
Crickhowell, NP8 1PU
Country-house style dining with Welsh emphasis
in cooking.

Republic of Ireland

CO CAVAN

CAVAN

🌹 Cavan Crystal Hotel

049 4360600 Dublin Road, Cavan
No surprises but everything as promised in the
innovative modern Irish cooking here – some
unusual twists to excellent ingredients.

CO GALWAY

GALWAY

🌹 Roundstone House Hotel

095 35864 Roundstone, Connemara, Galway
Close to Connemara mountains and overlooking
the Bay, superb sea views and delicious seafood
in informal dining room.

CO MAYO

WESTPORT

🌹 Knockranny House Hotel

098 28600 Westport
Simple, good cooking using local produce
enjoyed in popular elegant dining room with
superb views over Clew Bay and the town.
Own smokery.

KEY TO ATLAS

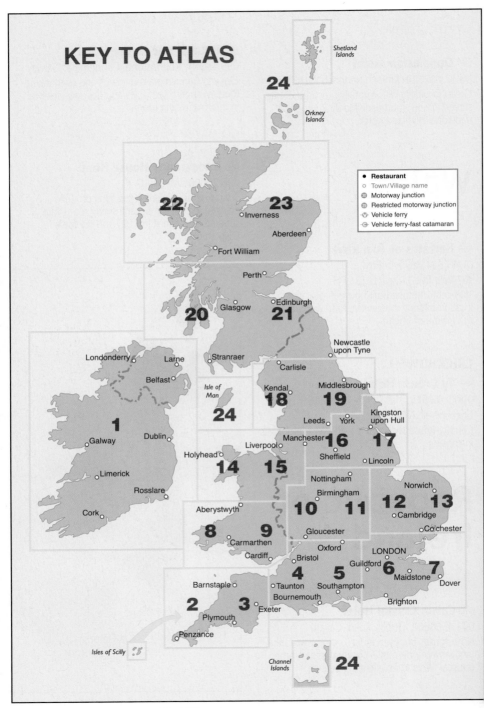

Shetland Islands

24

Orkney Islands

- ● Restaurant
- ○ Town/Village name
- ⊛ Motorway junction
- ⊛ Restricted motorway junction
- ⬦ Vehicle ferry
- ⬦ Vehicle ferry-fast catamaran

22   **23**
○ Inverness

Aberdeen ○

○ Fort William

Perth ○

○ Edinburgh
20   Glasgow ○   **21**

Newcastle upon Tyne

Londonderry ○   Larne ○   ○ Stranraer

Belfast ○   Carlisle ○

Isle of Man   Kendal ○   Middlesbrough ○
24   **18**   **19**

Leeds ○   York ○   Kingston upon Hull

1   Manchester ○ **16**   **17**
○ Galway   Dublin ○   Liverpool ○   Sheffield ○   ○ Lincoln

Holyhead ○   **14**   **15**

○ Limerick   Nottingham ○
Rosslare ○   Birmingham ○   Norwich ○
12   **13**
Cork ○   Aberystwyth ○   **10**   **11**   ○ Cambridge

Gloucester ○   ○ Colchester
8   **9**
Carmarthen ○   Oxford ○   LONDON
Cardiff ○   Bristol ○   Guildford ○ **6**   **7**
4   **5**   Maidstone ○   Dover
Barnstaple ○   ○ Taunton   Southampton ○
Bournemouth ○   Brighton ○
2   **3** ○ Exeter
Plymouth ○

Isles of Scilly

○ Penzance

Channel Islands   **24**

© Automobile Association Developments Limited 2005

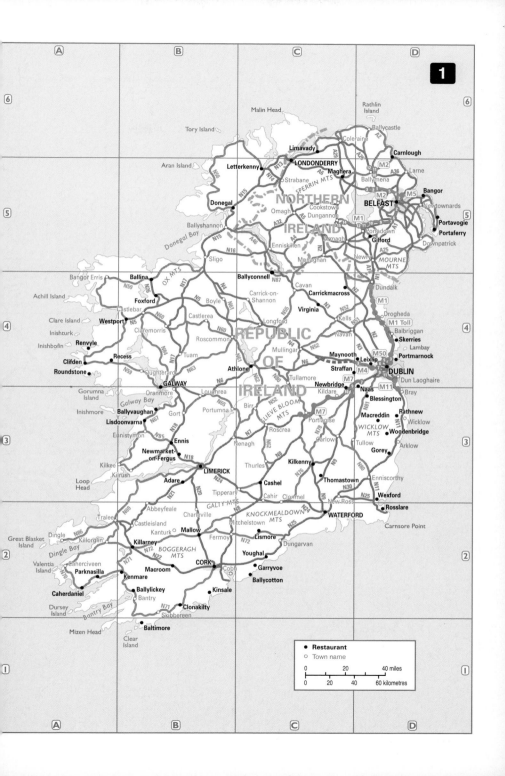

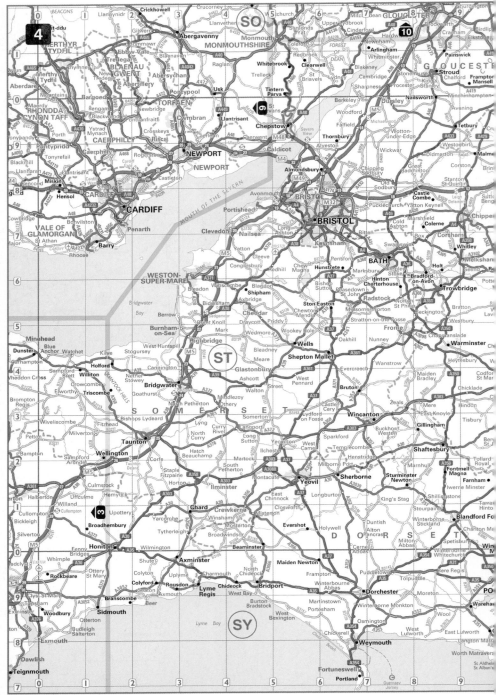

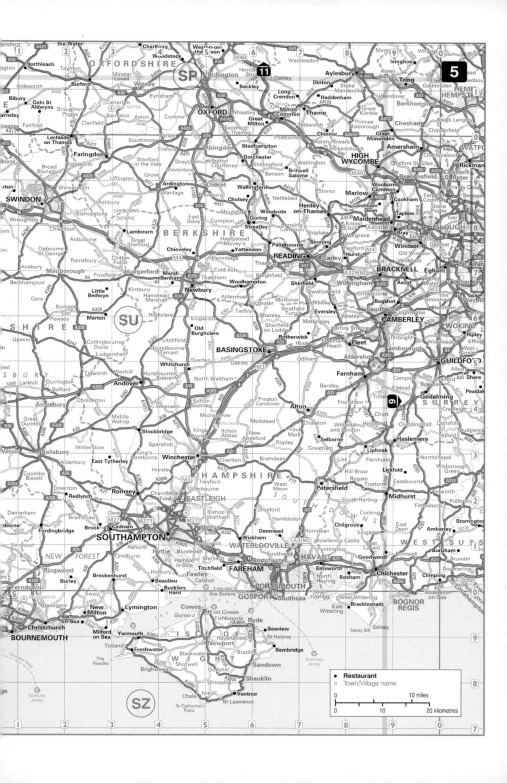

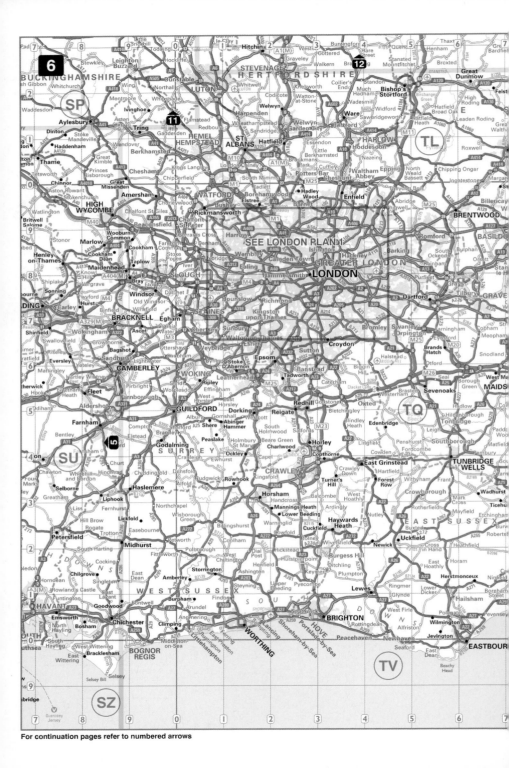

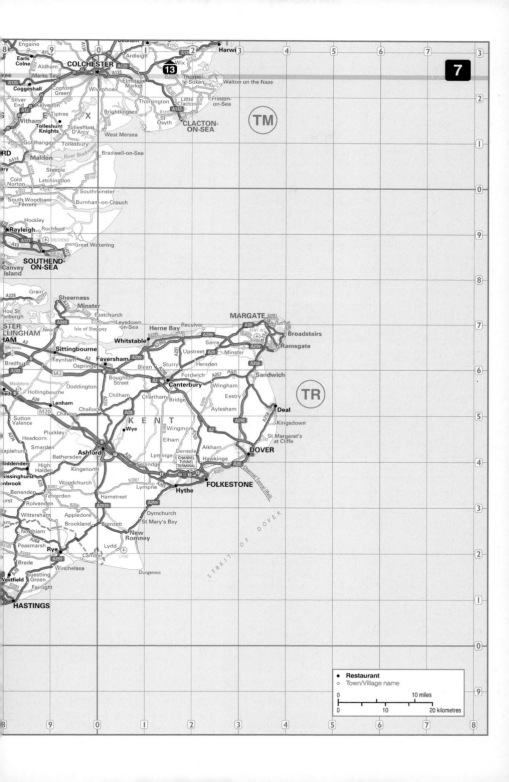

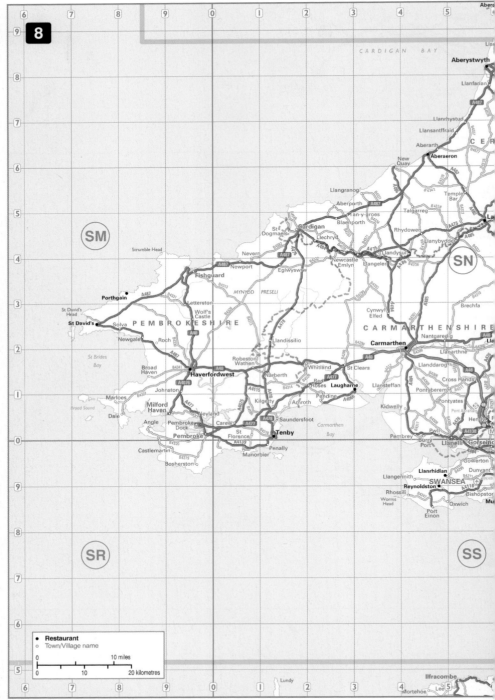

For continuation pages refer to numbered arrows

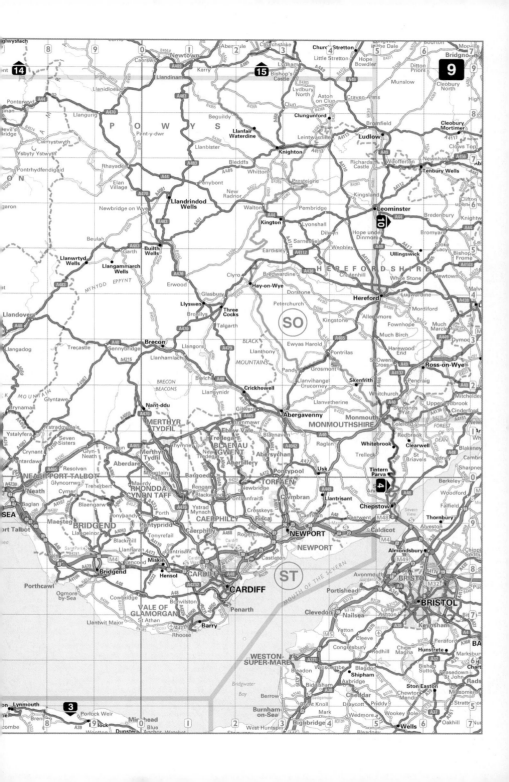

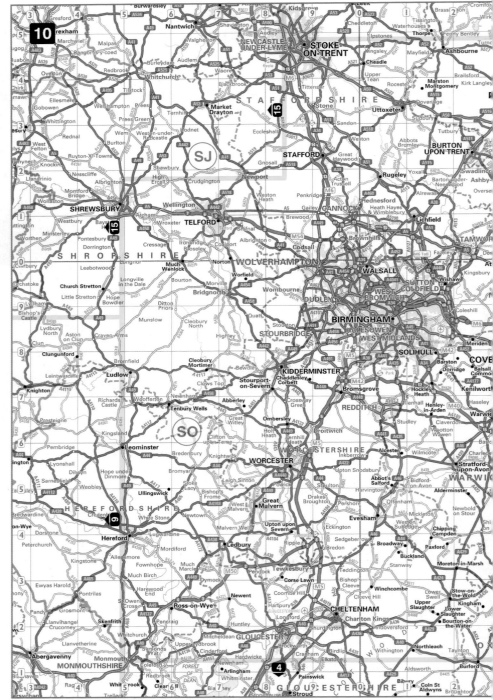

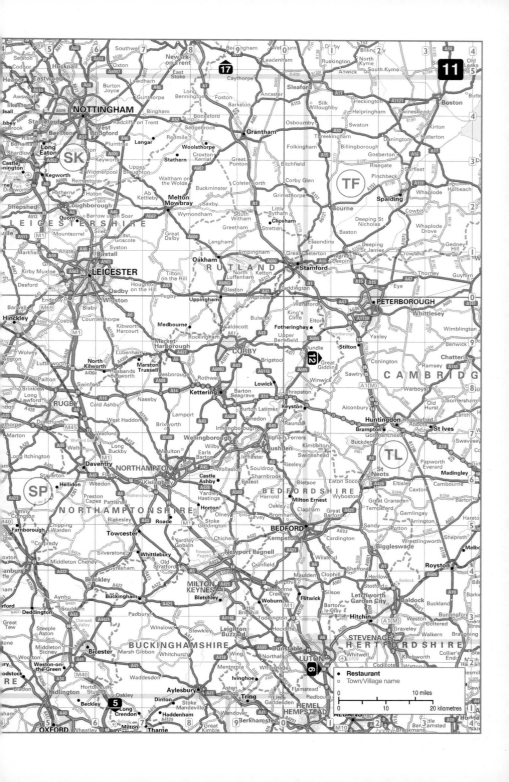

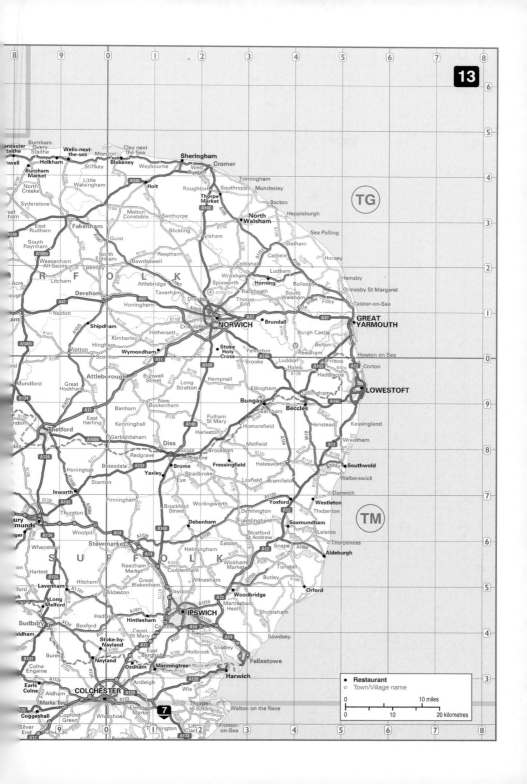

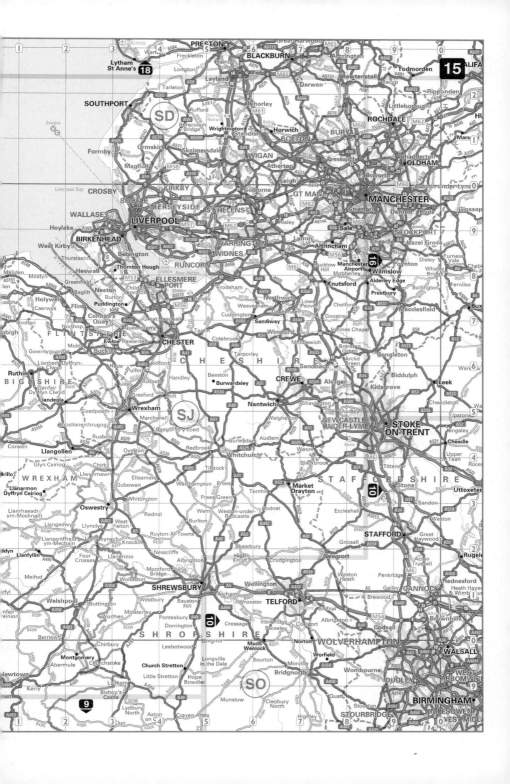

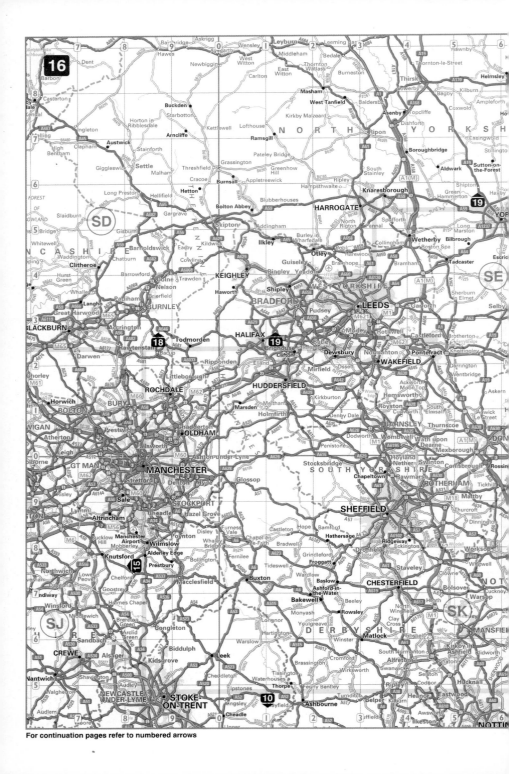

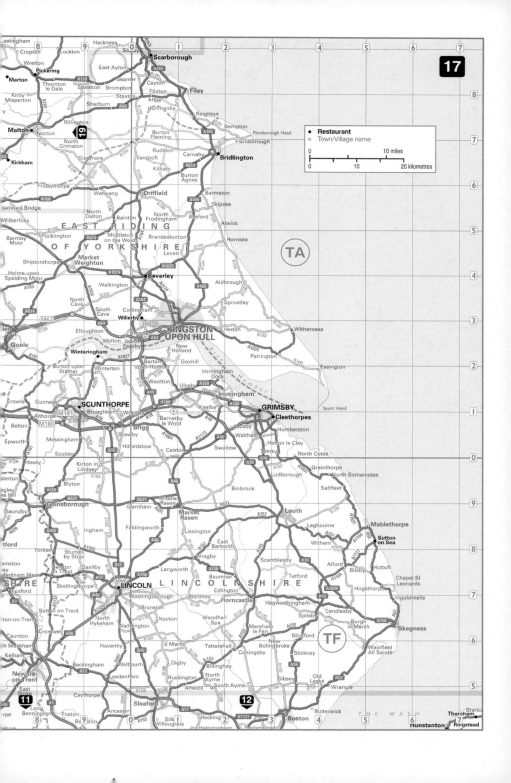

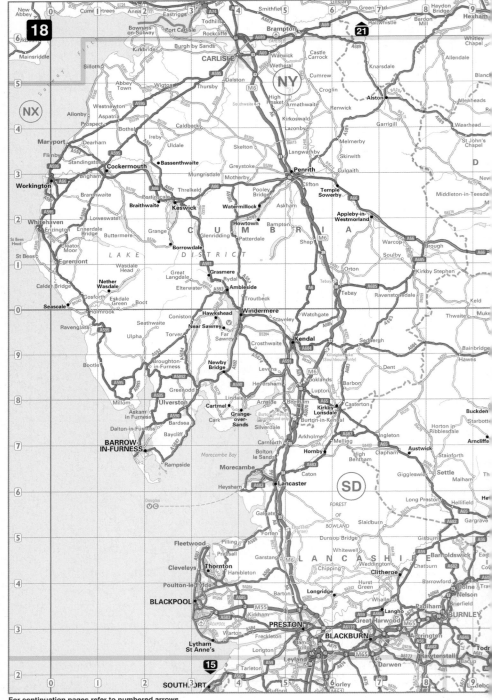

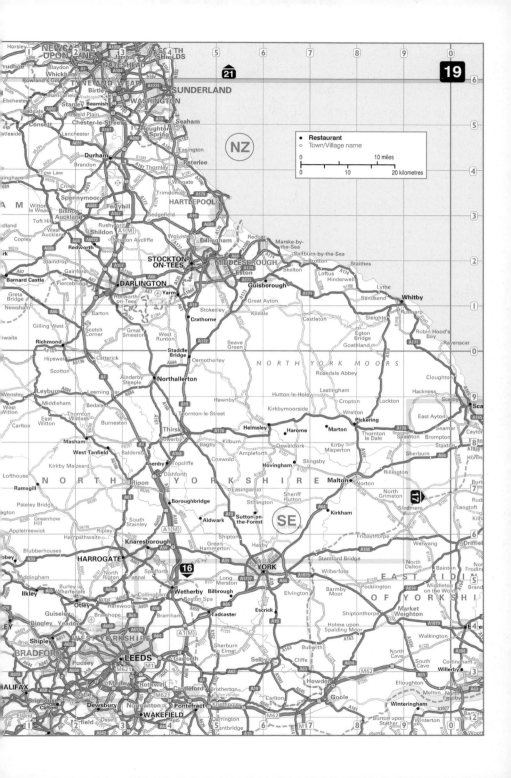

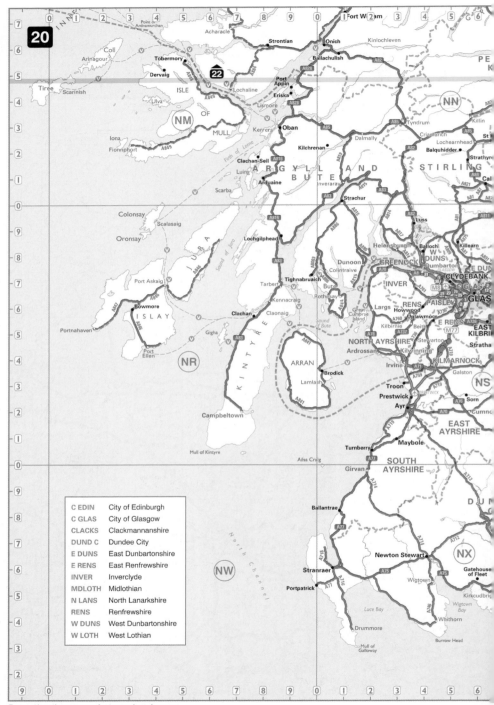

C EDIN	City of Edinburgh
C GLAS	City of Glasgow
CLACKS	Clackmannanshire
DUND C	Dundee City
E DUNS	East Dunbartonshire
E RENS	East Renfrewshire
INVER	Inverclyde
MDLOTH	Midlothian
N LANS	North Lanarkshire
RENS	Renfrewshire
W DUNS	West Dunbartonshire
W LOTH	West Lothian

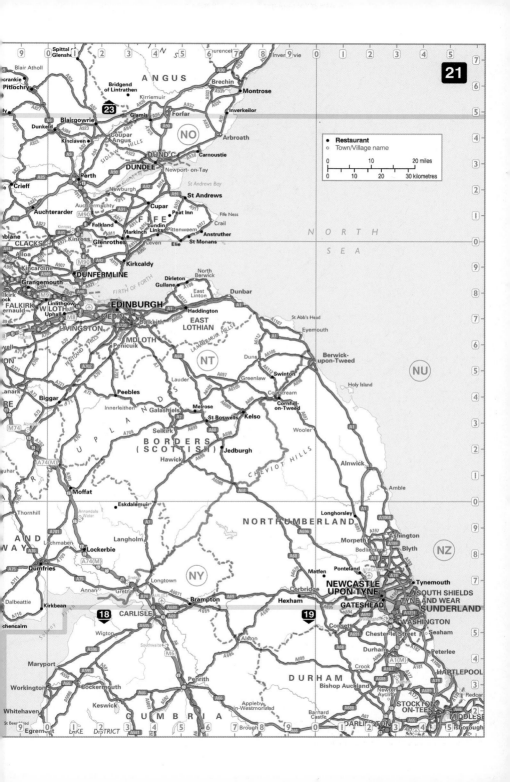

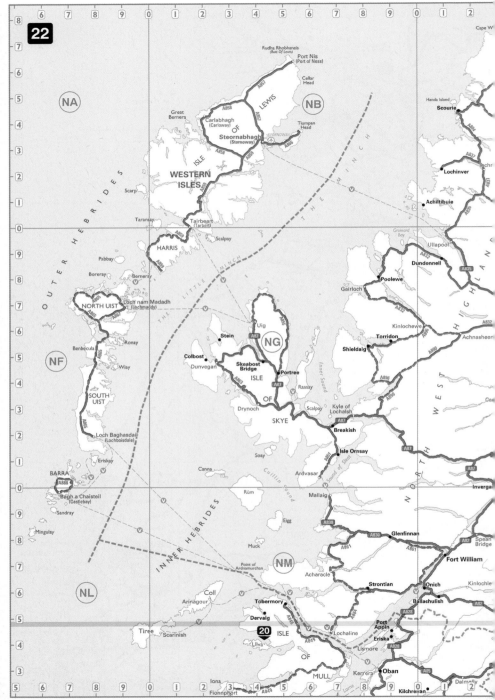

22

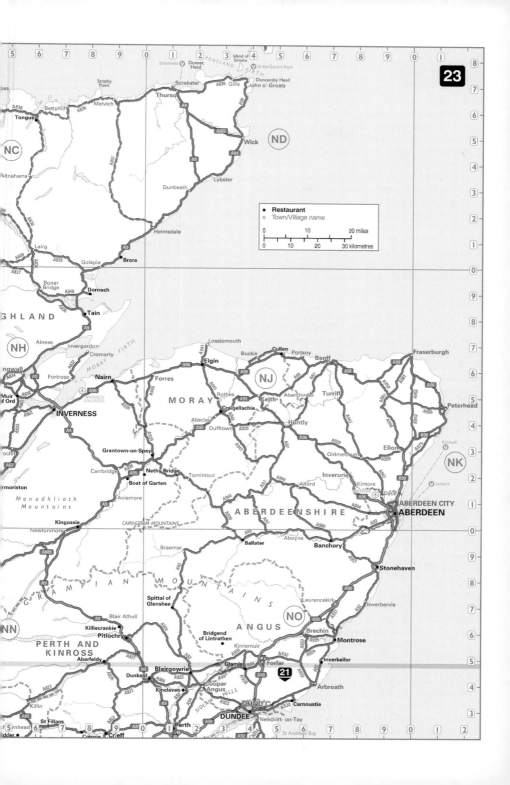

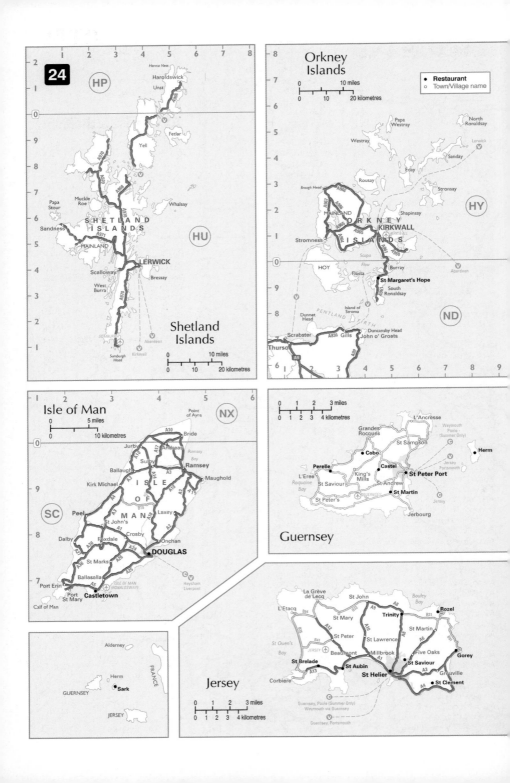

INDEX

D

INDEX

T

U

V

INDEX

Picture credits

Photos sourced from : Bananastock 1, 3t, 3cl, 3cr, 3b, 4, 16, 17t, 17b, 19
Brand X Pictures 17c, 21
Photodisc 14

Please send this form to:
Editor, The Restaurant Guide,
Lifestyle Guides,
The Automobile Association,
Fanum House,
Basingstoke RG21 4EA

or fax: 01256 491647
or e-mail: lifestyleguides@theAA.com

Please use this form to tell us about any restaurant you have visited, whether it is in the guide or not currently listed. Feedback from readers helps us to keep our guide accurate and up to date. Please note, however, that if you have a complaint to make during a visit, we strongly recommend that you discuss the matter with the restaurant management there and then so that they have a chance to put things right before your visit is spoilt. The AA does not undertake to arbitrate between you and the restaurant management, or to obtain compensation or engage in correspondence.

Date:

Your name (block capitals)

Your address (block capitals)

....

....

....

e-mail address: ....

Restaurant name and address: (If you are recommending a new restaurant please enclose a menu or note the dishes that you ate.)

....

....

....

Comments:...

....

....

(please attach a separate sheet if necessary)   **PTO**

We may use information we hold about you to write, e-mail or telephone you about other products and services offered by us and our carefully selected partners, but we can assure you that we will not disclose it to third parties.

Please tick here if you DO NOT wish to receive details of other products or services from the AA.

The Restaurant Guide 2006

Readers' Report Form

	YES	NO
Have you bought this guide before?	☐	☐

Please list any other similar guides that you use regularly.....................................
....
....

What do you find most useful about The AA Restaurant Guide?

....
....
....
....

Please answer these questions to help us make improvements to the guide:

What are your main reasons for visiting restaurants (circle all that apply)

business entertaining   business travel   trying famous restaurants

family celebrations   leisure travel   trying new food

enjoying not having to cook yourself   to eat food you couldn't cook yourself

other ....   because I enjoy eating out regularly

How often do you visit a restaurant for lunch or dinner? (circle one choice)
once a week   once a fortnight   once a month   less than once a month

Do you use the location atlas?...

Do you generally agree with the rosette ratings at the restaurants you visit in the guide? (if not please give examples)...
....

Who is your favourite chef? ....

Which is your favourite restaurant? ....

Which type of cuisine is your first choice e.g. French ....

Which of these factors are most important when choosing a restaurant?

Price   Service   Location   Type of food   Awards/ratings

Decor/surroundings   Other (please state):...

Which elements of the guide do you find most useful when choosing a restaurant?

Description   Photo   Rosette rating   Price   Other.........................

Please send this form to:
    Editor, The Restaurant Guide,
    Lifestyle Guides,
    The Automobile Association,
    Fanum House,
    Basingstoke RG21 4EA

Readers' Report Form

or fax: 01256 491647
or e-mail: lifestyleguides@theAA.com

Please use this form to tell us about any restaurant you have visited, whether it is in the guide or not currently listed. Feedback from readers helps us to keep our guide accurate and up to date. Please note, however, that if you have a complaint to make during a visit, we strongly recommend that you discuss the matter with the restaurant management there and then so that they have a chance to put things right before your visit is spoilt. The AA does not undertake to arbitrate between you and the restaurant management, or to obtain compensation or engage in correspondence.

Date:

Your name (block capitals)

Your address (block capitals)

....

....

....

e-mail address: ....

Restaurant name and address: (If you are recommending a new restaurant please enclose a menu or note the dishes that you ate.)

....

....

....

Comments:...

....

....

(please attach a separate sheet if necessary)   **PTO**

We may use information we hold about you to write, e-mail or telephone you about other products and services offered by us and our carefully selected partners, but we can assure you that we will not disclose it to third parties.

Please tick here if you DO NOT wish to receive details of other products or services from the AA.

Readers' Report Form

	YES	NO
Have you bought this guide before?	☐	☐

Please list any other similar guides that you use regularly.................................
....
....

What do you find most useful about The AA Restaurant Guide?

....
....
....
....

Please answer these questions to help us make improvements to the guide:

What are your main reasons for visiting restaurants (circle all that apply)

business entertaining   business travel   trying famous restaurants

family celebrations   leisure travel   trying new food

enjoying not having to cook yourself   to eat food you couldn't cook yourself

other ....   because I enjoy eating out regularly

How often do you visit a restaurant for lunch or dinner? (circle one choice)

once a week   once a fortnight   once a month   less than once a month

Do you use the location atlas?..

Do you generally agree with the rosette ratings at the restaurants you visit in the guide? (if not please give examples)..
....

Who is your favourite chef? ....

Which is your favourite restaurant? ....

Which type of cuisine is your first choice e.g. French ....

Which of these factors are most important when choosing a restaurant?

Price   Service   Location   Type of food   Awards/ratings

Decor/surroundings   Other (please state):....................................

Which elements of the guide do you find most useful when choosing a restaurant?

Description   Photo   Rosette rating   Price   Other........................

Please send this form to:
Editor, The Restaurant Guide,
Lifestyle Guides,
The Automobile Association,
Fanum House,
Basingstoke RG21 4EA

**Readers'
Report form**

or fax: 01256 491647
or e-mail: lifestyleguides@theAA.com
Please use this form to tell us about any restaurant you have visited, whether it is in the guide or not currently listed. Feedback from readers helps us to keep our guide accurate and up to date. Please note, however, that if you have a complaint to make during a visit, we strongly recommend that you discuss the matter with the restaurant management there and then so that they have a chance to put things right before your visit is spoilt. The AA does not undertake to arbitrate between you and the restaurant management, or to obtain compensation or engage in correspondence.

Date:

Your name (block capitals)

Your address (block capitals)

....

....

....

e-mail address: ....

Restaurant name and address: (If you are recommending a new restaurant please enclose a menu or note the dishes that you ate.)

....

....

....

Comments:...

....

....

(please attach a separate sheet if necessary)   **PTO**

We may use information we hold about you to write, e-mail or telephone you about other products and services offered by us and our carefully selected partners, but we can assure you that we will not disclose it to third parties.

Please tick here if you DO NOT wish to receive details of other products or services from the AA.

Readers' Report Form

	YES	NO

Have you bought this guide before? ☐ ☐

Please list any other similar guides that you use regularly............................
....
....

What do you find most useful about The AA Restaurant Guide?

....
....
....
....

Please answer these questions to help us make improvements to the guide:

What are your main reasons for visiting restaurants (circle all that apply)

business entertaining   business travel   trying famous restaurants

family celebrations   leisure travel   trying new food

enjoying not having to cook yourself   to eat food you couldn't cook yourself

other ....   because I enjoy eating out regularly

How often do you visit a restaurant for lunch or dinner? (circle one choice)

once a week   once a fortnight   once a month   less than once a month

Do you use the location atlas?...

Do you generally agree with the rosette ratings at the restaurants you visit in the guide? (if not please give examples)...
....

Who is your favourite chef? ....

Which is your favourite restaurant? ....

Which type of cuisine is your first choice e.g. French ....

Which of these factors are most important when choosing a restaurant?

Price   Service   Location   Type of food   Awards/ratings

Decor/surroundings   Other (please state):...

Which elements of the guide do you find most useful when choosing a restaurant?

Description   Photo   Rosette rating   Price   Other............................

Please send this form to:
Editor, The Restaurant Guide,
Lifestyle Guides,
The Automobile Association,
Fanum House,
Basingstoke RG21 4EA

or fax: 01256 491647
or e-mail: lifestyleguides@theAA.com

Please use this form to tell us about any restaurant you have visited, whether it is in the guide or not currently listed. Feedback from readers helps us to keep our guide accurate and up to date. Please note, however, that if you have a complaint to make during a visit, we strongly recommend that you discuss the matter with the restaurant management there and then so that they have a chance to put things right before your visit is spoilt. The AA does not undertake to arbitrate between you and the restaurant management, or to obtain compensation or engage in correspondence.

Date:

Your name (block capitals)

Your address (block capitals)

....

....

....

e-mail address: ....

Restaurant name and address: (If you are recommending a new restaurant please enclose a menu or note the dishes that you ate.)

....

....

....

Comments:..

....

....

(please attach a separate sheet if necessary)   **PTO**

We may use information we hold about you to write, e-mail or telephone you about other products and services offered by us and our carefully selected partners, but we can assure you that we will not disclose it to third parties.

Please tick here if you DO NOT wish to receive details of other products or services from the AA.

Readers' Report Form

Have you bought this guide before? YES ☐ NO ☐

Please list any other similar guides that you use regularly......................................
....
....

What do you find most useful about The AA Restaurant Guide?

....
....
....
....

Please answer these questions to help us make improvements to the guide:

What are your main reasons for visiting restaurants (circle all that apply)

business entertaining   business travel   trying famous restaurants

family celebrations   leisure travel   trying new food

enjoying not having to cook yourself   to eat food you couldn't cook yourself

other ....   because I enjoy eating out regularly

How often do you visit a restaurant for lunch or dinner? (circle one choice)

once a week   once a fortnight   once a month   less than once a month

Do you use the location atlas?...

Do you generally agree with the rosette ratings at the restaurants you visit in the guide? (if not please give examples)...
....

Who is your favourite chef? ....

Which is your favourite restaurant? ....

Which type of cuisine is your first choice e.g. French ....

Which of these factors are most important when choosing a restaurant?

Price   Service   Location   Type of food   Awards/ratings

Decor/surroundings   Other (please state):..

Which elements of the guide do you find most useful when choosing a restaurant?

Description   Photo   Rosette rating   Price   Other..........................

Why not search online?

Visit **www.theAA.com** and search around 8,000 inspected and rated hotels and B&Bs in Great Britain and Ireland. Then contact the establishment direct by clicking the 'Make a Booking' button...

...it's as easy as that!

Whatever your preference, we have the place for you. From a farm cottage to a city centre hotel — we have them all.

AA

FOOD LOVERS

wouldn't it be lovely...

...to live next door to a great little restaurant where the owner cooks everything from scratch, the menu changes monthly and uses only the finest produce (such as rare breeds meat)? Well now it doesn't matter where you live as we do all that and deliver to your door anywhere for menus call 01981 550500
www.downfromthehills.co.uk

---

 the gift of oil   www.thegiftofoil.co.uk

surprise your senses

with our amazing oils & vinegars

01204 559555

 **ARBLASTER & CLARKE**

Wine Tours Worldwide

Including
Champagne Weekends
Luxury stays in Bordeaux Châteaux
Exciting trips to Chile & Argentina
Vineyard Walks
Independent Opera Breaks

To speak to our specialists or request a brochure call

01730 893344
www.winetours.co.uk

Personalised menus, high quality ingredients, private lunches, art and design events, corp and dinner events

Chic staff and stylish flowers

Janie fraser
tel.02086749264
mob:07977447980
jfrosemary@hotmail.com

GRAIG FARM ORGANICS
AWARD-WINNING ORGANIC FOOD
DELIVERED TO YOUR DOOR

GRAIG FARM Large selection of food, including meat, fish, dairy, fruit & veg, groceries, etc.

BEST HOME DELIVERY SERVICE 2005
Soil Association Organic Awards

ORGANIC FOOD AWARDS 1993-2004

01597 851655
www.graigfarm.co.uk

Smoke your Own Food

We stock Food Smokers, Sausage Making Kits, Cheese, yogurt, & buttermaking Supplies,

Ascott Kitchen and Garden
www.kitchenandgarden.co.uk
Free Catalogue
0845 130 6285

Sheepdrove Organic Farm

ORGANIC BEEF LAMB PORK CHICKEN TURKEY & MEAT BOXES

Direct from our Farm
Delivered Nationwide

Order by phone or online
01488 674747
www.sheepdrove.com

Sheepdrove Organic Farm
Lambourn, Berks RG17 7UU

---

www.islandseafare.co.uk
Manx Mail Order
SEAFOOD

Based on the Isle of Man we offer a next day courier service direct to your door for UK addresses
Wide range of fresh local and exotic seafood

❖ **Fresh Fish**
❖ **Live and Cooked Lobsters**
❖ **King and Queen Scallops**
❖ **Smoked Salmon**
❖ **Fresh Cooked Crab**
❖ **Manx Kippers**
❖ **Gift Hampers**

Order online
www.islandseafare.co.uk
or call us on
01624 834494

BEST RESTAURANT
in your town

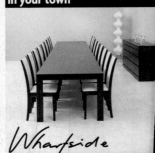

 *Wharfside*

Choose from over 100 different dining tables
call 01372 3798...
or visit www.WHARFSIDE.CO.U...

To Advertise on these pages call Vicky at Big Frog Ltd. on 0207 819 9999 www.bigfrogltd.co.uk **BigFrog**